THE

MEDICAL AND SURGICAL

HISTORY

OF THE

CIVIL WAR

VOLUME V

[Formerly entitled THE MEDICAL AND SURGICAL
HISTORY OF THE WAR OF THE REBELLION. (1861-65.)]

BROADFOOT PUBLISHING COMPANY
WILMINGTON, NORTH CAROLINA
1991

"Fine Books Since 1971."
BROADFOOT PUBLISHING COMPANY
1907 Buena Vista Circle
Wilmington, North Carolina 28405

THIS BOOK IS PRINTED ON ACID-FREE PAPER

ISBN NO.   0-916107-86-8

WAR DEPARTMENT,
Surgeon General's Office,
Washington, D. C., *January* 17, 1888.

Brigadier General JOHN MOORE,
Surgeon General, U. S. Army.

General:

I have the honor herewith to submit the Third and concluding Part of the Medical History of the War of the Rebellion. The *First Part*, published in 1870, consisted of a consolidation by departments and regions of the monthly reports of sick and wounded of the various regimental organizations, with appended extracts from special reports of medical officers, giving a view from the medical standpoint, of the movements of our armies and the many deadly struggles that took place between the opposed forces. The *Second Part*, published in 1879, was devoted to a thorough discussion of the alvine fluxes based on the materials, documentary and anatomical, collected by our medical officers during the war. Surgeon J. J. Woodward, its distinguished author, brought to his task a comprehensive knowledge of those records of the past, which form the historical basis of the professional opinions of the present day, on the nature and causation of these important diseases. Moreover, his intimate familiarity with the materials which had accumulated in the Army Medical Museum, and the enthusiasm with which he prosecuted their study, peculiarly fitted him for the work of laying before the profession the results of that study. Unfortunately, failing health and ultimately death, prevented the further progress of the work by the mind and hand that had conducted it thus far with such consummate ability. In July, 1883, the late Surgeon General Crane expressed to me his desire that I should undertake the *Third Part* of the work; and, in view of my reluctance to assume this heavy responsibility, he gave me to understand that his wish in this instance was intended to carry the weight of an order. No conditions were imposed as to the matter or manner of the volume to be written, save that the valuable plates which Dr. Woodward had prepared, illustrative of the pathological changes in the intestinal tunics, should be embodied in the work. Since that time I have given my best endeavor to the fulfilment of this duty; and in presenting the completed results of these years of labor, I beg that their shortcomings and errors may be attributed to lack of judgment rather than to a want of careful and earnest consideration.

I have the honor to be, General,
Very respectfully, your obedient servant,

CHARLES SMART,
Major and Surgeon, U. S. A.

TABLE OF CONTENTS

OF

VOLUME V

OF THE

MEDICAL AND SURGICAL HISTORY OF THE CIVIL WAR

CHAPTER I. ON THE MEDICAL STATISTICS OF THE WAR.

CHAPTER II. INTRODUCTORY TO THE PRESENTATION OF THE CAMP FEVERS.

CHAPTER III. ON THE PAROXYSMAL FEVERS.

CHAPTER IV. ON THE CONTINUED FEVERS.

LIST OF ILLUSTRATIONS.

LIST OF STATISTICAL TABLES AND TABULATED STATEMENTS.

THE
MEDICAL AND SURGICAL HISTORY

OF THE

WAR OF THE REBELLION (1861-'65).

PART III, VOLUME I.

BEING THE THIRD MEDICAL VOLUME.

CHAPTER I.—ON THE MEDICAL STATISTICS OF THE WAR.

I.—SICKNESS AND MORTALITY AMONG THE U. S. FORCES.

The First Part of this Medical Volume of the History of the War is mainly composed of a series of Tables giving the figures reported by various commands as expressing the facts connected with the occurrence of sickness and deaths from certain specified diseases among the troops composing them. To derive any information from these Tables other than that borne upon their face, as for instance, to compare their items one with another, or with similar statistics from other sources, it is necessary to convert their figures into others expressive of their relation to some common standard. But before deducing ratios of sickness and mortality in designated diseases from the figures tabulated, it may be well to recall some points connected with them that definite ideas may be obtained of their probable value.

1st. As to mortality actual and reported.—On page xxxvii of the Introduction to the First Part, it is shown by a comparison of data drawn from various sources that the actual mortality of our armies from May, 1861, to June 30, 1866, may be assumed to be closely approximated by the following figures:

MORTALITY.	WHITE.	COLORED.	TOTAL.
Killed in battle	42,724	1,514	44,238
Died of wounds, etc	47,914	1,817	49,731
Died of disease	157,004	29,212	186,216
Died, unknown causes	23,347	837	24,184
Total	270,989	33,380	304,369*

* According to Dr. JOSEPH JONES (see *Richmond and Louisville Med. Jour.*, Vol. IX, 1870, p. 259), the deaths in the Confederate armies during the war did not fall short of 200,000, three-fourths of which number were due to disease and one-fourth to the casualties of battle. The data from which these conclusions were derived are said to have been critically examined and considered correct by the former Adjutant General of the Confederate States, S. COOPER, of Alexandria, Virginia.

If the deaths from unknown causes in this statement be distributed among the three causes specified in the proportion which the figures of each bear to their total, the deaths from disease will be found to amount to 171,806 among the white troops, and to 29,963 among the colored troops, giving a total of 201,769 deaths from disease.

Looking now at Table C,* which gives a general summary of the sickness and mortality among the white troops during the war, it will be found that, excluding 37,237 deaths attributed to wounds, accidents and injuries, there were reported 128,937 deaths from diseases that are specified and 449 from diseases that are not specified, making a total of 129,386 deaths reported as from disease.

But since the total mortality from disease was 171,806, it is evident that 42,420 deaths, or 24.7 per cent. of the total, were not reported, and that 42,869 deaths, or 24.9 per cent. of the total, were not attributed to their special causes. Hence, if it be desired to obtain from the Tables in the First Part of this work an approximation to the absolute mortality from any specified disease, we may assume, in the absence of other and accurate data, a *pro rata* distribution of the 42,869 deaths from unspecified diseases and multiply the number in the tables by 1.33, since the number of deaths tabulated and reported as due to specified causes, to wit, 128,937, is to the whole number of deaths attributed to disease, 171,806, as 1 : 1.33. Thus, taking acute and chronic diarrhœa and dysentery by way of illustration, it is found that the deaths reported as from these diseases numbered 37,794; but the actual mortality caused by them must have been considerably greater, to-wit, about 50,226.†

Again, looking at Table CXI,‡ which gives a general summary of the sickness and mortality of colored troops during the war, it will be found that in the strength represented, 27,499 deaths were reported from specified diseases. This number is less by 2,464 than the actual mortality, 29,963, in the strength present and absent. The tables, therefore, embrace 91.8 per cent. of the mortality statistics of the colored troops. If an approximation to the actual mortality be desired in the case of any given disease, it may be obtained from the figures in the statistical tables by the use of the factor 1.09. Thus, in the case of the alvine fluxes, the tables give a mortality of 6,764, but the actual mortality was probably about 7,373.||

2D. As to MORTALITY RATES.—Although the figures given in the tables constitute but 75.3 and 91.8 per cent. of the total mortality among the white and colored troops respectively, it is to be remembered that the strength in which this tabulated mortality occurred was only a part of that which furnished the total. The tabulated deaths took place among the men in the field and garrisons, and among the floating population of the general hospitals in which the sick from the field and garrisons were treated, when, for military or medical reasons, it was deemed expedient to send them to a distance from their commands. The untabulated deaths of white and colored soldiers, 42,420 and 2,464, respectively, occurred firstly, in commands the reports of which were not received, or if received were not embodied in the tables on account of some defect which rendered them valueless for the computation of rates; secondly, among men separated from their commands by the fortune of war and held as prisoners by the enemy; and thirdly, among those not borne as present numerically in the strength of their commands on account of temporary absence on furlough or various special duties.

---

* Part First, p. 641.   † See Dr. WOODWARD'S calculation, p. 3 of Part II, where the actual mortality in this instance is figured as 49,885.
‡ Part First, p. 712. || Dr. WOODWARD'S calculation puts the number at 7,380.

With regard to untabulated deaths due to unrendered or rejected reports, the assumption seems warranted that, had these reports been received in a condition to admit of their incorporation in the tables, it is not likely that the rates calculated from the latter would have been materially altered, since the numbers tabulated were in themselves so large, and constituted so large a percentage of the deaths that occurred in the field, garrisons, and general hospitals. Dr. WOODWARD estimated that, in a general way, the tables covered about nine-tenths of the class of facts which they were intended to embrace.

With respect to the deaths that occurred among prisoners of war, they are with propriety excluded from data forming the basis of an inquiry into the mortality rates affecting our armies in the field, since, as is well known, the circumstances surrounding these unfortunate men were such as predisposed to a higher rate of mortality. Had full returns of the deaths among them, with a knowledge of the numerical strength present in the prisons during the war, been preserved, they would have served as materials for an interesting study; but it would not have been advisable to consolidate them with the mortality statistics of men under wholly different conditions.

Similarly, it seems proper to exclude from consideration the deaths that occurred among the large number of men absent from their commands on furlough and by reason of other causes, as this class was for the time being removed from the influence of the causes and conditions which favored mortality among the men on active service. It is highly improbable that the deaths among them were relatively as numerous as among men on field duty. Although many men were furloughed because they were sick, and undoubtedly many deaths occurred among such cases, the majority of those thus furloughed were convalescents looking for improvement and return to health during their temporary sojourn at home. The number of these absent from their commands cannot be obtained; but had it been possible to have ascertained all the facts, their consolidation with the matter of the statistical tables of Part First would have introduced an element which would have required elimination before the rates affecting the troops on active service could have been deduced.

We may therefore accept the conclusion that death rates based on the tabulated figures, notwithstanding the incompleteness of the latter, will furnish a fair index to the mortality caused by the morbific influences to which the army was subjected during the years of the war.

3D. AS TO THE CASES OF SICKNESS, ABSOLUTE AND REPORTED.—The tabulated statistics show the occurrence among white troops of 5,417,360 cases in which the disease is specified and 7,187 cases of unspecified disease, making a total of 5,424,547 cases of disease, exclusive of 400,933 cases of wounds, accidents and injuries comprised in Class V of the official reports. This number of cases of disease is far from including the whole of those furnished by the army during the war. The tabulated mortality among the white troops has been shown to be deficient by 24.7 per cent. The deficiency in the tabulation of the cases is even greater, as it includes not only cases among prisoners of war and others absent from their commands as well as those in commands which failed to make the required reports, but also the many cases that occurred among the floating population of the general hospitals. The strength of these hospitals was reported regularly; but it was found impossible, as already explained,* to ascertain the number of cases of sickness that

---

* Introduction, Part First, p. XXIV.

originated in them or the number of cases that were received without having been previously reported on regimental returns.

The same remarks are applicable to the 605,017 cases of specified diseases which are reported in the tables as having occurred among the colored troops.

4TH. AS TO SICK RATES.—But although the statistical tables give only an unknown percentage of the sickness which affected our armies, their application to the calculation of correct rates is not impaired thereby. They give, we may assume, a fairly accurate representation of the attacks of sickness that occurred in those commands in "field and garrison" from which reports were received. The large number of men, a mean strength of 431,237 white and 61,132 colored troops, under observation, warrants the belief that the rates deduced from the reports would not be materially altered if to these reports had been added the mean strength and total cases of sickness of commands which failed to report, or sent in reports which were valueless in this connection by the omission of needful data. The remarks already made with regard to mortality rates among prisoners of war and others absent from their commands are equally applicable here. Supposing the necessary figures for calculating the ratio of cases to strength among them to be available, the propriety of consolidating these rates with those from troops in active service would be subject to question, as tending to complicate the point at issue by the introduction of results due to other conditions. For similar reasons it would have been proper to have excluded from the tabulated reports the cases originating in the general hospitals, as the conditions affecting the inmates of these hospitals were certainly very different from those which determined attacks of sickness in the field. As it is, those cases were not reported. A complete medical history of any war necessarily involves the separate presentation of the facts reported from the various classes of men and their comparison with those gathered from the men present for duty with the flag; but the difficulties in the way of obtaining the necessary data are so great that it is doubtful if such a history will ever be written. While regretting the want of records covering the attacks of sickness in the whole number of men who were enrolled for service, it suffices at present to point out that this want does not affect the value of the sick rates deduced from the reports which form the main part of the First Part of this work.

5TH. THE RATES OF FATALITY IN SPECIFIED DISEASES.—In comparing the number of deaths from a given disease with the number of cases of the same disease to ascertain the percentage of fatal cases caused by it, a point of importance comes up for appreciation. It has been shown that neither the deaths nor the attacks tabulated form the respective totals of these occurrences, but only an uncertain though comparatively large portion of them, and it has been argued that this want of absolute figures does not detract from the value of the death rates and sick rates as deduced respectively from the strength given in connection with the figures of each, to wit: the strength present in the field and garrison in connection with the cases, and the strength present in the field, garrisons, and general hospitals in connection with the deaths. But in considering the ratio of deaths to cases their abnormal relationship, consequent on their derivation from different numbers of men, must not be forgotten. The cases occurred in the strength present in the field and garrisons; the deaths in the strength present in the field, garrisons, and general hospitals. The strength which furnished the cases, 431,237, in the instance of the white troops, was smaller than the strength, 468,275, which furnished the deaths. If the cases which originated in the hospitals were known, their addition to the others would establish a normal ratio between the cases and deaths. Or, if the deaths which occurred among such cases were known, a similar result would be obtainable by deducting them from the tabulated deaths. But, as it was found impossible to rectify this matter by either of these methods, there exists this want of relationship between the deaths and cases.

In calculating from the tabulated figures the rate of fatality of a given disease, a figure of unknown and probably different value for each disease, caused by the unrecorded cases among the hospital population, tends to increase the percentage of fatal cases.

The fatality of cases originating in the general hospitals was probably greater than that of those occurring among men in active service, for although the latter had a greater exposure to many of the causes of disease, they had at the same time a greater power of resistance against these morbific influences. The exposures of the field may be regarded also as having tended to multiply cases and to correspondingly lessen the fatality of disease among the troops as compared with the rates affecting a hospital population. If, therefore, we assume that the same rates prevailed among the floating population of the hospitals as in the commands from which their population was derived, we shall ascertain a portion of the error which is involved in a calculation of rates from the deaths and cases in the tables already published.

On this assumption the deaths attributable to diseases originating in the hospitals and those attributable to diseases originating in the field and garrisons would be respectively proportioned to the number of men present in each; and the factor .921, obtained by dividing the strength present in the field and garrison by the total strength in the field, garrison, and general hospitals, when applied to the rates of fatality calculated from the cases and deaths recorded in the First Part of this work, would reduce these rates by the elimination of the deaths assumed to have taken place among cases that originated in the hospitals. In this way a part of the error is indicated, the true rate of fatality being lower even than this corrected rate. Thus, in the case of typhoid fever among the white troops,* where 75,368 cases in the field and garrison are associated with 27,056 deaths in the field, garrison, and general hospitals a mortality of 35.9 per cent. is obtained; but this, for the reason given, is certainly higher than the true rate of fatality. Multiplied by the factor .921 the percentage becomes reduced to 33.0, and this probably expresses the very highest figure at which we may put the mortality from typhoid fever as deduced from the tabulated statistics. When we come to consider the continued fevers it will be found that this corrected percentage is open to question; but the present object is merely an illustration of an inaccuracy which affects the rates of fatality when deduced from the published figures.†

The factor .921, based on the mean strength for the whole period of the war, has necessarily a generic character. The error which it is intended to define varied month by month and year by year in the same command, and differed in different commands during the same periods in proportion to the number of men constituting the hospital population. In the following pages the rates of fatality will be calculated from the figures as reported in the First Part of this work. Those who desire greater precision in individual cases

---

* Table C, p. 636, First Part.

† Dr. GEORGE L. PEABODY, in an article on the *Treatment of Typhoid Fever*, in the Philadelphia Medical News, March 29, 1884, tabulates the typhoid fever cases as reported in the First Part of this work, and calculates the fatality among white troops at 35.9 per cent. of the cases, without observing that the cases and deaths did not occur among the same number of men.

may make use of the average factor above stated, or calculate the factor specially applicable to the case in point in accordance with the statement given of the principle involved.

GENERAL AND ANNUAL RATES OF SICKNESS AND MORTALITY.—The number of cases of disease reported among the white troops during the period, May 1, 1861, to June 30, 1866, was 5,424,547, and the number among the colored troops during the three years ending with the latter date was 605,017, making a total of 6,029,564 reported cases of disease.

During the same period the deaths reported as from disease numbered 129,386 among the white and 27,499 among the colored troops, making a total of 156,885; but, as has been already explained, if it be desired to obtain numbers which will express the absolute mortality from disease in our armies, the factor 1.33 must be used in the case of the white, and 1.09 in the case of the colored troops, to provide for the addition of 42,420 deaths among the former and 2,464 deaths among the latter, as the proportion of deaths from unknown causes which may with propriety be ascribed to disease. There were, therefore, during the war and the year that followed it 171,806 deaths among the white and 29,963 deaths among the colored troops, making a total in the United States Armies of 201,769 deaths which were attributed to disease.

The cases and deaths available for the calculation of rates of sickness and mortality are equivalent to 12,579 cases and 276 deaths in every 1,000 of the white troops during the five and one-sixth years covered by the reports, and 9,897 cases and 430 deaths in every 1,000 of the colored troops during the three years similarly covered. Disease among the latter is thus seen to have been not only of more frequent occurrence but considerably more fatal than among the former. This may be better seen by presenting the statistics of the colored troops on a basis of five and one-sixth years of service, when the numbers are found to be 17,044 cases and 740.6 deaths, equivalent to 135.5 cases and 268.4 deaths respectively for every 100 cases and every 100 deaths among the white troops. The greater liability of the colored troops to disease and death is also clearly shown by the presentation of the statistics in the form of annual rates. The average annual numbers among white soldiers per 1,000 of mean strength were 2,435 cases and 53.4 deaths; in the colored command the corresponding numbers were 3,299 and 143.4.

TABLE I.

Showing the Annual Movement of Sickness and Death among the White and the Colored Troops, expressed in ratios per 1,000 of mean strength.

| | FOR THE YEAR ENDING JUNE 30TH— | | | | | | | | | | | | AVERAGE ANNUAL RATE PER 1,000. | |
| | 1861. | | 1862. | | 1863. | | 1864. | | 1865. | | 1866. | | | |
	Cases.	Deaths.	Cases.	Deaths.	Cases.	Deaths.	Cases.	Deaths.	Cases.	Deaths.	Cases.	Deaths.	Cases.	Deaths.
White Troops	3,822	10.8	2,983	49.	2,696	63.	2,210	48.	2,273	56.	2,362	42.	2,435	53.4
Colored Troops							4,092	211.	3,205	140.	2,797	94.	3,299	143.4

It may be inquired how these figures compare with the records of other armies. To institute a satisfactory comparison between the sickness and mortality of armies of different nationalities is difficult, especially in dealing with the records of war service. Besides differences in nomenclature and in methods of reporting, which interfere with just comparisons in time of peace, the war records are usually more or less indefinite in certain items of information, as of strength present, needful to the calculation of comparative rates.

There is, however, little to be gained by comparing the statistics of one campaign with those of others conducted under wholly different conditions. Each may be advantageously studied for the special lessons inculcated, but unless similar general conditions coincided with particular conditions which were not similar, there is no profit in the comparison. The medical histories of the French and English armies before Sevastopol present many fruitful comparisons, but it is of little moment to place the 94.9 deaths* per 1,000 of strength which occurred from disease in the English ranks in January, 1855, by the side of our average annual rate of 53.4, or to note that during that one month diseases of the stomach and bowels, chiefly diarrhœa and dysentery, caused among the British troops as many deaths, 62.7 per 1,000 strength,† as were occasioned by all diseases in our armies during 1862–3, the year of their highest mortality, 63 per 1,000. For similar reasons it is needless to enter into detailed comparisons between the rates above mentioned and the 14.30‡ deaths per 1,000 of strength, equalling an annual rate of 24.51, which occurred from disease during the seven months of war, August, 1870, to February, 1871, inclusive, in the Prussian army.

The standard of comparison for each army should be its own average sick and death rates derived from the records of a series of years during which it was exposed to no specially unfavorable conditions, or, preferably, the best annual record furnished by its history, as all deviations from that record indicate, when their causes are investigated, not only how they may be avoided in the future, but how the standard itself may be improved.

The difference between such a standard and the disastrous experience of the English during the first half of the Crimean war was a measure of the virulence of the unusual morbific agencies to which their army was exposed.

* *Medical and Surgical History of the British Army which served in Turkey and the Crimea during the War against Russia in the years* 1854-6. Official publication, London, 1858, Vol. II, p. 44.

† *Op. cit.*, last note. Table B.

‡ Calculated from the figures given by Dr. ENGEL in the *Zeitschrift des Kön Preussichen Statisteschen Bureaus Jahrgung* 12, Berlin, 1872, p. 250. The mortality from disease in the German army during the war of 1870–71 was as follows:

MORTALITY.	NUMBER.	RATES PER 1,000 MEAN STRENGTH.
Deaths from acute internal diseases :		
Dysentery	1,971	2.31
Typhus	6,935	8.14
Gastric Fever	158	0.18
Small-pox	249	0.29
Inflammation of the air-passages and lungs	491	0.57
Other diseases	515	0.61
Deaths from chronic internal diseases :		
Consumption	521	0.61
Other internal diseases (chronic)	246	0.29
Sudden death (from disease)	93	0.10
Cases in which the disease was not given	553	0.64
Cases in which the cause of death was not given	415	0.56
TOTAL	12,147	14.30

The strength (850,585) from which these rates were calculated was obtained from Dr. ENGEL'S statement of the total number of deaths from disease and injury (40,743) and of the rate (47.90) per thousand of mean strength to which this total corresponded.

The difference between the ordinary death rate from disease in the German army, 5.64 in 1868 and 4.76 in 1869,* and the war rate of 1870, already instanced, shows the operation of insanitary causes which might be specified with more or less accuracy by detailed comparisons. The German record during this war is noteworthy as having presented a death rate from disease considerably smaller than that resulting from the casualties of battle. The total death rate, 47.90 per thousand strength, in the seven months of active operations consisted of 33.60 from violence and 14.30 from disease, the latter being equal to an annual rate of 24.51 per thousand. But when this record is compared with its proper standard, the mortality of the German army in time of peace, it will be observed that a very notable increase took place in the deaths from disease on account of the exposures incident to the seven months of war. The death rate, in fact, became quadrupled.

When our own war statistics, as given above in annual rates per 1,000 of strength, are compared with similar figures derived from reports covering eighteen years of the history of the army,† it will be found that the morbific influences to which our troops were subjected were such as to increase the annual death rate from disease by 34.50 per 1,000 of mean strength. The peace rate, 18.98 per 1,000, became nearly tripled by the war influences. Our war rate does not appear great when viewed in relation to the mortality rates of previous years and to the English and German figures instanced as expressing the mortality

* These rates were obtained from the *Sanitäts Bericht ü. d. Preuss. Armee*, 1868–69, pp. 40, 142–145, 203, and 298–301. The mean strength during 1868 was 250,376 and the mortality from disease 1,413; the strength during 1869 was 248,246 and the mortality 1,183.

† The records of the Surgeon General's Office show that, excluding deaths from wounds, accidents and injuries, and also those from Asiatic cholera and yellow fever, the annual mortality rate of the United States army during eighteen years of peace which preceded the outbreak of the civil war averaged 18.98 per 1,000 of strength, the extremes being 8.4 in 1845 and 39.6 in 1849. The deaths in excess of the minimum were due for the most part to diarrhœa and dysentery, continued and remittent fevers. The following table has been compiled to show the death rates from disease that prevailed in the army before the war. The years 1847–48 are not included, as the troops were then on active service in Mexico.

YEAR.	STRENGTH.	DEATHS FROM—			DEATH RATE FROM—	
		All Diseases.	Cholera.	Yellow Fever.	All Diseases.	Exclusive of that from Cholera and Yellow Fever.
1840	10,116	241	....	10	23.8	22.8
1841	9,748	367	....	6	37.6	37.0
1842	10,000	291	....	28	29.1	26.3
1843	9,863	156	....	12	16.2	14.6
1844	8,570	95	....	11	11.1	9.8
1845	8,590	72	....	....	8.4	8.4
1846	9,083	175	....	....	19.3	19.3
1849	9,148	721	367	52	78.8	39.6
1850	8,970	268	60	3	29.9	22.9
1851	9,242	280	91	....	30.3	20.5
1852	9,203	208	26	....	22.6	19.8
1853	9,994	266	94	4	26.6	16.8
1854	8,095	224	18	83	27.7	15.2
1855	9,367	305	104	20	32.6	19.3
1856	14,434	356	58	2	24.7	20.5
1857	12,701	167	....	14	13.1	12.0
1858	14,510	202	6	....	13.9	13.5
1859	15,510	240	....	72	15.5	10.8
Average	10,397	257	....	....	24.72	18.98

The figures of this table may be compared with those for the years 1866–83, given in note   upon page   , as well as with those in Table I of the text.

induced by war conditions. It is the mortality rate of our army in the years of peace preceding the war that compares unfavorably with the analogous German rate, and gives the high rate of death from disease when that consequent on the aggregation of our troops in large masses and the exposures incident to field service are superadded. Our army was scattered at posts in all parts of the country which afterwards became the theatre of war, and was exposed to the same miasmatic agencies which subsequently attracted more notice on account of the large number of men constituting the commands. The peace rate of 18.98 shows the insanitary conditions to which our troops were subjected during those eighteen years. The increase to 53.48 during the war is the measure of the mortality directly referable to its morbific influences.

But when, instead of the average of many years, the best annual record furnished by the history of our army is accepted as a standard, the influence of the war in giving potency to the causes of disease becomes very manifest. The rates 8.4 in 1845, 9.8 in 1844, and 10.8 in 1859 are much below the average of the eighteen years. Favorable conditions conduced to this relatively light mortality. But these favorable conditions were, as will be shown directly, in great part susceptible of attainment in other years. The average of these rates, 9.33, may therefore be accepted as indicating the unavoidable mortality from disease in a body of men constituted and circumstanced as was our army before the war; and the large increase of 44.15 deaths per 1,000 of strength annually is necessarily referred for causation to the war influences.

The war rates assume a larger relative magnitude when the rates which have prevailed among our troops since the war is made the basis of comparison.* The average annual

* The following table exhibits the mortality rates, exclusive of those from wounds, accidents and injuries and also those from Asiatic Cholera and Yellow Fever in the army since the war, and may be compared with that given in the note to page 8, *supra*.

TABLE *showing the Annual Death Rates among the White Troops of the United States Army since the close of the War of the Rebellion.*

YEAR.	MEAN STRENGTH.	DEATHS FROM—			DEATH RATE FROM—	
		All Diseases.	Cholera.	Yellow Fever.	All Diseases.	Exclusive of that from Cholera and Yellow Fever.
1866–7	40,183	1,529	747	7	38.05	19.29
1867–8	45,022	1,188	139	427	26.39	13.82
1868–9	37,197	376	2	1	10.11	10.03
1869–70	28,660	249		19	8.69	8.03
1870–1	29,373	355		46	12.09	10.52
1871–2	24,116	263		20	10.91	10.08
1872–3	24,897	247	2		9.92	9.84
1873–4	25,786	218	6	16	8.45	7.60
1874–5	21,939	158		2	7.20	7.11
1875–6	21,718	169		30	7.78	6.40
1876–7	23,383	179		2	7.66	7.57
1877–8	20,813	122			5.86	5.86
1878–9	21,848	162		10	7.41	6.96
1879–80	22,096	126			5.70	5.70
1880–1	21,174	131		2	6.19	6.09
1881–2	20,725	141			6.80	6.80
1882–3	20,922	146		3	6.98	6.83
Annual average	26,462	338.7	52.7	34.4	12.80	9.51

mortality from disease for the seventeen years, 1866-7—1882-3, was but 9.51 per 1,000, although the country occupied by the troops and the unavoidable causes of disease to which they were exposed were the same as in the years preceding the war. This rate, taken as a standard, refers the large annual mortality of 43.9 directly to the exposures incident to the war. But if the average rate of the ten years, 1873-4—1882-3, be made the basis of comparison, the war influences become correspondingly magnified. This rate, 6.74, is but slightly in excess of the minimum, 5.70, in 1879-80. The causation of this great diminution in the death rate of our soldiers of late years is readily appreciated. After the war the regular troops were distributed mainly over the undeveloped West to hold the Indians in check and promote the settlement of the country. The old posts which had been occupied before the war were in ruins, and the new conditions developed by the advance of civilization westward required the establishment of garrisons in positions which had formerly been unoccupied. Military policy rather than hygienic considerations usually dictated the selection of the site, and in many instances the stations were established in unhealthy river bottoms for the sake of being near to a water supply. The quarters built by the troops were of the most primitive character, the materials at command being only such as the country afforded. Practically, our soldiers during the years 1867 and 1868 were in the field, and hence the high death rate. But in the years that followed, posts which experience had shown to be unhealthy were abandoned, and money was appropriated for the construction of barracks at such stations as appeared likely to require permanent occupation. The conditions became gradually changed from those attending a state of war or active field service to those of garrison duty in time of peace, although occasional campaigns against hostile Indians kept the mortality rate higher than a purely peace rate should be. The average rate of the past ten years testifies to the efforts of the Medical Department on behalf of the soldier, and the earnest and intelligent co-operative action of military commanders.

The popular idea that our armies suffered severely from disease during the campaigns of the civil war is thus well sustained by the statistics, in view of the fact that no notable epidemic of imported pestilence, as of typhus, cholera, or yellow fever, contributed to their mortality. Had our camps been unhappily visited by these scourges, our annual mortality of 53 per 1,000 of strength would have appeared light in comparison with the terrible record which would have formed the text of a medical history of the period.

SICKNESS AND MORTALITY AS CAUSED BY VARIOUS DISEASES AND CLASSES OF DISEASE.— It has been already stated that among the white troops the cases of disease reported during the five and one-sixth years embraced in the statistical records numbered 12,579 and the deaths 276 in every 1,000 men of mean strength, these figures being equivalent to the annual rates of 24.34 and 53.48 respectively. It has also been stated that among the colored troops during three years of service there were recorded 9,897 cases of sickness and 430 deaths from disease in every 1,000 men of mean strength, figures equal to the annual rates of 3,299 and 143.4 respectively. The following table is designed to give a general view of the distribution of these cases and deaths under specific and generic headings. The first two columns of each division of the table represent the sickness and deaths that occurred during the whole period, the figures being ratios per 1,000 men of mean strength; the last two columns show to what extent the specified diseases contributed to the totals of the cases and deaths that were reported as from disease.

TABLE II.

Showing the Comparative Frequency of, and Mortality from, the Diseases that prevailed among the White Troops of the U. S. Army during the period from May 1, 1861, to June 30, 1866, and among the Colored Troops during the period from July 1, 1863, to June 30, 1866.

DISEASES.	WHITE TROOPS.				COLORED TROOPS.			
	Cases per 1,000 of mean strength.	Deaths per 1,000 of mean strength.	Cases per 1,000 of total cases of disease.	Deaths per 1,000 of total deaths from disease.	Cases per 1,000 of mean strength.	Deaths per 1,000 of mean strength.	Cases per 1,000 of total cases of disease.	Deaths per 1,000 of total deaths from disease.
Continued Fevers	208.16	59.91	16.55	216.82	68.98	37.36	6.97	86.84
Typho-malarial Fevers (a)	115.65	8.67	9.19	31.37	123.16	20.35	12.44	47.31
Malarial Fevers	2,698.78	17.38	214.55	62.91	2,488.73	30.08	251.47	69.93
Diarrhœa and Dysentery	3,675.93	80.71	292.23	292.10	2,518.14	105.81	254.40	245.97
Diphtheria (a)	16.87	1.53	1.34	5.53	12.69	.95	1.28	2.22
Eruptive Fevers	240.82	23.26	14.85	84.19	276.86	53.08	27.97	128.04
Other Miasmatic diseases (b)	404.60	5.33	32.16	19.28	396.90	8.98	40.13	20.88
Total Miasmatic diseases	7,306.84	196.79	580.87	712.21	5,885.46	258.62	534.68	601.19
Syphilis, Gonorrhœa and Orchitis	423.85	.29	33.69	1.05	233.22	.50	23.56	1.16
Scurvy	71.22	.82	5.66	2.96	265.28	6.07	26.80	14.11
Rheumatism, acute and chronic	590.71	1.01	46.96	3.67	525.50	3.67	53.10	8.55
Consumption	31.30	11.29	2.49	40.85	21.77	18.94	2.20	44.04
Itch	74.39	....	5.91	....	51.63	....	5.22	....
Diseases of Nervous System	394.29	9.49	31.34	34.33	391.53	12.75	39.56	29.04
Diseases of Eye and Ear	272.75	.02	21.68	.06	158.33	.03	16.00	.07
Diseases of Circulatory Organs	58.22	3.54	4.63	12.81	25.50	7.31	2.58	16.98
Acute Bronchitis and Catarrh (b)	901.57	2.53	71.67	9.16	531.91	4.07	53.75	9.46
Inflammation of Lungs and Pleura	215.78	32.73	17.15	118.47	381.27	86.62	38.52	201.35
Other diseases of Respiratory Organs	235.32	2.97	18.71	10.74	151.03	6.35	15.26	14.76
Total Respiratory Organs	1,352.67	38.23	107.53	138.36	1,064.22	97.04	107.53	225.57
Diseases of the Digestive Organs	1,306.10	8.85	103.83	32.04	887.77	15.19	89.70	35.31
Urino-genital disease	69.28	.92	5.51	3.32	49.34	2.05	4.98	4.76
Diseases of Bones and Joints	18.73	.10	1.49	.36	15.54	.23	1.57	.55
Boils, Abscesses and other Integumentary diseases.	440.17	.46	34.99	1.67	192.37	.42	19.44	.98
GRAND TOTAL	12,579.04	276.30	1,000.00	1,000.00	9,896.89	430.2	1,000.00	1,000.00

(a) Cases were reported under this heading only during the period from June 30, 1862.

(b) In the composition of this table the figures reported under the heading Epidemic Catarrh have been dropped from the class of miasmatic diseases and consolidated with the diseases of the respiratory organs, as there seems good reason for believing that influenza was at no time prevalent among the troops. See *infra*, page 725.

Among the white troops diarrhœa and dysentery occurred with great frequency and occasioned a large mortality. These intestinal affections were the cause of more than one-fourth of all the entries upon the sick reports; and it is a singular coincidence that their reported cases bear to the reported cases of all diseases the same ratio, 292 per thousand, that the deaths occasioned by them bear to the total deaths from disease. Malarial fevers followed in order of frequency, having constituted, if typho-malarial cases are included, about one-fourth of the whole number of cases of disease. These caused nearly one-tenth of the total deaths, a mortality almost reached by the eruptive fevers, which, however, occasioned only 14.8 of every thousand of the cases. But in order of gravity the continued fevers, consisting mainly of typhoid cases, took the second place, having caused 216 deaths in every thousand from disease, although contributing only 16.5 cases to every thousand cases of all diseases. To the miasmatic diseases as a class were attributed considerably more than one-half, 581 cases per thousand of all diseases, of the entries on sick reports, and nearly three-fourths of the mortality, 712 deaths in every thousand. The only other classes of disease which furnished high rates of prevalence, diseases of the digestive and of the respiratory organs, agreed closely in their number of cases, 103.8 of the former and 107.5 of the latter, contributed to every thousand of all diseases; but the deaths caused by the diseases of the respiratory organs assumed a higher proportion, 138.4 per thousand, on account of the gravity of the pneumonic cases. Scurvy as an individualized disease caused less than 6 in every thousand of the cases and less than 3 in every thousand of the deaths.

The second part of the table presents the parallel facts deduced from the medical statistics of the colored troops. Among the colored, as among the white troops, diarrhœa and dysentery occurred with great frequency and fatality. The ratio of cases of these intestinal affections to the total number of cases of disease was 254.4, and of deaths caused by them to the deaths caused by all diseases, 245.97 in every thousand of each respectively. Malarial fevers constituted one-fourth of the whole number of cases of disease, and caused, if typho-malarial fevers are included, somewhat more than one-tenth of the deaths. But inflammation of the lungs occupied the second place in the order of gravity, the deaths from this cause having formed 201.3 of every thousand from all diseases. The eruptive fevers occasioned 128 of every thousand deaths. The continued fevers did not occupy so prominent a place in the medical records of the colored troops as in those of the white regiments; the cases formed only 6.97 of every thousand cases of all diseases, and the deaths 86.84 of every thousand deaths from disease, as compared with 16.55 and 216.82, the corresponding numbers from the records of the white troops. Miasmatic diseases as a class caused 594.68 of every thousand cases and 601.19 of every thousand deaths. Scurvy attained a decided prominence among the colored troops as compared with its prevalence among the whites. It was nearly as frequent as the eruptive fevers, 26.80 cases having been recorded in every thousand cases of disease; and a comparatively large number of deaths were attributed to it, 14.11 of every thousand from all cases, as against 2.96 among the white troops.

Incidentally a comparison may be instituted between the sickness and mortality of the white and the colored troops by noting the figures in the third and fourth columns of Table II, in connection with the corresponding figures in its seventh and eighth columns. The first two columns of each division of this table are insusceptible of comparison, as they do not refer to equal periods of time, but in the following table the average annual rates of sickness and death in the white and the colored commands are strictly comparable.

From this table the greater sickness and the very much larger death rate among the colored troops may be appreciated and referred to the disease or classes of disease that occasioned them. There occurred on the average annually in every thousand of the colored men 143.4 deaths from disease as compared with 53.48 among the white troops; and as the sickness of the former, although large, was not proportionally increased, the greater fatality of disease among them is manifested.

Malarial diseases caused 829.58 cases as against 522.34 among the white troops, and 10.03 deaths as against 3.36, whilst at the same time cases reported as typho-malarial were more numerous and very much more fatal among the colored commands. Evidently, from these figures, the latter did not possess that insusceptibility to the malarial influence that has been sometimes claimed for them.* Indeed, an insusceptibility to the typhoid poison rather than to the malarial influence appears suggested, for the average annual number of

TABLE III.

Showing by Average Annual Rates per 1,000 of mean strength the Comparative Frequency of, and Mortality from, the Diseases that prevailed among the White and Colored Troops of the U. S. Army.

DISEASES.	WHITE TROOPS.		COLORED TROOPS.	
	Cases.	Deaths.	Cases.	Deaths.
Average annual rate for all diseases	2,434.64	53.48	3,298.96	143.4
Continued Fevers	40.29	11.60	22.99	12.45
Typho-malarial Fevers	22.38	1.68	41.05	6.78
Malarial Fevers	522.34	3.36	829.58	10.03
Diarrhœa and Dysentery	711.46	15.62	839.38	35.27
Diphtheria	3.92	.34	4.23	.32
Eruptive Fevers	46.61	4.50	92.29	18.36
Other Miasmatic diseases	78.31	1.03	132.30	2.99
Total Miasmatic diseases	1,414.22	38.09	1,961.82	86.21
Syphilis, Gonorrhœa and Orchitis	82.04	.06	77.74	.17
Scurvy	13.78	.16	88.43	2.02
Rheumatism, acute and chronic	114.33	.20	178.54	1.23
Consumption	6.06	2.18	7.26	6.31
Itch	14.40	....	17.21	....
Diseases of Nervous System	76.31	1.84	130.51	4.25
Diseases of Eye and Ear	52.79	.004	52.78	.01
Diseases of Circulation	11.27	.69	8.50	2.44
Acute Bronchitis	174.49	.49	177.30	1.36
Inflammation of Lungs and Pleura	41.76	6.34	127.09	28.87
Other diseases of Respiratory Organs	45.55	.57	50.34	2.12
Total diseases of Respiratory Organs	261.80	7.40	354.74	32.35
Diseases of Digestive System	252.79	1.71	295.92	5.06
Urino-genital diseases	13.41	.18	16.45	.68
Diseases of Bones and Joints	3.63	.02	5.18	.08
Boils, Abscesses and other Integumentary diseases	85.19	.09	64.12	.14

cases of the continued fevers was only 22.99 among the colored men, while it reached 40.29 among the white troops. Nevertheless, the annual death rate from these fevers, typhoid mainly, was somewhat larger among the colored men, 12.45, than the white commands, 11.60; thus indicating the unlikely coincidence of a diminished prevalence and a largely augmented virulence. This anomaly is probably due to the aggregation of a larger proportion of true typhoid cases in the 41.05 cases reported as typho-malarial from the colored commands than in the 22.38 cases similarly reported from the white regiments. Diarrhœa and dysentery, the eruptive fevers, diseases of the lungs—in fact, with the partial exception of the continued fevers, all the diseases that were specially prevalent in our camps occasioned more sickness and more deaths among the colored troops than among corresponding numbers of the white troops. Miasmatic diseases as a class caused 1,961.82 cases and 86.21 deaths, as compared with 1,414.22 cases and 38.09 deaths among the whites. Even those, such as

* See *infra*, page 84, in continuation of this subject.

syphilis, gonorrhœa and orchitis, consumption, diseases of the eye and ear, diseases of the circulation and acute bronchitic attacks, which were not of more frequent occurrence among the colored troops were, nevertheless, attended with a higher mortality than among the whites.*

Sick- and mortality-rates of U. S. white troops during the war as compared with those of other bodies of men of the military age.—Table IV and the plate which faces this page have been designed to illustrate the various points that appear of interest under this heading. Special attention may be invited to some of the more prominent of these.

Five of the red lines representing annual mortality rates among our white troops during the war are projected into the closed-up divisions of the plate. Evidently the diseases indicated by them caused the main portion of the total mortality. The length of these lines as compared with that of the correlated lines of other colors, gives expression to the influences which the conditions of war impressed on the mortality from these affections. The diseases thus prominently brought into notice are those already recognized in Table II as having occasioned so many of the deaths among our soldiers. Of the 53.48 deaths that occurred annually in every thousand men of the average strength present, diarrhœa and dysentery caused 15.62; the continued fevers, not including those reported as typho-malarial, 11.60; diseases of the respiration, pneumonia chiefly, 7.40; the eruptive fevers, 4.50; and the malarial fevers, 3.36. The only other lines that are projected into the denser portion of the plate are the black line indicating the mortality, 5.32, from diarrhœa and dysentery among our troops before the war, and the green line representing that from the continued fevers, 3.39, among the French troops. The former was due to that want of sanitary supervision and care for the health of the troops which permitted scurvy to show as a well-defined cause of death among them, while it scarcely appears among the other bodies of men tabulated, except in our own armies during the war, when the unusual nature of the conditions suffice to explain, and in a measure to condone, its appearance. The latter was due to the influence of local epidemics during the years taken for comparison, and especially to the prevalence of continued fevers among the troops in Algeria.

The increased mortality during the war from what has been called typho-malarial fever is well marked by comparison with the death rate from the same disease since the war; but, as will be shown hereafter, febrile cases presenting essential differences were aggregated under this heading.

The large death rate, 11.60 per thousand of strength, from the continued fevers during the war period, when compared with their relatively insignificant mortality in our army since the war, 0.61, in the German army, 0.98, or among our civil population of the military age, 0.49, implies of necessity a vastly increased prevalence as well as fatality. Both of these facts may be verified from the data in Table IV. A precisely analogous series of facts delineated under the heading of the eruptive fevers is suggestive of one of the probable causes of the increased prevalence and fatality of the continued fevers. The main factor in the development of an epidemic of the eruptive fevers is not so much the introduction of the contagion, although this of course is essential, but the accumulation in the population of a sufficient number of susceptible individuals to afford material for the

---

* This tendency of the colored troops to succumb to morbific influences was brought forcibly to the notice of the writer in 1864 by Assistant Surgeon J. T. Calhoun, U. S. Army, then in charge of a field hospital for their treatment at City Point, Virginia. "I do not know what to do with these colored men," he said, "I cannot keep them up. They do not have the stamina of our white men. They just go to their beds and die."

A Comparison of the Annual Mortality Rates
caused by certain Specified Diseases in Various Bodies
of Men of the Military Age.

Rates per Thousand of Strength.

Continued Fevers.

Malarial Fevers.

Typho-Malarial Fever.

Diarrhœa and Dysentery.

Eruptive Fevers.

Diseases of the Respiratory Organs.

Diseases of the Nervous System.

Diseases of the Circulatory Organs.

Diseases of the Digestive Organs.

Consumption.

Rheumatism

Scurvy.

U.S. Civilians.
U.S. Army during the War.
U.S. Army before the War.
U.S. Army since the War.
German Army } years of peace.
French Army

1.   2.   3.   4.   5.   6.   7.   8.   9.   10.   11.   12.   13.   14.   15.   16.

operation of the morbid agency. This is well recognized by the recurrence of the epidemic visitation after a certain lapse of time has permitted the community to accumulate a large proportion of persons hitherto unaffected; and in the case of small-pox, by the institution of effective preventive measures based on the destruction of the susceptibility rather than on the exclusion of the contagion. Regiments recruited in country districts that had been unvisited by these fevers for a number of years, presented material for their rapid spread on the introduction of the contagious principle. Similarly, regiments from localities that had been free from typhoid, were liable to suffer severely from this disease on account of the susceptibility of the men composing them.

The mortality lines of our armies during the war period are exceeded by those of other bodies of men in the two instances, consumption and scurvy. The males of our civil population have a higher death rate from the first-mentioned disease as a result of the selection for service and discharges for disability that tended to free the army from such cases. Our own troops, before the war, had a higher rate from scurvy, owing to deficient supplies and their isolation at stations at and beyond the frontier of civilization.

Diseases of the digestive system gave a larger mortality among our troops during the war than among other bodies of men. The records show this to have been mainly due to the fatality of cholera morbus and dropsy from hepatic disease.

Diseases of the nervous system had also a comparatively large mortality, which, however, was equalled in our own army before the war.

Active service during the war slightly increased the mortality from diseases of the circulatory system; but the records of the French army ascribe to these diseases a nearly similar death rate.

Rheumatism contributed but little to the mortality in our camps, scarcely more than was the result of the conditions existing at the military posts of earlier times.

From Table IV, on the next page, may be gathered some interesting points regarding prevalence not shown by the mortality lines.

Thus, according to the figures, the number of cases of sickness among our troops was relatively greater before the war than during its progress. Certainly, in its early service in the Indian country, our small army was exposed to many of the influences that subsequently contributed to the war rates of sickness. It will be observed, however, that the number of serious cases, i. e., of diseases yielding a high mortality, was invariably greater during the war than before it; hence the smaller figures of which our war rates consists, 2,434.64 cases annually per thousand of strength as against 2,886.01 in earlier years, must be attributed to the failure of our medical officers during the active progress of a campaign to record cases of trivial ailments rather than to an actual diminution in their number.

Again, the frequency of cases of disease in our army since the war appears to have been more than double that of the German army during corresponding years of peace, 1,474.26 per thousand of strength as compared with 660.78. Here the gravity of the affection recorded as a case of sickness forms an element of difference. In our service every man excused from military duty on account of sickness, however trivial, counts as one case upon the record; but since the mortality rate of the German army is not decreased in proportion to its sickness, as compared with our rates, it may be inferred that in their service the trivial cases are not recorded.

TABLE IV.

Average Annual Sick and Death Rates per thousand of mean strength in the U. S. Army before, during and since the war, and in the German and French armies, with the Annual Death Rate for males of the military age in the United States, as calculated from the returns of the census year 1880.

	White male population, 20 to 44 years of age, in certain parts of the United States.(a)	Total male population of the United States, white and colored, 20 to 44 years of age.(b)	U. S. Army, White Troops for 5½ years of War.		U. S. Army, White Troops for 18 years before the War (c)		U. S. Army, White Troops for 10 years since the War.		German Army for four years, 1874-'5 to 1877-'8.(d)		French Army for four years, 1875-'78.(e)
Strength represented	1,906,276	8,987,358	431,237		10,397		....		324,195		459,420
	Deaths.	Deaths.	Cases.	Deaths.	Cases.	Deaths.	Cases.	Deaths.	Cases.	Deaths.	Deaths.
Average annual rate for all diseases	6.97	6.87	2,434.64	53.48	2,886.01	18.98	1,474.26	6.74	660.78	4.38	8.78
Continued Fevers	.49	.54	40.29	11.60	21.30	1.29	3.23	.61	14.35	.98	3.39
Typho-malarial Fevers			22.38	1.68	....		2.58	.34	....		....
Malarial Fevers	.19	.26	522.34	3.36	596.63	1.76	226.68	.32	24.79	.009	.38
Diarrhœa and Dysentery	.22	.27	711.46	15.62	457.34	5.32	224.56	.47	21.88	.10	.26
Diphtheria	.04	.05	3.92	.34	....		.55	.02	1.18	.04	.05
Eruptive Fevers	.09	.06	46.61	4.50	7.48	.19	2.81	.06	4.86	.07	.39
Other Miasmatic Diseases			78.31	1.03	(f)	(f)	(f) 8.48	(f) .13	....		....
Total Miasmatic Diseases			1,414.22	38.09	1,112.74	8.56	468.89	1.96	67.07	1.20	4.48
Syphilis, Gonorrhœa and Orchitis	.02	.02	82.04	.06	87.86	.08	87.62	.05	41.56	.006	.004
Scurvy			13.78	.16	26.37	.28	.42	.005	.10	.009	.004
Rheumatism, acute and chronic	.04	.04	114.33	.20	114.33	.18	116.54	.06	26.21	.05	.09
Consumption	2.94	2.33	6.06	2.18	3.53	1.84	4.08	.72	3.77	.74	....
Itch			14.40	....	....		.29	....	7.75		....
Diseases of Nervous System	.64	.56	76.31	1.84	82.26	1.77	111.52	.79	4.17	.21	.48
Diseases of Eye and Ear			52.79	.004	59.04	.01	34.42	.005	41.08	.02	.004
Diseases of Circulation	.46	.33	11.27	.69	3.04	.23	7.70	.67	2.10	.06	.18
Acute Bronchitis	.08	.05	174.49	.49	299.59	.19	208.83	.06	43.64	.03	.18
Inflammation of Lungs and Pleura	.77	.97	41.76	6.34	27.28	1.36	10.54	.84	17.61	.72	1.02
Other Diseases of Respiratory Organs	.13	.12	45.55	.57	....		11.42	.20	....		.32
Total Diseases of Respiratory Organs	.98	1.14	261.80	7.40	326.87	1.55	230.79	1.10	61.25	.75	1.51
Diseases of Digestive System	.35	.32	252.79	1.71	128.46	.04	191.20	.69	30.82	.009	.29
Urino-genital Diseases	.33	.18	13.41	.18	....		15.44	.24	6.34	.08	.04
Diseases of Bones and Joints	.04	.03	3.63	.02	....		3.92	.03	7.13	.06	.09
Boils, Abscesses and other Integumentary Diseases.	.04	.05	85.19	.09	129.91	.10	118.09	....	42.78	.006	....

(a) The mortality returns of the Tenth U. S. Census, 1880, were not published at the time this table was calculated; but by the courtesy of the Superintendent the writer was furnished with page proofs of Table XI, *Statistics of Mortality*, giving the deaths in certain grand groups by age and sex, with distinction of color and specification of cause, from which he calculated the rates for his comparative table of annual rates in men of the military age. The grand groups, Nos. 2, 8 and 11 of the topographical divisions made by the Census Office, have a population of 1,906,276 white males between and including the ages of 20 and 44 years. They are: 2, the Middle Atlantic Coast, comprising the District of Columbia, the State of Delaware, and part of New York, New Jersey, Maryland and Virginia; 8, the Interior Plateau, embracing parts of New York, Pennsylvania, Virginia and North Carolina; and 11, the Southern Interior Plateau, including parts of South Carolina, Georgia, Alabama, Mississippi and Tennessee.

(b) The figures in this column were calculated from page proofs of Table VII of the *Statistics of Mortality* of the Tenth Census, which gives the mortality of the United States from each specified disease and class of diseases, with distinction of age and sex but not of color.

(c) The average rates in this column are from the statistics of the years 1840 to 1859 inclusive, but not including the years 1847 and 1848, during which the troops were on active service in Mexico. Yellow fever and cholera prevailed during certain of these years, but the influence of these epidemics has been excluded in calculating the rates. There were 317 deaths from yellow fever and 764 from cholera, which, if included, would raise the average annual death rate from 18.98 to 24.72.

(d) These rates were calculated from the *Statistischen Sanitätsbericht über die Königlich Preussische Armee*. Care was taken in the computation to so aggregate the figures given under specified diseases as to render them strictly comparable with the United States statistics.

(e) As the French *Statistiques Médicales de l'Armée* do not report the number of men excused from duty and treated in quarters, their recorded cases are not susceptible of comparison with those of the United States or German army.   (f) Not including yellow fever.

Notwithstanding the great frequency of malarial attacks during the war, 522.34 cases annually per thousand of strength, it will be observed that these were even of greater frequency among our troops during the years that preceded it, 596.63 per thousand. The material reduction of late years in malarial sickness, 226.68 per thousand, is due to the abandonment of unhealthy stations.*

Venereal diseases and those affecting the urino-genital organs were nearly as frequent in our army during the war as in earlier years.

Scurvy during the war gave annually per thousand of strength 13.78 cases, or only about one-half of the number, 26.37, recorded by our medical officers before the war.

The war records, compared with those of our army before and since the war, do not show an increased prevalence of rheumatism, nor of diseases of the nervous system, nor of bronchitic attacks; pneumonic cases, however, were more frequent and by far more fatal.

Diseases of the circulation were somewhat increased, and those of the digestive system considerably augmented in number during the period of the war.

SICKNESS AND MORTALITY AS INFLUENCED BY SEASON, LOCALITY, ETC.—The regimental monthly reports, compiled from the morning reports of the medical officers on duty, are the ultimate elements of which the statistics of sickness and death in our armies were composed; but these lost their individuality when they were converted into departmental returns. The data in these departmental tables were intended to show, when converted into comparative figures, the influence of season, locality and military operations as affecting the prevalence and fatality of the diseases specified. The influence of season can be determined with accuracy, but that exercised by locality and military operations is not so well defined.

A series of regimental histories giving in parallel sentences an account of the conditions affecting the health of the men during the progress of their service, and the prevalence of disease and death among them, would have been a desirable addition to the materials for a medical history of the war. The want of these has been in part replaced by the special reports rendered by medical officers, although generally in these more attention was given to the details of hostile movements, battle scenes and surgical service, than to the less exciting contests with the more deadly enemy, disease. By the consolidation of the regimental into departmental returns the numerical statements lost a great part of their value. Certain sections of the departments were healthy, others unhealthy, and the consolidation of the regimental reports obliterated the records of special localities and gave results for each department depending on the character of that section of it in which the majority of the regiments were concentrated. Besides this, even the boundary lines of departments were subject to constant variation consequent on changes in the military policy, the assignment of new commanders, etc. Departmental reports must therefore be considered in connection with the localities which were the theatre of military operations, rather than as figures applying generally to the section of country included in the department. This renders it difficult to attain to an accurate estimate of the relative value of region as influencing disease and mortality.

Moreover, military operations carried the troops from one part of a department to another, and frequently to some other department. They entailed upon the soldier fatigues, exposures and privations which tended to sickness and death. The pernicious influences of service in one department came thus in many instances to be credited to a wholly different locality. A synopsis of the history of the operations in each department precedes the annual statistical tables in the First Part of this work, and many of the movements and the influences exercised by them have already been given in free extracts from the reports of the medical officers who served with the commands. Nevertheless, it will readily be appreciated that the ratios of disease and death calculated from the figures in the departmental tables express only in a general way the conjoint influence of locality and military operations.

The following table presents a general view of the annual movement of sickness and death among the white and the colored troops in the several regions:

TABLE V.

Showing the Annual Prevalence of Sickness and the Mortality from Disease in the several Regions, expressed in ratios per 1,000 of mean strength.

| | FOR THE YEAR ENDING JUNE 30TH— | | | | | | | | | | | |
| | 1861. | | 1862. | | 1863. | | 1864. | | 1865. | | 1866. | |
	Cases.	Deaths.	Cases.	Deaths.	Cases.	Deaths.	Cases.	Deaths.	Cases.	Deaths.	Cases.	Deaths.
White Troops.												
Atlantic Region	3,930	11.4	2,719	32	2,553	42	2,137	33	2,221	53	2,292	42
Central Region	3,432	7.2	3,495	81	2,841	85	2,262	58	2,328	61	2,549	48
Pacific Region	......	......	2,171	10	2,133	9	1,816	11	1,864	12	1,749	14
Total white	3,822	10.8	2,983	49	2,696	63	2,210	48	2,273	56	2,362	42
Colored Troops.												
Atlantic Region	......	......	......	......	......	......	3,461	83	3,122	111	2,574	100
Central Region	......	......	......	......	......	......	4,373	269	3,248	156	2,842	93
Total colored	......	......	......	......	......	......	4,092	211	3,205	140	2,797	94

The commencement of service was in all instances characterized by the highest ratio of sickness.

Among the white troops the first year gave a mortality rate as low as 10.8 per thousand of strength; but this rate is calculated on observations covering only the months of May and June, as the troops were being hastily called into service. The third year, ending June 30, 1863, gave the highest death rate, 63 per 1,000. The rate fell to 48 in the fourth year, and rose to 56 in the fifth year. In the year following the war the sick rate preserved its war height, but the mortality fell to 42.

Among the colored troops the sick rate fell from 4,092 during the first year of their service to 2,797 during the last, and the death rate from 211 to 94.

The rates in the Pacific region corresponded with those in the army as a whole since the war. The troops in that region were, in fact, during the war exposed to no greater fatigues or privations than the army encountered when at the close of the war it was distributed over the west.

The high death rate of the troops in the Central region is one of the chief points developed by this table. In this region during the year of greatest prevalence the deaths were to the cases as 1 : 43, and during the year of least prevalence as 1 : 39. In the Atlantic region, omitting the figures for 1861 as representing only a part of a year, the corresponding proportions were 1 : 85 and 1 : 65. The fatality rates or the deaths in a given number of cases, as well as the mortality rates or the deaths in a given number of men, were greater in the Central than in the Atlantic region. Unfortunately it is impossible to learn precisely in which of the departments of the Central region this large excess of deaths took place. The statistical tables in the First Part of this work record the deaths which occurred among the troops serving in each department; but the deaths that occurred in the general hospitals among soldiers of one department are consolidated with those of men belonging to other departments in a series of tables giving the deaths in the general hospitals of the region. We must, therefore, endeavor to appreciate the influence of locality on the mortality by an examination of its influence on the prevalence of disease. The following table was constructed to facilitate this examination:

TABLE VI.

Showing the Annual Prevalence of Sickness from all Diseases in the several Military Departments, expressed in ratios of 1,000 strength.

WHITE TROOPS.	FOR THE YEAR ENDING JUNE 30TH—					
	1861.	1862.	1863.	1864.	1865.	1866.
	Cases.	Cases.	Cases.	Cases.	Cases.	Cases.
Middle Department	....	3,099	2,117	2,002	2,363	....
Department of the Shenandoah	....	2,201	....	....	....	....
Army of the Potomac	....	2,844	2,609	1,563	1,963	....
Department of the Rappahannock	....	2,204	....	....	....	....
Department of Virginia	....	2,432	2,583	2,823	2,729	....
Department of North Carolina	....	2,410	2,985	4,012	3,110	....
Department of the South	....	3,095	2,249	2,796	2,395	....
Department of the East	....	....	2,335	2,217	2,219	....
Department of Washington	....	....	2,524	2,401	2,273	....
Middle Division	....	....	....	....	1,788	....
Atlantic Region	3,930	....	....	....	....	2,292
Total in Atlantic Region	3,930	2,719	2,553	2,137	2,221	2,292
Department of Western Virginia	....	2,802	2,005	1,293	....	....
Department of the Cumberland	....	3,415	2,936	1,747	....	....
Department of Tennessee	....	3,991	2,858	2,614	....	....
Department of the Gulf	....	3,855	3,996	2,923	2,703	....
Department of the Northwest	....	2,889	2,394	2,035	2,109	....
Department of Missouri	....	3,301	2,296	2,249	2,494	....
Northern Department	....	....	3,383	3,029	2,508	....
Department of the Ohio	....	....	2,202	1,931	....	....
Department of Arkansas	....	....	....	2,829	3,428	....
Military Division of the Mississippi, Part 1	....	....	....	....	2,361	....
Military Division of the Mississippi, Part II	....	....	....	....	1,688	....
Central Region	3,432	....	....	....	....	2,549
Total in Central Region	3,432	3,495	2,841	2,262	2,328	2,549
Department of New Mexico	....	1,738	2,218	1,693	1,658	....
Department of the Pacific	....	2,575	2,076	1,900	1,964	....
Pacific Region	....	....	....	....	....	1,749
Total in Pacific Region	....	2,171	2,133	1,816	1,864	1,749
Army of the United States	3,822	2,983	2,696	2,210	2,273	2,362

Perhaps the first point that will attract attention in this table is the gradual diminution in the sick rates as the war progressed. The years of the war, though nominally five, were in reality but four, that ending June 30, 1861, having embraced only two months of service. In a general way, as may be seen by the regionic or army totals, the rate of sickness decreased during the first three years and became somewhat increased during the fourth year. Locality had nothing to do with this except in so far as in some instances to occasion an exception to the general rule, as in the Departments of Virginia and North Carolina, where the sickness increased progressively during the three years on account of continued exposures in malarious sections. The diminished sick rate must be attributed to the weeding out by death and discharge for disability of the inferior material necessarily present in all new levies. The term of service of many of the regiments expired during the third year of the war, when the hardy veterans composing them were in many instances replaced by raw troops who, in becoming inured to active service, swelled the sick rates during the fourth year.

The lowest rate, 1,293, was furnished during the third year by the high grounds of Western Virginia. The low rate of 1,563 was given during the same year by the veterans of the Army of the Potomac. The battle of Gettysburg began the year, and the desperate struggle that led from the Wilderness to Petersburg during May and June, 1864, ended it; but the greater portion of this period was spent in what was regarded by the troops as a picnic in summer quarters on the Rapidan, or hutted during the succeeding winter and spring in a healthy locality. All the conditions were favorable to a light sick report. Many of the men were anticipating a sojourn at home on the expiration of their term of service. Even the exhausting movements which closed the year, the constant skirmishing, and the battles fought in quick succession at the Wilderness, Spottsylvania, the North Anna, Cold Arbor and Petersburg, while undoubtedly the cause of much sickness, tended to reduce the sick rate as preserved on the records which medical officers made up at intervals from memory or pencilled notes, overlooking the slighter ailments that would have been recorded in quieter times and noting only those more serious cases that had been despatched with the wounded to the general hospitals.

The highest rate, 4,012, was furnished during the third year by the continued exposure of the troops in the malarious regions of the Department of North Carolina.

The high mortality rates in the Central region corresponded with high sick rates which are particularly displayed in the reports from the Departments of the Tennessee and the Gulf. The prevalence as well as the virulence of the morbific influences was greater in the Central than in the Atlantic region. The influence of locality on the prevalence of particular diseases will be discussed in the chapters relating to the diseases in question.

To express the relation of season to sickness and mortality in the various regions, and in the army as a whole, Tables VII, VIII, IX and X have been constructed; but, as it is a work of some labor to gather from such tables the relative value of the figures contained in them, the diagram facing page 24 has been prepared, and to it accordingly attention is invited.

The sickness is expressed in monthly rates per thousand of strength on the left side of the plate and the mortality on the right; but the scales have been so proportioned that the sick rate may be read as well on the right by appending a cipher to the printed numbers. The narrow red line represents the sick rate among the white troops of the army, the broader line the death rate, while the yellow lines indicate the correlated figures for the colored troops.

Monthly Death Rates among White Troops from

1. All diseases, 2. Diarrhoea and dysentery, 3. Typhoid fever,
4. All malarial fevers, 5. Inflammation of the lungs and pleura. 6. Eruptive fevers.

Year ending June 30, 1862.
Year ending June 30, 1863.
Year ending June 30, 1864.
Year ending June 30, 1865.
Year ending June 30, 1866.

July, Aug., Sep., Oct., Nov., Dec., Jan., Feb., Mar., Apr., May, June

(1) (2) (3) (4) (5) (6)

TABLE VII.

Monthly ratio of Sickness per 1,000 of mean strength among the White Troops, U. S. Army, by regions, for the period from June 30, 1861, to June 30, 1866.

YEAR ENDING—	REGION.	JULY.	AUGUST.	SEPTEMBER.	OCTOBER.	NOVEMBER.	DECEMBER.	JANUARY.	FEBRUARY.	MARCH.	APRIL.	MAY.	JUNE.	MONTHLY AVERAGE FOR THE YEAR.
June 30, 1862	Atlantic	385	370	297	268	257	232	201	184	167	206	198	227	227
	Central	283	389	346	326	303	315	348	253	261	294	269	252	291
	Pacific	157	193	200	197	230	154	128	205	194	141	226	187	181
	Total	324	364	306	285	271	257	239	202	195	245	233	239	249
June 30, 1863	Atlantic	311	235	239	285	240	228	222	181	180	149	163	158	213
	Central	245	220	263	270	263	244	256	236	240	210	192	219	237
	Pacific	186	256	215	172	181	159	172	146	152	169	154	181	178
	Total	279	228	250	275	251	235	238	209	211	182	179	196	225
June 30, 1864	Atlantic	184	244	234	197	176	151	148	135	158	166	147	206	178
	Central	238	268	222	192	169	143	153	138	169	168	190	227	188
	Pacific	178	161	175	186	190	158	140	113	142	138	134	124	151
	Total	217	257	226	194	172	146	151	137	164	167	174	218	184
June 30, 1865	Atlantic	269	276	235	212	189	168	158	140	141	136	170	181	185
	Central	258	263	230	195	160	174	165	146	179	176	183	190	194
	Pacific	132	143	145	159	154	144	160	153	159	189	162	166	155
	Total	260	265	230	201	172	171	162	144	162	158	177	185	189
June 30, 1866	Atlantic	199	214	227	223	177	150	113	124	142	149	188	207	191
	Central	232	253	246	224	185	144	138	134	154	137	170	224	212
	Pacific	149	160	166	183	154	149	113	96	136	141	155	146	146
	Total	215	233	232	219	177	147	125	123	146	142	172	199	197

TABLE VIII.

Monthly ratio of cases of Sickness per 1,000 of mean strength among the Colored Troops, by regions, for the period from June 30, 1863, to June 30, 1866.

YEAR ENDING—	REGION.	JULY.	AUGUST.	SEPTEMBER.	OCTOBER.	NOVEMBER.	DECEMBER.	JANUARY.	FEBRUARY.	MARCH.	APRIL.	MAY.	JUNE.	MONTHLY AVERAGE FOR THE YEAR.
June 30, 1864	Atlantic	292	517	569	403	294	274	257	247	286	228	253	278	298
	Central	494	441	410	430	388	342	333	301	347	363	346	377	364
	Total	459	458	451	422	361	323	309	282	328	319	317	342	341
June 30, 1865	Atlantic	341	349	298	293	234	226	289	219	208	177	292	264	260
	Central	356	264	343	284	255	249	227	206	234	241	259	261	271
	Total	351	359	328	287	248	241	252	211	224	216	271	262	267
June 30, 1866	Atlantic	259	231	264	251	198	154	168	152	161	122	92	154	215
	Central	311	316	286	280	203	185	165	158	141	129	125	157	237
	Total	300	298	282	275	202	181	165	157	145	127	120	157	233

Table IX.

Monthly ratio of Deaths from disease per 1,000 of mean strength among the White Troops, U. S. Army, by regions, for the period from June 30, 1861, to June 30, 1866.

Year ending—	Region.	July.	August.	September.	October.	November.	December.	January.	February.	March.	April.	May.	June.	Monthly Average for the Year.
June 30, 1862	Atlantic	1.95	2.04	1.78	2.01	2.66	3.23	2.90	2.40	2.52	3.12	2.85	3.00	2.67
	Central	.97	2.82	3.49	4.55	6.20	6.58	8.84	8.82	10.24	6.37	7.18	6.42	6.76
	Pacific	1.33	.89	1.26	1.21	1.60	1.00	.19	.41	.88	.49	.51	.77	.88
	Total	1.49	2.15	2.21	2.82	3.79	4.29	4.52	4.11	4.79	4.58	4.93	4.61	4.11
June 30, 1863	Atlantic	3.80	5.19	4.06	4.52	4.76	4.69	3.88	3.08	2.74	2.04	1.44	1.65	3.47
	Central	6.62	5.55	5.36	5.60	7.48	8.00	8.09	9.67	9.35	7.09	5.17	4.79	7.07
	Pacific	.72	.55	.56	.79	1.02	.81	.49	1.02	.32	1.15	.70	1.03	.76
	Total	4.96	5.25	4.58	5.01	6.09	6.21	5.93	6.39	6.11	4.76	3.52	3.56	5.27
June 30, 1864	Atlantic	2.45	2.74	2.63	3.02	2.51	2.46	3.03	2.63	3.51	2.95	1.87	2.93	2.73
	Central	6.67	7.53	5.84	4.18	4.06	3.50	3.94	4.25	5.51	4.98	3.92	4.41	4.87
	Pacific	.33	.65	.63	.94	1.00	1.28	1.25	1.28	1.01	1.08	.71	.81	.93
	Total	4.97	5.60	4.51	3.71	3.44	3.10	3.58	3.61	4.71	4.13	3.12	3.82	4.02
June 30, 1865	Atlantic	5.54	6.75	5.16	5.76	3.87	4.90	3.80	3.51	4.38	3.33	3.08	3.95	4.44
	Central	6.82	6.10	6.05	5.35	3.96	4.41	5.00	4.75	5.89	5.04	3.48	3.28	5.06
	Pacific	.65	.65	.53	1.08	.58	1.41	.88	1.30	1.11	1.63	1.17	.91	.99
	Total	6.17	6.25	5.58	5.46	3.86	4.57	4.41	4.11	5.11	4.15	3.24	3.53	4.71
June 30, 1866	Atlantic	5.06	3.62	4.26	4.42	3.05	1.84	1.24	1.06	1.84	1.14	1.05	.90	3.52
	Central	5.07	4.72	5.42	4.46	3.44	2.66	1.79	1.38	1.66	1.31	1.06	.82	4.01
	Pacific	.98	.99	1.39	1.09	1.98	1.49	.93	1.11	.85	.95	.77	.70	1.13
	Total	4.92	4.10	4.62	4.07	3.07	2.15	1.43	1.22	1.54	1.19	.99	.82	3.51

Table X.

Monthly ratio of Deaths from sickness per 1,000 of mean strength among the Colored Troops, by regions, for the period from June 30, 1863, to June 30, 1866.

Year ending—	Region.	July.	August.	September.	October.	November.	December.	January.	February.	March.	April.	May.	June.	Monthly Average for the Year.
June 30, 1864	Atlantic	2.22	4.58	7.40	7.08	4.48	7.31	7.54	9.03	9.41	6.32	5.77	5.77	6.90
	Central	29.19	31.40	31.02	32.63	16.84	15.40	18.48	20.24	22.16	25.52	21.38	20.75	22.44
	Total	24.15	25.31	24.91	25.06	13.22	13.12	15.09	16.41	18.07	19.25	16.54	15.40	17.60
June 30, 1865	Atlantic	8.60	7.38	8.89	8.62	6.67	6.76	9.08	11.75	10.35	8.36	11.23	13.31	9.23
	Central	20.70	18.50	16.87	13.39	10.01	10.93	15.24	12.14	12.11	10.33	10.70	9.01	12.99
	Total	16.71	14.79	14.14	11.63	8.81	9.33	12.77	11.99	11.45	9.55	10.89	10.04	11.66
June 30, 1866	Atlantic	11.11	7.24	8.59	12.09	7.15	5.18	8.16	6.73	7.45	4.64	4.21	2.91	8.30
	Contral	9.50	9.52	7.90	7.92	6.02	7.26	6.74	6.62	8.07	7.57	3.00	3.51	7.72
	Total	9.85	9.01	8.02	8.62	6.23	6.96	6.91	6.63	7.97	6.99	3.18	3.41	7.82

The largest monthly ratio of cases among the white troops occurred in August, 1861, shortly after the enlargement of the army to meet the military necessities of the time. This ratio amounted to 364 cases per thousand of strength. The exposures, fatigues, altered diet and other changes in the conditions affecting the men incident to their new mode of life as soldiers, coincided at this time with the period of greatest annual prevalence of malarial disease, and the large amount of sickness indicated by this ratio was the result. A reference to the diagram showing the prevalence of diarrhœa and dysentery* will manifest the great influence that this class of camp diseases exercised on the general sick rate of the army at this time. Their extensive prevalence in the Atlantic and Central regions, in which most of the troops were massed, contributed much to the height of the general sick wave as shown on the diagram under present consideration, or more especially on Table VII, which it illustrates.

The irregular prominence of the line in April, July and October, 1862, appears due to excess of diarrhœal cases,—in the Central region during the first-mentioned month, and in the Atlantic region during the others. As diarrhœa, dysentery and the malarial fevers occasioned more than one-half of all the cases of disease, 507 of every thousand cases† that were reported from the white commands, the concurrence of their periods of maximum prevalence gives prominence in the autumnal months of subsequent years to the line indicating the prevalence of disease in general. But in none of these years did the monthly ratio at all approach the height reached during the autumn of the year 1861: thus the highest ratio recorded in 1862 was that of July, 279, while August, in the three following years, gave the highest monthly rates, respectively 256, 265 and 233 per thousand of strength.

The minimum as well as the maximum of prevalence in the year ending June 30, 1862, was higher than in the subsequent years. This is attributable mainly to the frequency of diseases of the respiratory organs and to diarrhœas, which continued to affect the troops in the Central region, and but little to the malarial influence which in this year, as will be seen hereafter,‡ was at its minimum. The minima of the several years were as follows: 195 in March of 1862, 179 in May of 1863, and 137, 144 and 123 respectively in February of the three following years.

Speaking generally, the amount of sickness among the white troops was much less in the last year than in the first, the average monthly rate of the latter, 249, being greater than the highest monthly rate of the former, 233 per thousand. A glance at the diagram will, however, show these variations in the level of the rates more satisfactorily than a lengthened description. It may be added that the narrow red line, the subject of the foregoing remarks, corresponds closely in its course with that indicating the prevalence of disease among the white troops in the Atlantic region. The rates of the Central region, when plotted diagrammatically, give a line which runs parallel to the red line but on a somewhat higher level. The rates of the Pacific region, when delineated in this manner, occupy a lower level, and fail to manifest in their irregularities the existence of the marked autumnal elevations which form so striking a feature of the lines for the other regions.

The mortality from all diseases among the white troops, represented on the diagram by the thicker red line, increased from a low rate during the first month to its maximum, 6.39, in February, 1863. After this it fell during March and April to 3.5 in May and

June. The line is very irregular in the remainder of its course; but in each of the subsequent years there may be distinguished a large autumnal and a smaller spring elevation, the latter usually occurring during the month of March. The plate facing page 20 affords a satisfactory explanation of most of these irregularities in the level of the mortality line. The sudden rise in the rate during the autumn of 1861 was due almost wholly to typhoid fever, but in November and December of that year and January, 1862, pneumonia and the eruptive fevers aided considerably in its elevation. The mortality from typhoid fever continued to augment and uphold the general death rate, although the former allies of this disease declined in virulence as the spring advanced. Meanwhile diarrhœa, and a little later the malarial fevers, began to contribute materially to the rate. During the period from November, 1862, to March, 1863, when the monthly death rate amounted to about 6 per thousand of strength, all the diseases delineated formed notable percentages of the total. In the subsequent years the autumnal increase corresponded with larger rates from diarrhœa, typhoid and malarial fevers, while the smaller prominences in the spring months were caused by a maximum rate among the pneumonic cases and eruptive fevers, with a large minimum rate among the diarrhœal diseases and typhoid fever.

But to return to the diagram on the opposite page: The sick rate of the colored troops, indicated by the thin yellow line, was highest immediately after their enrollment in 1863, when nearly one-half of the command was reported as having been taken sick during each of the months July, August and September. Autumnal exacerbations were encountered during each of the subsequent years; but on the whole the health of these troops improved so remarkably that during the last quarter of the year ending June 30, 1866, their sick rates were somewhat lower than those of the white troops.

Their death rates, indicated by the heavier yellow line, followed a generally parallel course—high at first, about 25 per thousand of strength monthly during the first four months of service, and afterwards declining to the minimum of 3.18 per thousand in May, 1866; but at no period of their service did the death rate of these troops fall below that of the white commands.

DISCHARGES ON ACCOUNT OF DISABILITY FROM DISEASE.—The sick and mortality rates by no means express the whole of the loss to the army occasioned by disease. Large numbers of men were discharged as unfit for military service on account of disease that in a majority of instances originated in the line of duty.

The records of the Adjutant General's Office are understood to embrace certificates of disability on which 275,738 white soldiers of the regular and volunteer army were discharged, but the Surgeon General's Office has reports of only 215,312 such cases. Of these, 48,374 were based on wounds, accidents and injuries; 4,439 on deformities, immaturity and senility, disabilities which existed prior to enlistment; and 25,915 on causes that were not specified. Dropping these, there remain 136,584 certificates in which the disease is stated. But if the cases in which the disease was not stated and those reported to the Adjutant General, but not to the Surgeon General of the Army, were distributed *pro rata* among the discharges occasioned by wounds, by conditions which should have prevented enlistment, and by disease, the number referred to the last cause would be increased to 198,849, equal to an annual loss of 82.2 men in every thousand of strength.

The files of the Adjutant General's Office include certificates pertaining to 9,807 colored men, while those in the Surgeon General's Office number only 8,223; and of these

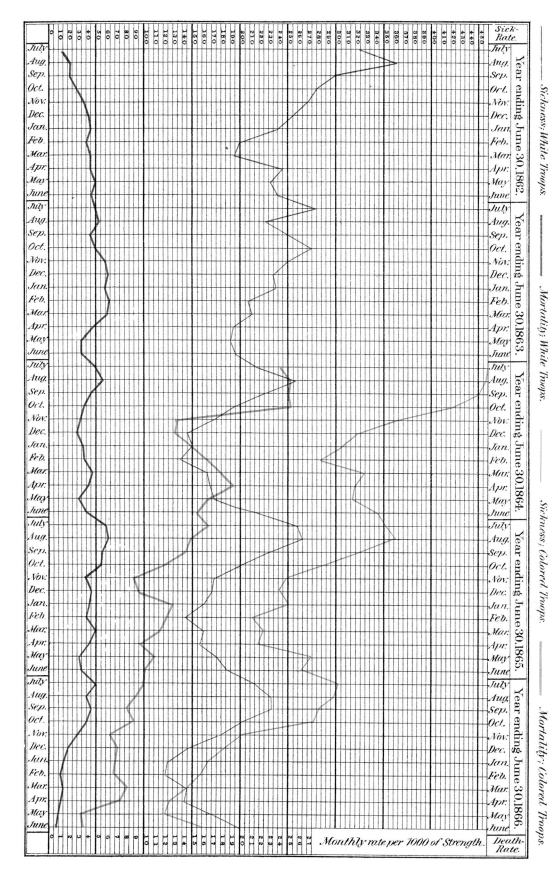

Diagram showing the Prevalence of Disease and the Mortality caused thereby among the White and the Colored Troops of the United States Armies during the years of the War and the year following the War, expressed in monthly rates per thousand of strength present.

——— Sickness; White Troops.　　　——— Mortality; White Troops.　　　——— Sickness; Colored Troops.　　　——— Mortality; Colored Troops.

Monthly rate per 1000 of Strength.

1,479 are based on wounds, 687 on causes which should have rejected the recruit, and 1,226 on unspecified causes. Dropping these, there remain 4,831 certificates in which the disease is specified. But if these figures were treated as in the case of the white troops, the number of discharges due to disease would be augmented to 6,771, equal to an annual loss of 35.3 men in every thousand of strength.

These heavy losses were not wholly due to the diseases incident to military service. Many of the disabilities existed prior to enlistment; for instance, not all of the men discharged for consumption contracted the disease in the service, nor did all of those discharged for hernia become ruptured in the performance of military duty. Ignorance, carelessness and intentional fraud at the recruiting depôts were at first responsible for the enrollment of this worse than valueless material; afterwards liberal bounties induced men to conceal infirmities in order to secure acceptance. In garrison or winter quarters their disabilities were in many instances not manifested; but when exposed to the hardships of a campaign they swelled the sick list, crowded the hospitals, and were eventually discharged. Dr. TRIPLER reported that of 3,939 discharges for disability from the Army of the Potomac during the last quarter of the year 1861, 2,881 were for disabilities that existed at the time the men were enlisted.* Medical officers serving in the field had their duties materially increased by the presence of cases of this character. Some adverted to the fact apparently to explain the large number of discharges reported from their commands; others entered a vigorous protest against the gross negligence of the recruiting authorities. A few extracts are herewith submitted, and as these are by no means exceptional cases, it will be appreciated that a considerable percentage of the disabilities were not fairly attributable to the service of the soldier:

I consider the careful inspection of the volunteers before acceptance a matter of the greatest importance. The great number of discharges for disqualifying defects among the three-months men that have come under my own notice, convinces me either that the men were not inspected at all, or else that the duty must have been performed by inexperienced officers. The incumbrance and dead weight of the men of this description with our columns has been a serious and constantly accumulating impediment to its motions.—Surgeon CHARLES S. TRIPLER, U. S. Army, Medical Director, Department of Pennsylvania, Charlestown, Va., July 18, 1861.

The number of men discharged from service within the last month or two is very large, owing chiefly to the fact that a great many were sent here without undergoing a proper physical examination at the time of their enlistment. For example, some thirty or forty cases of hernia have been sent away, and in almost every instance the disability existed previous to enlistment. I observe, also, that a large number of boys may be found among the troops who are physically incapable of enduring the hardships of a soldier's life in the field.—Surgeon J. M. CUYLER, U. S. Army, Medical Director, Fortress Monroe, Va., August 3, 1861.

In regard to the condition of the companies, they are, with one or two exceptions, composed chiefly of men who hold respectable positions at home as farmers, mechanics, &c., and who possess some degree of pride concerning cleanliness and proper behavior. It is to be regretted, however, that in the haste of preparation and departure, quite a number were enlisted whose physical condition was such that they ought to have been rejected. A large proportion were examined in the country towns by physicians not regularly appointed, and some were not examined at all. This may help to account for the fact that, while the number of sick in the hospital is not very great, the list of those in quarters is larger than it should be.—Assistant Surgeon J. FOSTER HAVEN, jr., U. S. Vols., Camp Foster, Poolesville, Md., September 30, 1861.

The 28th Pennsylvania Volunteers, numbering ten companies, left Philadelphia July 26, 1861, with orders to proceed to Harper's Ferry. They had never been regularly examined by a surgeon, and a number of diseased men had been enrolled. These have constantly made the sick list larger than it otherwise would have been. Eleven of these men have been discharged, and certificates of disability made out for fifteen others.—Surgeon H. EARNEST GOODMAN, 28th Pa. Vols., November 14, 1861.

I joined the regiment after it was mustered into service and found over one hundred enlisted men that should have been rejected by the Medical Inspector before their enlistment. As a consequence of this I have been compelled to recommend a large number of men for discharge on certificate of disability. There yet remain a few cases that I doubt not before long will be decided unfit for the duties of a soldier.—Surgeon WM. R. THRALL, 27th Ohio Vols., December 31, 1861.

---

* See page 47, Appendix to the First Part of this work.

The men in some of the batteries were not properly examined when enlisted, and I have found it necessary to recommend some for discharge on account of hernia, tuberculosis, ununited fractures, &c.—*Ass't Surgeon* WILLIAM A. BRADLEY, jr., *U. S. A., Camp Dupont, Va., December* 31, 1861.

GENERAL: An evil too great to pass unnoticed I now bring to your attention.

Yesterday and to-day I examined eighteen recruits just sent on from New Jersey, and all mustered into service before their arrival. I have unconditionally rejected eight. Of the remainder, one, a butcher, might be made useful as such, although, owing to an old injury, he is utterly unfit for the ordinary duties of a soldier. His case is, therefore, under advisement and awaiting your decision.

One half of these recruits were thus unable to stand the test of a physical examination, while among the whole there were but three or four well-formed and able-bodied men.

In this examination nice distinctions regarding corns, flat feet, unsymmetrical form, &c., were not made. Indeed, I approved of one man on account of previous service whose left elbow-joint has not perfect freedom of motion on account of a former fracture.

Most culpable negligence seems to prevail at the recruiting stations. The medical examination at Trenton or elsewhere can scarcely be better than a farce; at least my experience within the past two days seems to authorize such an opinion. The expense to the Government, and the injury to our cause, resulting from such shameful neglect require no formal expression.

I would suggest that the attention of the authorities of your State be invited to this matter, advising that medical examiners be instructed in their business by spending a week in the office of the medical officer of the regular army who inspects recruits in New York City.

I append a list of the causes requiring the rejection of the eight recruits in question:

1. Over age and fistula in ano of long standing. 2. Dislocation of the clavicle. 3. Hernia. 4. Large scrotal hernia. 5. Movement of right shoulder limited by previous dislocation, knock-knees and large variocele on left side. 6. Total blindness of right eye and imperfect vision of left eye. 7. Left shoulder crippled from an old injury. 8. Syphilis and pulmonary trouble; chest badly formed and general configuration imperfect. To these are added the two men disapproved, but retained for the decision of the commanding general: 1. Louis Loeb, the butcher, who is too fat and heavy for a soldier; his feet and legs are œdematous, and he suffers from an old and severe injury of the right side. 2. Samuel Williams, a trained soldier, but with imperfect motion of the left elbow, resulting from a previous fracture.—*Letter dated October* 11, 1861, *from Brigade Surgeon* GEORGE SUCKLEY, *to Brigadier Gen'l* P. KEARNEY, *commanding* 1*st Brigade New Jersey Vols., near Alexandria, Va.*

The table on the opposite page shows many points of interest connected with the diseases which were the chief causes of disability. The first column of each of its divisions gives for the white and the colored troops respectively the total number of discharges for the specified diseases during the periods covered by the statistics, five and one-sixth years in the one case and three years in the other. The second column expresses these facts in ratios per thousand of strength. The third column shows to what extent each disease contributed to the totality of the discharges for specified diseases, while the last column, giving the mean annual ratio of discharges per thousand of strength, enables a comparison to be made between the disabilities of the white and the colored troops and the frequency of the consequent discharges.

The prominent causes of discharge among the white troops were consumption, diarrhœa and dysentery, and debility, which respectively occasioned 149.4, 127.3 and 106.2 of every thousand discharges for disease. Typhoid and malarial fevers are directly credited with but few discharges; but the disability in a large proportion of the 14,500 debilitated and the 2,224 dropsical men was no doubt due to these morbific agencies. Rheumatism and heart disease, which together caused scarcely one death per thousand of strength annually, contributed largely in diminishing the effective force of the army, the former having constituted 86.2 and the latter 77.9 of every thousand discharges on account of disease.

The relations between death and discharge, as the result of disease, may be ascertained by an examination of Tables II and III in connection with that now under consideration. The white troops lost annually by death from disease 53.48, the colored troops 143.4 in every thousand men; but these rates, while correctly expressing the facts of the

TABLE XI.

Discharges for Disability from Disease in the United States Army from May 1, 1861, to June 30, 1866, with ratio per 1,000 of mean strength in Field, Garrison, and General Hospitals, ratio per 1,000 of total discharges and mean annual ratio per 1,000 of strength.

DISEASES.	WHITE TROOPS.				COLORED TROOPS.			
	Number of discharges during the 5⅛ years.	Ratio per 1,000 of the mean strength in field, garrison and general hospitals.	Ratio per 1,000 of total discharges for specified disease.	Mean annual ratio per 1,000 of strength.	Number of discharges during the 3 years.	Ratio per 1,000 of the mean strength in field, garrison and general hospitals.	Ratio per 1,000 of total discharges for specified disease.	Mean annual ratio per 1,000 of strength.
All diseases	198,849	424.7	....	82.2	6,771	105.9	....	35.3
Specified diseases only	136,584	291.7	1,000.0	56.5	4,831	75.6	1,000.0	25.2
Typhoid Fever	909	1.9	6.7	.37	10	.2	2.1	.05
Malarial Fevers	853	1.8	6.2	.35	30	.5	6.2	.16
Diarrhœa and Dysentery	17,389	37.1	127.3	7.19	359	5.6	74.3	1.87
Eruptive Fevers	427	.9	3.1	.18	3	....	.6	.02
Debility	14,500	31.0	106.2	5.99	540	8.4	111.8	2.82
Syphilis	1,779	3.8	13.0	.74	86	1.3	17.8	.45
Rheumatism	11,779	25.1	86.2	4.87	874	13.7	180.9	4.56
Dropsy	2,224	4.7	16.3	.92	109	1.7	22.6	.57
Consumption	20,403	43.6	149.4	8.43	592	9.3	122.5	3.09
Scrofula	907	1.9	6.6	.37	147	2.3	30.4	.77
Epilepsy	3,872	8.3	28.3	1.60	174	2.7	36.0	.91
Insanity	819	1.7	6.0	.34	34	.5	7.0	.18
Paralysis	2,838	6.1	20.8	1.17	69	1.1	14.3	.36
Ophthalmia	1,463	3.1	10.7	.60	25	.4	5.2	.13
Deafness	1,157	2.5	8.5	.48	38	.6	7.9	.20
Heart disease	10,636	22.7	77.9	4.40	161	2.5	33.3	.84
Varicose Veins	1,969	4.2	14.4	.81	69	1.1	14.3	.36
Varicocele	1,390	3.0	10.2	.57	25	.4	5.2	.13
Asthma	1,220	2.6	8.9	.50	42	.7	8.7	.22
Bronchitis	3,729	8.0	27.3	1.54	96	1.5	19.9	.50
Inflammation of Lungs	1,092	2.3	8.0	.45	25	.4	5.2	.13
Inflammation of Pleura	495	1.1	3.6	.20	18	.3	3.7	.09
Hæmorrhage from Lungs	634	1.3	4.6	.26	4	.1	.8	.02
Hernia	9,002	19.2	65.9	3.72	358	5.6	74.1	1.87
Inflammation of Liver	1,354	2.9	9.9	.56	29	.4	6.0	.15
Piles	1,555	3.3	11.4	.64	43	.7	8.9	.22
Inflammation of Kidneys	1,069	2.3	7.8	.44	27	.4	5.6	.14
Anchylosis	1,838	3.9	13.5	.76	105	1.6	21.7	.55
Diseases of Spine	1,547	3.3	11.3	.64	31	.5	6.4	.16
Ulcers	1,138	2.4	8.3	.47	46	.7	9.5	.24

official records, do not convey with accuracy the relations of death to disease. In view of the number of men discharged for diarrhœa and dysentery it is evident that the mortality rates for these intestinal affections would have been greatly increased had the undoubtedly serious cases that led to the issue of these certificates been followed up to their termination. In view also of the disproportion between the discharges from the white and the colored commands, the mortality from disease, as above expressed, requires modification. Among the former 82.2, among the latter only 35.3 men were discharged annually from every thousand present. No doubt many of these went home to die. If it be assumed that more deaths occurred among the 82.2 discharged white men than among the 35.3 colored men, the difference between the mortality rates of the two will be lessened. But even if the whole number of cases in each instance died ultimately of the disease which occasioned the disability, the greater mortality among the colored troops would still be evident, for the sum of the deaths and discharges among them numbers 178.7 annually per thousand of strength as against 135.68 among the white troops.

The infrequency of discharge among the colored troops may be attributed chiefly to their peculiar condition at that disturbed period of their history, and to the more rapidly fatal course which disease certainly ran when these men became its subjects. While 7.19 whites were annually discharged on account of diarrhœa and dysentery, 5.99 on account of debility and 8.43 on account of consumption from every thousand men, in the hope that the change of climate, scene and surroundings consequent on a return to their northern homes would tend to prolong existence, the corresponding figures for the colored troops were only 1.87, 2.82 and 3.09. The cases represented by the difference between these figures were retained in hospital until the occurrence of the fatal event, in some instances because of the imminence of that event, in others because of the homeless condition of the colored soldier.

TRANSFERS TO THE VETERAN RESERVE CORPS.—The list of men discharged for disability would have been considerably larger but for the establishment of the Veteran Reserve Corps. This command absorbed a large number of men who would otherwise have been discharged. From certain tables appended to a report of Surgeon J. H. BAXTER, U. S. Volunteers, Chief Medical Officer, Provost Marshal General's Bureau, dated April 28, 1864, it is found that among officers the principal disabling cause was wounds received in battle. Of 636 officers transferred, 426, or two-thirds of the whole number, were the subjects of gunshot wounds which prevented their participation in active or field service. Among the enlisted men, however, disablement by disease was more extensive than by wounds. Of a total of 25,031 transferred in 1863, 6,067, or 242.3 per thousand, were occasioned by gunshot wounds, and 2,037, or 81.4 per thousand, by injuries mainly also, perhaps, caused by gunshot. Deducting these cases from the total it is found that 16,927 were transferred on account of disease. Chronic diarrhœa and general debility were the chief causes of disablement in these cases, the former having occasioned the transfer of 2,292 men, or 135.4 per thousand of the total from disease, and the latter 1,916, or 115.0 per thousand. Consumption, which figured so largely in discharges, was found in only 217 of the transfers, or in 12.8 per thousand of those for disease. But disease of the heart, rheumatism and hernia contributed as largely to the constitution of the Invalid Corps as to the list of discharges. Heart disease occasioned 1,735 transfers, or 102.5 per thousand of the total from disease, rheumatism 1,363, and lumbago 427, a total of 1,790 cases, or 105.7 per thousand, and hernia 1,017, or 60.1 per thousand.

II.—MEDICAL STATISTICS OF THE CONFEDERATE ARMIES.

The sources of the little information we possess concerning the prevalence and fatality of disease in the Confederate armies have already been noted in connection with the subject of diarrhœa and dysentery.* They consist of the monthly returns of sick and wounded of the Army of the Potomac for the nine months from July, 1861, to March, 1862, the reports of certain general hospitals in Virginia for the four months, September to December, 1862, the original registers of the Chimborazo Hospital, Richmond, Va., extending from October 17, 1861, to March 31, 1865, and the figures published by Dr. JOSEPH JONES, of New Orleans, La., as compiled from the records of the Surgeon General of the Confederate States Army.

The Returns of the Army of the Potomac give 151,237 as the number taken sick and wounded during the nine months in an average strength of 49,394 men. The cases of sickness numbered 148,149, equivalent to three entries per man, 3,019 per thousand, during the nine months, or to four entries per man, 4,025 per thousand, for the year. The United States Army of the Potomac during the same nine months had 2,136 cases per thousand of strength, equivalent to an annual rate of 2,848 cases. The deaths on the Confederate returns number 2,016, but they are given only as the total number that occurred among the sick and wounded; their distribution among the specified diseases and wounds is not known.

The hospital reports show 48,544 admissions, of which 34,890 were for specified diseases; but the deaths, 1,899, are not distributed.

The registers of the Chimborazo Hospital, Richmond, Va.,† which have been carefully examined and freed from duplication of cases originating in transfers from ward to ward, show a total of 77,889 admissions; 14,661 of these are recorded under the headings of Class V of the U. S. sick reports, comprising wounds, accidents and injuries, 12,057 have no entry in the column of diagnosis, 50 are reported as malingerers and 771 as convalescents, without specification of the disease or injury. There remain 50,350 cases of specified sickness, but the result in 26,501 of these cases is unknown, as 14,464 were transferred to other hospitals, 5,537 were furloughed, while in 6,500 no disposition is recorded. Of the cases with known results, 23,849 in number, 19,457 were returned to duty, and to these may be added 998 terminated by desertion; 2,717 died and 677 were discharged. The mortality was therefore 11.39 per cent., equivalent to one death in every 8.8 terminated cases. An abstract of the cases in this hospital is given on the following page.

Some interesting data bearing on the mortality of disease in general, and of some specified diseases, may be gathered from the various publications of Dr. JOSEPH JONES.‡

* Page 26, Part Second of this work.

† Reference was made in a foot-note on page 28 of the Second Part of this work to a partial statement of the statistics of this hospital by Dr. JOSEPH JONES (*Richmond and Louisville Med. Jour.*, June, 1870, p. 650), and reasons were assigned for preferring to them the more complete statistics compiled from the hospital registers. Another partial statement of the statistics of this hospital was published by S. E. HABERSHAM—*Obs. on the statistics of Chimborazo Hospital, with remarks upon the treatment of various diseases during the recent civil war.*—*Nashville Jour. of Med. and Surg.*, N. S., Vol. I, 1866, p. 416—but Dr. HABERSHAM'S table covers only the period from October, 1861, to November, 1863, while the registers include the facts up to March 31, 1865. The former foots up only 36,847 admissions for all diseases, with 2,963 deaths, while the latter give 77,889 cases and 3,944 deaths.

‡ JONES—*Observations on the losses of the Confederate armies from Battle, &c.*—*Richmond and Louisville Med. Jour.*, October and November, 1869, and March and June, 1870. *Essay on the prevalence of Pneumonia and Typhoid Fever in the Confederate forces,* and on *The diseases of the Federal prisoners confined at Andersonville,* published in the *Medical Volume of the Memoirs of the United States Sanitary Commission,* New York, 1867. *Pneumonia in the Confederate Army,* in Vol. I of his *Medical and Surgical Memoirs,* New Orleans, 1876.

Table XII.

An Abstract of the cases of Specified Diseases, with recorded terminations, and of the Deaths among such cases at the Chimborazo Hospital, Richmond, Va.

SPECIFIED DISEASES.	Number of cases with known results.	Deaths among the number of cases with known results.	Percentage of fatal cases.	Deaths per 1,000 deaths from the total of specified disease-causes.
Continued Fevers	2,153	885	41.11	325.7
Malarial Fevers	1,988	125	6.29	46.0
Eruptive Fevers	760	166	21.84	61.1
Diarrhœa and Dysentery	4,644	455	9.80	167.5
Debility and Anæmia	5,780	117	2.02	43.1
Consumption	189	52	27.51	19.1
Rheumatism	1,984	80	4.03	29.4
Scurvy	119	8	6.72	2.9
Bronchitis and Catarrh	1,099	89	8.10	32.8
Pneumonia and Pleurisy	1,568	583	37.18	214.6
Other specified diseases	3,565	157	4.40	57.8
Total specified diseases	23,849	2,717	11.39	1,000

He states that the reports of sick and wounded filed in the Office of the Surgeon General of the C. S. A., exclusive of those from the Trans-Mississippi department, gave the following figures up to December 31, 1862:

	ON FIELD RETURNS.		ON HOSPITAL REPORTS.		TOTAL DEATHS.
	Cases.	Deaths.	Cases.	Deaths.	
All diseases and wounds	848,555	16,220	441,689	19,359	35,579
Gunshot wounds	29,569	1,623	47,724	2,618	4,241
All diseases and wounds except gunshot wounds	818,986	14,597	393,965	16,741	31,338

Dr. Jones has, however, pointed out that, on account of the repeated transfers of patients from one hospital to another, the number of cases shown by the hospital reports as admitted for treatment bears no ascertainable relation to the actual number of patients admitted from the field. This will readily be acknowledged, in view of the fact that while a total of only 108,068 cases were sent from the field to general hospitals, no less than 441,689 cases were reported as admitted on the hospital registers.

But since the system of reports in the Confederate army was similar to that employed in our own service, and since the hospital cases in both services were derived from similar sources, consisting of those from the field, those originating in the hospital population, and an indefinite number from men and commands on detached or special duties, the number of cases borne on the field reports of each service may be compared with the corresponding number of deaths in field and hospital, with the view of contrasting the relative mortality from disease in the two armies. In accordance with Dr. Jones' figures, 31,338* deaths in

---

* These numbers should probably be 31,238 and 819,286; see the totals in Table XIII of the text. Dr. Jones' statistics are full of inaccuracies, the result apparently of careless preparation and proof-reading.

field and hospital corresponded with 818,986 cases of disease and injury other than gunshot wounds. The deaths constituted 3.82 per cent. of the cases, or in other words, were to the cases as 1 : 26. In recasting our statistics* to conform to the classification adopted by Dr. JONES in his statement tabulated above, it is found that from the commencement of the war to December 31, 1862, the total number taken on sick report for all causes except gunshot wounds was 1,709,416 cases, of which 34,326 died, the deaths constituting 2 ver cent. of the cases, or being to them in the proportion of 1 : 50.

The following table contrasts the ratios calculated from Dr. JONES' figures with those obtained from the statistics of our army for the same period:

TABLE XIII.

A Comparison of the Prevalence and Fatality of Disease in the Opposing Armies from the Commencement of the War to December 31, 1862.

	CONFEDERATE FORCES.					U. S. FORCES.				
	Total cases.	Total deaths.	Ratio of cases per 1,000 cases of all diseases.	Ratio of deaths per 1,000 deaths from all diseases.	Percentage of mortality.	Total cases.	Total deaths.	Ratio of cases per 1,000 cases of all diseases.	Ratio of deaths per 1,000 deaths from all diseases.	Percentage of mortality.
Continued Fevers	36,746	12,225	45	391	33.27	51,923	11,571	30	337	22.28
Malarial Fevers	115,415	1,333	141	43	1.15	274,053	2,603	160	76	.95
Eruptive Fevers	44,438	2,274	54	73	5.12	38,888	2,050	23	60	5.27
Diarrhœa and Dysentery	226,828	3,354	277	107	1.48	482,764	6,040	283	176	1.25
Pulmonary affections	42,204	7,972	51	255	18.89	196,567	4,607	115	134	2.34
Rheumatism	29,334	....	36	....	....	88,475	122	52	3	.14
All other diseases	324,321	4,080	396	131	1.26	576,746	7,333	337	214	1.32
Total diseases and injuries exclusive only of gunshot wounds.	819,286	31,238	1,000	1,000	3.81	1,709,416	34,326	1,000	1,000	2.01

It is greatly to be regretted that Dr. JONES has not published the mean strength for the period corresponding to his sick reports. He has given, it is true, the mean strength represented by the field reports of the Confederate Army for each month of 1862 and for the first six months of 1863,† but as no mean strength for 1861 is tabulated, and as there is no way of ascertaining what portion of the figures given in his text belongs to that year and what portion to 1862, it is impossible to compute trustworthy ratios of cases to strength for either year.‡ Nevertheless, by making use of the sick report of the Confederate Army

---

* Published in Tables III, XXIV and XLVII, Part First of this work.　　† *Richmond and Louisville Medical Journal*, Vol. VIII, 1869, p. 351.

‡ Nor can any assistance be obtained in this connection from an interesting article published originally in the *New York Tribune*, and subsequently reprinted in the *Historical Magazine—Muster-rolls of the Confederate Army for 1862, 1863 and 1864. The Historical Magazine and Notes and Queries concerning the Antiquities, History and Biography of America.* Morrisania, New York, Vol. II, N. S., 1867, page 103. Mr. HENRY B. DAWSON, the editor of this magazine, invited the attention of the Surgeon General to the article cited, as likely to prove useful in connection with the data collected by Dr. JONES. Unfortunately the statements in this article referring to the year 1861 are too fragmentary to be used in computing ratios. Indeed they could not be safely so used were they as complete as the figures for 1862, contained in the same article. This will be readily understood on comparing the strengths reported for 1862 with those given by Dr. JONES. Thus, the article in question contains a table purporting to give "approximately and in round numbers the strength and disposition of the different Confederate armies at several important periods during the war." Two of these periods fall within the year 1862. The first, for July 20, 1862, does not include the Trans-Mississippi department, and gives the total strength of the "Armies of East and West" at 289,000 present, of whom 217,000 are reported "for duty." Now the table of Dr. JONES, referred to at the commencement of this note, which also does not include the Trans-Mississippi department, gives the "mean strength, officers and men," for July, 1862, at 79,999. The second period for which the total strength of the "Armies of East and West" are given in the *Historical Magazine* is September, 1862; this includes the Trans-Mississippi department. Deducting the force reported for that department there still remains, according to the magazine article, a force of 228,000 present, of whom 195,000 are reported for duty. But Dr. JONES gives the "mean strength, officers and men," for September, 1862, at 125,408. Nor does this enormous discrepancy indicate any unfaithfulness on the part of either authority. The magazine writer attempted to give a correct notion of the whole Confederate force; Dr. JONES necessarily intended only to give the actual mean strength of that part of the Confederate force represented by the sick reports to which he had access. Ratios computed from the cases and deaths derived from the latter, and the strengths derived from the former source, would understate the sickness and mortality of the Confederate armies to an indefinite extent.

of the Potomac, preserved by Dr. WILLIAMS, and of certain figures published by Dr. JONES,* it is possible to calculate sick rates for a part of the Confederate forces during certain periods prior to July, 1863, the aggregate monthly strength represented being 123,257 men. In Table XIV the information gathered concerning these forces is presented and calculated into ratios per thousand strength, which are placed for comparison in juxtaposition with the rates furnished by the white troops of the United States Army during the year 1863.

TABLE XIV.

Cases of Sickness and Wounds reported from certain of the Confederate Armies during portions of the years 1861, 1862 and 1863, with the strength present during the periods covered by the statistics, and the calculated annual rates per thousand of strength, in juxtaposition with the corresponding rates of the United States Army for the year ending June 30, 1863.

	Army of the Potomac, July, 1861, to March, 1862.	Department of South Carolina, Georgia and Florida, January, 1862, to July, 1863.	Confederate forces at Mobile, Ala., January, 1862, to July, 1863.	Department of Tennessee, June, 1862, to May, 1863.	Army of the Valley of Virginia, January, 1862, to October, 1862.	Aggregate.	ANNUAL RATES PER THOUSAND OF MEAN AGGREGATE STRENGTH. Confederate Army.	ANNUAL RATES PER THOUSAND OF MEAN AGGREGATE STRENGTH. U. S. Army.
Number of months	9	19	19	12	10	....		
Average monthly strength	49,394	25,732	6,752	40,282	15,582	123,257		
Cases of disease and wounds	151,237	157,113	58,453	226,721	53,198	646,722	4,563	2,861
Gunshot wounds	....	....	....	....	....	....	159(a)	93
Cases of disease	....	....	....	....	....	....	4,404	2,768
Continued Fevers	10,197				....	10,197	275	125(b)
Malarial Fevers	16,781	41,526	13,940	36,665	3,876	112,788	796	460
Diarrhœa and Dysentery	36,572					....	987	543(b)
Pneumonia	3,233	2,220	1,161	6,974	1,034	14,622	103	34
Pleurisy	734	445	135	1,158	211	2,683	19	17
Laryngitis	231	373	45	221	101	971	7	10
Phthisis	315	184	191	902	85	1,677	12	9
Tonsillitis	1,312	1,428	408	858	514	4,520	32	30
Acute Bronchitis and Catarrh, including cases reported as epidemic	19,455	18,862	3,500	11,575	5,408	58,800	415	192
Chronic Bronchitis	....	373	176	855	235	1,639	16	16
Asthma	....	251	111	290	36	688	7	6
Acute Rheumatism	....	1,953	1,189	4,732	1,518	9,392	90	76
Chronic Rheumatism	....	2,047	854	5,195	1,040	9,136	87	76

(a) See the text for the derivation of this rate.

(b) To effect an allowable comparison between the Union and Confederate figures indicating prevalence, this annual rate is based on the reports of the Union Army of the Potomac for the nine months, July, 1861, to March, 1862, inclusive.

The imperfection of the data here presented is obvious; only in the figures of the Confederate Army of the Potomac are the cases of disease separated from those of wounds received in battle. But as the gunshot casualties in this army during the nine months covered by the records do not fairly represent the frequency of these injuries, the rate derived from them cannot with propriety be applied to the consolidated figures from the

* See pages 571–589 of the *Medical Volume of the U. S. Sanitary Commission Memoirs*, New York, 1867.

other departments.   Fortunately, Dr. JONES has put on record figures which show the relation of gunshot wounds to cases of disease in the greater part of the Confederate forces during the first year and a half of the war.   The total number of cases of wounds and disease reported by him was 848,555, of gunshot wounds 29,569.   These figures authorize the statement that the tabulated annual rate of disease and wounds, 4,563 per thousand strength, included about 159 injuries received in battle.   The annual rate for disease alone is thus seen to have been 4,404, which may be compared with the corresponding rate of 2,768 among the Union forces.   Continued and malarial fevers, diarrhœa and dysentery, bronchitis and pneumonia, were apparently the chief causes of the increased rate among the southern troops.   An expression of the mortality rate per thousand of strength cannot be directly obtained from the data presented.   But since the sick rate has been found to number 4,404 cases annually per thousand of strength, while the fatality rate was 3.8 per cent., the annual number of deaths per thousand strength must have been 167.3, a rate larger even than the average annual mortality among our colored troops.   Exception may be taken to this calculation as the sick and fatality rates used are derived from different sources, but it serves to indicate in a general way the greater relative mortality among the smaller number of combatants on the southern side.

In brief, so far as comparison can be made with the statistics at command, disease was not only more fatal among the Confederate forces, but the number of cases in proportion to the strength present was considerably greater among them than among the United States troops.

III.—PREVALENCE AND MORTALITY OF DISEASE AMONG THE UNION TROOPS IN CONFEDERATE PRISONS.

The fragmentary character of the evidence relating to the diseases of the Federal prisoners in the hands of the Confederates has already been indicated.*   The statistics at command are derived from the original registers of the hospitals attached to the Andersonville and Danville prisons and certain tables prepared by Dr. JOSEPH JONES from official records, and published in his article on the diseases of the Andersonville prisoners.†   The records of the Adjutant General's Office, U. S. Army, according to a communication from that office dated June 22, 1878, include the cases of 30,564 Federal soldiers who died while prisoners of war.

The Andersonville register, extending from February 24, 1864, to April 17, 1865, inclusive, shows the number of admissions from the stockaded prison to have been 17,875, but as 458 of these are reported as having been cases of wounds and injuries, and 1,430 have no diagnosis entered against their names, the cases of specified diseases number only 15,987.   The result in 946 of these cases is not recorded, so that the number of cases of specified disease that may be traced to their termination is reduced to 15,041.   Of these 11,086 died, or 73.7 per cent. of the whole number.   This enormous mortality is an index

---

* See page 31, Second Part of this work.
† There are also in the Office of the Adjutant General a list of 142 deaths that occurred among sick and wounded prisoners at Cahawba, Ala., and two hospital registers, one from Hospital No. 13, and the other from a ward of Hospital No. 21, Richmond, Va. But these registers are valueless for statistical purposes, as so many of the patients received were speedily sent elsewhere; and in the case of the register of Hospital No. 21, the disposition of so many of the cases is unrecorded. The register of Hospital No. 13 extends from June 2, 1863, to February 14, 1865, and contains a record of 695 admissions disposed of by transfer in 621 cases, by death in 67, and by desertion, etc., in 7 cases. The register of Hospital 21 extends from November, 1863, to February, 1865. Of 1,358 admissions it is not stated what became of the patients in 508 instances: 230 were transferred, 226 paroled, 173 returned to quarters and 3 detailed; one is said to have escaped and 217 to have died.

of the condition to which the unfortunate men became reduced before they were admitted to this so called hospital. The professional mind is shocked in endeavoring to realize the scenes presented in an establishment the wards of which formed the portals of the grave to three out of every four soldiers who had the misfortune to enter them. Indeed, it appears that large numbers died uncared for in the prison and were removed to hospital simply for record and interment. Sometimes the deaths in the prison outnumbered those in the hospital. The reports for the week ending September 20, 1864, show the occurrence of 336 deaths in the former and 334 in the latter establishment. At this particular time one-half of the fatal cases were already terminated when taken up on the hospital register. The average number of deaths that occurred daily during the occupation of the depot was thirty; but as many as a hundred deaths were recorded in a single day. Certainly the most fatal field of the war was that enclosed within the stockade at Andersonville, Georgia.

Ratios calculated from the hospital register have a melancholy interest as indicating the manner in which these men were cut down in the flower of their manhood. They have no bearing on the fatality of the specified diseases as the number of those sick within the stockade is not known; but the information yielded concerning the relative prevalence of certain grave diseases is as definite as if complete records of the sickness were at command. The accompanying table gives a summary of the facts gathered from the register:

TABLE XV.

Summarizing the Records of the Hospital at Camp Sumter, Andersonville, Georgia.

	Cases admitted into hospital.	Cases with results unrecorded.	Total cases with recorded results.	Died.	Ratio of cases per 1,000 cases admitted with specified diseases.	Ratio of deaths per 1,000 deaths from specified diseases.	Percentage of fatal cases.
All diseases and injuries	17,875	1,001	16,874	12,541	....	....	....
Wounds and injuries	458	47	411	163	....	....	....
Not specified	1,430	8	1,422	1,292	....	....	....
Specified diseases	15,987	946	15,041	11,086	1,000	1,000	73.7
Continued Fevers	283	2	281	241	17.7	21.7	85.8
Malarial Fevers	254	13	241	163	15.9	14.7	67.6
Eruptive Fevers	164	2	162	82	10.3	7.4	50.6
Diarrhœa and Dysentery	7,352	376	6,976	5,605	459.9	505.6	80.3
Debility	333	36	297	192	20.8	17.3	64.6
Dropsy	498	19	479	383	31.2	34.5	80.0
Consumption	35	....	35	26	2.2	2.3	74.3
Rheumatism	202	30	172	83	12.6	7.5	48.2
Scurvy	5,662	377	5,285	3,614	354.2	326.0	68.4
Bronchitis	205	4	201	141	12.8	12.7	70.1
Pneumonia and Pleurisy	553	64	489	322	34.6	29.0	65.8
Other diseases	446	23	423	234	27.9	21.0	55.3
Total specified diseases	15,987	946	15,041	11,086	1,000	1,000	73.7

Diarrhœa and dysentery caused somewhat less than one-half, and scurvy somewhat more than one-third of the total number of cases. Under these two headings were entered

814.1 of every thousand cases, leaving only 185.9 cases in the thousand for distribution among all other diseases. These cases also occasioned the greater part of the mortality. Diarrhœa and dysentery caused 505.6 and scurvy 326.0 deaths in every thousand deaths from all diseases, leaving only 168.4 in the thousand for distribution among other fatal diseases.

Dr. JONES has fortunately preserved a monthly return of the cases and deaths in the stockade and hospital for the six months from March 1 to August 31, 1864, giving also the mean monthly strength during the period.* From this paper annual rates of sickness and mortality per thousand of strength may be calculated. Some idea of the relative prevalence of specified diseases and of the mortality caused by them may likewise be obtained from the information thus preserved. In the following table the facts gathered from the paper in question are so arranged as to admit of comparison with the analogous facts from the records of our troops in the field, the Confederate forces and other bodies of men already submitted in Tables II, III, IV, XIII and XIV.

TABLE XVI.

Giving a general view of the Sick and Death Rates from prominent diseases and classes of diseases among the Federal prisoners at Andersonville for the period extending from March 1 to August 31, 1864. Average present 19,453 prisoners.

	Total cases recorded.	Total deaths recorded.	Annual rates of cases per 1,000 strength.	Annual rates of deaths per 1,000 strength.	Cases of specified diseases per 1,000 of all diseases.	Deaths from specified diseases per 1,000 deaths from all diseases.	Percentage of fatal cases.
All diseases and injuries	42,686	7,712	4,388.6	792.8			
Wounds and injuries	238	21	24.4	2.2			
Not specified	474	565	48.8	58.0			
Specified diseases	41,974	7,126	4,315.4	732.6	1,000	1,000	17.2
Continued Fevers	753	199	77.4	20.5	17.9	27.9	26.4
Malarial Fevers	2,966	119	305.0	12.2	70.7	16.7	4.0
Eruptive Fevers	236	80	24.2	8.2	5.6	11.2	33.9
Diarrhœa and Dysentery	16,772	4,529	1,724.4	465.6	399.6	635.6	27.0
Debility	955	170	98.2	17.5	22.8	23.9	17.8
Dropsy	1,556	319	160.0	32.8	37.1	44.8	20.5
Consumption	114	33	11.8	3.4	2.7	4.6	28.9
Rheumatism	866	20	89.0	2.0	20.6	2.8	2.3
Scurvy	9,501	999	976.8	102.8	226.4	140.2	10.5
Bronchitis	2,808	90	288.6	9.2	66.9	12.6	3.2
Pneumonia and Pleurisy	979	266	100.6	27.4	23.3	37.3	27.2
Other diseases	4,468	302	459.4	31.0	106.4	42.4	6.8
Total specified diseases	41,974	7,126	4,315.4	732.6	1,000	1,000	17.2

The annual sick rate per thousand of prisoners was 4,388.6, or nearly double that of our white troops. Nevertheless, it was not so high as the rate which, according to Table

* *Memoirs of United States Sanitary Commission*, p. 524. Dr. JONES, *op. cit.*, p. 567, specifies the strength for each of the six months and gives the average strength as 21,120 men. There is an error either in the items or in the calculated average. But as the items are expressed by the same numbers in another part of his article, p. 502, it seems probable that the error is in the calculation, the correct strength for the six months being 19,453.

XIV, prevailed in certain portions of the Confederate forces. This demonstrates merely that the methods adopted in reporting sick men in the Confederate ranks was not observed in the case of the Andersonville prisoners. The number of sick was certainly vastly in excess of the number of recorded cases. When Dr. JONES inspected the stockade in September, 1864, he found two thousand sick exclusive of those admitted into the prison hospital, and as there was but one medical officer to attend to this enormous number of patients,* and to the cases brought daily to his notice among the mass of the prisoners, the impossibility of preserving an accurate record of the cases is manifest. Large numbers of the prisoners who had never been entered on the sick list were suffering from severe and incurable diarrhœa, dysentery and scurvy. Slighter ailments, such as dictated the relief of a soldier on active service from military duty and his entry on sick report, were of necessity unnoticed. Hence the annual ratio of sick per thousand persons present, and the ratio of deaths to cases, as represented in the table, are certainly far from accurate, and are not admissible for comparison with the records of the Confederate troops on active service. Nevertheless Dr. JONES instituted the comparison and concluded that the diseases referable to exposure without proper clothing and shelter were as prevalent among the Confederate troops as among the Federal prisoners. The following by Dr. J. C. BATES, who was on duty at the prison hospital from April 22, 1864, to March 26, 1865, is of interest in this connection:

"I regret to say that the supply of wood was not sufficient to keep the prisoners from what we term freezing to death. They would not, perhaps, actually freeze to death, but a patient whose blood is thin, and his system worn down, is very susceptible to the influence of cold. In the absence of sufficient food, sufficient stimulus, and especially in the absence of fuel, many of the patients (I speak now of what I saw in my own ward) would, during the night, become so chilled that in the morning, passing round, I would remark to my steward, 'Last night did the work for that poor fellow—he will die;' or 'This one will die; I cannot resuscitate him with the means in my hands, his system is so reduced.' Lying upon the ground during those chilly nights (the weather was not freezing, but sufficient to thoroughly chill the whole system), the patient would reach a condition in which resuscitation was a matter of impossibility after he commenced going down hill from this exposure. I have seen a number die in that way."— *Report on the Treatment of Prisoners of War by the Rebel Authorities, 2d Sess., 40th Cong., p. 118.*

The figures expressing the relations of individual diseases to the total cases of specified diseases are modified by the exclusion of the many cases of slight ailments which were unnoted, and by the errors in diagnosis consequent on the disposition of so many cases by one medical officer. On September 18, 1864, 906 new cases were reported as taken on sick report; but as none were so reported on the two following days, it may be assumed that these three days were spent in the transfer of the men in question to the sick report. Ten hours daily of uninterrupted labor on the part of the medical officer would have afforded about two minutes for the diagnosis and treatment of each case; but this officer was not at liberty to allow so much time to the new cases, for the 1,102 cases carried forward from the previous day claimed some share of his attention. Naturally, under such conditions, the diagnosis and management of a majority of the cases devolved upon the intelligence of the probably unskilled men who, having given their parole, were granted the freedom of the post and filled subordinate offices in its domestic economy.

Overlooking the influence of inaccurate diagnosis, the annual death rate tabulated may be accepted as a close approximation to the actual mortality. In this consists the chief value of the extracts made by Dr. JONES from the records. During the six months 7,712 deaths occurred in the average strength of 19,453 prisoners present, equaling an

---

* "At this time only one medical officer was in attendance, whereas at least twenty medical officers should have been employed."—JONES, *op. cit.*, p. 512.

annual rate of 792.8 per thousand, or the extinction of the whole 19,453 in about fifteen months. By comparing those columns of Tables XV and XVI which give expression to the total number of deaths, it will be found that the mortality was much greater during the first six months than during the last eight months, 7,712 deaths having been recorded during the former period, which number was increased to but 12,541 by the addition of those that occurred later. This might indicate that disease became less prevalent or less fatal as time progressed, or that the number of men in confinement became considerably reduced. In the absence of a knowledge of the strength present this point cannot be settled; but it is of interest to observe that while the greater number of the specified diseases participated in this diminished mortality there was one very marked exception. Thus: deaths from continued fevers, numbering 199 in the first six months, became increased to 241 during the whole period, an addition of only 42 fatal cases for the last eight months. Malarial fevers, numbering 119, became correspondingly increased by 44. Only 2 deaths from the eruptive fevers occurred in the last eight months, as against 80 in the earlier period. Diarrhœa and dysentery ended fatally in 4,529 cases during the first six months, and in 5,605 cases during the whole period, an addition of only 1,076 deaths for the last eight months. And so of most of the diseases specified. But scurvy, which occasioned 999 deaths in the first period, had by the end of the second period increased the number of its victims to 3,614 by an addition of 2,613 cases.

The aggravation of the scorbutic element, as time progressed, is manifested by these figures. Of the 7,712 deaths that took place in the first period, diarrhœa and dysentery caused 4,529, or 636 of every thousand, and scurvy 999, or 140 of every thousand. Of the 4,829 deaths that occurred during the second period, diarrhœa and dysentery caused 1,076, or 223 in every thousand, while scurvy caused 2,613, or 541 in every thousand. At first more than one-half of the victims fell before the causes of diarrhœa and dysentery, but later scurvy assumed the role of chief executioner. Together they occasioned more than three-fourths of the total mortality.

Dr. JONES says: The effect of scurvy was manifest on every hand, and in all its various stages, from the muddy pale complexion, pale gums, feeble, languid, muscular motions, lowness of spirits, and fetid breath, to the dusky, dirty, leaden complexion, swollen features, spongy, purple, livid, fungoid, bleeding gums, loose teeth, œdematous limbs, covered with livid vibices and petechiæ, spasmodically flexed, painful and hardened extremities, spontaneous hæmorrhages from mucous canals, and large, ill-conditioned, spreading ulcers covered with a dark purplish fungous growth.

In some of the cases of scurvy the parotid glands were greatly swollen, and in some instances to such an extent as to preclude entirely the power of articulation. In several cases of dropsy of the abdomen and lower extremities supervening upon scurvy, the patients affirmed that previous to the appearance of the dropsy they had suffered with profuse and obstinate diarrhœa; and that when this was checked by a change of diet from Indian-corn bread, cooked with the husk, to rice, the dropsy appeared. The severe pains and livid patches were frequently associated with swellings in various parts, and especially in the lower extremities, accompanied with stiffness and contractions of the knee-joints and ankles, and often with a brawny feel of the parts, as if lymph had been effused between the integuments and aponeurosis, preventing the motion of the skin over the swollen parts. * * *

The scorbutic ulcers presented a dark, purple, fungoid, elevated surface, with livid, swollen edges, and exuded a thin, fetid, sanious fluid instead of pus. Many ulcers which originated from the scorbutic condition of the system appeared to become truly gangrenous, assuming all the characteristics of hospital gangrene.

From the crowded condition, filthy habits, bad diet, dejected and depressed condition of the prisoners, their systems had become so disordered that the smallest abrasion of the skin, from the rubbing of a shoe, or from the effects of the hot sun, or from the prick of a splinter, or from scratching a mosquito's bite, in some cases took on a rapid and frightful ulceration and gangrene.

Dr. JONES was surprised at the comparative absence of typhoid and typhus fevers, notwithstanding the prevalence of the conditions that are supposed to produce them, and attributes this to the immunity derived from a previous attack, or to an insusceptibility resulting from continued exposure. According to the records continued fevers constituted only 17.9 of every thousand cases. They were thus comparatively rare, but this arose from the increased prevalence of diarrhœal and scorbutic cases rather than from the actual infrequency of typhoid. An annual rate of 77.4 cases of the continued fevers per thousand of strength was recorded; and, as has been already shown, the figures representing the prevalence of disease within the stockade greatly understate the facts. This rate is considerably higher than the average annual rate among our white or colored troops; although, as might be expected, it falls below that shown on Table XIV, as prevailing in the camps of the Federal and Confederate Armies of the Potomac when typhoid was epidemic in many of the new regiments. Continued fevers caused 26.4 deaths annually in every thousand prisoners, as compared with 11.6 deaths among our white troops.

Malarial fevers were infrequent among the prisoners; but as their percentage of fatal cases was much larger than among the United States or Confederate troops, 4 per cent. as against 1.15 and .95 respectively,* it is probable that numbers of intermittent and remittent attacks were not recorded.†

The other diseases specified were presumably of more common occurrence among the prisoners than among our troops in active service; certainly they were more fatal.

Bronchitis, which in the field gave an annual death rate of .49 per thousand of strength, caused a rate of 9.2 among the prisoners, while the corresponding rates for inflammation of the lungs and pleura were 6.3 and 27.4.

This extensive prevalence and terrible fatality of disease among the Andersonville prisoners creates no surprise when the unsanitary conditions affecting them are taken into consideration. These were officially investigated by Dr. JONES, and are fully developed in the report of the Committee of the House of Representatives on the treatment of prisoners of war by the rebel authorities during the War of the Rebellion.‡

The Andersonville stockade and prison hospital were established on a naturally healthy site in the highlands of Sumter County, Ga. The former enclosed twenty-seven acres, consisting of the northern and southern exposures of two rising grounds, between which lay some swampy bottom and a stream running from west to east. In August, 1864, nearly 33,000 prisoners were crowded together on this area, which afforded but little more than 35 square feet for each. But even this limited space was not wholly available, as six acres of the bottom land had by this time become unfit for occupation. Each prisoner had therefore scarcely 28 square feet of surface on which to conduct all the operations of nature. The Confederate guard occupied the fortified exterior of the stockade.

No shelter from the sun, wind or rain, the dews of night or the frosts of winter, was furnished by the Confederate government. Fresh arrivals of prisoners were driven into the stockade and left to find so many feet of foul surface for their occupancy among the army of ragged, vermin-covered, emaciated and dying men already there. The pines and other small trees that had originally sparsely covered the enclosure had been cut down. Fragments of tent-canvas, blankets, oil-cloth and clothing were stretched upon sticks as a protection from the hot sun. Some of the men burrowed in the ground and others built huts of the mud removed from these burrows.

The sinks were built over the lower portion of the stream, but the volume and flow of the water was insufficient to carry off the excreta. Heavy rainfalls causing the stream to

---

*See Table XIII *supra* p. 31.   †See *infra*, note *, page 109.
‡*Report No. 45, House of Representatives, 3d Sess., 40th Congress*, Government Printing Office, Washington, D. C., 1869.

overflow spread the foul accumulations over the adjoining bottom lands, converting them into a quagmire of fermenting filth the stench from which has been represented as horrible, sickening and indescribable. Speaking of the stream as it issued from the stockade, JONES says:

As these waters, loaded with filth and human excrement, flow sluggishly through the swamp below, filled with trees and reeds coated with a filthy deposit, they emit an intolerable and most sickening stench. Standing as I did over these waters in the middle of a hot day in September, as they rolled sluggishly forth from the stockade, after having received the filth and excrement of twenty thousand men, the stench was disgusting and overpowering; and if it was surpassed in unpleasantness by anything, it was only in the disgusting appearance of the filthy, almost stagnant, waters moving slowly between the stumps and roots and fallen trunks of trees and thick branches of reeds, with innumerable long-tailed, large white maggots, swollen peas, and fermenting excrement, and fragments of bread and meat.

But the pollution of the soil was not confined to the bottom-lands. Many of the men were so prostrated by diarrhœa and scurvy that they were unable to reach the low-grounds on every call of nature, and the general surface of the enclosure became covered with their morbid dejections. The ground was honey-combed with small pits a foot or two in depth, which were used as latrines and emitted an intolerable stench. Later, the tattered clothes of these men became the receptacle for their involuntary discharges; and ultimately the foul and wasted forms were carried out for burial. In the vicious atmosphere of this prison-pen myriads of flies and mosquitoes were developed, which would have made life a misery even to healthy men.

There is one form of disease which is almost too horrible to be witnessed, yet we cannot understand the wretchedness of the prison without looking upon it. This is not a solitary case, but we shall find numerous ones before we leave this living charnel-house. We instinctively pause as we reach the awful sight before us, holding our breath lest we inhale the terrible stench that arises from it. Here is a living being who has become so exhausted from exposure that he is unable to rise from the ground, suffering from diarrhœa in its last form. He is covered with his own fæces; the vermin crawl and riot upon his flesh, tumbling undisturbed into his eyes and ears and open mouth; the worms are feeding beneath his skin, burying themselves where his limbs, swollen with scurvy, have burst open in running sores; they have even found their way into his intestines and form a living, writhing mass within him. His case has been represented to the surgeons, but they have pronounced him incurable, and he is left here in his misery, in which he will linger for three or four days more.*

But all the sick in the stockade were not left thus to die when their strength had failed them. The 1,292 fatal cases in which no diagnosis was made may be supposed to represent those exceptional cases in which the medical officers on duty became first aware of the sickness by a knowledge of the death. It will be observed that such exceptions constituted one-tenth of the total mortality.†

In fact, an effort was made to aggregate the sick of the stockade, nearly 2,000 in number at the period of JONES' visit, in four long sheds open on all sides and situated at the north end of the enclosure. Here the haggard, helpless, hopeless miserables lay side by side on the boards or upon such ragged and vermin-covered blankets as they possessed, without bedding—without even straw—while foul emanations and swarms of flies constituted their atmosphere.

The Confederate Congress in May, 1861, passed a bill providing that the rations furnished to prisoners of war should be the same in quantity and quality as those issued to the enlisted men in the Army of the Confederacy. The daily ration per man officially consisted of one pound of beef or three-quarters of a pound of bacon, and one and one-

* Op. cit., last note, page 40.
† It appears that Andersonville, Ga., was not the only prison in which the sick were left to die in quarters without the care or knowledge of the surgeon. A letter to this office from the Adjutant General's Office, dated June 22, 1878, states that for the month of December, 1864, alone, the Confederate "burial report" at Salisbury, N. C., shows that out of 1,115 deaths, 223 or 20 per cent. died in prison quarters and were not accounted for in the report of the surgeon.

quarter pounds of corn-meal, with an occasional issue of beans, rice, molasses and vinegar. Although this may have been the issue at first, there is no doubt that it was diminished at a later period. Isaiah H. White, chief surgeon of the prison, in a report dated August 6, 1864, speaks thus of the diet of the prisoners:

> The ration consists of one-third pound of bacon and one and a quarter pounds of meal. The meal is unbolted, and when baked the bread is coarse and irritating, producing diseases of the organs of the digestive system [diarrhœa and dysentery]. The absence of vegetable diet has produced scurvy to an alarming extent, especially among the old prisoners.

It is also well established that this miserable diet was generally not only of an inferior but of a dangerous quality. The beef was often tainted, the bacon decomposing, and the meal musty, innutritious and irritant, the cob having been ground up with the grains. Moreover, the ration was frequently issued to the prisoners imperfectly cooked. Nearly three months after the establishment of the prison the surgeon in charge reported to the commanding officer that—

> The bakery and other culinary arrangements have just been completed, up to which time there had been an inadequate supply of cooking utensils, and in consequence thereof the articles of diet have been insufficiently cooked.

Frequently the food was issued in the raw state. Those of the prisoners who had the strength and energy to cook their allowance, lacked the necessary fuel and kitchen utensils, while many were incapable of the effort had all the facilities been afforded. The issue had, therefore, to be devoured in this condition, if the pangs of hunger were acute and the individual had not as yet reached the stage of apathy that preceded death. Many also were incapable of eating the ration even if properly cooked, on account of the condition of their teeth and gums. Lieutenant-Colonel D. T. Chandler, Assistant Adjutant and Inspector General, in his report of an inspection of the prison on August 5, 1864, says of the rations and their preparation:

> The sanitary condition of the prisoners is as wretched as can be, the principal cause of mortality being scurvy and chronic diarrhœa, the percentage of the former being disproportionately large among those brought from Belle Isle. Nothing seems to have been done, and but little if any effort made, to arrest it by procuring proper food. The ration is ⅓ pound of bacon and 1¼ pounds of unbolted corn-meal, with beef at rare intervals, and occasionally rice. When to be obtained—very seldom—a small quantity of molasses is substituted for the meat ration. A little weak vinegar, unfit for use, has sometimes been issued. The arrangements for cooking and baking have been wholly inadequate, and though additions are now being completed, it will still be impossible to cook for the whole number of prisoners. Raw rations have to be issued to a very large proportion, who are entirely unprovided with proper utensils, and furnished so limited a supply of fuel they are compelled to dig with their hands in the filthy marsh before mentioned for roots, &c.

But as this monotonous diet, inferior in quality, insufficient in quantity, and having its intrinsic harmful properties aggravated by the absence of facilities for its proper preparation was undoubtedly the cause of the diarrhœa, scurvy and starvation, which killed three-fourths of the prisoners who were buried at Andersonville, and contributed largely to the fatal event in the remainder of the cases, all details concerning it have a high etiological value. The following is therefore submitted from the Report of the Committee of the House of Representatives, already cited:

> The rations consisted of corn-meal, bacon, fresh beef, peas, rice, salt and sorghum molasses. The corn-meal was unbolted, some of it ground with the cob, and often filled with sand and gravel. Much of it had apparently been put up while warm, and had become sour and musty either during transportation or while in store. The bacon was lean, yellow, very salt and maggoty; it had been brought to us unpacked, and was covered with dirt and cinders; it was so soft with rust that it could easily be pulled in pieces with the fingers. The beef was slaughtered near the prison, to which it was brought and thrown down in a pile in the north cook-house, where it lay until it was issued to the prisoners. Here, in the hot climate, it was soon infested with flies and maggots, and rapidly changed into a greenish color, emitting an offensive odor peculiar to decaying flesh; it was very lean, but the heat

rendered it quite tender before it was served up. The article denominated black peas, or cow-peas, was brought in sacks, apparently just as it had left the threshing ground of the producer, having never been winnowed or cleansed of the fine pods or dirt which naturally mingles with all leguminous plants while growing in the field; besides, they were filled with bugs, and many of them were so eaten as to leave nothing but the thick, tough skin of the pea in its natural shape. The rice was sour or musty, and had apparently been put up in a half-dried state, when it became heated and wholly unfitted for use.

There were two cook-houses used in connection with the prison. The first of these was in process of erection when the detachment to which I belonged entered the pen, and went into operation about the middle of May. It was located on the north side of and near the swamp west of the prison, and was subsequently enclosed by the defensive stockades. At the time it was built it was supposed to be of sufficient capacity to perform all the cooking necessary for the prisoners, and contained three large brick ovens, and several kettles set in brick-work, for boiling the meat and peas or rice; but it being found inadequate to supply the wants of the men, another building was constructed some time in the latter part of August. It was located about a hundred yards north of the defences, on a line with the west wall of the prison. This was designed and used exclusively for boiling the peas and the meat, and contained perhaps a dozen large potash kettles set in brick-work. The old cook-house was thereafter used for baking the corn-meal. A strong force of paroled prisoners was appointed to perform the work in these cook-houses, but with constant labor was unable to supply our wants, and about one-half of the rations were issued raw.

The meal was prepared for baking by first pouring it in quantity into a large trough made for the purpose. A little salt was then added, when water enough was poured in to make it of the proper consistency, and the whole stirred with sticks to mix it thoroughly. The dough was baked in sheet-iron pans twenty-four by sixteen inches in surface and two and one-half inches deep. The whole was divided into pones containing about a pound, and each of these pones constituted a day's ration of bread for one man. The utmost cleanliness could not be observed in mixing this "stuff;" the meal, as above stated, was partly corn and partly cob, and often contained materials that were neither of these; the water was dipped in quantity from the creek, and no means of cleansing it were furnished; and these, with the haste necessary to be made in preparing the dough, conspired to make the mixture unpalatable and sickening, particularly when cold. The prisoners who had charge of the cook-house undoubtedly tried to prepare the food as well as they could, but all of their efforts were in vain with such limited facilities as they had.

The peas and rice were boiled in the north cook-house; they were turned from the bags as they were brought to the prison, without cleansing or separating from the chaff and dirt, into the large potash kettles containing the water in which the meat had been boiled; the cooks here, as in the south cook-house, had no means of cleansing the raw material, and had they possessed the facilities they had no time to devote to the purpose. To winnow, semi-weekly, a sufficient amount of peas for 16,000 rations, allowing a third of a pint to each, requires a long time even with the aid of the best machines; but for twenty men to pick over by hand this vast amount is simply impossible. Of these cooked rations there were daily issued to each prisoner about a pound of bread, a fourth of a pound of bacon, or four or six ounces of beef (including the bone) in place of the bacon, and a teaspoonful of salt; twice a week a pint of peas or rice were issued in addition, and occasionally a couple of tablespoonfuls of sorghum molasses. Sometimes a sort of mush was made to take the place of the pone, but, although it was a change from the monotonous corn-bread, it was so unpalatable that the bread was preferred. About half of the rations were issued raw; * * * one-half of the prisoners receiving raw food one day and cooked the next. I have here given the quantity issued during the early part of the season; but as the hot weather advanced and the number confined here increased, the daily allowance diminished until it became but a mere morsel to each man. * * * * *

Some time in the afternoon the ration-wagon drove into the stockade laden with corn-meal, bacon and salt, which were thrown down into a heap in an open space about midway the enclosure. It was a horrible sight to witness the haggard crowd gathered about this precious pile, while the commissary superintended its division among the squad sergeants; gazing, meanwhile, with wolfish eyes upon the little heap as it diminished, or following their sergeant-commissary back to his quarters, as famished swine follow clamorously the footsteps of their master as he carries their food to the accustomed trough. The rations were distributed by the division-sergeant to the mess-sergeant, who then divided them among the men. To avoid quarrelling during the last distribution, it was the custom among all the messes for the mess-sergeant to separate the rations into as many small parcels as there were men in the mess; one man of the mess was placed a short distance off, with his back towards the parcels, in such a position that he could not see them; the mess-sergeant then pointed to one, with the words, "Who has this?" to which the man replied announcing the name of the recipient, when it was given to him. In this manner the whole number was gone through with, with satisfaction to all.

Iron bake-pans, like those used by the Confederate soldiers, had been issued to the prisoners who first arrived at this place, in which to bake their own meal and fry their bacon; but nothing of the kind was ever given out afterwards, to my knowledge. The United States soldiers, as is well known, were never provided with other cooking utensils than mess-kettles and mess-pans, both too large to be transported in any other way than upon army wagons. At the time of our capture, in numerous instances, the tin cups and plates which we had were taken from us; our knives, it will be remembered, were confiscated at Danville; nothing, therefore, was left in our possession with which to cook our raw food after it was given us. How to accomplish this necessary feat was a grave question. We made shift, however, with chips, half canteens, tin cups that had escaped confiscation, and pieces of sheet-iron, to bake one side of the stuff, while the other was scarcely warmed through. The solder of the tin, melting and mingling with the bread, added another to our almost innumerable hardships. But with all our care and labor, the rations were at last devoured in a half-cooked state—a fact which aided in the increase of the frightful misery that subsequently occurred, quite as much as the small quantity that was issued.

The prison hospital covered about five acres of ground. It was established in a grove of forest trees which afforded a grateful shade to the unhappy and suffering men. Its atmosphere was polluted by the foul effluvia from the stockade; but irrespective of this, its own emanations rendered it as unfit for occupation as was the general pen. The men were crowded together in old and ragged tents; neither beds nor straw were furnished, and the patients lay in bunks or on the ground, often without even a blanket over them. Sick men, unable to visit the latrines, made use of small wooden boxes in the lanes behind the tents.

Millions of flies swarmed over everything and covered the faces of the sleeping patients, and crawled down their open mouths, and deposited their maggots in the gangrenous wounds of the living and in the mouths of the dead. Myriads of mosquitoes also infested the tents, and many of the patients were so stung by these pestiferous insects that they appeared as if they were suffering from a slight attack of measles.   *   *   *   *   *

The cooking arrangements were of the most miserable and defective character. Two large iron pots similar to those used for boiling sugar-cane were the only cooking utensils furnished by the hospital for the cooking of near two thousand men; and the patients were dependent in great measure upon their own miserable utensils. They were allowed to cook in the tent-doors and in the lanes, and this was another source of filth and another favorable condition for the generation of flies and other vermin.*

The rations of the hospital appear to have differed from those of the stockade only in having an occasional addition of potatoes. Indeed, it would seem that but for the shelter of the ragged tents, the shade of the trees and the increased area, the hospital patient had little advantage over the prisoner in the stockade. The supply of medicines was generally deficient, often exhausted, and medical comforts were unknown.

At the time of Dr. JONES' visit one medical officer attended to the sick in the stockade while three were on hospital duty. Generally, however, the medical staff consisted of six or eight for the prison and four or five for the hospital. These officers labored faithfully to alleviate the misery and suffering by which they were surrounded, but unfortunately they were powerless to effect a change in the methods of the establishment.

Day after day, for weeks and months, those surgeons labored, breathing the unwholesome air, and in constant contact with those horrible diseases; but they were patient, faithful men, and their sympathy with the victims often benefited them as much as the medicines they prescribed.   *   *   *   I gladly record the little acts of kindness performed by them, for they were verdant spots in that vast Sahara of misery. DRS. WATKINS, ROWZIE, THORNBURN, REEVES, WILLIAMS, JAMES, THOMPSON, PILOTT and SANDERS deserve, and will receive, the lasting gratitude of the prisoners who received medical treatment at their hands during that memorable summer at Andersonville.†

The medical profession owes a debt of gratitude to the gentlemen mentioned in the above extract, and to their colleagues on duty in the prison hospital, in that their labors, however fruitless on behalf of the unfortunate men confined at Andersonville, have permitted one unsullied paragraph to appear on that foulest page of American or any other history. The papers published by Dr. JONES, and by the Committee of the House of Representatives, show that Dr. I. H. WHITE, the surgeon in charge of the prison camp, repeatedly called the attention of his superiors to the deplorable condition of the prisoners, appealing for medical and hospital supplies, additional medical officers, an adequate supply of cooking utensils, hospital tents and even for straw for bedding. It is true his requisitions and recommendations should have been put in stronger language; but he probably recognized how utterly fruitless and unprofitable would be appeals to the humanity of an authority whose inhumanity rendered such appeals necessary. The following extract from his report, dated August 6, 1864, to General JNO. H. WINDER, the Commandant of the prison, shows him neither insensible to the suffering around him nor ignorant of the causes that made the prison-pen a charnel-house.

*JONES, page 520.   †H. M. DAVIDSON, 1st Ohio Light Artillery, page 49 of the report of the Committee already cited.

The evils within the power of the proper authorities to correct:

I. *The crowded condition of the prisoners.*—The number within the stockade should not exceed fifteen thousand. This would allow ample room for the remainder to be camped in order, with streets of sufficient width to allow free circulation of air and enforcement of police regulations. All that portion of the camp on the north side of the stream could then be used for exercise, where roll-call could also be held, thereby materially aiding the commandant of the interior.

II. *Construction of barracks and hospital accommodation.*—There should be no delay in the construction of barracks; with the greatest amount of energy it will be difficult to complete them before the cold weather comes on, when they will be required more than at present. Too great stress cannot be placed on the necessity for the construction of proper accommodations for the sick. There are at present two thousand two hundred and eight in hospital, all poorly provided for, and some three hundred without any shelter whatever. There are also at least one thousand men now in stockade who are helpless, and should be at once removed to hospital. Their removal is prevented by the absence of accommodations. The construction of hospitals should be at once begun, and in the meantime the sick should be at once transferred to some point where they can be properly provided for. An officer should be employed to arrange the stream passing through the stockade. The bottom-land should be covered over with sand, the stream be made deeper and wider, the walls and bottom covered with plank; the same arrangements to continue outside, conducting the drainage freely to the creek beyond, and if necessary, build a dam to prevent the overflow of the banks. The stream from stockade to the railroad should also be improved, and the use of it by the troops outside should be prohibited. Sinks should be at once arranged over the stream of such a nature as to render them inviting; at present, those who have an inclination to use them have to wade through mud and fæces to use them. At the upper part of the stream proper bathing arrangements should be constructed.

III. *Enforcing stringent police regulations.*—Some stringent rules of police should be established, and scavenger wagons should be sent in every day to remove the collections of filth. A large quantity of mouldy bread and other decomposing matter scattered through the camp and beyond the dead-line should be removed at once. If necessary, sentinels should be instructed to fire on any one committing a nuisance in other places than the sinks.

IV. *Establishment of regulations in regard to cleanliness.*—It should be the duty of Confederate sergeants, attending roll-calls, or others, to see that all the men of their command bathe at stated intervals, and that their clothes are washed at least once a week. For this purpose soap should be issued to the prisoners.

V. *Improvement in rations.*—The meal should be bolted and sifted before being used. Arrangements should be speedily made by which rice, beans and other anti-scorbutics should be issued during the present season; green corn might be issued in lieu of bread ration, if not regularly, at least three times a week. If possible, the prisoners should be supplied with vinegar, and with an occasional issue of molasses in lieu of the meat ration, which would tend greatly to correct the scurvy which prevails to a great extent.

The deaths at Camp Sumter, Andersonville, Ga., during the fourteen months of its occupation numbered about 13,000, when the unrecorded cases are taken into consideration. But these figures greatly underrate the mortality consequent on the treatment to which the prisoners were subjected. Thousands of men died after their liberation from this and other southern prisons. There are no records on file showing the subsequent history of the Andersonville captives; but the following communication indicates the probabilities with respect to them, in detailing the condition of those exchanged from Richmond, Va.:

I have the honor to make the following general report of the condition of patients (sick and wounded) who arrived at and were admitted to this hospital from "Belle Island," Va., per flag-of-truce steamer "New York," via City Point, Va., on the 29th instant:

This vessel left City Point with one hundred and eighty-nine sick and wounded. Before she arrived at Fortress Monroe four men died; on the trip from Fortress Monroe to this place four more died—leaving one hundred and eighty-one to be admitted.

Language is inadequate to express fully the condition of this number, and none but those who saw them can have any appreciable idea of their condition. I do not pretend to particularize, for every case presented evidences of ill-treatment: every one wore the visage of hunger, the expression of despair, and exhibited the ravages of some preying disease or the wreck of a once athletic frame.

I only generalize, therefore, when I say their external appearance was wretched in the extreme. Many had neither hats nor shoes, few had a whole garment; many were clothed merely with a tattered blouse or the remnant of a coat, and a poor apology for a shirt. Some had no under-clothing, and, I believe, none had a blanket. Their hair was dishevelled, their beards long and caked with the most loathsome filth, and their bodies and clothing swarmed with vermin.

Their frames were in most instances all that was left of them. A majority had scarcely vitality to enable them to stand. Their dangling, bony, attenuated arms and legs, sharp, pinched features, cadaveric countenances, deep, sepulchral eyes, and voices that could hardly be distinguished (some, indeed, were unable to articulate) presented a picture which could not be looked upon without calling forth the strongest emotions of pity.

Upon those who had no wounds, as well as on the wounded, were large foul ulcers and sores, principally on their shoulders and hips, produced by lying on the hard ground; and those that were wounded had received no attention, their wounds being in a filthy, offensive condition. One man, who died on the trip from Fortress Monroe, told the surgeon previous to death that his wound had not been dressed since the battle of Gettysburg, Pa., where he was wounded in the head, having both tables of the posterior part of the skull fractured.

. Most of the cases were suffering with diarrhœa—some of them with involuntary evacuations—their clothes being the only receptacle for them, and they too weak to remedy the difficulty. This being the case, you can, of course, imagine the stench emitted from them. Many had pneumonia; some in the advanced stages were gasping for breath. Delirious with fever, many knew not their destination or were not conscious of their arrival nearer home; or racked with pain, many cared not whither they went or considered whether life was dear or not; in some life was slowly ebbing, from mere exhaustion and the gradual wasting of the system. How great must be the mortality, then, of these men, and how dreadful among those still suffering the horrors of imprisonment. Every man who could, rejoiced over his escape, deplored the scenes through which he had passed, and mourned the lot of those he had left behind. Weak and debilitated, they wished but to die among their friends, a wish which, unfortunately, will be realized in too many instances.—*Letter of Acting Assistant Surgeon* S. J. RADCLIFFE, *U. S. A., Medical Officer of the day, at the U. S. General Hospital, Division No. 1, Annapolis, Md., reporting to the Surgeon in charge the condition of the sick and wounded admitted October 29, 1863, from Belle Isle, via City Point, Va.*

The records of the prison hospital at Danville, Va., extending from November 23, 1863, to March 27, 1865, furnish a total of 4,332 cases admitted. As 157 of these were cases of wounds and injuries and 7 cases in which no diagnosis was recorded, the number remaining as due to specified diseases is 4,168. But since there is no record of what became of 429 of these cases, the number of terminated cases of specified disease is reduced to 3,739, of which, 1,074 or 28.7 per cent. were fatal. An examination of the following table will discover the absolute and relative mortality of the prominent diseases for comparison with the Andersonville record, already presented, and with the records of our Northern prisons, to be submitted hereafter.

TABLE XVII.

Summarizing the Records of the Prison Hospital at Danville, Va., Nov. 23, 1863, to March 27, 1865.

	Cases admitted into hospital.	Cases with results unrecorded.	Total cases with recorded results.	Died.	Ratio of cases per 1,000 cases admitted with specified diseases.	Ratio of deaths per 1,000 deaths from specified diseases.	Percentage of fatal cases.
Total cases	4,332	437	3,895	1,084	....	....	....
Wounds and injuries	157	6	151	10	....	....	....
Not specified	7	2	5	0	....	....	....
Specified diseases	4,168	429	3,739	1,074	1,000	1,000	28.7
Continued Fevers	69	12	57	12	16.7	11.1	21.1
Malarial Fevers	235	19	216	17	56.4	15.8	7.9
Eruptive Fevers	880	258	622	165	211.1	153.6	26.5
Diarrhœa and Dysentery	1,418	51	1,367	451(a)	340.2	420.0	32.8
Debility	178	18	160	13	42.7	12.1	8.1
Dropsy	62	6	56	24	14.9	22.4	42.9
Consumption	18	1	17	7	4.3	6.5	41.2
Rheumatism	348	17	331	18	83.5	16.8	5.4
Scurvy	91	2	89	6	21.8	5.6	6.7
Bronchitis	269	12	257	31	64.5	28.9	12.1
Pneumonia and Pleurisy	314	19	295	88	75.3	81.9	29.8
Other diseases	286	14	272	242	68.6	225.3	89.0

(a) Dr. WOODWARD, on page 35, Part II of this work, gives the number of deaths from diarrhœa and dysentery as 592 instead of 451. The record shows that while in 1,367 terminated cases there occurred 451 deaths, by following out the histories of the cases other than diarrhœa and dysentery 141 of these are found to have proved fatal by the supervention of the prevailing intestinal flux. This accounts, for instance, for the high death-rate attaching to the cases tabulated under the caption of "other diseases."

Diarrhœa and the eruptive fevers, small-pox chiefly, occasioned the largest number of admissions as well as of deaths. Diarrhœas constituted 340.2 of every thousand cases of disease, and caused 420 of every thousand deaths from disease. But scurvy, which exercised so fatal an influence at Andersonville, was less manifest here, as it occasioned only 21.8 of every thousand cases and 5.6 of every thousand deaths. The general percentage of fatal cases of disease in this prison was only 28.7, as compared with 73.7, the Andersonville percentage. Evidently the prisoners at Danville were treated with comparative humanity, although the mortality among the cases was nearly three-fold that reported among the Confederate soldiers treated in the Chimborazo Hospital at Richmond, Va.* The ratios of sickness and deaths to the strength present were no doubt correspondingly augmented among the prisoners, although in the absence of data it is impossible to give any other than this vague expression of the facts.

IV.—PREVALENCE OF DISEASE, AND MORTALITY THEREFROM, AMONG THE CONFEDERATE TROOPS IN UNITED STATES PRISONS.

The rebel soldiers that died in our Northern prisons numbered, according to the monthly reports on file in the Surgeon General's Office, 30,716. Death in 5,569 of these cases was the result of wounds; in 404 the cause was unknown, and in 1,152 unstated. There remain, therefore, 23,591 deaths reported as from specified diseases.

The Confederate prisoners were confined in a number of prison camps, many of which have already been mentioned.† The statistics of nine of these camps have been examined, consolidated and tabulated to indicate the diseases and classes of disease that were the principal causes of the sickness and mortality among the prisoners. The records of these nine camps include 18,808 deaths from specified disease, or about 80 per cent. of the whole number of deaths reported as caused by disease. The statistics of the smaller camps might readily have been added to these, but their addition would have materially increased the size of the tabular statements without adding correspondingly to their value. Everything of interest susceptible of illustration by mere figures relative to the diseases of the prisoners may be gathered from the figures given below. Table XVIII consolidates the data of each prison; Table XIX consolidates the data of the whole, and deduces ratios by which comparisons may be instituted.

On comparing the latter consolidation with Table XIII it will be found that the items making up the total number of cases of disease among the prisoners did not differ much from those constituting the total among the Confederate troops in the field. Thus the two classes of disease, diarrhœa and dysentery and the malarial fevers, which caused the largest number of cases among both these bodies of men, have their prevalence expressed by very similar figures. Among the Confederate forces cases of diarrhœa and dysentery constituted 277 of every thousand cases of disease, while the malarial fevers numbered 141 in the thousand. Among the prisoners the corresponding figures were 268 and 157. The eruptive fevers formed 54 of every thousand among the troops on service, and 68 among the prisoners; pulmonary affections 51 among the former, 58 among the latter; and rheumatism 36 and 34 respectively.

---

* See Table XII.　　　　　　　† Pages 36–40, Part II, of this work.

TABLE XVIII.*

Showing the number of Cases of certain Specified Diseases and Classes of Disease, and of Deaths attributed to them, among the Confederate Prisoners of War at the principal Prison Depôts, for the period covered by the records of each prison.

	Camp Douglas, Illinois, from February, 1862, to June, 1865.		Alton, Illinois, from September, 1862, to June, 1865.		Rock Island, Illinois, from February, 1864, to June, 1865.		Camp Morton, Indiana, from June, 1863, to June, 1865.		Johnson's Island, Ohio, from June, 1863, to June, 1865.		Camp Chase, Ohio, from February, 1864, to June, 1865.		Elmira, New York, from July, 1864, to June, 1865.		Fort Delaware, Delaware, from August, 1863, to June, 1865.		Point Lookout, Maryland, from September, 1863, to June, 1865.	
Number of months recorded	41		34		17		25		25		17		12		23		22	
Mean strength present	5,361		1,008		6,030		2,865		2,114		3,570		6,591		6,406		9,610	
	Cases.	Deaths.	Cases.	Deaths.	Cases.	Deaths.	Cases.	Deaths.	Cases.	Deaths.	Cases.	Deaths.	Cases.	Deaths.	Cases.	Deaths.	Cases.	Deaths.
All diseases and injuries	70,088	4,009	29,095	1,475	13,678	1,604	9,122	1,187	3,697	161	24,687	1,771	10,455	2,931	44,388	2,218	44,934	3,704
Wounds, injuries and unspecified diseases	1,279	80	329	20	225	15	259	12	126	5	741	32	277	4	817	19	1,399	65
Specified diseases	68,809	3,929	28,766	1,455	13,453	1,589	8,863	1,175	3,571	156	23,946	1,739	10,178	2,927	43,571	2,199	43,535	3,639
Continued Fevers	1,116	351	190	70	52	54	55	42	93	26	115	53	239	140	432	156	267	217
Malarial Fevers	10,151	233	7,206	177	2,384	52	1,954	119	417	10	4,258	34	628	65	4,725	175	6,864	161
Eruptive Fevers	4,671	823	2,632	537	1,797	436	548	85	160	17	1,865	362	1,368	388	2,593	472	1,033	333
Diarrhoea and Dysentery	13,455	698	5,580	229	3,874	363	2,241	315	1,855	46	4,063	226	4,379	1,394	9,659	644	20,474	2,050
Anaemia	585	4	465	27	47	8	68	4	35	1	402	24	202	17	792	38	613	33
Consumption	259	113	47	27	26	76†	34	26	14	7	24	12	23	13	32	11	76	46
Rheumatism	3,212	37	518	7	700	1	190	5	106	1	988	0	360	9	1,494	19	772	16
Scurvy	3,745	39	390	6	439	14	778	6	58	0	828	5	356	20	6,351	94	3,312	167
Bronchitis	1,628	27	400	4	391	25	178	1	57	1	240	1	116	19	965	34	513	21
Pneumonia and Pleurisy	4,655	1,296	1,134	276	1,464	397	1,351	495	99	25	1,681	954	1,882	773	1,128	401	925	425
Other diseases	25,332	308	10,204	95	2,279	163	1,466	77	677	22	9,482	68	625	89	15,400	155	8,686	170
Total specified diseases	68,809	3,929	28,766	1,455	13,453	1,589	8,863	1,175	3,571	156	23,946	1,739	10,178	2,927	43,571	2,199	43,535	3,639

*The figures representing the mean number of prisoners present at each depot for the periods specified were calculated from the data in the monthly sick reports. They differ somewhat from the strength given in the Monthly Returns of Military and Political prisoners on file in the office of the Adjutant General of the Army, but as the former have already been used in the discussion of diarrhoea and dysentery in the Second Part of this work, it has been deemed advisable to retain them, especially as the differences are inconsiderable and the effect on the ratios insignificant. The mean numbers present, according to the statistics of the Adjutant General's Office, are as follows:—Camp Douglas, Illinois, 5,538; Alton, Illinois, 1,017; Rock Island, Illinois, 5,736; Camp Morton, Indiana, 2,844; Johnson's Island, Ohio, 2,402; Camp Chase, Ohio, 3,734; Elmira, New York, 6,390; Fort Delaware, Delaware, 6,288; and Point Lookout, Maryland, 9,463.

† At Rock Island *post mortem* evidence was always taken as to the cause of death while no corresponding change was made in the diagnosis of the case, bronchitis, pneumonia, etc., as originally entered on the hospital registers; hence the anomaly in the recorded deaths from consumption.

TABLE XIX.

In which the facts of Table XVIII are consolidated and expressed in average annual rates per thousand of strength, with the ratio of cases of specified diseases to cases of all diseases, of deaths from specified diseases to deaths from all diseases, and the percentage of fatal cases of specified disease. Average strength present 40,815 men.

DISEASES.	Total number of cases.	Total number of deaths.	Annual ratio per thousand of average strength.		Cases per thousand cases of all diseases.	Deaths per thousand deaths from all diseases.	Percentage of fatal cases.
			Cases.	Deaths.			
Continued Fevers	2,559	1,109	31.4	13.6	10.5	59.0	43.3
Malarial Fevers	38,587	1,026	472.7	12.6	157.7	54.6	2.7
Eruptive Fevers	16,667	3,453	204.2	42.3	68.1	183.6	20.7
Diarrhœa and Dysentery	65,580	5,965	803.4	73.0	268.1	317.1	9.1
Anæmia and Debility	3,209	156	39.3	1.9	13.1	8.3	4.9
Consumption	535	331	6.6	4.1	2.2	17.5	61.9
Rheumatism	8,340	95	102.2	1.2	34.1	5.2	1.1
Scurvy	16,257	351	199.1	4.3	66.4	18.7	2.2
Bronchitis	4,488	133	55.0	1.6	18.3	7.1	3.0
Pneumonia and Pleurisy	14,319	5,042	175.4	61.7	58.5	268.1	35.2
Other diseases	74,151	1,147	908.3	14.1	303.1	61.0	1.5
Total specified diseases	244,692	18,808	2,997.6	230.4	1,000	1,000	7.7

But although this similarity existed among the cases, showing that the diseases prevailing in the prisons were precisely those that were at the same time affecting the Confederate soldiers who were not prisoners, the fatality in the cases of the confined men was 7.7 per cent. as against 3.8 per cent. in the Confederate ranks. No doubt the relative mortality was considerably greater among the prisoners than among the men on service, but the increase shown by the statistics is in the main due to a failure to take up certain cases on the sick report, the deaths consequently forming a larger percentage of those that were taken up. The annual number of cases of disease entered on the surgeons' reports per thousand prisoners was 2,997.6; the annual number among the troops in the field per thousand of strength was 4,404. The apparently greater prevalence of disease in the field was obviously due to the entry of men on sick report for slight ailments necessitating temporary excuse from military duty; and the greater fatality of disease, as figured by the statistics of the prisons, resulted in part from the absence of such cases from the records. Prisoners with slight ailments did not require the surgeon's signature to excuse them from duty, as in general they had none to perform.

On the assumption that as many trivial cases occurred among the prisoners as among the Confederate ranks—and it can hardly be supposed that there were fewer—the percentage of fatal cases would be 5.2 instead of 7.7. On the assumption that the trivial cases outnumbered those occurring in the ranks, the prison rate of fatality would be proportionately lessened.

The actual increase in the percentage of fatality was occasioned by the greater prominence of diarrhœa and dysentery, the eruptive fevers and pneumonia as death causes. The continued fevers constituted a larger proportion of the mortality among the troops on service than among the prisoners. This is explained by the greater prevalence of these fevers in the regiments, where they contributed 45 to every thousand cases of disease, instead of 10.5 as among the prisoners.   Nevertheless, the fatality of the prison cases was greater, 43.3 per cent., than that of those occurring in the ranks, 33.27 per cent.

The terrible prominence of diarrhœa, dysentery and scurvy as causes of sickness and death at Andersonville* is not manifested on the records of our northern prisons.   Diarrhœa and dysentery, which occasioned 505.6, and scurvy, which occasioned 326.0 of every thousand deaths at Andersonville, are seen by the above tabulation to have caused in our prisons only 317.1 and 18.7 respectively.   The large number of deaths from these diseases among the unfortunate Federal prisoners reduced the proportion caused by other diseases; thus, according to their records, the continued fevers are held responsible for but 21.7 and the malarial fevers for only 14.7 of every thousand deaths, as against 59.0 and 54.6 among the captured Confederates.   Not that these and many other diseases were more prevalent or more fatal in the northern prisons; the deaths were merely more generally distributed among the various causes.

But the death rates per thousand of strength afford a more ready means of appreciating the relative mortality among these men.   The inmates of the nine prisons tabulated lost annually by disease 230.4 out of every thousand present, as contrasted with 53.48 among our white troops; 143.4 among our colored troops; 167.3† in the rebel armies, and 732.6 among the Andersonville prisoners.   The chief causes of these stated mortalities are shown in—

TABLE XX.

Contrasting the Mortality Rates, per thousand of strength, among the White and the Colored Troops of the U. S. Army and the Union and the Confederate Prisoners of War.

Mortality rate per 1,000 strength from—	Northern prisons.	Andersonville.	White troops.	Colored troops.
All diseases	230.4	732.6	53.48	143.4
Diarrhœa and Dysentery	73.0	465.6	15.62	35.27
Pneumonia	61.7	27.4	6.34	28.87
Eruptive Fevers	40.5	8.2	4.50	18.36
Continued Fevers	13.6	20.5	11.60	12.45
Malarial Fevers	12.6	12.2	5.04	16.81
Scurvy	4.3	102.8	0.16	2.02

The causes of the large mortality from diarrhœa and dysentery, pneumonia and the eruptive fevers, will be better understood by investigating the sanitary surroundings of the captives as described in the monthly reports of the Medical Inspectors.   From these documents the following accounts have been compiled:

PRISON-CAMP AND HOSPITAL AT CAMP DOUGLAS, NEAR CHICAGO, ILLINOIS.—This camp was established in January, 1862, and closed in September, 1865.   Its situation was within one-fourth of a mile of the shore of Lake Michigan, and about one and a half miles from the southeastern suburbs of the city of Chicago.   The site was a flat and treeless prairie about fifteen feet higher than the level of the lake.   It had been previously used as a fair-ground. The enclosed area measured 80 acres, nearly one-half of which was set apart for prisoners, the remainder for the garrison and hospital.   The soil was a sandy loam on a substratum of blue clay.   As the surface of the camp was not favorable to drainage it was often, in the wet weather of its earlier history, softened and muddy, unpleasant

---

* See Table XV, page 34.   † See *supra*, page 33.

and unhealthy. The buildings were at first poorly constructed wooden shanties arranged in parallel lines, east and west, with avenues between. The whole camp was in form a parallelogram, one long and one short side being used for prisoners, the other short side for officers and the other long side for offices. The average size of these buildings was $48 \times 25 \times 10$ feet, with kitchen in the rear 8 feet distant. These kitchens were small and were used also as mess-rooms. The whole camp was surrounded by a high wooden fence, and the barracks being in close proximity to it, very little fresh air, according to Dr. KEENEY's report for September, 1862, found its way into the dark, dingy and poorly ventilated quarters. In the month mentioned 7,798 prisoners of war were confined in this camp.

An extensive fire which occurred shortly after this destroyed a large number of the barracks; the buildings by which they were replaced were of a much better character in all particulars. The inspection report for December, 1862, says of this: "Some of the barracks have been burnt and others more substantial have been built in their places. The recent conflagrations have been attended with one salutary effect, in the immense destruction of animal life, in the form of lice, and had less of the filthy and rickety quarters been spared still greater salutary effects would have been the result."

The report for June, 1864, says that these quarters were "one-story high, frame, illy constructed, floors raised four feet from the ground, ridge ventilation and openings at side and ends ample in number." Their condition was further improved subsequently, for the report for October, 1864, says of them: "Fifty-two in number, each $70 \times 24 \times 7.8$ feet, with kitchens $20 \times 24 \times 7.8$, attached, in good order; eight new ones in course of construction."

In January, 1865, they were described by Dr. COOLIDGE as follows: "The prisoners of war are confined within an area of about forty acres, surrounded by a strong oaken barricade twelve feet in height, surmounted by a railed platform for sentinels. The prison barracks are one-storied, ridge-ventilated buildings erected on posts four to six feet from the ground, to prevent escape by burrowing. These barracks are sixty-four in number, four of which are for convalescents exclusively; thirty-one have been built since January, 1864. They are arranged in streets of suitable width, and are all of the same dimensions, viz: 90 feet long, 24 feet wide and about 12 feet to eaves. * * * Each barrack is subdivided into a kitchen and dormitory, the former 20×24, the latter 70×24, the dormitories fitted up with wooden bunks three tiers in height. In several of the barracks at the time of my inspection there were 165 men, each having a cubic space of 142 and a superficial area of 10 square feet. The prisoners of war confined in this camp, January, 1864, numbered 5,649, and 7,652 were received during the year, making a total of 13,301. The cases of sickness treated during the year amounted to 23,037, and the deaths to 1,156, of which 416 were from small-pox. The number of prisoners present December 31, 1864, was 11,780, of whom 577 were sick in hospital and 1,547 in quarters."

The prison hospital building, in common with that of the post, was described, in September, 1862, by Dr. KEENEY as follows: "The hospitals are pretty much the same as the men's barracks; though isolated from them they occupy grounds in the square. They are more thoroughly ventilated, but still are very defective in this particular; on an average 23 patients occupy a ward where 7 should be, allowing 1,000 cubic feet of air to each patient."

In the report for the following month Dr. KEENEY says: "The hospital accommodations of this camp have reached their utmost limit, * * sickness is on the increase." He recommended that the serious cases be transferred from the camp hospitals to the general hospitals at Chicago, and this appears to have been done.

The building is described in the inspection report for June, 1864, as follows: "One building, two stories high, with two wings, newly built, well-constructed frame, enclosed by a high board fence, well ventilated by the ridge and base, windows and high stories; 180 beds, and 117 in pest hospital; air-space, 800 cubic feet in hospital and 1,200 in pest hospital; total beds, 297."

The pest hospital was composed of two buildings, isolated and comfortable in every way.

The report for October, 1864, says: "Buildings, two two-story pavilions, two one-story pavilions, and one barrack for convalescents, all in good condition; six wards, 325 beds; air-space, 650 cubic feet; superficial feet, 54 each; overcrowded." At this date there were 7,361 prisoners of war in camp, 397 in hospital and 860 in quarters.

In January, 1865, Dr. COOLIDGE described the buildings as follows: "The prison hospital is within the garrison grounds but outside the prison square, enclosed with a strong oak fence. It consists of a central building with two wings, all two stories in height; four wards in each wing; the lower are 99 feet long, 27 feet wide and 12 feet high, well lighted and ventilated by cold-air shafts opening in the floor and vertical shafts in the walls, opening some near the floor, others near the ceilings. The upper wards are $99 \times 27 \times 11$ feet, well lighted and ventilated by shafts opening at the ridge. At time of inspection each of these wards had 60 beds occupied, so that each bed had 500 feet of air-space and 45 feet of area. * * * In addition to the hospital proper there was a single barrack ward 80×20 feet, with 30 beds for erysipelas."

The pest hospital was about one mile from the camp, and consisted of two ridge-ventilated frame buildings, 204×28 and 10 feet to eaves; divided into three wards, 150 beds. During the year 1864 1,519 of the prisoners were admitted with small-pox or varioloid, and 416 of these died. During the same period 144 cases were admitted from the Union troops at the post, and of these 24 were fatal.

Few alterations were made in these hospitals after this date except in minor points, all of which tended to improvement.

The diet of the prison-camp was the ordinary army ration with vegetables added. Some complaint was made of a scarcity of these by Dr. KEENEY, who said in September, 1862,—"I am inclined to believe the prisoners have been stinted in vegetable matter. The best indication of this is the appearance of the scurvy lurking about the command. There are many cases of incipient scurvy in camp." But the inspection reports of later dates speak of the rations as good and sufficient.

The diet in the prison hospital was rendered superior to that of the prison by the addition of delicacies purchased by the hospital fund, which appears to have been expended in this manner as fast as it accrued.   Dr. COOLIDGE reports for January, 1865, as follows: "The purchases by the hospital fund were as follows: (Some items only.) Milk, 1,237 gallons; potatoes, 167 bushels; dried apples, 427 pounds; butter, 994 pounds; chickens, 20 dozen; oysters (cans), 5 dozen—a great contrast to the treatment of our men in rebel prisons."   Excellent soft bread was issued from the post bakery at all times to the prisoners in camp and hospital.

An abundant water-supply was brought from the lake to the camp by the city water-pipes.

The drainage of the camp was at first imperfect.   Dr. KEENEY speaks of it thus: "The drainage is exceedingly bad.   The commanding officer and the surgeon have repeatedly submitted plans of drainage to the department, urging the necessity of such as a means for preserving the health of the camp.   As yet, nothing has been done but to permit long open sewers, extending for nearly a quarter of a mile, both in front and rear of the quarters, containing the garbage and other refuse of the kitchens of months' standing, to add their miasms to the already noxious air pervading the camp."   Again, in October, 1862: "The grounds are so low that no drainage, without much expense, can be had. Every rain converts the camp into a mud-hole, and in consequence of the flatness of the ground and the want of drainage, all the filth and refuse of the company quarters, of the men's sinks, and of the hospital, are to be removed *only* by the process of evaporation.   Already there exists in and around the company quarters and hospital sufficient animal and vegetable matter to contaminate the whole camp and generate fevers of the most malignant type." This condition of affairs appears, however, to have been remedied, for the report for June, 1864, speaks of the drainage as "naturally bad, but artificially good."   The camp was well graded, and a system of sewers built which could be flushed into the lake.

The sinks at early dates were shallow pits, many of them merely surrounded by a few poles and brush insufficient to afford privacy.   Dr. KEENEY, in his report for September, 1862, says: "The sinks are numerous, near the men's quarters and badly constructed; they are not sufficiently deep, nor are they filled up often enough and renewed. The wood-work is not close enough, consequently the mephitic gases are wafted to the quarters, hospitals and over the parade grounds.   This stench is intolerable."   At a later period these privies were built over a large sewer and the excreta effectually removed by flushing.

PRISON AND HOSPITAL AT ALTON, ILLINOIS.—The prison at Alton, Ill., was opened in January, 1862, and closed in June, 1865.   Its site was that of the Illinois State Penitentiary, on the hillside at the northern end of the city of Alton, overlooking the Mississippi river, high, dry, well-drained and considered healthy, though subject to malaria from the river bottom at certain seasons of the year.

The buildings, nearly all of limestone, formed a square which was surrounded by a high wall.   Many of the smaller buildings, used as executive offices, etc., were isolated.   The north side of the prison was formed by a building containing 256 cells, arranged in four tiers in the interior, each tier consisting of two rows facing the north and south walls respectively.   The cells were each $7 \times 7 \times 3\frac{1}{2}$ feet = 171.5 cubic feet; they were ventilated and lighted by the gratings which formed their doors.   They were used only for refractory prisoners or when the prison was crowded, which the inspection reports show to have often been the case, particularly in the earlier months of its occupation. Bunks were erected along the corridors, between the central cell structure and the walls of the building.   In addition to this there were two large rooms, each $45 \times 15 \times 10$, occupied as quarters, one of them at one time exclusively by Confederate officers.

Dr. LE CONTE in his report for May, 1863, says: "In the main building many of the cells are occupied by men who are not confined therein, but sleep there for want of better place."   He recommended that "the capacity of the prison should be considered as not greater than 1,000, and that not more than that number should be confined within it at one time."   The prison had been built to accommodate 300 convicts, and at the time of Dr. LE CONTE's visit it contained 1,500 prisoners.   Dr. KEENEY in his report for July, 1863, says: * * * "Fifteen hundred prisoners, both Federals and Rebels, have each about 100 cubic feet of *impure air* for respiratory purposes.   This deficiency of pure air alone is a sufficient cause to explain the great mortality within its enclosure."   In August, 1863, there were 1,200 prisoners; in October, 1863, 1,446; and in November, 1863, 1,800.

In order to afford increased accommodations for the prisoners, tents were at times erected, and the prison hospital was removed from the permanent stone building to one specially erected of wood, thus giving additional space for the inmates of the prison.

The reports at first speak of the hospital as consisting of one large ward in the basement of the penitentiary. In April, 1863, the hospital department was removed into a separate brick building in the prison yard, having room for 70 beds.   An additional building was used as a pest-house.

In August, 1863, out of 117 sick in the hospital 60 were small-pox patients, and to properly isolate these a new building was erected at "Sickleyville," on an island in the river about three-quarters of a mile from the town of Alton.   This building was of wood, well built and comfortably arranged; capacity, 100 beds with 670 cubic feet of air-space per bed.

In order to afford increased accommodations for the relief of the over-crowding in the prison quarters, a new two-story wooden pavilion building was erected inside the prison enclosure as a hospital, and all the permanent buildings were henceforth used as quarters.   This new prison hospital was divided into two wards, $183\frac{1}{2} \times 40 \times 13 = 95,420$ cubic feet each, the lower story being used for executive purposes, the upper only for the sick.   A fine and well-appointed bath-room was attached to this ward; in fact the hospital arrangements were complete in every particular.   The small-pox ward on the island was $200 \times 26 \times 13$ feet clear = 67,000 cubic feet, and had 67 beds.   It was well constructed, one story, with roof and side ventilation.   Thus the hospital accommodations at this place were at length made comfortable and complete.

The rations of the prisoners in quarters and hospital are reported as abundant and good.   The hospital fund, as it accrued, was liberally expended in the purchase of delicacies for the use of the sick, the surrounding farms furnishing vegetables in abundance.

The water-supply was at first hauled from the river to the prison by teams; later a steam force-pump was employed and an abundant supply was obtained.

The sinks were at first shallow pits situated too near the quarters, often over full and foul-smelling. At this time no water-closet was attached to the hospital, and the excreta had to be removed by hand. But these defects were remedied. The report for April, 1865, says of those attached to the hospital—"Water-closets clean and buildings good." The remarks on those of the prison are less satisfactory: "Water-closets and sinks ample but as foul as possible." In fact the condition of the sinks in the prison was generally severely criticised by the medical inspectors. The bathing facilities were characterized as "ample and good, with good furniture and fixtures."

The drainage was naturally good and the sewerage satisfactory during the early occupation of the prison; but in April, 1865—"most of the sewers having been clogged with trash, have been opened their entire length, and are open gutters of fæces, slops and all kinds of filth. The sewers not thus opened are choked; consequently the whole establishment stinks intolerably and the stench extends to the private residences in the vicinity of the prison walls. It is proposed to put earthen sewers here, and the work should be done at once."

The following extracts show the condition of this prison when at its worst:

Dr. KEENEY, November, 1862: "The quarters are poorly ventilated, and some have no ventilation at all.

The grounds and quarters are in a shocking condition. The prisoners are permitted to lounge about in their filth, with no other duty to perform seemingly than to amuse themselves by slaughtering the vermin crawling about their filthy persons. This seems to be their general avocation and amusement.

The kitchens are shining with grease, the floors seldom washed, the tables and other kitchen furniture also filthy.

The cooking arrangements are good; the ranges large and ample for all purposes.

The rations furnished are of the best quality, excepting flour, which is bad. But there is a great disproportion between animal and vegetable matter, a deficiency of the latter. Unless more vegetable matter is furnished scurvy will soon make its appearance.

The grounds around the company quarters and kitchens are the common receptacles for bones, damaged meat, mouldy bread, etc.

The prisoners do their washing on a slope where all the soapy water runs upon the ground and dries up under their feet.

The sinks are located in their midst and are exceedingly foul; the pits but three or four feet deep. There is no drainage to them, consequently they soon become filled up, and if not often removed they become an intolerable nuisance; such is the case now. I have called the attention of the commanding officer to this, and have recommended them to be filled up and new pits dug twenty feet deep and walled up.

I also find prisoners occupying the cells where the air is cold and damp and without ventilation, and where pneumonia and rheumatism were fast increasing. As these occupants were not condemned to the cells, I recommended the commanding officer to remove them immediately to a large open room where the sun's rays might occasionally brighten their dingy walls.

As above stated, there are 1,040 prisoners inside these walls. Sick in hospital 60; in quarters 70; total 130. The prevailing diseases are erysipelas, pneumonia, dysentery, typhoid fever and diarrhœa. The prevalence of the last disease arises from the sour bread furnished by dishonest contractors, under the administration of an inefficient commanding officer.

The hospital accommodations consist of one open ward with low ceiling and badly ventilated. The walls are dingy, the floors dirty, the bedding filthy, and the patients unwashed and alive with vermin.

The medical attendants, four in number, are Confederate prisoners of no account as medical practitioners. Dr. HARDEN has not time to give his attention to individual cases. The ward is now crowded, one bed riding another. In this loathsome ward each patient has about 200 cubic feet of foul air for respiratory purposes. Among the sick I found some eight or ten cases of erysipelas fast running into a contagious form. It is on the increase."

Dr. KEENEY, July, 1863: "The percentage of deaths has been as high as 30. Through the able administration of its present commander, Major HENDRICKSON, U. S. Army, and its present medical officer, Assistant Surgeon WALL, 77th Ohio Volunteers, the mortality has been reduced to 12 or 15 per cent.

The general state of police of the entire prison is now almost faultless, including the two wards used for hospital purposes. The rations are issued in abundance and of the best quality, and the cooking is both well done and served. The patients in hospital, some 85, are well provided with underclothing from the Government, and are amply supplied with everything to make them comfortable as far as the present capacity of room will permit. In this there is a sad deficiency, and humanity demands an immediate change for the better. In one ward, in the very midst of these 1,500 prisoners, there are 20 or more cases of small-pox under treatment; in the other and only ward are typhoid and malarious fevers, erysipelas, scabies, pneumonia, etc., etc.

Erysipelas often makes its appearance, assuming a contagious form from the vitiated air and animal poisons constantly being eliminated from the body. In fact, all forms of disease that would be mild with plenty of pure air, have in these dingy and loathsome rooms assumed the most virulent forms and baffled medical treatment.

In order to check in a measure this great and unnecessary mortality from disease, I have recommended the commanding officer to procure immediately a suitable building a mile or so from the prison and city, and have it fitted up for the accommodation of the small-pox cases.

As this loathsome disease seems a constant inmate of the prison in spite of vaccination, it will be necessary to keep up the small-pox hospital continually, and to employ an able physician to attend to this hospital alone. The persistence of small-pox in the prison is due to constant importations of the disease.

I have also recommended that the best ventilated and most isolated rooms now occupied by the well prisoners be appropriated to the erysipelatous and other contagious diseases, and the room now occupied by the small-pox cases be turned over to the well prisoners as soon as it is in proper condition to receive them.

I would also call your attention to the great necessity of immediately authorizing Major HENDRICKSON to employ two able physicians, one to attend to the small-pox hospital as soon as opened, and the other to assist Dr. WALL to attend the prison hospital. The duties in this hospital are too much for one man to do justice to the numerous bad cases of disease.

If these suggestions are carried out the condition of the sick will be ameliorated and the percentage of death lessened."

PRISON-BARRACKS AND HOSPITAL, ROCK ISLAND, ILLINOIS.—This prison was established November 13, 1863, and discontinued about August, 1865; the prison hospital was opened in December, 1863, and closed in June, 1865.

Rock Island, embracing about 1,000 acres, is situated in the Mississippi river between the cities of Rock Island, Illinois, and Davenport, Iowa. The soil is a stiff loam on a limestone foundation. Its well-wooded and undulating surface was considered to offer a healthy site for a prison-camp.

The barracks consisted of eighty-four one-story wooden pavilions, each of which was considered suitable for the accommodation of one hundred men. They were well built and comfortably arranged, ventilated by the ridge and well lighted; their floors were raised from the ground, and were comfortably bunked. They were built in streets 100 feet wide, crossing each other at right angles, and there was a central avenue 200 feet wide. Each barrack was 100 feet long, 22 feet wide and 10 feet high, but 20 feet of each was partitioned off to form a kitchen and mess-room. The whole area, 1,200 × 850 feet, was enclosed by a strong wooden fence 12 feet high, with a railed platform near the top on which the guard patrolled.

Dr. TOWNSHEND reports the result of his inspection in January, 1864, thus: "The prisoners on the island number 6,500. They are comfortably quartered in barracks well built and well arranged for comfort and security. The appearance of the men is highly creditable to themselves and to the officers having them in charge. In good weather the prisoners are employed in various duties, which secure to them the benefits of out-door exercise; these duties are therefore regarded by them as a privilege. The discipline of the prison is admirable, being efficient without being harsh."

The prison-hospital buildings, from January to April, 1864, consisted of a number of the barrack pavilions inside the prison enclosure. At the last-mentioned date ten of these barracks were used as hospital wards; but in May a new prison hospital was opened for the reception of patients. The buildings consisted of seven one-story frame pavilions arranged *en echelon*, tolerably well constructed, with ridge ventilation along the entire length of the roof. Each ward contained 50 beds and had a lavatory, bath and water-closet attached.

The increasing necessity for additional hospital accommodations caused seven additional pavilions of the same pattern to be erected, and the inspection report of January, 1865, describes them as follows: "The prison hospital is situated on elevated ground near the centre of the island. It consists of an administrative building two stories in height, 60 × 40 feet, and fourteen pavilion wards, each 140 × 24, 10 feet high at the eaves and 14 feet to the ridge, a small space being partitioned off for nurses and attendants; 50 beds to each ward, giving a cubic space of 645 feet to each bed." A kitchen and mess-hall was also erected, 112 × 40 feet, situated between the two rows of wards; to this building was also attached a well-supplied laundry.

In addition to the above there was a small-pox hospital consisting of six pavilion wards, each 150 × 24 and 12 feet high to the eaves. Each ward contained 50 beds, and gave 864 cubic feet and 72 square feet per bed. These buildings were isolated from the hospital proper, being situated on the Illinois side of the island. They were well drained and supplied with every convenience.

Notwithstanding the natural advantages of the site and the substantial and complete character of the buildings at this place the rates of sickness and mortality appear to have been high, chiefly due to an outbreak of small-pox. Dr. TOWNSHEND'S report, already quoted, says: "The present condition of the hospital may be considered good; but much suffering has occurred, and many deaths during the present month from causes beyond the control of the officers in charge. Many of the prisoners arrived during the extreme cold weather, a large proportion of whom were subsequently attacked with pneumonia. The same cold weather interfered with railway communications and prevented the receipt of hospital stores and medicines. In addition to the above, many of the prisoners were found to have small-pox, and, of course, had subjected many others to exposure. These unforeseen difficulties appear to have been met with the utmost promptitude by the medical officers and the post commander."

The diet of both the prison and the hospital was always of good quality, ample means being afforded for cooking the rations. No complaints appear under these headings in any of the inspection reports. In the hospital the fund was liberally expended in the purchase of delicacies for the use of the sick. Good light bread and corn bread, with potatoes three times a week, were issued to the prisoners.

The water-supply was abundant and of fair quality. It was pumped from the Mississippi river into a reservoir and distributed to the camp and hospital by pipes. An artesian and three ordinary wells inside the prison enclosure furnished a good supply in addition to that from the river.

The sinks were at first simply pits, from which the accumulations were removed by carts and thrown into the river. At later dates these were abandoned and a large latrine was constructed in the prison, communicating with the river by means of a trench. Daily flushing swept the deposits into the river. The sinks in the hospital were provided with zinc buckets, which were emptied twice daily.

H. Faber del.

PRISON BARRACKS AND HOSPITAL

AT ROCK ISLAND ILL.

P. Moras Lith. Phila.

1 Stockaded Prison. 2 Prison Hospital. 3 Pest house.

4 Barracks of the Guard. 5 Hospital for the Guard.

The drainage of the camp and hospital was naturally good on account of the rolling surface of the ground; and this was improved from time to time until the drainage system was considered excellent. Between the prison and the hospital there was a slough or bayou of some extent which was partly filled up and drained. Complaint was sometimes made in the inspection reports of the unsatisfactory character of the drainage in cold weather when the drains were frozen up.

The following, by Assistant Surgeon M. KING MOXLEY, U. S. Vols., is dated February, 1864:

"The prevalence of small-pox and its proportionally great mortality is a subject of serious consideration. The disease made its appearance about the last of December. The number of those affected increased so rapidly that men had to be allowed to remain in barracks after the eruption appeared, thus infecting the whole prison. Three small houses were used as a pest hospital. Each was capable of containing ten patients, but three times as many were crowded into them. Two large buildings were erected soon after I assumed charge, January 13, 1864. These held 50 patients each, allowing over 800 cubic feet of air per man. But as the number of cases augmented to an alarming extent, I asked the commanding officer for the erection of another similar building. Five days elapsed before the order was given to build. Meanwhile the cases increased on my hands; there was no place to put them but in one of the barracks used for hospital purposes in the prison enclosure; this was filled in two days. Surgeon A. M. CLARKE, U. S. Vols., Acting Medical Inspector, found me with 38 cases in the barracks, the accumulation of two days, although I was removing them at the rate of twenty a day and crowding the pest-hospital in hopes of soon getting into the new building. Had this building been erected when asked for, no case would have been left in the barracks an hour after being reported. Another of the prison-barrack buildings was then taken, and then another, and one more barrack used as a ward in the hospital, making four used as small-pox wards within the enclosure. About February 22, for several days as many as thirty-five new cases were reported daily, and during the last two weeks of February there was an average of 20 cases each day. Three new barracks at the pest-house were erected, making six in all. One of the small houses previously used is now used as a kitchen. The four barracks in the hospital and prison are now cleared of the small-pox; all the patients are in the six barracks and two small houses. There are at this time, February 29, 430 cases; each building, intended for 50 men, contains 70, including the nurses. A house is being erected as a dormitory for nurses; this will leave more room for the patients daily reported. There has been a scarcity of clothing for convalescents returning to prison, although I made a timely application for a supply. Hence, many had to be retained who could have made way for new cases. The great mortality results from several causes: 1st. Over-crowding, which could not be avoided. 2d. Want of proper bedding, rough cots with straw being the only beds that could be procured, though now there are in use about two hundred bed-sacks which were obtained from the quartermaster. 3d. Want of clothing to give the patients a change on coming into hospital, in view of their previous want of cleanliness. 4th. Insufficient vaccination. Nearly every prisoner had a large ugly scar on his arm, the result of impure virus imposed on him while in the Southern army. This did not protect him in the least. Prisoners have been received on whom the eruption appeared the next day following their arrival, thus showing that they had contracted the disease before coming here."

PRISON AND HOSPITAL AT CAMP MORTON, NEAR INDIANAPOLIS, INDIANA.—This depot, used as a camp for Union troops from April, 1861, was opened as a prison for rebels January 26, 1862, and closed in August, 1865. It was established on the State fair-ground, one mile and a half northwest of Indianapolis, Indiana. The site was a level plain, undulating but slightly in some parts, and hence possessing very poor natural drainage. The soil was an alluvial clay on a subsoil of gravel. The area enclosed for prison purposes was at first about twenty acres, subsequently increased to thirty, and was abundantly shaded by fine forest trees. The great objection to the site was the absence of running water, which deficiency was repeatedly noted by the various medical officers who inspected the post.

The prison barracks at first consisted of a number of poorly constructed wooden buildings which had been erected and used by Union troops. They are described in July, 1864, as "nine dilapidated barracks, each 150×24 and 10 feet high." The ventilation of these was by ridge openings running along the entire length of the roofs and by openings in the walls and doors at the ends and sides. They were fitted with three tiers of bunks. At this date there were also 210 condemned tents in use for the accommodation of the prisoners. Nevertheless these quarters were much crowded, there being only 60 to 80 cubic feet per man in the barracks, while five men were crowded in each "A" tent and nine men in each bell tent. A small isolated building within the enclosure was used for a few cases of variola that occurred. This crowded condition continued until September, 1864, when the prison area was increased by adding to it about ten additional acres of ground. In November, 1864, six men were crowded into each "A" tent while new pavilion barracks were in process of erection. In May, 1865, the barracks were stated as thirteen in number, each 150×18 feet and 9 feet high, giving "sufficient space." Little change appears to have occurred after this date.

Hospital buildings were at first extemporized by the occupancy of some of the prison-barrack buildings already described. It appears that at this time many of the sick and wounded were sent to the Indianapolis City Hospital for treatment. In June, 1863, the stated capacity of these buildings was 83 beds, occupied by 100 men, many of whom were on double beds. The report for July, 1863, says: "Enlarged hospital accommodations are much needed at this place. The present facilities are too limited and are often crowded beyond their capacity." In these buildings the air-space was often reduced to 350 feet per man. Few facilities were afforded for bathing; bath-tubs were in position, but as water had to be carried a distance of one hundred yards in buckets, they were seldom used. To expand the hospital a number of tents were pitched, but these also soon became crowded.

In December, 1863, the hospital department was much improved by the erection of two new pavilion buildings, by which the air-space was increased to 550 cubic feet. In July, 1864, these buildings were described as follows:

"The hospital buildings are four in number, one 114×20 and 12 feet high; one 100×20 and 12 feet high; one 40×20 and 11 feet 3 inches high; and one 99×24 and 14 feet high. Furniture good and sufficient. In addition a mess-room 30×24 feet, 12 feet high, and good kitchen accommodations."

The diet in both prison and hospital was good and sufficient; vegetables were freely used and the hospital fund liberally expended in the purchase of delicacies for the sick. Soft bread of excellent quality was issued daily from the post bakery.

The water-supply, derived from wells, was sufficient for the requirements of the camp. Drainage at first was imperfect. A ditch of irregular depth ran through the camp and carried off the rainfall. In dry weather stagnant water collected here and there in the deeper parts of its irregular bottom. These were repeatedly denounced by inspecting officers, and as a result the ditch was ultimately straightened deepened and converted into a main drain with which laterals from the area of the camp were connected.

The sinks were simply pits in the ground within the enclosure, and often so near the quarters of the prisoners as to be offensive. Lime was used daily as a disinfectant.

The condition of the camp during the last year of its occupation is not known, as no detailed accounts of a later date than July, 1864, have been found on file.

The figures for Camp Morton, presented in Table XVIII, do not include the statistics anterior to June, 1863. An estimate of the mortality previous to that date is contained in the report of Dr. HUMPHREYS for September, 1864, as follows: "There have been treated in the City Hospital of Indianapolis 846 rebel sick and wounded. They were all of the Fort Donelson prisoners; out of this number 75 died. The men were broken down in health by previous hardships and exposure. The limbs of many were frosted while working in the trenches at Fort Donelson. The prevalent diseases amongst them were typhoid fever and typhoid pneumonia, occurring in persons in whom the vital forces had been reduced to the lowest possible degree; many 'dropped dead' while walking about their quarters, without having manifested any disease, organic or functional, except great general debility. In persons of this class, while moving about looking apparently in medium health, the action of the heart and arteries would be so feeble as to be scarcely perceptible in pulsations at the wrist. These men were subsisted and treated medicinally and surgically in the same manner as the sick and wounded of the United States forces; the same air-space in hospital, and every facility afforded our own troops were given to the rebels. The records of the number of rebel prisoners received at Camp Morton since the commencement of the war are incomplete. Colonel BIDDLE of the 71st Indiana Infantry has been in command of the camp since the 28th of January, 1863. This officer reports the number of prisoners of war in this camp since the above date to June 10, 1863, to be 4,604. The sick in hospital out of this number were 591; of whom 43 died. About one-half of the 591 treated were wounded, among whom were many cases of hospital gangrene. The total number of rebel prisoners brought to Camp Morton since the war began exceeds 10,000. From the undertaker who personally superintended all the interments of the rebel dead at this post, I learned that the total number of deaths up to May 8, 1863, amounted to 353; total number of hospital cases treated in the period referred to 1,685."

PRISON-CAMP AND HOSPITAL AT JOHNSON'S ISLAND, NEAR SANDUSKY, OHIO.—The inspection reports of this prison-camp present a most gratifying picture of its sanitary condition. It was opened some time in 1862 and closed in October, 1865.

The island, three and one-eighth miles from Sandusky, Ohio, has an area of 360 acres. Its natural advantages as a depot for prisoners of war were very great; the soil was alluvial on a limestone basis; the drainage excellent; water from the lake abundant and of good quality, and the salubrity of the site unsurpassed.

The buildings in the camp, frame structures two stories high, with bunks along the sides, were well lighted and ventilated by doors and windows, and at a later date by artificial openings. They accommodated 2,000 men, giving an air-space of 300 feet per man. Their capacity was largely increased in 1864. The prison-camp was surrounded by a high board fence, enclosing an area of 15 acres. Officers were mainly confined in this prison.

The prison hospital was a two-story frame building, giving 700 feet of air-space to each of 80 beds. It was divided into four wards with lavatories in each. Bathing facilities were afforded by the abundant water-supply from the lake. The supply of bedding was abundant. The diet was similar to that furnished to the Union soldiers in the post hospital. Ice was furnished in abundance. Vegetables and delicacies were freely used. The medical officer in charge was assisted by Confederate surgeons confined in the prison.

The sinks at first were excavations in the ground, but later box-sinks, capable of being drawn out and emptied into the lake, were substituted for the old vaults.

The natural advantages of the site rendered but little artificial aid necessary to perfect the drainage. Garbage was stored in barrels and carted daily from the camp.

The following extract from the report of Surgeon T. WOODBRIDGE, 128th Ohio, in charge of the hospital, sums up the conditions affecting the prisoners under his care in a few words. The report is that for June, 1863: "The rations are of good quality and the cooking excellent. We have plenty of vegetables and an abundance of fresh fish; pure air; pure water; plenty of wood; a police system rigidly enforced; a natural salubrity unsurpassed. We are as perfect in what pertains to hygiene as possible."

PRISON-CAMP AND HOSPITAL AT CAMP CHASE, NEAR COLUMBUS, OHIO.—The precise date of the establishment of this camp and hospital is not shown by the records of the Surgeon General's Office. It was used as a prison-camp for political and military prisoners early in 1862, but the reports on file antedating January, 1863, are valueless. The hospital was not closed until December, 1865, although few prisoners remained after July of that year.

Camp Chase prison was situated in the southeastern part of the enclosed camp, four miles from Columbus, Ohio, on the National road. The site had previously been a race-course and fair-ground; it was treeless and nearly flat or somewhat basin-like, and surrounded by forests, which made it close and warm in summer. The soil was stiff, clayey and water-holding, poorly drained and destitute of running water.

The buildings in the prison-camp at early dates were poorly constructed wooden barracks, needing constant repairs to render them habitable. Dr. HUMPHREYS considered them little better than the huts ordinarily in use for the protection of domestic animals. They were divided into three sets, known as prison No. 1, for officers, and Nos. 2 and 3 for enlisted men. Each prison was separated from the other, and the whole was surrounded by a close board fence, fifteen feet high, with an elevated platform for the guard. These old barracks were fitted with three tiers of bunks, and the space per man was very small. To accommodate the large numbers of prisoners received, tents were pitched in the avenues between the barrack buildings, and the crowding was great. The dimensions of these buildings and the particulars of their construction are not clearly stated. At the inspection in September, 1863, the quarters were crowded; at this time there were confined 1,753 prisoners, of whom only 27 were sick—25 in hospital and 2 in quarters.

During 1864 the prison underwent a radical change: its area was increased, its buildings remodelled, and some of a better character erected. Division No. 1 of the prison consisted of two barracks, No. 2 of seventeen barracks and No. 3 of twenty-seven, making a total of forty-six barracks. Each was 100 × 22 × 12 feet, and was intended to accommodate 192 men, giving 137 cubic feet per man. They were all of the pavilion pattern, with door and windows at the sides, floors well removed from the ground, ridges ventilated, and the tiers of bunks reduced to two.

The prison-hospital building in 1862 and the early part of 1863 consisted of a small one-story wooden barrack, 79 × 20 × 12 feet, divided into two wards, having 600 feet of air for each of 36 beds. It was situated within the enclosure and too near the high close fence for good ventilation. It was well supplied with furniture and cooking apparatus, lavatories and sponge-baths. The capacity of the hospital was increased about December, 1863, by the erection of a new pavilion, which, however, was of an inferior character. It was built of old lumber preserved from some condemned buildings. Its size was 84 × 12 feet and only 8 feet high, allowing a little over 400 cubic feet of air per bed. Both of these buildings were afterwards condemned and abandoned. New and superior hospital pavilions were erected outside the prison enclosure. They consisted of six wards each 100 × 25 × 12 feet, affording 850 feet of air-space to each of 216 beds.

In addition to these, three isolated buildings south of the prison enclosure constituted the pest-hospital. Two were used for small-pox and one for erysipelatous patients. The small-pox hospital was 240 × 24 × 12 feet, having a capacity of 120 beds, to each of which it afforded a cubic space of 576 feet. These buildings were of the pavilion pattern, well constructed and supplied with everything needful for the comfort and well-being of the patients. The attendance was good and careful and the supplies ample and of good quality.

In a special report dated March 14, 1865, Dr. COOLIDGE compared the barrack occupancy of the Union troops and Confederate prisoners.

BARRACKS FOR—	No.	Length.	Width.	Height.	Bunks.	No. of men to each.	Air-space.	Area.
		Feet.	Feet.	Feet.			Feet.	Feet.
United States paroled	18	100	24	12	48	192	150	12.5
United States garrison	20	60	24	14	48	96	210	15.0
United States recruits	20	60	24	14	48	96	210	15.0
Confederate prisoners	46	100	22	12	48	192	137	11.4

The diet in the prison-camp was the army ration with the addition of vegetables, potatoes, onions, etc., the post bakery at all times furnishing a good supply of light bread. There appears to have been a prisoners' fund, but no account of its expenditure is on record. The kitchens of the prison-barracks were furnished with brick furnaces having cast-iron tops with holes for kettles. There were few complaints made by the inspectors under this head, the whole appearing to be quite satisfactory.

The prison-hospital diet was of the same quality as that of the prison, with the addition of such delicacies as were purchased by the hospital fund, which was expended as fast as it accrued, and, according to the inspection reports, it appears to have been ample for the purpose.

The supplies in both prison-camp and hospital are spoken of throughout as having been good and sufficient.

The water-supply was derived from wells, which in the early months of the occupation were not commended, although they were regarded at a later period as capable of yielding an abundant supply of good but somewhat hard water for drinking and cooking; it was, however, never sufficient for bathing or washing purposes, and on a few occasions, after prolonged dry weather, the low water in the wells rendered some precautionary economy advisable.

In consequence of the nearly level surface of the camp great difficulty was experienced in effecting a satisfactory drainage. The system consisted of a main drain or ditch running through the prison-camp from west to east, with lateral branches opening into it. But, as in the absence of running water these drains could not be satisfactorily flushed, they became foul and emitted disagreeable odors. On the remodelling of the camp and hospital buildings the drains were planked or boxed, and provision was made for flushing the system by means of water from a cistern. The defective drainage of this camp, arising from its physical conformation, was noted in almost every inspection report, and the advisability of removing the prisoners to another and healthier site was frequently suggested.

The sinks at first were merely pits in which lime and ashes were used as deodorizers. Much difficulty was experienced in keeping them in good condition. They were afterwards filled up lest they should contaminate the water-supply, and new sinks were constructed over the drains, which were flushed periodically. Garbage was collected in barrels and carted off regularly.

PRISON-CAMP AND HOSPITAL AT ELMIRA, N. Y.— Elmira barracks were built at the beginning of the war as a general recruiting depôt; but in July, 1864, Division No. 3, of the barracks, called afterwards Camp Chemung, was converted into a prison-camp. This division was situated on the river-bank a mile and a quarter west of the town. The site was believed to be healthy; it was level, and having a sandy soil resting on a stratum of coarse gravel a few feet below the surface, afforded good underground drainage. At the date mentioned twenty of the old barrack buildings were considered fit for the occupation of the prisoners and ten new ones were constructed. The former, 88 × 18 × 8 feet, were intended to accommodate each one hundred men. The latter, 80 × 25 × 12 feet, were each fitted with bunks for one hundred and forty-eight men. Mess-halls and kitchens were suitably furnished. The barracks were built of pine; they were well lighted, warmed by stoves and provided with ridge-ventilation. The bakery could turn out six or seven thousand rations per day. Good water was obtained from two wells, and any deficiency was supplied from the river. Lavatories and baths were not at first specially provided. Drainage was by means of pits dug to the porous subsoil. The sinks were covered pits, which were filled up when necessary.

The grounds of the camp, comprising thirty-five acres, were surrounded by a fence twelve feet high with a platform four feet from the top. In August, over a thousand tents were pitched, each to accommodate five persons. In one inspection report the drainage is said to have been into an open pond within the camp, thus forming what was called a perfect pest-hole; but on the recommendation of the inspector this pond was afterwards drained and an underground sewer constructed, while defects in the surface drainage were remedied from time to time. Nevertheless the grounds were frequently reported as in a muddy condition during wet seasons.

The prisoners were insufficiently clothed, there being at the same time a great want of blankets, especially among the prisoners in quarters. A supply is said to have been received on one occasion from the Confederate authorities. Sometimes the want of clothing was incompatible with the maintenance of health, and hospital patients, after having sufficiently recovered to be up, were obliged to keep their beds for want of pantaloons. Needs of this kind, and others less urgent, on becoming known, were relieved by the issue of hospital clothing. Bedding was supplied in quarters only to the sick, and consisted of sacks of straw and a blanket. The men in confinement here had the full prison ration as supplied at the other prison depôts. They had also a fair supply of vegetables purchased by the prison fund. Desiccated vegetables were at first furnished, but as they were not acceptable to the prisoners, fresh onions and potatoes were substituted. Inspector LYMAN reports on November 11, 1864, that onions and potatoes were supplied on three days out of five, and in each of his subsequent reports speaks of the supply of vegetables as sufficient. On one occasion he reported the beef as of inferior quality, but generally the diet is represented as good and well cooked, the kitchen being under the supervision of a special officer.

On the arrival of the prisoners, and while the hospital was in course of erection, the sick were treated in a pavilion set apart for their reception. Medical supplies and accommodations were deficient at this time. An inspection report dated July 15, 1864, says: "They are absolutely without the necessary medical and hospital supplies. Requisitions were made three weeks ago. Until the day of my inspection the sick were laid on the naked bunks from the inability to obtain straw. This was finally procured by the commanding officer after considerable difficulty, and arrived during my inspection. When the requisition for medicine and hospital supplies is filled they will be in every respect suitably provided in a sanitary view." In August, medicines were reported abundant; but the sickness was large and the mortality great. "This," said the inspector, "is due to the broken-down condition of the prisoners on their arrival." There were at this time 9,170 prisoners, of whom 553 received hospital attendance and 558 were prescribed for at sick-call.

The medical staff consisted of a surgeon in charge and eleven or twelve assistants. Confederate surgeons sometimes assisted in attending to the sick. Visits by the medical officer were made twice a day, and in special cases oftener; and any complaint against a medical attendant of inattention or harshness was promptly investigated. Competent persons were selected from among the prisoners to compound prescriptions and to act as nurses and cooks.

In August the hospital consisted of three wards of seventy beds each, and one of eighty-two beds, with 624 cubic feet of space per bed. On October 4th there were 9,063 prisoners, of whom 3,873 slept in the barracks and 5,190 in 1,038 tents. The air-space in the larger barrack buildings was 111 cubic feet per man, in the smaller buildings 92.5 cubic feet. There were 1,560 men on the sick report. The hospital had been extended, consisting now of six new wards averaging 62 beds each, with 654 feet of air-space per bed, and four barrack-buildings averaging 70 beds, with 342 cubic feet per bed.

On November 11, an additional hospital ward of 62 beds, with 654 feet of space per bed, had been completed, and one of the old 70-bed wards was vacated for use as quarters.

In January, 1865, with a view to diminish the sickness and lessen the mortality, the Medical Inspector made the following recommendations: "1st. That additional wards be constructed and provision be made for hot-water bathing of the sick. It is impracticable to give this thoroughly in the wards, and it is very much needed. 2d. That hospital clothing be allowed, which would afford an opportunity for cleansing the woollen and underclothing of the patients. 3d. That all the old barracks be provided with additional windows. In the winter season the men confine themselves to the wards as much as possible for warmth, and the closing of the doors and windows renders these barracks too dark. 4th. That more cubic and superficial space be allowed by the erection of additional barracks. The type of disease among the prisoners is that which results from over-crowding: there is no acute disease, everything assumes a typhoid type."

The condition of the camp at the date mentioned is thus described: "The whole appearance of this camp is greatly improved since the last inspection. The sick in hospital and quarters are now vigilantly watched; the food is good and well cooked; coal stoves have been substituted for wood, and the police of the barracks is quite as good, and, I think, better than in most regimental barracks." Small-pox broke out among the prisoners about this time. From December 1, 1864, to January 24, 1865, there had been 397 cases. To isolate these properly a small-pox hospital had been improvised with tents; but a new pavilion was being constructed to replace it. During January 5,600 vaccinations and revaccinations were performed. To replace, and afford better shelter than the tents, twenty-four new barracks, each 100 × 24 × 12 and 3 feet pitch of roof, had been completed by the middle of March, and six more were in course of construction. These are said to have given 180 cubic feet of air-space per man. At this period there were 1,738 on the sick-list in a total of 5,934 prisoners, and many of those in quarters were very sick and stood as much in need of suitable ward-accommodation as those in hospital, into which, for want of room, they could not be received. "The condition of the patients is pitiable," says the inspector; "the diseases are nearly all of the typhoid type, and much of the sickness is justly attributable to crowd-poisoning. In addition to this, the clothing during the winter was insufficient. The deep mud prevents the exercise of the prisoners in the open air, and there is no occupation for most of them to relieve, in a measure, the depressing influence of prison-life. The Fort Fisher prisoners, especially, arrived in cold weather very much depressed, poorly clad, and great numbers were soon taken sick with pneumonia and diarrhœa, rapidly assuming a typhoid character. The surgeon was recommended to press constantly upon the commandant the necessity for appropriating some of the best barracks for additional wards, the *immediate* completion of the floor-ventilation, the alteration already commenced in the hospital latrines, and the free use of permanganate of potash throughout the barracks and of bromine in the wards. I would renew the recommendation, made in my January report, that additional light be given to the old barracks, and greater facilities for warm and cold bathing as prophylactic measures." Subsequently, up to June 22, 1865, the date of the last report, the sanitary condition of the camp and buildings is reported as having been good. The number of prisoners continued to diminish and the ratio of mortality grew steadily less.

PRISON DEPÔT AT FORT DELAWARE, DELAWARE.—This fort assumed importance as a prison depôt in June, 1863, when 8,400 men captured by General Grant in his operations against Vicksburg were sent to it for confinement. On June 3, Medical Inspector E. P. VOLLUM, U. S. Army, inspected the post in accordance with instructions from the Surgeon General, to determine the character and extent of the hospital accommodations to be provided. At this time barracks for 8,000 men were in course of erection. The condition of the post and prisoners when at its worst, that is, shortly after the arrival of this large body of men, is fully depicted in the following report by Assistant Surgeon C. H. ALDEN, U. S. Army, dated July 11, 1863, on the causes of the sickness and mortality in the camp:

"Fort Delaware is situated on an island in the Delaware river, below Philadelphia and nearly opposite Delaware City. The island has an area of about 90 acres and the soil is of a low marshy nature. Fort Delaware proper is a large casemated work of granite and brick, which accommodates but a small part of the inhabitants of the post. It has within it the different offices of the post, officers' quarters, rooms where the officers, prisoners of war, are confined, and guard-house for the prisoners of the U. S. troops. Outside the fort are numerous wooden buildings of more or less recent date, accommodating the rank and file of the prisoners of war, workmen, the hospitals, sutler's store, etc., with a few cottages for officers' quarters, and a number of tents occupied by the troops composing the guard. There are now some 7,100 prisoners confined on the island, including about 300 officers. The guard numbers about 800 men.

The barracks for the prisoners of war are two in number, the old and the new, each composed of one-story wooden buildings enclosing a rectangular piece of ground. They are ordinary shed-buildings with shingle roofs. The ventilation of these buildings is very defective. The old barrack has small windows along the side at considerable intervals, and a ridge ventilator along the whole length of the building. The new barrack, though somewhat higher, is still worse in its facilities for ventilation, the ventilators at the ridge being only occasional and placed at considerable intervals. The interior is arranged with a central aisle and on either side three tiers of bunks or rather shelves, inclining towards the centre. The prisoners lie on these shelves with their heads directed to the exterior of the building. In the old barrack are confined 3,500 men, a number, it seems to me, far too great for its capacity. A rough estimate, but I believe a tolerably correct one, shows that each occupant has less than 100 cubic feet of air, in connection with which should be remembered the small opportunity offered for the renewal of the air. The new barrack is not yet entirely occupied, owing to a portion of the building having given away and requiring repair. This will in a measure account for the crowding of the old barrack, which will, I was assured, be relieved as soon as the new is in condition to be occupied. There are also attached to the barracks mess-halls and kitchens. The mess-halls have long narrow tables at which the prisoners stand at meals. The barracks, mess-halls, kitchens and the prisoners themselves were in a very dirty condition; some portions of the buildings much more so than others.

The island is intersected by several ditches and inlets, but the drainage is very imperfect, and the grounds inside the prisoners' barracks were rendered very muddy by the recent rains. The water is now excluded from the moat around the fort to enable the workmen to build the counterscarp. The filth received into this moat from the drains and privies of the fort is therefore not removed by the water and lies exposed and decomposing, causing most disagreeable effluvia on a warm day. The water-closets for the prisoners, as well as for all those living outside of the fort, are on the edge of the island projecting over the water.

The water on the island is chiefly rain-water of good quality. At intervals along the outside of the barracks are tanks for the collection and storage of the rain-water. Of these there are a large number, and many of them appeared pretty full from the recent rains. There are also tanks connected with the hospitals and other buildings around the fort. Under the casemates of the main work are a series of large cisterns which are designed to be filled by the rain-fall on the parapets percolating through the earth, sand and gravel (forming a filtering arrangement), down into them. They are of large capacity, but at present have a small supply in them. When rain-water is scarce it has been the practice to send for water by vessel to the Brandywine; some of the water now on the island is from this source. The water of the Delaware river, which surrounds the island, is, I learn from credible persons who have lived there some years, considered entirely fit for drinking in the winter and early spring. At other seasons it is somewhat brackish. If taken at low-water, however, it is not even in summer considered decidedly injurious. As far as I could learn, and I took the statements of several officers and of the prisoners themselves, the supply of rain-water has as yet been sufficient for the garrison, and has been enough also to afford drinking water to the prisoners. The latter use the river water in part, if not entirely, for cooking purposes. With the present number of persons on the island the supply of water on hand would certainly fall short soon. Measures are, however, being taken, by bringing water from the Brandywine and by pumping up (by steam apparatus) water from the river, throwing it over the parapets and allowing it to filter through into the cisterns beneath, to obtain a good supply. A condensing apparatus has also been ordered.

The ration issued to the prisoners is the ration issued to the U. S. Army before the late increase in quantity. The meat is brought, already butchered, from the main land, and appears to be of good quality. The bread is partly baked on the spot and partly procured from Delaware City. The latter is very good, but the former, though of tolerable quality generally, appeared in one or two instances a little sour. Besides this, hard bread is also supplied to the prisoners.

There are five hospitals on the island, one for the garrison and four for the prisoners of war, all outside the fort. They are frame buildings. Two are old, badly ventilated and poorly adapted for the purpose; the three others are mere sheds, which have, however, the advantage of being tolerably ventilated through the chinks of the rough boarding. One of the wards of the post-hospital was particularly small, and though it had but 17 men in it, they had an allowance of less than 300 cubic feet of air per man; it was besides badly ventilated. Two hospital tents are also occupied by sick prisoners of war. All the hospitals, but more particularly those of the prisoners, were in poor police; the grounds around them particularly so. There was a great deficiency, or rather an almost entire want of stores, clothing and medical supplies of all kinds; bedding was also very insufficient. There were no bedsteads for most of the sick prisoners of war. A sufficiency of stimulants for immediate use is, I was informed, obtained through the Quartermaster's department.

Assistant Surgeon H. R. Silliman, U. S. Army, is in charge. It is due to him to say that he was assigned to this post but a few days ago. I have no doubt he will immediately make efforts to have the defects above mentioned corrected. He informs me that four days since he made requisition for all necessary supplies on the Medical Director at Baltimore. The books and records of the hospital were in much confusion, or rather none were, I believe, kept except a register of the sick of the garrison and a morning report.

This want of correct records makes it difficult to obtain exactly the number of sick, deaths, etc., but the following data are believed to be tolerably accurate: There are 210 sick prisoners of war, among whom are included a few wounded just received from the battlefields in Pennsylvania. The morning report shows that there are 69 of the garrison sick, 24 being in hospital and 45 in quarters. The chief, and I may say almost exclusive, disease is chronic diarrhœa. Hospital reports reveal the fact that the disease and the incident mortality is almost entirely confined to the members of the rebel regiments from Alabama, Mississippi, and other southern states, taken prisoners by General Grant's army around Vicksburg. A large part of these men came hither broken down, emaciated and already the subjects, for some weeks or months, of this disease. The long journey from Vicksburg to this place seems to have exhausted all their vital powers, and many died soon after their arrival. There is very little sickness and hardly any mortality among the prisoners of war brought from General Lee's army, or any other source than the army around Vicksburg. All are equally exposed of course to any imperfect hygienic influences existing on the island; but the fact that the sickness and mortality are almost entirely confined to the prisoners from Vicksburg, shows, I think, that the conditions under which they are now placed are chargeable neither with their sickness nor mortality.

It is important to bear in mind that the majority of the prisoners have been upon the island but a few days. The want of ventilation, the over-crowding and bad police of the prisoners' barracks, which I have mentioned, have not as yet had time to produce any marked effect on their health. I cannot but conceive, however, that serious results will ensue, if these causes are allowed to operate for any length of time, especially at this season.

I deem it my duty, in view of the pressing necessity of the subject, to call the attention of the commanding general to the want of ventilation of the barracks, the over-crowding and the want of police. The prospect of a deficient supply of water had fully engaged his attention, and he was using his best efforts to provide for it. He requested me to point out the fact that the tanks attached to the barracks should have been double the size, also the need of a water-tank boat for bringing water, and suggested that the new hospital for 600 beds, now in progress of contruction, should have tanks twice the size of those contracted for.

The attention of the medical officer in charge was called to the urgent necessity of taking measures to provide hospital stores and medical supplies. He was advised to make an immediate special requisition on Surgeon Murray, the Medical Purveyor at Philadelphia, for such articles as were most needed, stating the emergency. He was also advised to have the hospitals and the grounds around them thoroughly policed, applying for a detail of men, if necessary, and to have the buildings whitewashed inside. It was recommended to obtain additional hospital tents and remove into them the sick from the crowded wards of the garrison hospital, and also to have a pig-sty near one of the hospitals taken away. Several benevolent individuals having offered contributions, he was advised to accept and invite them, especially of underclothing and hospital stores. This seems to be the more necessary, as at present there is no hospital fund with which to purchase extras.

The subject of allowing the prisoners to bathe unfortunately escaped my attention. I was informed, however, by one of the officers of the post, that it had not been permitted for the officers, and the condition of the men certainly indicated that they have not enjoyed any greater privileges in this respect. If occasional bathing could not only be allowed but compelled, it would of course contribute materially to the health of the prisoners, and there seems to be no good reason why, under proper and sufficient regulations, this could not safely be provided for."

PRISON-CAMP AND HOSPITAL AT POINT LOOKOUT, MARYLAND.—This camp was established in August, 1863, on the eastern side of the point at some distance north of the site of the Hammond General Hospital. In his report for July of that year Medical Inspector General J. K. BARNES, U. S. Army, mentioned the proposed settlement of ten thousand prisoners in the vicinity of the hospital, and called the attention of the Surgeon General to the fact that at least 700 of the beds of this establishment would be required for the use of the sick among this number of prisoners. The point was sandy and sparsely dotted with shrubby vegetation. The site was considered healthy. The prison-area was surrounded on three sides by a stockade; on the east side it opened on Chesapeake Bay. One or two gun-boats guarded the water-front of the camp. The prisoners were sheltered in Sibley and A tents, which were pitched in regular lines separated by well-graded streets. One division of the prisoners occupied cracker-box huts, built by themselves out of such timber as was obtainable on the point and shingle-like fragments of the empty hard-bread boxes. At first the sick were sent to the Hammond Hospital, but after a time a prison hospital, in which cases of a less severe character were treated, was established within the stockade. The water-supply was from a number of wells which yielded each from 500 to 1,000 gallons daily, but diarrhœa was sometimes attributed to its use. The soil of the camp-site was kept unusually free from excremental taint, as the sinks were built over the waters of the bay, which promptly carried off the deposited filth.

The first, and perhaps the only, report of special interest from this camp contains a protest against over-crowding. It was written by Surgeon JAS. H. THOMPSON, U. S. Vols., Surgeon in charge, June 30, 1864: "Several thousand prisoners captured during the present campaign have been received into camp during the month of June. Many of these were suffering from exhaustion and diseases incident to an active campaign. It will be perceived by a reference to the mortuary report that most of the deaths during the month occurred among these new arrivals. The types of all diseases occurring in camp have been more aggravated than during previous months. Wounds, though generally progressing favorably, have in several instances proved troublesome from gangrene and proneness to secondary hæmorrhages. Only one case of variola has occurred and fifty-five cases of measles; the latter disease is increasing, the former nearly extinct. Requisition has been made for vaccine lymph to protect the new arrivals.

Subjoined is an extract from a report forwarded to the commanding officer of the Post June 23, 1864:—

' I have the honor to call the attention of the commanding officer to the already crowded condition of the prisoners' camp at this post, and as sanitary officer of the camp to respectfully protest against the reception of additional numbers of prisoners, there being now fully fourteen thousand persons within the camp, and nearly twenty thousand on the point, including the U. S. Hammond General Hospital with one thousand three hundred wounded men, the contraband camp of indefinite numbers, the Quartermaster's department and troops of the garrison. In addition to these are the Quartermaster's stables with, I suppose, two hundred and fifty horses and mules.

The reasons why I am urged to make this protest are:

1st. The limited area of the camp and of the occupied surface of the point.

2d. The already insufficient and injurious quality of the water. According to the results of analysis the water of some of the wells is unfit for use, and to this I attribute largely the increased prevalence and fatality of disease during the past month.

3d. Though the police of the camp is, and has been for several months past, most excellent, still every precaution against epidemic disease, with this over-crowding of the camp not only continued but rumor says yet to be increased, will, I fear, prove futile, and we may see ere the summer is past an epidemic that will decimate not only the ranks of the prisoners, but affect alike all the inhabitants of the point,—

I therefore recommend to the consideration of the commanding officer:

1st. That no greater number of prisoners or troops than at present occupy the ground be allowed upon the point.

2d. That condensers be at once put up to furnish a sufficient quantity of pure water.

3d. The diminished issue of salt pork and the largely increased issue of fresh vegetables; this in consideration of the scorbutic tendency and character exhibited in the majority of diseases occurring in the camp.

4th. The *immediate* construction of barrack-hospitals for the accommodation of two hundred sick.' "

The condensers were not furnished, but to supply the increased necessity for water a number of new wells were dug. Free issues of vegetable food were made to the prisoners and a post-hospital of six wards was commenced outside the stockade. Large numbers of the prisoners were employed under guard on this and other work in the vicinity of the camp. The details for such duty were eagerly coveted as furnishing occupation and change of scene, and entitling the laborer to extra rations or special issues of tobacco, as might be desired.

By orders dated August 31, 1864, from headquarters of the military district in which the camp was situated, the provost marshal was charged with the duty of inspecting the camp and hospital of the prisoners of war. Daily inspections were enjoined, and weekly reports required, covering such points as personal cleanliness, clothing and bedding, quarters, kitchen and messing, police, sinks and drainage, hospital wards and attendants, etc.

From a perusal of these reports, now on file in the office of the Adjutant General of the Army, it is evident that few prison-camps were in better condition than this depot at Point Lookout. During the warm months the prisoners were required to bathe and change their underclothing once a week. In fact, many took frequent advantage of the general permission to bathe in the waters of Chesapeake Bay. During the winter the facilities for personal cleanliness were not so satisfactory. The water-supply from wells, twelve to twenty feet deep, was at first sufficient for all the needs of the camp; but as fresh commitments were made new wells had to be dug, and on a few occasions of large and unexpected increments of the population, as for instance, on April 16, 1865, when over 5,000 were received, precautions had to be taken against waste of water until new sources of supply became available.

Besides the ordinary body-clothing, every prisoner was furnished with an overcoat and blanket and a change of underclothing. On each of the weekly reports are noted the number of prisoners received and the articles of clothing, etc., issued. Sometimes, when a large commitment was made, the clothing on hand was insufficient for the supply of the new arrivals. Thus, although during the week ending October 16, 1864, 1,000 overcoats, 1,800 blankets, 402 blouses, 202 pairs of drawers, 168 pants, 650 shirts, 650 pairs of shoes and 380 pairs of socks were issued, it is stated that to make the prisoners comfortable and provide each with a blanket, further issues of 4,000 shirts, 3,000 pants, 2,500 pairs of shoes and 1,500 blankets were imperatively required. Requisitions for needful articles were as a rule promptly honored. The quartermaster had on hand at this time a large number of pants, but as they were of the regulation blue color it was deemed inadvisable to distribute them. The similarity in the dress of the guard and prisoners would have facilitated escape, particularly as over 900 of the prisoners were daily employed on the public works outside the stockade. During the winter some of the prisoners received extra articles of clothing from their friends in the south, and on February 19, 1864, twelve bales of blankets and one case of socks arrived from New York through the Confederate Agency for the supply of prisoners. These, and subsequent supplies from the same source, were distributed by a committee of prisoners to whom this duty was assigned. The report of March 5 states that two other lots of clothing had been received from General BEALE, the rebel agent in New York, and that of March 26 has the further statement that "the supplies of clothing furnished by the Rebel authorities are quite liberal and timely."

The quarters consisted of Sibley tents, twelve men to a tent, and A tents with four men in each. No description is given of the character of the make-shift shelters constructed of cracker-boxes and fragments of old lumber, but as permission to build was regarded as a favor, it seems as if these compared favorably in point of comfort with the tents, one-third of which, towards the end of the occupation of the camp, were reported as unserviceable.

Six kitchens, with large mess-halls attached, were used in the preparation and consumption of food. The rations were uniformly of good quality and well cooked. At the time these inspections were instituted vegetables were issued freely to counteract the tendency to scorbutic manifestations among the prisoners, and these issues appear to have been kept up to the end.

The camp was preserved in an excellent state of police. All cleaning was completed before 9 A. M., at which time the prisoners formed line in their respective divisions and were inspected by the provost marshal. To supplement the sinks, boxes were in use for the convenience of the prisoners during the night. These were removed in the early morning by the police parties.

At the suggestion of Surgeon THOMPSON nine hospital wards of sixty beds each were built outside the stockade; they were reported finished on October 30. There were in addition one hundred and twenty hospital tents floored with lumber and fitted up with hospital beds. Wards were set apart for the treatment of measles, small-pox and erysipelas. These, with a full staff of medical officers and attendants and ample supplies of medicines and medical comforts, were provided for the cure of the prisoners when sick and as a relief to the wards of the Hammond Hospital, which, however, continued to keep its doors open for the reception of prisoners when, as was usually the case, the prison-hospital failed to accommodate their number. On December 18 Surgeon THOMPSON insisted on the necessity for increased hospital facilities, but no action was taken on this recommendation as the Hammond Hospital at all times acted the part of a prison-hospital.

Occasional remarks on the reports of the provost marshal by Brigadier General JAMES BURNES, commanding the prison-camp, testify to the existence of a uniformly satisfactory condition of affairs. "I have," he says on the report of November 6, "nothing particular to add to the statement of the inspecting officer except my general testimony to the kindness manifested by the different officers connected with the duties of the government and discipline of the camp. Fortunately the general good conduct of the prisoners renders unnecessary any act of severity towards them, and is at the same time sufficient testimony as to the mode of their treatment."

The following extract from a report of Assistant Surgeon J. C. McKEE, U. S. Army, dated July 1, 1862, shows the insanitary conditions at one of the minor or temporary prison-camps—that established near Springfield, Illinois:

"CAMP BUTLER, ILLINOIS, is situated on the Great Western Railroad, six miles from the town of Springfield. The camp is established on a rather high and rolling piece of ground, surrounded by a high board fence, enclosing some fifteen acres of land. It was originally intended as a camp of instruction for volunteers. The barracks were built for two regiments. They are mere shells, single boards forming the sides and roofs; the sides very low, about eight feet in height; the roofs covered with tarred paper. Erected by contract they afford protection neither from storms nor heat. During this month the thermometer has been steady at 102° for days in my own room. The effect of such intense and continued heat on the sick and well in these miserably constructed barracks has been prostrating in the extreme. The prisoners of war, over two thousand in number, occupy the rows of barracks on the right; in front of these there are two rows of tents on a main street also occupied by them. Four of the barracks in this row are used as hospitals, part of another as a drug store. A line of sentinels surrounds all, leaving ample room for the prisoners to exercise; but they are generally indifferent to this and to their personal cleanliness. Two other hospitals outside of these lines are now allotted to convalescents on account of the shade. On my arrival here in May I found the hospitals, six in number, in a miserable sanitary condition. No one had taken the authority or trouble to better this. The floors were filthy; deodorizing agents were not thought of; slops and filth were thrown indiscriminately around. The sick were crowded in wooden bunks; some on the floor, many without blankets, and nearly all without straw, either new or old. No attention was paid to ventilation or drainage. The stench of the wards was horrid and sickening. Food was abundant but badly prepared; medicines were deficient. The stewards were ignorant and negligent of their business; the nurses and cooks insubordinate and inattentive to the wants of their sick companions. The condition of the prisoners, many of whom had been broken down in service prior to their capture, opened a favorable and unlimited field for the development of low types of disease, and accordingly typhus and typhoid fevers, pneumonia, erysipelas, etc., raged with violence and great fatality.

To carry out my plans of improvement required much explanation and persuasion. I was successful in what I undertook for the comfort of these unfortunate sick. Floors were scrubbed; lime applied freely on the walls and floors; ventilation and drainage attended to. A fever hospital (making seven) was established; another hospital was used for pneumonia; another for erysipelas. The surgeons (prisoners of war) were assigned to their own hospitals; stewards and nurses were encouraged to emulate each other in the cleanliness of their wards—all with the happiest effects. Cooks were supplied with necessary kitchen furniture; barrels were procured for slops; water was furnished in abundance for the sick; wards were limited to the number of 30 patients. The hospital fund procured many necessary articles such as ice. The Medical Purveyor at Chicago sent me a full supply, according to the Standard Supply Table, for six months. A drug store, under an excellent druggist, was established. A quantity, sufficient for a change, of shirts, drawers and sheets was obtained from the Quartermaster; fresh straw and bed-sacks were also secured. Under these changes the difference in the mortality of my hospitals was remarkable and exceedingly gratifying. During the month of May one hundred and twenty-three died, whilst in June only thirty died.

Of twenty-four cases of camp fevers (typhus) four died; of fourteen cases of typhoid two died; of thirty-three cases of common continued fever two died. In two cases I was unable to diagnose whether they were typhus or typhoid until after a *post-mortem* examination. The former disease was sudden in its attacks; in two cases the patients died on the third day. Ammonia, tonics and stimulants had to be used in large quantities. One case (I thought of fatal relapse) was saved by blistering the whole length of the spine with ammonia and mustard. Typhoid or enteric fever was treated much in the same way, with the addition of oil of turpentine, of which I cannot speak too highly. Quinia had to be employed freely among these men in nearly all diseases. They generally come from miasmatic districts. I can speak with the highest satisfaction of the use of muriated tincture of iron in the treatment of erysipelas; alternated with quinia it controlled the disease in all its forms. I found local applications, as of iodine and nitrate of silver, unsatisfactory in their results, not controlling the spread of the disease. I abandoned their use and applied emulsion of flaxseed, saving pain and trouble to my patients. The two fatal cases reported were complicated with other diseases."

Having obtained from this investigation of the reports of the medical inspectors some idea of the unhygienic surroundings of the prisoners at these depôts, the following table, contrasting their mortality-rates from all diseases and from certain prominent classes of disease, may be consulted with advantage:

TABLE XXI.

Comparing the Annual Sickness and Mortality from certain Specified Diseases at the Principal Depôts for Rebel prisoners.

NAME OF PRISON.	Camp Douglas, Ill.	Alton, Ill.	Rock Island, Ill.	Camp Morton, Ind.	Johnson's Island, Ohio.	Camp Chase, Ohio.	Elmira, New York.	Fort Delaware, Del.	Point Lookout, Md.	All these depôts.
Annual sick-rate per 1,000 strength ...	3,757	10,072	1,575	1,485	811	4,735	1,544	3,549	2,471	2,997.6
Annual death-rate from—										
Continued Fevers	19.2	24.5	6.4	7.0	5.9	10.4	21.2	12.7	12.3	13.6
Malarial Fevers	12.7	62.0	6.1	19.9	2.3	6.7	9.9	14.2	9.2	12.6
Eruptive Fevers...................	36.7	188.0	51.0	14.3	3.8	71.6	58.9	38.5	18.9	42.3
Diarrhœa and Dysentery	38.1	80.2	42.5	52.8	10.5	44.6	211.5	52.4	116.3	73.0
Scurvy	2.1	2.1	1.6	1.0	0.0	1.0	3.0	7.7	9.5	4.3
Pneumonia and Pleurisy..........	70.7	96.6	46.4	82.5	5.7	188.6	117.3	32.7	23.7	61.7
All diseases......................	214.5	509.4	186.1	196.8	35.4	343.2	444.1	179.1	206.6	230.4
Percentage of fatal cases.............	5.7	5.0	11.8	13.2	4.4	7.2	28.8	5.0	8.4	7.7
Annual death-rate from disease per 1,000 men admitted.	44.1	55.0	98.0	46.7	9.8	75.2	241.0	45.4	46.4	65.7

The average death-rate from disease, 230.4 annually per thousand prisoners present, was exceeded at the three depots, Alton, Ill., Elmira, N. Y., and Camp Chase, Ohio. At the first named of these prisons the high rate of 509.4 annually per thousand, calls for special inquiry into the conditions that produced it. Excepting scurvy, every one of the diseases mentioned in the above table had at this post a death-rate higher than among the prisoners generally. The exception suggests that here the inmates had a better and more varied diet than was served at prisons where the death-rate from disease was below the average, as at Fort Delaware and Point Lookout; the diet, at least, was apparently not responsible for the great mortality. This large death-rate seems at first sight an argument against the use of permanent brick or stone buildings, like this convict prison, as depots for the safe-keeping of prisoners of war. The annual rate from the eruptive fevers, 188, as against 42.3, the average among the prisoners in all the depots, might be held as illustrating the ravages of small-pox when such close ill-ventilated buildings become infected. The death-rate for the continued fevers, 24.5, nearly double that of the same fevers among the prisoners as a whole, might be regarded as further testimony to the influence of crowd-poisoning within substantial walls as compared with the influences developed by similar crowding in tents and cheaply constructed wooden pavilions. But when it is observed that malarial fevers also were largely more fatal than at any of the other depots, although the penitentiary was on a high, dry and well-drained site, it must be concluded that the facts, so far as presented, do not include everything bearing upon the mortality-rate per thousand of strength at this post.

The vast number of cases, 10,072, taken sick annually at Alton in an average strength of 1,008 men, equivalent to ten entries on sick report per man during the year, also requires explanation. This is found in the fact that the strength present was not a settled population; it consisted of constantly varying elements. Detachments of prisoners were received, bringing with them their sick to augment the sick report, while generally only the well men, those fit to travel, were exchanged, released on oath or enlisted into the service, the sick remaining to swell the mortality lists of the post. The number of persons committed to this depot was 9,330, and as the average strength was only 1,008, the stay of each prisoner must have been of comparatively short duration. Practically the strength present was changed 9.2 times during the period of its occupation as a military prison, or 3.2 times annually. When the deaths are viewed in connection with these facts, Alton will be found to have been by no means the terrible pest-hole suggested by the enormous rate of its cases to the average of its strength, or by the annual demise of more than one-half of its population.

All the other depots except Fort Delaware and Johnson's Island had a larger percentage of fatal cases of disease than the Alton penitentiary. The Fort Delaware rate of 5.0 per cent. equalled that of Alton; only at Johnson's Island was the rate of fatality smaller, 4.4 per cent. The ratio of deaths to cases among prisoners is, however, not of much value, as uncertain numbers of slight cases were not taken upon the report. But when the deaths are considered in relation to the number of persons who entered the penitentiary, the annual rate of 55.0 per thousand will be found less than the average rate of all the prisons, 65.7 per thousand.

Alton may not, therefore, be considered as having been the worst specimen of our northern prisons. On the contrary, but for the heavy mortality of its small-pox epidemic, it would have compared favorably with any of the others except the depot at Johnson's Island, Ohio.

Similar changes, to some extent, took place at all the other prisons; and their influence must be considered in estimating the unhealthiness of these depots from the death-rates expressed as ratios of the average strength present. A statistical table contained in a report of the Adjutant General of the Army, appended to the Report of the Committee on the Treatment of Prisoners of War, gives the total number of commitments to each of the prison depots: Camp Douglas, Ill., received 26,060 men; Alton, Ill., as already stated, 9,330; Rock Island, Ill., 11,458; Camp Morton, Ind., 12,082; Johnson's Island, Ohio, 7,627; Camp Chase, Ohio, 16,335; Elmira, N. Y., 12,147; Fort Delaware, Del., 25,275; and Point Lookout, Md., 42,762.*

When the deaths are calculated as annual ratios per thousand of these commitments, the depot at Elmira, N. Y., and not that at Alton, Ill., stands forth as the most insalubrious of these prison-camps. Not only had it a high mortality-rate, 444.1 annually per thousand of strength, but the percentage of fatal cases, 28.8, was more than double that of any other depot. The latter rate, like the corresponding figures from the Andersonville prison, gives no true expression to the ratio of deaths to cases, but it indicates such an extensive prevalence of disease that only the serious cases, too often destined to be fatal, were taken up on the registers of sick. The death-rate was equally high when viewed in relation to the commitments, 241.0 annually per thousand, as compared with 55.0 at Alton, or 65.7, the average of the prison-camps. Diarrhœa and dysentery, which caused more deaths at this depot, in proportion to the strength present, than were occasioned by all diseases at some of the other camps, and pneumonia, which produced a rate nearly double that of the average of the prisons, were the diseases which gave Elmira its unenviable notoriety. From the reports of the medical inspectors it is evident that while a large mortality was undoubtedly referable to over-crowding, insufficient hospital accommodation and insufficient protection from the cold of a northern climate in the earlier history of the depot, the main influence underlying all these and raising them into strong relief, was the broken-down condition of the men at the time of their commitment: most of them suffered from diarrhœa of a chronic character. Of the 1,394 deaths attributed to diarrhœa and dysentery on the records of this camp, 1,376 were reported as from chronic diarrhœa and only 6 from acute diarrhœa, 7 for acute dysentery and 5 for chronic dysentery.

Turning from the high rates prevalent at Elmira, it is a pleasure to point out the 35.4 per thousand of strength which constituted the annual mortality-rate at Johnson's Island, Ohio, its fatality rate of 4.4 per cent. of the cases and its 9.8 deaths annually for every thousand commitments.

The absence of Confederate records showing the general condition of the men on active service deprives us of the ability of learning from that source their probable state of health at the time of their capture. The few statistics presented in Table XIV indicate that the Confederate sick-rate was considerably greater than that of the Union forces, and that diarrhœa, dysentery and pulmonary affections, exceedingly prevalent in both armies, were more prevalent among the southern troops. In Table XIII these diseases were observed to yield at the same time a much larger percentage of fatal cases in the rebel ranks, the deaths from pulmonary disease constituting as much as 18.89 per cent. of the cases as compared with the federal rate of 2.34 per cent. The unbolted corn-meal, which formed the farinaceous staple of the Confederate ration, was certainly a prolific cause of intestinal

---

* *Op. cit.*, page 760 *et seq.*

irritation, especially in troops subject to the influence of strong predisposing conditions. The high rates in pulmonary affections may readily be referred to the exposures of the poorly clad and imperfectly protected southern soldiers during service in a northern and less genial climate than that to which they were accustomed. No information is on file concerning the prevalence of scurvy in their ranks; but that it was present to a greater extent than among the federal troops may be taken for granted, in view of the liberal ration of the latter, the efficiency of their supply system and their greater facilities for purchasing by private funds. It seems, indeed, highly probable that much of the scurvy reported on the sick lists of the prison-camps affected the prisoners at the time of their capture. At Johnson's Island, Ohio, where no death from scurvy took place, and where the abundance and variety of the diet negatived the idea of its development in the prison, there were, nevertheless, fifty-eight cases reported among the inmates, most of whom were officers of the rebel army. These cases must have reached the island in the scorbutic condition which necessitated their appearance on the sick list. And if scurvy affected the officers, its presence to a greater extent among the men cannot be doubted.* To the better condition of the officers of the Southern army, as compared with that of their men when the fortune of war consigned them to Johnson's Island, Ohio, must be in great part attributed the slight amount of sickness and mortality that affected them during their detention. They were subject to the same rules and regulations, and had the same ration as the prisoners in other camps. They had 300 feet of air-space in quarters, a more liberal allowance than was commonly furnished; but, as will be seen directly, the mortality among the prisoners generally cannot be ascribed to the limitation of bed-space.

The presumption is that, at the time of their capture, many of the prisoners were suffering from diseases resulting from insufficient diet and from the exposures and continued fatigues incident to the military movements preceding the disaster that brought about their captivity.

But no doubt exists as to their condition on their arrival at the prison. This is recorded by many of the inspecting officers. In fact, "the debilitated condition of the men from previous hardships and exposures," or words of similar tenor are of frequent occurrence in all reports relating to the sickness and mortality of the prisoners, as in those from Elmira already noted. To this is sometimes added a reference to the depressed mental condition consequent on their status as prisoners of war. Dr. ALDEN states very decidedly that the mortality from diarrhœa and dysentery among the prisoners at Fort Delaware in July, 1863, was almost entirely confined to the men from Alabama, Mississippi and other southern states taken by General GRANT's army around Vicksburg. Most of these men arrived in a broken-down condition, emaciated, and already the subjects of the disease for some weeks or months, while at that time the prisoners from General LEE's army, also confined at Fort Delaware, were in good condition. Dr. ALDEN's inference that the influences to which the prisoners were subjected at Fort Delaware were not to be charged with the sickness and mortality then occurring among them seems thoroughly sustained.

The following extract from a report on the sanitary condition of the depot at Hart's Island, New York Harbor, dated June 21, 1865, by GEORGE H. LYMAN, Medical Inspector,

---

* Dr. JONES says: "The large armies of the Confederacy suffered more than once from scurvy; and as the war progressed, secondary hæmorrhage and hospital gangrene increased to a great extent from the deteriorated condition of the blood, dependent on the prolonged use of salt meat; and but for the extra supplies received from home, and from the various benevolent State institutions, scurvy, diarrhœa and dysentery would have committed still greater ravages."—U. S. San. Com. Memoirs, p. 481.

U. S. Army, is submitted as a special illustration of the point in question, while showing at the same time that the insanitary influences affecting the prisoners at the smaller depots were similar in character to those already described as characteristic of the larger prison-camps:

The chief cause of the mortality is to be found in the fact that large numbers of the prisoners arrived at the depot broken down, in advanced stages of disease, some in fact moribund, and others past all hope for treatment.

The New Berne detachment, captured chiefly in the Carolinas, were nearly all broken down on arrival. It is said that less than 100 of them could be considered as well men or even in fair health. The surgeon then in attendance having been relieved, more precise information on this point is not now available; but it is certain that the largest percentage of sickness and mortality occurred in that detachment.

The largest proportion of deaths occurred from chronic diarrhœa brought with them, and pneumonia, which began to appear a few days after their arrival. The men being poorly clad, the weather wet and cold, and the barracks provided with no other bedding than such as the prisoners brought with them, the pneumonic cases developed rapidly, and the reduced vitality of the patients favored a typhoid type of that disease, increased probably to some extent by the crowded and unventilated condition of the barracks. These appear by measurement to have afforded 102 cubic feet of air-space to each man, and with no other ventilation than that afforded by the doors and windows on one side. Quite recently openings for ventilation have been made upon the other side of the barracks, it constituting the outer wall of the prison enclosure.

The rations have been good and in the quantity ordered by the Commissary General cf Prisoners, which is sufficiently liberal. The hospital ration has been such as is used in our own hospitals.

The drainage from the barracks is superficial but good. The sinks are outside the camp and over tide-water. The water for cooking and drinking is abundant and of excellent quality; it is derived from wells.

The prisoners have had access, under guard, to the beach, and have availed themselves of it freely for salt-water bathing. They have also been *required* to take daily exercise.

Over-crowding was regarded by the inspectors as the most serious of the insanitary conditions bearing on the prisoners during the period of their detention. But this comprehended more than the mere limitation to so much dormitory space. Under it were gathered all the evil consequences of suddenly assigning a large number of men to a camp which had not been systematically arranged for their reception. The prisoners were generally destitute of clothing and blankets, and one-tenth of them on arrival required hospital treatment. The exposures consequent on their destitute condition speedily increased the disparity between the hospital accommodations and the requirements of the sick. The wards became crowded, and the more recently developed cases had to remain in the still more crowded general quarters of the prisoners, lacking the comforts which the hospital provided for its less unfortunate inmates, and adding grievously to the harmful influences of the quarters containing them. Generally, also, healthful exercise was prevented by the mud and dust begotten of the surface-soil by the tramping of many feet in the ordinary occupations of prison life. Defective police and inadequate arrangements for the disposition of excreta rendered the external air in many places foul and sickening. A hastily dug series of pits often emitted their polluted exhalations in close proximity to the quarters, because if placed at a greater distance the sick men, especially at night, would fail to reach them. The prisoners had foul air without and fouler air within their quarters. Under these circumstances the extension and aggravation of diarrhœal cases, and the typhoid type assumed by febrile diseases such as pneumonia, naturally followed. The evils directly referable to the commitment of an excess of depressed, debilitated and destitute men to a given camp were the causes of the large sick and mortality rates that prevailed. Over-crowding, as restricted to a limitation of bed-space, was a concomitant but minor evil, as it alone would have required some time to produce its typhous effects.

Without exception, the officers in charge of these camps and hospitals, and the medical inspectors in their monthly rounds, recognized the conditions in fault; and their earnest efforts at improvement are worthy of all commendation, since they saved many lives to our re-united country and preserved our annals stainless.

The history of each of these camps shows at first a period of overwork, anxiety and grave responsibility on the part of the officers in charge when their failure to provide for the urgent necessities of the occasion would have been attended with disastrous results. In no instance does it appear that the food-supply was at any time deficient; but clothing, bedding, shelter and kitchen utensils for those who were well, and hospital accommodation, supplies and comforts for those who were sick, had often to be provided at short notice and under various difficulties. Hospital clothing was issued to the destitute until the arrival of authorized supplies. Tents were obtained for use until barracks were built. Barracks were used as hospitals until special buildings were erected. Sinks were dug for the excreta until some less objectionable method of disposal was planned and carried into effect. Trenches were opened for drainage until a covered system was provided. Nor did the improvements end when all were sheltered and fitted out with comparative comfort. New barrack buildings were constructed after improved plans, and the old were destroyed or retained to increase the available air-space. New hospitals with better conveniences replaced the old, which became converted into increased barrack-room. Lavatories and baths and the accessibility and abundance of the water-supply for flushing and other purposes received attention. In fact, from the establishment of the prison-camp until its disuse at the close of the war, the improvement of its sanitary condition was progressive and uninterrupted.

The sites selected were usually such as were considered healthy; that at Elmira had been used from the beginning of the war as a recruiting depot, and the twenty barrack buildings formerly occupied by the recruits formed the nucleus of the prison-camp,—nor was this a solitary instance of the kind. The bed-space allotted to each man in quarters was sometimes less than one hundred cubic feet, as at Fort Delaware where three tiers of bunks ran along each wall of the pavilion separated by a central or median aisle. Over-crowding to this extent was, however, not confined to the prison-barrack buildings. The wooden shelters built for the Union regiments at depots which were considered permanent were fitted up with similar shelves. The experiences of the war educated our people in sanitary matters. At an early period of its progress medical inspectors urged, with some hope of success, a reduction of the bunks to two tiers in the prisoners' quarters as well as in those of our own troops. Their request must not be esteemed a measure of what these officers considered needful. They did not ask for all they wanted, but only for what they might be likely to get.*

That the mortality among the Confederate prisoners was due, as suggested above, to other causes than the mere limitation of barrack-space, is shown conclusively by some of the reports. In the summary of the sanitary history of Camp Chase a tabular statement is given of the occupancy of the barrack buildings by the Confederate prisoners and their Union guard, showing that the latter had an air-space of 150 to 210 feet and an area of 12 to 15 feet per man, while the former had 137 cubic feet and 11.4 of superficies. There occurred in January, 1865, while the buildings were thus occupied, 8 deaths among 1,683 Union troops, or 1 in 210, and 283 deaths among 7,583 prisoners, or 1 in 26.79; in the following month the deaths among 6,414 Union soldiers numbered 36, or 1 in 178, while of 8,259 prisoners 495 died, or 1 in 16.68. These enormous differences in the death-rates cannot be attributed to the comparatively trivial differences in the air-space.

---

* The double-tiered bunk was not finally expelled from its last retreat in a western military post until ten years after the war.

Small-pox followed diarrhœa, dysentery and pneumonia in order of importance as a cause of death among the prisoners, having occasioned 32.1* of the 230.4 deaths that occurred annually from disease in every thousand of the average strength present. Nothing is on record concerning the prevalence of this disease in the southern armies. Table XIII shows that among the unknown number of the Confederate forces there were up to December, 1862, 44,438 cases and 2,274 deaths from the eruptive fevers, as compared with lower figures among the certainly larger number of the Union troops. But these statistics include measles, etc., as well as small-pox. Nevertheless its frequent occurrence among them may be inferred in view of the fact demonstrated by its ravages in the prisons,—the insufficiency of their protection by vaccination. Certainly in some instances it was apparently introduced into the prisons from the Confederate ranks. The eruption is reported as having broken out on some of the prisoners within a day or two after their arrival at the depot.

Our medical officers' appear to have faced the emergency with spirit, isolating, sometimes with difficulty, as at Rock Island, and protecting by vaccination, also with difficulty sometimes, as at Camp Douglas and Alton, until the scourge was controlled. In reporting the condition of Camp Douglas in June, 1864, Dr. HUMPHREYS says:

Of those prisoners who have been vaccinated in prison with virus that produced no bad effects in United States troops, 668 have healed tardily, while 912 vaccinated are suffering from phagedenic or indolent or irritable ulcers. This difference in the results from the use of the same virus in federals and rebels must be attributed to the cachectic and scorbutic condition of the latter.

In a report for January, 1863, Dr. WALL, the surgeon in charge at Alton, remarks as follows:

Epidemics both of small-pox and erysipelas visited us, the former with fearful violence, and what rendered it very unfortunate for us, the vaccine virus that we obtained from St. Louis, Mo., proved worthless,—thus rendering abortive for a while our attempts to stay its progress by vaccination. I am confident that if we had been successful in procuring good virus we would have modified the epidemic to a very great extent.

The probability of a marked scorbutic taint in the southern troops has already been suggested as accounting for much of the sickness and mortality directly charged against scurvy by the prison records. The ration furnished by our Government to its prisoners of war was more liberal in its quantity and variety than that issued by the Confederate Government to its soldiers on active service. Other things being equal, scurvy was therefore more likely to affect them before than after their capture.

The Confederate ration, in accordance with Army Regulations, consisted of:

Three-fourths of a pound of pork or bacon, or one and one-fourth pounds of fresh or salt beef; eighteen ounces of bread or flour, or twelve ounces of hard bread, or one and one-fourth pounds of corn-meal; and at the rate, to one hundred rations, of eight quarts of peas or beans, or in lieu thereof ten pounds of rice, six pounds of coffee, twelve pounds of sugar, four quarts of vinegar, one and one-half pounds tallow, or one and one-fourth pounds adamantine, or one pound of sperm candles; four pounds of soap, and two quarts of salt. On a campaign or on marches, or on board transports, the ration of hard bread is one pound. * * * When the officers of the medical department find anti-scorbutics necessary for the health of the troops the commanding officer may order issues of fresh vegetables, pickled onions, sour-krout, or molasses, with an extra quantity of rice and vinegar. (Potatoes are usually issued at the rate of one pound per ration, and onions at the rate of three bushels in lieu of one of beans.) Occasional issues (extra) of molasses are made—two quarts to one hundred rations—and of dried apples of from one to one and one-half bushels to one hundred rations.

During the early period of the war, when the full ration was issued, scurvy was comparatively rare. At later dates the supply department became unable to furnish coffee; corn-meal had to be largely substituted for wheaten bread or flour; fresh beef was irregu-

---

larly supplied, and the issues of rice, beans, molasses, vinegar, potatoes, dried apples and vegetables generally were diminished in frequency and in quantity. Scurvy appeared in consequence, manifested, according to Dr. JONES:

> In the frequency of night-blindness, in the numerous accidents after vaccination, in the increase of secondary hæmorrhage and hospital gangrene after wounds, as well as in the actual manifestations of the disease, indisposition to exertion, spongy gums, uncertain and ill-defined muscular pains, and obstinate diarrhœa and dysentery.[*]

The Subsistence Department of the United States Army allowed the same money value for the subsistence of the Confederate prisoner of war as for the Federal soldier. In other words, the ration allowed to the prisoner was the same in all its parts as that allowed to the United States volunteer. But the experience of our army had demonstrated that the troops seldom consumed the whole of their ration. Arrangements were therefore made by which the money value of the unconsumed portion accumulated in the hands of the subsistence officers, forming a fund by which the diet of the men might be varied by the purchase of articles not kept for issue by the subsistence department as a formal part of the ration. A surplus of bacon or coffee could by this means become converted into fresh vegetables if needful for the health of the command. Cooking utensils and articles of mess-furniture for the comfort and convenience of the men were also authorized to be purchased with this fund. A similar system was adopted at the hospitals, and milk, eggs, chickens, oysters, fruit, vegetables or other articles not issued by the subsistence or medical departments of the army, and needful for the use of the sick, were obtained by means of the money value of the bacon, flour, coffee or other articles of issue which they did not consume.

This system, in use in the forts and garrisons of the United States, was extended to the prison-camps and their hospitals. The Commissary General of Prisoners published from time to time the articles and quantities to be issued for consumption by the prisoners, and the difference between the money value of the ration thus issued and that of the full ration allowed by law to the United States soldier was set aside as a prison fund for the purchase of such articles as were necessary for the health and comfort of the prisoners, and not expressly provided for by the Army Regulations.

The saving on the ration was the chief but not the only source of the prison fund. The sutler or camp-trader was taxed a small amount for his privilege of trade, and this tax made a part of the general fund, as did also all current money left by deceased prisoners of war or accruing from the sale of their effects, and all current money clandestinely forwarded to prisoners or found concealed by them.

The following table shows the ration in kind allowed to the prisoners by circulars of the dates mentioned from the office of the Commissary General of Prisoners, together with the full ration of the United States troops at the same dates, and the difference in the value of the two rations credited to the prison fund. Prior to April 20, 1864, no specific instructions were published limiting the quantities of the constituents of the ration to be issued, but commanding officers of prison-camps were directed to withhold from the ration all that could be spared without inconvenience to the prisoners, as a basis of a fund for their benefit. After the establishment of a special prison-issue, commanding officers were authorized to report to the Commissary General of Prisoners, if at any time it seemed advisable to them to make any change in the scale:

---

[*] *Mem. U. S. Sanitary Commission*, p. 624.

	PRISONERS OF WAR.			U. S. Troops, 1864.	PRISONERS OF WAR.		U. S. Troops, 1865.
	April 20, 1864.	June 1, 1864.	Employed on public works, June 13, 1864.†		January 13, 1865.	Employed on public works.	
Pork or bacon, or	10 oz.	10 oz.	12 oz.	12 oz.	10 oz.	12 oz.	12 oz.
Fresh or salt beef	14 oz.	14 oz.	16 oz.	20 oz.	14 oz.	16 oz.	20 oz.
Flour or bread (soft), or	18 oz.	16 oz.	18 oz.	22 oz.	16 oz.	18 oz.	18 oz.
Hard bread, and	14 oz.	14 oz.	16 oz.	16 oz.	10 oz.	12 oz.	12 oz.
Corn-meal	18 oz.	16 oz.	18 oz.	20 oz.	16 oz.	18 oz.	20 oz.
To each 100 rations:—							
Beans or peas, and	6 qts.	12½ lbs.	14 lbs.	8 qts. (15 lbs.)	12½ lbs.	15 lbs.	15 lbs.
Rice or hominy	8 lbs.	8 lbs.	10 lbs.	10 lbs.	8 lbs.	10 lbs.	10 lbs.
Coffee, green, or	7 lbs.	....(*)...	7 lbs.	10 lbs.	....(*)...	7 lbs.	10 lbs.
Coffee, roasted and ground, or	5 lbs.	....(*)...	5 lbs.	8 lbs.	....(*)...	5 lbs.	8 lbs.
Tea	18 oz.	....(*)...	16 oz.	1½ lbs.	....(*)...	1 lb.	1½ lbs.
Sugar	14 lbs.	....(*)...	12 lbs.	15 lbs.	....(*)...	12 lbs.	15 lbs.
Vinegar	....	3 qts.	3 qts.	4 qts.	2 qts.	3 qts.	4 qts.
Candles, adamantine	5 candles.	....	....	1¼ lbs.	....	....	1¼ lbs.
Soap	4 lbs.	4 lbs.	4 lbs.	4 lbs.	2 lbs.	4 lbs.	4 lbs.
Salt	2 qts.	3¾ lbs.	3¾ lbs.	3¾ lbs.	2 lbs.	3¾ lbs.	3¾ lbs.
Molasses	1 qt.	....	1 qt.	1 gall.	....	....	....
Potatoes (fresh)	30 lbs.	15 lbs.	30 lbs.	100 lbs. three times a week.	....	....	....
Pepper	....	....	....	....	....	....	4 oz.
Average cost price ....cts..	16. 48	13. 63	20. 31	26. 24	16. 81	24. 20	27. 73
Credit per ration to prison fund ....cts..	9. 76	12. 61	5. 93	....	10. 92	3. 53	....

* Sugar and coffee or tea were issued to the sick and wounded only, every other day, on the recommendation of the surgeon in charge, at the rate of twelve pounds of sugar, five pounds of ground or seven pounds of green coffee or one pound of tea, to every hundred rations.

† Prisoners employed on public works other than the proper police duties of their camps were allowed, if mechanics, ten cents per day, and if laborers five cents per day, from the prison fund, which allowance was authorized to be paid in tobacco to those who preferred its expenditure in that way.

Disbursements charged against the prison fund were made by the Commissary of Subsistence on the order of the commanding officer, and all such expenditures of funds were accounted for by the commissary on his monthly statement of the prison fund, showing the issues made and the articles and quantities purchased, the prices paid, the services rendered, etc. Among the articles authorized to be purchased by this fund were all table furniture and cooking utensils, articles for policing purposes, bed-ticks and straw, and the means of improving or enlarging the barrack accommodations. Extra pay was allowed from it to clerks who had charge of the camp post office, who kept the accounts of moneys deposited by the prisoners with the commanding officer or who were otherwise engaged in labors connected with the prisoners.

The hospital fund accumulated from the savings of the ration of the sick men was disbursed on the recommendation or requisition of the surgeon in charge, approved by the commanding officer. It was kept separate from the fund of the hospital for the troops. Disbursements from it were chiefly for the purchase of articles of diet, but when the fund was sufficiently large, it was permitted to be expended for shirts and drawers for the sick, the expense of washing clothes, articles for policing purposes and all articles and objects indispensably necessary to promote the sanitary condition of the hospital.

Clothing was not charged against the prison fund. The commanding officer, through his quartermaster, made requisition on the nearest depôt for such clothing as was absolutely necessary for the prisoners, and the papers were submitted for the approval of the Commissary General of Prisoners. The articles when furnished were issued by the quartermaster under the supervision of an officer detailed for the purpose, whose certificate that the issue had been made in his presence was the quartermaster's voucher for the clothing issued. From April 30 to October 1 neither drawers nor socks were allowed except to the sick. When army clothing was issued the buttons and trimmings were removed and the skirts cut short to prevent those wearing such articles from being mistaken for United States soldiers.

The efficiency of the ration allowed the prisoners of war depended, as in the case of United States troops, on the method of its management, and on the market price of vegetables in the neighborhood of the camp. The portions of the ration issued were certainly insufficient to prevent the appearance of scurvy, for that disease was manifested among our own troops on the full ration during the war, and has been observed since the war at western posts where vegetables were scarce and correspondingly high-priced. Assuming the ration as issued to have contained a sufficiency of the nutritive elements to repair the waste generated by the internal work of the body and the slight amount of outward manifestations of force exerted by the prisoners in their enforced confinement, the want of variety in the diet would in time have produced a distaste for the food and developed the scorbutic condition. Their protection from this depended on the proper application of the prison fund. Every guard was apparently placed on the expenditure of this fund. The subsistence officers purchased only on the approval of the commanding officer, and their action was reported in detail at monthly intervals to superior authority. Inspecting officers usually devoted particular attention to the condition of the prison and hospital funds and the details of their expenditure. In many of the reports the extra articles of diet purchased during the month are itemized; in others, when a scorbutic tendency was detected, larger purchases of such articles were recommended. Generally, however, the issued rations supplemented by the purchases were considered by these able and impartial officers as an ample provision against the scorbutic taint. It may therefore be concluded that had the prisoners been healthy on their arrival, instead of broken down physically by previous hardships and depressed mentally by present conditions and anxieties, their sick and mortality lists would have been no more burdened with scorbutic cases than were those of our own men who underwent the strain of active service upon the same allowances.

In summing up the results of this study of the inspection reports of the prison depots, it may be said that the hardships and exposures entailed on the men by the military events that ended in their capture were the main causes of the disease and mortality with which they were afflicted during their subsequent confinement. The hurried marches, want of sleep, deficient rations and exposures in all kinds of weather, by night and by day, that precede and attend the hostile meeting of armies result in larger losses by disease than those that are directly attributed to the engagement. And as the wounded of a defeated army are more exposed to capture than the uninjured, so the exhausted and debilitated rather than the vigorous become included in the lists of prisoners of war.

Fatigues and exposures en route to the prison depots supplemented those already endured in exhausting their strength and producing sickness. The prisoners seldom carried from the field a sufficiency of clothing and blankets to protect them from ordinary weather-changes, and to these the journey frequently added changes of a climatic character.

The depression of spirits consequent on defeat and capture, the home-sickness of the prisoners, the despondency caused by scenes of suffering around them, the gloomy and vacuous present, and the uncertainty of the future, conspired to render every cause of disease more potent in its action.

The sudden aggregation of these men at camps unprepared for their reception developed many insanitary conditions which combined with pre-existing causes in evolving sickness and stamping it with a greater virulence. The most prominent of these were: the temporarily defective police of the camp, which contributed to the spread of diarrhœa and dysentery; the insufficient protection in quarters, which induced inflammations of the respiratory organs and gave them a typhoid character by the over-crowding; and the insufficient hospital accommodation, which, in leaving the sick in quarters, tended to the development of new cases, or, in taking them into hospital, lessened the chances of recovery of those already there.

But the evil influences exercised by the camp conditions would not have been followed by the same sickness and mortality had the ground and shelters been crowded to the same extent with well-disciplined troops awaiting the opening of a campaign. The broken health and broken spirits of the inmates were the main factors in the production of disease and death.

CHAPTER II.—INTRODUCTORY TO THE PRESENTATION OF THE CAMP FEVERS.

The fevers which prevailed in our armies were reported at the beginning of the war under the respective headings of *typhus, typhoid* and *common continued fevers, remittent fever* and *quotidian, tertian, quartan* and *congestive intermittent fevers.* Each of these names indicated, with more or less precision, a particular series of morbid phenomena. The aggregation of symptoms which gave the disease in each instance its individuality might be stated from an extensive personal knowledge of the clinical and pathological views held by the medical men who dealt with these febrile cases, but this would be admissible only in the absence of general and more trustworthy data. The lines defining each of these specially reported fevers might be drawn from the clinical records of the regimental and general hospitals of the time; but the presentation and study of these must be made later and in other connections. Nor is it necessary that this study should be attempted at the present time, for the clinical and other facts implied by the titular diagnoses of our medical men in 1861, in febrile cases, may be gathered from a brief reference to the important discoveries concerning the non-identity of certain fevers which had been made some years before, to the character of the fevers prevalent in this country at the outbreak of the war, and to the volumes on practice of medicine which were furnished by the Medical Department of the Army to its officers as books of reference.

Typhus and Typhoid Fevers.—Many observers from the time of Willis and Syden-ham described epidemics of fever differing notably in their characteristics from those of the typhus, which, under such names as *pestilent, malignant, putrid, contagious, camp, ship, jail* and *hospital* fevers, prevailed from generation to generation as a well-known scourge. These anomalous cases were afterwards named *slow, mild, nervous fevers,* or *low continued fevers;* and their occurrence was considered due to some peculiarity of the epidemic constitution from meteorological or other alterations in the condition of the atmosphere.*

At the beginning of the present century it was stated by PROST, on the authority of autopsical observations, that these fevers had their seat in the mucous membrane of the

---

* SYDENHAM suggested this peculiarity of the epidemic constitution as arising "from some certain secret and hidden alterations taking place within the bowels of the earth and pervading the atmosphere; or that, perhaps, it might chiefly depend upon some influence of the heavenly bodies." *Sydenham Society's Sydenham*, London, 1850, Vol. II, p. 191.

intestine; and for some years afterward it was taught in the French schools that they were essentially an enteritis. In 1813 PETIT and SERRES showed that the lower part of the ileum was specially affected, and that the disease, thus differing in its site from an ordinary inflammation, must be of a specific character. BRETONNEAU'S observations in 1818–27 localized the inflammation in the solitary and agminated glands, and demonstrated a want of correspondence between the severity of the local lesion and the gravity of the general symptoms. He regarded the disease as an internal exanthem,—*dothienenterite*.

Two years later, in 1829, the observations of LOUIS recognized the lesion of the intestinal glands as the essential or characteristic of the specific fever which he described as the *typhoid affection*. The profession in America became familiar with LOUIS' work through Dr. BOWDITCH's translation published in 1836.

Meanwhile pathologists in England failed to discover the glandular lesions in their fever cases except occasionally in such as presented some variations from the type of true typhus. BRIGHT in London, and ALISON in Edinburgh, in 1827, reported cases in which were found the intestinal lesions of the French observers. Thus, while the French pathologists considered the glandular lesions essential to typhus as it occurred under their observation, the British regarded them only as a comparatively rare and accidental complication. These opposing views were reconciled by a demonstration, made in Philadelphia, of the non-identity of the British and French fevers. At this time the continued fevers of the United States were neither so contagious nor so deadly as those of Britain. In the preface to his translation of HILDENBRAND on Contagious Typhus, published in 1828, Prof. S. D. GROSS said of our so-called typhus: "Nor is it perhaps precisely of the same nature and characterized by the same symptoms as the typhus of Europe." But Drs. GERHARD and PENNOCK of Philadelphia, who had studied the typhoid affection under LOUIS, and seen British typhus in London, recognized in the former the prevailing continued fever of their own country, and were able to identify the latter when it appeared in an epidemic form in Philadelphia during their service at the hospital Blockley. Their experience of this outbreak* established its identity with the contagious typhus of Britain, and showed the characteristics which distinguished it from the familiar typhoid or *dothienenterite*. These were the activity of its contagion, the suffusion of the eyes, the dusky-red color of the countenance, the stupor, the petechial eruption and the absence of special abdominal symptoms, together with the general progress of the individual case as manifested in the succession of the symptoms. In 1839 Dr. SHATTUCK of Boston insisted on the existence of two fevers in London similar to those described in Philadelphia by GERHARD. His paper, read before the Medical Society of Observation of Paris, was made the basis of an argument by M. VALLEIX on the error of the English in confounding their fevers, one of which was identical with the Parisian typhoid.

As a result of these investigations LOUIS, in the second edition of his work issued in 1841, recognized that the typhoid affection of Paris was a different disease from the contagious typhus of Britain; and in our country BARTLETT in 1842 and WOOD in 1847, described typhus and typhoid as distinct affections. Some opposition was raised to these new doctrines, but its influence was slight. Professor DICKSON of Charleston, S. C., in his Elements of Medicine published in 1855, adhered to the view that fever had but a single cause, and that the variations in its manifestations, which had given rise to such names as

---

* *American Journal Medical Sciences*, February and August, 1837.

typhus gravior and *mitior*, *putrid* and *nervous* fevers, *cerebral* and *abdominal typhus*, were due to variations in the intensity or concentration of the poison and to influences exerted on the condition or predisposition of the subject; as, for instance, where ochlesis gave to each of the forms the character of putridity or malignancy. He quoted approvingly from CAMPBELL:* "It is undeniable that the two diseases are inseparably bound together in ties of the strongest and most indissoluble, though mysterious affinity; the necessity which any theory may involve of separating them is enough of itself to declare its absurdity." Nevertheless he was constrained to treat of typhus and typhoid in his Elements under two separate heads, in deference to the almost universal usage in America at the time.

Dr. BARTLETT had already shown, in discussing the locality of typhoid fever, that it was the common continued fever of our Eastern States, and that it occurred, although perhaps with less frequency, in the West and South, where intermittents and remittents prevailed; but most of the instances cited by him were of epidemics occurring in towns. Some years later Dr. JAS. E. REEVES brought prominently to the notice of the profession the fact that enteric fever was of common occurrence in sparsely settled rural districts as well as among urban populations.†

The works on Practice of Medicine supplied to the Medical Department of the Army in 1861 were those by WOOD,‡ WATSON|| and BENNETT.§ In the first the distinction between typhus and typhoid was clearly given, and the name *enteric* fever was suggested in place of typhoid to emphasize the distinction. Dr. WATSON, influenced by Dr. JENNER's presentation of the arguments,¶ had recently subscribed to the doctrine of non-identity; and in the volume under consideration he taught the notable differences which existed in the symptoms and course of the two diseases, as well as in their comparative fatality and exciting causes, regretting that the affinity of the names imputed a similarity in the diseases, and approving Dr. BUDD's suggestion to replace the name *typhoid* by *intestinal fever*. In Dr. BENNETT's lectures the views of JENNER were given, but the author did not support them. He recognized typhoid and typhus clinically, but considered them as "evidently produced by variations in the intensity or the nature of the exciting cause."

It appears evident from these considerations that our medical officers, in identifying a case of idiopathic fever as typhoid, had well-defined ideas concerning the aggregation and sequence of symptoms to which this term should be applied. Of typhus they had practically no knowledge; but they had such conceptions of this disease and of the characteristics which distinguished it from typhoid that, when a diagnosis of typhus was given, it necessarily meant that the disease differed so materially in some points from the familiar typhoid fever as to suggest that the unfamiliar typhus of Britain was under observation.

Common Continued Fever.—Many medical officers no doubt looked upon this appellative on the sick reports as an obsolete term. The studies and observations which developed a knowledge of typhoid fever as a separate disease showed so many instances of obscurely marked fever in connection with well-marked epidemics, that these lighter cases were considered due to the prevailing typhoid cause, peculiarities in its manifestations being referred to variations in the individual constitution. Thus, while separating a specific

* P. 285 of his *Elements*.
† In the Buffalo *Medical Journal*, 1856, and in a *Practical Treatise on Enteric Fever*, Philadelphia, Pa., 1859.
‡ *A Treatise on the Practice of Medicine*, by GEORGE B. WOOD, M. D., Philadelphia, 1847.
|| *Lectures on the Principles and Practice of Physic*, by THOMAS WATSON, M. D., edited by D. F. CONDIE, M. D., Philadelphia, 1858.
§ *Clinical Lectures on the Principles and Practice of Medicine*, by J. HUGHES BENNETT, M. D., F. R. S. E. American edition. New York, 1860.
¶ In the *Edinburgh Monthly Journal of Medical Science*, Vols. IX and X, 1849–50.

typhoid from a specific typhus because individual or epidemic constitutional peculiarities seemed insufficient to account for the notable differences in the average cases of each, they hesitated to push the argument and thereby separate fevers of short duration, unaccompanied by typhoid symptoms, from the cases of fully developed typhoid fever. Others, on the contrary, recognized in these febriculæ or ephemeral fevers a distinct clinical entity, and reported them as common continued fever irrespective of etiological considerations. The unknown or suspected cause, whether conceived to be the poison of typhoid or of typhus modified in some way, a specific poison differing from these, or a non-specific irritant, had no weight in the formation of the diagnosis. Dr. Wood recognized an idiopathic fever resulting from causes of irritation having nothing specific or peculiar in their mode of operation—an inflammatory fever, the synocha of Cullen, but without any local lesion other than an occasional slight inflammation of the fauces wholly insufficient to account for the intensity of the general symptoms. Bennett and Jenner also recognized a febricula, though differing in opinion as to its nature, the former considering it a modified typhus and the latter an essential fever due to a specific cause. The clinical features of the cases reported under the name of common continued fever may therefore be readily appreciated.

Remittent Fever.—The paroxysmal fevers of the West and South were well known at the outbreak of the war, even to those of the profession whose practice anterior to their military service had been in non-malarious localities. The importance of these fevers, and the national character of the great medical schools of the North, called for as thorough a discussion of the malarial fevers as of those which constituted the common fever of the North and East. The text-books gave prominence to the endemic fevers. The American edition of *Watson's Practice* contained an article by Dr. Condie on remittent fever to fit the work for its new sphere of usefulness. The medical journals showed that the energies of the profession were as much engaged on malarial disease as on typhus and typhoid. The medical officer from the North was therefore well prepared to recognize malarial remittents when presented to him, and perhaps better qualified than the southern practitioner to recognize the to him familiar typhoid fever when occurring in the habitat of malaria. Bartlett had shown that typhoid fever was to be found in such localities, and Wood, in speaking of the diagnosis of enteric fever, called special attention to the miasmatic remittent as one of the diseases liable to be confounded with it, especially when the remittent was protracted or attended with 'typhus' symptoms. The figures, reported by our medical officers during the war under the heading remittent fever, may therefore be accepted as giving a fair expression of the prevalence of this form of fever. Mistakes in diagnosis no doubt occurred,—remittent fever may have been recorded as typhoid, especially when it assumed an adynamic form, and, on the other hand, typhoid may have been set down as remittent in localities where the latter was endemic; this will be considered hereafter. It is sufficient for the present to know that the name remittent fever was given to a definite and generally appreciated clinical picture.

Intermitting Fevers.—The intermittents, including the congestive form, were usually characterized by such marked and well-known peculiarities that the conditions indicated by the diagnosis are easily understood.

On June 30, 1862, two changes affecting the method of reporting idiopathic febrile diseases were made in the sick reports. The first involved the disuse of the term common continued fever. No instructions were issued regarding the disposition to be made of such cases as had heretofore been reported under this designation; but from what has been stated above concerning the tendency developed by the study of typhoid fever, it may be assumed that many of the cases were thereafter reported under that heading while the remainder may have found place under *Other Miasmatic Diseases*. During the year ending June 30, 1862, when the term common continued fever was in use, there were reported under it, per thousand of strength, 42 cases, 1.25 per cent. of which were fatal, while under the term other miasmatic diseases there were reported only 27 cases, with .41 per cent. fatal. During the following year, when no special provision was made for the classification of the cases formerly reported as common continued fever, the cases returned as other miasmatic diseases rose to 50 per thousand and their fatality to 2.84 per cent. A large number of the common continued cases may, therefore, have been returned under this indefinite heading.

The second change consisted of the insertion in the reports of a new term, *Typho-malarial*. The writer has not been able to find the report of the Board that recommended these changes, and is, therefore, ignorant of the arguments which led to the abolition of the one term, but Dr. WOODWARD has detailed the circumstances attending the introduction of the other.* In the autumn and early winter of 1861 the medical officers of the army called attention to the fact that the camp fevers then coming under observation differed in many particulars from the enteric fevers which they had treated in civil practice before the war.† A Board consisting of Surgeon A. N. McLAREN, U. S. A., Surgeon G. H. LYMAN, U. S. Vols., and Assistant Surgeon M. J. ASCH, U. S. A., was convened, December 16, to investigate and determine whether the fever then prevailing in the army was to be considered an intermittent or bilious remittent fever in its inception, assuming in its course a typhoid type, or a typhoid fever primarily. The board examined the fever in several of the division hospitals of the Army of the Potomac. It communicated by circular letter with many medical officers whose commands could not be conveniently reached. The replies received, in their general tenor, confirmed the opinion which the board had formed on the basis of its personal observation, that while a certain number of cases of ordinary typhoid existed in the army, the large majority of the febrile cases were bilious remittent fevers which, not having been controlled in their primary stage, had assumed that adynamic type which is present in enteric fever. This officially pronounced adynamic remittent prevailed extensively during the Peninsular campaign of the following year and was familiarly known as *Chickahominy fever*. Dr. WOODWARD had served with the army in this campaign, and had formed the opinion that these fevers were hybrid forms resulting from the combined influence of malarial poisoning and the causes of typhoid fever, modified in individual instances in accordance with the preponderance of one or the other of these influences and occasionally by the presence of a scorbutic taint. At this time he was detailed a member of a board to revise the form of sick report in use in the army, and actuated by the strength of his opinions, he induced the board to recommend the insertion of the term typho-malarial in the blank form for the monthly sick report as a suitable designation for the complex conditions which he believed to be present in these cases. He afterwards regretted that he had not also urged upon the board the preparation of a circular

* *Typho-malarial Fever: Is it a Special Type of Fever?* Philadelphia, 1876, pp. 10–12.
† For an illustration of the characters of the fevers occurring at the time specified, refer *infra*, p. 216 *et seq.*, to the admirable clinical records of the Seminary Hospital, Georgetown, D. C.

letter to accompany the new sick report, explaining why this term had been adopted, and calling for special reports with regard to the cases which it was intended to designate. This omission was indeed unfortunate, as it left the medical officers without a guide for the use of a term not only of indefinite meaning but absolutely of double meaning. These fevers, in accordance with the views then current, were either remittents with low or typhous symptoms, or they were cases of enteric fever with accidental malarial complications. The uncertainty attaching, in the absence of the necessary instructions, to the value of the first part of the compound word, permitted it to be used as a diagnostic title for both of these series of cases. Indeed it was perhaps better suited to meet acceptance as a designation for low remittents than for cases of true typhoid marked by malarial symptoms, for the compound term *typhoid-pneumonia* was familiar as a household word at the time, and no meaning was conveyed by it involving the presence of the specific poison of enteric fever. Nevertheless Dr. WOODWARD subsequently claimed that the prompt acceptance of the term typho-malarial showed how widely the opinions he had formed were shared by the medical officers of the army. But the sense of the profession cannot be thus construed in support of the view of a specific enteric essential in the typho-malarial cases reported at that time. During the month of July, 1862, the first month of the use of the new term, 2,283 cases were reported, while Dr. WOODWARD's opinions were unknown except to a few personal friends. Indeed his views were not published until the issuance, on September 8, 1863, of *Circular* No. 15, Surgeon General's Office, Washington, D. C. In this the meaning designed to be attached to the term typho-malarial was for the first time made known in the following words:

> Moreover, while a certain amount of uncomplicated enteric and remittent fevers certainly did occur, especially at the commencement of the war, the vast majority of the camp fevers of the army were of a mixed character, exhibiting undoubted enteric phenomena variously combined with the periodicity and other peculiarities of malarial disease, and still further modified by the tendency to incipient scurvy, which is the ordinary concomitant of camp diet. To indicate this mixed nature, the term typho-malarial fever, which I had the honor to suggest to the Department in June, 1862, appears appropriate, and, at the present time, is coming into very general use.

Up to the close of the month of August, 1863, shortly before the publication of this circular, 27,399 cases of typho-malarial fever had been reported in a total of 49,871 such cases during the war. In other words, more than one half of the cases were reported during the fourteen months which intervened between the appearance of the term on the reports and the publication of a casual reference to the meaning designed to be attached to it.

The nomenclature of the fevers as officially given in the army sick reports at the beginning of the war gave expression to species with marked clinical distinctions. Uncertainties attached to the etiology of the small percentage reported as common continued fever, but the nature of the uncertainties was fully appreciated—and the segregation of the cases rendered them available for special study. The removal of this term from the sick report complicated the statistics thereafter furnished by doubts as to the disposition made of ephemeral and other febrile cases not distinctly typhoid. What proportion of these were sent to swell the lists of typhoid, how many complicated with the effects of malaria were added to the typho-malarial list, and how many were dropped out of consideration altogether by being placed among other miasmatic diseases, are questions which constantly recur in studying the statistics of fever furnished after June 30, 1862. The insertion of the term typho-malarial was also a grievous complication. The true value of the statistics given under this heading can never be known in the absence of a complete record of all the cases. Such cases as were reported with more or less of detail will be presented hereafter, and the figures themselves, and those allied to them, will be examined in this connection. In the meantime a consideration of the conditions under which the diagnoses were made will show that clinically typho-malarial cases may have presented great diversity, from the severe and protracted remittent ending fatally with great prostration, low delirium, stupor and coma, and the equally severe cases of typhoid fever ending fatally in like manner, but with some modification in their progress from concurrent malarial poisoning, to the mild enteric and abortive cases viewed doubtfully as typhoid, and diagnosticated, when such diagnosis was officially admissible, as common continued fever, yet recorded with propriety, in accordance with the views of Dr. WOODWARD, as cases of typho-malarial fever, in the presence of indications calling for the exhibition of quinine as an antiperiodic.

CHAPTER III.—ON THE PAROXYSMAL FEVERS.

I.—THE STATISTICS OF THE MALARIAL FEVERS.

I.—MALARIAL FEVERS AMONG THE U. S. FORCES.

PREVALENCE AND MORTALITY.—During and immediately after the war, one-fourth of all the reported cases of disease among the white troops was of a malarial character. There were 224 cases of malarial fever in every thousand cases of reported disease. Typho-malarial fever is included in this statement, as, irrespective of the views entertained concerning its typhoid element, its malarial factor was definitely recognized by all parties. It seems proper, therefore, to consider it in a discussion of the prevalence of malarial disease, although it may be needful to know more about it before its mortality can with propriety be admitted to weigh in the scale with that due to the purely malarial fevers.

The simple intermittent constituted by far the greater proportion of these febrile cases, 2,003 cases per 1,000 of mean strength having been reported in a total of 2,814 of malarial disease; in other words, a distinct period of intermission was recognized in five-sevenths of the paroxysmal fevers. These figures represent only the number of cases in which intermittent fever was the most obvious abnormal condition present. They by no means express the extent to which this disease prevailed, even in that part of the army represented in the statistical tables. As the system of reporting provided no method of recording complications, it very generally happened that cases of intermittent fever complicated with serious diarrhœa, dysentery, pneumonia or other grave affections, were reported under the head of these disorders without any mention of a co-existing malarial affection. But, although understating the facts, the statistics convey a clear idea of the extensive prevalence of this form of malarial disease. Out of 1,213,685 cases of malarial fever 863,651 were cases of simple intermittent. How many of these were first attacks, and how many recurrences in individuals already affected by the malarial influence, cannot be determined. It is probable that the majority of the primary attacks are included in the number, for a soldier who experienced an ague-fit for the first time was usually disposed to be alarmed at the violence of the symptoms, and to seek medical assistance, even if the nature of the duties required of him at the time was such as to render it needless for him to report for the purpose of being relieved from their performance. On the other hand, it is certain that many of the recurrences which took place were not reported. Men became accustomed to attacks of this kind, and visited the dispensary after the paroxysm, not to report as sick, but to procure a supply of quinine to prevent a return; even when on important duty which they were incapable of performing during the attack, such men would be temporarily excused by their company officers, the medical officer of the command remaining in ignorance of the recurrence.

In more than one-half of the agues the cycle of morbid phenomena was completed in twenty-four hours. Tertians followed closely in order of frequency. Quartans were comparatively rare, forming only one-twentieth of the whole number. Of the 2,003 cases of simple intermittents occurring per 1,000 of mean strength among the white troops during the five and one-sixth years covered by the statistics, 1,037 were quotidians, 870 tertians and 96 quartans.

Congestive fever was fortunately of infrequent occurrence, it having furnished but 32 cases per thousand of strength, constituting 3 of the 224 cases of malarial disease which were recorded in every thousand cases of all diseases.*

Remittent fever gave 664 of the total of 2;814 cases of malarial disease which occurred per thousand of mean strength, or 53 of the 224 malarial cases recorded per thousand cases of all diseases. Excluding the typho-malarial cases, the 664 remittents formed part of 2,699 cases of pure malarial fevers which occurred in every thousand men of the command, or 53 of the 215 pure malarial fevers recorded in every thousand cases of disease. In simpler figures, the remittents formed one-fourth or 24.6 per cent. of the purely malarial fevers, and a little less than this, or 23.7 per cent. of all malarial fevers, including the cases recorded as typho-malarial.† These typho-malarial cases, 115 per thousand of strength, formed only 9 of the 224 malarial cases which occurred in every thousand cases of disease.

The deaths reported among the white troops as occasioned by malarial fevers numbered 12,199; but if to these be added a due proportion of the 42,869 deaths from unspecified diseases, the number becomes augmented to 16,225. Of the 12,199 deaths specially referred to malarial fevers, 4,059 were considered due to typho-malarial manifestations, 3,853 to remittent, 3,370 to congestive and 917 to simple intermittent fevers.

Although congestive fevers were infrequent and remittents formed only one-fourth of the purely malarial fevers, the deaths from these forms of malarial affection were in striking contrast with those from the simple intermittents. The latter numbered less than 2 per thousand of strength, and the former somewhat over 7 and 8 per thousand respectively. Of 1,000 deaths from all diseases, 94 were caused by malarial fever, 31 of these being due to typho-malarial, 30 to remittent, 26 to congestive and 7 to simple intermittent fevers.

In the last column of the table which follows is shown the light rate of mortality in the intermittents, one death in every thousand cases of quotidian or tertian ague, and one

---

* The relative frequency of the types of intermittent fever expressed as percentages of the total number of intermittent cases which occurred in each of the military departments will be found in Table XXXIII *infra*, p. 98.

† The table mentioned in last note gives also the relative frequency of the forms of malarial fever expressed as percentages of the total number of malarial cases which occurred in each of the departments.

death in every five hundred of the quartans. The greater mortality in the last-mentioned form is at variance with the opinion which regards the quotidian as an expression of a higher degree of the malarial poisoning than is present in the tertian or quartan. Many of these deaths might be passed to the credit of congestive fever, as the fatal result was due to the occurrence of a paroxysm of an aggravated type; while others with equal propriety might be transferred to remittent fever, as, although the case was intermittent originally, and so reported, the fatal issue did not take place until after the fever had assumed the remitting type.

Remittent fever gave a fatality-rate of 1.31 per cent., or one death in 76 cases, and congestive fever 24.65 per cent., or one death in 4 cases. But notwithstanding this high rate of the congestive fevers, such was their infrequency as compared with the less dangerous forms of the disease, that the deaths from the purely malarial diseases amounted only to seven-tenths of one per cent., or, including the deaths from typho-malarial fever, to one death in every hundred cases.

TABLE XXII.

Statement of the Frequency and Mortality of the several forms of Malarial Fever, giving the totals reported from May 1, 1861, to June 30, 1866, with the ratio of cases to strength and to cases of all diseases, and the ratio of deaths to strength, to deaths from all diseases and to cases of Malarial Fever.

WHITE TROOPS.

DISEASE.	Number reported during the period from May 1, 1861, to June 30, 1866.		Ratios per 1,000 of strength.		Cases per 1,000 of cases of all diseases.	Deaths per 1,000 of deaths from all diseases.	Percentage of fatal cases.
	Cases.	Deaths.	Cases.	Deaths.			
Quotidian Intermittent	447,258	452	1,037	.96	82	3.49	.10
Tertian Intermittent	375,170	381	870	.81	69	2.95	.10
Quartan Intermittent	41,223	84	96	.18	8	.64	.20
Total simple Intermittent	863,651	917	2,003	1.95	159	7.08	.16
Congestive Fever	13,673	3,370	32	7.20	3	26.05	24.65
Remittent Fever	286,490	3,853	664	8.23	53	29.78	1.31
Total pure Malarial Fevers	1,163,814	8,140	2,699	17.38	215	62.91	.70
Typho-malarial Fever	49,871	4,059	115	8.67	9	31.37	8.14
Total Malarial Fevers	1,213,685	12,199	2,814	26.05	224	94.28	1.00

But although the mortality from these fevers was comparatively light, their influence in detracting from the efficiency of the army must have been very great. We have no means of ascertaining how many men constantly on sick report would represent this loss, nor can we learn how many were permanently removed from active service by discharge on account of the pernicious influence of the fever-poison on the constitution. The statistics show that 373 men were discharged for remittent fever and 480 for intermittent fever;

but when it is recognized that there were 2,224 cases in which dropsy figured as the cause of disability necessitating discharge, 14,500 having debility as the nominal cause, and 25,915 in which the cause was not stated, we are left to speculate upon the influence which these fevers may have exercised in the production of temporary and permanent disablement to our armies.

The malarial fevers as they affected the colored troops are shown in the following table:

TABLE XXIII.

Statement of the Frequency and Mortality of the several forms of Malarial Fever, giving the totals reported from July 1, 1863, to June 30, 1866, with the ratios of cases to strength and to cases of all diseases, and the ratios of deaths to strength, to deaths from all diseases and to cases of Malarial Fever.

COLORED TROOPS.

DISEASE.	Number reported during the period from July 1, 1863, to June 30, 1866.		Rates per 1,000 of strength.		Cases per 1,000 of cases of all diseases.	Deaths per 1,000 of deaths from all diseases.	Percentage of fatal cases.
	Cases.	Deaths.	Cases.	Deaths.			
Quotidian Intermittent	63,992	58	1,047	.91	106	2.11	.09
Tertian Intermittent	51,045	54	835	.85	84	1.96	.10
Quartan Intermittent	3,923	15	64	.23	7	.55	.30
Total simple Intermittent	118,960	127	1,946	1.99	197	4.62	.10
Congestive Fever	2,536	794	42	12.42	4	28.88	31.31
Remittent Fever	30,645	1,002	501	15.67	50	36.43	3.27
Total pure Malarial Fevers	152,141	1,923	2,489	30.08	251	69.93	1.26
Typho-malarial Fever	7,529	1,301	123	20.35	12	47.31	17.27
Total Malarial Fevers	159,670	3,224	2,612	50.43	263	117.24	2.02

In comparing this table with that given for the white troops, it must be remembered that while the latter includes the statistics of five and one-sixth years the former embodies the records of only three years of service. If it be assumed that the rates of prevalence and mortality which were found in these three years among the colored troops would have prevailed had the observations been continued for five and one-sixth years, the ratio of cases per thousand of strength would have been 4,498 as compared with 2,814 among the whites, and the deaths 86.88 as compared with 26.05, or, in other words, for every 100 cases occurring among a given number of white soldiers in a certain time, 160 cases would have occurred among the same number of colored troops in the same period, and for 100 deaths from malarial fever occurring among the white, 334 deaths would have been recorded in the same time among the same number of colored troops. This is definitely shown in Table XXVI, where the sickness and deaths for both races are tabulated as annual averages.

But the element of time does not affect the comparative value of the figures in the last three columns of the table at present under consideration. Thus the increased mortality which has just been indicated is in the last column distributed among the various forms of fever. Of 100 cases of congestive fever among the colored troops 31.31 died, or 1 in 3.2 cases, as against 1 in 4 among the whites; of the same number of remittent cases 3.27 died, or 1 in 30, as against 1 in 76 among the whites; of 100 typho-malarial cases 17.27 died, or 1 in 5.8, as against 1 in 12 among the whites. The influence of this increased mortality in the more dangerous forms of malarial fever among the colored troops was such that the percentage of fatality of the malarial fevers as a class among the colored men is found to be as large again as that which obtained among the white soldiers: thus, the purely malarial fevers gave a mortality of 0.7 per cent., or 1 in 143 cases among the latter, and 1.26 per cent., or 1 in 79 among the former; while, if typho-malarial fever is taken into consideration, its greater fatality among the blacks will be found to raise their percentage of fatal cases to 2.02 as compared with 1.00 among the white troops. But it may not be inferred from these facts that negro troops are more liable to malarial seizures, and more prone to succumb to the malarial influence than white troops, until it has been shown that both bodies of men were exposed to similar influences.

The tabulated statistics of malarial disease have reference solely to the fevers. It is not possible to ascertain the actual number of men who suffered from chronic malarial poisoning during the civil war. Most of them were undoubtedly reported under the head of the intercurrent diseases which were developed during the progress of the cachexia. Large numbers were registered as cases of general debility or other diseases of the miasmatic order. Under these headings 101,892 cases with 1,981 deaths were reported among the white troops, and 11,887 cases with 535 deaths among the colored troops; moreover, there were 14,500 white, and 540 colored, soldiers discharged the service for debility. Under the head of anæmia 21,892 cases, 438 deaths and 347 discharges on certificates of disability were reported among the white troops; 2,771 cases, 258 deaths and 35 discharges among the colored. Men broken down by the most diverse morbid conditions were included in these figures; and although all who had opportunity of observing large numbers of such cases during the war will testify to the frequency with which the malarial cachexia occurred among them either as the chief morbid condition or as a complication, there is no possibility of giving even an approximate numerical expression of the fact. It may be added that, according to the tables in the *First Medical Volume*, 1,977 cases, 17 deaths and 171 discharges on account of *diseases of the spleen* were reported among the white troops, and 55 cases, 3 deaths and 3 discharges among the colored men; and although the majority of these cases were instances of malarial enlargement of the organ, it cannot be supposed that the numbers represent any very considerable proportion of the actual cases, which were usually recorded under other heads, such as intermittent fever, debility and anæmia. Nor is it possible to determine the number of cases of malarial cachexia that terminated in dropsy, though it must be believed that a large number recorded as *general dropsy*, *abdominal dropsy*, and *dropsy from hepatic disease* had this origin. Under these headings 7,337 cases and 398 deaths were reported among the white troops; and 2,224 men are said to have been discharged for *dropsy*. Under the same headings 1,427 cases, 272 deaths and 109 discharges were reported among the colored troops.

Of neuralgia, another manifestation of malarial poisoning, 58,774 cases were noted among the white, and 6,018 among the colored troops. A number of these cases may have been due to malaria, but it is difficult to believe that the majority were so, for neither in their geographical distribution nor in the season at which they were most prevalent do the figures reported agree with the distribution of the reported cases of intermittent fever.*

The occurrence of malarial fever in connection with diarrhœa and dysentery has already been shown.†

Annual variations in prevalence and mortality.—Turning now to Table XXIV, illustrating the relative frequency and mortality of these febrile affections among white troops during the several years covered by the statistics, it is found that their prevalence increased gradually to the fourth year, or that ending June 30, 1864, when the war maximum was attained, diminished somewhat during the fifth year, and experienced a marked increase during the sixth, or year succeeding the war. This marked advance to the fourth year, and slight diminution during the fifth year, was due to the influence of the mass of the intermittents on the figures representing the prevalence of the other forms; for both congestive and remittent fevers were slightly more prevalent during the second year than during any other of the years of the war.

TABLE XXIV.

Relative Frequency of cases of Malarial Fevers, and Deaths caused by them, during the several years of the war and the year following the war, expressed in annual rates per 1,000 of mean strength.

WHITE TROOPS.

DISEASES.	1860–1.		1861–2.		1862–3.		1863–4.		1864–5.		1865–6.	
	Cases.	Deaths.	Cases.	Deaths.	Cases.	Deaths.	Cases.	Deaths.	Cases.	Deaths.	Cases.	Deaths.
Quotidian Intermittent	56.17	....	144.36	.11	163.01	.21	230.51	.17	221.93	.21	364.92	.32
Tertian Intermittent	59.63	....	95.81	.11	134.23	.18	210.44	.19	184.38	.12	295.58	.26
Quartan Intermittent	10.25	....	12.62	.01	16.07	.06	22.87	.03	19.39	.03	24.70	.01
Total simple Intermittents	126.05	....	252.79	.24	313.31	.45	463.82	.39	425.70	.36	685.20	.59
Congestive Fever	5.20	.02	7.99	1.25	6.45	1.55	6.16	1.53	4.90	1.12	8.20	2.26
Total	131.25	.02	260.78	1.49	319.76	2.00	469.98	1.92	430.60	1.48	693.40	2.85
Remittent Fever	43.60	....	143.26	1.28	140.38	1.76	114.12	1.27	127.84	1.86	159.70	2.57
Total pure Malarial Fevers	174.85	.02	404.04	2.77	460.14	3.76	584.10	3.19	558.44	3.34	853.10	5.42
Typho-malarial Fever	....	....	....	....	38.00	1.78	18.93	1.71	22.91	2.27	16.62	2.54
Total Malarial Fevers	174.85	.02	404.04	2.77	498.14	5.54	603.03	4.90	581.35	5.61	869.72	7.96

The increased prevalence of malarial fever during the year succeeding the war was probably due to the occupation of Southern and malarious territory by the army, and the concurrent discharge from service of troops stationed in Northern and less malarious sections. Although this increase is observable in all the forms of malarial fever, each reaching a higher figure per thousand of strength than in any of the previous years, the intermittents constituted absolutely and relatively its greater portion. As will be seen hereafter in Table XXXII, the troops in the Department of Arkansas had the highest malarial record, and among them intermittents were relatively more frequent and remittents less frequent than among troops in less malarious localities.

---

* See article on Neuralgia, *infra*, page 874.   †In the second part of this work, pp. 287, 398, 495 and 637.

Typho-malarial fever, however, during these years did not follow the course of the unmodified malarial fevers. Its presence was not reported during the first two years, embraced in Table XXIV. During the year ending June 30, 1863, there were 38 cases per thousand of strength. In the following year, when malarial fevers were at their war maximum, typho-malarial fever fell off one-half, to 18.93, increasing slightly during the last year of the war, and subsiding to its minimum when the pure malarial fevers were at their maximum during the year succeeding the war.

In general the mortality of the malarial fevers increased with their increased frequency: thus, in the year after the war, with 853 cases per thousand of strength there were 5.42 deaths, while in 1861–2, with 404 cases the deaths were 2.77. But in the typho-malarial fevers an increased mortality was associated with a diminished prevalence: in the year 1862–3, with 38 cases per thousand of strength, the corresponding death-rate was 1.78, while in 1865–6, with 16.62 cases, the ratio of deaths rose to 2.54.

Similar results are obtained by an examination of the statistics from the colored commands, as given in—

TABLE XXV.

Relative Frequency of Cases of Malarial Fevers and of Deaths caused by them among the Colored Troops during two years of the war and the year following the war, expressed in annual rates per 1,000 of mean strength.

DISEASES.	1863–4.		1864–5.		1865–6.	
	Cases.	Deaths.	Cases.	Deaths.	Cases.	Deaths.
Quotidian Intermittent	362.60	.46	308.67	.29	398.94	.19
Tertian Intermittent	276.50	.41	235.19	.26	345.34	.21
Quartan Intermittent	23.96	.13	21.57	.08	19.02	.04
Total simple Intermittent	663.06	1.00	565.43	.63	763.30	.44
Congestive Fever	23.62	7.76	11.12	3.42	9.97	2.33
Total	686.68	8.76	576.55	4.05	773.27	2.77
Remittent Fever	147.04	6.43	173.48	4.72	173.73	5.04
Total pure Malarial Fevers	833.72	15.19	750.03	8.77	947.00	7.81
Typho-malarial Fever	56.15	10.85	37.47	5.51	34.21	5.49
Total Malarial Fevers	889.87	26.04	787.50	14.28	981.21	13.30

These figures cover only the last two years of the war and the year succeeding the war. The year ending June 30, 1864, yielded a higher ratio of cases than that which followed it, but, as in the case of the white troops, not so high a rate as was attained after the cessation of hostilities. Here also the preponderance of the intermittents is the cause of the varying tides in the annual progress of these fevers; for, while the congestive cases were most prominent during the first year, corresponding in this respect with the intermittents generally, the remittents were least prominent during that year.

Typho-malarial cases were most prevalent, 56 per thousand of mean strength, during the first year of the service of the colored troops, diminishing to 37 and 34 per thousand during the two following years.

Relative prevalence and mortality among the white and the colored troops.—The following table consolidates the data of the last two tables, giving the annual average ratios per thousand of strength as deduced from the experience of five and one-sixth years of service by the white troops and of three years of service by the colored troops:

TABLE XXVI.

Relative Frequency among the White and the Colored Troops of Cases of Malarial Fevers and of Deaths caused by them, as shown by the average number annually recorded, reduced to ratios per 1,000 of strength.

DISEASES.	WHITE TROOPS.		COLORED TROOPS.	
	Cases.	Deaths.	Cases.	Deaths.
Quotidian Intermittent	200.73	.19	348.93	.30
Tertian Intermittent	168.39	.16	278.33	.28
Quartan Intermittent	18.50	.03	21.40	.08
Total simple Intermittent	387.62	.38	648.66	.66
Congestive Fever	6.14	1.39	13.82	4.14
Total Intermittents	393.76	1.77	662.48	4.80
Remittent Fever	128.58	1.59	167.10	5.23
Total pure Malarial Fevers	522.34	3.36	829.58	10.03
Typho-malarial Fever	(a) 26.15	(a) 1.95	41.04	6.79
Total Malarial Fevers	(a) 544.72	(a) 5.04	870.62	16.82

(a) As the annual rates of typho-malarial fever among the white troops are derived from the statistics of four years while the rates of the totality of the malarial fevers cover five and one-sixth years of observation, the latter differ somewhat from the sum of the rates of the purely malarial and typho-malarial fevers.

The greater prevalence of all forms of malarial fever among the colored troops is as well shown in the various items of this table as in the totals of 544.72 cases per thousand of mean strength among the white, and 870.62 among the colored men. These figures are as 100 to 160. The greater mortality among the negroes is equally well shown, and is especially marked in the more serious forms, giving an average annual total of 16.82 deaths per thousand of strength as compared with 5.04 among the white troops; figures which are in the ratio of 334 to 100. As has already been seen,* the deaths formed 1.00 per cent. of the cases in the white and 2.02 per cent. in the colored regiments.

These statistics indicate that the colored race exhibited a greater susceptibility to the malarial poison than was shown by the white commands, or that the colored troops

---

* Tables XXII and XXIII, pp. 79 and 80, *supra.*

were exposed to influences of a more deleterious nature.* It would, however, be injudicious to attach weight to a comparison of the annual averages given in Table XXVI as bearing on the relative liability of the white and the colored troops to the malarial influence. Large numbers of the white troops served in departments which were comparatively salubrious, and the influence of their records is felt in diminishing the average annual rate for the white commands as a whole. The black men, on the contrary, were aggregated in malarious districts. Those serving in the Atlantic region were mainly distributed in the Departments of the South, of North Carolina and of Virginia, and those on duty in the Central region held fortresses along the Mississippi bottom and in the Department of the Gulf. Manifestly, in making a comparison to determine relative prevalence, locality must be taken into consideration. The records do not enter with sufficient minuteness into the conditions of service of the white and the colored commands to enable their relative susceptibility to be determined. In fact the question was seldom touched upon by our medical officers. The writer is aware that the officers on duty at the Field Hospital for colored troops at City Point, Va., were of the opinion that although the colored people under similar conditions of exposure might be less liable to seizure than the whites, they were assuredly much less able to resist the febrile influence when the attack was developed. Surgeon JOHN FISH, 17th regiment Corps d'Afrique, appears to have entertained the belief that the negro was as liable to malarial attacks as the white soldier.†

The 17th regiment Corps d'Afrique was recruited at Baton Rouge, and first mustered August 10, 1863. Its strength at that time was 510 men. We left Baton Rouge on steamer for Port Hudson, September 18, 1863, and have been on duty here ever since. The most frequent diseases have been diarrhœa and dysentery, intermittent fever, typhoid fever, scurvy, pneumonia and rheumatism.

I had supposed the black man to be peculiarly exempt from diseases due to malarial influences; but I should not expect to have encountered a greater number of cases of intermittent fever in a body of white troops equalling ours in number than we have actually had.—*Port Hudson, La., Feb.* 25, 1864.

---

* Some writers have claimed for the negro race an immunity from malarial disease. Thus FERGUSON in his article *On the Nature and History of the Marsh Poison*, Trans. Royal Society, Edinburgh, Vol. IX, says:—"The adaptation of the negro to live in the unwholesome localities of the torrid zone, that prove so fatal to Europeans, is most happy and singular. From peculiarity of idiosyncrasy he appears to be proof against fevers; for to him marsh miasmata are in fact no poison, and hence his incalculable value as a soldier, for field service in the West Indies. The warm, moist, low, and leeward situations, where these pernicious exhalations are generated and concentrated, prove to him congenial in every respect. He delights in them, for he there enjoys life and health, as much as his feelings are abhorrent to the currents of wind that sweep the mountain tops; where alone the whites find security against endemic fevers. One of the most obvious peculiarities of the negro as compared with the European is his thick oily skin, rank to a degree; and from this circumstance the theorist, when he speculates upon the mode of reception of the marsh poison into the constitution, whether by lungs, stomach, or skin, may draw a plausible conjecture in favor of the last."

† Dr. E. ANDREWS, in a letter published in the Chicago Med. Examiner, Vol. III, 1862, p. 481,—speaks of the prevalence of intermittent and remittent fevers among the troops near Memphis, Tennessee, during the summer of 1862, and remarks that he constantly observes these fevers among the negroes, whose powers of resistance he conceives to have been greatly over-estimated. See also an interesting paper by Dr. SANFORD B. HUNT—*The Negro as a Soldier*, The Quarterly Jour. of Psychological Medicine, Vol. I, 1863, p. 161 *et seq.* These fevers were, moreover, exceedingly common among the colored people who received medical assistance from the Freedman's bureau. In an article entitled *Remarks concerning some of the diseases prevailing among the freed people in the District of Columbia* (Bureau Refugees, Freedmen and Abandoned Lands), American Journal of the Medical Sciences, 1866, p. 366, Dr. R. REYBURN, Surgeon U. S. Volunteers, cites the occurrence among these colored people of 2,776 cases of remittent and intermittent fevers in a total of 7,949 cases of sickness and wounds, or about 35 per cent. of the whole, as a sufficient answer to and refutation of the statement so often reiterated in our text-books, that the negroes are not subject to, and do not suffer from, malarial disease. "Now it may be that in Africa, and in the West Indies they do not suffer to the same extent as unacclimated whites do, but they certainly are not exempt from these diseases in this country; and as far as our own opinion goes, we are strongly inclined to the belief that this so-called exemption has no foundation in fact and is unworthy of credence." The only testimony in favor of any supposed immunity of the colored troops from these diseases during any part of the war is contained in a report by Medical Inspector N. S. TOWNSHEND, U. S. A., cited in the American Med. Times, Vol. VII, 1863, p. 65. This report is on file in the office of the Surgeon General and is dated May 19, 1863. It relates to an inspection of Forts St. Philip and Jackson, near the mouth of the Mississippi river, and contains the following paragraph: "Of the troops at the forts four-fifths are of the 13th Maine, and one-fifth Louisiana negroes. The comparative exemption of the latter from diseases of malarial origin is most marked. Of the entire white force 10.8 per cent. had intermittent or remittent fever, while of the colored troops only .8 per cent. suffered from those diseases. In respect to other diseases their liability appeared nearly equal." This statement is no doubt true so far as the time and place referred to are concerned, though it cannot be verified because in the report of sick and wounded at this post for the month of May, 1863, by Surgeon JAS. M. BATES of the 13th Maine, the figures for the white and colored troops of the garrison, viz: eight companies of the 13th Maine and one battery of Louisiana heavy artillery, are unfortunately consolidated. But whatever may have been the cause of the temporary condition reported, the subsequent separate reports of the colored troops at this post show no such immunity from intermittent or remittent fevers. In this connection reference may be made to the statement of A. G. TEBAULT with regard to the "Negroes of Virginia," as cited by T. P. ATKINSON—*Report on the anatomical, physiological and pathological differences between the white and the black races, etc.*, Trans. of the Third Annual Session of the Med. Soc. of Virginia, held at Staunton, Nov., 1872, Richmond, 1873, Appendix E, p. 112, "Cases of intractable intermittent are rarely seen among them, and never of chronic enlargement of the spleen, or the quartan ague."

But this is an opinion based upon one-sided experience. To ascertain the fact, statistics are required from white and colored commands camped or operating in the same localities at the same time. In their absence, the following table may be of interest as presenting the rate of prevalence among the colored troops during the fourth and fifth years of the war in juxtaposition with the rates prevailing among the whites during the same period in the same departments or sections of the country.*

TABLE XXVII.

A Comparison of the Prevalence of Malarial Fevers among the White and the Colored Troops serving in the same localities during the two years from July 1, 1863, to June 30, 1865, the figures given being the average annual ratios per 1,000 of strength.

	WHITE TROOPS.				COLORED TROOPS.			
	Remittents.	Intermittents.	Typho-malarial.	Total Malarial.	Remittents.	Intermittents.	Typho-malarial.	Total Malarial.
Department of Virginia	88	676	25	789	(a)	(a)	(a)	(a)
Department of North Carolina	244	1,364	33	1,641				
Department of the South	108	497	46	651				
The above Depts. of the Atlantic Region	129	786	33	948	140	412	44	596
Department of the Gulf	147	779	24	950	(a)	(a)	(a)	(a)
Division of Mississippi and Department of Tennessee	144	542	16	702				
Department of Arkansas	166	1,107	18	1,291				
The above Departments of the Central Region	147	664	18	829	176	715	44	935
Total in these sections of the Atlantic and Central Regions	143	692	22	857	164	615	44	823

(a) The statistics of the Colored Troops having been consolidated by regions, it is impossible now to distribute the cases among the several Departments.

From this table it appears that in those departments of the Atlantic region in which white and colored troops served during the period stated, malarial fevers prevailed more extensively among the white men, they having presented 948 cases per thousand of mean strength annually as compared with 596 among the colored troops. In the departments of the Central region, however, the colored men suffered more than the whites. The aggregate rates in these various sections show the fevers as somewhat more prevalent among the white troops—857 per thousand annually as against 823 among the colored men.

* The Mortality Tables of the Tenth U. S. Census, 1880, do not furnish satisfactory information concerning the relative prevalence and fatality of malarial fevers among the white and colored population. The returns are known to be very incomplete. A comparison with the death records of the registration offices of the States of Massachusetts and New Jersey showed a deficiency on the part of the census tables of 26.42 per cent. of the whole number returned by them in the former, and of 34.45 per cent. in the latter, State. This would not affect a calculation intended to give expression to the relative frequency of death from any specified cause in the two races were the deficiency equally distributed; but it is recognized by Dr. BILLINGS, p. 1706, *Compendium of the Tenth Census of the United States*, 1880, that in the sections of country having the largest colored population the greatest deficiencies were found, and that these were probably greater among the colored than among the white population. With the knowledge that the ratios for the colored people were in all likelihood greater than is represented by the figures, the following table may be examined:

The statistics do not furnish the necessary data for determining the relative mortality among white and colored commands operating in the same departments.

		POPULATION.	Total deaths from malarial fever.	Deaths per 100,000 living.
Group 2 of Census Tables, Middle Atlantic Coast	White	3,857,503	1,284	33
	Colored	518,632	238	46
Group 8 of Census Tables, Interior Plateau	White	4,990,587	791	16
	Colored	724,096	374	51
Group 11 of Census Tables, Southern Interior Plateau	White	1,653,096	1,410	85
	Colored	1,972,449	1,784	90

The second group comprises Delaware, the District of Columbia and parts of New York, New Jersey, Maryland and Virginia; the eighth includes parts of New York, Pennsylvania, Virginia and North Carolina; and the eleventh, parts of South Carolina, Georgia, Alabama, Mississippi and Tennessee. According to this tabulation the colored race is more liable to death from malarial fevers in these sections of the United States; but that this does not depend on distinctions of race seems indicated by the fact that although in the more malarious regions the death-rate of both races is increased, the relative increase is much greater among the whites. Until proved otherwise it may be assumed that the higher death-rate among the negroes is due to greater exposures.

The mortality figures returned by the health officers of certain cities have been tabulated below as bearing on the point at issue. These figures having been obtained by a regular system of registration, based in most instances on the requirement of burial permits, are probably very nearly accurate; and as they represent deaths which occurred within certain restricted limits of territory, they may be considered as possessing better qualifications for a comparative inquiry than the figures of the census reports:

Comparison of the Death-rate from Malarial Disease among the White and Colored population of certain cities of the United States, from data taken from the Consolidated Mortality Report of the National Board of Health for the year 1881. Bulletin of the Board, Vol. III, pp. 324–327.

CITIES AND TOWNS.	POPULATION.		Deaths from malarial disease.		Ratio of deaths per 100,000 of living.	
	White.	Colored.	White.	Colored.	White.	Colored.
District of Columbia	120,000	60,000	78	84	65.0	140.0
Norfolk, Virginia	11,933	10,033	17	21	142.5	209.3
Richmond, Virginia	35,756	28,047	11	10	30.8	35.7
Lynchburg, Virginia	7,484	8,475	2	4	26.7	47.2
Petersburg, Virginia	10,000	12,000	3	7	30.0	58.3
Wilmington, North Carolina	6,893	10,468	6	13	87.0	124.3
Charleston, South Carolina	22,712	27,287	9	9	39.6	33.0
Augusta, Georgia	12,364	10.659	6	5	48.5	46.9
Atlanta, Georgia	21,086	16,335	5	3	23.7	18.3
Savannah, Georgia	15,007	15,674	30	24	199.9	153.1
Mobile, Alabama	16,837	14,368	19	11	112.8	70.7
Selma, Alabama	3,345	4,184	8	22	239.1	525.8
Columbus, Mississippi	2,760	2,470	1	2	36.2	81.0
Natchez, Mississippi	3,421	3,637	2	1	58.5	27.5
Vicksburg, Mississippi	5,975	5,839	19	20	318.0	342.5
New Orleans, Louisiana	158,379	57,761	237	119	149.6	206.0
Shreveport, Louisiana	3,739	7,278	16	27	428.0	371.0
Baton Rouge, Louisiana	2,917	4,300	5	7	171.4	162.8
Galveston, Texas	16,900	5,353	10	5	59.2	93.4
San Antonio, Texas	17,525	3,036	12	2	68.5	65.9
Nashville, Tennessee	27,004	16,457	11	15	40.7	91.1
Memphis, Tennessee	18,622	14,971	20	27	107.4	180.3
St. Louis, Missouri	328,232	22,290	345	42	105.1	188.4
	868,891	360,922	872	480	100.4	133.0

It is not possible, in view of these figures, to decide whether the negro is less susceptible to the malarial influence than the white race; but the assertion may be allowed,

In twenty-three United States cities which contain a notable colored population, the death-rate from malarial fever among the white people in 1881 was in nine cities larger than that of the colored people; but the excess in the other direction was so great in the remaining fourteen cities that in a total population of 868,891 white and 360,922 colored, the deaths were 100 in every 100,000 of the former and 133 in every 100,000 of the latter. It is probable that local conditions were involved in the production of the various death-rates given in this table; for although in some towns that are notably malarious, as Shreveport, Louisiana, and in others that are not so, as Atlanta, Georgia, the death-rate among the colored people was less than among the whites; in some that are notably malarious, as Selma, Alabama, and Vicksburg, Mississippi, and in others that are not so, as Richmond and Lynchburg, Virginia, the death-rate among the colored people was greater than among the whites. The only inference that may with propriety be drawn from these municipal statistics is that which has been reached in the text from a comparison of the figures relating to malarial fevers in the white and colored commands during the war: that the colored race suffers greatly from these fevers, but whether to greater or less extent than the white race, cannot be determined in the absence of a thorough knowledge of the surroundings and exposure. Manifestly, since in any of these cities the colored people may or may not have been aggregated in unhealthy localities, nothing can be said of their relative liability to malarial fevers until a comparison is made of the prevalence of these fevers in the two races in certain wards or sections of the city having the same medical topography.

Our army experience since the war presents statistics which ought to be of more value in this connection than those heretofore adduced. Certain posts have been occupied by a mixed garrison of white and colored troops. The two commands have been similarly quartered, clothed and rationed; they have performed the same guard, fatigue, escort and scouting duties, and have necessarily been exposed to the same malarious influences. Moreover, the same medical authority has supervised the record of the sickness of both races. The facts tabulated below may therefore be accepted as obtained under conditions which permit the relative liability of the white and colored races to be as satisfactorily tested as if they had been specially arranged for the experiment. Unfortunately, however, owing to the small number of posts garrisoned by mixed commands, the strength represented is small.

TABLE *exhibiting the Prevalence of Periodic Fevers at different Posts in the Department of Texas.*

POSTS.	Troops.	Year.	Mean strength.	Remittent Fever.	Quotidians.	Tertians.	Quartans.	Typho-malarial Fever.	Annual rate of cases of Malarial Fever per 1,000 strength.
Fort Bliss, Texas	White	1878–9	60	....	16	....	......	16	266.6
	Colored		52	....	11			11	211.5
Fort Bliss, Texas	White	1879–80	54	....	14			14	259.3
	Colored		26		4			4	153.9
Fort Brown, Texas	White	1876–7	340	18	91	4		113	332.4
	Colored		56		5	1		6	107.1
Fort Clark, Texas	White	1876–7	256	11	14	10	......	35	136.7
	Colored		120	3	3	1	1	8	66.6
Fort McIntosh, Texas	White	1878–9	98	3	31	1		35	357.1
	Colored		99	....	37			37	373.7
Fort McIntosh, Texas	White	1879–80	65	4	7	1		12	184.6
	Colored		137	4	22			26	189.8
Fort McKavett, Texas	White	1876–7	263	5	14	10	......	29	110.3
	Colored		59	....	2	1		3	50.8
Fort McKavett, Texas	White	1877–8	164	3	21	5		29	176.8
	Colored		30	1	....			1	33.3
Fort Ringgold, Texas	White	1876–7	199	30	113	8		151	758.8
	Colored		74	3	24			27	364.9
Fort Ringgold, Texas	White	1877–8	155	21	18	2	......	41	264.5
	Colored		78	12	4	1		17	217.9
Fort Ringgold, Texas	White	1878–9	126	10	8	4		22	174.6
	Colored		119	19	10	1		30	252.1
Fort Ringgold, Texas	White	1879–80	107	1	11	3	......	15	140.2
	Colored		166	5	12	1		18	108.4
Total White			1,887	106	358	48	......	512	271.3
Total Colored			1,016	47	134	6	1	188	185.0

At Forts Bliss, Brown, Clark and McKavett, Texas, there was a greater prevalence among the white troops; at Fort McIntosh the white and colored troops suffered at about the same rate; while at Fort Ringgold, in the year 1878–9, there were more malarial cases among the colored than among the white soldiers. But in dealing with such small numbers as are represented at each of these posts the records of a single garrison do not have much value, as they may be affected by unknown local conditions. The totals tabulated show a less degree of prevalence among the colored troops, the annual rate per thousand among them being 185.0, while among the white troops it was 271.3.

that the colored troops did not suffer in a marked degree as compared with the white men, although it is not unlikely, from the then generally accepted belief in their partial immunity, that they were often stationed in localities that would have proved specially dangerous to white men. It is probable, therefore, that if strictly comparable figures were obtained they would show the black man to be less susceptible to malarial attacks than the white soldier.

Seasonal variations in Prevalence.—The following table shows the monthly rates of malarial cases among the white troops, and permits a comparison to be made between the rates among the troops operating in the several regions.

Looking first at the totals in the army, the purely malarial fevers (the intermittents and remittents) are seen to have a distinct maximum and minimum of prevalence in each year. These seasonal variations will be more readily followed by a reference to the diagram facing page 90. The maximum in the year ending June 30, 1862, was attained in the months of September and October, 1861, when the monthly ratios were 61.3 and 60.7 respectively, and the minimum in January, February and March, 1862, when the ratios were respectively 18.8, 18.2 and 17.0. In October of 1862 the maximum, 62.6, was again reached, after which the fevers subsided rapidly, and comparatively few cases occurred during the months of January, February, March and April, 1863, the ratios for these being 29.4, 26.8, 28.6 and 29.3. A steady increase in the number of cases reached its maximum in August and September, with ratios of 88.5 and 80.7 per thousand of strength. The fall to the minimum in January and February, 1864, was as

TABLE XXVIII.

Showing the Seasonal Variations in the Prevalence of Malarial Fevers among the White Troops in the several regions during the years of the War and the year following the War, expressed in monthly ratios per 1,000 of mean strength.

YEAR ENDING JUNE 30, 1862.

DISEASE.	REGION.	1861.						1862.						FOR THE YEAR.
		JULY.	AUGUST.	SEPTEMBER.	OCTOBER.	NOVEMBER.	DECEMBER.	JANUARY.	FEBRUARY.	MARCH.	APRIL.	MAY.	JUNE.	
Intermittent (including Congestive) Fever ..	Atlantic ...	10.2	27.6	39.4	34.6	22.2	14.2	7.9	8.5	6.9	12.3	15.2	15.8	195.9
	Central....	38.9	67.0	56.9	65.5	41.7	30.7	21.9	17.2	19.1	26.7	27.6	27.1	379.9
	Pacific	8.2	20.6	18.2	21.7	20.1	13.9	7.2	10.1	8.8	10.0	8.9	13.0	161.8
Intermittent in all the regions........................		22.2	35.9	43.2	44.2	28.4	19.6	11.7	10.8	10.5	18.9	21.2	21.2	260.8
Remittent Fever	Atlantic ...	2.8	9.9	15.9	16.0	13.7	9.3	5.7	6.7	5.3	8.5	15.8	14.2	124.4
	Central....	13.5	31.6	26.3	18.4	18.6	13.3	11.3	10.0	9.5	12.6	15.7	17.9	182.1
	Pacific	.9	.4	1.3	7.4	3.1	4.5	1.2	1.8	4.3	8.5	1.7	8.9	55.0
Remittent in all the regions........................		7.2	14.3	18.1	16.5	14.9	10.5	7.1	7.4	6.5	10.4	15.8	15.9	143.2
Intermittent and Remittent..................	Atlantic ...	13.1	37.5	55.2	50.6	35.9	23.5	13.5	15.1	12.2	20.8	31.0	30.1	320.3
	Central....	52.4	98.5	83.2	83.9	60.3	44.0	33.2	27.2	28.7	39.3	43.4	45.0	562.0
	Pacific	9.1	21.0	19.5	29.1	23.2	18.5	8.4	11.9	13.1	18.5	10.6	21.9	216.9
Total Malarial in all the regions		29.4	50.2	61.3	60.7	43.3	30.1	18.8	18.2	17.0	29.3	37.0	37.1	404.0

MALARIAL FEVERS

YEAR ENDING JUNE 30, 1863.

DISEASE.	REGION.	1862.						1863.						FOR THE YEAR.
		JULY.	AUGUST.	SEPTEMBER.	OCTOBER.	NOVEMBER.	DECEMBER.	JANUARY.	FEBRUARY.	MARCH.	APRIL.	MAY.	JUNE.	
Intermittent (including Congestive) Fever ..	Atlantic ...	20.4	21.4	24.4	30.8	19.4	12.9	11.3	8.6	9.2	10.4	15.3	18.8	191.2
	Central	32.3	36.8	56.3	61.2	46.0	33.9	28.5	26.9	29.2	28.6	29.1	44.0	440.8
	Pacific	12.5	17.4	17.6	11.4	11.1	8.0	8.2	6.0	7.3	8.2	7.7	9.8	124.5
Intermittent in all the regions...........................		25.4	28.8	39.3	46.3	33.2	23.1	19.9	17.9	19.5	20.3	23.0	34.3	319.8
Remittent Fever	Atlantic ...	21.4	16.1	13.4	16.7	10.5	8.0	8.0	6.6	6.7	6.8	8.5	9.0	123.3
	Central....	19.0	18.1	18.4	16.3	12.6	10.3	11.2	11.2	11.6	10.9	12.2	14.9	158.3
	Pacific	2.4	6.6	15.0	7.0	5.7	2.7	1.5	.7	1.8	4.0	3.6	3.2	53.6
Remittent in all the regions............................		19.9	16.9	15.8	16.3	11.5	9.1	9.5	8.9	9.1	9.0	10.5	12.5	140.4
Intermittent and Remittent................	Atlantic ...	41.8	37.5	37.8	47.5	29.9	20.9	19.3	15.2	15.9	17.2	23.8	27.8	314.5
	Central....	51.3	54.9	74.7	77.5	58.6	44.2	39.7	38.1	40.8	39.5	41.3	58.9	599.1
	Pacific	14.9	24.0	32.6	18.4	16.8	10.7	9.7	6.7	9.1	12.2	11.3	13.0	178.1
Total in all the regions.................................		45.3	45.7	55.1	62.6	44.7	32.2	29.4	26.8	28.6	29.3	33.5	46.8	460.2
Typho-malarial Fever.....................	Atlantic ...	6.1	4.1	3.3	3.4	3.8	3.8	4.2	2.9	2.7	2.5	2.7	3.5	42.3
	Central....	4.8	4.5	3.2	3.2	2.3	1.9	2.8	3.9	3.3	2.6	2.1	2.0	34.8
	Pacific	2.0	2.3	1.6	2.2	.9	3.4	.2	.8	.7	1.3	.7	2.2	18.0
Typho-malarial in all the regions		5.4	4.3	3.2	3.3	3.0	2.9	3.4	3.4	3.0	2.6	2.3	2.6	38.0
Intermittent, Remittent and Typho-malarial	Atlantic ...	47.9	41.6	41.1	50.9	33.7	24.7	23.5	18.1	18.6	19.7	26.5	31 3	356.8
	Central....	56.1	59.4	77.9	80.7	60.9	46.1	42.5	42.0	44.1	42.1	43.4	60.9	633.9
	Pacific	16.9	26.3	34.2	20.6	17.7	14.1	9.9	7.5	9.8	13.5	12.0	15.2	196.1
All the regions		50.7	50.0	58.3	65.9	47.7	35.1	32.8	30.2	31.6	31.9	35.8	49.4	498.2

YEAR ENDING JUNE 30, 1864.

DISEASE.	REGION.	1863.						1864.						FOR THE YEAR.
		JULY.	AUGUST.	SEPTEMBER.	OCTOBER.	NOVEMBER.	DECEMBER.	JANUARY.	FEBRUARY.	MARCH.	APRIL.	MAY.	JUNE.	
Intermittent (including Congestive) Fever..	Atlantic ...	27.6	44.7	52.0	47.8	38.8	23.5	19.4	17.1	21.0	24.2	22.2	24.5	359.7
	Central....	66.3	84.6	74.7	58.2	42.6	30.4	28.6	27.4	32.1	33.8	34.8	37.6	541.0
	Pacific	13.8	15.7	25.3	25.1	15.7	10.7	8.0	7.4	10.4	10.6	11.8	11.6	161.8
Intermittent in all the regions		51.6	69.0	65.3	54.0	40.8	27.7	25.1	23.4	27.7	29.7	30.1	32.7	470.0
Remittent Fever	Atlantic ...	11.2	17.6	15.3	12.3	7.7	4.8	3.8	3.7	4.6	5.5	5.1	10.7	99.8
	Central...	19.3	21.0	15.7	10.0	7.1	4.9	5.0	5.5	6.3	7.7	9.8	13.5	123.6
	Pacific	5.0	5.1	6.8	11.3	11.6	3.6	2.7	.9	2.2	3.0	5.4	5.6	61.4
Remittent in all the regions		16.2	19.5	15.4	10.4	7.4	4.9	4.6	4.8	5.6	6.8	8.2	12.4	114.1
Intermittent and Remittent	Atlantic ...	38.8	62.3	67.3	60.1	46.5	28.3	23.2	20.8	25.6	29.7	27.3	35.2	459.5
	Central....	85.6	105.6	90.4	68.2	49.7	35.3	33.6	32.9	38.4	41.5	44.6	51.1	664.6
	Pacific	18.8	20.8	32.1	36.4	27.3	14.3	10.7	8.3	12.6	13.6	17.2	17.2	223.2
Total in all the regions		67.8	88.5	80.7	64.4	48.2	32.6	29.7	28.2	33.3	36.5	38.3	45.1	584.1
Typho-malarial Fever.....................	Atlantic ...	4.4	4.2	3.0	2.8	1.8	1.2	1.3	.7	.7	.9	1.2	3.1	24.6
	Central....	2.9	3.2	1.9	1.4	1.2	.8	.6	.5	.7	.7	1.0	1.5	16.1
	Pacific	.8	.2	.3	.1	.4	.2	.2	.4	.1	.1	.2	.1	3.0
Typho-malarial in all the regions		3.4	3.5	2.3	1.9	1.4	1.0	.8	.6	.7	.7	1.0	2.0	18.9
Intermittent, Remittent and Typho-malarial	Atlantic ...	43.2	66.5	70.3	62.9	48.3	29.5	24.5	21.5	26.3	30.6	28.5	38.3	484.1
	Central....	88.5	108.8	92.3	69.6	50.9	36.1	34.2	33.4	39.1	42.2	45.6	52.6	680.7
	Pacific	19.6	21.0	32.4	36.5	27.7	14.5	10.9	8.7	12.7	13.7	17.4	17.3	226.2
All the regions..		71.2	92.0	83.0	66.3	49.6	33.6	30.5	28.8	34.0	37.2	39.3	47.1	603.0

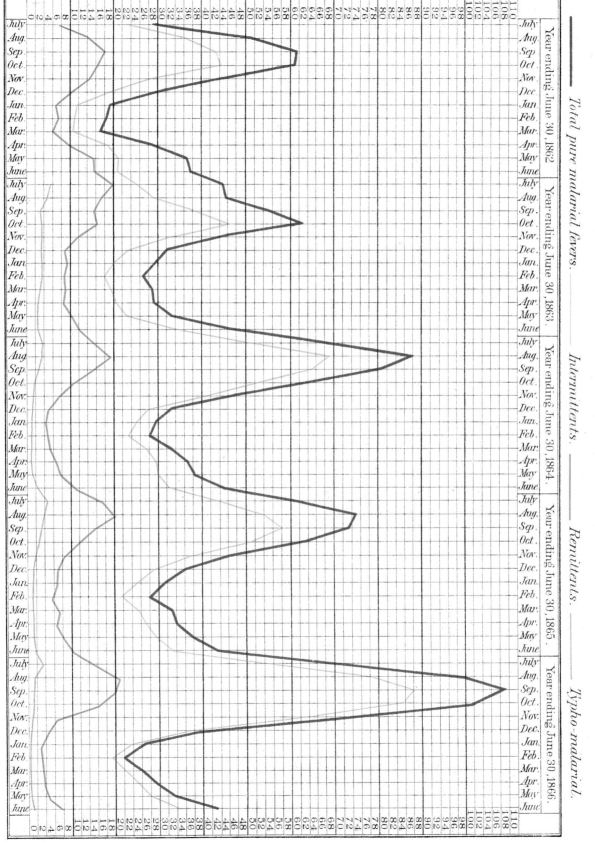

Diagram showing the Monthly Ratio of Cases of Malarial Fevers among the White Troops,
per thousand of strength present

Total pure malarial fevers. ——   Intermittents. ——   Remittents. ——   Typho-malarial. ——

YEAR ENDING JUNE 30, 1865.

DISEASE.	REGION.	1864.						1865.						FOR THE YEAR.
		JULY.	AUGUST.	SEPTEMBER.	OCTOBER.	NOVEMBER.	DECEMBER.	JANUARY.	FEBRUARY.	MARCH.	APRIL.	MAY.	JUNE.	
Intermittent (including Congestive) Fever..	Atlantic ...	32.6	41.3	52.9	51.0	39.1	24.6	18.6	16.6	19.6	20.0	26.9	28.0	359.3
	Central....	52.8	62.4	62.8	53.3	36.8	32.5	29.7	26.3	31.3	33.6	34.1	38.1	495.8
	Pacific	8.0	14.9	12.9	16.4	11.4	8.5	9.2	9.6	9.2	13.4	12.0	17.3	142.8
Intermittent in all the regions		43.9	53.8	57.9	51.6	37.2	28.8	24.7	21.6	25.6	26.8	29.4	32.9	429.5
Remittent Fever.....................	Atlantic ..	17.4	17.4	16.0	13.7	9.4	6.7	6.8	5.8	6.8	6.7	7.6	9.9	119.3
	Central....	18.5	22.8	15.5	10.8	8.4	7.9	7.6	7.1	8.2	8.0	9.8	11.7	137.3
	Pacific	5.4	8.6	3.8	8.3	1.8	1.2	2.6	1.9	2.6	2.4	3.8	4.1	46.9
Remittent in all the regions		17.8	20.6	15.5	12.0	8.7	7.3	7.2	6.4	7.5	7.3	8.7	10.7	127.8
Intermittent and Remittent	Atlantic ...	50.0	58.7	68.9	64.7	48.5	31.3	25.4	22.4	26.4	26.7	34.5	37.9	478.6
	Central....	71.3	85.2	78.3	64.1	44.2	40.4	37.3	33.4	39.5	41.6	43.9	49.8	633.1
	Pacific	13.4	23.5	16.7	24.7	13.2	9.7	11.8	11.5	11.8	15.8	15.8	21.4	189.7
Total in all the regions..................		61.7	74.4	73.4	63.6	45.9	36.1	31.9	28.0	33.1	34.1	38.1	43.6	557.3
Typho-malarial Fever..................	Atlantic ...	7.6	6.6	4.8	4.0	2.9	1.6	1.4	1.3	1.5	1.4	1.7	1.6	34.4
	Central....	2.1	2.3	1.7	1.2	.7	1.1	.8	.4	1.0	1.2	.8	1.4	14.9
	Pacific	....	.1	.4	1.1	.5	.2	.4	....	.1	....	....		2.6
Typho-malarial in all the regions		4.2	3.8	2.9	2.4	1.6	1.3	1.1	.8	1.2	1.2	1.2	1.5	22.9
Intermittent, Remittent and Typho-malarial	Atlantic ...	57.6	65.3	73.7	68.7	51.4	32.9	26.8	23.7	27.9	28.1	36.2	39.5	513.0
	Central....	73.4	87.5	80.0	65.3	44.9	41.5	38.1	33.8	40.5	42.8	44.7	51.2	648.0
	Pacific	13.4	23.6	17.1	25.8	13.7	9.9	12.2	11.5	11.8	15.9	15.8	21.4	193.3
All the regions		65.9	78.2	76.3	66.0	47.5	37.4	33.0	28.8	34.3	35.3	39.3	45.1	580.2

YEAR ENDING JUNE 30, 1866.

DISEASE.	REGION.	1865.						1866.						FOR THE YEAR.
		JULY.	AUGUST.	SEPTEMBER.	OCTOBER.	NOVEMBER.	DECEMBER.	JANUARY.	FEBRUARY.	MARCH.	APRIL.	MAY.	JUNE.	
Intermittent (including Congestive) Fever ..	Atlantic ...	45.9	66.5	88.0	92.7	63.3	39.0	18.5	16.8	20.4	28.4	38.3	34.7	658.7
	Central	63.4	91.3	96.1	90.3	73.0	40.9	31.7	25.4	29.5	25.2	29.2	42.2	808.9
	Pacific	18.8	23.9	42.7	41.4	37.5	22.8	12.9	7.4	12.0	18.7	18.1	21.7	285.0
Intermittent in all the regions............		54.7	78.2	88.1	85.6	63.9	37.0	23.6	18.9	22.3	24.9	27.9	34.7	693.4
Remittent Fever	Atlantic ...	13.4	16.7	21.8	16.0	6.5	4.6	2.4	2.1	3.1	4.5	5.1	8.7	144.8
	Central....	19.3	26.1	21.7	19.3	8.2	5.1	3.5	4.1	3.9	4.4	6.2	11.5	197.2
	Pacific	3.4	3.5	5.0	4.7	3.2	3.1	2.2	2.5	3.2	2.5	2.6	2.3	39.0
Remittent in all the regions		16.3	21.3	20.2	16.4	6.8	4.6	2.9	3.1	3.5	4.0	5.0	8.3	159.7
Intermittent and Remittent	Atlantic ...	59.3	83.2	109.8	108.7	69.8	43.6	20.9	18.9	23.5	32.9	38.4	43.4	803.5
	Central....	82.7	117.4	117.8	109.6	81.2	46.0	35.2	29.5	33.4	29.6	35.4	53.7	1,006.1
	Pacific	22.2	27.4	47.7	46.1	40.7	25.9	15.1	9.9	15.2	21.2	20.7	24.0	324.0
Total in all the regions.................		71.0	99.5	108.3	102.0	70.7	41.6	26.5	22.0	25.8	28.9	32.9	43.0	853.1
Typho-malarial Fever..................	Atlantic ...	1.4	1.7	1.6	1.7	.5	.2	....	.3	....	....	.1	.2	13.0
	Central....	4.5	1.7	1.0	1.1	.9	.3	.1	....	.05	....	.1	1.2	22.5
	Pacific	.6	.1	....	....	.2	.1	....	....	....	.1	.1	.5	1.5
Typho-malarial in all the regions		3.1	1.6	1.1	1.2	.6	.2	.1	.1	.02	.05	.1	.7	16.6
Intermittent, Remittent and Typho-malarial	Atlantic ...	60.7	84.9	111.4	110.4	70.3	43.8	20.9	19.2	23.5	32.9	38.5	43.6	816.5
	Central....	87.2	119.1	118.8	110.7	82.1	46.3	35.3	29.5	33.4	29.6	35.5	54.9	1,028.6
	Pacific	22.8	27.5	47.7	46.1	40.9	26.0	15.1	9.9	15.2	21.3	20.8	24.5	325.5
All the regions		74.1	101.1	109.4	103.2	71.3	41.8	26.6	22.1	25.82	28.95	33.0	43.7	869.7

rapid and equable as the antecedent increase, the ratios for these months, 29.7 and 28.2, being very similar to those of the preceding year. The maximum was again reached, 74.4 and 73.4, in August and September, and the subsequent minimum, 28.0, in February, 1865. During the year succeeding the war the highest figures, 99.5, 108.3 and 102.0 were reached in August, September and October; the fall to the minimum, 22.0, in the following February being as sudden as was the rise which preceded it.

The intermittents had similar waves of prevalence; in fact, the contour of the general malarial waves was mainly due to the preponderance of fevers of this type. But remittents also followed the same general course, having their maximum in July, August or September,—18.1 per thousand strength in September, 1861; 19.9 in July, 1862, and 19.5, 20.6 and 21.3 in August of the three following years. The minima corresponded with January, February and March, and often included December on the one hand and April on the other; thus the average monthly ratio for these five months was 8.4 in the year 1861–2; 9.1 in 1862–3; 5.3 in 1863–4; 7.1 in 1864–5; and 3.6 in 1865–6.

It is noticeable that only in the year ending June 30, 1862, was there a distinctly marked occurrence of vernal fevers, as notable among the remittents as among the intermittents, but in both cases this vernal rise culminating in May, was separated from the autumnal increase not by a diminution in the number of febrile cases in June, but only by the failure of that month to show an increase corresponding with that of May on the one hand or July on the other. A tendency to a stasis in the advance of the febrile wave occurred also in April or May of the other years, and was most defined among the intermittents in 1864.

The great prevalence in the autumn of 1863, and again in 1865, must be considered due to the meteorological conditions of those years favoring the evolution of the disease-poison or to the operations of the troops carrying them into more dangerous localities. But these high waves were composed largely of recurrences; for the corresponding winter seasons were not characterized by that increased prevalence which would have resulted from the relapses occurring in a larger body of men subject to attack under the influence of chill, fatigue and other so-called predisposing causes. The ratios of the winter months may be regarded as giving expression to the relative numbers of men under the influence of the malarial poison in each year, for there are not wanting reports such as that of Surgeon J. M. BATES, 13th Maine Volunteers, to establish the principle that winter attacks were generally recurrences.

Every case of intermittent fever has occurred in those who were affected with the disease during last summer and fall. The attacks have shown a very general tendency to recur every seventh, fourteenth, or twenty-first day. Two companies that came from Ship Island, Mississippi, about the middle of February, have as yet given no indication of the disease, showing that the malarial influence is not sufficiently strong at this season of the year to induce the disease in those not previously affected.—*Forts Jackson & St. Philip, La., March, 1864.*

In view of this principle, it may be recognized as a fact that in October, 1862, our armies became as fully saturated with the malarial poison as in any of the after years; for while the minimum in March of that year was as low as 17.0 per thousand of strength, the succeeding minimum, which was considerably higher, did not differ much from those which followed it.

Typho-malarial fevers, which are included in the table and on the diagram, were most prevalent in the year ending June 30, 1863, diminishing gradually in the after years. The waves of prevalence were abrupt, culminating in July and falling gradually during the autumn months.

But the study of these seasonal variations for the several years may be much facilitated by their consolidation into the average figures of Table XXIX and the corresponding lines of the diagram facing page 94.

TABLE XXIX.

Average monthly number of Cases of the several varieties of Malarial Fever among the White Troops from July 1, 1861, to June 30, 1866, expressed as ratios per 1,000 of mean strength.

DISEASES.	JULY.	AUGUST.	SEPTEMBER.	OCTOBER.	NOVEMBER.	DECEMBER.	JANUARY.	FEBRUARY.	MARCH.	APRIL.	MAY.	JUNE.	ANNUAL AVERAGE.
Quotidian Intermittent..........	22.00	29.00	30.00	27.00	19.00	13.00	10.00	10.00	11.00	12.00	13.00	16.00	204.00
Tertian Intermittent............	18.00	24.00	23.00	21.00	16.00	11.00	9.00	8.00	10.00	11.00	12.00	13.00	171.00
Quartan Intermittent...........	1.92	2.22	2.72	2.39	1.79	1.18	1.31	1.10	1.07	1.14	1.01	1.53	18.82
Total simple Intermittents....	41.92	55.22	55.72	50.39	36.79	25.18	20.31	19.10	22.07	24.14	26.01	30.53	393.82
Congestive Fever..............	.82	.94	.89	.70	.47	.42	.39	.32	.32	.37	.39	.45	6.24
Total Intermittents..........	42.74	56.16	56.61	51.09	37.26	25.60	20.70	19.42	22.39	24.51	26.40	30.98	400.06
Remittent Fever..............	17.18	19.23	16.11	13.55	9.96	7.56	7.10	6.79	7.26	8.07	10.17	12.61	130.89
Total pure Malarial Fevers...	59.92	75.39	72.72	64.64	47.22	33.16	27.80	26.21	29.65	32.58	36.57	43.59	530.95
Typho-malarial Fever (a)......	4.07	3.52	2.64	2.45	1.98	1.71	1.85	1.66	1.65	1.50	1.51	2.04	26.15
Total Malarial Fevers........	63.99	78.91	75.36	67.09	49.20	34.87	29.65	27.87	31.30	34.08	38.08	45.63	557.10

(a) From July 1, 1862, to June 30, 1866.

From these the purely malarial fevers, and the intermittents which constituted so large a proportion of them, are seen to have attained their maximum in August and September. They decreased rapidly during October and November, and slowly thereafter to their minimum in February. Their increase was slow and equable from March to June, and without any vernal wave other than that involved in the gradual formation of the autumnal increase. During July the cases occurred with greater frequency, leading to the maximum in August.

The remittents prevailed as a single annual wave, rising in March, culminating in August, and falling, more abruptly at first but more equably than the intermittents, to a minimum during the winter months.

It is noticeable also that the autumnal increase affected the intermittents and the remittents alike, i. e., both of these types of fever contributed to the annual maximum of malarial fevers the same percentage of increase on their respective minima. Thus in the intermittents the difference between the minimum, 19.42, and the maximum, 56.61, is 37.19, an increase of nearly two hundred per cent. on the minimum; while the difference between the minimum, 6.79, and the maximum, 19.23, of the remittents is 12.44, also an increase of nearly two hundred per cent. on the minimum.

The seasonal curve of typho-malarial prevalence rose abruptly in June to its maximum in July, fell gradually during August, September and October, and thereafter remained at about the same level until the next June rise.

A similar table constructed from the statistics of the colored troops shows the maximum of the purely malarial fevers as having been reached in August, September and

October, after which the fall was rapid to the minimum in February. A notable increase in May, with a less marked rise in June, gives a suggestion of a vernal wave as well among the remittents as among the intermittents. The remittents, as in the case of the white troops, decreased in the autumn before a corresponding decrease occurred in the number of the accompanying agues.

The typho-malarial curve differed from that of the remittents in falling less rapidly during September and October.

TABLE XXX.

Average monthly number of Cases of the several varieties of Malarial Fever among the Colored Troops from July 1, 1863, to June 30, 1866, expressed in ratios per 1,000 of strength.

DISEASES.	JULY.	AUGUST.	SEPTEMBER.	OCTOBER.	NOVEMBER.	DECEMBER.	JANUARY.	FEBRUARY.	MARCH.	APRIL.	MAY.	JUNE.	ANNUAL AVERAGE.
Quotidian Intermittent..........	34.00	41.00	50.00	49.00	33.00	25.00	20.00	17.00	19.00	17.00	21.00	20.00	349.00
Tertian Intermittent............	25.00	32.00	36.00	39.00	30.00	20.00	18.00	16.00	14.00	16.00	15.00	18.00	278.00
Quartan Intermittent..........	1.93	2.26	2.97	2.95	1.98	1.04	1.14	1.24	.91	1.53	2.01	1.50	21.39
Total simple Intermittents....	60.93	75.26	88.97	90.95	64.98	46.04	39.14	34.24	33.91	34.53	38.01	39.50	648.39
Congestive Fever	1.56	1.57	1.93	1.99	.94	1.17	.85	.72	.93	.45	.88	.83	13.83
Total	62.49	76.83	90.90	92.94	65.92	47.21	39.99	34.96	34.84	34.98	38.89	40.33	662.22
Remittent Fever	23.20	23.08	21.61	17.51	12.10	8.57	7.77	7.46	8.51	9.05	13.61	15.08	167.10
Total pure Malarial Fevers ...	85.69	99.91	112.51	110.45	78.02	55.78	47.76	42.42	43.35	44.03	52.50	55.41	829.32
Typho-malarial Fever..........	6.34	6.87	6.11	4.44	1.90	1.66	1.97	1.56	2.13	1.96	2.95	3.29	41.06
Total Malarial Fevers........	92.03	106.78	118.62	114.89	79.92	57.44	49.73	43.98	45.48	45.99	55.45	58.70	870.38

Seasonal Variations in Mortality.—This has been illustrated by the plate facing page 20, on which are delineated the monthly variations in the level of the malarial death-rate in juxtaposition with the corresponding variations in the mortality from certain of the more fatal classes of disease and from diseases in general. The autumnal prominences are clearly defined, particularly in the last three years, the culminating points being in August in 1863 and 1864, when 1.14 and .94 per thousand are reached, and in September, 1865, when a rate of 1.18 is shown. The autumn waves in 1861 and 1862 do not have so distinct a culmination. These death-rates will be found to correspond precisely with the variations in the line of prevalence in the diagram facing page 90; whence it may be inferred that in general these fevers caused death within the month of the attack.

Influence of Region on Prevalence.—Table XXVIII, already presented, shows the seasonal variations in prevalence as affected by the climatic and other influences of the region in which the white troops operated during the several years of the war. The malarial fevers were more frequent in the Central than in the Atlantic region, while in the Pacific region the ratio of cases was much smaller than in either of the others. During the year succeeding the war the increased prevalence of these fevers affected the troops in all the regions. In the Central and Atlantic regions this was due to the occupation of southern and malarious territory; in the Pacific region it was owing in part to the estab-

Diagrams showing the Average Annual Curves of Prevalence of the Malarial Fevers among the White and the Colored Troops during the War, in Monthly Rates per Thousand of Strength.

——————— Total pure malarial fevers.   ——————— Remittents.
——————— Intermittents.   ——————— Typho-malarial.

White Troops.   ### Colored Troops.

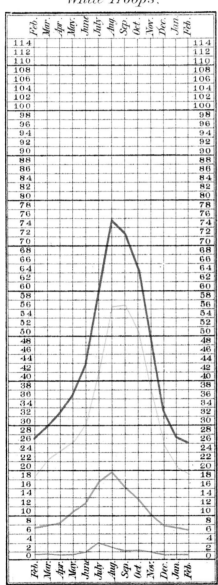
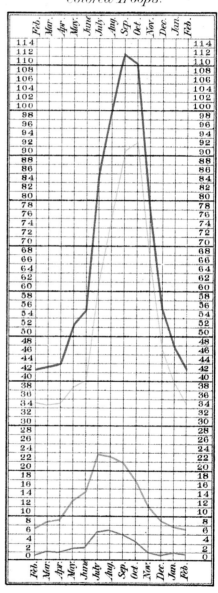

lishment of new posts in unhealthy bottom lands, and in part also to the distribution over this region of regular troops subject to intermittent relapses from previous service in the Southern States.

In Table XXXI the statistics of the malarial fevers among the white troops in each of the regions have been consolidated into average monthly ratios. From these, or from the accompanying diagram, it will be seen that the malarial waves in the three regions presented a general similarity of contour. In all the minimum was reached in February and the maximum in August, September and October. A distinct vernal wave, affecting alike the remittents and the intermittents, is presented by the ratios of the Pacific region.

TABLE XXXI.

Average monthly number of Cases of the several forms of Malarial Fever among the White Troops in the several Regions, expressed in ratios per 1,000 of strength, calculated from the cases which occurred from July 1, 1861, to June 30, 1866.

ATLANTIC REGION.

DISEASES.	JULY.	AUGUST.	SEPTEMBER.	OCTOBER.	NOVEMBER.	DECEMBER.	JANUARY.	FEBRUARY.	MARCH.	APRIL.	MAY.	JUNE.	ANNUAL AVERAGE.
Quotidian Intermittent	14.4	20.6	24.4	23.4	16.3	9.7	7.2	6.6	7.2	8.4	10.6	11.1	152.4
Tertian Intermittent	13.0	16.6	17.8	17.4	12.6	7.8	5.8	5.2	6.3	7.6	9.1	9.8	123.3
Quartan Intermittent	1.1	1.2	2.2	1.8	1.2	.7	.5	.4	.5	.6	.5	1.0	11.3
Congestive Intermittent	.4	.5	.5	.7	.4	.5	.4	.3	.2	.2	.2	.2	4.4
Total Intermittent	28.9	38.9	44.9	43.3	30.5	18.7	13.9	12.5	14.2	16.8	20.4	22.1	291.4
Remittent	15.8	16.3	15.5	14.6	10.1	7.2	6.3	5.7	5.9	6.7	8.9	10.8	117.9
Total pure Malarial	44.7	55.2	60.4	57.9	40.6	25.9	20.2	18.2	20.1	23.5	29.3	32.9	409.3
Typho-malarial	5.4	4.6	3.5	3.4	2.9	2.4	2.6	1.8	1.7	1.6	1.9	2.7	33.5
Total Malarial	49.8	59.3	63.5	60.6	42.9	27.9	22.2	19.6	21.5	24.9	30.8	35.0	436.8

CENTRAL REGION.

DISEASES.	JULY.	AUGUST.	SEPTEMBER.	OCTOBER.	NOVEMBER.	DECEMBER.	JANUARY.	FEBRUARY.	MARCH.	APRIL.	MAY.	JUNE.	ANNUAL AVERAGE.
Quotidian Intermittent	28.2	35.9	35.1	30.8	21.4	16.0	13.3	12.5	14.4	15.5	15.5	19.5	250.7
Tertian Intermittent	23.1	29.4	28.2	25.3	18.6	14.4	12.7	11.5	13.6	13.6	14.5	16.1	215.6
Quartan Intermittent	2.6	3.0	3.3	2.9	2.4	1.6	2.0	1.7	1.6	1.6	1.4	1.9	25.4
Congestive Intermittent	1.1	1.3	1.2	.8	.5	.4	.4	.4	.4	.5	.5	.6	7.9
Total Intermittent	55.0	69.6	67.8	59.8	42.9	32.4	28.4	26.1	30.0	31.2	31.9	38.1	499.6
Remittent	18.9	22.0	17.1	13.0	10.0	8.0	8.1	8.0	8.7	9.3	11.3	14.2	144.9
Total pure Malarial	73.9	91.6	84.9	72.8	52.9	40.4	36.5	34.1	38.7	40.5	43.2	52.3	644.5
Typho-malarial	3.2	2.9	2.1	1.9	1.4	1.2	1.4	1.6	1.7	1.5	1.3	1.7	21.6
Total Malarial	77.1	94.4	86.9	74.5	54.2	41.4	37.8	35.7	40.2	41.7	44.3	53.8	664.2

PACIFIC REGION.

DISEASES.	JULY.	AUGUST.	SEPTEMBER.	OCTOBER.	NOVEMBER.	DECEMBER.	JANUARY.	FEBRUARY.	MARCH.	APRIL.	MAY.	JUNE.	ANNUAL AVERAGE.
Quotidian Intermittent	6.8	11.9	17.2	15.5	13.8	8.9	5.6	4.9	4.7	6.7	6.7	9.4	111.5
Tertian Intermittent	4.6	5.0	6.6	7.8	5.5	3.8	2.8	2.6	4.0	4.6	4.6	4.2	55.5
Quartan Intermittent	.9	.9	.7	.6	.6	.4	.9	.4	1.0	.8	.3	1.2	8.6
Congestive Intermittent	.2	.7	.3	.2	.1	.2	.1	.1	.1	.1	.3	.2	2.6
Total Intermittent	12.5	18.5	24.8	24.1	20.0	13.3	9.4	8.0	9.8	12.2	11.9	15.0	178.2
Remittent	3.8	5.7	6.6	7.6	5.0	3.0	2.1	1.6	2.8	3.7	5.1	4.6	50.6
Total pure Malarial	16.3	24.2	31.4	31.7	25.0	16.3	11.5	9.6	12.6	15.9	17.0	19.6	228.8
Typho-malarial	.8	.6	.5	.8	.5	.9	.2	.3	.2	.3	.2	.5	5.8
Total Malarial	17.0	24.7	31.8	32.4	25.4	17.0	11.5	9.9	12.7	16.2	17.1	20.1	233.7

DIAGRAM *showing the Seasonal Prevalence of the Malarial Fevers in the Atlantic,* Central† and Pacific‡ Regions.*

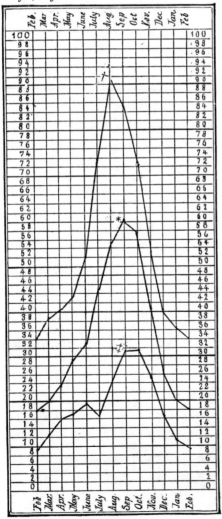

The concurrence of an elevated temperature and high ratios from malarial fevers, so well marked in the seasonal variations in prevalence, is noted also in the geographical distribution of the cases. Table XXXII, which follows, exhibits an increased prevalence in the departments of the southern part of the Atlantic coast, as compared with those on the northern part of that coast. The increase from an annual rate of 144 cases per thousand of strength in the Department of the East, through the Middle and other coast departments, to 1,035 in North Carolina and 930 in the Department of the Gulf, shows in a general way the connection of these fevers with temperature as affected by latitude. In the interior their increased prevalence in the river towns, as compared with the higher ground constituting the water-shed, may be seen in the 538 cases in the Department of the Missouri, the 865 cases in the Department of Tennessee and the 1,287 cases in the Department of Arkansas, as against 227 in Western Virginia and 265 in the Department of the Ohio; while the country bordering the great lakes gave 526, as against 238 in the northwest.

In compiling this table it was found that the highest malarial sick-rate for any one year was presented by the Department of North Carolina, in which during the year 1863–4 there were recorded 23,848 cases in a strength of 10,226 men, or 2,353 cases per thousand.

TABLE XXXII.

Showing the Prevalence of Malarial Fevers in the Departments on the Eastern and Southern Coasts of the United States, and in those of the high and low grounds of the Central Region, expressed in annual ratios per 1,000 of strength, calculated from the statistics of the four years ending June 30, 1865.

	Intermit- tent.	Remit- tent.	Typho- malarial.	Total Malarial Fevers.
Department of the East	108	32	4	144
Middle Department	172	81	11	264
Department of Virginia	503	110	37	650
Department of the South	396	131	31	558
Department of North Carolina	828	179	28	1,035
Department of the Gulf	738	148	44	930
Department of West Virginia	146	71	10	227
Department of the Northwest	150	82	6	238
Department of the Ohio	187	66	12	265
Department of the Cumberland	306	135	15	456
Northern Department	386	126	14	526
Department of Missouri	390	136	12	538
Department of Tennessee	661	181	23	865
Department of Arkansas	1,103	166	18	1,287

But while the seasonal wave was made up of a proportionate increase of the intermittent and remittent cases, the increase in the number of malarial cases, which coincided with lower latitudes and lower grounds in the same latitudes, was largely composed of intermittent cases. It is evident that the 32 remittents in the Department of the East do not bear the same relation to the 108 intermittents of that command that the 166 remittents of the Department of Arkansas bear to its 1,103 intermittents. Although remittents increased in their absolute number with an increase in the total of malarial cases, their number as a percentage of that total became diminished in the more malarious localities. This is readily gathered from Table XXXIII, in which the various types of fever that occurred in each department are tabulated as percentages of the total number of its malarial cases.

At first sight it appears as if no relationship existed between the prevalence of the remittents and intermittents; for of the two departments, the East and New Mexico, which had less than 200 cases of malarial fevers annually per thousand of strength, the one had 75 per cent. of intermittents and 22 of remittents, while the other had 61 per cent. of the former and 35 of the latter. But if an examination is made of the figures from such departments as the South, the Missouri, the Northern Department and Part I of the Mississippi Division, which had an annual rate of from 500 to 600 malarial cases per thousand of strength, the intermittents will be found to have constituted from 71 to 73 per cent. of the total and the remittents from 23 to 25 per cent. It is noteworthy also, that these figures agree with the averages from the army as a whole, for with 539 malarial cases annually per thousand of strength in all the departments the percentage of intermittents was 71.71 and that of the remittents 24.01.

TABLE XXXIII.

Showing—1, The relative prevalence of the Malarial Fevers among the White Troops in the several Departments and Regions during the four years ending June 30, 1865, expressed as ratios per 1,000 of strength; 2, The relative frequency of the forms of these Fevers, expressed in percentages of the total number of cases; and 3, The relative frequency of the varieties of Intermittent Fever, expressed as percentages of the total number of Intermittent cases.

Average annual ratio of Malarial cases per 1,000 of strength.	DEPARTMENTS AND REGIONS.	Total number of Malarial cases.	Percentage of Intermittent.	Percentage of Remittent.	Percentage of Typho-malarial.	Total number of Intermittent cases.	Percentage of Quotidians.	Percentage of Tertians.	Percentage of Quartans.	Percentage of Congestive fevers.
144	Department of the East	6,330	75.07	22.29	2.64	4,752	45.27	49.77	4.48	.48
264	Middle Department	12,275	65.04	30.56	4.47	7,984	58.20	37.04	3.31	1.45
284	Department of the Shenandoah	4,560	69.99	30.06	.. (a) ..	3,189	64.36	33.68	1.38	.60
329	Middle Military Division	15,297	64.64	30.13	5.23	9,889	52.89	43.67	2.52	.92
390	Department of Washington	40,349	62.51	26.15	11.34	25,224	47.34	47.29	4.34	1.04
315	Army of the Potomac	138,494	52.73	38.43	8.84	73,031	51.50	41.27	4.83	2.40
288	Department of the Rappahannock	4,075	53.50	46.50	.. (a) ..	2,180	43.53	47.16	6.05	3.26
650	Department of Virginia	67,249	77.43	16.90	5.68	52,068	51.33	43.48	3.85	1.34
1,035	Department of North Carolina	64,389	80.00	17.21	2.79	51,512	58.75	38.07	2.44	.74
559	Department of the South	36,175	70.82	23.50	5.68	25,619	47.73	45.56	4.77	1.94
422	Atlantic Region	389,193	65.64	27.71	6.65	255,448	52.26	42.27	3.94	1.54
238	Department of the Northwest	4,706	63.07	34.59	2.34	2,967	61.61	33.27	4.04	1.08
526	Northern Department	20,085	73.35	24.03	2.62	14,732	50.55	42.37	5.38	1.70
227	Department of West Virginia	14,075	64.19	31.22	4.59	9,035	50.08	46.00	2.78	1.14
538	Department of the Missouri	54,093	72.54	25.31	2.15	39,239	48.79	42.72	6.34	2.15
265	Department of the Ohio	22,645	70.44	25.07	4.49	15,950	52.08	42.23	4.16	1.54
456	Department of the Cumberland	107,603	67.03	29.75	3.22	72,129	52.13	41.02	5.19	1.65
865	Department of the Tennessee	211,229	76.43	20.88	2.69	161,445	51.74	41.36	5.13	1.77
595	Military Division of the Mississippi, Part I	65,004	73.46	23.44	3.10	47,756	52.53	41.15	4.93	1.39
457	Military Division of the Mississippi, Part II	40,855	70.43	27.20	2.37	28,775	50.37	44.92	3.84	.88
1,287	Department of Arkansas	73,477	85.74	12.85	1.41	62,999	49.21	43.26	6.14	1.39
930	Department of the Gulf	115,290	79.38	15.87	4.74	91,517	44.23	49.00	5.10	1.66
648	Central Region	729,062	74.97	22.00	3.03	546,544	50.03	43.18	5.19	1.62
195	Department of New Mexico	2,987	60.73	35.15	4.12	1,814	62.72	27.62	7.72	1.93
212	Department of the Pacific	5,052	77.16	20.70	2.14	3,898	59.81	33.78	5.44	.98
207	Pacific Region	8,039	71.05	26.08	2.87	5,712	60.73	31.83	6.16	1.28
539	Total in the Regions	1,126,294	71.71	24.01	4.28	807,704	50.85	42.77	4.79	1.59

(a) These departments became merged in others before the introduction of the term *typho-malarial*.

If, however, the specially malarious localities are examined, it will be found, as indicated in the presentation of Table XXXII, that the remittent fevers did not form so large a percentage of the total as in the departments where the malarial influence was manifestly not so extensively prevalent. Thus, in the Department of Arkansas scarcely 13 per cent. of remittents occurred in 1,287 malarial cases annually per thousand of strength, in the Gulf department 16 per cent. in 930, in North Carolina 17 per cent. in 1,035 and in Tennessee 21 per cent. in 865; in the whole of the Central region 22 per cent. in 648, and in the whole of the Atlantic region 28 per cent. in 422.

In other departments, as the East, New Mexico, etc., where, with similar totals giving expression to the malarial influence, the remittents and intermittents were not similarly distributed, it is probable that the percentages of each may have been largely determined by the existence of those conditions which are recognized as predisposing causes. The highest proportion of remittents occurred in the Armies of the Potomac and Rappahannock. Predisposing causes such as fatigue, exposure to weather changes, loss of sleep, improper food, impure water, etc., were undoubtedly at their maximum among the actively engaged troops of those commands.

The typho-malarial cases, while more frequent in a malarious locality than in one comparatively free from malarial disease, do not appear to have exhibited any fixed relationship to the malarial fevers. Thus, the Department of Arkansas had the lowest percentage of typho-malarial cases, although presenting the highest annual total of malarial fevers, and the Department of Washington and Army of the Potomac gave by far the highest percentage of typho-malarial cases, although they were below the average as regards the prevalence of malarial disease.

The statements of medical authors as to the relative frequency of the types of intermittents are somewhat at variance. Thus, BROWN* represents the tertian as most frequently met with, the quartan standing next, and the quotidian as in some degree rarer than the latter. COPLAND† also gives the tertian the greatest, and the regular quotidian the least, prevalence. Climate and season have no doubt an influence on the production of these varieties. HERTZ‡ says that in temperate climates the tertian occurs most frequently, and that the short types approaching the continued form prevail in the tropics and in the temperate climates during the hot season. Indian experience appears to sustain this view. SULLIVAN§ gives the order of frequency as quotidian, tertian and quartan. MAILLOT and E. COLLIN‖ have published statistics of prevalence among the French troops in Algeria which show a similar order of frequency. Our own statistics give the following percentages: Quotidians 50.85, tertians 42.77, quartans 4.79 and congestive attacks 1.59.

On the assumption that the short types are most common in hot weather and in hot climates, quartan agues ought to be most frequent where the total of malarial disease is smallest. But the table just presented shows similar percentages of this type of fever in the Department of the East and in that of the South, in the Northern Department and in that of the Gulf, while the Department of Arkansas had many quartans and the Department of the Cumberland comparatively few. The tertians were more frequent than the quotidians in the Department of the East; but the same statement holds good with regard

---

* JOSEPH BROWN in the *Cyclopædia of Practical Medicine*, Phila., Pa., 1845, Vol. II, p. 206.
† *A Dictionary of Practical Medicine*, by JAMES COPLAND, London, 1858, Vol. I, p. 935.
‡ HERTZ in *Ziemssen's Cyclopædia*, Amer. Transl., New York, 1875, Vol. II, p. 595.
§ *Endemic Diseases of Tropical Climates*, by JOHN SULLIVAN, M. D., London, 1877, p. 33.
‖ F. C. MAILLOT—*Traité des Fièvres Intermittentes*, Paris, 1836—gives, on p. 414, a table showing the occurrence in the military hospitals at Bone of 2,338 clearly defined intermittents, of which 1,582 were quotidians, 730 tertians and 26 quartans. E. COLLIN—in his *Recherches sur les affections de la rate*, published in Recueil de Mémoires de Médecine, etc., 2e Série, T. IV, Paris, 1848—states, p. 116, that of 6,636 cases observed at Philippeville in Algeria, 3,523 were quotidians, 916 tertians, 58 quartans, 303 erratic of variable type and 1,836 remittents.

to the Department of the Gulf. A closer inspection of the data from which this table was made up gives greater prominence to the irregularity in this respect. While the nature of the disease-poison is no doubt the main factor in determining the type of the disease, it is probable that predisposing conditions exercise a strong influence on the resulting fever. Congestive fever constituted .48 per cent. of the intermittents in the Department of the East; .60 in the Shenandoah; .92 in the Middle Military Division, and .98 in the Department of the Pacific, in each of which the malarial total was comparatively small: 1.66 in the Department of the Gulf, and 1.39 in Arkansas, in which the totals were large; but it constituted only .74 per cent. in the highly malarious Department of North Carolina, and 1.93 in the comparatively healthy territories of the Department of New Mexico. Since, however, the highest proportionate number of congestive cases was found in the Army of the Potomac, 2.40 per cent., and in the Department of the Rappahannock, 3.26 per cent., it may be assumed, as in the case of the remittents, that these pernicious fevers were largely due to the fatigues, exposures and deprivations incident to active operations.

The distribution of the malarial fevers during the war, presented in numbers in the last two tables, has also been illustrated by the tinted map which faces this page. It is impossible to show on a single map of this, or perhaps of any size, the many changes which the exigencies of the moment necessitated in the boundaries of the various military departments. For this reason no attempt has been made to secure such official accuracy in their outlines as would be required were the map intended as an illustration of a military study. Nor is this needful, for the depth of tint indicating the prevalence of malarial fevers in a given department was determined not by the malarial character of the department as a whole, but only by that of the part, oftentimes a small one, occupied by the Union forces. The lines and circles of solid color show in what parts of the various departments our armies operated during the years of the war,—red, yellow, blue and green respectively representing the portions held during the years ending June 30, 1862, '63, '64 and '65. In certain of the home departments, as the Northern Department and those of the East and Northwest, no lines of position are given, as the troops serving in these military commands were scattered generally over the country at recruiting depots and camps of instruction, etc.

The Departments of the Rappahannock and Shenandoah and the Middle Military Division are not represented on the map. The first two temporarily formed independent commands in the section of country which was for most of the time known as the Department of the Potomac, and the last, during the latter part of the war, included West Virginia and the Valley of the Shenandoah. Nor does the Military Division of the Mississippi appear on the map. Part I of this Division included, during the last year of the war, the country composing the Departments of the Ohio, Cumberland, and Tennessee and such parts of the neighboring States as were occupied by the army under General Thomas; while Part II comprised the territory passed over by General Sherman's army in its march through Georgia to the Atlantic Coast, and thence northward to Washington, D. C.

The map shows in a general way the greater frequency of the malarial fevers in the southern portions of the Atlantic and Central regions. Apparent exceptions were due to easily explained circumstances. Thus, in the Atlantic region the troops in the Department of the South suffered less than those of the North Carolina command, because the greater portion of the former occupied during most of the war comparatively healthy sites on coast

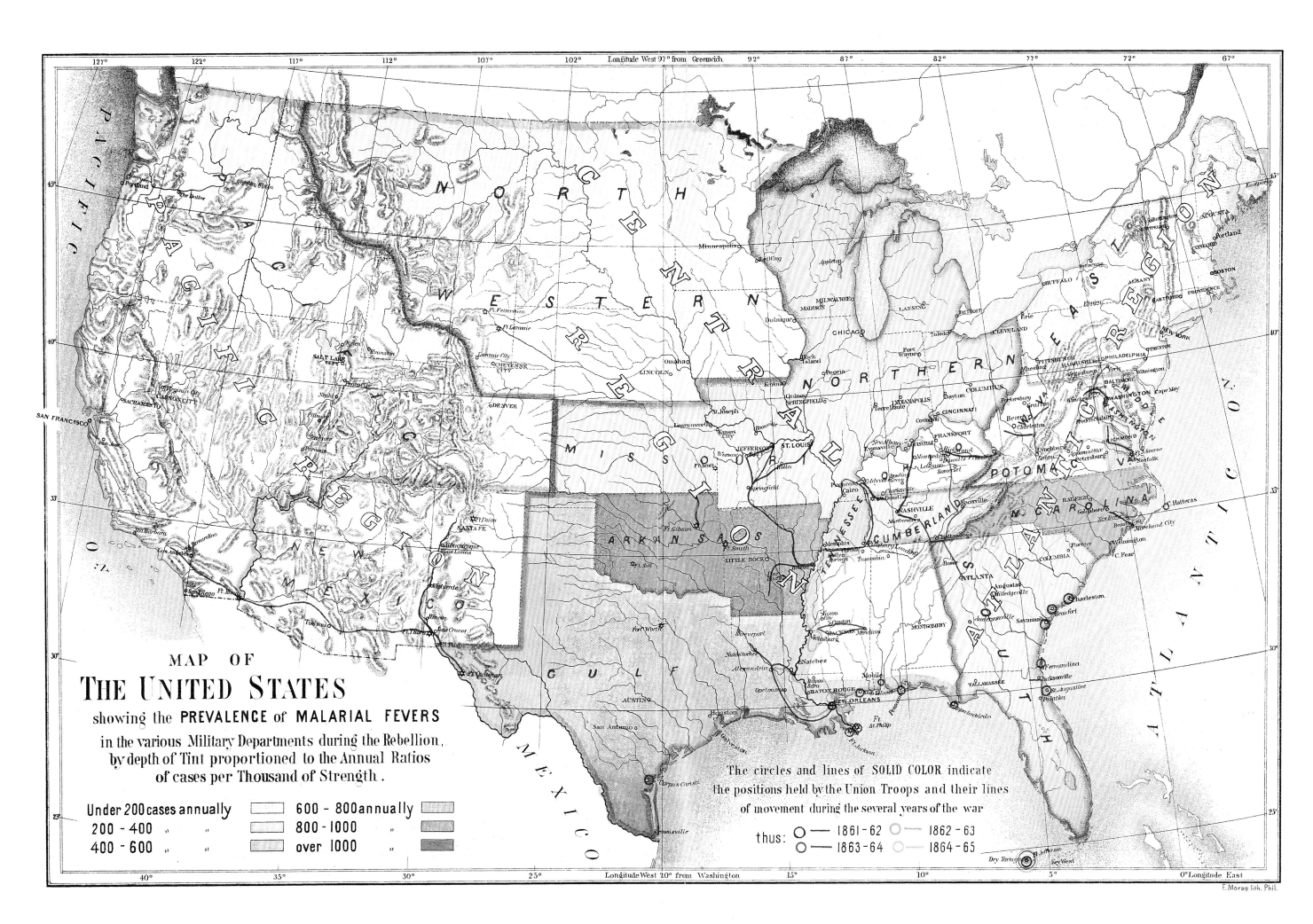

MAP OF
THE UNITED STATES
showing the PREVALENCE of MALARIAL FEVERS
in the various Military Departments during the Rebellion,
by depth of Tint proportioned to the Annual Ratios
of cases per Thousand of Strength.

Under 200 cases annually
200 - 400   „   „
400 - 600   „   „

600 - 800 annually
800 - 1000   „
over 1000   „

The circles and lines of SOLID COLOR indicate
the positions held by the Union Troops and their lines
of movement during the several years of the war

thus: ⊙ — 1861-62   ⊙ 1862-63
      ⊙ — 1863-64   ⊙ 1864-65

Longitude West 97° from Greenwich

Longitude West 20° from Washington

0° Longitude East

F. Moras lith. Phil.

islands. Had the fortune of war carried them into the more malarious districts, they would undoubtedly have had an experience similar to that of the rebel troops that held those districts.* Thus, also, in the Central region the depth of color expressive of prevalence is greater in the Department of Arkansas than in that of the Gulf, on account of the occupation by the troops of the unhealthy bottom lands in the former section of the country.

It would be interesting in this connection to discuss the geographical distribution of the malarial fevers among the civil population of the United States and the garrisons of our military posts in times of peace. Information on the latter head will be found in FORRY's book[†] and in the publications of the Surgeon General's Office.[‡] As to the former, the works of DRAKE and HIRSCH [§] may be consulted. Both these writers have relied to a considerable extent on the military statistics compiled by FORRY and COOLIDGE.

Throughout the Atlantic region malarial fevers were, during the war, most prevalent in the swampy districts and lowlands adjoining the sea and bordering the water courses: they became milder in the dryer and more elevated districts of the interior, and disappeared in the highlands of the Appalachian chain and the mountainous districts of New England and New York; but south of Pennsylvania they were found in the river valleys at a considerable elevation.

In the Central region the malarial influence was most intense in the lowlands bordering the Gulf of Mexico and along the rivers that discharge into its waters; thence it extended northward with diminishing intensity to the vicinity of the great lakes, where it again became markedly prevalent. On the East it penetrated toward the headwaters of the streams arising in the Appalachian range, and on the West it became gradually milder towards the Rocky Mountains, finally disappearing on the lofty slopes of that system, though still existing to some extent in its elevated valleys.

In the Pacific region the relative prevalence of the malarial influence corresponded closely with that which obtained in the Atlantic region on the same isothermal lines.

---

* Compare the statements of the frequency of the malarial fevers among the Confederate troops in these very districts, given in a subsequent part of this chapter, p. 105, on the authority of Dr. JOSEPH JONES. See also the testimony of KOLLOCK, cited by J. F. POSEY—*Report on the topography and epidemic diseases of the State of Georgia*, Southern Med. and Surg. Jour., Vol. XIV, 1858, p. 191—with regard to the freedom from miasmatic fevers of those sea islands on the coast of Georgia, which have "few or no brackish ponds or lagunes as compared with the opposite main." For further remarks on the medical topography of this part of the Southern States, see a reference to the report of the Confederate Surgeon SAMUEL LOGAN, *infra*, page 171.

† SAMUEL FORRY—*The Climate of the United States*, 2d Edit., New York, 1842. See also, by the same author, *Statistical Researches elucidating the Climate of the United States and its relation with diseases of Malarial origin*, etc. The Amer. Jour. of the Med. Sci., N. S., Vol. II, 1841, p. 13, and the *Endemic influences of the United States*, in the same volume, p. 293.

‡ See the *Statistical Reports on the Sickness and Mortality in the Army of the United States:* the first, *from January,* 1819, *to January,* 1839, Washington, 1840, Edit. by FORRY; the second, *from January,* 1839, *to January,* 1855, Washington, 1856, edited by R. H. COOLIDGE; the third, *from January,* 1855, *to January,* 1860, Washington, 1860, edited by the same; also the two reports edited by Assistant Surgeon (now Surgeon) J. S. BILLINGS, U. S. A., viz: *Circular No.* 4, Surgeon General's Office, Washington, Dec. 5, 1870,—*A Report on Barracks and Hospitals, with descriptions of Military Posts,* and *Circular No.* 8, Surgeon General's Office, Washington, May 1, 1875—*A Report on the Hygiene of the United States Army, with description of military posts.*

§ DANIEL DRAKE—*On the Principal Diseases of the Interior Valley of North America,* Cincinnati, 1850; also, the same work, Second series, Philadelphia, 1854. A. HIRSCH—*Handb. der historisch-geographischen Pathologie,* Erlangen, 1860, Bd. I, S. 11 *et seq.* See also, besides the several essays cited by HIRSCH, the following: OLIVER WENDELL HOLMES—*Facts and traditions respecting the existence of indigenous intermittent fever in New England:* being the Boylston Prize dissertation for the year 1836. Boston, 1838.—An interesting paper, giving a good deal of evidence to show that at various times during the previous century, and even earlier, intermittent fever prevailed more extensively in New England than it did at the time it was written, or indeed for a number of years previously. J. W. HEUSTIS—*Medical facts and inquiries respecting the cause, nature, prevention and cure of fever in the Southern States, etc.,* Cahawba, Alabama, 1825. R. S. HOLMES, late of the Medical Staff, U. S. Army—*On Malaria in connection with Medical Topography.* The St. Louis Med. and Surg. Jour., Vol. V, 1848, p. 519—compares the topography of certain military posts in Florida, Portland and Holton, Maine, Prairie du Chien on the Upper Mississippi, and certain points in Mexico. E. D FENNER—*Southern Medical Reports,* New Orleans and New York, Vol. I, 1849, Vol. II, 1850. JOHN F. POSEY—*Report upon the Topography and Epidemic Diseases of the State of Georgia,* Southern Med. and Surg. Jour., Vol. XIV, 1858, pp. 106 and 191. J. C. HARRIS of Alabama—*An Essay on the climate and fevers of the Southwestern, Southern Atlantic and Gulf States.* The New Orleans Jour. of Med., Vol. XXIII, 1870, p. 401 *et seq.*; also Charleston, S. C., 1872. H. BRONSON—*History of intermittent fever in the New Haven region, with an attempt to distinguish the known from the unknown causes.* Proceedings of the Connecticut Medical Society, 2d Series, Vol. IV, 1872-5, p. 29. A. W. BARROWS—*On Malarial fever in New England.* (President's Address.) Same proceedings, 1877, p. 22. See also the *Reports on the Epidemics and Climatology* of various States, made to the Section of Meteorology, Medical Topography and Epidemic diseases, scattered through the volumes of *Transactions of the American Medical Association* prior to and including the year 1873: subsequently, many of the reports to the section of State Medicine and Public Hygiene [organized in 1873] in the same *Transactions.*

In each of these regions the malarial influence became in a general way more intense towards the south; but local conditions everywhere exercised a controlling or modifying power. Malarial fevers were less prevalent in well-drained rolling districts, elevated plateaux and mountain slopes, while they increased in frequency and severity on low plains, in moist river valleys and in swampy lands. In fact, their distribution during the war corresponded intimately with that already outlined by FORRY and COOLIDGE, and with the indications of the mortality tables of the Census Reports* and of the deaths returned by municipal boards to the National Board of Health.†

II.—MALARIAL FEVERS AMONG THE CONFEDERATE TROOPS.

Prevalence.—The consolidated monthly returns of the Confederate Army of the Potomac, preserved by Dr. T. H. WILLIAMS, have served for the computation of ratios indicating the monthly prevalence of malarial fevers in that army from July, 1861, to March, 1862, inclusive. In the table on the following page these ratios are given in juxtaposition with those for the Federal Army of the Potomac during the same months.

These figures show that malarial fevers were even more prevalent in the Confederate than in the Federal Army of the Potomac. The average monthly strength represented by the Confederate sick reports was 49,394 men, among whom occurred the monthly ratio of 38 malarial cases per thousand, while the average strength represented by the Federal sick reports was 111,169 men, and the monthly ratio of malarial cases 28.

It is not possible to contrast statistically the mortality of the two armies from these fevers during the period in question, as the Confederate returns give the number of deaths only under the heading "total from all causes."

---

* In this connection the following table has been compiled from the Statistics of the Census years 1870 and 1880. The figures tabulated represent deaths from malarial fevers per 100,000 living persons:

ATLANTIC REGION.	1870.	1880.	CENTRAL REGION.	1870.	1880.	PACIFIC REGION.	1870.	1880.
Rhode Island	3	1	Wisconsin	5	10	Utah	13	8
Vermont	4	9	West Virginia	6	8	Oregon	15	18
Massachusetts	4	4	Dakota	......	12	California	25	18
Connecticut	5	· 6	Nebraska	13	22	Nevada	38	6
Maine	6	4	Iowa	14	27	New Mexico	47	121
New Hampshire	7	5	Ohio	14	17	Washington Territory	......	11
Pennsylvania	7	9	Michigan	21	20	Arizona	......	15
New Jersey	9	29	Kentucky	25	45	Colorado	......	15
New York	10	20	Indiana	31	47	Idaho	......	15
District of Columbia	16	47	Minnesota	34	4	Montana	......	20
Delaware	18	24	Illinois	35	36	Wyoming	......	29
Maryland	20	28	Tennessee	45	59			
Virginia	21	39	Missouri	61	83			
North Carolina	42	69	Kansas	66	72			
South Carolina	52	73	Alabama	76	104			
Georgia	60	69	Mississippi	77	91			
Florida	114	112	Arkansas	91	140			
			Texas	114	93			
			Louisiana	115	92			

† See note on p. 87, *supra*.

The cases embraced in the reports of Dr. WILLIAMS consisted of 9,954 intermittents and 6,827 remittents. Of the former, 5,713 were quotidians, 3,769 tertians, 389 quartans and 83 congestive cases.

TABLE XXXIV.

A Comparison of the Prevalence of Intermittent and Remittent Fevers in the Confederate and Federal Armies of the Potomac from July 1, 1861, to March 31, 1862.

	CONFEDERATE ARMY.							U. S. ARMY.						
	MEAN STRENGTH.	Number of Cases.			Ratio per 1,000 strength.			MEAN STRENGTH.	Number of Cases.			Ratio per 1,000 strength.		
		Intermittent.	Remittent.	Total Malarial.	Intermittent.	Remittent.	Total Malarial.		Intermittent.	Remittent.	Total Malarial.	Intermittent.	Remittent.	Total Malarial.
July, 1861	21,577	299	330	629	14	15	29	17,709	165	63	228	9	4	13
August, 1861	50,525	1,674	1,716	3,390	33	34	67	50,608	1,607	584	2,191	32	11	43
September, 1861	58,360	1,739	1,739	3,478	30	30	60	85,408	3,514	1,340	4,854	41	16	57
October, 1861	58,918	1,864	1,347	3,211	31	23	54	113,204	3,984	1,756	5,740	35	16	51
November, 1861	55,099	1,405	664	2,069	26	12	38	133,669	3,011	1,922	4,933	23	14	37
December, 1861	56,700	1,148	477	1,625	20	9	29	152,759	2,151	1,474	3,625	14	10	24
January, 1862	57,089	687	262	949	12	5	17	167,267	1,170	982	2,152	7	6	13
February, 1862	54,810	650	171	821	12	3	15	153,308	1,344	1,148	2,492	9	7	16
March, 1862	31,470	488	121	609	15	4	19	126,588	793	664	1,457	7	5	12
Monthly average	49,394	1,106	759	1,865	23	15	38	111,169	1,971	1,104	3,075	18	10	28

The consolidated monthly reports for certain general hospitals in Virginia during the last four months of 1862 give, in a total of 34,890 admissions for disease, 3,095 admissions for malarial fevers, distributed as follows: Remittents 931, or 30 per cent. of the malarial total, quotidians 623, tertians 1,309, quartans 215 and congestive cases 17. Unfortunately the mortality from these cannot be ascertained from the reports.

According to Dr. JONES, the reports of sick and wounded for the years 1861 and 1862, filed in the office of the Surgeon General of the Confederacy, exclusive of those from the Trans-Mississippi department, gave a total of 819,286 cases of disease and injury, not including gunshot wounds, while the cases of malarial fever numbered 115,415, or one case of malarial fever in 7.1 of the cases constituting the total. The corresponding figures* from the records of the United States troops give 1,709,416 cases of all diseases and injuries exclusive of gunshot wounds, and 274,053 cases of malarial fever, or one case in every 6.2 of the total. These rates indicate that the proportion of malarial cases to the whole number taken on sick report was greater among our men than among the Confederates. But it would be unsafe to conclude from this that the ratio of the paroxysmal fevers to strength was at all less with them than with us. Indeed, in the few instances in which it has been possible to ascertain the ratios of cases to strength in certain portions of the Confederate army, they have been found to be actually greater than in the corresponding parts of the United States forces. Among the statistics preserved by Dr. JONES is a table relating to the Confederate Army of Tennessee, the figures of which may be compared with those of the Federal Army of the Tennessee for the same year. The table covers fourteen

---

* See Table XIII, *supra*, page 31.

months, from April, 1862, to May, 1863, inclusive; but the mean strength for the first two months is unfortunately not given. Dr. Jones remarks, also, that the returns for July, September and October, 1862, are "incomplete." They represent, however, a sufficiently large part of the force to give a fair notion of the prevalence of the disease under consideration in the whole army. In the following table the malarial statistics of these armies are contrasted:

TABLE XXXV.

A Comparison of the Prevalence of Intermittent and Remittent Fevers in the Confederate and the United States Armies of the Tennessee from June 1, 1862, to May 31, 1863.

| | CONFEDERATE ARMY. | | | | | | | U. S. ARMY. | | | | | | |
| | MEAN STRENGTH. | Number of Cases. | | | Ratio per 1,000 strength. | | | MEAN STRENGTH. | Number of Cases. | | | Ratio per 1,000 strength. | | |
		Intermittent.	Remittent.	Total Malarial.	Intermittent.	Remittent.	Total Malarial.		Intermittent.	Remittent.	Total Malarial.	Intermittent.	Remittent.	Total Malarial.
June, 1862	40, 675	3, 269	2, 487	5, 756	80	61	141	66, 042	2, 541	1, 574	4, 115	38	24	62
July, 1862	10, 658	982	927	1, 909	92	87	179	80, 647	3, 045	1, 927	4, 972	38	24	62
August, 1862	30, 025	2, 161	1, 593	3, 754	72	53	125	70, 997	3, 245	1, 725	4, 970	46	24	70
September, 1862	9, 311	543	97	640	58	11	69	82, 972	5, 898	1, 702	7, 600	71	21	92
October, 1862	15, 082	902	230	1, 132	60	15	75	111, 891	7, 338	1, 669	9, 007	65	15	80
November, 1862	33, 791	1, 310	268	1, 578	39	8	47	136, 503	6, 783	1, 643	8, 426	50	12	62
December, 1862	48, 958	1, 695	398	2, 093	35	8	43	133, 119	4, 643	1, 405	6, 048	35	10	45
January, 1863	50, 604	1, 795	491	2, 286	35	10	45	143, 942	4, 771	1, 891	6, 662	33	13	46
February, 1863	63, 494	2, 213	613	2, 826	35	9	44	141, 158	4, 566	1, 715	6, 281	32	12	44
March, 1863	61, 226	3, 103	908	4, 011	50	15	65	146, 790	5, 076	1, 919	6, 995	35	13	48
April, 1863	64, 441	3, 734	1, 418	5, 152	58	22	80	143, 367	4, 695	1, 736	6, 431	33	12	45
May, 1863	55, 121	4, 030	1, 498	5, 528	73	27	100	140, 277	3, 911	1, 565	5, 476	28	11	39
Monthly average	40, 282	2, 144	911	3, 055	53	23	76	116, 475	4, 709	1, 706	6, 415	40	15	55

In the case of these confronting armies, as in the case of the Confederate and Federal Armies of the Potomac previously contrasted,* the Confederates had actually a larger proportion of cases than was reported by thé Federal Army. Other statistics published by Dr. Jones point in the same direction. The rebel command serving in the river batteries below the city of Savannah, Ga., reported from October, 1862, to December, 1863, inclusive, a mean strength of 878 officers and men, with 3,313 malarial cases, of which 2,824 were intermittents and 489 remittents. As this command occupied the low rice lands of the Savannah river its experience may serve to indicate what our own troops in the Department of the South would have suffered had they been advanced by the fortune of war from the comparatively healthy coast islands to the lowlands of the main. Looking only to the statistics of the year 1863, Dr. Jones's figures give 2,214 intermittents and 461 remittents, a total of 2,675 cases of malarial fever in a mean strength of 873 men. In ratios per 1,000 of strength these are equivalent to 2,536 for the intermittents, 528 for the remittents and 3,064 for all the malarial fevers. Among the United States troops in the Department of the South the ratio of malarial cases for the year ending June 30, 1863,

---

* Page 103, *supra.*

was but 528, that of the intermittents being 359 and of the remittents 169; while for the following year the malarial ratio was 594, the intermittent ratio being 492 and the remittent 102.

Equally instructive is the contrast between our reports from the Department of the South and those published by JONES as from the Confederate troops serving in the Department of South Carolina, Georgia and Florida, from January, 1862, to July, 1863, inclusive. The mean strength of the command during this period was 25,723 men, and the cases of malarial fever 41,539, of which 35,925 were intermittents and 5,614 remittents. Considering only the figures for the fiscal year ending June 30, 1863, the following results are obtained, which may be compared with the ratios just stated as from the Federal Department of the South: Mean strength 26,185; number of intermittents 30,322, or 1,158 per 1,000 of strength; remittents 3,665, or 140 per 1,000; total of malarial fevers 33,987, or 1,298 per 1,000.

Another table presented by JONES embodies the statistics of the Confederate troops in and around Mobile, Ala., for the period from January, 1862, to July, 1863, inclusive: Average strength 6,752; malarial cases 13,668, of which 10,500 were intermittents and 3,168 remittents. The figures for the year ending June 30, 1863, give a mean strength of 7,659, and a total of malarial fevers amounting to 10,878, of which 8,635 were agues and 2,243 remittents. The ratios obtained from these numbers, respectively 1,420, 1,127 and 293 per 1,000 of mean strength, exceed those for the same year from our Department of the South, and even those for the same period from our more unhealthy Department of the Gulf, which reported per 1,000 of strength 863 cases of malarial fever, 696 being intermittents and 167 remittents.

The Army of the Valley of Virginia, during the ten months, January, 1862, to October, 1862, inclusive, had 3,885 malarial cases in an average strength of 15,582 men. The figures for the first six months of this period may be contrasted with those of the Federal troops in the Department of the Shenandoah. An equally trustworthy comparison cannot be made for the remaining four months, because during that period the Federal reports for the district in question have not been separately tabulated.*

---

* We may, however, contrast the figures furnished by Dr. JONES for the Confederate Army of the Valley of Virginia during the months of July, August, September and October, 1862, with those of the Federal troops in the Middle Department for the same period; for on the breaking up of the Department of the Shenandoah the sick reports of the troops which remained in it were consolidated with those from the Middle Department.

A Comparison of the Prevalence of Intermittent and Remittent Fevers in the Confederate Army of the Valley of Virginia and the U. S. Middle Department of the Atlantic Region for the period from July 1 to October 31, 1862.

| | CONFEDERATE ARMY. | | | | | | U. S. ARMY. | | | | | | |
| | MEAN STRENGTH. | Number of Cases. | | | Ratio per 1,000 strength. | | | MEAN STRENGTH. | Number of Cases. | | | Ratio per 1,000 strength. | | |
		Intermittent.	Remittent.	Total Malarial.	Intermittent.	Remittent.	Total Malarial.		Intermittent.	Remittent.	Total Malarial.	Intermittent.	Remittent.	Total Malarial.
July, 1862	15,589	473	239	712	31	15	46	12,357	266	150	416	22	12	34
August, 1862	15,643	434	305	739	28	19	47	9,135	214	82	296	23	9	32
September, 1862	21,123	348	127	475	16	6	22	19,101	235	139	374	13	7	20
October, 1862	34,200	632	351	983	19	10	29	21,531	473	193	666	22	9	31
Monthly average	21,639	472	255	727	22	12	34	15,531	297	141	438	19	9	28

TABLE XXXVI.

A Comparison of the Prevalence of Intermittent and Remittent Fevers in the Confederate Army of Virginia and the U. S. Department of the Shenandoah from January 1, 1862, to June 30, 1862.

	CONFEDERATE ARMY.							U. S. ARMY.						
	MEAN STRENGTH.	Number of Cases.			Ratio per 1,000 strength.			MEAN STRENGTH.	Number of Cases.			Ratio per 1,000 strength.		
		Intermittent.	Remittent.	Total Malarial.	Intermittent.	Remittent.	Total Malarial.		Intermittent.	Remittent.	Total Malarial.	Intermittent.	Remittent.	Total Malarial.
January, 1862	9,278	23	13	36	3	1	4	17,143	123	85	208	7	5	12
February, 1862	8,193	16	9	25	2	1	3	21,498	155	96	251	7	5	12
March, 1862	7,418	6	7	13	1	1	2	27,437	261	127	388	9	5	14
April, 1862	9,554	31	3	34	3	31	4	14,072	181	92	273	13	6	19
May, 1862	16,731	291	48	339	17	3	20	9,508	82	50	132	9	5	14
June, 1862	18,099	310	210	520	17	12	29	14,391	177	76	253	13	5	18
Monthly average	11,545	113	48	161	10	4	14	17,341	163	88	251	9	5	14

These statistical fragments indicate that malarial fevers were more prevalent among the Confederate than among the Federal soldiers.

Mortality.—For want of data on the rebel side it is not possible to determine the relative mortality from these fevers in the opposed armies; but, as bearing on the question, we have Dr. JONES's statement that the records of the Surgeon General's Office for the years 1861 and 1862 gave 1,333 deaths in connection with 115,415 cases of paroxysmal fever and 31,238 deaths from all causes excepting gunshot injuries. Table XIII, already presented, shows that these figures are equivalent to 43 deaths from malarial fever per thousand deaths from all the included causes, and to a fatality rate of 1.15 per cent., or one death in 86.2 cases, while the corresponding figures from the records of the U. S. troops are equal to 160 deaths from malarial fever per thousand deaths from all causes, and to .95 per cent. of fatal cases, or one death in every 105.3 recorded attacks.

According to these figures the ratio of deaths to the recorded cases was greater among the rebel than among the northern troops; but there is no certainty that the recorded cases in the two armies bore the same relation to the number of cases that actually occurred. It appears not unlikely that this larger ratio of deaths to recorded cases may have originated in a failure to report the lighter agues. The familiarity of the Southern people with malarial disease suggests that many attacks which would have appeared on the sick reports, had they occurred among Northern men, may have been suffered without excuse from duty in the Confederate camps. It will be noticed, also, that the large ratio per thousand deaths from all causes constituted by the deaths from malarial fevers among the U. S. troops, as compared with the small corresponding ratio on the Confederate records, is opposed to the view that the fatality of these diseases was greater among the rebel troops.

The summary which Dr. JONES has given of the field reports from the Department of South Carolina, Georgia and Florida, is available for estimating the gravity of the malarial fevers, as he has fortunately published in connection with it a tabular consolidation of the hospital reports from that department for the same period. From these it is found that

41,539 cases of malarial fever corresponded with 227 deaths, or one death in every 187 cases, constituting a smaller percentage of fatal cases, .55, in this malarious department than the average percentage, .70,* among the Union troops in all the departments.

The opinion that the rate of fatality of the malarial fevers as a class was smaller among the Confederates than among the Union troops gathers support from a study of the totals in the following table, which show that the percentages of the different types of fever were not the same in the two armies:

TABLE XXXVII.

Showing—1, The Relative Frequency of the Forms of Malarial Fever among the Confederate Troops as compared with their Frequency among the Troops of the United States, expressed in percentages of the total number of Malarial Cases; and, 2, The Frequency of the Varieties of the Intermittents, expressed in percentages of their totals.

COMMAND.	PERIOD UNDER OBSERVATION.	Total number of Malarial Fevers.	Intermittent as per cent. of Total.	Remittent as per cent. of Total.	Total number of Intermittens.	PERCENTAGE OF TOTAL INTERMITTENTS.			
						Quotidian.	Tertian.	Quartan.	Congestive.
Garrison of Savannah, Ga. ____Confed.	} Oct., '62, to Dec., '63, { 15 months.	3,313	85	15	2,824	47	51	1	.07
Department of the South____U. S.		17,821	78	22	13,946	48	45	6	1.00
Department of South Carolina, Georgia and Florida ____Confed.	} Jan., '62, to July, '63, { 19 months.	41,539	86	14	35,925	50	47	3	.50
Department of the South ____U. S.		14,842	69	31	10,294	53	39	6	2.00
Garrison of Mobile, Ala____Confed.	} Jan., '62, to July, '63, { 19 months.	13,940	77	23	10,772	36	60	3	.80
Department of the Gulf____U. S.		26,783	81	19	21,576	43	52	3	2.00
Army of Tennessee ____Confed.	} April, '62, to May, '63, { 14 months.	40,133	70	30	28,099	47	45	6	2.00
Department of the Tennessee____U. S.		84,868	73	27	61,803	50	42	6	2.00
Army of Virginia ____Confed.	} Jan. to Oct., 1862, 10 { months.	3,885	66	34	2,573	46	45	7	2.00
Department of the Shenandoah, Middle Department____U. S.		3,257	67	33	2,167	62	33	4	1.00
Army of the Potomac____Confed.	} July, '61, to Mar., '62, { 9 months.	16,781	59	41	9,954	57	38	4	.90
Army of the Potomac____U. S.		27,672	64	36	17,739	50	40	5	5.00
Total Confederate____		119,591	76	24	90,147	48	47	4	.90
Total United States ____		175,243	73	27	127,525	49	43	5	3.00

The remittents, for instance, constituted a larger proportion of the malarial cases among the Union than among the Confederate troops. It must be remembered, also, that only the remittents and intermittents occurring in the Federal forces are here tabulated, the typho-malarial cases having been omitted as the Confederate reports had no corresponding heading. No doubt some of our typho-malarial cases, had they been in the hands of southern officers, would have been reported among the remittent fevers, as some of the remittents of the Confederate surgeons might, on account of a dry dark tongue or other symptoms, have been called typho-malarial had they occurred in the practice of northern medical men. It may therefore be assumed that if the same medical views had determined the diagnosis of all the cases tabulated above, the difference between the percentages of remittents in the two armies would have been greater. Had the diagnosis been made by our northern medical men the remittents of the Confederate army would have been dimin-

---

* Table XXII, *supra*, p. 79.

ished by the abstraction of a certain number of typho-malarial cases, while, had the southern officers made the record, the remittents of our army would have been increased in the absence of the typho-malarial group.   On either supposition the preponderance of grave cases of malarial fever, shown by the table as having existed among the Union troops, would have been augmented.   The greater percentage of congestive cases among our troops is also suggestive of a larger mortality.   Indeed, these percentages may be used to determine approximately the average gravity of the malarial fevers among the Confederate troops.   If it be admitted that the various types of paroxysmal fever, as they occurred among the Confederates, were attended by the mortality which characterized them in their attacks upon our soldiers, as shown in the last column of Table XXII,* the influence exercised on the mortality by the smaller proportion of remittent and congestive cases among them may be estimated.   The deaths thus calculated formed .57 per cent. of the cases,† or one death in every 175 cases among the Confederate troops, and .97 per cent., or one death in every 103 cases that occurred among the United States soldiers for the periods stated in the table above presented.   It seems probable, therefore, that although attacks of malarial fever were of more frequent occurrence among the Confederates, the gravity of these attacks, including the consequent mortality, was less than among the Union troops.

III.—MALARIAL FEVERS AMONG THE PRISONERS OF WAR HELD BY THE REBEL AUTHORITIES.

It might reasonably be supposed, from the situation of the principal places of confinement, that malarial fevers of local origin would not have prevailed so largely among our captured men as among our troops on active service; but the statistics bearing on this question are not of a satisfactory character.

Dr. JONES has endeavored to show that the Federal prisoners in the Andersonville stockade suffered less from these fevers than the rebel troops serving in South Carolina, Georgia and Florida, or even in such an elevated and comparatively healthy region as the Valley of Virginia.‡   A reference to Table XVI,§ compiled from figures published by him, will show that during the six months of 1864, March to August inclusive, there were reported among the prisoners 2,966 cases of malarial fever, 119 of which were fatal.   Of the cases 1,170 were quotidians, 775 tertians, 195 quartans, 8 congestive fevers and 818 remittents.   The intermittents caused 64 deaths and the remittents 55.   The monthly ratio of cases per thousand of strength was 23, a number considerably smaller than the average monthly ratio among our white troops in the Atlantic region for the months stated, as may be seen by a reference to Table XXVIII.‖   Dr. JONES, however, recognized the

---

* See page 79, *supra*.
† In every hundred cases of pure malarial fever there were—

AMONG THE UNION TROOPS.		AMONG THE CONFEDERATE TROOPS.	
35.8 Quotidians with	.0358 deaths.	36.0 cases with	.036 deaths.
31.4 Tertians with	.0314 deaths.	35.3 cases with	.0352 deaths.
3.6 Quartans with....................................	.0073 deaths.	3.0 cases with	.0060 deaths.
2.2 Congestive with..................................	.5398 deaths.	0.7 cases with	.1664 deaths.
27.0 Remittents with...............................	.3537 deaths.	25.0 cases with	.3275 deaths.
100.0 Malarial with	.9680 deaths.	100.0 cases with	.5711 deaths.

‡ See his *Investigations upon the diseases of the Federal Prisoners*, etc., cited in note, page 29, *supra*.
§ Page 35, *supra*.   ‖ Pages 89, 90 and 91, *supra*.

fact that his figures did not embrace the whole number of cases that occurred within the stockade during the six months.* Their deficiency may be appreciated by an examination of the original hospital register of the prison, now on file in the office of the Adjutant General of the Army. This document shows the number of deaths caused by these fevers between February 24, 1864, and April 17, 1865, to have been 163; of which 149 occurred during the period covered by JONES' compilation, being 30 in excess of those reported by him.

But the register throws no direct light on the number of cases. Only a small minority of the malarial fevers occurring among the prisoners in the stockade were admitted to hospital. While Dr. JONES' statement embraces 2,966 cases in a period of six months, the hospital register acknowledges the admission of only 254 cases in a period of over fourteen months, which included the six months aforesaid. The character of the admitted cases may be inferred from the fact that 163 of their number terminated fatally. There were 160 intermittents with 101 deaths, 88 remittents with 59 deaths, and 6 congestive cases with 3 deaths: in 13 of the cases no disposition is recorded.†

Dr. JONES has pointed out that after a considerable increase in the prevalence of the malarial fevers among the prisoners during the month of May, when the maximum ratio of 77 per thousand was attained, the cases thereafter diminished to a ratio of 17 per thousand in July and 15 in August. Although the figures which he has published have no absolute value, it is probable that they give a fair expression to the relative prevalence at different times, especially as confirmatory evidence is obtained from the mortality as recorded in the hospital register, which shows 149 deaths from malarial fevers during the six months ending August 3, 1864, and but 14 deaths during the subsequent eight months. In explanation of this, he has suggested that the morbific influences generated by the overcrowded and filthy condition of the stockade neutralized or destroyed the malarial poison;‡ and in view of the well-known infrequency of malarial fevers in densely peopled cities this suggestion appears probable enough.

The only other statistics bearing on the prevalence of malarial fevers among Federal prisoners in the South are from the register of Division No. 2 of the hospital at Danville, Va. This record extends from November 23, 1863, to March 27, 1865. There were 4,332 admissions and 1,084 deaths, of which but 233 cases and 17 deaths are attributed to malarial fevers. Such figures suggest similar conditions, so far as concerns the occurrence of these fevers, to those which existed at Andersonville.

IV.—MALARIAL FEVERS AMONG THE PRISONERS OF WAR HELD BY THE UNITED STATES.

The alphabetical registers of the Surgeon General's Office record the deaths of 1,134 Confederate prisoners from malarial fevers in a total of 23,591 deaths from all diseases; of these 122 were attributed to simple intermittents, 169 to congestive, 489 to remittent and 351 to typho-malarial fever. These figures afford no basis for calculating the relative

* He remarks, in speaking generally of the statistics of the Andersonville prisoners,—"No classified record of the sick in the stockade was kept after the establishment of the hospital without the prison. This fact, in conjunction with facts already presented, relating to the insufficiency of medical officers, and the extreme illness, and even death, of many of the prisoners in the tents in the stockade without any medical attention or record beyond the bare number of the dead, demonstrate that the figures, large as they appear to be, are far below the truth." P. 530, op. cit. When, however, he comes to discuss the frequency of malarial fevers among these prisoners, he takes a somewhat modified view: "While it is evident from the results of the examinations recorded in the fourth chapter that these statistics are below rather than above the absolute numbers, still it does not appear that the errors were greater in this class of diseases than in the others, and in fact, from the nature of malarial fever, we should be disposed to consider them less." P. 566, op. cit. On the contrary, it would seem that in an establishment where the medical attendance was insufficient, as at Andersonville, such comparatively mild forms of disease as ordinary intermittent fever would have been most likely to escape report.

† See Table XV, p. 34, supra.   ‡ Op. cit., p. 568.

frequency or fatality of malarial disease among the prisoners; but the following table, compiled from the monthly reports of sick and wounded from the principal prison depots, is of value in this connection:

TABLE XXXVIII.

Cases of Malarial Fever with resulting mortality, reported from the principal Prison Depôts as having occurred among the Confederate Prisoners of War; with the annual ratios per thousand of strength present.

	Camp Douglas, Ill., Feb., 1862—June, 1865.	Alton, Ill., Sept., 1862—June, 1865.	Rock Island, Ill., Feb., 1864—June, 1865.	Camp Morton, Ind., June, 1863—June, 1865.	Johnson's Island, Ohio, June, 1863—June, 1865.	Camp Chase, Ohio, Feb., 1863—June, 1865.	Elmira, New York, July, 1864—June, 1865.	Fort Delaware, Del., Aug., 1863—June, 1865.	Point Lookout, Md., Sept., 1863—June, 1865.	Total in the nine Prison Depôts.
Average number of prisoners present......	5,361	1,008	6,030	2,865	2,114	3,570	6,591	6,406	9,610	40,815
Intermittent cases.........................	5,864	5,234	1,365	1,032	228	2,527	321	2,498	5,209	24,278
Remittent cases...........................	4,124	1,250	1,009	416	135	1,728	305	653	1,620	11,240
Typho-malarial cases......................	163	722	10	506	54	3	2	1,574	35	3,069
Total Malarial Fevers.................	10,151	7,206	2,384	1,954	417	4,258	628	4,725	6,864	38,587
Deaths from Intermittents................	48	30	17	12	3	14	5	27	57	213
Deaths from Remittents..................	134	25	23	9	3	11	59	57	103	424
Deaths from Typho-malarial.............	51	122	12	98	4	9	1	91	1	389
Total deaths from Malarial Fevers	233	177	52	119	10	34	65	175	161	1,026
Annual ratios per thousand of strength for cases of—										
Intermittent Fever......................	320.5	1,832.9	159.8	172.9	51.8	499.7	48.7	203.5	295.4	297.4
Remittent Fever........................	225.4	437.9	118.1	69.7	30.7	341.7	46.3	53.2	91.9	137.7
Typho-malarial Fever...................	8.9	252.9	1.2	84.8	12.2	.6	.3	128.2	2.0	37.6
All Malarial Fevers....	554.8	2,523.7	279.1	327.4	94.7	842.0	95.3	384.9	389.3	472.7
Annual ratios per thousand of strength for deaths from—										
Intermittent Fever......................	2.6	10.5	2.0	2.0	.7	2.7	.8	2.2	3.3	2.6
Remittent Fever........................	7.3	8.8	2.7	1.5	.7	2.2	8.9	4.6	5.9	5.2
Typho-malarial Fever..................	2.8	42.7	1.4	16.4	.9	1.8	.2	7.4	.0	4.8
All Malarial Fevers...................	12.7	62.0	6.1	19.9	2.3	6.7	9.9	14.2	9.2	12.6

The ratio of cases to strength at Johnson's Island and Elmira was very small; at Rock Island and Camp Morton it was less, and at Camps Chase and Douglas more, than the ratio for the United States troops in the Northern Department—526 per thousand annually. At Fort Delaware and Point Lookout the ratios were somewhat less than that furnished by our own troops in the Department of Washington—390 per thousand. Only at Alton, Illinois, was the ratio such as to suggest the existence of intense local malarial influences. Here the proportion of cases was greater than in any part of our army except the Department of North Carolina during the third year of the war.* But when the facts relating to the frequent changes in the individuals composing the average number present at this post are understood,† the large rates may be accounted for without assuming the

---

* See *supra*, p. 96.   † See *supra*, p. 62.

existence of malarial influences of local origin; and indeed the prison, according to the reports of the inspectors, was on a dry, elevated and generally healthy site.

The deaths from the purely malarial fevers in our army, as shown by Table XXVI, were 3.36 per thousand of strength annually, or, including the deaths from typho-malarial fever, 5.04 per thousand. These figures are exceeded by the mortality rates of all the prisons except Johnson's Island. On the other hand the annual mortality rate among our colored troops, 10.03 for the purely malarial fevers, or 16.82 including the typho-malarial group, was considerably greater than the average of the prison rates, 7.8 for the pure malarial fevers or 12.6 inclusive of the typho-malarial cases.

The extent to which these fevers prevailed among the Confederate armies renders it probable that many of the cases that occurred among the prisoners were recurrences of a disease contracted in the field before their capture.

II.—CLINICAL RECORDS OF MALARIAL DISEASE.

The clinical records of the war contain but few cases of malarial disease, and these, as a rule, are exceedingly meager in details, seldom giving more than an identification of the patient and a statement of the diagnosis, treatment and result. A description of the symptoms as they varied from day to day in the progress of the fever, or as influenced by remedies, was rarely attempted. But a word or two occasionally introduced, indicating deterioration of the constitution, length of time during which the disease had been in progress, or the existence of notable complications, give an interest to the records by impressing an individuality on many of the cases.

The absence of details is not surprising, in view of the great prevalence of malarial fevers. Disease which is of daily occurrence is not usually noted by the profession unless presenting some difference in its symptoms from those generally accepted as characteristic. Thus, from the very absence of records it may be concluded that the intermittents, remittents and congestive fevers which were so prevalent in our armies, presented little to distinguish them from the same diseases as observed by our medical men in their practice before the war.

Moreover, intermittent cases were mainly treated in the field where medical officers had few facilities for note taking. Remittents seldom got farther away from active service than the hospitals at the base of supplies except by furlough during convalescence, for death occurred from the violence of the morbific agency, or a cure was effected by specific medication, during the period occupied by treatment in the field or at these base hospitals. The temporary character of the latter and their liability to be at any time crowded with wounded from the field of battle constitute a sufficient explanation of the paucity of clinical histories among their records. It was only at the general hospitals, the permanent establishments situated at a distance from the conflicting armies, that clinical records of disease were kept; and malarial cases seldom reached the wards of these except as instances of chronic malarial poisoning, or debility, or as complicating other diseases having a lengthened course, such as diarrhœa or typhoid fever.

The following cases may not, therefore, be considered as illustrating malarial diseases under their ordinary aspects, but as presenting certain exceptional features which led to their being recorded, the exceptional feature in some instances consisting of nothing more remarkable than the presence of the case in the wards of a general hospital in which clinical records were kept with more or less regularity. Nevertheless, most of the cases may be taken as typical of a class or series, for it seems unlikely that any one of them would have been unique if the records of the whole vast number of cases had been preserved.

A quotidian intermittent.—CASE 1.—Private Patrick Shehan, Co. H, 146th Ill. Vols., was admitted September 23, 1864, with quotidian intermittent fever. Quinine was given every four hours for three or four days, and afterwards vegetable tonics. He was furloughed November 1, and on his return on the 18th was sent to his command for duty.—*General Hospital, Quincy, Ill.*

A quotidian with relapses.—CASE 2.—Private J. M. Hinchee, Co. K, 33d Ill. Vols.; age 19; was admitted October 12, 1863, having been affected with intermittent fever since September 19. On the 18th he had a chill, for which eight grains of quinine were given in divided doses. The chill returned daily until the 21st. It recurred on November 3, and again on the 15th, but by continuing the quinine no further relapse took place up to December 8, when he was returned to duty.—*General Hospital, Quincy, Ill.*

A tertian with relapses attributed to over-eating, &c.—CASE 3.—Private Anthony Monsieur, Co. C, 13th Ill. Cav.; age 30; was admitted August 19, 1863, with tertian ague. His skin was sallow, conjunctivæ yellowish, tongue coated, bowels loose, pulse full and strong. Quinine, blue-pill and opium were given, and when the paroxysms were checked, strychnia was administered. He improved rapidly under this treatment, but as he was given to excesses in eating and drinking, several relapses occurred. He was ultimately returned to duty with his regiment October 13, 1863.—*General Hospital, Quincy, Ill.*

A quartan with slow recovery after several relapses.—CASE 4.—Private James Wright, Co. F, 21st Ill. Vols.; age 21; was admitted September 25, 1863, having a chill every third day. His skin was sallow, tongue coated and bowels loose. Strychnia, blue-pill and capsicum were prescribed. He improved slowly, suffering several relapses; ultimately Fowler's solution proved effectual and the patient was returned to duty February 14, 1864.—*General Hospital, Quincy, Ill.*

Debility from recurring attacks of ague.—CASE 5.—Private William Lambert, Co. G, 19th Mass. Vols., a feeble-looking boy, was admitted October 10, 1861, much prostrated from repeated attacks of ague. He had one paroxysm after admission. He took fifteen grains of quinine at once and three grains three times a day afterwards. He was confined to bed by weakness for some time; but after this, when able to walk out a little, his improvement was more rapid. He was returned to duty on November 29.—*Regimental Hospital 19th Mass. Vols.*

CASE 6.—Private George Frazer, Co. D, 7th Va. Vols.; age 20; was admitted May 23, 1865, from Lincoln Hospital, Washington, D. C. He had contracted intermittent fever in March in the pine swamps at Humphrey's station before Petersburg, Va. On admission he was very weak and anæmic. Fowler's solution in five-drop doses was given three times a day until the 31st. On June 7 he was placed on hospital-guard duty, and on July 12 was returned to duty with his command.—*Satterlee Hospital, Philadelphia, Pa.*

CASE 7.—Corporal Jno. W. Moore, Co. K, 13th Iowa Vols.; age 24; was admitted Sept. 23, 1863, with debility from intermittent fever. He was placed on duty in the ward as he had no chills, and his tongue was clean and appetite good. Quinine and iron were prescribed. About October 20 he had a rigor with high fever every few days. Quinine and strychnia were given. On November 20 the chills continued, and there was some diarrhœa, for which nitrate of silver and opium were ordered. By December 25 he was gaining strength slowly. The diarrhœa was checked by January 10, 1864, but the chills continued. Fowler's solution was given. He was returned to duty March 22.—*General Hospital, Quincy, Ill.*

Cases complicated with diarrhœa and dysentery.—CASE 8.—Private Dennis O'Brien, Co. C, 56th Ill. Vols.; age 37; was admitted October 11, 1862, with intermittent fever and diarrhœa, with which he had been affected since September 29. He was treated with quinine, blue-pill, opium and turpentine emulsion. He improved steadily and was returned to duty on the 27th.—*General Hospital, Quincy, Ill.*

CASE 9.—Private Frank Gad, Co. A, 84th Ill. Vols.; age 17; was admitted Sept. 18, 1864, having been sick for two weeks with quotidian intermittent and dysentery, the paroxysms occurring about 3 P. M. The bowels were loose and the tongue coated white. Five grains of quinine with three of Dover's powder were given every three hours. A relapse occurred on October 9. The patient was returned to duty October 27.—*General Hospital, Quincy, Ill.*

CASE 10.—Private Thomas L. Dixie, recently discharged from Co. A, 38th Iowa Vols., was admitted August 29, 1863, much prostrated by chills and fever and a diarrhœa of ten or twelve stools daily, from which he had suffered since July 3. The diarrhœa and chills were checked on September 4, and his appetite improved. He went home on the 8th.—*Union Hospital, Memphis, Tenn.*

Ague with diarrhœa, anæmia and enlarged spleen.—CASE 11.—Private James J. Wolfe, Co. G, 10th Ill. Cav., was admitted August 30, 1863, with intermittent fever and diarrhœa. He had been subject to diarrhœa for more than a year, but the ague dated only from July 1. On admission he was emaciated and anæmic; he had some diarrhœa, a short hacking cough, a weak pulse, 95, an anxious countenance, a systolic cardiac murmur and a spleen which extended three inches below the false ribs; he had, however, a good appetite. He gained strength and ultimately, on October 23, was returned to duty.—*Union Hospital, Memphis, Tenn.*

Ague with diarrhœa and debility; slow recovery.—CASE 12.—Private Jno. J. Hand, Co. E, 127th Ill. Vols.; age 21; was admitted September 23, 1863, with intermittent fever. He had a chill every day followed by high fever; he had also dyspnœa and pain in the hypochondrium; tongue covered with a white fur; appetite moderate. Quinine and tincture of iron were prescribed. Diarrhœa supervened on October 10, and was treated by nitrate of silver and opium; the aguish paroxysms continued to recur. At the beginning of November he was furloughed for two weeks. At the end of the month he was much debilitated, having from three to five discharges from the bowels daily. In December one-sixteenth of a grain of strychnia was given three times a day. Improvement was very slow. He was not returned to duty until March 9.—*General Hospital, Quincy, Ill.*

Ague followed by dysentery.—CASE 13.—Horace Hastings, drummer, Co. E, 19th Mass. Vols., was admitted on November 2, 1861, with quotidian intermittent. One fifteen-grain dose of quinine was given, followed by five grains three times a day. The chills were suppressed, but the patient had some bloody and painful discharges from the bowels. While taking Dover's powder and acetate of lead the passages became reduced to two daily, but were accompanied with much pain, protrusion of the rectum and free hæmorrhage; he had also some tenderness in the epigastric region, which was relieved by sinapisms. The tongue became clean and the diarrhœa checked on November 14, and the patient was returned to quarters on the 16th.—*Regimental Hospital 19th Mass.*

Ague protracted and complicated with jaundice.—CASE 14.—Private James J. Ray, Co. I, 10th Wis. Vols.; age 26; was admitted March 3, 1863, emaciated, feeble and jaundiced, with a thickly coated tongue, small appetite and very rapid pulse. He had been taken with intermittent fever in August, 1862, and had done no duty since that time. After his admission he was attacked with excruciating pains in the bowels. He was treated with gelsemium, taraxacum, iodide of potassium and extract of cinchona. He improved rapidly, gaining in flesh and strength, and was returned to duty August 31, 1863.—*General Hospital, Quincy, Ill.*

Ague followed by jaundice and diarrhœa.—CASE 15.—Sergeant Charles Legrist, Co. E, 35th Mo. Vols., had an attack of intermittent fever early in August, 1863; jaundice and diarrhœa supervened. He was admitted October 1 with increasing debility and a diarrhœa of twelve stools daily. He failed rapidly and died on the 10th.—*Union Hospital, Memphis, Tenn.*

Protracted ague followed by carbuncle.—CASE 16.—Private A. Lydick, Co. D, 78th Pa. Vols.; age 44; was admitted March 10, 1863, having been unfit for duty on account of intermittent fever since August, 1862. At the date of admission he was feverish and had on his back a large and painful carbuncle. Tonics were given and creasote dressing applied. In healing, the carbuncle left him stooped very much, and the cicatrix was very tender. He was transferred November 25 to the 27th Company, 2d Battalion, Invalid Corps.—*General Hospital, Quincy, Ill.*

Protracted ague followed by ulcers of leg.—CASE 17.—Private John Hogan, Co. E, 119th Ill. Vols.; age 23; was admitted August 10, 1863. This patient had intermittent fever from May, 1862, to March 9, 1863, when the chills ceased with the appearance of a sore upon his left leg. On admission his leg was swollen, red and firm, presenting between the ankle and the upper third many open suppurating sores. Under the use of iodide of potassium, rest and bandages, he improved. In January, 1863, having overstayed a pass he was reported as a deserter, and on his return was transferred to the care of the provost marshal.—*General Hospital, Quincy, Ill.*

Ague with consumption supervening.—CASE 18.—Private M. E. Williams, Co. A, 87th Ill. Vols.; age 26; admitted August 20, 1863. This man was taken with intermittent fever in November, 1862, and did no duty from that time. On admission he complained of pain in left subclavicular region, where there was dulness on percussion; his respiration was hurried and difficult, pulse frequent; he had hectic fever, night-sweats and colliquative diarrhœa. Cod-liver oil, porter, quinine and aromatic sulphuric acid were employed in the treatment. Afterwards he improved somewhat while taking syrup of wild cherry. On November 11 he was transferred to Cincinnati for discharge.—*General Hospital, Quincy, Ill.*

Tertian becoming quotidian and afterwards remittent.—CASE 19.—Lieutenant H. M. Rideout, 10th U. S. Art'y, was admitted November 3, 1863. He had been attacked ten days before with a severe chill, followed by fever and headache; two days after this he had a second chill with fever and some delirium. The fever was accompanied with much pain in the back, anorexia, gastric irritation, prostration and constipation. The chill recurred daily during the next three days. After the fifth chill there had been only imperfect remissions of the fever. The patient had been on duty for eight months in the low swampy lands of Louisiana. On admission his pulse was 120 and skin hot, dry and pallid. Ten grains of blue pill were given, and quinine and capsicum ordered every three hours. Under this treatment the fever abated and there was no recurrence of the chills. On November 9 there was slight fever, the pulse 96 and somewhat corded, but this condition lasted only a few hours. He was returned to duty on the 30th. —*Hospital, Natchez, Miss.*

Intermittents becoming remittent.—CASE 20.—Sergeant John L. Hopper, Co. I, 119th Ill. Vols.; age 28; was admitted October 31, 1862, with remittent fever, having been sick for four days with intermittent fever. On admission the tongue was clean but red at the tip, pulse 96, skin hot but moist, bowels loose; the patient complained of much thirst and pain in the back and stomach. He was treated with quinine and aromatic powder, morphia and carbonate of soda. Medication was stopped on November 4, and he was returned to duty on December 1.—*General Hospital, Quincy, Ill.*

CASE 21.—Sergeant Jas. M. Price, Co. G, 26th Mich. Vols.; age 31; while en route with his regiment for New York City on account of the draft riots, was taken, while in Washington, D. C., July 13, 1863, with intermittent fever, which recurred daily. On admission on the 18th he was much prostrated, having just passed the sweating stage of that day's paroxysm. One grain of quinine was prescribed for administration every hour until symptoms of cinchonism were produced. He took eleven grains, and next day the skin was hot and dry, the tongue coated, and the urine high colored and scanty; towards noon there was a remission. On the 21st the disease was distinctly remittent. Quinine was given during the remissions and acetate of ammonia during the exacerbations. In a day or two the fever ceased and did not recur, but the patient was quite feeble, anæmic and without appetite. On the 28th he stayed up dressed for a short time. Tincture of iron was given. He was returned to duty on September 7.—*Act. Ass't Surg. G. M. Smith, U. S. Army, Ladies' Home Hospital, New York City.*

Intermittent fever becoming continued and accompanied with diarrhœa.—CASE 22.—Private Orlando Wood, General Steel's escort, taken sick with intermittent fever, followed by a continued fever and diarrhœa after recurrences of the intermittent, was admitted October 11, 1862. He was very sallow. Quinine, blue pill and opium were given for the fever and turpentine emulsion for the diarrhœa. The patient improved rapidly from his entry into hospital, and was discharged on the 28th on account of an old fracture of the femur.—*Hospital, Quincy, Ill.*

Intermittent followed by typhoid fever.—CASE 23.—Private O. S. Raymond, Co. F, 28th Wis. Vols.; age 19; was admitted June 21, 1863, with typhoid fever. He was attacked with intermittent fever June 1, while in camp at Helena, and the fever assuming a typhoid type, he was removed to this hospital. On admission his tongue was dry and brown, the edges and tip red; pulse 85; skin dry and harsh; bowels irritable and tympanitic. He was furloughed August 19 and returned to duty September 11.—*Lawson Hospital, St. Louis, Mo.*

Cases of remittent fever.—CASE 24.—Private George Vaden, Co. B, 24th Tenn.; age 20; was admitted November 6, 1864, with remittent fever, having been sick for six days before admission. Quinine, capsicum and morphia were given. He had no fever in the morning after the 7th, but every evening up to the 16th, some febrile action was manifested, and the tongue remained more or less furred. Blue pill and Epsom salts were given on the 9th. Cough was troublesome on the 10th, and muriate of ammonia, ipecacuanha and opium were prescribed. After this, quinine, Dover's powder and capsicum were given, and a blister applied on the 15th. He was returned to duty on the 28th. —*Hospital, Rock Island, Ill.*

CASE 25.—Private E. W. Kirkland, Co. H, 4th Ala. Cav.; age 30; was admitted November 8, 1864, with remittent fever. He had been sick for eight days prior to his admission. When admitted he was greatly debilitated, but had no fever, which, however, returned at night for some time. Three grains each of quinine and Dover's powder, with one grain of capsicum, were given every three hours. Blue pill and Epsom salts were prescribed on the 10th, as the bowels were constipated and the tongue much furred. There was great irritability of stomach on the 13th. The quinine was combined with carbonate of ammonia and camphor, and whiskey was given. A blister was applied on the 16th, on account of pain in the left side. Treatment was continued until December 6. The patient was returned to duty on the 10th.—*Hospital, Rock Island, Ill.*

CASE 26.—Private Wm. R. Kimball, 2d Batt. V. R. C.; age 41; was admitted May 12, 1864, with remittent fever. He had headache, weakness, pain in the back and limbs, loss of appetite and much thirst. The fever was aggravated in the morning, and did not remit until some time in the night. His tongue was yellow-coated and his skin somewhat jaundiced; his bowels were quiet. Quinine and blue pills were administered, and on the 20th the patient was improving slowly. On June 11 he was placed on light duty in the ward, and on the 18th was returned to duty.—*Act. Ass't Surg. D. C. Owens, U. S. Army, Hospital, Quincy, Ill.*

Remittent with relapse.—CASE 27.—Private Louis Eberhard, Co. E, 111th Pa. Vols.; age 47; was admitted April 27, 1865, from David's Island, New York Harbor, as a convalescent from remittent fever. He was in good general health, although somewhat debilitated. Full diet was ordered, but no medication. On May 18 he was placed on fatigue duty. On June 14 he re-entered the ward, having been sick for six days before presenting himself for treatment. His pulse was full, strong and bounding; skin hot and dry; tongue furred; breath fœtid; stools light colored; he suffered also from headache. Blue-mass was ordered on the 15th, to be followed by citrate of magnesia. Two copious stools were procured, and on the 17th he was in better condition, although the fever continued with anorexia and foul tongue. Blue pill, ipecacuanha and quinine were given in small doses every four hours, and on the 20th the patient was able to sit up. The medicine was omitted on the 21st, and on the 28th the man was well and walking about.—*Satterlee Hospital, Philadelphia, Pa.*

Remittent with hepatic complication.—CASE 28.—Private Charles Laihn, Co. E, 16th Ill. Cav.; age 42; intemperate; was admitted July 31, 1863, with remittent fever. A day or two before admission he was taken with a chill followed by the usual symptoms of common remittent fever, but accompanied with pain, tenderness, slight fulness and hardness in the region of the liver. He was treated with quinine, chalk with mercury and Dover's powder, sinapisms to the ankles and a blister to the hepatic region. The fever began to subside on August 2, but the pain and fulness in the side continued. On the 7th a half drachm of iodide of potassium with extract of hyosciamus was given after each meal instead of the quinine and mercurial, and the blister was reapplied to the side. He improved but slowly, his bowels meanwhile being very torpid and requiring the use of laxatives and enemata. The iodide was omitted on September 10, and on October 10 the patient was returned to duty.—*Act. Ass't Surg. F. K. Bailey, U. S. Army, Hospital, Quincy, Ill.*

CASE 29.—Private George Hurst, Co. D, 25th Ind. Vols., was admitted October 12, 1863, having had diarrhœa and fever for three days. He was greatly prostrated; his mind dull; countenance suffused; lips and tongue coated black; pulse 110 and quick; skin hot. Next day he was delirious. One ounce of brandy was given every hour. On the 14th the fever was found to remit in the morning, becoming increased in the afternoon. Mercury with chalk and rhubarb was given, and during the night the bowels were opened twice. Next day there was less fever; quinine was prescribed in three-grain doses three times a day. On the 16th there was less fever, but the patient vomited frequently. Ten grains of quinine were given at once, and the mercury, chalk and rhubarb were repeated with carbonate of soda. On the following day the bowels were opened several times, and the mind became clearer. The skin and conjunctivæ became yellow-colored on the 19th, and on the 20th he had epistaxis, but was otherwise improving. He was transferred, December 15, to Adams Hospital, Memphis [and afterwards to Jefferson Barracks, St. Louis, Mo., February 22, 1864]. He was ultimately returned to duty May 25.—*Union Hospital, Memphis, Tenn.*

Remittent with scurvy.—CASE 30.—Private Samuel W. Flemming, Co. I, 201st Pa. Vols.; age 23; was admitted November 4, 1864, with remittent fever from which he had been suffering for some time. He was quite prostrated, being unable to speak above a whisper; his tongue was pale, gums spongy and bowels moved with great frequency; he was anæmic and had some cough. On the 6th he was delirious; the tongue black; the teeth covered with sordes; the bowels were moved less frequently, but there was great tenderness in the right iliac region. Turpentine was prescribed. On the 10th the patient was much improved. He was returned to duty January 14, 1865.—*Hospital, Alexandria, Va.*

Remittent with dysentery supervening.—CASE 31.—Private Albert Frane, Co. C, 24th Ind. Vols., was admitted September 21, 1863, with dysentery. [On August 8 this man had an attack of remittent fever and continued sick for four weeks, at the end of which period he was much debilitated. He was furloughed, but while bound home-ward had an attack of dysentery and piles, much blood passing with the stools.] On admission he was very weak, emaciated, and had abdominal pain and tenderness, with twelve to fifteen bloody stools daily; his appetite was poor; tongue thickly coated brown; pulse 95 and weak; skin hot; mind dull. On the 23d pain in the umbilical region was somewhat relieved by sinapisms. The stools were frequent but not bloody on the 24th, when delirium and dysphagia supervened. He died on the morning of the 25th, the stools becoming less frequent for some hours before death.—*Union Hospital, Memphis, Tenn.*

Remittent fever with cerebral symptoms.—CASE 32.—Private Henry Taylor, Co. B, 85th Pa. Vols.; age 50; was admitted November 3, 1862, convalescing from remittent fever. As his general health and strength improved symptoms of cerebral congestion appeared. Of medium height, thick set, with a short and full neck and turgid countenance, he was more or less constantly affected with headache, disturbed vision and tinnitus aurium. Epistaxis, with temporary relief, was of frequent occurrence; the bowels were constipated. On the day after admission the patient was bled from the arm to the extent of fifteen ounces, with prompt and decided relief of the prominent cerebral symptoms. Low diet was enjoined, and under the repeated use of active hydragogue cathartics the cerebral symptoms gradually yielded; but the patient continued to have at times slight returns of epistaxis, which always gave relief, his pulse becoming reduced in force and volume. He was recommended for return to his regiment February 14, and left the hospital to join it on March 4. On this case the attending physician remarks: "After the summer's experience of hypæmia, cachexia and adynamia, conditions so almost universally present in disease as observed at the military hospitals, and requiring as they did a supporting and tonic treatment, it was with curious interest that we recognized this exceptional case of hyperæmia demanding depletion from the general circulation, conjoined with low diet and active catharsis."—*Satterlee Hospital, Philadelphia, Pa.*

CASE 33.—Ass't Surg. Samuel S. Garrigeus, 29th Mich. Vols.; age 36; was admitted October 11, 1864. He was taken, while at Detroit on the 7th, with a severe chill which lasted an hour, and was followed by two hours of fever. On the 8th and 9th he had fever but no chills. On the morning of the 10th he took eight grains of blue pill and a Seidlitz powder, which procured an evacuation but caused much nausea and vomiting. On admission he had fever, anorexia, great thirst, offensive breath, white furred tongue, constipated bowels and headache, and he had slept but little from the time of the attack; pulse 120, respiration 30. Sweet spirits of nitre and extract of ipecacuanha, barley-water and cream of tartar were given, with a Dover's powder at bedtime; next day quinine was administered. The fever, headache and constipation continued, and on the 14th the patient was delirious during the greater part of the day. Eight grains each of calomel and rhubarb were given, followed by a saline cathartic, which moved the bowels. Next day he was conscious, his pulse regular and slow. Tea, toast, soups and panada were given. After this he improved in condition; but on the 25th he had symptoms of cerebral congestion, which were relieved by cold to the head and mustard to the feet. These attacks recurred during the early part of November, but by avoiding excitement and errors of diet they ceased to trouble him. On October 31 Fowler's solution was given in fluid extract of cinchona and continued for three weeks.—*Officers' Hospital, Louisville, Ky.*

CASE 34.—Private John McCammant, Co. B, 84th Ill. Vols., was admitted August 24, 1862, with remittent fever. During the night following admission he was a little delirious, but next morning he was quiet. A blister was ordered, as he complained of soreness in the bowels. About 2 P. M. of this day, as he was resting quietly and engaged in conversation with a friend from camp, he suddenly sprang from his bed and jumped through the scuttle-way from the upper to the lower floor of the hospital, a distance of about thirty feet. He struck on his head and right shoulder. He was taken up unconscious and died thirty-six hours after. A clot seemed to have formed behind the right orbit as the eye-ball soon became considerably protruded. No *post-mortem* examination was made.—*Hospital, Quincy, Ill.*

Remittent with diarrhœa in a paroled prisoner.—CASE 35.—Sergeant Samuel S. Cook, Co. B, 27th Conn. Vols.; age 38; was admitted May 17, 1863, with remittent fever and diarrhœa. He was taken prisoner at Fredericksburg, Va., May 3, and marched to Richmond. He had a chill two days before his capture, followed by diarrhœa and fever. On admission his tongue was furred and dry; he had headache and pain in the back; his pulse was 80 and feeble, but his general appearance was not bad; one stool was passed in the twenty-four hours. Quinine was given in five-grain doses every four hours. On the 19th his bowels became loose, yielding four stools on that day and on the 20th, six or seven on the 21st and only two on the 22d. On the 23d the diarrhœa ceased and there was no fever. The patient quickly regained his strength and was returned to duty on June 13.—*Act. Ass't Surg. E. J. Radcliffe, U. S. A., Hospital, Annapolis, Md.*

Remittent with a probable typhoid element.—CASE 36.—Sergeant J. N. Richardson, Co. E, 2d West Tenn. Cav.; age 22; was admitted September 24, 1863, with remittent fever. He had been a prisoner on Belle Isle since July 4, during which period he suffered from diarrhœa and chills. "This, like many other cases of fever among paroled prisoners from the South, has been very much *sui generis* and difficult to classify, having symptoms of malarial remittent and of typhoid. It has been characterized by irregular remissions, the pulse sometimes as high as 130, sometimes as low as 80, irregular diarrhœa, delirium, swellings under the chin and of the parotid and frequent micturition. He was treated with quinine, blue pill and opium, effervescing mixture, chlorate of potash and sinapisms. He began to improve in strength and flesh in November and made rapid progress to health. He was transferred to Ohio January 6, 1864."—*Act. Ass't Surg. A. Claude, U. S. A., Hospital, Annapolis, Md.*

CASE 37.—Sergeant William J. Goode, Co. F, 16th Ill. Cav.; age 25; was admitted July 21, 1863, with severe fever, tongue coated, skin hot and dry, pulse frequent, bowels irritable. Quinine, Dover's powder and turpentine emulsion were prescribed. By August 2 the fever had lessened, but the bowels were more relaxed, and there was abdominal tenderness; the tongue was coated except at the tip, which was red; the stomach was irritable; the skin moist. Medicine was withheld. On the 14th the patient was improved but feeble; the bowels continued loose and the abdomen tender. Elixir of calisaya was given. The fever returned on the 19th, and recurred nightly, although the administration of quinine was resumed, until the end of the month, when profuse sweatings took place towards morning. The fever at this time was recorded as having become "somewhat typhoid." On September 3 the tongue was red at the tip but thickly coated at the base; bowels loose; pulse 60, feeble and compressible; appetite poor. Aromatic sulphuric acid was given until the 14th, when it was replaced by the elixir. The patient was pale and feeble on the 16th, but able to walk about. On the 22d there was some fever at night, and the tongue was red and coated but not dry; diarrhœa continued. On October 1 the roof of the mouth was sore and spongy. Next day a blister was applied on account of pain and soreness in the left hypochondrium. After this he improved rapidly, and deserted on the 16th.—*Hospital, Quincy, Ill.*

Recorded as typhoid but treated as remittent.—CASE 38.—Private Matthew Baird, Co. C, 3d Mich. Vols.; age 23; was admitted October 19, 1861, as a case of typhoid fever. About October 5 he had been seized with pain in the head and bones, fever and chills; he had some nausea and vomiting at first, and a diarrhœa which continued for two days; the headache lasted four days; during the second week his urine had to be removed by catheter. On admission his pulse was 62 and of fair strength, skin soft and warm, tongue pale, moist and slightly coated, brownish in the center, teeth and gums clean, appetite good; he had tinnitus aurium and giddiness, but no pain, eruption nor sudamina; one thin watery stool was passed, but there was no tenderness, borborigmus nor tympanites, and the abdomen was soft; there was no cough and the urine was normal. Quinine was prescribed in full doses three times daily. Next day the face was calm and natural; the pulse 64, steady and of fair strength; the skin soft and warm; the tongue slightly pale and flabby, but moist and clean; the appetite good; one thin fœtid stool was passed. On the 22d the quinine was reduced to two grains three times daily, and during the night the patient had a chill, but next day its effects disappeared. On the 28th he rested badly and had some diarrhœa, but there was no tenderness nor tympanitis; the tongue was pale and moist and the appetite fair. The skin and conjunctivæ became jaundiced on the 31st. Small doses of calomel and opium were given. On November 4 he slept well; his mind was clear, countenance calm, bowels regular and appetite good. He was transferred to Annapolis, Md., on the 18th.—*Seminary Hospital, Georgetown, D. C.*

Remittent following typhoid.—CASE 39.—Private Sidney Nafus, Co. F, 143d Pa. Vols.; age 22. [This man entered Stanton Hospital, Washington, June 15, 1863; Diagnosis—debility; and was transferred to Satterlee Hospital, Philadelphia, on the 17th; Diagnosis—chronic dysentery. He was returned to duty August 28, but contracted typhoid fever October 2, and was confined to bed for four weeks. On November 23 he was admitted to Douglas hospital, Washington, as a convalescent from typho-malarial fever, and on the 27th was transferred to Satterlee Hospital; diagnosis—intermittent fever.] On December 13 he was reported as much improved, and the quinine and carbonate of iron, which he had been taking, was omitted. On the 18th he had a paroxysm of fever, which was repeated next day; pulse 120; tongue coated and somewhat dry; skin moist; headache; tenderness in the epigastric and right hypochondriac regions. Quinine in three-grain doses was given every two hours. The fever continued, but with diminishing intensity for a week, the skin being sallow and dry, the tongue white coated, the bowels regular or constipated. The medicine was omitted on the 28th; but on January 1, 1864, the heart's action became much increased, pulse 138 and skin hot and dry. Digitalis was given and a blister applied to the chest. Next day the skin was cool and the pulse reduced to 96. After this he was treated occasionally with digitalis, but he remained weak for a long time. He was put on guard duty April 25.—*Satterlee Hospital, Philadelphia, Pa.*

Continued fever quickly changing to remittent and intermittent.—CASE 40.—Private George H. Gardner, Co. G, 19th Me. Vols.; age 19; was admitted December 16, 1862, with varicocele. After some time he became affected with sore throat and pain in the ears, and presented symptoms which the attending physician was inclined to attribute to the presence of the typhoid fever poison. On January 5, 1863, the first day on which these were noticed, the skin was hot, face flushed, tongue furred, pulse tense and rapid and there was considerable gastric disturbance. On the 6th these symptoms were much increased. On the 7th the fever was accompanied by diarrhœa with tenderness in the abdomen, pulse about 95, tongue coated but moist, red on the edges. Neutral mixture and sweet spirits of nitre were given. Next day there were two rose spots; the abdominal tenderness was increased; the mouth not so moist, but not dry; both ears were discharging freely, and there was great drowsiness. On the 9th there was no diarrhœa, but the abdomen continued painful, especially on pressure; the fever was much increased, the pulse having risen to 120; but towards noon there was a decided remission, lasting about three hours, during which the skin was cooler and the patient in a pleasant sleep. At noon on the 10th a distinct chill was followed by a fever of about three or four hours duration. Quinine in three-grain doses was given every three hours. Tenderness and pain in the abdomen continued. The chill recurred at noon of the 11th, but was not so violent as on the previous day; the patient complained of great pain in the right shoulder, and was unable to move the arm, which was very sensitive to pressure, but without redness or swelling; he also complained of pain on percussion over the liver; the eyes were not at all yellow but natural, and there was diarrhœa. The quinine was continued. No chills nor fever occurred on the 12th; the pain in the shoulder continued, but there was no more pain over the liver than over any other part of the abdomen, in which there were acute flying pains seemingly neuralgic in character. Next day the patient was much better: tongue cleaner, appetite returning, shoulder less painful and fever absent. Quinine was continued in two-grain doses every four hours. On the 15th he sat up for a short time, but the pain in the shoulder was troublesome and was felt even as late as the 30th. "The above case is presented as a curious instance of what was apparently typhoid fever in its commencement, changing to remittent and then to intermittent fever in the short space of a week."*—*Satterlee Hospital, Philadelphia, Pa.*

Remittent followed by intermittent.—CASE 41.—Private Thomas Gaitly, Co. E, 19th Mass. Vols., had a paroxysm of intermittent fever on November 9, 1861. He had been recently discharged from hospital on recovery from remittent fever. He was readmitted on the 10th and had a marked paroxysm on admission. Fifteen grains of quinine were given at a dose, with five grains in a half ounce of whiskey to be taken thereafter three times daily. On November 12 there was no return of the chill; the patient's appetite was good and he felt well but weak. He was returned to quarters.—*Regimental Hospital 19th Mass. Vols.*

Remittent ending fatally.—CASE 42.—Private Christopher Commars, 69th Co. 1st Batt. V. R. C.; age 22; was admitted November 11, 1863, with remittent fever. He said he had been sick for six days, but had continued on duty although he suffered from a chill on the 10th. On the 11th he had a severe chill and was seen by the medical officer of the day, who ordered him into the ward. Two grains of quinine were given three times a day. On the 12th he had vomiting, and pain and tenderness in the left side of the chest. The quinine was omitted and three grains of calomel ordered every four hours until four powders had been taken, with a Seidlitz powder after the last dose. The bowels were moved on the 13th, but the vomiting continued until death on the 15th. During his sickness the patient expressed no anxiety as to its result; he was confident that he would be able to return to duty in a few days.—*Act. Ass't Surg. Henry M. Dean, U. S. A., Lincoln Hospital, Washington, D. C.*

CASE 43.—Private David Kensinger, Co. I, 8th Tenn. Vols.; age 19; was admitted May 10, 1864, suffering from remittent fever and debility. Quinine in five-grain doses three times a day was prescribed and an enema of castor oil administered. On the 13th the patient had a hot skin and frequent pulse, with much prostration, wakefulness, restlessness, loathing of food, nausea and vomiting, but no pain. Carbonate of ammonia and brandy were prescribed. On the 14th there was a slight abatement of the fever in the morning and an exacerbation in the evening, which became more marked on the evening of the 15th. On the 19th there was much nervous disturbance, restlessness and jactitation. On the 21st the stools became frequent and the tongue dryer and darker. On the morning of the 22d the tongue was not so dry as during the preceding paroxysm, but in the evening the patient became delirious. After this each successive exacerbation was more severe and protracted, and each remission less decided until death took place on the 28th. Clammy sweats, collapsed features, involuntary passages and imperceptible pulse preceded death for several hours.—*Act. Ass't Surg. J. H. Coover, U. S. A., Hospital, Annapolis, Md.*

Malarial congestions.—CASE 44.—Private H. Straight, Co. C, 154th N. Y. Vols.; age 25; was admitted December 12, 1862, with jaundice, chronic nephritis, enlargement of the spleen and dulness on percussion over the summit of the left lung, with some rude respiration and a dry hacking cough. His sickness began during the Peninsular campaign with a severe attack of remittent fever. He was much emaciated and had anorexia, lassitude and mental dulness; his stools were deficient in bile; his urine was albuminous; the pulse about 90; rigors and exacerbations occurred every evening. Iodide of potassium and bicarbonate of potash were prescribed, each in five-grain doses three times daily, with fluid extract of taraxacum in teaspoonful doses and the application of tincture of iodine over the enlarged spleen. By December 20 the jaundice was somewhat lessened and the stools tinged with bile, but the cough was aggravated, the sputa nummular and blood-stained, and the patient complained of flying pains through the body and of constant nausea. On enquiry it was found that his father had died of tuberculosis. An anodyne expectorant mixture was prescribed. Ten days later, while the jaundice was disappearing the nephritic symptoms became prominent. Tincture of iron with quinine in two-grain doses three times a day was added to the previous treatment. By January 8 the nausea had ceased and the appetite was better; the albumen in the urine was decreasing in quantity although the patient complained of great pain over the region of the kidneys and along the ureters. The iodine mixture was omitted and the following substituted: Ten grains of bicarbonate of potash, three drops of liquor potassæ, five drops of tincture of cannabis indica and one drachm of extract of uva ursi to be

* It is possible that an explanation of the anomalous course of the constitutional disturbance in this instance might have been discovered by a closer examination and report of the progress of the aural inflammation. Diffuse inflammation of the ear is often accompanied with much febrile action, headache and seeming mental dulness, which is in reality a disinclination to be disturbed by enquiries. The fever subsides on the establishment of a discharge from the ear, but slight exposures not unfrequently cause a sudden suppression of the discharge with a recurrence of the febrile condition often-times preceded by rigors and gastric disturbance. The local inflammation with its symptomatic fever superimposed on a case of specific fever of so mild a character as to be indicated only by a fugitive diarrhœa, some abdominal tenderness and two rose-spots, might be regarded as accounting for the changes which constitute the anomaly in this case.

taken in a tablespoonful of mint-water three times a day. On January 14, 1863, the splenic enlargement and lung symptoms continued unchanged, but otherwise the patient's condition was much improved. By January 25 the albuminuria had ceased and the patient had gained flesh but was still very weak. Cod-liver oil was substituted for the potash mixture; the quinine and iron were continued and iodine was applied over the spleen. On February 8 the pulmonary symptoms had almost disappeared and the patient's strength was returning. He was sent to his regiment for duty on the 14th.—*Satterlee Hospital, Philadelphia, Pa.*

CASE 45.—Private Robert Wilson, Co. D, 1st Ky. Vols.; age 24; was admitted May 27, 1861. He had been sick for two weeks with inflammatory rheumatism, for which he had taken colchicum, quinine and opiates. On admission he had fever and delirium, pain in the chest, with roughened respiratory murmur, vomiting and relaxation of the bowels; his tongue was large, moist and white; skin moist, extremities cool; pulse 128 and feeble. One grain of quinine with three of Dover's powder was given every three hours. He was very restless and did not sleep during the following night; his bowels were moved frequently and sometimes involuntarily, the stools being dark green and watery, and there was much gurgling on pressure in the right iliac region. At midnight a pint and a half of dark-colored urine was drawn off by catheter; sudamina appeared on the abdomen and lower part of the chest. Next morning the pupils were dilated, the right to a greater extent than the left, and there was dulness of hearing. A pint of urine was withdrawn. There was a good deal of pain in the chest, but the bowels were quiet until 2 P. M., after which the stools were frequent, dark and watery; the delirium increased and the tongue became so swollen as to cause much suffering. He died at 7 P. M. No autopsy. [After death a medical officer stated that this man had been seized two weeks before with a paroxysm resembling a congestive chill; that he had been bled from the arm, and that reaction had been established with much difficulty.]—*Marine Hospital, Cincinnati, Ohio.*

Remittent followed by congestive fever.—CASE 46.—Private James S. West, Co. D, 16th Ill. Vols., had a very severe attack of remittent fever from which he recovered and was detailed on hospital duty. On July 3, 1862, while thus employed, he was taken with a congestive form of intermittent fever. Mercurial cathartics and enemata were given, with quinine, iron and pepsin, without avail, for the congestive paroxysm returned daily, and finally the patient sank into a completely typhoid state and died August 1st.—*Hospital, Quincy, Ill.*

Congestive fever.—CASE 47.—Private John Boman, Co. B, 5th Ill. Cav., was admitted September 1, 1863, having had diarrhœa for three days. Early on the following morning he was found unconscious, with sluggish respiration, quick feeble pulse and clammy yellow skin. He had vomited viscid dark-green matters and passed involuntary stools which were offensive and bloody. A tablespoonful was given every hour of a mixture containing thirty grains of quinine in two ounces of cinnamon-water acidulated with aromatic sulphuric acid. At 4 P. M. the pulse was better. Fifteen grains of chlorate of potash were ordered to be taken every four hours with stimulants and beef-tea. He rallied much during the night, but in the morning relapsed into his previous condition. The administration of quinine was resumed, but death occurred at 5 P. M.—*Union Hospital, Memphis, Tenn.*

CASE 48.—Private Edwin Graves, Co. D, 86th N. Y. Vols.; age 26; was admitted March 17, 1862; diagnosis—typhoid fever. He was taken sick about March 12 with pain in the chest, headache, nausea, feeling of general swelling and much debility, succeeded by a chill, fever and profuse perspiration, which symptoms recurred daily about 11 A. M.; he had also much annoyance from a numb feeling in his fingers. On admission the pulse was rapid and quick; the skin hot and moist; the tongue moist, red and slightly coated; the patient's appetite was poor and he had some diarrhœa and pyrosis. He stated that the chill and fever occurred at the same time in rapid alternations in different parts of the body, the paroxysm lasting two or three hours. Twenty-four grains of quinine were directed to be taken during the day. He was delirious during the 18th; his pulse rapid and weak; skin natural; tongue moist and coated white. Punch and beef-essence were given every two hours. He died delirious on the morning of the 19th.—*Seminary Hospital, Georgetown, D. C.*

Malarial rheumatism.—CASE 49.—Sergeant Michael Leffey, Co. F, 119th Pa. Vols.; age 24; was admitted March 20, 1863, having been affected with intermittent fever since early in January. On admission he had pain in the back and left side and tenderness over the lumbar vertebræ; he had tremors, and was unable to stand erect. He was treated with quinine, powdered iron, morphine and camphor, with tincture of aconite as a local application. He was transferred to Christian street hospital April 21 [where his case was diagnosed chronic rheumatism, and whence he was discharged June 2, because of general debility].—*Satterlee Hospital, Philadelphia, Pa.*

Malarial neuralgia, debility and œdema.—CASE 50.—Private Martin L. Robertson, Co. K, 4th Me. Vols.; age 23; was admitted December 12, 1862, for torpidity of the liver, which was treated with mercurials and salines. During his convalescence he had a severe attack of tonsillitis ending in suppuration of both glands. Soon after this he was seized with violent pains in the head and face, assuming the forms of supra- and infra-orbital neuralgia, the paroxysms of which were distinctly periodic, sometimes quotidian and again on alternate days. During the exacerbations he complained of numbness on the right side, with prickling of the skin of the face and a sense of fulness in the head. Cups on the back of the neck and purgatives gave some relief to the symptoms, but dimness of vision followed, with unpleasant illusions. Extract of belladonna applied around the eyes relieved the pain slightly; but it was soon thought advisable to have recourse to cinchona, the disease being conceived to be dependent upon the action of malarial or miasmatic poisoning contracted on the Rappahannock, but remaining until now latent in the patient's system. Quinine was perseveringly tried for some time, but it failed to arrest the paroxysms (as had been previously observed in some analogous cases in the hospital). Fowler's solution in five-drop doses was substituted, and after a few days the neuralgic symptoms began to yield sensibly to its influence (as had also happened in similar cases where the cinchona had failed). After exhibiting the medicine for a week, slight sickness of the stomach seemed to suggest its discontinuance, and it was accordingly laid aside for a short time, when it was again resumed with benefit at intervals. The original hepatic disorder reappeared, requiring a repetition of the mercurials. The strength of the patient had failed considerably, but his nutrition was pretty well maintained. On March 28 he had a severe bilious attack, requiring mercurials and laxatives, to which it soon yielded, but he was left with some wandering neuralgic pains in the head, arms and other parts of the body. The nervous system was impaired in power, and it seemed impossible to rally his strength and spirits. Tincture of iron was given after the suspension of the Fowler's solution. On April 2 the neuralgic pains were very nearly gone, but his system remained enfeebled and his spirits despondent. At this time he was transferred by order to a hospital in Maine.—*Satterlee Hospital, Phila., Pa.*

CASE 51.—Private Jno. V. Martin, Co. G, 13th Wis. Vols., was admitted December 8, 1864, as a marked case of anæmia following intermittent fever. He had occasional attacks of neuralgic supraorbital pain severe in character, with serous effusion around the eyes, sometimes almost filling the orbit; the sclerotic was very white and the eyes watery. He was improving rapidly and promising a speedy return to health, when a recurrence of the intermittent fever was followed by a return of the supraorbital pain and the anæmic condition. After rallying from this another recurrence was productive of similar results. He was treated with quinine, iron and wine. A prescription which appeared of value in this case consisted of forty grains of chlorate of potash, twelve of citrate of quinine and iron and two of powdered capsicum, taken in four doses during the day.—*Hospital, Quincy, Ill.*

CASE 52.—Private Daniel W. Huff, Co. H, 104th Pa. Vols.; age 29; was admitted September 1, 1864, suffering from enlarged spleen and general debility induced by malarial disease. He had severe neuralgic pain in the back and limbs; his feet and legs frequently became very much swollen, which condition, as it could be traced to no marked lesion of the viscera, was referred to weakness of the circulation and anæmia. The treatment consisted of a general alterative and supporting course. Iodide of potassium, iron in various forms, vegetable bitters, mineral acids, stimulants, counter-irritation and anodynes were employed in accordance with the indications. No improvement, however, was apparent; in fact he seemed to decline. After remaining in hospital three and a half months he was discharged from the service December 16, 1864.—*Hospital, Alexandria Va.*

III.—SYMPTOMATOLOGY OF MALARIAL DISEASE.

I.—INTERMITTENTS AND REMITTENTS.—The cases submitted above illustrate the recurrence of the intermittent paroxysm daily, every second day, or every third day, with the frequent relapses which occurred in the progress of the disease and the congestions of the abdominal organs as manifested by enlarged spleen, diarrhœa, dysentery and jaundice. The debility and anæmia consequent on the prolonged action of the morbific cause are incidentally mentioned, and as a result of the altered condition of the blood, boils and ulcers are noted among the sequelæ of the disease. Consumption appears to have found favorable conditions for its development in systems broken down by the continued influence of the ague-poison. The identity of the cause of the intermittent and remittent fevers is indicated by the interchangeable character of these fevers, tertians developing into quotidians, and these into remittents and congestive fevers, and the remittents becoming intermittent in their favorable progress. The remittents also appear to have assumed a typhoid character; but whether this was due to the presence of a specific poison or to some depressing agencies developed in the system by the malarial influence is not manifest from these records. On the other hand remittent is seen to have followed typhoid fever; and here also it is not evident that there was any connection in this other than the accidental sequence of the disease causes.* The relapses that occurred in remittent cases are illustrated as well as the frequent association of diarrhœa, dysentery and hepatic congestion with the febrile phenomena. The concurrence of scurvy is also observed. The tendency to an adynamic condition is noticeable in so many that a hyperæmic case in which bloodletting was used in the treatment on account of acute cerebral congestion was considered worthy of special comment by the reporter. More or

---

* S. K. TOWLE, Surgeon 30th Mass. Vols., in his *Notes of Practice in the U. S. Army General Hospital at Baton Rouge, La., during the year* 1863, published in the *Boston Medical and Surgical Journal*, Vol. LXX (1864), pp. 49–56, alluding to the complicated character of the diseases observed in his hospital, says: "Indeed, the symptoms of many of the cases would indicate rather a combination of diseases than any one disease—fevers being inexplicably combined with diarrhœa or dysentery, and vice versâ, so that one would hardly know under which class to make the record. And again, with the different variety of fevers, the record will often depend upon the period of observation; an intermittent, with well-marked stages, will, if neglected, often in a few days become an equally well-marked remittent, or typho-malarial, or a little further on will prominently exhibit advanced typhoid symptoms; or perhaps a few weeks or months later die from chronic diarrhœa or dysentery."

less of congestion of the brain, lungs, liver, spleen and kidneys was occasionally recognized, and in some of these cases the internal congestion was so sudden and violent as to cause speedy death. Rheumatism and neuralgia are also suggested as consequent upon the malarial influence.*

But nothing is said of the aggregation of symptoms which led to the diagnosis of intermittent or remittent, as the case might be. The presumption is that in general there occurred no special alteration from well recognized characteristics. In fact in some of the sanitary reports it is definitely stated that nothing unusual was presented by the malarial diseases under observation. In the intermittents the onset of the disease may be assumed with or without preliminary feelings of languor, weariness, indisposition for physical exercise or mental work, depression of spirits, yawning, aching in the bones and soreness in the muscles, with creeping or chilly sensations along the spine, loss of appetite and perhaps nausea, which had been noted as having recurred for days prior to the advent of the regular paroxysm. We may assume the cold stage as having presented its chills, developing perhaps into rigors, and accompanied with goose-skin, shrunken features and lividity of the lips and nails, and with internal congestions manifested by nausea and irritability of stomach, epigastric pain, splenic or hepatic uneasiness, hurried respiration, rapid, irregular or slow pulse, irritability of temper, headache, confusion of mind, drowsiness or even stupor and coma; the gradual accession of reaction, the alternations of flushings and chills until in the full development of the hot stage the cheeks became flushed, the skin hot, the mouth dry, the tongued furred, the respiration accelerated and the pulse full and strong, or frequent and feeble, if the patient was reduced by previous attacks of this or other enervating disease; and lastly, concurrent with the outbreak of free perspiration, the gradual subsidence of these symptoms and the re-establishment of a comparatively normal condition until the commencement of a succeeding paroxysm. We may assume also the various irregularities frequently presented, especially by the cold stage, it having been sometimes almost absent or indicated only by depression of spirits, yawning or some other comparatively trifling symptoms quickly followed by fever.

In the remittents we may assume a preliminary stage of such malaise as seemed due to hepatic disorder, followed by a chill and the development of a febrile condition, with anorexia, thirst, nausea and bilious vomiting, epigastric or hepatic tenderness, pains in the back and limbs, hot, dry and perhaps jaundiced skin, hurried breathing and frequent pulse with throbbing headache, tinnitus aurium and occasional delirium. We may infer also constipation, a fœtid or bilious diarrhœa or, even, dysenteric symptoms, as presented by the bowels and a large, coated and furred tongue, cleaning as a favorable issue was promised, or becoming dark colored as hiccough, low delirium, involuntary stools, clammy perspirations, collapse, stupor and coma indicated impending death; while the exacerbations and remissions are implied in the name.

On examining the cases that have been presented enough may be found to warrant the acceptance of the above remarks.

The skin was sallow or pallid in the protracted cases; and in the paroxysmal recurrences when its condition is mentioned, it was hot and dry or moist, according as the notes were taken during the exacerbations or remissions; occasionally it is said to have been jaundiced. The pulse is represented as rapid in the majority of the cases, and

---

* Although neuralgia was frequently regarded as a clinical associate of malarial fevers, or indeed as the legitimate offspring of the malarial poison, the cases reported on the monthly reports had no autumnal tides of prevalence to indicate their connection with or dependence upon the cause of the paroxysmal fevers. (See diagram facing page 874 of this volume.) To account for this we must assume that all neuralgic cases in any way connected with malaria must have been reported under the heading of *miasmatic diseases*, or which seems more probable, that neuralgia was less frequent in its association with malarial disease than was currently supposed.

when its volume, impulse and resistance are not specifically stated, feebleness may be inferred as its characteristic, for emaciation, debility, prostration or anæmia is noted in twenty-three of the cases. The pulse is reported in case 40 as tense; but in this the malarial character of the attack is not satisfactorily established. It is stated to have been full and strong in three cases, one of which, 3, was a case of tertian ague, the second, 27, a relapse in a remittent case, and the third, 32, a remittent reported as being of an unusually sthenic type.

The tongue in twenty-five cases in which its appearance is recorded was clean in one; white or furred in fourteen; pale in one; large and white in one; soft, pale, moist and coated in one; brownish in the centre and afterwards becoming pale and flabby in one; dark-brown or black in three; red at the tip in two, and at the edges in one. The clean tongue was recorded in a chronic case, 7, during the absence of paroxysmal manifestations; the pale tongue in the scorbutic case, 30, in which it afterwards became black and was accompanied with delirium. The brown or black tongue appeared also in three cases, 29, 31 and 43, in which there was likewise delirium with much prostration, and in the last two instances a fatal issue. The tongue was red at the edges in the anomalous case 40, and at the tip in two cases, in one of which, 20, there was nothing to suggest that it was other than a remittent attack, while in the other, 23, the specific poison of typhoid fever was considered to be present.

The condition of the tongue in malarial fevers is usually stated by medical writers as white or yellow-coated, becoming dry and of a brown or black color when the case assumes a serious aspect; as for instance Horton, Martin, Aitken, Copland, Watson, Bartlett and others,[*] many of whom speak of the edges and tip as being of a brighter red than natural. The descriptive clause, *red at the tip and edges*, is suggestive of the condition of the tongue in typhoid fever, and, indeed, in Horton's statement of the pathological changes in his febrile cases the patches of Peyer were sometimes found inflamed and ulcerated. There is a probability, therefore, that specific typhoid may have been present in many of the tedious and low forms of fever that occurred in the practice of our medical men before the war; and that the condition of the tongue in such cases may have been embraced in the account of the symptoms of remittent as given by Jones, Doniphan, Boling and others.[†]

But in Sir J. R. Martin's description the red edges and tip are distinguished from a similarly stated condition in enteric fever by the words *loaded, clammy* and *moist*, as applied to the tongue generally. His account of the disease corresponds with that given of the Rio Grande remittents by Dr. Peck in the report presented below,[‡] in which the red tip and edges of the tongue are specially mentioned. In the Bengal fever, as in that of the river bottoms of New Mexico, there is seldom evidence of a co-existing enteric lesion. Hence a tongue with red edges and tip may be considered present in fevers of a purely malarial origin, although during our war this condition was seldom noticed. The tongue was generally soft and flabby, somewhat enlarged, broadened, thickened and indented at the margins, of a pale, livid or bluish tint, and more or less coated or furred white, yellow or brownish, according to the severity of the pyrexial attack.

---

* J. A. B. HORTON, M. D., in his treatise on *Diseases of Tropical Climates*, London, 1879, p. 66, says of the tongue as it appears in the marsh remittent fevers, that "it is more or less furred, redder than natural at the tip and edges." And again, on p. 68: "The tongue at the commencement of the disease is generally covered with a thick whitish or yellowish-white fur, thicker towards the centre, having a feeling of being large and flabby, and marked on its periphery by impressions of the teeth; the edges are usually red, but in a more advanced stage the coating assumes a darkish brown appearance. Sometimes the tongue is dry, presenting several furrows, accompanied with severe thirst." Sir JAMES RANALD MARTIN, in his *Influence of Tropical Climates*, London, 1861, p. 314, speaking of the remittent fevers of Bengal, states that "The tongue is red at the tip and edges, loaded, clammy, and moist; at other times, with a bitter or bad taste, the organ is but little changed from the healthy appearance." AITKEN, in his *Science and Practice of Medicine*, describes as follows: "The tongue, in the mild form of the disease (fever and ague), is clean in the cold stage, white in the hot stage, and again cleans after the sweat has flowed. In severe cases the tongue is white during all the stages, and also during the apyrexia, while in the worst cases the tongue is brown in all the stages."—American edition, 1866, Vol. I, page 483. COPLAND'S *Dictionary of Practical Medicine*, London, 1858, Vol. I, p. 948, says that the tongue in remittent fever is "clammy, moist or flabby and coated, and afterwards dry, rough or brown," and on page 935, that the tongue of intermittent fever "is white and loaded." CONDIE, in the American edition of WATSON'S *Practice*, Philadelphia, 1858, p. 502, in his article on Bilious Remittent Fever, says: "The tongue is usually moist, red at the sides and edges, and coated on its upper surface with a whitish, light brown or yellowish fur, which often acquires considerable thickness." BARTLETT, in his *Fevers of the United States*, 3d edition, Philadelphia, Pa., 1852, p. 361, says: "The tongue is generally more or less thickly covered with a yellowish or dirty white fur—the color being probably occasioned in many cases by the fluids ejected from the stomach. The edges of the tongue are often somewhat redder than natural. During the early periods of the disease the tongue usually retains its moisture; but in grave cases, especially, and after the third or fourth paroxysm, it frequently becomes parched and dry, dark brown or nearly black on the dorsum, more intensely red on its edges, and sharpened at its point." GEORGE B. WOOD thus gives the appearance of the tongue in a fully-formed case of remittent fever: "The tongue is now thickly and uniformly covered with a white or yellowish-white coating, which, as the disease advances, often becomes brown or blackish, especially in the centre. In moderate cases the tongue is usually rather moist throughout the disease; but, in those of a higher grade, it not unfrequently becomes dry or dryish, and sometimes chapped or fissured upon the surface. It is occasionally disposed to be dry in the paroxysm, and to become moist in the remission. At the sides, when not covered with fur, it is usually red, and not unfrequently indented by the teeth, in consequence of being somewhat swollen."—See *Practice of Medicine*, Philadelphia, Pa., 1847, Vol. I, p. 258.

† JOSEPH JONES, in *Observations on some of the Physical, Chemical, Physiological and Pathological Phenomena of Malarial Fever*, Philadelphia, 1859, says, p. 297: "In almost every case the papillæ of the tongue were enlarged, and of a bright red color. In the mildest cases the tongue was only slightly coated with white and light yellow fur, and the tip and edges were redder than normal. In the severest cases the tip and edges of the tongue assumed a bright red color, and the tongue was much drier than in the milder cases." * * "The fur on the tongue in many cases was thick, and of a brownish-yellow color." And further: "In the active stages of remittent fever the tongue, in many cases, especially if it be the first attack of fever, presents upon those portions which are clean a brilliant scarlet color, and dry, glazed surface; the papillæ are enlarged; the fur which frequently coats the tongue is of a yellowish or brownish-yellow, and sometimes black color, and almost always dry; the tongue, in many cases, feels, when the finger is passed over it, as dry and harsh as the surface of a rough board." D. A. DONIPHAN, M. D., in *Remarks on the Bilious Remittent Fever of certain portions of Louisiana*, describes the tongue in the early stages as red on the tip and edges, covered on the dorsum with a white or pale yellow coat, stating that in the advanced stage it "changes to a brown or dark brown dorsum, while the tip and edges are red, and present a glazed appearance."—See *Western Lancet*, Lexington, Ky., 1846, Vol. IV, p. 212. WM. M. BOLING, M. D., of Montgomery, Alabama, in *Observations on Remittent Fever as it occurs in the Southern part of Alabama*, says: "The tongue in the first exacerbation may remain moist, sometimes almost natural; but in most cases the edges will be redder than in perfect health, and the dorsum covered with a thin yellowish or dirty white fur." * * "In the third or fourth exacerbation it is apt to become dry, at least on the dorsum, though the edges remain moist, and still later it becomes parched, rough and cracked."—*Am. Jour. of Med. Sci.*, Philadelphia, N. S., Vol. XI, 1846, p. 297.

‡ Page 124.

Thus, Surgeon S. K. Towle, 30th Mass. Vols.,* referring to the diagnosis of fever cases, says: "The white, thick, pulpy, rounded tongue will dumbly speak of malaria." Surgeon E. C. Bidwell, 31st Mass. Vols.,† had already made note of the thickening and rounding of the sides of the tongue, and considered this condition an unmistakable evidence of the presence of the malarial poison in the system.

Dr. T. C. Osborn of Alabama,‡ has described and figured a condition of the tongue which he claims to be a pathognomonic symptom of malarial disease existing in all cases, both acute and chronic. Its essential feature is that the tongue presents a more or less wide, smooth margin, with slightly flattened and crumpled sides and edges. The color amounts ordinarily to a very faint bluish tinge, which is often lost or merged in the various tints or furs produced by other diseases. According to Osborn the crenated or crumpled condition of the edges is not due to the impression of the teeth, for the transverse lines are closer together than would happen if this was their cause, and they are observed in infancy and old age, when no teeth are present.

The appetite in the cases which have been presented is said to have been good in two instances, 7 and 11, but in both the reports were made during the progress of recovery. Ordinarily, in acute attacks of malarial disease, there was anorexia or impaired appetite with nausea and perhaps vomiting, these symptoms being noted in fifteen of the cases. Thirst appears less frequently, having been recorded only in two cases. Disordered digestion was manifested in two cases, 27 and 33, by fœtor of the breath. Constipation is mentioned in seven and diarrhœa or dysentery in twenty-two of the cases in which the condition of the bowels is recorded.

Abdominal pain or tenderness is usually reported as having been in the epigastric, hypochondriac or umbilical regions. In one instance, 30, the scorbutic case, the right iliac region is stated to have been tender. The abdomen was tympanitic in one case, 23, in which typhoid fever was considered to have been present.

Headache is reported in nine cases, in two of which delirium also is said to have existed; but as there are six cases in which delirium occurred, although headache, if present, was not reported, the frequent presence of cerebral symptoms in these malarial fevers must be accepted. Epistaxis in one of the cases, 32, in which the delirium was accompanied with tinnitus aurium and disturbed vision, gave temporary relief to these special symptoms; but in case 29 the spontaneous bleeding from the nose did not take place until after the delirium had begun to subside. Ringing in the ears was present also in cases 38 and 40; in the former a diagnosis of typhoid fever was entered, but the patient was treated successfully by quinine; in the latter an aural inflammation gave a sufficient explanation of the tinnitus.

The delirium in a few of the cases, as in 32 and 33, appeared due to cerebral hyperæmia, but in the larger number it was manifestly of an asthenic character, and the concurrent symptoms were in some instances such as to suggest the use of the word typhoid for their expression. In 29 the patient was greatly prostrated and his lips and tongue coated black; in 30 he was unable to speak, his tongue was black, his teeth covered with sordes, and there was tenderness in the right iliac region; in 36 there were "symptoms of typhoid" and swelling of the salivary glands; in 43, clammy sweats, involuntary passages, collapsed features and imperceptible pulse; and in 45, involuntary passages, gurgling on pressure on the right iliac fossa, dilated pupils and dulness of hearing. Whether these symptoms were manifestations of the malarial agency or indicative of the typhoid fever-poison cannot be decided by the records, although it seems likely that an adynamic condition may have existed independent of the specific poison of enteric fever, for in 29 and 43 there appears nothing to warrant the supposition of a specific typhoid element.

The characteristics of the intermittents consisted of the persisting tendency to recurrence induced by continued exposure to the influences determining the primary attacks, the liability to a fatal issue by a change to the remittent type or by the sudden onset of a pernicious attack, and the gradual production of that depraved condition of the system known as chronic malarial poisoning.

The remittents were characterized chiefly by the accompanying asthenia, and as this was present in cases free from diarrhœal, pneumonic or marked cerebral symptoms, as well as in those in which one or more of these symptoms gave increased gravity to the attack, it must be referred to a deterioration in the constitution of the subjects caused by the malarial or some antecedent influence. The frequency of diarrhœa as a concomitant must

---

* In his paper cited *supra*, p. 119.

† This officer, in an article entitled *Diagnosis of the Malarial Diathesis: New Test Symptom*," says: "It is a very peculiar and abnormal appearance of the tongue, in which its under surface appears to have trespassed upon the upper, the papillæ of the latter being supplanted by the transverse *rugæ* of the former. The sides are thickened and rounded, the normal well-defined edge being obliterated, and the line of demarcation moved nearer to the mesial line. This appearance of the sides may be associated with any and every possible appearance of the remaining papillary surface, clean or coated, thick or thin, light or dark, just as the malarious disease may be attended by any and every variety of morbid condition of the system. Through all this variety it is perfectly distinct, and, when once learned by actual inspection, is unmistakable."—*Boston Med. and Surg. Jour.*, Vol. LXVIII, 1863, p. 36.

‡ T. C. OSBORN—*Remarks on a peculiar appearance of the tongue in malarial disease.*—The *Western Jour. of Med. and Surg.*, Vol. VIII, 1851, p. 109—also by the same, *A peculiar appearance of the tongue in Malarious disease.*—*Trans. of the Amer. Med. Assoc.*, Vol. XX, 1869, p. 175 [with colored plate]—and *A new variety of Malarial Fever.*—*New Orleans Jour. of Med.*, Vol. XXI, p. 664. The reference to a trespass of the under on the upper surface in Dr. BIDWELL'S article is a singular coincidence, if he was unaware of Dr. OSBORN'S paper published in 1851, in which occurs the following: "The most fixed condition of this symptom is an appearance of *indentation* or *crimpling*, transversely, which is apparently confined to the subjacent tissue, while the superficial tegument is moist, smooth, and transparent. In a word, it seems to be a continuation or encroachment of the inferior surface upon the superior and lateral borders of the tongue, greater as we approach the root of the organ."

be attributed to the simultaneous action of the causes of the alvine fluxes and the malarial poison. Where so many men were affected with diarrhœa a certain percentage of diarrhœal complications was to have been expected among the remittents, irrespective of the action of the malarial poison on the integrity of the alimentary mucous membrane. But as it is certain that the coincidence of diarrhœa and periodic fever was greater than could be accounted for by these considerations, we are at liberty to consider it either as due directly to the malarial agency or as a further illustration of the proposition that the malarial influence, other conditions being equal, is more readily manifested in the debilitated than in the strong and healthy. The diseased action as it affected the lungs, excluding from consideration the supervention of pernicious chills, was not manifested by any urgent or prominent symptoms; it appeared rather to progress insidiously as in the course of typhoid fever. If cases occurred such as were described by MANSON in 1857 under the name of malarial pneumonia, and by GAINES of Mobile in 1866,* who proposed for them the title of remittent *pneumonic fevers*, they were not recorded by our officers as manifestations of malarial disease. The incidence of the disease-poison on the liver was very generally manifested by bilious vomiting and not unfrequently by jaundice; in some instances this latter symptom was so strongly marked as to suggest the idea of yellow fever.† The kidneys did not come into prominence in the symptomatology. The urine was affected during the febrile condition, and in the jaundiced cases it participated in the general coloration, but it is not often mentioned as having been albuminous or sanguinolent.

The following extracts from special reports refer to the symptoms of the intermittents and remittents:

Surgeon M. R. GAGE, *25th Wis. Vols.; Columbus, Ky., March* 31, 1863: Bilious fever, as we have seen it in our present location, presents the following symptoms: For many days before the patient gives up he complains of languor, bitter taste in the mouth, slight feelings of nausea, disinclination for food, sometimes constipation, and very generally a considerable degree of heavy, dull pain over the eyes. A chill, more or less severe, generally precedes the attack, followed by increased heat of the entire surface, and slight or severe pain in the lumbar region; the skin becomes hot and dry, the countenance flushed, the eyes red and watery, the pulse quick and breathing hurried; extreme irritability of the stomach is a frequent and distressing symptom, and for many days sometimes, a persistent accompaniment, nearly everything in the form of ingesta being rejected. There is commonly considerable thirst, a marked decrease in the urinary secretion, which is highly colored and has a strong odor, and after the disease has continued for a time the skin shows a yellow hue, which tint also extends to the eyes. An exacerbation and remission of the fever takes place during the twenty-four hours, each succeeding exacerbation, perhaps, acquiring greater severity. The symptoms above described, greatly intensified, with a more continuous exacerbation and less distinctly marked remission, constitute the severer form of the disease. To allay the pain in the head and back, which is often distressing, mustard applied to the nape of the neck and the small of the back, together with cold applied to the head, often affords prompt relief. If the suffering is intense and the case more urgent, cupping the temples and back of the neck is of the first importance, and should by no means be neglected; so also the cups may be applied to the epigastrium, if, as is sometimes the case, a feeling of death-like oppression is a constant and serious symptom. Cathartics are at once resorted to, the prescription generally used being as follows: Four grains of podophyllin, ten grains of bicarbonate of soda and ten grains of calomel, divided into six powders, one of which is taken once in two hours. This combination ordinarily produces very free catharsis, and, together with the means already brought into use, often affords prompt and permanent relief, and places the case in a condition to move through the course of the disease in safety, if the latter is not effectually cut short. Bathing the entire surface in water to which a little soda has been added, and of such a temperature as to feel comfortable to the patient during the exacerbation, is a matter

---

* Report of O. F. MANSON on *Malarial Pneumonia.—New Orleans Medical News and Hospital Gazette*, Vol. 4, 1857–58, p. 400 *et seq.* *Malarial pneumonia.* An Essay read before the Mobile Medical Society, March 5, 1866, by E. P. GAINES, M. D.—*New Orleans Med. and Surg. Jour.*, Vol. XX, p. 12 *et seq.* MANSON describes this form of pneumonia, which he considers the prevailing type of the disease in the South, as a severe remittent fever with pneumonic symptoms superadded. The lungs become permeated with a blood-tinged serum rather than consolidated by exuded plasma. He considers the condition as one of congestion, for it often occurs with cold skin, flagging pulse and colliquative diarrhœa, manifestations which he regards as inconsistent with the existence of the inflammatory process. GAINES says that cases ushered in with a severe chill are dangerous, as the lungs may be overwhelmed by the sudden congestion; but the fatality generally depends more upon the febrile disease than upon the pulmonary inflammation which accompanies it. In a few cases he bled for the sake of the immediate relief given to the congested lungs, and he had experienced no evil after-effects from the bleeding; but cupping answered in the majority of cases. This was followed by calomel, and if the fever became high, by veratrum viride. When the remission recurred large doses of quinine were given.

† See Surgeon TOWLE'S *Notes* cited *supra*, p. 119.

of no small moment, and affords a pleasant relief from the intense heat of the skin and helps to keep that great depurative organ in a condition the better to perform not only its ordinary functions but the large increase of duty now incumbent upon it. The effervescing draught, spirit of mindererus, sweet spirits of nitre, Hoffmann's anodyne, Dover's powder and ipecacuanha are remedies of some importance, and may be administered with advantage by an election of cases, and if their exhibition be properly timed. Blisters are useful after the force of the exacerbation has been reduced in those cases where any considerable head, gastric or pulmonary difficulty remains.

Surgeon A. F. PECK, *1st New Mexico Mounted Vols.; Los Lunas, New Mexico, Sept. 30, 1862*: Intermittents are of the quotidian type; remittents approach very closely in character to continued fever. The cold stage, so well marked in the intermittent fevers of the different sections of the United States, is but slightly developed on this river (the Rio Grande) as far as I have observed; it amounts to no more than chilly sensations in different parts of the body, after which the stage of pyrexia supervenes and lasts for several hours, when the sweating stage begins and the fever declines. The tongue is heavily coated with a white fur; there is great thirst with sometimes nausea and vomiting; all disposition for food is lost; the breathing is hurried and often irregular, with feelings of weight and oppression in the epigastrium; the pulse is full, strong and frequent. The nervous system is much disordered; there are severe pains of a neuralgic character in the back, loins and extremities; the secretions are diminished, the skin being dry and hot and the urine scanty. In the course of a few hours the sweating stage makes its appearance, when all the febrile symptoms gradually abate. As it advances the skin becomes cool, the excitement of the circulation subsides, the headache disappears and the patient falls into a calm sleep, from which he awakens free from fever.

The symptoms of remittent fever differ in many particulars from those above enumerated: For several days previous to an attack the patient describes himself as feeling languid and weak, with pains in the body generally, epigastric uneasiness, deficiency of appetite, disordered taste and slight soreness in different parts of the body. This state of system continues until a regular paroxysm of fever makes its appearance, which continues with little or no abatement in the twenty-four hours. In many cases the only sign of a remission is a slight diminution in the fulness of the pulse, the frequency remaining the same, while the pains in the body may be less violent and the skin not so hot as a few hours before. The tongue, at first covered with a yellowish-white fur, in the course of two or three days assumes a dark and dry appearance in the centre with edges and tip very red; great thirst; intense pains, especially in the head and back; sometimes diarrhœa and at others constipation; urine scanty and very dark; respiration hurried and difficult; skin sometimes of a yellowish hue.

The treatment that I adopt for these two diseases, which are undoubtedly identical in character but different in intensity, is as follows: If the bowels are confined I give three or four compound cathartic pills or half an ounce of sulphate of magnesia; if there is diarrhœa, castor oil half an ounce with half a drachm of oil of turpentine to be taken at once. After the bowels are thoroughly cleansed I give fifteen to twenty grains of sulphate of quinine morning and evening. If the patient has fever the next morning I repeat the quinine, giving twenty grains of the sulphate rather than fifteen, as I find that this quantity answers much better, given at once, than a greater quantity in divided doses. By this method of administration its full sedative and febrifuge effects are produced. I never have known two, or at most three, twenty-grain doses of the sulphate (and often much less is required) fail in this valley to reduce the fever and produce complete convalescence. In a few cases I have thought it necessary to resort to alterative doses of mercurials combined with opium or Dover's powder at night to procure rest; and if the urine should be very deficient in quantity I give sweet spirits of nitre, half a drachm to a drachm, three or four times in the twenty-four hours. If there should be much prostration I give essence of beef with wine or brandy, as circumstances may dictate. Method of administering sulphate of quinine, with some of its attendant results: I never wait for an intermission or a remission; if the bowels are open I give it at once, in the height of the fever, in from fifteen to twenty-grain doses, and repeat if necessary in three or four hours. When the symptoms are of an alarming character I very often combine the sulphate with a cathartic and give both at once, and if in three or four hours no sedative impression is made I give an additional quantity. In ordinary cases I never have found it necessary to give more than two twenty-grain doses in the twenty-four hours, although I have seen many cases in which I have given double or triple this quantity with the very best results. The immediate results of the administration of the sulphate in large doses during the fever are so gratifying that I cannot refrain from noting some of them. In from one to three hours the sedative effects of the medicine begin to appear. The pulse, before full, bounding and rapid, now becomes soft, less frequent and more regular; the skin, that before was hot and dry, now begins to be cool and moist; the countenance, that was anxious and restless, now bears the marks of composure and rest; the respirations, that were hurried and oppressed, are now easy and free; the tongue begins to show signs of returning moisture; the urine becomes copious; and lastly, the whole nervous system is quieted and the patient enjoys sweet repose.

Surgeon M. D. BENEDICT, *75th New York; Santa Rosa, Fla., April 3, 1862*: We have had since March 1 a large number of cases of remittent fever, mostly of mild type, although a few have shown a stronger tendency to congestion. It seems like a fever of acclimation, and in its treatment quinine is our main dependence.

Ass't Surg. J. H. SCHEETZ, *47th Pa. Vols.; Beaufort, S. C., August 31, 1862*: Remittent fever, which prevailed to a considerable extent, was characterized by a daily exacerbation and remission. Most of the cases presented the following symptoms: A general feeling of lassitude for two or three days, with partial loss of appetite, followed by alternating chills and flushes of heat, cephalalgia, referred principally to the supraorbital regions, sharp and lancinating in character, but sometimes dull, aching and heavy; eyes generally suffused; skin sallow, hot and dry during exacerbation, moist and flaccid during remission; tongue coated; thirst; anorexia; pain in the back and extremities; bowels usually torpid, but in some disposed to looseness; tenderness over the right hypochondriac and epigastric regions; nausea frequently and sometimes vomiting; pulse from 85 to 115 per minute; urine generally high-colored and occasioning frequent complaints of scalding.

The treatment found most beneficial was to administer a mercurial purgative in cases with torpid bowels; when nausea was present twenty grains of ipecacuanha were added to the mercurial. After the evacuation of the intestinal canal quinia in five-grain doses was given four to six times daily. Diarrhœa was treated with opium or Dover's powder alternating with the quinine.

Surgeon G. W. PHILLIPS, *75th Ill. Vols.; Perryville, Md., December* 31, 1862: Many cases of miasmatic disease were complicated with diarrhœa, bronchitis and hepatic derangement. The paroxysms in most of the cases were not distinct—occurring at a certain hour, and made up of distinct stages, as of chill, fever and sweating—but light chills, followed in a short time by flushes of fever, but without subsequent perspirations. The febrile action was not high; skin hot but not burning; pulse frequent and often weak and small. A sense of great muscular prostration attended all these cases; congestion of the kidneys was also common. They were treated with free doses of quinine.

Surgeon J. L. MULFORD, *48th N. Y. Vols.; Fort Pulaski, Ga., September* 1, 1862: The cases of malarial fever this month have been of a mild form. The symptoms are nausea and vomiting, great lassitude and weakness, pain in the back part of the head with a heaviness over the vertex, pain in the knees, high-colored urine, dark-colored stools, and slight pain in the liver. In all cases I think the difficulty arises from an inactive liver. The treatment has been mercurial purgatives and castor oil, followed by five-grain doses of quinine in aromatic sulphuric acid.

Surgeon H. EARNEST GOODMAN, *28th Pa. Vols.; Point of Rocks, Md., September* 30, 1861: I have observed a peculiar disease among the men, beginning with a dull headache for several days, and then characterized by a harsh, dry skin, dry tongue, feeble pulse, extreme debility, no appetite, probably a little fever once in several days, and with more of a tendency to constipation than diarrhœa. After one or two weeks spent in this condition the patients brighten up, eat ravenously, and soon return to a healthy state. I have classed these cases under the head of remittent fever; but the fever is seldom perceptible to the touch.

Ass't Surg. D. L. HUNTINGTON, *U. S. Army; Fort Monroe, Va., September* 30, 1862: The prevalent diseases have been those of miasmatic origin and those depending on a deranged state of the portal circulation. The bilious fevers have been mild and easily managed. Intermittents have proved more obstinate, and in many cases have continued a long time, quinine having seemed to exercise but little of its peculiar power. In these cases a resort to Fowler's solution has been of great advantage. I have noticed a marked tardiness of recovery in these cases of miasmatic disease, which I have attributed partly to the fact that the poison still remains in the system, though held in abeyance for the time, and partly to the enervating effects of the climate. It is proper to state that but little of the disease has originated here; it was contracted during the campaign on the peninsula or previous to enlistment.

Surgeon A. W. WRIGHT, *58th Pa. Vols.; Suffolk, Va., November* 1, 1862: We had also a number of cases of a peculiar type of remittent fever. A man would complain of a few ordinary bilious symptoms for a day or so, doing light duty, when his messmates would report him as crazy. In a day the following symptoms would be developed: Dry tongue; quick pulse, 110–120; slight heat of skin; good appetite; some tendency to diarrhœa; wildness of expression; nervousness; constantly moving about, lying down only when ordered to; embracing every opportunity to escape the care of nurses, and talking rationally, although occasionally mildly delirious. These symptoms lasted about two weeks, when the patient suddenly awoke to a consciousness of his condition. Convalescence was rapid. I had six cases of this kind, and all recovered except Private Putnam of Company G, who became insane and was sent to the Asylum at Washington. The disease sometimes assumed another form: The man would have a slight chill, then fever, quick pulse, dry tongue, either copious perspiration standing in drops all over the body or great coolness of surface, delirium, great perspiration and death in twenty-four to fifty-six hours. I had two such cases in Oak Grove Camp and lost one of them.

II.—THE PERNICIOUS FEVERS.—In the form of sick report used during the civil war the term *congestive intermittent fever* was employed as the equivalent of the designations *pernicious intermittent fever, congestive fever* and *congestive chills*, to indicate that dangerous form of intermittent, characterized especially by the intensity and severity of the cold stage, which had long been recognized as of frequent occurrence throughout the malarious districts of our Southern States. Such attacks occurred not only in persons who were for the first time exposed to a highly malarious atmosphere, but also among those who had suffered more or less from the malarial influence before the supervention of the congestive seizure; indeed it is probable that a majority of the deaths recorded by our medical officers as from simple intermittents were really due to the occurrence of this pernicious type of the disease. It assumed various forms, one of which appears to have been observed with much frequency. In it were presented grave symptoms of disturbance of the brain and nervous system; excessive headache, drowsiness, even coma, occasionally convulsive phenomena and sometimes delirium, accompanied its onset. In some cases the nervous disorder manifested itself in the form of epileptiform convulsions, as observed by Surgeon GEORGE COOPER, U. S. Army, while Medical Director of the Department of the South.*   In other instances unusual manifestations were recorded, as by Surgeon G. RUSH, 101st Pa. Vols., who published two cases of pernicious fever in which unconsciousness and insensibility were associated with so little disturbance of the organic functions that in the first case which occurred the patient was suspected of malingering.†

Frequently the severity and prolonged duration of the chill or of the condition of collapse that followed it, corresponded to what has been described as the algid variety of pernicious fever.   Dr. WOODWARD‡ mentions having seen at the siege of Yorktown a number of cases in which the collapse was profound and extremely prolonged.   In other cases congestion of the lungs appeared to determine the fatal issue.   Although vomiting and diarrhœa were frequent concomitants of the simple intermittents and remittents, it does not appear that the concurrence of these symptoms, constituting a choleraic variety of the disease, was often observed in our pernicious cases.   When the incidence of the disease fell on the intestinal mucous membrane profuse hæmorrhage was the more common result, as in the cases described in Surgeon MERRITT's report submitted below.§   The hæmaturic variety of hæmorrhagic malarial fever, which has attracted so much attention in the Southern States since the close of the war, does not seem to have been observed among our soldiers.   But in some of MERRITT's cases intense jaundice, which, with blood in the urine, is regarded as the characteristic symptom of the hæmaturic variety, appeared in connection with the hæmorrhagic extravasations from the intestinal mucous membrane.‖   In other instances the hæmorrhagic tendency was shown by petechiæ and vibices.   Dr. WOODWARD's cases, which

* See the report of Surgeon COOPER, p. 231 of the Appendix to Part I of this work.   Some of the cases referred to by Surgeon D. W. HAND, U. S. Vols., as occurring during the summer of 1863 in the 27th Mass. Vols., near New Berne, N. C., must also have presented marked cerebral symptoms, for he says: "I have reason to believe that some of these cases were mistaken for cerebro-spinal meningitis by the medical officers in attendance."

† In the Philadelphia *Med. and Surg. Reporter*, Vol. X, 1863, page 368: Private C., of Co. C, and private K., of Co. I, 101st Pa. Vols., who had presented nothing unusual during the night and previous day, were found on the morning of Sept. 25, 1863, in a state of insensibility.   Both lay motionless and no movement could be excited in either of them; their temperature was natural "or perhaps a little higher;" their skin moist or perspiring; pulse 80, regular and moderately full; countenance placid.   The eyes were open and looked natural, the pupils acting under the influence of light; they would follow an object moved before them, and away to a considerable distance, and close quickly when a sudden movement was made near and towards them.   To restore the patients blisters were applied to the cervical and dorsal portions of the spine, and carbonate of ammonia and quinine were administered.   For thirty-six hours they remained in this unmoved condition, the pulse meanwhile becoming weaker and the urine voided involuntarily.   Beef-extract was given as nourishment.   Two drops of croton oil were put on the tongue and copious dejections were followed by improvement in both cases.   The hearing was somewhat restored, and when the men's names were loudly called they made muttering efforts to speak.   Forty-eight grains of quinine were administered to private K. in twenty-four hours.   He recovered.   Private C. died fifty-two hours after the attack.   *Post-mortem* examination found the brain and its membranes normal.   Plymouth, North Carolina, where the regiment was stationed at this time, is surrounded by cypress swamps; 90 per cent. of the officers and men had been affected by miasmatic fevers.

‡ *Camp Diseases of the United States Armies*, Philadelphia, 1863, p. 174.

§ Page 142.

‖ The following sketch of hæmorrhagic malarial fever, as it appears in our medical literature since the war, is of interest in connection with Surgeon MERRITT's cases: In the autumn of 1867 Dr. T. C. OSBORN, of Greensboro', Ala.—*New Orleans Jour. Med.*, 1868, XX, p. 644—observed ten cases of a variety of malarial fever characterized by chills, nausea and vomiting, followed by sudden bronzing of the skin and hæmaturia; five of these proved fatal, in some instances with suppression of urine and uræmic convulsions.   In the recoveries convalescence was tedious.   All the patients were thoroughly imbued with the malarial poison, having been subject to intermittent attacks for a long time before the development of these unusual manifestations.   A few months later Dr. J. D. OSBORN, in an essay on Malignant Congestive Fever, read before the Greensboro' Medical Society and published in the *New Orleans Jour. Med.*, Vol. XXII, p. 61, added but little to the description of the disease already given by his father.   But from his paper it is understood that the new disease had become epidemic, and that the country people called it yellow fever.   His cases occurred during the period from September to April.   About the same time Dr. H. C. GHENT, of Port Sullivan, Texas, in a letter published in the *Richmond and Louisville Med. Jour.*, Vol. V, p. 271, described the disease as it occurred in his part of the country in 1866–67, and from the recurring chills, blood in the urine and the name, black jaundice, applied to the disease, as well as its fatality and occurrence only in cachectic individuals, it is apparent that the new malarial fever of Greensboro', Ala., was endemic in certain parts of Texas.   The next paper of importance which appeared was read by R. F. MICHEL, of Montgomery, Ala., before the Medical Association of the State of Alabama in March, 1869.   In it he defines the disease as "a malignant malarial fever following repeated attacks of intermittent, characterized by intense nausea and vomiting, very rapid and complete jaundiced condition of surface as well as most of the internal organs of the body, an impacted gall-bladder and hæmorrhage from the kidneys.   These phenomena presented themselves in an almost uninterrupted link, attended by remissions and exacerbations.   It is a fever peculiar to the United States."   In the record of an autopsy on a case of death from this disease, contributed by Dr. MICHEL, the brain was natural, its veins comparatively empty and its membranes jaundiced.   The thoracic organs were yellow-colored but otherwise normal.   The omentum and its fat were saffron-colored; the stomach filled with dark grumous bile and its mucous membrane thickened and injected, especially near the pylorus; the intestines normal.   The spleen was firm and solid, weighed nineteen and a half ounces and was about three times its normal size.   The liver was slightly enlarged, firm, solid and of a dark chocolate color; the gall-bladder was filled with an almost solid pasty pear-shaped mass, the smallest particle of which tinged a basin of water the color of saffron.   The kidneys were enlarged and of a pale-reddish color, but dark-green on section.   Dr. MICHEL embodied the impacted gall-bladder in his definition of the disease, but in subsequent cases it

were very fatal, presented these characteristics.   Perhaps the depravation of the blood which gave origin to the petechial blotches was due, as suggested by him, to the concurrent action of a scorbutic taint; but this must be considered doubtful, for, as will be seen hereafter, these

was found to contain a thick greenish-black bile, the impaction in this case being only an aggravation of the usual condition; the spleen also has been found to be more frequently softened and filled with disorganized blood than firm and solid.

The new disease was attributed by J. D. OSBORN to the uncared-for condition of the country. Dr. WM. A. GREENE, of Americus, Ga., in the *Richmond and Louisville Med. Jour.*, 1872, Vol. XIII, p. 149, in an article entitled Miasmatic Hæmaturia, speaks of the almost entire neglect of drainage consequent on the changed condition of agricultural pursuits since the war. Dr. NORCOM, of Edenton, N. C., in his address on Hæmorrhagic Malarial Fever, read before the State Medical Society in 1874, gave expression to similar opinions: "Before the war, the Southern States were in a high state of cultivation and the lands thoroughly drained, hence the malignant forms of malarial disease, as a general rule, were not known except in very low badly-drained swamp lands. Within the past eight years, owing to so much land lying waste, defective drainage and the general unsanitary condition of the country, the malarial poison has acted with intense virulence, and caused the disease we are now considering." In fact the morbid state was generally regarded as malarial in its origin, but no satisfactory explanation of its evolution was presented. Dr. E. D. McDANIEL, of Camden, Alabama, considered this question in his article on Hæmorrhagic Malarial Fever in the Transactions of the State Medical Association, 1874, p. 297. He says: "Why should those localities which, years ago, showed the most unequivocal and extreme influences of malaria by annual autumnal visitations of congestive or pernicious intermittent, remittent and pseudo-continued malarial fevers, almost putrid in general intensity, have not, in those times, presented with considerable frequency and in considerable numbers cases of this now justly dreaded scourge? And why did those same localities, soon after the earliest November frosts, become in old times as healthful, so far as fevers are concerned, as mountain tops, while the insatiate malaria of to-day relentlessly pursues its bleeding victims in mid-winter, when the air is filled with snow-flakes and the forests are hung with icicles? And why are some places once so salubrious that they knew no malarial fevers at all, or if any, only the mildest intermittents, then popularly regarded as trivial and almost harmless, now not exempt from even this the direst of all malarial ills—the very summation of all extreme malarial manifestations? * * * * I have seriously pondered this whole subject, and I am fully convinced that the grave, new order of symptoms now occurring in malarial fever in Alabama and the adjacent States, even in localities not heretofore known as specially insalubrious, is not due to any marked increase in the quantity, intensity or extension of malaria; for with exception, perhaps, of 1867 and 1868, the average numerical manifestations of malaria have been fewer since the advent of the icterode hæmorrhagic period than they were before that period set in. Nor to any allotropic or otherwise modified condition of malaria, be this chemical or dynamical, or sporoid in its nature; nor to any marked deterioration of the blood and constitution due to depression of spirit or exhaustion of body, but to a *wide-spread* epidemic influence." It is to be regretted that none of the observers gave any consideration to the character of the water-supply in these virulent manifestations of malarial disease. The violence of the morbid action occurring at a time when exhalations from a malarious soil were not available in explanation, and the occasional appearance of two or more cases in the same household indicating a local cause, in the absence of contagious qualities, are facts suggestive of water-infection.

The publication of the articles which have been mentioned attracted the attention of the profession to the hæmaturic fever, and a number of papers on the subject have since appeared in the journals recording cases and discussing the pathology and treatment of the disease. But first it was denied that OSBORN'S new disease was a hitherto unobserved expression of malarial poisoning. Dr. J. C. FAGET, in the *New Orleans Med. Jour.*, 1869, p. 768, in reviewing MICHEL'S paper, called attention to the facts that this disease, although new to the majority of our Southern practitioners, had been described by DUTROULAU and other French authorities as occurring in the colonies in Madagascar, Cayenne and the West Indies, and that he himself in 1859 and 1864 had treated of Hæmorrhagic Paludal Fever, and specially of its hæmaturic form. The hæmatemesic variety, he contended, had been frequently seen in New Orleans, but had been generally confounded by medical men with yellow fever. Indeed, J. C. CUMMINGS, of Monroe, Ala., in the *New Orleans Med. News and Hosp'l Gaz.*, 1859–60, Vol. VI, p. 811, records six cases which differ in no respect from those afterwards described by OSBORN and others, and refers to the prevalence of the disease during previous seasons. NORCOM instanced McLEAN'S article on malarial fevers in *Reynold's Practice* to show the familiarity of that writer with a hæmorrhagic variety of the disease. The cases which are described at length by our Southern brethren dwell upon the blood in the urine and in the serum which collects after the application of blisters; but other hæmorrhages appear to have been rare, although mention is occasionally made of bleeding from the nose, mouth and stomach. Dr. FAGET, as already intimated, considers that hæmorrhage from the stomach is a frequent expression of the morbid action. "And when I speak of large clots of blood, still red, let no one imagine that I then saw blood coming from the nasal fossa or from the gums, swallowed, and, afterwards, ejected before undergoing the influence of the acid of the gastric juice. By no means. I beg that I may have the credit of examining things closely, and that I may not be charged with having committed an error of so grave a character." Hence NORCOM so enlarges the lines used by MICHEL in defining the disease that its name of necessity becomes Hæmorrhagic Malarial Fever instead of Malarial Hæmaturia as given by those whose field of observation had been restricted to the one hæmorrhagic manifestation. He says: "A malignant malarial fever, the result of frequent attacks of intermittent, or of a prolonged and exhausting remittent, characterized by hæmaturia, hæmatemesis, epistaxis, enterorrhagia, metrorrhagia or hæmorrhage from the gums and fauces, or from two or three at the same time; most distressing and incessant nausea and vomiting, and complete jaundiced condition (greenish-yellow hue) of body. The cold stage, though not always, is generally well marked, and the paroxysms oftenest recur about every ten or twelve hours, but far more frequently the fever is uninterrupted by intermission or remission." A few years later, in 1874, the work of BÉRENGER-FÉRAUD, *De la Fièvre Bilieuse Mélanurique des Pays Chauds comparée avec la Fièvre Jaune*, and in 1875, his chapter on *Melanuric fever* in his *Traité Clinique des Maladies des Européens au Sénégal*, show the existence of a disease which corresponds in its general features with the American hæmaturic fever with the exception that the dark color of the urine is attributed to the presence of a large quantity of biliary matters. Relying upon the accuracy of M. BÉRENGER-FÉRAUD'S observations and experiments, the writer of a review of his work in the *American Jour. Med. Sciences*, New Series, Vol. LXIX, p. 163, throws doubt upon the hæmaturia so frequently reported by our American practitioners, and suggests that they may have been deceived by the biliary coloring matters with which the system is so thoroughly pervaded. Dr. FAGET begged that he might have the credit of examining things closely. If our other observers did not emphasize in like manner it is probably due to the fact that they could not realize that their testimony as to blood in the urine would be questioned, constituting as this condition did, with the concurrent jaundice, the pathognomonic symptom of the disease under observation. M. BÉRENGER-FÉRAUD regards melanuric fever as differing only from other expressions of acute malarial poisoning in having an excessive secretion of bile replacing the more usual perspirations or choleraic discharges. Our American writers allow the presence of bile in the urine, as the whole system seems deluged with it, but they are positive as to the presence of blood, not only as manifested by a coloration due to the dissolved hæmatine of disorganized blood corpuscles, in which case the symptom is regarded as an effort to restore the blood to its normal constitution by the elimination of the debris of its destroyed corpuscular elements, but as shown by the presence of the red corpuscles themselves, and even in many cases by unmistakable blood-clots which must be regarded as the result of a true hæmorrhage from ruptured capillaries during a stage of active congestion. McDANIEL regards the hæmorrhage as due to interrupted cutaneous action such as explains the hæmaturia in rheumatic, catarrhal and scarlatinal cases. The sudden appearance of jaundice when there is no apparent obstacle to the free passage of bile from the system by the alimentary canal has been referred for explanation, by Professor JOYNES in the *Richmond and Louisville Med. Jour.*, Vol. XXIII, p. 222, to the following from NIEMEYER'S chapter on Hæmatogenous Icterus in his *Text-Book of Practical Medicine*, Vol. I, p. 684: "The views regarding the occurrence of jaundice without retention and reabsorption of bile have totally changed since the observations of VIRCHOW, KÜHNE and HOPPE-SEYLER have shown that bile-coloring matter may be formed from the free coloring matter of the blood without the action of the liver; and we may induce artificial jaundice in animals by injecting substances that dissolve the blood corpuscles. There is now no doubt that some of the formerly enigmatical forms of icterus are due to the disintegration of blood corpuscles, and the transformation of the freed coloring matter circulating in the blood into bile-coloring matter. This is particularly true of those cases of icterus occasionally caused by poisoning from chloroform or ether; for, as experiment proves, these substances possess the power of dissolving blood corpuscles. . . . . This mode of origin is very probable, though not absolutely proved, for other varieties of jaundice, as in that

blotches in fulminant malarial cases were found oftentimes in men who had been robust and healthy until struck down by the pernicious influence. Surgeon JACKSON, 11th Pa., Vols., in a report, hereafter presented, describes a number of cases which occurred in a command camped in and around Annapolis, Md., in the winter of 1861. Some of the regimental surgeons reported these cases under the head of *typhus fever*, others called them *spotted fever:* Surgeon JACKSON designated them at first as *malignant .congestive fever*, and afterwards simply as *congestive fever*, and his reports indicate that he looked upon them as congestive intermittents modified by the overcrowded condition of the buildings occupied by his regiment as barracks. The petechial spots, the uncoagulated condition in which the blood was found in the fatal cases, and the early period at which *post-mortem* putrefaction set in, strongly favor the view that the disease was cerebro-spinal meningitis; but the absence during life of the usual brain symptoms of cerebro-spinal fever is opposed to this view. In many of the fatal cases the mind was clear to the last. Moreover the necropsies made by Surgeon JACKSON show that although the cerebral membranes were congested they were free from deposits of lymph or pus. It might be urged that winter is not the season at which cases of congestive intermittent fever would be likely to occur; but the statistics of the war show that as a matter of fact. congestive intermittents did occur at all seasons of the year, and in JACKSON's own regiment as well as in other regiments in the vicinity, cases of ordinary intermittent fever were occurring side by side with the pernicious cases under discussion; as indeed ordinary intermittents were occurring during the same months in all parts of our armies. The dangerous hæmorrhagic fever since prevalent in the South is of frequent occurrence during the winter months. The cases observed by Dr. J. D. OSBORN, which formed the basis of his paper calling attention to the hæmorrhagic form, occurred between the months of September and April. Again, the mortality of the Annapolis cases does not correspond with the usual mortality of cerebro-spinal meningitis. The monthly sick reports of the 11th Pa. Vols. show that during January, 1862, there were 7 cases and 3 deaths in the regiment; during February 17 cases and 1 death; during March 2 cases and no deaths: in all 26 cases and 4 deaths. During the same period there were 13 cases of quotidian intermittent fever and 11 of remittent fever, one of the latter fatal. Surgeon JACKSON attributed the small number of deaths among his petechial cases after January not merely to the improved hygienic condition of the regiment, but to the fact that he had recognized the malarial character of the disease and resorted to the appropriate treatment.

occurring after snake-bites, in that observed constantly in yellow fever, quite often in recurrent (relapsing) fever, septicæmia and puerperal fever, and more rarely in other infectious diseases, and acute diseases accompanied by severe fever." Commenting on this extract Professor JOYNES remarks: "The destructive action of the malarial poison upon the blood-discs is so well proved that none will question it; and if we admit that under such intense and concentrated action of the morbific agent as that which induces an attack of hæmorrhagic malarial fever, this destructive effect is unusually rapid and extensive, the applicability of the above view to the icterus occurring in this disease becomes at once obvious, and the relationship between that symptom and the hæmaturia receives important elucidation." Recent researches have cleared away much of the difficulties that surrounded this subject. Thus, PONFIC—*Hæmoglobinuria—Berlin Klin. Wochen.*, 1883, No. 26—sustains by further experimental evidence the view that the destruction of the red corpuscles within the vessels is the essential element of the process. Having introduced blood dissolved by freezing into the veins of an animal, he found that the remains of the destroyed corpuscles were taken up by the spleen while the coloring matter was removed by the liver; but when there was an excess of hæmoglobine the kidneys participated in the excretion. When the blood has been so deteriorated that the action of these organs is insufficient to remove the detritus the patient becomes jaundiced by the metamorphosis of hæmoglobine into bilirubin within the current of the circulation.

The treatment adopted for the disease is based upon the recognition of its malarial causation. Quinine is given in free and repeated doses, by the stomach, if the gastric irritation can be allayed sufficiently for its introduction in this way, or failing this, by the rectum or hypodermic injection. Many practitioners consider an evacuant dose of calomel of advantage preparatory to the administration of quinine. NORCOM allays the vomiting by the hypodermic injection of morphine, and refers to the fears entertained by many lest the opium lead to suppression and uræmic convulsions, mentioning some cases where uræmic symptoms, which had already appeared, yielded after the exhibition of the morphine. BÉRENGER-FÉRAUD also approves of the use of opiates. Medication is seldom addressed specially to the hæmorrhage. But some writers have objected to the generally accepted methods. Thus McDANIEL urges as the first care of the practitioner in these cases the control of the hæmorrhage from the kidneys by the restoration of cutaneous action, which he endeavors to effect by the application of hot air and vapor-baths, &c., or by alternating these with cold affusions as stimulants to the general surface. He is doubtful as to the benefit to be derived from quinine, and instances the aggravation or recurrence of the hæmaturia under its influence. Other practitioners have also claimed that quinine was injurious. MALONE, in the *Mississippi Valley Med. Monthly*, Vol. I (1881), p. 62, while he does not believe that quinine will produce the disease, thinks that he has often seen it precipitate an attack in those predisposed. He regards the fever as due to the presence of a micro-organism, and claims great success for the hyposulphite of soda in thirty-grain doses with one fluid drachm of extract of buchu given every three hours.

III.—CHRONIC MALARIAL POISONING.—Those soldiers who had been long exposed to malarial influences frequently became the subjects of a peculiar form of cachexia known as *chronic malarial poisoning* or *malarial cachexia*. It was generally observed in men who had already suffered from acute attacks of malarial disease, but it appeared also as a primary affection in those who had never been attacked by fever.* This chronic disorder was essentially an anæmia accompanied by more or less of hepatic disorder and enlargement of the spleen. The complexion was early modified, acquiring a peculiar yellowish pallor, which was usually unaccompanied by any icteroid tinge of the conjunctiva. The skin became dry and harsh, the lips livid and the tongue large, flabby, pale or of a faintly bluish tint, indented on the sides, and generally fissured on the dorsum, which was thinly covered with a whitish or yellowish coat. The patient lost his appetite and suffered from pains and aches in the bones and muscles, and frequently from neuralgia. In some, muscular debility was associated with tremors, which prevented the individual from assuming the erect position. Choreic movements and paralysis agitans are also referred to as having occurred. The patient became dull in mind, depressed in spirit, homesick, indisposed to undertake any work involving even slight exertion and unable to carry it out from physical disability. The heart appeared to be early influenced by the debility affecting the muscular system; probably many cases of sudden death were due to heart-failure.† At first the bowels were constipated, but generally, on account of the conditions of camp life, diarrhœa supervened and became very intractable.

That a notable alteration in the quality of the blood was one of the first results of malarial poisoning, was manifested by the anæmic appearance of the patients. This blood-change was intimately connected with the generally accompanying enlargement of the spleen; but the enlargement was not in all cases proportioned to the cachectic condition. In most instances the increase in bulk of the spleen could be detected by careful physical exploration, and in some it was very marked. Disorder of the liver and kidneys could also generally be discovered in these cases. In many, œdema of the feet and legs, and even ascites, appeared, due to organic changes in the viscera in some instances, but in others, in which no organic lesions could be discovered, the serous transudation must be attributed to the altered condition of the blood and the weakness of the circulation.

IV.—POST-MORTEM RECORDS AND PATHOLOGY OF MALARIAL DISEASE.

I.—POST-MORTEM RECORDS.—A full history of the attack is seldom given in these cases, but *ante-mortem* notes, when taken, were of the same general character as those already submitted in the clinical records. The tongue was coated or furred, dry during the fever, moist at other times, occasionally brown in color. Diarrhœa was a prominent symptom, but sometimes constipation was present, with anorexia, thirst, vomiting, jaundice and

---

* Sir JOSEPH FAYRER in his *Tropical Diseases*, London, 1881, p. 222, says: "Malarious enlargement of the spleen, and the attendant or consequent cachexia, are frequently, but by no means constantly, the result of repeated recurrences of malarious periodic or remittent fever in those long exposed to such influences; and when the patient has previously suffered from ague it is to be expected that whilst the *spleen remains affected, so long* will the person be liable to *recurrence* of paroxysms of fever. These, however, are not by any means the most serious or obstinate cases of splenic cachexia; on the contrary, they are often more tractable and amenable to remedial measures than others apparently of a less formidable though more chronic nature, which not infrequently present themselves in a marked form where no fever has previously occurred."

† Surgeon TOWLE, of the 30th Massachusetts, in his paper cited *supra*, p. 119, says: "In August, 1862, a patient convalescing in my regimental hospital from malarial fever, who had recovered sufficiently to walk out of doors, by a mistaken order of his commanding officer, was stripped and washed with water brought from the river. In the midst of the washing he fell back, gasped feebly a few times, and before I reached him, though near by, he was dead." Dr. TOWLE regarded the fatal consequences as due to the inability of the enfeebled and enervated heart to overcome the check received by the circulation.

abdominal pain. The pulse was frequent, ultimately becoming imperceptible. There were pains in the head, back and limbs. Delirium, cough, dyspnœa, hiccough, profuse sweats, involuntary discharges and coma led to the fatal result in remittent cases. Convulsions were occasionally regarded as the manifestation of a cerebro-spinal engorgement due to the malarial poison. The symptoms in some cases are of interest as suggesting the *ante-mortem* formation of heart-clot.

The autopsies in the nine cases, recorded below, of death from intermittent fever, show that the fatal result depended on congestion of certain of the internal organs, the hyperæmia in some instances leading to the formation of inflammatory products. No one organ appears to have been specially liable to injury by the malarial influence; for in one or more of these cases the brain, lungs, heart, stomach, intestines, liver, spleen and kidneys are reported healthy, while in others they were found in an abnormal condition, to which the symptoms observed during life may with propriety be referred. In case 53 the force of the disease-poison was expended on the lungs, causing fatal congestion, and although fever of a paroxysmal type had persisted for some time, and the symptoms had at one time assumed a typhoid character, no diseased condition was observed in the intestines; the stomach was normal and the liver healthy; the brain and spleen were not examined. As there is no clinical record in 54, the *post-mortem* appearances must be taken in connection with the diagnosis of intermittent fever. The stomach and intestines were healthy, as were the lungs, but the heart, liver and especially the spleen were markedly altered. The recurrence of aggravated paroxysms in 55 caused the patient to fall into an adynamic condition marked by sordes, imperceptible pulse, profuse perspirations, hiccough, stertor, insensible pupils and involuntary passages; and these symptoms were associated with congestion of the brain and left lung, pericardial adhesions, notable alteration in the liver and spleen and patches of congestion in the ileum. In 56, which presented diarrhœa, vomiting and jaundice, the small intestine was of a purple color, the stomach ecchymosed, the liver altered in color and the lungs congested in their posterior portions; but the brain, heart and spleen were normal. In 57, after the suppression of the paroxysms, the patient instead of recovering his usual health became morose, apathetic and ultimately comatose, while affected with cough and diarrhœa, symptoms which might be considered obscurely suggestive of typhoid fever or of that fever as masked by the presence of the malarial cachexia. But the autopsy revealed such indications of repeated congestion of the brain as might be conceived to account for the cerebral symptoms, while the intestines presented no other lesion than patches of congestion in the ileum and of black pigment in the sigmoid flexure; broncho-pneumonia and nutmeg liver were present, yet the spleen was normal. A special interest attaches to this case, as the manuscript bears, in Dr. WOODWARD's hand-writing, the words "Typho-malarial fever. *Note.*"—as indicating that it was intended to occupy a prominent place in the expression of his views regarding this fever. It seems evident, however, by a reference to the time which elapsed between the suppression of the paroxysms and the date of death, that there was no specific typhoid element in the case, else the agminated glands would have been found extensively ulcerated. Case 58 is from the clinical stand-point an undoubted typho-malarial fever, if such a fever is susceptible of diagnosis. A continued adynamic fever persisted after the suppression of the chills, but the intestines were not altered from the healthy condition. In 59 the necropsical record indicates that the force of the disease was expended on the lining membrane of the intestinal canal. In 60 there was latent pneumonia, with heart-clot and affection of the liver, spleen and kidneys; and in 61 a coincidence of tubercular disease and malarial manifestations.

CASE 53.—Private Thomas W. Parker, Co. F, 3d Md. Cav., was admitted from Prince street prison October 10, 1864. The patient stated that he had suffered for some time from regular paroxysms of ague. His condition on admission indicated great nervous depression. Quinine and whiskey were prescribed, and the bowels moved by compound cathartic pills. Six days later the fever assumed a typhoid type, but this was speedily followed by an improvement, the tongue becoming moist and clean, the pulse 85 and the skin natural. On the 21st, after having been unusually comfortable and even lively during the morning, he complained in the afternoon of dyspnœa, for which counter-irritants were applied, and as there was some cough, an expectorant mixture was given. At 5 P. M., after eating a good meal of bread and milk, he was suddenly seized with intense dyspnœa; in the course of half an hour convulsions set in, and he died shortly after. Stimulants, friction of the extremities, etc., were tried without effect. *Post-mortem* examination eighteen hours after death: Both lungs were much congested throughout, with the exception of a small portion of the anterior border of each; they contained no tubercles, nor was any other lesion observed in them. Nothing abnormal could be detected in the stomach or intestines. The liver was healthy. The other organs were not examined.—*Third Division Hospital, Alexandria, Va.*

CASE 54.—Private Patrick Bradley, 17th Ind. Bat'y; age 25; was admitted October 11, 1862, with intermittent fever, and died November 9. *Post-mortem* examination: There were pleuritic adhesions on the left side; the pericardium contained four ounces of serum; the heart was enlarged and fatty. The stomach was normal; the liver greatly enlarged and congested; the gall-bladder distended and ulcerated near its duct; the spleen much enlarged, softened and infiltrated with pus in its upper part. The circular fibres of the colon were strongly contracted in its entire length.—*H. Pierce, Ass't Surg., 150th N. Y., Stewart's Mansion, Baltimore, Md.*

CASE 55.—Private John McVea, Co. B, 10th U. S. Inf.; age 32; was admitted October 20, 1865, having been sick five weeks, first with diarrhœa for two weeks and afterwards with chills and fever. He had a chill daily at 3.30 P. M., for which five grains of quinine were ordered at 8, 10, 12 and 2 o'clock. During the paroxysms the patient's intellect was clouded and his replies delayed; he fainted on sitting up; passed his urine involuntarily; had pain in the head, back and limbs; the heart's action was tumultuous; the pulse too rapid to count, and most frequent at the commencement of the sweating. Some roughness of the heart-sounds were observed. The tongue was coated, dry during fever, moist at other times; the bowels were open. On the 22d the quinine was repeated, but the chill and fever recurred in a more aggravated form. The patient was very weak; had sordes on his teeth; pulse scarcely perceptible at the wrist; urination involuntary. Whiskey was given and mustard applied to the epigastrium. Next day he had hiccough, stertor, profuse sweats, vomiting of small blood-clots, dysphagia, insensible pupils and involuntary passages; crepitation was heard over the lower part of the left side of the chest. He died at 2.30 P. M. *Post-mortem* examination twenty hours after death: Right arm flexed and rigid; left arm flaccid. There was a quantity of serum in the ventricles of the brain; the brain-substance was of a darker ash color than usual, and sections presented many points of black engorged vessels. The right lung was healthy; the lower lobe of the left lung much congested, nearly hepatized. The pericardium contained three ounces and a third of light-pink serum; the apex of the heart adhered to the pericardium by a lymph-patch the size of a shelled almond; the right ventricle of the heart was unusually flaccid, the mitral valve thickened and of a dull yellow color. The omentum was thin and dark lead color. The liver weighed eighty-five ounces; it was of a dull slate color. The spleen was pulpy, weighed twenty ounces and a half. Some patches of congestion were observed in the ileum. The kidneys were large but healthy.—*Douglas Hospital, Washington, D. C.*

CASE 56.—Private Leonard Bennett, Co. D, 199th Pa. Vols., was admitted June 30, 1865, suffering from intermittent fever. There was great emaciation with a yellow tinge of the conjuctiva and skin, anorexia, occasional vomiting, five or six loose passages daily and restlessness; the tongue was moist and slightly furred; pulse 70 and feeble. He died August 15. *Post-mortem* examination twenty-four hours after death: Body emaciated and rigid. Brain normal. Lungs intensely congested in their posterior portions. Heart normal. Liver of light color superficially, blackened anteriorly and below; bile yellow and granular. Spleen firm and of normal size; pancreas normal. Stomach presenting blood-spots in its mucous membrane. Small intestines generally discolored and very offensive; jejunum black or dark purple; ileum cherry-colored in its upper part, darker below. Kidneys large.—*Ass't Surg. George M. McGill, U. S. A., Hick's Hospital, Baltimore, Md.*

CASE 57.—Private James Hight, Co. D, 23d Ohio Vols.; age 23; was admitted January 18, 1865, with tertian intermittent fever. He had chills at irregular intervals succeeded by profuse sweating; his intellect was unnaturally dull; he would not eat nor try to help himself though he appeared strong; he had no pain; pulse regular and compressible. The chills yielded readily to quinine, but he remained without appetite or energy. After the first week he declined gradually, becoming morose in disposition and absent-minded, and affected with cough and diarrhœa. On February 20 he was reported as emaciated and imbecile; he had no diarrhœa but passed his stools in bed. On March 1 he rallied so as to answer simple questions correctly; but he had dyspnœa, much expectoration and extensive crepitus in both lungs. On the 5th he became half comatose with quick short breathing, and died on the evening of that day. *Post-mortem* examination thirteen hours after death: Much emaciation; blister mark on back of neck. There was effusion under the cerebral membranes, which were not injected but pale; the arachnoid at the foramen of Bichat was thick, opaque and white; the ventricles were distended with serum; there was a cream-colored spot of softening, apparently covered by serous membrane, on the ventricular wall formed by the right corpus striatum; the middle commissure was remarkably firm, as it stretched out to nearly an inch in length and so remained without breaking across; the substance of the cerebrum was hard, that of the cerebellum and cord soft. The anterior mediastinum was emphysematous. The bronchi in the right lung and in the lower lobe of the left lung, especially behind and below, were dilated, of a dark purple color and filled with a pus-like fluid, while the lung-tissue around them was here and there dark and solid, the affected lobes as seen from the surface being sunken and of a dark lead color. The heart contained a fibrinous clot. The liver was large and finely marked with nutmeg foliations; the spleen normal. There were patches of reddening along the ileum, and pigment patches in the sigmoid flexure.—*Third Division Hospital, Alexandria, Va.*

CASE 58.—Horace Hill, a robust muscular man, age 25 years; colored; was admitted November 7, 1865, with quotidian intermittent fever; tongue yellow-coated; appetite poor; pulse during the intervals of the paroxysm 84, full and of good strength; bowels quite regular; urine scanty and of high color; no difficulty of breathing; no œdema of the feet and legs. After treatment for two days the chills left the patient, but a febrile pulse remained; two days later sordes appeared on the teeth and lips, and the tongue became exceedingly dry; mental torpor and slight delirium were manifested. There was fulness and slight tenderness on pressure in the right hypochondrium and greater precordial dulness than natural. Moderate vomiting took place about noon of the 13th, and in a few minutes the patient suddenly and unexpectedly died. *Post-mortem* examination sixteen hours after death: The right ventricle of the heart much dilated; spleen greatly enlarged and softened; liver much enlarged; kidneys fatty; other organs normal.—*Surgeon Edwin Bentley, U. S. Vols., L'Ouverture Hospital, Alexandria, Va.*

CASE 59.—Private W. P. Jones, Co. M, 3d U. S. Art'y, was admitted September 5, 1863, and died on the 10th, of intermittent fever. *Post-mortem* examination twenty-four hours after death: Both lungs were congested and adherent. The heart was hypertrophied and coated on its exterior with a thick layer of adipose tissue. The liver was slightly enlarged, its concave surface congested and of a dark bluish color, which extended about one-eighth of an inch into the substance of the organ. The spleen was congested and dark colored. The intestinal canal contained a black mixture of coagulated blood and mucus; its mucous membrane was deeply congested and almost black.—*Act. Ass't Surg. J. A. Murphy, West End Hospital, Cincinnati, Ohio.*

CASE 60.—Quartermaster-Sergeant William L. Billman, Co. H, 3d Pa. Art'y; age 38; was admitted January 22, 1864, with intermittent fever and died March 7. He was able to walk about up to the evening of his death; he was present at inspection, undressed himself and went to bed apparently feeling well. *Post-mortem* examination twenty-four hours after death: Both lungs were in the third stage of pnuemonia; there were adhesions on both sides and three ounces of liquid in the left pleural sac. The pericardium contained four ounces of liquid. The aortic valves were thickened; on one of them was a considerable quantity of adherent fibrin; the left side of the heart contained coagula of fibrin. The liver was hypertrophied; the spleen large and soft; the left kidney much larger than the right, and the pelves of both kidneys contained pus. [No. 336, Medical Section, Army Medical Museum, is the heart from this case.]—*Act. Ass't Surg. B. B. Miles, U. S. A., Jarvis Hospital, Baltimore, Md.*

CASE 61.—Private William T. Griffey, Co. G, 1st Conn. Cav.; age 23; was admitted January 12, 1864, with intermittent fever. He died April 7. *Post-mortem* examination: The right lung was tuberculous. The left pleural sac and the pericardium contained effused serum. The liver was enlarged and tubercles were diffused through its substance; it weighed four pounds ten ounces. The spleen was soft and friable; it weighed sixteen ounces.—*Act. Ass't Surg. B. B. Miles, U. S. A., Jarvis Hospital, Baltimore, Md.*

In the next case the intermissions disappeared and the patient became affected with remittent fever; yet the *post-mortem* appearances did not differ from those already described. The stomach, lungs and kidneys had suffered, but the other thoracic and abdominal organs were not perceptibly altered.

CASE 62.—Private Henry Morton, Co. E, 56th Mass. Vols. (colored); age 30; was admitted December 16, 1864, from field hospital, with intermittent fever. The paroxysms were checked by quinine, and the patient was soon able to walk about. About December 31 he had an attack of diarrhœa, which was readily controlled by astringents. A few days later his ague recurred, and persisted in spite of the administration of quinia. The disease assumed the pernicious form, the remissions being but slight; the respiration became hurried, and delirium setting in, he died January 9, 1865. *Post-mortem* examination: The left lung was congested. The mucous membrane of the stomach was of a dark yellow color and much softened. The kidneys were congested. No other abnormal appearances were observed. The brain was not examined.—*Act. Ass't Surg. F. Stoddard, L'Ouverture Hospital, Alexandria, Va.*

The twelve cases which follow are illustrations of remittent fever. In 63, the diagnosis, originally quotidian intermittent, was changed in the progress of the case to typhoid fever; but there was no diarrhœa during life, and no intestinal lesion was discovered at the necropsy; delirium was present, and there was an effusion of jaundiced serum in the ventricles and under the membranes of the brain. Delirium is mentioned as having been present in one other case, but in it the brain was not examined. The lungs were congested in two cases, 63 and 72, tubercular and splenified in one case, 69, and hepatized and infiltrated with pus in a fourth case, 73; in four cases they were unaffected; in one they were not examined, and in three their condition is not stated. The heart does not appear to have been subject to notable alteration; it is reported as normal in six cases and in the others its condition is not stated. The stomach contained a muddy-green liquid in two instances, 69 and 70. In all the cases except 63 the intestines were more or less affected. In two, 68 and 74, both the large and small intestines are said to have participated in the morbid action; in five, 64, 65, 67, 70 and 72, in which the intestines are stated to have been congested, inflamed or ulcerated, it is probable that the large and the small intestine were both intended to be included in the statement, for in 71 the inference that the large intestine was affected is fully warranted by the phraseology—"the intestines were ulcerated, the ulcers in the small intestine being of large size." In 70 the mucous membrane of the intestine was in part almost gangrenous, the duodenum ulcerated and the peritoneum inflamed; in 73 the intestines were congested and the ileum extensively inflamed; in 66 the small intestine presented signs of inflammation, but the condition of the large intestine is not recorded; in but one, 69, of the twelve cases is it definitely stated that although the small intestine was congested the large intestine was in its normal condition; in none was there any affection of Peyer's glands, but the solitary follicles near the ileo-cæcal valve were prominent in one instance, the case last mentioned.

The liver is reported as normal in two cases; in a third case nothing is stated regarding its condition; in nine cases it is variously described as large, fatty, pale, fawn-colored, bronzed, soft, congested, etc.

The condition of the spleen was normal or not stated in six cases; it was enlarged, soft or dark colored in five cases, and contained a purulent collection in one case, 74.

CASE 63.—Sergeant Owen Crossman, Co. H, 28th Mich. Vols.; age 45; was admitted February 5, 1865. Diagnosis—quotidian intermittent fever, changed on the 8th to typhoid fever. He had suffered from chills every night for two weeks, but had none after his admission. He was much emaciated and depressed in mind; had a slight dry cough but with easy and natural breathing; uneasy feelings in the upper part of the abdomen; darting pains in the abdomen and thorax; anorexia; thirst; his skin was dry but covered at times with a clammy sweat; bowels regular. On the 14th he had profuse perspiration, delirium and involuntary passages. He died next day. *Post-mortem* examination twenty-two hours after death: Skin jaundiced. Much effusion under arachnoid at vertex; brain-substance quite hard, most of the vessels having yellow spaces between tracks of black fluid blood; lateral ventricles full of liquid; choroid plexus showing bulbs of yellow liquid about the size of peas along its posterior lower edge; locus niger very dark and broad. A little high-colored but clear serum in the pericardium; small yellow fibrinous clots in the heart. Right lung so congested posteriorly by hypostasis as to sink in water, soft, gray-colored and adherent to walls of chest by many white bands; left lung dark but crepitant posteriorly, firmly adherent. Liver pale and fatty; gall-bladder the size of a butternut; spleen very large and soft, anæmic; kidneys pale.—*Third Division Hospital, Alexandria, Va.*

CASE 64.—Private John Gavallence (command not stated); age 27; was admitted July 8, 1863, from Alexandria jail, having been sick six weeks with bilious remittent fever. From his delirious mutterings he was supposed to be a rebel deserter. He did not rally sufficiently to converse rationally, but died on the 12th. *Post-mortem* examination ten hours after death: Liver and spleen somewhat enlarged; Brunner's glands enlarged; mucous coat of intestines extensively inflamed, but with no ulceration.—*Act. Ass't Surg. A. P. Crafts, Third Division Hospital, Alexandria, Va.*

CASE 65.—Marcellas F. Dixon, citizen of Missouri; age about 20; was admitted December 6, 1864, with remittent fever. He afterwards had erysipelas, and on recovery from this was attacked with diarrhœa and laryngitis. He died January 28, 1865. *Post-mortem* examination four hours after death: There was a tough frothy mucus in the trachea and bronchi; the larynx did not exhibit definite signs of inflammation. The pericardium contained effused serum. The right lung was adherent. The bowels were congested but not ulcerated; the mesenteric glands were enlarged.—*Act. Ass't Surg. J. B. Young, U. S. A., Rock Island Hospital, Ill.*

CASE 66.—Sergeant Charles M. Gould, Co. M, 3d Va. Cav.; age 20; was admitted June 5, 1863, with remittent fever. Quinine was administered with apparent success, but during convalescence the patient being imprudent in his diet, was attacked with diarrhœa, and died June 22. *Post-mortem* examination six hours after death: The liver was fawn-colored. The spleen was soft and measured eight inches by five. The small intestine contained some undigested food and its mucous membrane was slightly inflamed.—*Third Division Hospital, Alexandria, Va.*

CASE 67.—Private William Cornog, Co. A, 51st Pa. Vols.; age 34; was admitted August 7, 1864, with remittent fever. He was very ill when admitted, and for three days before death, on the 18th, suffered constantly from singultus. *Post-mortem* examination: The lungs and heart were normal. The thoracic cavity contained four ounces of serum and the abdominal cavity four ounces and a half. The liver, spleen and pancreas were normal. The kidneys were large and white, weighing six ounces and a half each. The intestinal mucous membrane was slightly ulcerated.—*McDougall Hospital, Fort Schuyler, N. Y. Harbor.*

CASE 68.—Private L. D. Johnson, 2d Ohio Battery, was admitted May 10, 1863, with remittent fever, having been sick since March. He died May 14. *Post-mortem* examination: Thoracic viscera normal. Liver large. Kidneys large, soft and fatty, weighing seventeen ounces. Mucous membrane of small intestine thickened and softened; large intestine congested.—*City Hospital, St. Louis, Mo.*

CASE 69.—Private John Ingraham, Co. C, 17th U. S. Inf'y; age 23; was admitted November 23, 1863, with remittent fever. He died November 26. *Post-mortem* examination: Body not much emaciated; rigor mortis well marked. There was some venous congestion in the membranes of the brain. The right lung weighed thirty-three ounces; its upper lobe contained tubercles, some of which were cretefied, and beneath these a cavity the size of a horse-chestnut; the middle lobe was healthy; the lower lobe splenified. The left lung weighed twenty-four ounces; it was firmly bound to the thoracic parietes by old adhesions, which also obliterated the division of the lobes; the posterior portion of its lower lobe was splenified and contained some tubercular deposits. The bronchial glands were large and black. The right auricle of the heart was greatly distended by fluid blood; there were no clots in any of the cavities. The liver was bronzed and weighed fifty-two ounces; the gall-bladder contained twenty-five drachms of bile. The spleen was firm and of a dark mahogany color. The pancreas was quite white but not very firm; it weighed three ounces. The kidneys were very much congested. The stomach was enormously distended with a muddy-green liquid. The mucous membrane of the small intestine was congested throughout and intensely purple; the valvulæ conniventes were prominent; Peyer's patches were not elevated; the solitary follicles near the ileo-cæcal valve were conspicuous, their summits being of a deeper purple than the adjacent mucous membrane. The large intestine was normal.—*Ass't Surg. Harrison Allen, U. S. A., Lincoln Hospital, Washington, D. C.*

CASE 70.—Private Elias Henderson, Co. A, 10th East Tenn. Cav.; age 46; was admitted September 11, 1863, having been sick in camp five days. His skin was yellow, urine high-colored, bowels moved slightly three to five times per day, abdomen somewhat tender, especially in the right hypochondriac region; pulse 80 and weak. He was much prostrated, vomited very frequently, and ejected food almost as soon as taken. Hiccough came on next day and continued with jaundice, vomiting, abdominal pain and increasing prostration until death occurred on the 20th. *Post-mortem* examination ten hours after death: The heart and lungs were not examined. The stomach contained about six ounces of dark grumous liquid, and was highly injected near the pylorus; four inches below the pylorus an ulcer three lines in diameter penetrated the coats of the intestine, which contained in this locality about an ounce of sanious pus. The mucous membrane of the intestinal canal was inflamed and in some parts almost gangrenous. There was some peritonitis, evidently recent. The pancreas was enlarged and scirrhous; the spleen softened; the liver somewhat enlarged and its peritoneal coat inflamed; the gall-bladder filled with dark inspissated bile; the kidneys normal.—*Hospital No. 2, Nashville, Tenn.*

CASE 71.—Private Dallas Sechler, Co. H, 92d Ill. Vols.; age 20; was admitted September 8, 1864, with remittent fever, and died on the 14th. *Post-mortem* examination on day of death: Lungs and heart normal; liver congested and softened; spleen eighteen ounces; kidneys normal; intestines ulcerated, the ulcers in the small intestine being of large size.—*Field Hospital, Chattanooga, Tenn.*

CASE 72.—Private Francis Felton, Co. M, 9th Ohio Vols.; age 27; was admitted August 27, 1864, with remittent fever, and died September 23. *Post-mortem* examination on day of death: Lungs somewhat congested; heart, spleen and kidneys normal; liver pale and soft; mucous membrane of intestines congested, softened and showing many ulcers, large and small.—*Field Hospital, Chattanooga, Tenn.*

CASE 73.—Private Orrin P. Tracy, Co. H, 3d Pa. Art'y; age 29; was admitted March 25, 1864, with remittent fever, and died April 8. *Post-mortem* examination: Extensive pleural adhesions on both sides; right lung infiltrated with pus; upper lobe of left lung hepatized; three ounces of effusion in pericardium; liver four pounds ten ounces and a half; left kidney ten ounces and a half, right seven ounces and a half, all normal in appearance. Intestines much congested and presenting extensive marks of inflammation in the ileum. No ulceration of Peyer's patches.—*Act. Ass't Surg. B. B. Miles, U. S. A., Jarvis Hospital, Baltimore, Md.*

CASE 74.—Private H. H. Wade, Co. A, 18th Mass. Vols., was admitted August 7, 1862, in a dying condition, probably from malarial fever. Death occurred next day. *Post-mortem* examination: Body much emaciated. The heart and lungs were healthy. The liver was sound. The spleen was moderately enlarged and its substance natural in appearance except that a part of the organ was reduced to a thin sanious puruloid liquid forming an abscess about as large as a goose's egg. This abscess was in contact with the diaphragm, the left extremity of the stomach and the edge of the left lobe of the liver, and was separated from the peritoneal cavity by adhesion of the spleen to the parts mentioned. The stomach was exceedingly contracted but healthy. The mucous membrane of the ileum and colon was inflamed, but the agminated glands were natural.—*Act. Ass't Surg. J. Leidy, Satterlee Hospital, Philadelphia, Pa.*

In the six cases, 75–80, the fever became complicated with dysentery, pneumonia, pericarditis or peritonitis. The brain was healthy in the only case in which it was examined. The heart was natural in two cases and unnoted in the others. In three the mucous membrane of the intestines was congested or ulcerated; in one the duodenum and pancreas were ulcerated. The stomach contained a mud-like liquid in two cases, 75 and 79, and its mucous membrane was thickened and slate-colored in one case, 80. The spleen was normal in one, unnoted in three, and enlarged in two cases. The liver was affected in three cases and unnoted in the others.

CASE 75.—Private Asa L. Patten, Co. I, 144th Ohio Vols.; age 24; was admitted February 6, 1865. Bilious malarial fever, with dysentery. Died February 8. *Post-mortem* examination six hours after death: Body very much emaciated. Heart containing a large fibrinous clot; liver enlarged; stomach distended with almost half a gallon of a dark grumous liquid; intestines congested and ulcerated; blood watery and degenerated—*Act. Ass't Surg. W. Bryan, Stanton Hospital, Washington, D. C.*

CASE 76.—Private Michael McCuskey, Co. F, 9th Ohio Cav.; age 18; was admitted February 22, 1864, with remittent fever, from which he recovered but remained weak and did not leave his bed. On March 25 pleuro-pneumonia set in, and death occurred on the 30th. *Post-mortem* examination seventeen hours after death: The lower lobe of the left lung was hepatized, exuding a red frothy liquid on section; the lower lobe of the right lung was hepatized; the right lung was covered with unorganized lymph; each pleural cavity contained twenty ounces of reddish serum. The heart was healthy; the liver presented the nutmeg appearance; the spleen and kidneys were large and congested; the mesenteric glands enlarged.—*Hospital No. 8, Nashville, Tenn.*

CASE 77.—Recruit Casper Christenson, 66th N. Y. Vols.; age 40; was admitted March 7, 1864, with remittent fever, for which quinine and brandy were given, but he did not improve. Two days before his death his left leg and ankle became enormously swollen and painful, and next day the right leg became similarly affected. He died March 18. *Post-mortem* examination forty-eight hours after death: There were old pleuritic adhesions on both sides. The pericardium contained about two ounces of bloody serum, and there were other evidences of recent pericarditis. Some old ulcers were observed in the intestines.—*Third Division Hospital, Alexandria, Va.*

CASE 78.—Private Uriah K. McFarland, Co. E, 4th Ind. Cav.; age 36; was admitted July 24, 1863, with chronic diarrhœa. He recovered and was doing light duty, when on December 25th he was attacked with remittent fever. He improved after the use of quinine for three days; his appetite returned and he was able to walk about, when, on January 5, 1864, the chill recurred and was followed by fever; bowels somewhat constipated. Three compound cathartic pills were given at once, and the quinine was again resorted to in six-grain doses. Next day he had a burning pain in the epigastrium, increased by pressure and deep inspiration, incessant nausea and vomiting, a white furred tongue, feeble pulse, 130, and short and hurried respiration. Morphia and warm fomentations were employed. On the 7th small and repeated doses of calomel and opium were given, and a blister was applied to the epigastrium, but the vomiting continued, and on the 8th hiccough, restlessness and great anxiety were added to the symptoms. On the 9th delirium supervened and the extremities became cold. He died next day, the vomiting and hiccough having ceased for some hours before death. *Post-mortem* examination eighteen hours after death: The peritoneum was much thickened; the omentum adhered to the intestines and anterior wall of the stomach; the serous coat of the large and small intestines was disorganized; the coats of the stomach were thickened; the spleen was twice the normal size, softened and friable.—*Hospital, Madison, Ind.*

CASE 79.—Private Samuel Clancy, Co. B, 1st N. Y. Vols. Admitted July 26, 1862. Diagnosis—pernicious fever. Died August 1st of peritonitis. Shortly before death this man vomited a considerable quantity of a dark olive-brown, muddy liquid. *Post-mortem* examination: The peritoneum was inflamed throughout its whole extent. Pseudo-membrane was found on the intestines, but they were not agglutinated. The stomach contained about a pint and a half of the mud-like liquid above mentioned. The mucous membrane presented a small patch of inflammation, but elsewhere appeared neither softened nor otherwise unhealthy. The mud-like liquid, examined microscopically, exhibited an abundance of epithelial cells but no distinct appearance of blood.—*Act. Ass't Surg. J. Leidy, U. S. A., Satterlee Hospital, Philadelphia, Pa.*

CASE 80.—Private Lewis T. Fisher, Co. K, 149th Pa. Vols.; age 20; was admitted March 26, 1864. Diagnosis—remittent fever. Died April 25. *Post-mortem* examination nine hours after death: Brain, lungs and heart healthy. The mucous membrane of the stomach was thickened and slate-colored. The intestines were much congested, and their serous coat, which was of a slate-blue color, was adherent to the abdominal walls. The upper half of the duodenum was extensively ulcerated and almost perforated in some places. The liver was much softened in the neighborhood of the gall-bladder; the spleen firm and healthy; the pancreas somewhat ulcerated along its attached surface. The left kidney was enlarged and much congested.—*Lincoln Hospital, Washington, D. C.*

Typhoid symptoms are spoken of in the two cases which follow, accompanying in the first case a relapse which was complicated with inflammation of the parotids, and in the other a pneumonic abscess; but in neither does the *post-mortem* record indicate the presence of an affection of the patches of Peyer.

CASE 81.—Private Adam Hauser, Co. G, 38th N. Y. Vols.; age 25; was admitted October 14, 1862, with remittent fever, which assumed a typhoid form, with dry tongue, diarrhœa and low delirium. During convalescence a relapse occurred, accompanied by inflammation and suppuration of the parotid glands. He died November 21. *Post-mortem* examination eighteen hours after death: Extreme emaciation. The lungs were healthy. The pericardium contained about four ounces of serum. Nothing abnormal was noted in the liver; the gall-bladder was moderately filled with bile. The spleen was enlarged and softened. The intestines were distended with flatus; their peritoneal coat was highly injected and their mucous coat softened. The kidneys and bladder were healthy.—*Third Division Hospital, Alexandria, Va.*

CASE 82.—Private Louis Buckmyer, Co. I, 37th Ohio Vols., was admitted October 24, 1862, with chronic diarrhœa terminating with symptoms resembling those of typhoid remittent fever. He died November 13. *Post-mortem examination*: Body extremely emaciated. There were pleuritic adhesions on the left side posteriorly, and an abscess of considerable size in the lower lobe of the right lung. The liver was enlarged. The mucous membrane of the small intestine was injected, softened and ulcerated.—*Third Division Hospital, Alexandria, Va.*

In the next case the patient, during convalescence from an attack of intermittent, appears to have been taken with true typhoid fever, developing diarrhœa and rose-colored spots at the end of the second week and ending fatally on the sixteenth day. The mucous membrane of the small intestine was ecchymosed and the agminated glands enlarged but not ulcerated.

CASE 83.—Corporal William T. Reeves, Co. L, 10th Ky. Cav., was admitted April 23, 1863, with intermittent fever. He had an attack of hiccough which continued for three days with but short intermissions; but he speedily convalesced under anodynes and quinine, and on May 10 was up and walking about the ward. On the 12th he was seized with colicky pains, which, on the two following days, became very severe, but were relieved by cathartics and opiates. From the 16th to the 20th he complained of headache and had considerable irregular fever. By the 24th diarrhœa had developed, with tenderness of the bowels and some mental confusion. Next day the tongue became dry, and on the following day glazed; stupor had set in, and there was tympanites of the abdomen with gurgling under pressure and an eruption of rose-colored spots, well marked, over the whole of the body. He died on the 27th after copious perspirations, great prostration and increased stupor. *Post-mortem* examination twelve hours after death: The rose-colored spots, which were very numerous on the trunk and also on the limbs, presented a purpuric appearance. The small intestine was mottled with purple, and there were two or three spots which seemed ready to slough; Peyer's glands were enlarged and inflamed but not ulcerated. The spleen was very large; the liver and the thoracic viscera healthy.—*Act. Ass't Surg. J. B. Smith, Washington Park Hospital, Cincinnati, Ohio.*

In the next case the patient, during the debility consequent on intermittent attacks, became sick with fever which proved fatal about the seventeenth day, the tongue in the meantime becoming dry, brown and fissured and the teeth covered with sordes. Peyer's glands usually become ulcerated at an earlier period of the disease than this; but, as in the last case, death on the sixteenth day did not give ulceration of the patches as a *post-mortem* lesion although the disease was apparently enteric fever, it is probable that the poison was present in this case also; and in this connection it may be inquired if the occasional deposits of tubercle recorded as discovered in the ileum were not typhoid enlargements of the agminated and solitary glands. In 85 the relapse, which was accompanied with typhoid symptoms, may perhaps be regarded as an attack of enteric fever.

CASE 84.—Private James Coady, Co. B, 24th Vet. Res. Corps; age 21; was admitted February 2, 1865, with debility from malarial disease. The patient had a haggard look, but complained of nothing but weakness and inability to sleep; his tongue was slightly coated with white fur, bowels somewhat loose, pulse 90, skin natural. He said he had recently suffered from intermittent fever. Wine-bitters and quinine were given, with Dover's powder at night. He slept well during the following night, but in the morning he was feverish, his tongue dry and brown in the centre, his bowels loose, and he complained of pain in the right iliac region; there was also some cough, with pain in the right breast and dulness on percussion over the upper third of the right lung. Acetate of ammonia and brown mixture were given and the quinine continued. During the next few days the typhoid symptoms became more marked; deafness, fissured tongue and sordes. Milk-punch was ordered. He died on the 19th. *Post-mortem* examination: There were old pleuritic adhesions on both sides, but particularly on the right. The right lung was infiltrated with tubercle, some of which was softened, and there was some intercurrent pneumonia; the mucous membrane of the bronchial tubes was thickened and of a dark-purple color. The liver was large and somewhat cirrhosed; the spleen dark-brown and soft. There were patches of inflammation and occasional deposits of tubercle in the ileum. The mesenteric glands were enlarged.—*Third Division Hospital, Alexandria, Va.*

CASE 85.—Private John Herman, Co. F, 59th N. Y., was admitted September 9, 1864, jaundiced; convalescing from remittent fever. He was up for several days, but a relapse occurred and the disease assumed a typhoid character. Diarrhœa set in with much fever and tenderness over the abdomen. Death, on October 16, was preceded by low delirium, involuntary stools and retention of urine. *Post-mortem* examination: Lungs healthy; heart loaded with fat; liver of proper consistence but abnormally yellowish-brown; intestines injected with blood; Peyer's patches somewhat diseased but only slightly ulcerated; kidneys congested.—*Act. Ass't Surg. Henry Gibbons, jr., U. S. A., Douglas Hospital, Washington, D. C.*

In 86 a reference is made to typhoid symptoms, and the necropsy appears to have been held with the intent to discover whether these clinical features were dependent on enteric fever. The cases 87 to 91 are apparently of a similar character; no mention is made of typhoid symptoms, but the anatomical lesions in the small intestine differ from those above described as present in malarial fever and agree with those found in 83, in which enteric fever seems to have seized upon a convalescent from malarial disease. Although these cases appear to indicate that many others giving a record of typhoid symptoms were probably of an enteric nature, it may be noted, on the other hand, that, in cases 53, 55, 57, 58, 63, 64, 81 and 82, these symptoms were apparently unconnected with a specific lesion.

Case 86.—Charles Lassell, Co. L, 14th N. Y. Heavy Art'y; age 28; was admitted June 15, 1864, with remittent fever. On the 20th typhoid symptoms, including diarrhœa, were developed, and he died on the 22d. *Post-mortem* examination twenty hours after death: Some of Peyer's patches were enlarged and some inflamed, but none ulcerated. —*Third Division Hospital, Alexandria, Va.*

Case 87.—Private George Williams, 4th Mich. Vols.; age 19; was admitted August 10, 1862. Remittent fever. Died August 11. *Post-mortem* examination next day: The body was much emaciated. The thoracic organs were healthy. The spleen exhibited a remarkable number of the so-called Malpighian bodies, which were of uniform size, white and about the size of yellow mustard-seed. The liver, stomach, kidneys and pancreas were healthy. The mucous membrane of the intestines was more or less inflamed throughout, the redness being moderate; the glands of Peyer and the solitary glands were more than usually prominent.—*Act. Ass't Surg. J. Leidy, Satterlee Hospital, Philadelphia, Pa.*

Case 88.—Private Ananias Spangler, Co. K, 204th Pa. Vols.; age 19; was admitted October 28, 1864, with remittent fever and died November 9. *Post-mortem* examination nineteen hours after death: Body emaciated; rigor mortis marked; suggillation posteriorly; muco-purulent matter escaping from nostrils; large but superficial abscess in perinæum. The pharynx and œsophagus were normal. The larynx and trachea were filled with muco-purulent matter, but the mucous membrane was healthy. The right lung was adherent to the thoracic parietes by recent lymph; its posterior portions were infiltrated with pus. The left lung, heart and pericardium were healthy. The liver was darker in color than usual, but was otherwise healthy; the gall-bladder contained six drachms of bile. The spleen, pancreas and kidneys were normal, as were also the stomach and the greater portion of the small intestine. The lower part of the ileum presented three or four ulcers which appeared to be in Peyer's patches; but the patches were not thickened and the ulcers seemed to be healing. The colon and rectum were normal.—*Act. Ass't Surg. Thomas Bowen, Second Division Hospital, Alexandria, Va.*

Case 89.—Private Charles Reed, Co. C, 185th N. Y. Vols., was admitted January 17, 1865. Diagnosis—remittent fever. Died on the 21st. *Post-mortem* examination: The right lung weighed thirty-two ounces; its upper lobe was adherent and hepatized; the left lung weighed twenty-five ounces and had a slight tubercular deposit near its apex. The heart weighed ten ounces and was healthy; the liver seventy-six ounces, pale; the spleen twenty-four ounces, soft; the stomach was injected in spots and had one ulcer on its posterior wall; the duodenum and jejunum were healthy; the ileum thickened; Peyer's patches and the solitary follicles enlarged and thickened; the solitary follicles of the colon enlarged and infiltrated; the mesenteric glands much enlarged; the kidneys normal, each weighing six ounces.—*Act. Ass't Surg. H. Loewenthal, U. S. Vols., Fifth Army Corps Field Hospital, Army of Potomac.*

Case 90.—Private Perley J. Blodget, Co. H, 5th Wis. Vols.; age 21; was admitted October 17, 1864. Diagnosis—remittent fever. Died November 1. *Post-mortem* examination forty-eight hours after death: Eight ounces of serum in right and two ounces in left pleural sac, one ounce in pericardium and a pint in the abdominal cavity. Spleen soft, dark, weighing about two pounds; liver and kidneys normal; Peyer's patches in the lower ileum, and the solitary follicles in the cæcum and upper colon much thickened and ulcerated; mucous membrane of colon inflamed. —*Second Division Hospital, Alexandria, Va.*

Case 91.—Private Peter Blair, Co. I, 125th Ohio Vols.; age 21; was admitted November 17, 1863. Intermittent fever. Died December 9. *Post-mortem* examination eighteen hours after death: Slight emaciation. Lungs healthy; heart nine ounces, valves slightly thickened; liver fifty-nine ounces, healthy; gall-bladder large and distended with bile; spleen fourteen ounces; kidneys seven ounces each, normal; stomach healthy; Peyer's patches much thickened, some ulcerated; large intestine presenting a few superficial ulcers.—*Hospital No. 1, Nashville, Tenn.*

The five cases which follow come under the heading of *congestive chills*. In 92 the patient died comatose from cerebral congestion; but the liver, spleen and lungs were also affected and the blood was diffluent. In 93 the œdema and congestion of the abdominal viscera must be regarded as the result of the malarial influence, for, had the condition of the heart been responsible for them, the right lung would not have been reported as healthy. Violent convulsions took the place of the chill in 94. In 95 the fatal chill was accompanied with difficulty of breathing; but the *post-mortem* record declares the brain, lungs, liver, stomach, intestines and kidneys of normal size and perfectly healthy; the spleen was enlarged and there was a thrombus in the right auricle. Whether the heart-clot was concerned in the production of the fatal seizure is uncertain. But in 96 death apparently resulted from the formation of fibrinous clots in the cavities of the heart. They probably originated during the chill, when a tendency to stasis in the heart, increased by the incompetency of the valves, gave opportunity for their deposit. The muffling of the heart-sounds must be referred to an internal obstruction, since there was no excess of liquid in the pericardium nor other external condition to account for it. The other symptoms described are consistent with the theory of the *ante-mortem* formation of the clots in this instance.

CASE 92.—Private Henry Wolfus, Co. I, 187th N. Y. Vols.; age 25; was admitted May 10, 1865. Diagnosis—intermittent fever and cerebral congestion. The patient was quite cold and comatose; pulse irregular; respiration noisy. There was no dulness on percussion except over the posterior and lower part of the left lung. Warmth was applied to the feet, cold to the head and a large stimulating enema was administered. He died next day. *Post-mortem* examination eleven hours after death: Lower lobe of right lung hepatized; liver congested; spleen congested and softened; venous blood diffluent; cerebral sinuses and veins turgid; three ounces of serum in arachnoid.—*Slough Hospital, Alexandria, Va.*

CASE 93.—Stephen McLaughlin, who was discharged from 2d U. S. Art'y August 17, 1865, on account of premature old age, asthma and general debility from twenty years' service, was admitted September 11, confused in mind and with tremors of the limbs and voice; pulse 136; he appeared to have been drinking to excess. His legs were œdematous; abdomen full, tense and fluctuating; auscultation disclosed roughness of the heart-sounds with increased impulse, the sounds being heard all over the left side; there was absolute dulness from a little below the nipple to midway between that point and the crest of the ileum; the respiratory murmur was absent at the base of the left lung, puerile at its summit and on the right side; the left side of the chest was contracted, the right side enlarged. At 2 P. M. on the day of admission he experienced a severe chill, for which brandy and quinine were given and mustard applied. He recovered, but the chill recurred at 2.30 P. M. on the following day and he died at 7 P. M. *Post-mortem* examination seventeen hours after death: Body bloated; skin of the head dark and livid; a thick greenish liquid flowing from the mouth. The brain was normal. The right lung was healthy. The left pleural cavity was partly obliterated by adhesions, but contained in its sacculi serum and lymph; the lung was diminished to half its size, the lower lobe being very friable and having its air-cells filled with a prune-juice liquid. The pericardium contained four ounces of serum. The heart weighed fourteen ounces and a half; the ventricle was hypertrophied, the middle valve somewhat thickened and the curved margins of the pulmonary and aortic valves hardened. The liver was enlarged and softened; the spleen, weighing twenty-two ounces and a half, was pulpy. The peritoneum was darkly injected and contained ten ounces of serum. The stomach and intestines, which were much distended with gas, had their mucous lining congested. The kidneys were nodulated on the surface and contained several cysts somewhat larger than a pea.—*Douglas Hospital, Washington, D. C.*

CASE 94.—Private Otto Ziegera, Co. G, 1st U. S. Vet. Vols.; age 25; was admitted September 13, 1865, and died September 19. He stated that he had been suffering from remittent fever. On admission his skin was of natural temperature and perspiring freely, but he had headache and his appetite was poor, tongue furred, pulse intermittent and countenance anxious. In four days he had improved so much as to be able to walk about. On the 17th he was said to have had a violent convulsion, which was considered as a congestive chill by the attending medical officer, who found the patient next morning collapsed, almost speechless, and covered with a profuse cold perspiration. During the day he rallied, but on the morning of the 19th he had another violent convulsion and expired in an hour.* Previous to death he had been eating watermelon and boiled eggs. *Post-mortem* examination eight hours after death: Rigidity marked. The arachnoid was opaque and presented numerous white spots of small size, chiefly over the

* A case in which the fatal chill assumed convulsive features is given by Act. Ass't Surgeon HENRY M. LYMAN, U. S. A., as having occurred in Hospital No. 2, Nashville, Tenn. The patient was admitted June 26, 1862, having the appearance of being well nourished; but at the same time there was an unusual paleness of the tongue and palpebral conjunctiva. Prior to admission he had complained continually of rheumatism and debility. Quinine and iron were prescribed. During the two weeks following his entrance into hospital he was twice attacked by malarial fever, which was readily suppressed by quinine. On July 17 he began to suffer much from pains which he called rheumatic, and at the same time his surface was covered with a fœtid perspiration; the latter continued through the day and following night. A scruple of Dover's powder was given during the day, and next morning a scruple of quinine was administered. After this he continued well until the night of the 23d, when the fœtid perspiration again appeared and lasted through the following day. Ten grains of Dover's powder every four hours were "ordered till the cessation of the fœtor." Quinine was again prescribed; but whether it was taken or not was uncertain, because of the prejudice of the patient against the remedy. Subsequently he expressed himself well until the 27th, when he complained of pains in his limbs, of a burning sensation in his stomach such as he never felt before, and of insatiable thirst. A scruple of quinine was prescribed for him, which, however, he did not take. He walked about the ward conversing with his comrades and presented nothing unusual in his appearance. He lay down on his bed and was soon seized with convulsive movements of the feet, arms and head, and stertorous breathing with frothing at the mouth; his surface grew purple and he died in a few minutes. The *post-mortem* examination, five hours after death, found considerable serous effusion under the arachnoid and about four ounces of fluid at the base of the brain, with much softening on the lower surface of its middle lobes. The lungs were healthy; the pleura presented nothing of any importance; the heart was normal; in the right ventricle was found a small white clot; the left ventricle was empty and contracted and the right auricle enormously distended with black fluid blood. Five ounces of clear serum were contained in the pericardium. The duodenum externally exhibited a pinkish hue; the ileum and colon were of a darker appearance. The spleen was normal in size and of a slate color, and the liver of a dark chocolate hue. Everywhere throughout the body the blood was found uncoagulated. This case of congestive fever was presented in the Second Part of this work, p. 239, as Case 776 of the diarrhœal and dysenteric series.

sulci on the right side of the cerebrum; the pia mater was congested. The substance of the brain was of normal consistence; it presented many puncta; the lining membrane of the lateral ventricles was opaque, but the cavities contained no serum; the floor of the fourth ventricle was congested and showed some small ecchymoses. Both lungs were marked in spots with melanic matter, the foreign substance of which could be felt by passing the finger over the pleura covering it; the right lung was congested by hypostasis posteriorly and inferiorly, and the substance at the summit of the left lung was puckered, tough, inelastic and of the same specific gravity as water. The heart contained loosely-formed black clots. The liver was normal in specific gravity and consistence; the spleen enlarged, soft, flaccid, weighed fifteen ounces; the pancreas was large; the kidneys and suprarenal capsules normal. The ileum and lower portion of the jejunum were colored yellow with bile; the large intestine presented internally a blackish color which was not associated with softening, ulceration or any appreciable lesion.—*Geo. M. McGill, Ass't Surg., U. S. A., Hicks Hospital, Baltimore, Md.*

CASE 95.—Private David Calvin Legrone, Co. D, 40th Ala.; rejected frontier man; age about 23; was reported on the morning of the 6th of December, 1864, as having intermittent fever. Five grains of quinine were directed to be taken night and morning. Next day he had no fever and made no complaint, remaining up till 9 P. M. He then went to sleep, but in about two hours awoke with a chill and difficulty of breathing and died in about half an hour. *Post-mortem* examination sixteen hours after death: The brain, lungs, liver, stomach, bowels and kidneys were of normal size and perfectly healthy. There was a thrombus in the right auricle of the heart and about three or four ounces of serum in the pericardium. The spleen was about twice the usual size and very soft, dark colored and engorged with blood.—*Act. Ass't Surg. W. B. Matthews, U. S. A., Rock Island Hospital, Ill.*

CASE 96.—Private George Evans, 6th Kansas Cav. (a Delaware Indian), weight 180 pounds, was admitted February 23, 1863, with a large ulcer, of several years' standing, on the right leg. This healed kindly under treatment with ointment of carbonate of zinc and adhesive strips. The patient, however, was taken on March 14 with a severe chill which lasted several hours, and was followed by fever, with a full and laboring pulse, 120, dyspnœa and great anxiety of expression. The fever gradually abated and with it the force and frequency of the pulse; but frequent palpitations supervened with consequent loss of sleep. Next morning the pulse was so small and frequent that it could not be counted; there was a suffocating feeling at the præcordia, with a pain which extended to the left shoulder; the countenance continued distressed; the dyspnœa increased; frequent vomiting of greenish matter occurred throughout the day; the sounds of the heart were muffled and indistinct; the bowels open and stools healthy; the urine normal; the skin moist and warm; the intellect clear. The pulse became imperceptible at the wrist and death took place at 3 A. M. of the 16th, forty-two hours after the accession of the chill. The treatment consisted of five grains of quinine every three hours, with opiates, Hoffmann's anodyne, nitrate of bismuth and mustard cataplasms. *Post-mortem* examination thirty-five hours after death: Rigor mortis well marked. The lungs were healthy throughout. The pericardium contained one ounce of serum. The right cavities of the heart contained dark clotted blood and a large white clot which projected into the veins and pulmonary artery; the left cavities also contained a fibrinous clot, which extended several inches into the aorta; these clots had numerous attachments to the walls of the heart; the valves of the left side were thickened and incomplete. The spleen was enlarged, soft and pulpy; the other abdominal viscera were healthy.—*Hospital, Fort Scott, Kansas.**

The following case, discovered among the records after the others had been placed and numbered, is inserted here as of interest in connection with those just recorded:

Private Philip Kiser, Co. M, 3d Ky. Cav.; age 20; was admitted November 29, 1864, with a gunshot wound of the left leg near the head of the tibia, received at Marietta, Ga., October 5, 1864. He was put upon light duty at the barracks until January 1, 1865, when he was admitted to hospital, having had a chill which was followed by fever, nausea and vomiting. When first seen, January 2, the vomiting continued. A sinapism was applied over the stomach, and mercury with chalk, morphia and camphor were administered in small doses every two hours. Next day the pulse was small and rapid, 50 per minute, the respiration thoracic and hurried, 35 per minute, and the abdomen exceedingly tender, particularly over the cæcum. On the 4th the vomiting persisted and the bowels were tympanitic, the pain and tenderness being much increased. Brandy-toddy or milk-punch was given hourly, and friction and artificial heat were applied to the feet. On the 5th the symptoms were aggravated; the respiration increased to 60 per minute; the pulse imperceptible at the wrist; the extremities cold and the general surface cyanotic. Death occurred on this day. *Post-mortem* examination eighteen hours after death: The calvaria was not opened. The pericardium contained five ounces of serum; the pleural surface of the left lung was thickened and its apex intensely congested but not hepatized; the right lung was healthy; the heart of normal size; firm clots were found in both ventricles, attached in some places to the auriculo-ventricular valves. The liver weighed sixty-two ounces; its left lobe was softened and crumbled easily on pressure; the gall-bladder was distended. The peritoneal cavity contained eight ounces of sanguineo-purulent serum; the omentum was inflamed and the surface of

---

* A similar case has been detailed by Dr. JOSEPH JONES: The patient was sallow, anæmic and subject to attacks of chills and fever. He had a chill attended with much embarrassment of respiration on the night of January 25, 1869, and was admitted into the Charity Hospital of New Orleans on the following day. There was great dyspnœa and much restlessness, but the respiratory murmur was audible enough. The heart's action was irregular, rapid and tumultuous and its sounds muffled; the arterial circulation was weakened, the pulse being small and intermittent and the surface cold; the venous system was engorged. Death took place suddenly at 1 P. M. of the 28th. The clot, consisting of distinct fibrinous laminæ free from blood corpuscles, was firmly attached to the muscular columns and cords of the right side of the heart; it sent a branching prolongation into the pulmonary artery. Dr. JONES is of opinion that the formation of heart-clot during life is very common in malarial fever.—See *Clinical Lecture—Heart-clot. New Orleans Jour. of Med.,* Vol. XXII, 1869, p. 469.

the intestine reddened and coated with lymph. The cardiac end of the stomach was highly congested. The spleen weighed fourteen ounces and was softened. The kidneys were small and healthy.—*Act. Ass't Surg. D. W. Flora, U. S. Army, Hospital, Madison, Ind.*

Cases 97–99, from their rapidly fatal course and the purpuric blotches which characterized them, were regarded as cases of *spotted fever*.

CASE 97.—Private Alonzo A. Lumbert, Co. H, 7th Wis. Vols.; age 19; was admitted from Haddington Hospital, Philadelphia, Pa., July 26, 1864, suffering from partial paralysis of the left arm, resulting from a gunshot wound received at the battle of the Wilderness May 6. The ball had entered on the anterior surface of the arm a little below the shoulder-joint and emerged near the spine of the ninth dorsal vertebra. The patient improved under treatment, gradually gaining the use of the arm, until August 11, when he was seized with nausea, headache, weakness and pain in the lower limbs. Next morning he had a chill followed by fever, pain in the bowels and slight diarrhœa; the nausea, headache and debility were increased; the tongue was coated with a white fur. He was treated with two-grain doses of quinine every three hours. There was no improvement on the 13th; in the evening he vomited frequently and complained of great weakness. Next day the vomiting continued; he was restless; his extremities were cold, face and lips bluish, pupils slightly dilated, pulse imperceptible at the wrist, but his mind remained clear. Circular purplish spots, which were not elevated, made their appearance on the face and right arm; they disappeared under strong pressure and returned slowly when the pressure was removed. Brandy was given freely and bottles of hot water applied to the lower extremities. About 11 P. M. convulsive movements of the limbs occurred, with retraction of the head and muscular twitchings of the face. Death took place within half an hour of the convulsive seizure. *Post-mortem* examination four hours after death: Body well developed; rigor mortis marked; slight discolored spots were observed on the face, right arm and lower extremities; there was also some suggillation posteriorly. The vessels of the pia mater were greatly congested and some exudation of lymph marked their course, especially in the vicinity of the longitudinal sinus; the brain was of natural consistency, the puncta vasculosa numerous; there was no exudation at the base of the brain nor effusion into the ventricles; the cerebellum was less congested than the cerebrum; the pons and medulla appeared to be normal. The surface of the spinal cord in the cervical region had a pinkish hue, due to congestion of the pia mater; its substance was natural in consistence and color. The lungs were engorged with blackish fluid blood, which exuded on section. The heart was rather small and was filled with black fluid blood, which was frothy in the right but not in the left cavities. The liver was of natural size, but darker than usual in color and engorged with fluid blood. The spleen was rather large and congested and its parenchyma firm. The mucous membrane of the stomach presented a number of ecchymosed spots; portions of the small intestine were much congested and the solitary follicles and glands of Peyer were enlarged; the mesenteric glands were engorged with dark blood. The kidneys were likewise engorged with blood.—*Act. Ass't Surg. Charles Carter, U. S. A., Turner's Lane Hospital, Philadelphia, Pa.*

CASE 98.—Private Charles Octmier, Co. G, 79th Pa. Vols.; age 45; was admitted May 17, 1865, with diarrhœa of six weeks' duration, two to six stools daily, but with no pain nor fever; his feet were œdematous, which condition was ascribed to hard marching. Delirium of an acute character was developed on the 20th, the patient talking loudly, making frightful grimaces and constantly seeking to leave his bed. Next day at 8 A. M. his pupils were dilated and he was unable to recognize any one; pulse rapid and feeble; tongue dry and parched; stools and urine passed involuntarily; a purple petechial rash appeared over the body, especially on the abdomen. At 9.30 A. M. he slept quietly. Two hours later he was in collapse and gasping for breath; pupils much contracted. He died at 1 P. M. *Post-mortem* examination twenty-three hours after death: There was much emaciation. The lungs were adherent on both sides, congested posteriorly and contained crude tubercle and several chalky concretions; the apex of the right lung contained also a small vomica about the size of the thumb-nail. There were two ounces of yellow transparent serum and two yellow coagula in the pericardium; on the surface of the heart was a serous effusion which appeared around the auricular appendices as a jelly. There were three ounces of a turbid, reddish liquid in the abdominal cavity; the mesenteric glands were softened; the liver was small and soft; the spleen semi-fluid; the kidneys normal; the stomach eroded and ecchymosed; Peyer's patches exhibited the shaven-beard appearance; the rectum was much ulcerated; the bladder distended with urine.—*Douglas Hospital, Washington, D. C.*

CASE 99.—Private Louis Gross, Co. H, 9th Invalid Corps; age 42; admitted November 19, 1863. On admission this man had much fever and a hacking cough, with an expectoration of frothy mucus. A cough mixture and solution of acetate of ammonia were ordered. Next day at 7 A. M. he had a hemorrhage from the bowels; at the same time the superficial capillaries of the thighs and abdomen became congested, and the capillaries of the whole surface of the body were soon affected in like manner, assuming in patches the appearance of hemorrhagic extravasation. Whiskey was administered every half hour, but he sank rapidly and died at 10 A. M. *Post-mortem* examination five hours after death: Extravasations of blood over the entire surface of the body. Bright-red spots on the surface of both lungs; extensive pleuritic adhesions over the left side. Right auricle and ventricle of the heart considerably dilated, the auriculo-ventricular opening being large enough to permit the passage of three fingers; the mitral valve thickened and feeling like cartilage. Liver weighing seventy-two ounces; gall-bladder distended; spleen normal. Mucous membrane of stomach, ileum and colon presenting bright-red spots similar to those on the surface of the lungs; the descending colon containing a large quantity of fluid blood; the last twelve inches of the ileum presenting old ulcers, and the lower part of the ileum and the large intestine generally much congested; kidneys healthy.—*Act. Ass't Surg. Lloyd Dorsey, Harewood Hospital, Washington, D. C.*

In connection with these cases the following reports are of interest:

Surgeon R. M. S. JACKSON, 11*th Pa. Vols.; Annapolis, Md., January* 31, 1862.—The cases of unusual interest in this report are those of a disease now popularly called *spotted fever*, and catalogued as *malignant congestive fever.* The following are some of the leading features of the cases, all of which presented great uniformity of nosographic points, there being but few premonitory symptoms. First a severe chill with extreme oppression; violent pains in the head and limbs, the latter complained of as an "awful soreness," or as "stinging" and "burning;" expression of terror and alarm in the countenance, particularly noticeable in the eyes; cold skin; most of the cases pulseless at the wrist when first examined. Spontaneous vomiting occurred in some, and in one case constant inclination to go to stool, with but little or nothing passed from the bowels. Spots appeared in from four to ten hours after the attack, the patients dying generally from ten to twenty hours after the appearance of the spots; one case lingered three days. The shortest time from attack to death, including appearance of spots, was sixteen hours. The spots were of various sizes and shapes, first appearing on the feet and legs; some were of a stellated or radiating form, bright red; others roundish and irregular, of a bluish color, and from a mere point in size to a quarter of an inch in diameter. They gradually extended over the whole trunk, superior extremities and face, at last appearing on the eyelids as small blood blisters. These spots, as death approached and after death, became larger, more diffuse and of a bluish or purple color. In some of the cases there were large blotches of the size of the hand or larger, connected together irregularly over the body and limbs; in some, after death, the face became of a livid color, puffy and swollen, the eyes protruding, lips turgid and flabby, a frothy mucus boiling from the mouth and a sanious substance issuing from the nose and ears. Before death some of the cases had the mottled appearance of persons who had been bitten by venomous reptiles.

The *post-mortem* appearances very soon after death exhibited a dissolved condition of the blood and a putrefactive tendency of the fluids and solids. Cadaveric odors were emitted by some of the bodies almost immediately after death, while the abdomen became enlarged by distending gases and the face presented a bloated appearance, with frothy boilings from the mouth, already described. The brain revealed the marked *post-mortem* appearance of *dissolved* or *dead* blood; its inferior portions showed a gradually increased saturation of the membranes and cerebral substance, the bloodvessels blackening almost the entire surface. The sinuses and large veins being punctured discharged their contents of inky blood in a state of perfect dissolvedness. The hyperæmia from hypostasis was particularly marked, the blood appearing to sink from gravity by percolation like water through the tissues. The membranes of the brain showed no evidence of inflammation, only passing engorgement. The substance of the brain, exposed by slicing it down from the vertex to the base, seemed unaltered in mechanical consistence, but darker of hue in both medullary and cineritious substances. The cut vessels penetrating the cerebral mass exhibited the same condition as those of the periphery. The ventricles were full of a light straw-colored serum, no doubt the effect of a mere mechanical transudation of the watery portion of the blood from relaxed vessels and tissues. It was evident that no inflammation *could* have existed in the brain or its investing membranes, for the mental manifestations were clear in many cases to the last. The cavity of the abdomen showed some effusion; its contents presented the same general tendency to ecchymosis of tissue as existed on the skin and other organs. The stomach exhibited no evidence of inflammation, but the same dark and mottled appearance predominated. The inner surface was of a dark-yellowish muddy color, as if slightly stained by bile, but contained only mucus and undigested material recently swallowed in the shape of beef-tea, brandy, etc. The whole bowel was of a dark mottled color, the large intestine being distended with gas. The liver was normal but of a darker brown color than usual.

The troops of this regiment came from Harrisburg on the Susquehanna river. This is a well-known malarious region, the Juniata and Susquehanna rivers having been long noted for their autumnal fevers. Most of the men enlisted had come from districts of the State where these diseases are unknown and were thus, as is a well ascertained fact, more liable to attacks of miasmatic affections. Before leaving Harrisburg, where the regiment remained from the latter part of August until the 27th November, 1861, the principal diseases were clearly of malarial origin—intermittent and remittent fevers assuming a typhoid form. A number of typhoid cases were left at Harrisburg; many of these died. On our arrival at Annapolis over one hundred men were on the sick-list, nearly all of whom were taken sick at Harrisburg. For one month after our arrival at Annapolis the troops had no vegetables, as they could not be procured. They were crowded into the buildings of St. John's College, where many other regiments had been quartered at different times. These buildings had never been cleansed, renovated or disinfected in any way. The deleterious influence of over-crowding was thus added to the transported poison. Efforts were made to get lime and disinfectants in vain, and as the troops were constantly expected to move from this station no radically reformatory measures with regard to the vicious condition of the post were persevered in. * * * When the troops were supplied with vegetables the scorbutic condition of the blood of many of the men was soon changed and the health of the regiment was speedily improved. [On the monthly report of sick and wounded from this regiment for January, 1862, signed by Surgeon Jackson, are 7 cases and 3 deaths reported under the head of *other fevers,* and on the list of deaths the three deaths are ascribed to *febris maligna congestiva.*]

Surgeon R. M. S. JACKSON, 11*th Pa. Vols.; Annapolis, Md., March* 1, 1862.—The cases of interest in the accompanying report for February, 1862, are of the class of fevers: Congestive 17, intermittent 9, remittent 8. The occurrence of such a number of intermittent and remittent cases with clearly defined features is significant as showing a rational *genesis* for the whole class. The cases of congestive fever were clearly the old form of "spotted fever." The symptoms were the same, with a slight modification in some of the characteristic points. Many of the cases exhibited the same style of maculation, the same intensity of quickly locked and gorged congestions of the splanchic cavities, the same disposition to fatal first chill, etc. One striking modification was observed: Some of the cases without spots on the extremities, but with the same symptoms otherwise, showed a remarkable swelling of the *integuments of the head and face*. This bloated puffy look was the most striking appearance, together with a dingy blueness of the integument in other parts of the body, while the injected condition of the vessels of the conjunctiva produced a regular chemosis or elevated ring around the cornea. Only one of these cases proved fatal.

The improved condition of the general health of the troops, from a proper supply of food or mixture of vegetable matter in their rations, accounts for the increased power of resistance to disease; bloodless and scorbutic constitutions having become more highly vitalized, the surgeon's efforts to arrest the destroying powers have been of more avail. A clear apprehension of the true pathology of the disease having been established, the remedies employed have had marked success.

Surgeon SAMUEL A. SABINE, *9th N.Y. Art'y.; Fort Mansfield, Md., February* 8, 1864.—You will observe in my report for January that there have been taken on the sick report seven cases of congestive intermittent fever, of which four have died. I find that the disease occurs most frequently among the new recruits, and from observation I have ascertained that the locality from which they were taken appears to have a controlling influence. A large number came recently from Onondaga County, N. Y., which abounds in malarial poison exhaled from the numerous swamps in that portion of the State. Four out of the seven cases of congestive fever have occurred among these recruits. The symptoms of this disease are extremely varied, indeed no two cases are the same; yet a similarity exists which enables the careful observer to detect the same *materies morbi* exerting its influence with deadly effect upon the brain and nervous system. In some cases the symptoms are identical with those occurring in the congestive fevers of the West, while in others there is no perceptible chill from first to last. But a better idea of the symptoms may be obtained by reporting a few of the cases:—

1. John Boyer, Ordnance Serg't, 47 years of age; married; in the service seventeen years; always healthy. Was called to see him about 8 P. M. and found him in a profuse sweat, his clothes being completely saturated; pulse 115, small and soft; tongue clean; extremities inclined to be cold; respiration normal; countenance pale and anxious. About 5 o'clock he had eaten a hearty supper, soon after which he went for a pail of water; on returning was attacked with faintness, indescribable sensations and pain in the epigastrium and right side of the chest. Sinapisms were applied to the extremities and stimulants directed to be given at frequent intervals until the pulse grew stronger. I placed him in charge of a competent person and left him. He soon became comfortable; took something to eat and drink during the night; told his wife he felt so well she must go to bed. She did so, and he was perfectly quiet and comfortable until 6 A. M. when, while standing upon the floor, he was again seized with the same feeling as at first and died immediately. No autopsy.

2. Albertus Cowan; 20 years of age; healthy. He was taken with a chill on the morning of January 14 and continued to get worse until night, when he became insensible and was brought to hospital. He moaned constantly, and when disturbed was violent. The pulse was 64 and intermitted occasionally; it was slow and had but little force; respirations 35 and some catching of breath; no stertor; skin natural in color and but slight coolness of surface; pupils dilated and insensible to light. He could not be aroused nor induced to swallow anything. Directions were given to have his head shaved and blistered. At 6 P. M. some slight improvement was manifest; the pulse was stronger and the respiration improved. The blister had drawn well, and some beef-tea and stimulant had been given during the evening, but the patient remained perfectly unconscious. On January 16 there was a decided improvement. He was semi-conscious, and took beef-tea in sufficient quantities; pulse 70 and regular. Ordered thirty grains of quinine in two powders, four hours apart. On January 17 the improvement continued. It was noticed that there was a slight strabismus of the left eye. The blister was re-applied to the scalp. On the 20th the pupils had resumed their natural size and the strabismus was entirely removed. After this he gradually improved until the present time, but has had symptoms of remitting fever. He convalesces slowly.

3. Garrett S. Prosse, 20 years of age; healthy. He had been in the service but two or three days when he was attacked in the same manner as Cowan. I did not see him until twenty-four hours after the attack, as the men composing the company were all new recruits and their officers were not notified of his illness He did not become insensible until about eight hours after the chill. His pulse was 60, slow, soft and with but little force; respiration 34 and sighing. A brisk cathartic was given which moved the bowels thoroughly; but his condition did not improve. He died on the third day. No autopsy.

In all the cases that recovered there has been a tendency to remitting or intermitting fever during convalescence, which has invariably been slow.

Surgeon DAVID MERRITT, *55th Pa. Vols.; Beaufort, S. C., May* 10, 1863.—We have also had in the regiment a few cases of congestive, or as it is termed by some writers, pernicious fever. In most of them there has been very little time in which to do anything by way of medication, so rapidly has the disease resulted in death. In these cases the congestion has manifested itself in various ways: In one case spinal congestion was evinced by the prolonged spasms which occurred with hardly any intermission; in other cases spinal irritation or spinal meningitis; in others, congestion of the brain at a very early period, with obliquity of vision, sardonic grin and evidences of a disposition to convulsions; in others, intense congestion of the lungs, which, upon examination after death, were found engorged with dark venous blood; in others, congestion of the bowels, accompanied by extravasation of venous blood from the mucous membrane of the intestine and by softening of the mucous membrane to a remarkable degree. One case, sent to General Hospital No. 3, Beaufort, S. C., Ass't Surg. F. T. DADE, U. S. Vols., in charge, I particularly remember: Private John Moyer, Co. H, 55th Pa. Vols., came to me after surgeon's call and asked for "a dose of physic," as his bowels had not been moved for three days. He did not appear to be sick. I gave him at one dose twenty grains of mercury with chalk and fifteen grains of powdered rhubarb. This was taken at about 8 A. M. At 2 P. M. I was summoned to his tent and found him in a state of syncope, from which he rallied under the administration of stimulants. About 3 P. M. he was removed to hospital, and died the same night at about 9 o'clock of intestinal hæmorrhage, a pool of dark venous blood beneath him in the bed. Persulphate of iron had vainly been given by enema, and sulphate of quinia, capsicum, ether, brandy, etc., administered internally. By invitation of Dr. DADE I was present at the *post-mortem* examination twelve hours after death. The brain was slightly congested. The lungs were nearly normal and not noticeably changed. The heart was normal. The liver presented the nutmeg appearance; on section it was found to be considerably congested. The spleen was *very much enlarged, very friable and much congested.* One of the kidneys presented an extravasation of blood on its surface. The stomach was *slightly* congested. The intestines contained a quantity of extravasated blood; Peyer's glands and the solitary follicles were somewhat congested and the mucous coat of the whole intestinal canal was so much softened that it was possible, with the handle of the scalpel, to *scrape off the mucous coat* and leave the *muscular* coat denuded.

Another patient died during the chill, living only about ten minutes after being brought to the regimental hospital on a stretcher from his quarters, where, less than three hours previously, he had been joking with one of the drummer boys. This was Private Edward Riley, of Co. D. Another case, Private Philip Miller, of Co. H, died comatose a few days after admission to regimental hospital, the whole external surface of his body presenting an icteroid hue before death. Another, Private Irwin Little, of Co. I, died soon after admission to regimental hospital, and in this case the surface of the body became jaundiced immediately after death. This man, like the others, was treated with quinine, capsicum, brandy, etc.; calomel was given with a view to stimulating the secretion of the liver, and mustard applied to the surface of the body and limbs.

Surgeon W. M. SMITH, 85th *N. Y. Vols.; New Berne, N. C., February* 22, 1863.—Two men died in hospital at Suffolk of remittent fever with meningeal complications. *Post-mortem* examination showed that the arachnoid surface of the falx cerebri was much congested, having *plastic exudation* at several places on its surface. In one case the right lateral ventricle contained one ounce of turbid serum tinged with blood; the left ventricle contained six drachms of serum less turbid than bloody. The arachnoid surface of the tentorium cerebelli and the visceral layer of the arachnoid covering the cerebellum were greatly congested.

Surgeon W. H. GRIMES, 13th *Kansas Vols.; near Springfield, Mo., February* 2, 1863.—Many of the men were taken with high grades of bilious fever and several died of congestion of the brain. In these cases the most active treatment was pursued: the patients were bled, cupped, blistered; had calomel and the bitartrate of potash and antimony, and other remedies as the indications demanded; yet we were unsuccessful. We began to doubt our powers of diagnosis, but the citizens told us that congestion of the brain is a common disease in this region, and that their doctors bleed and give large doses of calomel.

Ass't Surg. J. W. MASON, 12th *Corps d'Afrique; Port Hudson, La., February* 23, 1864.—Nearly all the cases that came under my observation in the months of October and November, 1863, were the result of zymotic influences; these, coöperating with the scorbutic taint that had been largely developed in the regiment, produced, in even the ordinary incidental diseases, an adynamic condition of the system. Many laboring under this pathological condition were attacked with typho-malarial or congestive fever. The typho-malarial cases were in most instances amenable to treatment, but a large proportion of the congestive cases proved fatal. The most prominent point of interest developed in this unmanageable disease was a loss of vital force. As an unusual thing the disease was ushered in with a slight chill, but generally this was not apparent. In some cases the patients would soon become cold and pulseless; and no treatment, however vigorous, succeeded in establishing reaction. Death closed the scene in a few hours, or the patients lived for several days conscious and without pain, and then died quietly, as though they had fallen into a gentle slumber.

Lastly, two cases of chronic malarial poisoning are given, with some references from New Berne, N. C., to this condition among the troops operating there in 1863. In both cases the blood was evidently greatly altered. In one, the spleen weighed sixty-eight ounces and the veins contained soft greenish-white clots, while in the other there was diffluent blood in the pleural cavity and the liver and spleen were disorganized.

CASE 100.—Private Levi Beech, Co. D, 1st Mich. Cav.; age 36; was admitted October 27, 1864, with a contusion of the left side caused by the kick of a horse. He was feeble; the spleen was much enlarged, occupying nearly the whole of the left lumbar region and parts of the umbilical and left inguinal region. He had suffered from ague eight years before for fourteen months, the disease intermitting occasionally for about a week at a time. After admission his appetite was variable, and he lost flesh although his bowels were regular. He was treated with citrate of iron and quinia, stimulants and nourishing diet. He was able to be about the ward and out of doors; occasionally he had some cough. About noon on December 31 he became speechless and unable to swallow. He died at 6 P. M. *Post-mortem* examination: No rigor mortis. The brain was normal; its membranes somewhat adherent to the medulla and pons. The right cavities of the heart were distended and a greenish-white, soft, almost pus-like clot floated in the ventricle. The right lung was somewhat congested and adhered by old firm fibrinous bands; the left lung was congested by hypostasis; one or two glands at the root of the left lung contained cheesy and chalky matters. The liver was large and bloodless; its portal veins filled with soft yellow clots. The spleen weighed sixty-eight ounces and adhered to the diaphragm and stomach; its veins contained soft greenish clots; a secondary spleen the size of an unhusked walnut was found at the head of the pancreas. The mesenteric glands were indurated and about the size of a pea. The ileum and colon were normal. The psoæ muscles were softened and their surfaces blackened. The external iliac arteries contained blood. The kidneys were white and fatty. Microscopically the greenish-white clots of the heart and bloodvessels consisted of granules and polynucleated cells, many of the latter a little larger than a blood corpuscle, but the majority much larger.—*Third Division Hospital, Alexandria, Va.*

CASE 101.—Corporal S. Cininion, Co. K, 44th N. C.; died June 13, 1863. The patient had been sick for some time and died suddenly and unexpectedly. *Post-mortem* examination: The right lung was adherent to the costal pleura. The heart was very soft but contained no clot. The thoracic cavities on either side contained three ounces of uncoagulable blood, the red corpuscles of which, under the microscope, were seen to be broken down, stellated and withered, the serum of a yellowish-red color and the white corpuscles very numerous, seemingly from the absence of the red. The liver and spleen were pultaceous and disorganized. The kidneys were flabby.—*Ass't Surg. H. Allen, U. S. A., Lincoln Hospital, Washington, D. C.*

Surgeon F. J. D'AVIGNON, 96th N. Y. Vols.; *New Berne, N. C., February* 28, 1863.—The low diet, constant exposure, want of rest and severe labor from which the regiment suffered during the summer of 1862, while before Richmond and at Harrison's Landing, so reduced the vitality of the men that the influence of the miasmatic atmosphere of the swamps, the intense heat and the impure water used, met but feeble resistance. It was a common thing for healthy robust men to lose thirty, forty and even fifty pounds of flesh in a few days; and the sunken eyes, emaciated form and languid step demonstrated the existence of agencies beyond the influence of medicine. The ordinary remedies for disease seemed of no avail.

Surgeon ISAAC F. GALLOUPE, 17th Mass. Vols.; *New Berne, N. C., February* 20, 1863.—In the latter part of June, 1862, intermittent fever and other malarial diseases began to appear in this command, increasing in severity and prevailing more extensively as the season advanced, until November, when the regiment was quartered in town. Notwithstanding the extreme prevalence and severity of miasmatic diseases but few deaths occurred. During the months of August and September several hundred cases were reported, but of these only five proved fatal. In many cases, however, paralysis agitans, chorea and ascites resulted. In other cases the constitution was completely broken down and the men were discharged the service. No treatment was of any avail except by quinine, and this was most effectual. When cinchonism was rapidly produced the disease was promptly and almost invariably broken up. It was rare that a patient would have a second paroxysm after coming under treatment.

Besides the relatively small number of cases presented above, it is recorded in thirty-eight of the cases embraced in the chapter on the alvine fluxes that the patients were suffering or had recently suffered from intermittent fever;* and references to remittent fever occur with equal frequency. In view, however, of the enlarged spleens and other more or less characteristic conditions found at the *post-mortem* examination of the diarrhœal cases, it is probable that a much larger number of them than is shown by the clinical notes were concurrently affected by the malarial influence.

II.—PATHOLOGICAL ANATOMY AND PATHOLOGY OF MALARIAL DISEASE.—In summarizing the pathological appearances presented by the recorded cases of malarial disease, it seems proper to exclude the nine cases, 83–91, in which typhoid fever is suggested by the clinical history or morbid anatomy. There remain FORTY cases of death from malarial affections in which *post-mortem* investigations were held.

The STOMACH.—In **twenty-one** of the cases the condition of the stomach is not stated; it was normal in **five** and constricted in **one**. In **thirteen** cases a morbid condition is specified thus: In *four* the organ contained a green grumous or mud-like liquid; in *two* its mucous membrane was congested; in *one* softened; in *one* slate-colored; in *one* thickened, and in *four* ecchymosed.

The INTESTINAL CANAL.—In **six** of the forty cases the intestines were reported healthy; in **nine** their condition was not stated. In **thirteen** of the remaining twenty-five cases the large and small intestines, so far as can be ascertained from the phraseology of the reports, were both affected.† *Five* of these cases, 59, 64, 65, 73 and 93, were much congested or inflamed, but not ulcerated; in the first-mentioned, for instance, the canal was almost black from the engorged condition of the capillaries, and coagulated blood was found in its interior. In *one* of the thirteen cases, 81, the mucous membrane was softened and in *seven* ulcerated; in two of the latter, 70 and 80, the duodenum alone was ulcerated, although the canal generally was highly congested; in 67 the ulcerations were reported as slight; in 77 as old; in 71 and 72 as large and small, and in 75 as associated with a congested condition of the mucous membrane. In **six** of the twenty-five cases the condition of the small and the large intestine is specifically stated: In 74 both were inflamed, but the patches of Peyer were not diseased; in 99 both were much congested and ecchymosed; in 57 and 94 deposits of black pigment were found in the large intestine, while the ileum in the former was but slightly congested and in the latter merely stained with bile; on the other hand the patches of Peyer in 98 presented

---

* See, in the Second Part of this work, cases 95, 103, 104, 171, 189, 191, 194, 196, 243, 260, 272, 305, 316, 373, 389, 396, 401, 410, 433, 517, 552, 601, 614, 639, 686, 704, 735, 738, 742, 747, 758, 776, 809, 852, 854, 857, 858, 859.

† In Algeria, where the French troops were exposed to influences similar to those affecting our soldiers in the malarious districts of the South, the lesions of chronic dysentery were, according to LAVERAN, constantly found in cases of fever when death occurred a long time after the commencement of the malarial affection.—*Recueil de Mémoires de Médecine de Chirurgie et de Pharmacie Militaires,* 1 série, t. LII, 1842, p. 83.

the pigmented appearance, while the rectum was ulcerated ; in 68 the mucous membrane of the ileum was softened and thickened, that of the colon congested. In the remaining *six* of the twenty-five cases the small intestine or ileum only was affected : In 55, 66 and 97 it was congested, and in the last-mentioned case the patches of Peyer and the solitary glands were enlarged ; in 82 it was ulcerated ; in 69 congested to a purple color, which presented a deeper tint in the apices of the solitary glands, although the patches of Peyer were unaffected ; in 56 also there was a deeply colored congestion, which was specially marked throughout the jejunum.

In two of the cases, 78 and 79, in which the condition of the mucous lining is not stated, there was peritonitis, and in two, 70 and 80, in which the mucous lining was congested, there was, in addition to peritoneal inflammation, in one ulceration of the duodenum and in the other ulceration of the duodenum and pancreas. Some serous effusion was found in the peritoneum in two other cases, and in several there was more or less injection and darkening of the serous coat and omentum.

It would appear from these records that although inflammatory tendencies in the intestinal canal were not an invariable consequence of malarial disease, they occurred with more frequency than might reasonably be referred to the concomitant action of diarrhœal causes as distinct from the malarial poison ; and further, that the incidence of the disease was not localized on any particular part of the tract, but affected alike the large and the small divisions of the gut. The slight preponderance of cases in which the small intestine was affected may be referred to diarrhœal causes, as in MAILLOT's cases, given below,* the preponderance seems to have been due to the inclusion of typhoid fever.

In this absence of partiality for a particular region of the intestine as the site of its manifestations, the malarial poison differs essentially from the typhoid. The lower part of the ileum, as will be seen hereafter, was the site of typhoid developments when no other part of the canal was affected ; and when a greater extent of the canal was involved this part of the ileum was more intensely affected than others. But in the cases at present under consideration the duodenum, jejunum and colon were found, one or all, to be at times implicated without a corresponding intensity of the inflammatory action in the ileum.

Another and striking difference will be observed between the action of the malarial poison and that of the typhoid disease on the intestines. In the latter the inflammatory action was circumscribed and its force expended on the closed glands of the mucous tract, which were destroyed by ulceration or sloughing, while the general surface was not necessarily involved. In the former, on the contrary, the action was general over the parts of the intestine implicated and not confined to a particular anatomical component ; and if the closed glands were affected they were not specially so, but only as forming a part of the congested tract. Moreover, while in the typhoid cases the mucous lining of the intervals between the glands was sometimes darkened or reddened with congestion, the engorgement was never so diffuse or intense as in the malarial cases in which the intensity of the congestion was often manifested, as in 97–99, by ecchymoses, or as in 59, by the escape of blood into the canal from its engorged and blackened membrane.

---

* The following summary of MAILLOT's observations are given for comparison with the text.—See *Traité des Fièvres Intermittentes*, Paris, 1836, p. 283 *et seq.* Among the observations that I have collected and reported there are twenty-eight cases of *post-mortem* inquiry. In all these the digestive organs were examined ; in a single case the head was not opened, and in another case the chest ; in twenty-one cases the condition of the spinal cord is recorded. The different organs presented the following abnormities : *Digestive Organs.*—Twenty-seven times the mucous membrane of the stomach offered something worthy of note ; only once was it in a normal state. The alterations were : Gray slate-colored softening, without vermilion-colored injection, five times ; gray slate-colored softening, with punctated vermilion injection, in a case of quotidian fever which became typhoid ; dirty-gray softening, with vermilion injection, eleven times ; dirty-gray softening, without vermilion injection, in a case in which death did not occur until after twenty-three days of apyrexia ; russet-colored softening four times ; red-brown softening twice ; blackish softening, without injection, once ; in a case of rupture of the spleen, the mucous membrane of the stomach presented only a very slight recent injection with a gray tint ; finally, in a case of typhoid fever, there was found that red color, with softening, peculiar to acute gastro-enteritis. The *small intestine* presented the following changes : Fifteen times softening with a gray, brown or slate-colored tint with or without recent injection ; once the red softening of acute enteritis ; twelve times vestiges of honey-combed patches, of which three presented the shaven-beard appearance ; eleven times an abnormal development of the solitary follicles ; twice the circular whitish patches depressed ; once only ulcerations ; twice intussusceptions without redness ; four times there were no lesions, and once the condition of the small intestine was not recorded. The *large intestine* presented anatomical lesions less frequently than the stomach and the small intestine. In eleven cases it offered nothing of note ; in three its condition was not mentioned ; its changes of texture and color were similar to those in the small intestine with the exception of the honey-combed patches, which cannot be formed there.

The condition of the LIVER was not stated in *four* of the cases; in *eight* it was reported normal. Enlargement is mentioned in *sixteen* cases, of which *one* was reported in addition to be pale and with soft yellow clots in its vessels, *one* congested, *one* soft, *one* tubercular, *one* bluish, *one* slate-colored and *one* as presenting nutmeg foliations. In *one* the liver was congested, in *one* congested and softened and in *two* softened; in *one* it presented the nutmeg appearance; in *one* it was fatty, in *one* pale and soft, in *one* fawn-colored, in *one* partly blackened, in *one* bronzed, in *one* dark-colored and engorged with fluid blood and in *one* pultaceous. In one case the gall-bladder was found to be ulcerated.

Dr. STEWARDSON,* after a series of necropsies in cases of remittent fever, came to the conclusion that a change in the color of the liver from a reddish-brown to a mixture of gray and olive was the anatomical characteristic of the disease in the series which he had studied, and probably also in all cases, as this series was made up of cases extending over three successive seasons, and originating not in a single locality but in different and widely separated places. The organ was described in individual cases as of the color of bronze, of a mixture of bronze and olive or of a dull lead-color externally and bronzed with a reddish shade internally. *Post-mortem* records antedating STEWARDSON's observations, made occasional mention of an engorged and dark-colored liver in cases of malarial fever; and in 1847 MECKEL† referred the coloration to pigment in the blood, where it was found later by other investigators.

FRERICHS,‡ in 1854, during an epidemic of fever in Silesia, resulting from an overflow of the Oder, observed deposits of pigment in the liver and spleen, and frequently in the brain and kidneys. The liver was steel-gray, blackish or chocolate-colored, sometimes presenting brown insulated figures on a dark ground. The pigment to which this coloration was due consisted of granules, larger masses and true pigment-cells in the capillary networks of the portal and hepatic veins, and in many cases in the arteries. It was noticed also that while there was enlargement from congestion in acute cases, the organ was frequently diminished in size.§ Some years later Dr. J. FORSYTH MEIGS‖ made a series of observations in the wards of the Pennsylvania Hospital which he presented as attesting the accuracy of FRERICHS' views.

The *post-mortem* notes given above show such variety in the color of the organ that it is impossible to consider the bronzed or gray and olive liver as a constant pathognomonic lesion. MAILLOT¶ and E. COLLIN ** show similar autopsical results; and DUTROULAU, while regarding congestion, with augmentation of volume and consistence, as the prominent condition, refers also to fatty degeneration and changes in color from altered secretions, and especially from the presence of pigment formed in the liver itself or derived from the spleen.††

The SPLEEN‡‡ was normal in *seven* cases, while in *eight* its condition was not reported. There was

---

* See *Observations on Remittent Fever founded upon cases observed in the Pennsylvania Hospital*. Am. Jour. Med. Sciences, Vol. I, N. S., 1841, p. 289.

† H. MECKEL.—*Ueber schwarzes Pigment in der Milz und dem Blute einer Geisteskranken*. Allg. Zeitschr. für Psychiatrie, Bd. IV, 1847, S. 198— first observed black pigment-cells in the blood of an insane patient who died of phthisis: it is not known whether he had intermittent fever. The spleen, liver and brain were rich in pigment. VIRCHOW—*Zur path. Physiologie des Bluts*. Archiv, Bd. II, 1849, S. 587—observed pigment-cells in the blood of the heart of a man dead of malarial cachexia.

‡ *A Clinical Treatise on Diseases of the Liver*. New Sydenham Soc., London, 1860, Vol. I, p. 317.

§ "In all the cases which terminated fatally (38) the liver contained a quantity of pigment; in ten it appeared enlarged and congested and in eight atrophied; in nine cases the cells contained much oil; lardaceous matter could be detected in three cases, but only in small quantity. Except in one case, pigment was always found in the spleen; three times this organ was lardaceous, and in thirty cases its volume exceeded the usual limit." Op. cit., p. 334.

‖ *On the Pathological Appearances presented in Marsh Fever*. Am. Jour. Med. Sci., Vol. L, N. S., 1865, p. 305.

¶ Thus MAILLOT: In five instances the condition of the *liver* was not indicated; in five it presented nothing abnormal; nine times it was congested; three times friable; once brittle; three times yellowish, pale and soft; once greenish-yellow, and once it had the aspect of a cake of chocolate.

** In COLLIN's 52 cases of pernicious fever the liver was normal in size in six cases and hypertrophied in forty-six; in ten of the latter it was softened and in two indurated. The color was altered in nineteen cases to such tints as dark-brown, chocolate, bistre, fawn-color and earth-color; but he notes his failure to observe the morbid coloration mentioned by STEWARDSON in his Pennsylvania Hospital cases.—Recueil de Mémoires de Médecine de Chirurgie et de Pharmacie Militaires, 2e série, t. IV, 1848, p. 128.

†† DUTROULAU.—*Traité des Maladies des Européens dans les pays chauds*. Paris, 1864, p. 196.

‡‡ MAILLOT speaks of the spleen thus: In five cases its condition was not indicated; in one only it appeared normal; twenty-one times it was larger than usual, in one instance without change of color or texture; thirteen times it was of the color of the dregs of wine; seven times chocolate-colored; in one case it was broken and reduced to a wine-colored pulp, and in one in which it resembled a cake of chocolate, its fibrous membrane was easily detached and crackled like a sheet of parchment.

enlargement in **nineteen** cases, accompanied in *twelve* with softening or pulpiness,[*] in *two* with congestion, in *one* with abscess[†] and in *one* with infiltration of pus. **One** spleen was congested and softened, **one** congested and dark-colored, **one** soft and small, **one** semifluid, **one** pultaceous and **one** firm and of a dark mahogany-color.

The connection between enlargement of the spleen and periodic fevers has been recognized from the earliest times, but as late as 1828 M. GENDRIN noted the fact that medical authorities may be searched in vain for a thorough description of the changes in the spleen in subjects dead of intermittent fever. He endeavored to determine the anatomical characters of these changes by massing and comparing the isolated facts recorded in special papers and works on pathological anatomy. His results showed that the spleen was either tumefied, with or without induration, or softened, with or without tumefaction.[‡] M. NEPPLE,[§] in 1841, arrived at similar conclusions from a study of cases, but he added also that the stagnation of the blood in the spleen tended to hypertrophy, acute and chronic inflammations, softening and degeneration of tissue, which were often fatal. More recently DUTROULAU[||] summarized the alterations in the spleen as simple congestion causing augmentation of volume, hypertrophy of tissue from repeated congestions, and changes in the contained blood involving diffluence and accumulation of pigment, with disorganization of the splenic tissue when the blood has attained an extreme degree of dyscrasia. The cases presented by our medical officers during the war illustrate the various splenic conditions from the normal to disorganization without, and occasionally with, the intermediation of inflammatory action; but no mention is made of pigmentary deposits in the organ,[¶] as the microscope was seldom used in their *post-mortem* investigations.

Medical writers generally consider the changes in the spleen as the most frequent and characteristic of those occurring in malarial fevers. In all of LAVERAN's cases the spleen was enlarged and more or less softened.[**] In but one of MAILLOT's cases was it normal. Nevertheless in the cases presented by our medical records there are seven instances of normal spleen in thirty-two cases in which its condition was reported. PIORRY[††] found it healthy in six of twenty-seven cases of intermittent fever. HASPEL[‡‡] also observed it

---

[*] ROKITANSKI in his *Pathological Anatomy*, B. III, S. 381, says that in obstruction of the circulation the blood, accumulated and retained in the spleen, creates a condition of hyperæmic turgescence with a dark-red color of the organ, and by its continuance produces hypertrophy of the fibrous tissues as well as of the pulpy substance. This turgescence is always characterized by some increase in consistence, firmness and density. The changes of tissue following such turgescence may be very different, inasmuch as they depend on the constitution of the blood, and therefore may sometimes occur as an induration and sometimes as a softening.

[†] COLLIN—*Recueil des Mémoires de Méd. Militaires*, 2e série, 1855, t. XV—*Ruptures de la Rate*—considers that external violence often acts as the determining cause in the production of suppurative inflammation. BLANC also, in his *Abscès de la rate dans la cachexie paludéenne*, Paris, 1879, agrees with COLLIN, as enlarged spleens are so common and abscess so rare in malarious subjects, and especially since the points where abscess is determined are those most exposed to violence from without or from the traction caused by the weight of the enlarged organ. These points are the superior extremity, the external face and the anterior margin; but the organ may be converted into a capsule filled with pus, in which case it is impossible to determine the point of initiation.

[‡] The following is a rendition of M. GENDRIN's conclusions: 1. The spleen is frequently affected in intermittent fever, and this affection has for its principal characteristic an augmentation of volume. 2. The augmentation of volume is always somewhat large and frequently considerable. 3. The tumefaction is sometimes carried so far as to incommode mechanically the functions of the digestive organs. 4. The augmentation of volume extends in all directions, but particularly in length. 5. The tissue of the tumefied spleen is augmented in density, but there is no alteration in its texture; its vessels remain permeable. 6. The tumefied spleen may experience a certain degree of displacement by its own weight. 7. The softening is the immediate effect of certain intense periodical fevers or the result and termination of some old splenic engorgement. 8. The softening is of two kinds: 1st. Idiopathic, or not seemingly dependent on any morbid affection of a different nature; 2d. Inflammatory, and dependent upon the inflammation of the organ. 9. There seems to exist a direct relation between certain lesions of the spleen and certain alterations of the blood. 10. The engorged and softened spleen in fevers may be ruptured by causes directed against it and operating against its tissue mechanically or through augmentation of the congestion of which it is the seat. 11. The rupture may be spontaneous from the simple progress of the malady. 12. The chronic engorgement of the spleen following intermittent fever is a frequent cause of fatal gastro-intestinal hæmorrhage. 13. When this accident occurs the spleen is softened and engorged with blood, more or less black, as if it were ruptured; the gastro-splenic veins are dilated, varicose and sometimes ruptured. 14. The spleen is directly and immediately emptied by hæmorrhage into the digestive passages from the gastro-splenic vessels. 15. This disgorgement may be salutary, because it may destroy the morbid condition of the spleen.—*Journal Général de Méd.*, Paris, 1827, t. C, p. 36.

[§] *Journal de Médecine de Lyon*, t. 1, 1841, p. 367.   [||] *Op. cit.*, p. 195.

[¶] FRERICHS describes the spleen as bluish-black or dark-brown in color, either uniform or speckled, from deposited pigment. *Op. cit.*, p. 318.

[**] LAVERAN, *Documents pour servir a l'Histoire des Maladies du Nord de l'Afrique. Mémoires de Méd. Militaires*, 1e ser., t. LII, 1842, p. 85.

[††] *Gazette Médicale de Paris*, 1833, p. 398.

[‡‡] HASPEL.—*Maladies de l'Algérie*, Paris, 1850, t. II, p. 318.

occasionally in its normal condition, especially when the fatal fever had not been of long duration. Indeed, he considers the absence of splenic lesions in pernicious fevers as frequent and remarkable, referring to BAILLY and JACQUOT for illustrations. DUTROULAU believes the spleen to be normal in 20 per cent. of the endemic fevers of hot climates.

The KIDNEYS were normal in *nine* cases recorded by our medical officers, and not mentioned in *sixteen*. They were large in *two* cases; large and white in *one;* congested in *five;* fatty in *three;* flabby in *one;* pale in *one;* in *one* case they contained cysts and in *another* pus.*

The condition of the HEART was not stated in *twenty-one* of the cases; it was recorded as normal in *ten* cases, leaving only *nine* for special mention—thus: Hypertrophy in *one* case, dilatation in *one*, enlargement and fatty degeneration in *one*, flaccidity in *one*, softness in *one* and valvular lesions in *four* cases. Whitish fibrinous clots were noted in the cardiac cavities in six instances, chiefly on the right side; in one case greenish clots were found on the right side, in another loosely formed black clots on both sides, and in another black fluid blood, which was frothy in the right but not in the left cavities. The PERICARDIUM was partially adherent to the heart in one case, and in twelve cases there was an effusion of from one to four ounces of serum, which was tinged with blood in two cases and in one instance contained yellow coagula.

According to the French observers† changes in the muscular tissue of the cardiac walls are frequently noted. DUTROULAU, indeed, regards the alterations in the heart as second in importance only to those in the spleen. M. VALLIN‡ conceives the alteration to consist of a primary transformation of the interfibrillar protoplasm into albuminous granules which cloud the striæ, cause swelling and end in fatty degeneration.

The LUNGS§ in the recorded cases were normal in *nine,* tubercular in *three,* more or less congested in *ten,* inflamed in *seven* and ecchymosed in *one;* in *ten* their condition was not mentioned. There were adhesions in four of the cases in which the state of the lung-tissue was not recorded, and a small pleuritic effusion in one in which the lungs were normal. The pleura was adherent also in three cases in which the lungs were congested and in four in which they were inflamed, and there was effusion in two of the pneumonitic and one of the tubercular cases.

The BRAIN in *twenty-eight* of the forty cases was probably not examined by our medical officers, as no mention is made of its condition. An examination in *twelve* instances showed a normal condition in *five.* In *one* case there was venous congestion; in *three* cases the brain was engorged with blood and presented effusion under the membranes or in the ventricles; in one of these the serum was jaundiced, the blood black and the cerebral tissue firm, and in another the brain-substance was of a darker ash-color than usual. In *three* cases there were indications of inflammatory action, in one injection of the meningeal vessels with some exudation near the longitudinal sinus, in another a similar injection with opacity of the arachnoid, and in the third case thickening of the membranes, effusion and circumscribed softening of the cerebral tissue.

MAILLOT found the brain affected so frequently‖ that he regarded malarial fevers as

---

* DUTROULAU says of these organs, that when blood and albumen have been observed in the urine with some persistence the *post-mortem* examination shows either pigmentation of the cortical substance or a lardaceous degeneration with an accumulation of pigment. *Op. cit.*, p. 197.

† Thus MAILLOT: The *heart* in six cases was flabby and pale; once flabby with yellowish coloration; once flabby with dilatation of the left ventricle, and four times the walls of this ventricle were hypertrophied. LAVERAN—The heart was of diminished consistence in nine of fourteen cases. *Op. cit.*, p. 84. COLLIN's experience also shows the heart as frequently affected. In his fifty-two cases of pernicious fever it was normal in two-fifths; its volume was augmented in three-tenths, and in one-half it was flaccid and of a dull livid color. These characters were even more prominent in the chronic cases: In sixty-one cases the physiological condition was noted only in one-fourth, flaccidity with a dull or onion-peel color in two-thirds and augmented volume in four-ninths. *Op. cit.*, p. 139.

‡ M. E. VALLIN, *Des altérations Histologiques du cœur et des Muscles Volontaires dans les fièvres pernicieuses et remittentes. Recueil de Mémoires de Méd. Militaires*, 3me sér., t. XXX, Paris, 1874, p. 12 *et seq.*

§ MAILLOT continues: In one case the chest was not opened; in one, also, it offered nothing abnormal. Thirteen times the pleura presented old adhesions, but the lungs were sound; in one case there was hepatization of the apex of the right lung, and in another some spoonfuls of russet-colored serum in the left cavity. LAVERAN says that in his cases the lungs were always engorged and the bronchial tubes oftentimes filled with blood-tinged mucus. *Op. cit.*, p. 85. In COLLIN's fifty-two pernicious cases the lungs were normal in only two instances; they were deeply congested in the majority and splenified in one-fifth of the subjects. *Op. cit.*, p. 135.

‖ MAILLOT's summary is as follows: *Membranes of the brain.*—Five times the arachnoid was generally opaque (once this general opacity coincided with the development of Pacchioni's glands; once, with the same alteration, there were adhesions to the dura mater and a gelatinous subarachnoid infiltration); three times the opacity was confined to the sulci between certain convolutions; in one case of algid icteric fever the arachnoid had a yellowish tint; in one case of quotidian fever which had become typhoid there was a collection of purulent serum in the cavity of the arachnoid. In eleven cases the pia mater was more or less vividly injected, the arachnoid not being so; in six other cases these membranes were simultaneously the seat of a vermilion-colored injection; in the majority of the cases the superficial vessels of the encephalon were markedly congested; several times the injection of the different membranes was sufficiently fine to form more or less extensive patches of an intense and brilliant red. *Brain.*—Twenty-two times the brain was more or less injected; generally of a density and firmness which seemed much more pronounced than natural. Ordinarily it showed a closely punctated red coloration; in some cases of comatose and delirious fevers the cerebral mass was so intensely congested that on compressing it the blood issued from its cut surface as if from a saturated cloth. Eight times we noted a dark coloration of the gray matter, which in five cases was even blackish; six times the choroid plexus was of a dark red color; ten times the ventricles contained a sanguinolent serum. In a comatose fever the brain was soft, although much injected; in a case of algid icteric fever it was slightly injected, of ordinary consistence and yellowish in color; in three other cases it was also slightly injected, but without change of color or consistence. The nervous substance of the cerebellum presented less frequently than its membranes alterations analogous to those in the brain and its membranes. *Membranes of the spinal cord.*—Fourteen times the spinal pia mater was the seat of a vermilion injection; five times the arachnoid and the pia mater were simultaneously injected; in a case of algid icteric fever both had a yellowish color; in another

due to an irritation having for its anatomical character a hyperæmia of the nervous matter and its membranes. The dark coloration of the brain-substance was observed by him and others, especially by Bright,* who illustrated the condition, long before Frerichs drew attention to it and connected it with other pigmentations in malarial cases. More recently Hammond has suggested the possibility of recognizing this condition during life.†

In one of the forty recorded cases the PAROTID GLANDS were inflamed, and in one the PSOÆ MUSCLES were blackened and disorganized.‡

The GENERAL MASS OF THE BLOOD is specially mentioned in two cases as having undergone change; in one it was diffluent and in the other watery and degenerated. In a third case blood, which had escaped into the pleural cavities, was uncoagulable, its red corpuscles broken down, stellated and withered, its white corpuscles relatively numerous and its serum of a reddish-yellow color. But an altered condition of the blood is suggested by the records of many other cases: as by the occasional blood-tinge shown by the effusion into the pericardium; the loose black clots in the heart; the black blood with which the cerebral veins and occasionally those of other organs were loaded, the vessels in one instance having presented yellow specks between tracts of black fluid blood; the soft, greenish, pus-like coagulation which had taken place in the heart and portal veins of one subject, the fibrinous heart-clots of several cases, and the frequent softening and occasional degeneration of the liver and spleen, apparently unconnected with inflammatory processes. Unfortunately the microscope was seldom used, and the records therefore give but little information as to the details of this altered condition.§

their condition was not stated. *Medullary substance.*—In four cases the cord was generally injected and more than ordinarily firm; in one case it was less firm than natural; in one the injection was very slight; three times it presented a normal consistency without injection; in two cases the injection was general, but much more marked in the cervical and lumbar regions; in one it was of a yellowish tint without other change; in four there was general injection with red dorsal softening; in three the softening, dorsal also, was white; in another the white softening had its seat in the cervical region; finally, in one case the injection of the gray matter, generally more pronounced than that of the white matter, was very intense in the cervical arch, and extended to the red softening in the dorsal portion.

* Bright—*Reports of Medical Cases*, London, 1831, Case CI, Vol. II, p. 217, Plates XVII and XIX. The cortical substance of the brain was almost of the color of black lead, and the minute circulation of the cineritious substance was so loaded with venous blood as to give one general purple-gray color. The medullary matter was of a uniform dead gray-white color, which appeared to be given by innumerable fine gray specks and short hair-like vessels resembling the appearance produced by scraping the nap of fine cloth upon a sheet of paper.

† In an article on *Pigmentary Deposits in the Brain resulting from Malarial Poisoning*, in the *Trans. Amer. Neurological Association*, 1875, Dr. W. A. Hammond pointed out that in affections of the nervous system having a malarial origin, and in which presumably there are cerebral pigmentary deposits, similar formations may often be detected in the retina by ophthalmoscopic examination. See also a contribution to the study of the nature and consequences of malarial poisoning.—*St. Louis Clinical Record*, Vol. IV, 1877, p. 129.

‡ M. Vallin discovered cloudy swelling, obscuration of striæ and fatty degeneration in the fibres of the recti muscles, especially towards their lower part. See article already referred to in connection with changes in the muscular tissues of the heart.

§ The altered condition of the blood was studied by Becquerel and Rodier—*Recherches relatives à la composition du Sang, dans l'état de santé et dans l'état de maladie. Compt. rend.*, Paris, 1844, XIX, p. 1083; and by Léonard and Foley in 1845—*Recueil de Mém. de Méd., &c., Militaires*, t. LX. The latter reporters made analyses of the blood in sixty-six cases of Algerine fever. Their results show, p. 191, a watery condition due to diminution of globules, albumen and inorganic constituents of the serum, without augmentation of fibrin, unless, as in rare cases, the congestion of the organs had developed into inflammation. Dr. Joseph Jones gives the following as the results of his investigation into the character of the changes in the blood: "1. In malarial fever the specific gravity of the blood and serum is diminished. The specific gravity of the blood ranges in this disease from 1030.5 to 1042.4, and the specific gravity of the serum from 1018 to 1023.6. In health, on the other hand, the specific gravity of the blood varies from 1055 to 1063, and the specific gravity of the serum from 1027 to 1032. 2. In malarial fever the colored blood-corpuscles are greatly diminished. In health the dried corpuscles may vary from 120 to 150 parts in the 1,000 of blood, and the moist blood-corpuscles from 480 to 600. In malarial fever, on the other hand, the dried colored corpuscles range from 51.98 parts to 107.81, and the moist blood-corpuscles from 207.92 to 323.63. The careful comparison of these analyses of malarial blood with each other reveals the fact that the extent and rapidity of the diminution of the colored corpuscles corresponds to the severity and duration of the disease; a short but violent attack of congestive or of remittent fever, in its severer forms, will accomplish as great a diminution of the colored blood-corpuscles as a long attack of intermittent fever, or the prolonged action of the malarial poison. 3. In malarial fever the relation between the colored corpuscles and liquor sanguinis is deranged. Thus in healthy blood the relative proportions of moist blood-corpuscles in the 1,000 parts and liquor sanguinis may vary from 480.00 to 600.00 of the former, and from 520.00 to 400.00 of the latter; whilst in malarial fever the globules vary from 207.92 to 323.63, and the liquor sanguinis from 792.08 to 676.37. 4. The fibrin of the blood is diminished to a marked extent in some cases of malarial fever, and is altered in its properties and in its relations to the other elements of the blood and to the bloodvessels. 5. The organic matters of the liquor sanguinis, and especially the albumen, is diminished in malarial fever. Thus the solid matters of the serum may vary in health from 90 to 105; whilst in malarial fever they vary from 62.78 to 80.22 parts in the 1,000 parts of blood."—*Medical and Surgical Memoirs*, New Orleans, 1876, Vol. I, p. 586. Dr. Jones makes no mention of pigment in the blood although aware of Frerichs' views, which he discusses in connection with the autopsies of his cases of chronic malarial poisoning, in both of which the liver and spleen, and in one the brain, were densely loaded with black pigment. American pathologists do not appear to have prosecuted the study of the blood-changes. Hutchinson, in an article on a case of enlarged spleen, with remarks on the malarial cachexia, in the *Med. News and Abstract*, Vol. XXXVIII, 1880, p. 449, reports a microscopical examination of the blood as follows: "The red corpuscles are irregular in shape and size, and form themselves poorly into rouleaux. Most of them show a tendency to alter in shape—to become double convex. The white corpuscles also vary in size and are slightly increased in number, a few more of them being seen in a field than in health, but the blood is not leucocythæmic. There is no evidence of pigmentation." Dr. Richard Heschl—*Ueber Pigmentbildung nach Febris intermittens. Zeitschr. der kais. kön. Gesellschaft der Aerzte zu Wein*, Bd. I, 1850, S. 338—describes the pigment as consisting partly of dark-brown and partly of dark-violet bodies about as large as blood corpuscles, some enclosed in cells and the others isolated or adherent in masses of twenty or thirty granules, generally lying close to the coats of the vessel. A subsequent article—*Ueber das Wechselfieber und die capillaren Blutungen in der Melanämie. Oesterreichische Zeitschrift für Praktische Heilkunde*, Wein, Bd. VIII, 1862, S. 810 et seq.—gives among others the following conclusions: The peculiar pigment of intermittent fever comes neither from an arrest of blood in the vessels, which Virchow holds as one of the conditions of its occurrence, nor from hæmorrhage, but from the coloring matter of the blood leaving the blood-corpuscles. The coloring matter is communicated to the coats of the vessels, and may there be found at first as a reddish, and later, oftentimes as a dark-brown substance; while the corpuscles not entirely deprived of their coloring matter continue to circulate with the rest of the blood as small reddish-looking bodies. The principal seat of this pigment-formation in severe cases is the brain, and in mild cases the liver or spleen. This peculiar hue of the coloring matter of the blood is due to the action of malaria, as it is observed only in cases of disease arising from this cause. Dr. Jul. Planer—*Ueber das Vorkommen von Pigment im Blute. Zeitschr. der k. k. Ges. der Aerzte zu Wien*, 1854, Bd. I, S. 126 et seq.—found pigment in the spleen, liver and brain of the subjects of intermittent fever. Blood taken from the living subject contained a multitude of

The varying and sometimes healthy condition of each of the organs presented in these records gives assurance that no one of them is entitled to have its changes from the normal state regarded as pathognomonic of malarial disease. The opinion of MAILLOT connecting the disease with a hyperæmic condition of the nervous matter and its membranes, that of· STEWARDSON, holding the bronze coloration of the liver as essential, and that of many French writers, associating the febrile manifestations with enlargement of the spleen, are rendered equally untenable by this one consideration. MAILLOT considered the hyperæmia to be the cause of the fever and not simply an accompanying anatomical fact. STEWARDSON was content to regard the liver-change as pathognomonic, without insisting on its being the cause of the morbid phenomena, since there was no evidence that it existed at the commencement of the fever and the early symptoms could not be traced to it as their source. The enlargement of the spleen, so long known to be associated with malarial disease, and the softening and occasional inflammatory appearances presented by it are undoubtedly suggestive of an intimate relationship between the fevers and the changed condition of the organ. AUDOUARD* held the tumefaction to be the effect of a congestion which preceded and determined the fever. At that time medical opinion generally considered malarial fever as an affection of ·the nervous system, the particular seat of which remained involved in obscurity, while the affection of the spleen was regarded as connected with an obstacle to the circulation in the portal system not pertaining exclusively to intermittent fever.† Following AUDOUARD, PIORRY concluded that the tumefaction was essentially a

---

brown and black masses similar to those often seen in *post-mortem* blood. But cell-like pigment bodies were constantly found. Dr. PLANER admits that the subject of pigment-formation is as yet far from being understood to its full extent, and that there is nothing in his observations to enable us to decide upon the manner or place of its formation. FRERICHS describes the pigment found in the blood as usually in the form of small rounded or angular granules, sometimes sharply defined and at others surrounded by a brownish or pale margin. They are occasionally isolated, but more frequently held together in small aggregations by a pale hyaline connecting substance. The groups are rounded, elongated or irregularly branched. True pigment-cells are also observed, although in smaller numbers than the granules and granular masses. The color is usually deep black, more rarely brown or ochre-colored, and least frequently reddish-yellow. The pigment exists in greatest abundance in the blood of the portal veins. He regards it as formed chiefly in the spleen, as the spindle and club-shaped cells with rounded nuclei in the blood resemble those which are found along with free granules in the spleen. But he conceives that the liver also may be concerned in the production of the pigment, as in one case of death after a protracted quartan the spleen was enlarged, lardaceous and completely free from pigment, while the liver contained considerable quantities. A. KELSCH—*Contribution à l'Anat. Path. des Maladies Palustres endémiques. Archives de Phys. normale et path.*, 2ᵉ série, t. II, 1875, p. 691. This investigator counted the number of blood-corpuscles in seventy cases of acute and chronic malarial poisoning at the hospital at Phillipeville in 1874–5 and found an invariable diminution in the number of the red corpuscles (oligocythæmia). Twenty to thirty days of simple remittent, quotidian or tertian fever reduced the number from five millions to one million, or even as low as half a million per cubic millimeter. He observed that a quotidian or remittent fever, on its first invasion, would reduce the number of globules as much as two millions per cubic millimetre in four days or even one million in a single day. But usually, as soon as the oligocythæmia was established, at one to two million globules per cubic millimetre, it remained stationary or nearly so. The white globules were also generally diminished in number, and proportionally even more than the red, notwithstanding the enlargement of the spleen; their number was one to one, two or three thousand red; but there were exceptions to this: in a few cases the white corpuscles were relatively more numerous than in health. He counted in particular instances 1 to 192, 118 or even 112 red. These blood-changes are more rapid during the first few days of the fever; they continue, but more slowly, for a longer period, and then remain stationary or nearly so. While the red corpuscles were found to be diminished in number their transverse diameter was increased, in some instances to 11, 12 and even 13 micromillimetres; the smallest mean in fourteen cases, in each of which one hundred globules were measured, was 7.889 and the largest mean 9.429 micromillimetres. In pernicious fever there is a rapid diminution in the number of the red corpuscles, amounting to from half a million to a million a day at the beginning of new cases; but in those that supervene on previous malarial anæmia the decrease is less rapid, from 100,000 to 200,000 a day. In these cases the white corpuscles are relatively and absolutely increased in number; there may be as many as 1 to 200 or even 70 red, in this respect differing from the blood in ordinary agues. He observed pigment in the white corpuscles of the blood twenty-four times in twenty-four cases of pernicious fever. In forty-seven chronic cases he had twenty-one negative and twenty-six positive results; of the latter twelve were observed during life, the others after death. He never found pigment in the peripheral vessels unless the portal and splenic veins, the liver, spleen and bone-marrow were saturated; on the contrary, in fourteen autopsies he found it in these internal parts, although there was none in the peripheral vessels. In eight cases of ordinary ague, on pricking the finger immediately after a paroxysm, he found the pigment five times. In a later paper—*Nouvelle Contribution à l'Anat. Path. des Maladies Palustres endémiques. Archives de Phys. normale et path.*, 2ᵉ série, t. III, 1876, p. 191—KELSCH states that during the intermittent attack the leucocytes diminish in greater proportion than the red corpuscles. The diminution is rapid and continuous, reaching as low as one-half or one-third of their number before the attack. One or two days are required for their re-establishment. The swelling of the spleen is coincident with their disappearance; but these phenomena are not proportionate. In the cachectic cases the leucocytes are diminished, but not in proportion to the splenic enlargement.

* *Jour. Gén. de Méd.*, t. LXXXIII, Paris, 1823, p. 245.

† At a later date Dr. EISENMANN, in an article on the proximate cause of enlargement of the spleen in intermittent fever and fevers generally, in the *Archiv für die gesammte Medicin*, B. V, Jena, 1843, S. 401, refers the tumefaction of the spleen to the chill. He was led to this opinion by reading the histories of two cases, one of hepatic phlebitis brought on by a fish-bone, which, in its progress from the stomach, had transfixed the superior mesenteric vein, and the other a case of rupture of a metastatic abscess into one of the hepatic veins. In both there were repeated chills with splenic enlargement. He considers, therefore, that since we have tumefaction of the spleen in varieties of fevers which in their origin, nature and indications are wholly different, we may enquire whether this enlargement does not belong to the fevers as such, originating in the febrile movement, no matter on what cause the latter is dependent. During the chill the capillaries are greatly contracted and the blood partly or wholly excluded from them, in consequence of which

congestion, although inflammatory changes might in progress of time appear, and was inclined to view the fever as connected with the condition of the spleen.* NELET[†] strengthened this view by reporting a case in which an inflammation of the spleen caused by external violence was immediately followed by intermittent fever which was cured by quinine. COHADON[‡] in his thesis argued in behalf of PIORRY's theory, that intermittents are due to a pathological condition of the spleen and of the portions of the nervous system which correspond with that organ. PÉZERAT,[§] however, was the most outspoken advocate of the view that intermittents are due to an inflammation of the spleen. His principal argument was the existence of tumefaction and pain in the organ, but it was shown by NEPPLE,[‖] NIVET[¶] and others, that while this pain is absent in many intermittent cases it is present with tumefaction in other diseases, as typhoid fever, in which there are no intermittent symptoms. The very character of the fever was an obstacle to the acceptance of PÉZERAT's views, as the tendency of inflammation, once established, is to progress not to intermit. Moreover, GENDRIN had already shown that the tumefaction occurs without inflammation or other material change in the intimate structure of the organ. The enlargement was therefore held to be the effect, not the cause, of the febrile manifestations. Finally, DUTROULAU[**] argued that while the state of the spleen is the most frequent and marked characteristic of malarial fevers, and sometimes one of the causes of grave symptoms, it is neither the point of departure nor the seat of the febrile phenomena.

But before, and during the continuance of, this contest as to the connection of splenic engorgement with the intermittent phenomena, there was an underlying idea that the condition of the blood stood in a peculiar relation to the organ and occasioned its congestion. One of GENDRIN's conclusions points to vitiation of the blood. NIVET held that in intermittents, as in scurvy and typhoid fever, in which also there is engorgement, the disease is general and the blood probably altered. Even PIORRY regarded a change in the blood as antecedent to the pathological condition of the spleen. Some light was thrown upon this point by the discovery of the pigmented condition of certain of the viscera in malarial fevers. FRERICHS considered that the disorganization of the blood was effected in the spleen, suggesting in explanation that during the stasis which takes place in the blood-current as it passes from the arterial system into the splenic sinuses, a stasis which is augmented in the congested state of the organ consequent on malarial fever, conglomerate masses of blood corpuscles are transformed into pigment, which is afterwards arrested in the capillaries of the liver, brain, kidneys, &c. The spleen, however, could not be considered the only organ actively concerned in the disorganization, as much pigment had been found, in one case, in the liver, while there was but little in the lardaceous spleen. But

---

the larger vessels and heart become overloaded. In this turgescence the spleen has a great share, as it seems designed for the reception of blood in a disordered state of the circulation, to obviate thereby the dangers arising from such disturbance. He alludes to the fact that splenic enlargement may arise from disordered circulation resulting from heart disease, as shown by BRERA—(*Rapporto della clinica di Padova*, 1812, p. 12); NASSE—(*Horn's Archiv*, 1819, August, S. 120), and SOUCHOTTE, (*Mém. de la Soc. de Méd. Prat. de Montpellier*, t. XX, p. 243-254)—and inquires why there should not be an overcharging of the spleen with blood, and a consequent enlargement, in a disturbance of the circulation due to spasm of the capillaries in the chill of fevers. He concludes that since all the facts and direct observations indicate that the chill causes the splenic engorgement, this condition will be found in every fever which begins with a chill, and will be most marked in intermittents, because in them the chill is not only more severe than in other febrile diseases but more frequent in its recurrences. So also in the fever arising from purulent infection, where the chills return frequently the enlargement of the spleen will be marked; but in those having only a single chill the augmentation naturally cannot be so great. Besides the character of the fever the tone of the tissues seem to have an influence on the enlargement; for in adynamic fevers in which the tissues have lost their tone the spleen will make less resistance to the blood forced upon it in the cold stage, and in time will have less power to remove the accumulated blood, than in sthenic cases in which the tissues remain vigorous. In irritative and inflammatory fevers the splenic enlargement need be sought for only while the chill lasts, and no great increase need be expected, while in asthenic forms it is not only great but of longer duration.

* *Mémoire sur l'état de la rate dans les fièvres intermittentes.* *Gazette Médicale*, 1833, p. 393.

† *Archives Générales de Médecine*, 2e serie, t. V, 1834, p. 137.   ‡ COHADON—*Collection des Thèses*, Paris, 1847, t. III, No. 31.

§ *Archives Générales de Médecine*, 2e série, t. V, 1834, p. 199.   ‖ NEPPLE—*Gazette Médicale*, t. IV, 1833, p. 613.

¶ NIVET—*Annales de Méd. Belge*, t. II, 1838, p. 25.   ** *Op. cit.*, p. 195.

the valuable researches of KELSCH appear to warrant his conclusion that the pigment is formed in the mass of the circulating blood and is deposited therefrom in the substance of those organs when a stasis in the circulation affords conditions favorable for sedimentation. He regards the splenic melanosis as secondary to the appearance of the pigment in the blood because in two of his cases there was little deposit in the spleen while the blood was charged with masses of pigment, and because the deposition of this melanæmic pigment is conducted in the same manner as that of other matters, such as cinnabar, which have been artificially introduced into the circulation.* In a later paper KELSCH† concludes from his many observations that the presence of this pigment in the blood is a pathognomonic sign of acute malarial poisoning; that it is not found in chronic cases in the absence of febrile accessions, and that it is an intermittent phenomenon allied to the other intermittent manifestations of acute impaludism, with which it appears and disappears.

In summarizing the *post-mortem* records left by our medical officers it is evident, not only that the condition of no one organ is the cause of malarial manifestations, but that these are due primarily to a morbid condition of the blood. In this way only may death be accounted for in cases characterized by alteration of the blood with but little enlargement of the liver or spleen. In this way also may be explained the pigmentary deposits associated with stasis of the blood, from engorgement as in the spleen, or from congestion or inflammatory conditions in other organs as the liver, brain or intestinal canal.

The change in the blood is presented as of two different characters: one in which it was thin and watery with a tendency to effusion and separation of fibrin; and the other in which it became black and disorganized. The former was its condition in intermittent and chronic cases, as indicated by such symptoms as anæmia, debility and effusion, and by the *post-mortem* appearances in those cases in which death occurred less from the intensity of the poisonous influence than from some accidental circumstance, as heart-clot in cases 95 and 96, or from the effects of some complication, as in case 75. The latter was its condition during pernicious attacks. These changes were produced in the blood by the operation of the malarial influence. If they are regarded instead as due to the action of the enlarged or softened spleen, which was so frequently present, the disorganization of the blood would be proportioned to the splenic alteration. But the presence of blood capable of continuing life in a patient whose spleen weighed sixty-eight ounces, case 100, is inconsistent with the idea of the participation of this organ in the disorganizing process. In other cases death occurred from altered blood although the spleen weighed only a few ounces more than usual. The notably enlarged spleen is a characteristic of chronicity; it corresponds to a mildness of the poison, as where the disease occurs in temperate climates, or to an accommodation of the system to pernicious doses, where it occurs in highly malarious localities. On the other hand, in some of the fatal remittents the spleen was found to be unaffected. Instead, therefore, of regarding this organ as an active agent in the disorganization of the blood, its action may plausibly be considered as conservative, preventing dangerous congestions in other organs by its enlargement, and preserving the blood from that diffluent and black condition which is the concomitant and probable cause of the more dangerous pyrexial manifestations. It may be that the action of the spleen is mechanical: as suggested by

---

*LANZI and TERRIGI—*Il miasma palustre*, Roma, 1875—connect malarial diseases with certain dark-colored granules found in the cells of microscopic algæ, which in the winter cover the Roman Campagna, but die under the heat and dryness of the summer and are converted into a dark-colored *humus*. The dust particles from this are affirmed to be identical with the black pigment of malarial disease, and to act as a ferment when introduced into the human system.

†A. KELSCH—*Contribution à l'histoire des maladies palustres—De la Melanémie—Archives Gén. de Méd.*, 7me serie, t. VI, 1880, p. 385.

KELSCH, the pigment-masses may be removed from the circulating blood by a process of sedimentation; but the hypertrophy which is so frequently found in chronic cases appears to indicate that there is a vital action involved in the removal of the malarial poison from the blood and in the regeneration of the latter after its disorganization by the morbific agent.

V.—CAUSATION OF MALARIAL DISEASE.

The following extracts from sanitary reports have been selected from many of a similar tenor as indicating the views of our medical officers on the causation of malarial disease:

Surgeon F. L. DIBBLE, 6th Conn. Vols., Dawfuskie Island, S. C., March 31, 1862.—The regiment remained at Hilton Head, S. C., during the first twenty days of January, 1862, when it was ordered to embark—about 800 strong—on the steamer *Cosmopolitan.* The boat at best was not capable of accommodating over four hundred men for any length of time. From some unexplained cause the command was kept on the crowded transport for five days in the harbor of Port Royal and for fifteen more in Warsaw Sound, when it was ordered to encamp on Warsaw Island, Ga. The side of the island where the troops were landed did not afford sufficient dry land to lay out a regular encampment, and the tents of the men were huddled together without regard to order. What we saw of the island was one vast swamp. The climate is nearly the same as at Hilton Head, generally mild and equable. The disease that particularly affected the regiment at this place was the congestive or pernicious fever of the coast, which raged for the first five days after we landed with almost incredible violence. Of the fatal cases not more than two lived twenty-four hours after the commencement of the attack. While at Warsaw Island the only duty exacted of the troops, besides the usual guard and picket duty, was about three hours daily drill. The command remained on shore about nine days, when it was ordered to re-embark on the little transport, and there we lay lazily at anchor for the eleven succeeding days in Warsaw Sound. At the expiration of this time General Sherman, by advice of the Medical Director, ordered the return of the regiment to Hilton Head. It should be stated, however, that when the order came to return no fatal case had occurred for the previous twelve days. For the next twenty days the regiment remained at Hilton Head, when it was ordered to the support of General Viele at Dawfuskie Island, S. C. [The report of sick and wounded from this regiment for the quarter ending March 31, 1862, gives a mean strength of 932 officers and men, among whom were 22 cases of congestive fever with 11 deaths.]

Surgeon JAS. H. THOMPSON, 12th Me. Vols., New Orleans, La., October 1, 1862.—The vicinity in which the abovementioned companies were stationed is, if possible, more marshy and unhealthy than the rest. The marshes are irregularly intersected with deep sluggish bayous and lagoons; this fact, in connection with the effluvia from the canals or sewers before mentioned, explains the large number of intermittent and continued fevers reported.

Surgeon JAMES BRYAN, U. S. Vols., opposite Vicksburg, June 27, 1863.—The vicinity of the great swamps near the Mississippi permitted the malaria to be borne by the prevailing winds to the locality of our hospital, and convalescents and patients from this cause were liable to new attacks and relapses. The only efficient preventive, judiciously administered, was quinine. This was found a sure prophylactic; but becoming scarce we had to resort to cinchona, which, in larger doses, we found to be equally effectual both as a prophylactic and a remedy.

Surgeon S. K. TOWLE, 30th Mass. Vols., December 31, 1862.—July 1, 1862, the regiment was in bivouac on the swampy point opposite Vicksburg, where it had been about ten days. This whole locality had just emerged from an overflow of many weeks' duration, and was still barely passable through mud and water from ankle to armpit deep, the slope of the level being the only place upon which the men could sleep. About the 10th the bivouac was changed to alongside the canal or cut-off being dug across the bend of the river through a heavily wooded swamp—thus adding the deleterious influence of large quantities of fresh soil of vegetable origin, daily thrown up, to that already experienced from the thick deposit of the long flood. This position was occupied to the end of the month, when the place was evacuated. During this time the men had no tents, but were required to build booths of branches as a partial protection from rains and heavy dews, and to construct platforms of poles two or three feet high upon which to sleep. Moreover, the duties were very severe. At first, on account of the mud and water in laying out the canal and cutting the trees from its course, many of the men were wet day and night; after this, digging the cut-off entailed similar hardships and exposures. There were also frequent alarms at night and much guard, picket and scouting duty, exposing them greatly to both dew and sun. Drills were also ordered, after the first few days, from 5 to $7\frac{1}{4}$ A. M. (practically before breakfast) and again for two and a half hours in the afternoon. The diet was exclusively, as it had been with but slight exceptions since leaving Massachusetts in January, salt meat and hard bread, and many of the men exhibited in consequence the preliminary symptoms of scurvy. All the circumstances tended to depress the spirits, and there was no prospect of any change for the better unless the entire object of the expedition was abandoned.

As the immediate result of this long exposure to intense malaria under circumstances tending to still further increase disease, a malignant form of remittent fever became very prevalent, with a strong tendency to take on the congestive type. Out of the eight hundred picked men (one hundred and fifty feeble and second-rate men had been left behind) eighteen died in the swamp, while at the time the regiment left that position more than half of the entire force was on the sick list, two hundred being in hospital and more than that number sick in quarters. The hospital accommodations were negro huts and steamboat decks, with no beds, bedding, stores or provisions other than rations, obtainable excepting by seizure.

During August the regiment was at Baton Rouge, La., where on the 5th it took part in the battle, losing four killed and eighteen wounded. The sick list during this month was never below four hundred, almost entirely from malarial diseases, chiefly remittent fevers. In September and October the regiment was encamped near Carrollton, La., on the so-called Metairie ridge, near the swamp extremity of the fortifications defending New Orleans from attack from up-river. This ridge at the point of encampment is but a few feet above the heavily wooded swamp within gunshot on either side, and with the exception of the fresh deposit of decaying vegetable matter, was but little if any improvement over the swamp opposite Vicksburg, producing the same class of diseases, although somewhat less pernicious in type. At Baton Rouge and Carrollton the men got vegetables enough to eradicate the scorbutic symptoms, and the labor and exposure were less; but the sick list did not fall at any time much below four hundred, and generally three hundred were in the hospital. Nearly all those who had remittent fever from the exposure at Vicksburg had repeated attacks at Carrollton, and of the few who had escaped up-river not one, officer or private, escaped illness from the effect of malaria at the latter locality. Although the general type of malarial disease was somewhat less severe at Carrollton than at Vicksburg, the men had become so debilitated by repeated attacks that the mortality was no less. There also resulted a class of chronic cases, with diarrhœa, anasarca and anæmia, tending apparently irresistibly to death by exhaustion of the vital powers. Hospital accommodations were much better than while up the river, and gradually became quite good, while the facilities for a proper diet were also much improved.

In November and December the regiment was quartered at the U. S. barracks four miles below New Orleans, where, with but nominal duty, little exposure, good diet, dry airy quarters and a generally cheerful and contented feeling, the men have steadily improved in health and strength. But while this has been true in general terms of the regiment, there have been many relapses, and in many cases the system has seemed so thoroughly poisoned by long exposure, under the most unfavorable circumstances, to malarious influences as intense as could be found in the South, that no response would follow the exhibition of stimulants or the most nutritious food, but death would inevitably occur from exhaustion or debility alone.

The treatment followed has been simple from necessity, if not from choice; for the majority of the cases have been treated in the regimental hospital with only the limited variety of supplies furnished for field service. Sulphate of quinine has, of course, been the great reliance, and in no case of intermittent fever, in which anything approaching a fair trial could be had, has it failed in effecting a prompt cure. Cases of malarial fever treated in houses (contrary to the results of my experience with typhoid fever on the Potomac) have progressed much more favorably and rapidly than those in tents, and cases in Sibley tents have proved less tractable and more liable to a relapse than those in wall tents with a fly. Indeed, in this climate, in summer a fly is indispensable for comfort either in the hot sun by day or the heavy dews at night. Capsicum has proved of great value in conjunction with quinine, especially in cases requiring stimulants, as after the first most of them did. Mustard in the form of large poultices was more useful than when applied with baths, and, especially in the congestive cases, was of the first importance. Of stimulants, ale was the most universally beneficial, and but few instances were noted in which it failed to act kindly.

The total mortality in the regiment during the six months, in general as well as regimental hospitals, was two hundred and two, or *one-fifth* the aggregate strength July 1, which was one thousand and eleven. Of these 114 died during the quarter ending September 30 and 88 during the last quarter. The aggregate, December 31, 1862, is seven hundred and thirty.

Surgeon J. M. ALLEN, 54th Pa. Vols., May 31, 1862.—The regiment is on duty in the valley of the Potomac. This region of Virginia is proverbial for almost every variety of miasmatic fever, and when the peculiar nature of the climate, hot days and cold nights, is taken into consideration in connection with frequent overflows and rank undergrowth, the cause may be easily explained. The diseases incident to the vicinity are remittent, intermittent, typhoid and congestive fevers, pneumonias, diarrhœal and bronchial affections.

Surgeon ROBERT MORRIS, 9th N. Y. Vols., Key West, Fla., April 1, 1862.—The ponds in this vicinity are a fruitful source of disease; for the rains wash into them a large quantity of vegetable matter, which, during the process of decomposition, evolves so much malaria or bad air that the odor is very offensive, particularly when the wind blows over them towards the camp. One of these ponds, that nearest the encampment, has recently been filled up, and no doubt the salubrity has been thereby much increased.

Surgeon A. W. WOODHULL, 9th N. J. Vols., Carolina City, N. C., June 1, 1863.—Some of the posts at which portions of this regiment have done picket duty have been extremely unhealthy. Particularly is this true of Havelock, a post on the railroad, eight miles from Newport barracks and sixteen miles from New Berne, N. C. It is situated in a low wet swamp on the border of Slocum's creek, which is here dammed for water-power. In the spring of 1862 the dam washed away, leaving a large extent of surface which had been covered with water. This place became extremely unhealthy, developing intermittent and remittent fevers in great abundance. The record shows that 98 per cent. of the men of this regiment, who had been stationed there more than ten days, were attacked by one or the other of these fevers. For a time they were kept subdued by administering daily portions of quinine, but the supply being suddenly cut off, they reappeared with greater frequency and increased severity. It is believed that a sufficient supply of quinine will prevent at such places the prevalence of these fevers to any serious extent.

Surgeon A. W. McCLURE, 4th Iowa Cav., near Helena, Ark., September 30, 1862.—On July 1 we were encamped on the White river at Jacksonport, Ark., perhaps the most malarious locality in the State. Our fevers were then, as they had been for some months previous, of a malignant character. On the 6th we moved down the river on short rations. Miasmatic fevers prevailed to a considerable extent, but of a mild character. About the last of July we reached this place. Our brigade has since been encamped six miles west of the town in a position as salubrious as any in this vicinity, although the low cotton-lands extending to the south afford fertile soil for the production of malaria, and our men have not been proof against its withering influence. Intermittent and remittent fevers have readily yielded under the use of quinine; but the atmosphere is so impregnated with poison that there exists a strong tendency to a return or relapse. After a repetition of the attacks, or even after a severe and protracted first attack, diarrhœa has supervened, attended with cachexia, and we have found it necessary to remove the patients to northern hospitals; nearly all such cases, however, have recovered by being thus removed and put upon a liberal diet.

Surgeon H. F. CONRAD, *174th Pa. Vols., Beaufort, S. C., April 30, 1863.*—The camp we now occupy is situated on Port Royal, one of the sea islands, a sandy plain. Immediately in the rear of our location passes an inlet from Coosaw river. This inlet is about one-fourth of a mile wide. When the tide is in it is filled with water, but is left bare when the tide recedes. Long swamp grasses cover its bed, giving rise to an increased miasmatic influence from the decomposed vegetation. As the warm weather advances a still greater quantity of the miasmatic poison will be generated. The prevailing disease is intermittent fever, which has increased considerably within the last two weeks, and is generally of the quotidian type. It has so far readily submitted to active treatment. I generally commence with a purgative dose of calomel, followed, if necessary, by a dose of oil, rhubarb or salts. I then put the patient on sulphate of quinine, from twelve to twenty grains daily, divided into three or four doses. This seldom fails to check the paroxysms; yet I generally continue the quinine for some time to prevent the recurrence of the disease. I observe that it requires larger quantities of quinine to act efficiently in this climate than in our northern States, no doubt from the miasmatic influences being more powerful in this region than in the north. I have not as yet had any case of bilious remittent fever, but anticipate its prevalence as the summer months advance.

Surgeon S. N. SHERMAN, *34th N. Y. Vols., Seneca Mills, Md., October 1, 1861.*—Chills and fever have resulted, but only in those doing guard duty on the river; and of those attacked few fail of a rapid recovery when quinine is liberally used and strict confinement to camp enjoined. With the approach of the frosts of autumn the number of attacks decrease and the recoveries are more speedy. But for diseases of malarious origin the health of the regiment would be good.

Asst. Surg. JAMES B. HUNTER, *60th Ind. Vols., on the condition of certain regiments near Thibodeaux, La., August 31, 1864.*—It is worthy of remark that the sick reports of the 18th N. Y. Cav. and 4th Iowa Bat. show a much larger percentage of cases of intermittent fever than those of the 16th and 60th Ind. Vols. for the same time and under nearly similar circumstances as far as camps and duties are concerned. The question suggests itself whether the difference in favor of the last two regiments is not due, at least in part, to the fact that they are using the wedge-tent while the other commands have only the imperfect protection of the shelter-tent, in which, in bad weather, the men cannot keep their clothing or blankets even tolerably dry, and under which they are constantly exposed during the night to currents of air probably charged with malarious poison. [In another regiment, the 33d Ill., in which intermittent and remittent fevers have been the prevalent diseases, prophylaxis has been attempted with fair success by the administration to the portion of the command most exposed of a spirituous infusion of willow bark.]

Asst. Surg. ALEXANDER INGRAM, *U. S. Army, 2d U. S. Cav., Sharpsburg, Md., September 1, 1862.*—The first two months of the quarter were passed on the Peninsula, where the men were exposed to excessive heat and miasm. Add to these agencies the influences of water tainted with alluvial and animal matters, and the exhalations from the various unwholesome accumulations incident to a crowded camp, and the essential causes of sickness in the command will be comprised. These various causes resulted in irregular malarial diseases, nearly every case being benefited by the administration of quinine,—intermittent fevers, remittent fevers and diarrhœas characterized by torpidity of the liver. That the malarial fevers did not assume a typhoid type, as was the case in many commands, I attribute to the superior cleanliness of the men in person and camp, and temperance in diet and drink, they being old and disciplined soldiers.

Surgeon CHARLES J. NORDQUIST, *83d N. Y. Vols., near Sharpsburg, Md., October 10, 1862.*—On October 21, 1861, the command was ordered to the scene of the Ball's Bluff disaster, and while at Conrad's ferry it was exposed to a drenching rain-storm for eighteen hours. The men were without shelter of any description, and remained in their wet clothing for forty-eight hours; this, in connection with the insanitary conditions of their camp at Muddy Branch, decaying vegetable matter, a clayey, moist soil and muddy, brackish water, caused a marked change in their health. Remittent, intermittent, bilious and typhoid fevers prevailed to an alarming extent, and fully one-third of the regiment succumbed to the evil influence exerted on their systems by the above-mentioned causes.

These reports, as also occasional references in those published in the first part of this work,* indicate the belief of our medical officers in the identity of origin of all the so-called malarial diseases from simple languor and loss of strength, with slight splenic enlargement or hepatic derangement, to the congestive fevers which were so speedily fatal. The essence of these various and clinically dissimilar morbid phenomena was conceived to be an emanation from certain soils, especially those which were rich in vegetable matter undergoing the

*See, for instance, in the Appendix the reports of TRIPLER, p. 46; COOPER, pp. 232–3; HAND, p. 239; FRINK, p. 318, and WHITEHILL, p. 334.

natural process of decomposition under the combined influence of heat and moisture.   Hence swamps, marshes, river-bottoms liable to flood, bayous, lagoons, ponds, dams and canals were deemed sufficient to account for the presence of disease, especially towards the close of the summer season, when the heat was believed to operate indirectly, by lowering the water-level and exposing larger surfaces of moist soil, as well as directly in promoting the generation and evolution of the malarial miasm.

The disease-cause was recognized as moving, cloud-like upon, and for some distance along, the slopes which faced its marshy source; and as capable of being carried in dangerous concentration for considerable distances by winds passing over such extensive swamps as are found in the Mississippi bottom.   Its greater concentration or more malignant character at night was illustrated by the frequency with which men were seized while on night duty.   Dr. HUNTER, indeed, refers to the greater prevalence of the disease among men who slept in shelter-tents, the open ends of which gave free exposure to the air, than among those who, other things being equal, were better protected by the wedge or 'A' tents.

It is manifest, however, that the presence of absolute swamps or marshes was not considered essential to the development of the miasm, as it was attributed to cotton-lands and other soils where vegetation was rank.   FRINK noted the prevalence of intermittents in some regiments camped in a strip of timber on rather low ground.   The cutting down of trees for firewood or for the building of huts, corduroy roads, breastworks, bomb-proofs, abatis and other military works was frequently followed by the development of malarial fevers.   As in civil life similar consequences have often been ascribed to the clearing of timbered lands, the exposure of the soil to an increased solar heat was regarded as the cause of the newly developed insalubrity.   And, as in the inception of agriculture in a new country, the removal of undergrowth and the upturning of the soil are so frequently followed by malarial manifestations or the aggravation of pre-existing diseases, it seems likely that no inconsiderable proportion of such diseases in our armies may have been owing to the clearing of the surface and disturbance of the soil incident to the process of going into camp.   It is certain that many of our medical officers recognized this possibility, and were as earnest in their efforts to preserve the natural integrity of a camp-site which appeared free from malarial factors, as to drain and improve one which was manifestly insalubrious.

But a soil capable of evolving malaria under the theory of organic decomposition was reputed, in one exceptional instance, as exercising no injurious effect on the health of the troops camped near it:—

Ass't Surg. GEORGE H. HORN, 2d Cal. Cav., Camp Independence, Owen's Valley, Cal., April 1, 1863.—The great extent of swamp-land might be supposed to cause miasmatic disease.   No case has, however, been known to arise. All the causes favorable to the development of such diseases exist.   Their absence can only be accounted for by the extreme dryness of the atmosphere and the quantity of saline materials in the soil and water.

It is probable, however, that the swamps of Owen's Valley are as malarious as those of the river-bottoms in Arizona, where the climate, soil and vegetation are of a similar character, and that the absence of malarial manifestations reported by Dr. HORN was due to the absence of exposure.   After the establishment of Fort McDowell, Arizona Territory, on the dry mesa sloping towards the Verde river-bottom, the garrison remained free from malarial disease for over a year.   At the end of this period Indian hostilities called detachments of the garrison into the field, and coincident with their exposure in temporary camps in the river-bottoms malarial fevers appeared among them.   Camp Independence was established three miles from Owen's river, on high ground bearing only scattered patches of bunch-grass and sage-bush. At the time Dr. HORN made his report the post had not been garrisoned for more than a year. Its later records show the presence of malarial fevers.

On the other hand, malarial diseases of a pernicious character are reported in one instance where the surroundings are said to have been inconsistent with the theory of organic decomposition :—

Surgeon W. W. BROWN, 7th N. H. Vols., Fort Jefferson, Tortugas, Fla., June 30, 1862.—There seems to be no cause for malarial disease, as the waters of the Atlantic Ocean constantly bathe the walls of the fort; yet three or four cases of very severe and malignant congestive fever occurred in rapid succession, though nothing of that character has since appeared.

The records of Fort Jefferson show the prevalence of malarial affections;* but, although there is little surface-growth, the absence of organic matter in the soil may not be admitted. On the contrary, the soil appears rich in the elements of vegetable growth; for at Key West, where a similar coral-sand is raised a few feet above the salt-water level, it is covered with a thick chaparral, and produces under cultivation nearly all the tropical fruits and vegetables.†

A review of the observations bearing on the relation between vegetation and malarial disease appears to indicate that the poison of the disease is elaborated during the reduction of nitrogenous organic matter into the inorganic form in which it is available for absorption by growing plants, and evolved from the surface as malaria when the living vegetation fails to absorb all the richness of the prepared nutritive material. Thus, in the diurnal changes, malarial exhalation ceases when the vitality of the plant is at its maximum under the influence of the sun's light and heat, and becomes active during the night, the period of vegetable repose. Our spring fevers occur when, with the northward advance of the sun, the earth becomes heated before its surface is covered with the new vegetation. During the summer, when vegetable life is in full activity, malarial diseases do not increase in proportion to the increasing heat of the season. In the autumn the hot sun and occasional rains continue the processes going on in the soil, but the natural decay which succeeds to the fructification of the annuals interferes with absorption and malarial diseases assume an increased prevalence and malignancy.

The association of autumnal fevers with vegetable decay led to the belief that the putrefaction or decomposition of vegetable tissues was directly connected with the febrile occurrences. But it is well known that free exposure to the effluvium from decomposing vegetable masses does not develop malarial affections. It is only when this vegetable matter has been mixed with soil and is undergoing the fermentative processes which result in the nitrification of organic ammonia that the presence of malaria is manifested. Seasonal observations made in the tropics give testimony agreeing with that of the temperate zones. The dry season is the analogue of our winter; but while with us soil-fermentation is held in check by cold, in the tropics moisture is the lacking factor. With the first showers of the rainy season some cases of fever occur. ALIBERT‡ explained these sudden developments by enunciating his sixth proposition: "Rains which fall in very hot weather may contribute to the production of malignant intermittents by setting at liberty putrid vapors which had been confined beneath the hardened surface of the earth." But they correspond to our vernal intermittents, and may be referred to the same cause, the presence of the conditions needful to soil-fermentation and the absence of growing vegetation. As the

* "The prevailing diseases are malarial fevers, usually mild, and catarrhal affections."—Hygiene of the U. S. Army. Circular No. 8, S. G. O., Washington, D. C., 1875, p. 140.
† Work last quoted, p. 144.   ‡ALIBERT—A Treatise on Malignant intermittents. Caldwell's translation, Philadelphia, 1807, p. 182.

rains continue the country becomes covered with an exuberant verdure, and the malarial manifestations are lessened, but only to break out with increased virulence when this annual growth wilts and decays at the end of the rainy season.*

Malaria may therefore be considered due to a want of relation between the nutritive elements of the soil and its living vegetation. When thus viewed, malarial developments following a removal of the natural growth in the preparation of the ground for agricultural purposes are readily explained. Their subsequent disappearance when, by drainage and cultivation, a proper relationship has been established between the soil and its crop, is an obvious consequence. Exhalations from a parched soil bearing a withered vegetation, as noted by FERGUSON in rocky ravines, river-bottoms and bare open hollow lands in the Iberian Peninsula, are also understood, as well as his remark that a healthy condition of soil in these pestiferous regions was infallibly regained by the restoration of the marshy surface to its utmost vigor of vegetable growth.† There was underlying moisture in these rocky ravines and temporarily dried up water-courses. So at Fort Jefferson, Fla., a rich organic soil with underlying moisture, a high temperature and absence of living vegetation may be accepted as the conditions which permit of malarial exhalation.

Oftentimes men in the full vigor of health were struck down by the miasmatic influence, but in general the operation of predisposing conditions was recognized. These are variously enumerated, but all undoubtedly acted by lowering the vital powers and rendering the system less able to withstand the influence of a superadded miasm. Most of the conditions affecting the soldier on active service were of a depressing or exhausting tendency. He was often hungry; his food was not unfrequently poorly cooked; the issues of hard bread and fresh meat at times occasioned diarrhœa; the sameness of diet developed a scorbutic taint. One reporter, indeed, regarded the ration as the most powerful of the predisposing factors, the excess of its carbonaceous elements inducing a congestion of the portal system which opened the way to malarial attacks.‡ While generally warmly clothed, the soldier was often chilled at night, or after profuse perspiration or exhaustion from fatigue. He was exposed to rains, and had to remain in his wet clothes for days at a time, sleeping on the wet ground without shelter. At other times the exhaustion was consequent on forced marches or excessive labor under an oppressive sun. The water-supply was generally surface collections, often foul naturally, and usually tainted by the inflow of the surface washings and drainage of neighboring camps. Lastly, a state of mental depression arising from absence from home, domestic concerns, impending personal or public danger, etc., was considered as adding to the predisposition.

Hot days and cold nights are mentioned by Surgeon ALLEN as predisposing the system to malarial attacks; but OLDHAM's theory, that malaria is chill,§ is sufficiently disproved by DIBBLE's report from Dawfuskie Island, N. C., where, in a mild and equable climate, the command became subject to some of the most malignant of the malarial affections.

The influence of predisposing conditions in determining the type of the fever is suggested by a study of Table XXXIII, where the indicated prevalence of congestive and remittent cases in the Potomac Department seems explicable only on the assumption that the fatigues, exposures and privations of the troops operating between Washington and Richmond

---

* For an excellent description of the seasonal occurrence of these fevers at Sierra Leone and neighboring points on the African coast, see BOYLE on the *Diseases of Western Africa*, London, 1831.

† *On the Nature and History of the Marsh Poison. Trans. Royal Society*, Edinburg, 1823, Vol. IX, p. 273.

‡ FRINK—*Appendix to Part First of this Work*, p. 318.   § *What is Malaria?* by C. F. OLDHAM, London, 1871.

rendered them more liable, when exposed to the malarial influence, to become affected with an aggravated type of the disease than men who, though exposed to more concentrated miasms, were in better condition to resist their prostrating influence.

Several of the reporters refer to impurity in the drinking-water as occasioning a predisposition to malarial affections. In the early history of medical science paroxysmal fevers and enlarged spleens were referred to the action of impure water. But as the doctrine of an aërial miasm, enunciated by LANCISI, explained many things which had been obscure, it met with general acceptation, and the possibility of water-infection was forgotten by the profession although it continued as a strong belief in the minds of the uneducated in all malarious countries. This theory, however, of an air-borne swamp-poison failed to account for all the cases that occurred, unless on the supposition that the evolving surface was sometimes so minute as to be readily overlooked.* Meanwhile an occasional instance was reported in which the disease was apparently due to the drinking of an infected water, as for example the well known case of the Argo.† But as malarious waters, supposing them to exist, are usually and for obvious reasons found in localities presenting all the conditions needful to the evolution of an aërial poison, the disease, when it did occur, was referred to the latter as a matter of course, while the existence of the former remained unsuspected. The recognition of water as an agent in the transmission of malarial disease has been gradually effected. Professor PARKES, giving weight to a number of cases which he mentions, accepted the theory and speculated on the connection between the disappearance of malarial fevers in England and the coincident use of purer supplies of drinking water.‡ Professor LÉON COLIN, from his experience in Algiers, denies that marshy waters produce intermittent fevers; but as the troops under his observation were operating in a notoriously malarious country the difficulties in the way of arriving at a positive conclusion must have been very great. His testimony cannot be considered as authorizing a stronger statement than the denial of the occurrence of cases which might not be plausibly referred to malarial exhalations.

A country where malaria is not exhaled from the soil, at least in quantity or concentration sufficient to produce intermittents, would seem necessary to relieve observations on malarious waters from the objection caused by the alleged presence of the aërial poison, and

---

* Thus MACCULLOCH, in his *Essay on Malaria*, Philadelphia, 1829, p. 28: "If it is acknowledged or proved that marsh or swamp, whether fresh or salt, is generative of malaria, it is also a very common opinion that a certain extent of this soil, and generally a considerable one, is necessary to the production of disease. This is an error; and it must be classed among the dangerous ones, as being productive of false security." He then adverts to the analogy between malaria and contagion, arguing that the quantity of malaria necessary to produce its peculiar disease or diseases must be indefinably small, for it is well known that often from a very limited spot the poison will proceed through the air or on the winds to distances of three or four miles, exhibiting, notwithstanding the dilution which must take place in transit, almost as much virulence as in its native marsh; and he cites the hills of Kent as infected by emanations from the marshes of Erith, Northfleet and Gravesend. "The conclusion," he says, "is obvious; and there is nothing in it which seems to admit of dispute, since it is almost a question of arithmetic. If the produce of a hundred square feet or acres or of any scale and number of parts can, under a dilution of one thousand or ten thousand times, excite disease, then must, in the inverse ratio, the produce of the one-thousandth or the ten-thousandth portion of that space be capable, before dilution, of producing the same effects; or a single blade of grass acting on water (if this be the cause) may be as efficacious as an acre; supposing, of course, that it is actually applied to that part of the body which can suffer from its action." TOMMASI-CRUDELI holds that malaria may be generated in quantities sufficient to produce intermittent fever by the garden mould of flower-pots kept in bedrooms, and on the authority of Professor VON EICHWALD, instances the case of a Russian lady whose aguish relapses, having been referred to this cause, were permanently cured by the removal of the flower-pots.—*Practitioner*, Vol. XXVII, pp. 387-8.

† PARKES in his *Practical Hygiene* summarizes and remarks on this case as follows: "The case of the Argo, recorded by BOUDIN,—*Traité de Géographie et de Statistique Médicales*, 1857, t. I, p. 142,—is an extremely strong one. In 1834, 800 soldiers in good health embarked on three vessels to pass from Bona in Algiers to Marseilles. They all arrived at Marseilles the same day. In two vessels there were 680 men without a single sick man. In the third vessel, the Argo, there had been 120 men; thirteen died during the short passage (time not given), and of the 107 survivors no less than 98 were disembarked with all forms of paludal fever, and as BOUDIN himself saw the men there was no doubt of the diagnosis. The crew of the Argo had not a single sick man. All the soldiers had been exposed to the same influences of atmosphere before embarkation. The crew and the soldiers of the Argo were exposed to the same atmospheric conditions during the voyage; the influence of air seems therefore excluded. There is no notice of the food, but the production of malarious fever from food has never been suggested. The water was, however, different—in the two healthy ships the water was good. The soldiers on board the Argo had been supplied with water from a marsh, which had a disagreeable taste and odor; the crew of the Argo had pure water. The evidence seems here as nearly complete as could be wished."

‡ "Is it not possible," he says, "that the great decline of agues in England is partly due to a purer drinking water being now used? Formerly, there can be little doubt, when there was no organized supply and much fewer wells existed, the people must have taken their supply from surface collections and ditches, as they do now, or did till lately, at Sheerness."

the tendency to refer all morbid phenomena to its influence. The writer was at one time stationed in such a country, at Fort Bridger, on the northern slope of the Uintah Mountains in Wyoming T'y, where intermittents were undoubtedly imported diseases which tended to longer intervals and ultimate recovery.* Nevertheless, in this country, a remittent fever was well recognized as indigenous. It was known to the settlers as *mountain fever*, and although in most cases recovery was rapid under mercurial purges and quinine, the patient, if not subjected to specific treatment, would fall into an adynamic condition to which the name of *typhoid* or *typho-malarial* was occasionally applied. That this fever was malarial in its origin was the general opinion of the medical men familiar with it, although the source of the exhalation was not evident and although, moreover, the disease did not correspond in its period of prevalence with the remittents of notoriously malarious regions. It occurred with greatest frequency during the months of May, June and July, but appeared occasionally in all the other months *except* September and October,† the months of special prevalence of the ordinary autumnal fever.

This remittent was traced by the writer to the use of the river-water constituting the supply of the post.‡ He found that this water contained a larger quantity of organic matter than was usual in good river-waters, and that the maximum and minimum of the prevalence of the fever corresponded in time with the maximum and minimum of the organic impurity in the water-supply. During the period of increased impurity the bed of the stream was more or less flooded and the water turbid from the spring rains, and especially from the melting of the snows on the mountains. As the post was seven thousand feet above the sea-level, and on the northern exposure of the mountain range, its springs were late, the thaw beginning only toward the end of April and lasting well into July. During the period of diminished impurity, as scarcely any rain fell on the mountains which at this time were free from snow, the small volume of clear water which ran in the bed of the stream must be regarded as percolated waters contributed by the mountain springs.

This led to a more extended survey of the history of mountain fever, which developed in every instance a similar relationship to organic impurity in the water. Thus hunters, miners, cattle-herders, surveying parties and soldiers on scouting duty, who made use of a surface-water supply charged with vegetable impurities, were more frequently affected with remittent fever than permanent settlers who had provided themselves with a pure supply from wells and springs. That the remittents which affected these nomads were not directly due to malarial exhalations was manifest from their occurrence when the ground was covered with snow and the temperature far below the freezing point. At Camp Douglas, Utah, such remittents were observed only among soldiers who had been absent from the station on scouting duty. On account of the small size of the stream on which this post depended for its water-supply, and the possibility of its drying up at times during summer, a storage reservoir had been built. This was large enough to permit of an efficient sedimentation; but to prevent the unnecessary filling up of the basin by the intrusion of solids the instructions to the man in charge looked to the admission of water only when it ran without turbidity in the stream. The exclusion of the snow-waters and heavy rainfalls, thus effected, gave a comparatively pure spring-water at all times for the use of the post. Moreover, the gradual disappearance of these mountain remittents with the progress of

---

* *Hygiene of the U. S. Army.—Circular* No. 8, S. G. O., 1875, p. 319.

† See work last cited, p. 320, where a table of monthly sick rates is presented, embracing the eight years 1866–73.

‡ SMART.—*On Mountain Fever and Malarious Waters. Am. Jour. Med. Sci.*, Vol. LXXXV, 1878, pp. 1–27.

settlement was of some weight in the argument. In the early days of trans-continental travel, when the overland journey implied months of weary marching and a water-supply from rivers, ponds, dams, etc., the disease was common and dangerous; but when the journey was accomplished by steam in a few days, and the settlements furnished with a better water-supply, the remittent occurred only in those whose mode of life imposed on them the conditions common to all in the earlier days.

Soldiers on scouting duty are particularly liable to this remittent. They are exposed to climatic influences, over-fatigue, loss of sleep, anxieties, insufficient and badly cooked food and impure water. These are precisely the harmful agencies to which our troops were subjected during the civil war, except that in the latter instance there was in addition an exposure to malarial exhalations which was considered the efficient cause of all malarial manifestations. But since the troops on Indian service in Wyoming and other Territories are liable to a remittent which may not be attributed to emanations from the soil, it is possible that some of the remittents which affected our soldiers during the war may have been due to other causes than an air-borne malarial poison. And if so, this cause must have been an impure water; for the troops at Fort Bridger were also affected by the remittent, and they had nothing in common with the soldiers on scouting duty except the water-supply from the running stream, at times charged with vegetable impurities. They were well fed, well clothed and sheltered, and had no exposures nor fatigues other than those borne by their comrades at posts where there were no remittents, but where there was at the same time a better water-supply.

In view of these facts and considerations, to which may be added a few instances of probably malarious waters more recently recorded,* it seems not unlikely that a certain percentage of the malarial diseases which affected our armies was due to the introduction of the malarial poison into the system by means of the drinking-water.

The writer was, and is, inclined to believe that the cases due to water-impregnation were included among those characterized by adynamic tendencies, because remittents instead of intermittents occurred at Fort Bridger, and these, when neglected, assumed a typhoid character. It may readily be allowed, however, that where the water is strongly charged with the poison the morbid developments may be rapid and pernicious, as in the cases on

---

* See SMART on *Water Analysis*, in the *Annual Report of the National Board of Health*, Washington, D. C., 1880, p. 502, where sample No. 45, sent by Dr. GAINES of Mobile, on account of malarial remittents having occurred among the persons using it, was found to contain .35 part organic ammonia per million. No. 46 of the same report, from a cistern in a well-paved and non-malarious section of New Orleans, was furnished by Dr. C. B. WHITE, Medical Director of the Citizen's Auxiliary Sanitary Association, that lead, if present, might be detected, as the persons using the water had been affected with many anomalous symptoms. No lead was found, but the impurity of the water, .70 of organic ammonia, was such that the analyst believed himself dealing with swamp-water furnished for the purpose of testing his results. Pending the analysis a severe case of remittent fever was developed in the house in the person of a woman who had not been in a malarious neighborhood for many months. Suspicion was aroused in the minds of the people and the cistern was closed. When the analyst reported the water as a veritable swamp-water, the occurrence of this fever was made known to him. According to the *Report of the National Board of Health*, 1882, p. 293, Dr. E. D. COONLEY, of Mariner's Harbor, Staten Island, N. Y., was called on a Wednesday to see the case of a girl six years of age who died after a convulsive seizure which had been preceded by twenty-four hours of chill, headache and vomiting. No autopsy was held. On the following Sunday another child of the same family had a chill followed by febrile excitement. The chill recurred next day, and death took place after delirium and convulsions. As the remaining children, three in number, were now showing symptoms of congestive fever, Dr. COONLEY ordered the family to move into another house about thirty rods distant and situated upon higher ground. The ground on which the vacated house stood was so low that occasionally it was surrounded by the tide. The well was only about six feet deep, and about a month before the death of the first child it was completely filled by a very high tide. This was baled out, and afterwards, when the water came into the well, a green scum was noticed on the surface of it. The door-yard was kept in a filthy condition. This was the only water used from the time the well was baled out until the second child died; and the mother stated that these two children drank a good deal of the water. The remaining children promptly began to recover under specific treatment and were fully restored to health. Dr. COONLEY referred the cases to the use of the well-water. The analyst's report on this sample, the history of which was unknown to him, may be summed up in the remarks appended to the analytical details—"bad, probably ditch-water." See also the *British Medical Journal*, November 8, 1884, to which Mr. WHALLEY, a member of the Indian Civil Service, contributed, p. 942, an interesting memorandum concerning the propagation of malarial fevers by impure drinking-water. Along the base of the Himalayas, in the northwestern provinces of India, lies a belt of marsh and forest called the Terrai, which for many years has been uninhabitable owing to the malarial fevers which prevail there. Continuous efforts have been made by the government of the provinces to reclaim and populate this tract, but with only partial success. The strife between enterprise and malaria is continually carried on, but at the cost of a fearful sacrifice of human life. The people have for ages believed in the transmission of the fever by means of the drinking-water, and this belief, it is stated, has at last been accepted in its

the Argo and in those recorded by Dr. COONLEY.* The occurrence of hæmaturic fever in the winter months is suggestive of a water origin,† as are also the congestive chills which occur in some instances without an apparently adequate exposure to concentrated miasms. These cases may not be all referred to differences in the physiological condition of the individual, due to variations in nutrition or hygienic surroundings, since differences in the type of the disease are manifestly less dependent on such idiosyncratic conditions than on season and locality, and, as in the case of the mountain fever, on the nature of the poison or on its mode of introduction into the system.

The agency of the water-supply in the transmission of the malarial poison has an important practical bearing. A water free from vegetable organic matter is indicated as a means of prevention. But, in addition, a study of the data collected concerning the effects of impure water shows that while surface waters have malarial possibilities, filtered or percolated waters have not been suspected of causing paroxysmal fevers.‡ Filtration appears to remove the malarial poison. The conditions of active field service do not always admit of well-digging or systematic artificial filtration, and hence the occasions are of frequent occurrence when an extemporized filtration by the regiment, company or individual would probably prevent much sickness, disability and death.

Although the connection between vegetable matter in a water and a possible malarial character of the latter has been established, there is no ground for assuming that the vegetable impurity is the cause of these remittents. Infusions of putrescent vegetable substances have been taken into the stomach without the production of malarial symptoms.§ But as malaria is generated in soils rich in vegetable matter, a water contaminated by the one will be likely to be charged with the other, whether that water is stagnant on the surface of the malarious soil or an air-cleansing precipitation on a non-malarious region. It is not difficult to understand the absorption of malaria by moisture in swamps, marshes and other localities where exist the conditions recognized as needful to the generation of the poison. It seems probable, however, that the processes of nature result in a general

entirely, though hesitatingly, by most of the medical profession in India. The illustrations given by Mr. WHALLEY are convincing: "A party of workmen were sent two or three years ago, in the month of October, to repair a bridge over a stream called the Chūkā, and they were dependent on the stream for their drinking-water. Out of the thirty men only three escaped fever, and several died. Since then a deep masonry well has been constructed at a few hundred yards distance from the bridge; and the forest guards, who are located there and drink only the water of the well, find the station as healthy as any other. Again, a village named Bahrwa, two or three miles from the forest border, where the supply of drinking-water was obtained from shallow wells fed by the infiltration of the surface drainage, had been repeatedly settled and deserted, owing to the fatal character of the fever which prevailed there. Six years ago the landlord went to the expense of constructing a masonry well forty feet deep, reaching down to the spring level, and closed all the shallow wells previously used. Since then the village has become known as one of the healthiest villages in the neighborhood. The Forest Department now constructs deep masonry-wells at all the forest stations, and by this precaution is enabled to maintain a permanent staff of guards at stations where formerly the men were invalided and had to be relieved every fortnight. Moreover, the villagers in the vicinity show their appreciation of the measure by resorting to these wells for their supply of drinking-water during the malarious season. There seems therefore to be little doubt that in this tract the chief cause of malarious fever is the drinking-water, which has been exposed to some poisonous action above ground. The streams which enjoy the most deadly reputation all take their rise in the dense forest, and are overhung for a portion of their course by a thick screen of overarching trees and bushes. Streams which are bordered by sand or boulders are generally innocuous. Unhealthy villages are found mostly along the shallow depressions which convey the surface-water of the forests to the rivers. Both facts seem to point to the conclusion that the malaria contained in the water is generated by the decaying vegetation; and the fact that the malarious season begins in April and becomes most deadly in October, which has been used to establish another theory, does not militate against this, for these periods are coincident with the periods when the forest trees shed their leaves. But, however this may be, there is no question that many places noted for malaria have now become healthy, and the change has been sharply marked, and contemporaneous with the construction of masonry-wells." Surgeon E. G. RUSSELL, Bengal Medical Service,—*Malaria and Injuries of the Spleen*, Calcutta, 1880,—also gives from his experience in India many instances of the association of malarial diseases with the use of water draining from jungles, terrais or marshes at the base of mountain ranges, and their disappearance on the substitution of a better water-supply.

* See last note.

† See note *supra*, p. 126.

‡ The purer supply which in all countries has succeeded the use of impure surface collections, and which has coincided with the diminished prevalence of malarial disease, has been in the first instance derived from wells or springs. The water of these has often been convicted on more or less positive evidence of the propagation of typhoid fever; but in no case has a well-water been arraigned for the causation of malarial disease unless there has been an evident inflow of surface washings. In Professor MALLET'S investigation into the value of the processes of water analysis—*Annual Report of the National Board of Health*, Washington, 1882—nineteen natural waters were reported, in each of which there seemed fair ground for believing that disease had actually been caused in the persons of those drinking them; but of these Dr. COONLEY'S case, noted above, is the only instance of a well-water suspected of malarial infection, and in it a surface inflow was clearly established.

§ See experiments of PARENT-DUCHATELET and ANDRAL, noted in the Second Part of this work, p. 610.

diffusion of malaria in the surface waters of the earth. If malarial exhalations be not destroyed by atmospheric agencies they must accumulate as a part of the heterogeneous materials which would collect to a suffocating turbidity in the aërial ocean but for their precipitation from time to time with the rain and snow. The fogs or mists which gather over marshes are known to be specially pernicious from the condensation or concentration of evolved malaria accompanying the fine precipitation of the atmospheric moisture. It is but a step further to assume its condensation and precipitation with the rainfall and snow.*

---

* Dr. Woodward, in a note on p. 610 of the Second Part of this work, says that he will have occasion hereafter, when discussing the etiology of malarial fevers, to refer to the arguments brought forward by Dr. Smart in favor of the probable presence of malaria in the snow. There is thus presented to the writer the delicate task of criticising his own work and opinions from Dr. Woodward's point of view. Fortunately his article on *Mountain Fever and Malarious Waters, Am. Jour. Med. Science*, Jan., 1878, was submitted while in manuscript to Dr. Woodward, who, in a letter to Assistant Surgeon General C. H. Crane, U. S. A., dated May 1, 1877, entered his objections to the theory: 1st. "Let me point out," he says, "that if Dr. Smart's analyses are correct, the snow that falls at Camp Douglas contains as much organic ammonia as Wanklyn, whose process he employs, found in the Thames at London Bridge, and more than he found in some of the worst London drinking-water. I confess it easier for me to believe that Dr. Smart has fallen into some error in his manipulations than to believe this. The process is acknowledged to be one of extreme delicacy, in which it is easy for an inexperienced manipulator to fall into error, so that I cannot help suspecting the extraordinary results obtained." Dr. Woodward's want of faith in the accuracy of the analytical results prevented him from giving the subject that consideration which it would otherwise have received from him; thus only may we account for the hasty and superficial views on which his further objections were based. 2d. "Nor am I better satisfied with the hypothesis by which Dr. Smart accounts for the presence of so much organic matter in the air of the Rocky Mountain region. The prevailing winds of the continent are from the west to the east, the great majority of the storms move in that direction, and they ought to carry the organic matter blown with the air from the surface of the continent *away* from the Rocky Mountains instead of towards them. 3d. Moreover, if Dr. Smart's hypothesis is correct, the *vernal* intermittents in the Rocky Mountain region ought to predominate in number and severity over the autumnal ones. So far as I know, however, the reverse is the case. The statistics of the Pacific region, including the stations in New Mexico, Colorado and the slope between the Rocky Mountains and the Pacific Ocean, show malarial diseases to be as distinctly autumnal as in the other regions. 4th. Even Dr. Smart's post of Camp Douglas is no exception to this rule. The annual number of cases of intermittent and remittent fever occurring at it is usually very small, but in 1866-'69, '71, '72-'73 and '74 there were a good many cases. Those of 1869 were all imported from Florida; the others originated on the spot, and give a distinctly autumnal curve in every year except 1874, in which the vernal fevers predominated. 5th. As to mountain fever, I have never seen a case, and know it only from the testimony of others. From what I have thus learned I am obliged to conclude that Dr. Smart's observations refer to certain mild *vernal* epidemics, and are hence partial and incomplete. The more severe epidemic observed by Dr. Vollum in 1871 at Camp Douglas was an autumnal one, and as his account of it is interesting and differs in many respects from that of Dr. Smart, I submit a copy of the remarks on his sick report for September, 1871. * * * 'During this month an epidemic of intermittent and remittent fever accompanied by diarrhœa, dysentery and tonsillitis has prevailed at this place and in the neighboring settlements. The officers' and soldiers' families were chiefly affected, but the severest cases occurred among the troops. The number of cases among the families was, intermittents 23, typhoid fever 4. Among the women and children symptoms resembling hysteria often appeared and tended much to disguise the cases. In many of these cases there was a strong tendency to sink into a typhoid condition; and the typhoid cases reported among the troops commenced as intermittent. Among the officers' and soldiers' families there were four cases of typhoid fever that commenced in the same way. This epidemic is styled by the resident physicians as the mountain fever, the tendency of which seems to be to pass on from the symptoms of a simple intermittent to those of true typhoid fever. Its habits in the intermittent or remittent stage are similar to malarial fever elsewhere in the United States, and it is controlled by quinine if pushed in ten-grain doses three times a day for a week or ten days. I have a belief that if this treatment, accompanied by good nourishment and moderate stimulation, were adopted early enough, the typhoid symptoms would be prevented and the case kept within the bounds of intermittent or remittent fever.'"

In reply to these arguments the writer submits:—1st, That an experience of many years in the processes of water analysis, including numerous examinations of rain-water and snow-falls in various parts of the country, warrants a belief in the substantive existence of the vegetable matter reported by him in the river, rain and snow-waters of Fort Bridger, Wyoming Territory, and Camp Douglas, Utah Territory. 2d. That the prevailing winds are from the west to the east is acknowledged; but this cannot be considered as proof that the rain and snow-falls in the Rocky Mountains are especially free from organic matter, when they are known by direct experiment to contain an unusually large quantity. There are currents and counter-currents in the air, as in the ocean, and we cannot predicate what may be going on in the higher strata of the aërial ocean from the direction of the currents at its bottom. 3d. There are many malarious valleys in the Rocky Mountain region and in the vast section of country known as the Military Division of the Pacific, where intermittents are produced by exhalation as in other swampy districts; and as these predominate so greatly over the mountain fever cases, malarial diseases in the Pacific region may be expected to be as distinctly autumnal as they are in the Mississippi Valley. There is, indeed, no general season for mountain fever. Its appearance in a given locality is due to local conditions. At Fort Bridger it is vernal in its visitations, since that is the season during which the stream is specially contaminated. On account of the high elevation and northern exposure the immense masses of snow which choke up the mountain gorges during the winter take a long time to melt and drain off, during which period the river is swollen to two or three times its average size and its waters are discolored and turbid. At Camp Douglas, however, the conditions are wholly different. The stream is small, it being one of a dozen which run a short course down the mountain side to a main stream, the Jordan river; the exposure is southern, the altitude lower, and the winter climate much less severe than on the mountains above Fort Bridger, so that snow does not accumulate, but falls, melts and is carried off several times during the course of the season, from November to May, rendering the stream swollen and turbid for a week or two at a time; and so, during the summer and autumn, a thunder-cloud creeping along the mountain range will flood the creek for a day or two, or if the mountain showers are repeated at short intervals, for a week or two, thus disseminating the probable cause of mountain fever all over the spring, summer and autumn, if the turbid and impure waters are used as a drinking-supply. Hence the time of visitation at Fort Bridger may not be the time of visitation at another station. The time corresponds with the flooding of the stream with snow and rain-water, and not with any special month or season of the year. Nor can this time be ascertained from the record of the rainfall at a post, as it is the fall on the radicles of the stream which is in question: the stream at Camp Douglas, for instance, is not unfrequently turbid from mountain showers while the post and its vicinity are dusty and parched for lack of rain. 4th. The annual number of cases of malarial disease occurring at Camp Douglas is usually very small, but in certain years there were a good many. In 1869 the intermittents were imported from Florida, and in the other years characterized by their presence there were very notable changes in the constitution of the garrison. The statement that the cases which occurred in these years originated on the spot is not sustained by a close inspection of the history of the post. Some of them originated, to the knowledge of the writer, while the men were absent on Indian service. From the impossibility of distinguishing in many instances the imported from the indigenous malarious cases among those which appear on the records of former years, it cannot be determined that the latter are vernal or autumnal, nor which is of more importance, that they do or do not correspond with the impure condition of the water-supply. 5th. Dr. Vollum attributed his cases in 1871 to rotting wood in the old barrack quarters, and to dampness and want of ventilation and sunshine, factors which certainly do not enter into the causation of many undoubted cases of mountain fever. An improvement in the health of the garrison was coincident with the construction of the water-reservoir; but as at the same time new and commodious quarters were built, the writer did not admit this increased healthfulness of the post into his original argument in favor of the transmission of malaria by the water-supply. Inasmuch,

Malaria is not an unstable organic gas, for were it so its dissipation in the air would be followed by its destruction, and its subsequent condensation in the marsh mists would be impossible. It has therefore a certain stability, and its presence in the rain may be as readily accepted as its presence in the mists, if the same morbid phenomena follow the ingestion of the rain-water as follow an exposure to the mists. This stability, in view of the oxidizing influences of the air, is suggestive of a vital resistance on the part of the miasm, and lends countenance to the views of those who regard as the essential of malarial disease a specific germ, which will be eventually, if it has not been already, identified.*

RELAPSES.—In some instances in which the individual had already suffered from the disease the so-called predisposing causes operated so strongly as to be apparently the determining cause of a relapse or recurrence. It was observed, in commands affected by the malarial poison, that a suddenly developed increase in the number of the intermittent cases frequently resulted from exposure to chill, as from wet clothes, weather changes or incau-

---

however, as Dr. WOODWARD has brought the epidemic forward in this connection, it may be pointed out that while the local conditions mentioned by Dr. VOLLUM may, and undoubtedly had their influence on the character and progress of the disease, they were not the essential, for he expressly states that the epidemic was not confined to the post, but implicated the neighboring settlements, all of which, it may be remarked, made use of water from the Camp Douglas stream or from others running a parallel course and subject to the same contaminating influences.

*The latest attempts at identification have been by KLEBS and TOMMASI-CRUDELI—*Studi sulla Natura della Malaria.* Roma, 1879. These estinvigators announced the discovery of a bacillus which they found constantly present in the swamp-mud of the Roman marshes. This bacillus was susceptible of cultivation in fish-gelatine, and when injected into rabbits produced a fever similar to that which occurs in the human subject when exposed to paludal exhalations. It consisted of short rods 5 to 10 micromillimetres in length which evolved into tortuous filaments, jointed by the formation of clear spaces at regular intervals in their protoplasm; spores were developed in the centre or at the extremities of the joints. They considered this microphyte as the cause of malarial fever, and named it B. malariæ. But other observers have failed to identify it. STERNBERG, who was sent by the National Board of Health to investigate this subject in the malarious environs of New Orleans, found in the marsh-mud, among many other bacterial forms, some which seemed to answer the description given of the B. malariæ, but similar forms were found in dust from the city squares of New Orleans, and also in culture experiments at Baltimore, where malaria was not in question. Moreover, the inoculation experiments on rabbits were held by him to be inconclusive, as the temperature curve in the rabbits operated on had in no case a distinctly paroxysmal character, while healthy rabbits sometimes showed as marked variations in temperature as those delineated in the charts of KLEBS and TOMMASI-CRUDELI. The changes in the spleen which these experimenters found at the autopsy of the inoculated rabbits, and attributed to the malarial influence, were shown by STERNBERG to occur in death from septicæmia produced by the inoculation of human saliva—see *Supplement No. 14, National Board of Health Bulletin,* Washington, 1881. We must therefore conclude with him that the evidence on which KLEBS and TOMMASI-CRUDELI based their claim to a discovery is not satisfactory. Nevertheless Dr. JULIUS DRESCHFIELD, Pres. Microscopical Section, Manchester Medical Society, exhibited at one of the meetings of the section specimens of blood taken from a sailor suffering from intermitting attacks of fever. The blood contained bacilli of exactly the same character as those described by TOMMASI-CRUDELI. During the intermissions the bacilli disappeared, but their spores could be readily distinguished.—*British Med. Jour.,* Vol. 1, 1884, p. 462. While LANZI and TERRIGI (see note *supra,* p. 152) regard the pigment granules in the blood of malarial cases as resulting from a fermentative action produced by similar granules derived from the decomposition of an *Alga miasmatica,* LAVERAN—*Nature Parasitaire des Accidents de l' Impaludisme,* Paris, 1881—insists that these pigment granules are connected with the life-history of a microparasite which flourishes in the blood and which has heretofore been regarded by KELSCH and others as a pigment-bearing leucocyte. In examinations of the blood in sixty malarial cases during his service in Algiers LAVERAN found the pigment granules in forty-two cases. The large proportion of negative results was due to prolonged treatment in these instances by the sulphate of quinine. But the interest in his observations attaches to the cellular envelope enclosing the pigment granules. It was distinguished under three forms, which he has figured. In the first the cells are elongated, somewhat pointed at their ends and often incurved (banana-shaped); sometimes, however, they are oval; the pigment grains are loosely aggregated or disposed in an annular form toward the centre of the cell. In the second the cells are spherical, and in size sometimes even larger than a red blood-corpuscle; the pigment grains are usually arranged in a ring concentric with the circumference of the cells. These spherical bodies are furnished with three or four slender filaments each about three times as long as the diameter of a red blood-corpuscle. When in rapid motion the filaments undulate like the anguillula and their action impresses a movement on the neighboring corpuscles. In the third form there are various deviations from the spherical outline; the cells are larger than those of the filamented series, and while the contained pigment grains are irregularly disposed the annular arrangement is sometimes noticed. LAVERAN regards these three kinds of cells as representing different phases of the evolution of the same parasite, the second form furnished with mobile filaments being considered the perfect state of the organism, while the third form is regarded as the cadavers of the parasitic elements and as identical with the pigmented elements found in the organs of persons who have died of pernicious fevers. Recently TOMMASI-CRUDELI, MARCHIAFAVA and CELLI—*Indian Medical Gazette,* Vol. XXI, p. 7, Calcutta, January, 1886—have shown that the appearances regarded by LAVERAN as due to an exotic organism in the blood are in reality the result of degenerative changes in the red blood-corpuscles. The globular protoplasm appears to become absorbed or converted into a hyaline material showing amœboid changes of form, and the hæmoglobin is transformed into melanotic particles which exhibit oscillatory movements in the interior of the corpuscle now represented by a diaphanous spherule. The mobile filaments of LAVERAN have been observed by these investigators, but are believed to consist of globular protoplasm modified in a way as yet unknown. The corpuscles ultimately become disintegrated and the black particles in various degrees of aggregation are set free in the current of the circulation. CAMILLO GOLGI—*Fortschritte der Medicin,* B. IV, 1886—has also seen changes in the blood similar to those described, consisting of the development of colorless plasmic bodies in the red blood-corpuscles. As these bodies enlarge melanotic particles are found scattered within their substance. All trace of the normal constitution of the blood-corpuscle becomes lost in its transformation into a colorless globule containing particles of pigment. The latter ultimately tend to the centre of the globule, appearing as a dark nucleus around which the colorless substance undergoes fission in radiating lines, the resulting cellules presenting a semblance to the rays of a composite flower. When this stage of development has been reached a febrile attack is imminent. Afterward the cellules and the central mass of pigmented matter are liberated into the current of the blood. At Pavia, GOLGI examined forty cases with negative results in two only. Most of his fevers were quartans; and he claims that the long intervals between the paroxysms afforded time for the complete development and fission of the altered corpuscles, results which are not observed in fevers which have shorter intervals. Whether the destruction of the red blood-corpuscles and the associated pigmentary changes result from the action of the bacillus malariæ or of the alga of LANZI and TERRIGI, or are independent of both, does not appear to have been determined; but TOMMASI-CRUDELI regards them as of great practical importance in the diagnosis of obscure cases of malarial infection in continued and subcontinued fevers.

As the germ theory of malarial disease explains so many of the morbid phenomena and is at the same time consistent with what is known of the natural history of the disease-essence, there is a strong tendency to accept it in advance of the isolation and identification of the specific micro-organism.

tious cooling after the perspirations of fatigue duty. That these attacks were not due to fresh accessions of the poison was evidenced by their occurrence after the temporary chill of a bath undertaken as a luxury or in the interest of personal cleanliness. Relapses were also oftentimes referred to errors of diet. They occurred at any time after the primary attack; but in cases in which the operation of a predisposing cause was not manifest a tendency to recurrence at weekly intervals was generally conceded: thus MERRITT speaks of warding off the hebdomadal chill by arsenite of potash.* No observations were recorded on this point; nor were they possible on an extended scale, as treatment interfered with the natural progress of the morbid phenomena.†

VI.—PREVENTION OF MALARIAL DISEASE.

GENERAL CONSIDERATIONS.—From what has been said under the head of causation, it is clear that the protection of the troops from the malarial influence is the all-important preventive measure. It is true that on active service the imperative military necessity often requires the sacrifice of life by disease in the occupation of an important but unhealthy locality, as it calls for exposure to death on the line of battle; but in both instances a thorough knowledge of the ground may permit it to be held with a minimum of loss. Dr. WOODHULL shows that the disease in the 9th N. J. Vols. was due to the occupation of a camp near a broken dam presenting a large extent of bottom land as a malarial exhalent. The 6th Conn. Vols., in DIBBLE's report, became seriously damaged by its camp in the swamps of Warsaw Island. These and various other reported instances may have been unavoidable results of the military necessity; but it is certain that the health of many commands suffered from the occupation of unhealthy camp-sites which were afterwards abandoned although the military conditions remained unchanged. Thus we find Dr. TRIPLER effecting

* See MERRITT's report, infra, p. 180.

† FORRY in his Climate of the United States, New York, 1842, p. 283, says: "That intermittent fever has a tendency to a septenary revolution is a fact that was frequently verified in Florida under the author's observation; and this too in a manner so unequivocal that it attracted the attention of the common soldier. At these septenary periods, after the seventh, fourteenth or twenty-first paroxysm, the disease has a disposition to terminate spontaneously. It is at these periods that febrifuge remedies act with the greatest success; and as regards relapses, it is then too that a vast majority occur,— a circumstance of such frequent occurrence in Florida that soldiers would voluntarily come to the hospital to obtain medicine to prevent its return." These statements are somewhat paradoxical: The influences operating at the septenary periods not only cause the subsidence of an attack in one who is suffering, but have power to determine the occurrence of an attack or relapse in one who is not suffering. The doctrine of a periodicity dependent on lunar influence has been long entertained by able observers, especially in India. Dr. FRANCIS BALFOUR in his Treatise on Putrid Remitting Intestinal Fevers, Edinburgh, 1790, developed the theory of sol-lunar influence. In accordance with his views daily remissions and aggravations, septenary returns and seasonal prevalence were due to the combined influence of the sun and moon, the febrile state being greater at the diurnal meridional periods than during the intermeridional intervals; at the novi-lunar and pleni-lunar periods than during the intervening periods, and especially at the lunar periods of the equinoxes as compared with those of the inter-equinoctial intervals. He states that the sol-lunar influence in fever is felt at Bonaris and other places not less than three hundred miles distant from the reach of the tides, and that consequently LIND's idea that these, and not the agencies by which they are caused, are connected with the progress of fever is sufficiently refuted. Sir J. R. MARTIN in his Influence of Tropical Climates, London, 1861, quotes the observations by which Mr. FRANCIS DALY, of the Madras army, arrived at the conclusion that there is a sol-lunar influence as argued by Dr. BALFOUR; and W. MOORE in his Diseases of India, London, 1861, pp. 87–8, says: "Indeed a very short practice in the tropics will convince the most sceptical that individuals who have suffered from malarious fevers are more or less affected at either the full or change of the moon. Many experience return of fever at these times; others, feelings of uneasiness or malaise, but not amounting to actual ague; and this predisposition to become periodically affected may remain for months and even years, and may recur at uncertain periods, the intervals being passed in perfect health. That the moon per se has any effect in inducing this state may well be questioned; but that the amount of mud surface exposed by the low ebb-tides and the consequent greater exhalation taking place may act as an excitant, is at least probable in the neighborhood of the sea-coast. In far inland districts some other solution of the mystery is, however, requisite; and MOREHEAD inclines to the opinion that when the coincidence of febrile disease and lunar phases is noted, there will generally be found present an appreciable atmospheric change of temperature, of moisture or of direction of winds, which he apprehends is the determining cause of the febrile disturbance." Nevertheless, in the Annals of Military and Naval Surgery, &c., London, 1863, Dr. H. GIRAUD, on page 184, states that the want of reliable evidence on the subject of the moon's influence on periodic fever having been brought to the knowledge of the commander-in-chief, orders were issued requiring that the records of paroxysms should be kept in every medical charge in the Bombay Presidency during the year 1861, with a view to determine the question. The result showed 56,175 paroxysms as occurring in 146 medical charges at 44 stations, and it is concluded from these that paroxysms of fever do not occur more frequently at the springs than at other periods of the month.

the removal of the troops from the flats near Arlington, Va., to the higher grounds beyond the first ridge overlooking the Potomac river, that they might have the protection of its crest from the malarious currents uprising from the bottom lands.*

The predisposing conditions or so-called causes were also unavoidable in many instances, but not in all. Exposures to excessive heat, cold, rain, fatigue, etc., might not be avoided in the face of the enemy, but their influence was at times unnecessarily felt in camp. At one period the men of the Army of the Potomac were turned out for duty long before sunrise and breakfast, but Dr. TRIPLER, recognizing that this had much to do with the prevalence of malarial fevers, obtained an order that reveille should not be sounded until after sunrise, and that hot coffee should be issued immediately after roll-call.

A dry camp-site, good water and food, suitable clothing, the avoidance of unnecessary drills and fatigues during hot weather, and of exposure to nocturnal chills, particularly when the troops are fasting, will not only lessen the prevalence of malarial diseases in commands which have unfortunately been exposed to the miasmatic influence, but when combined with temperance, cleanliness and that regularity of life which old and well disciplined soldiers find to be not inconsistent with active service in the field, will probably, as suggested by Ass't Surg. INGRAM, prevent the development of typhoid symptoms in the manifestations which do occur.

The experience of our medical officers is opposed to the idea of an accommodation of the system to the malarial poison with the concurrent retention of a normal degree of health. The febrile accessions might fail to recur, but the patients continued anæmic, weak and languid, if they did not become subject to the more active manifestations of chronic malarial poisoning, so long as they remained exposed in the malarious country. Medical Inspector W. H. MUSSEY, U. S. A., touches this subject in a report of an inspection of the Department of North Carolina, dated April 13, 1863:

> Much has been said upon the subject of acclimation, which, in these localities, would be nothing more nor less than a complete saturation of the system with malaria, so that intermittent fever would be the normal condition of those acclimated. But there must be acclimation to the new life of the camp, and this is important. It is essential to keep the soldier up to the highest point of resistance to the malarial influences. Care in the quality of the food, the proper mixture of vegetables, the cookery, the administration of prophylactics, attention to cleanliness, raising the bed above the ground, avoiding unnecessary exposure in the night, wearing flannel, and the administration of coffee and a lunch, are the best means of securing this resistance.

PROPHYLACTIC USE OF QUININE.—The attention of the medical officers of our armies was directed to the prophylactic use of quinine at the very outset of the war. In the *Rules for preserving the health of the soldier*, prepared by Dr. WM. H. VAN BUREN of New York, for the United States Sanitary Commission, and issued July 13, 1861,† the daily use of quinine was recommended in localities where ague and fevers were prevalent. Later in the year a pamphlet by the same author‡ was also issued giving a digest of the evidence on which the recommendation was founded.

> This embraced the personal experience of the author in Florida during April, 1840, that of his friend Dr. J. S. Newberry on the Isthmus of Panama and elsewhere, a letter from President David Hoadley of the Panama railroad company, setting forth the beneficial results of an issue of quinine in wine to the crews of merchant vessels visiting Aspinwall, a letter from William Laird of Liverpool, relating the successful use of quinine as a prophylactic by the

---

* Appendix to Part First of this work, p. 46.

† U. S. Sanitary Commission Doc. No. 17, reprinted in *Military Med. and Surg. Essays*, edited for the Commission by WM. A. HAMMOND, Philadelphia, 1864, par. 25, p. 168: "It is wise and prudent, when ague and fevers are prevalent, that every man should take a dose of quinine bitters at least once in twenty-four hours. This will surely serve as a safeguard against an attack of disease; it has been practised in Florida and elsewhere with undoubted benefit."

‡ WILLIAM H. VAN BUREN—*Quinine as a Prophylactic against Malarious disease*, Sanitary Commission Doc. 31, New York, 1861, reprinted *op. cit.*, last note, p. 93 *et seq.* From a note appended to the original pamphlet it appears that this essay was approved for publication September 30, 1861.

crews of a line of steamers plying between Liverpool and the coast of Africa, the testimony of Bryson * and Hayne †
of the English Navy, De Saussure ‡ of Charleston, S. C., and of several African travellers, § besides sundry favorable
opinions and recommendations from various sources showing the confidence with which the measure was regarded
in various quarters.‖

It was declared to be a fact well established in the experience of American physicians,
that the daily use of three to six grains of quinine by those who are exposed to the danger
of malarial poisoning will in most instances avert an attack, or failing this, will render the
disease milder and prevent the development of the malarial cachexia.

In accordance with these recommendations quinine dissolved in whiskey was frequently used as a prophylactic by our medical officers, but no systematic records of the results
were kept; nor does it appear that the method was anywhere employed with persistence
on a considerable scale. The difficulty of transporting the whiskey needed for the purpose
often interfered with the continuance of the experiment, and at other times the quinia
itself could not be obtained in sufficient quantity. Many medical officers were led by
their observations to form a favorable opinion of the efficacy of this prophylactic method,
and in the Sanitary Commission's Memoirs may be found the testimony of Surgeons Isaac
F. Galloupe, S. B. Thrall, F. H. Milligan, S. W. Abbott, W. S. Willes, H. Z.
Gill and Professor Paul F. Eve.¶ Moreover, Dr. Flint expressly states that no testi-

* Alexander Bryson—On the Prophylactic influence of Quinine. Med. Times and Gaz., 1854, Vol. I, p. 6—refers to a standing rule in the Navy enjoined
by the 9th article of the Surgeons' Instructions, that men sent on shore in tropical climates should take daily in the morning a drachm of powdered bark
in wine as a prophylactic, and states that this measure had fallen into disuse partly on account of the doubts of the medical officers and partly because
of the nauseous character of the dose. He then speaks favorably of the use of amorphous quinine in wine, citing the reports of a number of medical
officers on the African station to the effect that boats' crews using this prophylactic either wholly escaped or had milder attacks. He admits the occasional failure of quinine-wine as a preventive of fever, but holds that it has been of most essential service. He had previously recommended its use, and
given some evidence in its favor in his Report on the Climate and Principal Diseases of the African station. London, 1847, p. 218.

† L. J. Hayne—On the Endemic fevers of Africa and the Prophylactic use of Quinine. Med. Times and Gaz., 1855, Vol. I, p. 280—cites the case of a boat's
crew exposed on the Ponga river for two days and nights : 32 officers and men who used the prophylactic daily had but four slight cases of fever. As a
contrast to this he instances the exposure for seven or eight days on the Lagoon at Lagos of 34 officers and men who only took the quinine every other
day, and had seventeen severe cases ; while an officer and man on shore at Sierra Leone for eight days took no quinine, and both had remittent fever.
But it will be observed that the men who suffered least had been exposed the shortest time, and that the localities were not the same.

‡ H. W. De Saussure—Quinine as a Prophylactic of Intermittent and Remittent fevers. Charleston Med. Jour. and Review, Vol. XV, 1860, p. 433—testifies
to the success of this measure on the rice plantations and elsewhere in South Carolina, citing the English naval experience, and contrasting the fatality
of remittent fever in the first Niger exploring expedition with the comparative good health of the second expedition, in which quinine was used as a
prophylactic. An account of the first has been given by J. O. McWilliam—Med. Hist. of the Expedition to the Niger during the years 1841-2, comprising an
account of the fever which led to its abrupt termination. London, 1843. The second has been chronicled by William Balfour Baikie—Narrative of an
Exploring voyage up the rivers Kwo'ra and Bi'nue (commonly known as the Niger and Tsádda) in 1854. London, 1856. See Appendix G, p. 452, and also an
article by the same author—On Remittent fever, especially as it appears on the West coast of Africa, etc. Edinburgh Med. Jour., Vol. II, 1856-7, p. 803.

§ Such as W. B. Baikie, see last note. T. J. Hutchinson—Impressions of Western Africa, London, 1858, p. 229. The article on Intermittent fever in
the Encyclopædia Britannica, and Du Chaillu—Equatorial Africa, Chap. XVIII, p. 369—to which the editor has added a reference to the observations of
Mouat among the Andaman Islands—Annals of Military and Naval Surgery and Tropical Medicine, etc., London, 1864, p. 193.

‖ He cites George B. Wood—A Treatise on Therapeutics, etc., Philadelphia, 1856, Vol. I, p. 260 ; and also the recommendations of several English army
medical officers of high position and reputation, whose views, however, do not appear to have been carried far enough to yield definite practical results.
The first of these is the letter of Director-General A. Smith of the Army Medical Department, July 27, 1855, to the Inspector General of Hospitals in the
Crimea, recommending the prophylactic use of quinia, and remarking : "Having now at command sufficient of this drug, specially provided for that
service, to furnish five grains per diem to every member of a force of 35,000 men, I beg you will take such measures as you think proper with a view to
induce the medical officers to employ that remedy."—Report of the Commissioners appointed to inquire into the Regulations affecting the Sanitary condition of the
Army, etc., London, 1858, Appendix 79, p. 70. The Med. and Surg. History of the British Army which served in Turkey and the Crimea, etc., London, 1858,
makes no mention of the adoption of this measure ; but in the appendix to Vol. I, p. 504, Sir John Hall, Inspector General of Hospitals, in reply to
one of the queries of the Director General, wrote in January, 1857, that "In malarious districts, quinine, or quinoidine in solution, which is preferable
from the form it is in, given as a prophylactic in either wine or spirit, is very beneficial, but soldiers do not like it, and I have heard them declare that
it had occasioned the complaints they were laboring under at the time." The second is the recommendation of Director-General J. B. Gibson of the
Army Medical Department, submitted to the Minister of State for War during the preparation for hostilities in China in 1859, that a stock of quinine-
wine be provided for issue during the unhealthy months, or when the soldiers are required to proceed up rivers or to encamp in the vicinity of marshy
ground,—with the instructions to use quinine-wine contained in ? 8 of the New Medical Regulations for Field Service issued to the Expeditionary Army
(in China) during the same year.—Army Med. Department, Statistical, Sanitary and Medical Reports for the year 1859, London, 1861, p. 181. But in the volume of
the same reports for 1860, London, 1862, p. 393, is found an official statement of the Practical results bearing on the Medical Department deducible from the
operations in China, from which we learn : "That the experiment of quinine as a prophylactic against malaria was not tried in this campaign on a sufficiently extended scale to warrant reliable results." It is true that Wm. R. E. Smart—Obs. on the Climatology, Topography and Diseases of Hong-Kong and the
Canton river station, Trans. Epidem. Soc., London, Vol. I, 1860-1, p. 231—speaks of the "comparative exemption" secured by quinine for the crews of
the gunboat flotilla on the Canton river, but he gives nothing more precise than the statement that "they seemed not to suffer disproportionally from
malarious fevers, excepting those of the intermittent type." It would appear, too, from his remarks that the quinia was given "on the slightest occasions of indisposition" rather than to the well men. The last of these citations is a mere suggestion for the use of this measure by H. C. Reade—
Remarks on the Topography of the Military stations in British Guiana, etc., Volume for 1859, cited supra, p. 243.

¶ Sanitary Memoirs of the War of the Rebellion, collected and published by the U. S. Sanitary Commission. Medical,—edited by Austin Flint, New York,
1867, p. 134. See also an article headed Quinine as a Preventive of Malarial disease. San. Com. Bulletin, Vol. I, 1864, p. 215; also Amer. Med. Times, Vol.
VIII, 1864, p. 248, in which the inspector of the Sanitary Commission in the Department of North Carolina and Virginia, J. W. Page, reports great benefit
from the issue of a quinine ration to regiments in the vicinity of New Berne, N. C.

mony adverse to this method of prophylaxis had been received by the Commission. Reports favorable to the issue of quinine were made to the Surgeon General's Office by certain medical officers, and some communications were received by Dr. WOODWARD in response to a letter requesting information on the subject. These are herewith submitted.

Surgeon C. N. CHAMBERLAIN, *10th Mass. Vols., Washington, October* 1, 1861.—The fevers were of a bilious remittent type, some rapidly assuming a typhoid form. At first they were of a very severe character, and four treated in our regimental hospital proved fatal. One became convalescent and left the hospital for his quarters, but owing to imprudence he suffered a fatal relapse. Another was delirious from the first, his skin literally covered with petechiæ and vibices; he had severe congestions of the head and bowels, and sank after an illness of ten days. The third and fourth had all the phenomena of ordinary typhus fever, and both died of severe and repeated hemorrhages from the bowels. As the epidemic progressed the type of the disease became milder, although we still have occasionally cases of a severe character. The treatment employed has been usually a mild laxative of castor oil and oil of turpentine, often preceded by five grains of blue pill; full doses of quinine, and an occasional Dover's powder, after the operation of the cathartic. This has sufficed to arrest very promptly the large proportion of the cases, while it mitigated the others, excepting the few cases more emphatically typhoid in their tendency which ended fatally.

After witnessing the salutary effects of quinine as a remedy, I determined to employ it as a prophylactic, provided a sufficient quantity could be procured. An appeal to the Sanitary Commission secured twenty-three gallons of whiskey containing three grains of quinine per ounce of liquor. The men were allowed to take daily one or two ounces, and I was happy to witness its results in reducing the morning report of the sick from fifty or sixty to twenty daily. After the supply was exhausted the reports exhibited an increase of the disease. I am prepared to recommend emphatically the use of quinine as a prophylactic under circumstances parallel to our own. A second small supply, furnished also by the Sanitary Commission, has been of great service.

Medical Inspector JOHN WILSON, *U. S. A., Army of the Potomac, October* 31, 1864.—The ordinary endemic diseases of the region have touched the Army of the Potomac [before Petersburg] with unwonted gentleness during the usually sickly autumnal months. This, at least in a measure, is due to the vigilant surveillance kept over the police of the camps and the cleanliness of the person of the soldier, and also to the excellent manner in which the army has been fed and clothed. In the more malarious localities occupied by our troops during the months of September and October, a ration of whiskey and quinine was given daily with excellent effects as a prophylactic.

Asst. Surg. ALFRED A. WOODHULL, *U. S. A., in charge of Battalion of 2d and 10th U. S. Infantry, September* 30, 1862.—The whiskey ration that was at one time attempted is, in my opinion, not only unprofitable but absolutely detrimental when it is issued indiscriminately, even under the worst aspect of military life on the Chickahominy. It is unprofitable, because on those occasions when it would be of service, if at all, it is often impracticable to issue it. If useful, it is chiefly in the depression and exhaustion induced by wet and cold, immediately after a fatiguing march; but as these are the very times when the wagons are not up, it is impossible to obtain it until the occasion for its use has passed. The transportation of the required amount would greatly burden the Quartermaster's department, an item in the movements, and consequently in the health, of the army not to be overlooked. Its habitual issue would unquestionably tend to the production of intemperate habits in some and foster those of others that a campaign might otherwise dissipate. While accustoming men to a stimulant, to be deprived of at those times they would most need it (as indicated above), would be doing a double injury. The addition of quinine does not seem to counterbalance the evil, and so great a consumption of that valuable drug appears to be a waste which nothing but the most certain benefits should authorize. To leave the issue of quinine to the legitimate channel of the medical department is much more rational than its indiscriminate administration by battalions. Of course these remarks refer to the circumstances of the Army of the Potomac, and not to those climates where perpetual cinchonism is the condition of life to the white.

Surgeon J. G. BRADT, *26th Mass. Vols., New Orleans, La., March* 31, 1863.—The rainy season continued through the last quarter, and probably had an effect upon the health of the regiment, as shown by a considerable increase in the number of cases of intermittent fever. Wet days, followed by sudden changes to warm, muggy weather, have invariably increased the prevalence of this fever; but all the cases occurred among men who had previously suffered from the disease. I consider that the city is comparatively free from the miasm to which malarial fevers owe their origin, and that these fresh cases are merely the reappearance of an old trouble which had been lying dormant in the system. To test the value of whiskey and quinine as a prophylactic, I procured fifteen gallons of whiskey and added one ounce of quinine to the gallon. This mixture was served out to the guard at night at the rate of one ounce per man. In wet weather a ration was also served out at midnight. I am positive that it prevented a great number of attacks of chills.

Surgeon DAVID MERRITT, *55th Pa. Vols., Beaufort, S. C., May* 10, 1863.—The issue of a ration of whiskey and quinine while the regiment was on Edisto Island was of great service to the health of the command. At Beaufort the ration has only been issued to the men on picket duty. I am a strong advocate of the measure, and the oral testimony of other medical officers corroborates my opinion.

Asst. Surg. E. A. THOMPSON, *12th Me. Vols., Baton Rouge, La., February,* 1863.—Most of the cases of intermittent fever which occurred during the winter were observed in the companies that were exposed to malaria during last summer while on detached service at Lake Pontchartrain. We are now issuing rations of quinated whiskey to the men on picket and extra duty with marked benefit.

Medical Inspector E. P. VOLLUM, *U. S. A., Louisville, Ky., December* 31, 1863.—I have to state that from my experience with quinine-whiskey as well as with simple quinine, I am led to believe that it is a prophylactic against malarial fevers. When troops are about to enter or abide in a region well known to be malarious, I would advise the moderate use of quinine-whiskey, to be continued in diminished quantities as long as it is evident that the troops are in danger of attack; but I would discountenance its general issue except at such seasons and in such regions as are markedly malarious.

Medical Inspector A. C. HAMLIN, *U. S. A., Washington, D. C., November,* 1863.—My observations have not been conducted on an extensive scale, but the results have convinced me that the use of quinine-whiskey in prophylactic doses produces a prompt and energetic action, and supports the organic forces in resisting the pernicious influence of malaria and neutralizing the paludal poison; but when paludal cachexia is once fairly established the administration of quinine seems to be without much force. I will also state that I consider the best mode of administering this drug to be in solution in the red wines, by reason of their tonic effect upon the muscular fibre; and I believe, with the distinguished chemist Henry, that the red wines of Burgundy are best adapted to the purpose.

Surgeon A. P. MAYLERT, *U. S. Vols., Louisville, Ky., November* 4, 1863.—I think that the issue of quinine or some antiperiodic as a prophylactic would be not only humane but an economical measure for the Government. Alcohol is doubtless the best menstruum for its administration, and pure old whiskey the best form of alcohol; but inasmuch as it would be impossible to obtain the latter, I would recommend that diluted rectified spirits, *i. e.*, pure diluted alcohol, be used for this purpose. I regard alcohol when properly administered as prophylactic to a limited extent, but when improperly used, as is too often the case, its effect is doubtless the reverse. I would therefore recommend that in any such combination the alcohol should bear as small a proportion to the antiperiodic as may be.

Surgeon T. H. BACHE, *U. S. Vols., Washington, D. C., November* 3, 1863.—I know quinine-whiskey is of great use as a prophylactic against malarial fevers. However, I am opposed to the mixture, and think its general issue would cause much harm, owing to the fondness of many for whiskey. I am in favor of a mixture without whiskey, though I would in some cases have recourse to whiskey as well as to quinine.

Surgeon E. SWIFT, *U. S. A., Chester, Pa., November* 22, 1863.—In June, 1847, at Vera Cruz, Mexico, I recommended two grains of sulphate of quinia in about two ounces of whiskey, to be taken by the officers every morning at the moment of rising. This could not be administered to the men for want of a sufficient supply of the liquor. The army was, however, generally healthy, and I did not discover any marked difference between officers and men. In Texas I frequently recommended this prophylactic in malarious districts, and credited it with an influence in warding off disease. So fully convinced was I of this that, as Medical Director of the Army in Kentucky in December, 1861, I urged General Mitchell to approve a daily issue of quinine-whiskey, but the advance of the army into Tennessee prevented me from making satisfactory observations. In a circular published to the Army of the Cumberland by order of General Rosecrans, I find the following directions, viz: "Hot coffee should be issued to the soldier immediately after rising in the morning, and in inclement weather quinine and whiskey in the evening."

Favorable testimony is also found in some of the reports printed in the Appendix to the First Part of this work,* and in certain articles published by army medical officers in the medical journals.† Unfortunately this testimony is in no instance based upon statistics showing the comparative effect of like exposures upon commands using the quinine and others not using it. On the other hand no reports condemning the prophylactic use of quinine have been published,‡ although doubts have occasionally been expressed as to its

---

* See, for instance, that of Surgeon C. S. TRIPLER, Medical Director, Army of the Potomac, pp. 47-8, in which he states that, having received favorable reports of the effects of quinine and whiskey as the result of an experimental issue made by his medical officers, he recommended its use to those regiments whose condition seemed most to demand it, and was induced thereafter to keep it constantly on hand in the Purveyor's store. See also p. 67, where Surgeon J. B. BROWN, Medical Director, 4th Army Corps, expresses himself satisfied that had a liberal supply of quinine been obtainable for prophylactic purposes and treatment, one-half of the sickness that prevailed in his command during the advance on Williamsburg, Va., in 1862, would have been prevented. Also, on pp. 78-9, Assistant Surgeon HARVEY E. BROWN, U. S. Army, states that his regiment, the 70th N. Y. Vols., while on the Peninsula, was seriously threatened with intermittent fever, but that a liberal administration of quinine dissolved in whiskey to the whole command checked the progress of the disease. Also, on pp. 232-3, Surgeon GEO. E. COOPER, U. S. Army, after referring to the generally received opinion that white men could not live on the low marshy grounds bordering the rivers of the southeastern coast, and to the feeling of anxiety consequent on the issue of orders to construct and garrison fortifications on these bottom lands, states that: "The medical officers on duty in the batteries were instructed to issue to the men quinine and whiskey as a prophylactic, and with beneficial effect it was used, as the statements of the medical officers informed me. While referring to the prophylactic use of quinine, I would state that in such cases as came under my own observation I saw much good resulting from it. Many men who seemed to be imperceptibly almost succumbing to the malarious poison were in a short time giving indications of perfect health. I would strongly recommend its use in all malarious districts, for though the expense is considerable the benefit following will, I think, more than compensate for the outlay."

† See letter from Brigade Surgeon GEO. H. LYMAN—*Boston Med. and Surg. Jour.*, Vol. LXV, 1862, p. 312—in which the prophylactic use of quinine is highly commended; see also the same journal, LXIX, 1863, p. 169, where Surgeon GEORGE DERBY, 23d Mass. Vols., relates his experience with this drug in his regiment at New Berne, N. C., and vicinity, and strongly commends its use as a prophylactic.

‡ If we except the following: A board of surgeons consisting of Drs. G. H. GAY, C. D. HOMANS, R. M. HODGES, specially detailed by the Governor of Massachusetts to inspect the condition of the Massachusetts regiments of the Army of the Potomac, then before Yorktown, visited that army during April, 1862, and made a report, *Boston Med. and Surg. Jour.*, Vol. LXVI, 1862, p. 354, to the Surgeon General of the State, in which they remark: "Malaria was said to be acting powerfully, and therefore quinine must be administered in large doses. The ill effect from this large dosing was found to be much greater than that from any supposed malarial influence. The improvement in every instance where the quinine was either entirely stopped or given in greatly reduced quantities was too marked and too continued to leave a shadow of a doubt as to the exciting cause of the persistent headache and diarrhœa. The good effect of stimulants, brandy or whiskey, was immediately seen when we had some to give." This paragraph is cited by the editor

value.* In view of the general tenor of the testimony, it must be allowed that quinine exercised a protective influence. Nevertheless, as the practice of administering it for its prophylactic virtues was generally abandoned in the later years of the war, it must be conceded that the results achieved did not equal the expectations which were at first entertained. But a consideration of the well-known temporary action of the drug on the system will readily explain its failure to protect where the exposure in a malarious country was so prolonged as during our civil war. An intermission in the use of the quinine, by leaving a command exposed to the miasm, necessarily put an end to the prophylactic experiment. The sickness of those who became affected by the malarial influence and the idiosyncratic immunity of others under similar exposures rendered unnecessary, in many instances, the further expenditure of quinine as a preventive, and led to the gradual abandonment of the method by our medical officers. Practically, therefore, the prophylactic use of quinine in our armies was a failure; but it does not follow that the method, so far as employed, was not of value. On the contrary, all who adopted it give positive evidence on this point. Men were saved from attack and preserved in perfect health for the active service of the time-being by the use of the drug. That it did not continue to save them after its use was intermitted does not detract from the value of the protection already rendered. That it did not save from attack every one to whom it was administered is no argument against its prophylactic use. Its efficacy even as a remedy is unequal, some cases requiring more, some less, for the suppression of the morbid phenomena, and in certain instances in which the morbific influence is overwhelming, quinine, although well known to be of remedial value, is unfortunately of no value. Its efficacy as a preventive may not be supposed to be more equable than its remedial power. The malarial influence may be so overpowering that the prophylactic dose may be as inefficient for prophylaxis as the remedial dose for cure. From these considerations it would seem that the quinine which was used with a view to prophylaxis was of value in preserving health temporarily, and that the disuse of the method was due not to a recognition of its want of value, but to the difficulty attending its successful prosecution in cases of prolonged exposure, especially as the periods of active service which led the troops into dangerous bivouacs and surrounded them with predisposing conditions were precisely those in which there was the greatest liability to a failure in the issue of the prophylactic doses.

Nor must it be forgotten, in a discussion of the prophylactic value of quinine, that although, owing to conditions of continued exposure, the attempt to protect whole commands was given up during the later years of the war, the protection of individuals from relapses continued to be practised to the last, not by issues of quinine and whiskey, but by the administration of the drug in repeated doses, covering several days at a time, or by larger doses given at specified periods. The success of this mode of treating relapses, really a prophylactic use of the drug, bears strongly on its value when used under favorable conditions for the protection of healthy men from the miasmatic influence.

---

of the *Chicago Medical Journal*, Vol. XIX, 1862, p. 416, who remarks: "Is not this monstrous 'quinine prophylaxis nonsense about played out'? The word of its promise is not even kept to the ear, and the humbug proves dangerous as well as expensive." The report of the Massachusetts physicians is not understood, however, to refer specifically to the use of quinia as a prophylactic, but rather to its alleged abuse in the treatment of the sick. The prophylactic use is probably objected to in the remarks of ALEX. LE B. MONROE—*Letter to the Surgeon General of the State of Massachusetts, Boston Med. and Surg. Jour.*, Vol. LXVII, 1862-3, p. 21—who, writing of a brief tour of duty in the Army of the Potomac during June and July, 1862, says: "We found a great many patients who had suffered from over-dosing with quinine administered in whiskey."

*J. J. WOODWARD—*Outlines of the chief Camp Diseases, etc.*, Philadelphia, 1863, p. 168 *et seq.*—speaks doubtingly of the prophylactic value of quinine, first, on account of its failure to become an accepted method of prevention in the army, and secondly, on the claim that its continued use establishes a tolerance of the remedy by which its curative powers are to a great extent lost. "The general use of quinine-whiskey as a preventive of malarial disease is therefore to be regarded as unadvisable. * * * Quinine should be reserved for employment as a therapeutic measure in the treatment of the actual symptoms of malarial disorders when they appear in individual cases."

The experience of the war appears to teach that, when a command is to be temporarily exposed in a specially dangerous locality, quinine should be issued for the sake of such protection as it may give; but that when the command is to be stationed for a long time in a malarious section, prevention should be attempted by the judicious selection of camp sites and the avoidance of predisposing causes, while quinine is reserved for remedial exhibition on the first manifestations of the malarial poison in the system, and for special prophylactic doses under conditions of unwonted exposure or in anticipation of relapses.

The whiskey ration is brought incidentally into question by its connection with the quinine. Dr. WOODHULL has expressed the prevailing sentiment of our medical officers with regard to it. As a matter of fact, the campaigns of the civil war were made on hot coffee, with a rare issue of whiskey under special conditions of fatigue or discomfort. The sanitary reports are therefore generally silent on the subject of the whiskey ration *per se*.

On the Confederate side attention was directed at an early period of the war to the prophylactic use of quinine by Dr. JOSEPH JONES, who cited in support of his favorable opinion the accounts of its successful employment by English naval vessels on the African coast.* This essay was subsequently embodied, with some additional matter, in a report made by JONES to the Surgeon General of the Confederate Army in August, 1864.†

From this report it appears that quinia had not been employed as a prophylactic to any extent in the Confederate Army chiefly because of a scarcity of the drug. Nevertheless it had been used on a small scale with decided benefit in certain malarious localities. Ass't Surg. J. N. WARREN, 25th South Carolina,‡ stationed on James Island, S. C., gave four and a half grains daily to two hundred men of his regiment, from April to October, 1863. Four cases of malarial fever and one of typhoid occurred among these men. The remainder of the regiment, between three and four hundred men, did not take the prophylactic, and over three hundred cases of paroxysmal fever, with twenty-three of typhoid, occurred among them. Surgeon SAMUEL LOGAN,§ chief surgeon of the 2d and 3d Military Districts, Department of South Carolina, Georgia and Florida, tried quinia in four-grain doses daily as a prophylactic during the summer and autumn of 1863, in portions of several small commands stationed in malarious districts of South Carolina. The coast line is indented with numerous bays, inlets and salt-water creeks, which contribute to the formation of a series of islands consisting of light sand supported by a clay stratum a few

* JOSEPH JONES—*Sulphate of quinia administered in small doses during health the best means of preventing Chill and fever, and Bilious fever, and Congestive fever,* in those exposed to the unhealthy climate of the rich lowlands and swamps of the Southern Confederacy. *Southern Med. and Surg. Jour.,* Vol. XVIII, August, 1861, p. 593. "Under these exposures I have found that sulphate of quinia, taken in from 3 to 5 grains twice during the day, would in most cases prevent the occurrence of malarial fever, and if it failed to ward it off entirely the attack would be of a very slight character." In support of this position he cites the prevalence and fatality of malarial fevers among Europeans in Africa before the introduction of the use of quinia as a prophylactic, and contrasts this with the comparative immunity in the case of certain English naval vessels on the west coast of Africa during 1856 and 1857.—See *Statistical report of the health of the Royal Navy for the year 1856,* London, 1858, pp. 100 to 116; also the same for the year 1857, London, 1859, pp. 78–85.

† *Quinine as a Prophylactic against Malarial fever: being an appendix to the Third report on Typhoid and Malarial fevers, delivered to the Surgeon General of the late C. S. A., August, 1864. Nashville Jour. of Med. and Surg.,* Vol. II, 1867, p. 441 *et seq.* Dr. JONES adverts to the great prevalence of intermittent and remittent fevers in the command stationed in and around Fort Jackson on the Savannah river. This command had a mean strength of 878 men, and during the twelve months "from October, 1862, to November, 1863, 2,808 cases of malarial fever were treated." He assumes that these men might have been protected at a cost of $4,390 by each using an ounce of quinine during the period stated. On the other hand he supposes that had no prophylactic been used the proper treatment of the cases reported would have required on an average 50 grains of quinia each, or about 300 ounces, costing at $5 per ounce $1,500. The additional cost of the quinia required for prophylaxis would thus be $2,890; but against this he offsets the pay of the men on the sick-list. Assuming 100 men to be constantly off duty in the unprotected command, their pay per annum, estimated at $13,200, would give a balance of $10,310 as a saving to the Confederacy by using the quinia as a prophylactic. Besides the reports of Surgeons WARREN and LOGAN, mentioned in the text, Dr. JONES reprints a report by Surgeon OCTAVIUS WHITE, dated James Island, S. C., May 7, 1862, in which the writer refers to the English naval experience, and recommends the prophylactic use of quinia by the troops on James Island and in St. Andrew's Parish; also a letter from Dr. D. DU PRE, dated Nashville, Tenn., May 10, 1867, mentioning the case of six individuals exposed to malarial influences who attributed their escape from fever to the use of quinia.

‡ Surgeon WARREN's observations were made at the instance of Dr. JONES.

§ SAMUEL LOGAN, P. A. C. S.—*Prophylactic effects of quinine. Confed. States Med. and Surg. Jour.,* Vol. I, p. 81. This article was republished by its author in the *Richmond Med. Jour.,* Vol. II, 1866, p. 412.

feet below the surface.   Towards the interior the light sea-island soil gives place to level tracts of stiffer earth, sandy, but mixed with red clay, on which the undergrowth is extremely luxuriant.   These lowlands are intersected by swamps, some bearing rice, and all composed of an alluvium on blue clay.   Beyond this the pine barren region, a dry, porous sand with clay underlying it at a considerable depth, becomes gradually changed into the rolling ground which leads up to the mountain slopes.   Malaria prevails in the sea-islands, in the low-levels and in the lower part of the pine barrens.   The higher parts of the last, and some of the first are exempt from fevers; but as the Union troops occupied all the healthy portions of the shore, the rebel lines of defence ran through the unhealthy low-lands just within the belt of sea-islands.   During the summer months most of the troops were moved to the healthy pine lands, but some, chiefly cavalry commands, were retained for outpost duty in the sickly low grounds.   To these quinine was administered as a prophylactic; but it was not taken by all, although all were exposed to similar influences.   This failure on the part of some to make use of the quinine gives a value to Dr. LOGAN's statistics by permitting a comparison to be made between the sick rates from malarial disease among those who did and those who did not use the drug.   His results were as follows:

Total number who took no quinine 230; had fever 134; ratio per 1,000 of fever cases to patients 582.60, or 1 in every 1.71 patients; ratio per 1,000 of severe cases to total cases 313.43, or 1 in every 3.19 cases.   Total number who took quinine irregularly, 246; had fever 96; ratio per 1,000 of fever cases to patients 390.24, or 1 in every 2.56 patients; ratio per 1,000 of severe cases to total cases 291.66, or one in every 3.71 cases.   Total number who took quinine regularly 506; had fever 98; ratio per 1,000 of fever cases to patients 193.67, or one in every 5.16 patients; ratio per 1,000 of severe cases to total cases 326.53, or 1 in every 3.06 cases.   It would seem from these statistics that although not an absolute prophylactic, the degree of protective power possessed by the agent fully warrants its use. If four-fifths of the fever cases are prevented, it should surely be used.   It may be well to explain that under the head of *number who took quinine irregularly* are included those who would forget or neglect to take it some three or four days in the week, or take it one day and forget it the next, or omit it for a week at a time.

On the other hand it has been stated by Dr. HERRICK of Louisiana, that quinia was issued in a spirit ration to the crews of the Confederate fleet in Mobile Bay during the summer of 1863, by order of the Confederate States naval commandant, but the result of the trial was not satisfactory and it was soon discontinued.*

It is not difficult to add to the list of authorities brought forward by VAN BUREN and JONES in support of the prophylactic virtues of quinia.   On this side of the question may be cited the papers of MERRITT, ROGERS, HERRICK, BARTHOLOW, VIVENOT, JILEK and HAMILTON, and the favorable opinions expressed by EASTON, DUTROULAU, STILLÉ, H. C. WOOD and HERTZ.†   Moreover, favorable notices of the successful employment of the measure on the West Coast of Africa may be found in the official volumes containing the statistical returns of the health of the Royal Navy subsequent to those cited

* S. S. HERRICK—*Quinine as a therapeutic agent.* Trans. Amer. Med. Association, Vol. XX, 1869, p. 618.

† J. KING MERRITT—*Quinine as a Prophylactic in Malarious regions.* Amer. Med. Times, Vol. III, 1861, p. 305. STEPHEN ROGERS—*The Protective or prophylactic preventive and some points in the Curative uses of Quinine, etc.* Trans. Med. Society, N. Y. State, 1862, p. 181; also, *The Prophylactic and the Therapeutic uses and abuses of Quinia and its salts.* Trans. Med. Association, Vol. XX, 1869, p. 187. Both MERRITT and ROGERS instance their experience on the Isthmus of Panama as authorizing their favorable opinion. S. S. HERRICK—cited in last note. ROBERTS BARTHOLOW—*Army hygiene.* Proceedings Connecticut Med. Society, Vol. III, 2d series, 1868–71, p. 76; also, *Quinine and its salts,* in same Vol., p. 96; also, *A Practical Treatise on Materia Medica and Therapeutics,* New York, 1876, p. 131. RUDOLF RITTER VON VIVENOT, JUN.—*Ueber die prophylaktische Anwendung des Chinin gegen Malaria-intoxikation.* Med. Jahrb., Wein, 1869, S. 39. In this paper the writer relies almost wholly on the essay of Van Buren, cited note ‡, p. 166, *supra,* and the English naval experience, which he gleans chiefly from the work of C. FRIEDEL—*Die Krankheiten in der Marine, geographisch und statistisch, nach den "Reports on the Health of the Royal Navy,"* dargestellt, Berlin, 1866. A. R. VON JILEK—*Bietrag zur Prophylaxe gegen Marlariafieber.* Wochenblatt der k. k. Gesellschaft der Aerzte in Wein, April 27, 1870 (No 17), S. 177. J. BUTLER HAMILTON—*Remarks on the value of Quinine as a Prophylactic.* Indian Med. Gaz., Vol. VI, 1871, p. 233. This author relates that at Jubbulpore, in 1866, he gave three grains of quinine every second day to each of 135 men under his immediate charge; few cases of fever and no deaths occurred among them, the average number in hospital not exceeding four per cent. of the command.   At the same time and place 500 men of the 23d R. W. Fusileers, who did not use the quinia prophylaxis, were attacked with severe remittent fever, having at one time as many as 150 of their number sick in hospital, and 150 more convalescent from the fever, encamped on the hill close by: "The number of deaths I cannot remember, but I think they were about 20." A. F. DUTROULAU—*Traité des Maladies des Europ_ens dans les pays chauds,* 2e edit., Paris, 1868, p. 253. J. A. EASTON—*General observations on poisons, etc.* Glasgow Med. Jour., Vol. VI, 1858, p. 273. ALFRED STILLÉ—*Therapeutics and Materia Medica,* 3d edit., Philadelphia, 1868, Vol. I, p. 454. H. C. WOOD—*Treatise on Therapeutics,* 2d edit., Philadelphia, 1876, p. 73. HENRY HERTZ—*Malarial diseases,* in Ziemssen's Cyclopædia of the Practice of Medicine, Vol. II, Amer. transl., New York, 1875, p. 657.

in the paper of VAN BUREN. These notices are indeed so laudatory as to warrant the anticipation that the statistics would show a considerable and permanent reduction in the frequency of malarial fevers among the sailors of this station after the general introduction of the prophylactic use of quinine under the auspices of BRYSON in 1854; but an examination of the actual figures does not show any such reduction, although of late years the mortality has been very materially diminished.

The shore operations of the Ashanti war led to a high rate of prevalence of malarial fevers among the men of the British Navy and undermined the faith of their medical officers in the prophylactic virtues of quinine. Staff Surgeon THOMSON expressed a doubt,* Staff Surgeon LUCAS gave an unhesitating denial,† Surgeon Major GORE, on the staff of the quartermaster general, declared that his unfavorable opinion was shared by European residents in West Africa,‡ and Sir ANTHONY D. HOME, principal medical officer, regretted that he had been unable to recognize any value in quinine given in prophylactic doses, for it seemed neither to ward off attacks nor to mitigate their severity.§

MOREHEAD, from his observations in India, entertained the opinion that the evidence in favor of the power of quinia to prevent intermittents and remittents in malarious districts was by no means conclusive.‖ LIVINGSTON, during his expedition to the Zambesi river, found that those of his men who took quinine as a preventive were attacked with fever as frequently as those who did not attempt thus to secure protection.¶ LÉON COLIN's experience in Algeria and Italy led him to an equally unfavorable opinion.** The method was tried without success among the Russian troops in the Caucasus.†† VIVENOT's essay‡‡ suggested its use in the Austrian army and navy during the year 1869, when JILEK obtained

---

*Surgeon JAMES THOMSON, of the *Amethyst*—*Statistical report for 1874*, pp. 180 and 184—writes: "Whether any prophylactic treatment can be completely successful in this climate is a problem for the future. I confess to considerable disappointment in the present case, although I think it probable that the daily administration of four-grain doses of quinine had a modifying influence. It is, moreover, worthy of remark that I have heard of no case having a fatal termination."

†Surgeon LEONARD LUCAS, of the *Argus*—*Statistical report for 1873*, p. 196: "A question arises, does quinine given as a prophylactic prevent an attack of remittent fever? I unhesitatingly say no. Take the case of those marines landed at Elmina to guard the place. Quinine was administered to them daily, yet within a month all these men returned on board with fever. It is true Fort St. Jago is unfit for men to live in; but those billeted in the castle fared no better. It does not follow that men landed for a day, who had quinine before leaving their ship, escaped fever in consequence, because men have also been landed without any quinine and have fared equally well. It remains to be proved whether its administration as a prophylactic tends to render the attack of fever milder in character."

‡ALBERT A. GORE—*A Contribution to the Medical History of the West African Campaigns*, London, 1876, p. 164—gives specific illustrations of the failure of the quinia-prophylaxis, as for instance: "Quinine was served out to the marines who started for Elmina on the 12th June—five grains in half a gill of rum all round, the same quantity at daylight in port wine; all these men had severe attacks of remittent fever. After wet and damp nights it was always given to the sentries with no better effect."

§Deputy Surgeon General Sir ANTHONY D. HOME, K. C. B., &c.—*Medical history of the War in the Gold-coast Protectorate in 1873. Army Medical Department Report for the year 1873*, Vol. XV, London, 1875, p. 229: "With regret, and heartily wishing that my opinion may be overthrown by those of others, I have to say that I did not recognize any value in quinine given prophylactically; it neither seemed to ward off attacks nor to mitigate the severity of malarious fevers in those attacked. With the exception that in some men a daily three-grain dose produced transient deafness, and in a few others nausea, no untoward symptom followed the use of the medicine. On the other hand I was unable to agree with the startling opinion seriously propounded to me by some men of the West India regiment encamped at Napoleon, that the quinine they took daily as a prophylactic had given them the ague from which they suffered."

‖CHARLES MOREHEAD—*Clinical Researches on Diseases in India*, 2d edit., London, 1860, p. 149—speaks of the alleged success of two-grain doses of quinine in preventing malarial fevers in the 92d Highlanders during its service in the jungly tracts along the southern base of the Sautpoora hills during November and December, 1858, but shows that other detachments of the same expedition belonging to the 18th Royal Irish, the 3d Dragoon Guards and the Bombay Horse Artillery were equally fortunate, although they took no quinine.

¶DAVID and CHARLES LIVINGSTON—*Narrative of an Expedition to the Zambesi, etc.*, New York, 1866, p. 82: "Whether we took it daily, or omitted it altogether for months, made no difference; the fever was impartial, and seized on the days of quinine as regularly and severely as when it remained undisturbed in the medicine chest, and we finally abandoned the use of it as a prophylactic altogether." In a paper of earlier date by DAVID LIVINGSTON and JOHN KIRK—*Remarks on the African fever on the lower Zambesi. Med. Times and Gaz.*, Vol. XIX, N. S., 1859, p. 473: "The result of our experience has been to discontinue the daily use of quinine."

**LÉON COLIN—*Traité des Fièvres Intermittentes*, Paris, 1870, p. 424; also, *Considérations générales sur l'étiologie des fièvres intermittentes, Arch. Gén. de Méd.*, VIme série, t. XV, 1870, p. 34. See also his report to the Minister of Public Works, April 4, 1881—*Bull. de l'Acad. de Méd.*, t. X, 1881, p. 1398. He insists that quinine is not properly an "anti-miasmatic medicine"; it only acts against certain symptoms of the malarial intoxication, especially the febrile symptoms. He recommends that it be reserved for the sick, and given to them in sufficient doses. According to BÉRENGER-FÉRAUD—*Maladies des Européens au Sénégal*, Paris, 1875, t. I, p. 244—the French military surgeons in Algeria are divided in opinion as to the prophylactic virtue of quinia, some being for and some against it.

††COLIN, in *Bull. de l'Acad. de Méd.*, cited in last note.

‡‡See note †, p. 172, *supra*.

somewhat favorable results in a detachment of marines at Pola on the Adriatic;* but a similar experiment at the same time and place by the surgeon in charge of the 29th infantry gave about the same proportion of cases among those who took the quinine as among those who did not; and equally unsatisfactory results were obtained in the case of several small cavalry detachments on the Danube, as also, during the same year, among the troops forming the large garrison of Komorn.†

The evidence bearing on the virtues of quinia as a prophylactic against malarial fever is therefore by no means uniformly affirmative; but in the instances of failure or of doubtful benefit there is always that prolonged exposure which, as we have seen, led to the disuse of the method in our armies during the war. Bérenger–Féraud recognized the difference between temporary and prolonged exposures in this connection, and even specified that if the exposure was to be continued for more than twenty days, prophylaxis need not be attempted.‡ Moreover, some of the instances of failure may perhaps be attributed to the inadequacy of the quantity given. Quinine as a prophylactic has usually been administered in comparatively small doses. A grain and half to three grains daily as used by Jilek, and two grains daily as at Komorn and elsewhere in Austria, might well be regarded as inefficient; yet Hamilton, with three grains every other day, reports one of the most brilliant instances of success.§ Most of those who in this country have recommended the quinine prophylaxis have insisted on a daily dose of four or five or even more grains.

Herrick advocated the view that the most effectual plan is not to make daily use of quinia, but to resort to it in decided doses on the first appearance of malarial symptoms.‖ This opinion, which was based on his experience of intermittent fever in his own person, corresponds with that which has been given above as to the proper mode of meeting the dangers attending the prolonged exposure of an army in malarious districts.

Similar in principle was the plan pursued by the medical officers of the English army during the war of 1879 in Zululand. Surgeon General Woolfryes reports that during the sickly season quinine was administered three times a week to all the debilitated men.¶

The opinion expressed by Hamilton that quinoidine used for the purpose in view is more efficacious than quinine, is not as yet supported by adequate evidence.**

Besides the doubts that have occasionally been thrown upon the power of quinia to prevent malarial fevers, the serious objection has been urged that those who take the drug

*Jilek—op. cit., note †, p. 172, supra. The quinia was given in 1½ to 3-grain doses daily in rum; 500 men took it from June 1 to September 20, 1881, among whom there were 91 cases, while among 236 men who did not take it there were 68 cases. Jilek thinks, too, that the cases among those who took the quinia were milder than among those who did not.

†These facts are reported in an article Erfahrungen über die prophylaktische Anwendung von Chinin und Ext. nucis vomicæ gegen Malaria-Intoxikationen, Allg. Militärärztliche Zeitung, 1870, No. 10 u. 11, S. 76 et seq. Two grains were given daily in spirits of wine. At Komorn, between January 1 and August 25, 1869, there were 1,449 intermittents in a mean strength of 5,360 men, or 270 per 1,000 for the time named. This is spoken of as less than the usual proportion of cases at the post, but as there were neither floods nor prolonged heats during 1869, it was considered doubtful whether the lessened prevalence was really due to the quinine.

‡L. J. B. Bérenger-Féraud—Op. cit., note **, p. 173, supra, t. I, p. 246.

§Hamilton—cited p. 172, supra.

‖Herrick—loc cit., note *, p. 172, supra, says: "In 1864 the writer had occasion to test the value of quinine as a preventive of intermittent fever in his own person, and became convinced that the most effectual plan was not to make a daily use of it, but to resort to it in decided doses on the first warning. It is only necessary to exercise constant vigilance, for a paroxysm is generally preceded by unmistakable signs of malaise for a day or two previously, and the attack can be warded off by a few timely doses of quinine."

¶Surgeon General J. A. Woolfryes—Medical History of the war in Zululand in 1879; Army Medical Department Report, 1879, London, 1881, p. 299: The strength of the regular troops of this command was 13,333 officers and men, of whom 2,941, or 220 per 1,000, were taken on sick report with fevers between January 4 and October 3; the proportion of malarial fevers is not stated.

**J. Butler Hamilton—Report on the action of Quinoidine and Cinchonine as regards their influence on Malarious fevers; Indian Med. Gaz., Vol. VI, 1871, p. 50—gave to each soldier of a detachment of 80 men at Allahabad, from August 3 to November 16, 1870, three grains of quinia daily; to each of a detachment of 67 men the same quantity of cinchonine, and to each of a third detachment, also of 67 men, the same quantity of quinoidine. In the first detachment there were 7 cases of ague, or 87 per 1,000; in the second 13 cases, or 194 per 1,000; in the third 5 cases, or 77 per 1,000; whence he concludes that quinoidine ranks highest and quinine next in prophylactic virtue. On the other hand Gore—p. 164, op. cit., note ‡, p. 173, supra—reports that the men of the West India regiment who occupied the camp at Napoleon during the Ashanti war took daily a solution of quinoidine without deriving any particular benefit.

habitually acquire in time a tolerance of its action, in consequence of which its power as a remedy becomes lost.* But, as during our war there frequently occurred cases in which, without the previous administration of quinine as a prophylactic, this remedy failed to break up the paroxysms, necessitating a recourse to arsenic and other antiperiodics, it is possible that this tolerance to the habitual use of the drug may have been really due to some peculiarity in the individual or in the attack. It has also been represented that gastric and intestinal irritation, loss of appetite, headache and even diarrhœa result from its continued use.;† but although these accidents undoubtedly occur in some highly susceptible individuals, it is not unlikely that in most cases the medicine is undeservedly blamed for symptoms referable to the coincident malarial and other morbid influences. This explanation unquestionably applies to the opinion sometimes expressed by soldiers,‡ that the fevers and other serious results of malarial intoxication from which they suffer are caused by the medicine employed to prevent them,—an opinion sustained by MALONE and McDANIEL in this country, and by the Sicilian physician TOMASELLI and others, whose error has been sufficiently exposed by the criticism of BÉRENGER–FÉRAUD.§

PROPHYLACTIC USE OF OTHER MEDICINAL AGENTS.—Several other medicaments have been said to act as prophylactics against intermittent fever. The only one of these mentioned in the official reports as having been tried during the civil war was the bark of the willow. Assistant Surgeon HUNTER, in a report of his inspection, August 31, 1864, of certain regiments in camp near Thibodeaux, La., states that a spirituous infusion of willow-bark had been used by the 33d Ill. Vols. with fair success;‖ but the monthly report of sick and wounded of this regiment, on file in the Surgeon General's Office, shows that during the month stated no less than one-third of the men were taken sick with intermittent or remittent fever.¶

In the Confederate armies the *Cornus florida* or dogwood was used in some instances

---

* STILLÉ in his *Therapeutics and Materia Medica*, Philadelphia, 1874, Vol. I, p. 519—refers to this toleration of the medicine and its loss of remedial power as dangers inherent in daily doses continued for any length of time, and quotes Dr. GRAVES (*Dublin Quarterly Jour.*, February, 1846, p. 72) as perhaps the first to call attention to this subject. Dr. GRAVES, after a comparative trial of several methods of administering quinine in a case of obstinate quartan ague, concluded that it was best to withhold the remedy until premonitions of a fit occurred, and then to give it in large doses; for if continued throughout the apyretic interval "the system becomes accustomed to its impression and is less powerfully affected than when it is taken only at such times as the derangement which it is adapted to remedy is about to occur." It appears to the writer that the tolerance and loss of power are by no means proved by Dr. GRAVES's experiment. The allowable conclusion does not reach further than the greater efficacy of large as compared with small and repeated doses, which is now a well recognized fact in all malarious districts. See, for instance, a reference to Dr. CHARLES McCORMICK's experience, noted on p. 179, *infra*. Nor does Dr. WOODWARD give any ground for the assertion as to the loss of antiperiodic power. J. J. WOODWARD—*Outlines of the Chief Camp Diseases*, Philadelphia, 1863, p. 171 : "The system in time acquires a tolerance of the action of quinia, and when acute malarial affections supervene, as they frequently do, the grand therapeutic agent on which the surgeon relies is found to have lost its curative power to a great extent." BARTHOLOW—*Army hygiene*, cited note †, p. 172, *supra*—says : "Quinine loses its power by long continued use ; its antiperiodic power is not exhibited satisfactorily in cases of chronic malarial poison, and hence its prophylactic power is feeble in the same morbid state." ROGERS—*Trans. Amer. Med. Ass.*, 1869, p. 200,—expresses the opinion that insusceptibility to the therapeutic effects of quinia is seldom met, except in those who have used it continuously, and recommends, therefore, that "considerable intervals of abstinence" should be practiced by those who employ it prophylactically. Surgeon A. G. DELMEGE, of the British navy, who had charge of a detachment of Royal marines landed at Cape Coast Castle during the Ashanti war of 1873—*Statistical Report*, 1873, p. 206,—states that the officers of the Army Medical Staff who had served for long periods on the coast advised him to give quinine as a prophylactic only to those of his men who were especially exposed, as by its constant use "such a tolerance of it was created that when attacked with fever it would require enormous doses to produce any effect." GORE—p. 164, *op. cit.*, note ‡, p. 173, *supra*—states that it is a general idea among the English residents in West Africa "that when taken *de die in diem* it loses its power as a remedy."

† Such symptoms were referred to the quinine in the report from Komorn, cited p. 174, *supra*, although only two grains daily were given.

‡ As for example by the English soldiers in the Crimea, according to Sir JOHN HALL, cited in note ‖, p. 167, *supra*, and during the Ashanti war, according to Sir ANTHONY HOME, note §, p. 173, *supra*.

§ MALONE and McDANIEL expressed the belief that while quinine did not cause malarial hæmaturia it determined an attack or recurrence in those liable to the affection from continued exposure to the malarial influence. See note on *hæmorrhagic malarial fever*, *supra*, p. 128; and also SALVATORE TOMASELLI—*L'intossicazione chinica*, etc., Catania, 1877—abstracted in the *Bull. de l'Acad. de Méd.*, 2ᵉ série, t. VI, 1877, p. 756; G. B. UGHETTI—*L'intossicazione chinica e la febbre biliosa ematurica*, Lo Sperimentale, 1878, p. 614; and the paper of KARAMETZAS in the Bull. of the Medical Society of Athens, session of Nov. 18–30, 1878. BÉRENGER-FÉRAUD—*L'intoxication quinique et l'infection palustre*, Archives de Méd. navale, t. XXXI, 1879, p. 355—has thoroughly exploded this charge, and shown that the untoward symptoms attributed to quinia are really those of hæmaturic remittent fever. A similar explanation of the views expressed in TOMASELLI's paper was offered in the Acad. of Medicine, Bull., vol. cited *supra*, p. 778, by LE ROY DE MÉRICOURT.

‖ See his report, p. 155, *supra*.

¶ The report is signed by Assistant Surgeon H. T. ANTIS, of the 33d Illinois Volunteers: Mean strength of the command 631 officers and men; 197 cases of intermittent fever and 20 of remittent are reported—total 217; of the intermittents 5 were congestive, and two of these died.

instead of quinine as a prophylactic. Circular No. 12, issued from their Purveyor's Office August 22, 1862, refers to an arrangement by which whiskey medicated with dogwood and other indigenous barks was to be used by the troops as a protective against malaria.* Dr. JOSEPH JONES reports that this compound tincture was issued by the purveyors to troops serving in swampy districts, and was employed with good effect in preserving them from malarial fevers.†

VII.—TREATMENT OF MALARIAL DISEASE.

GENERAL CONSIDERATIONS.—Prior to the introduction of cinchona bark into medical practice the system by which these fevers were treated was palliative and uncertain, depending chiefly on the special symptoms manifested by the individual case. The primary congestions suggested the propriety of bloodletting, but the subsequent deterioration of the blood, so marked as to have originated the name *putrid fever*, caused much opposition to this measure. The introduction of cinchona as an element in the treatment was opposed by those who considered bloodletting essential, and advocated by such as looked specially to the putrescent character of the developed disease. At first the bark was regarded as an antiseptic, and was given in conjunction with camphor and wine; but, as early as 1765, Dr. JAMES LIND trusted to it alone as a specific antidote to the disease-poison.‡ Its value was also urged by HUNTER, CLARK and others.§ But in 1804 its use

* This circular is quoted from Dr. JONES's article cited in the next note: "Although no orders have been issued to that effect, some of the purveyors appear to be under the impression that they should make a mixture of the indigenous barks (dogwood, &c.) and whiskey. The arrangement intended by the Surgeon General and Commissary General is, that the Commissary Department shall furnish the whiskey to the troops, giving each man one drink a day. The Purveying Department was to furnish the barks to mix with the whiskey, to make a species of army bitters, as a preventive against malaria, &c. The arrangement is merely an issue of whiskey by the Commissary Department to the troops, and the Purveying Department furnish the bark to mix with it. This office has not yet been instructed whether the mixture is to be made at the purveying depot or at the commissary depot. Therefore whiskey will not be issued in other than the medical preparations that have been or may be ordered as regular issues."

† As, for instance, to the Eutaw (25th South Carolina) regiment, whilst it was encamped upon James' Island, in a notoriously malarious locality. This regiment had a mean strength of about eight hundred officers and men. During the summer and autumn of 1862 one-third of the command was at times upon the sick-list with the various forms of malarial fever. "The assistant surgeon of this regiment, J. W. WARREN, of South Carolina, communicated to the author, during his inspection of the sick upon James' Island, some interesting facts upon the prophylactic powers of certain indigenous remedies. A compound tincture, or medicated whiskey, prepared by the Medical Purveyor from the dogwood, cherry, poplar and willow barks, was administered daily, in the proportion of one-half to one gill to each man during two weeks in the month of September, 1862. Under the use of this tonic mixture the number of new cases of malarial fever diminished one-half, although as the autumnal season advances upon James' Island malarial fevers increase in number and severity. The supply of this medicated whiskey being limited, at the end of two weeks it was exhausted, and in the course of eight days the cases of malarial fever had increased from thirty-six to eighty. A fresh supply having been obtained its use was again commenced, and in the course of five days the number of cases of malarial fever fell to the original number." Dr. JOSEPH JONES—*Indigenous remedies of the Southern States, &c.*, No. 2, Dogwood.—*St. Louis Med. Reporter*, 1868, p. 306.

‡ An *Essay on Diseases incidental to Europeans in Hot Climates*, by JAMES LIND, M. D., F. R. S., Sixth Ed., London, 1808, p. 323 *et seq.*: "The preparation of the body requisite previous to the administration of the bark is not considerable. It is sufficient to cleanse the stomach and alimentary canal by an emetic or purge. * * * The bark may be administered at any period of the disease. When the ague is slight it need not be given till a second fit has evinced the true nature of the disease; but when the ague is severe there is frequently an absolute necessity of administering it upon the first intermission, even with scarce any preparation of the body: instances have occurred, on unhealthy spots in England, of agues having been so malignant after hot summers that a return of the fit sometimes proved fatal." * * * After adverting to the opinion that an ague must continue some time before it is completely formed, and that till such time it is highly dangerous to apply any remedy, he continues: "The advantage of administering the bark as early as possible in the disease fully appeared in the year 1764 and the two following years, during an uncommon prevalence of remitting and intermitting fevers, which spread themselves over the greater part of England and furnished me with a number of patients laboring under all the symptoms of these diseases. * * * I never prescribed the bark until the patient was free from the fever; and then without regard to a cough or any other chronical indisposition I ordered it to be given in large doses. I have given the bark in every circumstance attending intermitting fevers during their remission, but never gave it during the fit."

§ JOHN HUNTER—*Observations on the Diseases of the Army in Jamaica*, London, 1788—speaking of the cure of intermittents, says, p. 208: "When the intermissions were complete the bark was given directly without any previous evacuations in order to cleanse the stomach and bowels, which is to be considered as rather recurring to an old than giving in to a new practice. There was no inconvenience arose from omitting the vomiting and purging, usually made to precede the bark; on the contrary it was so much time gained." HUNTER refers to SYDENHAM's use of bark in this manner. JOHN CLARK—*Observation on the Diseases which prevailed in long voyages to hot countries, particularly on those in the East Indies*,—London, 1809: "As soon as the intestinal canal has been thoroughly cleansed the cure [of the remittent fever] must entirely depend on giving Peruvian bark in as large doses as the patient's stomach will bear, without paying any regard to the remissions or exacerbations of the fever. If the remissions be distinct the bark, indeed, will have a more speedy effect in subduing the fever; but even if it become continued, by a regular and steady perseverance in the medicine it will be effectually prevented from growing dangerous or malignant."

was checked by the experience of Dr. James Johnson,* who, finding that his first case of remittent at Calcutta rejected the remedy and died with an engorged liver and congested brain, had recourse in his succeeding cases to venesection and evacuants. Moreover, the beneficial effects of twenty-grain doses of calomel taken by himself during an attack accompanied by dysenteric symptoms† led him to urge this practice, which for many years afterward sent Europeans back from India with their constitutions shattered by repeated salivations.

As the evils of the mercurial system were developed, bleeding was resorted to freely and repeatedly as the only efficient remedial measure. Meanwhile, in 1820, quinine was discovered and its use introduced into England and France, but several years elapsed before it was employed by the Indian practitioners in those dangerous remittents for which bleeding to relieve congestions, free purgation to remove vitiated secretions, and calomel and opium to act on the secretory and excretory functions, constituted the standard treatment, although Sir J. Annesley and Twining‡ made use of small doses of quinine, when full remissions

* The Influence of Tropical climates on European Constitutions, by James Johnson, M. D., Second Ed., London, 1818, p. 48—after referring to the instructions for treatment given in the works of Drs. Clark and Lind, he describes his first case as follows: "A young man, of a good constitution, in the prime of life and health, had been assisting with several others to navigate an Indiaman through the Hoogly. The day after he returned he was seized with the usual symptoms of this fever. I did not see him till the cold stage was past; but the reaction was violent; the headache intense; skin burning hot; great oppression about the præcordia, with quick hard pulse; thirst and nausea. An emetic was prescribed, and towards the close of its operation discharged a quantity of ill-conditioned bile, both upwards and downwards; soon after which a perspiration broke out, the febrile symptoms subsided, and a remission, almost amounting to an intermission, followed. I now, with an air of confidence, began to "throw in" the bark, quite sanguine in my expectations of soon checking this formidable disease. But, alas! my triumph was of very short duration; for in a few hours the fever returned with increased violence, and attended with such obstinate vomiting that although I tried to push on the bark through the paroxysms, by the aid of opium, effervescing draughts, &c., it was all fruitless; for every dose was rejected the moment it was swallowed, and I was forced to abandon the only means by which I had hoped to curb the fury of the disease."

† Op. cit., in last note, p. 208: "I was bled, and took an ounce of castor oil immediately; a few hours after which six grains of calomel and one of opium were taken, and repeated every five hours afterwards, with occasional emollient injections. The day passed rather easier than the preceding night; the tormina were somewhat moderated by the medicine; but I had considerable fever, thirst, restlessness and continual calls to stool; nothing, however, coming away but mucus and blood. As night closed in the exacerbation was great. The opium lulled me occasionally, but I was again delirious; and the phantoms that haunted my imagination were worse than all my corporeal sufferings, which were, in themselves, indescribably tormenting. The next day I was very weak; and so incessant were the griping and tenesmus that I could hardly leave the commode. The tenesmus was what I could not bear with any degree of fortitude; and, to procure a momentary relief from this painful sensation, I was forced to sit frequently in warm water. The calomel and opium bolus was now taken every four hours, with the addition of mercurial frictions. An occasional lavement was exhibited, which gave much pain in the exhibition, and I each day took a dose of castor oil, which brought off a trifling feculence, with inconsiderable relief. My fever was higher this day than yesterday, with hot, dry, constricted skin. As night approached my debility and apprehension of the usual exacerbation brought on an extreme degree of mental agitation. The surgeon endeavored to cheer me with the hope of ptyalism, which, he assured me, would alleviate my sufferings—I had then no local experience in the complaint myself. As the night advanced all the symptoms became aggravated, and I was convinced that a fatal termination must ensue unless a speedy relief could be procured. I had no other hope but in ptyalism; for my medical friend held out no other prospect. I sent for my assistant and desired him to give me a scruple of calomel, which I instantly swallowed, and found that it produced no additional uneasiness; on the contrary I fancied it rather lulled the tormina. But my sufferings were great; my debility was increasing rapidly, and I quite despaired of recovery! Indeed I looked forward with impatience to a final release! At four o'clock in the morning I repeated the dose of calomel, and at eight o'clock (or between 60 and 70 hours from the attack) I fell, for the first time, into a profound and refreshing sleep, which lasted till near midnight, when I awoke. It was some minutes before I could bring myself to a perfect recollection of my situation prior to this repose; but I feared it was still a dream, for I felt no pain whatever! My skin was covered with a warm moisture, and I lay some considerable time without moving a voluntary muscle, doubtful whether my feelings and senses did not deceive me. I now felt an uneasiness in my bowels and a call to stool. Alas, thought I, my miseries are not yet over! I wrapped myself up, to prevent a chill, and was most agreeably surprised to find that, with little or no griping, I passed a copious, feculent, bilious stool, succeeded by such agreeable sensations—acquisition of strength and elevation of spirits—that I ejaculated aloud the most sincere and heartfelt tribute of gratitude to Heaven for my deliverance! On getting into bed I perceived that my gums were much swollen and that the saliva was flowing from my mouth. I took no more medicine, recovered rapidly and enjoyed the best state of health for some time afterwards."

‡ James Annesley, of the Madras Medical Establishment—Researches into the Causes, Nature and Treatment of the more prevalent Diseases of India and warm climates generally, London, 1828, Vol. II, p. 490 et seq.—recommends in agues the moderation of the cold stage, if severe, by the hot or vapor bath, frictions and the internal administration of camphor, ammonia, ether, wine, brandy and water or other stimulants. When the vascular excitement of the hot stage is excessive, general or local bleeding is suggested, especially in the plethoric and when accompanied with determination to the head and delirium, or to the liver and spleen, with symptoms of inflammatory action in those viscera. Cooling diaphoretics, as the nitrate of potash, acetate of ammonia, camphor julep, antimonials, etc., are also recommended as promoting the speedy supervention of the sweating stage. When the paroxysm has ceased an emetic is given, and its operation encouraged by the free use of diluents, after which a full dose of calomel, fifteen or twenty grains, is administered, followed by a purging draught, and if these fail to act within a few hours, their operation is assisted by a cathartic enema. "Having thus promoted discharge of the morbid secretions and fæcal accumulations, and removed local congestions by bloodletting, we may resort to the exhibition of bark so as to prevent the accession of the paroxysm. Unless purgatives have been employed previously to the exhibition of bark, so as effectually to carry off morbid accumulations, and unless local determinations of blood and congestions are removed by general or local depletions, we shall resort to this most valuable medicine to little purpose; for it will either not be retained on the stomach, or it will fail of producing its febrifuge effects if retained, and occasion obstruction and enlargement of the liver and spleen." Quinine, although in use in England, had not been introduced into medical practice in India at the time Annesley wrote. Similarly in remittent fever: "Bark may be resorted to in the remissions. But care should be had not to give this medicine during active demonstrations to the head, liver, lungs or spleen until such complications have been removed by vascular depletion, either general or local, and by the judicious employment of whatever means the particular circumstances of individual cases may require."—On the effects of Bloodletting in the cold stage of Intermittent fever, by W. Twining, Esq., Trans. Med. and Physical Society of Calcutta, 1831, Vol. V, pp. 58-100. Twining adopted and advocated the method introduced by Mackintosh of Edinburgh, of bleeding in the cold stage to relieve the heart and large vessels from

were established, to prevent a return of the paroxysm.   Even as late as 1861 Sir J. R. MARTIN gave the administration of quinine a secondary place in the list of remedial agents.*   But during this time Dr. HARE was urging the antidotal power of quinine in these malarial fevers.   He obtained successful results from thirty-grain doses, and from an extensive and systematic experimental practice of this method, advocated its use in the pernicious fevers of India to the exclusion of other remedial means excepting the occasional use of small doses of calomel when there was gastric irritability.†   Nevertheless the value of the treatment by quinine may not be considered as fully established in Indian practice, for HORTON, in 1879, did not consider the remedy admissible until portal and abdominal congestion and epigastric irritation had been relieved and the febrile action moderated.‡

In France, MAILLOT, from an experience of many thousand cases of pernicious inter-mittents, urged an immediate recourse to quinine in large doses.§   But perhaps to American medical men is due the credit of having been the first to use quinine in large doses and irre-spective of preliminary evacuant treatment, as antidotal to the malarial poison; for PERRINE

<hr>

their state of engorgement, to unload the lungs and remove congestion of the brain and spinal marrow; but as he did not consider that venesection superseded the necessity of using other remedies, according as the nature of the existing symptoms and the course of the disease might demand, he occasionally used the sulphate of quinine or powdered bark combined with purgatives. See also his *Diseases of Bengal*, Calcutta, 1832, p. 627, where he says: "In every description of remittent fever we must watch the changes which take place; and when the pyrexia abates administer sulphate of quinine for the purpose of preventing a return of the exacerbation; in most cases where the cerebral symptoms are not urgent and continued the effect of this remedy is undoubted."

* Sir J. R. MARTIN—*The Influence of Tropical Climates*, London, 1861, p. 430: "Quinine, the great febrifuge, justly administered acts purely as a nerve tonic to the cerebrospinal and visceral sympathetic system.   Exhibited in extravagant doses it is toxical and not therapeutic."   And again, on page 360: "Subject only to the limitations already stated, bleeding—early bleeding—whether general or local, *and always practised at the very outset of the stage of reaction*, is very generally necessary in the severer forms of Bengal remittent fever; then come full doses of calomel and sudorifics, short of producing salivation, with saline purgatives, antimonials and refrigerants, and quinine in the intervals."

† E. HARE—*On the Treatment of Malarious fevers*.   *Med. Times and Gazette*, London, 1864, p. 540: "In 1843 I was sent to Segowlie, on the borders of the Nepal Terai, the most deadly in India, and there remained for four years.   I was called to a distance on one occasion to see a medical gentleman with cholera.   He died, and left me a valuable medical library, in which I found the now scarce works of LIND and HUNTER.   Their practice was new to me, and I read them with eagerness.   I had seen enough of the standard practice to be dissatisfied with it, especially in some recent cases I had treated of the Terai fever.   They all died.   No remission took place; there were head symptoms, and I durst not give quinine.   In fact, it was so utterly for-bidden by all authorities that it never occurred to me to give it.   I tried to salivate, but the fever was so active that my patients were dead before the mercury had time to affect them.   It then struck me as remarkable that since the discovery of quinine no one had tried it in the same way as LIND and HUNTER had used bark, from the dread of increasing congestion and inflammation, and a case quite hopeless under the common treatment soon offered itself to me, and I determined to try quinine. * * * I found a young lad of about 20 lying quite insensible on a native bed.   The natives said that he was traveling on a pony in the Terai, had fallen off insensible in their village, and fearing he should die there and cause suspicion they had brought him to the nearest doctor.   I immediately mixed one scruple of quinine in some wine, and by giving him a teaspoonful at a time made him swallow the whole of it.   I repeated it every four hours three times that day.   Early in the morning he was sensible.   I gave him another dose and some arrowroot and milk.   He took the same doses throughout this day, with some soup, and the next to my delight he was out of danger, having taken two and a half drachms of quinine in forty-eight hours, and without much inconvenience. * * * In the first place, no blood was drawn either by lancet or leeches.   Bleeding, therefore, is not necessary, and the disease not inflammatory.   No opium; no purgative to bring away bad secretions; no drug of any kind is required, except quinine, for the successful treatment of malarious fever.   Quinine also may be given in the largest doses, whether there are head symp-toms, delirium, coma or pain in the liver.   Whether it be in the hot stage or cold quinine is not only safe for all forms of malarious fever, but its certain cure; and in cases where there is danger to life the earlier and the larger the doses of quinine which can be given to the patient the better. * * * * Quinine, therefore, may with reason be pronounced as a direct antidote to the poison of malaria, and not simply as an antiperiodic and adapted only to stop periodicity, for it always cured equally well those fevers in which there were no periods, but which continued without the slightest remission during the twenty-four hours."

‡ J. A. B. HORTON—*The Diseases of Tropical Climates and their Treatment*, London, 1879—speaking of quinine as useful in preventing the recurrence of the paroxysm, says, p. 93: "This valuable remedy requires some caution in its administration in this disease; in large doses it should on no account be given when the paroxysm of fever is on the patient, and more especially when there are signs of gastric or cerebral inflammation or congestion, with scanty or depraved secretions, full and hard pulse, as it may lead to the fixing of the inflammatory and congestive tendency to the brain.   Quinine is safe, and should be administered when there is a complete remission; when there is no sign of venous congestion; when the pulse is reduced in fre-quency and force; when the skin is moist and the secretions free."

§ *Traité des fièvres ou irritations cérébro-spinales intermittentes d'après les observations recueillies en France, en Corse et en Afrique*, par F. C. MAILLOT, Paris, 1836.   See pp. 360 *et seq.*, where he speaks to the following effect: Many practitioners, still under the influence of obsolete ideas, are accustomed to use laxatives and purgatives to prepare the stomach for the reception of quinine.   This custom is generally followed in Italy and in several marshy districts of France, Holland and Germany.   TORTI, in applying this method, acted consistently with his principles; in a great number of cases, however, he was forced on account of the gravity of the symptoms to expedite matters and give quinine without employing this hackneyed preparation; which fact, it seems to me, ought to have put him in the right path, or, at least, shown him the uselessness of this medication.   In ordinary intermittent fevers the employment of laxatives sometimes suspends the attack, but more often its only effect is to put off for a time the use of quinine—which must always be had recourse to in the end.   The more energetic purgatives and emetics increase the congestions which take place in the digestive mucous membrane of which the coating of the tongue is merely an indication; they may rapidly raise these irritations to a higher degree—to inflammation. * * * In fact while laxatives are being administered pernicious attacks often take place; but even admitting that purgatives and emetics do not increase the gastro-intestinal irritation, they have the greater inconvenience of permitting attacks to occur, which by their violence and continuance always add to the dangers of the disease and to the difficulty of its treatment.   It is clear that when our predecessors used purgatives and emetics to prepare the stomach to receive quinine, they followed rather their medical theories than the teachings of experience. * * * Having observed several thousand cases, I think that immediately after and sometimes before bleeding, sulphate of quinine ought to be used whatever may be the symptoms.   Neither the persist-ence of the arterial excitement nor the signs of gastro-enteritis ought to bar its employment.   All the morbid phenomena will disappear as if by enchant-ment in a few hours.

in 1826 advocated the employment of large doses at any period of the fever,* and this practice was common among our army medical officers during the Florida war.†

During the War of the Rebellion quinine was the *sine quâ non* of treatment for malarial disease. Other drugs and remedial measures were used as called for by particular conditions of system; but other antiperiodics were seldom employed except in cases in which quinine after a fair trial failed to eradicate the disease.

In addition to the notes of treatment found in the clinical and *post-mortem* records submitted in this chapter, and to the references which appear in the sanitary and special reports already printed,‡ the following extracts are presented as bearing on this subject:§

Ass't Surg. W. W. GRANGER, *3d Mo. Cav., Rolla, Mo., October,* 1862.—Our cases of intermittent fever, both quotidian and tertian (except two), have yielded readily to quinine combined with capsicum in equal proportions. In the two exceptional cases the system, through frequent use, had apparently lost its susceptibility to the effects of quinine, either alone or in combination with stimulants or opiates. These cases finally yielded to emesis, induced an hour or two in advance of the expected chill, and followed as soon as the stomach would tolerate it with one-fourth of a grain of sulphate of morphia, two grains of capsicum and one-fourth of a grain of sulphate of copper, given every three hours during the intermission. One of the cases presented the unusual phenomenon of inversion of symptoms, that is, the precedence of the hot stage, followed by the cold. I think decided advantage resulted in this case from the use of quinia alone in the intermission, and the administration of capsicum in ten-grain doses as soon as the sweating stage arrived, continuing every hour till the chill had passed off.

There were sixteen cases of remittent fever, twelve of which began with languor and indisposition to action, constipation, full and frequent pulse, dizzy sensations, pain in the head and, as the patient expressed it, in the bones and flesh generally. Five of these experienced much restlessness during the later stages. Convalescence was reached in from four to sixteen days and was rapid in nearly every case. Treatment consisted of a purgative of calomel and powdered rhubarb, followed in six or eight hours by castor oil and turpentine or salts, when necessary. After free evacuation, quinine in full doses was administered during the remission; and during the accession bathing, cold or tepid as proved agreeable, Dover's powder, nitrate of potash and sweet spirit of nitre were relied on with satisfactory results. I found nothing better than cold or tepid sponging as a sudorific, anodyne and refrigerant in remittent fever; and when the fever was associated with irritation of the kidneys, a cold wet cloth over the lumbar region acted satisfactorily as a diuretic. In cases characterized by much restlessness, sponging was an efficient anodyne, and almost indispensable when cerebral disturbance contraindicated the use of opiates. Under this course the remissions became longer, the febrile accessions lighter; the circulation resumed its natural character, the skin

---

* HENRY PERRINE—*Fever treated with large doses of Quinine in Adams county, near Natchez, Mississippi. Philadelphia Jour. Med. and Phys. Sci.*, 1826, Vol. 13, pp. 36–41—relates several cases of remittent fever treated by bleeding and quinine, the latter in eight-grain doses, repeated at intervals: in one case characterized by stupor and insensibility 64 grains were taken in the twenty-four hours, and apprehensions of danger were removed. He concludes: "My observations so far, exhibit the following as one of the successful modes of treating our autumnal fevers, whether congestive or inflammatory. Bleeding whenever the symptoms require it. A dose of from 6 to 12 grains of sulphate of quinine every two or three hours, at any period of the fever, until its symptoms in the pulse and skin are subdued. Then purgatives to obtain copious consistent evacuations from the bowels, until they regain their usual power. Subsequent attempts to form fever should be counteracted by a large dose of quinine."

† The *Statistical Report on the Sickness and Mortality in the Army of the United States*, by R. H. COOLIDGE, Assistant Surgeon, U. S. A., Washington, 1856, gives, p. 638 *et seq.*, a special report by CHARLES MCCORMICK, dated October 11, 1841, in which he brings to the notice of the Surgeon General's Office his treatment of intermittent fever by large doses, fifteen or twenty grains, of quinine administered immediately after the sweating stage, with the view of suppressing the occurrence of further paroxysms. Two years before the date mentioned he had been so unsuccessful in arresting intermittent paroxysms with the sulphate of quinine in two-grain doses every hour, although as much as twelve, eighteen and twenty-four grains had been taken during the apyrexia, that he gave up its use and resorted to relaxants, such as tartar emetic, ipecacuanha and opium. But soon thereafter he resumed the use of quinine, giving it in from four to six grains every hour until its peculiar effects on the brain were produced, when he found himself invariably successful in controlling the intermittent. This led him to give it in single doses of ten, fifteen or twenty grains, according to the violence of the symptoms. He used in similar doses with benefit in remittents, claiming to have given it at all times of the paroxysm in many hundreds of cases without witnessing any alarming or dangerous effects from its administration in this manner. The practice of using quinine in such large doses, and during the stage of febrile excitement, having excited much attention, and the propriety of such treatment having been questioned, Surgeon General LAWSON issued a circular to medical officers of the army asking for their experience of this method of treating malarial fevers. Fifty-seven replies testified to the value of the method. Some of the replies, as those of B. F. HARNEY, R. S. SATTERLEE, R. C. WOOD, BURTON RANDALL, J. J. B. WRIGHT, B. M. BYRNE, J. H. BAILEY, D. C. DELEON, T. C. MADISON, R. F. SIMPSON and JOHN BYRNE, are published in the Statistical Report above mentioned. See, also, an article *On the Treatment of Intermittent fever*, by AUSTIN FLINT, in the *American Jour. Med. Sci.*, Vol. 11, New series, 1841, pp. 277–292. Dr. FLINT gives an analysis of 33 cases occurring in soldiers lately from Fort Gratiot, Michigan, in which he gradually increased the dose of quinine until twenty, thirty and in one case forty grains were administered within half an hour. He gives also a number of cases from civil practice illustrating the efficiency of this method. He argues that the system requires no preparatory process for the reception of the quinine, and that "the most rational policy is manifestly to strike at once at the *fons et origo* of the difficulty."

‡ See in the Appendix to the First Part of this work the reports of HAND, p. 239; HEWITT, p. 313; FRINK, p. 318, and WHITEHILL, p. 334; also in the present Vol. those of GAGE, p. 123; PECK, p. 124; HUNTINGTON, p. 125; MERRITT, p. 142; GALLOUPE, p. 144; TOWLE, p. 153; etc.

§ Few articles on the treatment of malarial fevers appeared in the journals during the war. THOMAS T. SMILEY, writing from Hilton Head, S. C., October 15, 1862, furnishes the following paragraph on *Intermittent fevers* in the *Boston Med. and Surg. Jour.*, Vol. LVII, 1862–63, p. 270: "The cases admitted into the hospital have not been numerous, and have presented no aggravated features. After a proper attention to the stomach and bowels, they have generally yielded speedily to the exhibition of quinine, in doses of from three to five grains, repeated more or less frequently, and combined with alcoholic stimulants, or not, according to the previous habits or condition of the patient. In a few cases the disease has assumed a congestive form, when quinine was administered in much larger doses." S. S. THORN, in a letter published in the *Med. and Surg. Reporter*, Vol. VIII, 1862, p. 280, refers to the treatment of intermittents.

its moisture and the system its tone. Aromatic sulphuric acid was used as a tonic. The four remaining cases differed in having no constipation at the beginning, and in greater mildness throughout, yielding in from four to six days to quinine during remission, and five grains of Dover's powder during accession, given every five hours, and followed by the acid tonics during convalescence.

Surgeon EZRA READ, 21st Ind. Vols., Camp Dix, Baltimore, Md., September 5, 1861.—In the treatment of intermitting fever I have relied upon sulphate of quinine in full doses, giving from one to two scruples in twenty-four hours to arrest the periodicity. During convalescence I have continued the same in five-grain doses every morning, and have had no relapses and no unfavorable results from visceral enlargements.

Surgeon JNO. W. SCOTT, 10th Kansas Vols., September 30, 1862.—As was to have been expected, most of the cases were malarial fevers, chiefly of a remittent type; a few assumed a decidedly typhoid character, and to these was due most of the mortality. Pure intermittents were of rare occurrence, there being in almost every case more or less febrile action in the intervals; but this, as a rule, occasioned no delay in the administration of antiperiodics, as the combination of diaphoretics with quinia sufficed to counteract any unduly stimulant effect of the latter,—and the cases yielded to treatment with the usual facility. The fevers, remittent and intermittent, have shown during the past summer a much slighter tendency to relapse than usual; and we have met with none of those cases of enlargement of the abdominal viscera and general debility which are so often the result of continued attacks of autumnal fevers in this climate. Doubtless this marked exemption from the usual sequelæ of ague has direct relation to the fact that so few cases of the disease have occurred. The cause which produces by its intensity a great number of cases must, by its persistent action, occasion relapses in constitutions debilitated by previous attacks.

Surgeon D. W. HENDERSON, 96th Ohio Vols., Louisville, Ky., November 19, 1862.—The regiment left Camp Bates [four miles from Covington, Ky.] October 8, 1862, marching to Falmouth, Ky. * * * In all cases of intermittent fever larger doses of quinine are required here than north or in home practice, twenty-five to thirty grains being generally needful to accomplish the desired object.

Surgeon DAVID MERRITT, 55th Pa. Vols., Beaufort, S. C., May 10, 1863.—We have had in the regiment very many cases of intermittent fever which have yielded promptly to the following mode of treatment: First, I give an emetic consisting of two grains of tartar emetic and twenty of powdered ipecacuanha in conjunction with capsicum. Then, as soon as the stomach becomes quiet, I administer ten grains of calomel combined with twenty of jalap. After the bowels have been freely opened I give large doses of sulphate of quinia, which generally arrest the paroxysms speedily. In some cases I have given the solution of arsenite of potassa to ward off the hebdomadal chill and its sequences, but generally I keep on with the sulphate of quinia in two-grain doses three times daily, or it may be in larger doses and oftener, knowing well that the mere arrest of the paroxysm is only an apparent and not a real cure. I may also mention that in several cases of intermittent fever I have cut the chill short and prevented a paroxysm, both since being with this regiment and when in Iowa (near the Mississippi river above Dubuque), by the mere administration of the emetic above mentioned, with the exception that in these cases more of the capsicum was added to the other ingredients. I have frequently given quinine in twenty-grain doses since arriving at this place with the effect of a speedy arrest of the intermittent paroxysm, and then, by continuing the remedy in smaller doses, have been much gratified with the result. With regard to the sulphate of cinchonia I cannot bear very favorable testimony, and would much rather depend upon the sulphate of quinia, with which, if it produces gastric distress, I administer a few drops of tincture of opium. We have also had in the regiment numerous cases of remittent fever, many of which have been complicated by periodical congestion of the bowels, manifested by mucus and bloody stools, in some cases simulating dysentery. The uncomplicated cases have been mild, and readily yielded to treatment. An emetic was first given, if indicated, then a mild cathartic, followed by blue mass and Dover's powder, neutral mixture or a solution of acetate of ammonia, and finally sulphate of quinia.

Surgeon B. F. HARRISON, Independent Battalion, N. Y. Vols., Morris Island, S. C., January 9, 1864.—[This battalion arrived at Hilton Head, S. C., February 1, 1863, and subsequently, to the date of the report cited, served in the Department of the South.]

There is probably no point in which the medical history of the battalion is more peculiar than in the small amount of quinine which has been used. I commenced my service with it at Yorktown, Va., on August 18, 1862. At that time intermittents prevailed, and no quinine was on hand. I borrowed one ounce, and before the first of January, 1863, had obtained thirty ounces from the medical purveyor. Since the commencement of the year (1863) to the 16th of November, I obtained thirty ounces more from the purveyor, and of this we have now fourteen ounces on hand, so that not more than forty-six ounces have been consumed during fifteen months, whilst at the same time there have been regiments in the field by the side of us, doing no harder service and having no greater number of men than ours, which have used an ounce a day for a considerable portion of this period. In one regiment in particular, which was in camp near us in Virginia, and has been with us almost constantly since, there were, according to the sick reports, three or four times as many cases of intermittent fever during the month of October of this year as we had. This and many other circumstances have convinced me that the consumption of quinine in the army is larger than is useful, and perhaps, even injuriously large, as well as a source of large and useless expenditure. I never give quinine as a prophylactic in a case where the paroxysmal character of the disease has not been distinctly manifested. My practice is, when the intermittent paroxysm has once exhibited itself, if the patient is still in the cold stage, to give half an ounce or an ounce of whiskey with some hot drink, and, if there are no violent symptoms, to let the paroxysm pass, modifying or assuaging some of the most uncomfortable manifestations as may seem necessary. About two hours before the next paroxysm is expected I give eight or ten grains of quinine in one dose; and if the paroxysm is kept off, I give two or three grains less two hours before the next paroxysm is expected; and if that does not occur I again diminish the dose by two or three grains, and again repeat two hours before the next paroxysm is expected, and thus give from two to five doses, by which time the disease has usually disappeared. But I am not always so fortunate as to control the disease in this prompt and easy manner, and sometimes twelve grains are necessary to "break the chill;" and oftentimes the system is out of order in other ways, the tongue coated, the appetite gone, the digestion disordered, and in other respects the patient may be suffering from conditions which should be attended to; all the functions should be brought into the most healthy condition.

Surgeon CLAIBOURNE J. WALTON, 21st Ky. Vols., Army of the Tennessee, December 31, 1862.—The intermittent and remittent fevers observed in this regiment have yielded readily to the use of quinine. Twenty grains given at one dose usually prevent the return of the paroxysm in intermittent cases. The same quantity given in five-grain doses during the twenty-four hours (without regard to the remission) and continued in some cases for two days, with or without mercury, is sufficient to relieve a remittent.

Surgeon JOHN WRIGHT, 107th Ill. Vols., Elizabethtown, Ky., December 31, 1862.—The intermittent fevers observed in this regiment have been generally treated with antiperiodic doses of quinine, preceded by a cathartic in cases of constipation, and associated with opium in cases of diarrhœa. Sixteen to twenty grains of quinine, given during the intermission, sufficed to prevent a return of the chill. Remittents have been treated on the same plan, the quinine being given during the remission, and with favorable results, the remission in a few days becoming an intermission. Occasionally there has been great irritability of the stomach; in such cases large doses of laudanum appeared to answer well.

In INTERMITTENTS the sulphate of quinine was usually administered in doses of three to five grains, repeated every few hours during the intermission. Where the disease was common and deaths from sudden congestions rare, these doses were given three or four times a day, with the intention of favorably modifying and ultimately suppressing the succeeding paroxysms. But where the occasional occurrence of fatal congestions infused into the case a possible danger to life, the remedy was administered with especial intent to immediately suppress the morbid manifestations. To this end the dose was repeated at such intervals that ringing in the ears or other symptoms of cinchonism might be produced, or failing this, that a specified quantity might be taken, before the time when the next paroxysm was conceived to be due. Thus, in case 55, five grains were ordered for administration at 8, 10, 12 and 2 o'clock, to anticipate a paroxysm expected at 3.30 P. M. The quantity needful to effect this object varied with the section of the country which gave rise to the disease. Thus, while WRIGHT says that sixteen to twenty grains, given during the intermission, were sufficient to prevent a return of the chill, HENDERSON states that twenty-five to thirty grains were generally required to accomplish this. But the quantity varied also in individual cases, some requiring more some less; and these peculiarities becoming known in primary attacks, dictated the quantities prescribed in subsequent relapses.

The danger attaching to the recurrence of the chill led to the very general adoption of the practice of giving one or more large doses as being more efficient than the repetition of a smaller dose. The large dose was usually administered early in the intermission, that time might be afforded for its full absorption and efficient action before the period of the expected return. Thus the medical officer of the 19th Mass. Vols., in cases 5, 13 and 41, gave fifteen grains at once, and continued the remedy thereafter in three- or five-grain doses at intervals. PECK gave fifteen to twenty grains morning and evening; MERRITT, WALTON and others twenty grains. HARRISON, who comments on the unnecessary expenditure of quinine in some commands, states that a practice leading to economy of the drug in his own charge consisted in the exhibition of ten-grain doses to ward off expected chills; but he allows that he was not uniformly successful, and that twelve grains had sometimes to be given. A few reports referring to methods of administration speak of the use of evacuants prior to the exhibition of quinine; but that this was not usual in practice may be gathered from the clinical records, where the remedy is generally ordered at once and unaccompanied by a cathartic. When called for by the condition of the tongue or bowels, blue pill and opium were combined with the quinine, or a mercurial was given, followed by Epsom or Rochelle salts, or the citrate of magnesia; capsicum was frequently used as an adjuvant, especially in the Western armies. Emetics were seldom given; but MERRITT and GRANGER refer to their successful use in preventing recurrences. When gastric irritability interfered with the administration of quinine, opium was considered of value; Hoffmann's anodyne, ice and sinapisms were also used to overcome occasional vomiting. Diarrhœa as a complication was treated with Dover's powder, opium or aromatic powder in conjunction with quinine or camphor, or with opium combined with acetate of lead or nitrate of silver. During the paroxysm little was done other than to make the patient as comfortable as possible and to abridge the febrile stage by the use of hot drinks.

Quinine was used as freely to prevent anticipated relapses as to suppress expected paroxysms after the relapse had occurred. For this purpose small doses were occasionally continued for several days; but more generally the patient was directed to report at the end of the first, second and third weeks for the administration of a large dose in anticipation of a relapse at those periods; or he was cautioned to be on the outlook for premonitory symptoms and instructed to report for treatment immediately on their appearance. An occasional dose of blue pill, when the tongue was furred, was also given as a part of this prophylactic system.

Strychnia was sometimes employed in obstinate cases, as in case 4, in which it was combined with blue pill and capsicum. But when quinine failed to prevent relapses, medical officers generally had recourse to Fowler's solution, which was often found beneficial. After the paroxysms were controlled quinine was not unfrequently resumed in roborant doses with other vegetable tonics and the tincture of iron; or the citrate of iron and quinine was employed. Surgeon TOWLE considered the removal of the patient from the malarious atmosphere of the greatest importance in treating obstinate fevers, and urged the advisability of having such cases removed from the exposures incident to camp life in tents, stating that many cases in his practice which had proved refractory to quinine recovered when the patients were tranferred from a tent to the better protection of a house.*

REMITTENTS.—In the treatment of remittents the sulphate of quinine was generally used, often with capsicum or blue pill and opium, in five or more grains, repeated four or five times in the twenty-four hours. Frequently a mercurial cathartic, followed by a saline, was given; but the administration of quinine was not delayed for the action of the bowels. The specific remedy was prescribed during the pyrexial periods as well as during the remissions, but when the latter were well marked, larger doses were administered during their continuance, while acetate of ammonia, spirit of nitre and neutral mixture were employed during the exacerbations. Local congestions were not permitted to interfere with the administration of quinine, as they were believed to originate in the miasmatic influence, and were found to be relieved when the latter became counteracted or modified by specific medication. Turpentine emulsion was frequently used in the diarrhœa accompanying these cases. Dover's powder was often given to restrain the bowels, promote perspiration and secure rest. In some instances of hemorrhage from the intestines, enemata containing persulphate of iron were employed. Vomiting was controlled as in the intermittent fevers.

---

* S. K. TOWLE, Surgeon 30th Mass. Vols.—*Notes of Practice in U. S. A. General Hospital*, Baton Rouge, La., during the year 1863. *Boston Med. and Surg. Jour.* Vol. LXX, 1864, pp. 49–56. "While on the Potomac I was so well pleased with the progress of typhoid cases in hospital tents that I thought them as good as houses; but since being in this department I have become convinced that cases of malarial disease do very much better in buildings than in tents—the canvas protecting the patients much less than boards from the two great excitants to the action of miasmatic poison, the heat of the sun and the chilly heavy dews of night."

Sinapisms or blisters were applied on account of pain in the hypochondriac or umbilical regions; and calomel, opium and taraxacum were administered when indications of jaundice appeared. Active catharsis, as by calomel, rhubarb and salines, was used in the few sthenic cases which occurred, in conjunction with low diet, cold to the head, mustard to the feet, and very exceptionally, bloodletting. Digitalis was sometimes employed with the quinine when there was much cardiac excitement. Aromatic sulphuric acid was used to restrain excessive perspirations, and carbonate of ammonia and alcoholic stimulants when the prostration was great.

CONGESTIVE FEVER.—In congestive cases the sole reliance was on quinine. Dr. GAL-LOUPE* expressed the general opinion in saying that in these cases no treatment was of any avail except that by quinine; and that when cinchonism was rapidly produced the disease was promptly and almost invariably broken up. Large and repeated doses were given, irrespective of the condition of the patient as to collapse, fever, intermission, head symptoms or intestinal inactivity or derangement. Other measures were employed as adjuncts during the stage of collapse, as mustard emetics, capsicum, alcoholic or ethereal stimulants, stimulating enemata, hot frictions and sinapisms or the hot bath. HEWITT recommended the application of iodine to the spine, which was assumed to do good by relieving passive congestion of the cord, thus enabling the organ to generate and transmit power sufficient to remove local obstructions and restore integrity of vital function.†

CHRONIC MALARIAL POISONING.—Quinine was also given in cases of chronic malarial poisoning, but in these it was by no means so efficacious as in the acute manifestations of the disease. D'AVIGNON, speaking of such cases at New Berne, N. C., says that the ordinary remedies were of no avail; and in case 52, reported above, iodide of potassium, iron in various forms, vegetable bitters, mineral acids, stimulants, counter-irritants and anodynes were employed for three and a half months, during which the patient seemed rather to decline than improve. Removal to a non-malarious climate was apparently essential to recovery from this condition of chronic poisoning. The deteriorated blood had to be improved before the general health could be re-established, and this could not be effected so long as the individual remained exposed to the influences which had caused his disability. This was well recognized by our medical officers, and furlough, discharge from service or removal for treatment to some northern hospital was their usual prescription. Iodide of potassium internally and iodine applied to the region of the spleen, with tincture of iron and small doses of quinine, or the citrate of iron and quinine, and the best diet procurable, constituted the routine treatment of such cases, special symptoms receiving attention as they became prominent. At the Satterlee Hospital, Philadelphia, Fowler's solution succeeded in allaying supraorbital neuralgia in several instances in which quinine gave no beneficial result,‡ while extract of belladonna applied locally was a means of temporary relief. At Quincy, Ill., this neuralgia was favorably affected by forty grains of chlorate of potash, twelve of citrate of quinine and iron and two of capsicum, given in four doses during the day.

UNTOWARD EFFECTS OF QUININE.—The medical records of the war make no mention

---

* See his report, *ante*, p. 144.

† See his report in the Appendix to the first part of this work, p. 313.

‡ An Assistant Surgeon (name not given)—*Effects of latent Malaria, roused into activity by an exciting cause. Med. and Surg. Reporter*, Vol. X, 1863, p. 100—describes several cases of periodic neuralgia in soldiers brought to hospital from the Army of the Potomac, in which arsenic succeeded after quinia had failed. See, also, letter from Surgeon GEORGE B. WILLSON, 3d Mich. Vols., from Camp Michigan, Va., Feb. 25, 1862, *Boston Med. and Surg. Jour.*, Vol. LXVI, 1862, p. 109,—in which he describes some cases of periodic neuralgia relieved by quinine and some by Fowler's solution.

of harmful effects from the use of large doses of quinine in suppressing malarial fevers. Giddiness, deafness, ringing in the ears and even temporary prostration were frequently experienced, but these were regarded as desirable symptoms, indicating that the remedy had been absorbed and was pervading the system with its antidotal influence.   Nausea was sometimes produced, but was considered as of little moment in comparison with the great benefit to be derived from the administration.   The absence of specially dangerous symptoms or undesirable sequelæ attributable to quinine might well be accepted, in view of its extensive employment during the war, as establishing the harmlessness of the remedy when exhibited in large doses in malarial fever.*   It must be admitted, however, that large doses may be a source of danger by the direct sedative action of the drug on the nervous and circulatory systems, especially in cases having a tendency to heart-failure from temporary enfeeblement or degeneration of tissue.   Dr. D. S. Lamb of the Surgeon General's Office, U. S. Army, published recently the case of a child of three years, in which, at the end of the first week of a mild attack of typhoid fever, death was caused in little over an hour by syncope following the ingestion of forty-two grains of quinine.†   Stillé cites several cases of death from quinine, in which the autopsy showed congestion of the brain and lungs, and in some degree also of the stomach.‡   The toxical effects of quinine must therefore be held in view; and their notable absence from the records of the war be attributed to that judicious use of the remedy which relieved diseased conditions and even recovered the patient from impending death without injuring the system by an excess.

OTHER REMEDIAL AGENTS.—The sulphate of cinchonia was occasionally used during the war, but no systematic observations were made on its efficacy as compared with that of quinia.   The opinion formed was unfavorable to its use.   Surgeon MERRITT, for instance, states that he preferred quinine to cinchonine, but does not give the grounds of his preference.   Certain experiments in this country, and recent observations in India, lead to the belief that cinchonia is energetic and in adequate doses a sure remedy.§   Nevertheless, from

---

* The medical officers mentioned in note † p. 179, *supra*, were requested to testify on this subject.   The 7th inquiry of General LAWSON's Circular was as follows: "Since the practical introduction of quinine in large doses, the statistics of this bureau exhibit a much higher ratio of diseases of the bowels—as, for instance, diarrhœa and dysentery,—and also a much higher average of mortality from the same diseases.   It remains therefore to be determined how far this result is due to this cause, or to the operation of other agents."   In reply, Surgeon R. C. WOOD stated that—"I have always been opposed to the administration of quinine in very large doses, and have no doubt but that dysentery and diarrhœa have been aggravated by the excessive use of this remedy."   But the experience of the others did not sustain Dr. WOOD's opinion.   They attributed the increase in the bowel affections to the conditions existing during the Florida war, and conceived that quinine was efficient as a remedy in those diseases.   Thus Surgeon R. S. SATTERLEE reported: "I have not the least hesitation in saying that the constant and long exposure of the soldiers in Florida to the influence of malaria, and their suffering from fevers, both remittent and intermittent, was the cause of the great mortality as well as the great number of cases of dysentery and diarrhœa that occurred there, and by no means the use of quinine; on the contrary, I have often seen intermittent and chronic dysentery, both in the same case, at the same time checked by that remedy."   Assistant Surgeon B. M. BYRNE is the only officer who refers to other evil effects from the use of quinine: "I have, however, met with several cases of *nervous* affections, which evidently resulted from the administration of large quantities of this medicine.   I have witnessed four cases in which partial deafness was experienced for upwards of three months; one in which the deafness was *permanent*; and one in which almost total blindness was occasioned for several days, and in which perfect vision was not restored for some months.   These cases were all clearly attributable to the administration of quinine in large quantities.   I have, besides these, met with numerous other cases of nervous derangement of a chronic character, such as slight spasmodic affections, frequent attacks of vertigo, palpitation of the heart, cephalalgias, nervous tremors, &c., which, it appeared to me, could be fairly ascribed to the same cause.   In nearly all these cases the remedy had been exhibited in doses of from ten to thirty grains; and in several of them, as high as two hundred grains had been administered within ten days."

† *New York Med. Jour.*, Vol. XXXIX, 1884, p. 549.

‡ *Therapeutics and Materia Medica*, by ALFRED STILLÉ, M. D., Philadelphia, Pa., 1874, Vol. I, p. 206.

§ *Observations upon one hundred cases of intermittent fever in which the sulphate of Cinchonia was used as a substitute for quinia*, by A. PAUL TURNER, M. D., *Am. Jour. Med. Sciences;* New Series, Vol. XLVII, 1864, p. 396.   Dr. TURNER, after referring to MAGENDIE, GITTERMANN, CHOMEL and others who, after slight inquiry rejected the pretensions of cinchonia as a febrifuge, cites BALLY, who, in 1825, succeeded in immediately checking twenty-five out of twenty-seven intermittents, while the refractory cases yielded on a judicious perseverance in the remedy.   He recalls the favorable opinions of MARIANI, WUTZER, DUFRESNE, POTIER and BARDSLEY, and invites special attention to Professor WILLIAM PEPPER's success in promptly checking eleven out of fifteen cases, two of those remaining having yielded to a second administration of the remedy.   Of his own cases seventy-nine had no paroxysm after the first exhibition of the medicine, fifteen had one paroxysm but not two, four had two but not more, one had three or more paroxysms, and in one the cinchonia, as administered, was without effect in averting the disease.   The maximum quantity used during a single intermission was thirty grains, and the largest dose given at one time was fifteen grains.   It was usually given in three-grain doses every hour during the intermission, until about twenty grains had been taken. Vertigo and buzzing in the ears were observed in most of the cases; nausea and vomiting occurred in five and cephalalgia in six.   See, also, *Report of 57 cases of intermittent fever treated by the sulphate of cinchonia,*—J. C. WELLS,—*Cincinnati Med. Observer*, Vol. I, 1856, p. 15, and *Table of 102 cases of intermittent fever treated with the sulphate of cinchonia,*—G. MARTIN, in *Trans. College of Physicians*, Philadelphia, 1853–'56, Vol. II, pp. 434–436.   JOSEPH DOUGALL, M. D.,

the slow progress made by this remedy into public favor, it seems unlikely that it will displace quinine as the special antidote to the poison of malarial fever.

The case-books of the Pettigrew hospital, Raleigh, N. C., Surgeon E. BURKE HAYWOOD in charge, give the details of the treatment of intermittents by turpentine applied to the chest over the fourth and fifth ribs. The application was made an hour before the accession of the cold stage, with a view to prevent the recurrence of the paroxysm. Mention has occasionally been made in the medical journals of the internal use of turpentine in intermittents;* but there are few references to its use as an external application. Nevertheless its employment in this way was advocated by some Southern practitioners, as appears from a letter written in 1855 by R. A. FONTAINE of Georgia,† in which he reports the successful treatment of an intermittent by anointing the entire chest, stomach and axillæ with turpentine, as recommended by J. C. NOTT of Mobile. Prior to its use at the Pettigrew hospital it had been employed at Savannah, Ga., in 1862, by STILES KENNEDY,‡ with very successful results. The patient was directed to appear at the steward's tent forty-five minutes before chill time, when a bandage of cotton cloth eight inches wide, soaked in turpentine, was wound around his chest; his linen was buttoned closely down over the bandage, after which he was wrapped in a blanket and kept under medical supervision. At the time this practice was begun there were sixty-two intermittent cases on the register. Of this number fifty received immediate relief—that is, the expected paroxysm was suppressed; nine resulted in cure on the second application, and three on the third; but during these three days eight new cases were reported, all of which were cured on the first application. Fowler's solution was administered in each case to prevent relapse. In his subsequent experience Dr. KENNEDY found the turpentine a prompt and efficient remedy when used in this way. In some instances failure occurred from irregularity in the return of the chill, as when, by anticipating the period of its recurrence, no time was given for the preventive treatment by turpentine. In two cases of failure the oil made no impression on the skin, and in four or five cases remittent fever supervened.

It appears that the favorable results obtained by Surgeon KENNEDY, when reported to

---

Surgeon Madras Army—*The febrifuge properties of the cinchona alkaloids—cinchonia, quinidia and cinchonidia. Edinburgh Med. Jour.* Vol. XIX, Part I, 1873, pp. 193–209. From observations on 108 intermittent cases Dr. DOUGALL concludes that after quinine, quinidia is the most powerful as an antiperiodic, cinchonidia next to it, and cinchonia the least active; but that even cinchonia is energetic, and in adequate doses a sure remedy. In the first trials the alkaloids were given during the intermission. "Ere long they were given indiscriminately during paroxysm and intermission. At length it became apparent that they were most serviceable when administered during the paroxysm only." Head symptoms were less common than with quinine; but nausea and bilious purging were frequent concomitants, the latter appearing to facilitate the cure. It does not appear from the history of the cases that mercurials or other evacuants were administered. The doses were usually five grains, with an occasional large dose of twelve grains. See also a *Report on, and Statistical details of, the treatment of six hundred cases, of malarious fever, in the Bhopal Battalion Hospital, by cinchona febrifuge or mixed alkaloids,* by F. ODEVAINE. *Indian Medical Gazette,* 1878, Vol. XIII, p. 69. The maximum quantity administered in twenty-four hours in any one case was twenty-one grains, which was usually given in three doses. The average quantity for all the cases from the commencement of treatment to discharge was 36.59 grains. The maximum number of days under treatment was thirty-three, the minimum one, and the average 4.55 days. Of the total 466 were quotidians, 116 tertians, 15 quartans and 3 remittents; and the average number of grains in each case of the first variety was 37.26; of the second 33.58; of the third 35.33, and of the last 54.33. But the antiperiodic was continued on the average in each case 1.65 days after the arrest of the paroxysm, and as for this protective purpose an average of 14.88 was used, the average quantity which sufficed to arrest the paroxysms amounted only to 21.71 grains. This quantity of the mixed alkaloids was estimated to contain only 1.35 grains of quinine; whence it was assumed that the combination of the alkaloids gave rise to an increased specific effect. In tertians and quartans Fowler's solution was given on the days of intermission, the cinchona febrifuge having been used only on the days of expected paroxysms. The mixed alkaloids did not cause nausea, vomiting or head symptoms in a larger number of cases than occurs with quinine. The writer's small experience of cinchonia is not so favorable as that noted above: In 1868 he supplied a detachment of troops at a malarious station in the San Pedro bottom, Arizona Territory, with sulphate of cinchonia, in the absence of the quinia salt. The men, who were accustomed to the use of the latter, pronounced against the new medicine as prone to cause vomiting and as being less efficacious than quinine.

*M. F. COLBY—*Effects of Spirits of Turpentine in a case of intermittent. Boston Med. and Surg. Jour.,* 1828, Part 2, Vol. I, p. 712—gave two-thirds of a tablespoonful of turpentine in molasses at the beginning of the cold stage, which was immediately suspended; vomiting occurred, and the hot and sweating stages were not distinctly marked. On subsequent occasions the remedy was followed by suppression of the paroxysms without nausea or other unpleasant result.

†See *Atlantic Medical and Surgical Journal,* 1858–59, Vol. IV, p. 444.

‡ *Turpentine as a remedial agent* by STILES KENNEDY, M. D., of Hallstown, Del., in the *Med. and Surg. Reporter,* Philadelphia, 1867, Vol. XVI, p. 458: "As to the mode of action of the oil of turpentine, I submit, 1st. The pain produced by it calls the whole attention of the mind. 2d. The impression on the nervous centres. 3d. The stimulant effect." Mustard was frequently used by Dr. KENNEDY, but he found that the skin became sore, swollen and irritated under its use, while the turpentine yielded no such undesirable results.

the Surgeon General, C. S. A., led to a series of experiments on this mode of treatment in several sections of the Confederacy. Seven cases were reported in the *Confederate States Medical and Surgical Journal*, January 7, 1864;* in these the expected accession was prevented, but the chill recurred on the seventh or fourteenth day. The *Journal*, the official organ of the Surgeon General, expressed a desire for a larger experience of this economical method of treatment, and requested that reports of cases be promptly forwarded. In response to this, seventy returns, involving over 400 cases, were received from different hospitals and posts, and the announcement was made that with few exceptions the remedy was regarded by the reporters as one of great power, if not positive efficiency, in preventing a return of the paroxysm. Nevertheless, in a later issue† the editor hesitated to accept these favorable experiences, considering that the turpentine had no special advantage over other powerful revulsives, such as blisters, alcoholic stimulants, narcotic medicines, sudden shock as from a plunge in cold water, exciting news, etc., which sometimes stave off chills, although they are seldom used for this purpose therapeutically. The results at the Pettigrew hospital were not so satisfactory as those reported by KENNEDY; but whether this was owing to the smaller surface exposed to the action of the turpentine or to a difference in the character of the cases is unknown; certainly in many instances the failure was not due to irregularities in the type of the disease. A report from the Chimborazo hospital, Richmond, Va., shows that this mode of treatment was employed in its wards, and proved successful in some cases, although in many others it merely retarded the access.

At the Pettigrew hospital there was also tried a mixture of tincture of opium‡ and solution of ammonia as a substitute for quinine in the treatment of intermittent fevers. A draught containing thirty drops of each was given a short time before the expected onset. Of thirty-three cases detailed below thirteen were treated by turpentine applied by means of a roller bandage around the chest; *one* of these was successful on the first application:

CASE 1.—Private J. B. Kelly, Co. F, 50th N. C., had a quotidian chill Nov. 7, 1864, at 8 p.m. Next day at 7 P. M. the roller was applied for an hour, and there was no chill. The operation was repeated on the 9th and 10th, and there was no recurrence of the chill. Three ounces of turpentine were used without injury. He was returned to duty on the 28th.

Three were successful on the second application:

CASE 2.—Private D. D. Stubbs, Co. F, 21st S. C., had a quotidian chill June 28, 1864, at 3 P.M. At 1.30 P.M. the next day turpentine on a roller bandage was applied and continued for three hours. The chill however recurred. The application was repeated on the following day, and the chill was suppressed. No strangury or injury to the tissues resulted. Three ounces of turpentine were used.

CASE 3.—Private M. B. Manners, Co. K, 10th N. C., had a tertian chill Sept. 7, 1864, at 7.30 A. M. The application was made on the 9th at 5.30 A. M. and continued for two hours. A slight chill occurred; but after a second application there was no recurrence. No injury to the tissues or other bad effect followed. Two ounces of turpentine were used.

CASE 4.—Private M. Steen, Co. A, 13th Art'y Batt., had a quotidian chill Sept. 19, 1864, at 11 A. M. At 10 A. M. next day the application was made and continued an hour without success; but after the repetition of the application on the 21st there was no chill. Five ounces of turpentine were used.

One on the third application:

CASE 5.—Private C. M. Dowd, Co. H, 1st Junior Reserves, had a tertian chill Sept. 20, 1864, at 3 P. M. On the 22d at 2 P. M. the application was made and continued for one hour; it was repeated on the 24th, with partial success. The chill recurred on the 26th. The application was renewed, and there was no chill thereafter. Six ounces of turpentine were used.

---

* *Confederate States Med. and Surg. Journal*, Richmond, 1864, Vol. I, p. 7;—*On the external application of the oil of turpentine as a substitute for quinine in intermittent fever, with report of cases.*

† *Op. cit.*, last note, *Editorial*, p. 119.

‡ Opium has been frequently used in conjunction with quinine to relieve the patient from the head symptoms occasionally produced by the latter, to restrain the bowels when diarrhœa or dysentery accompanied malarial fever, or, as we have already seen, to allay gastric irritability which might threaten the rejection of quinine. But it has sometimes been used alone, as for instance : *Eight cases of simple intermittent and six of remittent fever successfully treated by the exhibition of partially denarcotized opium.*—W. S. SINN of Chili, Hancock, Ill.—*Nashville Med. Jour.*, 1854, Vol. VII, p. 379.

While in *eight* it was found advisable to have recourse to quinine:

CASE 6.—Private H. L. Lawson, Co. I, 18th S. C., had a tertian chill at noon of June 8, 1864. On the 10th at 11 A. M. a roller bandage wet with turpentine was applied and continued for three hours. The chill, however, continued to recur every second day. The amount of turpentine used was ten ounces. No injury to the tissues or strangury occurred. He was finally treated with quinine.

CASE 7.—Private D. W Greenlee, Co. K, 50th N. C., had a quotidian chill Nov. 8, 1864, at 6 A. M. Next day at 5 A. M. the roller was applied for an hour and no chill occurred. On the 10th a chill occurred at 2 A. M. Quinine was administered on the 11th and 12th, and there was no recurrence of chills. He was anæmic, and was therefore given tincture of iron and infusion of quassia. Two ounces of turpentine. He was returned to duty on the 27th.

CASE 8.—Private B. J. Pollard, Co. D, 50th N. C., had a quotidian chill Nov. 7, 1864, at 9 A. M. Next day at 8 A. M. the roller was applied for one hour, and repeated on the 9th, and no chill occurred. On the 10th the roller was not applied, and a chill occurred at 10.30 A. M. He was then given quinine until the paroxysms ceased, and was continued on tonic treatment for debility. Two ounces of turpentine were used. He was furloughed on the 14th for sixty days.

CASE 9.—Private T. J. Turner, Co. F, 50th N. C., had a quotidian chill Nov. 7, 1864, at 2.30 P. M. The paroxysms were so irregular that the roller was applied but once, on the 9th at 11 A. M., for one hour, one ounce of turpentine being used. A chill had occurred on the 8th at 12.30 P. M., and recurred on the 9th at 3 P. M. Quinine was then used and the paroxysms ceased. He remained under treatment for diarrhœa.

CASE 10.—Private H. W. Canisse, Co. G, 50th N. C., had a quotidian chill Nov. 8, 1864, at 2 A. M. On the 9th at 1 A. M. the roller was applied for an hour. At 1 P. M. the chill recurred. The operation was repeated at noon on the 10th, but a chill occurred at 10 P. M. Two ounces of turpentine were used. On account of the irregularity of the chills, quinine was given, three grains every two hours, and a cure effected. He was retained on tonic treatment because of debility following intermittent fever.

CASE 11.—Private J. C. Hutchings, Co. G, 50th N. C., had a quotidian chill Nov. 7, 1864, at 11 A. M. The chill recurred irregularly. The first application was on the 8th, at 10 A. M., for an hour. He was treated in the same manner as Canisse. Two ounces of turpentine were used. He continued in the hospital taking tonics for debility.

CASE 12.—Private G. L. Black, Co. G, 50th N. C., had a tertian chill Nov. 8, 1864, at 1 P. M. A quotidian character was afterwards assumed. The roller was applied on the 10th and 11th for two hours, without success. Two ounces of turpentine were used. Quinine was then resorted to. He remained under treatment for debility.

CASE 13.—Private J. C. Strickland, Co. D, 11th S. C., had a quotidian chill Oct. 8, 1864, at 10 A. M. Next day at 9.30 A. M. the roller was applied for half an hour. A chill, however, occurred. The application was repeated on the 10th and no chill occurred. Next day he had fever, which continued several days. He was given quinine, two grains every three hours, and the paroxysms were finally checked. On the 18th a chill occurred at 9 P. M. The roller was applied at 8.30 P. M. on the 19th, 20th and 21st, without success, but on the 22d the chill was arrested and did not recur. Eight ounces of turpentine were used without any injurious effects.

Of the twenty remaining cases *one* was treated successfully by turpentine with the subsequent addition of opium and ammonia:

CASE 14.—Private R. Clarke, Co. D, 9th Pa. Reserves, had a quotidian chill Nov. 9, 1864, at 10 A. M. Next day at 9 A. M. the roller was applied for an hour, and there was no chill. On the 11th laudanum and ammonia were used in addition to the roller. No chill occurred. Having chronic diarrhœa he was retained in the hospital. Two ounces of turpentine were used.

Two were treated with success by opium and ammonia without the use of the turpentine bandage:

CASE 15.—Private Jacob W. Cobb, Co. H, Bonaud's Georgia battery, had a chill June 6, 1864, at 6 P. M. Next day at 5.30 P. M. laudanum and solution of ammonia, of each thirty drops, were given. The chill did not recur. The dose was repeated on the 8th, and there was no further recurrence of chill. A tablespoonful of infusion of dogwood was given every three hours through the day. He was returned to duty, cured, on the 16th.

CASE 16.—Private G. G. Davis, Co. H, Bonaud's Georgia battery, had a chill June 6, 1864, at noon. The next day at 11 A. M. thirty drops each of laudanum and solution of ammonia were given, and the chill did not return. Infusion of dogwood was administered every three hours.

Six were treated at first with the turpentine bandage; but the chills persisting, opium and ammonia were resorted to with beneficial results:

CASE 17.—Private J. B. Woodliss, Co. E, 1st N. C. Cav., had a quotidian chill Oct. 2, 1864, at 1 P. M. Next day at noon the usual application was made and continued for one hour; but the chill recurred. On the 4th the operation was repeated and laudanum and ammonia in the usual dose administered, after which the chill did not recur. There were no injurious effects from the turpentine, two ounces of which were used. He was returned to duty on the 15th.

CASE 18.—Private George W. Thompson, Co. F, 2d Junior Reserves, had a tertian chill Oct. 15, 1864, at 8 A. M. On the 17th at 7 A. M. the roller was applied and continued for an hour. On the 19th a chill occurred. The roller was repeated and laudanum and ammonia administered. No further chills occurred. Two ounces of turpentine were used, without injurious effect. He was returned to duty on the 24th.

CASE 19.—Private Wm. S. Davis, Co. G, 50th N. C., had a quotidian chill Nov. 10, 1864, at 11.30 A. M. Next day at 10.30 A. M. the roller was applied for one hour over the fifth and sixth ribs, and was repeated on the 12th without success. On the 13th laudanum and ammonia were administered, after which there was no recurrence of chill. Three ounces of turpentine were used without injury. He was returned to duty on the 30th.

CASE 20.—Private G. W. Wren, Co. A, 50th N. C., had a quotidian chill Nov. 7, 1864, at noon. Next day at 11 A. M. the roller was applied for an hour. A slight chill occurred. The same treatment was pursued on the 9th and 10th, a chill occurring each day. On the 11th laudanum and ammonia were added. There were no further chills. Four ounces of turpentine were used. He was treated for anæmia with muriate of iron and infusion of quassia.

CASE 21.—Private J. C. Snead, Co. A, 13th N. C. Art'y, had a quotidian chill Sept. 20, 1864, at 1 P. M. The roller was applied at noon and continued for an hour. It was repeated thus for four consecutive days, but without preventing the recurrence of the chill. On the 24th laudanum and ammonia, of each thirty drops, were given while the bandage was on. A slight chill occurred. On the 25th this treatment was repeated, and there were no chills afterwards. Ten ounces of turpentine were used. Oct. 14, at 5 A. M. he had a tertian chill. On the 16th at 4 A. M. the application was made and continued for one hour; at the same time laudanum and ammonia were given. No chill occurred thereafter. One ounce of turpentine was used. He was returned to duty on the 19th.

CASE 22.—Private W. P. Wilson, Co. I, 1st N. C. Reserves, had a quotidian chill Sept. 20, 1864, at 2 P. M. Next day at 1 P. M. the application was made for one hour, and repeated daily till the 24th, without success. On the latter date the usual dose of laudanum and ammonia was given, and the chill did not occur. This treatment was repeated the next day, and there was no chill afterwards. Ten ounces of turpentine were used.

In *five* cases treated by turpentine externally, in conjunction with opium and ammonia internally, four were successful on the first day and one on the second day:

CASE 23.—Private W. H. Roberts, Co. D, 20th Ga. battery, had a tertian chill Aug. 31, 1864, at 10 A. M. At 9.30 A. M., Sept. 2, the roller was applied for an hour over the fourth and fifth ribs, and at the same time were given laudanum and solution of ammonia, of each thirty drops. The chill did not recur. The roller and the laudanum and ammonia were repeated on the 4th. No further chills occurred. There was no injury to the tissues nor other bad effect from the turpentine. The amount used was ten ounces. He was returned to duty on the 23d.

CASE 24.—Private James R. Dean, Co. B, 1st Junior Reserves, had a quotidian chill Oct. 24, 1864, at 3 P. M. Next day at 2 P. M. the roller was applied for an hour, with the laudanum and ammonia internally. The chill did not recur. The same treatment was repeated on the 26th, and there were no chills afterwards. Two ounces of turpentine were used. He was furloughed on the 29th.

CASE 25.—Private J. S. Tribble, Co. B, 8th Georgia, had a tertian chill Oct. 2, 1864, at 6 P. M. On the 4th at 5 P. M. the roller was used for one hour, in connection with the laudanum and ammonia. The chill did not recur. One ounce of turpentine was used. He was much debilitated from diarrhœa.

CASE 26.—Private J. M. Wilson, Co. H, 50th N. C., had a quotidian chill Oct. 3, 1864, at 2 P. M. Next day at 1.30 P. M. the roller was applied for half an hour, and laudanum and ammonia used. There was no chill. The treatment was repeated at the end of the week, and there was no recurrence of chill. One ounce of turpentine was used. As he was anæmic he was given Vallet's mass and quinine for a week. On the 20th he was returned to duty.

CASE 27.—Private John Broadbent, Chappell's Train Guard, had a quotidian chill Oct. 2, 1864, at 3 A. M. Next day at 2.30 A. M. the roller was applied for half an hour without, however, preventing a chill. Laudanum and ammonia were also used. On the 4th the treatment was repeated, and there was no chill. No injurious effect followed the use of the turpentine, of which two ounces were used. He was returned to duty on the 18th.

And in *six* recourse was had to quinine after a conjoint trial of the new methods:

CASE 28.—Private J. S. Inge, Chapman's Guard, had a quotidian chill Oct. 1, 1864, at noon. At 11.30 A. M. next day the roller was applied for half an hour, in connection with laudanum and ammonia internally: a chill occurred. Next day it was developed an hour earlier. On the 4th it occurred at 10 A. M.; the treatment having been commenced at 9 A. M. 5th, The chill occurred at 10 A. M.; treatment repeated. 6th, The chill, which was less severe, occurred at 10.30 A. M., the same treatment having been pursued. 7th, The laudanum and ammonia were omitted. The chill began at 11 A. M. and receded half an hour daily until the 10th. On that day fifteen grains of quinine were given but without success. Next day three grains every two hours were given until eighteen grains had been taken, and there was no chill. Smaller doses of quinine were used until the 15th; no chill. Twelve ounces of turpentine were used without injury to the tissues. He was returned to duty on the 18th.

CASE 29.—Private J. G. Stephenson, Co. D, 50th N. C., had a quotidian chill Nov. 7, 1864, at noon. Next day at 11 A. M. the roller was applied for an hour, and the chill did not recur. On the 9th the application was repeated. There was no chill, but some fever. A chill occurred on the 10th. The application was repeated at 10.30 A. M. of the 11th, and at the same time laudanum and ammonia were given, but without success. 12th, Two grains of quinine every two hours were given. A chill occurred. 13th, The treatment was repeated and no chill occurred. Four ounces of turpentine were used without injury. He remained anæmic for some time, and was given infusion of quassia one ounce three times daily; 23d, he was returned to duty.

CASE 30.—Private J. D. Woodall, Co. C, 50th N. C., had a quotidian chill Nov. 7, 1864, at 4 P. M. At 3 P. M. the next day the roller was applied for two hours, but the chill occurred at 9 P. M. On the 9th the application was made at 5 P. M.; there was slight fever afterwards. On the 10th the treatment was repeated, but the chill occurred, receding three hours. 11th, Laudanum and ammonia were added, but without effect. 12th, Quinine was given, and there was no chill. He was anæmic, and was retained in hospital. Five ounces of turpentine were used.

CASE 31.—Private S. Laws, Co. I, 1st N. C. battery, had a quotidian chill Nov. 7, 1864, at 9 P. M. Next day at 8 P. M. the roller was applied for one hour, but the chill occurred at 11 P. M. On the 9th and 10th this treatment was repeated without preventing the chill. 11th, Laudanum and ammonia were added without effect. On the 12th and 13th quinine was employed, and no chill occurred. Four ounces of turpentine were used without injury. As he was anæmic tincture of muriate of iron, twenty drops three times daily, was given.

CASE 32.—Private William Huntingdon, Co. I, 50th N. C., had a quotidian chill Nov. 7, 1864, at 10 A.M. The next day at 9.30 A.M. the roller was applied for one hour. The treatment and results were as in the case of Laws. Four ounces of turpentine were used. He was returned to duty on the 27th.

CASE 33.—Private A. Britt, Co. D, 50th N. C., had a quotidian chill Nov. 7, 1864, at 1 P.M. At noon next day the roller was applied for an hour and there was no chill. On the 9th and 10th the application was repeated, and a chill occurred each day. 11th, Laudanum and ammonia were added to the other treatment, but without avail. On the 12th and 13th quinine was used. An infusion of quassia, one ounce three times daily, was given for seven days. Three ounces of turpentine were used without injury. He was returned to duty on the 20th.

In addition to these the records of the Pettigrew hospital state that—

A number of cases were treated with the turpentine roller as an adjuvant to quinine, greatly reducing the quantity of the latter administered.

The following is from the case-book of the Chimborazo hospital, Richmond, Va.; the writer's name is not given:

Intermittent fever, the common ague of this country, has been quite prevalent this winter, and quinine, almost the only remedy employed against it internally, has not prevented relapses. The turpentine stupe has proved useful in some cases, applied an hour before the expected paroxysm, but in many others it has only retarded the access of the paroxysm. The acetates, citrates and tartrates of soda or potash, so highly commended as adjuvants to the antiperiodic treatment by Golding Bird, have not been employed, nor has sufficient care been taken to repeat the antiperiodic remedy, whether quinine, arsenic or other, at intervals of seven days. The individual cases have presented no points of particular interest except that of Pitts, who died of the congestive or pernicious form. He was a fine, tall, robust fellow, recently from the Army of Virginia. He was rational but taciturn on admission, and though without typhoid symptoms, gave the idea of a profound cerebral impression. Each evening he was seized with what was spoken of as convulsive movements, quite violent, during which he struck to the right and left and had to be held by main force: it was supposed that he sought to jump out of the window. This maniacal delirium was succeeded by intense fever. After a few nights he became very cold at the evening access and shook violently. During the intervals he remained taciturn and did not seem to recognize his friends. The treatment employed was insignificant. A few small doses of quinine, cupping to the temples, a blister to the nucha, etc. Nothing made any impression, and he died within a week.

The prevalence of malarial diseases in the Confederate Armies, together with the scarcity of quinine resulting from the blockade of the Southern ports, gave origin to a continued effort to utilize such indigenous remedies as were popularly credited with antiperiodic powers. In fact, in the first year of the war Dr. JOSEPH JONES called attention to the advisability of investigating the properties of native plants with a view to finding a substitute for quinine.* Of these the *Pinckneya pubens* or Georgia bark and the *Cornus florida* or dogwood, had an extensive trial. The former is a small tree closely allied to the cinchonas, growing on the wet and boggy margins of the streams which intersect the pine barrens from New River, S. C., to Florida. Dr. JONES reports it as having been used in conjunction with dogwood and wild cherry as a tonic and antiperiodic. In view of its reputed virtues the Surgeon General, C. S. A., directed his medical purveyor to have it collected for experiment. The only published report on its use, that rendered by Medical Director A. M. FAUNTLEROY, does not sustain its claim for notable febrifuge powers.†

---

* *Indigenous remedies of the Southern Confederacy, which may be employed in the treatment of malarial fever. Southern Med. and Surg. Jour.*, Augusta, Ga., 1861, Vol. XVII, pp. 673 and 753. In this paper Dr. JONES insists on the examination and employment of Southern remedies, not as a temporary expedient in the absence of quinine, but as a permanent advance toward the establishment of absolute independence. He reviews the various remedies which may be employed in the treatment of the most common and important of Southern diseases, citing the evidence on which the reputation of each has been established. As of value in malarial fevers, the following remedial means and measures are discussed : The inner bark of the *Pinckneya pubens* or Georgia bark ; the bark of the root, stem and branches of *Cornus florida* or dogwood ; the bark of other species of dogwood, as *C. circinata*, the round-leaved dogwood, and *C. sericea*, the swamp dogwood ; the bark of the poplar or tulip-tree, *Liriodendron tulipifera* ; the bark of certain magnolias, as the small magnolia or sweet bay, *Magnolia glauca* ; the cucumber tree, *M. acuminata* ; big laurel, *M. grandiflora*, and umbrella tree, *M. tripetala* ; the bark of the persimmon, *Diospyros Virginiana* ; the bark of the catalpa, *Bignonia catalpa* ; Virginia snake-root, *Aristolochia serpentaria* ; Indian quinine or ague weed, *Gentiana quinquefolia* ; thoroughwort, boneset or Indian sage, *Eupatorium, perfoliatum* and wild horehound, *E. rotundifolium* ; willow bark, *Salix alba* and *S. nigra* ; the root of the yellow jessamine, *Gelseminum sempervirens* ; the root of milkweed, *Asclepias syriaca* ; chloride of sodium ; hydrochlorate of ammonia ; nitric acid ; arsenious acid ; ligature of the extremities and cold affusions and douches.

A. M. FAUNTLEROY, Medical Director, Wilmington, N. C.—Report of additional cases of febris intermittens treated with the extract of Pinckneya pubens. Confederate States Med. and Surg. Jour., Vol. I, p. 134—concludes thus : "The extract has undoubted antiperiodic properties ; still it is too slow in its action to be used as a substitute for the sulphate of quinine. It has, with one exception, always produced diaphoresis. Its therapeutical action

The *Cornus florida*, a small tree common on moist gravelly soils in the Northern and Middle States and along the borders of swamps and bottom lands in the South, was also employed under official auspices.* Dr. JONES says he used the decoction and tincture to a considerable extent during the war, and found the remedy of value in the treatment of malarial fever. In severe cases the paroxysm was arrested by quinine and the treatment subsequently continued with dogwood. Its use is incidentally mentioned in some of the cases given above from the records of the Pettigrew hospital. But it does not appear that any formal reports testifying to its efficacy were rendered; for as these were requested by the medical authorities, it may be assumed that, had any such been returned, they would undoubtedly have been published. The medical journals are also silent on the subject. We may therefore conclude, with Dr. KENNEDY, that although the dogwood and other bitter infusions furnished by the Confederate States Army Medical Purveying Department possessed an antiperiodic power which, under favorable conditions, would cure ague, there were certain objections to their use, and in no case could they be valued as a substitute for quinine.†

CHAPTER IV.—ON THE CONTINUED FEVERS.

I.—THE STATISTICS OF THE CONTINUED FEVERS.

I.—IN THE UNITED STATES ARMIES.

PREVALENCE AND MORTALITY.—The uncertainties attaching to the statistics of the Camp Fevers from the abolition of the term *common continued fever*, and the institution of the new term *typho-malarial*, have already been indicated.‡ The figures representing the typhoid cases of the later years do not comprise the whole of the cases that occurred in the commands from which they were reported, for some were certainly included in the typho-malarial statistics. Indeed, in accordance with the intent of the new term, each case reported under it should have been essentially a typhoid case. But a comparison of the rates of fatality of the two series of cases manifests that in its acceptance by the profession the new term had a more extended signification than was purposed by its author. The percentage of deaths in typhoid cases among the white troops was 35.90, among the colored troops

---

is principally that of a tonic, and it deserves a position in the front rank of vegetable tonics. From the tardiness of its action, and its effect upon the vascular system, together with its manifest invigoration of the digestive organs, I am induced to think its energy as an agent is displayed through the organic nervous system."

* A circular from the Surgeon General's Office, C. S. A., dated Dec. 5, 1862, printed by JONES in his article on *Indigenous Remedies of the Southern States—St. Louis Medical Reporter*, 1868, Vol. III, p. 261 *et seq.*—gives a formula "for a compound tincture of the indigenous barks, to be issued as a tonic and a febrifuge, and substituted, as far as practicable, for quinine. * * * Dried dogwood bark, 30 parts; dried poplar bark, 30 parts; dried willow bark, 40 parts; whiskey 45 degrees strength. Two pounds of the mixed bark to one gallon whiskey. Macerate fourteen days and strain. Dose, one fluid ounce three times a day."

† Dr. STILES KENNEDY gives his opinion of these indigenous remedies incidentally in introducing the subject of turpentine externally applied. See note *supra:* "While in Savannah, November, 1862, I assumed control of the medical department of the 47th Georgia regiment in order that its surgeon might visit his sick wife in Griffin. Several companies of this regiment had been exposed during the summer months to the effluvia of the rice fields on the Savannah river, and at first 'sick-call' I found over one hundred cases of 'chills.' No quinine was being issued at this time by the Confederate purveyor, but instead of this potent remedy, infusion of *Pinckneya pubens*. Spanish willow and dogwood were sent in large quantities with full directions for their use, and the hope was expressed that I would be able to return a favorable report of their effects. And I will state here, that when the patient is in comfortable quarters in town, away from exposure and malarial influences, with sufficient tone and calibre of stomach to bear repeated drenchings of these nasty infusions, there is no difficulty in curing intermittent fever. But my troops were in the field and on picket-duty every day. * * * The infusions failed during a severe trial."

‡ *Supra*, p. 75 *et seq.*

55.69, while in typho-malarial cases the corresponding rates were 8.14 and 17.27. During the fourteen months, July, 1862, to August, 1863, inclusive, following the introduction of the term, and while yet in ignorance of the value intended to be officially attached to it, medical officers of white troops reported 27,399 cases, or more than one-half of the total number of cases, 49,871, embraced in the statistics; of these only 1,585 died, or 5.08 per cent. Had enteric fever been assuredly present in all these cases a further deterioration of the blood by a coincident malarial fever must be regarded as a desirable complication in typhoid epidemics. But, after the public announcement of the intent of the term, the suddenly increased gravity of the cases reported under it must be understood as meaning that a certain proportion of the medical officers of the army became aware of the value intended to be attached to *typho-malarial*, and restricted its use accordingly to cases which appeared to them to present a specific typhoid element. The 22,472 cases reported subsequently to August, 1863, included 2,474 fatal cases, the percentage of fatality being 11.01. The probable proportion of true typhoid cases embraced by the typho-malarial statistics will be suggested hereafter when the clinical and pathological features of the cases thus reported have been submitted and fully considered.* But although the whole of the typho-malarial cases were not typhoid fevers modified by coexisting malarial influences, they were probably all of a more or less continued type; and while their statistics have been presented in connection with the paroxysmal fevers in view of their malarial element, it seems proper to again submit them in the present connection in view of their continued, if not in all cases truly typhoid, character.

The following table summarises the reported statistical facts:

TABLE XXXIX.

Statement of the Frequency and Fatality of the Continued Fevers, giving the totals reported from May 1, 1861, to June 30, 1866, among the White Troops, and from July 1, 1863, to June 30, 1866, among the Colored Troops; with the ratio of cases to strength and to cases of all diseases, and the ratio of deaths to strength, to deaths from all diseases, and to cases of the continued fevers.

SPECIFIED FEVERS.	Number reported during the period stated.		Ratio per 1,000 of strength.		Cases per 1,000 of cases of all diseases.	Deaths per 1,000 deaths from all diseases.	Deaths per 100 cases.
	Cases.	Deaths.	Cases.	Deaths.			
Among White Troops from May 1, 1861, to June 30, 1866:							
Typhoid Fever	75,368	27,056	175	57.78	13.90	209.11	35.90
Common Continued Fever	11,898	147	28	.31	2.19	1.14	1.24
Typhus Fever	2,501	850	6	1.82	.46	6.57	33.99
Typho-Malarial Fever	49,871	4,059	115	8.67	9.19	31.37	8.14
Total	139,638	32,112	324	68.58	25.74	248.19	23.00
Among Colored Troops from July 1, 1863, to June 30, 1866:							
Typhoid Fever	4,094	2,280	67	35.67	6.77	82.91	55.69
Typhus Fever	123	108	2	1.69	.20	3.93	87.80
Typho-Malarial Fever	7,529	1,301	123	20.35	12.44	47.31	17.27
Total	11,746	3,689	192	57.71	19.41	134.15	31.41

* See *infra*, p. 375.

Among the white troops there were reported 139,638 cases of the fevers specified, and of these 32,112 were fatal, making 324.0 cases and 68.58 deaths per thousand of strength present during the five and one-sixth years covered by the statistics. Although the cases formed only about one-fortieth of the total cases of disease, 25.74 per thousand, their fatality was such that the deaths constituted one-fourth of the deaths from all diseases, or 248.19 per thousand. This was due to the relatively large proportion and grave character of the typhoid cases. The percentage of fatal cases among those reported as typhus was large, 33.99, but the number of cases being comparatively small, this fever was charged with only 6.57 of the 248.19 deaths from continued fevers presented by every thousand deaths from all diseases. The cases of typho-malarial fever, on the other hand, assumed an importance from their number, although they furnished only 31.37 deaths as compared with 209.11 caused by typhoid in every thousand deaths from disease.

Among the colored troops nearly two-thirds of the total number, 11,746, of cases of continued fever were reported as typho-malarial fever. The ratio of typho-malarial to typhoid cases among the white troops cannot be obtained from the upper division of the table, as the periods during which the cases occurred were of unequal duration. But a

TABLE XL.

Expressing the Frequency and Mortality of the reported forms of the Continued Fevers as percentages of the total cases and deaths caused by such fevers.

WHITE TROOPS.

SPECIFIED FEVERS.	Total number of cases.	Total number of deaths.	Cases of specified fevers in total of febrile cases.	Deaths from specified fevers in total deaths from all the forms.
May 1, 1861, to June 30, 1862—				
Typhoid Fever	22,062	5,665	63.4	94.2
Typhus Fever	841	204	2.4	3.4
Common Continued Fever	11,898	147	34.2	2.4
Total of specified forms	34,801	6,016	100.0	100.0
July 1, 1862, to June 30, 1866—				
Typhoid Fever	53,306	21,391	50.8	82.0
Typhus Fever	1,660	646	1.6	2.5
Typho-malarial Fever	49,871	4,059	47.6	15.5
Total of specified forms	104,837	26,096	100.0	100.0
COLORED TROOPS.				
July 1, 1863, to June 30, 1866—				
Typhoid Fever	4,094	2,280	34.9	61.8
Typhus Fever	123	108	1.0	2.9
Typho-malarial Fever	7,529	1,301	64.1	35.2
Total of specified forms	11,746	3,689	100.0	100.0

reference to Table XL, on the opposite page, will show that during the three years in which both typho-malarial and typhoid cases were reported the former constituted less than one-half of the total. It will be seen hereafter that this greater prevalence of typho-malarial fever among the colored troops was associated with a diminished prevalence of typhoid, the average annual number of cases of continued fever among them having been nearly the same as among the white commands. Hence the deaths from typho-malarial fever constituted a larger proportion of the deaths from continued fever, and of the deaths from all causes, among the negroes than among the whites, and the deaths from typhoid fever a smaller proportion, although the percentage of cases that terminated fatally was considerably greater among the former than among the latter. It will be observed also that among the colored troops the deaths from the continued fevers constituted a smaller proportion of the deaths from disease, 134.15 per thousand, than among the whites, 248.19 per thousand, notwithstanding the similar rates of prevalence among both and the larger rate of mortality among the negroes. This may be seen, by Table II,* to have been caused by the relatively greater mortality from diseases of the respiratory organs.

During the period when common continued fever held a place in the official nosological system typhoid cases formed 63.4 per cent. of the continued fevers among the white troops, typhus 2.4 and common continued fever 34.2 per cent.,† while typhoid was charged with 94.2 per cent. of the deaths; subsequent to that period typhoid contributed a little more and typho-malarial a little less than one-half of the cases, typhus forming only 1.6 per cent., while the deaths attributed to typhoid were reduced to 82.0 per cent. of those from the continued fevers by the substitution of the larger percentage from typho-malarial fever for the smaller percentage formerly referred to common continued fever.

Among the colored troops 64.1 per cent. of the febrile cases were reported typho-

TABLE XLI.

Relative Frequency of Cases of the Continued Fevers, and of Deaths occasioned by them, during the several years of the war and the year following the war, expressed in annual rates per thousand of strength present.

WHITE TROOPS.

DISEASES.	1860–1.		1861–2.		1862–3.		1863–4.		1864–5.		1865–6.	
	Cases.	Deaths.	Cases.	Deaths.	Cases.	Deaths.	Cases.	Deaths.	Cases.	Deaths.	Cases.	Deaths.
Typhoid Fever	14.00	2.46	78.62	19.55	52.36	15.89	16.32	6.63	16.96	8.99	12.97	6.23
Typhus Fever	2.89	.43	2.94	.69	1.55	.57	.56	.18	.57	.19	.32	.21
Common Continued Fever	18.63	--------	42.13	.51	--------	--------	--------	--------	--------	--------	--------	--------
Typho-malarial Fever	--------	--------	--------	--------	38.00	1.78	18.93	1.71	22.91	2.27	16.62	2.54
Total Continued Fevers	35.52	2.89	123.69	20.75	91.91	18.24	35.81	8.52	40.44	11.45	29.91	8.98

COLORED TROOPS.

DISEASES.	1860–1.		1861–2.		1862–3.		1863–4.		1864–5.		1865–6.	
Typhoid Fever	--------	--------	--------	--------	--------	--------	41.67	16.35	20.24	13.34	9.74	5.99
Typhus Fever	--------	--------	--------	--------	--------	--------	1.56	1.30	.55	.46	.13	.12
Typho-malarial Fever	--------	--------	--------	--------	--------	--------	56.16	10.85	37.47	5.51	34.21	5.49
Total Continued Fevers	--------	--------	--------	--------	--------	--------	99.39	28.50	58.26	19.31	44.08	11.60

* Page 11, *supra*.　　　　† The relative frequency of the reported forms is given with more of detail in Table XLVII.

malarial, 34.9 typhoid and 1.0 typhus, while the deaths under these headings were respectively 35.2, 61.8 and 2.9 per cent. of the whole number attributed to these fevers.

Table XLI, presented on the last page, shows the annual variations in prevalence and mortality. The columns for 1860–61 may be overlooked, as their figures are based only on the reports for the last two months of the fiscal year.

As the war progressed these fevers became less frequent among the white troops. The first year gave 123.69 cases per thousand of strength; the last year of the record gave only 29.91. But this decline suffered, in 1864–65, a slight interruption, specially marked among the typho-malarial cases, and probably due to the substitution of fresh troops for men who withdrew to their homes on the expiration of their term of service. The death-rate was similarly interrupted in its fall from 20.75 to 8.98 per thousand of strength.

No interference occurred in the gradual subsidence of these fevers among the colored troops from a rate of 99.39 per thousand strength in the first year to 44.08 in the last, nor in the fall of the mortality-rate from 28.50 to 11.60.

But although the annual mortality expressed as a ratio of the strength present diminished with the reduction in the number of the cases, the decrease of the one was not exactly proportioned to the other. Nor was this disproportion due to the association of lessened virulence with diminished prevalence. On the contrary, the gravity of the cases increased to the close of the war. During the first complete fiscal year 17.4 per cent. of the febrile cases among the white troops terminated fatally; during the last year 31.8 per cent.; during the year following the war 30.9 per cent. Table XLII illustrates the increasing gravity of the individual cases during annual periods which, according to Table XLI, were characterized by a diminution of the prevalence of these fevers and of the mortality caused by them in the army as a whole.

TABLE XLII.

Showing the Annual Percentages of Fatality of the Continued Fevers.

WHITE TROOPS.

Year ending June 30—	1861.	1862.	1863.	1864.	1865.	1866.	Rates for the whole period.
Typhoid Fever	17.5	25.7	32.6	44.2	59.5	49.4	35.90
Typhus Fever	15.0	24.5	39.7	35.2	37.8	67.8	33.99
Common Continued Fever	0.0	1.2	----	----	----	----	1.24
Typho-malarial Fever	----	----	5.0	9.9	11.2	15.7	8.14
Total	8.1	17.4	21.3	25.9	31.8	30.9	23.00

COLORED TROOPS.

Year ending June 30—	1861.	1862.	1863.	1864.	1865.	1866.	Rates for the whole period.
Typhoid Fever	----	----	----	40.3	70.3	63.2	55.69
Typhus Fever	----	----	----	85.7	89.1	100.0	87.80
Typho-malarial Fever	----	----	----	19.9	15.7	16.5	17.27
Total	----	----	----	29.5	35.3	27.1	31.41

The rates here presented cannot be accepted as accurate. The want of relation between the cases and deaths borne on the reports has already been explained. The cases that occurred in the large population of the general hospitals were not taken up on the reports, but all the deaths were noted. The mortality among this unknown number of cases adds considerably to the calculated rates of fatality. The limits of the error may be fairly defined for certain diseases, but in the instance of typhoid fever, other cases than those that originated in the hospitals were unrecorded. Vast numbers of ailing men were sent to the general hospitals from the field, especially when the army was on the eve of a move. Few of these were entered as typhoid fever on the field reports, although had they continued longer under observation this diagnosis would have been authorized; and in many instances, unfortunately, opportunity was afforded after death for its verification. The number of these unreported cases must have been very large, for the experience of medical officers in charge of general hospitals near the base of operations of troops on field service testifies to the frequency with which typhoid fever reached their wards without appearing on the antecedent records. In view of these unregistered cases, which contributed largely to the recorded deaths, it is impossible to ascertain the actual percentage of fatality of the continued fevers.

The ratios of typhoid fever are modified also by the withdrawal of so many of the cases into the typho-malarial group, while those of the typho-malarial fevers are valueless from the uncertainty as to the nature of the fevers thus reported and the certainty that, as may be inferred from the ratios themselves, not all of the cases possessed a typhoid element. The comparatively small percentages of fatality sometimes recorded for typhus are explained by the entry of the cases in accordance with the diagnosis under the typhus heading, and of the resulting deaths, in view of *post-mortem* revelations, under the heading typhoid—the typhoid rate thereby becoming augmented at the expense of the other.

But although of little value as indices of the fatality of the continued fevers, the ratios presented above are admissible evidence of the increased gravity of the cases as the war progressed; for the statistics from which they were calculated were gathered under similar conditions.

The average annual rates per thousand of strength show, in Table XLIII, a similarity

TABLE XLIII.

Comparison of the Frequency of Cases of the Continued Fevers, and of the Deaths occasioned by them, among the White and the Colored Troops, as shown by the average numbers annually recorded, reduced to ratios per thousand of strength; the figures for the White Troops based on the statistics of the period May 1, 1861, to June 30, 1866, and those for the Colored Troops on the statistics of the three years July 1, 1863, to June 30, 1866.

DISEASE.	WHITE TROOPS.		COLORED TROOPS.	
	Cases.	Deaths.	Cases.	Deaths.
Typhoid Fever.	33.83	11.18	22.32	11.89
Typhus Fever.	1.12	.35	.67	.56
Common Continued Fever.	37.07	.44		
Typho-malarial Fever.	26.15	1.95	41.06	6.79
Total Continued Fevers.	62.67	13.27	64.05	19.24

in the rates of prevalence among the white and the colored troops, 62.67 and 64.05 per thousand respectively; but the mortality was greater among the colored than among the white men, 19.24 as compared with 13.27. This increased mortality was caused by the typho-malarial cases, they having occasioned 6.79 deaths per thousand of strength as against 1.95 among the whites. The mortality from typhoid was similar in both, but the cases having been less numerous among the colored men their larger percentage of fatality, already noted, is explained. The slight prevalence of cases reported as typhus, 1.12 among the white and .67 among the colored soldiers, accounts for an annual mortality which was less among the white troops than that from common continued fever, notwithstanding the high rate of fatality that attended the typhus cases.

PREVALENCE AS RELATED TO SEASON AND LOCALITY.—To reduce the size of Table XLIV, and at the same time to simplify figures, the data on the seasonal and regionic prevalence of the fevers reported typhus have been consolidated with the statistics of the typhoid cases. This might have been done with propriety in all the tables of this section; for, as will be shown hereafter,* the greater number of the cases reported as typhus were in reality cases of typhoid fever; but it was deemed advisable to present in certain of these tables the rates of the reported cases of typhus by way of intimating to some extent the modification of the typhoid cases by crowd-poisoning, as the typho-malarial cases similarly, but perhaps less certainly, indicate their modification by the malarial influence.

TABLE XLIV.

Showing the Variations in the Prevalence of the Continued Fevers among White Troops in the various Regions during the years of the War and the year following the War, expressed in monthly ratios per thousand of mean strength.

YEAR ENDING JUNE 30, 1862.

DISEASE.	REGIONS.	1861. JULY.	AUGUST.	SEPTEMBER.	OCTOBER.	NOVEMBER.	DECEMBER.	1862. JANUARY.	FEBRUARY.	MARCH.	APRIL.	MAY.	JUNE.	FOR THE YEAR.
Typhoid and cases reported as Typhus	Atlantic	2.3	4.6	5.8	7.1	9.1	8.3	5.8	4.6	3.2	6.0	5.9	7.8	74.0
	Central	1.8	2.8	9.4	12.1	13.2	9.8	10.4	7.1	6.0	6.9	8.7	6.3	99.8
	Pacific	.2	------	------	2.5	1.4	1.0	.3	.5	.8	------	------	.4	8.1
In all the regions		2.0	4.0	6.5	8.6	10.2	8.5	7.0	5.1	3.9	6.3	7.2	7.0	81.6
Common Continued Fever	Atlantic	3.4	4.5	4.2	4.7	5.3	2.3	2.4	2.6	2.4	3.5	3.5	4.3	41.4
	Central	1.0	2.7	4.0	6.1	4.3	3.7	2.2	1.7	1.7	3.6	4.8	4.9	45.2
	Pacific	.4	.9	3.8	1.2	1.0	.8	.6	1.1	1.3	.7	4.1	3.3	16.5
In all the regions		2.1	3.9	4.2	5.0	4.8	2.8	2.3	2.4	2.2	3.5	4.1	4.6	42.1
All the Continued Fevers	Atlantic	5.7	9.1	10.0	11.8	14.4	10.6	8.2	7.2	5.6	9.5	9.4	12.1	115.4
	Central	2.8	5.5	13.4	18.2	17.5	13.5	12.6	8.8	7.7	10.5	13.5	11.2	145.0
	Pacific	.6	.9	3.8	3.7	2.4	1.8	.9	1.6	2.1	.7	4.1	3.7	24.6
In all the regions		4.1	7.9	10.7	13.6	15.0	11.3	9.3	7.5	6.1	9.8	11.3	11.6	123.7

* *Infra*, p. 324.

YEAR ENDING JUNE 30, 1863.

DISEASE.	REGIONS.	1862.						1863.						FOR THE YEAR.
		JULY.	AUGUST.	SEPTEMBER.	OCTOBER.	NOVEMBER.	DECEMBER.	JANUARY.	FEBRUARY.	MARCH.	APRIL.	MAY.	JUNE.	
Typhoid and cases reported as Typhus	Atlantic	8.5	6.3	2.8	7.4	7.4	6.3	5.5	4.8	4.8	3.0	2.6	2.4	61.7
	Central	4.7	4.6	3.5	4.4	4.6	4.6	4.8	4.9	4.8	3.5	2.4	1.8	48.1
	Pacific	.2	2.3	3.1	2.7	2.1	.7	.6	.4	.3	------	------	.3	13.0
In all the regions		6.7	5.3	3.1	5.8	5.8	5.4	5.1	4.8	4.7	3.2	2.5	2.0	53.9
Typho-malarial Fever	Atlantic	6.1	4.1	3.3	3.4	3.8	3.8	4.2	2.9	2.7	2.5	2.7	3.5	42.3
	Central	4.8	4.5	3.2	3.2	2.3	1.9	2.8	3.9	3.3	2.6	2.1	2.0	34.8
	Pacific	2.0	2.3	1.6	2.2	.9	3.4	.2	.8	.7	1.3	.7	2.2	18.0
In all the regions		5.4	4.3	3.2	3.3	3.0	2.9	3.4	3.4	3.0	2.6	2.3	2.6	38.0
All the Continued Fevers	Atlantic	14.6	10.4	6.1	10.8	11.2	10.1	9.7	7.7	7.5	5.5	5.3	5.9	104.0
	Central	9.5	9.1	6.7	7.6	6.9	6.5	7.6	8.8	8.1	6.1	4.5	3.8	82.9
	Pacific	2.2	4.6	4.7	4.9	3.0	4.1	.8	1.2	1.0	1.3	.7	2.5	31.0
In all the regions		12.1	9.6	6.3	9.1	8.8	8.3	8.5	8.2	7.7	5.8	4.8	4.6	91.9

YEAR ENDING JUNE 30, 1864.

DISEASE.	REGIONS.	1863.						1864.						FOR THE YEAR.
		JULY.	AUGUST.	SEPTEMBER.	OCTOBER.	NOVEMBER.	DECEMBER.	JANUARY.	FEBRUARY.	MARCH.	APRIL.	MAY.	JUNE.	
Typhoid and cases reported as Typhus	Atlantic	2.9	3.0	2.8	2.0	1.5	1.2	1.3	.9	1.0	1.0	.9	1.4	19.6
	Central	2.0	2.2	1.9	1.3	1.1	.9	1.2	.7	1.0	1.0	1.0	1.5	15.7
	Pacific	.3	.3	.1	1.0	1.3	.3	.4	.2	.2	------	.5	.3	4.8
In all the regions		2.3	2.5	2.2	1.5	1.3	1.0	1.3	.7	1.0	1.0	1.0	1.5	16.9
Typho-malarial Fever	Atlantic	4.4	4.2	3.0	2.8	1.8	1.2	1.3	.7	.7	.9	1.2	3.1	24.6
	Central	2.9	3.2	1.9	1.4	1.2	.8	.6	.5	.7	.7	1.0	1.5	16.1
	Pacific	.8	.2	.3	.1	.4	.2	.2	.4	.1	.1	.2	.1	3.0
In all the regions		3.4	3.5	2.3	1.9	1.4	1.0	.8	.6	.7	.7	1.0	2.0	18.9
All the Continued Fevers	Atlantic	7.3	7.2	5.8	4.8	3.3	2.4	2.6	1.6	1.7	1.9	2.1	4.5	44.2
	Central	4.9	5.4	3.8	2.7	2.3	1.7	1.8	1.2	1.7	1.7	2.0	3.0	31.8
	Pacific	1.1	.5	.4	1.1	1.7	.5	.6	.6	.3	.1	.7	.4	7.8
In all the regions		5.7	6.0	4.5	3.4	2.7	2.0	2.1	1.3	1.7	1.7	2.0	3.5	35.8

YEAR ENDING JUNE 30, 1865.

DISEASE.	REGIONS.	1864.						1865.						FOR THE YEAR.
		JULY.	AUGUST.	SEPTEMBER.	OCTOBER.	NOVEMBER.	DECEMBER.	JANUARY.	FEBRUARY.	MARCH.	APRIL.	MAY.	JUNE.	
Typhoid and cases reported as Typhus	Atlantic	2.9	2.9	1.7	1.9	1.9	1.5	1.6	1.6	1.2	1.0	1.3	1.6	20.4
	Central	2.1	2.0	2.4	1.4	1.2	1.0	1.3	.8	1.0	.7	.7	.8	15.8
	Pacific	.3	.1	.8	.7	.3	.4	.6	.3	.2	.4	.5	.3	4.8
In all the regions		2.4	2.2	2.1	1.6	1.5	1.2	1.4	1.2	1.1	.9	1.0	1.2	17.5
Typho-malarial Fevers	Atlantic	7.6	6.6	4.8	4.0	2.9	1.6	1.4	1.3	1.5	1.4	1.7	1.6	34.4
	Central	2.1	2.3	1.7	1.2	.7	1.1	.8	.4	1.0	1.2	.8	1.4	14.9
	Pacific	------	.1	.í	1.1	.5	.2	.4	------	------	.1	------	------	2.6
In all the regions		4.2	3.8	2.9	2.4	1.6	1.3	1.1	.8	1.2	1.2	1.2	1.4	22.9
All the Continued Fevers	Atlantic	10.5	9.5	6.5	5.9	4.8	3.1	3.0	2.9	2.7	2.4	3.0	3.2	54.8
	Central	4.2	4.3	4.1	2.6	1.9	2.1	2.1	1.2	2.0	1.9	1.5	2.2	30.7
	Pacific	.3	.2	1.2	1.8	.8	.6	1.0	.3	.2	.5	.5	.3	7.4
In all the regions		6.6	6.0	5.0	4.0	3.1	2.5	2.5	2.0	2.3	2.1	2.2	2.6	40.4

YEAR ENDING JUNE 30, 1866.

DISEASE.	REGIONS.	1865.						1866.						FOR THE YEAR.
		JULY.	AUGUST.	SEPTEMBER.	OCTOBER.	NOVEMBER.	DECEMBER.	JANUARY.	FEBRUARY.	MARCH.	APRIL.	MAY.	JUNE.	
Typhoid and cases reported as Typhus	Atlantic	1.7	1.9	1.7	2.6	1.5	.8	.5	.6	.7	.4	.4	.4	17.9
	Central	1.2	1.2	1.2	1.2	.6	.3	.3	.4	.4	.3	.5	.3	11.2
	Pacific	.4	.7	.5	.8	.3	.2	.3	1.0	.7	1.3	1.0	.5	7.5
In all the regions		1.4	1.4	1.3	1.7	1.0	.5	.4	.6	.6	.6	.6	.4	13.3
Typho-malarial Fever	Atlantic	1.4	1.7	1.6	1.7	.5	.2	------	.3	------	------	.1	.2	13.0
	Central	4.5	1.7	1.0	1.1	.9	.3	.1	------	------	------	.1	1.2	22.5
	Pacific	.6	.1	------	------	.2	.1	------	------	------	.1	.1	.5	1.5
In all the regions		3.1	1.6	1.1	1.2	.6	.2	.1	.1	------	------	.1	.7	16.6
All the Continued Fevers	Atlantic	3.1	3.6	3.3	4.3	2.0	1.0	.5	.9	.7	.4	.5	.6	30.9
	Central	5.7	2.9	2.2	2.3	1.5	.6	.4	.4	.4	.3	.6	1.5	33.7
	Pacific	1.0	.8	.5	.8	.5	.3	.3	1.0	.7	1.4	1.1	1.0	9.0
In all the regions		4.5	3.0	2.4	2.9	1.6	.7	.5	.7	.6	.6	.7	1.1	29.9

The striking irregularities in the monthly rates of prevalence of the continued fevers as a class may be more readily observed by means of the plate facing page 199 than by the tabulated figures. There are six notable prominences on their line of prevalence: one, the highest, culminating in November, 1861; the second, less acute, spreading over the months of May, June and July, 1862; the third, still more obtuse, covering the last

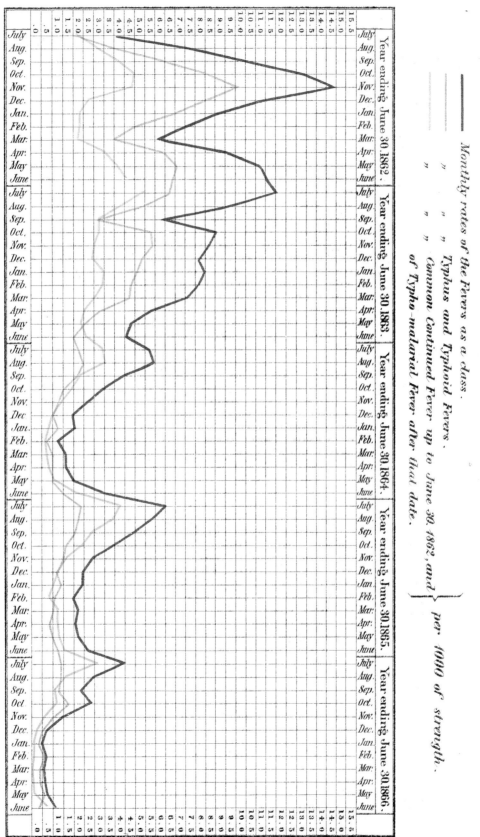

Lines indicating the Prevalence of the Continued Fevers among the White Troops.

——————— Monthly rates of the Fevers as a class.

" " " Typhus and Typhoid Fevers.

" " " Common Continued Fever up to June 30. 1862, and
" " " of Typho-malarial Fever after that date.

} per 1000 of strength.

three months of 1862 and January and February of 1863; the other three prominences are acute and culminate in August, 1863, and in July of 1864 and 1865.

Evidently something more than mere seasonal change was involved in the production of the first of these waves of prevalence, for while in September, 1861, the line tends to the summit of the first elevation, in September, 1862, it forms the angle of the deep sulcus between the second and third, and whilst it falls in the winter months of 1861, the corresponding months of 1862 sustain it on the crest of the third epidemic wave. On the other hand, the prominences occurring in July and August of 1863, 1864 and 1865 suggest by their regularity a seasonal influence, which is seen by the green line to have been due to the prevalence of typho-malarial fever.

The elevations of the line indicating typhoid fever show that the poison of this disease was the principal cause of the irregular waves of febrile prevalence during the early period of the war. The sudden aggregation of young men in camps where they were exposed to influences favorable to the spread of this disease accounts for its rapid increase from May to November, 1861. During this period the troops which furnished the statistics were increased from sixteen thousand to three hundred thousand men, under President LINCOLN's call of April 15 for 75,000 men for three months and the closely following act of Congress, approved July 22, calling for 500,000 men for three years. This suggests the explanation of the irregularities in the second and third prominences of the line of prevalence of the continued fevers. In November, 1861, the epidemic among those who responded to these calls was at its height, 15.03 monthly per thousand of strength, after which it subsided rapidly to 6.14 in March, 1862. But meanwhile the army became augmented in response to a requisition for 300,000 three-years' men; and this second aggregation was followed by a second epidemic which, as the volunteers responded less promptly than on the first call, had a less prominent but more prolonged acme, yielding in May 11.30, in June 11.55 and in July 12.11 cases in every thousand men, after which the disease again subsided to 6.33 in September. About this time the call for 300,000 nine-months' men occasioned the third epidemic wave by the fresh material thus brought into the camps; but as the men arrived more slowly than on the former requisitions the monthly rate during the acme in October, 9.07, was not so high as during the previous visitations. Nevertheless the susceptible men of the new levies did not escape, but were seized with fever as they arrived, giving monthly rates of 8.80, 8.29, 8.52 and 8.22 for the four months next following. In March the epidemic began to subside, and as no large bodies of new troops were added to the army after this date until the expiration of the term of service of the three-years' men, the only prominences in the line of prevalence are those already noted as occurring towards the end of summer, and evidently occasioned in great part by the malarial element of the fevers reported as typho-malarial. It is probable, however, that into the first of these, that culminating in August, 1863, there entered febrile cases from the regiments that responded to the call issued June 15, for men for temporary service in protecting Maryland and Pennsylvania from invasion; and it is equally probable that the high rates of July and August, 1864, were in part the effect of the replacement of discharged veterans by fresh levies.

It appears, therefore, that outside of the influence exercised on the rates of prevalence of the continued fevers by the absorption of certain malarial cases the statistics afford no information concerning variations due to seasonal changes. If any such were present they were of so slight a character as to be swamped in those arising from the one great cause of variation—the number of men present susceptible to the action of the febrile poison.*

From this view of the line of prevalence of the continued fevers, and from what has been said of the increasing gravity of the cases as the war progressed, it will be readily understood that the line of mortality, while presenting prominences similar to those on the line of prevalence, would not, if drawn, be separated from that line throughout its course by the same multiple of its own height, but by a lesser multiple at points near the end than at points near the beginning. The monthly variations in the mortality rates from typhoid fever have already been illustrated on the tinted diagram facing page 20.

The lines of prevalence and mortality among the colored troops are traced on the plate facing this page. Typhoid cases formed a larger proportion of the strength present at the beginning of the term of service than at subsequent dates; but the line of prevalence is irregularly elevated as fresh regiments were mustered into service. The line expressing the prevalence of the continued fevers as a class presents three very notable seasonal prominences, due principally to the presence of fevers reported as typho-malarial.

In treating of the paroxysmal fevers the seasonal variation was emphasized by consolidating the rates for the corresponding months of the several years into a line expressing the average rate for each of the months or the average annual curve; but in the case of the fevers now under consideration the prominences due to the aggregation of susceptible material are the main factors in determining the contour and level of the line obtained by such a consolidation. The average line for the white troops, as shown on the diagram on the opposite page, exhibits a notable elevation in July, 7.14 per thousand strength, due to the malarial element of the fevers, and a smaller elevation stretching over the months of October and November, due, so far as shown by the data, to the incomplete levelling of the epidemic prominences.

The average annual curve of prevalence among the colored troops presents a marked elevation in July, August and September, 9.31, 9.45 and 8.64, respectively, per thousand men present. This is evidently due mainly, but not wholly, to malarial influences; for while typho-malarial fever certainly contributed to the elevation, typhoid fever was also more prevalent then than at other seasons. In view of the greater prevalence of typhoid in the first July of their service, as delineated in the plate facing this page, the composition of the prominence under consideration may be appreciated.

* There are many observations in the literature of typhoid showing its increased prevalence in the late autumn and winter months, its diminished prevalence in the spring and its presence at all seasons: but in this country there have been few statistics gathered on the large scale. The National Board of Health collected and published weekly mortality returns during the period from January, 1880, to May, 1882. Cities and towns aggregating a population of about eight millions were represented in these returns. The absolute figures as reported in the instance of typhoid fever have been converted into monthly rates expressed as annual rates per thousand of population, and from them the accompanying diagram has been drawn.

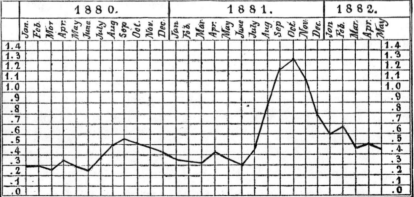

DIAGRAM *showing by annual rates per thousand the seasonal variations in the mortality, and hence in the prevalence of typhoid fever, among a United States population of about eight millions.*

Lines indicating the Prevalence and Mortality of the Continued Fevers among the Colored Troops.

———————— Monthly rates of the Fevers as a class.
————————   „   „   „ Typho-malarial Fever.
————————   „   „   „ Typhoid Fever.   } per 1000 of average strength.
————————   „   Death Rates from all the Fevers.

In Dec. 1864 the death line runs into that of typhoid prevalence, the two in the remainder of their course being almost coincident.

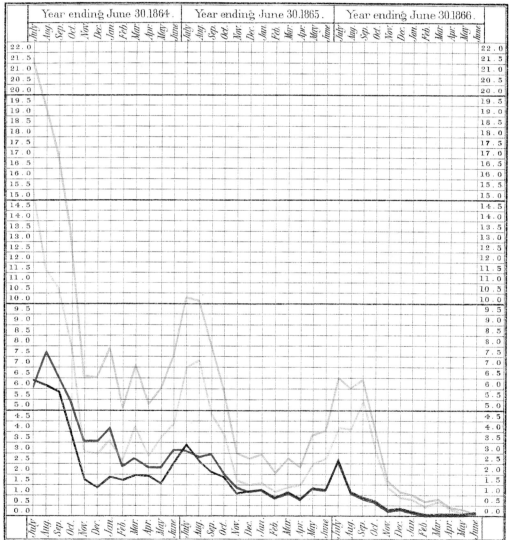

DIAGRAM *showing the average annual curves of prevalence and mortality of continued fevers.*

The upper unbroken line shows the rate of prevalence of the fevers as a class, the lower the death-rates caused by them. The dotted line represents the prevalence of typho-malarial fever, and the space between it and the line above it the prevalence of typhoid fever.

WHITE TROOPS.

COLORED TROOPS.

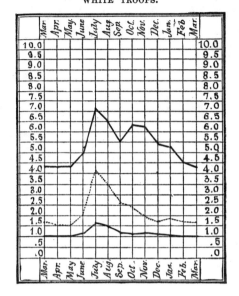
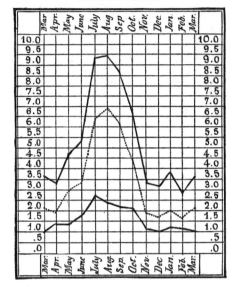

The data from which these curves have been constructed are submitted in the two tables which follow:

TABLE XLV.

Seasonal Variations in the Prevalence and Mortality of the Continued Fevers among the White Troops, expressed in average monthly rates per thousand of strength, obtained by the consolidation of the figures for the corresponding months of each of the years covered by the statistics.

DISEASES.	JULY.	AUGUST.	SEPTEMBER.	OCTOBER.	NOVEMBER.	DECEMBER.	JANUARY.	FEBRUARY.	MARCH.	APRIL.	MAY.	JUNE.
Cases of—												
Typhoid Fever (a)	2.98	2.80	2.61	3.50	3.78	3.43	3.22	2.64	2.46	2.35	2.33	2.40
Typhus Fever (a)	.15	.12	.08	.09	.09	.07	.08	.08	.10	.09	.08	.10
Common Continued Fever (b)	2.16	3.92	4.14	5.02	4.82	2.76	2.33	2.33	2.20	3.49	4.14	4.56
Typho-malarial Fever (c)	4.07	3.52	2.64	2.45	1.98	1.71	1.85	1.66	1.65	1.50	1.51	2.04
All the Continued Fevers (d)	7.14	6.47	5.47	6.35	6.24	5.37	5.23	4.48	4.28	4.25	4.35	4.99
Deaths from—												
Typhoid Fever (a)	1.34	1.20	.89	.91	1.00	.96	.89	.85	.84	.84	.86	.93
Typhus Fever (a)	.04	.03	.02	.02	.03	.03	.02	.04	.05	.03	.03	.03
Common Continued Fever (b)		.02	.04	.03	.03	.02	.03	.02	.01	.09	.06	.10
Typho-malarial Fever (c)	.27	.30	.27	.18	.14	.10	.13	.12	.13	.10	.10	.16
All the Continued Fevers (d)	1.64	1.51	1.16	1.09	1.16	1.08	1.03	.99	1.00	.97	.98	1.10

(a) The rates for typhoid and typhus are the average rates of the five years July 1, 1861, to June 30, 1866.
(b) The common continued fever rates are those for the year ending June 30, 1862.
(c) The typho-malarial rates are the averages of the four years July 1, 1862, to June 30, 1866.
(d) The rates for these fevers as a class are the averages of the facts recorded during the five years aforesaid; they are of necessity not the sum of the rates of the specified fevers, as neither common continued fever nor typho-malarial fever was reported during the whole of the five years.

TABLE XLVI.

Seasonal Variations in the Prevalence and Mortality of the Continued Fevers among the Colored Troops, expressed as average monthly rates per thousand of strength, obtained by the consolidation of the figures for the corresponding months of each of the three years, July 1, 1863, to June 30, 1866.

DISEASES.	JULY.	AUGUST.	SEPTEMBER.	OCTOBER.	NOVEMBER.	DECEMBER.	JANUARY.	FEBRUARY.	MARCH.	APRIL.	MAY.	JUNE.
Cases of—												
Typhoid Fever	2.94	2.55	2.40	2.14	1.46	1.47	1.82	1.18	1.45	1.34	1.61	1.97
Typhus Fever	.03	.03	.14	.07	.02	.04	.04	.05	.06	.02	.09	.08
Typho-malarial Fever	6.34	6.87	6.10	4.44	1.89	1.67	1.97	1.56	2.13	1.95	2.95	3.29
All the Continued Fevers	9.31	9.45	8.64	6.65	3.37	3.18	3.83	2.79	3.64	3.31	4.65	5.36
Deaths from—												
Typhoid Fever	1.58	1.23	1.22	1.14	.69	.68	.89	.84	.68	.88	.86	1.21
Typhus Fever	.08	.07	.07	.01	.01	.02	.02	.02	.06	.07	.08	.06
Typho-malarial Fever	1.02	1.11	.87	.97	.38	.30	.27	.28	.22	.45	.48	.46
All the Continued Fevers	2.68	2.41	2.16	2.12	1.08	1.00	1.18	1.14	.96	1.40	1.42	1.73

The regionic figures in Table XLIV show that the lines of prevalence in the Atlantic and Central regions conform in their general course to that already submitted from the army as a whole. Each presents three irregular prominences in the earlier part of its course not referable to seasonal or regionic influence, but to the aggregation of men under the calls for troops; and each shows subsequently three other prominences, apparently seasonal in their recurrence, and corresponding with an increase in the typho-malarial rates. The line of prevalence in the Pacific region is less regular, but even in it the general contour of the line of the army may be observed. These have been traced on the diagram which faces this page.

The highest rate of prevalence in the Atlantic region was 14.6, in July of the second epidemic wave; the highest in the Central region, 18.2, was in October of the first epidemic wave; the highest, 4.9, in the line of the Pacific region, was reached in October of the third wave. Although the Central region contributed the highest monthly rate and the highest annual rates during the first and last years, the high annual rates furnished by the fevers of the Atlantic region during the three intervening years gave that region the highest average rate.

The inconsiderable number of troops in the Pacific region, 10,172, when the maximum rate was yielded, is naturally suggested as a possible cause of the small size of this maximum and of the generally low level of the line of prevalence in that region. But the Central region furnished its maximum of 18.2 when only 81,387 men were present, while the maximum of the Atlantic region was only 14.6, although the strength for the month amounted to 227,419 men. Again, the annual rate for the first year was greater in the Central region, 145 per thousand of strength, than in the Atlantic region, 115.4, although in the latter the average strength was 176,650, as compared with 105,108 in the former. The mere aggregation of troops in a region has therefore apparently but little influence on the prevalence of these fevers. Nor does the narrowing of the limits from the region to

Lines indicating the Prevalence of the Continued Fevers in the three Regions.

Atlantic Region
Central Region
Pacific Region } *Monthly rates per 1000 of strength.*

Year ending June 30, 1862.
Year ending June 30, 1863.
Year ending June 30, 1864.
Year ending June 30, 1865.
Year ending June 30, 1866.

the department develop in the statistics of the latter any special influence of locality or of aggregation on the occurrence of the continued fevers. It is evident that for an explanation of all the facts we must go behind these aggregations to the susceptibility of the material of which they were composed.

TABLE XLVII.

Showing the relative Frequency of the reported forms of the Continued Fevers among the White Troops in the several Departments and Regions during the four years of war service from July 1, 1861, to June 30, 1865.

DEPARTMENTS AND REGIONS.	Years of active service embraced by the statistics.	Total number of cases of the Continued Fevers.	Average annual ratio of cases per thousand of strength.	Reported forms of Fever as percentages of the total number of cases.					
				During the year ending June 30, 1862, when Common Continued Fever was reported.			During the three years from June 30, 1862, to June 30, 1865, when Typho-malarial Fever was reported.		
				Typhoid.	Typhus.	Common continued.	Typhoid.	Typhus.	Typho-malarial.
Department of the East	2d, 3d & 4th	909	27	----------	--------	----------	78.0	3.6	18.4
Middle Department	1st, 2d, 3d & 4th	3,285	71	62.1	6.4	31.5	73.9	5.9	20.2
Department of the Shenandoah	1st	1,114	69	66.0	1.6	32.4	----------	--------	----------
Middle Military Division	4th	1,654	35	----------	--------	----------	49.5	2.1	48.4
Department of Washington	2d, 3d & 4th	10,818	105	----------	--------	----------	56.7	1.0	42.3
Army of the Potomac	1st, 2d, 3d & 4th	37,053	84	64.0	1.4	34.6	48.4	1.0	50.6
Department of the Rappahannock	1st	1,385	98	60.9	7.2	31.9	----------	--------	----------
Department of Virginia	1st, 2d, 3d & 4th	7,182	69	54.6	4.9	40.5	40.9	.6	58.5
Department of North Carolina	1st, 2d, 3d & 4th	4,713	102	65.8	1.5	32.7	43.2	1.7	55.1
Department of the South	1st, 2d, 3d & 4th	4,664	72	45.6	.5	53.9	31.0	.6	68.4
Atlantic Region		72,777	79	62.1	2.0	35.9	49.7	1.3	49.0
Department of the Northwest	1st, 2d, 3d & 4th	799	40	57.1	35.7	7.2	84.0	2.0	14.0
Northern Department	2d, 3d & 4th	1,581	41	----------	--------	----------	64.3	2.4	33.3
Department of West Virginia	1st, 2d & 3d	6,091	99	70.1	2.3	27.6	68.5	1.4	30.1
Department of Missouri	1st, 2d, 3d & 4th	5,310	53	62.9	3.8	33.3	61.1	3.2	35.7
Department of the Ohio	2d & 3d	2,968	56	----------	--------	----------	64.3	1.4	34.3
Department of the Cumberland	1st, 2d & 3d	13,327	62	68.9	2.7	28.4	61.0	1.3	37.7
Department of the Tennessee	1st, 2d & 3d	15,467	63	67.8	2.0	30.2	50.8	1.8	47.4
Military Division Mississippi, Part I	4th	3,928	36	----------	--------	----------	48.3	.5	51.2
Military Division Mississippi, Part II	4th	1,599	18	----------	--------	----------	38.8	.7	60.5
Department of Arkansas	2d & 3d	1,801	33	----------	--------	----------	39.7	2.8	57.5
Department of the Gulf	1st, 2d, 3d & 4th	10,145	82	31.2	7.3	61.5	38.4	2.9	58.7
Central Region		63,016	56	66.0	2.8	31.2	52.6	1.9	45.5
Department of New Mexico	1st, 2d, 3d & 4th	284	19	15.7	--------	84.3	40.6	1.9	57.5
Department of the Pacific	1st, 2d, 3d & 4th	352	15	42.4	1.9	55.7	52.0	4.1	43.9
Pacific Region		636	16	31.8	1.1	67.1	46.7	3.1	50.2
Total in all the Regions		136,429	65	63.6	2.4	34.0	51.1	1.6	47.3

On account of the greater prevalence of the continued fevers during the early period of the war, comparisons in this connection can be instituted with propriety only on the statistics of those departments that were kept intact during the four years of active war service. It would be inadmissible, for instance, to contrast the annual rate of 18 per thousand among the veteran soldiers of the Military Division of the Mississippi, who marched from Atlanta to the coast, with the 72 per thousand furnished by the troops who operated on the seaboard of the department through which the march was made, because the latter rate includes the larger figures of the early period; while the former is unaffected by them.

Looking only at those departments from which reports were furnished during the whole period of active operations, the rates of 69 in the Department of Virginia, 84 in the Army of the Potomac and 102 in the Department of North Carolina, all of which commands were contiguous geographically, indicate that departmental locality exercised no marked influence on the number of cases.

Again, as to aggregation in the departments. The comparatively low rate in the Department of the Northwest, and the small number of troops operating within its limits, support the idea suggested by similar conditions in the Departments of the Pacific region, especially in view of the larger rates, already instanced, in departments which contained a larger number of men. But when the statistics of these are compared with each other it is found that the fever rates did not increase in proportion to the strength present. In the Army of the Potomac, with an average strength of 109,734 men, the average annual rate of prevalence was 84 per thousand, while the adjoining territorial command, the Department of North Carolina, gave a rate of 102 in a strength of only 15,541 men.

The consolidated statistics now under consideration are incompetent to show precisely whether concentration in a locality exercised an influence on the prevalence of the fevers. As the rate was greater in the Department of North Carolina than in the Army of the Potomac it would seem that local conditions were more efficient than mere concentration in promoting their spread; for the small number of troops in the department mentioned rendered impossible such a concentration of forces as was found in the camp of the Army of the Potomac. But the influence of susceptible material in the ranks was so great that conclusions drawn from figures merely are necessarily of doubtful value. This influence has been seen in the elevation of the line of prevalence following the arrival of fresh troops. It may also be observed in the table now submitted, by comparing the rates in the Department of the Shenandoah, 69, and in the Department of the Rappahannock, 98, gathered during the first year of the war, with the rates in the Middle Military Division, 35, and in the Military Divisions of the Mississippi, 18 and 36, collected during the fourth year of service. The highest rate, 105, in the Department of Washington, appears exceptional, as it does not include the records of the first year. But this department was in a measure a camp of organization and equipment for new and undisciplined regiments, which were subsequently transferred, as the occasion required, to other points for active service. Young soldiers passed through it on their way to the front; hence the high rates yielded by its reports. The rate in this department during the fourth year, 73.6, was higher than that of the Shenandoah in the first year of the war. In the third year, when there were fewer changes in the personnel, the rate fell to 63.8. The rate for the second year was 151.0. During the first year the reports from the troops in Washington and its vicinity were consolidated with the returns from the Army of the Potomac, which furnished a rate of 126.2 per thousand of strength.

In the other columns of this table may be observed the relative frequency of the reported forms of fever expressed in percentages of the whole number of febrile cases. During the period when the term common continued fever was in use typhoid fever constituted nearly two-thirds of the cases except in the Pacific region and the Department of the Gulf, where, on the contrary, common continued fever formed this proportion of the whole. During the period when the term typho-malarial was in use, about one-half of the febrile cases were reported as typhoid. A small percentage, larger generally in the earlier than in the later years, appeared as typhus. The unusual percentages of typhus and common continued fevers returned from the Department of the Northwest during the first year of the war originated in the inconsiderable number of cases entering into the calculation, only fourteen, of which five were said to have been typhus and one common continued fever.

It is worthy of note, as bearing on the disposition made of the continued febrile cases after the term common continued fever was removed from the reports, that those departments from which a large percentage of that form of fever was reported were subsequently characterized by a large percentage of typho-malarial cases. Thus, while common continued fever formed 34.0 per cent. and typho malarial 47.3 per cent. of the reported forms in the Army as a whole, the Departments of the South, the Gulf, Virginia and New Mexico gave, in both instances, percentages largely in excess of the average. Nevertheless, a high percentage of common continued fever in the Department of the Pacific was not followed by a correspondingly high typho-malarial figure; and, on the other hand, as equally exceptional, a high percentage of typho-malarial fever in the Army of the Potomac and in the Department of North Carolina was not preceded by corresponding figures under the heading common continued fever.

Lastly, variations in the percentages of typho-malarial fever may be noted as having been wholly unconnected with the prevalence of the continued fevers as a class. This may be illustrated by taking as a standard the figures furnished by the Army of the Potomac. In that army 84 febrile cases occurred annually in every thousand men, and of these 50.6 per cent. were typho-malarial cases. But in the Departments of West Virginia and North Carolina a greater number of cases than 84 occurred annually, while the percentage of typho-malarial cases in the one department was greater, and in the other smaller, than in the Army of the Potomac; and on the other hand, in the Departments of Missouri and the South a number of cases considerably less than the standard, 84, occurred annually, while the percentage of the typho-malarial cases, as in the other two departments instanced, was in one greater and in the other smaller than in the Army of the Potomac.

The statistical relations of typho-malarial fever to the purely malarial fevers have already been shown in Tables XXXII and XXXIII.

II.—IN THE CONFEDERATE ARMY.

Evidence has already been cited in Table XIV establishing the fact that in the early period of the war the Southern troops operating in Virginia suffered more from the continued fevers than the soldiers of the Army of the Potomac opposed to them, the annual rates of cases per thousand of strength having been respectively 275 and 125. From the following table, which contrasts the prevalence of these fevers in the two armies during a period of nine months, it is found that the monthly average of cases in each was about the same; but as the United States Army had more than twice the strength of the other the ratio of cases to strength was correspondingly smaller, 10.4 monthly per thousand as against 22.9 in the Confederate ranks. It may be observed also that this greater ratio in the rebel army was due chiefly to an epidemic that prevailed during the months of August, September, October and November, following the increase of the strength present from 21,577 to 58,918 men, and that at the close of the record in March, 1862, the rate of prevalence was small and almost identical in the two armies. Both commands during this period were composed of raw levies unaccustomed to camp life. Both were similarly rationed, quartered and disciplined, for the officers who organized them had been comrades in their military education and experiences. It would seem, therefore, that local conditions were not responsible for the greater prevalence of fever in the Confederate camps.

The U. S. Army of the Potomac was largely recruited from the urban population of the New England and other Eastern States. In its ranks there was certainly a larger proportion of city men than in the Southern Army. This appears to have a bearing on the greater frequency .of typhoid fever in the latter, in view of the well-known facts that a majority of the enteric cases in cities occur in young people recently from country districts, and that an army encampment is in many of its sanitary relations an extemporized city.

Increased rates prevailed also in the Union Army as its strength was augmented by the arrival of fresh troops, but the monthly rate did not rise above 15.9, while in the Confederate camp the rate in September was 45.2 per thousand of strength.

TABLE XLVIII.

Number of Cases of the Continued Fevers in the Confederate and Federal Armies of the Potomac from July 1, 1861, to March 31, 1862, with the ratio per thousand of mean strength for each month.

MONTHS.	CONFEDERATE TROOPS.						UNITED STATES TROOPS.					
	Mean strength represented by the reports.	Number of cases of—			Total number of cases.	Ratio of cases per thousand strength.	Mean strength represented by the reports.	Number of cases of—			Total number of cases.	Ratio of cases per thousand strength.
		Typhoid.	Typhus.	Common Continued.				Typhoid.	Typhus.	Common Continued.		
July, 1861	21,577	190	2	31	223	10.4	17,709	39	6	101	146	8.2
August, 1861	50,525	1,716	4	390	2,110	41.8	50,608	311	1	317	629	12.4
September, 1861	58,360	1,801	299	546	2,646	45.2	85,408	504	50	437	991	11.6
October, 1861	58,918	947	221	437	1,605	27.2	113,204	818	34	520	1,372	11.2
November, 1861	55,099	853	132	370	1,355	24.6	133,669	1,456	13	663	2,132	15.9
December, 1861	56,700	566	77	307	950	16.8	152,759	1,351	32	341	1,724	11.3
January, 1862	57,089	398	38	215	651	11.4	167,267	1,098	17	384	1,499	9.0
February, 1862	54,810	283	39	160	482	8.8	153,308	772	12	423	1,207	7.9
March, 1862	31,470	86	1	88	175	5.6	126,588	360	8	310	678	5.4
Monthly average	49,394	760	90	283	1,133	22.9	111,169	745	19	388	1,153	10.4

The only other figures that reveal the numerical status of the continued fevers in the Confederate forces are certain monthly rates calculated and published by Dr. JONES.* These are submitted in juxtaposition with the rates of the white troops of the U. S. Army for the same monthly periods, typho-malarial statistics being included after June, 1862.

---

* Page 666, Vol. I of his published Memoirs.

TABLE XLIX.

A Comparison of the Prevalence of the Continued Fevers in the Union and Confederate forces during the nineteen months, January, 1862, to July, 1863, inclusive, expressed in monthly ratios per thousand of strength. Typho-malarial cases are included in the statistics of the Union Armies after June 30, 1862.

MONTHS.	CASES OF THE CONTINUED FEVERS EXPRESSED IN MONTHLY RATES PER 1,000 OF STRENGTH.		MONTHS.	CASES OF THE CONTINUED FEVERS EXPRESSED IN MONTHLY RATES PER 1,000 OF STRENGTH.	
	Confederate.	Federal.		Confederate.	Federal.
January, 1862	13.8	9.26	November, 1862	6.4	8.80
February, 1862	11.7	7.46	December, 1862	10.7	8.29
March, 1862	11.6	6.14	January, 1863	8.9	8.52
April, 1862	14.4	9.77	February, 1863	6.1	8.22
May, 1862	13.7	11.30	March, 1863	8.1	7.71
June, 1862	30.2	11.55	April, 1863	11.0	5.80
July, 1862	27.8	12.11	May, 1863	9.0	4.80
August, 1862	18.3	9.63	June, 1863	6.4	4.61
September, 1862	8.5	6.33	July, 1863	9.9	5.27
October, 1862	8.2	9.07	Average monthly rates	7.9	11.2

These figures, so far as they go, strengthen the conclusion derived from the statistics of the Confederate Army of the Potomac, that the Southern troops suffered more from the continued fevers than the Union Army during the epidemics consequent on the aggregation of susceptible material. Their high rates during the months of June, July and August, 1862, followed the Conscription Act of the Confederate Congress, passed April 16, calling out all white men between the ages of eighteen and thirty-five. Their lower rates during the later months cited above, and the lessened prevalence of typhoid in our own camps towards the close of the rebellion, sustain Dr. JONES in his assertion that "typhoid fever progressively diminished during the progress of the war, and disappeared almost entirely from the veteran armies."*

The Confederate death-rate from these fevers cannot be obtained for comparison, but it must of necessity have been considerably higher than the Union rate. While in each camp nearly the same number of cases (see Table XLVIII) were reported as typhoid, the number of cases of common continued fever was smaller and of typhus larger in the Confederate than in the Union Army. Thus, in the former a hundred cases of fever consisted of 67 of typhoid, 25 of common continued and 8 of typhus; in the latter the percentages were 64.6 of typhoid, 33.7 of common continued and only 1.7 of typhus cases. Moreover, it has been shown in Table XIII† that up to December 31, 1862, the number of fatal cases among the Confederate forces was 33.27 per cent. of the whole, as against 22.28 per cent. among the Union troops during the same period. This, in connection with the greater rates of prevalence in the Southern camps, indicates with certainty that the mortality rates, if known, would be considerably higher than those calculated from the Federal statistics. In fact, if the rates of fatality just cited be applied to the rates of prevalence in the Armies of the Potomac, the average mortality rate in the rebel army will be found to have been 7.62 monthly per thousand of strength, as compared with 2.32 among our Northern troops.

The number of cases that terminated fatally in the Chimborazo hospital, Richmond,

---

* *Op. cit.*, p. 665.　　　　　† *Supra*, p. 31.

Va., was 885 or 41.11 per cent.* of the total of 2,153 febrile cases with known results, typhoid fever claiming 661 deaths or 47.6 per cent. of 1,388 cases, and common continued fever 224 deaths or 29.3 per cent. of 765 cases.

III.—AMONG THE UNION SOLDIERS, PRISONERS OF WAR.

It has already been shown that at Andersonville, Ga., the rate of prevalence of the continued fevers, 77.4 annually per thousand men present, was higher than the average annual rate among our white or colored troops, and that the mortality rate, 20.5, was nearly double that among our white troops. Nevertheless the rates among the prisoners were very much lower than those calculated for our army during the early periods of epidemic visitation.

The 753 cases and 199 deaths in Table XVI† consisted of 126 cases reported *febris continua communis*, with 10 deaths, equalling 7.9 per cent. of fatality; 155 reported *febris continua simplex*, with 4 deaths, equalling 2.6 per cent., and 472 reported *febris typhoides*, with 185 deaths, equalling 39.2 per cent,—the whole equalling 26.4 per cent.

The cases in Table XV,‡ 281, of which 241 were fatal, were distributed thus:

	Returned to Prison.	Transferred.	Died.	Total Cases.
Fever, Continued, - - - - - - - - - -	6	--	3	9
" " Common, - - - - - - -	1	--	18	19
" Typhoid, - - - - - - - -	32	1	220	253
Total, - - - - - - - - -	39	1	241	281

No case of typhus fever was reported.

---

* See Table XII, p. 30, *supra.*—Dr. JONES, page 664 of his *Medical and Surgical Memoirs*, Vol. I—has published some figures concerning typhoid and common continued fevers which are reproduced in the following tabulation:

Statistics of the Continued Fevers in certain of the Confederate General Hospitals.

NAME OF HOSPITAL.	PERIOD COVERED BY THE STATISTICS.	TYPHOID AND COMMON CONTINUED FEVER.		Per cent. of deaths in cases of Typhoid and Common Cont'd Fever.	Total deaths from disease and wounds.	Ratio of deaths from these Fevers per 1,000 deaths from all causes.
		Cases.	Deaths.			
General Hospitals in Virginia out of Richmond	January, 1862, to February, 1863	6,245	1,619	25.90	5,516	293.5
General Hospitals in Richmond, Va	September, 1862, to April, 1863			26.31		249.4
General Hospitals in Virginia	April, 1863, to August, 1863	2,863	509	17.78	2,705	188.2
General Hospital of Charlotteville, Va	July, 1861, to September, 1863	1,312	313	23.86	868	360.6
General Hospital, No. 1, Savannah, Ga	December, 1861, to January, 1864	204	93	45.59	333	279.3
General Hospital, No. 2, Savannah, Ga	June, 1862, to January, 1864	239	42	17.57	125	336.0
Guyton Hospital, near Savannah, Ga	May, 1862, to January, 1864	105	11	10.48	46	239.1
Total		10,968	2,587	23.59	9,593	269.7

These rates of fatality have absolutely no value. They vary from 10.48 per cent. in one hospital to 45.59 per cent. in another; the experience of seven hospitals averaging 23.59 per cent. of fatal cases. It is to be remembered, however, that the cases enumerated were not *bona fide* cases, but in many instances duplications of cases already recorded. On the transfer of a man from hospital to hospital his name was entered as a new case on the register of the hospital to which he was transferred. The influence of this duplication may be in part appreciated when it is known that for every case recorded as sent from the field to the general hospitals there were more than four admissions on the hospital registers. Dr. JONES in the *Richmond and Louisville Medical Journal*, Vol. VIII, p. 347, acknowledges that: " The large number received into hospitals, as shown by these returns, can only be accounted for in the repeated transfers of patients during convalescence, from one hospital to another." To calculate rates of fatality when the deaths are unmodified facts and the cases a multiplication of facts by an unknown number, is manifestly absurd. These registers should have been carefully revised, excluding all admissions, which were merely transfers, from the list of cases, as was done at this office with the records of the Chimborazo Hospital. It is impossible to tell how many of the 10,968 cases of fever in the seven hospitals were due to transfers during convalescence; but were the number known and deducted from the total the percentages of fatal cases would no doubt be very different from those tabulated. The figures in the last column are of little value for purposes of comparison, as deaths from wounds, of necessity a very variable number, are included in the thousand deaths which form the basis of the calculation.

† *Supra*, p. 35.   ‡ *Supra*, p. 34.

IV.—AMONG THE CONFEDERATE SOLDIERS, PRISONERS OF WAR.

In Table XIX* the annual rates of prevalence and mortality of these fevers among the rebel prisoners were stated as 31.4 and 13.6 respectively per thousand prisoners. But these numbers do not include the fevers reported as typho-malarial. When the 37.6 cases and 4.8 deaths returned as the annual prison rates of this fever are added to those of typhoid, typhus and common continued fever, the rates for these fevers as a class become 69.0 and 18.4, smaller than the average annual rates of the rebel troops on active service but larger than those of the Union forces.

The following table exhibits the statistical relations of the continued fevers at certain of the prison depôts:

TABLE L.

Number of Cases of the Continued Fevers, with the resulting Mortality, reported from the principal Prison Depôts as having occurred among Confederate Prisoners of War, with the annual rates per 1,000 of strength.

	Camp Douglas, Ill., Feb., 1862, to June, 1865.	Alton, Ill., Sept., 1862, to June, 1865.	Rock Island, Ill., Feb., 1864, to June, 1865.	Camp Morton, Ind., June, 1863, to June, 1865.	Johnson's Island, Ohio, June, 1863, to June, 1865.	Camp Chase, Ohio, Feb., 1864, to June, 1865.	Elmira, N. Y., July, 1864, to June, 1865.	Fort Delaware, Del., Aug., 1863, to June, 1865.	Point Lookout, Md., Sept., 1863, to June, 1865.	Total in the nine principal depôts.
Average number of prisoners present	5,361	1,008	6,030	2,865	2,114	3,570	6,591	6,406	9,610	40,815
Cases:										
Typhoid	1,114	185	51	54	93	115	235	414	265	2,526
Typhus	--------	5	1	1	--------	--------	4	(b) 18	2	31
Common Continued	2	--------	--------	--------	--------	--------	--------	--------	--------	2
Typho-malarial	163	722	10	506	54	3	2	1,574	35	3,069
Total Continued Fevers	1,279	912	(a) 62	561	147	118	241	2,006	302	5,628
Deaths from—										
Typhoid	351	67	52	41	26	53	140	156	216	1,102
Typhus	--------	3	2	1	--------	--------	--------	--------	1	7
Typho-malarial	51	122	12	98	4	9	1	91	1	389
Total Continued Fevers	402	192	(a) 66	140	30	62	141	247	218	1,498
Numerical ratio per 1,000 of strength for the cases of—										
Typhoid (including Typhus and Common Continued)	60.9	66.5	6.1	9.2	21.1	22.7	36.3	35.2	15.1	31.4
Typho-malarial	8.9	252.8	1.2	84.8	12.3	.6	.3	128.2	2.0	37.6
Total Continued Fevers	69.8	319.3	7.3	94.0	33.4	23.3	36.6	163.4	17.1	69.0
For the deaths from—										
Typhoid (including Typhus and Common Continued)	19.2	24.5	6.3	7.0	5.9	10.4	21.2	12.7	12.3	13.6
Typho-malarial	2.8	42.7	1.4	16.4	.9	1.8	.2	7.4	.1	4.8
Total Continued Fevers	22.0	67.2	7.7	23.4	6.8	12.2	21.4	20.1	12.4	18.4

(a) The number of cases registered on admission as ague, bronchitis or other slight febrile affection and credited to the continued fevers on the occurrence of a fatal issue, has more than offset the recoveries among those admitted originally as cases of the continued fevers.

(b) In these cases the deaths, in accordance with *post-mortem* revelations, were charged to typhoid, the diagnosis on the record remaining unchanged.

* *Supra*, p. 47.

Of the 5,628 febrile cases noted in this table 44.9 per cent. were reported typhoid, 54.5 typho-malarial and only 0.6 typhus. Of the cases reported as typhoid and typhus 43.3 per cent. were fatal; of those regarded as typho-malarial 12.7 per cent.; of the whole number of febrile cases 26.6 per cent.

Typhoid, notwithstanding the smaller number expressing the totality of its cases, was the prevailing fever at two-thirds of the depôts. Typho-malarial predominated at Alton, Camp Morton and Fort Delaware; but on account of the uncertainty·attaching to the nature of these cases the large annual rates at Alton, 319.3 cases and 67.2 deaths per thousand of the average strength, cannot be accepted as indicating a typhoid epidemic of unusual virulence within the walls of the prison. The frequent changes in the constituents of the average number present must be remembered, in connection with these high rates, as modifying and materially reducing them.* The deaths, which numbered 16.9 per cent. of the typho-malarial and 36.8 of the typhoid cases, imply a doubt of the presence of typhoid in many of the cases of the former series. Indeed, had this camp experienced an epidemic of typhoid or other continued fever due to its insanitary conditions, the fatality of its febrile cases would have been greater instead of considerably less than that of the continued fevers in the prisons generally. The percentage of fatal cases at Alton was 21.0; in the nine prisons tabulated the percentage was, as already stated, 26.6. But as malarial fevers were prevalent at this point, in the apparent absence of local conditions for their development, it is probable that many of the typho-malarial cases, which constitute nearly four-fifths of the whole number on the record, were adynamic remittents imported from southern fields of service.

The comparative infrequency of the continued fevers among the prisoners on both sides, notwithstanding the insanitary elements of their environment, which included the presence of the typhoid poison, must be ascribed to the same cause that preserved the camps of the veteran armies from visitation—a want of susceptibility on the part of the individuals composing the aggregation.

II.—CLINICAL RECORDS OF THE CONTINUED FEVERS.

The clinical records of the continued fevers are, as might be expected, contained principally in the case-books of the various general hospitals. Field reports treated of such cases only in exceptional instances, as when, during winter quarters, a medical officer retained his typhoid cases rather than expose them to the dangers attending transportation to a distance. Usually. however, cases of enteric fever were sent from the field on the first favorable opportunity.

The recorded cases, as a rule, are more or less imperfect. On arriving at the general hospital the patient was frequently unable to give an account of the early history of his case. In some hospitals no attention was paid to the clinical records. In others the case-books were kept, but in so perfunctory a manner that they show little to indicate the nature of a particular case other than the entry of the disease as determined by the examination on admission and some fragmentary details of the medication prescribed. Fortunately, however, some of these books were carefully kept, and from them ample materials may be gathered for a representation of the continued fevers as they were seen and treated by our

* See *supra*, p. 62.

medical officers during the war. But to obtain a clear view of the subject the study of a large number of cases is needful, not only to supplement the incomplete details of one case by those of another, but chiefly because of the variety presented by the cases. A certain aggregation and sequence of symptoms might be selected for presentation as illustrative of a certain grade and type of the febrile manifestations, but such an arrangement would be purely artificial and arbitrary. Some medical officers refer briefly to their cases on the medical descriptive lists as having been typical instances of the fever as diagnosticated. This was due either to a limited experience or to preconceived views of the general course of the disease. There were in fact no typical cases: the fevers presented an infinite variety. As has been seen, even the line separating the paroxysmal from the continued fevers was not defined, and among the latter every gradation was found, from the mild attack in which the patient hardly recognized that he was sick, and the abortive case with its early convalescence, to that in which a fatal issue appeared from the beginning to be the only probable termination; and from the cases which progressed with some regularity toward their favorable or unfavorable ending, to those which were beset with alternations of hopefulness and uncertainty, prolonged for months by the continuance of intercurrent or the supervention of sequent disease. Only a few of the mild or abortive cases are detailed in the case-books. Such cases were treated in the field, where clinical records were not kept. When they occurred in the general hospitals they seem, owing to the prevalence of more serious cases, to have reached their termination without attracting special attention, and the diagnosis *typhoid*, entered probably on a mental review of the history, constitutes their only record.

I.—COMMON CONTINUED FEVER.

To the same causes which possibly account for the absence of details in mild cases of typhoid fever may be attributed the absolute want of clinical records in cases of common continued fever. Although no less than 11,898 febrile cases, 147 of which proved fatal, were reported under this heading during the first fourteen months of the war, no official record has been preserved of the symptoms and progress of any one of them. When details of febrile cases are recorded in the case-books, the diagnosis is typhoid fever. But among the *Medical Descriptive Lists* there is one case which appears as *simple continued fever*. Remissions are definitely acknowledged as having occurred in this case.

Private William R. Snyder, Co. G, 2d N. C. Battery, was admitted August 8, 1863, as a case of simple continued fever. He had been left on the field at Gettysburg as a nurse when Lee's army retreated. About August 1 he was seized with severe headache and loss of appetite. On admission he was very feeble; pulse 120 and weak; tongue moist but with a brown fur in the centre; skin hot and dry; bowels constipated. On the 15th the fever subsided by the occurrence of remissions; the patient's bowels were alternately loose and constipated. By September 1 he was considered fit to be sent away, having been able to walk about the grounds for the previous ten days. He was treated with small doses of quinine, spirit of nitre and blue-pill.—*Ass't Surg. H. C. May*, *145th N. Y. Vols., Hospital, Gettysburg, Pa.*

There are also on these lists thirty-seven febrile cases which were reported as *continued fever*.* These are all of a later date than the order calling for the disuse of the term *common continued fever*, and may therefore be regarded as contributions to the clinical history of that fever furnished by officers who were unacquainted with the requirements of existing orders. Unfortunately most of the descriptive lists are barren of information except as to

---

* To these may be added the case which, from the softening of the mucous membrane of the large intestine, was submitted by Dr. WOODWARD as No. 465 of the diarrhœal series, p. 193 of the Second Part of this work, and also the cases 249, 288 and 301 of the *post-mortem* records of the continued fevers to be hereafter presented. In these the characteristic lesions of typhoid were observed.

dates of admission and of recovery or death, with or without notes of treatment. Of these cases seven, which give more or less testimony as to the condition of the patient, are herewith submitted:

CASE 1.—Private Benjamin Midler, Co. G, 147th N. Y. Vols.; age 16; was admitted June 18, 1863, with a severe attack of continued fever which had lasted two weeks. He is reported as improving slowly on the 26th; as markedly improved on July 2, and as returned to duty August 8.—*Act. Ass't Surg. T. Turner, U. S. Army, 3d Division Hospital, Alexandria, Va.*

CASE 2.—Private J. E. Vosburg, Co. H, 137th N. Y. Vols.; age 18; was admitted June 17, 1863, in the advanced stage of an attack of mild continued fever. On the 20th the tongue, which had been slightly brown and dry, became clean, the febrile excitement abated and the appetite returned. He was returned to duty July 1.

CASE 3.—Private Charles Robinson, Co. I, 137th N. Y. Vols.; age 21; was taken while in camp, June 7, 1863, with continued fever of a mild type. On admission on the 17th he complained of severe headache, and his tongue was slightly brown in the centre and red on the edges. On the 21st he had diarrhœa; but was convalescent on the 26th, and returned to duty July 6. He was treated with diaphoretics, opiates and astringents.—*Act. Ass't Surg. Benjamin Wilson, U. S. A., 3d Division Hospital, Alexandria, Va.*

CASE 4.—Ass't Engineer Jas. Flinn, U. S. Navy; age 22; was admitted July 14, 1863, having been sick for fourteen days with continued fever. He had slight delirium at night and a diarrhœa of six or eight light-colored stools daily; but there was no tenderness of the abdomen. The tongue was white furred; appetite deficient; he had a slight bronchial cough. He took a mixture of dilute phosphoric acid and ipecacuanha, and was sponged over the whole surface of the body twice daily with cold sea-water. He was able to be up on the 18th, and was returned to duty August 1.—*Act. Ass't Surg. T. H. Liebold, U. S. A., Hospital, Point Lookout, Md.*

CASE 5.—Private Sherman Hopkins, Co. L, 6th Mich. Cav.; age 30; was admitted September 8, 1864, with continued fever. On the 12th the patient is reported as presenting all the symptoms of typhoid fever and as being much reduced. He had muttering delirium, slight diarrhœa and great tenderness over the abdomen; tongue thickly coated; teeth covered with sordes; pulse 136. He seemed to improve a little for a day or two; but during the afternoon of the 14th he began to gasp for breath and his extremities became cold. He died next morning.—*Act. Ass't Surg. W. Kempster, U. S. A., Patterson Park, Baltimore, Md.*

CASE 6.—Private Benjamin Shuester, Co. D, 2d Mass. Cav.; age 23; a paroled prisoner from Savannah, Ga., was admitted December 19, 1864. He was much emaciated, and complained of headache and soreness in his bones. He had a chill on the 25th; was restless during the night, and next day his bowels were loose; pulse 125; eyes red; face flushed; skin dry; tongue coated and tremulous. The diarrhœa continued severe until the end of the month and was accompanied with much abdominal pain. On January 2, 1865, the patient became drowsy; on the 5th a petechial eruption was observed on the chest and abdomen; there was much tympanites and great tenderness of the bowels; pulse 120; respirations 38. On the 8th the tongue was dry and covered with sordes and thin watery passages came from the bowels. He became delirious on the 11th, and from the 12th to the 15th, when he died, he was moaning constantly.—*Act. Ass't Surg. H. A. Maughlin, U. S. A., Annapolis, Md.*

CASE 7.—Private J. L. Austin, Co. D, 37th N. C.; age 25; was admitted from Fort Delaware October 16, 1863, having been taken sick with continued fever about a week before his arrival. He suffered from pains in his right foot and thigh, probably connected with an open sore of gangrenous appearance near the roots of the toes; these pains occurred in severe paroxysms and prevented sleep. By the 28th the local inflammation was subdued, but the fever became aggravated in the evenings. After this he became much debilitated; his tongue was moist but red in color, subsequently becoming dry and brown; and he had a diarrhœa of about three stools in the twenty-four hours. By November 16 he was greatly emaciated, and on this day he had twitchings of the muscles and involuntary discharges. Death took place on the 19th.—*Act. Ass't Surg. W. A. Harney, U. S. A., Point Lookout, Md.*

II.—TYPHO-MALARIAL AND TYPHOID FEVERS.

The bedside records of typho-malarial fever are represented in the case-books by but three cases, which, moreover, do not appear characteristic of the diseased conditions for which the name was suggested; for in the first there is, in view of our knowledge of the symptomatology of malarial fevers, a remittent fever with nothing to indicate a specific typhoid, in the second, another remittent, but of a graver type, and in the third, as will be seen hereafter, a typhoid fever with nothing in the record to indicate a malarial complication.

CASE 1.—Sergeant Egbert H. Little, Co. A, 38th Wis. Vols.; age 20; was admitted July 26, 1864. About July 1 he contracted diarrhœa, which yielded to treatment; on the 14th he had severe headache followed by a decided chill, and afterwards by high fever, which recurred daily for a week. On the 17th he was admitted to the 3d Division Hospital of the Ninth Army Corps, and on the 22d transferred to this hospital, arriving as above stated. He was very feeble, and had a tendency to low fever every afternoon; his bowels were constipated and appetite lost. A ten-grain dose of blue-mass was given on admission, and three grains of quinine with tincture of iron were prescribed for administration three times a day. On August 7 he continued to have headache and fever every afternoon, and his bowels were constipated and appetite poor. On the 21st the quinine was omitted; three compound rhubarb pills were given, and neutral mixture and acetate of ammonia prescribed for use every three hours. The diaphoretic mixture was omitted on the 25th, and the iron and quinine resumed. After this the patient improved gradually and was returned to duty October 18.—*Satterlee Hospital, Philadelphia, Pa.*

CASE 2.—Private William Smith, Co. K, 154th Ind. Vols.; age 24; was admitted June 24, 1865, with typho-malarial fever. He had been sick for ten days with constant nausea and frequent vomiting of dark-green bile, headache, pain in the loins and diarrhœa; his tongue was large, flabby and coated with a thick brown fur; pulse 90, soft and compressible; skin dry. The diarrhœa continued, coma supervened, and on the 30th convulsions were followed by death.—*Cumberland Hospital, Md.*

CASE 3.—Private David Markly, Co. A, 126th Ohio Vols.; age 23; was admitted September 3, 1863. He was attacked with typho-malarial fever in camp at Castle Garden, New York, on August 31, but the symptoms were not very marked. Quinine and milk diet were ordered. A diarrhœa of five or six stools daily set in on the 4th, and slight delirium on the 6th. Sudamina appeared on the 9th, on which day there was bleeding from the nose. Milk-punch and beef-tea were prescribed. There was a slight papular eruption on the 10th, and rose-colored spots on the 13th. The diarrhœa had meanwhile abated and the general condition of the patient improved. Convalescence was uninterrupted; he was returned to duty November 29.—*Central Park Hospital, N. Y.*

In addition to these there are among the medical descriptive lists thirty-seven cases reported as typho-malarial fever. Twenty of these are destitute of value as they give no statement of the actual condition of the patient; the others are given below. In 1 and 2 the fever had subsided before admission, as also in case 3, in which a diarrhœal sequel proved fatal. Cases 4–8 were mild febrile attacks which, before the introduction of the new term, would have been recorded as common continued fever: there is nothing in the record of case 4 to exclude a diagnosis of mild remittent fever, especially if the patient had been exposed to malarial influences; but cases 5–8, in the Central Park Hospital, were evidently mild attacks of typhoid fever. The Fairfax Seminary cases, 9–12, represent the last stages of typhoid fever or of an adynamic remittent without the presence of specific typhoid, if the existence of such a diseased condition be admitted. Cases 13–16, in the Douglas and Stanton Hospitals, show more distinctly the presence of a malarial element. Case 17 was apparently a pernicious malarial fever.

CASE 1.—Private R. L. Keeth, Co. D, 7th Conn. Vols., was admitted Sept. 28, 1863, with typho-malarial fever. When admitted he was weak, but the fever had subsided, the tongue was cleaning and the appetite improving. On October 14 he was placed on light duty and recommended for transfer to the Invalid Corps on account of an oblique inguinal hernia.

CASE 2.—Private B. Earl, Co. H, 142d N. Y. Vols., was admitted Oct. 1, 1863, with typho-malarial fever. The fever had subsided but the patient was greatly debilitated, and there was general œdema and effusion into the peritoneal and pleural cavities. One grain of iodide of iron and two grains of powdered squill were given every six hours in the form of pill. This course was continued until November 1, when the patient was reported as doing very well—his bowels regular, secretions normal, appetite good and effusion removed. He was returned to duty November 24.—*Charles T. Reber, Act. Ass't Surg., U. S. A., Hospital No. 14, Beaufort, S. C.*

CASE 3.—Sergeant Thomas Julien, Co. I, 62d N. Y. Vols.; age 27; was admitted June 14, 1863, with typho-malarial fever. He had diarrhœa and was somewhat emaciated, but slept well. On July 20 the diarrhœa became uncontrollable, the matters passed being thin and slimy. Death occurred August 2.—*Act. Ass't Surg. M. H. Picot, U. S. A., Lincoln Hospital, Washington, D. C.*

CASE 4.—Private John Roach, Co. C, 26th Pa. Vols.; age 16; was admitted Oct. 9, 1863, with typho-malarial fever. He complained of weakness, loss of appetite, pains in the back and limbs and fever at night; his pulse was feeble, tongue coated and bowels regular. He was able to be up on the 15th, and was returned to duty on the 27th. Treatment consisted of tonics, quinine and milk diet.—*J. P. Rossiter, Act. Ass't Surg., U. S. A., 2d Division Hospital, Alexandria, Va.*

CASE 5.—Private Elam Dye, Co. H, 126th Ohio Vols.; age 21; was admitted Sept. 5, 1863, with typho-malarial fever, with which he had become affected seven days before admission. His fever was continued. He had no chills nor eruption; his tongue was furred but moist; skin hot and dry; bowels constipated. He had headache but his mind was not affected. A slight bronchitis retarded his convalescence. He was returned to duty November 29.

CASE 6.—Private Hector S. Hunt, Co. D, 126th Ohio Vols.; age 22; was admitted Sept. 5, 1863, with typho-malarial fever. A week before this date he had been attacked while in camp at the Battery, New York, with fever followed by diarrhœa. The fever lasted only for two or three days after admission, but the diarrhœa continued until the 10th. After this he was placed on light duty. He gained strength rapidly, and was returned to field service October 15.

CASE 7.—Private William Craig, Co. H, 126th Ohio Vols.; age 21; was admitted Sept. 5, 1863, with typho-malarial fever, having had continued fever without diarrhœa for eight days before his admission. He had slight headache and much pain in the back and limbs; his skin was hot and dry; tongue moist and lightly furred; pulse 88; bowels regular; there was no eruption. He had some delirium during the night on the 8th and 9th, but after this his case progressed favorably. He was treated with quinine, pills of rhubarb and soda, milk-punch, and tepid sponging of the body and limbs. He was returned to duty November 29.—*S. Teats, Act. Ass't Surg., U. S. A., Central Park Hospital, N. Y.*

CASE 8.—Private David A. Maskley, Co. A, 126th Ohio Vols.; age 23; was admitted Sept. 3, 1863, with typho-malarial fever. He had been sick in camp at Castle Garden for seven days before admission. He had diarrhœa from the 4th, and afterwards slight delirium. Epistaxis occurred on the 9th, on which day sudamina appeared. A slight papular eruption, which faded somewhat under pressure, but which did not seem to be the specific eruption of typhoid fever, was discovered on the 10th. The typhoid eruption, however, was well marked on the 13th. The diarrhœa ceased on the 17th, after which convalescence was progressive. He was treated with quinine, camphor and opium, and milk-punch. He was returned to his command November 29.—*S. Smith, Act. Ass't Surg., U. S. A., Central Park Hospital, N. Y.*

CASE 9.—Sergeant William H. Smith, Co. B, 6th Md. Vols.; age 25; was admitted August 19, 1863, as a case of typho-malarial fever. He was much exhausted by the fatigues of his journey to hospital; pulse 120, feeble and vibrating; skin dry; bowels very loose, but not tender; lips and teeth covered with sordes. Delirium and subsultus tendinum set in on the 22d, with involuntary passages and some tenderness of the bowels. On the 26th he appeared to be improving, being at times rational, but the prostration increased and death occurred on the 30th. The treatment consisted of the administration of neutral mixture, acetate of lead and opium, small doses of quinine, turpentine emulsion and milk-punch; the general surface was sponged repeatedly with diluted alcohol, and mustard was applied to the abdomen.

CASE 10.—Private George W. Hamilton, Co. G, 6th Md. Vols.; age 22; was admitted August 19, 1863, in a dying condition from typho-malarial fever. He had diarrhœa with involuntary stools, fulness and tenderness of the abdomen and sordes on his lips and gums. He became delirious on the 21st and much prostrated. He died next day. Neutral mixture, astringents, stimulants and sponging with warm water and alcohol were used in the treatment.— *George S. Bennett, Act. Ass't Surg., U. S. A., Fairfax Seminary, Va.*

CASE 11.—Private Alfred Chase, Co. F, 35th N. J. Vols.; age 19; was admitted May 16, 1865, with typho-malarial fever. He had been ailing for some days prior to admission, but had not been confined to bed. In a few days, however, cerebral symptoms set in, accompanied with a profuse diarrhœa, and the patient sank rapidly, dying on the 23d. He was treated at first with acetate of ammonia and afterwards with moderate doses of quinine, opiates and stimulants.—*J. D. Smith, Act. Ass't Surg., U. S. A., Fairfax Seminary, Alexandria, Va.*

CASE 12.—James McQueen, unassigned recruit, was admitted May 19, 1865, with typho-malarial fever. He was received from the provisional camp, Virginia, in a critical condition. His sickness had lasted ten weeks. When admitted he was under the influence of a chill, which was followed by fever and profuse perspiration. He was delirious most of the time. His tongue was coated and very red; bowels regular; pulse 110 and feeble, and he experienced much difficulty in urinating. Three grains of quinine and Dover's powder were directed to be given every three hours, and twenty grains of calomel at night, followed by a full dose of castor oil and opium in the morning. Brandy was added to the treatment on the 22d, on which day the fever and perspirations continued, with difficulty of swallowing and much gastric irritability. Hiccough and subsultus tendinum appeared on the 23d, with increasing perspiration and involuntary passages on the 26th. He appeared a little better on the 27th, taking some nourishment, although the delirium and the involuntary passages continued. Death took place on the 29th.—*Fairfax Seminary, Va.*

CASE 13.—Private Daniel McCumber, Co. H, 26th Mich. Vols., was admitted November 4, 1863, with typho-malarial fever. The patient was incoherent, constantly endeavoring to get out of bed. He had fever of a remittent type and diarrhœa; pulse 120; respiration feeble. He perspired freely at times, but the delirium continued, the pulse became weaker, and death took place on the 13th.—*P. R. Holly, Act. Ass't Surg., U. S. A., Douglas Hospital, Washington, D. C.*

CASE 14.—Sergeant Horace Hammond, Co. F, 124th N. Y. Vols.; age 36; was admitted June 14, 1863, with typho-malarial fever. The patient had suffered with slight chills and feverishness, recurring several times during the day, for several days following June 8. On admission he had no intermittent symptoms and the case was supposed to be incipient typhoid, but its mixed character soon became evident. He was treated with milk-punch and beef-essence, to which, on August 22, quinine was added at the rate of sixteen grains daily. At the end of three weeks he was able to walk about, although weak and having a slight diarrhœal tendency. He was returned to duty August 24.—*C. C. Lee, Ass't Surg., U. S. A., Douglas Hospital, Washington, D. C.*

CASE 15.—Private James Wheeler, Co. I, 141st N. Y. Vols.; age 29; was admitted July 26, 1863, with typho-malarial fever, having been sick since the 19th with fever of a typhoid type. The tongue was red and moist; the pulse frequent and feeble; the bowels loose and tender. He was treated with opiates and aromatic sulphuric acid. On August 2 there was a distinctly marked remission; but the diarrhœa continued and the patient became enfeebled. Quinine was given. Perspirations and remissions recurred, but delirium set in on the 7th and death took place on the 10th.

CASE 16.—Corporal N. K. Stille, Co. A, 168th N. Y. Vols.; age 19; was admitted July 28, 1863, with typho-malarial fever. He had been sick since the 22d with headache, pain in the back and bowels, and diarrhœa. His pulse was frequent and full and tongue coated and dry, but with red edges. He had remissions with profuse perspirations at the end of the month, having been taking quinine meanwhile in doses of ten to thirty grains daily; and during the first week of August he had some febrile movement every afternoon; but his tongue became moist and clean and his bowels constipated. On August 22d he was sent to New York for muster out.—*George A. Mursick, Act. Ass't Surg., U. S. A., Stanton Hospital, Washington, D. C.*

CASE 17.—Private John Ennis, Co. E, 9th N. Y. Cav.; age 19; was admitted on the afternoon of May 4, 1864, with typho-malarial fever. Surgeon E. M. PEASE of the 9th N. Y. Cav. stated that the patient had been sick for three days. He had delirium with stupor and subsultus tendinum; his pulse was rapid and full and his tongue coated with a long yellow fur. He continued in low delirious condition until death at 3.30 A. M. of the 6th. Stimulants and beef-tea were given, and a fly-blister was applied to the nape of the neck.—*J. M. Wallack, Act. Ass't Surg., U. S. A., Hospital No. 6, Beaufort, S. C.*

Outside of these cases, and a few clinical notes to be presented hereafter in connection with the *post-mortem* records, there has been filed in this office nothing that will indicate the probable history of the 57,400 cases (white 49,871, colored 7,529) reported as typho-malarial fever during the period extending from June 30, 1862, to June 30, 1866.

SEMINARY HOSPITAL CASES.—The case-books of the Seminary Hospital, Georgetown, D. C., were kept with much care during the autumn and winter of 1861, while the establishment was under the supervision of Surgeon JOSEPH R. SMITH, U. S. A. These books contain an admirable series of fever cases received from the Army of the Potomac. As the term typho-malarial had not been introduced at this time, the cases were entered on the record as typhoid or remittent, in accordance with the views then held by the attending surgeons as to the symptomatology of the camp fevers. Later in the war the relative proportions of these fevers became changed, the percentage of pure typhoid cases undergoing a diminution, partly from an actual decrease in prevalence and partly from the complication of the typhoid manifestations with those due to a more extensive prevalence of malarial disease among the troops; but there are no grounds for supposing that the fevers which occurred immediately after June 30, 1862, differed in type from those that occurred immediately before that date. An examination of the records of the Seminary Hospital will therefore show, among the typhoid and remittent fevers, those which at a later date would have been reported as typho-malarial, in accordance with the views of the late Dr. WOODWARD.

The case-books contain the histories of *one hundred and twenty-three* cases of fever. The entries were made daily, and in some instances twice a day, at the morning and evening visits. The utmost care appears to have been taken in recording every thing of note in connection with each case; but this very care renders the records unpresentable in their original form in a work of this kind: the continued repetition of the condition of the skin, tongue, pulse, etc., and the persistence of cerebral, pulmonary and intestinal symptoms, day after day on the records, while giving the cases their value, render them unnecessarily tedious. As presented below they appear in a condensed narrative form, care having been exercised to omit no statement which tends in any way to convey an appreciation of the patient's condition. They have been arranged as follows:

Fifty-one cases of fever, entered as *typhoid*, in which there is no ground for acknowledging the presence of a prominent malarial complication. Ten of these were fatal.

Seven cases of fever, entered as *remittent*, in which there is nothing to indicate the presence of the typhoid poison. None of these terminated fatally.

Thirty-five cases of fever, entered as *typhoid*, in which the records give more or less evidence of the coexistence of malarial disease. Seven of these were fatal.

Eleven cases of fever, entered as *typhoid*, in which intermittent fever preceded the development of the symptoms which authorized the diagnosis. Seven of these were fatal.

Eight cases of fever, entered as *typhoid*, in which remittent fever seemed to precede or accompany the typhoid manifestations. One of these proved fatal.

Eight cases of fever, entered as *remittent*, in which the records give more or less evidence of the coexistence of the typhoid poison. One death occurred among these.

Two cases of fever, entered as *typhoid*, but in which the malarial disease only is prominent.

One case, entered as *typhoid*, but which was probably a case of pericarditis.

This classification of the fever cases of the Seminary Hospital is the result of a careful analysis of the history of each. The symptoms apparently regarded as characteristic of typhoid fever by our medical officers were separated from the aggregate, while holding in view the clinical phenomena of malarial fever as deduced from the cases presented in the third chapter of this volume. A defined periodic character of the chills, fever or perspirations, epigastric pain, gastric irritability, hepatic tenderness, jaundice, densely coated or large and flabby tongue, constipation or, concurrent with diarrhœa, an umbilical or general abdominal tenderness, and a manifest influence of quinine on the febrile condition, were regarded as indicating the presence of the malarial poison in the system. Certain symptoms in the Seminary Hospital cases appeared common to both forms of fever, either as the result of the febrile action or of the specific influence of its cause. Increased heat, circulatory excitement, diminished secretions, cerebral disturbance amounting to delirium, stupor or coma, hemorrhagic extravasations or other general manifestations of a depraved condition of the blood, were therefore excluded from consideration as indefinite in their indications. There remained a set and sequence of symptoms, to be particularized hereafter, which our medical officers evidently regarded as pathognomonic of typhoid fever.

Of the one hundred and twenty-two cases in the records of this hospital, excluding the case of mistaken diagnosis, one hundred and seven were regarded as typhoid and fifteen as remittents by the physicians in attendance. But on arranging them in accordance with a typho-malarial symptomatology, there are found to be fifty-one cases of typhoid fever, seven of remittent and sixty-four of typho-malarial fever, fifty-six of the last having been drawn from the record of typhoid cases and eight from that of the malarial fevers.

The fifty-one typhoid cases furnished ten deaths or 19.6 per cent., and the sixty-four typho-malarial cases sixteen deaths or 25.0 per cent.; none of the pure remittents died. These results differ markedly from the percentages obtained from the numerically reported cases. As may be seen by Table XLII, typhoid fever during the war gave a mortality of 35.9 in every hundred cases, while typho-malarial fever was credited with only 8.14 per cent. of fatal cases.

Although fifty-six of the sixty-four cases of typho-malarial fever were reported as typhoid, it is evident, from the record of treatment, that the medical officers were not ignorant of the presence of the complication nor of the importance of removing it by specific medication. But as malarial fever gave a small mortality and typhoid fever a large one, the more dangerous disease was naturally entered on the record as the diagnosis. These cases illustrate the true typho-malarial fever of the autumn of 1861, as well as those which occurred at a later date; but it is manifest, from the mortality rates to which reference has been made, that they do not give information concerning all the classes of cases which were afterwards reported as typho-malarial.

FIFTY-ONE TYPHOID CASES.

CASE 1.—*An incomplete record.*—Private Henry A. Hitchcock, Co. B, 3d Vt. Vols.; age 25; was admitted Oct. 1, 1861, as a case of typhoid fever. On the 2d he was dull, stupid, deaf, and had fulness of the head, tinnitus aurium and some delirium and subsultus; his skin was hot and dry; tongue pale, red at tip but coated gray in the centre; he had also some diarrhœa, slight tympanites and acute iliac tenderness. Quinine was given. Next day the skin was moist and but one stool was passed; the acute tenderness continued. He was returned to duty on the 28th.

CASE 2.—*A light febrile attack, unmarked by specific symptoms.*—Private Fospeld Black, Co. C, 1st Long Island Vols., was admitted September 14, 1861, having been sick for twelve days. The disease began with chills, which were followed by fever, pain in the head and bones, buzzing in the ears, epistaxis, anorexia and weakness. On admission he slept well after a bath, and next morning his tongue was coated yellowish-white, skin hot but moist, bowels regular; he was a little drowsy and had some cough. Dover's powder was given at night. He rested well, and on the 16th had a good appetite and quiet bowels, but his tongue was white. Castor oil produced two stools. No further medication was required. His tongue became clean. He was returned to duty on the 30th.

CASE 3.—*Slight intestinal symptoms and rose-colored spots, but progress not reported in detail.*—Private Joseph Caldwell, Co. K, 9th Pa.; age 21; was admitted September 19, 1861, as a case of typhoid fever. He had been sick for a week, at first with chills and afterwards with pain in the head and bowels, diarrhœa and fever, which last was worse in the evening and on alternate days. He had taken but little medicine. On the day of admission he had six stools, with tenderness in the right iliac region and rose-colored spots on the chest and abdomen, disappearing on pressure; the pulse was 74 and strong; the skin warm and moist; the tongue smooth, fissured, red, dry, quite clean anteriorly but with a brown fur posteriorly. On the 20th the eyes were suffused, the cheeks flushed, the pulse 80 and full, skin dry and warm, the tongue dry, brown and fissured; epistaxis, anorexia, thirst, one thin fœtid stool and slight tenderness of the abdomen are also noted. The details of the case are not recorded. The patient was returned to duty October 20.

CASE 4.—*Weakness, giddiness, drowsiness, perspiration, sudamina and rose-colored spots.*—Private James F. Tomb, Co. H, 12th Pa.; age 19; had headache, weakness and diarrhœa on August 28, 1861, and was admitted September 4 as a case of typhoid fever. On the morning of the 5th there was slight fever, the pulse 80, weak, the skin dry and hot, the tongue red, flabby and coated. Quinine was ordered with Dover's powder at night. He rested well during the night, and next day had no fever; pulse 72, tongue heavily coated, skin warm and moist, bowels slightly relaxed; nor did the fever recur in the evening. The following is the daily record of observations in this case: 6th, Morning: rested well; pulse 62; tongue heavily coated; skin warm and moist; one stool; no fever. Evening: pulse 72; skin warm and dry; tongue very red, coated white; one stool; no fever. Gave ten grains of Dover's powder. 7th, Morning: rested well; pulse 76; drowsy; tongue coated brown, red at tip; skin warm, natural; bowels quiet; appetite fair. Evening: pulse 60; skin warm and moist; no fever; tongue slightly coated; bowels quiet; appetite good. 8th, Morning: rested well; drowsy; pulse 56, weak; tongue pale, slightly coated white; skin cool, moist; no fever; giddiness; bowels quiet; appetite fair; walking about. Evening: pulse 50; tongue coated, pale; skin cool, moist; appetite good; stronger; bowels quiet; sleepy. 9th, Evening: sleepy; pulse natural; tongue pale; one thin small stool; skin natural. 10th, Morning: rested well; slept much; pulse 102, strong; tongue coated white, moist; skin moist, warm; rose-spots; profuse sudamina; bowels natural. Gave wine of cinchona. Evening: pulse 85 when standing; skin warm and dry; tongue slightly coated; profuse sudamina; one large stool. 11th, Morning: rested well; pulse 88, sitting; tongue pale, coated at base; skin cool; sudamina profuse; three stools; no pain; appetite good; no rose-spots. Evening: walking about; some weakness; profuse sudamina. Ordered rest. 12th, Morning: rested well; pulse 78, quick, compressible; tongue slightly coated gray; skin warm, moist; no fever; profuse sudamina; no tenderness; one large stool; walking around; weak. Evening: pulse 80, sitting; tongue pale, slightly coated grayish; skin natural, covered with sudamina; one natural stool; appetite good. 13th, Transferred to hospital at Baltimore, Md.

CASE 5.—*The mind continued affected after the other symptoms had disappeared.*—Private Charles Whitfield, Co. B, 1st Mich.; age 25; admitted March 2, 1862. Diagnosis—typhoid fever and chronic bronchitis. On the 4th he was quite deaf, drowsy and delirious; he was hoarse and had a frequent cough with free expectoration; his cheeks were hot and flushed, and he had much thirst; pulse rapid and weak; tongue somewhat dry, quite red and with enlarged papillæ; stools not frequent but loose; abdomen tender. Two watery stools were passed on the 5th. The tongue became moist on the 6th, the appetite returned and the bowels were quiet, but the other symptoms remained unchanged. On the 7th the deafness lessened and the hoarseness and cough diminished; pulse 90, good; skin natural; tongue moist, fissured, clean; bowels unmoved; but the mind continued affected for some time longer. On the 13th he replied naturally to questions, but had curious hallucinations which returned occasionally for several days after this, and the deafness continued for some days longer. During this time the bowels were regular or inclined to constipation. Milk-punch and tincture of iron were used. He was able to walk about on the 27th. On April 26 he was discharged for disability.

CASE 6.—*Deafness; successive crops of rose-red eruptions; bowels quiet but for castor oil; skin moist; date of onset undefined.*—Private Charles Cheney, Co. G, 9th Pa. Vols. Admitted Sept. 19, 1861. Diagnosis—typhoid fever. No note of the case was taken until the 23d, when the patient was reported as quite weak and without appetite; his pulse 85 and quick; face flushed; eyes suffused; sense of hearing somewhat dulled; skin natural, showing an eruption which was not considered characteristic; tongue brown in the centre and moist at the edges; bowels quiet. Tincture of iron was ordered three times daily, turpentine emulsion every three hours, and Dover's powder at night. He slept some during the night and perspired towards morning, when the eruption of the previous day was found to have disappeared and been replaced by an abundance of rose-colored spots; there was some borborygmus, but no stool and no tenderness or tympanites of the abdomen. The patient was thirsty and his tongue red, dry and slightly furred, but there was less deafness. In the evening castor oil was given, after which he slept badly and had five passages from the bowels during the night with some umbilical pain; he perspired towards morning. Next day the tongue was red, dry and glossy, and the eruption fading. On the evening of the 25th acetate of lead and tannin were given with Dover's powder. On the 26th the pulse was 80, the skin soft and natural, the eruption disappeared, the tongue yellowish and slightly furred, the appetite improved and the bowels quiet. Some rose-spots appeared on the 27th and 28th, disappearing on the 30th. The bowels remained unmoved from the 26th until the 30th, when there was one stool; after this they continued unmoved until October 3, when the record closes,—the patient's skin being in natural condition, his tongue clean but a little dry in the centre and his appetite good. He was transferred to Annapolis, Md., on the 10th.

CASE 7.—*Drowsiness; abdominal symptoms slightly marked; rose-colored spots on 6th day; convalescent on the 15th.*—
MED. HIST., PT. III—28

Private G. W. Beeman, Co. A, 4th Mich Vols.; age 19; was admitted Oct. 30, 1861. Diagnosis—typhoid fever. He had chills on the 25th, followed by fever and diarrhœa, for which quinine had been given. On the evening of admission he was drowsy, his face slightly flushed, pulse 85 and of good strength, skin dry and warm, showing a few rose-colored spots on the abdomen and chest, tongue red, smooth, dry and glossy, teeth blackened with sordes, bowels quiet; he had no appetite, some abdominal tenderness and gurgling, but no meteorism. Milk-punch, turpentine emulsion and beef-essence were prescribed on November 2. The skin became covered with sudamina on the 4th and the appetite was improved. A full dose of castor oil on this day produced one large evacuation. On the 7th the patient was looking bright and lively, and on the following day was up and walking about. He was transferred to Annapolis Md., on the 18th.

CASE 8.—*Headache and dizziness; bowels quiet notwithstanding purgative medicines, but right iliac region tender; rose-spots on the 14th day, with convalescence succeeding.*—Corporal B. F. Gale, Co. A, 4th Mich.; age 20; was seized about Sept. 9, 1861, with weakness, pain in the head and back and fever, and was admitted as a case of typhoid fever. In the evening his pulse was found to be 92, quick and strong, skin natural, tongue red at tip but coated slightly in the middle, bowels quiet and appetite poor. Ten grains each of calomel and jalap were given. Next day the pulse was 74, the skin natural and moist, the tongue white in the centre and red at the edges, and the bowels quiet. Quinine was ordered. In the evening the pulse was 66 and the skin and tongue unchanged. One stool was passed in the morning; no tenderness. The patient had slight headache and dizziness. The bowels remained quiet during the following days, but some tenderness was manifested in the right iliac region. The skin continued warm and moist and the tongue unchanged, although the patient developed some appetite. On the 20th he was sitting up. On the 21st he had tinnitus aurium and some thirst, but the pulse was 64, tongue clean and appetite good. On the 22d a few rose-colored spots appeared, the patient's condition otherwise remaining unaltered. He was improving generally when, on October 1, he was transferred to hospital at Annapolis, Md.

CASE 9.—*Deafness; dizziness, but mental faculties clear; diarrhœa; rose-colored spots on the 10th and 12th days, fading on 14th, when convalescence followed; to duty on 27th day.*—Private George N. Barber, Co. G, 14th N. Y.; age 18; was admitted Sept. 20, 1861, having been taken sick a week before with weakness, pains in the head, back and bowels, and epistaxis. Diagnosis—typhoid fever. On admission the pulse was 114, the skin hot and moist, the face flushed, the tongue gray in the centre and red at the tip and edges; there was diarrhœa, with irritability of the stomach and much tenderness in the right iliac region; the patient was sometimes affected with dizziness, but his mind was clear. Blue-pill was given. On the 21st he had five stools with persisting tenderness and gurgling, anorexia, a slight cough, epistaxis and deafness; his face was flushed, skin hot and moist, tongue red at tip, whitish-gray at base. On the 22d the epistaxis recurred; the tongue was dark-red at the tip, brown at the base, and its papillæ were prominent; the skin was warm and dry and presented one or two rose-colored spots; one stool was passed and the tenderness continued; pulse 76. Quinine in eight-grain doses was given three times daily, with morphia at night. The eruption faded next day, but appeared again on the 24th. The tongue began to clean on the 22d and the skin softened on the same day, after which, although the bowels continued relaxed and tender for a few days and the throat became slightly sore on the 27th, there was a steady improvement, and the patient was returned to duty October 9.

CASE 10.—*Deafness; muscular twitchings; rose-colored eruption; abdomen tender, scaphoid; improvement after the second week.*—Private William Patterson, Co. K, 6th Wis.; age 28; was admitted Oct. 2, 1861, with typhoid fever. The condition of the patient is not stated until six days after admission, when his pulse was weak and compressible, 110; countenance haggard; cheeks sunken; eyes suffused; tongue slightly coated brown and very dry and fissured, as the mouth was open much of the time; he was very deaf and difficult to arouse; he spoke with much effort, and had exquisite tenderness in the epigastric and right iliac regions and spasmodic twitchings of the arms. Whiskey-punch was given every hour. Next day the eruption appeared over the abdomen and the tenderness was very much lessened; sinapisms were applied where the tenderness had been acute. The abdomen became scaphoid on the 10th, the tongue clean and very red, the face much sunken and the eyes suffused and surrounded by dark areolæ; pulse 104; the patient had much thirst, cough and hurried respiration. Next day the countenance was more natural and the tongue moist. On the 12th the expression was better, the eyes clearer, and there was less epigastric and umbilical pain. The sinapisms were repeated on this day. After this the patient gradually improved, although for some days the skin continued dry and husky, the bowels somewhat relaxed, about two thin stools daily, and the right iliac region slightly tender. On November 1, when he was transferred to Annapolis, Md., his pulse was natural, appetite good and bowels regular.

CASE 11.—*Bronchitis prominent.*—Private J. Little, Co. H, 3d Mich. Vols.; age 26; was admitted October 19, 1861. Diagnosis—bronchitis. About October 12 he was taken with pain in the head, neck, back and limbs, and with loss of appetite. Throughout the progress of this case there was cough with much yellowish expectoration and some dyspnœa. Rose-colored spots appeared on the day of admission, and continued to erupt until the 30th. There was headache with dizziness, ringing in the ears and for a short time deafness; the tongue was moist, white in the centre and red at the tip and edges; the pulse was usually 80; the skin hot; the bowels relaxed, two to four stools daily being passed; the abdomen tympanitic and tender, especially in the right iliac and umbilical regions. On the 31st, on the disappearance of the eruption, the skin was of the natural temperature, so recorded for the first time; the tongue coated, but the appetite good; one stool was passed; there was slight headache, and the cough persisted, with asthmatic paroxysms at night. He was transferred to Annapolis, Md., on November 1, and discharged on the 13th on account of "fever."

CASE 12.—*Symptoms generally not strongly marked; free rose-colored eruption from 7th to 18th day; dysuria from 20th to 28th day; convalescence rapid.*—Private J. E. Hollom, Co. H, 6th Me.; age 22; of large frame and stout habit, was taken about Sept. 3, 1861, with pain in the head, back and shoulders, slight fever, epistaxis and diarrhœa. He was admitted on the 9th as a case of typhoid fever. The patient was weak; his tongue coated at the base, pale at tip and moist; skin hot and dry, showing a profusion of rose-colored spots; his cheeks were flushed, quite red, and he had cough and hoarseness, but his bowels were quiet. Dover's powder was given. He rested well, but next morning the fever ran high; pulse 104; skin hot and dry; face much flushed; tongue purple at the tip, coated, pale; large numbers of rose-spots on the abdomen, thighs and back, disappearing on pressure; one thin stool; borborygmus; anorexia. Squill and tartar emetic were given to allay the cough. In the evening the flushed condition of the face continued and the patient became drowsy,—pulse 108, but the skin began to be moist; four small thin stools were passed; but there was no abdominal pain, tenderness nor borborygmus. Next day the skin was perspiring and covered with rose-spots, the pulse had fallen to 92, and the patient's drowsiness was dissipated and his cough lessened; he had epistaxis. In the evening he sat up for a short time. On the 12th he had four small stools and some tympanites, but no pain nor tenderness. In the evening the face was flushed, eyes injected, skin hot and dry, but the mind perfectly clear. The diarrhœa abated gradually, and on the 15th he had one natural passage; on which day the skin was in natural condition, the tongue dark-red and slightly coated and the mind clear; the patient's face was flushed, and he had some cough and hoarseness; the rose-spots continued on the surface and did not disappear finally until the 20th. On the 22d the patient complained of dysuria, occurring suddenly after beginning to urinate, and accompanied by the passage of a few drops of blood and pain in the end of the penis; this continued more or less until the 30th. On October 2 he was employed in light duty about the ward, and was returned to duty on the 20th.

CASE 13.—*Dizziness and drowsiness; intestinal symptoms slight; no rose-colored spots; defervescence about end of second week; convalescence on 24th day.*—Private W. T. Smith, Co. C, 1st Long Island Vols.; age 20; was admitted Sept. 14, 1861. Diagnosis—typhoid fever. Ten days before admission he had chills, followed by fever, increasing debility, pain in the head and bones, anorexia and slight diarrhœa. He rested well after a bath and Dover's powder, and on the 15th the pulse was 88, tongue moist, red at the tip and sides, brown in centre, bowels regular, skin dry and warm. In the evening he was drowsy and had a sense of heaviness over the eyes; the bowels were quiet. Sulphate of magnesia was given with the effect of moving the bowels twice. After this the bowels remained quiet, but with some tenderness and gurgling in the right iliac region. The tongue became somewhat dry on the 18th, but regained its moisture in a few hours. The skin became moist on the 20th, the appetite returned, and the sense of heaviness in the head was removed. On the 22d turpentine emulsion and one ounce of brandy were ordered for administration every three hours. He rested poorly on the 24th and had some nausea and less appetite. Castor oil was administered, and repeated on the 26th and on the 29th, after which one drachm of extract of senna was given daily for some days on account of headache and dizziness. He was able to sit up on the 27th, and was transferred to Annapolis, Md., on October 10th. No rose-colored spots were observed in the case.

CASE 14.—*Headache; no diarrhœa; successive crops of eruption; convalescence following free perspirations on the 27th day.*—Corporal Joel E. Yaw, Co. H, 1st Long Island; age 19; had chills, fever and headache on Sept. 9, 1861, and was admitted on October 1st as a case of typhoid fever. On admission his pulse was 95, full and strong; skin slightly above the natural temperature and covered with elevated rose-colored spots on the chest and abdomen; tongue moist and heavily coated brown in the centre; appetite poor. Quinine was given on the 2d, tincture of iron on the 3d, and turpentine emulsion, three times daily, on the 4th. One stool was passed daily. On the 5th he was perspiring freely, and the chest and abdomen were covered with rose-spots and sudamina; on this and the following day he had a slight diarrhœal attack. After this he gradually improved and was transferred to Annapolis, Md.

CASE 15.—*Mental dulness; delirium; eruption; diarrhœal affection not prominent as a symptom; skin moist; date of onset not defined.*—Private Frederick P. Seclor, Co. A, 9th Pa.; age 24; had suffered from fever and ague in June, 1861; but since then had done his duty uninterruptedly until September 19, when he was admitted as a case of typhoid fever. In the evening the patient was weak and had headache; the bowels were quiet, but there was some tenderness in the right iliac region and intestinal gurgling; face flushed; eyes bright; breath offensive; pulse 88; skin hot and moist; head cool and sweating; tongue grayish-yellow in the centre, red and clean at the edges. Ten grains of calomel and jalap were given. Next day, with a continuance of the symptoms stated, the patient became dull and stupid and had muscæ and tinnitus. On the night of the 21st there was delirium, and the characteristic eruption appeared on the 22d, on which day also he had two stools with some tympanites and tenderness; his tongue was black at the base, reddish-white in the centre and red at the tip. Turpentine emulsion and wine were given. Next night he was again delirious, and on the 23d dull, the skin unaltered save by the fading of the eruption from the chest and abdomen, the bowels quiet, slightly tympanitic but free from tenderness, and the tongue cleaning. Dover's powder was given in small doses, with stimulants. An enema was administered on the 24th, with two grains of blue-pill and one of quinine every three hours. By the 26th the eruption had disappeared, but the patient continued dull; the skin was moist, the tongue cleaning. The bowels were moved once on this day and on the 27th, and some tenderness and tympanites remained; but after this the tongue became clean, the appetite good and the bowels natural. The patient was returned to duty October 20.

CASE 16.—*Date of onset not specified; delirium; rose-colored spots; diarrhœa persists after the occurrence of profuse perspirations.*—Private Harrison Woods, Co. K, 5th Wis.; age 26; was admitted October 1, 1861, with typhoid fever. He had been taken about September 1 with diarrhœa followed by fever. On the day after admission his face was flushed, eyes injected, pulse 100, skin hot, covered with perspiration, tongue moist, red, appetite not wholly lost; he had some headache but no diarrhœa nor cough. Tincture of iron was ordered three times daily. On the 3d rose-colored spots were noticed; the skin continued moist but the tongue was dry, red and glossy. Emulsion of turpentine was given. Next day sudamina appeared, and the patient was dull mentally, quite deaf and at times delirious. Rose-colored spots were very numerous on the 6th and 7th. The bowels were moved two or three times daily, and there was more or less of right iliac, umbilical and even general abdominal tenderness and meteorism. The tongue became moist on the 10th, the face less flushed and the eyes clearer. The delirium disappeared on the 12th, but the deafness and tinnitus aurium, together with the diarrhœa causing three to five stools daily, continued up to the time of the patient's transfer to Annapolis on November 1st. A large crop of rose-colored spots appeared on the 20th and a few more on the 24th. [This patient was returned to duty November 9.]

CASE 17.—*Deafness and aphonia the prominent symptoms; diarrhœa; rose-colored spots on the 6th day; improvement on the 21st.*—Private W. H. Harrington, Co. G, 22d Mass.; age 19; was taken sick March 1, 1862, with headache, nausea, debility, pains in the limbs and diarrhœa, and was admitted next day as a case of typhoid fever. No details are given until the 6th, when he was reported as weak, dull looking, very deaf and aphonic; he had epistaxis, cough, accompanied with epigastric pain, and rose-colored spots on the abdomen and chest. His skin was hot and dry; face congested; eyelids puffy; tongue moist and coated; stools frequent and watery. Quinine was given. The symptoms continued, being at times more or less aggravated, until the 21st, when the deafness was much diminished, the voice nearly recovered, the tongue cleaning and the bowels regular. A discharge issued from the left ear on the night of the 16th. On the 27th the general health was improving rapidly. On the 29th the patient was walking about. On April 15 he was discharged from the service on account of a contusion, the particulars of which do not appear on the record.

CASE 18.—*Cerebral symptoms slight; diarrhœa abated after occurrence of perspirations; rose-colored spots on 13th and 15th days and on 17th and 22d, accompanied by sudamina and followed by convalescence.*—Private Joseph Husang, Co. E, 19th Iowa; age 19; had a chill followed by fever on August 27, 1861, and was admitted Sept. 4 as a case of typhoid fever. On the morning of the 5th he had slight fever and anorexia; pulse 84, skin dry, tongue coated brown in the middle and dry; the mind was clear. Quinine was given. In the evening there was moderate fever, the pulse 84 and strong, face flushed, skin dry and hot, tongue very red, flabby and coated white, appetite poor, bowels moved four times; the patient was weak and dizzy and had headache. Dover's powder was ordered. No marked change took place on the two following days; the face became flushed towards evening. On the 7th the skin was somewhat moist, and next day an eruption of rose-spots was observed. On this day, the 8th, he had six thin painless stools; he became restless, talking in his sleep, and in the evening drowsy. Pills of acetate of lead and opium were administered. On the 9th a slight cough was developed with mucous and sibilant râles; the abdomen became somewhat tender and the rose-spots disappeared. In the evening the pulse was 68; the tongue moist and heavily coated brown at the base; the skin warm and moist; the bowels were moved once during the day without pain, but some tenderness was present; anorexia continued and epistaxis was noted. Next day there was one painless stool; a few rose-spots appeared; and in the evening, while the skin was perspiring the tongue became dryer and there was some cough, flushing of the face and headache. Friction with alcohol was applied to the skin. The perspiration continued on the 11th, during which there was one stool at night and one during the day, and the patient became weak and exhausted. Aromatic sulphuric acid was ordered and the body sponged with alcohol and nitro-muriatic acid. On the 12th the skin became dry and a profuse characteristic eruption appeared. The lead and opium was omitted. Next day night-sweats were reported and some improvement in the appetite; but the tongue continued dry and brown. Blue-pill three times daily and oil of turpentine were ordered. On the 14th the tongue was cracked, and although there had been no night-sweats, the skin was warm and moist; the bowels were quiet and the appetite improved; in the evening there was a slight cough with diminution of the appetite. The night-sweats returned on the 16th, when also the tongue became moist and less coated, the bowels remaining quiet. Whiskey-punch was ordered. Next day the skin and tongue again become dry; rose-spots and sudamina appeared and the bowels were moved twice; a slight flushing of the face was noted in the evening, as also on the evening of the following day. On the 19th the tongue assumed a gray, moist coating; the skin was warm and sweating; the bowels moved once; rose-spots were present but no sudamina, no tenderness nor tympanites. From this time he gradually improved. Thus, on the 24th, the report is as follows: Rested well; pulse 98; tongue red, moist, slightly coated; bowels regular; appetite good. He was able to walk about on October 1 and was transferred to Annapolis, Md.

CASE 19.—*Admitted delirious and in low condition about the 21st day; free perspirations occurred two days later, after which convalescence was gradually established.*—Private John Cross, Co. E, 14th N. Y. State militia; age 23, and of stout habit; had been sick three weeks when admitted Sept. 14, 1861, with typhoid fever. He was delirious and affected with great muscular debility and twitchings; pulse 120; skin hot and moist; face hot and dark-red; tongue coated brownish-white and fissured; body emitting a peculiar odor. Next day there was less delirium; but the subsultus continued with great roaring in the ears; the pulse was 104, tongue brown and slightly fissured, teeth covered with sordes, skin hot and dry, face flushed, on one side purplish-red, and abdomen tender on pressure. Turpentine emulsion and stimulants were ordered. In the evening the tongue was dry and coated posteriorly, and the delirium and subsultus persisted. Dover's powder was administered. On the 16th copious perspiration, with subsidence of the delirium and subsultus and increase of appetite was noted; the patient was weak and had great thirst, dryness of tongue and some incontinence of urine. In the evening the skin was warm and perspiring, the mind much clearer, the subsultus absent, the pulse 104, the tongue cleaner and moist and the bowels quiet. The Dover's powder was continued. He rested well, and on the 17th the tongue was white, pulse 100 and skin moist. Aromatic sulphuric acid was given. In the evening the pulse was 100, the tongue white and less fissured and the bowels regular. Next day sudamina appeared with free continued perspirations, great thirst for acid drinks, high-colored urine and regular bowels. After this the daily record varies but little, showing a good appetite, tongue moist, clean or with yellow or brown patches, the skin natural or moist, the bowels quiet except when sometimes moved after the administration of extract of senna, and the sleep sound. Some deafness and tinnitus were noted for a day or two. The patient was transferred to Annapolis, Md., October 1, where he was entered as a case of continued fever, and whence he was returned to duty October 21.

CASE 20.—*Record commencing about third week; perspirations accompanying subsidence of the fever.*—Private D. P. Smiley, Co. F, 11th Pa. Cav.; age 19; was said to have contracted diarrhœa on Sept. 9, 1861, and was admitted on the 30th. Diagnosis—typhoid fever. He was weak, had a slight cough, a diarrhœa yielding two stools daily and but little appetite; pulse 100 and quick; skin natural; tongue moist, but coated in the centre. Next day he was dull; had some headache and tenderness in the right iliac region. On October 2d the tongue was dry, brown and fissured in the centre. No change was noted on the 3d, but on the 4th his pupils were dilated; he was delirious and had a wild look. The delirium abated somewhat on the 6th; the tongue became dry, red and fissured by the 10th, but the appetite improved and the bowels continued unmoved for several days, the pulse beating 75 to 80 per minute, although there was some abdominal tenderness and tympanites, with flushed cheeks, injected eyes and nocturnal delirium. The patient perspired during the night, and next morning the tongue was red at the tip and edges and coated white in the centre; there was less delirium and the appetite was good. On the 12th the tongue was moist and clean but for a yellowish streak on each side of the centre. One stool was obtained on the 14th, after the administration of two compound cathartic pills. The tongue on the 17th was moist and clean but for some white patches. The patient steadily improved and was returned to duty November 13.

CASE 21.—*Headache; epistaxis; delirium; sordes and rose-colored spots on the 12th day; perspirations and convalescence on the 29th.*—Private Jno. Stoddard, Co. A, 13th N. Y. Vols.; age 25; was admitted Nov. 1, 1861, having been sick for a week before admission with headache, epistaxis, anorexia, thirst and cough. On the 2d the patient's eyes were suffused, face congested, pulse 100, full and strong, skin hot, tongue red at the tip and edges and coated yellowish in the centre; appetite poor; he had epistaxis during the day and one passage from the bowels, which gurgled and were tender on pressure, particularly on the right side; he had also some cough with yellowish blood-streaked sputa. The epistaxis did not recur, and next day he had headache, which was accompanied by mental hebetude on the 4th and by delirium on the 5th. An eight-grain dose of quinine, turpentine emulsion three times a day, and six grains of calomel with one of opium at night, were prescribed on the 4th. Rose-colored spots appeared on the chest at this time, as also dryness of the tongue and blackening of the teeth and lips from sordes. The delirium lasted only one day, but the dulness of mind persisted. A diarrhœa of three or four stools daily was perhaps due to the calomel, which was repeated on the 5th. Much abdominal tenderness and tympanites were also present; the appetite, however, continued good and the thirst was lessened. The tongue became moist and covered with white patches on the 6th, swollen and coated on the 7th and 8th and clean on the 10th; but the skin did not become moist until the 21st. On the 22d there was profuse perspiration. Complaint was made of earache on the 25th. Three days later the patient was able to leave his bed. On December 3, when transferred to Baltimore, Md., he had tinnitus aurium and cough and his bowels were slightly relaxed.

CASE 22.—*Date of onset unrecorded; cerebral, pulmonary and intestinal symptoms; rose-colored spots; convalescence.*—Farrier Alexander Wenrich, Co. K, 2d Pa. Cav. Admitted Nov. 5, 1861. Diagnosis—typhoid fever. On the day after admission he was delirious and slightly deaf; had frequent and involuntary stools, some cough and the respiration increased to 22; his eyes were injected; face congested; pulse 100, quick, bounding and intermittent; skin hot; tongue red and slightly coated yellowish-white. Hoffmann's anodyne, tincture of valerian, turpentine and astringents were prescribed, with morphia at night. Sordes appeared on the teeth on the 7th, on which day two stools were passed; beef-essence, punch and morphine were ordered. He was stupid on the 9th; had headache and tinnitus on the 10th, two stools and slight tympanites and tenderness in the right iliac region, but the tongue was moist and cleaning and the cough slight. Rose-spots appeared on the chest on the 11th. The delirium did not quiet down until the 16th, after which he slept well and had a good appetite. He was transferred to Alexandria, Va., Dec. 20th.

CASE 23.—*Deafness and mental dulness; intestinal symptoms; perspirations and rose-colored spots on 19th day; sordes and delirium on the 20th and 21st; convalescence on the 33d day.*—Private William O'Brien, Co. G, 13th N. Y.; age 20; contracted typhoid fever Oct. 15, 1861, and was admitted November 1. Next day there was headache and deafness, tinnitus and hebetude; the face was congested; pulse 78; the tongue was dry, swollen and coated yellow; the patient had no appetite, much thirst, relaxed bowels and some tympanites and abdominal tenderness; profuse sweating had occurred during the night, and on the chest and abdomen a few rose-colored spots were discovered. On the 3d sordes appeared on the teeth, and on the 4th delirium supervened, the patient making frequent attempts to leave his bed; the tongue became red at the tip and edges. There was less deafness, and the mind became clearer on the 6th, but the delirium did not entirely subside until the 11th. On the 16th the tongue was clean, pulse 75, and there was no abdominal tenderness. The case was treated from the 3d with milk-punch, beef-essence and emulsion of turpentine. He was transferred to Annapolis, Md., on the 18th [and returned to duty Dec. 16].

CASE 24.—*Presenting delirium, unconsciousness, floccitatio, subsultus, slight diarrhœa, rose-spots, sudamina, bed-sores and vibices. Improvement manifested about 35th day.*—Private William E. Thompson, Co. C, 9th Pa. Vols.; age 19; was taken about August 22, 1861, with pain in the head and back, epistaxis, chill, fever and diarrhœa, and was admitted September 12 as a case of typhoid fever: pulse 100, quick; skin hot and dry; tongue dry at the tip and coated gray at the base; the patient was dull-looking and had subsultus, relaxed bowels, right iliac tenderness and intestinal gurgling. Dover's powder was given. On the 13th the skin was hot but moist with perspiration; rose-colored spots appeared. Next day the skin was again hot and dry, but covered with profuse sudamina; the cheeks were flushed, the tongue dry, smooth, cracked and protruded with difficulty, and the patient stupid but restless. Toward evening on the 15th a few more rose-spots came out; sordes appeared on the teeth; the bowels continued slightly relaxed and there was right iliac tenderness; the patient was haggard; he turned his head from side to side, muttered, and had subsultus tendinum. No change occurred on the 16th, but on the 17th more rose-spots made their appearance and the patient became drowsy. On the 19th his pupils were dilated and he was unable to articulate. Next day the pulse was 112, irritable and full; the skin dry and husky; the rose-spots and sudamina had disappeared;

the tongue was rough, dry and brown; the gums and teeth covered with sordes; right iliac tenderness, meteorism, gurgling and relaxation of the bowels continued, and the patient muttered and groaned, but had no subsultus. He was greatly emaciated and prostrated, and for some days lay on his back with his eyes half-closed; sometimes partly delirious, picking at the bed-clothes, and at other times unconscious. Meanwhile the pulse became more rapid, rising to 128 on the 23d, and the circulation of the skin languid. He vomited on the evening of the 22d, and after this his bowels became more quiet. Bed-sores appeared over the sacrum. Turpentine, Dover's powder, astringents and stimulants had been used in the treatment. On the 25th the pulse was 114 and stronger, the tongue cleaning and the mind clearer, but the skin continued hot and dry, and vibices appeared profusely on the chest; the bowels remained quiet. The patient was sponged with alcohol and turpentine; warm bottles were applied to the feet and soft pads to the sacrum over the sores. In the evening the eyes became brighter and the skin moist, the pulse having meanwhile fallen to 100. Next day the patient was tranquil, the tongue moist and cleaning at the edges; the bowels were moved by an enema. A purulent discharge came from the right ear. The left ear became similarly affected on the 28th. The appetite returned on the 29th, and after this improvement continued. The patient was furloughed October 31.

CASE 25.—*Delirium; involuntary stools; sordes; rose-colored spots; convalescence coincident with free perspiration.*— Private W. H. Barnett, Co. D, 14th N. Y.; age 26; was admitted Oct. 2, 1861, as a case of typhoid fever. On the 6th he was reported as weak and having suffused eyes, quick pulse, 115, hot and dry skin, moist, brown and slightly fissured tongue, anorexia, relaxed bowels and iliac tenderness. Turpentine emulsion and camphor with sweet spirit of nitre were ordered. Next day the patient was quite delirious and had three involuntary stools; sordes appeared on the teeth and six rose-colored spots on the skin. Milk-punch and tincture of opium were ordered. On the 8th the rose-colored spots increased in number and the delirium was somewhat lessened; the five stools passed were not involuntary; some irritability of stomach was manifested. Sudamina appeared on the 10th with a fresh crop of rose-colored spots, and the tongue became red at the tip and edges. On the 11th epistaxis occurred and the patient was stupid. Next day headache accompanied the delirium, the other symptoms continuing as already stated. On the 14th the tongue was somewhat moist and the appetite improved. On the 15th the pulse had fallen to 80, the diarrhœa lessened, epistaxis recurred and the patient was more rational. Next day there was only one passage from the bowels, but the right iliac tenderness continued with some tympanites and gurgling. Rose-colored spots appeared on the 18th and again on the 21st; on the former day the headache and delirium were greatly lessened, and on the 19th the tongue was clean and the appetite good; but some general tenderness continued in the abdomen and there was some cough. A free perspiration occurred during the following night, after which the progress of convalescence was steady. He was transferred to Annapolis, Md., November 1 [whence he was returned to duty on the 22d].

CASE 26.—*Cerebral and intestinal symptoms; rose-colored spots from the 11th to the 34th day; improvement on the 26th day, coincident with subsidence of febrile heat and appearance of moisture on surface.*—Private Hugh Murphy, Co. I, 3d Vt.; age 22; had measles in July, 1861, and on Sept. 25 was taken with a heavy cold, chills, headache and diarrhœa. On admission, Oct. 3, his case was diagnosed one of typhoid fever. He slept well, but his eyes were suffused and he had some pain in the head, anorexia and slightly relaxed bowels; his tongue was moist and coated yellowish in the centre; skin natural; pulse 90 and full. Rose-colored spots appeared on the chest and abdomen on the 5th and were very profuse on the 7th, when the skin became hot and dry, the lips parched and the tongue red and glossy at the tip and edges and dry at the base and centre; five stools were passed on this day, and there was much tympanites but no tenderness. By the 10th the eyes had become injected, the cheeks flushed, the tongue dry and dark and the teeth covered with sordes; the patient was stupid and at times delirious; meteorism and borborygmus accompanied the diarrhœa. Up to this time emulsion of turpentine and Dover's powder had been used in the treatment; quinine was now given in two-grain doses every hour. The bowels were moved nine times on the 11th and the right iliac region was markedly tender. Tincture of iron was given on the 12th. Deafness was noticeable on the 13th. This condition of mental hebetude, deafness, occasional delirium, flushed face, hot and dry skin with eruption of rose-colored spots, dry and dark tongue and marked diarrhœa continued until the 20th, when the skin lost its heat, the tongue its dryness and the stools became less frequent; the patient was troubled with some cough during this period. The skin was reported moist for the first time on the 24th. The eruption did not disappear until the 28th. The tongue continued moist and but slightly coated, the skin natural, the appetite good and the bowels moved but once daily until Nov. 1, when the patient was transferred to Annapolis, Md. [whence he was returned to duty on Dec. 2].

CASE 27.—*Diarrhœa; muttering delirium; coma vigil; sordes; dark-red spots, persisting under pressure, on the 17th day, after which improvement was progressive.*—Private Andrew Scriber, Co. C, 14th N. Y.; age 22; was admitted Sept. 20, 1861, having been taken sick two weeks before with chills, pains in the head and bones and great muscular debility. Diagnosis—typhoid fever. His pulse on admission was 118 and soft, face flushed dark-red, countenance anxious, skin hot and dry, tongue thickly coated gray in the centre, red at the tip and sides, gums and teeth covered with sordes; there was some diarrhœa with tenderness of the abdomen and tympanites; the patient lay with his eyes and mouth partly open, muttering incoherently when roused. On the 21st he was dull, stupid and difficult to arouse; pulse 90 and quick, skin hot and moist, tongue brownish-gray. He had six stools during the day, accompanied with gurgling but no tenderness. Turpentine emulsion and enemata of laudanum were ordered. On the 22d he was restless; pulse 112, small; skin hot and dry, with here and there dark-red spots which did not disappear on pressure; tongue brown and dry in middle, moist and red at edges. The diarrhœa was checked by the enemata, but there was some tenderness of the abdomen and intestinal gurgling. Brandy was given. On the 23d the eruption had disappeared; two stools were passed; the sordes persisted about the lips, but the tongue was cleaning from the edges. The sordes disappeared on the 25th. Next day the tongue was clean; there was some appetite, and the patient looked and said he felt well; but he was restless and wanted to go out. He had three stools; pulse 84. In the evening the pulse rose to 100, the face was flushed, the skin hot and dry, and there was borborygmus with right iliac tenderness and one stool. On the morning of the 28th the pulse was 82; the skin warm and moist; the tongue moist, red at the tip and slightly coated. His appetite was good on the 29th. He had four stools on the 30th, but no tenderness; his countenance was natural, his skin warm and soft, and he was gaining strength. On October 20 he was detailed on extra duty.

CASE 28.—*Dizziness; deafness; diarrhœa; eruption on the 9th day, not disappearing on pressure; manifest improvement coincident with epistaxis on 16th day; hemorrhage from bowels on 19th day, with subsequent inflammatory action in the pulmonary and urinary organs, and delirium lasting until the 33d day, when improvement was again manifested.*—Private James Scoffield, Co. K, 6th Wis.; age 20; became subject about Sept. 25, 1861, to faintness and feelings of weakness, chills, fever, diarrhœa, pain in the head and back and anorexia. He was admitted October 2 as a case of typhoid fever. His face was flushed darkly; eyes suffused; expression dull and heavy; pulse 100, strong and full; skin hot, dry, smooth and without eruption; tongue slightly moist, red at the tip and thickly coated grayish-white in the centre; bowels relaxed but not tender; he was somewhat deaf and had a slight cough. Next day the patient was drowsy and had headache with dizziness and increasing deafness; the skin hot and slightly moist, showed a few spots which did not disappear on pressure; the bowels were moved four times and were tender. No change took place until the 7th, when tinnitus aurium and epistaxis were noted, the tongue having become clean, dry, red and fissured. On the 9th the tongue became very rough, red and grayish-white in the centre; epistaxis recurred; four stools were passed, and there was slight tenderness in the right iliac region; the urine was scanty and very dark-colored. Next day epistaxis again occurred, the pulse was 100 and strong, the skin soft although hot and dry; the expression was less anxious, the eyes clearer, the hearing improved and the tongue moist and cleaning in the centre, but the patient complained of headache and pain in the back and side, a dry hacking cough and much thirst; he had two thin stools with much tenderness and gurgling and slight meteorism. On the 13th a profuse hemorrhage occurred from the bowels; the patient became very pale and stupid, pulse 120, skin hot and husky, tongue moist, fissured and slightly coated; the abdomen was soft and tender. Next day the pulse was 104, the skin dry and husky, the tongue dry, dark, cracked and rough, the countenance pinched and somewhat anxious, the teeth and gums covered with sordes; the bowels moved three times during the night, about eight ounces of blood coming away with one of the passages. No hemorrhage took place on the 15th, but the patient had subsultus tendinum and some bronchitic cough. His expression on the 16th was wild; he was very wakeful and complained much of pain in his heels and legs. On the 17th he perspired profusely and had frequent epistaxis but no stool; the bladder was so distended as to require the employment of the catheter; the tongue was dry, furred and scaly; pulse 112, feeble; mind dull; countenance anxious; respiration normal. Two stools were passed on the 18th; the bowels were tympanitic and acutely tender; the skin was dry but at times moist and perspiring; the delirium present was not of a violent character. From this date until the 27th the patient was dull, drowsy and more or less delirious, sometimes crying out loudly; the skin was dry and husky but occasionally moist; the tongue dry, fissured and scaly and the teeth black with sordes; two or three stools were passed daily, and there was much right iliac and hypogastric tenderness, with meteorism and borborygmus; the catheter had to be used, and the urine withdrawn was strongly alkaline, containing blood, mucus, pus, epithelium and excess of phosphates. Some sibilant râles were heard in the upper parts of both lungs, and the respiration at one time became increased to 28 per minute. He was emaciated and very weak; but on the 27th the mind became clearer. On the 28th the eyes were bright, the skin warm and sweating, the tongue moist and cleaning, the bowels quiet, the abdominal tenderness much diminished, but still acute in the right iliac and hypogastric regions. On the 29th some appetite was manifested. The teeth and gums were clean on November 1. Micturition was free and natural on the 4th, but for some days after this he had at times much pain in the penis and bladder. On the 9th bed-sores are mentioned; the skin was hot and dry; the tongue dry, smooth and fissured; the bowels were quiet, but tenderness continued in both iliac regions; the appetite was good. No further record was made except that on the 20th the patient was transferred to Annapolis, Md. This case was treated with turpentine emulsion on October 7th, Dover's powder on the 9th, acetate of ammonia on the 10th, extract of buchu on the 11th, and thereafter with quinine, opium and stimulants.

CASE 29.—*Deafness and headache; abdominal tenderness and tympanites, but no movement except by castor oil; rose-colored spots on the 12th to 21st day; defervescence by free perspirations on the 27th, and convalescence on the 36th day.*—Private F. Klussman, Co. I, 35th Pa. Vols.; age 23; was admitted Oct. 30, 1861. Diagnosis—typhoid fever. His illness began on Oct. 20, with chills and fever, anorexia and thirst. On the 31st he was very weak and did not sleep, the eyes dull, cheeks flushed, pulse 85, skin hot, chest and abdomen covered with a profuse rose-colored eruption, tongue red at the tip and edges but coated white in the centre, teeth covered with sordes; he was deaf and had tinnitus aurium, anorexia, thirst, extreme tenderness of the abdomen and tympanites although but one stool was passed; there was also some cough. Quinine and turpentine emulsion were prescribed. Next day the tongue became dry in the centre; on the 2d there was epistaxis, and on the 3d headache and inability to sleep, the tongue having meantime become dry, swollen and fissured at the edges. Beef-essence and milk-punch were prescribed, and as there had been no movement of the bowels for some days, castor oil was given; the abdomen was tympanitic and tender and gurgled under pressure. The tongue became moist on the 6th, the skin moist on the 7th, but free perspiration did not occur until the 16th, when the appetite returned. The headache became relieved about the 10th, at which time the last crop of the eruption faded. The patient was able to be up on the 25th, and was transferred to Baltimore on Dec. 3. Except on the day of admission, no passage was obtained from the bowels of this patient without the aid of castor oil.

CASE 30.—*Delirium, diarrhœa and rose-colored spots; improvement dating from the 38th day, when the tongue became moist.*—Private Andrew Schick, Co. E, 1st Pa. Art., was taken about Aug. 20, 1861, with a cold; he suffered for a week from diarrhœa with severe pain in the head, and fever which became aggravated in the middle of the day. He was admitted Sept. 19 as a case of typhoid fever. The patient was stupid, deaf and delirious; the stools thin; the right iliac region so tender that he objected to having the abdomen touched; the pulse 128, small and feeble; the skin hot but soft and presenting an occasional rose-colored spot with sudamina on the neck; the tongue red at the tip and gray in the centre and at the base. A half-ounce of castor oil was given. Next day three stools were passed, the skin was hot and dry, and there was much thirst; otherwise little change was presented. Quinine was given on the 27th. Next day there was less fever; the pulse fell to 95 and was stronger; the tongue was moist, but the skin continued dry; the mind became clearer. The improvement progressed on the 29th. The pulse on the 30th was 106; the tongue clean; appetite good; bowels quiet and natural. Whiskey-punch was given. The patient was returned to duty November 1.

CASE 31.—*Date of onset unrecorded; rose-colored spots; delirium; chest complications interfere with defervescence about end of 4th week, and prolong the case for two or three weeks.*—Private Christian B. Krieger, Co. I, 4th Mich.; age 22; admitted Aug. 31, 1861. Diagnosis—typhoid fever. He was weak and feverish, and had diarrhœa, tympanites and well-marked rose-spots; pulse 110; tongue dry and brown but red at the tip; teeth covered with sordes. Brandy-punch, beef-essence and astringents were given. Next day he was slightly incoherent, and on September 4 delirious. The record does not again state his condition until the 13th, when there was fever with much thirst, delirium, tinnitus aurium, muscæ volitantes, a moist brown tongue and dry hot skin. Dover's powder, beef-essence and brandy were given at this time. On the 15th, the patient's general condition remaining the same, his pulse rose to 106, his tongue became dry, and in the evening his urine was passed involuntarily. On the 16th the presence of bronchitis was reported. Next day his tongue began to clean in patches, and on the 18th was moist, glossy and nearly smooth, the appetite improved and the bowels quiet; but the delirium did not abate until the following day, when in the evening it recurred, accompanied with abdominal tenderness and tympanites, some cough, hurried respiration, 30, and dryness of the tongue, which was protruded with difficulty. On the 21st he rested well; his face was pale and sunken but bright; his tongue remained dry, red and glossy, and was slightly coated in patches; the teeth were covered with sordes; the cough continued; but the hearing was good, the bowels quiet, the urine normal and the appetite good. Next day delirium was again added to these symptoms, and on the 23d some deafness and subsultus tendinum. On this day the tongue again became moist, but dried on the 24th in the centre although remaining red and moist at the edges. Turpentine emulsion was ordered. This condition continued until the 26th, when the delirium became lessened, the face and lips pale, the expression anxious, the eyes clear and bright, the pulse 96, the skin dry and husky but of natural temperature, and the tongue clean, soft and moist, but with some sordes remaining on the teeth. Some perspiration is mentioned on the 27th as occurring on the skin for the first time in the history of the case. Delirium recurred on the 29th, with slight failure of the appetite and cough, the tongue remaining moist and the bowels undisturbed. After this the skin was natural, moist, or occasionally dry, the tongue clean or slightly patched with yellow, the pulse from 72 to 96, the appetite good; but the bowels became relaxed, yielding two, three or four stools daily. While in this condition he was transferred to Annapolis, Md., October 10. [This man ultimately recovered and was returned to duty with his regiment.]

CASE 32.—*Muttering delirium; sordes; intestinal effusion; rose-colored spots on 14th day; petechiæ on 15th; pains in the feet; slight improvement on the 17th, but record incomplete.*—Private C. D. Emons, Co. D, 7th Wis. Vols.; age 18; was admitted Oct. 30, 1861. Diagnosis—typhoid fever. He was taken sick about the 22d with diarrhœa, chills, weakness and loss of appetite. On admission his face was flushed, pulse 100 and of fair strength, skin hot and dry, tongue thickly coated, teeth black with sordes, breath very offensive; he had much thirst, relaxed bowels and some tenderness in the right iliac region, with borborygmus and tympanites; he muttered in his sleep. Oil of turpentine, compound catechu powders and whiskey-punch were prescribed. Delirium became a prominent symptom for a few days, during which the pulse was strong and slightly above 100, the face dusky, the eyes much injected and the tongue red at the tip, blackened and fissured; but on Nov. 4 the delirium lessened, the pulse fell to 86; he slept well during the previous night, the teeth and gums were cleaner and the skin was soft and presented a few rose-colored spots. On the 5th the pulse was 88 and feeble; petechial spots appeared on the skin; the tongue was very dry and thickly coated brown. The patient was drowsy and difficult to arouse; one stool was passed, and the bowels were tender and gurgled on pressure. On the 7th the mind became clearer and the eyes were less injected, but otherwise there was little change in the condition; he complained of pain in the feet. The record gives no further details. He was transferred to Baltimore, Md., on December 3.

CASE 33.—*Muscular pains as a sequel of the fever.*—Private Benjamin F. Reynolds, Co. K, 86th N. Y.; age 29; admitted Feb. 18, 1862. Diagnosis—typhoid fever. On March 5 he was dejected and languid, complaining of rheumatic pains in the lower extremities; his skin was natural; pulse 90 and good; tongue moist and clean; bowels unmoved. Stiffness and pain in the legs increased until the 10th, the bowels meanwhile requiring aperients for their regulation. After this date he improved and was transferred to Annapolis, Md., on the 24th.

CASE 34.—*Date of onset undefined; mental dulness; eruption; sordes; perspiration followed by delirium; improvement, but record unfinished.*—Private Henry Klummer, Co. I, 35th Pa. Vols.; age 20; was admitted Oct. 30, 1861, as a case of typhoid fever, presenting dulness of mind, dull and somewhat injected eyes, congestion of the face, a full strong pulse beating 90 per minute, a hot skin showing a few rose-spots on the chest and abdomen, a dry, fissured and brown-crusted tongue, sordes on the lips and teeth, anorexia, thirst and some tympanites. Beef-essence, quinine and turpentine emulsion were prescribed. No change took place until November 2, when the skin was bathed in perspiration and some deafness was noted. Delirium set in on the 3d, on which day the patient had three stools. The tongue seemed cleaning on the 7th and the delirium lessened, but the condition otherwise was as related. On the 9th, after passing a better night than usual, he showed a return of appetite. Next day he was intelligent. On the 11th the tongue was red at the tip and edges, dry and brown in the centre and the skin was hot, but the patient slept well, had a good appetite, and his bowels were quiet. The record gives no further details. He was transferred to Baltimore, Md., on December 3.

CASE 35.—*Giving a view of the patient for ten days during convalescence from a protracted attack of fever.*—Private Alfred G. Bates, Co. A, 3d Mich.; age 24; became affected with typhoid fever in June, 1861, and was admitted Sept. 28. He felt pretty well, but he had some cough with expectoration, and pain in the head, back and limbs; his face was slightly flushed and his eyes dull; pulse 96, full and strong; skin hot and soft; tongue white in centre; appetite small; bowels quiet but somewhat tender and tympanitic. He slept poorly the first night, but very well after that. His tongue was more or less coated white or yellowish in the centre and red at the tip and edges; his appetite improved. His bowels were not relaxed; small doses of blue-pill and compound extract of colocynth, castor oil and sulphate of magnesia had to be prescribed to move them. At one time he had some difficulty in micturition. When transferred to Annapolis, Md., on October 10, his skin was of the normal temperature, tongue moist and clean, appetite good and bowels quiet.

CASE 36.—*Delirium; diarrhœa; rose-spots, vibices and bed-sores; pneumonic complications delay convalescence until after the 40th day.*—Private George Felter, Co. B, 9th Pa. Vols.; age 22; was taken sick about Sept. 1, 1861, and admitted on the 19th with typhoid fever. The notes of the case on the 20th are: pulse 96; skin hot and dry; high fever; tongue coated white in centre, red at tip and edges, slightly moist; acute iliac tenderness; tympanites; constipation; enlargement of the thyroid gland. Ordered: enema of soapsuds; emulsion of turpentine; Dover's powder at night. On the 21st: pulse 120, full and soft; skin hot and moist; tongue dark-red at the margins, dry and brown in the centre; characteristic rose-spots; no sudamina; less tympanites; tenderness of abdomen on pressure; borborygmus; subsultus; delirium; drowsiness; decubitus dorsal; respiration 30. Gave wine whey four times daily with beef-essence. On the 22d, morning: delirium; subsultus; pulse 118, full and soft; few rose-spots; skin hot and dry; tongue very red and moist; respirations hurried; submucous and sibilant râles in upper part of both lungs; decubitus dorsal; acute general abdominal tenderness; tympanites less; borborygmus; one stool. Ordered: one-fourth of a grain of morphia; cold applications to head. Evening: pulse 120; face flushed; skin hot and dry; tongue dry; rose-spots; high fever; delirium; deafness. No change took place until the 24th, when there was some diarrhœa. On the 25th the tongue became slightly moist and cleaner, the delirium gave place to dulness, vibices appeared on the chest, the urine and fæces were passed involuntarily and a large bed-sore formed over the sacrum. The tongue became again dry on the 26th, and the lungs were found consolidated in their lower portions. On the 27th the pulse was 113 and strong, the face flushed, the skin hot and dry, the respirations 40, with submucous and sibilant râles in the upper part of the right lung and a short dry cough. A blister was applied to the upper part of the chest. The bowels were quiet on the 28th. The tongue became moist on the 29th, red at the tip and gray in the centre; the skin was warm, dry and soft; the bowels were quiet, but there was tenderness on both sides, with tympanites and borborygmus; the sacral sore was healing and the patient rational. The chest was again blistered; tonics and stimulants were administered. The stools became involuntary on the 30th, with acute right iliac tenderness and some anxiety of expression; pulse 106; surface circulation sluggish; respirations 40; some cough and much dyspnœa. The patient became restless on October 1. Vibices appeared on the abdomen on the 2d; some diarrhœa occurred, the stools being involuntary; delirium occasionally returned at night. On the 4th there was some improvement in the chest-symptoms. On the 7th the face was slightly flushed; the pulse 114, steady; the skin hot and dry, moist in some places; the tongue moist, red at tip, coated in centre; the bed-sores showing points of granulation; the stools involuntary at long intervals, with borborygmus and some tympanites but no tenderness; micturition involuntary. On the 8th, 9th and 10th the pulse fell respectively to 108, 106 and 100, one or two stools occurring daily with some tenderness—the skin continuing hot and dry, but the tongue becoming cleaner and its edges moist. On the 10th the eyes were bright and the countenance cheerful. The pulse fell to 90 on the 11th; the condition of the tongue improved and the appetite returned. On the 17th the tongue was clean and moist but redder than natural; the bowels were regular; the appetite good; a slight cough yet remained. The record, which is continued in detail up to the 27th, shows the occurrence of an occasional thin stool but the tongue preserved its clean and red condition, the appetite was good and the sleep sound at night; no further reference is made to the healing of the bed-sores. This patient was transferred to hospital at Alexandria, Va., December 20.

CASE 37.—*Skin generally moist and intestinal symptoms not prominent; some delirium and pulmonary trouble; crops of rose-colored spots from 13th to 31st day; convalescence on the 37th day.*—Private Martin A. Stowell, Co. A, 3d Vt.; age 24; was admitted Oct. 1, 1861, having been sick since September 24 with pain in the head, back and limbs, and diarrhœa. Quinine had been taken. On the day after admission he was looking natural although his face was somewhat congested; pulse 100, full and strong; skin hot and moist; tongue moist, white at the edges, dry and brown in the centre; he had some headache and abdominal tenderness. Spirit of nitre, camphor and tincture of iron were ordered. A six-grain dose of blue-pill was given on the following day, and repeated on the 4th, with two grains of extract of colocynth. On this day there was some delirium; the tongue was moist and yellow coated and the skin covered with perspiration. This was followed by frequent stools on the 5th, but the diarrhœa did not persist. During the remainder of the patient's sickness the bowels were moved twice daily for two weeks and once daily thereafter to the termination of the record. Rose-spots appeared on the chest on the 6th, the tongue became red at the margins and brown-coated in the centre, and there was slight tenderness in the right iliac region. More rose-spots erupted on the 8th; the tongue became dry, red and cracked, and there was tenderness in the left iliac and umbilical regions with borborygmus. On the 11th a few rose-spots appeared. On this day turpentine emulsion was prescribed. Delirium returned on the 13th and continued at times until the 18th, during which time the tongue, skin and pulse were unaltered, although a slight cough was developed. But on the 18th the tongue became slightly moist, and next day it was moist and clean, the pulse 72, regular, the skin of natural temperature although still showing some rose-colored spots, the appetite good, the abdomen tender and tympanitic over the transverse colon. Some rose-spots appeared on the 24th. On the 30th the patient was dressed and sitting up. On November 1 he was transferred to Annapolis, Md. [whence he was discharged on the 29th because of debility].

CASE 38.—*Delirium and rose-colored spots on the 9th and following days; intestinal symptoms not severe. A favorable change on the 16th day is interrupted by the occurrence of pneumonia; improvement on the 32d day.*—Private Hiram Billington, Co. F, 2d Me.; age 29; admitted Oct. 7, 1861. Diagnosis—typhoid fever. He was taken with headache on Oct. 1 and with pain in the back on the 3d, but had no chill, diarrhœa nor eruption. On the evening of the 7th he was somewhat dull, his face flushed dark-red, pupils dilated, head hot and painful in the temporal regions where the arteries throbbed strongly; tongue red at the tip and coated in the middle; skin hot and moist; he had pain in the back, slight cough, abdominal tenderness and slight relaxation of the bowels; pulse 100. Cold water was applied to the head and five grains each of calomel and jalap given at once. Next day he had two thin stools, his tongue was cleaning and his pulse lowered to 90, but to the headache, flushed face and other symptoms of the previous day some deafness was added. Quinine was ordered. The dilatation of the pupils continued on the 9th with increasing dimness of vision and muscæ volitantes; the patient muttered in his sleep, and even when awake his mind was at times disturbed; he had a dry cough and pain in the chest, but his respiration was not accelerated; his bowels were moved twice, and he had acute tenderness in both iliac regions but no borborygmus nor tympanites; his skin was hot and moist and showed a few rose-colored spots on the chest and abdomen; his tongue was quite red, moist and clean, and he had anorexia and great thirst; pulse 88; urine chemically and microscopically normal. He was very drowsy on the 10th and had violent delirium in the afternoon. Next day a few more rose-spots came out, the skin became warm and dry and the tongue very dry, hard and fissured; two thin stools were passed with gurgling but no tympanites. On the 12th the red spots had become darker in color; there was less delirium, but the eyes were somewhat suffused and the expression stupid. Turpentine emulsion and spirit of Mindererus and of nitre were given. On the 13th the mind was clear and the countenance natural, but there was some dizziness at times; pulse 80, steady; skin soft and warm; tongue dry in the centre, moist at the edges, quite pale and slightly coated; the anorexia continued, but the thirst was lessened; three stools were passed. The bowels were moved but once on the 14th and were quiet on the 15th, on which day a few more rose-spots appeared. During the night he slept well, and on the 16th the skin was moist and warm; the tongue cleaning from tip and edges but still coated in the centre; the bowels continued quiet. Citrate of iron and quinine was given. During the ten days which followed there was but little change in the patient's condition; the bowels were quiet or moved once daily, with more or less of tenderness; the skin was warm and moist in the day-time and frequently bathed in perspiration at night, and the tongue was moist; but on the 25th, after a sleepless night, the tongue became dry and fissured, and complaint was made of cough and pain in the præcordia, near which submucous and sibilant râles were heard. A blister was applied, and on the 27th one drachm of Epsom salt and a half grain of tartar emetic were given three times daily. Next day there was mucous expectoration with dulness over the lower part of the left lung, and the patient became delirious. Brandy-punch was substituted for the tartar emetic mixture. On the 29th the patient was very drowsy, moaned frequently and muttered in his delirium; his tongue was coated with scales, dry in the centre, pale and moist at the edges; the teeth and gums were thickly covered with sordes; the skin was hot and moist; pulse 96; respiration 33, short, quick and somewhat labored; râles were heard in the lower parts of the lungs, and to a less extent in the upper parts; the expectoration was rust-colored; the bowels were moved twice and were tender and tympanitic. Calomel and opium in repeated doses were ordered on the 30th. On the 31st there was much cough with rusty sputa. A slight improvement was manifested on November 1. He slept well during the following night, and on the morning of the 2d looked bright although very weak; some thirst continued, but there was a slight appetite, and the teeth, gums and lips were clean; the tongue was moist, deeply fissured and covered with white patches; the urine contained a trace of albumen. Slight salivation occurred on the 4th, on which day the urine was found to be normal. The last entry with regard to the case, dated on the 7th, shows the patient as having rested well during the preceding night and as being bright and cheerful at the morning visit, the pulse 88 and of good strength, the skin soft and warm, the tongue soft, moist, fissured and coated; some cough continued and the bowels were moved twice, but there was no tenderness. He was transferred to hospital at Alexandria, Va., on December 20.

CASE 39.—*Pneumonia occurring after the appearance of profuse perspiration and rose-spots.*—Private Warren G. Butler, Co. I, 2d Me.; age 22; was admitted March 2, 1862. Diagnosis—pneumonia. This man had measles with severe sore throat in September, 1861. On the 4th he had headache and deafness; his cheeks were flushed and hot; pulse weak and rapid; skin hot and moist, showing on the abdomen some eruption, which disappeared on pressure; tongue dry and coated; two watery stools were passed; cough was troublesome, the respiration natural. Next day there was profuse perspiration and great thirst, the tongue remaining dry and coated; the bowels were constipated and the patient suffered from tormina and frequent nausea, tinnitus aurium and dizziness; the breathing became rapid and the cough aggravated. Ten grains of calomel were given with three of jalap. On the following day there was much tendency to stupor; four watery stools were passed during the night, after which the bowels became quiet. Little change occurred during the next two or three days. On the 10th profuse perspiration occurred; the expectorated matters were exceedingly viscid. Milk-punch, cod-liver oil and carbonate of ammonia were given. On the 11th the skin was natural, the pulse rapid and weak, the tongue moist, clean and tremulous, but the appetite remained poor; three watery stools were passed and the cough continued. During the next two days the quantity of the sputa diminished. On the 13th there was occasional nausea, and on the 14th the deafness was increased, although otherwise the patient seemed better, as the bowels were regular, the skin natural, the cough lessened and the sputa less viscid and more frothy. The deafness increased until the 19th, after which it lessened; the cough prevented sleep at night and the appetite did not return; the tongue was clean but unnaturally red in co.or. On the 25th, the last day on which the symptoms were entered, the appetite was improving. The patient was furloughed on April 8.

CASE 40.—*Pneumonia precedes the febrile attack, which is not characterized by severe symptoms.*—Private Elijah Marsh, Co. D, 7th Wis. Vols., was admitted Oct. 30, 1861. Diagnosis—typhoid fever. On October 9 he had pain in the bowels but no diarrhœa, pain in the chest and cough with rusty sputa. On the 27th he had a chill followed by some fever, but without headache or confusion of mind, epistaxis or diarrhœa. On admission the skin was husky, tongue dry and smooth, teeth blackened, pulse 80; there was difficulty of swallowing from soreness of the fauces; he had two thin yellowish stools with acute tenderness in the right iliac region, but no tympanites nor gurgling; he had little appetite and was very weak; some cough was also present. Turpentine emulsion and whiskey-punch were prescribed. Next day he had soreness in the bones, occasional dizziness and mental dulness. On November 1 the tongue became moist, clean at the tip and edges but covered with a grayish fur at the base; on this day he expectorated some blood. There was some headache on the 2d; but the patient slept well on the 3d, and next day there was moisture and sudamina on the skin, while the tongue had again become dry and brown and there was much abdominal tenderness; two stools were obtained on this day by means of castor oil. The tongue on the 6th became again moist and clean at the tip and edges and the skin dry; two offensive stools were passed; there was some cough and the respirations at this time were increased to 34 per minute; two rose-colored spots were discovered on the chest. The record gives no further details, closing with the statement that the patient was returned to duty on December 1.

CASE 41.—*Increasing drowsiness; deafness; delirium; relaxed bowels; no eruption. Killed on the 12th day by springing from a window to the ground.*—Private Henry Hickman, Co. B, 83d Pa. Vols.; age 20; was admitted March 2, 1862. Diagnosis—typhoid fever. He became sick on February 23 with headache, chilliness, cough and pains in the limbs, for which Epsom salt was given. On admission he had much pain in the right side; he slept fairly at night, but was drowsy during the day; he had much thirst, slightly flushed cheeks, dejected countenance, full and rapid pulse, hot and dry skin, a moist tongue coated in the centre and one thin scanty stool; his respiration was hurried. A blister was applied over the right lung; three-fifths of a grain of calomel and one-tenth of a grain of opium were given every hour. The drowsiness increased on the 5th and there was some deafness. Twenty-four grains of quinine were directed to be taken during the day. He became delirious on the 6th, and at night rose from bed, sprang from a window and was killed by the fall.

CASE 42.—*Deafness; delirium; diarrhœa; cough; eruption; death on 20th day from pulmonary congestion.*—Private C. A. Bartlette, Co. H, 5th Vt. Vols.; age 23; was admitted Nov. 1, 1861. Diagnosis—typhoid fever. His illness began about October 15 with pain in the back and limbs, anorexia and diarrhœa. On November 2 he was wakeful, his eyes dull, face congested, pulse 100, skin hot and dry, showing the characteristic eruption, tongue dry, red at the tip and edges and coated yellow in the centre; he was very deaf and had buzzing in the ears, much right iliac tenderness and some cough with yellowish sputa. Next day he was stupid and delirious, frequently attempting to leave his bed; his pulse was imperceptible and his breathing laborious. He died on this day. Turpentine, milk-punch and beef-essence were prescribed, with sinapisms to the abdomen.

CASE 43.—*Delirium; diarrhœa; iliac tenderness; no rose-colored spots; coma; death on 29th day.*—Private William Etzel, Co. C, 2d Pa. Cav.; age 29; was admitted Nov. 5, 1861. Diagnosis—typhoid fever. He had been in good health until October 22, when he was seized with chills followed by fever, epistaxis, pains in the back and limbs, lassitude, anorexia and thirst. On the 6th his countenance was anxious, eyes dull and suffused, face congested, pulse 95, skin hot, tongue slightly moist, red at the tip and edges, coated white in the centre, appetite good, thirst considerable; he was somewhat deaf and spoke in a whisper; one stool was passed during the previous twenty-four hours, and there was much iliac tenderness with some tympanites; the respirations were 20 per minute and there was some cough. One drachm of emulsion of turpentine was prescribed, to be taken every four hours. On the 8th the tongue was dry and yellow in the centre and the teeth covered with sordes; he slept well and had a good appetite. He became dull and stupid on the 10th and had three stools with much tenderness and tympanites, but no cough. On the 16th he was delirious and constantly picking at the bed-clothes. The diarrhœa continued, the tongue being moist and yellow-coated, pulse 90, skin hot; coma supervened, followed by death on the 19th.

CASE 44.—*Date of onset not defined; diarrhœa; headache; wakefulness; mental dulness; eruption; cough; inflammation of parotid; death 13 days after admission.*—Private John Kuenzle, Co. I, 35th Pa. Vols.; age 29; was admitted Nov. 5, 1861. Diagnosis—typhoid fever. He had been attacked some time before with chills followed by fever, headache, anorexia, thirst and diarrhœa. On the 6th he was wakeful, eyes suffused, cheeks slightly injected, pulse 100, skin hot and showing a few rose-spots on the chest, tongue dry and coated brown in the centre, teeth black with sordes; his appetite was poor and he had slight headache and tenderness in the parotid region; the bowels were relaxed and the abdomen tympanitic. Emulsion of turpentine was given every four hours; twelve grains of quinine and astringents were ordered, with Dover's powder at night. Next day the tongue was red at the tip and edges, brown in the centre and slightly moist; the quinine was repeated. He continued in this condition and under treatment by quinine until the 10th, when some cough was recorded. Next day he was dull mentally, and the cough was accompanied with white frothy sputa. No further details are given. He died on the 17th.

CASE 45.—*Diarrhœa; cough; sordes; rose-spots on 8th day, succeeded by others on the 11th, 14th and 17th days; deafness; delirium; epistaxis; otorrhœa on 22d day, with relief to all symptoms; death from pneumonia on the 31st day.*—Private Z. McLaughlin, Co. A, 3d Pa. Cav.; age 18; was admitted Oct. 20, 1861. Diagnosis—typhoid fever. He had been healthy until Oct. 14, when he was seized with chills followed by fever and sweating. On admission he had epistaxis, diarrhœa, anorexia, thirst and cough. Next day his eyes were dull and slightly injected; pulse 94 and quick; skin hot and dry, presenting a profusion of colored spots on the chest and some on the abdomen; tongue slightly moist, red at the tip and edges but coated white in the centre; lips black with sordes; two stools were passed during the twenty-four hours; there was some meteorism and also a slight cough. Tincture of iron was prescribed. Next day eight stools were passed, and there was some cough with expectoration of tenacious mucus. Turpentine emulsion, lead, tannin and opium were prescribed. The diarrhœa, which was attended with much tympanites, became checked in the course of a few days and the bowels thereafter remained quiet or with not more than one movement daily; the skin continued hot and dry throughout. Fresh crops of rose-colored spots appeared on the 24th, 26th and 30th, and were reported on November 2 as fading and unelevated; but on the 3d and 5th the chest is noted as covered with sudamina. Deafness was recorded on October 24; buzzing in the ears on the 27th; epistaxis and delirium on the 29th, the former recurring on the 31st and on November 3 and 4. On October 30 the patient was kept from sleeping by the cough, and there was much delirium, deafness and tinnitus; at this time the tongue was dry and its papillæ prominent. On November 1 the tongue was swollen, dry and brown. On the 3d the deafness was very great, but a discharge occurred from the ear, and with this the tongue became moist and the deafness lessened. On the 4th, when the last attack of epistaxis occurred, the pulse became so faint that it could scarcely be counted; but the appetite improved. On the 5th the tongue was moist and yellowish, pulse 100 and feeble; there was no abdominal tenderness and less cough. On the 8th the pulse was 105 and the respiration 22. Next day the pulse was 120. Death took place on the 12th with pneumonic symptoms.

CASE 46.—*Diarrhœa; drowsiness and deafness; bronchial and pneumonic accompaniments; rose-colored spots on 17th and vibices on 25th day; otorrhœa; pains in the legs; death on the 122d day.*—Private Mark Warner, Co. E, 1st Pa. Art.; age 26; was taken sick Sept. 1, 1861, with pain in the back and bones, headache and chills, and was admitted on the 16th. Diagnosis—typhoid fever. On admission his pulse was 94; tongue smooth and dry in the middle, moist at the edges; skin hot and moist; cheeks flushed; eyes dusky; bowels loose and tender; he had headache and was dull mentally. Catechu was used. Next day the characteristic rose-colored spots appeared on the chest and abdomen and sibilant and sonorous râles were heard over the chest, especially on the left side. Whiskey-punch and turpentine emulsion were prescribed. On the 18th the patient was drowsy and had acute tenderness in the abdomen and tympanites, although the bowels were quiet. An enema of soap-suds was administered. On the 19th the skin was moist and the mind less obtuse, the bowels loose, the tympanites reduced, but the tenderness was not lessened. The respirations were increased to 30 on the 20th; bronchitic sounds were heard over the whole of the chest, and a part of the lower lobe of the right lung was consolidated. Dover's powder was given. On the 21st the pulse was 108, soft and weak; skin hot and dry, showing a few fresh rose-colored spots; decubitus dorsal with flexed limbs; tongue smooth, glossy, dry; bowels relaxed, tender and tympanitic in the iliac regions; the patient was somewhat deaf, and complained of pains in the limbs. Vibices appeared on the skin on the 25th and 29th, sudamina on the 27th. The tongue became clean on the 26th and the appetite returned on the 30th, the chest symptoms meanwhile gradually becoming relieved; the pulse, however, continued accelerated, 100 to 112. On October 7 a discharge from the ear was treated with a solution of nitrate of silver; but it became more profuse and persisted up to the close of the detailed record. On the 9th the patient suffered much from pain in the legs, which were greatly emaciated; sponging with alcohol gave temporary relief; this pain also continued to the close of the record on October 17. After this date the only entry made was the announcement of death from typhoid fever on December 31.

CASE 47.—*Severe diarrhœa at the onset; delirium and great prostration; improvement on the 12th day coincident with eruption and epistaxis; recurrence of severe symptoms on the 33d day, and death on the 36th.*—Private F. Taylor, Co. I, 2d Mich. Vols.; age 23; was admitted Aug. 16, 1861, with rheumatism. He improved rapidly till Sept. 6, when he was seized with a severe diarrhœa, fever and pains in the head and bones. Sugar of lead, tannin and opium were prescribed. On the 11th tinnitus aurium, muscæ volitantes, slight deafness and headache were among the symptoms; the skin was hot and dry, pulse 116 and weak, tongue coated; seven stools were passed. On the 12th emulsion of turpentine was prescribed. On the 13th the tongue was dry and brown and the patient muttered in his sleep. He complained much of rheumatic pains in his bones; his bowels were moved five times during the night and nine times during the day. Beef-essence and brandy were given. He perspired much on the 15th, and the urine passed involuntarily. On the 16th he was very weak and had a cadaverous look; his tongue was dry, brown, glossy and red at the tip; the diarrhœa continued. On the 17th he was much prostrated, somnolent and indifferent to surrounding objects, but the bladder was more under control and the stools less frequent. He had epistaxis during the night, and next day the tongue became moist and clean in patches and some rose-colored spots appeared on the abdomen. He was brighter on the 19th, free from delirium, but with some headache, dizziness and deafness; the tongue was clean, dry, glossy and protruded with difficulty. On the 20th the eyes were bright, face pale and sunken, pulse 90 and weak, skin warm and moist, tongue dry and brown but red at the tip and sides, teeth and lips clean; he had some appetite; one stool was passed and the iliac regions were tender. He continued in this condition, the bowels comparatively quiet,—occasional headache, dizziness and slight deafness being the only cerebral symptoms until October 8, when diarrhœa again set in with delirium, dulness, deafness, great prostration and profuse sweating, ending in death on the 11th. A copious eruption of rose-spots appeared on September 24, vibices on the 28th, with fresh and numerous outcrops of the latter on October 4 and 8.

CASE 48.—*Probable relapse four months after primary attack. Diarrhœa; abdominal tenderness; eruptions; sordes; delirium; death.*—Private William Boardman, Co. D, 1st Pa. Rifles; age 29; was admitted Oct. 10, 1861. He stated that he had been sick since June, when he had an attack of enteric fever. On admission he had headache and was anxious looking, his eyes dull, cheeks flushed, pulse 90, quick and feeble, skin hot and dry, tongue slightly moist, red at the tip and edges, black and fissured in the centre; his appetite was fair. Dover's powder was prescribed. Next day he was reported as having had four movements of the bowels; his tongue had become white in the centre and his skin covered profusely with an eruption the character of which is not stated. Punch and tincture of iron were given. The eruption is mentioned on the following day and again on the 21st. During the progress of the case the bowels were relaxed, two stools being passed daily. The appetite continued good until the day of death. There was great tenderness in the abdomen, which was at first especially marked in the left iliac region, but afterwards became associated with various regions as the epigastric, umbilical, the track of the transverse and descending colon and on one occasion the right side; the tenderness was usually accompanied by meteorism and gurgling. The skin was hot and dry throughout except on one or two days, when it was reported as very dry but not hot. The tongue was dry, red, fissured and glazed, the lips covered with sordes and the teeth with tenacious mucus. On the 16th there was some headache with occasional delirium of a mild character, which afterwards became more continuous. On the 23d the patient is reported as having slept well as usual; his countenance was pale, face pinched, lips parched, skin and tongue dry, pulse 95 and feeble, the abdomen flat. Turpentine emulsion, cod-liver oil and quinine were prescribed. He died during the night.

CASE 49.—*Relapse. Head symptoms not marked; rose-spots from the 41st to the 59th day; vibices on 50th; bowel affection not prominent until cessation of perspirations; returned to duty in 160 days.*—Private M. R. Taggart, Co. A, 9th Pa. Vols.; age 34; was admitted Oct. 10, 1861, having been sick since Sept. 1 with what had been regarded as enteric fever, for which quinine had been given. On admission his eyes were dull, face congested, pulse 110, quick and full, skin hot and dry, tongue moist, red at tip and edges, coated white in the centre, appetite poor; he had some cough. Dover's powder was given. He slept badly during the night and next day was stupid and dull-eyed; a few rose-colored spots were found on the chest and many on the abdomen; the pulse was 100 and feeble; his bowels had not been moved. Tincture of iron was ordered to be taken three times daily and extract of senna in the evening. He slept well, and on the morning of the 12th the pulse was found to have fallen to 90; the eyes were bright and the flush had disappeared from the face; the bowels had not been moved, but there was much tenderness in the right iliac region. On the 13th the patient was covered with a profuse perspiration; pulse 120 and feeble; a slight epistaxis had occurred and one stool had been obtained. Tincture of digitalis and sweet spirit of nitre were ordered to be taken four times during the day. The perspiration continued on the 14th, and the appetite was found to be improved. Five grains of quinine were given every two hours. On the 15th the pulse had fallen to 90 and was more regular, the skin was hot but somewhat moist, the tongue dry, the appetite poor; the bowels had been moved twice. On the morning of the 16th the skin was dry, but there had been a profuse perspiration during the night; the tongue was red and clean but dry, and the appetite poor; one stool was passed, and the patient was troubled with cough. Profuse perspiration recurred nightly until the 22d. On the 17th the tongue became moist and covered with white patches. Next day a few rose-spots appeared on the abdomen; two stools were passed, and there was slight umbilical tenderness. On the 19th the profuse perspiration continued during the day; the pulse rose to 120; tympanites and borborygmus were present but no stool was passed. Several rose-spots and vibices appeared on the abdomen on the 20th; pulse 86; two stools were passed. The skin was soft and natural on the 21st, and next day the tongue was clean and moist and the appetite good. During the following week an occasional nocturnal perspiration was noted, but otherwise the condition of the patient was good. On the 29th some rose-spots appeared and three stools were passed. Four stools were recorded on the following day, and on the 31st nine stools, with dry tongue, heat of skin and accelerated pulse. Twelve stools were passed on November 1, on which day the patient was transferred to Annapolis, Md. [where his case was diagnosed typhoid fever, and terminated in a return to duty on March 19, 1862].

CASE 50.—*Diarrhœa; rose-rash; delirium; parotid inflammation; coma vigil; return of consciousness before death at end of third week.*—See case of Private Oscar Snow, Co. H, 3d Vt., No. 31 of the *post-mortem* records.

CASE 51.—*Chills; epistaxis; diarrhœa; tympanites; vibices; deafness, but no delirium or notable cerebral implication; temporary improvement followed by bed-sores, and death probably from pulmonary engorgement.*—See case of Private Benjamin Cunningham, Co. D, 86th N. Y., No. 34 of the *post-mortem* records.

SEVEN REMITTENT CASES.

CASE 52.—Private James Brown, Co. B, 26th Pa. Vols.; age 38; was attacked Aug. 20, 1861, with headache, chill and pains in the bones, and admitted Sept. 4 as a case of remittent fever, presenting constipation, anorexia and epistaxis, with high fever, the pulse being 100, the skin moist and the tongue heavily coated and of a yellowish-brown color. A dose of Epsom salt was taken at once, and quinine ordered three times daily. The bowels were moved twice during the night and once next morning, after which the pulse was found lowered to 60, the skin natural, the tongue pale, flabby and coated, and the abdomen sore. Dover's powder was given at night. The fever did not recur. The tongue continued pale, flabby and somewhat coated, but the appetite returned, and he was sent to duty on the 11th.

CASE 53.—Private James Baker, Co. D, 19th Ia. Vols., was admitted Sept. 4, 1861, having had a chill followed by fever without diarrhœa. Diagnosis—remittent fever. On the morning of the 5th his pulse was 70; skin moist and cool; tongue pale, flabby and slightly coated, and bowels loose from the action of Epsom salt; he had a dry cough with pain in the chest. Quinine was given. In the evening there was some heat of skin, but otherwise the condition of the patient was unchanged. The cough was somewhat troublesome on the 6th, but there was no fever. The tongue continued pale, flabby and more or less coated, but the appetite returned and on the 9th he was able to walk about. His bowels did not remain loose after the purgative action of the salt had ceased. No eruption appeared on the skin. He was returned to duty on the 14th.

CASE 54.—Private Frank Teats, Co. C, 5th N. Y. Cav.; age 22; was taken sick Sept. 19, 1861, with giddiness, chills, epistaxis and pain in the back, and admitted on the 23d as a case of remittent fever. His face was flushed, eyes suffused, pulse 85, quick and strong, skin hot and moist, tongue slightly white in the middle and red at the edges, appetite lost, bowels unmoved. He had headache, a slight cough and hurried respiration, 25 per minute. A small dose (one and a half drachms) of sulphate of magnesia with one-eighth of a grain of tartar emetic was given, and Dover's powder ordered to be taken at bedtime. He rested well, had one stool during the night, and next morning his countenance was natural. In the evening the face was again flushed, the eyes dull, pulse 92, tongue moist and white but with the papillæ at the tip projecting; appetite small. He had headache, cough with difficulty of expectoration, and a pain in the chest and abdomen from having taken capsicum by mistake. Six grains of quinine and three of Dover's powder were given every two hours until three such doses were taken. On the 25th there was no fever nor headache; the skin was warm and moist, the tongue moist and coated light brown, the pulse 98; the bowels were moved once; there was epistaxis at night. Next day the pulse was 78, and there was one stool with gurgling in the right iliac region and dysuria, but the cough had ceased and the appetite had returned. Extract of buchu was given. He was returned to duty on the 30th.

CASE 55.—Private Samuel Cunningham, Co. H, 12th Pa. Vols., was taken about Sept. 1, 1861, with weakness, headache, nausea and pain in the bones, and was admitted on the 5th as a case of remittent fever. His tongue was flabby, white-coated and red at the edges, pulse 90, face flushed, skin moist and hot, bowels constipated. His fever was reported to be worse in the morning than in the evening. A dose of Epsom salt was followed by six large thin stools. Quinine was given. Next day he had two small stools, and on the 7th his bowels were quiet. On this day the morning pulse was 84, the evening 68, full on both occasions; and there was headache with flushed face, a pale white-coated tongue and anorexia. Dover's powder was given at night. On the 8th the morning pulse was 66, the tongue coated white in the middle, the face slightly flushed and there was some giddiness. In the evening the pulse had risen to 74, the tongue was clean, and an eruption, stated as owing to the poison of the rhus toxicodendron, appeared in confluent patches. After this he rested well and had no fever. Bicarbonate of soda was applied to the eruption, which faded in four or five days. On the 12th the patient's appetite was good and he was walking about. On the 13th he was transferred to hospital at Baltimore, Md.

CASE 56.—Private John Hoadley, Co. B, 12th Pa. Vols., was taken with headache and pain in the bones about Aug. 29, 1861, together with a daily recurring chill and fever, and a diarrhœa causing about six stools daily. He was admitted September 5 as a case of remittent fever. The tongue was pale, flabby and coated, the face flushed, the skin warm and moist, the pulse 86, the bowels loose. A small dose of tincture of opium was given. Next day quinine was ordered, with Dover's powder at night. He had no chill after admission, but there was an evening exacerbation of fever, which on the 9th and 10th was accompanied by drowsiness and stupidity. On the morning of the 11th the remission was very marked, and in the evening the appetite became improved. On the evening of the 12th the tongue, which had been flabby and coated hitherto, became clean. The bowels were relaxed throughout the attack, but there was no tenderness except on the 9th, in the umbilical region. On this day also there was a slight cough with a stitch in the right side. The diarrhœa abated with the decline of the fever and the cleaning of the tongue. The patient was transferred to hospital at Baltimore, Md., on the 13th.

CASE 57.—Sergt. Byron Hinman, Co. G, 24th N. Y. Vols.; age 24; was admitted Sept. 25, 1861, with remittent fever which he had contracted about four weeks before. He had headache with flushed face, suffused eyes, a quick pulse, 82 per minute, and a warm but moist skin, a slight cough, anorexia and moist yellow-coated tongue. A six-grain dose of blue-pill was ordered, with Dover's powder at night. Next day there was some umbilical tenderness; sixteen grains of quinine were given in the forenoon and a small dose of castor oil; two stools were passed. On the 27th the face was not so much flushed and there was some return of appetite. The patient was dizzy and in the afternoon had a free perspiration. The quinine was repeated on the 28th, but the headache, anorexia and foul tongue were not removed until October 1, after a second mercurial dose with castor oil. He was returned to duty on the 9th.

CASE 58.—Private H. Hardridge, Co. F, 6th Wis. Vols., was admitted Oct. 30, 1861. Diagnosis—remittent fever. Since October 23 the patient had headache, weakness, pain in the back, some loss of appetite and much thirst. On the day of admission he had a slight chill followed by fever. Quinine was given. He rested well but not until after midnight, and next morning the skin was warm and moist but jaundiced, and the tongue soft, pale, moist and coated, the pulse 86 and bowels quiet. Calomel and morphia were given three times during the day. Quinine in six-grain doses three times daily was substituted on November 1 and continued until the 7th. The patient was returned to duty on the 15th.

THIRTY-FIVE TYPHOID FEVER CASES WITH MORE OR LESS EVIDENCE OF THE EXISTENCE OF MALARIAL AFFECTION.

CASE 59.—*Relapse manifested by diarrhœa, eruption, wakefulness and increased temperature.*—Sergt. George M. Cook, Co. G, 3d Mich. Vols.; age 23; was admitted Oct. 19, 1861. He had previously suffered from rheumatism, intermittent fever and enteric fever, and while convalescing from the last, about October 14, he was seized with a chill followed by fever and perspiration, wakefulness, thirst, diarrhœa and pain in the bowels. His case on admission was diagnosed typhoid fever. On the 20th he was wakeful, his eyes dull, cheeks not flushed, pulse 66, full and strong, skin somewhat above the natural temperature, tongue red, slightly moist and with a few yellowish patches in the centre, appetite poor; he had six stools with some general abdominal tenderness and tympanites. A few rose-colored spots appeared next day, but otherwise his condition was unaltered. On the 22d he slept well; the pulse rose to 74 and was regular and strong; the skin was of the natural temperature; the tongue flabby and patched with a white fur; the appetite continued poor and the diarrhœa active, the abdominal tenderness being more marked on the right side. After this the diarrhœa gradually lessened, the tongue became clean and the appetite good. Up to the end of the month he was troubled with a slight cough with yellowish expectoration. He was returned to duty Nov. 7.

CASE 60.—*Light febrile attack following intermittent fever, but not influenced specially by the action of the malarial poison; debility, drowsiness and diarrhœa.*—Teamster Edward C. Ledley, 2d Mich.; age 23; had chills and fever with diarrhœa since the middle of August, 1861, but attended to his duty as an ambulance driver until September 6, when he was admitted as a case of typhoid fever, presenting chills, increased local and general heat, anorexia, muscular debility and pain in the head and bones. On the 14th he was drowsy and had headache; pulse 78, tongue moist, red at the tip and brown in the centre, appetite returning. Next evening the headache continued and he had two stools; but after this the bowels became regular, the skin moist and warm, the tongue moist and clean, the pulse natural, the sleep sound and the appetite and strength improved. He was returned to duty on the 30th. Dover's powder and turpentine emulsion, with quinine towards the end, formed the medication.

CASE 61.—*Dizziness, wakefulness, rose-colored spots and diarrhœa; improvement about end of 2d week.*—Private A. A. Rich, Co. G, 5th Vt. Vols.; age 17; was admitted Nov. 1, 1861. Diagnosis—debility. He had been sick about a week, first with chills, afterwards with fever. On admission he was wakeful and had headache, dizziness, buzzing in the ears, anorexia, thirst, vomiting, diarrhœa and cough. Next day the wakefulness continued; pulse 100, quick, full and firm; skin hot and presenting a few rose-colored spots on the chest; there was slight headache with tinnitus aurium; the tongue was slightly moist and furred white, but red on the tip, edges and central line; the appetite was good, but there was considerable thirst; the bowels were slightly relaxed, tympanitic and tender on pressure in the umbilical and left iliac regions; there was also some cough with frothy sputa. He slept well during the following night, and on the morning of the 3d the pulse was reduced to 80, but otherwise the symptoms continued as already stated. Treatment was by sulphate of quinine and astringents. On the 6th the diarrhœa became suddenly aggravated, five stools having been passed in the twenty-four hours, accompanied with abdominal tenderness and gurgling. Next day three stools were passed and on the 8th one stool. Improvement was progressive after this, but on the 18th, when the patient was transferred to Baltimore, Md., there was still some heat of skin, with slight abdominal tenderness and some cough. [He was returned to duty Jan. 27, 1862.]

CASE 62.—*Slight diarrhœa; dizziness; rose-spots on 10th day; improvement at end of 2d week.*—Private George W. Olney, Co. A, 4th Mich.; age 18; became sick about Sept. 9, 1861, with weakness, headache, diarrhœa and slight fever without chills, and was admitted on the 16th. Diagnosis—typhoid fever. He had epistaxis; his pulse was 70 and full; skin warm and moist; tongue pale, flabby and slightly coated white; bowels quiet. Ten grains each of calomel and jalap were prescribed. He had three passages from the bowels during the night, and next day the skin was warm and sweating. Rose-colored spots appeared on the 18th, and the tongue began to clean; there was some dizziness but no mental dulness; two thin large stools were passed, and there was tenderness in the right iliac region. On the 19th the pulse was 76; tongue tremulous, pale at the edges and coated in the middle; bowels quiet; skin hot and moist. Quinine was given. Next day the skin was natural; there was no tenderness nor tympanites; the countenance was pleasant and the eyes bright. A few dark rose-colored spots appeared on the 22d. The bowels remained quiet until the 23d, when they were moved seven times, but there was no accompanying tenderness, meteorism nor gurgling; the appetite was good, the tongue pale, gray in the centre but cleaning at the tip. Opiate enemata controlled the diarrhœa and the patient improved on tonics and stimulants. He was able to walk about on October 1, when he was transferred to Annapolis, Md.

CASE 63.—*Mental dulness; rose-spots on the 9th day, disappearing on the 16th; bowel affection slightly marked.*—Private John Dickerson, Co. A, 4th Mich.; age 24; was taken about Sept. 9, 1861, with pain in the bones, back and head, fever which was said to be worst at noon, and diarrhœa. He was admitted on the 16th. Diagnosis—typhoid fever. In the evening the fever was slight; pulse 74; skin warm and dry; face flushed; tongue red at the edges, coated yellowish at the base and in the middle, moist and with prominent papillæ; a bitter taste was felt in the mouth; one stool was passed during the day, and there was some umbilical tenderness. Two grains each of calomel and jalap were given. Next day the pulse was 70 and small; the skin dry; the tongue dry, heavily coated and brownish; the cheeks flushed; the patient was weak and dull; his bowels had been moved once; a few characteristic rose-spots were seen. Quinine was ordered. During the next week there was little change in the patient's condition; his eyes were injected and half closed and he was dull and drowsy, answering questions in a low tone; the face was flushed and the skin hot, dry, husky and profusely spotted with the rose-colored eruption; the tongue, heavily coated and brown, became moist on the 19th; the bowels quiet and neither tender nor tympanitic; there was some headache with dizziness at this time. On the 22d the patient was dull; his pulse 86 and feeble; face flushed; skin hot, moist and spotted; tongue red at tip and gray in centre; he vomited once during the day and had one stool. Next day the pulse was 82 and weak, the eyes suffused, the skin warm and moist, the tongue gray in the centre and red at the tip, the bowels quiet and not tender. On the 24th the pulse was 78, the skin warm and soft, the tongue moist and slightly coated gray, the appetite good. Wine was occasionally given. He was returned to duty October 24.

CASE 64.—*Onset obscured by presence of tonsillitis; headache, deafness and tinnitus; disease marked chiefly by abdominal symptoms; diarrhœa alternating with perspirations.*—Private G. W. Conger, Co. B, 19th Ind.; age 20; was admitted Sept. 4, 1861, with a high grade of inflammatory fever, presenting marked remissions and accompanied with flushed face, bloodshot eyes, hot and moist skin, yellow-coated tongue, regular bowels, anorexia and slight tonsillitis. Quinia and a gargle were ordered. On the 7th the fever lost its remittent character and was accompanied with headache, dry tongue and frequent stools; pulse 80. Turpentine emulsion, beef-essence and milk were substituted for the quinine. On the 14th diarrhœa, tympanites and tinnitus aurium were noted; pulse 88. Dover's powder was given at night. The patient rested well and had some appetite next morning; the bowels were quiet, but the skin was hot and dry and the pulse 108; a slight eruption had appeared on the penis and scrotum. In the evening the pulse was 106, the tongue moist and slightly coated; the patient had two stools and some tympanites during the day. The Dover's powder at night was continued. On the 16th the bowels were regular and there was some appetite;

pulse 75 and skin moist. On the 17th the tongue was cleaning, the appetite good, the pulse 80 and the bowels regular. Dover's powder was continued. On the 18th the report is varied by noting abdominal tenderness with one stool, and on the 19th by dryness of skin, the tongue continuing moist, slight deafness, cough, respiration increased to 24 per minute and bowels tympanitic, slightly tender in the right iliac region and moved twice. Twelve grains of quinine were given. Copious sweating occurred during the night and sudamina appeared, the bowels again becoming regular and the respiration natural. On the evening of the 22d pain recurred in the abdomen with two stools, dryness of skin, some headache and increase of the pulse to 100. Next day two stools were again reported, but the skin had recovered its moisture and the tongue was natural. On the 24th there was slight deafness but no cough nor pain; the tongue and skin were in natural condition and the appetite good. Again on the evening of the 26th, with an acceleration of the pulse and dryness of skin, there was abdominal pain with borborygmus, followed by free perspiration during the night. From this date to October 1, when he was transferred to Annapolis, Md., the patient slept well, had a good appetite, moist and clean or yellow-patched tongue and natural skin; but there was more or less abdominal pain with from two to four stools daily.

CASE 65.—*Date of onset obscured by sequelæ of measles; deafness and tinnitus aurium; diarrhœa and rose-colored spots; convalescence.*—Private C. Mills, Co. E, 6th Wis.; age 22; had measles in August, 1861, and about September 1 was taken with chills, fever, diarrhœa, cough and headache, for which calomel and opium had been administered. He was admitted October 1. Diagnosis—typhoid fever. Turpentine emulsion and astringents were ordered. He slept but little, and nex' day was looking dull and had slight headache and congestion of the face; pulse 90, quick; skin natural; tongue moist, heavily coated brown; appetite moderate; he had a bad cough with slight expectoration; three stools were passed and micturition was difficult. Cough mixture was given with small doses of blue-pill and opium every two hours. On the 3d the skin was moist and covered on the left side of the chest and abdomen with a profusion of rose-colored spots. Next day deafness and tinnitus aurium were noted. On the 5th the pulse was 85, full, the skin cool and moist, the tongue moist and having a yellowish patch in the centre, the appetite poor; one stool was passed, and there was some tenderness in the left iliac region; respiration was natural although there was much cough and free expectoration. Four stools were passed on the 6th, six on the following day, and three daily after this until the 11th, when there was but one; during this time the expression was dull, the face somewhat congested, the tongue moist, white and flabby, and the appetite poor. On the 11th the tongue became clean and the appetite good. Tincture of iron was ordered. He slept well during the night, and next day his eyes were bright, cheeks not flushed, pulse 90, regular, skin natural, tongue moist, slightly coated white, appetite good. On the 14th he was transferred to Baltimore, Md.

CASE 66.—*Chill and remitting fever; rose-spots on 12th day; drowsiness; sordes; cough; diarrhœa and iliac tenderness; record unfinished.*—Private J. M. Foster, Co. A, 6th Wis. Vols.; age 21; was admitted Nov. 1, 1861, as a case of typhoid fever. Late in September he had measles, and on October 24 was taken with a chill followed by fever, weakness, anorexia, pain in the back and bones, nausea, vomiting and diarrhœa, which continued up to the date of his admission. He said he felt better about noontime daily. On November 2 he was dull, his eyes slightly suffused, pulse 112, quick and of fair strength, skin soft and moist, tongue soft, coated in the centre and at the tip, teeth covered with sordes; he had anorexia, much thirst and a diarrhœa of four stools daily, with some abdominal tenderness and some cough. Quinine in five-grain doses was given three times daily. Next day his condition was unchanged but on the 4th the pulse became reduced to 100 and lost its quickness and strength, the skin was hot and covered with minute rose-colored spots, the tongue moist and brown, eyes injected and the respiration labored. The patient continued dull and drowsy on the 6th, and the diarrhœa persisted, with some tenderness in both iliac regions; but the tongue appeared cleaner at the edges and the respiration was natural. On the 7th the pulse was 108 and weak, the skin dry, husky and covered with rose-colored spots, the tongue dry and brown, the gums and teeth blackened, the bowels loose, tympanitic, tender and gurgling on pressure. The record leaves the patient in this condition on the 8th, and closes with the remark that he was transferred to Philadelphia, Pa., Feb. 15, 1862.

CASE 67.—*Headache; epistaxis; hebetude; abdominal symptoms not marked; rose-spots on the 9th day, with perspirations and sudamina about the beginning of the 3d week, accompanying defervescence.*—Sergeant John Evans, Co. H, 12th Pa., had a chill on the morning of Aug. 30, 1861, followed next day by fever which increased towards evening, and was associated with headache and pains in the bones and small of the back. To these symptoms, on September 2, epistaxis, lassitude and a tendency to stupor were added; but the bowels remained regular and urination free. On the 4th he was admitted to hospital as a case of typhoid fever: pulse 78, skin hot and dry, tongue coated white, bowels constipated and tender on pressure. Two grains each of compound cathartic mass and blue-pill were given at once, with sulphate of quinia, by which the bowels were moved three times. He rested well during the night, and on the morning of the 5th his pulse was 80, skin warm and moist, but his tongue was dry, red, coated and flabby, and he complained of pain in the limbs. During the day he had three small thin stools, and in the evening the pulse was 72, the tongue red, flabby and coated white, the skin dry and warm; there was also some dizziness. A ten-grain dose of Dover's powder was given. During the progress of the disease there was but little variation in the pulse; it did not go over 80, and on the 11th fell to 64, coincident with a warm moist skin and the development of an abundant crop of sudamina on the abdomen and shoulders. The skin was warm and generally dry, but sometimes it felt moist; it was covered with perspiration on the 11th and 14th, after which latter date it was generally either cool or natural. The tongue became brown-coated and dry on the 7th coincident with the occurrence of anorexia and some obtuseness of the intelligence followed by drowsiness; it became moist again, but very red and coated on the next day, when also the appetite showed signs of return, and a few rose-spots were noted on the abdomen, with slight tenderness and borborygmus in the right iliac fossa, but it was not until after the appearance of the sudamina on the 15th and 16th that the mental hebetude was removed. The bowels were not notably loose at any time save immediately after admission, as already related; but there was a tendency to laxness, as two drachms of castor oil on the 9th produced two thin stools:—on the other hand, ten grains each of calomel and jalap on the 14th, after yielding three thin stools, created no further disturbance of the intestinal tract. During the night of the 6th he had a colic, which was relieved by the application of mustard. On the 16th, as a slightly jaundiced hue of the face was apparent, small doses, two grains each, of blue-pill and quinia were given with port wine three times daily. After the 20th the patient did some light duty about the ward, and was returned to his command October 5.

CASE 68.—*Mental dulness; sordes; vibices; right iliac and hepatic tenderness, but no diarrhœa nor rose-colored spots; improvement about the end of the 3d week.*—Private W. Patchen, Co. F, 74th N. Y. Vols.; age 18; was admitted Nov. 2, 1861, having been taken sick two weeks before with chills, anorexia and pain in the back. The case on admission was diagnosed typhoid fever. On the 3d the patient was dull and stupid, his eyes suffused, cheeks congested, pulse 100, skin hot and dry, tongue dry and clean, lips and teeth covered with sordes, appetite lost; there was some tenderness and gurgling in the right iliac region: twelve grains of quinine were given at once, followed after a time by a half-ounce dose of castor oil and by turpentine emulsion every three hours. Next day one stool was passed; the patient had some cough and hepatic tenderness, and vibices appeared on the chest. On the 6th he had tinnitus aurium. On the 8th he seemed better; his tongue was red at the tip and edges and coated white in the centre; his bowels had been moved but once since the day following his admission. He improved gradually after this, and was transferred to Baltimore, Md., December 3.

CASE 69.—*Flabby tongue; gastric irritability; recurring epistaxis; diarrhœa and general abdominal tenderness; headache; delirium; sordes; prostration; inflammation of parotid; rose-spots and ribices; discharged on account of typhoid fever.*—Private Patrick Devine, Co. K, 3d Vt.; age 18; was admitted Oct. 1, 1861, with typhoid fever. He had been taken, September 26, with headache, chills, fever, diarrhœa and epistaxis (which last had been of frequent occurrence during the previous month), and on the 28th with retention of urine. On October 2 the patient's face was congested; his eyes dull and heavy; pulse 112, quick and strong; skin hot and dry; tongue moist and coated brown; teeth covered with sordes; stomach irritable and unable to retain food or medicine; he had headache and pain in the back, with tenderness over the whole of the abdomen and slight borborygmus. Repeated doses of calomel and opium, with turpentine emulsion, were given. Quinine, extract of buchu and sweet spirit of nitre were administered on the 4th, and beef-essence, milk-punch and astringents on the 6th, as diarrhœa began to be a prominent symptom. On the 7th the pulse was 90 and strong, the skin natural, the tongue slightly moist, red at the tip and edges, heavily coated brown and fissured in the center and at the base; eight stools were passed, and micturition was difficult. Rose-colored spots appeared on the following day; there was some mental dulness with headache and occasional delirium; cough was troublesome, and the diarrhœa was accompanied with general abdominal tenderness which was especially acute in the right iliac region. Epistaxis occurred on the 11th and next day the bowels were quiet. With the moderation of the diarrhœa the tongue became flabby and remained dry and brown-coated in the centre, although the appetite improved. Epistaxis recurred on the 14th with some headache and delirium; the tip and edges of the tongue became red, the lips covered with sordes and the bowels relaxed to five stools daily. Next day the nose bled again, some rose-colored spots appeared, and the patient was unable to protrude his tongue on account of swelling of the parotid gland. Epistaxis, profuse perspiration and vibices on the neck and chest, with headache and increased swelling of the parotid, but no delirium, were noted on the 17th; the diarrhœa continued with general tenderness and some meteorism, especially marked in the right iliac region. Vibices were numerous on the abdomen on the 18th, and fresh rose-spots appeared on the 20th, 22d, 23d, 25th and 28th: during these days the diarrhœa moderated, but the tenderness continued, being sometimes general and at others specially marked in the umbilical and right or left iliac regions; some headache and cough were noted but no delirium; the appetite was good, the skin generally moist, and the tongue moist and but slightly coated; the patient continued unable to protrude his tongue. Epistaxis recurred on the 28th and on November 2d, 4th, 6th and 8th, during which days there was some heat and dryness of skin, with headache and tinnitus, relaxation of the bowels, abdominal tenderness and coated tongue, the appetite continuing good and the cough subsiding; pulse 80 to 100. No change took place in his condition up to the 18th, when he was transferred to Annapolis, Md. [whence he was discharged on the 29th on account of typhoid fever].

CASE 70.—*Severe diarrhœa and abdominal pain; free perspirations; mental dulness; rose-spots from 15th to 30th day; tongue flabby and yellow-coated; improvement in 5th week.*—Private Byron Steinback, Co. A, 1st Pa. Art.; age 21; became affected on Sept. 25, 1861, with headache, pain in the back and limbs and diarrhœa, on October 2 with chills and fever, and on the 6th with epistaxis and some retention of urine. He was admitted on the 9th, on the evening of which day he was found to be weak, having had ten stools, with general abdominal tenderness and some retention of urine; a few rose-spots were scattered on the chest and abdomen; the face was slightly flushed, the eyes injected and suffused and their lids closed, the skin of natural temperature, pulse 80, tongue moist, red at the tip and edges, coated yellow on the dorsum, appetite deficient; he had some cough and pain in the limbs. On the 10th there was much thirst; the skin was hot and dry; four new rose-spots had appeared; the tongue was moist and flabby, red at the tip and edges and heavily coated yellow in the centre; six stools were passed. Tincture of iron was given three times daily. On the 11th the skin was covered with perspiration, the rose-spots had increased in number, the bowels were moved twice and there was tenderness at the umbilicus and in the iliac regions, markedly on the right side, with some tympanites and borborygmus. Turpentine emulsion was given every three hours. On the 12th the patient was reported as having slept well; he was dull and stupid; his eyes dull and injected; cheeks somewhat flushed; pulse 75, regular; skin hot, dry and profusely covered with rose-colored spots; tongue slightly moist, red at the tip and edges, coated yellow in the centre; lips and teeth covered with sordes; appetite poor; his bowels were moved five times, and there was much abdominal tenderness, notably about the umbilicus. Astringents were given, but the diarrhœa continued. On the 15th, 16th and 17th profuse perspirations were noted, and rose-spots, perceptible to the touch, continued to erupt. A few of these spots appeared on the forehead on the 22d and a few more on the chest two days later. On the 22d the diarrhœa was controlled: one stool only was passed instead of three, four or more, as on previous days; but the general abdominal and extreme umbilical tenderness was not relieved until some days later. Meanwhile the tongue became clean, the skin natural and the appetite good. The cough, which had affected the patient more or less from his admission, now assumed prominence as a symptom, and was accompanied with mucous expectoration. He was transferred November 1 to Annapolis, Md. [whence he was discharged from the service on the 29th because of debility].

CASE 71.—*Headache; deafness; diarrhœa; cough; rose-colored spots following paroxysmal fever.*—Private F. Cameron, Co. F, 74th N.Y.; age 23; was admitted Nov. 2, 1861, as a case of typhoid fever. He became sick about October 1 with chills, fever and sweating, epistaxis, headache, anorexia, thirst, diarrhœa and irritability of stomach. When admitted his eyes were dull and somewhat injected, cheeks slightly flushed, pulse 75, regular but weak; a few rose-spots on the chest; tongue red, dry and fissured in the centre; lips and teeth covered with sordes; appetite poor; he was a little deaf and had buzzing in his ears; one stool was passed with much right iliac and umbilical tenderness and tympanites; he had also a slight cough with some whitish expectoration. He slept none during the night and had but one stool on the 3d; the tenderness lessened and the cough ceased. Beef-essence, punch and turpentine emulsion were given. After this the bowels continued quiet, and on the 7th the tongue began to clean and the appetite to return. He was transferred to Annapolis on the 8th [whence he was discharged for disability on the 29th].

CASE 72.—*Cerebral manifestations slight; rose-spots on the 8th day with successive crops to 22d day; diarrhœa ceasing on occurrence of free nocturnal perspirations on 17th day.*—Private Peter Martin, Co. B, 3d Vt. Vols.; age 18; was seized Sept. 28, 1861, with chills, fever and pain in the head, back and limbs, for which he was admitted October 3. His pulse was 85, full and strong; skin natural; tongue moist and furred yellowish. He was somewhat dull and had pain in the head, anorexia and relaxed meteorized bowels. Blue-pill was given with opium every two hours. Rose-colored spots appeared on the chest and abdomen on the 5th, and on the 7th were very profuse. The tongue, from being covered with a thick yellow fur, became red at the tip and margins, remaining coated on the dorsum. The diarrhœa caused three or four stools daily, and was accompanied by tympanites and right iliac, umbilical and, indeed, general abdominal tenderness. Sixteen grains of quinine were given on the forenoon of the 7th. The headache, anorexia and other symptoms as stated continued until the 14th, when, after a free perspiration during the night, the pulse fell to 66, the bowels became quiet and the appetite returned; the tongue, however, remained coated heavily with a moist yellow fur at the base and centre. A small dose of blue-pill was given on the 16th, but the fur was not removed until the 23d. Rose-spots appeared on the 16th and again on the 19th. Nocturnal perspirations were recorded on the 17th and 19th. Some cough occurred during the progress of the case. The patient was returned to duty on the 28th.

CASE 73.—*Dizziness and slight headache; diarrhœal tendency not marked; rose-colored spots on the 10th, 19th and 30th days, and vibices on 19th.*—Corporal J. B. Morgan, Co. E, 1st Pa. Rifles; age 24; was healthy until about Oct. 1, 1861, when he had chills, fever and profuse sweating, with pain in the head, dizziness, epistaxis, pain in back, limbs, shoulder and chest, some cough, diarrhœa and retention of urine. He was admitted October 10 as a case of typhoid fever. The pulse on admission was 90 and quick; the skin hot and dry, exhibiting a profuse eruption; the tongue was slightly moist, red and clean; the appetite poor; the bowels unmoved but somewhat tender and tympanitic; the patient had slight headache, cough and pain in micturition. Wine and cinchona bark were ordered. The eruption faded, but no other change took place until the 13th, when the tongue became dry. One ounce of Epsom salt was given. Three stools were passed on each of the two following days, and the tenderness became more marked in the right iliac region; otherwise there was no change. The Epsom salt was repeated on the 16th. Three stools were passed on the 17th and one on the 18th. Vibices appeared on the chest and rose-spots on the abdomen on the 19th. A few more rose-spots were detected on the 30th. During this period the skin was generally of the natural temperature, the tongue moist, red and clean and the appetite good. On November 1 the patient was transferred to Annapolis, Md., where his case was entered as one of debility, and whence he was returned to duty on December 2.

CASE 74.—*Dulness and drowsiness for a day or two; diarrhœa and dry skin persisting; rose-colored spots and vibices; tongue flabby and coated yellow; moist skin, and convalescence on 38th day.*—Private William Morrison, Co. E, 1st Pa. Rifles; age 38; had a chill about Oct. 1, 1861, followed by fever and perspiration, slight headache, anorexia and some cough. He was admitted on the 10th as a case of typhoid fever. Next day he was dull and drowsy, but without any sign of congestion about the face; his pulse was 80 and feeble, skin hot and dry, tongue slightly moist, red at the tip and edges and heavily coated with yellowish fur in the centre; he had intense abdominal tenderness, but only one stool during the previous twenty-four hours. Emulsion of turpentine and tincture of iron were ordered in repeated doses. On the 12th the eruption appeared; the skin was of natural temperature, the tongue slightly moist but coated with yellowish fur, and the appetite good; two stools were passed, and the patient had some abdominal tenderness and cough. He slept well and next day was brighter mentally. From this time till the end of the month his general condition remained unchanged. The tongue was flabby and always more or less yellow-furred; the appetite usually good; the bowels moved from one to seven times daily, with general and occasionally umbilical and left iliac tenderness, and with slight tympanites on the 10th and 29th; the skin, usually hot and dry, showed some vibices on the 19th and 20th; on the 22d rose-colored spots appeared on the face and did not fade until the 29th, when some epistaxis occurred; there was more or less cough with some mucous expectoration; the pulse beat generally about 75 per minute. On the 30th quinine was ordered in three-grain doses every two hours. Next day the pulse was lowered from 80 to 60, and the diarrhœa increased from one to seven stools; otherwise the patient's condition appeared unaltered. Astringents were given, and in the course of four or five days the diarrhœa became lessened to one or two stools daily. On November 4 a boil appeared on the patient's forehead. On the 7th the skin is recorded for the first time as being moist; pulse 75; tongue cleaning; appetite good; bowels tender and moved twice. Cod-liver oil and wine were ordered on the 10th. The daily record of symptoms ceases on the 11th. The patient was transferred to Alexandria, Va., December 20.

CASE 75.—*Successive crops of rose-colored spots from 10th to 36th day; perspirations; diarrhœal tendency slight; gastric irritability; convalescence on 38th day.*—Private S. B. French, Co. B, 6th Wis.; age 25; is said to have had typhoid fever in 1859. On Sept. 24, 1861, he was taken with chills and fever, headache, pains in the back and limbs and diarrhœa, for which quinine was given. He was admitted October 1. Next day his face was somewhat congested, eyes bright, pulse 100, quick and strong, skin hot and moist, edges of the tongue dry and its centre covered with a brown crust, appetite small; three stools were passed, and there was some cough with viscid mucous expectoration. Turpentine emulsion and astringents were given. Rose-colored spots appeared on the 3d and continued to erupt at intervals until the 29th. The skin was generally moist; but on the 6th and 7th free perspiration occurred accompanied with sudamina; tinnitus aurium also was noted at this time, and the pulse fell to 75. The bowels were moved once or twice daily, and there was more or less tenderness, chiefly umbilical and left iliac. Five stools were passed on the 10th and again on the 15th, but the tendency to diarrhœa was not marked, for three grains of blue-pill repeated twice on the latter day, and six grains of compound cathartic pill repeated twice on each of the two following days, did not aggravate it; the bowels were generally moved twice, but sometimes only once daily to the end of the record. Profuse nocturnal perspiration occurred on the 15th and following days. The tongue on the 8th became red at the tip and edges and brown or yellowish-brown in the centre; on the 10th it became slightly dry in the middle; on the 17th red, moist, flabby and with prominent papillæ, and after this more or less coated to the end. The appetite continued good from the second day after admission, but on the 26th and 27th there was some irritability of stomach. Quinine was given at this period in three-grain doses every two hours. On the 29th the patient slept well; his eyes were bright; cheeks not flushed; pulse 78, regular; skin hot and moist, a few rose-spots appearing on the breast and abdomen; tongue red at the tip and edges, yellowish coated and fissured in the centre; appetite good; one stool was passed; the stomach continued irritable, and there was some cough with yellow expectoration. On the 31st he was sitting up; the gastric irritability and the cough had ceased. On November 1 he was transferred to Annapolis, Md. [whence he was discharged on account of atrophy of the leg, March 28, 1862].

CASE 76.—*Record imperfect during first four weeks; delirium; diarrhœa; rose-spots from 29th to 39th day; convalescence on 40th day.*—Private Peter Courtwright, Co. B, 1st Pa. Rifles; age 27. This man stated that he had suffered from some kidney trouble at the age of 20, and afterwards from both liver and kidney disease. About Sept. 12, 1861, he had chills followed by fever and sweating, with epistaxis, pain in the back and limbs and anorexia. He was admitted October 10, when he seemed stupid; his eyes were dull; cheeks flushed; pulse 90 and quick; skin hot and dry; tongue moist, red at the tip and edges, coated whitish in centre; appetite poor; the bowels quiet, but with some gurgling and slight tenderness in the left iliac and umbilical regions; a few rose-spots were noted. Dover's powder was given. On the 11th and 12th the general condition remained unaltered; the skin lost its heat but continued dry. Tincture of iron was ordered to be taken three times a day. On the 13th the eyes were dull, injected and suffused and the cheeks slightly flushed; the pulse had fallen to 60; a few rose-spots appeared on the chest and abdomen; three stools were passed, and there was pain on urinating. Profuse perspiration occurred during the night, and in the morning the patient looked bright but there was some mental derangement; the pulse was 46, full and firm; six stools were passed. Astringents were ordered. The condition on the 15th is not recorded, but on the following day there were more rose-spots, delirium, tinnitus aurium, six stools and umbilical tenderness; pulse 68. Tenderness and tympanites over the tranverse colon accompanied six stools recorded on the 17th. There was less delirium on the 18th; the face had become pale and the eyes sunken; one stool was passed. Three stools were reported on the 19th and six on the 20th, on which day also some rose-spots appeared. On the 21st, after sleeping well, the patient's tongue, which had heretofore been red at the tip and edges and more or less coated in the centre, was found to be clean and natural, his skin of normal temperature, pulse 70 and appetite good; two stools were passed. After this he improved, but a diarrhœa, causing about three stools daily, persisted until November 4, when the bowels were reported regular. He was able to be up and to walk about October 30th, and was returned to duty November 10.

CASE 77.—*Delirium, diarrhœa and involuntary stools; eruption of rose- and dark-colored spots; improvement about end of 4th week, but debility with flabby tongue continuing after defervescence.*—Private B. T. Conglin, Co. G, 5th Wis. Vols.; age 22; was taken about Sept. 16, 1861, with epistaxis, headache, pain in the limbs and back and diarrhœa, and was admitted October 1 as a case of typhoid fever. On the 2d his face was congested and he looked dull; his pulse 90, quick and strong, skin normal and tongue moist, brown and with prominent papillæ; he had some pain in the back and anorexia, but no movement from the bowels; the abdomen was covered with dark spots (vibices?) and showed a few rose-spots, which latter disappeared on pressure; he was delirious. Emulsion of turpentine was given every two hours, tincture of iron three times daily and beef-essence as required. Five involuntary stools were passed on the 3d, and astringents were administered. The passages were frequent but passed voluntarily on the 4th; the abdomen and chest were covered with dark-colored spots imperceptible to the touch and disappearing on pressure; the tongue was dry and brown and there was some hoarseness. The stools became again involuntary on the 5th, and the teeth and lips covered with sordes. The patient's face was congested, eyes dull, skin hot and showing the remains of the dark-red spots. He had anorexia, slight tympanites and iliac tenderness; pulse 100. Beef-essence and punch were ordered, with Dover's powder in the evening. Involuntary micturition and defecation, with much tenderness, were noted on the 6th; pulse 112. The tongue was clean, red and dry on the 7th; the appetite improved and there was but one stool. During the three or four days which followed the tongue became moist and flabby, with prominent papillæ; the appetite continued to improve; the bowels were quiet, but there was much umbilical and some iliac tenderness. On the 12th the pulse fell from 110 to 80, the eyes became bright and the delirium ceased. Next day the tongue was moist and clean and the appetite good; but until the end of the month flabbiness and prominent papillæ were reported. The patient was free from diarrhœa, but the abdomen was occasionally tender; at times he had headache. He was transferred to Annapolis, Md., November 1, as a case of debility [and was returned to duty Feb. 3, 1862].

CASE 78.—*Record imperfect at beginning and end of case; headache; diarrhœa; abdominal tenderness; rose-colored spots.*—Private Gottfried Scrieber, Co. I, 6th Wis.; age 30; had some lung trouble in July, 1861, from which he had not entirely recovered, when about October 15 he was taken with chills followed by fever and sweating, with headache, tinnitus aurium, pain in the back, chest and limbs, lassitude, anorexia, thirst, diarrhœa, retention of urine and some cough. He was admitted November 7. Diagnosis—debility. On the 8th rose-colored spots appeared on the chest and abdomen, and there was much tenderness in the umbilical and left iliac regions with a burning feeling in the epigastric region. Blue-pill with opium, followed by castor oil, was prescribed. The skin on the 9th was covered with perspiration; the bowels were moved twice. On the 10th there were some rose-spots, a burning feeling in the stomach, tenderness in the umbilical and left iliac regions, but no passage from the bowels; the tongue was very red at the tip and edges. Eight grains of quinine were given with turpentine and tincture of iron. This patient was transferred on the 18th to Annapolis, Md. [Diagnosis—typhoid fever. Returned to duty Feb. 3, 1862.]

CASE 79.—*Cerebral symptoms not marked; constipation; bilious vomiting; rose-spots on 14th and 18th days.*—Private Thomas Connell, Co. K, 3d Vt.; age 22; caught cold Sept. 27, 1861, and had headache, pain in the loins and limbs and anorexia. He was admitted October 3d as a case of gastritis. His eyes were suffused; pulse 95, full and strong; skin moist but somewhat hot; tongue dry, red and glossy; constipation, anorexia and great irritability of the stomach were present. Sulphate of magnesia and antimony were given, and ten grains of calomel in the evening. The Epsom salt was repeated on the 5th. Next day two grains of quinine were given every two hours, and tincture of iron on the 7th. One stool was obtained on this day; the gastric irritation had somewhat lessened; pulse 70. On the 9th the pulse fell to 45, the skin was of natural temperature, the tongue red, clean and moist but rather flabby, the appetite moderate and the bowels unmoved. Rose-colored spots appeared on the 10th; the appetite was poor; the bowels unmoved and tender. Two compound cathartic pills were given, with turpentine emulsion, every three hours, and two grains of quinine every hour. Next day one stool was obtained, and there was marked tenderness with gurgling in the right iliac and umbilical regions. Some irritability of stomach, cough, pain in chest, suffusion of eyes and congestion of face were noted on this day; pulse 50; skin natural; tongue moist, red and clean. On the 13th, the bowels having continued unmoved and tender in the interval, a cathartic enema was given; this was followed on the 16th by an ounce and a half of castor oil. Three stools were passed on the 17th, three on the 18th, and seven, twelve and fifteen on the following days, after which two stools were recorded daily for several days, with some abdominal tenderness. Rose-spots were noted on the 14th. The patient was sent to Annapolis, Md., November 1 [whence he was returned to duty December 2].

CASE 80.—*Date of origin unknown; unconsciousness; rose-colored spots; moist tongue; diarrhœa; rapid convalescence.*—Private George Robinson, Co. B, 14th N. Y.; age 19; admitted Sept. 27, 1861, having been affected with diarrhœa for two months. Diagnosis—typhoid fever. He was partly comatose and difficult to arouse; pulse 80, firm, strong; face congested; eyes suffused; skin hot and soft; tongue moist, gray; abdomen tender and bowels moved twice. Calomel with kino was given. Next day the abdomen and chest were covered with rose-colored spots; the tongue was moist and coated, except at the tip and edges, with a rough brown fur; three stools were passed, and the abdomen was tympanitic and tender especially in the umbilical region; there was some purulent expectoration streaked with blood, but not much cough. No change took place until October 1, when sudamina appeared on the chest; the stomach became irritable, the bowels remaining undisturbed. Next day the patient looked better and had some appetite; his tongue was white at the tip and edges and brown at the base and centre. Turpentine emulsion was prescribed on the 4th. Profuse perspiration occurred on the 5th with sudamina, and on the 9th rose-colored spots appeared in fresh crops, which by the 11th were very profuse; headache, tinnitus aurium and deafness affecting the left ear accompanied the eruption, and the tongue, which had before been flabby and more or less patched with yellow, became red at the tip and edges and yellow-coated in the centre; he slept well, however, his appetite remaining good and his bowels undisturbed. On the 14th he was considered convalescent, and on the 21st was returned to duty.

CASE 81.—*Unconsciousness; muscular twitchings; involuntary passages; sordes; diarrhœa during convalescence.*—Private Luther Howard, Co. B, 72d N. Y., was admitted Sept. 29, 1861, having been sick for two weeks. Diagnosis—typhoid fever. He was partly unconscious and unable to speak except occasionally; the face was congested, the eyes slightly injected, the facial muscles disturbed and those of the extremities twitching involuntarily in almost choreic movements; he had headache and some laryngeal trouble; the skin was soft and moist; the pulse 88, firm; the abdomen tender. Camphor and opium were given. Next day he was partly comatose, his face congested, pulse 100, full and strong, skin hot and soft; no stool was passed, but the abdomen was tympanitic and tender; no urine was voided for sixteen hours; the muscular twitchings continued, and the patient was unable to open his mouth or speak. Emulsion of turpentine, sweet spirit of nitre, valerian and Dover's powder were ordered. On October 1 sordes appeared on the teeth, the tongue was coated dark brown and the mouth filled with dark tenacious mucus; the patient was indifferent, but ate food when offered to him; the bowels were unmoved. Five grains each of calomel and jalap, with twelve of quinine, were given him. One small stool was obtained next day, and the patient was less stupid; he was very deaf, but answered questions correctly when put to him in a loud voice. On the 3d he protruded his tongue with less difficulty and the choreic movements were lessened, but there was some dysphagia and the stools were passed involuntarily. On the 4th he was rational; the tongue slightly moist; bowels tender and moved once, but not tympanitic. Turpentine emulsion, brandy, Fowler's solution and Epsom salt were given. Two involuntary stools were passed on the 6th, but the dysphagia was lessened, the twitchings had ceased and the patient was able to articulate well and masticate his food. Beef-essence and astringents were ordered. Some headache and delirium were present on the 8th; the tongue was dry and tremulous, showing yellow patches and prominent papillæ, and the bowels were loose. After this the skin was usually hot and dry or of the natural temperature, although on the 18th there was some perspiration at night. The tongue was moist, clean or patched with white or yellow, and usually flabby and with prominent papillæ; but on the 13th it was red at the tip and edges and coated yellow in the centre. The appetite was good, and for several days was recorded as excessive. The bowels were loose, yielding two or three passages daily, with occasional tympanites and tenderness mostly in the right iliac region. He slept well, but was occasionally troubled with a little cough. Epistaxis occurred on the 30th, and on November 4, 5 and 6 there was some headache with dizziness and twitchings of the eyeballs. He was transferred to Annapolis, Md., on the 18th [as a case of typhoid fever, and was returned to duty December 27].

CASE 82.—*Ague; gastric irritation; rose-colored spots; cerebral symptoms slightly marked; perspiration and periodic epistaxis.*—Private Fred. Shaffer, Co. G, 72d N. Y.; age 23; became affected in July, 1861, with ague which lasted for six weeks, after which he was confined to bed with abdominal pains. He was admitted September 29 as a case of typhoid fever. For some days after admission he rested well at night, but had from two to six stools daily with, but sometimes without, tympanites and abdominal tenderness, chiefly marked in the umbilical and left iliac regions; he had some congestion of the face and headache, and the pulse ranged from 85 to 100, being usually somewhat more rapid at the evening visit; his skin, which was natural or slightly moist with the lower pulse and usually hot and dry with the higher, presented a few rose-spots and a profuse eruption; he was troubled with anorexia and great irritability of the stomach; his tongue was moist and white or yellow-coated, or dry and brown; he had some difficulty in micturition and afterwards retention of urine. He was treated with turpentine emulsion, Dover's powder, astringents and small doses of calomel and opium. On October 5 he was restless at night; his face was congested, eyes dull, pulse 95 and weak, but his skin was cool and covered with perspiration. Next night he slept well and in the morning looked better; pulse 80, regular; skin natural; tongue moist, clean; appetite good; but the stomach continued irritable and much green matter was vomited; four stools were passed. Tincture of iron and astringents were given. From this time forward the record shows the presence of occasional headache with dizziness and tinnitus aurium. The stomach continued irritable, but after the occurrence of epistaxis on the 10th and free perspiration on the 11th, this symptom became less prominent and disappeared. The epistaxis recurred on the 13th, 15th, 17th and 21st. The tongue was always moist and generally clean, but flabby and with prominent papillæ. The bowels were loose, giving two or three passages daily, with decreasing tympanites, gurgling and general abdominal tenderness, sometimes particularly marked in the umbilical and right iliac regions; towards the end of the month the stools became reduced to one daily. On the 25th quinine in two-grain doses was given three times daily. The patient was transferred to Annapolis, Md., November 1 [as affected with typhoid fever, on account of which he was discharged from the service on the 25th].

CASE 83.—*Chills; diarrhœa; umbilical pain; free perspirations; no notable cerebral symptoms.*—James Tobin, attendant; age 29; was admitted Sept. 11, 1861, having been taken sick ten days before with headache, constipation, pains in the bones and a chill and fever, for which quinine was administered. On the day after admission he was restless and had an anxious expression; he perspired during sleep, but when awake his skin was hot and dry; pulse 74; tongue pale but red at the tip and edges; four thin stools had been passed during the twenty-four hours, and there was slight pain, chiefly umbilical and during micturition; he had also a stitch in the side and some pain in the breast. Quinine was given. In the evening the pulse was 78, the skin hot but sweating and the tongue pale, flabby and somewhat brown; four stools were passed during the day. Acetate of lead and opium were prescribed. Next morning the pulse had fallen to 56 and the patient was sweating profusely. In the evening there was a slight accession of fever; only one stool was passed during the twenty-four hours. For some days after this the perspiration continued profuse, especially at night, although aromatic sulphuric acid was administered; the bowels remained quiet and the tongue flabby and coated gray or brown at the base. Blue-pill was given three times on the 15th, and in the evening of the 16th ten grains of calomel, which produced three painful stools, but the bowels thereafter became again quiet although tender especially in the right iliac region. The perspirations continued. Morphia was given at night and the patient was sponged with alcohol. On the 18th some pustules appeared on the abdomen. Next day he is reported as looking stout and healthy, with bright eyes and clear mind, although there was some headache and pain in the back and breast, with a slight gray coating on the tongue. Three grains of calomel and a half grain of opium were given three times. The record concludes on the 21st, the patient still perspiring at night and having the umbilical region tender.

CASE 84.—*Death, probably from perforation of the intestine, on the 28th day.*—Sergeant David Puckett, Co. E, 5th U. S. Cav.; age 27; was admitted Oct. 18, 1861, having been sick since the beginning of the month with headache and pain in the limbs, back and epigastrium. A cathartic, to be followed by quinine, was prescribed. On the day after admission the patient was wakeful, his eyes dull and yellow-tinged, cheeks flushed, pulse 110, full and strong, skin hot, tongue slightly moist, red at the tip and edges but heavily coated yellowish-white in the centre; he had anorexia, thirst, three passages from the bowels during the twenty-four hours, much umbilical tenderness and tympanites, a slight cough and difficult micturition. Sinapisms were applied to the abdomen and emulsion of turpentine given every three hours, with extract of buchu as required. On the 20th the pulse fell to 90, but the condition of the patient was otherwise unchanged. A powder containing three grains of calomel, one grain of opium and one-eighth of a grain of tartar emetic was given every three hours. Next day the tongue became dry; seven stools were passed and the hypogastric and iliac regions were highly tympanitic and tender. On the 22d the diarrhœa continued, eight stools having been passed; cerebral symptoms were manifested, as headache, hebetude, dizziness and tinnitus; the stomach became irritable and the tongue dry, red at the tip and edges and brown in the centre. On the 23d no change was recorded except the passage of urine without pain for the first time in several days. Lead, opium and tannin with tincture of iron were prescribed. On the 24th the patient was dull, lying with his eyes half closed in a semi-delirious condition; no stool was passed, but there was much vomiting. Two grains of calomel and a half grain of opium were ordered for administration every hour. On the 26th, having slept well at night, the patient was brighter, his mind less obtuse, and there was less abdominal tenderness; but the tongue was heavily coated yellow and the anorexia, thirst and vomiting persisted. Next day five grains of calomel and a quarter of a grain of sulphate of morphia were given, but no marked change was apparent until the 27th, when the patient was partly unconscious and delirious, lying with his eyes rolled up and mouth open, his breathing hurried, pulse 125, tongue dry and coated brown and stomach rejecting everything; there was extreme tenderness of the abdomen and much meteorism. Stimulants were administered by enemata. Death took place on the morning of the 28th.

CASE 85.—*Remittent fever; symptoms of typhoid fever not distinctly manifested; fatal by peritonitis on the 25th day.*—Private Mason Hitchcock, Co. A, 19th Ind. Vols.; age 33; had a chill Aug. 28, 1861, with pain in the bones, back and calves of the legs, relaxation and tenderness of the bowels, and fever which was worse in the evening. He was admitted on the morning of September 5, when his pulse was 80, skin warm and moist, tongue pale and coated and colon tender on pressure. Quinine was given. He had a chill at 2 P. M., and in the evening the skin was hot and dry and the tongue very red, flabby and coated. On the 6th, 7th and 8th he had no fever at the morning visit; but in the evening the skin was hot and dry and the bowels somewhat relaxed and tender; his complexion was sallow and his mind rather dull. He was treated with Dover's powder and small doses of blue-pill. After the 9th there was slight fever at the morning visit, but the patient was able to be up and walk around a little until the 12th; the tongue was dry, brown, yellow and white by turns, but usually red at the tip; the pulse was weak, 80 when lying, 100 when standing; the bowels were moved from one to three times daily, and there was always some tenderness along the track of the colon. On the 15th two bloody stools were passed and the patient was much depressed, the colon tender, the tongue thickly coated yellow, the skin hot and sweating, pulse 86. A blister was applied over the colon and opium and tannin prescribed. The bowels remained quiet until the 17th, when an enema of soap was administered. At this time there was some tenderness in the right iliac region. On the 18th the stomach was irritable and the pulse ran up to 120. Vomiting continued next day and was accompanied with acute tenderness in the epigastrium; the patient lay on his back with his legs drawn up. On the 21st the pulse was 140, tongue nearly clean but very dry, skin hot, abdomen tender. In the evening the body became covered with a profuse sweat, the extremities cold, the features pinched, the pulse imperceptible, the heart's action irregular, speedily ending in stupor and death. No rose-colored spots were discovered in this case although specially looked for.

CASE 86.—*Defervescence on the 22d day checked by chest complications; return to duty delayed to 80th day by diarrhœal sequelæ.*—Bugler Henry L. Case, Co. H, 4th Mich.; age 22; was admitted Sept. 6, 1861. Diagnosis—typhoid fever. This patient had good health up to August 26, when he was taken with pain in the head and bones, chills and fever, somnolence, great thirst and epistaxis. His case was not taken up in detail until the 13th, when the morning record shows him to have rested well during the preceding night; he was very weak but had some appetite, regular bowels, a thickly coated brown tongue, a pulse beating 98 per minute and a slight cough: the evening record shows a white tongue, bad taste in the mouth, some fever, bowels regular, abdomen tender and slightly tympanitic, cough, tinnitus aurium and muscæ volitantes. On the 14th anorexia was added to the symptoms already stated. Next day he became dull, complained of heaviness over the eyes, and in the evening seemed drowsy. On the evening of the 16th the tongue became moist and white, but this was not followed by any general improvement; on the contrary, on the evening of the 17th the fever increased with slight nausea, the pulse running up to 106, while next day a pain on deep inspiration was developed. But on the 19th the pulse again fell to 92 and the skin became moist and sweating. There was some tenderness in the epigastrium on the 20th, in the hypochondrium on the 22d and in the right iliac region on the 23d, in addition to the abdominal tenderness which had existed from the time of admission. On the 21st the patient became somewhat deaf in the left ear, and next day his eyes became dull. The abdominal tenderness was relieved on the 24th, when, also, the tongue began to clean in patches, but thirst continued until the 27th. The patient slept badly on the night of the 24th, the only night which furnished such a record, for usually he rested well, and next morning his pulse was 96 and he had a soreness in the chest. On the 26th the tongue was moist and only slightly coated, which improvement was followed next day by a brightening of the eyes, abatement of the thirst and a return of the appetite. The bowels, which to this time had remained quiet rather than lax, now became loose, giving two, three or four stools daily, with iliac tenderness and a yellow fur upon the tongue; but in progress of time this diarrhœa abated and on November 1 the patient was transferred to Annapolis, Md., whence he was returned to duty on the 13th. He was treated at first with Dover's powder and sweet spirit of nitre, and afterwards, on the 23d, with turpentine emulsion and iron, opium, acetate of lead and tannin.

CASE 87.—*Headache, dizziness, deafness, delirium and muscular twitchings; relaxation, tenderness and tympanites of the bowels; pneumonia; no rose-colored spots.*—Private Sidney D. Way, Co. I, 2d Vt.; age 18; was admitted Sept. 27, 1861, having been taken three weeks before with intermittent fever, cough and pain in the breast. The case was diagnosed typhoid fever. The patient was weak, his cheeks flushed, countenance anxious, pulse quick, 120, skin hot and dry; he had some pain in the head and chest, with deafness and muscular twitchings; there was anorexia with a moist white tongue, and relaxed bowels with much tympanites and general abdominal tenderness. Small doses of blue-pill and opium were given on the 28th and turpentine emulsion on the 29th. During the next four days his condition was but little altered; the deafness increased, and delirium, dizziness and aphonia were manifested; three or four passages from the bowels were recorded every twelve hours; the cough occasionally became troublesome, and was accompanied with a mucous expectoration; the respirations were at one time as high as 36 per minute. On the morning of October 2 the patient, having slept well during the previous night, was found with the skin of natural temperature and bathed in perspiration, sudamina on the right side and over the abdomen, the tongue moist and slightly coated yellow, and the pulse 95 but strong and quick; two stools had been passed during the night and a little blood expectorated, after which the cough became less troublesome; respiration 28, with much crepitation anteriorly on the left side and a little on the right side. Next day, however, the pulse was again accelerated, 113, and the skin hot and more or less dry, the other symptoms continuing as already described until the 6th, when with a freely perspiring skin the pulse fell to 90, and the patient had less cough and some improvement in the voice. After this the pulse again rose to 105, the skin becoming hot and dry, but the tongue remaining moist and yellow-coated; the cough and expectoration of mucus and blood continued, with dulness over the lower lobe of the right lung posteriorly and mucous and submucous râles above, and with crepitation over the left lung posteriorly; the diarrhœa and abdominal tenderness continued as already reported. By the 11th the pulse had risen to 118, and the patient was quite deaf and complained of headache. On the 12th the tongue, still continuing moist and yellow-coated, became red at the tip and edges; some sordes formed upon the lips, and tormina accompanied the diarrhœal passages. From this time to the end of the month the condition varied little from day to day, but a gradual alleviation of the symptoms of the lung and bowel complaints was observed. A free perspiration which occurred on the 20th was followed by a reduction of the pulse on the 21st and the manifestation of some appetite. The abdominal tenderness became lessened and the passages less frequent until the 31st, when, for the first time, the daily record shows that no stool was passed during the previous twenty-four hours. On November 1 the pulse was 80 and feeble, the skin natural, the tongue pale, the appetite good; the cough was less troublesome and there had been but one stool. His condition had not changed materially on the 9th, when he was discharged from the service on account of debility; the cough persisted with occasional relaxation of the bowels and abdominal tenderness, but with a good appetite and natural skin.

CASE 88.—*Diarrhœa; bilious vomiting; perspirations; no rose-colored spots; dizziness; pulmonary complications on the 15th day; improvement on 28th.*—Private Dwight Tousely, Co. E, 3d Mich. Vols.; age 30; was admitted Oct. 19, 1861. Diagnosis—typhoid fever. On the 12th, after undergoing much fatigue, he was taken with headache, weakness and slight diarrhœa. He slept well after admission, and on the morning of the 20th his countenance was natural, pulse 88 and strong, skin perspiring, tongue moist, pale-red at the tip and edges and brownish in the centre; he had some appetite, slight thirst, two thin watery stools, some right iliac tenderness, borborygmus and slight tympanites. Quinine administered in a full dose at noon was vomited along with much phlegm and greenish-watery liquid. On the evening of the 21st he again vomited a greenish mass mixed with the rejected ingesta; he had dizziness and tinnitus aurium. The tongue on the 23d was covered with white scales; on the following day it was raw, red in the centre, pale and slightly coated at the sides; it became scaly again on the 25th, and the pulse rose to 94. On the 26th the pulse was 120 and feeble, the patient delirious, his countenance haggard and anxious, skin warm, moist and at times sweating profusely, tongue moist and cleaning from the tip and edges; he had no pain, but there was much tympanites, which was relieved by an enema; râles and creaking sounds were heard in the upper part of the chest, and the respirations were increased to 25. The pulse fell to 96 on the 27th, and on the 28th the patient appeared somewhat better; his mouth and fauces were covered with aphthæ. He had a chill on the afternoon of the 29th, and on the 30th was very nervous, although the tongue was cleaning, appetite good, bowels quiet and respiration normal. His condition did not improve materially until November 8, the tongue being occasionally dry and brown or moist and cleaning, the skin husky and the pulse accelerated. After that date, however, he slept well, had a good appetite, no thirst, soft skin and quiet bowels; some tenderness remained in the right iliac region; he had sore throat, but no cough, and his respiration was normal. He was transferred to Annapolis, Md., on the 18th.

CASE 89.—*Date of onset not defined; persisting diarrhœa and vomiting of bilious matter; rose-colored spots; sordes; muttering delirium; involuntary passages; cold perspirations; death on 16th day after admission.*—Private Charles Green, Co. C, 1st Long Island; age 18; was admitted Sept. 14, 1861, having been suffering for some time from weakness, pain in the bones, heat of skin, thirst and diarrhœa. On admission his stomach was irritable. He rested well during the night, and next day, although he had a brown and thickly coated tongue and a bad taste in his mouth, his appetite was good, pulse 92 and skin hot and moist. Dover's powder was given. The tongue became dry and red at the tip on the 16th; the bowels were moved six times and were tender; the pulse rose to 108 and there was some deafness. He muttered continually during sleep on the 17th; the diarrhœa and irritability of stomach continued. In the evening rose-colored spots appeared on the chest and abdomen and sordes on the teeth; the lips were livid, and a peculiar odor emanated from the body. The muttering during sleep increased, and on the evening of the 18th the patient was delirious on awaking; nausea returned and he vomited twice. During the night he vomited five times a thin greenish-yellow matter of a highly offensive odor. Mild delirium continued during the 19th, and the urine was passed involuntarily; the matter vomited became of a lighter color; the diarrhœa persisted notwithstanding the administration of astringents, and there was intestinal gurgling with umbilical tenderness. Calomel in one-grain doses was given. Next day the gastric irritability was quieted and the diarrhœa lessened. In the evening he was restless and wakeful, his skin hot and dry, but his face covered with a cold perspiration, pulse 120, weak and tremulous; he had subsultus tendinum and passed one stool involuntarily. A similar stool was passed on the 21st, during which the prostration increased. The right iliac region is noted as having been tender on this day. He died on the 22d.

CASE 90.—*Diarrhœa; delirium; sordes; pneumonic complication; eruption; slightly marked improvement on 15th day, after which free perspirations alternated with diarrhœa; vibices; epistaxis; peritonitis; death on the 31st day.*—Teamster

Jas. H. Perkins, quartermaster's department; age 23; a Virginian; was admitted Sept. 30, 1861. Diagnosis—typhoid fever. He had been taken with diarrhœa on the 25th and with head-pain and rheumatism on the 27th. On admission his face was flushed, eyes bright, pulse 96, quick and strong, tongue moist and slightly coated white; his bowels had been opened three times during the previous twenty-four hours, and the iliac regions were tender and tympanitic; he had also some cough. Calomel, opium and tartar emetic were prescribed. On October 1 the bowels were quiet, but there was some pain in the chest when coughing, with dulness over the lower lobes of the lungs. Small doses of calomel and quinine were given. He had three stools on the 2d. Next day the pulse ran up to 112, and complaint was made of headache and backache. Tincture of iron and camphor with opium were prescribed. He vomited twice on the 4th. His skin became moist on the 5th, and on the following day was covered with a profuse perspiration; but there was some delirium and much twitching of the tendons. On the 6th emulsion of turpentine was administered. On the 7th the pulse was 105, quick and strong, the skin natural, the tongue moist and heavily coated yellow; four stools were passed; the transverse and descending portions of the colon were tympanitic and the umbilical region tender; he had some cough, with slight pain in the right side below the nipple, and there was dulness on percussion over the lower lobes of both lungs, especially marked on the right side. On the 8th the skin was hot and dry and the bowels loose. On the 9th the patient was wakeful at night and dull and stupid during the day; the pulse 120, quick and strong; the skin hot and dry, showing some eruption (the character of which is not stated); the tongue red, fissured at the edges and coated dark-brown in the centre; the teeth and lips covered with sordes; he had, moreover, deafness, delirium, anorexia and diarrhœa. He continued in this condition until the 15th, when the tongue became moist, yellowish at the centre and red at the tip and edges, and the delirium and deafness were somewhat less marked; the pulse had fallen to 100. The skin was bathed in perspiration on the 16th and 17th, and this condition recurred on the 19th, 21st, 23d and 25th. Three or four stools were passed on the alternate days when the skin was hot and dry, but on the days when the skin was moist the bowels remained quiet except on the 21st, when they were moved six times. On the 19th vibices appeared on the skin and on the 23d became very numerous. On the 21st the pulse rose again to 120, and there was epistaxis with low delirium and increased deafness. The epistaxis recurred on the 22d. The patient became almost pulseless on the 25th; his skin was bathed in perspiration, and there was acute pain in the abdomen. He died on this day.

CASE 91.—*Relapse of typhoid; fever, perspiration, delirium, diarrhœa and tenderness; rose-rash; death three days after the occurrence of what was regarded as a congestive chill.*—See case of Private James Beckwith, Co. F, 2d Me., No. 16 of the *post-mortem* records.

CASE 92.—*Chills, diarrhœa and tenderness; nausea and vomiting; epistaxis and hemorrhagic stools; deafness; temporary improvement; death from parotid inflammation and gangrenous erysipelas.*—See case of Private James M. Forman, Co. H, 33d Pa., No. 103 of the *post-mortem* records.

CASE 93.—*Chill and perspiration; diarrhœa, tenderness, rose-rash and mental confusion; temporary improvement followed by inflammation of the larynx and lungs, hemorrhagic stools and death.*—See case of Private D. F. McLachlan, Co. G, 14th N. Y., No. 110 of the *post-mortem* records.

ELEVEN TYPHOID FEVER CASES IN WHICH AGUISH PAROXYSMS PRECEDED THE DEVELOPMENT OF THE CONTINUED FEVER.

CASE 94.—*Intermittent fever; relaxation of the bowels and abdominal tenderness; no cerebral nor special typhoid symptoms, but no particulars are given of the patient's condition for some days preceding death.*—Private Andrew Landon, Co. C, 74th N. Y. Vols.; age 18; was admitted Nov. 2, 1861. Diagnosis—typhoid fever. His health had been good until about a month before admission, when he contracted intermittent fever. On the 3d his eyes were bright, cheeks flushed, pulse 100, quick and small, skin hot and dry, tongue faintly yellow; he had some appetite, some thirst, two stools and slight epigastric tenderness. On the 5th a blister was applied on account of increasing tenderness with some tympanites in the umbilical and iliac regions. At this time he was taking twelve grains of quinine daily with tincture of iron. On the 8th he was wakeful, the pulse rose to 120, the skin continued hot and the tongue coated; the tenderness had decreased, but the bowels were slightly relaxed and there was some cough. Emulsion of turpentine and beef-essence were prescribed. On the 10th there was much tympanites and three stools were passed. Whiskey-punch and astringents were ordered. On the 11th the eyes were bright, face pale, pulse 120 and quick, skin hot and dry, tongue dry and red but slightly yellow in the centre, appetite good. Acetate of lead and tannin were prescribed, but death took place on the 17th.

CASE 95.—*Chills, fever and perspirations; eruption on 18th day; relaxation of bowels; iliac and epigastric tenderness; delirium; death on 35th day.*—Private John Dietrich, Co. B, 35th Pa. Vols.; age 19; was admitted Nov. 5, 1861. Diagnosis—typhoid fever. He had been healthy till Oct. 20, when he was taken with chills, fever, perspirations, pain in the head, back and limbs, lassitude, anorexia, thirst, vomiting, diarrhœa and cough with expectoration. On the 6th he was wakeful, eyes suffused, cheeks flushed, pulse 120, quick and bounding, skin hot, perspiring and covered with eruption and sudamina on the chest and abdomen, tongue moist and white-coated, bowels slightly relaxed, tympanitic and tender in the iliac and epigastric regions; he had some appetite, much thirst, slight cough and somewhat accelerated respiration. Quinine and tincture of iron were prescribed, with sinapisms to the abdomen. On the 7th the tenderness and tympanites were lessened. The mustard was repeated and Dover's powder given at night. He had some headache on the 8th and became delirious on the 10th. Here the record closes abruptly with the announcement of death on the 23d. Turpentine emulsion was administered on the 8th.

CASE 96.—*Cerebral symptoms strongly marked; intestinal and pulmonary symptoms obscured; death on 19th day.*—Corporal S. H. Forsyth, Co. A, 3d Pa. Cav.; age 33; was taken sick Sept. 7, 1861, with chills, nausea and vomiting, which recurred for three days. He was admitted on the 14th. Diagnosis—typhoid fever. He had pain in the head and bones, increased heat of skin, tinnitus aurium, dulness of intellect and occasional epistaxis. A bath was ordered for him and Dover's powder at night. He rested well, his bowels remaining quiet although somewhat swollen and tender; the tongue was brown and dry. Turpentine emulsion was given every two hours. On the 16th the pulse was 106 and strong, tongue brown, bowels regular but tympanitic, skin hot and dry, showing some rose-colored spots; there was anorexia and occasional epistaxis. He was restless during the night, and on the 17th became somewhat delirious, dull and drowsy; the pulse was 106 but weaker; the bowels regular but distended. A few rose-colored spots appeared on the 18th, and one dark-colored stool was passed. The tongue was tremulous and protruded with difficulty on the 19th, and the teeth were black with sordes. In the evening the tongue was dry, red at the tip and edges and black in the centre and at the base. Beef-essence and whiskey-punch were prescribed. On the 20th the eyes were suffused, pupils contracted, pulse 116, skin hot and dry but soft, teeth and lips covered with sordes, breathing labored, bowels quiet but tympanitic and gurgling on pressure. In the evening the pulse had risen to 126; a slight perspiration bedewed the forehead and arms and a few rose-colored spots appeared on the chest and abdomen; the delirium was accompanied by some deafness and muscular twitchings, but the respiration had become quiet and natural. Two days were passed without material change, but on the 23d the respiration became increased to 35; the skin was moist and hot, hands cold and clammy, pulse 136, small and tremulous, bowels quiet but largely meteorized, urine passed involuntarily. Tincture of capsicum was given and a blister and bandage applied to the abdomen. On the 24th the pulse reached 144 and was very feeble; the face was covered with sweat, the hands cold and damp, the feet warm; the patient was somewhat conscious but very deaf, and he had some difficulty in swallowing. A tube was passed to relieve the tympanites. On the 25th he was unconscious, muttering in his delirium, pulse 148, features pinched, forehead flushed, nose and lips blanched, eyes sunken and injected, cornea dull and partly glazed, extremities pulseless, heart's action feeble, skin of body warm and bedewed with perspiration, hands shrunken, damp and cold, tongue dry, brown and badly fissured, lips and teeth covered with dark-brown sordes; he was very deaf, had violent subsultus, dysphagia, involuntary urination and excessive tympanites, but no movement of the bowels; respiration was slow and labored. He died on this day.

CASE 97.—*Preceded by quotidian chills; date of onset undefined; diarrhœal affection severe; delirium; prostration; death.*—Private Jacob Benson, Co. B, 1st Pa. Cav.; age 23; suffered with quotidian chills during August, 1861, and on September 7 was admitted. Diagnosis—typhoid fever. The patient was weak, dull and stupid; pulse 104, skin hot and dry, tongue dry, brown and heavily coated, bowels relaxed and painful. Whiskey and beef-essence were administered. Six thin stools were passed during the next twenty-four hours; the right iliac region was tender. Turpentine emulsion, Hoffmann's anodyne and morphine were prescribed. On the 9th delirium, epistaxis, rose-colored spots and three thin dark stools were noted, and on the 10th sordes, subsultus, difficulty in protruding the tongue and aggravation of the diarrhœa. Enemata of starch and laudanum were used, but the diarrhœa persisted, giving five or six stools daily until the end. A profuse eruption of rose-colored spots and sudamina appeared on the 14th. The stools were passed involuntarily on the 16th, and afterwards the abdomen was tympanitic and tender in the right iliac region. Carbonate of ammonia was prescribed on the 17th. Next day the stomach was irritable, the respiration labored, skin congested, eyes dull, half opened and with contracted pupils. On the 19th a few rose-colored spots appeared; the pulse was 120, soft and compressible, and the features shrunken. Death took place on the 20th.

CASE 98.—*Chills and fever with, subsequently, the gradual accession of symptoms of enteric fever; diarrhœal attack on 17th day; rose-spots and delirium on 18th; inflammation of parotid on 24th; aggravation of diarrhœa on 28th and death on 30th day.*—Private James Roe, Co. F, 1st Mich.; age 22; was admitted Sept. 28, 1861, having been taken sick about a week before with chills and fever, for which quinine and alteratives had been administered. On admission he was weak, had anorexia and headache, but his skin was natural, tongue moist and slightly coated, pulse 72 and bowels quiet. Up to October 5 there was no marked change in the patient's condition; the coating of the tongue became somewhat thickened; the skin was dry, hot on the 3d, perspiring on the 4th; the bowels were quiet or moved once daily, and there was some tenderness in the right iliac region; the headache continued and there was slight cough. On the 6th the patient vomited some dark-colored matters. On the 7th he was restless for the first time since admission; the bowels were moved four times and the tongue was moist, red at the tip and edges and dark-brown at the centre and base. On the 8th he was delirious; pulse 90 and quick; skin hot and dry, showing a few rose-spots, disappearing on pressure, and mingled with profuse eruption (character not stated); tongue dry, flabby, red at the tip and edges, coated brown in the centre; appetite very good; he had one stool, some tympanites and slight gurgling in the right iliac region. No change was manifested save increasing dulness of mind and prostration until the 13th, when the tongue became slightly moist and the delirium lessened. During this period the teeth were covered with sordes and the mouth filled with tenacious mucus. On the 14th the parotids became swollen. Next day the pulse was 120 and feeble and the bowels quiet but tender and distended; the patient, nevertheless, when aroused from his low delirium, expressed himself as feeling quite well. The tongue became moist and its coating yellowish-white on the 16th, and on the following day the patient was more rational; the eruption was present up to this date. A sharp diarrhœa of seven stools occurred on the 18th and the pulse reached 140. A blister was applied to the abdomen. On the 19th vibices appeared; the tongue could not be protruded on account of the parotid swelling; the bowels were moved once only, but they were generally tender and much meteorized. Death took place on the 20th.

CASE 99.—*Typhoid fever following intermittent; intestinal symptoms not marked; death from pneumonic complications.*—Private A. W. Armagust, Co. I, 33d Pa. Vols., was admitted Oct. 2, 1861. Diagnosis—typhoid fever. About September 28 he had been taken with headache and chills, which recurred every night. He felt well on the morning after admission, but in the evening the pulse became accelerated and strong, the skin hot and dry and the tongue red, clean at the tip but coated at the base; he had three stools during the day, with some soreness of the abdomen, but no tympanites nor gurgling. Quinine was given. He is reported as having slept well on the 4th and as having had no chill on the 5th; on the 6th his condition is not stated. On the 7th he had headache and was restless; countenance natural; pulse 86, steady; skin hot and dry but soft; tongue moist, red and quite clean; he had pain in the bones, two stools and abdominal tenderness, but no tympanites. He had one stool on the 8th. Small doses of calomel, quinine and opium were given. The headache was worse on the 9th; there was a feeling of pressure on the brain with buzzing in the ears and deafness; four stools were passed; the tongue was dry, red at the tip, furred in the centre and coated gray at the base. Sweet spirit of nitre was prescribed. On the 10th the bowels were quiet and continued so to the end with but little complaint of abdominal tenderness or tympanites. Emulsion of turpentine and Mindererus' spirit were administered. On the 11th the skin was hot but moist; the tongue continued dry and the appetite did not return, although there was marked improvement in the cerebral and abdominal symptoms. On the 15th the patient was restless, and there was some cough for the first time in the progress of the case; the cough grew worse, and on the 17th brown mixture was prescribed. Next day there was anxiety of countenance and much cough, but neither accelerated respiration nor pain. On the 20th the patient was slightly delirious. Whiskey-punch and citrate of iron and quinine were given. On the 22d his face was pale, countenance dull, pulse 82, steady, surface circulation good, skin dry and husky but not hot, tongue slightly brown and dry in the centre, whitish and moist along the sides, red at the tip and edges, teeth and gums clean; he had some appetite, no thirst, and a cough with slight wheezing and gurgling sounds in the lower parts of the lungs; at times also he had some dizziness and tinnitus. On the 23d the respiration became increased to 26; the pulse to 102; the abdomen was soft and natural. He died on the 29th. No eruption was noticed in this case.

CASE 100.—*Chills; pale, coated tongue and offensive breath; jaundice and epigastric pain; bowels quiet; cerebral symptoms not marked; record unfinished.*—Private George H. Peters, Co. F, 4th Mich. Vols.; age 21; of weakly constitution, was admitted Nov. 1, 1861, as a case of typhoid fever. On October 23 he was taken with headache and chills which lasted for three days, and with anorexia, weakness, diarrhœa, cold feet, tinnitus aurium and fever, for which Epsom salt and quinine had been administered. On admission he was dull and unable to collect his thoughts on account of a fulness in the head and ringing in the ears; his pulse was 98 and strong, skin warm and soft, left cheek flushed darkly, tongue dry and moist by turns, pale, clean at the tip and thickly coated whitish-gray at the base; he had no appetite but much thirst, acute epigastric and right iliac tenderness, tympanites, but no diarrhœa; respiration was normal, but the breath was very offensive; there was also some pain in urinating. Brandy-punch and beef-essence were given with quinine, calomel and opium three times daily. A few rose-colored spots appeared next day. On the 4th the skin was dry, warm and somewhat jaundiced; the tongue red at the tip and edges, pale and coated white in the centre and at the base, the bowels meanwhile remaining tympanitic and tender but unmoved. He slept well during the night, and on the 5th his mind was clear and eyes intelligent, skin dry, tongue moist, pale and slightly coated in the centre, breath free from all offensive odor. On the 6th a few more rose-colored spots appeared, but the bowels remained quiet, and the slight tenderness present was in the epigastric region; the abdomen was soft. He had two stools on the 7th. Turpentine was administered. On the 8th the skin was warm and soft and presented a few dark-red spots which were imperceptible to the touch and disappeared on pressure; pulse 56, small and compressible; tongue moist and thickly coated in the centre. At this time he did not sleep well and his appetite continued poor. Here the record leaves him, concluding with a statement of his transfer to Annapolis, Md., on the 18th.

CASE 101.—*Recurring chills; cerebral symptoms slightly marked; gastric irritability; diarrhœa and abdominal tenderness.*—Private Frederick Doser, Co. B, 24th N. Y. Vols.; age 24; had been troubled with liver complaint since 1856, and about Sept. 16, 1861, was taken with intermittent fever, which persisted notwithstanding the use of quinine and opium. He was admitted on the 30th as a case of typhoid fever. His eyes were dull, pulse 96, skin natural, tongue moist but furred white; he had pain in the bones and anorexia, cough and pain in the chest, three stools daily with tympanites, iliac tenderness and some gurgling. Opium, antimony and blue-mass in small doses were given every three hours. Next day the pulse was 112, skin somewhat hot, eyes injected and suffused, tongue moist, furred in the centre and red at the edges, bowels much meteorized and tender at the umbilicus. Quinine was given with turpentine emulsion in place of the mercurial. The quinine was continued on the 2d and tincture of iron ordered on the 3d, the pulse having meanwhile fallen to 85, the tongue become cleaner and the appetite improved. A diarrhœa of four stools daily set in on the 4th, followed on the 5th by epigastric pain, intestinal gurgling, tenderness in the right iliac region and in the course of the transverse colon, and on the 6th by loss of appetite and irritability of the stomach. Seven stools were passed on the 9th and three on the 10th, after which the attack gradually declined; during this time there was some head-pain with dizziness and tinnitus aurium, and the tongue remaining red at the tip and edges became covered elsewhere with yellowish patches. Conjunctivitis, which appeared on the 11th, was treated with a zinc wash. On the 14th the pulse was 56 and regular, the skin natural, the tongue moist and clean and the appetite good. The patient was transferred to Annapolis, Md., November 1.

CASE 102.—*Recurring chills and diarrhœa; perspirations; nothing but rose-spots on the 13th day as specially characteristic of typhoid fever.*—Private A. Stoughton, Co. C, 5th Vt. Vols.; age 18; was admitted Nov. 1, 1861, as a case of typhoid fever. On October 23 the patient had chills which recurred for several days, fever, general pains, weakness, anorexia and diarrhœa. On November 2 his eyes were bright, countenance calm, pulse 88 and of fair strength, skin warm and perspiring, tongue clean at tip, moist and slightly coated at the base and in the centre, lips and teeth clean, appetite fair, abdomen soft and respiration normal; one stool was passed in the twenty-four hours. A full dose of quinine was given three times daily. On the 3d he was reported as having slept well; pulse 84, appetite good, skin natural, tongue cleaning; two stools were passed. On the following day, without any other change in the symptoms, rose-colored spots appeared on the chest and abdomen; he had one stool on this day, and after this his bowels were reported as regular. He was returned to duty on the 11th.

CASE 103.—*Recurring chills; diarrhœal tendency; mental dulness; rose-spots on 14th day, immediately followed by convalescence.*—Private Samuel Bissinette, Co. A, 4th Mich.; age 22; was seized about Sept. 9, 1861, with daily chills accompanied by headache, pain in the back and legs, anorexia and costiveness. He was admitted on the 16th. Diagnosis—typhoid fever. In the evening the patient was weak and had no appetite; the pulse was 80; skin hot and moist; tongue coated white, but red at the tip and edges; one stool was passed; the right iliac region was tender, and complaint was made of pain in the back and legs. Ten grains of calomel and jalap were given. Eight dejections occurred during the night, and next morning the skin and eyes were jaundiced. Quinine was given. In the evening the pulse was 74, the skin warm and moist, the tongue coated gray but red at the tip, the bowels quiet; there was acute right iliac tenderness and mental dulness with tinnitus aurium. Next day the bowels remained quiet and the tenderness ceased; but pain in the head and in the back was noted. The abdominal tenderness returned on the 19th, when, also, the tongue was nearly clean but dry, the cheeks flushed and the pain in the back so acute as to require sinapisms. The bowels were quiet on the 20th and without pain or tympanites; the tongue coated gray; the skin moist. Two stools were passed on the 21st; the tongue was white, the skin hot and dry, and there was some thirst and cough, but the appetite was good. A few rose-spots appeared on the 22d, the tongue being pale and moist, the pulse 80. In the evening of this day he was dull; pulse 64. He perspired during the night, and next day the skin was warm and moist, the tongue pale and clean and there was no tenderness, tympanites nor eruption. A few dark spots were found next day on the abdomen and chest. After this improvement was steady. The patient was walking about on the 29th, and was transferred to Annapolis, Md., October 1.

CASE 104.—*Recurring chills and fever; diarrhœa; slight delirium; great prostration; vibices and gangrene of blistered surfaces; death.*—See case of Private Daniel Plummer, Co. H, 33d Pa., No. 93 of the *post-mortem* records.

EIGHT TYPHOID FEVER CASES PRECEDED OR ACCOMPANIED BY REMITTENT FEVER.

CASE 105.—*Record given in full. The existing malarial attack appears to have ended on October 7, when the pulse had fallen to 80 and the skin and tongue were in natural condition, leaving the patient, however, with a diarrhœa, suggesting a congested and perhaps ulcerated condition of the bowels, and some pulmonary engorgement. The typhoid fever is unmarked by prominent symptoms; its influence, other than in the appearance of the rose-colored spots, seems only to have prolonged the period needful to a return to health. It is noticeable that on October 16, while the rose-spots were yet fading, the patient was permitted to be out on pass.*—Corporal Christopher Beninger, Co. D, 3d Mich.; age 26; had been liable to attacks of intermittent fever since 1858. He was admitted Sept. 28, 1861, as a case of typhoid fever. He had been taken sick three days before with chills, fever and pain in the back, and had taken quinia; face flushed, eyes dull, lids dropped; pulse 104, small, easily compressed; skin moist, slightly above natural temperature; tongue moist, slightly coated white; anorexia and irritability of stomach manifested by unsuccessful efforts at vomiting; tenderness over entire abdomen, slight tympanites in right iliac region, no stool; dull, heavy head-pain; nervous twitchings of muscles; no cough but respiration hurried, 30 per minute. During the examination a violent chill came on; the extremities became cold, the pulse small and at times imperceptible at the wrist, the cheeks cold, the breathing hurried and interrupted, the eyes turned upward; some stupor was also noted. Quinia, opium and calomel were ordered to be given every four hours. 29th, *morning:* Slept some; face congested; eyes suffused; pulse 120, quick, feeble; some pain in head and limbs; some deafness and stupor; skin of natural temperature; tongue dry, brown, moist at edges; anorexia; epigastric and general abdominal tenderness; tympanites; derangement of liver; no cough. Milk-punch, beef-essence and blue-mass and opium were ordered. *Evening:* Feeling better; face flushed; eyes suffused; head dull and heavy; pulse 120, full and strong; skin moist; tongue moist at edges, brown and dry in centre; anorexia; slight tenderness in abdomen, particularly in right iliac region; some tympanites and borborygmus; no stool; no cough. Dover's powder was given. 30th, *morning:* Slept well; cheeks congested; eyes dull; head-pain; pulse 112, quick, small; skin hot and moist; tongue moist at edges, dry in the centre; anorexia; tympanites; slight tenderness in right iliac region, marked in left; much soreness in right hypochondriac region; two stools. Ordered three grains of calomel, one of opium and one-sixth of a grain of antimony every three hours. *Evening:* Drowsy; face congested; eyes dull; head-pain; pulse 112, strong; skin above the natural temperature, covered with perspiration; tongue slightly moist at tip and edges, dry and brownish in centre; four stools; slight tympanites; tenderness in left iliac region. Ordered astringents. October 1, *morning:* Head-pain; pulse 112, quick, strong; skin moist, slightly above the natural temperature; tongue moist at edges, dry and white in centre; appetite small; several stools; some cough; pain in right lung; respiration 30. Ordered beef-essence and astringents. *Evening:* Ordered one grain of quinia and two grains of Dover's powder every three hours. 2d: Slept some; face congested; eyes dull; slight head-pain; pulse 105, quick and strong; skin hot and moist; tongue moist, coated white in patches in centre; some appetite; slight tenderness; no tympanites; paroxysms of coughing; mucous expectoration streaked with blood; respiratory murmur in lower lobes of right lung entirely lost. Veratrum viride and sweet spirit of nitre were ordered to be taken every hour. 3d: Slept some; head-pain and slight delirium; pulse 112, quick, strong; skin somewhat hot; tongue moist, clean but for a few yellowish patches in centre; some appetite; two stools; much cough; viscid mucous expectoration streaked with blood; respiration 35; respiratory murmur absent over lower part of right side; some dulness on percussion on both sides. 4th: Slept but little; some head-pain; pulse 108, strong; skin hot; tongue moist, covered with yellowish patches in centre; vomiting; anorexia; three stools; some cough; mucous expectoration streaked with blood; respiration 30 but deeper; dulness decreased in left lung, increased in right. Fifteen drops of veratrum viride were given during the day. 5th: Slept well; pulse 85, full; skin soft but rather warm; tongue moist, slightly coated in centre with yellowish patches; some appetite; three stools; but little expectoration; respiration 26. Milk-punch and Dover's powder were given. 6th: Slept well; head-pain; pulse 90, full; skin of natural temperature, covered slightly with perspiration; tongue moist, coated white in centre; appetite good; some tympanites; right iliac tenderness; two stools; slight cough and expectoration; respiration 25. 7th: Slept well; looking better; pulse 80, natural; skin and tongue natural; two stools; slight cough; respiration 25; respiratory murmur absent on left side below third rib. 8th: Not so well; countenance and skin natural; pulse 85, quick; tongue moist and clean; appetite good; three stools; some cough; slight expectoration of mucus slightly tinged with blood; respiration 35; some crepitation and absence of respiratory murmur on left side, lower portion; mucous râles in middle lobe of right lung, vesicular murmur in upper portion. 9th: Slept well; pulse 80, weak; skin natural; appetite improving; two stools; respiration 26. 10th: Restless; eyes more natural, cheeks less congested; pulse 80, quick; skin natural; tongue moist, clean; appetite moderate; cough slight; two stools. Tincture of iron ordered three times daily. 11th: Stronger; slept some; eyes bright; face slightly flushed; pulse 85, quick; skin natural; tongue moist, clean; appetite good; three stools; cough slight. 12th: Slept well; looking better; cheeks congested; pulse 90, strong, wiry; skin of natural temperature, an occasional rose-spot appearing; tongue moist, clean; slight tenderness in right iliac region; two stools; no cough. 13th: Slept well; looking bright; pulse 90, quick; skin a little above the natural temperature; slight pain in right lung; tongue moist and clean; appetite good; six stools; no cough. 14th: Slept well; looking bright; pulse 110, quick, corded; skin of natural temperature, an occasional rose-spot appearing; tongue slightly coated yellowish in centre; appetite moderate; three stools; moderate tenderness in right umbilical and left iliac regions. 15th: Slept some; pulse 80, regular, corded; skin of natural temperature, showing a few rose-spots, disappearing on pressure; tongue moist, coated yellowish-white in centre; appetite good; three stools; some umbilical tenderness; some pain in middle of right side on deep inspiration. 16th: Out on pass. 17th: Slept well; pulse 85, quick; skin of natural temperature; tongue moist, coated slightly white in centre; appetite moderate; two stools. 18th: Wakeful; pulse 86, somewhat irregular; skin covered with perspiration; slight headache; tongue moist, clean; appetite poor; two stools; some epigastric pain and tenderness. 19th: Slept well; pulse 62, regular; skin natural; tongue moist, clean; appetite moderate; three stools; pain on deep inspiration. 20th: Slept well; pulse 86, regular; skin and tongue natural; appetite good; two stools. 21st: Slept well; pulse 90, quick; skin and tongue natural; buzzing in ears; appetite good; two stools. 22d: Slept well; bright; pulse 90, somewhat quick; tongue clean; appetite good; two stools; some abdominal tenderness. 23d: Slept well; pulse 90, natural; still some pain in right side of chest. 24th: Wakeful; pulse 90, quick; skin moist; tongue white; appetite moderate; two stools; less tenderness. 25th: Slept well; pulse 90, quick; skin natural; tongue clean; appetite good; two stools; some general tenderness. 26th: Returned to duty.

CASE 106.—*Remittent fever not amenable to treatment by quinine; record deficient, but typhoid fever suggested by diarrhœa, tenderness in the right iliac region, brown tongue and subsequent discharge for debility.*—Private James Ellison, Co. F, 19th Ind.; age 24. This man contracted tertian ague about Aug. 20, 1861. The chills were broken up by quinia. He was admitted September 4 as a case of typhoid fever. On the morning of the 5th the fever was slight, the pulse 72, skin natural, tongue flabby and coated yellowish-brown, appetite good, bowels somewhat relaxed and tender on pressure. Quinia was ordered. In the evening there was a moderate fever with flushed face, hurried respiration, hot and dry skin and a burning in the mouth and throat; the bowels were moved twice during the day. Dover's powder was given. He rested well during the night, and next morning was sweating and without fever; but in the evening the skin became hot and dry, the tongue pale, dry and slightly coated, and seven loose stools had been passed accompanied with umbilical pain. A similar remission and exacerbation occurred on the 7th, the dejections on this day being thin, small and lumpy. The remission on the morning of the 8th was not so well marked, although the bowels had not been disturbed during the night; the mind was clear. On the 9th, in the morning, the face was flushed, the pulse 68, the tongue pale, flabby and coated in the centre and at the back, the skin warm and dry; one thin stool had been passed without pain but with borborygmi. In the evening the pulse was 86, the skin warm and dry, the tongue pale and coated brown in the middle; there were no rose-spots; three thin small stools had been passed without pain; the appetite was improving. Dover's powder with small doses of blue-pill and citrate of iron and quinine were ordered. The 10th gave a similar record, but in the evening the tongue was dry and coated brownish, and in connection with four thin small stools passed during the day, it is stated that there was some right iliac tenderness. The blue-pill and iron were omitted and the Dover's powder and quinine continued. On the 11th an acetate of lead and opium pill was given three times, but the diarrhœa continued with slight fever in the evening, and a moist tongue, coated brown in the centre, up to the 13th, when he was transferred to hospital at Baltimore, Md. [He was discharged October 15 on account of general debility.]

CASE 107.—*Recurring chills; diarrhœa; rose-colored spots; gastric irritability; improvement about end of 4th week.*—Private R. M. Robinson, Co. C, 9th Pa. Vols.; age 19; was admitted Sept. 19, 1861, with typhoid fever. About three weeks before his admission he had been taken with chills and pain in the head and bones; the former recurred at intervals of several days with fever at night and continued diarrhœa. On the evening of the 19th the patient was weak but looked well; pulse 78, eyes bright and clear, skin warm but dry and covered on the abdomen and chest with characteristic rose-spots, tongue dry, smooth, glossy and nearly clean; but he had pains in the head, back and limbs and in the hypogastric and right iliac regions, with distended bladder and dysuria. Castor oil, acetate of potash and sweet spirit of nitre were given. He slept badly and had epistaxis at night. Next day the pain in the back and limbs was severe; the skin was dry and warm, the tongue dry, cracked and yellowish-brown in color, the stomach slightly irritable, the bowels tender; one stool was passed. On the 23d a second crop of rose-colored spots appeared on the surface; the bowels were quiet and the tenderness much relieved. The tongue became clean on the 25th. On the 30th the patient was considered convalescent. He was transferred to Annapolis, Md., November 1 [and was returned to duty December 12].

CASE 108.—*Mild typhoid grafted on remittent fever.*—Private R. R. Lassey, Co. A, 4th Mich.; age 28; was seized with headache, weakness and nausea about Sept. 6, 1861, and on the 16th was admitted as a case of typhoid fever. In the evening the patient's face was flushed and he had nausea and loss of appetite, pulse 92, skin warm and moist, tongue moist, yellowish and heavily coated, bowels quiet. Ten grains each of calomel and jalap were given; two dejections followed, and next morning the tongue was cleaner at the tip and edges. Quinine was ordered. In the evening there was no fever, the skin was cool, moist and perspiring; one stool was passed during the day, and there was tenderness in the right iliac region. On the morning of the 18th there was no fever, the skin being cool and moist, and the abdominal tenderness relieved; but in the evening the patient had one thin, large stool, and the right iliac region became acutely tender. Dover's powder was prescribed. On the 19th there was tympanites and the iliac region continued tender, but the skin remained cool and moist and the bowels quiet. The condition of the patient was changed on the 20th only by the diminution of the tympanites; one stool was passed during the day. On the 21st there was deafness with anxiety of expression; there was also some thirst, but the appetite was good and skin natural. The tongue was clean on the 22d, the pulse 68, small and soft, the skin natural, the bowels quiet and neither tender nor tympanitic, but the face was somewhat flushed. In the evening rose-spots made their appearance, and a second crop on the 24th. Wine and bark were ordered. He was reported as walking about on the 30th, and was transferred to Annapolis, Md., October 1.

CASE 109.—*Mild typhoid grafted on remittent fever.*—Private Eli Sulgrave, Co. D, 19th Ind.; age 18; had a chill about Aug. 25, 1861, and was admitted September 4. Diagnosis—typhoid fever. He had headache, pain in the bones and back, and slight diarrhœa with fever, which was aggravated daily about noon. On the morning of the 5th there was tinnitus aurium but no fever; the pulse was 78, skin cold and moist, tongue coated, pale and flabby, appetite good, bowels regular. Quinine was ordered. In the evening the pulse was 72 and strong, tongue pale, flabby, red at the edges and white at the base and centre. During the day he had one thin stool and was weak and giddy. Dover's powder was given at night. Until the 11th the patient continued without change, a slight febrile action occurring every evening, manifesting itself in flushing of the face, but the pulse in no instance rose higher than 80; there was one stool daily, with, on one occasion, pain in the left iliac fossa. He usually rested well and had a fair appetite, although his tongue continued pale, flabby and coated. On the 11th a few rose-spots appeared, which faded next day, but were replaced by others and an eruption of sudamina; the pulse was 68, the skin cool, bowels quiet and not tender, tongue coated brownish but red at the tip. On the 13th he was sent to hospital at Baltimore, Md. [He was afterward transferred to the 20th Ind. and served until the close of the war.]

CASE 110.—*Mild typhoid grafted on remittent fever.*—Private E. S. Elmer, Co. K, 14th N. Y.; age 22; was admitted Sept. 24, 1861, having been taken sick three weeks before with diarrhœa followed by bilious remittent fever. On admission he had severe headache with flushed face, injected eyes and accelerated pulse. He slept little during the following night; in the morning he was covered with sweat, pulse 108, full but weak, tongue slightly yellow, bowels moved once, respiration natural; his appetite was good, but he had much thirst and was somewhat dizzy. Two grains of blue-mass and a half grain of quinine were ordered to be given every two hours. On the 26th he was not so well; his face was flushed, eyes much suffused and countenance anxious; the dizziness was increased and there was delirium; the tongue was heavily coated yellow and the appetite lost; there was also retention of urine, but the skin was moist and profusely covered with sudamina; there had been but one stool, and the patient had no pain nor tenderness. Castor oil and extract of buchu were ordered. In the evening the skin was hot but bathed in perspiration, the pulse 96, strong, the tongue coated and moist, the bowels tender and slightly tympanitic. On the 27th the face was not flushed; the skin was soft and natural, the respiration normal, the tongue moist, yellow in the centre, and the appetite good; two stools were passed and there was some right iliac tenderness; a few rose-colored spots appeared on the abdomen. One drachm of turpentine emulsion was given every three hours, with twelve grains of quinine in the forenoon. In the evening the cheeks were flushed, the eyes suffused, the pulse 96, the skin dry and hot, the tongue moist and heavily coated gray, the appetite good; two stools were passed and tympanites, borborygmus and tenderness were present. Sweet spirit of nitre and Dover's powder were given. No stool was passed on the 28th; the skin was natural, pulse 92, strong, the tongue moist and yellow, the appetite moderate; there was some difficulty in micturition but no abdominal pain nor tenderness. In the evening four or five rose-colored spots appeared on the abdomen and chest. Next day the skin was soft but rather above the natural temperature, the tongue moist and yellow-coated but red at the tip and edges; there were twelve dull red spots on the abdomen, which was slightly tympanitic but not tender. He vomited during the following night and had three stools with some tympanites and left iliac tenderness. Lead, opium and tannin were given. Slight relaxation of the bowels continued up to October 10, when the patient was sent to hospital at Annapolis, Md.

CASE 111.—*Chill; remitting fever; slight diarrhœa; moist skin; flabby tongue; rose-spots on 15th day; drowsiness; perspirations; sordes; record imperfect; death.*—Private Henry Martindale, Co. F, 19th Ind. Vols.; age 24; was taken Aug. 28, 1861, with headache, pains in the bones, languor and chill. He took quinia and had no recurrence of the chill; but the fever which followed was generally worse in the morning. He was admitted September 4. Diagnosis— typhoid fever. On the 5th: Pulse 76; skin warm and moist; tongue heavily coated, pale and flabby; slight diarrhœa; pain in the back. Quinine was given. *Evening:* Skin warm, dry; tongue flabby and coated white; four thin small stools, but no pain or tenderness in the bowels; appetite fair. Dover's powder at night. On the 6th and 7th the symptoms were unchanged. On the 8th the mind was somewhat dull; the patient continued to be up and to walk about occasionally. Sugar of lead and opium were given. No material change took place until the 11th, when the warm and moist skin showed sudamina and some rose-colored spots on the abdomen, the tongue at this time being pale, flabby and coated gray, the bowels but slightly relaxed and the appetite good. Whiskey-punch was prescribed. The patient was drowsy on the 12th, and on the following day the tongue became brown and cracked but remained pale at the tip, the skin hot and dry, the breathing hurried, and the bowels moved eight times but free from pain and distention. On the 14th the tongue was dry and the countenance haggard. Two grains of quinine and one of calomel were prescribed for administration three times daily. Profuse perspirations occurred on the 15th, but the diarrhœa continued and sordes appeared on the teeth. Turpentine emulsion was given. On the evening of the 16th there was some tenderness of the abdomen and the patient kept tossing his head from side to side. On the 18th the pulse was 80, weak and small, tongue heavily coated, brown in the middle and red at tip and edges, skin hot and moist, bowels not tender but quite loose, especially at night. On the 19th there was some tenderness in the right iliac region. Ten stools were passed on the 22d, and on the following day the abdomen was tympanitic. The record closes abruptly with the announcement of death on the 28th.

CASE 112.—*Coincidence of remittent fever and typhoid.*—Arminius Tyler, attendant; age 21; was admitted Sept. 9, 1861, having been sick since the 1st with headache, pain in the back and fever, aggravated at night, but not preceded by a chill. On admission his face was flushed, pulse 79, tongue white and coated, skin warm and sweating; he had epistaxis and a few rose-colored spots on the abdomen. Next day the tongue was moist, brown-coated in the centre and red at the tip and edges; the bowels were quiet but tender on pressure. Quinine was taken during the day and Dover's powder at night. On the 11th the patient was dull and prostrated, pulse 68 and feeble; but in the evening there was much restlessness with high fever, pulse 90 and strong. Next morning a remission occurred, followed by an exacerbation in the evening; the tongue was pale, flabby and coated brown, and the bowels continued quiet. On the 13th the evening exacerbation was not so marked, but the tongue was heavily coated gray and the skin and conjunctivæ were jaundiced. Blue-mass was given in addition to the quinine. On the 15th two large stools were passed, and in the evening three free, thin and painless stools. Aromatic sulphuric acid was prescribed. On the 16th the pulse was 62, the tongue pale and heavily coated gray, the bowels quiet, the jaundice disappearing; there were rose-colored spots and a profusion of sudamina on the skin, which perspired freely. Rose-colored spots appeared again on the 18th; the bowels continued quiet and the evening accession became less manifest; night-sweats were profuse. On October 1 the patient had so far recovered as to be placed on light duty.

Eight Remittent Fever Cases with More or Less Evidence of the Co-existence of Typhoid Fever.

CASE 113.—*Diagnosis—remittent. Delirium, stupor, deafness; diarrhœa; rose-colored spots and bed-sores.*—Private Bennett Pepper, Co. H, 62d N. Y.; age 19; was taken sick early in February, 1862, with headache, nausea, vomiting and pains in the back and limbs, and was admitted on the 27th as a case of remittent fever. On March 5 he was delirious, drowsy and inclined to stupor; he had tinnitus aurium and twitching of the mouth, puffy eyelids, flushed cheeks, rapid and weak pulse, hot and dry skin, moist but much coated tongue, sordes on the teeth, some appetite, much thirst, a diarrhœa of four watery stools daily, which were sometimes passed involuntarily; respiration was hurried and there was some cough. Beef-essence, turpentine emulsion and tincture of opium were prescribed. On the 6th there was profuse perspiration with sudamina. Next day the delirium abated and the patient replied rationally but with difficulty; the tongue was coated but moist, and was permitted to remain protruded indefinitely; the bowels were regular but meteorized and tender and the abdomen showed some rose-colored spots; the breath was very offensive from ozæna. There was much tendency to stupor on the 9th, with occasional delirium. Free perspiration with sudamina occurred again on the 10th, and the urine was excessive in quantity; cough persisted and there was some dulness on percussion a little below the clavicle on the right side. The skin became hot and dry on the 12th and the watery stools returned; respiration was hurried and the breath very offensive. The mind became clear on the 14th, and on the following day the skin was natural, the tongue clean, the pulse good, but the bowels continued loose. The diarrhœa, however, subsided on the 16th, on the occurrence of copious sweating with sudamina, and the cough was much relieved; earache, developed on this day, was noted also on the 17th, when the skin again became hot and dry and the tongue somewhat coated. Some sore spots on the back and hips were observed on the 18th, and next day the patient was placed on a water-bed. He became deaf at this time, but his general condition improved, and on the 28th he was able to walk about. He was discharged April 26 because of general debility.

CASE 114.—*Diagnosis—remittent fever. Diarrhœa and abdominal pain; deafness, delirium and prostration; record incomplete.*—Private Edwin White, Co. H, 86th N. Y. Vols.; age 18; was admitted March 2, 1862, with remitting fever, headache, giddiness, nausea and constipation. The record is silent as to his condition until the 13th, when he was dull and dejected and talked much in his sleep, having a hot and dry skin, a dry tongue, rough and coated but clean and moist at the edges, some pain in swallowing, diarrhœa, abdominal pain and slight iliac tenderness, with headache and flushed cheeks, rapid pulse and occasional epistaxis. The fever increased towards evening and was followed by a chill. From the 14th to the 18th he had delirium at night but was rational during the day; his bowels were slightly relaxed, the stools thin and watery, and there was much abdominal tenderness. Quinine was ordered on the 14th, tincture of iron and turpentine emulsion on the 15th; epistaxis was noted on the 16th and deafness on the 17th. On the 18th delirium gave place to dulness and stupidity, which increased until on the 21st the patient was unable to protrude his tongue well and swallowed with difficulty; there was epistaxis; cough became troublesome and the expectoration was tinged with blood, which was conceived to be owing to the epistaxis. From this time to the 30th, when the daily record ends, there was little change in the symptoms. The patient was discharged for debility May 10.

CASE 115.—*Symptoms of typhoid in a case entered as remittent; discharged on account of rheumatism.*—Private L. Pettit, Co. D, 3d Mich. Vols.; age 22; of delicate constitution and liable to pulmonary troubles, was admitted Oct. 19, 1861, as a case of remittent fever. Next day his eyes were bright, cheeks slightly flushed, pulse 74 and regular, skin somewhat above the natural temperature, tongue moist, fissured and faintly coated yellow, appetite good; he had a slight cough, pain in the back and limbs, relaxed bowels, tympanites and general abdominal tenderness, marked in the right iliac region. Two rose-colored spots were discovered on the 21st, the symptoms otherwise remaining as stated. Twelve grains of quinine and two of opium were given daily in divided doses, with Dover's powder at night. On the 24th the skin became moist. Next day he was wakeful, his eyes dull and cheeks congested. Two drachms of sulphate of magnesia with one-twelfth of a grain of tartar emetic were given in the morning and two compound cathartic pills at night. After this he seemed to improve, his pulse, tongue and skin becoming natural and appetite good. He slept well, and on the 29th was out of bed and dressed; but on this day his eyes were bright, cheeks somewhat flushed, pulse 80, and he had pain in the hip, knee and ankle-joints, which continued until his transfer, November 1, to Annapolis, Md. [Diagnosis—rheumatism; patient discharged from service on the 29th.]

CASE 116.—*Diagnosis—remittent. Diarrhœa and rose-colored spots; no cerebral symptoms.*—Private Oscar H. Field, Co. C, 24th N. Y. Vols.; age 30; was taken Sept. 23, 1861, with intermittent fever, and admitted on the 30th as a case of remittent fever, presenting a quick strong pulse, 100, continuous headache, a red and slightly coated tongue and capricious appetite. Dover's powder was given. The patient vomited during the night; next day the tongue was dry, red at the edges and brown in the centre, and the teeth covered with sordes. Turpentine emulsion was given every two hours, with small doses of opium, ipecacuanha and nitre. On October 2 wine and cinchona were ordered in repeated doses; at night the patient perspired a little. On the 3d the skin was of natural temperature and presented some rose-colored spots, which were perceptible to the touch and disappeared on pressure; the bowels, which had been quiet since admission, were on this day moved four times. He rested well at night, and on the 4th had a natural skin, moist and slightly brown tongue and feeble pulse, 90 per minute; three stools were passed. During the following week the patient continued without much change. On the 5th there was some ringing in the left ear, with slight headache on the following day; on the 10th marked deafness with tinnitus aurium. The bowels were somewhat relaxed at this time, the pulse from 80 to 100, the skin natural and the tongue brownish and inclined to be dry or, occasionally, moist and yellow-coated except at the edges, which were red. On the 11th fifteen grains of quinine, with six of blue-pill and two of opium, were given in two doses at an interval of two hours, with four grains of quinine every two hours thereafter. During the night profuse sweating occurred, and next day there was no stool. On the 14th the patient was transferred to Baltimore, Md.

CASE 117.—*Diagnosis—remittent. Bowels loose and tympanitic; no characteristic symptoms of typhoid.*—Private O. Gunderson, Co. B, 6th Wis. Vols.; age 19; was admitted Nov. 8, 1861, having been attacked about the 1st with chills and fever, headache, pain in the back and limbs and anorexia. On admission he was wakeful and suffering from headache, his countenance anxious, eyes dull, cheeks flushed, pulse 100 and thread-like, skin about the natural temperature, tongue red and moist at the tip and edges, dry and coated yellow in the centre, appetite lost and bowels loose and tympanitic; he had some cough with whitish expectoration. One drachm of sweet spirit of nitre was given every hour. Small doses of blue-pill and opium were prescribed on the 9th and repeated on the 10th and 11th, with twelve grains of quinine each day, and with eight grains on the 12th, on which day beef-essence and emulsion of turpentine were also administered. The tongue, however, remained coated yellowish-white and the appetite poor up to the 19th, when the last notes were entered on the record. The patient was transferred to Baltimore, Md., December 3.

CASE 118.—*Remittent fever followed by typhoid.*—Private A. Whipple, Co. A, 4th Mich. Vols.; age 19; was admitted Oct. 30, 1861, as a case of remittent fever. On October 8 he had chills and fever which continued a week, with weakness, anorexia, nausea and vomiting, and during this period he felt better in the morning than in the evening. He was treated with quinine, rhubarb and capsicum. On admission his cheeks were slightly flushed, countenance calm, eyes bright, conjunctivæ yellow, pulse 99, full and strong, skin yellow, warm, dry, soft and without eruption or sudamina, tongue moist, red at the tip and coated grayish in the centre, appetite deficient; the bowels were moved five times, and there was abdominal tenderness with slight gurgling but no meteorism. Calomel and full doses of quinine were prescribed. During the night the patient was delirious at times, and on the following day he had some deafness and tinnitus aurium. The quinine was continued and the calomel omitted. On November 1 the tongue was moist, pale and coated somewhat in the centre and at the base. Next day two rose-colored spots were noticed and sordes appeared on the teeth. Milk-punch, beef-essence and turpentine emulsion were prescribed. On the 4th the patient's condition was unchanged; he was very delirious, his face much flushed, pulse 98 and strong, skin very hot and showing some rose-colored spots, tongue dry in the centre but moist at the edges; he had no cough, but mucous and sibilant râles were heard in some parts of the chest; the bowels were moved by an enema of castor oil and turpentine and the tympanites which had been present was thereby reduced. He was dull and stupid on the 5th and had subsultus tendinum. Next day some petechial spots appeared. No further details are given. The patient was transferred to Annapolis, Md., on the 18th.

CASE 119.—*Typhoid fever following remittent fever; prognosis favorable until the advent of peritonitis.*—Private Abraham Haner, Co. D, 14th N. Y. Vols.; age 21; was admitted Sept. 23, 1861, as a case of remittent fever. He had been epileptic from infancy to the age of 19, when the fits ceased. He was taken two weeks before admission with a convulsion. Quinine was given but the convulsions recurred. On admission his face was flushed, eyes injected, bowels loose and abdomen painful. A slight fever was present on the 25th; appetite deficient, thirst considerable, pulse 88, full and strong, skin warm and moist (he had perspired profusely at night), tongue light-brown and fissured; he had a little headache and dizziness. Acetate of ammonia was prescribed with five drops of Fowler's solution four times daily. He did not sleep well at night, and on the 26th was restless, his cheeks flushed, eyes suffused, pulse 96, skin hot and moist, tongue brown and dry in the centre, fissured and moist at the edges; he had headache and slight delirium, pain in the stomach, pain and great tenderness in the iliac region, some cough and difficulty in retaining urine. The acetate of ammonia was continued and turpentine emulsion was ordered for administration every two hours. In the evening the skin was moist, the pulse 102, the tongue yellowish. Hoffmann's anodyne was prescribed in drachm doses every four hours. He slept but little during the night, and on the 27th the pulse was 96, skin hot and dry, tongue dry in the centre, moist at the edges; he had headache, anorexia, tympanites on the right side, tenderness in the right iliac region and his bowels had been moved six times. Turpentine emulsion and Fowler's solution were renewed and pills of opium, lead and tannin prescribed. In the evening the pulse was 104, the skin hot and moist but with no eruption nor sudamina, the tongue rather yellow in the centre but less fissured; the headache was lessened and the diarrhœa reduced to one stool, but the tenderness and tympanites continued. Sweet spirit of nitre and wine of antimony were administered during the night. He slept well and perspired early in the morning; no stool was passed. On the 28th the skin was hot and moist, tongue brown, dry and fissured in the centre, its edges moist and white; the anorexia, headache and cough persisted, and there was partial retention of urine, with pain in the hypogastrium. Extract of buchu was given. In the evening the face was flushed, eyes bright, pulse strong and regular, skin soft but somewhat hot, tongue moist, white and fissured; bowels moved once, tender and tympanitic; the cough had subsided and the appetite was returning. Dover's powder was ordered. He slept well during the night, and on the 29th the face was somewhat flushed, eyes injected, pulse 88 and strong, skin hot and moist, tongue brown and dry in the centre, moist at the edges, the bowels quiet but a little tender and tympanitic. In the evening there was slight headache; the bowels were moved once, but the tenderness and distention continued; the appetite was good. Tincture of opium and essence of peppermint were administered. On the 30th the skin was soft and its temperature decreased; the tongue moist at the edges, brown and dry in the centre, the appetite moderate; three stools were passed and there was much tympanites with marked tenderness in the right iliac region and some in the left side. On October 1 the skin was natural, the tongue slightly coated in the centre and fissured, the appetite good and the bowels quiet. He improved after this, so that from the 3d to the 6th no note of his condition was recorded. On the 7th the pulse was 85, skin natural, tongue moist but red at the tip and edges, yellow and fissured in the centre; bowels moved three times. No marked change occurred until the 10th, when the skin became hot and dry, followed on the 11th by a profuse eruption of rose-colored spots; on this day the tongue was slightly moist, yellow in the centre, the appetite good and the bowels quiet, but the abdomen was tender and tympanitic, especially in the umbilical and right iliac regions. Tincture of iron was prescribed. Fresh crops of rose-colored spots appeared at intervals until the 28th, when they faded. The heat of skin gradually lessened until on the 16th it became normal; two days later the skin was moist. The bowels were moved once or seldom twice daily, but a good deal of tenderness and distention was noted in the umbilical and right iliac regions. On the 20th extract of senna was administered and two passages followed its exhibition. The patient usually slept well and his appetite was good; the tongue was moist and clean, faintly furred or yellow-coated in the centre. He appeared to be doing well when, on the 29th, he was seized with extreme tenderness of the abdomen. After a wakeful night his eyes on the 30th were dull, cheeks flushed, pulse 100, skin hot, tongue moist, brown and fissured, lips and teeth covered with sordes; he had some deafness and mental dulness, anorexia and thirst; there was no diarrhœa, but much general abdominal tenderness and some tympanites. A blister was applied to the abdomen and calomel and opium prescribed for administration every three hours. On the 31st the pulse was 140 and irregular and the skin bathed in perspiration, but the abdomen was less tender. Death took place on this day.

CASE 120.—*Remittent fever and a recurrence of remittent overlapping the typhoid case.*—Private E. J. Tice, Co. G, 14th N. Y. Vols.; age 23; had chills, perspirations, pain in the head and umbilical tenderness on Sept. 28, 1861, and was admitted October 2 as a case of remittent fever. On the evening of admission the patient's pulse was not accelerated, but his face was flushed, eyes injected and skin hot; his tongue was moist and coated white, appetite deficient, bowels tender and moved once during the day. Blue-pill and opium were given. Next morning the tongue was coated yellow and bowels moved; pulse 80, strong; skin perspiring. Quinine was ordered to be taken at the rate of sixteen grains a day, with Dover's powder in the evening. This condition of slight fever with yellow-coated tongue, anorexia and some headache continued for several days; but in the meantime the bowels became quite loose, meteorized and tender, especially in the right iliac region. On the 8th the tongue was red at the tip and edges and yellowish-white in the centre, the appetite improved and the pulse lowered to 60. Tincture of iron was ordered. During the following week the bowels were less affected, only one or two stools being passed daily; the skin was of the natural temperature and sometimes perspiring, the appetite good, but a slight headache persisted. A chill occurred suddenly on the 16th, and next day the pulse was 100, full and strong, the skin hot and dry, the tongue slightly moist, white at the sides, yellow in the centre, the appetite poor, the bowels moved once, the abdomen tender, especially in the right iliac region. Blue-pill and opium were given in repeated doses. On the 18th the pulse fell to 70 and several rose-colored spots appeared on the skin; but the tongue continued coated until the 28th, Fowler's solution having been given in the meantime, and the headache, relaxed bowels and abdominal tenderness lasted for ten days longer. The patient was transferred, November 18, to Annapolis, Md. [as a case of typhoid fever; he was returned to duty with his regiment December 2].

TWO CASES ENTERED AS TYPHOID, BUT IN WHICH ONLY THE MALARIAL ELEMENT WAS PROMINENT.

CASE 121.—*Malarial symptoms prominent; the presence of enteric fever not clearly established.*—Private Matthew Baird, Co. C, 3d Mich. Vols.; age 23; was admitted Oct. 19, 1861, as a case of typhoid fever. About October 5 he had been seized with pain in the head and bones, fever and chills; he had some nausea and vomiting at first, and a diarrhœa which continued for two days; the headache lasted four days; during the second week his urine had to be removed by catheter. On admission his pulse was 62 and of fair strength, skin soft and warm, tongue pale, moist and slightly coated brownish in the centre, appetite good; he had tinnitus aurium and giddiness, but no pain, eruption nor sudamina; one thin watery stool was passed, but there was no tenderness, borborygmus nor tympanites, and the abdomen was soft; there was no cough and the urine was normal. Quinine was prescribed in full doses three times daily. Next day the face was calm and natural, the pulse 64, steady and of fair strength, the skin soft and warm, the tongue slightly pale and flabby but moist and clean, the appetite good; one thin fetid stool was passed. On the 22d the quinine was reduced to two grains three times daily, and during the night the patient had a chill, but next day its effects disappeared. On the 28th he rested badly and had some diarrhœa, but there was no tenderness nor tympanites; the tongue was pale and moist and the appetite fair. The skin and conjunctivæ became jaundiced on the 31st. Small doses of calomel and opium were given. November 4 he slept well; his mind was clear, countenance calm, bowels regular and appetite good. He was transferred to Annapolis, Md., on the 18th.

CASE 122.—*Death in eight days. Diagnosis—typhoid, but symptoms and treatment those of remittent fever.*—Private Edwin Graves, Co. D, 86th N. Y. Vols.; age 26; was admitted March 17, 1862. He was taken sick about the 12th with pain in the chest, headache, nausea, a feeling of general swelling and much debility, succeeded by a chill, fever and profuse perspiration, which symptoms recurred daily about 11 A. M.; he had also much annoyance from a numb feeling in his fingers. On admission the pulse was rapid and weak, the skin hot and moist, the tongue moist, red and slightly coated; the patient's appetite was poor and he had some diarrhœa and pyrosis; he stated that the chill and fever occurred at the same time in rapid alternations in different parts of the body, the paroxysms lasting two or three hours. Twenty-four grains of quinine were directed to be taken during the day. He was delirious during the 18th; his pulse rapid and weak, skin natural, tongue moist and coated white. Punch and beef-essence were given every two hours. He died delirious on the morning of the 19th.

The last case of this series appears to have been one of mistaken diagnosis:

CASE 123.—Private Wm. H. Courtney, Co. B, 24th N. Y. Vols.; age 24; was taken Sept. 4, 1861, with pain in the shoulders and left side and also on breathing; he had chills and fever and had been blistered. He was admitted on the 18th. Diagnosis—typhoid fever. The pulse was 46, skin cool and moist, left side tender and dull, respiration short, decubitus on the sound side, tongue smooth, nearly dry, bowels constipated and tender in both iliac regions. Two grains of calomel and one-fourth grain of morphia were prescribed. Next day the pain was less sharp, the præcordia seemed elevated and the sounds of the heart were obscured. In the evening the patient was drowsy, pulse 50 and irregular, skin natural, tongue slightly coated gray posteriorly, red at the tip. Calomel in two-grain doses with opium was given every two hours. On the 20th there was acute tenderness in both iliac regions but the bowels continued constipated. On the 21st the breath became fetid, and on the following day the gums were swollen and tender. The mercurial was omitted. On the 24th chlorate of potash was given on account of the salivation. The patient was walking about and had a good appetite on the 30th, and was doing light duty in the ward on October 3. He was returned to duty on the 17th.

FEVER CASES FROM REGIMENTAL RECORDS.—The symptoms of typhoid fever assumed a prominence in the typho-malarial cases of the Seminary Hospital, and no doubt in those of other general hospitals, which was not shown in the cases occurring at the same time in the field. This difference in character was a consequence of the greater prevalence of remittent fevers at the front. Remittents seldom reached the general hospitals, as they proved fatal if pernicious, or recovered if of a mild type, under the influence of quinine, at the regimental or field division hospitals. Similarly, if the remittent fever masked an existing typhoid, the notable symptoms in a rapidly fatal case were those of the pernicious fever, while in a mild attack the treatment prior to the transfer to the general hospital had its effect on the malarial symptoms and left the case for the records of the hospital as one of comparatively unmodified typhoid. But even in the febrile cases treated in the field the symptoms of typhoid fever were sometimes so strongly developed as to leave no doubt concerning the nature of the disease. Not only was this the case in local epidemics occurring in non-malarious districts, but in commands which at the same time reported numerous cases of malarial fever, the presence of which led to a routine administration of quinine in all febrile cases. This may be illustrated by a series of cases from the records of the 27th Connecticut Volunteers. Fevers had prevailed in this regiment from the establishment of winter quarters at Falmouth, Va., after the battle of Fredericksburg. Thus, in January, 1863, there were reported on the monthly report of sick and wounded six cases of typhoid, seven of typho-malarial, three of intermittent and sixteen of remittent fever; but the details of none of these cases are preserved. In February and March, the months during which the recorded cases were treated in the regimental hospital, no typho-malarial cases were reported, the fevers being entered either as remittent or as typhoid. The histories of thirteen cases of typhoid are recorded; one of these, in which the body was examined after death, is presented as case 330 of the *post-mortem* records of the continued fevers;* the others are given below in the order of their admission for treatment. Appended to the record of the first case is a remark by the regimental surgeon, WM. O. McDONALD, as follows:

I regard this as a purer case of typhoid fever than that of Dolph, for this was uncomplicated. The rose-spots appeared on the seventh day of his stay in hospital, the disease having probably made some progress before any record was kept of the case.

CASE 1.—*Delirium; involuntary stools; abdominal tenderness; rose-colored spots; improvement from the end of the second week.*—Private H. E. Burnham, Co. H, 27th Conn. Vols., having been complaining for two or three days, was admitted Feb. 2, 1863. The pulse was 132, small and weak, and the muscles of the body were sore to the touch. On the 5th the tongue was dark-colored and there was some delirium. Sixty grains of quinine were administered in three doses during the day. On the 7th the bowels were moved twice and there was tenderness over the cæcum and ascending colon. Next day the pulse was 132, tongue dry, red and cracked, lips black; the patient was very delirious and had several involuntary passages from the bowels. Stimulants were given. On the 9th the pulse was 132, tongue a little more moist, bowels quiet and delirium lessened; six rose-colored spots were found on the abdomen. The patient was not so well next day; the tongue was dryer and darker; the abdomen was distended and gurgled on pressure in the right iliac fossa, and there were several ineffectual attempts at stool. On the 11th the tongue was dry as ever and the lips as black, but the patient was able to talk sensibly. After this the pulse gradually fell to 80, the tongue became clean and moist, the abdominal tenderness ceased and the appetite improved; but the return to health was slowly effected.

CASE 2.—*Low fever and hebetude; diarrhœa and abdominal tenderness; night-sweats and œdema of legs; recovery.*—Private William A. Morse, Co. H, 27th Conn. Vols., was admitted Feb. 2, 1863, after exposure on picket duty to cold, wet and stormy weather. Diagnosis—typhoid fever. Stupor; pulse 96; tongue dry and red; twelve stools; tenderness in the right iliac and hypogastric regions. 3d: Dull and stupid; pulse 88, full, soft; skin moist; tongue dry and red; one stool; tenderness; pains in the back and limbs. 4th: Looking better; pulse 84; tongue dry; much thirst; two stools. 5th: Pulse 72; tongue red, clean, moist; tenderness below umbilicus; one thin watery stool. 6th: Pulse 84; tongue red, bare, moist; one stool; less tenderness. The patient took ten grains of quinine five times a day during the first four days of his stay in hospital. 7th: Pulse 72, dicrotic; tongue red, dry, glazed; odor feverish; eyelids dusky; iliac and hypogastric tenderness. 8th: Tongue dry, glazed; face dusky; three stools. Whiskey was prescribed. 9th: Pulse 78; tongue moister; one stool. 10th: Two stools. 13th: Pulse 84; tongue glazed, bare; one stool. For some days anterior to this date the patient had been taking solid food. On the 27th aromatic sulphuric acid and quinine were given on account of night-sweats. These recurred on March 12, but were immediately controlled by renewing the acid medicine. He was very pale and anæmic; iron was prescribed. After this his legs became œdematous. He was not returned to duty until May 24.

CASE 3.—*Febrile attack during convalescence from jaundice;† diarrhœa and right iliac tenderness; mental dulness; moaning respiration; dusky skin; great prostration and tremulousness; death on 13th day.*—Private Joseph Hull, Co. I, 27th Conn. Vols.; intemperate; suffered in January, 1863, from an attack of jaundice from which he convalesced slowly. On February 18 he was taken into hospital. Fifty grains of quinine were prescribed for administration during the day. On the 19th the pulse, which had been very slow for some days, rose to 60, the lips were black, tongue red and dry, bowels quiet and free from pain. The quinine was omitted on the 20th. On the 21st the patient was drowsy, mind dull, speech thick, bowels moved twice and abdomen tender; deafness, which was probably in part induced by the quinine, became somewhat lessened. Beef-tea and stimulants were ordered. Little change took place until the 26th, when the bowels became more relaxed; on this day four watery stools were passed, the tongue was dry as a board, pulse 84, respiration moaning, hands tremulous. Next day the tongue became somewhat moist, the hearing improved and there was less dulness and wandering of the mind; the bowels were moved three times and the right iliac region was tender. On the 28th the pulse rose to 120, the respiration to 27; the tongue was dry and cracked but not very dark, the skin dusky or purplish; the patient slept with his mouth open and moaned with each breath; he was emaciated and extremely prostrated. Death took place March 2.

CASE 4.—*Bronchitis; slight diarrhœa and delirium; sordes; rose-colored spots about the 10th day; favorable signs at end of second week; distention and ecchymoses of the abdomen; bed-sores; pneumonic symptoms and death at the end of the fourth week.*—Private Charles L. Alling, Co. H, 27th Conn. Vols.; age 18; a slender boy, was first seen Feb. 18, 1863, suffering from a cold contracted while on picket duty. Veratrum viride was given daily until the 21st, when it was omitted and quinine substituted, sixty grains in divided doses during the day. He was admitted to hospital on the

* *Infra*, page 408, case of Private E. B. Dolph.

† Surg. J. T. WEBB, 23d Ohio Vols., in a letter dated Feb. 10, 1862, at Fayetteville, Va., and published in the *Cincinnati Lancet and Observer*, Vol. V, p. 171, makes the following statement: "At the close of this month jaundice made its appearance, and what is most remarkable, its advent among us appears to have eradicated all the different forms of fever, and since the 10th of January, just one month this day, not a single case of fever of any description has made its appearance. * * * For the first time since we have been in Western Virginia, a little more than seven months, one whole month has passed without a case of camp-fever occurring in our midst." Jaundice prevailed in the camp of the 27th Conn. Vols. at Falmouth, Va., during January, 1863, but its prevalence was not associated with that disappearance of fever which occurred in the experience of Surgeon WEBB. See *infra*, p. 875.

22d as a case of typhoid fever with bronchial complication. Small doses of ipecacuanha, opium and camphor were administered. On the 23d the pulse was 96 and the bowels tender but quiet. Three ten-grain doses of quinine were given during the day. On the 25th the tongue was dark at the base, red at the tip, the lips and teeth black, the bowels moved twice, the mind wandering. He had been taking beef-tea and quinine up to this time; whiskey was now added. A few indistinct rose-colored spots appeared on the 27th; speech was difficult and incoherent. There was some dysuria on the 28th, relieved by hot fomentations to the abdomen; the tongue was dry, dark and cracked; pulse 108. The patient had coughed more or less since his admission, but at this time the chest symptoms became more prominent. On March 2 the pulse was 120 and dicrotic, the abdomen tender, the bowels moved three times, the stools thin and watery; the hands and cheeks were purplish in color; speech somewhat less incoherent. On the 4th the pulse was 120, tongue slightly moist and softer than heretofore, face pale; the patient took some interest in his condition and suffered much from abdominal distention. Turpentine was prescribed. On the 5th the pulse was 108 during sleep, 132 while awake, respiration 23, tongue dry, abdomen distended and ecchymosed, skin over sacrum congested. On the 6th the pulse was 144, respiration 36, tongue dry, cracked, dark and bloody. No material change took place until the 8th, when the integuments over the sacrum formed a sloughing bed-sore. On the 10th much flatus was passed from the bowels with great relief to the patient; dysphagia was noted at this time. On the 14th the pulse was 128 to 132, respiration 36 to 40, pulse dicrotic, cheeks flushed, lips and nose white, tongue dry, brown and cracked; the distention of the abdomen was again a cause of much suffering and prevented the patient from taking his allowance of beef-tea and whiskey; the bowels were moved twice. On the 16th the dicrotism of the pulse ceased, the tongue became more generally moist, and the patient smiled in answer to a question. But delirium returned on the 19th, respiration became reduced to 26 and the lower jaw moved with each breath; the expectoration was rusty. Death took place on the 21st.

CASE 5.—*Bronchitis; tenderness over colon, but a large cathartic dose produced no injurious effect; pink spots on chest about 9th day; no cerebral symptoms until late in the attack, when the delirium noted was probably due to continued pain in the feet and morphia given for its alleviation; gangrene of the feet; death.*—Private Wm. F. Bernhardt, Co. K, 27th Conn. Vols., was admitted March 17, 1863. Diagnosis—bronchitis and probable fever. He had taken veratrum viride for two days. On the 18th the pulse was 96, respiration 20, tongue dry in the centre; there was some cough with expectoration and substernal soreness, and the right iliac and umbilical regions were tender. During the five following days two hundred and forty grains of quinine were taken in ten-grain doses, the tongue meanwhile becoming red at the tip and edges and somewhat moist and the cough and scanty mucous expectoration continuing. There was tenderness along the track of the colon but no movement of the bowels. Five compound cathartic pills were administered on the 21st, and two stools were passed on the following day. Some pink spots appeared on the chest on the 23d. On the 25th the tongue was moist and cleaning, the abdomen covered with sudamina, but the right foot was very painful and numb. For some days there was little change in the condition of the patient: Pulse 108; respiration 20, with slight cough and expectoration and râles posteriorly; tongue clean and moist; appetite good; face natural; bowels quiet and free from pain; feet very painful especially at night, requiring the administration of large doses of morphia to give rest and relief. Aconite and turpentine liniments were used but without benefit. On the 29th the dorsum of the right foot became purple and cold and the leg immediately above the ankle puffy; two days later the left foot became similarly affected. Small doses of tincture of iron, quinine and sweet spirit of nitre were prescribed and great attention was paid to the diet of the patient; hot bricks and flannel wrappings were applied to the feet. On April 7, in addition to the ecchymosis on the dorsum of the right metatarsus, a slough extended over most of the toes; the patient was delirious during the night. One grain of sulphate of morphia was prescribed for administration at bed-time, the dose to be repeated in an hour if required. The black line forming the margin of the ecchymosed and puffy patches spread gradually towards the ankles and toes; bullæ formed on their surface. On the 16th the end of the great toe and upper surface of the toes of the right foot were hard, horny, shrunken, dry and black, while the dark patches were slowly extending over both feet. The patient was transferred to Stanton hospital, Washington, D. C., on the 19th, where he died June 15 of "typhoid fever and gangrene of the feet."

CASE 6.—*Date of onset undefined; rose-spots; iliac and umbilical tenderness; pneumonia; numerous spots like small blood-blisters on the limbs and trunk; dusky skin, low delirium, tremulousness and subsultus; vomiting; epistaxis; bed-sores; recovery of intelligence for a week before death.*—Private S. H. Plumb, Co. C, 27th Conn. Vols.; age 22; had been treated in quarters for quite a long time before his admission into hospital, March 23, 1863, as a case of typhoid fever. The pulse was 88; respiration 16; tongue shrunken, furred and dry, the tip and edges red; eyes somewhat yellow; hearing dull; chest and abdomen covered with sudamina and a large crop of red and pink spots, disappearing on pressure; bowels moved once daily, and tender in the iliac and umbilical regions. There was free perspiration during the night of the 24th, and next morning some of the sudamina had coalesced into bullæ containing turbid yellowish-white liquid; one loose watery stool was passed. Twenty-five grains of sulphate of quinine were given three times daily with aromatic sulphuric acid. Next day there was no sweating, but the condition was otherwise not much changed; pulse 108; bowels moved twice; no abdominal tenderness; red spots disappearing; sonorous râles posteriorly on both sides of the chest. On the 27th the quinine was continued in ten-grain doses three times daily, but the acid was omitted; the expectoration was white, slimy and adhesive, with intermixture of scarlet blood; there was soreness over the ascending and transverse portions of the colon. On the 28th the patient was reported as having had some delirium in the early part of the night; the skin of the abdomen was desquamating. Small doses of ipecacuanha and opium were given. The quinine was omitted on the 29th; the chest was not tender on percussion, but the sputa contained bright blood. On the 30th the pulse was 96; respiration 16; tongue cleaner and less dry; bowels moved once; abdomen somewhat sore all over; sputa thick and adhesive, containing bloody masses;

small crepitation was heard in the left lung under the fourth rib. Carbonate of ammonia was prescribed. On the 31st he was again reported as having been delirious during the night. Some nearly pure blood was expectorated on April 1; the tongue was brown at the tip and centre, the lips dry, cracked and bleeding, the teeth covered with dark patches, the bowels moved once; the patient was again delirious during the early part of the night. Quinine in three-grain doses was given three times daily, with small doses of carbonate of ammonia and ipecacuanha and a full dose of morphia at bed-time. He perspired profusely on the 2d; his cheeks were somewhat flushed; many spots like small blood-blisters appeared on the limbs and shoulders and a few were present on the trunk; he was delirous and wanted to get out of bed. Beef-tea and whiskey were given at intervals during the day. The perspirations continued on the 3d; on this day some nausea was developed and the appetite, which had been very good hitherto, became affected; the expectoration was scanty, rust-colored and contained bloody masses; all kinds of murmuring, bubbling and rattling were heard in the chest; pulse 100; respiration 26 and irregular. On the 4th there was some vomiting, no stool, but some tenderness in the right iliac and umbilical regions; the small purplish ecchymosed spots were fading from the arms, but those on the abdomen were very numerous and presented a pur-pura-like appearance. On the 6th the pulse was 120, respiration 30 and irregular, tongue dry, brown, hard and fissured, lips dry and cracked, cheeks slightly flushed of a dusky-violet color; the stomach rejected solid food; one natural stool was passed; the purpuric eruption appeared on the back and hips. On the 7th the ecchymosed spots increased on the abdomen; there was frequent but scanty vomiting and an incoherent muttering, with tremulousness of the hands and incessant subsultus. Bed-sores on the hips and sacrum and continued vomiting were recorded on the 8th. Next day the eruption had nearly faded; the pulse was 96 and respiration 28, the lower jaw participating in the respiratory movement; a copious epistaxis occurred; the stomach was less irritable. On the 10th the face was pale and sunken, the hands and jaw twitched and there was occasional moaning on inspiration, but the lower jaw did not move as on the previous day. Next day he seemed to recognize the attending physician. On the 12th the tongue was somewhat moist and the patient brighter; he talked a little. From this time until death on the 18th he retained his intelligence, sometimes expressing his wants. The vomiting ceased and he swallowed the beef-tea, whiskey, etc., offered him without objection. As the left hip and back were raw and granulating, he lay usually on the right side. For two or three days the bowels were slightly relaxed. A peculiar odor, like that of spoiled meat, was noticed about his person. Cough was troublesome but useless, as it brought up nothing from the lungs. On the day before death the respiration suddenly rose to 44, the pulse being 120; on the day of death the pulse fell to 60, respiration being 48.

CASE 7.—*Deafness; delirium; perspirations; rose-colored spots; diarrhœa; recovery.*—Private Daniel Doolittle, Co. A, 27th Conn. Vols., was admitted on the evening of March 23, 1863. Next day the pulse was 84 and dicrotic, tongue clean and moist, skin moist, conjunctiva of right eye inflamed, throat sore; one thin dark-colored stool was passed and the abdomen, which was full and soft, was somewhat tender over the track of the colon; the patient was deaf and talked thickly in a dull delirium. Quinine in ten-grain doses was prescribed for administration five times a day and thirty grains of blue-pill were given at night. On the 25th there was free perspiration but no sudamina; one faint rose-spot was found on the chest; the lower eyelids were so dark as to seem ecchymosed; the bowels were moved twice; the patient was sullen and ate nothing; during the night he had been violently delirious. No medicine was given. On the 26th the pulse rose to 108, the tongue became somewhat dry and the delirium of a jocose character. Quinine in ten-grain doses was given three times a day with morphia at night. On the 27th the pulse was 120; the patient rested better at night, and although dull and stupid gave rational replies to questions; one thin stool was passed. On the 28th the tongue was furred at the base, clean at the tip and edges, pulse 96; delirium had returned during the night; two stools were passed and the abdomen was tender over the cæcum and the ascending and trans-verse portions of the colon. The prescriptions of the 26th were repeated. On the 29th the pulse was 72; a few elevated pink spots appeared on the abdomen and the upper eyelids seemed ecchymosed. The tongue was clean and moist on the 30th; three stools were passed and the bowels were tender. On the 31st the patient was rational and the spots fading, but the bowels continued loose and tender. On April 1 there was vomiting, the condition of the bowels remaining unchanged. Quinine in three-grain doses with whiskey, and at night morphia, were prescribed for administration. On the 2d a few spots appeared on the chest and abdomen; five stools were passed. On the 3d three stools, resembling pea-soup, were passed, and the patient was very thirsty; but after this the diarrhœa ceased, so that on the 9th a compound cathartic pill was given, which was not followed by any alvine movement until the 11th. Meanwhile the patient's appetite had returned; on the 7th he had been permitted steak for breakfast. He was transferred to division hospital on the 21st.

CASE 8.—*Delirium, perspirations, pink-colored spots; constipation until after the free administration of purgative medicines; recovery.*—Private Amos N. Benton, Co. C, 27th Conn. Vols.; age 36. This patient had suffered from jaun-dice, for which mercury and ipecacuanha had been taken. He fainted on the night of March 23, 1863, and was admitted next day. He became very delirious in the afternoon, expecting to die, and thinking that the attending physician had killed him. On the 25th the pulse was 96, respiration 24, tongue moist and brownish, skin sweating constantly and freely; he had a slight cough which had troubled him for two weeks before his admission. The delirium continued during the night but abated and ultimately ceased towards morning, the patient becoming rational. The skin was bathed in perspiration on the 26th, but was free from sudamina; the abdomen was swollen and there was some gurgling in the right iliac fossa. Quinine was given in ten-grain doses three times, and morphia ordered for use at bed-time. On the 27th some faint pinkish-colored spots were found on the abdomen. As the bowels had not been moved since admission, four compound cathartic pills were given. Next day the tongue was a little dry at the tip, the bowels were moved twice without pain, the perspirations continued and the patient was in a constant delirium. Two stools followed on the 29th, none on the 30th, but the perspirations and delirium remained unabated. The face was pale on the 31st and the patient sullen although not particularly delirious; the perspirations had ceased. Next day the sweating was renewed and continued until the bowels became disturbed. He was rational on the 3d and his appetite returned on the 4th; he complained at this time of his hips being sore; eight or ten spots or pimples appeared on the abdomen, fading on the following day, except one which developed into a pustule. As the bowels on the 5th had not been moved for six or seven days, three compound cathartic pills were given. Next day two stools were passed, and on the 7th six, which were small, bloody and accompanied with tenderness in the right iliac and epigastric regions. An ounce and a half of sulphate of magnesia was given, producing six copious watery stools on the 8th. During the three following days the bowels were moved twice daily. On the 11th and 12th the perspirations recurred, and quinine in three-grain doses, with aromatic sulphuric acid, was administered. On the 13th eight stools were passed and the patient perspired but little. An ounce and a half of sulphate of magnesia was given, and morphine prescribed for use at night to produce rest and quiet the bowels. Four stools were passed on the 14th but none on the 15th. Again on the 16th the bowels were moved four times. Meat and vegetables were omitted from the diet, the patient being placed on tea, toast and rice; one ounce of castor oil was given. On the 17th three stools were passed, and there was tympanites with gurgling and some tenderness of the abdomen. After this the bowels were moved twice daily until the close of the record. On the 18th tincture of iron was prescribed, and beefsteak and potatoes allowed. On the 20th the patient complained much of pain in his foot. On the 21st he was transferred to division hospital. During the continuance of this case there was some cough with frothy mucous expectoration, and at times some acceleration of the respiration.

CASE 9.—*Diarrhœa and umbilical tenderness; pneumonia; rose-colored spots; delirium; epistaxis; recovery.*—Private Patrick Glinn, Co. G, 27th Conn. Vols.; age 24; was admitted from quarters March 28, 1863. Next day the pulse was 96, respiration panting, tongue yellow, furred in the centre and moist, bowels tender, especially in the umbilical region, and moved six times; the patient had eaten nothing for four days. A full dose of castor oil was given. On the 30th the pulse was 104 and dicrotic, the respiration 28, the tongue furred white or yellowish-white but red and somewhat dry at the tip; the bowels were moved five times and continued tender. Quinine in ten-grain doses was given with opium three times a day. The diarrhœa persisted, giving daily three to five stools resembling pea-soup, until April 8, when it ceased; it was accompanied by tenderness in the epigastric region, tenderness and gurgling in the umbilical and right iliac regions. The respiration continued somewhat accelerated, about 24, and on the 1st the sputa became rusty, changing in a few days to yellow matter mixed occasionally with bloody lumps, and retaining this character until the 10th, after which the pulmonary symptoms lost their prominence. Some indistinct rose-colored spots appeared on March 31; eight were noted on the abdomen on April 1, and about fifty on the following day. On the 1st the quinine was diminished to three grains three times daily, with whiskey and morphine, beef-tea, toast and rice; carbonate of ammonia was prescribed on the 5th, but as it seemed to cause vomiting its administration was suspended. No delirium or other head-symptoms had been noted up to this time, but on the 7th there was deafness, and although the pulmonary symptoms were improving, the respirations being but 18 per minute, the face was of a dusky-purplish color. On the 8th the face was less dusky and the appetite returning. On the 9th there was epistaxis and the integuments over the sacrum were reddened. Sudamina appeared on the 11th, many of them occurring on the site of rose-colored spots which were yet present. At this date free perspiration began to occur at night and continued to the end of the period covered by the record. The eyes were jaundiced on the 12th, and two days later delirium occurred for the first time in the progress of the case. Quinine in small doses, with aromatic sulphuric acid, was given on the 16th. On the 18th the pulse was 72, the tongue clean, appetite good and bowels quiet; there were many rose-colored spots on the abdomen and the sudamina were shrinking. Steak was permitted to be used and tincture of iron prescribed. Next day the patient was transferred to division hospital.

CASE 10.—*Bronchitis; diarrhœa and abdominal tenderness, chiefly umbilical; febrile movement slight; rose-spots on 8th and 16th days; recovery.*—Private Frederick Buckley, Co. A, 27th Conn. Vols.; age 19; was taken with diarrhœa Dec. 1, 1862, and sent to general hospital. On his return to the regiment the disease recurred after exposure on picket towards the end of March, 1863. He was admitted to hospital on the 28th, and on the following day the pulse was 84, respiration 20 to 24, tongue furred white and its papillæ projecting; he had ten stools during the twenty-four hours, and there was tenderness over the entire course of the colon, particularly over the transverse colon. Quinine in five-grain doses was given three times a day. On April 1 the bowels were quiet, the tongue red at the tip and edges and less moist; there was cough with thick white expectoration; the abdomen was full, tender in the epigastric and umbilical regions and tender and gurgling on pressure in the right iliac region. On the 4th two pink-colored and slightly raised papules were observed on the abdomen. After this the patient improved; his bowels were but slightly relaxed and the tenderness diminished daily; the cough lessened and the respirations became of normal frequency, though continuing somewhat labored; his appetite returned and he was allowed meat twice daily. No cerebral symptoms are mentioned as having been present. Perspirations and sudamina were noted on the 12th, as also a few rose-colored spots on the abdomen, but the bowels continued quiet and free from tenderness except in the umbilical region; a cathartic pill on the 16th caused but one movement. The case was transferred to division hospital on the 19th. [This man was ultimately returned to duty from the Mower hospital, Philadelphia, July 20.]

CASE 11.—*Nausea and vomiting; slight diarrhœa and tenderness in the umbilical and iliac regions; pink spots on the abdomen and chest; recovery.*—Private Wm. A. Beard, Co. C, 27th Conn. Vols., having been feeling sick for a week, was admitted to hospital April 5, 1863. Next day the pulse was 96, respiration 20, tongue brown and dry in the centre, bowels slightly relaxed and tender on pressure in the right iliac fossa; he had anorexia, thirst, nausea and vomiting but no cough. Quinine in five-grain doses was given three times daily. The tongue became dry and rough as if baked or toasted, but the symptoms did not change much for the worse. The bowels were moved once or twice daily, the passages thin and watery; sometimes there was no movement during twenty-four hours, but tenderness, chiefly marked in the umbilical and iliac regions, was present. On the 10th the patient was reported as looking brighter and laughing. On the 11th one red pimple was found on the abdomen; it faded on the 14th; meanwhile there was some vomiting on the 12th. Three pink spots appeared on the abdomen and chest on the 15th, fading on the 18th. Some headache was reported on the 17th. On the 19th, when the patient was transferred to division hospital, the tongue was sticky and somewhat furred, the appetite fair and the bowels quiet and not tender. Roasted apples formed a part of the dietary throughout the progress of this case.

CASE 12.—*Recurring chills; abdomen concave and tender; rose-colored spots; nocturnal delirium; record incomplete.*—Private H. R. Ishell, Co. G, 27th Conn. Vols.; age 30; was admitted April 8, 1863, having been sick in quarters since March 20 with chills daily in the afternoon or evening. On the 9th the pulse was 72, respiration 24, lips cracked, tongue moist and white furred, bowels quiet but tender in the umbilical and left iliac regions; the patient was very nervous-looking and did not rest well. Quinine in four-grain doses was given three times daily, with diet of toast, roasted apple, tea, rice and beef-tea. On the 10th there was continuous headache and soreness in the chest in deep breathing. Next day about a dozen spots appeared on the abdomen. They were touched with nitrate of silver. On the 12th they were replaced by eight fresh spots; eleven others appeared next day, all of which were touched with nitrate of silver. The abdomen at this time was concave and tender and there was gurgling under pressure; sleep was disturbed by dreams. On the 14th the pulse was 88, respiration 16, tongue raw and glazed in the middle; three thin and watery stools were passed; six new spots appeared on the surface; the patient talked in his sleep. While in this condition he was transferred on the 19th to Division hospital; [he was discharged July 27.]

CASE 13.—*Febrile condition associated with bronchitis; stools infrequent but loose; tenderness over colon, but no tympanites nor rose-colored spots; cerebral symptoms slight; clinical history not suggestive of the typhoid affection.*—For this case see No. 330 of the *post-mortem* records.

It is difficult to determine to what extent the freedom of these cases from the acute manifestations of malarial disease was due to the lavish use of quinine in the medical service of the regiment. We may suppose that this treatment would have prevented chills and febrile accessions in the subsequent progress of the cases; but inflammatory processes following malarial congestions of the intestinal mucous membrane would have persisted for some time, giving rise to a more general abdominal tenderness than usually characterized unmodified typhoid fever. The tenderness so frequently noted in these cases in regions other than the right iliac may therefore be accepted, among other indications, as suggestive of a malarial complication. It is true that only in case 12 was the attack ushered in by recurring chills, but the concurrence of remittent fever in other members of the command, the existence of fevers reported as typho-malarial during the preceding month, and the method of treatment adopted by the medical officers, give sufficient countenance to the opinion that typhoid fever in these instances occurred in those who had been exposed to the malarial influence.

If the practice of keeping clinical records of fever cases had been generally, instead of exceptionally, followed, there would have been ample proof that in a large class of cases the symptoms were not such as to indicate with certainty the specific typhoid or malarial origin of the febrile phenomena. Fortunately Surgeon J. F. DYER, 19th Mass. Vols., has preserved in his regimental case-book a series of sixteen cases which illustrates the difficulty that was frequently experienced in making a diagnosis. Three of these cases have already been presented as Nos. 5, 13 and 41 of the malarial series; the others are given below. Cases 1 and 2 were regarded as remittents; in fact typhoid fever appeared to be excluded by the absence of symptoms specially indicative of that affection. No. 3, in which no diagnosis was entered, was of a similar character. In case 4 there was in addition some bronchial inflammation. No. 5, although reported as remittent, presented certain symptoms—abdominal pains, diarrhœa, faintings and continued ill health—which become of interest in connection with the cases accompanied by more pronounced indications of typhoid fever. A similar remark applies to the deafness in case 6. In 7, 8 and 9 the difficulty in discriminating between an adynamic remittent and a specific typhoid fever sufficiently accounts for the absence of a formally recorded diagnosis. The fatal case, 10, which in point of time was the first of the series, was reported as a case of typhoid. Case 11 was entered as a remittent, although presenting one or two equivocal rose-colored spots. But the rose-colored eruption in 12 appears to have suggested the presence of the typhoid poison not only in it, although the bowels were not relaxed, but in the fatal case 13, in which there was no rose-colored eruption.

CASE 1.—Private Charles C. Forbes; sharpshooter; was admitted Oct. 23, 1861, with fever and slight delirium, yellow-furred tongue, constipated bowels and offensive breath; he had an eczematous eruption between and under the eyes, and showed a morbid desire to lie with his head covered by the bedclothes. Quinine in three-grain doses was used three times daily, with occasional purgatives such as compound colocynth pills and fluid extract of senna; milk diet was ordered. On November 11 the tongue became cleaner and the appetite improved. Tincture of iron was prescribed on the 14th and beefsteak allowed on the 16th. But the bowels again became constipated, the tongue furred and the appetite impaired. Compound cathartic pills and other purgative medicines were employed. He walked a little on the 18th and seemed improving, when, on the 25th, his feet became painful and continued so up to December 4, the date of his transfer to general hospital.

CASE 2.—Private William Reinnells; sharpshooter; was admitted Oct. 24, 1861, with remittent fever. He had been in the hospital of the 20th Mass. regiment, but the crowded condition of that establishment necessitated his removal. He was dull and stupid, had headache, tinnitus aurium and pains in the limbs; his tongue was thickly furred, appetite capricious and bowels constipated. He was treated with quinine in three-grain doses three times daily, with nitrate of potash and occasionally some cough mixture; compound cathartic pills and other purgatives were also given. On the 11th he had a slight purulent discharge from the ear. Tincture of iron was prescribed for daily use on the 12th. Beefsteak was authorized on the 20th. Pain in the feet, complained of December 1, was not relieved on the 4th, the date of his transfer to general hospital.

CASE 3.—Corporal John Cushing, Co. H, 19th Mass. Vols., was admitted Nov. 16, 1861, having been unwell for about eight days with chills and headache. On admission the pulse was 90, tongue furred and bowels painful and tender. A half drachm of ipecacuanha was given, and fifteen grains of nitrate of potash prescribed for administration three times daily. On the 17th the umbilical region was tender, the pulse 72, skin warm and dry, tongue thickly furred in the centre and red at the tip and edges, appetite deficient; the patient had headache and buzzing in the ears but no epistaxis. His condition remained unchanged for several days. Fomentations were applied to the abdomen, and castor oil and extract of senna were given without inducing a movement of the bowels. On the 21st a half ounce of fluid extract of senna and two drachms of fluid extract of rhubarb produced one dejection, and on the 24th castor oil was followed by two movements. On the 25th the nitrate of potash was omitted and quinine given in three-grain doses instead. The bowels continued constipated throughout the progress of the case, but were moved at intervals of a few days by some laxative medicine. For about a week following the 26th the patient's feet were so painful as to prevent him from sleeping at night; frictions and afterwards poultices were applied to them. On the 29th the fur began to clean from the tongue and the appetite to return. Milk diet was used up to December 8, when beefsteak was allowed. On the 15th he was sent on furlough to promote convalescence.

CASE 4.—Private F. Chandler, Co. I, 19th Mass. Vols., was admitted Nov. 10, 1861, having been ill for a week with weakness, fever and headache. On admission his pulse was 112 and his tongue dry and streaked. An emetic of ipecacuanha was given, and at night a Dover's powder. During the night sleep was disturbed by pains in the bowels, which had not been moved since the day before admission; his tongue on the 11th was dry and patched with whitish fur. Three compound colocynth pills were given; but these produced no effect until the following day, when one stool was passed. Squill and paregoric were prescribed on account of cough. On the 15th the pulse was 86, moist and cleaning, but there was no appetite. Nitrate of potash, which had been given since admission, was replaced by three grains of quinine twice daily. From this time until the 23d the patient became weaker; he did not rest well at night; cough was troublesome and was accompanied with much mucous expectoration streaked with blood; the bowels were constipated, requiring occasional doses of castor oil or extract of senna to relieve them. On the 23d the tongue became very dry and cracked. On the 25th the nocturnal restlessness increased to delirium. After a free passage, induced by castor oil and extract of rhubarb on the 28th, the patient slept well; but next night he was kept wakeful by pain in the feet. This pain continued during November 30 and December 1, causing loss of sleep and slight delirium. His condition was improving on the 4th, when he was sent to division hospital.

CASE 5.—Private F. Lunt, Co. G, 19th Mass. Vols., was admitted Oct. 25, 1861, with remittent fever and neuralgia of the right side of the face. He complained much of cold feet and for some days of a faintness at the epigastrium. He was treated with three grains of quinine three times daily, but on November 9 Fowler's solution was substituted; purgatives were used to move the bowels. On the 10th he complained of headache, sore throat and coryza. On the 12th he fainted on two occasions when attempting to rise; the sounds of the heart were indistinct. Camphor and valerian were prescribed. The headache continued, and on the 13th the scalp was rubbed with tincture of aconite diluted with alcohol. On the 14th he had colicky pains and diarrhœa. The Fowler's solution was omitted on the 15th, four grains of quinine three times daily being substituted for it. On the 16th the patient fainted on rising to stool. The headache became somewhat lessened next day; three greenish stools were passed with much colicky pain. Four similar stools were recorded on the 18th. A ten-grain dose of calomel followed by castor oil caused frequent dejections, some being greenish in color and bloody. Opium was prescribed, but the colicky pains did not cease nor the blood disappear from the stools for several days. On the 27th headache was again complained of, and as the bowels had become inactive, compound colocynth and blue-pills were given. A blister was applied to the back of the neck on the 30th. On December 3 there was pain and discomfort in the stomach with acid eructations, for which rhubarb and bicarbonate of soda were prescribed. Next day the patient was transferred to general hospital. [He was discharged on the 13th on account of neuralgia.]

CASE 6.—Corporal J. C. Cronan, Co. G, 19th. Mass. Vols., took cold about Nov. 11, 1861, and had been constipated, without appetite and troubled with a cough since that time. He had taken purgative pills with effect. He was admitted on the 18th. Dover's powder was given. On the 19th the cough was urgent; the patient was deaf and had tinnitus but no headache nor epistaxis; the bowels were quiet and not tender but appetite was wanting. Small doses of tincture of opium, wine of antimony and chloroform were prescribed, with extract of valerian at night. Next day the teeth were covered with sordes and the tongue with a thin black fur. Fluid extract of senna was given. The patient had nausea on the 21st; the prescription of the 19th was omitted and quinine in three-grain doses substituted. This was omitted on the 23d, as it appeared to increase the nausea; nitrate of potash in fifteen-grain doses was given instead. The tongue became cleaner and the patient felt better on the 26th, but occasional purgatives were required for some time after this date. On the 30th he was able to sit up and his appetite was good. He was furloughed December 12.

CASE 7.—Ephraim, a colored servant, was admitted Nov. 9, 1861. He had been troubled with a cough for two or three days, anorexia, headache and pain in the back and limbs. On admission the tongue was thickly white-coated, the pulse 90 and full; the headache had ceased but there was much thirst and restlessness at night. Nitrate of potash in fifteen-grain doses was given three times a day with Dover's powder at night. One loose dejection was passed on the 10th and another next day. Thirst was a prominent symptom; currant-jam with water was used as a drink. On the evening of the 11th the skin became hot and dry and the tongue dry, white in the centre and red on the edges. The patient was delirious during the night, and on the 12th was stupid; sordes appeared on the teeth; the pulse was 100 and feeble. Quinine in three-grain doses was given three times a day and a half ounce of brandy every two hours; the nitrate of potash was omitted. During the night he escaped in his delirium from the ward and returned to quarters. Next day he had epistaxis, and in the evening one involuntary bloody dejection. Small doses of carbonate of ammonia were given every two hours. Four loose and bloody stools were passed during the night of the 13th and three on the following day; the extremities were cold and there was some muscular trembling. The carbonate of ammonia was replaced by turpentine. On the 15th the stools were frequent, thin and mixed with blood-clots or consisting chiefly of blood, but the delirium was somewhat lessened. On the 16th he became quite rational towards morning; his pulse was scarcely perceptible at the wrist, extremities cold; stools frequent, scanty and bloody; tongue cleaner and more moist. He rallied well on the 17th, and next day his appetite was voracious; but on the 19th he had pain in the bowels, headache and furred tongue, and there was some mental wandering, especially at night. This condition persisted for a week, during which the bowels remained unmoved. On the 25th his back was found to be excoriated, but on the 30th the excoriations were reported as healing. His bowels continued confined and he did not rest well at night, but his appetite was excellent and his strength returning, when on December 4 he was sent to division hospital on account of the removal of the regimental camp from Poolesville to Muddy Branch, Va.

CASE 8.—Private John Ross, Co. I, 19th Mass. Vols., was taken sick about Nov. 8, 1861, with chills, pains in the head and bowels and slight diarrhœa. On entering hospital on the 13th the patient was in a general perspiration; his tongue was red at the tip and edges and furred in the centre; he had no appetite, no epistaxis and no tinnitus; he said he usually felt better in the morning than at night. Quinine in five-grain doses was given three times a day. He had three or four dejections during the night, with pain in the bowels, but next morning felt very well. The diarrhœa was not restrained by Dover's powder or tincture of opium. On the night of the 16th involuntary watery discharges were passed, and during the 17th the patient slept most of the day, muttering dreamily. On the 18th his face was flushed, eyes suffused, tongue red and cracked; he groaned and talked in his sleep and was easily awakened; he had much headache, a short cough and pain in the umbilical region; the watery discharges persisted; the pulse was 96; skin hot and without any rose-colored spots. He had some nausea after taking an opiate on the 19th. He continued to sleep most of the time with his eyes half closed, moaning and muttering, but always rational when aroused. On the 23d he did not moan so much. On the 24th nausea and vomiting followed the use of quinine, which was thereupon suspended. In the course of a few days the diarrhœa became somewhat restrained, but the cough increased and was attended with much expectoration and some pain in the side; the tongue continued brown and cracked, the appetite failed and thirst increased. By December 2, however, he was able to sit up, and on the 13th he was returned to quarters.

CASE 9.—Sergeant J. Q. A. Ferguson, Co. B, 19th Mass. Vols., was admitted Nov. 26, 1861. He had been unwell for a fortnight, during which he had lost strength, and more recently had become stupid and partially deaf. On admission his face was flushed, eyes suffused, skin hot and dry, tongue moist and slightly coated, lips parched, pulse 86; he had some cough and substernal pain. Small doses of opium and ipecacuanha were prescribed. On the 27th, as the bowels had not been moved for three days, fifteen grains of compound extract of colocynth were given; two dejections followed its use. The tongue became clean and the patient walked about a little; his appetite was good, but he did not rest well, his pulse was accelerated and his lips parched. On December 1 he was delirious and deaf; on the 3d he had epistaxis. In this condition he was transferred to division hospital on the 4th on account of the breaking up of the regimental camp. [His name does not appear on the register of deaths.]

CASE 10.—Private Elias W. Phelps, Co. G, 19th Mass. Vols., was admitted Oct. 1, 1861, having been suffering for several days from fever, lassitude, want of appetite and pains in the head and bowels. On admission the patient was somewhat delirious, his pulse 96, tongue thickly covered with a dark fur and bowels unmoved for three days.

An ipecacuanha emetic was given. He was restless during the night, talking in his sleep and incoherent when awake. A purgative consisting of one blue-pill and one compound cathartic pill produced one free dejection; but in the evening the tongue was darker and the patient indifferent to everything when not specially addressed. On the 3d the delirium was increased, the stools involuntary, the pulse 120 and the tongue dry and dark. No rose-colored spots were discovered. Brandy was given at intervals. The diarrhœa and delirium continued; the teeth and lips became coated with sordes; the muscles twitched and the pulse increased in frequency while losing in strength until it became imperceptible. Death occurred October 5.

CASE 11.—Private J. Fitzgerald, Co. I, 19th Mass. Vols., was admitted Nov. 1, 1861, with well marked remittent fever, for which three grains of quinine were given three times daily. He complained of not sleeping well at night. Valerian and Hoffmann's anodyne were prescribed for use at bedtime. On the 12th the tongue was thickly coated, the teeth covered with sordes, pulse 96 and feeble; one stool was passed during the previous twenty-four hours; the appetite continued fair. One stool was passed on the 13th, but there was no gurgling nor tenderness in the iliac region; one or two equivocal rose-spots were observed; the tongue was dry; the patient slept a little during the day and muttered in his sleep. Brandy and tincture of iron were prescribed. He was somewhat delirious during the 14th; his face livid, hands cold, tongue red at the tip and edges, respiration short and loud, pulse 96; on this morning he tried to support himself and fell; one stool was passed. On the 15th the patient was stupid, spoke with difficulty and had muscular twitchings; the bowels were quiet. Next day he was delirious; the tongue was black, dry and cracked, the pulse very feeble, and the bowels unmoved. Death took place on the 18th.

CASE 12.—Private Edward Brailey, Co. D, 19th Mass. Vols., was admitted Oct. 11, 1861. He had been on picket duty on the banks of the Potomac and during the last two days had felt cold and feverish. He came to camp in a baggage wagon. His face was flushed, pulse 90, tongue covered with a thick white fur; he was restless at night and talked a good deal in his sleep. An emetic of ipecacuanha was given on admission and a Dover's powder at night. Next day the pulse was 96, skin hot, face flushed, eyes suffused, tongue dry and white, teeth covered with sordes, bowels moved twice, stools thin and watery. Sweet spirit of nitre was prescribed and quinine in two-grain doses three times a day. On the 13th the patient perspired a little at times and the skin of the abdomen showed some rose-colored spots; he had one passage and the abdomen was rather full, but there was no tenderness nor gurgling. Extract of valerian was given. Delirium came on gradually and continued until the 19th, when, after a good sleep, he awoke feeling better and more rational. During this period the bowels were rather constipated; the rose-colored spots were very thickly set and bright on the abdomen. He took port-wine and chicken-broth; brandy was rejected by the stomach. On the 20th he sat up in bed with aid to read a letter. After this his condition improved for some days, but the bowels remained unmoved and the tongue furred. An enema was given on the 23d, with castor oil in the evening and extract of senna on the following day; one alvine dejection was thus procured on the 25th, after eight days of torpidity. On the 26th the face was flushed, eyes suffused, pupils dilated, mouth dry and tongue covered with patches of thick white fur; headache was also present. Next day the tongue was clean but rather abnormally red in color; the patient complained of soreness from lying so long in bed. The bowels continued constipated, stools being obtained only at intervals of three or four days by the use of extract of senna, but about the middle of November four to six figs were eaten daily and under their use the bowels became more regular. On the 9th of this month complaint was made of tender feet, and this was continued until the 17th, when the tenderness diminished. He sat up for a short time on the 18th and during most of the day on the 19th. Beefsteak was now allowed in the dietary instead of the soups, broths and soda crackers to which he had been restricted up this time. He was furloughed December 12.

CASE 13.—Private James Kelly, Co. D, 19th Mass. Vols., was admitted Dec. 13, 1861, having been sick for three or four days with slight cough, anorexia and pains in the head and limbs; his tongue was dry and brown in the centre, pulse 86, bowels constipated. Ten grains each of blue-mass and colocynth were given at night. On the morning of the 14th it was reported that the patient had groaned during most of the night; his face was flushed and breathing short. Next day diarrhœa, epistaxis and tinnitus aurium were recorded as present. Tannin in five-grain doses was prescribed three times daily. On the 19th the passages became involuntary. On the 20th the tongue was dark-colored, the teeth black with sordes, diarrhœa profuse, pulse 100, respiration short and mind wandering. No rose-colored spots were found on the skin. Turpentine was substituted for the tannin. [The case-book gives no further information, but on the register of deaths this man is reported as having died of typhoid fever Dec. 20, 1861, at the regimental hospital, Muddy Branch, Va.]

FEVER CASES FROM VARIOUS RECORDS.—The following cases have been selected from the case-books of various hospitals and from the medical descriptive lists to further illustrate the character and consequences of the fevers which, although reported as typhoid, were probably in many instances more or less modified by the malarial influence.

Cases 1–5 are presented as specimens of a large class of records which give an account of the condition of the patient at some period, usually that of admission into hospital, but fail to carry out in detail the daily progress of the case. It is not difficult, however, to appreciate the course of such cases, especially when aided by a study of those which have been recorded in full; for, in addition to the result, there is given generally some short statement as to progress, or, in the absence of this, some hint as to the patient's condition is conveyed by recorded changes in the medication or diet.

CASE 1.—Sergeant Nahum L. Hayward, Co. F, 6th Conn.; age 30; was admitted from the field May 23, 1864, with typhoid fever. He was unable to give a satisfactory account of himself. He had headache, restlessness and anxiety of expression, incessant thirst and much diarrhœa; his tongue was dark, cracked and dry, pulse feeble and rapid, abdomen tympanitic and but slightly tender. The surface of the body was sponged with tepid water; cold was applied to the head and counter-irritation to the back of the neck; turpentine emulsion was given with milk-punch freely, beef-tea at short intervals and anodynes at night. The symptoms increased in violence; the patient became noisily delirious and died June 1.—*Hammond Hospital, Point Lookout, Md.*

CASE 2.—Private David F. Farr, Co. E, 8th Me.; age 21; was admitted Aug. 17, 1864, having been sick since July 27 with typhoid fever. He was much prostrated, tongue furred and dry, conjunctivæ injected. Quinine with brandy-punch and turpentine emulsion was given. Diarrhœa supervened on the 18th, but was checked two days later. The turpentine was omitted on the 23d, the brandy on the 25th, the quinine on the 28th. The patient was able to sit up on the 27th. He was furloughed September 3 and returned to duty November 28.—*Satterlee Hospital, Philadelphia, Pa.*

CASE 3.—Sergeant Edwin A. French, Co. B, 17th Pa. Cav., was admitted July 8, 1863, with typhoid fever. Countenance dusky; pain in back; abdomen slightly tympanitic; sudamina and tâches rouges; gurgling on pressure in right iliac fossa; pulse 90; tongue furred but moist; dry râles throughout chest; patient stupid. Gave Mindererus' spirit, quinia, beef-essence and milk-punch. 22d: Steadily improving, taking nine grains of quinine daily. August 1, convalescent. November 13, returned to duty.—*South street Hospital, Philadelphia, Pa.*

CASE 4.—Sergeant Walter A. Brooks, Co. I, 53d Mass., admitted Aug. 16, 1863; mind dull; abdomen tympanitic and covered with sudamina and petechiæ, gurgling in right iliac fossa; tongue dry and fissured, protruded with difficulty; teeth covered with sordes; face suffused; subsultus tendinum; much delirium. Gave an ounce of sherry wine every hour; beef-tea freely. Died August 20.—*Union Hospital, Memphis, Tenn.*

CASE 5.—Private Fabian Liszt, Co. C, 19th Pa. Cav.; age 22; was taken sick Aug. 10, 1863, a few weeks after enlistment, and was admitted on the 17th much exhausted, with brown furred tongue, hot and dry skin, pulse 120 and a diarrhœa of three or four stools daily. Dover's powder, neutral mixture and sweet spirit of nitre were prescribed. On the 20th the pulse was 100, the tongue moist and the bowels not so loose. Milk-punch was given. Small doses of blue-pill, opium and ipecacuanha were prescribed on the 22d, for which, on the 26th, neutral mixture was substituted. On September 10 full diet was allowed and small doses of quinine prescribed. He was returned to duty October 21.—*Turner's Lane Hospital, Philadelphia, Pa.*

In cases 6 and 7 the fever began to decline about the end of the second week; in case 8 it was prolonged for another week, apparently in connection with the intestinal lesion.

CASE 6.—Private E. T. Ellsworth, Co. G, 16th N. Y.; age 19; was admitted Oct. 10, 1861, having been treated for three days before admission with astringents and nutrients. The attack commenced with a chill. On admission he had pain in the head, back and abdomen, a slow and feeble pulse, hot and dry skin, heavily coated white tongue with clean tip and slightly reddened edges, thirst, slight cough, somewhat labored respiration and scalding during micturition. Next day the characteristic eruption came out on the face and abdomen. His appetite was improved on the 12th; the tongue natural and the skin perspiring on the 13th. Two days later the skin became dry and hot, the tongue white at the base and red at the tip and margins, the pulse full, but there was no diarrhœa; next day the febrile action abated. On the 22d he was considered convalescent, and on November 1 he was returned to duty.—*Hospital, Alexandria, Va.*

CASE 7.—Private Thomas J. Bitzer, Co. B, 1st Pa. Res., was admitted Sept. 3, 1862, with typhoid fever. On the 4th he had diarrhœa and profuse epistaxis. On the 6th the fever ran high; the pulse 120, full but compressible, the skin hot and dry, tongue moist and heavily coated, of a dirty brown color but red at the edges and tip; he had tympanites, mostly over the colon, anorexia, some headache and backache. Small doses of sweet spirit of nitre and fluid extract of ipecacuanha were given every hour and five grains of blue-pill with Dover's powder at bedtime. On the 7th the tongue was moister, the pulse full, slow and strong, the appetite better and no stool had been passed for two days; but on the forenoon of this day the fever returned and steadily increased; delirium, jactitation and tympanites over the small intestine were noted in the afternoon. Oil of turpentine and camphor-water were given every second hour, alternating with a diaphoretic mixture. In the evening the tongue became moist, the pulse soft, feeble and compressible and the skin bathed in perspiration. Next day there was retention of urine. A grain of quinine was given every hour and beef-tea and milk freely used. A few poorly defined rose-colored spots were found on the chest and abdomen on the 9th, and the right iliac fossa was tender and gurgled on pressure; the delirium increased in the afternoon of this day, but after a full dose of morphia and Hoffmann's anodyne the patient slept well, and next morning his appetite was better and there was an abundant crop of sudamina on the back and chest. On the 15th he was manifestly improving. On the 20th his appetite was excellent and the bowels had not been moved for five days. Powdered rhubarb in small and repeated doses was prescribed. He was returned to duty November 21.—*Hospital 16th and Filbert streets, Philadelphia, Pa.*

CASE 8.—Private David Old, Co. A, 9th Iowa Cav.; age 17; was admitted March 22, 1864, with bronchitis, and became sick with typhoid fever on the 30th. The pulse was small, 105 to 110, the tongue furred; the patient was restless and had headache, giddiness, chilliness, an unpleasant taste in the mouth, no appetite, scanty urine and no diarrhœa. During the second week the pulse was strong, 118 to 122, skin warmer, tongue dry, red at the tip and edges; there was also severe headache, with spinal and muscular pains and symptoms of pneumonia in the lower lobe of the right lung. After the tenth day minute rose-red spots appeared on the breast and abdomen, and there was some diarrhœa. During the third week the tongue was dry, brown and smooth, the teeth and gums covered with sordes, the lips dry, the skin hot and dry, the pulse 128 to 132; delirium, especially at night, deafness, pain in the right iliac region, tympanites, diarrhœa, disturbed sleep, anorexia and great thirst were present. In the fourth and fifth weeks the tongue was moister and cleaner, the pulse 90 to 86, the countenance brighter, the evacuations natural and the appetite improving. On May 2 the patient was sent to Keokuk, Iowa, as a convalescent.—*Lawson Hospital, St. Louis, Mo.*

Cases 9–17 illustrate the occurrence of intestinal hemorrhage, of perforation of the intestine and of complicating or sequent erysipelas, pneumonia and diarrhœa.

CASE 9.—*Intestinal hemorrhage.*—Private Robert H. Howe, Co. B, 140th Pa.; age 22; was admitted from Harewood hospital, Washington, May 6, 1862, as a convalescent from typhoid fever. On the 10th he had hemorrhage from the bowels. Sulphate of quinine, tincture of iron and milk-punch were used in the treatment. Severe hemorrhage continued up to June 11. On July 18 he was much better. Medicine was omitted on the 31st. The patient was furloughed August 8 and returned to duty December 10.—*Satterlee Hospital, Philadelphia, Pa.*

CASE 10.—*Violent diarrhœa and intestinal hemorrhage.*—Private David Jacoby, Co. C., 17th Pa. Cav.; age 24; was admitted July 7, 1863; he had been sick and under treatment in the hospital of his regiment since January for rheumatism. On admission he had fever, injected and watery eyes, epigastric tenderness, nausea and vomiting, eight stools in the twenty-four hours, abdominal pain and a thickly coated tongue, red at its edges. A poultice was applied; mercury with chalk and Dover's powder was prescribed every four hours, and acetate of ammonia with syrup of squill three times a day; beef-tea and wine-whey were also ordered. On the 11th the stools were occasionally bloody. A pill of acetate of lead and opium was given three times and oil of turpentine twice daily. The pain was relieved on the 12th and 13th, but returned on the 14th, with vomiting and dull headache; pulse 94. Subnitrate of bismuth was given. On the 15th the pulse was 110 and feeble; the vomiting had ceased, but the headache continued with tinnitus aurium and epistaxis. Opiate enemata were used in addition to the pills of lead and opium. On the 16th the stools became less frequent, but severe pain in the back and legs was reported. The diarrhœa became worse again next day. On the 20th the pulse was 115 and very weak; tongue dark and thickly coated; stomach irritable and the ejected matters bilious. On the 21st the patient was somewhat deaf and on the 22d delirious, with profuse diarrhœa, cold extremities and hemorrhage from the nose and mouth. The stools were involuntary and bloody on the 23d, and death occurred on the morning of the 24th.—*Mower Hospital, Philadelphia, Pa.*

CASE 11.—*Perforation of the intestine.*—Private Thomas A. Watson, Co. C, 58th Pa.; age 37; was admitted Aug. 17, 1864, from Petersburg, Va., having been sick since July 29. He was very weak and much exhausted; tongue dry and thickly furred; subsultus tendinum. Quinia and aromatic sulphuric acid, with brandy-punches and turpentine emulsion were given. Next day he was seized with a severe pain in the abdomen, which became worse on the 19th; his pulse was thready; he picked at the bedclothes. He died on the morning of the 21st.—*Satterlee Hospital, Philadelphia, Pa.*

CASE 12.—*Intercurrent erysipelas.*—Corp'l Daniel Austin, Co. G, 16th N. Y.; age 25; was taken about Aug. 7, 1861, with diarrhœa, which became worse and was accompanied by pain in the head, back and abdomen. He was admitted on the 22d as a case of gastro-enteritis. Next day his tongue was heavily coated in the centre but bright-red at the sides, teeth black with sordes, pulse 100, quick, bowels tympanitic but not tender, yielding frequent watery stools. In the evening the fever increased and the patient was at times delirious. On the 24th the eruption appeared on the face and abdomen; the tongue became dry and brown; the stools continued frequent. He was restless at night, and next day the tongue was fissured, abdomen prominent and mind disturbed. The eyes were fixed, the expression vacant on the 26th and the patient raved about Mount Vernon on the 27th, but became rational again on the 28th. On September 1 an erysipelatous blush appeared on the nose and extended over the cheek. Tincture of iron was given every three hours and the face painted with tincture of iodine. The swelling increased and by the 6th affected the hairy scalp; at this time there was some cerebral excitement. Wine and nourishment were given and the iodine reapplied. He was improved on the 13th and able to sit up on the 15th. Bed-sores were present on the right hip and on the sacrum. This patient was discharged May 31 because of disability from typhoid fever.—*Hospital, Alexandria, Va.*

CASE 13.—*Intercurrent pneumonia.*—Private Michael Laly, Co. K, 2d Mich., was admitted Oct. 21, 1861, as a case of typhoid fever. This man had been sick with continued fever for six days prior to his admission, during which time he was treated with diaphoretics and tonics. On the 22d his pulse was 84, tongue dry and brown, skin hot and dry. Three five-grain doses of quinine were given with blue-mass and ipecacuanha. Next day the pulse was 80, the skin cool and the tongue moist. Four two-grain doses of quinine were given with Dover's powder at bedtime. There was a diarrhœa of two or three stools daily from the 24th to the 28th, and the tongue became dry and brown in the centre. On the 29th the pulse was 90 and quick, the tongue dry and tremulous, the skin hot; stupor, much delirium, frequent dry cough, some uneasiness on inspiration and crepitation in the lower part of the left side of the chest were among the symptoms recorded on this day. Calomel, ipecacuanha and quinine with turpentine emulsion and chlorate of potash were prescribed, and a blister applied to the left side. Next day there was cough with bloody sputa; the patient could be roused from his muttering delirium to answer questions, but he replied slowly and protruded his tongue with hesitation; the diarrhœa ceased during this attack. The cough became less frequent and the expectoration viscid and rusty on November 1. Wine was ordered four times daily. During the following night a profuse epistaxis occurred. The tongue became moist on the 3d and next day the expectoration was more abundant and the drowsiness lessened; pulse 76; respiration 24. A blister was applied to the front of the chest. On the 7th the cough was lessened, the expectoration mucous, the countenance bright, the bowels regular.

Milk diet was ordered with an ounce of brandy every four hours. He recovered January 10, 1862, and was returned to duty March 7.—*Hospital, Alexandria, Va.*

CASE 14.—*Sequent pneumonia.*—Private James A. Evers, Co. C, 1st Del. Art.; age 18; was admitted Aug. 20, 1863, having been attacked with fever on board a transport from Alexandria to New York about the 18th. On admission the febrile action was marked, but the mind was clear and there was no diarrhœa, although the bowels were free; pulse 90. Profuse perspiration occurred on the 31st. No eruption was observed. On September 4 dulness and fine crepitation were marked over the right lung, and on the 6th two-thirds of the left lung was implicated. In the evening of this day the febrile action became heightened but free perspiration broke out towards morning; the expectoration was rust-colored, the tongue clean, pulse 86. On the 9th the condition of the patient had improved, although physical examination revealed no apparent change. By the 16th the area of dulness was much diminished and the expectoration free and without viscidity. Ten days later the patient was able to walk out, and on October 15 he was reported for duty.—*Central Park Hospital, N. Y. City.*

CASE 15.—*Sequent diarrhœa from injudicious diet.*—Private Albert Hill, Co. I, 126th N. Y., was admitted Dec. 12, 1862, from Emory hospital, Washington, D. C., as a convalescent from typhoid fever. He was placed on full diet. On the 14th a diarrhœa of two to six stools daily set in and continued until the 21st. On Jan. 5, 1863, the diarrhœa recurred after eating apples. The patient was restricted to milk diet and the intestinal trouble ceased. Full diet was restored on the 12th; but on the 16th there was a recurrence of the diarrhœa, necessitating treatment until February 7. He was returned to duty March 4.—*Satterlee Hospital, Philadelphia, Pa.*

CASE 16.—*Sequent diarrhœa and debility.*—Private Sylvester Chesebro, Co. K, 149th Pa.; age 23; was admitted June 18, 1863, from Stanton hospital, Washington, D. C., having suffered from typhoid fever since May 6. He was much emaciated and so debilitated that he was unable to stand without the aid of crutches; he had pain in the back, and his mouth and throat were slightly ulcerated. He was placed upon extra diet; a chlorate of potash gargle was prescribed. On June 20 the diarrhœa recurred with pain in the abdomen; but by the 26th this condition was relieved and the patient was evidently gaining strength. All medication was omitted and he was allowed full diet July 17. On the 28th he assumed light duties about the ward, and on August 18 was returned to duty with his command.—*Satterlee Hospital, Philadelphia, Pa.*

CASE 17.—*Sequent diarrhœa and pulmonary affection.*—Private Clinton Dayton, Co. I, 17th Conn., a convalescent from typhoid fever, was admitted Dec. 16, 1862, with diarrhœa and shooting pains in the chest. Pills of lead and opium were given three times daily, and on the 21st the diarrhœa was restrained. Tincture of iron was then ordered, but the diarrhœa returned on the 26th. Small doses of an emulsion of castor oil, laudanum, mucilage and turpentine were prescribed. On the 30th the diarrhœa was controlled, but its recurrence with some abdominal pain, Jan. 12, 1863, called for opium twice a day. On the 14th ten grains of blue-pill were given; on the 18th the opium was omitted. Meanwhile, as the cough was troublesome, an expectorant mixture was ordered on the 15th, and croton oil applied to the chest from February 2 to the 6th. The expectorant was omitted on the 9th, but was renewed on the 17th and continued until the 22d. On March 27 he was placed on guard duty; he was furloughed April 1, and returned to his command June 28.—*Satterlee Hospital, Philadelphia, Pa.*

Cases 18–29 show debility, bed-sores, deafness, œdema, anasarca and morbid conditions of the lungs, liver and kidneys consequent on fever.

CASE 18.—*Protracted debility.*—Private Samuel Watson, Co. K, 63d Ind.; age 39; was admitted April 6, 1865, debilitated from typhoid fever. [This man contracted typhoid fever in August, 1863, at Shephardsville, Ky.; he was admitted to hospital No. 1, Louisville, Ky., Jan. 26, 1864, with lumbago, and transferred to Madison, Ind., where his case was entered as chronic rheumatism; on March 23 he was assigned to Co. K, 19th Veteran Reserve Corps. He entered Judiciary Square hospital, Washington, D. C., April 9,—diagnosis: intermittent fever—and on the 26th was furloughed. He returned to Judiciary Square hospital March 23, 1865, and on April 6, as above stated, was transferred to Satterlee.] He was treated with quinine, iron, cod-liver oil and porter, and discharged from service May 26 on account of chronic pleurisy and protracted debility.—*Satterlee Hospital, Philadelphia, Pa.*

CASE 19.—*Debility and phthisis.*—Private Charles McCormick, Co. D, 4th Mich.; age 20; was admitted Aug. 10, 1862, debilitated from typhoid fever. On December 9 he became affected with diarrhœa, which was checked by chalk, opium and catechu on the 17th. A few days later bronchitis was manifested. In February, 1863, there was dulness with sonorous râles over the apex of the left lung. He was discharged on the 28th on account of phthisis.—*Satterlee Hospital, Philadelphia, Pa.*

CASE 20.—*Debility, deafness and bed-sores.*—Private John D. Magee, Co. D, 133d N. Y., had typhoid fever in June, 1861, followed by an enormous bed-sore involving all the supra-sacral tissues; he had not done any duty since the occurrence of this fever. He was admitted from Fairfax Seminary hospital, near Alexandria, Va., Dec. 16, 1862, and was placed on special diet with beef-essence and milk-punch. His appetite was impaired, bowels irregular; he complained of pain about the joints and of a slight cough. He was treated with sinapisms and expectorant syrups. On Feb. 9, 1863, it was noted that the patient had become partially deaf in one ear. He was discharged March 27 because of general debility and partial deafness of the right ear following typhoid fever.—*Satterlee Hospital, Philadelphia, Pa.*

CASE 21.—*Otorrhœa.*—Private H. Harpster, Co. K, 88th Ind.; age 21; while in hospital for an injury to his back, caused by a fall from a wagon, was taken with typhoid fever in April, 1863, and had a long and serious illness, during which he was much troubled with a purulent discharge from his ear. He was treated with turpentine emulsion, brandy and beef-tea. When transferred to Camp Morton, June 9, he was improving rapidly and gaining in flesh.—*Hospital, Quincy, Ill.*

CASE 22.—*Debility, deafness and œdema of feet.*—Private Albert Friedlander, Co. D, 157th Pa.; age 23; was admitted Feb. 23, 1865, with anæmia, deafness and œdema of the feet, and was discharged by order of the A. G. O. dated May 3d. [This man had a severe attack of typhoid fever in January, 1865, and passed through the Fifth Army Corps hospital at City Point, Va., to Patterson Park hospital, Baltimore, Md., where he arrived February 8 and was entered as a case of pneumonia. On the 23d he was removed to Philadelphia.]—*Satterlee Hospital, Philadelphia, Pa.*

CASE 23.—*Swelling of lower extremity.*—Private David D. Cline, Co. I, 180th Ohio; age 31; was admitted March 24, 1865, his left leg being œdematous. He had an attack of typhoid fever in January, and during his convalescence the leg became swollen. Arsenic and compression by bandages failed to remove the tumefaction. He was discharged from service June 5.—*Tripler Hospital, Columbus, Ohio.*

CASE 24.—*Debility and œdema of lower extremities.*—Corporal Hugh McCrossen, Co. A, 118th Pa.; age 24; was admitted Oct. 25, 1863, with debility following typhoid fever; he had also some cough. On the 30th his legs became œdematous and continued in this condition until November 22, with variable appetite and occasional feverishness and cough. For some days, about the end of this month, he suffered from tympanitic distention of the abdomen. On December 6 there was much palpitation of the heart after exertion. On the 7th the cough continued and the œdema of the legs reappeared, but on the 8th there was an improvement which progressed steadily until the patient's transfer to the Invalid Corps. In his treatment quinine in small doses, citrate of iron and quinine, compound tincture of cinchona, wild cherry, squill, morphine, Dover's powder, cod-liver oil, milk-punch and porter were employed.—*Satterlee Hospital, Philadelphia, Pa.*

CASE 25.—*Sequent diarrhœa and œdema of feet.*—Private John Vaus, Co. C, 82d Ill.; age 35; was admitted June 18, 1863, from Stanton hospital, Washington, D. C., as a convalescent from typhoid fever. He had been taken with the fever in March; diarrhœa followed, and about June 1 his feet began to swell. He was placed on quinine and tincture of iron in small doses, and due attention was paid to his diet; but the diarrhœa recurring, pills of Dover's powder and sulphate of iron, and afterwards turpentine in mucilage, were tried. Medication was continued to August 1, and the patient was returned to duty on the 26th.—*Satterlee Hospital, Philadelphia, Pa.*

CASE 26.—*Sequent diarrhœa and anasarca.*—Private Robert H. Davis, Co. A, 78th Ill.; age 27; was admitted Sept. 16, 1864, having suffered from a severe attack of typhoid fever June 16, 1863, followed by a persisting diarrhœa. On admission he had ascites and œdematous legs. He was discharged as wholly disabled December 8, 1864.—*Hospital, Quincy, Ill.*

CASE 27.—*Enlargement of liver and ascites.*—Private Henry C. Packard, Co. E, 6th Vt., was admitted Aug. 10, 1862, with typhoid fever. On October 3 the left lobe of the liver was enlarged and the patient affected with ascites. Nitro-muriatic acid and saline cathartics were used in the treatment. His appetite became very good, but otherwise there was little improvement. He was discharged December 29 because of enlargement of the left lobe of the liver, with ascites.—*Satterlee Hospital, Philadelphia, Pa.*

CASE 28.—*Inflammation of liver and probable abscess discharging into colon.*—Private Benjamin M. Richardson, Co. C, 93d N. Y.; age 24; was admitted Dec. 15, 1862. Diagnosis—diarrhœa. [He had contracted diarrhœa at Williamsburg, Va., in May. This lasted ten days, after which he was confined to bed for four weeks with typhoid fever; during convalescence he was much troubled with pain referred to the liver and stomach.] By January 12, 1863, the diarrhœa was checked, but the skin became yellowish and on the 19th jaundice was well marked and the liver enlarged. Small doses of mercurials were given. Diarrhœa recurred on February 1, but was quieted on the 6th by the use of krameria and paregoric. After this the stools became clay-colored, and on the 9th pain was developed in the right hypochondrium, which became so acute on the 15th that the poulticing which had been employed was discarded and a blister applied with relief to the patient for a day or two. On the 21st the pain returned and on the 24th a sharp diarrhœa set in, yielding from two to eleven stools daily until the 28th. After this he improved under the use of quinine, carbonate of iron and nitro-muriatic acid. He was placed on hospital guard April 10 and was returned to his command August 27.—*Satterlee Hospital, Philadelphia, Pa.*

CASE 29.—*Disease of the kidney.*—Private Thomas Buckley, Co. D, 6th Conn.; age 21; stated that he had never been intemperate in the use of liquors and was perfectly healthy before enlistment. In September, 1863, he had had typhoid fever and was sent to general hospital at Hilton Head, S. C. Two months elapsed before convalescence was established. A week after his return to duty he was admitted to the regimental hospital with œdema of the lower extremities. In about a month he was furloughed to his home, where he remained until his admission into this hospital, April 19, 1864. His face was puffy and pallid, his feet and legs œdematous; the urine was albuminous and contained granular casts. He was discharged from service August 12.—*Central Park Hospital, N. Y.*

Cases 30–50 illustrate the occurrence of inflammatory processes in various parts of the body, but especially in the lower extremities and parotid glands.

CASE 30.—*Muscular pains.*—Corporal Emanuel Davis, Co. K, 137th N. Y.; age 36; was admitted June 20, 1863, convalescing from typhoid fever which had disabled him since March 10. On admission he was troubled with subacute muscular pains affecting the left arm and leg and sometimes the right thigh. These pains were not continuous, but came on at intervals without premonitory symptoms or accompanying fever and lasted about twelve hours. Dampness and cold appeared to act as exciting causes. The joints, large and small, were also occasionally affected. The pains were increased by motion and relieved by pressure; the warmth of bed aggravated them. The patient was much debilitated, emaciated and low spirited. He was treated at first with a pill containing one-half grain each of powdered iron and extract of nux vomica and one-sixth of a grain each of quinia and calomel, given three times a day, with a liniment of ammonia, soap and chloroform; but after a few days the pills were omitted and a teaspoonful of a mixture consisting of one drachm of iodide of potassium, one fluid drachm of colchicum wine and two ounces of compound tincture of gentian was prescribed instead.   Two weeks after this treatment was instituted the patient began to improve, and on August 11 he was returned to duty.—*Act. Ass't Surg. Otto Rœhrig, U. S. A., Satterlee Hospital, Philadelphia, Pa.*

CASE 31.—*Rheumatic pains.*—Corporal Dudley S. Cutler, Co. F, 83d Pa.; age 20; was received June 12, 1863, from Lincoln hospital, Washington, D. C. [He had been treated for typhoid fever in regimental hospital until April 20, when he was transferred to Lincoln hospital.] On admission he complained of a dull heavy pain in the left hip and leg and seemed to have lost a good deal of flesh. Cups, blisters and liniments were employed with turpentine emulsion internally. [On August 1 he was removed to Sixteenth and Filbert streets hospital, Philadelphia, Pa. Diagnosis—chronic rheumatism. He was transferred to the 1st Battalion, V. R. C., September 23.]—*Satterlee Hospital, Philadelphia, Pa.*

CASE 32.—*Pain and swelling of feet.*—Private Peter Gates, Co. E, 1st Mich.; age 25; was admitted March 2, 1862. This man became affected with intermittent fever in November, 1861, and continued in ill health from that time. From the daily entries on the hospital record which cover the period to March 29, it is found that the case was regarded as one of typhoid fever, and that the patient was unable to walk, having a bed-sore on each hip and much swelling, tenderness and pain in his feet, but his tongue was moist and clean, appetite good, bowels regular, skin natural and pulse of fair strength. Stimulants and citrate of iron and quinine were given, but for some time there was no improvement in the condition of the feet. Severe frontal headache was noted as having been present on the 10th and 11th and as having recurred on the 15th, 20th and 29th. Quinine was prescribed on the 15th. At the time the last entry was made the bed-sores were healing and the swelling of the feet had subsided. The patient was discharged from service May 3.—*Seminary Hospital, Georgetown, D. C.*

CASE 33.—*Pain in foot and leg.*—Private William Camp, Co. D, 122d Ohio; age 19; was admitted Sept. 11, 1863. Diagnosis—intermittent fever. He had been sick for five days, during which the bowels were constipated. Three compound cathartic pills given on admission produced two copious stools at night. On the 12th the pulse was 90, full and strong, tongue coated, appetite deficient, skin hot and moist and urine scanty; there was pain in the head, limbs and back. Sweet spirit of nitre was prescribed. By the 15th the skin had become cooler and the headache diminished; epistaxis occurred twice on this day. Diarrhœa set in on the 16th, the stools being liquid and yellowish and the tongue dry and coated. Drowsiness and delirium were developed on the 18th and recurred particularly at night; the pulse ran up to 110 and the respiration to 32. Milk-punch was given and a blister applied to the chest; squill and seneka were also prescribed. The diarrhœa meanwhile persisted, and on the 22d three involuntary stools were passed. Subnitrate of bismuth was given. The patient rested well on the 27th, and next day was more rational; the chest symptoms also were much improved. The diarrhœa continued at the rate of three to five stools daily, with sometimes severe pain in the bowels, until October 16, and during this period the tongue was more or less coated and sometimes dry and the appetite poor. Wine, brandy, porter, milk-punch, wine-whey and whiskey with quinine were used. The appetite returned on the 23d, but the diarrhœa recurred on the 26th and again on November 17, its appearance on the latter date having been attributed to the use of apple-sauce. About October 1 the foot (side not stated) became very painful, but no further mention is made of this until November 13, when the leg was reported as much swollen, and hop fomentations were prescribed. On the 25th the left leg and foot were swollen and fomentations of pepper and hops were used. On the 27th chloroform, arnica and aconite were mixed with olive oil as a liniment for the left leg and foot, but after this no more information is given concerning their condition. The patient was furloughed Jan. 25, 1864. He returned February 24, and was sent to his command for duty May 3.—*Third Division Hospital, Alexandria, Va.*

CASE 34.—*Scorbutic complication; pain in feet and legs; boils.*—Private J. H. Penny, Co. A, 1st S. C.; prisoner of war; age 19; was admitted Nov. 10, 1863, as a case of continued fever. The tongue was red, streaked with white, the gums pale and swollen, the pulse frequent; he was very weak and had much pain in the limbs. On the 14th the bowels were moved five times and the tongue was dry, red and brown; nevertheless he began to improve from this date, so that by the 21st the tongue was moist and cleaning and the bowels regular. On the 27th the patient's condition continued favorable, but he had a troublesome bed-sore. On December 20 he remained weak and emaciated and had large unhealthy boils on various parts of the body which appeared in successive crops until January 6, 1864, when the last boil ceased to discharge. He also at this time suffered great pain in his feet and legs, which were swollen and cold; this was considered due to the severity of the weather. After January 9 this pain ceased and he steadily improved until April 27, when his exchange was effected.—*Act. Ass't Surg. W. A. Harvey, U. S. A., Hammond Hospital, Point Lookout, Md.*

CASE 35.—*Superficial abscesses.*—Private William Dundass, Co. C, 11th N. J.; age 25; was admitted from Summit House hospital, Philadelphia, Aug. 18, 1864, as a convalescent from typhoid fever, suffering from diarrhœa and abscesses in the right hypochondrium and over the epigastrium; his fever dated from June 10. Not until December 1 was the diarrhœa checked, by which time the abscesses were healed and the general health much improved. He was then placed on full diet with cod-liver oil, iron and quinine. On Feb. 16, 1865, he began to do guard duty, and on May 20 was discharged by order of A. G. O., dated May 3.—*Satterlee Hospital, Philadelphia, Pa.*

CASE 36.—*Abscess and contraction of leg.*—Private Aaron Chubbuck, Co. C, 2d Pa. Heavy Art.; age 18; was admitted Aug. 12, 1864, convalescing from a tedious attack of typhoid fever [regarded as remittent during the patient's stay at Harewood hospital, Washington, D. C.], which had left him with abscesses in the left thigh near the buttock. The leg was partially flexed and could not be extended without much pain. Iron and quinine were administered with full diet; pressure was applied to the leg from December 3 to January 5, 1865. On the 15th the leg was reported as much contracted, discharging and so painful as to be unable to bear extension on splints. On February 4 another abscess was reported as forming; this discharged on the 20th. On March 23 the patient suffered from a slight attack of varioloid. On June 20 he was discharged from service on account of lameness of the left leg.— *Satterlee Hospital, Philadelphia, Pa.*

CASE 37.—*Ulceration of toes.*—Private Israel J. Gromoble, Co. I, 148th Pa.; age 18; was admitted Sept. 23, 1863, from Finley hospital, Washington, D. C., as a convalescent from typhoid fever. On the 26th four of the patient's toes were found to be ulcerated and much congested. Incisions were made around the ulcers and warm-water dressings prescribed, with tincture of iron internally, porter and extra diet; a wash containing sugar of lead and opium and an alcohol and water lotion were subsequently employed. On October 18 the ulcers were granulating. All treatment was omitted on the 25th, and on November 16 the patient was returned to duty.—*Mower Hospital, Philadelphia, Pa.*

CASE 38.—*Ulceration of leg.*—Private James A. Humes, Co. H, 150th Pa.; age 20; was admitted Dec. 12, 1862, from Carver hospital, Washington, D. C., as a convalescent from typhoid fever. He was weak and emaciated and had slight tenderness in the right iliac region. Nux vomica in compound tincture of gentian was ordered. On Feb. 10, 1863, he had fever-sores on the leg, which were treated first with flaxseed poultice and afterwards with oakum dressing. On the 27th the patient's hair was falling out. On March 4 the nux vomica was omitted. A lotion of sulphate of zinc was applied on the 20th and pills of carbonate of iron and quinine were given three times a day, under which treatment the ulcers healed. On April 17 all medication was omitted and the patient was put on light duty. He was returned to his command June 28.—*Satterlee Hospital, Philadelphia, Pa.*

CASE 39.—*Sloughing of cornea.*—Private William A. Chase, Co. F, 161st N. Y., was left under the care of a nurse in regimental hospital on the departure of his command. He had been sick for several weeks and was believed to be dying. He was exceedingly emaciated and had delirium, diarrhœa, dry tongue, blackened with sordes, cough and jerking respiration. He was admitted Dec. 4, 1862, for better attendance and treatment. He was not removed from bed during the transfer, but was carried by relays of men, and was well protected from the cold by blankets, hot bottles and whiskey toddy. He was extremely weak but was restless and picked at the bedclothes; his breath was very offensive. The left cornea sloughed with escape of the contents of the anterior chamber, but the case progressed without much suffering and a cicatricial staphyloma was formed. On Jan. 9, 1863, he was fairly convalescent, and on March 16 was discharged from service on account of debility and loss of vision of the left eye.—*Elmira Hospital, N.Y.*

CASE 40.—*Superficial gangrenous patches.*—Corp'l J. H. Kourtz, Co. C, 130th Pa.; age 19; was admitted April 20, 1863, having been sick since the 1st. He was considerably emaciated and in bad nervous condition; his pulse 90, appetite poor, tongue white-coated, dry and cracked, and bowels moved five or six times during the twenty-four hours; he had a slight cough with thin gray sputa mixed with semi-solid masses of a dark-brown color, and there was dulness and slight crepitus in the right infraclavicular region. Suitable nourishment was ordered with sweet spirit of nitre and Dover's powder at bedtime. On the 24th two small pustules with inflammatory areolæ were observed above the left knee. A two-grain dose of quinine in sherry was given every two hours. By the 29th the centre of these spots had become gangrenous and evolved a very offensive odor; a similar but larger spot had also developed on the right forearm three inches above the wrist. Chloride of zinc solution was used locally. The spots enlarged slowly, and on May 3 a pustule with a large inflammatory base appeared on the mucous membrane of the left side of the lower lip. On the 5th there was low delirium; the left side of the face was swollen and the gangrenous spot on the lip was as large as a penny and increasing rapidly; the diarrhœa meanwhile continued. The patient became unconscious and died on the 8th.—*Act. Ass't Surg. O. P. Sweet, U. S. A., Lincoln Hospital, Washington, D. C.*

CASE 41.—*Gangrene of toes.*—Private William Wollcott, Co. H, 12th N. Y.; age 53; was admitted June 23, 1863, from Harewood hospital, Washington, D. C. [The records show that this man had typhoid fever at White Oak Church, Va., in March, and that he was received into Harewood hospital, April 21, whence he was transferred to Satterlee hospital, Philadelphia, Pa., as stated.] On admission he was found to have a diarrhœa causing four or five stools daily, and a gangrene, attributed to frost-bite while on picket, involving four of the smaller toes of the right foot and two of those of the left foot; he had also an ulceration of the left buttock which was supposed to have resulted from riding in ambulance wagons. On the 27th the sphacelated parts of the right toes separated leaving clean ulcers, and on July 4 the first joints of the second and third toes of the left foot were removed by operation. Water dressing was applied. On the 29th the patient was furloughed. On September 4 he was transferred to the Invalid Corps.—*Satterlee Hospital, Philadelphia, Pa.*

CASE 42.—*Gangrene of leg.*—Private E. D. Ellis, Co. H, 2d Vt.; age 20; was admitted June 29, 1862, with chronic bronchitis following typhoid fever. The patient, although lightly built and not very robust, had always enjoyed good health until attacked by typhoid fever on the Yorktown peninsula, where he remained in hospital until conveyed to this place. While on board the transport he noticed a pimple on the outer side of his left leg about two and a half inches above the ankle. As it did not create annoyance at that time the attention of the attending surgeon was not called to it until about a week after his admission. It was then painful and presented the appearance of an ordinary boil which had broken; warm fomentations were applied. In a day or two the edges began to slough, but under the influence of good diet and tonics, with the continuance of warm applications, the slough separated with but little loss of tissue, leaving a healthy ulcer. Granulation proceeded kindly and cicatrization was nearly completed when the surrounding tissues became red, swollen and painful. The general treatment was not changed, but a bread-and-water poultice was applied to the sore with much relief to the patient. The ulcer remained for a time quiescent, but thereafter the edges again took on violent inflammation and became gangrenous. Nitric acid was freely applied to the whole surface, but the processes of separation and granulation were carried on slowly. Gradually, however, the patient improved; his cough subsided; he gained flesh and became able to take exercise in the open air. Towards the end of December the ulcer was quite small and looked well; but at this time the patient partook freely of liquor while absent on pass, and, perhaps as a result of unnoticed violence, the gangrene reappeared and spread more rapidly than before. Caustic potash was applied, but the slough began to spread, involving the skin, fascia, muscles, tendons and even the bone. The general health became much impaired; the stomach loathed food and rejected whatever was taken into it; opiates, even in large doses, were insufficient to induce sleep, so that the patient rapidly lost flesh and became exceedingly irritable. To the whole gangrenous surface sulphate of zinc was freely applied and carefully retained in position by dry lint and strips of adhesive plaster; for an hour, or a little more, there was an increased aching in the parts, but comparative ease followed. In twelve hours a poultice of slippery elm was applied. Next day the slough began to soften, free suppuration took place and the patient's appetite and sleep improved. In a week nearly all the slough had separated and the granulations were progressing satisfactorily. The lower edge of the deeper portions of the ulcer still looked suspicious and required a re-application of the zinc sulphate, diluted, however, on this occasion by the addition of an equal part of powdered gum arabic. The result was beneficial, and at the date of the report the whole ulcer was filled with healthy granulations.*—*Satterlee Hospital, Philadelphia, Pa.*

CASES 43–50.—*Disorganization of the parotid gland.*—CASE 43.—Private Edward J. Wilson, Co. I, 138th Ill.; age 18; was admitted Oct. 1, 1864, with typhoid fever. He had high fever, dry skin, brown and dry tongue, sordes, anorexia, occipital pain, mental dulness, epistaxis, yellow watery stools seven or eight times a day and tympanites and tenderness of the abdomen. Dover's powder, quinine and calomel were given every four hours, and the skin was sponged three times a day with alkaline water. On the 11th the skin and tongue had become moist, the diarrhœa lessened and the appetite better, but the left parotid gland was swollen and painful. On the 14th the patient was delirious and refused food. On the 15th there was much dysphagia and the radial pulse was hardly perceptible. He died on the 18th.—*Hospital, Quincy, Ill.*

CASE 44.—Private B. F. Ross, Co. G, 78th Ill., was admitted Sept. 19, 1862. A severe diarrhœa complicated this febrile case. The patient had, moreover, recovered from an attack of mumps only a short time before his admission. Two or three weeks after admission and while under treatment for the fever the parotid of the left side, which had been most affected during the previous attack of mumps, became painful and swollen, increasing gradually to an immense size and remaining for some time very hard and resisting. When it had softened under continuous poulticing it was lanced in several places, and again after a few days more, without other issue than a few drops of dark-colored blood. After this the tumor began to discharge through the ear and then through the openings made with the lancet, the whole of the gland finally suppurating. Meanwhile a harassing cough set in and the diarrhœa could not be controlled. The patient died October 29.—*Hospital No. 1, Quincy, Ill.*

CASE 45.—Private James E. Taylor, Co. A, 111th N. Y.; age 18; was admitted Jan. 8, 1862, with an abscess of the parotid gland following an attack of typhoid fever. He was much emaciated. As the abscess discharged from the auditory meatus, an incision was made below the ear to give exit to the pus. Nutrients, tonics and stimulants were employed, but the patient died on the 21st.—*Third Division Hospital, Alexandria, Va.*

CASE 46.—Private John Kinnison, 48th Ind., a nurse, was placed on sick report July 13, 1863, on account of an attack of duodenitis, with hepatic complications, supervening upon a diarrhœa of two weeks' standing. Rest in bed, mild nourishment and Dover's powder were prescribed. During the next five days the bowels improved and pain on pressure ceased, but after this the left parotid became painful and swollen. There was severe dysphagia on the 19th. An abscess at the angle of the jaw was opened on the 24th and discharged freely; there was also a copious discharge from the external auditory meatus. Iron, quinine, opium, strong wine and good diet were employed. On August 20 he was furloughed.—*Union Hospital, Memphis, Tenn.*

CASE 47.—Private Abram W. Pearl, Co. H, 9th N. H.; age 45; was admitted Dec. 11, 1862, from Carver hospital, Washington, D. C., where he had been treated for typhoid fever since October. He had parotitis of the right side. Simple cerate was applied. On Jan. 30, 1863, he had some diarrhœa. He was placed on guard duty February 7, but three days later returned to the ward on account of severe pain in his feet. On the 13th he had some vertigo and on the 16th a recurrence of diarrhœa, which was not checked until the 26th. The pain in the feet continued until April 10. Shortly after this he was placed on duty in the kitchen and was not returned for field service until September 26.—*Satterlee Hospital, Philadelphia, Pa.*

CASE 48.—Private Robert Powell, Co. D, 10th Ill. Cav., was admitted Sept. 10, 1863, much emaciated and very weak from fever and diarrhœa; he could scarcely speak. He had a freely suppurating parotid abscess which opened externally and also into the external auditory canal. He died on the 21st.—*Union Hospital, Memphis, Tenn.*

CASE 49.—Private William Lyons, Co. B, 34th Ohio; age 17; robust and athletic; was admitted Aug. 11, 1864, having had diarrhœa for several days, causing five or six liquid stools daily. Astringents were employed, and next day he had but one stool, but the abdomen was tender, the skin hot and dry, the tongue moist and very glossy and the appetite lost; there was also some faintness. Quinine, iron and whiskey were prescribed. The bowels remained

---

* Act. Ass't. Surg. LLOYD DORSEY, *U. S. A., Med. and Surg. Reporter,* Philadelphia, Vol. X, 1863, p. 385, in a series of clinical notes gives the history of a case reported as scurvy with mortification of the left foot. The case had a decidedly febrile character throughout. The patient, B. W., Co. G, 33d Mass. Vols.; age 17; was admitted to Harewood hospital Nov. 19, 1862, with an urethral affection of two months' standing. Treatment entirely relieved his ailment when, on December 7, he was taken with debility, diarrhœa and febrile symptoms. On the morning of the 9th there was great delirium; the pulse 120, weak and irregular; the skin hot and dry; the tongue dry, rough and coated with sordes. Turpentine emulsion, quinine, wine and beef-tea were prescribed. During the two following days the symptoms showed little change. On the 12th the fever was subsiding and the delirium lessened, but both feet were greatly swollen, painful and covered with blisters of various sizes, while the legs were ecchymosed and the hands purplish; there was no hemorrhage from the mucous membranes and, aside from an excessive odor, nothing peculiar was noticed in the stools. After a few days the feet became less tumid, the vesications collapsed and the ecchymoses faded somewhat; but on the 21st the left foot began to slough and this morbid action continued to the close of the case. Meanwhile blotches appeared on the surface of the body, the pulse became feeble, the stools involuntary, and delirium recurred, ending this time in stupor. Death took place Jan. 3, 1863.

quiet, but on the 19th two stools were obtained, castor oil and turpentine having been given on the previous day. On the 21st the pulse was 116, tongue moist and with a slimy white coat, skin hot and dry, appetite deficient and stomach irritable, bowels moved five times; rose-colored spots appeared on the abdomen; rough and sibilant râles were heard in the upper lobes of the lungs. Turpentine, squill and ipecacuanha were given, with warm bricks to the feet, a blister to the chest and sinapisms to the epigastrium. On the 23d sordes appeared on the teeth and there was frequent epistaxis; the abdomen was tympanitic and covered with dark spots; the mind so dull that questions were answered with reluctance and indistinctly; both parotids were inflamed and painful. The patient was very restless and delirious on the 25th; his pulse was 132 and he was evidently sinking rapidly. He died on the morning of the 26th.—*Cumberland Hospital, Md.*

CASE 50.—Private Melvin Brown, Co. G, 23d Ohio; age 18; was admitted Oct. 17, 1864, having been sick for four months. He was much emaciated and unable to walk; he had no appetite; his abdomen was tympanitic and tender, bowels loose, tongue smooth, dry and shining, lips dry and parched, skin dry and hot, pulse 112. Quinine, iron, Dover's powder, beef-essence and stimulants were ordered, and glycerine applied to the tongue and lips. On the 22d crepitus was heard over the middle parts of both lungs. On the 24th epistaxis recurred about every two hours and the parotid glands began to swell. The submaxillary glands became involved on the 27th. Pus was discharged from the left ear on the 29th. Nevertheless the patient rested well at night, had some appetite and was hopeful. Carbonate of ammonia was given on account of the cough. Pus was discharged from the right ear on the 31st and the eye of that side was closed by the increasing swelling. Next day there was a bed-sore on the sacrum. The pulse became very weak and almost imperceptible. He died November 5.—*Cumberland Hospital, Md.*

Injury to the nervous system is suggested on more or less definite testimony by the eleven cases numbered 51–61.

CASE 51.—*Œdema and partial paralysis of right leg.*—Private Ernest Bowman, Co. B, 9th Pa. Res.; age 20; was taken sick at Harrison's Landing with typhoid fever, July 18, 1862, but when admitted, August 10, was so far recovered as to have no fever and but little diarrhœa. Shortly after admission his right leg became painful and swollen from œdema. In two weeks the swelling disappeared, but a partial paralysis remained for a considerable period.—*Satterlee Hospital, Philadelphia, Pa.*

CASE 52.—*Partial paraplegia.*—Private Richard H. Martin, Co. D, 16th Maine; age 28; was admitted May 28, 1864, as a convalescent from typhoid fever. [About Dec. 15, 1863, while near Culpeper, Va., he was taken with fever and delirium and became very weak; he was treated in the field division hospital and transferred Feb. 1, 1864, to Stanton hospital, Washington, D. C.] On admission his health was impaired and his lower extremities partially paralyzed; he could walk, but slowly and unsteadily. He was discharged August 15 because of this disability.—*Turner's Lane Hospital, Philadelphia, Pa.*

CASE 53.—*Paraplegia with atrophy of right leg.*—Private Chauncey Brown, Co. B, 97th N. Y., was admitted Sept. 3, 1862, as a convalescent from typhoid fever. He was much emaciated and debilitated and had a large bed-sore over the sacrum, severe pain in the back and paralysis of the lower limbs. By November 15 he could go about a little on crutches, for which, on December 4, he was able to substitute a cane, the bed-sore having healed, though there still remained some tenderness and wasting of the right leg. He was returned to duty on the 26th.—*South Street Hospital, Philadelphia, Pa.*

CASE 54.—*Paraplegia.*—Corporal John McGinnis, Co. C, 42d N. Y., was admitted Aug. 7, 1862, as a convalescent from typho-malarial fever contracted on the Peninsula. He did well under tonic treatment till September 30. Loss of power and sensation in the lower limbs gradually increased to an almost total paralysis. During the winter iodide of potassium and strychnia were given and the galvanic battery applied. The patient improved very much, but as he was unable to do duty he was discharged March 20, 1863.—*South Street Hospital, Philadelphia, Pa.*

CASE 55.—*Partial hemiplegia with contraction of right leg.*—Private William Criswell, Co. I, 12th Ky.; age 30; was admitted March 3, 1863, with some diarrhœa, a bad cough, pain in the back and partial hemiplegia. He suffered from typhoid fever in November, 1862, and had never fully recovered from the consequences of the attack. Cups were applied to the back and strychnia and capsicum administered. He improved rapidly, but continued lame in his right leg, which was somewhat contracted at the time of his transfer to Louisville, Ky., June 9.—*Hospital, Quincy, Ill.*

CASE 56.—*Hemiplegia.*—Private Nathan Smith, Co. M, 1st Wis. Cav.; age 34; was admitted Dec. 8, 1864, suffering from paralysis of the left side, which, according to the statement of the patient, was the result of an attack of typhoid fever. He was treated with one-fifteenth of a grain of strychnia and two-thirds of a grain of capsicum three times a day, but there was no improvement in his condition at the time of his discharge, April 8, 1865.—*Act. Ass't Surg. D. Lewis, U. S. A., Hospital, Quincy, Ill.*

CASE 57.—*Hemiplegia.*—Private Gilbert Leonard, Co. D, 27th N. Y., was admitted Oct. 30, 1861, having been sick for several weeks with typhoid fever. He had some diarrhœa and cough on admission, but the respiration was natural. On the evening of November 4 the respiration became increased to 26, the tongue dry, the pulse accelerated, and crepitation was detected in the lower part of the right lung. The sputa became streaked with blood on the 5th and rusty on the 6th. On the 9th the patient was very weak and swallowed with difficulty; he was scarcely able to expectorate; he slept with his eyes half open and was unable to speak. He was stronger on the 11th and his bowels were quiet, but the right side of the body was paralyzed. On the 12th he was much stronger and asked for food; his countenance was bright, tongue nearly clean and bowels regular. He gradually rallied from this low condition but the paralysis continued. Strychnia was given on December 1. On Jan. 1, 1862, he was able to walk with a cane; sensation in the arm was much improved but motion was impossible. He was discharged for disability on February 18.—*Hospital, Alexandria, Va.*

CASE 58.—*Paralysis of right arm and left leg, with atrophy of the latter.*—Private James Williamson, Co. G, 109th Pa.; age 18; was admitted April 24, 1865, as a convalescent from typhoid fever. [He was taken sick Sept. 2, 1864, at Camp Taylor, Arlington Heights, and treated in Augur hospital, near Alexandria, Va., for two months. He was unconscious for two weeks, during which he lost the power of moving his right arm and left leg. He was afterwards transferred successively to the Lincoln, Cuyler and Turner's Lane hospitals.] On admission his general health was good and he had recovered the use of his arm, but he could not flex the left foot; the left calf was atrophied to the extent of two inches and a half and there was some atrophy of the thigh. He was transferred May 10 to McClellan hospital, Philadelphia [whence he was removed to Mower hospital on July 20 and to Harrisburg for muster out on September 15].—*Turner's Lane Hospital, Philadelphia, Pa.*

CASE 59.—*Paralysis agitans.*—Private Thomas Dunlap, Co. K, 68th Pa.; age 23; was perfectly healthy before enlistment, and, so far as could be ascertained, had no hereditary predisposition to disease. He was admitted Dec. 12, 1862, as a convalescent from typhoid fever, much debilitated and with a constant trembling of the whole body. Under treatment by quinine and iron, beef-essence, milk-punch, oysters and eggs he increased in strength, but the paralysis agitans continued undiminished. He was discharged Feb. 11, 1863, on account of paralysis agitans and general debility supervening on typhoid fever.—*Satterlee Hospital, Philadelphia, Pa.*

CASE 60.—*Sequent cerebro-spinal fever.*—Private Arthur Potter, Co. M, 1st N. J. Cav.; age 19; was admitted Aug. 20, 1864, with severe uncomplicated typhoid fever, from which he convalesced rapidly. By September 23 he was walking about the ward; but on October 15 he was seized with headache, fever and constipation. Castor oil and turpentine were given and the urine withdrawn by catheter. He became semi-comatose on the 17th and died comatose next day.—*Satterlee Hospital, Philadelphia, Pa.*

CASE 61.—*Inflammation of spinal cord with paraplegia.*—Private William J. Pool, Co. A, 126th N. Y.; age 23; admitted Dec. 12, 1862, as a convalescent from typhoid fever. He was much emaciated, pale, greatly prostrated, but without apparent organic lesion; he had little appetite and slept badly, but under the use of quinine and compound tincture of cinchona, with generous diet and porter, his general health and strength after a little while began to improve. In about two weeks he expressed himself as feeling much better, but complained of great weakness of the legs, which gave way under him when he attempted to stand. Regarding this as a local expression of general debility, extract of nux vomica was given in quarter-grain doses three times daily; but this medicine was soon discovered to be injurious and its use was suspended. It was found that even when in bed the patient had very little power over his lower extremities, for when raised by the hand of an assistant they would fall by their own weight when the support of the hand was removed. The sensibility of the skin, as tested by pressure and pinching, was found to be remarkably deficient, but pressure in the lumbar region of the spine revealed great tenderness. These symptoms, with the experience furnished by the use of the nux vomica, were believed to indicate an inflammatory condition of the cord or its membranes, and the case was treated in accordance with this diagnosis. Blood to the amount of six ounces or more was immediately removed by cupping the loins; free catharsis was induced by compound powder of jalap, which was continued in doses of twenty grains night and morning for two or three days; dry cupping was used; the patient was restricted to a vegetable diet, and tonics and stimulants were withdrawn from the system of treatment. In a short time improvement was manifested by increased power in the lower limbs and by the return of the sensibility of the surface. On Feb. 11, 1863, he was able to raise both his legs in bed; in a fortnight or more he endeavored to use his legs out of bed, and with assistance was able to rest a little upon them but could not exercise any directing or controlling power. Week by week improvement was noted by the manifestation of some power regained, but the pressure of the feet upon the floor continued weak and uncertain for a time. On March 22 the patient was allowed a pass to go to the city partly on foot and partly on the passenger railway car. On April 25 he was transferred to the military hospital nearest his home in the State of New York. At this time he was able to make very good use of his legs and was strong and healthy in his general condition.—*Satterlee Hospital, Philadelphia, Pa.*

A spasmodic asthma appeared as a sequel in the following case:

CASE 62.—Private James Barnes, Co. G, 71st Pa.; age 17; a convalescent from typhoid fever; was admitted Dec. 8, 1864, with deafness and spasms of the diaphragm. He was much debilitated and anæmic. The diaphragmatic spasm, which occurred at first nearly every night, produced constriction of the chest and seriously interfered with the breathing; there was also some spinal tenderness between the shoulders. He was given salines, tonics and antispasmodics, and a blister was applied between the shoulders; but the spasms continued to recur until the following powder was tried: Cream of tartar half an ounce, muriate of ammonia one drachm, citrate of iron and quinia twenty-four grains, aloes twelve grains, strychnia one grain, mixed well and divided into twelve powders; one three times a day. This finally controlled the spasmodic action. He was returned to duty, still slightly deaf, April 13, 1865.—*Act. Ass't Surg. A. J. Dickerhoff, U. S. A., Hospital No. 5, Quincy, Ill.*

Cases 63–65 are presented as instances of relapse in typhoid fever; in 65 the diagnosis of typhoid does not appear to have been clearly established.

CASE 63.—Private Edwin O. Johnson, Co. I, 8th Mass., was admitted June 17, 1863. This patient had suffered from typhoid fever at Port Royal, but had so far recovered as to be able to be removed by steamer. On admission he was anæmic and had diarrhœa. Two days afterward he had fever and typhoid symptoms were gradually developed; the tongue became dry, the mind dull, an eruption, disappearing under pressure, was found on the abdomen, there was some epistaxis and the pulse became frequent and feeble. Involuntary stools followed, but there was no hemorrhage from the bowels until the 24th, on which day the patient died.—*Ladies' Home Hospital, N. Y. City.*

CASE 64.—Private John Thayer, Co. I, 9th Mich. Cav., was admitted July 16, 1863, with typhoid fever. An expectorant, a tonic laxative, a diaphoretic and a mouth-wash of chlorate of potash were prescribed. The patient was delirious on the night of the 21st and passed five copious watery yellow stools. Next day his pulse was 112 and tongue covered with sordes; the delirium was lessened; three stools were passed; there was some cough and mucous râles were heard over the lungs. The delirium recurred on the following night; the stools were passed involuntarily; pulse 100 and very feeble; skin cool. He rested well on the 23d and was free from delirium next day, but the diarrhœa continued until the 27th, the tongue meanwhile cleaning and the lung symptoms abating. After this his progress was satisfactory until about August 17, when a violent diarrhœa set in. On the 20th the tongue was dry and yellowish-white in color, the pulse had risen from 84 to 110, the bowels were tender and had been moved twelve times in the previous twenty-four hours, the stools being large, watery and sanguinolent. Stimulants and astringents were employed, but death took place on September 5.—*West End Hospital, Cincinnati, Ohio.*

CASE 65.—Private Peter Dickerhoff, Co. E, 115th Ohio; age 20; was admitted with typhoid fever Nov. 10, 1862. On the 3d he had been exposed to cold night-air after being overheated by marching at double-quick time. A rigor followed and diarrhœa set in causing four to six stools daily. Quinine was given. On admission his face was livid and anxious, eyes dull, skin dry and hot but without eruption, tongue somewhat furred, thirst urgent, appetite deficient, stools watery, pulse 104 and compressible; he had severe frontal headache, pains over the whole body and twitchings of the muscles. Neutral mixture was prescribed. On the 14th the stools became less frequent and more fæcal in character but very fetid. Next day the patient's eyes were brighter, pulse 94, soft and regular, tongue moist but much furred, skin moist, cool and without eruption; four fæcal stools were passed. Stimulants and chicken-broth were given. Little change occurred until the 21st, when there was an increase of the fever towards night. On the 22d there was less fever and the tongue was moist and less furred, pulse 90 and compressible. Frontal headache and five stools were reported on the 23d, and next day the headache was characterized as periodic. Quinine was given on the 25th and 26th, but brown mixture was substituted on the following day, as there was some cough with scanty expectoration. The patient continued to improve until December 6, when he relapsed somewhat in consequence of a frightful railroad accident near the building. On the 8th he was quite drowsy and had subsultus; pulse 90, weak and compressible; skin hot and harsh; tongue furred. Sulphate of quinia in one-grain doses was prescribed for use every two hours. On the 9th he was less drowsy, the bowels were more regular and the subsultus lessened. On the 14th there was difficulty in hearing, but after this he improved steadily and was sent to general hospital at Camp Dennison Feb. 12, 1863.—*West End Hospital, Cincinnati, Ohio.*

Two cases, represented as second attacks of the specific fever, are also submitted:

CASE 66.—Corp'l William H. Lake, Co. K, 126th N. Y., was admitted Dec. 12, 1862, on account of a sprained ankle. A few days after a case of typhoid pneumonia was transferred to the ward; he complained, Jan. 13, 1863, of some headache and nausea, and next day was in bed at the morning visit with vomiting, diarrhœa, coated tongue and anxious countenance. Mercurials were given and a Dover's powder at night. On the 15th astringents were ordered with quinine in two-grain doses four times daily. He passed a very restless night, and on the 16th the pulse was 120, skin dry and hot, tongue dry, face flushed and right iliac region tender. The quinine was continued with turpentine and stimulants added. Rose-colored spots appeared on the 20th, on which day there was also epistaxis, meteorism but no diarrhœa; the pulse was still rapid, about 100, the tongue somewhat dry but moist on the edges, the mind clear. [The patient stated, and his father subsequently corroborated the statement, that he had at a previous period suffered from typhoid fever with a relapse and a prolonged convalescence.] On beef-tea, chicken and oyster-soup, milk-punch, etc., with quinine, he progressed favorably, and was able to walk on February 12. He was furloughed on the 19th.—*Satterlee Hospital, Philadelphia, Pa.*

CASE 67.—Private David Lacy, Co. K, 136th Pa.; age 31; was admitted Dec. 16, 1862. He had suffered from pain in the breast, cough and hæmoptysis, weakness and diarrhœa since October 3. He stated also that two years before he had been affected with what was called typhoid fever by his physician. This attack, which had lasted several weeks, was characterized by delirium and diarrhœa, with tympanites, pain in the bowels and an eruption on the abdomen, great weakness, emaciation and prolonged convalescence. On December 22, a few days after his admission, he had a chill which was followed next day by fever, diarrhœa, debility, headache and hebetube, and on the 24th by epistaxis and great thirst but no nausea. On the 27th he had another aguish paroxysm, and three grains of quinine were given three times daily. On the 30th he was reported as having been somewhat delirious during the preceding night, walking undressed in the ward, trying to urinate into the stove, insisting that the doctor had sent for him, etc. On the 31st his tongue was cleaner, his pulse nearly natural; there had been no delirium during the previous night but six liquid stools had been voided. The same general condition was found on Jan. 1, 1863, but the expression was dull and next day the tongue was rather dry. On the 3d the eyes were injected, the skin harsh, the bowels nearly natural, pulse 84. The patient coughed much during the previous night and brought up mucus dotted with blood; percussion gave a dull sound and respiration was feebly heard over the lower third of the left lung, but there was no crepitus nor bronchial respiration. The quinine was suspended. Next day numerous rose-colored spots appeared on the skin of the abdomen and chest; the skin of the face had a varnished look; the mind was clear, the hearing slightly obtuse and there was slight headache. Sudamina appeared on the 5th in the iliac region and on the neck; the abdomen was moderately distended; one stool was passed; the matter expectorated was thick and rusty. The hearing was improved on the 6th and the tongue more moist. The progress of the case was steadily towards convalescence; dulness of hearing was, however, very noticeable until the 14th. The patient was able to leave his bed on the 23d, after which he gained rapidly in flesh and strength.—*Satterlee Hospital, Philadelphia, Pa.*

III.—TYPHUS FEVER.

Although 2,501 cases of typhus fever, 850 of which were fatal, were reported among the white troops, and 123 cases with 108 deaths among the colored troops, the case-books contain particulars of only six cases that were recorded under this heading, while the medical descriptive lists of but ten cases have been placed on file. Cases 1–6 from the case-books are submitted in full; cases 7–13 are abstracted from the descriptive lists. Three cases treated in September and October, 1863, at the St. James Hospital, New Orleans, La., are not presented, as the official papers, signed by J. V. C. Smith, Act. Ass't Surg., U. S. A., give no information except as to names, dates and results,—death in one instance, recovery in a second and transfer to another ward on account of an attack of erysipelas in the third.

Case 1.—Private Ira Martin, Co. I, 1st Mich. Sharpshooters; age 23; on his recovery from a gunshot injury of the arm was placed on light duty in the kitchen, and while thus employed was seized, Jan. 7, 1865, with a severe chill followed by high fever; his tongue was coated, mouth clammy, bowels constipated, and he had severe headache and pain in the back and limbs. Blue-pill and quinia were given. The fever abated but recurred at noon next day with increased violence. On the 10th the fever had become continuous; the eyes and skin were injected, and the latter presented spots on the chest and abdomen which were neither true petechiæ nor the characteristic rose-colored spots of typhoid fever. Next day the pulse was frequent, small and irregular, the tongue coated brown and the patient delirious. Quinine and stimulants were prescribed; but on the 12th the stools became involuntary and the surface livid. Death occurred on the 13th. [Acting Assistant Surgeon Wm. H. Grafton, U. S. Army, the attending physician, at first regarded this as a case of typhoid fever, but the injection of the surface and the subsequent collapse led him to change the diagnosis to typhus, the more so that the patient had access to a ward in which was a well-marked case of this fever.]—Hospital, Annapolis, Md.

Case 2.—Private William E. Tullis, Co. C, 134th Ohio; age 19; was admitted May 17, 1864, with measles. He recovered and was returned to duty June 25th, but being seized with acute diarrhœa and high fever was re-admitted on the 28th: pulse 110; face flushed; eyes suffused; mind confused and anxious. Astringents were prescribed. Next day he was restless, anxious, feverish and had several discharges from the bowels. On the 30th the pulse was 116, tongue red and smooth, face flushed and spotted, mind anxious, stools frequent and watery. Turpentine emulsion was prescribed. On July 2d the patient lost twelve ounces of blood by epistaxis; he was much exhausted; the delirium and diarrhœa continued. The nostrils were plugged anteriorly with lint saturated with persulphate of iron and tincture of iron was prescribed for internal use. On the 4th brandy was given every three hours. The diarrhœa ceased on the 7th; the tongue became moist and the mucous and salivary secretions increased in quantity and were of healthy appearance, but the delirium continued and the exhaustion was very great. On the 9th there were involuntary discharges from the bowels and bladder. Death occurred next day.—Cumberland Hospital, Md.

Case 3.—Private Isaac H. Starr, Co. F, 119th Ill.; age 23; was admitted Oct. 25, 1862, having been sick for about four weeks with fever. Diagnosis—typhus fever. On admission the tongue was dry and red, dark in the centre, pulse 92, skin dry and hot, bowels not painful but moved three or four times in twenty-four hours; he had much thirst and some cough. Turpentine emulsion and syrup of ipecacuanha were prescribed. He was restless and somewhat delirious during the night but perspired slightly towards the morning of the 26th; during the day he had occasional but slight epistaxis. Small doses of opium and quinine were added to the treatment. The skin continued moist, the stools became frequent, and on the 30th the tongue lost its dryness and began to clean, but the patient talked incoherently and was seized with a general tremor on moving. On November 1 he seemed somewhat better; the tongue was moist, pulse 78, but the tremors of the hands continued. The dose of turpentine was increased and whiskey was added to it. There was a slight improvement up to the 6th, when the mind again wandered and the tongue became dry, red and cracked transversely in the centre; the bowels were neither loose nor tender, but the recti muscles were somewhat tense. Next day there was tremulousness of the muscles of the face with subsultus; the patient was drowsy and his mind feeble; the bowels became loose on the afternoon of this day but were controlled by tannin and morphia. On the 8th the intelligence returned. The tongue and skin were moist on the 9th, but the former became somewhat dry next day, and in the afternoon while perspiring profusely a copious bloody dejection was passed from the bowels. Similar bloody stools recurred on the 11th, after which the pulse became feeble and the general appearance of the patient unfavorable. Opium, tannin, quinine and capsicum were given with whiskey, beef-soup and egg mixture; but the stools continued bloody or wine-colored, though less frequent; the pulse was very feeble and the features shrunken. Opiate enemata were also used. On the 14th there was nausea and a quantity of green liquid was vomited. Death occurred on the 15th.—Hospital, Quincy, Ill.

Case 4.—Private Isaac Howell, Co. D, 119th Ill.; age 20; was admitted Nov. 1, 1862, having been sick for eight days. Diagnosis—typhus fever. He had pain in the back and breast; his tongue was red and rather dry, pulse 88, skin warm and bowels open. Small doses of quinine and Dover's powder were prescribed. On the 2d the patient was incoherent and somewhat deaf; the stools, thin and dark-colored, were not accompanied with pain. Turpentine emulsion, sweet spirit of nitre and paregoric were prescribed in addition to the quinine and Dover's powder. On the 4th he was very wild during the night and attempted to leave nis bed. Wine was added to the treatment. The patient slept occasionally but his sleep was interrupted by startings; the mouth and lips became covered with sordes, the tongue foul and the body emaciated. The skin was moist on the 7th, but delirium of a violent character continued; his inspirations were deep and inclined to be stertorous. On the 8th he was exceedingly wild and incoherent; the pulse 90, tongue more moist but covered with sordes, skin bathed in a copious sweat, bowels quiet. Quinine, chlorate of potash and capsicum were prescribed with stimulants and beef-soup. In the evening he had involuntary stools and red spots appeared on his body and face; he was much prostrated and his features very haggard. On the 9th he seemed more natural and could protrude his tongue with less difficulty. He perspired copiously on the 11th, and recognized his mother who had come to see him; his bowels were quiet. On the 12th and 13th there was delirium with no favorable change in the general appearance; the tongue was moist but red, raw and rough. He died on the 14th.—*Hospital, Quincy, Ill.*

CASE 5.—Private Sanford C. Pruitt, Co. F, 25th Ind.; age 30; was admitted Feb. 2, 1865, with chronic rheumatism. April 28: Pulse 104 and full; tongue red and moist; pain in back; eruption over body; thirst; anorexia; slight headache. Diagnosis—typhus fever. Gave neutral mixture, milk and beef-tea. 29th: Pulse 115 and full; skin hot and dry; tongue red and dry in centre; thirst; one stool. Gave two grains of quinine every two hours. 30th: Pulse 116, feeble and irregular; tongue moist and red; no stool. Omitted quinine. May 1: Pulse 114 and feeble; tongue a little coated; no stool. 2d: Pulse 110; tongue natural; tinnitus aurium; no stool. 3d: Pulse 112; tongue moist; skin natural; urine natural; no stool. 4th: Pulse 104 and regular; tongue dry; skin natural. Gave oil of turpentine in emulsion. 5th: Pulse 100; tongue dry and furred; skin hot; no stool. 6th: Pulse 85 and regular; tongue moist; one stool. 7th: Pulse 78 and rather feeble; tongue moist at edges, a little furred; no stool; free pneumonitic expectoration. 8th: Pulse 86; tongue moist; no stool; listless and dull. 9th: Pulse 70; tongue clean; skin moist; one stool; convalescing. 10th: Transferred to Mower hospital, Philadelphia.—*Cuyler Hospital, Philadelphia, Pa.*

CASE 6.—Elijah Watts, contract nurse. April 29, 1865: Tongue coated but moist; pulse 102; skin dry and warm; eruption over body; three stools; thirst; restlessness; nervous tremors. Ordered neutral mixture and brandy every two hours and a tablespoonful every three hours of a mixture of a half drachm of quinine in one ounce each of syrup of rhubarb and water; arrow-root and milk diet. 30th: Delirium; pulse 125, feeble and irregular; tongue dry; skin hot; one stool. May 1: Pulse as before; tongue moist; skin warm; profuse epistaxis; tinnitus aurium. Discontinued brandy; gave a teaspoonful every two hours of one drachm of oil of turpentine in two ounces of mucilage. 2d: Pulse 115; tongue dry and clean; skin natural. 3d: Pulse 105; tongue moist; skin natural; delirium. Gave occasionally a teaspoonful of a mixture containing one drachm of chloroform in one ounce and a half of alcohol. 4th: Pulse 100; tongue parched; urine drawn off by catheter. 5th: Pulse 100; tongue and mouth very dry; inability to speak or protrude tongue; dull, somewhat comatose; eyes and mouth open. 6th: Pulse 98; tongue and mouth dry. 7th: Pulse 80; tongue and mouth moist; could protrude tongue and speak; rested better. 8th: Pulse 79; tongue cleaning; skin moist; breath and passages very fetid. 9th: Pulse 90; tongue cleaning; skin natural. The patient recovered. Contract annulled May 23.—*Cuyler Hospital, Philadelphia, Pa.*

CASE 7.—Private Rudolphus Grant, Co. B, 10th N. Y.; age 23; was admitted May 27, 1863, presenting all the diagnostic characters of typhus fever inclusive of the eruption. Treatment consisted of twenty drops of diluted sulphuric acid every two hours, with alcoholic stimulants and nourishment. On June 30 he was quite well excepting that he complained of headache and debility. He stated that he had been insane and an inmate of the Utica asylum for six months three years ago. He was delirious during the course of the fever and during convalescence, but he did not show evidence of insanity. He was returned to duty July 23.—*Act. Ass't Surg. Austin Flint, U. S. A., Lexington Avenue Hospital, N. Y.*

CASE 8.—Private John McManus, Co. C, 25th N. Y.; age 29; was wounded in the right arm at the battle of Fredericksburg, and had the forefinger of the left hand carried away by a shot. He was treated in Bellevue hospital, which he left well as regards his wounds March 28, 1863; but although without definite ailments, his general health was not good. On April 1, while at his home in this city, he was obliged to take to bed, having at this time chills followed by febrile movement. He soon became delirious, and in this condition was received into this hospital on the 22d. He talked incoherently and made frequent attempts to get out of bed; the pulse was 120 per minute and feeble; there was no diarrhœa and the abdomen was not tympanitic nor tender on pressure; the body and extremities were thickly covered with an eruption presenting the distinctive characters of the typhus eruption, dusky in color, not elevated and the redness not disappearing on pressure. Whiskey, half an ounce hourly, with essence of beef and milk, were prescribed. His condition remained unchanged on the 23d and the treatment was continued. Next day there was less delirium; pulse 100; skin moist. The whiskey was diminished to half an ounce every two hours. The improvement continued on the 25th; the pulse had fallen to 85 and the eruption had faded considerably. The whiskey was reduced to half an ounce every three hours. On the 27th the febrile movement and delirium had subsided and the eruption was nearly gone. The patient desired food. Convalescence progressed without any unfavorable symptoms, and on May 1 his case was reported as cured, but some diarrhœa delayed his return to duty until June 29.—*Act. Ass't Surg. Austin Flint, U. S. A., Ladies' Home Hospital, N. Y. City.*

CASE 9.—Private Martin Walker, Co. C, 10th N. Y. Cav., was admitted Feb. 11, 1864, with typhus fever. The eruption appeared soon after admission. He was treated with diluted sulphuric acid and whiskey, and a diet of beef-tea, eggs and milk. He was convalescent on the 26th and was reported for duty on March 1.—*Act. Ass't Surg. L. L. Tozier, U. S. A., Lexington Avenue Hospital, N. Y. City.*

CASE 10.—Sergeant Ebenezer C. Talcott, 4th Me. Battery; age about 35; was admitted July 11, 1863, in a semi-comatose condition ascribed doubtfully to typhus fever. A companion stated that the patient was delirious when put on board the boat at Sandy Hook, Md. The stupor gradually became more profound and death took place on the 16th.—*Act. Ass't Surg. John H. Hinton, U. S. A., Hospital, Lexington Avenue, N. Y. City.*

CASE 11.—Private Abraham Koof, Co. M, 10th N. Y. Art.; age 23; was admitted June 10, 1865, with typhus fever. The fever continued twenty days after his admission, and during this time there was much deafness and delirium. The eruption was marked and disappeared under pressure. There was considerable tympanites and diarrhœa but no hemorrhage from the bowels. Epistaxis occurred several times during the early part of the attack He suffered from bronchitis but not in a marked degree. On July 1 he was able to sit up and on the 9th was around the ward although suffering considerably from diarrhœa. Tonics, stimulants and opium with camphor were administered. On August 15 the diarrhœa continued and the patient was anæmic; he was able, however, at this time to walk in the yard. He was returned to duty November 29.—*Act. Ass't Surg. F. Everts, U. S. A., Central Park Hospital, N. Y. City.*

CASE 12.—Recruit John Talbot, unassigned; age 20; was admitted Oct. 1, 1864, with typhus fever. He was treated with alcoholic stimulants. On the 8th the patient became delirious; pulse 120; an eruption appeared on his chest. Two days later pneumonia set in and death took place on the 15th.—*Hospital, Elmira, N. Y.*

CASE 13.—Private William A. Wood, Co. K, 21st Mich.; age 25; was admitted May 20, 1865, as a case of typhus fever. On June 8 he had headache, pain in the back and pain with some soreness in the right hypochondrium; the tongue was slightly coated but quite red on the edges and tip; pulse 110. Soon after this delirium set in, and on the 11th the patient was nearly pulseless, his jaw quite stiff, subsultus strongly marked and skin covered with cold perspiration. Brandy and Hoffmann's anodyne were given. Next day he recovered his mind and seemed stronger, but the improvement was temporary. He died on the 16th.—*Act. Ass't Surg. C. A. Burnham, U. S. A., Hospital, Fairfax Seminary, Va.*

III.—SYMPTOMATOLOGY OF THE CONTINUED FEVERS.

I.—COMMON CONTINUED FEVER.

From the absence of clinical histories of cases of common continued fever it is impossible to speak from the records concerning the symptoms of the many cases which were reported under this title during the first fourteen months of the war. The single case of *simple continued fever* and the seven cases of *continued fever* that have been presented are insufficient to illustrate the disease.

It has already been shown that typhoid fever was recognized as the common continued fever of the United States, and that the tendency of medical opinion at the outbreak of the war was to regard all cases of continued fever which were not distinctly specific in their character as due to the poison of typhoid.* But the indefinite term common continued, which at one time included typhoid among other possible fevers, remained on the army sick reports, after the differentiation of typhoid, as a standing suggestion of the existence of

---

*This opinion seems to have become more extensively diffused since that time both in this country and in Britain: MACLAGAN gives expression to this view, *Edinburg Med. and Surg. Jour.*, April, 1871, where he says, p. 875: "Indeed, I think it may be stated generally that a febrile attack which is too long to be febricula, which is not ague and which is not due to local disease, must be enteric." Nevertheless MURCHISON, although regarding as typhoid fever most of the cases called by British practitioners simple continued fever, describes the clinical histories of four non-specific varieties: The first, *ephemeral fever*, is similar to a single paroxysm of ague. Chills or rigors are followed by a quick full pulse, flushed face, dry hot skin, white furred tongue, thirst, anorexia, constipation, scanty high-colored urine, severe headache, restlessness and sleeplessness or sometimes drowsiness and pains in the limbs. The symptoms subside suddenly, often with perspirations, in twelve, twenty-four or thirty-six hours. In the second, corresponding to the synochal grade of the inflammatory fevers of the old writers, the febrile action continues from four to ten days; the pulse is full, rapid and often hard or bounding; the headache acute and throbbing; sometimes there is delirium. Defervescence is attended with perspirations, epistaxis, vomiting or diarrhœa, and is so frequently associated with herpes on the lips or nose that the disease has been called *herpetic fever*. The *ardent continued fever* of the tropics constitutes his third variety, which is regarded as an exaggerated form of the synocha of Britain. As seen among the European troops at Calcutta in 1853 and in Burmah in 1854, the disease mostly affected young plethoric recruits recently arrived from Europe, and prevailed in the hot, dry months, when the temperature was never below 84° Fahr. The symptoms, which in many cases commenced immediately after incautious exposure to the direct rays of the sun, were chilliness; nausea or vomiting; accelerated, full and firm pulse; dry burning skin; flushed face; giddiness; intense headache; ringing in the ears; intolerance of light; muscæ volitantes; restlessness and sleeplessness; yellow furred tongue; parched lips; thirst; constipation; scanty high-colored urine. Acute delirium occurred about the fourth or fifth day, followed by unconsciousness, contraction of the pupils and sometimes complete coma, which ended in death between the sixth and ninth days if convalescence was not meanwhile established by a copious perspiration. He cites MOREHEAD and MARTIN in support of his assertion that the subsidence of the fever was occasionally followed by sudden or even fatal collapse. The fourth variety is introduced rather as a suggestion than as a clinically defined entity. It is called *asthenic simple fever*, and is said to be characterized by loss of appetite and strength; pulse rather feeble, ranging from 90 to 120; slightly furred tongue; confined bowels; headache and disturbed sleep. The symptoms continue for two or three weeks without any great change except increasing prostration. It is evident that the difficulty of discriminating between this variety and mild typhoid attacks would be very great, in fact, clinically the discrimination is impossible. The distinction could only be effected by the aid of etiological considerations.—*A Treatise on the Continued Fevers of Great Britain*, London, 1873, p. 679 *et seq.*

other non-symptomatic febrile conditions. It seems probable, however, that the common continued fever of the monthly reports consisted in great part of anomalous cases of typhoid. When the characteristic symptoms of typhoid were present in a given case its entry under the specific heading was assured; but when these were absent, obscured or modified, the term common continued fever afforded a convenient escape from a positive and specific diagnosis. When a febrile case did not run the prolonged course of typhoid; when it was unmarked by rose-colored spots and free from relaxation of the bowels or tenderness in the right iliac region; especially when in addition the cerebral symptoms did not appear to justify the appellation of typhoid, the indefinite term accommodated it with an appropriate position on the official record.

It is equally probable that there were reported under this heading many febrile cases of short duration which were treated in quarters or in the regimental hospitals. Such cases corresponded with the *simple continued, ephemeral* or *irritative** fevers of medical writers, presenting languor, lassitude, muscular weakness, headache, inability to collect the thoughts, wakefulness or dreamful sleep, perhaps even slight nocturnal delirium, constipation or diarrhœa, white-coated tongue, hot skin and feeble and rapid pulse. This condition lasted one or more days, was followed by perspirations or a gradual subsidence, and was seldom characterized by the tedious convalescence of the typhoid attack.

If it be allowed that cases of this character occurred among the troops, some of them must have assumed an adynamic form and represented with more or less fidelity the general outlines of the clinical picture of typhoid fever; for the influences to which the adynamic condition is usually attributed were in strong force in our camps and garrisons during the war. As distinguishing between such cases and typhoid fever there would have been the absence of rose-colored spots, a want of connection between the diarrhœal attack and the febrile condition, perhaps also the character of the alvine evacuations and the location of the intestinal tenderness, with the short duration of the primary fever in cases that had been closely watched from the commencement. These would have been correctly reported during the early months of the war as cases of common continued fever, although from the concurrent prevalence of undoubted typhoid they were liable to be regarded as expressions

---

* Under the title *Irritative Fever*, Dr. GEORGE B. WOOD includes all cases of idiopathic fever resulting from non-specific causes of irritation. An over excitement of one or more of the functions is induced, and this being propagated to different parts of the system may throw all the functions into a state of derangement capable of sustaining itself after the direct cause has ceased to operate. There must be a pre-existing disposition in the system to the febrile movement that it may be thus independently sustained. There is occasionally slight inflammation associated with the fever, most frequently in the fauces or in some portion of the alimentary or pulmonary mucous membrane, but this is wholly insufficient to account for the symptoms and is often wanting entirely; moreover, a truly symptomatic fever subsides immediately with the subsidence of the inflammation. He observes that when the febrile action is prolonged to the seventh or tenth day, it is apt to become somewhat remittent, relaxing in the morning and undergoing exacerbation in the afternoon or evening. It is usually sthenic. "But occasionally the general actions of the system, though excited, have the taint of feebleness. A low fever somewhat of the typhus character is developed, though infinitely less dangerous than the genuine typhus. The previously debilitated condition of the patient, a depraved state of his blood from bad living, or exposure for some time to depressing influences, as of certain epidemics, exhalations from privies, etc., may account for this adynamic character."—*A Treatise on the Practice of Medicine*, Philadelphia, 1847, Vol. I, p. 224. Under the term *Cess-pool fever*, Dr. ALONZO CLARK describes a febrile disease which has been traced in almost every instance to foul water or water made foul by the admixture of human excrement or to neglected privies. It is not always ushered in by a chill, but there is always a certain amount of fever and a diarrhœa lasting two, three or more weeks. The illustrative case which he records had no headache, epistaxis, tenderness or pain in the abdomen or iliac region, tympanites, sordes, nor rose-colored spots; delirium was moderate, the patient trying to get out of bed, saying he wanted to go home; the pulse became small and feeble, and the diarrhœa continuing, death took place from exhaustion about the end of the third week. Cases of this kind occur, according to the experience of Dr. CLARK, in every region of the country; and he holds that, so far as we can judge from the symptoms, they are not cases of the typhoid affection.—See *Med. Record*, Vol. XIII, New York, 1878, p. 303. Dr. I. A. WATSON of New Hampshire, in the *Report of the State Board of Health*, 1884, regards as cess-pool fever certain cases which originated in a poisoned well at Little Boar's Head. They seemed to be instances of blood poisoning, in their last stage resembling typhoid fever. A wealthy Philadelphian who had spent many summers at Little Boar's Head built a handsome residence there on an elevation about fifty feet above the sea-level and but a short distance from the water. The elevation consisted of seamy ledges with only a few feet of soil covering them. Instead of building a sewer to the ocean he constructed a cess-pool forty feet from the house. Sixty feet from this cess-pool, and apparently on the same level, was dug the well which was to supply the residence with water, but before a free supply of water was obtained it was necessary to dig ten feet into the ledge. The well and cess-pool were both constructed at the same time, and two weeks thereafter the well-water became polluted; but the family not recognizing the source and nature of the pollution continued to use the water until it became so tainted as to be repulsive. The owner and a lady visitor died from the febrile attack; the owner's daughter, a servant and a guest of the family recovered after a severe illness.

of the presence of the poison of that disease modified by peculiarities of individual constitution and local hygienic conditions. During the latter part of the war it may be assumed that they were reported among *other miasmatic diseases* by those who regarded them as due to an unknown miasm, or that they were added to the typhoid or typho-malarial list, according to the views entertained by the reporting officers of the absence or presence of a malarial factor in cases essentially enteric. The following extracts from sanitary reports have a bearing on this subject:

Surgeon THOMAS C. BAKER, *7th Me., Camp Lyon, Baltimore, Md., Oct.* 1, 1861.—From the time the regiment was mustered into service at Augusta till the close of the quarter ending September 30 only one death occurred. This was a case of typhoid fever. Among *other diseases of this class,* in the class of fevers, are eight cases, all of fever or feverishness, some of which approached common continued fever in their general characteristics.

Surgeon W. W. BROWN, *7th N. H., St. Augustine, Fla., March* 31, 1863.—I neglected to mention a variety of fever which seems rather peculiar to this place, and which made its appearance in our regiment in December last and continued to affect us somewhat during January and February, but entirely disappeared about the first of the present month. It usually commenced with the general symptoms of fever, and in most cases assumed the common continued type. It had no appearance of having had a miasmatic origin, but seemed to have been occasioned by the frequent and sudden variations of temperature which we experienced during those months, and to which all places on the Atlantic coast are subject, although the range of the thermometer may be small. About four-fifths of the cases were mild and required little treatment other than low diet and rest after having the primæ viæ thoroughly evacuated. The remaining fifth tended to a typhoid condition, with diarrhœa, and some of them assumed a very grave character, although all recovered with one exception. The typhoid cases were treated on general principles, but early required stimulants and nourishing diet, with occasional opiates to allay nervous irritation. There was more or less pulmonary inflammation in the severe cases, and the diarrhœa was very intractable. Stimulants were well borne, but quinine was neither required nor well adapted except during convalescence. We had in all over one hundred cases; in the fatal case involuntary evacuations with low delirium and subsultus of the tendons came on early, and our most active exertions proved unavailing.

Surgeon J. T. CALHOUN, *74th N. Y., near Alexandria, Va., June* 30, 1862.—But the stench from the battle-field [Fair Oaks] was most disgusting; and in such an atmosphere, in the month of June, were our men living. Every third day they were on picket, and in the interval they were frequently employed in the trenches. Skirmishing was of daily occurrence, and night alarms frequent and harassing; I seldom passed a day without having a wound to dress. The men were ill fed, overworked, exposed to frequent alarms and living in an atmosphere largely composed of poisonous gases exhaled from the imperfectly buried dead. A peculiar form of fever presented itself, characterized by an extremely weak pulse, great prostration, suffused eyes, vertigo and anorexia. Its duration was generally from four to five days. The treatment was usually a mercurial cathartic followed by ten-grain doses of quinine three times a day.*

Surgeon M. R. GAGE, *25th Wis., Camp Randall, Wis., Dec.* 31, 1862.—We have met with cases of continued fever which might properly be termed passive in character in contradistinction to those of a more absolute and active grade. These, although manifesting but little activity, it being in fact scarcely possible to determine the existence of fever in many of the cases, are liable to indefinite protraction. The treatment most efficacious in this class of cases consists of a calomel cathartic and then a judicious alterative, diaphoretic and refrigerant course. Recovery generally ensues as soon as the specific effect of the mercurial is produced. A full dose of calomel in the incipiency of the cases goes far towards interrupting and controlling the period of their continuance; the hepatic derangement is overcome, the pulse reduced, and the skin having resumed its natural function, a march is stolen upon the disease and convalescence is quickly induced. A stimulating plan has not been required; that generally pursued has been mildly antiphlogistic. During convalescence tonics and a more generous diet are allowed; in many instances at this period remedial agents are entirely withdrawn and the patient left to the recuperative forces of his purified and regenerated organism, together with the invigorating influences of a generous but carefully selected diet.

Ass't Surg. HENRY S. SCHELL, *U. S. A., Miner's Hill, Va., Sept.* 4, 1862.—Cases of fever were of constant occurrence during the quarter, and under whatever name registered, they were all of the same general asthenic character. So far as I can determine, few if any of those which assumed a decided periodic form originated primarily in this locality. Miasmatic affections seemed in most instances to be the result of the seeds of disease which had remained in the system from last year and were now quickened into activity by exposure to the vicissitudes of a campaign. The prevailing form of febrile disease I regarded as an ordinary irritative fever of an adynamic type, and many of the cases marked as remittent fever in the statistical report were of this kind; they assumed a sort of periodicity which was not well defined, but which rendered it difficult to decide upon their true nature. Every case which I have registered as common continued fever was of the same character as those which other surgeons in the division reported remittent fever, but which on several grounds I considered independent of malarial influences. 1st: The affection usually followed exposure to sudden changes of weather, hard duty or rapid and exhausting marching—as for instance, the expedition to Hanover Court House. In the light batteries the fever did not follow exposure on picket duty in the swamps of the Chickahominy because the men, once upon the ground, stretched the tarpaulins to make shelters for themselves and went as regularly and comfortably to bed as when in camp. With the infantry

---

* In the *Medical and Surgical Reporter*, Phila., Pa., Vol. IX, p. 399, Dr. CALHOUN refers to this fever, and considers the name typho-malarial an appropriate one for it.

pickets it was different; they, perhaps at a distance of not one hundred yards from the batteries, stood in water to the knees during the long watches of the night, and returned to camp after forty-eight hours utterly exhausted, and in a few days, it may be the next day, were burning with fever. 2d: The cases began with languor, debility or utter prostration, and in all instances gradually; the tongue was coated with a white fur, the bowels mostly loose, but sometimes there was alarming diarrhœa which clung to the patient long after the fever had disappeared and occasionally threatened to destroy him; there was considerable heat of surface, pulse about 100 or 110; in a few cases derangement of the liver was present; there was invariably a tendency to debility, which rendered the use of stimulants necessary from the beginning; towards the close of the disease the kidneys were often affected, and the mind was always implicated if the sickness became serious. 3d: Most of the cases were cured, if properly treated, in from four to ten days without the administration of quinine, which drug usually retarded recovery, when given in antiperiodic doses, by producing a diarrhœal aggravation of the existing debility. 4th: The treatment which I found most effective was to enjoin perfect rest and keep the bowels in as natural a condition as possible. Dover's powder was administered as a diaphoretic when there was much muscular soreness; the citrate of potassa was sometimes given. In all cases the patient was sustained with milk-punch, eggs, beef-essence, etc. Under this plan he was usually able to return to duty in a week or two after being attacked.

In estimating the causes of this disease I should enumerate the predisposing and the exciting. Among the former were the constant heat, to which the men were unaccustomed; the debilitating action of fatigues and privations; exposure to the effluvia of badly regulated sinks, half or totally unburied offal from slaughter-pens and excrement deposited in improper places, and the continued occupation of the same camping ground. The chief of the exciting causes were extraordinary toil, privations and vicissitudes of weather.

Surgeon GEORGE W. CLIPPINGER, *14th Ind., Cheat Mountain, Va., Dec. 31, 1861.*—The sickness was of a peculiar type, characterized by exhaustion of the nervous system with stagnation of the capillary circulation. This was attended by blueness of the skin, which might be considered pathognomonic. The face was of a dull leaden color and the features bloated and swollen. The particular viscus receiving the largest proportion of the blood thrown in from the surface of the body became at once the seat of disease. This was accompanied by frequency of the pulse, great lassitude, muscular and articular pains, anorexia, dry and husky skin, great thirst, red and parched tongue and violent pain in the head with more or less incoherence. These cases, known familiarly as "camp-fever," were officially reported as "continued fever." The causes were unquestionably protracted and exhausting labor, exposure to cold and incessant rains, insufficient clothing and sameness of food.

The treatment had in view the removal of congestion and restoration of the capillary circulation. When this was accomplished convalescence was hastened by the administration of tonics. Sulphate of magnesia with ipecacuanha was beneficial, particularly in the early stages. The fatal cases assumed the gravest appearances of typhoid fever; tenderness of the colon supervened, with gurgling in the cæcum and sigmoid flexure; intestinal hemorrhage occurred in many cases and in all that were fatal.

Ass't Surg. H. M. SPRAGUE, *U. S. A., Sept. 30, 1861.*—About September 1, after having been encamped for a week in an exceedingly foul locality, there broke out a severe epidemic which has given us our only fatal cases of disease. When this epidemic appeared there was nothing formidable in its external features. The men looked simply debilitated. Their history was that for several days, often two weeks, they had been suffering from diarrhœa, yellowish and watery, attended sometimes with griping and accompanied with debility, listlessness, drowsiness, pain in the bones, white tongue, slight heat of skin morning or evening and some acceleration of pulse, ranging from 94 to 106. The disease had the appearance neither of typhoid nor of remittent fever. *Post-mortem* examination of two bodies revealed some congestion of the bowels, with moderate enlargement of the mesenteric glands; no ulceration of Peyer's patches; no destruction of the mucous membrane; no inflammation of the rectum; the spleen was slightly engorged; the other organs healthy.

II.—TYPHOID FEVER.

It has been a matter of some difficulty to the writer to present the symptoms of typhoid fever as distinct from those of the so called typho-malarial fever. This has arisen from the want of records to show what constituted the characteristics of the cases reported under the latter heading.* But as Dr. WOODWARD in November, 1863, expressly stated that the term typho-malarial was meant to include only those cases in which typhoid fever had its symptoms more or less masked by the coexistence of manifestations of malarial poisoning,† the detailed cases presented in the "Clinical Records of the Continued Fevers"

---

* See page 212, *supra*.

† J. J. WOODWARD, *Ass't Surg., U. S. A., Outlines of the Chief Camp Diseases of the United States Army*, Phila., 1863, p. 74: "Under the designation of *Camp Fevers* may be included * * *typhus*; * * *yellow fever*; * * *typhoid fever* with or without scorbutic complications; *malarial remittent fever* with or without scorbutic complications; and a vast group of mixed cases, in which the malarial and typhoid elements are variously combined with each other and with the scorbutic taint, and for which the author proposed the name of typho-malarial fever." * * But, on p. 110, in discussing the nature of the disease, he gives utterance to the opinion that the so-called typho-malarial fever was not a merely modified typhoid, but a composite disease or new hybrid. "On the one hand typho-malarial fever is not to be regarded as a new disease in the ordinary acceptation of the term, that is, as an affection characterized by some new pathognomonic element. Nor, on the other hand, is it just to look upon it merely as a modified enteric fever, since the malarial and scorbutic phenomena which accompany it are predominant in many cases—perhaps, on the whole, in the greater number. Much rather should it be considered simply as a new hybrid of old and well-known pathological conditions, in which the exact train of symptoms is as variable as the degree of preponderance attained by each of the several concurring elements."

274   SYMPTOMATOLOGY OF

afforded the materials for determining the symptoms not only of the cases regarded as typhoid by the attending physicians, but of those which Dr. WOODWARD would have classified as typho-malarial. In the chapter on malarial disease, in this volume, the characteristics of malarial fevers have been illustrated. By studying these in connection with the fully recorded typhoid cases treated in the Seminary hospital, the latter have been divided into cases of pure and of modified typhoid.

The paroxysmal type of the malarial fevers stands prominently forth as a diagnostic mark of the complicated disease, manifesting itself by recurring chills and febrile exacerbations alternating with perspirations or a moist condition of the skin at a period of the clinical history when, in pure typhoid fever, the febrile action is continued and the skin dry and husky. But these signs of undoubted complication are liable to be lost in two directions. On the one hand typhoid fever is marked by daily remissions, which may be detected, in the absence of thermometric records, by notable changes in the pulse, general surface, tongue, secretions, etc.; on the other hand, the remissions in remittent fever may be so slight or transitory as to escape unnoted. Hence, although the absence of the paroxysmal type does not exclude the possibility of the coexistence of malarial disease, its slightly marked presence cannot be accepted as indicating malarial complications unless supported by other and less indefinite evidence. It is impossible to determine in all cases that an evening exacerbation is due to malarial influences, but when the paroxysmal feature is strongly developed a remittent or intermittent fever may be regarded as associated with the progress of the typhoid affection. The frequency of this coincidence, especially in men who had previously suffered from acute malarial disease, leads to the supposition that the typhoid onset itself or the exposures and unhygienic conditions which predisposed to it, acted as the determining cause of a recurrence of the paroxysmal fever. Moreover, it is generally accepted that in malarious subjects diseases which are not occasioned by malaria oftentimes exhibit a tendency to periodicity. Nevertheless there are not wanting on the records cases of apparently unmodified typhoid in which the previous history of the patients embraced a series of aguish attacks or other indications of malarial poisoning.

When the complicating element failed to manifest itself by paroxysms and perspirations, which do not belong to the history of typhoid fever, its expression was found in hepatic tenderness, gastric irritability, epigastric pain and other signs of interference with the normal action of the liver and upper portion of the alimentary tract. In the absence of these from the record a modification of certain of the symptoms of typhoid fever may sometimes be attributed to the malarious condition of the patient. If, for instance, the malarial poison has not been productive of intestinal congestion, diarrhœa, which is one expression of the local lesion of typhoid, may not be prominent as a symptom, and this is especially the case when the malarial influence is manifested by frequently recurring perspirations; the character of the stools may also be altered. At the same time it is to be remembered that diarrhœa is not present in all cases of distinctly pure typhoid fever; its absence does not, therefore, constitute an indication of malarial complication except when in conjunction with other testimony of a more or less suggestive character. On the other hand, if the malarial influence has expended its force on the mucous lining of the intestinal canal, there may be diarrhœa and tenderness with other strongly marked signs of the abdominal lesion of typhoid fever; the tenderness, however, is general, or specially noted in regions other than the right iliac,—frequently over the tract of the colon,—and the stools are often of a dysenteric character. But here again there is a want of value for diagnostic purposes inasmuch as typhoid fever engrafted on an antecedent diarrhœa or dysentery may give rise to such symptoms.

The recorded condition of the tongue furnishes in many instances satisfactory evidence of the presence of a malarial complication. In typhoid fever it had at first a slight coating of a white or yellow color, but redness of the tip and edges was generally manifested even at this period, and as the tongue dried and darkened on the dorsum the redness became more noticeable. When a malarial element was present this condition of the tongue did not generally obtain; it was pale, flabby and variously coated not only during the progress of the febrile phenomena but during convalescence.

The pneumonitic tendencies of typhoid fever were seldom altered by the presence of the malarial poison, although the latter had apparently a greater proclivity to the development of sudden and dangerous pulmonary congestions. Nor were the cerebral symptoms of typhoid materially changed by the presence of the complicating element except when this was prominently and perniciously developed, masking the continued type by its irregular paroxysms and changing the muttering delirium of the febrile condition into the coma of malarial congestion.

Extravasations of blood under the skin, constituting petechiæ and vibices, were common to the continued operation of both poisons; but an early appearance of such spots in typhoid cases, when combined with other testimony, is suggestive of malarial complication. Deterioration of the blood, from scurvy or ochlesis, was also occasionally concerned in the development of these spots.

Lastly, a rapid issue in fatal cases is indicative of malarial disease, since typhoid cases usually ran a progressive course while the paroxysmal fevers were often fulminant.

By giving weight to these considerations the febrile cases treated at the Seminary hospital have been arranged into two series, one of pure typhoid and the other assumed, on more or less satisfactory evidence, to have been complicated by the malarial poison. From these and other cases submitted above, as also from a series of fatal cases to be presented hereafter in connection with the *post-mortem* appearances, the following general description of the clinical progress of the typhoid fever of the war has been written.

Cases regarded and reported as typhoid fever began with feverishness, depression of spirits, muscular debility and unusual relaxation of the bowels. Oftentimes the soldier suffered in this way for several days, attributing his condition to some particular exposure or indiscretion in diet, the effects of which he hoped would speedily subside. Ultimately headache, pain in the back, aching in the bones and muscles, loss of appetite and increasing weakness wholly incapacitated him for duty and led him to report as sick. As the patients were mostly young and inexperienced soldiers, it frequently happened that they did not realize their loss of health, but continued their usual occupations in an apathetic manner until their appearance led to inquiries by more experienced comrades or company officers, when they were sent to the regimental surgeon. In nearly one-half of the cases the disease was ushered in by a chill which was immediately followed by fever and perhaps diarrhœa, but not by perspiration: Of fifty-one typhoid cases found in the records of the Seminary hospital the onset was by chill in twenty, without chill in eleven, while in the remaining twenty the manner of the attack was not recorded.* Of the twenty cases

---

* Of sixty-three cases in which MURCHISON noted the commencement, pains in the head and limbs, commonly aching but sometimes neuralgic, were among the earliest symptoms in fifty-six, and most of these patients also suffered from irregular chills, languor and giddiness; rigors occurred in only three of the cases. But in several instances, not included in the analysis, he observed decided rigors and in fact all the phenomena of ague during the first few days.—*Op. cit.*, p. 545.

that had an initiatory chill five were mild, eight severe and seven fatal; of the eleven that began with no marked sensations of chilliness three proved mild, six severe and two fatal. These numbers are not large, but so far as they go they indicate that the course of the disease is not affected by the mode of onset. It may be owing to an appreciation of this fact that few writers advert to the prognostic value of chill as an initial symptom of typhoid fever. Nevertheless LOUIS was inclined to regard a severe chill as suggestive of a severe attack, for his observations showed a greater frequency of chills among the severe than among the mild febrile cases.*

The course of the disease after this onset by defined chills or gradual accession differed much in individual cases. In some, probably in a majority of those which, anterior to the issue of the order removing common continued fever from the list of diseases on the monthly sick reports, would have been reported under that heading, the febrile condition did not at any time become more marked than during the first few days. The tongue was somewhat furred or white-coated, with the edges and tip of a deeper red than natural and with some tendency to dryness at the base and centre; the skin was dry, the face slightly flushed and the eyes injected, especially in the evening; the urine was scanty and the bowels relaxed or unusually susceptible to the action of laxative medicines; the pulse was seldom rapid, full or tense, but was occasionally dicrotic; slight epistaxis occurred at times; the cerebral manifestations were restricted to headache, restlessness, drowsiness and inability to concentrate the attention or follow up a train of thought; a bronchial cough often accompanied these symptoms. In a few days the febrile action subsided, the improved condition being first noticed after a sound and refreshing sleep, coincident with a cleaner tongue, diminished thirst and recovered appetite; occasionally perspirations, epistaxis or slight diarrhœa marked the defervescence. The patient, however, remained weak for a long time after the attack.

But in a majority of the cases the disease was prolonged for two or more weeks, during which time certain of the symptoms assumed a special gravity. The intestinal symptoms in some became especially noteworthy, consisting of a more or less active diarrhœa, with pain in the abdomen, tenderness on pressure, particularly in the right iliac region, gurgling and some tympanitic distention. The diarrhœa often subsided at the end of the second week, and this improvement was usually associated with an amelioration of the general symptoms, free perspirations and the appearance of sudamina. But when defervescence was effected gradually and without the occurrence of perspiration, relaxation of the bowels was prone to continue, with diminishing tenderness, perhaps for eight or ten days longer, during which recrudescence was not uncommon. The patient continued weak after the subsidence of the active symptoms, and at any period of the prolonged convalescence he was liable to dangerous recurrences of the diarrhœa from slight indiscretions in diet or other faults in the sanitary regimen.

The cerebral symptoms in other cases constituted apparently the special characteristic of the disease, for they were often present in the absence of diarrhœa and abdominal ten-

* Chills occurred in thirty-one of thirty-three fatal cases in which he was able to learn anything definite on this point; of forty-five severe though not fatal cases, all except three had chills or a greater sensibility to cold, while in thirty-one mild cases chills were reported in twenty-four only.— (*Recherches Anatomiques, Pathologiques et Thérapeutiques sur la maladie connue sous les noms de Gastro-entérite, Fièvre putride, adynamique, ataxique, typhoïde, etc.* CH. A. LOUIS, Paris, 1829, t. II, p. 259.) Nevertheless, if the fifty-eight cases recorded in the work just cited are examined in reference to this point, it will be found that chills are not recorded as frequently as the above statements would lead us to anticipate. Forty-five of these cases are regarded as undoubted typhoid, the observations 46–58 being variously classified as doubtful, simulated, etc. In twenty-two of the forty-five cases chills are noted as having occurred at the beginning of the attack, and in one on the fourth day of the fever; in the remaining twenty-two cases either no mention is made of the symptom or it is positively stated that it was not present.

derness. The wakefulness and restlessness which affected the patient during the first week of the disease increased at night, until sleep became disturbed by incoherent mutterings. During the day he was drowsy, and when aroused was found to be dull and stupid, held at attention for the moment but relapsing immediately into a semi-somnolent or mildly delirious condition. In such cases the tongue became dry and dark-colored, retaining however the redness of its margins, and with diarrhœa present the stools were often passed without the consciousness of the sufferer; the urine was also sometimes evacuated involuntarily, or retained, causing hypogastric distention and pain until removed by the catheter. In most cases at this period sordes accumulated on the teeth and gums. But at the close of the second week, coincident with a moist condition of the skin, epistaxis and sudamina, the tongue became moist, the mind clear, the appetite improved, and refreshing sleep, enjoyed for the first time since the occurrence of the attack, ushered in the period of convalescence.

Generally in cases which ran a two weeks' course to defervescence the rose-colored eruption, viewed by most of our medical officers as characteristic of the disease, was discovered on the chest and abdomen from the seventh to the fourteenth day. In several instances the appearance of this eruption about the end of the second week was associated with improvement, and was the only concomitant of defervescence entered on the record.

Death seldom occurred before the fourteenth day except as the result of accident connected with the febrile condition, as in case 41 of the Seminary series, in which the patient was killed by jumping from a window in his delirium, or by some intercurrent attack, as in 20 of the *post-mortem* records, in which pneumonia proved fatal on the thirteenth day.

When defervescence failed to take place about the fourteenth day the protracted course of the disease was usually due to the occurrence of intestinal or pneumonic complications. Diarrhœa became aggravated and prolonged the duration of the case for several weeks, or an exhausting attack was speedily followed by collapse and death. Intestinal hemorrhage increased the prostration of the patient, adding gravity to otherwise mild attacks and sometimes leading directly to a fatal issue. The suffering occasioned by abdominal distention appeared in some cases to be the cause of the failure to convalesce at the end of the second week; indeed death at a later period was occasionally due to exhaustion induced by a continuance of the abdominal distress. Peritonitis supervened in many cases, the mesentery becoming affected by the condition of the glands or the peritoneal coat of the intestines by the inflammatory processes in their interior tunics; but, more frequently, in cases protracted by the unfavorable progress of the abdominal lesions, the occurrence of exquisite pain, vomiting, hiccough, cold perspirations, collapse and death, indicated perforation of the intestine and the escape of its contents into the peritoneal sac.

With or without the continuance of diarrhœa the course of the disease was often prolonged by the development or aggravation of cough, pain in the chest, hurried breathing and the physical signs of pneumonitic processes. Patients subject to bronchial cough from the early days of the attack were specially liable to this complication; the mucous expectoration became purulent and bloody, sometimes viscid and rust-colored. In favorable cases the duration of the sickness was much lengthened by these attacks, and if no serious intestinal or cerebral symptoms were present, the lung disease assumed a prominence which led in many instances to a diagnosis of pneumonia by medical officers who had not observed the case from its commencement. In others in which an extensive and manifest implication of the lung was coincident with low delirium and great prostration the disease, in the absence of a knowledge of its previous history, was frequently reported as *typhoid pneumonia*.

Nevertheless, in most of the cases in which defervescence at the end of the second week was prevented by intestinal or pneumonic complications, a close study of the details of the daily record of progress reveals an effort on the part of nature to establish convalescence at that period. The tongue became less dry, the skin moist, the pulse less frequent, delirium subsided, or the patient was recorded as being more intelligent or less stupid or drowsy or as having passed a better night than usual. But this favorable change in such cases was transitory: with some aggravation of the existing cough, pain in the chest and accelerated respiration, or with increased tenderness and distention of the abdomen, with or without an exacerbation or recurrence of the diarrhœa, the tongue became again dry, the skin hot, and a febrile condition, proportioned to the extent and severity of the local lesions and the depressed vitality of the patient, was re-established.

When cerebral symptoms were specially prominent during the third week, the existence of serious intestinal lesions might not be manifested by their usual symptoms; generally, however, stools passed without the consciousness of the patient were loose and frequent and in a proportion of the cases hemorrhagic. Under similar cerebral conditions extensive congestion of the lungs or numerous foci of catarrhal pneumonia were at times developed without expressing their existence by local symptoms.

When complications prolonged the febrile condition into the fourth week the patient became greatly emaciated, his pulse rapid and weak and his prostration extreme. At any time during the course of the disease sudden death from failure of the heart's action or heart-clot was a possible occurrence. Fatal syncope not unfrequently attended the effort to rise to stool or followed the unconscious impulses of an active delirium. During or before this time there often occurred a swelling of the parotid glands, which usually terminated in suppuration and extensive disorganization, if the death of the patient did not meanwhile interfere with the progress of the local affection. Not unfrequently, also, at this time deafness and headache, both of which were often obscured by the presence of delirium or stupor, indicated the probable occurrence of inflammatory processes in the ear, a complication which sufficed of itself to prolong the apparent duration of the original febrile attack, for the untoward symptoms sometimes disappeared and convalescence was established on the free issue of purulent matter from the affected organ.

If the conditions mentioned did not prove fatal by the fifth week the activity of the morbid processes referable to the direct action of the typhoid poison in the blood appeared to subside; diarrhœa became less active or ceased; pneumonic symptoms improved; delirium and other cerebral manifestations abated. Sometimes the return of consciousness about this time, after many days of low delirium or stupor, gave rise to hopes of a favorable issue which were not realized, the patient dying shortly afterwards of asthenia but retaining his recently recovered intelligence to the last. In other cases the tongue became clean, usually of a lighter red than in health, and sometimes patched with white or yellow fur; the appetite returned, and the patient showed a languid though increasing interest in the affairs of life. But he was generally extremely prostrated, and bed-sores, which had formed latterly, were slow to heal and caused much suffering; in fact his condition was such that the slightest adverse influence was sufficient to precipitate a fatal issue.

Irrespective of the direct influence of the typhoid poison on the blood a morbid quality of this fluid necessarily resulted from the continuance of the febrile condition by its interference with the healthy action of the blood-forming and blood-purifying organs. This deterioration was occasionally manifested at a late period of the typhoid attack by the development of petechial spots and even of larger extravasations. Abscesses were formed in various situations, and sometimes these became gangrenous in character. Gangrene of the toes and feet, simulating that from frostbite and necessitating amputation, was recorded as a consequence of the typhoid affection.

Even in favorable cases convalescence was tedious, and in its duration generally proportioned to the severity of the antecedent attack. Muscular strength and mental power alike required a long period for the return of their former vigor. Nor was the convalescence progressive: Diarrhœa was a frequent and oftentimes dangerous accident. Chronic pneumonia resulting from processes set up during the febrile attack often proved fatal as a sequel. Pain in the muscles retarded the return to health, keeping the patient for months in hospital under treatment for so-called chronic rheumatism. Various paralyses also appeared in the list of the sequelæ. Rarely a well defined relapse occurred marked by the presence of rose-colored spots on the chest and abdomen, diarrhœa, tenderness in the right iliac region, tympanites, epistaxis, tinnitus aurium, deafness, delirium and such other symptoms as were present during the primary attack.

But an analysis of the symptoms presented by certain of the cases that have been submitted will be of more value than the above generalizations in conveying correct impressions of the typhoid fever which affected our troops.

TEMPERATURE.—At the present day the course of a case of typhoid fever may be represented by a temperature chart with a few notes to indicate the prominence of a particular class of symptoms and explain anomalous deviations in the temperature curve. This curve is generally divided into three stages: In the first, that of gradual accession or ascending oscillations, the temperatures on each morning and evening are about a degree of Fahrenheit's scale higher than those of the preceding day, but the morning temperature is usually about two degrees lower than the temperature of the previous evening. The daily rise begins about noon and reaches its height between 7 and 12 P. M.; the fall begins at midnight, and between 6 and 8 A. M. the lowest temperature of the day is recorded. The highest evening temperature is usually attained from the fourth to the eighth day, and is generally 104°, 105° or 106°. The second stage is that of stationary oscillations in which the morning and evening temperatures remain at about the same height on each day, the former being a degree or more lower than the latter. This continues in mild cases until about the twelfth day, when, coincident with absorption of the deposit in the intestinal glands, the morning remission is strongly emphasized, and the third stage or that of descending oscillations commences. During this stage the febrile heat is that of a declining remittent fever. In its latter part the morning temperature may be at or lower than the normal, rising in the evening considerably above it, and constituting an intermittent period in the defervescence of the typhoid fever. In more severe cases, with ulceration of the intestine taking place about the twelfth day, the second stage, that of stationary oscillations, is prolonged into the third week; but after that, in favorable cases, the temperature declines, as in the milder cases, by remitting and intermitting stages. Accidents and complications are manifested by deviations of the curve from this typical course.

A consideration of the thermometric chart and of its anomalies in complicated cases shows the clinical thermometer to be an instrument of value not only for diagnostic but for prognostic purposes.* But the thermometer was unfortunately not in use in our hospitals during the war. The records do not show at a glance the gradual accession of the fever by evening increments and morning remissions, its vibratory continuance between its morning and evening maxima nor its decline by remittent and intermittent stages. To place on record an appreciative view

* Considering it in the former light, LIEBERMEISTER, in Ziemssen's Cyclopedia, American translation, New York, 1874, Vol. I, p. 77, says: "The diagnosis of fever can usually be made from the fever-curve alone, and this is true not only of the simple cases, but also of the obscure and complicated ones, provided that the physician is acquainted with the ordinary deviations." One of the rules of thermometric diagnosis deduced by WUNDERLICH from his observations, was that the disease in which the temperature has not risen in the evening of the fourth day to 39.5° Cent. (103.1° Fh.) is not typhoid fever.—See C. A. WUNDERLICH On the Temperature in Disease, Sydenham Society's Transactions, London, 1871, p. 293. But MURCHISON teaches that a diagnosis of typhoid must not be excluded if the temperature does not reach 103° Fh.—See his treatise On the Continued Fevers of Great Britain, second edition, London, 1873, p. 516. Considering the temperature as an element of prognosis, LIEBERMEISTER, op. cit., p. 133, says that the histories of more than 400 cases in the hospital at Basil were tabulated with reference to the maximum axillary temperature, and that, "Of those patients in whom 104° or more was not observed, 9.6 per cent. died; of those in whom 104° was reached and passed, 29.1 per cent.; finally, of those in whose axilla the temperature rose to 105.8° and over, more than half died." And he insists also on the prognostic value of the daily fluctuations on the ground that a fever which shows notable remissions is more easily borne than one which remains at the same height. In this connection, E. SEGUIN's volume on Medical Thermometry, New York, 1876, p. 111, may be quoted: "The temperature indicates the severity of the disease about the middle of the second week, rarely earlier. A single observation does not do it, a whole day's observation gives it; but two or three days are still better. It indicates, best of all signs, the irregularities in the course; the complications that no other means can detect; a relapse after the patient has begun to recover; warns of the tendency towards death; regulates the potency of therapeutic operations; shows the tendency to convalescence with great definiteness, etc.; besides the most important fact that a large thermometric experience in typhoid fever has rendered possible the knowledge of its course and the certainty of its diagnosis and prognosis, which were absolutely impossible with the previous means of observation."

of the progress in a given case our medical officers had to observe and note the changes which took place in the general condition of the patient as manifested by the state of the surface, the tongue, pulse, respiration and muscular system, and by the extent and intensity of the cerebral implication as well as the influence exercised on the general condition by the progress of visceral and other local inflammatory processes. Enough of carefully detailed work of this character was performed, especially by the officers of the Seminary hospital, to authorize the statement that in their cases of typhoid fever the essential or primary fever tended to defervescence at the end of the second week. In many of the cases borne on the *Medical Descriptive Lists* which give little information other than that embraced in names and dates, improvement, quickly followed by convalescence, is noted about the fourteenth day. In one hundred and twenty-one recoveries from typhoid fever in Hospital No. 1, Nashville, Tenn., there were, according to a report of Act. Ass't Surg. B. BRANDIES, U. S. A., sixteen cases in which convalescence was pronounced at the end of the second week; these presented rose-colored spots and other symptoms regarded as pathognomonic. In twenty-five of the fifty-one cases of unmodified typhoid fever found in the records of the Seminary hospital the date of defervescence can be ascertained, and in eight of these, cases 2, 4, 7, 8, 9, 10, 13 and 27, a decided and permanent improvement was manifested about the period stated. But although defervescence may be said to have begun about this time, its progress was so gradual that convalescence, as marked by the ability of the patient to walk about the ward, was delayed for a week later. In these cases it must be assumed that the specific inflammatory processes in progress in the intestinal canal at this stage of the disease were so limited in their extent or degree that the constitutional disturbance accompanying them was insufficient to maintain the febrile condition, while at the same time the patient remained free from accidental or secondary lesions which, if present, would have been manifested by a maintenance or recurrence of the pyrexia.

It does not follow from the facts stated that the mild and uncomplicated cases of typhoid among our troops differed in their period of duration from those observed in civil practice before or since that time. Dr. JAS. E. REEVES, of Wheeling, West Va., in his delineation of the enteric fever of Virginia as presented to the practitioner shortly before the war, gives a table of the duration of the disease in sixty-four mild cases, *i. e.*, cases in which, in the absence of serious intestinal or pulmonary lesions, the attack ended with the cessation of the primary fever, or was prolonged, but in a mild form, by the existence of limited intestinal inflammation. The calculation was made from the time when the patients became unable to pursue their ordinary vocations to the cessation of febrile symptoms and the return of appetite. The duration was from nine to fourteen days in twenty-four cases, from fifteen to eighteen days in thirty-seven and over eighteen days in three cases.*

Observations of this kind were open to error at both extremes of the period. The insidious approach of the disease in many cases rendered the date of onset obscure, and in the absence of more delicate means of determining the cessation of the febrile movement than were used by our medical officers during the war, and by our medical men before that time, it was impossible to assign a date in all cases as that on which convalescence was established. The return of the patient to the state of health was so gradual and unmarked by striking phenomena that arbitrary lines had to be drawn. Thus, LOUIS considered the patient convalescent when he commenced to eat a little bread.† But on the other hand the onset was often distinctly marked by chills and other notable bad feelings, as headache, pain in the limbs and weakness, and although the date of convalescence might not be indicated with certainty, there was usually no difficulty in assigning a particular day as that on which the patient showed the first manifestations of improvement.‡

Since the war the duration of mild cases of typhoid fever, as usually stated, is three

---

* *A Practical Treatise on Enteric Fever*, by JAMES E. REEVES, M. D., Philadelphia, 1859, p. 102 *et seq.*

† CH. A. LOUIS, *Recherches Anatomiques, etc.*, t. II, note to page 12.

‡ Dr. AUSTIN FLINT in his *Clinical Reports on Continued Fever*, Buffalo, 1852, p. 116, argued that the day of convalescence might be determined from the general symptoms with sufficient accuracy for all practical purposes. "If a febrile movement, as determined by the heat of the skin, acceleration of pulse, etc., have ceased, clearness of the intellect returning, with refreshing sleep, and the patient has a desire for and a relish of food, he may be pronounced convalescent. Some one or more of the above conditions, in some instances, may be wanting, and, still, the other circumstances be such that convalescence may be properly declared. Judgment and some experience are requisite to decide correctly; and with every qualification on the part of the observer, it will not infrequently be a matter of some doubt as to the particular day which should limit the termination of the febrile career. Different practitioners would not fix upon the same day in all cases, owing to differences in the mode of estimating the circumstances upon which the opinion is based. Perfect exactitude and entire uniformity, in short, as respects this point, are not practicable; and yet sensible physicians, in the majority of instances, will act with sufficient correctness for all practical purposes."

weeks, or three periods of five or more days, corresponding with the ascending, stationary and declining stages as marked out by thermometric observation. The clinical thermometer has defined the date of convalescence as that on which the temperature does not rise above the normal at the hour of its usual post meridian increase. This instrument, by exactly defining the *close* of the febrile movement, has added to the duration of the disease as stated by physicians; but at the same time, by determining with equal delicacy and exactitude the *beginning* of the period of defervescence, it has shown the accuracy of our medical officers in noting slight changes indicative of improvement in mild and uncomplicated cases about the end of the second week. In point of duration there was no difference between these cases and those that since then have been studied thermometrically by the profession.

Cases in which the disease ran a longer course may be divided into two classes. The first were characterized by the occurrence of a short interval between the commencement of the decline of the primary fever and the accession of a fever symptomatic of secondary lesions. The second presented no sign of improvement at the end of the second week, the symptomatic fever having been developed prior to the subsidence of the specific or primary attack. The former were usually cases in which the recurrence of the fever was due to a late development of pulmonary complications. The latter comprised those in which diarrhœa or in some instances pneumonic symptoms were prominent from an early period, as in 17, 26 and 39 of the Seminary series. But sometimes the progress of the intestinal lesion was such as to permit a manifestation of temporary improvement to be shown about the usual time, an improvement which was speedily lost in the constitutional disturbance attending the progress of ulceration or sloughing of the agminated glands. Thus, in case 21, the tongue became moist on the thirteenth day, but the skin continued dry and the diarrhœa was prolonged until the twenty-ninth; in 47 a marked improvement was manifested on the twelfth day, corresponding with the occurrence of rose-colored spots, epistaxis and a moist condition of the tongue, but a mild degree of febrile action was continued for some time, and the case had a fatal issue by a sudden aggravation of the diarrhœal symptoms. In other instances the condition of the kidneys appeared to exercise an influence in the prolongation of the febrile movement: In case 28 a tendency to improvement about the sixteenth day was followed by fever symptomatic of inflammatory processes in the intestines, kidneys and lungs; in 12 the fever declined in part at an earlier date than the fourteenth day, although convalescence was delayed until the twenty-eighth day, a result chiefly due, so far as indicated by the symptoms, to the condition of the kidneys.

PULSE.—The pulse during the primary fever was not much accelerated. In many cases it ranged from 80 to 90, in others from 90 to 100, but it seldom rose above 100 per minute, even when the fever was at its acme. Thus in twenty-seven of the Seminary cases the pulse did not exceed 100 at any period of the attack, while many, characterized during their later stages by rapidity of pulse, recorded a less frequent beat in the progress of the primary fever. In eleven of the twenty-seven cases the rate did not exceed 90; in seven the rate was between 90 and 100, but did not reach the latter number, while in nine 100 was reached but not exceeded. This slightly accelerated pulse was generally quick; indeed the febrile condition was manifested rather by sharpness or increased impulse than by acceleration. It was oftentimes small and weak, rarely full and strong, and if so, only for a short time preceding the appearance of the eruption or the occurrence of a free perspiration, which changed its rate and quality. When defervescence took place toward the close of the second week, the pulse lost its sharpness, becoming at the same time less frequent and more feeble, but regaining strength, volume and sometimes frequency as convalescence advanced. When the primary fever was associated with a pulse-rate of 100 or more, there was generally a notable suffusion of the face, injection of the eyes and not unfrequently epistaxis, especially if the pulse, as in cases 12, 21 and 28, was at the same time strong and full. In seven of the Seminary cases in which the pulse-rate exceeded 100, the acceleration was chiefly due to the primary fever, although sometimes, as in 47, the prostration caused by an active diarrhœa rendered the pulse rapid and weak at an earlier period than usual.

It would seem from these analytical results that in the typhoid cases of the war, as illustrated by those treated in the Seminary hospital, the average frequency of the pulse was considerably less than in the disease as it attacks civilians. MURCHISON has published some statistics which may be used in effecting the comparison.* The pulse exceeded 100 in 85 per cent. of the cases mentioned by him, but in only 43 per cent. of the Seminary cases. Most authorities agree that, excluding certain exceptional instances, the gravity of the disease is proportioned to the frequency of the pulse.† This would imply that the typhoid of our soldiers was of a milder type than is generally encountered, a deduction which is negatived by the positive testimony furnished by the percentage of fatality. The relatively slow pulse must therefore be attributed to some other cause than the mildness of the affection.

The Seminary hospital records show that when the febrile condition was prolonged beyond the second week the pulse became frequent and feeble in proportion to the increasing prostration. Symptomatic fever was manifested by quickness, but occasionally, and especially in some pneumonitic cases, the frequent pulse was full, soft and irritable. During the persistence of low delirium, subsultus and involuntary passages, the pulse was rapid, 120–130, small and weak; occasional exceptions occurred, as in 48, in which, with typhoid delirium, it was 95 shortly before death. Usually in delirious cases the condition of the pulse was an index of the patient's strength; but in some exceptional instances, as in 42, violent muscular efforts were associated with an almost imperceptible radial beat.

Perspirations and epistaxis occurring at the end of the second week lowered the pulse-rate and lessened its impulse; but their recurrence at a later date, especially if frequent and profuse, induced the rapid pulse of typhoid prostration. This prostration, when the disease was prolonged by secondary fever, was as manifest in the action of the heart as in that of the voluntary muscles. Slight exertion was followed by aching in the limbs, great weariness and exhaustion; the patient's legs trembled under his weight when he rose from bed, and when unable to rise tremors might be seen in the movements of the hands or in the protruded tongue. Correspondingly the pulsations at the wrist became weak undulations that could not be counted; hypostasis occurred in the lungs and the activity of the capillary circulation in the skin became diminished; the hands and feet were cold and clammy, the face pale and features shrunken. This condition of prostration is well outlined in case 31 of the *post-mortem* records. In some instances, as in 150 of the same series, collapse occurred with a slow and imperceptible pulse. Many of the sudden deaths recorded as having taken place when the patient was at stool or subsequent to some violent delirious

---

* He states that the pulse exceeded the normal standard of frequency in all but one of one hundred cases. It exceeded 90 in ninety-seven cases; 100 in eighty-five cases; 110 in seventy cases; 120 in thirty-two cases; 130 in twenty-five cases; 140 in ten cases; and 150 in two cases.—*Op. cit.*, p. 518.

† Dr. JAMES JACKSON, in his *Report on the cases of typhoid fever or the common continued fever of New England, which occurred in the Massachusetts General Hospital from September, 1821, to the end of 1825*, Boston, 1838, gives on page 41 the following table of the frequency of the pulse in this fever:

	Average of {	Least frequent pulse.	Most frequent pulse.
In 290 cases, in all of which the pulse was sufficiently noted	- - - - - - - - - - - - -	77.07	106.44
In cases which terminated favorably, taken alone	- - - - - - - - - - - - -	74.16	102.68
In those which terminated unfavorably, taken alone	- - - - - - - - - - - - -	91.88	129.29
In the males among the fatal cases	- - - - - - - - - - - - - - -	85.50	124.29

LIEBERMEISTER states that the frequency of the pulse runs a course parallel to the height of the temperature.—*Op. cit.*, p. 82. MURCHISON gives positive data on this question: "As a rule those cases are most severe in which the pulse is quickest, and the prognosis is usually bad when, in an adult, the pulse persistently exceeds 120. Of thirty cases where I found the pulse never exceeded 110, not one died; whereas of seventy cases where it was above 110, twenty-one, or 30 per cent., died; of thirty-two cases where it was above 120, fifteen, or 47 per cent., died; of twenty-five cases where it was above 130, thirteen, or 52 per cent., died, and of ten cases where it was above 140, six died. Two of the patients who recovered after the pulse exceeded 140 were under ten years of age."—*Op. cit.*, p. 519. But LOUIS, in considering the fact that in 8 of 41 fatal cases and in 21 of 57 severe but not fatal cases the pulse did not rise above ninety beats per minute, came to the conclusion that a moderately accelerated pulse is of favorable omen as suggesting that the attack will not be prolonged, while a slow pulse awakens fear as to the length of the disease and its issue.—See his *Recherches*, t. II, p. 276.

effort are attributable to failure of the heart's action. Death from this cause also occurred unexpectedly during convalescence.

EPISTAXIS was noted in sixteen of the fifty-one Seminary hospital cases. In six it occurred during the early part of the attack and in three during the second week; in none of them did the loss of blood appear to influence the progress of the disease. Nevertheless, in seven cases in which it took place or recurred at the end of the second week or later, a favorable change was coincident. These cases were Nos. 12, 18, 25, 28, 45, 47 and 49. In the first three cases, as also in the relapse, 49, the epistaxis was closely associated with general symptoms of defervescence. In 28 and 47 the improvement was of a transitory character, as the secondary affections ultimately caused death. In 45 the loss of blood was so profuse that the pulse could not be counted; yet the patient rallied satisfactorily. The improvement in this case must be referred to a free discharge of pus from the ear rather than to the epistaxis, for previous losses had been followed by no amelioration of the patient's condition.

This proportion of cases is similar to that recorded in civil life by FLINT and MURCHISON;* epistaxis was, however, of more frequent occurrence in the experience of LOUIS.† In many cases the quantity lost was so small as to be without influence on the condition of the patient; sometimes it amounted only to a few drops. When it took place in the early period the febrile accession was uninterrupted by its occurrence. The cases in which there is a probable connection between the loss of blood and the defervescence which speedily followed are of interest in view of the positive assertions of so many observers that epistaxis occurs without relief to the symptoms.‡ When the febrile movement was at its height, the pulse full and comparatively strong, the skin hot, cheeks flushed and eyes injected, it is difficult to dissociate the flow, if sufficient to create an impression on the system, from the improvement which followed. But defervescence was in these cases about to commence, and would have commenced irrespective of the occurrence of the epistaxis, as is indicated by the progress of those cases in which the fever declined without an accompanying loss of blood. The epistaxis must therefore be regarded as essentially a coincidence which may have emphasized the first remission of the declining stage of the fever and rendered the improvement that subsequently followed more marked than it would otherwise have been.

Of the few *post-mortem* cases which are preluded by a summary of symptoms, epistaxis is mentioned only in six, in all at a late period of the disease. The loss of blood does not appear to have in any instance materially affected the progress of the case; the quantity was not estimated, but in 17 and 297 it would seem to have been small and mainly induced by the patient picking the nostrils with his fingers.

CONDITION OF THE SKIN.—In the majority of the Seminary cases the skin is said to have been hot and dry, and this condition persisted to the subsidence of the primary fever.

In the typhoid cases of civil life the skin is not unfrequently moist or perspiring, especially at night or towards morning, even before the occurrence of the strongly marked remissions which indicate the decline of the fever.§ There is here a distinction between the typhoid fever of the war and the disease as seen in civil practice. But it may be said that this distinction is an arbitrary one; that the Seminary cases did not in fact present this continued dry state of the skin, but only that proportion of them which has been separately submitted as illustrative of unmodified typhoid. If, however, those cases which

* Dr. FLINT found epistaxis in 8 of 30 cases. Usually it was slight, occurring at an early period, and producing no appreciable effect on the progress of the disease.—*Op. cit.*, p. 97. MURCHISON noted its presence in 15 of 58 cases: "All observers agree," he says, "in stating that the bleeding is never followed by any relief to the symptoms, while on the other hand it may be so profuse as to be the immediate cause of death." Several examples of death from epistaxis came under his notice.—*Op. cit.*, p. 543.

† LOUIS says that the epistaxis was less frequent in mild than in severe cases. It was present in 11 of 24 mild cases; 27 of 34 severe cases, and 11 of 16 fatal cases, and was nearly always without the slightest relief to the symptoms.—*Op. cit.*, t. II, p. 219.

‡ See the opinions expressed in the last two notes.

§ LOUIS says that the skin was almost always dry in one-fourth of his fatal cases, and was covered with more or less perspiration in the others after the evening exacerbation or during sleep at night; in the severe but not fatal cases similar conditions prevailed, and also in the mild cases, although the heat was less intense.—*Op. cit.*, t. II, p. 265. According to LIEBERMEISTER: "The skin is usually dry; sometimes, especially in the morning, it is moist and even covered with sweat, but this latter circumstance has no favorable significance." p. 90.

were characterized by softness of the skin, moisture or free and recurring perspirations, be closely examined, the majority will be found to have presented other symptoms of malarial implication. Moreover, in many of these the perspirations had a notable influence on the pulse and general febrile condition; while most authors agree that the occasional moisture on the skin of typhoid patients does not exercise any controlling influence on the course of the fever.* It would seem, therefore, that a hot and dry condition of the skin was in reality a characteristic of the cases of unmodified typhoid among our soldiers.

During the continuance of the primary fever the rose-colored eruption made its appearance usually from the seventh to the fourteenth day. The skin rarely became cool or moist before the eruption appeared; but it frequently happened, especially in the milder cases, that defervescence associated with free perspiration coincided with the discovery of rose-colored spots on the chest and abdomen.

In cases prolonged by the existence of secondary lesions the skin generally retained its febrile heat and dry husky state; but at times a moist condition alternated with this, and free perspirations were not uncommon. In this respect these cases did not differ from similar cases of typhoid as delineated by medical authorities. The perspirations were sometimes of nightly occurrence and so copious and exhausting as to suggest the necessity of special medication for their suppression. Occasionally improvement dated from their occurrence, but in other instances their favorable import was not so manifest, although, as will be shown hereafter, they may have exercised a beneficial influence on the morbid processes in progress in the intestinal canal. In cases characterized by extreme prostration, as in 47 of the Seminary cases, and in 19, 150 and 199 of the *post-mortem* series, profuse perspiration attended the fatal issue.

An eruption of **sudamina** was occasionally noted as an accompaniment of the perspirations, especially of those occurring at the beginning of defervescence. These miliary vesicles are mentioned in thirteen of the fifty-one cases, and in eight of these they were associated with a moist or perspiring state of the skin. It does not appear, however, that this condition was essential to their development, for in four of the cases, 7, 25, 30 and 45, the skin was not moist at the time of their appearance, nor had it been moist at any previous period of the attack, and in 46 the skin was dry at the time of the eruption and had been dry for some days before its appearance.

This eruption may not be regarded as of special significance, although it occurred occasionally as one of the concomitants of defervescence, for it often appeared in the history of fatal cases. It was present in case 39 of the necroscopic series; the breast and abdomen were covered with sudamina in 163, while the patient was in a comatose condition from which he did not recover; the vesicles were noted as a *post-mortem* appearance in 170; they were present also in other cases, as in 7, 38 and 118.

There is nothing in these facts to suggest a difference between the typhoid fever of our camps and that described by medical writers. Most authors and observers refer to sudamina as of more frequent occurrence in this than in any other acute disease.† The eruption is therefore regarded as possessing diagnostic value in so far as it tends to confirm a diagnosis already made. As an element of prognosis it is evidently valueless; although the opinion

---

* Dr. FLINT found that free perspirations occurred once, twice or several times in 33 of 60 cases. These were exclusive of the instances in which sweating was coincident with or occurred shortly before convalescence or as a precursor of death. He at first concluded that "we are not warranted in predicating expectations of speedy convalescence or of recovery upon either of these symptoms [moisture and free perspiration] disconnected from other circumstances, nor do these results afford any grounds for supposing that to induce moisture or sweating by therapeutical means will be likely to prove beneficial." This conclusion was derived from the observation that a moist condition of the skin was in a large proportion of instances not succeeded at a short interval by convalescence, and that perspirations occurred in nearly one-half of his fatal cases. But he subsequently changed this opinion on finding that free perspirations were followed by a fall in the pulse-rate, and that the average severity, as manifested by the pulse and the duration of the attack, was less in cases characterized by an occasional moist condition of the skin than in the febrile cases generally.—*Op. cit.*, p. 333. Unfortunately his observations on this head were not extensive. The opinion of LIEBERMEISTER, given in the last note, is that of the profession generally. See also page 295, *infra*, on the probable influence of perspirations on the diarrhœa.

† ENOCH HALE, in his *Remarks on the Pathology of the Typhoid Fever of New England*, read at the annual meeting of the Massachusetts Medical Society May 29, 1839, and published in the Transactions of the Society, says, p. 193, that this eruption was present in 75 of 197 cases treated in the Massachusetts General Hospital, absent in 15, while in 107 the records made no reference to its appearance. MURCHISON noted it in about one-third of his cases, p 515.

generally expressed by recent writers that it is associated with perspiration and has no special connection with the poison of typhoid fever may well be doubted.*

During the primary fever the face was generally flushed, a condition which in some instances was noted as aggravated at the evening visit. Sometimes the flush was described as dark-red or dusky, as in 19, 27, 28, 32 and 38 of the Seminary cases and in 17, 18 and 30 of the *post-mortem* series. At a later stage the face became pale and the features shrunken.

Rose-colored spots were observed in forty of the fifty-one cases treated in the Seminary hospital. They usually made their first and in some mild cases their only noted appearance just before the moistening of the skin and the abatement of the fever towards the close of the second week. The eruption may have been present in some of the eleven cases in which no record of its existence was made, for in one case, 1, the history is incomplete; in 2 and 5 the record begins about the period of defervescence; in 41 the patient died on the twelfth day from the effects of a fall; in 43 the record does not begin until the sixteenth day; in 19, 20 and 51 the patients were not admitted until late in the progress of the disease, and in 33 and 35 the results of the fever and not the fever itself were under observation; even in 13 there was time for the spots to have appeared and faded unnoticed, as the patient was not examined until the twelfth day. Thus in forty cases which were observed daily during the greater portion of the febrile continuance this eruption was present in all.

In the cases recorded in the books of other hospitals and on the medical descriptive lists the existence of lenticular spots is frequently noted, although more frequently, owing to insufficiency of detail, no mention is made of their presence; but only in two cases, 43 and 330 of the *post-mortem* records, is their absence specially reported. In the former the patient was not examined until the twelfth day; the latter is therefore the only case in which it is stated that rose-colored spots were not observed, although the patient was under medical supervision during the whole course of the disease. It is worthy of remark, however, that the soldier in this exceptional case was treated in quarters for six weeks as a case of bronchitis before he was taken into hospital; that after his admission the solicitude of his medical attendant was mainly aroused by the condition of the pulmonary mucous membrane, and that the diagnosis of typhoid fever was consequent on necroscopic revelations. Under these circumstances the statement that rose-colored spots were not observed in the progress of the case does not have a positive value.

We must conclude from these facts that cases of typhoid fever which were not characterized by the appearance of rose-colored spots were exceptional;† and that our medical officers were fully warranted in regarding the eruption as pathognomonic, since its occurrence had not been observed in connection with any other disease.‡ That it was looked for

---

* LOUIS recognized that the miliary vesicles were not always proportioned to the perspiration; in fact, he sometimes found them numerous when there had been little perspiration and absent when there had been much. Moreover, in forty cases of acute disease other than typhoid fever, attended with free perspiration, sudamina were found in but three cases, although special attention was directed to their detection. His observations led him also to consider them more numerous in severe than in mild attacks of typhoid fever. He therefore looked upon these vesicles as of much importance in the history of the fever, conceiving them to be dependent on some unknown condition of the skin which was more pronounced in serious than in slight cases.—*Op. cit.*, t. II, p. 244; see also second ed., 1841, t. II, p. 110. This opinion no doubt gave rise to the impression that they were of critical importance. Some practitioners have looked for them with anxiety about the period of defervescence; REEVES, p. 59, instances this fact, although himself attaching little importance to the eruption. Indeed the general tenor of medical opinion regards it as having no special significance: See CHOMEL, p. 25, and WOOD, p. 320. LIEBERMEISTER says that it is found in patients who have not perspired very freely, p. 94. MURCHISON, on the other hand, p. 515, believes that it usually appears with perspirations, and is, perhaps, equally common in all febrile diseases attended with sweating. M. J. VIRMONTOIS, in his thesis *Du Diagnostic et du Traitement de la Fièvre Typhoïde*, Montpellier, 1877, embodies the present view of the eruption as deduced from the literature of the subject, where he says: "Les sudamina ne constituent pas un caractère spécifique de la maladie: ils n'ont pas une grande valeur diagnostique; on les a rencontrés dans beaucoup d'autres maladies: pneumonie, rhumatisme articulaire aigu. Cette éruption est tout simplement liée aux sueurs plus ou moins abondantes du malade." J. C. WILSON has expressed the prevailing opinion in this country in his *Treatise on the Continued Fevers*, New York, 1881, p. 169, where he says: "They [the sudamina] are very common in typhoid fever, but are without specific character, and occur with perhaps equal frequency in other febrile affections." In the absence of observations on the frequency of sudamina in acute diseases, such as intermittent fever, pneumonia, acute rheumatism, etc., attended with perspirations, the statement of their connection with perspirations is hardly warranted; while the acknowledged frequency of the eruption in typhoid fever, and its appearance in that disease when the skin is not even moist, seems to authorize the doubt which has been expressed in the text.

† LOUIS found the *taches roses lenticulaires* in 26 of 35 fatal cases, but acknowledged that they may have been present in more than this number, as many of the patients came to the hospital at a period when perhaps the spots had disappeared. In 57 severe but not fatal cases they were present in all but 3, in two of which the patients did not come under observation until late in the disease, and in the third no examination of the surface was made except between the seventh and eleventh days,—t. II, p. 231. ENOCH HALE believed them to be always present. He says—in his *Remarks on the Pathology of the Typhoid Fever of New England*, Trans. Mass. Med. Soc., 1839, p. 191—"Of the 197 cases that I have analyzed for this paper, rose-spots are recorded in 177. In the greater part of the remaining 20 it is apparent from the record that sufficient attention was not given to them to render it by any means certain that they did not exist. Most of the omissions are in the earlier part of the period I have specified, before the importance of this appearance, as a diagnostic mark, was fully appreciated. In a few cases the patient was brought to the hospital at too late a period of the disease for them to be visible. With this exception I have, for a long time past, seen no case that could with any propriety be regarded as decidedly the typhoid fever, in which rose-spots were not found, and I think it is not assuming too much to consider them a constant attendant upon that disease." In three series of cases reported by Dr. FLINT the eruption was present in 23 of 30 cases, in 12 of 29 cases and in all of 14 cases. BARTLETT rarely failed to find it when properly looked for,—p. 60. According to MURCHISON, these spots were observed in 4,606 of 5,988 cases or in 76.92 per cent. of the typhoid cases admitted into the London Fever Hospital during twenty-three years, but in some of the remaining cases the fact of the spots not being observed was perhaps due to their not having been looked for with sufficient care,—p. 511. REEVES seldom failed to find them at some period of the disease,—p. 57. LIEBERMEISTER says they are frequently entirely wanting in slight undeveloped cases; but "whether there are well developed cases without any roseola throughout the entire course of the disease I am unable to decide; in all cases which I examined sufficiently often, I have found at least a few spots,"—p. 93.

‡ CHOMEL—*Leçons de Clinique Médicale*, Paris, 1834—probably influenced by the positive statement made by LOUIS in 1829, as to the occurrence of rose-spots in certain diseases other than typhoid fever, speaks of their eruption,—p. 21—as "aussi rare dans les autres affections aiguës qu'elle est commune dans la fièvre typhoïde, et que dans les cas rares où on l'observe dans le cours d'une pneumonie, d'une entérite, ou d'autres affections aiguës, jamais

with care in febrile cases is evidenced by such reports as 7 of the 27th Conn. record and 40 of the Seminary series, in which one or two rose-spots were recorded as having been discovered on the chest, or 11 of the 19th Mass., in which one or two equivocal spots are said to have been seen. Occurring in connection with an otherwise satisfactory complexus of symptoms, the presence of a few doubtful spots might be accepted as constituting a specific manifestation; but in obscure cases such an appearance could hardly be regarded as of diagnostic value. CHOMEL did not consider the eruption present unless fifteen or twenty spots appeared.* When LOUIS first looked for these *taches roses lenticulaires* in acute diseases other than the typhoid affection, he discovered them in twelve of fifty cases—once in two cases of pneumonia, twice in twelve of diarrhœa, once in three of rheumatism, three times in eight of catarrh, once in four of gastro-enteritis and four times in ten of gastric embarrassment;† but he afterwards concluded that he had in these instances mistaken ordinary pimples for the spots in question.‡ Since this close observer had to acknowledge an error of this kind, some hesitation may be shown in accepting one or two spots as a specific eruption unless the diagnosis has been completed, irrespective of their presence, by the concurrence of other symptoms.

The spots generally presented their usual well-known characters. They were circular or somewhat oval in outline, half a line to two lines in diameter, rose-red in color, slightly elevated and with well-defined margins; they disappeared on pressure. Their customary site was the chest and abdomen, but occasionally they were noted on the back and thighs. They were observed for the first time usually during the second week, but in some, as in cases 7 and 17, they appeared as early as the sixth day.§ In many instances the records take note of but one crop, which faded as defervescence progressed; fresh spots may, however, have erupted in these cases without having been noticed or recorded by the medical officer, for his interest would naturally have diminished as the favorable issue of the case became a certainty. In mild cases, when the spots appeared at an early day, fresh crops were developed during the second week as those first formed were fading. In prolonged cases a succession of spots was the rule, lasting, as in case 37, from the thirteenth to the thirty-first day, or as in 26, from the eleventh to the thirty-fourth day.

It does not appear that this eruption had a prognostic value or was connected with any special condition of the skin, for although in some, as in the case last mentioned, its recurrence corresponded with fever, delirium and diarrhœa, in others the symptoms during its continuance were by no means grave: In 37, rose-colored spots and abdominal tenderness were for some days before convalescence the only symptoms explanatory of existing weakness and disability, while in 4 the patient was able to walk and was in a fair way to recovery when the eruption appeared on the fourteenth day. Nor did the number of spots present at a given time bear any relation to the character of the attack: The eruption was profuse

elle n'est aussi abondante que dans la fièvre typhoïde, on concevra pourquoi nous attachons à cette éruption une si grande valeur pour le diagnostic de la fièvre typhoïde." LOUIS himself, as indicated in the text, after a longer experience in the study of the rose-colored spots, concluded that he had mistaken simple pimples for this eruption in the cases mentioned; for, after the publication of the first edition of his work, he vainly sought for the spots in patients affected with other acute diseases. MURCHISON, after describing the specific characters of the rose-colored spots, says, p. 513—"At the London Fever Hospital I have had occasion to examine many thousand cases of acute diseases of every form, and my opinion is that an eruption which presents all the characters above mentioned is peculiar to enteric fever."

*CHOMEL, page 18.   †LOUIS, Ed. 1829, t. II, p. 242.   ‡Ed. 1841, t. II, p. 107.

§MURCHISON says the spots appear from the 7th to the 12th day (inclusive)—p. 511. According to CHOMEL, p. 20, they erupted in twenty-seven cases as follows: In two cases from the 6th to the 8th day; in thirteen from the 8th to the 15th day; in seven from the 15th to the 20th day; in four from the 20th to the 30th day, and in one on the 37th day. JENNER, On Typhoid and Typhus Fever—Monthly Jour. Med. Science, Edinb., Vol. IX, 1849, p. 676—has expressed the opinion that except in cases of relapse rose-spots never appear after the 30th day, but MURCHISON met with several instances in which they appeared daily as late as the 35th day, and in one mild case he noted the almost daily appearance of fresh spots from the 14th to the 60th day—p. 547.

in the mild case 12 of the Seminary hospital as well as in 14 of the *post-mortem* series; it was scanty in the mild cases, 9 and 40 of the former, and equally scanty in cases 31 and 41 of the latter series.*

Occasionally the eruption was of a darker color than usual: In 27 and 28 of the Seminary series it was dark-red in color and did not disappear on pressure; in these cases the deeply flushed face, suffused eyes, heavy expression and intensity of the cerebral symptoms were suggestive of a typhous condition. In other instances the spots did not present what was regarded as their normal characteristics: In 2 of the *post-mortem* series some red blotches were observed on the face, arms and chest, and in 6 of the Seminary cases the typhoid rash was preceded by an anomalous eruption. Excluding the duskiness of the spots presented by certain of the cases there is nothing in these facts to base a distinction between the typhoid cases of the army and those seen elsewhere. FLINT observed that some typhoid spots disappeared but partially on pressure,† and many authors refer to eruptions which precede or accompany the rose-colored spots.‡

In none of the records of typhoid fever is mention made of the pale-bluish spots, the *taches bleuâtres* of the French writers.

Petechiæ seldom appeared on the skin. They are mentioned in case 32 of the Seminary series, in which they were noted on the fifteenth day, or one day after the eruption of the typhoid spots; this case recovered. They were also noted in 21, 36, 45 and 49 of the *post-mortem* series, situated usually on the chest and abdomen, but in the last-mentioned case extending to the thighs; their number was not recorded. Ecchymotic spots of larger size, reported as *vibices*, appeared at a late period of the attack in several cases, generally during or after the fourth week. They must be considered a grave prognostic; of the Seminary cases in which they were noted three cases, 24, 36 and 49, were severe, and three, 46, 47 and 51, were fatal.

As the rarity of ecchymotic spots in typhoid fever is generally conceded,§ the frequency

---

* Following LOUIS, who observed that in three-fourths of his fatal cases the rose-colored spots were few in number, Ed. 1829, t. II, p. 231, A. P. STEWART—in his article entitled *Some considerations on the nature and pathology of typhus and typhoid fever, applied to the solution of the question of identity or non-identity of the two diseases. Edinburgh Med. Jour.*, LIV, 1840, p. 326—was led to consider that the more copious the eruption the less the severity of the case. He found the spots few in number or absent, although carefully looked for, in a deadly epidemic which prevailed in Glasgow in 1836, and afterwards observed them more or less numerous in sporadic cases presenting a much less intense form of the affection. But after further inquiry he came to the conclusion that this opinion, although to a certain extent correct, was not of general application. THOS. B. PEACOCK observed—*Medical Times and Gazette*, XXXIV, London, 1856, p. 182—that the cases in which there is a copious eruption are of a sthenic type and terminate favorably; but he acknowledges that in many cases in which there is no eruption at all the disease is also mild, while in others it is severe and often proves fatal. MURCHISON disposes of the question by the statement that there is no relation between the presence or absence of the eruption and the severity of the fever,— p. 512. In this country DR. JAS. E. REEVES considered that the number of spots diminished in proportion to the extent of the intestinal changes. WILSON summarizes the prevailing opinion of the profession at the present day in his assertion that—"There is no relation between the abundance of the eruption and the severity of the symptoms,"—p. 168. As REEVES' experience was drawn from the country districts of a State, Virginia, which afterwards furnished the Seminary hospital with its typhoid cases, his remarks on the eruption may be of interest : "In mild cases of the disease, in which the diarrhœa is not troublesome, I have several times seen the patient spotted from head to foot. At other times the eruption was principally confined to the abdomen, chest and inner part of the thighs. In other instances it was scattered upon the extremities, even to the fingers and toes, while upon the trunk it was either entirely absent or only a spot here and there to be found. Again I have seen it thickly set upon the back ; and I am inclined to believe that it more frequently occupies this locality than is generally supposed. It is not so conveniently sought for in this region as upon the abdomen, chest and extremities ; and therefore results, perhaps, the rarity of its being spoken of as occupying this region. All this I have observed in mild cases of the disease. In the intermediate form of the disease I have occasionally observed it largely spread over the different parts of the surface, but this was rare when compared with its frequency in milder cases. In this form it is mainly confined to the abdomen, with, perhaps, a patch now and then to be seen upon the breast and shoulders. It is also somewhat later in its appearance than in the mild form. In cases of still greater severity—those belonging to the malignant form—it is, as a general rule, still more tardy in its appearance, and does not occupy as much surface at a time as is usually seen in the preceding forms. It has been in the worst cases of the disease that I have observed the smallest amount of this eruption. In a very few instances I have seen it thickly spread upon the abdomen, chest and shoulders, with a few spots on the back and thighs ; but in the majority of severe cases it occupied only the region of the abdomen. It does not always make its appearance upon all of the several parts of the surface named at the same time, but comes out in successive crops—sometimes abundant in one region, and at other times only one, two, three or four spots in the next locality. When the first patch begins to fade a second will make its appearance, and so on, until the eruption ceases or is lost in the larger and more livid discolorations known as petechia, which in very grave cases show themselves. The time occupied in this fading and recurrence of the eruption may vary from five to twenty-five days. The greatest duration of this process I have noticed, almost invariably, to occur in those cases which passed through the milder forms to the malignant, and particularly in those cases which terminated in death. In the majority of these cases but few spots could be found at a time after the most careful search."

† FLINT, *op. cit.*, p. 322.

‡ Thus HALE—p. 192—says that in some instances there are interspersed with the rose-colored spots true papulæ of the same color but larger, slightly elevated and hardened and not disappearing on pressure ; they are generally quite numerous, extending to other parts of the body than the abdomen and chest, and are occasionally attended with considerable itching. JENNER—*On the identity or non-identity of Typhoid and Typhus Fevers*, London, 1850, p. 12—called attention to a pale and delicate scarlet tint of the skin which sometimes preceded the typhoid eruption but never lasted more than a day or two ; the skin resembling in tint that of a person shortly after leaving a hot-bath.

§ MURCHISON met with petechial spots and vibices in rare cases, several of which recovered. To support his own testimony he cites TROUSSEAU, *Clinique Médicale de l' Hotel Dieu*, Paris, 1861, p. 159, as having recorded a case in which there were extensive vibices,—p. 515. WILSON, who has given to the profession in this country the latest complete view of the fever, says that true petechiæ are rare, and does not even refer to the occurrence of larger ecchymotic patches.

of their appearance in these Seminary hospital cases suggests a difference between them and the typhoid fever cases of civil life.

Continued pressure and the lowered vitality of the patient led to the formation of **bed-sores** over the sacrum, trochanters and other bony prominences during or after the fourth week of the attack. Cases 24, 28, 36 and 51 of the Seminary records may be mentioned as illustrations; but these observations are perhaps equally common in the clinical history of typhoid as seen elsewhere.*

Herpes labialis is not mentioned as having been present in any of the cases.†

A *peculiar odor* from the body was noted in case 19 of the Seminary records;‡ but the ammoniacal odor from the patient in some of the *post-mortem* series was probably due to involuntary micturition.

THE NERVOUS SYSTEM.—*Headache* was the most frequent cerebral manifestation observed in cases of unmodified typhoid fever. It is mentioned in thirty-six of the Seminary cases; *delirium* was recorded in twenty-nine, *deafness* in twenty-eight, more or less *stupor* in twenty-seven, *drowsiness* in fifteen, *tinnitus aurium* in sixteen, and *dizziness* in eleven. But these numbers do not express the relative frequency of such cerebral developments. When delirium alone was noted, it is probable that at some period of its course the case presented headache, drowsiness, hebetude of mind or deafness, which was not recorded or perhaps observed on account of the greater prominence of the delirious condition and the higher importance attached to it as an indication of gravity.

Headache was generally frontal; but in 38 of the Seminary series its seat was the temples. It was usually dull; in case 1 it was reduced to a mere sense of fullness, and in 13 to a heaviness over the eyes; but in many it was severe and distressing. Head pain was a symptom of the period of accession; in but one case, 40, is it expressly stated that there was no headache during this period. Occurring after or without chilliness it was accompanied by pains in the limbs and back, thirst, anorexia and other general symptoms of the febrile condition. It usually persisted during the first week, and was not unfrequently associated with dizziness, restlessness and inability to sleep. During the second week it subsided or was obscured by drowsiness, mental hebetude or delirium, which set in about that time. It is probable that in most instances there was a real abatement of this pain, for exceptionally, in some, as 22 and 25, it was a source of complaint when delirium was present.§ Sometimes headache was reported at a later stage; in 29 it occurred without delirium in the third week, subsiding as the last crop of eruption faded, and in 47, in conjunction with dizziness and deafness, it preluded a recurrence of delirium.

Drowsiness, which generally terminated the period of wakefulness and headache, was developed gradually; the patient became dull and stupid and was aroused with increasing difficulty. Frequently tinnitus aurium and deafness were associated with this mental dulness. In more severe cases delirium, usually of a quiet and asthenic character, was developed; drowsiness during the day gave place to restlessness at night, the patient muttered in his sleep and was incoherent for some time after he awoke, and, afterward, this condition of muttering delirium became continuous.

Delirium was present in twenty-nine of the fifty-one cases—in eight of ten fatal cases and in twenty-one of forty-one recoveries. In the fatal cases, 44 and 46, in which delirium was not reported the records are not carried out in detail to the end. Of the twenty favorable cases in which there was no delirium, the cerebral symptoms in two cases, 3 and 14, consisted of headache only; in 7 and 12 there was also drowsiness, to which tinnitus

---

* "Vitality is so feeble in the skin that blistered surfaces often slough, and gangrenous eschars are produced in parts exposed to continued pressure, as over the sacrum and upon the hips."—WOOD's *Practice*, Vol. I, p. 317.

† The rarity of *herpes labialis* in typhoid cases is acknowledged by FLINT where he says: "An herpetic eruption about the mouth was observed in one case. Lest the occurrence of this symptom may suggest a suspicion that the disease was, in this case, *remitting* fever, in which herpetic eruptions in that situation are apt to occur, it may be stated that no doubt could exist as to the diagnosis, the characteristic *maculæ*, together with other distinguishing traits being present,"—p. 75.

‡ CHOMEL—p. 40—says the whole cutaneous surface exhales a fetid odor. BARTLETT—p. 61—frequently noted a semi-cadaverous and musty odor, especially in the later stages. FLINT—p. 213—was unable to satisfy himself as to the existence of this odor. "The sisters at the hospital, and some of the students, have frequently assured me that they were sensible of a distinctive odor arising from the bodies of fever patients under my charge, but I have always failed to verify, to my own satisfaction, this diagnostic. It would be assuming too much to distrust the ability of others to recognize the disease by the olfactory sense, and the probable as well as the more modest inference is, that the ill success which has attended my efforts is due to a want of sufficient acuteness to appreciate impressions received from that source." WOOD says that a peculiar unpleasant odor often exhales from the body.—Vol. I, p. 317. MURCHISON's statement is that there is rarely any peculiar odor given off by the skin in enteric fever,—p. 518.

§ LOUIS argued that the cessation of headache on the development of somnolence or delirium is not always to be attributed to an incomplete perception, for many of his patients complained of pains in other parts of the body while giving assurance that they were free from headache,—t. II, p. 132.

was added in 2 and dizziness in 4, 13 and 18; dizziness and tinnitus were present in 8, stupor in 40 and 49 with dizziness in the former; deafness in 6, with tinnitus in 29, dizziness in 9, tinnitus and dizziness in 11, tinnitus, dizziness and stupor in 39 and stupor in 10 and 17. Cases 33 and 35 should not be admitted into this enumeration, as delirium is not known to have been absent from their history.

Dilatation of the pupil accompanied delirium in 20 and 38; but in 24 it was associated with drowsiness, inability to articulate, and other symptoms of the comatose condition, in connection with which it is mentioned in some of the *post-mortem* series, as in cases 18, 117, 297 and 299. Nevertheless there was no manifest obscuration of the mental faculties in case 34 of this series notwithstanding the great prostration of the patient and the dilatation of his pupils.*

Cerebral symptoms which did not culminate in delirium usually ceased with the decline of the primary fever, drowsiness becoming dissipated, the hearing less obtuse and the expression intelligent. Tinnitus aurium was in some instances no doubt caused by the administration of quinine.

The delirious condition lasted from one to many days; in case 28 there was an almost continuous delirium for three weeks. Usually it was manifested by quiet incoherent mutterings, although sometimes the patient became possessed with a desire to get up, and required constant watching but seldom restraint to keep him in bed. The soldier in case 41 was killed for want of this watchful care. In mild cases delirium was of short duration, subsiding with the other cerebral symptoms at the close of the primary fever. In protracted cases it oftentimes alternated with periods of stupor, from which the patient was aroused to incoherency with difficulty. The return of intelligence was frequently observed in the morning after a less troubled night than usual: on such occasions the patient's face was pale and shrunken, his eyes clear and bright. In other instances the delirium left headache with more or less of stupor and deafness for some time in its train, and in this event its recurrence was probable as an accompaniment of lung complication, aggravation of intestinal conditions, aural, parotid or other inflammations. But even when the intelligence was apparently unimpaired delirium was prone to return on the advent of these untoward complications. In fatal cases with strongly developed cerebral symptoms death occurred by coma and exhaustion; the patient becoming unconscious and greatly prostrated, the pulse almost imperceptible, the eyes glassy and half exposed, the lower jaw dropped, and the only visible movements those of respiration and muscular spasm. *Subsultus tendinum* was frequently associated with the delirious condition. Occasionally, in protracted cases, when delirium had given place to unconsciousness or coma vigil, the mind became clear for a short time during the extreme prostration which preceded death: 50 and 51 of the Seminary series are cases in point. In the *post-mortem* series death from coma is occasionally noted, as in 17, 18, 163, 171 and 235. Generally the cerebral symptoms of this series were similar to those observed in the Seminary hospital, but one or two anomalous cases may be noted: In 119 the restlessness which preceded the delirium persisted during its continuance in the aggravated form to which the term jactitation has been applied; in 25 there was extreme nervous agitation; in 160 the strangeness of the patient's manner led to the supposition that he was crazy,† and in 299 the symptoms were referred to congestion of the brain.

---

* Sir W. JENNER was the first to point out the dilated condition of the pupil in enteric fever as contrasted with the small pupil of typhus; of 23 fatal cases he observed dilatation in 7 and contraction in 2. MURCHISON—*Continued Fevers*, p. 541—says: "In fully three-fourths of my cases the pupils were abnormally dilated at some stage of the fever, and Dr. W. T. GAIRDNER has made similar observations at Edinburgh. Dilatation of the pupil may be observed after the tenth day in cases where there is no delirium or impairment of the mental faculties, or it may coexist with delirium, and especially with that condition approaching to hysteric coma already described."

† SKODA and OPPOLZER—*Le Mouvement Médical*, 1872, p. 154—say that it is not rare to find typhoid fever presenting only nervous phenomena and simulating a mental affection. In three cases in which MURCHISON was consulted the illness had at first been regarded as acute mania, and in two of these the removal of the patients to a lunatic asylum had been contemplated. He cites M. MOTET, *Archiv. Gén. de Méd.*, 1868, XI, p. 504, as having recorded a case of this kind in which the patient was actually sent to an asylum before the real nature of the malady was discovered,—p. 535.

At first sight it might be considered that the nervous symptoms of the Seminary cases did not differ in any respect from those generally recognized as characteristic of typhoid. Headache, restlessness, confusion of thought, giddiness, hebetude, somnolence, deafness, incoherence, muttering delirium and coma are daily under observation by the practicing physician. In the frequency of delirium, and the increased gravity which attached to its occurrence, the typhoid fever of our camps did not differ from that described by observers elsewhere.* Moreover the occasional exceptional or anomalous cases which have been mentioned are seen to have their parallels in the literature of the subject. But if the character of the delirium as it occurred among our troops be compared with that of typhoid delirium as usually described, it will be found that the former was generally less violent in its character than the latter. MURCHISON says delirium is at first often active and noisy, the patient screaming and shouting and being with difficulty kept in bed.† In JENNER'S cases it varied much in character, being sometimes so violent that the patients left their beds and even ran screaming through the wards, while at other times it showed itself by slight delusions only discovered to exist by accident.‡ BARTLETT states that in many cases, particularly such as are rapid in their march and of great severity, delirium is attended with cries and screams, and that the constant presence of attendants with occasionally no slight degree of force is required to keep the patient in bed.§ Among thirty-eight fatal cases recorded by LOUIS, delirium was accompanied in twelve subjects, especially during the night, with violent agitation, necessitating the use of the straight-jacket; it was so considerable in one patient that the strongest means barely sufficed to keep him in bed on the tenth day, the day preceding death. The greater number of his patients, ten out of twelve, uttered cries so loud as to prevent their comrades in the same ward from sleeping.‖ Indeed, the straight-jacket figures as one of the essentials of treatment in the practice of this great authority.

Now, although watchfulness on the part of hospital attendants was often required to prevent a patient from attempting to rise under the influence of some incoherent fancy, restraint was seldom needful in the wards of our general hospitals during the war. The intense prostration which characterized the attack rendered force unnecessary, even when the patient developed a persistence in the attempt to carry out his delirious impulses. Usually he was docile as a child, requiring only a kindly hand to be laid on him to allay his fears or soothe his irritation. Certainly the violent agitation which was a characteristic of so many of the cases instanced by the authors cited formed no part of the general clin-

---

*The recorded experience of LOUIS shows delirium to have been present in 38 of 46 fatal cases; in 39 of 56 severe cases, and in none of 31 mild cases,—t. II, p. 150. JACKSON noted its existence in 108 of 303 cases, and of these 75 had a favorable and 33 a fatal issue; the fatality among the delirious cases being 30.6 per cent. as against 13.86 per cent. among the cases as a whole. He considered it probable, however, that slight delirium occurred at night in many cases in which it was unobserved and remained in consequence unnoted as a symptom,—p. 47. MURCHISON found 67 of 100 cases to present delirium or mental confusion, but in many of these the delirium was slight and occasional, occurring chiefly at night, while at other times the patient was quite rational; of the 67 cases 18 were fatal, but in only 22 cases, of which 11 were fatal, was there at any time complete unconsciousness,—p. 534. According to LIEBERMEISTER, among the typhoid patients treated in the hospital at Basle in the years 1865–68, there were 983 in whom the disease ran its course without any specially noteworthy brain symptoms; of these 34 died, or about 3.5 per cent. Slight delirium, excitement of low grade, lasting for only a short time or appearing only during the night, occurred in 191 cases, of which 38, or 19.9 per cent. died; well-marked delirium occurred in 176 cases, of which 96, or 54 per cent. died; stupor and coma were present in 53 cases, of which 30, or 70 per cent died.

†MURCHISON, p. 534.

‡ "Ten of eighteen patients, i. e., more than one-half, or in the proportion of 55.5 per cent. of those who were delirious after they entered the hospital, and of whom notes on the point were made, left their beds to wander about the ward."—JENNER, p. 22. Dr. REEVES also, p. 38, refers to the occurrence of violent delirium: "When the delirium is violent it usually requires constant restraint to keep the patient in bed. He cries, laughs and makes use sometimes of the most obscene language. At other times he seems in a fit of anger, and in some imaginary encounter strikes at the bed-posts, the wall or at the attendants with all his strength; his consciousness being embarrassed 'by false presentations, illusions, phantasms—a condition in which he is haunted by *spectra* analogous to those visual and auditory sensations which arise in connection with disease in the optic or acoustic nerve; a state in which the centre of consciousness, abnormally excited, forges subjectively all manner of images of incident and circumstance, with a self-assurance of their objective reality.'—Simon's *General Pathology*, p. 153. A very common impression with such patients is that they are absent from home and surrounded by persons who take particular delight in doing them an injury to both person and property; and harassed by these impressions, they leap out of bed and, if not at once arrested, make for the door, or in the attempt fall exhausted upon the floor."

§BARTLETT, p. 66.   ‖LOUIS, t. II, p. 150.

ical history of the disease during the war. The patient was rarely noisy, but lay muttering in a low tone; when roused for the administration of food or medicine, he took without objection whatever was presented to him and sank back into his former condition. Active delirium was exceedingly rare, the only instance in the Seminary series being case 38, in which it was associated with dilated pupils and temporal headache.

THE DIGESTIVE SYSTEM.—*Anorexia* was a constant symptom of the primary fever It was manifested from the occurrence of the chill of onset or accompanied the hebetude, headache and pains in the limbs which marked the departure from the state of health. *Thirst* was also common, but it did not attain its maximum until about the eruptive period in cases which ran a course unobscured by the intensity of the cerebral symptoms. *Gastric irritability* was rarely noted among the earlier manifestations of the disease; it occurred only in the two cases, 9 and 17, and had no manifest influence on their progress.* In case 25 it was noted at the acme, and in 39 nausea was associated with the intercurrence of pneumonia. When vomiting occurred at a later period it was ominous of dangerous inflammatory conditions in the abdominal cavity, although in the only case, 24, in which it was noted as having affected the patient late in the history of the attack, it did not possess this sinister meaning. In cases 19, 32 and 226 of the *post-mortem* records vomiting was associated with perforation of the intestine, and in 243 with gangrenous conditions in the abdominal cavity. It was also noted at a late period in 165 and 166; in 280 it occurred earlier, but persisted to the end. Nausea in 150 was an accompaniment of the onset of peritonitis.

In only three of the Seminary cases, 15, 32 and 50, was the breath mentioned as having been offensive during the progress of the fever.

The *tongue* was at first moist, coated at the base with a white, gray or yellow fur, and with the margins and tip of an unnaturally red color. Gradually the base and centre lost their moisture and became brown in color and rough, the edges continuing as before. Sordes gathered on the teeth, lips and tongue, and were generally regarded as an exponent of the typhoid condition, in view of the great prostration, muttering delirium and semi-unconsciousness which were usually present with these accumulations. The dry, brown tongue became cracked, and blood which oozed from its fissures added to the mass of sordes. The patient when roused for the moment seldom expressed a desire for food or drink, but swallowed, although sometimes with difficulty, whatever was placed in his mouth. Later in the attack the tongue lost its dark fur, becoming red and glossy and afterwards moist, or it cleaned gradually, leaving brown or yellowish patches at the base or on each side of the mesial line far into the period of convalescence.† When cerebral symptoms were not strongly developed the patient sometimes showed a desire for food notwithstanding the dry,

---

*JACKSON, in his analysis of 303 cases, found nausea and vomiting to be frequent symptoms, particularly at the commencement of the fever,—p. 38. Dr. FLINT, on the contrary, considered that during the febrile career nausea and vomiting are not only absent in the majority of cases, but are unimportant as symptoms, occurring at irregular periods, seldom recurring or persisting and possessing no special significance,—p. 172. WOOD states that the stomach though often retentive is sometimes irritable.—Vol. I, p. 316. LOUIS found that in thirty fatal cases twenty had nausea, vomiting or pains in the epigastrium. Each of these symptoms regarded by itself he conceived to be of little value as an indication of the condition of the stomach, but his necropsical observations demonstrated that the mucous membrane of the stomach was more or less altered in all the cases (five) in which epigastric pain was associated with vomiting of bile,—t. II, p. 45. MURCHISON was inclined to regard vomiting at the commencement of the attack as a favorable symptom, but cites PEACOCK, *Lancet*, 1865, Vol. I, p. 117, as expressing an opposite opinion. WILSON says that nausea and vomiting occur in the early stages of a small proportion of the cases, and that so far as his own observation goes, early vomiting has been followed by the severest forms of the disease,—p. 171. All authorities agree as to the generally deadly signification of vomiting in the later stages when associated with other symptoms indicative of peritonitis or perforation.

† In JACKSON's cases the tongue was characterized as dry, dark or denuded,—p. 37. BARTLETT says that in a certain proportion of cases, severe as well as mild, it is but slightly altered in appearance; even in fatal cases, terminating early, it may be merely somewhat dry and coated. In mild cases it is often almost natural in appearance or covered only with a light yellowish coat, while in others of a similar grade of severity it is smooth, moderately red and moist with a tenacious adhesive matter which is common in the severe forms as well as in the mild. In grave or protracted cases it gradually becomes dry and brown along its middle and red at its tip and edges; later it becomes dark over its whole surface,—sometimes nearly black,—glazed, stiff and crossed by cracks and fissures. The dry crust peels off in flakes and patches, leaving the surface red and shining; sometimes there is a whitish aphthous exudation on the mucous coating of the tongue and mouth; at other times, late in the disease, the tongue is morbidly red, sometimes swollen, painful and tender and occasionally ulcerated,—p. 72. According to WOOD, the tongue, from being moist and clammy, often becomes quite dry, assumes a brown color and is at times gashed and sore. He regards its condition in the later stages as an element of prognosis: A favorable termination is indicated by the tongue becoming moist and clean; but in other instances, especially in severe and protracted cases, "instead of cleaning gradually from the edges it throws off its fur in flakes, generally at first from the centre or towards the base, leaving the surface smooth, red and somewhat shining, as if the papillary structure had been partially destroyed. This state of the tongue is sometimes preceded by soreness of the fauces; and the velum pendulum and half arches will, if examined, be found covered with an exudation which they are beginning to part with. This is usually a sign of an approaching amelioration of the symptoms. If the tongue when thus cleaned remain moist, convalescence may be pretty confidently expected, though it is always tedious. In some instances the tongue coats itself over again, and again becomes clean; and this change may take place more than once. Occasionally, too, an aphthous exudation appears upon the surface; but still, if the moisture continue, the prognosis is ultimately favorable. If, however, at any time during the above cleaning process, or even after it has been completed, the tongue should become permanently dry the symptoms are again aggravated and the patient again thrown into danger."—Vol. I, p. 317.

brown and fissured condition of the tongue: In case 43 of the Seminary series the appetite was good although the teeth were covered with sordes; and in 48 it is said to have been retained until the day of death.

In forty-eight of the Seminary cases in which the condition of the **Tongue** was recorded during the progress of the fever, it was red at the tip and edges and variously coated brown, gray, yellow or white on the dorsum in thirty-two cases. Indeed it may be said that these characteristics were present in thirty-four cases, if the description given in case 3, "smooth, fissured, red, dry, quite clean anteriorly, but with a brown fur posteriorly," and that in 22, "red and slightly coated yellowish-white," be accepted as equivalent to *red at the tip and edges.** Of the remaining cases the tongue was dry, brown and fissured in 10, 19 and 24; red, dry and glossy in 6, 7 and 16; smooth, glossy and dry in 46; brown in 14 and 50; moist and coated in 17 and 41; dry and coated in 39; dry, red and with enlarged papillæ in 5; and yellowish-white when first noted, and afterwards white in 2.

In two cases, 4 and 18 of the thirty-four in which what may be called the characteristic tongue of typhoid was present, it is mentioned as having been at one period flabby. In the first of these the early appearance of moisture on the skin, and the benefit following the administration of quinine, suggest the possibility of a malarial complication; but in the other the flabbiness of the tongue was unaccompanied by other suggestive symptoms.

The tongue when protruded in the earlier stages of the disease was often tremulous, participating in the debility which affected the muscular system. In the later stages it was protruded with difficulty, and the mouth was frequently coated with a tenacious glutinous mucus.

Sordes gathered on the teeth and lips of twenty-one of the fifty-one cases, and five of these had a fatal termination. Five of the thirty cases which did not present these accumulations were likewise fatal: 41, killed in his delirium; 42, died of pulmonary congestion; 47, from a recrudescence of the diarrhœal affection; 51, from exhaustion, and 46, from some unstated conditions several months after the primary attack.

From these facts it may be inferred that although sordes and the generally accompanying dry, dark tongue were symptoms of great gravity, the disease was nearly as prone to end fatally in their absence as in their presence.

The condition of the mouth and tongue was alone sufficient to account, in many cases, for the dysphagia or disinclination to swallow which was sometimes manifested; but owing to the difficulty of examining the throat in patients laboring under typhoid prostration, it is probable that inflammation and ulceration of the fauces and pharynx were more frequently present than appears from the records.† Dysphagia in case 40 was due to pharyngeal inflammation; but in other instances, as in 197 of the *post-mortem* cases, it must be attributed mainly to the deep stupor in which the patient was plunged.

Diarrhœa was present at some period in the progress of most of the cases, varying from a slight relaxation of the bowels to an attack giving six, eight or more stools daily. Occasionally the intestinal affection was manifested by a want of consistence of the passages rather than by their frequency. The discharges were usually thin, small and yellowish, sometimes watery, often fetid, and generally painless.‡

---

* The recognition of this condition of the tongue as characteristic of typhoid fever has the authority of Sir W. JENNER, who says that: "The small dry tongue with red tip and edges, smooth, pale brownish-yellow fur, and fissured—the surface seen between the fissures being of a deep red—may be considered differentially as a diagnostic sign of typhoid fever."—*Monthly Journal of Med. Science*, Edinb., Vol. X, 1850, p. 310. "I have observed, indeed have learned to regard it as almost characteristic, that the tongue in typhoid fever shows at the tip a wedge of reddish or brownish surface free from coat."—J. M. DACOSTA in *Trans. College Physicians*, Phila., 1877, p. 104.

† JACKSON found a difficulty in deglutition more or less strongly marked in 21 of his 303 cases, and of these four were fatal. He considered that were he to count only those cases in which the dysphagia was very great this symptom would be an indication of much danger,—p. 38. Of thirty-two grave but not fatal cases in which LOUIS examined the mouth and fauces with care, there was inflammatory redness in twenty-one; the tonsils were swollen in three of these cases, the velum in two, the pharynx to some extent in one; the roof of the palate was in one instance covered with a number of whitish pellicles which were easily separated from it; ulceration was present in three cases, the pillars of the fauces being affected in two and the lower lip in the third,—t. II, p. 90. And in connection with these signs of inflammation most of the patients complained of pain, pricking sensations, dryness and more or less difficulty in swallowing. But among his fatal cases there were several in which the pharynx and œsophagus were more or less seriously affected with no symptom to indicate their altered condition. In explaining this anomaly by the presence of delirium, he took occasion to remark that an obstinate refusal to drink on the part of a delirious patient may be regarded as an index of the state of the throat and generally of the organs of deglutition,—t. II, p. 130.

‡ "The stools may be only one or two daily, or more frequent, up to ten, twelve, or more. They are generally yellowish or brownish, and apparently healthy except in consistence. This is one of the remarkable features of the disease. While in other severe fevers the discharges are almost always greatly altered, in this they often remain nearly natural, with the exception alluded to, throughout the complaint."—WOOD, Vol. I, p. 319. BARTLETT compares the liquid, turbid and yellowish stools to new cider; but says that in a considerable number of cases they are of a dark-brown color, fetid and offensive,—p. 75. MURCHISON represents the stools as liquid and of the color of yellow ochre, offensive and often ammoniacal in odor and alkaline in reaction,—p. 524. WATSON characterizes them as somewhat like pea-soup,—p. 1097. LIEBERMEISTER says: "The stools are thick or watery, light-brown or yellow, often like pea-soup; after standing they separate into two layers; the upper is a turbid brownish fluid, the lower is a brownish flocculent mass; the reaction of the fluid is alkaline; it contains little albumen. In the sediment we find fragments of food, detritus, mucous corpuscles, fungous spores, accidental substances, often crystals of triple phosphate,"—p. 92.

Omitting cases 33 and 35, there are forty-nine cases in the Seminary records in which the condition of the bowels was stated from day to day. In forty-five of these the diarrhœal tendency was more or less marked; nevertheless in nine of them at some period of their history it was deemed advisable by the medical attendants to adopt some means to effect a movement of the bowels: In two, 36 and 46, enemata of soapsuds were employed with the intent of relieving abdominal pain and distention associated with constipation in the one case and a quiescent condition of the bowels in the other; in the former no recorded effect was produced, and diarrhœa did not occur until several days later; in the latter the enema appeared to determine a condition of relaxation. In 30 and 40 castor oil was administered without producing any over-active effect; but in 6 its exhibition was followed by umbilical pain and a necessity for the administration of acetate of lead and opium. In 38 and 39 calomel and jalap were employed without apparent harm to the intestinal tract. In 9 and 13 blue-pill and Epsom salt were administered, but the induced action did not persist. Of the four cases which were not characterized by marked diarrhœal tendencies the bowels are said to have been regular in one, the mild febrile attack, 2, in which castor oil was given towards the conclusion of the case; in two cases, 8 and 15, the bowels were quiet and calomel and jalap did not cause undue action; in the fourth of these cases, 29, there was notable constipation, no passage having been procured during the stay of the patient in hospital except by the use of castor oil.

It is somewhat difficult to compare the relative frequency of diarrhœa in typhoid cases reported by different observers when numerical statements only are made the basis of the comparison. This appears due to a bias given to the clinical records by the pathological knowledge of the reporter. The recognition of an intestinal lesion as the anatomical essential of the disease and the connection of diarrhœa with an ulcerated condition of the intestinal mucous membrane have probably led many physicians to regard and report as diarrhœa in typhoid fever that which would not have been recognized by so formidable a title had it occurred in the course of a pneumonia or other acute disease. Laxness of the bowels, or even a tendency to relaxation, manifested by a diminished consistence of passages of natural frequency, may by some have been considered as establishing the diarrhœal condition. To draw conclusions from statements regarding the frequency of diarrhœa it is needful to know precisely to what conditions of the bowels the term was applied. It is clear that Louis recognized one passage daily as a typhoid diarrhœa; he graded this symptom as *fort, modéré* and *faible*, and the last included cases that might not by every one be considered diarrhœal.*

Nevertheless, in view of the acknowledged absence of diarrhœa in a notable proportion of typhoid cases observed in civil practice, there appears no room to doubt that the cases which occurred among our soldiers during the war, as illustrated by those preserved in the records of the Seminary hospital, were characterized as a whole by the prevalence of a more severe and protracted diarrhœa than is usually associated with the disease.†

---

*Louis's statistics bearing on the frequency and severity of diarrhœa in typhoid fever are as follows: Of 120 cases diarrhœa was present in all but two. Of 32 fatal cases an active diarrhœa of eight to ten or more stools in the twenty-four hours was present in 18; a moderate diarrhœa of from four to six stools daily in 7; and a mild diarrhœa of one or two stools daily, rarely more, also in 7. In 57 severe but not fatal cases the diarrhœa was violent in 14 patients who had from eight to twenty stools daily; less severe in 22 cases with two to four stools daily; and moderate in 21 others in which the number of the stools is not indicated. The diarrhœa in 31 mild cases was less intense and of shorter duration than in those already stated; it was considerable in 4 cases, absent in 2, while in the remaining 25 the degree of severity is not stated in direct terms, but the presumption is that it did not exceed one or two stools daily,—t. II, pp. 17, 23 and 25. HALE, in his analysis of the cases of the Massachusetts General hospital, concluded—p. 223—that the principal difference between the typhoid fever of New England and that of Paris, as delineated by LOUIS, was the greater frequency of diarrhœa in the latter. In his hospital cases he found diarrhœa in 167 of 297 cases, or in 56 per cent.; and in 197 cases of which he had the histories in detail the proportion was still less, 96 cases or 49 per cent. But he found a similar difference in regard to the prevalence of diarrhœa in other acute diseases according as they were recorded in Massachusetts or Paris; LOUIS reported 61 cases of diarrhœa in 273 of acute disease other than typhoid fever, which is nearly 30 per cent., while in 159 cases of similar disease in New England, diarrhœa was present in only 18 cases, or 11 per cent. From these facts he concluded that the more frequent occurrence of diarrhœa in the fever of Paris was not to be attributed to any peculiarity in the characteristics of the disease itself as compared with the typhoid of New England, but to some more general cause affecting other acute diseases in an equal proportion. It is possible that the more general cause may have been, to some extent at least, a want of precision in the application of the term diarrhœa.

† MURCHISON considers diarrhœa to be absent in fully one-fifth of the cases,—p. 524. See also the preceding note giving the observations of LOUIS and HALE. In FLINT's *Clinical Reports on Continued Fever* he states that diarrhœa more or less in degree or duration was present in 12 of 13 cases of typhoid fever, in 7 of which it was mild or slight, in 1 severe and in 4 subsequent to the operation of cathartics,—p. 80; in 9 of 18 cases and in 14 of 29 cases,—p. 173; and in 13 of 14 cases, in all of which it was mild and easily restrained by opiates,—p. 316. With few exceptions, probably not more than three or four, no cathartic or laxative medicine was administered in the cases analyzed by Dr. FLINT, consequently the condition of the bowels as respects frequency of the dejections and other symptoms were such as belong to the disease uninfluenced by medical interference. The facts contained in the histories of some of his cases he considers to be of interest and importance, and believes that they will be a surprise to some of his readers as showing that oftentimes instead of diarrhœa a state of absolute constipation was present. He gives several cases in illustration, of which the following is quoted as a specimen: "*Case 3.* In this case the bowels had not moved for *three* days prior to admission. They remained quiescent for *two* days after admission

In general terms, the gravity of the affection was proportioned to the severity of the diarrhœa.* In mild cases the diarrhœal attack was slight; in severe cases it was aggravated, and death in many instances was precipitated by its violence. The frequent occurrence of involuntary passages shows that an implication of the cerebral system did not interfere with this manifestation of the morbid condition of the intestinal tract. But there were many exceptional cases in which, with moderate diarrhœa, perforation of the intestinal tunics took place and death resulted from the escape of fæcal matters into the peritoneal cavity. The subject of perforation will be submitted to better advantage in connection with the *post-mortem* records. Cases also proved fatal from the gravity of pulmonary lesions without being of necessity associated with an aggravated diarrhœa.

Hemorrhage from the bowels occasionally added to the exhaustion consequent on the diarrhœa and prostration due to the specific action of the fever-poison. In case 28 of the Seminary series the bleeding was profuse, and occurred about the end of the third week, no doubt from an invasion of the vascular walls by the ulcerative process; the case terminated favorably. It is probable that bleeding in small quantity, dependent on a congested state of the intestinal mucous membrane, occurred in some instances at an early date without exercising any marked influence on the progress of the disease; but it is certain that the profuse hemorrhages of a later period were symptomatic of grave, immediate and possible dangers. Occasionally severe hemorrhage occurred in cases which were otherwise free from alarming symptoms; of this Brigade Surgeon GEORGE H. LYMAN has furnished an instance.† Fatal exhaustion sometimes followed the loss of blood, as in case 27 of the *post-mortem* records. But if the patient rallied from the loss, the possibility of a fatal recurrence or of peritonitis with or without perforation, as suggested by the depth of tissue necessarily involved in the ulcerative process before a hemorrhage of this character could take place, was such as to occasion the most serious forebodings.‡ It is probable also that fatal exhaustion was sometimes the result of hemorrhage which did not manifest its existence by the

---

and moved spontaneously on the *third* day, i. e., on the *sixth* day after the last preceding movement. On the day following another dejection occurred, which was moulded and perfectly natural in appearance—a phenomenon which is not likely to fall under the observation of practitioners who are accustomed to administer cathartics daily, or every other day, during the progress of the disease!"—p. 175.

* MURCHISON is very positive on this point. He says, p. 524: "Twelve years ago I found that in 34 cases, where the diarrhœa from its severity or duration was noted as excessive, 10 died; but that only 10 died out of 59 cases in which the diarrhœa was moderate or slight. Since then I have had under my care more than two thousand cases of enteric fever, and no fact appears to me to be better established than that the severity and danger of this disease are in direct proportion to the intensity of the diarrhœa." NATHAN SMITH in 1824, writing of the fever as it prevailed in New England, expressed a similar opinion: "The danger of the disease is in proportion to the violence of the diarrhœa; when the patient has not more than four or five liquid stools in the twenty-four hours it is not alarming, as it does not seem to weaken him much, but if they exceed that number serious consequences may be apprehended,"—p. 37.

† See his letter to the *Boston Med. and Surg. Journal*, Vol. LXV, 1862, p. 389: "One case of continued fever so mild in its type as to call for little or no treatment was complicated with intestinal hemorrhage to an alarming degree."

‡Hemorrhage from the bowels occurred in 31 of JACKSON's 303 cases, and of these 20 terminated favorably while 11 died. "In some instances the hemorrhage was followed by relief, and in a few by well marked and permanent relief. But in most there was great weakness and sense of exhaustion in consequence of it,"—p. 39. Notwithtanding his statement as to the relief occasionally obtained, this author's observations show distinctly the increased danger in cases attended with hemorrhage, for while the general death-rate based on his 303 observations was 13.86 per cent., the rate among the hemorrhagic cases was 35.5 per cent. Hemorrhage amounting to over six ounces occurred in 58 of 1,564 cases under MURCHISON's care, or in 3.77 per cent. In 18 of 60 hemorrhagic cases the antecedent symptoms were mild, and in 8, of which 6 were fatal, the bowels up to the occurrence of the hemorrhage had been constipated. Of the 60 cases the bleeding commenced towards the close of the second week in 8; during the third week in 28; during the fourth in 17; during the fifth in 1; during the sixth in 3; during the seventh in 1, and during the eighth in 1, while in 1 case the date of its occurrence was not recorded. In three cases where it took place on the sixteenth, eighteenth and nineteenth days, it recurred on the forty-ninth, thirty-second and forty-fourth days. This author never observed benefit from its occurrence, but on the contrary has frequently seen patients die unexpectedly by syncope a few hours after a copious bleeding. He therefore agrees with BRETONNEAU, CHOMEL, LOUIS, JENNER, BELL and others in regarding it as a dangerous symptom, although he cites some authors who taught otherwise: GRAVES, in his *Clinical Lectures*, Dublin, 1848, Vol. I, p. 266, as speaking of certain cases in which the occurrence of hemorrhage was thought to be productive of marked benefit; KENNEDY, *Edinburgh Med. Jour.*, 1860, p. 226, as of a similar opinion, and TROUSSEAU, *Clinique Médicale*, Paris, 1865, t. I, p. 225, as urging that it is a less dangerous symptom than is generally thought, inasmuch as in seven years he had known only three cases to prove fatal,—pp. 525–29. LIEBERMEISTER, although failing to concur with GRAVES and TROUSSEAU as to the favorable import of hemorrhage from the bowels in this fever, does not on the other hand regard it as having so dangerous a significance as was formerly thought. His mortality statistics agree with those of JACKSON given above: 38.6 per cent. of his hemorrhagic cases died, while the general rate was only 11.0 per cent. Nevertheless he points out that a patient seldom dies as the direct result of hemorrhage or during the collapse that immediately follows it, and he considers the statistics inconclusive, since bleeding occurs most frequently among the gravest cases in which the mortality without hemorrhage would still be highest. He concludes, therefore, that "while intestinal hemorrhage must be regarded on the whole as affecting the prognosis unfavorably, yet each individual case must be judged on its own merits,"—p. 149.

presence of blood in the stools.*   Although no clinical history is recorded in case 176 of the *post-mortem* series, the possibility of the occurrence of death without external manifestations of erosion of the intestinal vessels, other than those involved in the supervention of sudden collapse,† is strongly suggested by the condition of the colon, which was found filled with blood for eighteen inches of its length.

Diarrhœa occurring during the course of the primary fever was associated with heat and dryness of skin, and in mild cases its subsidence was concomitant with the decline of the pyrexia.   Moreover, when it persisted at a later period along with a persistence of the febrile action in more dangerous cases, its abatement or absolute cessation was often coincident with the appearance of moisture on the skin and especially of free perspirations.   Thus in eleven of the Seminary cases a moist condition of the skin was followed by more or less quiescence of the bowels, and in one, 49, the recurrence of acute diarrhœa was associated with suppressed perspirations and increased heat of skin.   On the other hand, in five instances, 16, 27, 34, 46 and 47, looseness of the bowels persisted notwithstanding the occurrence of perspirations; in two, 14 and 37, it followed their appearance, and in one, 26, it abated with diminution of the febrile heat some days before the skin became moist.‡

Although diarrhœal stools were usually passed without pain, the patient generally suffered from pain or tenderness in the abdomen at some period of the disease.   In many instances the tenderness was limited to the situation of the ileo-colic junction, and although in others the suffering was not thus localized, it was nevertheless more acutely felt in that region than in other parts of the abdominal cavity.   It was frequently associated with tympanitic distention and gurgling on pressure.§   These symptoms usually accompanied the diarrhœa, sometimes preceded it, and often persisted after its subsidence.

Tenderness was present in thirty-nine of the forty-nine Seminary cases, *tympanites* in twenty eight and *gurgling* in nineteen.

Tenderness was recorded as having affected the abdomen generally in eighteen of the thirty-nine cases, but in ten of these certain regions were, in addition, specifically indicated as the seat of suffering; in *three* the right iliac region was particularized, in *two* the right iliac and umbilical and in *five* both iliac regions,—one of these having the umbilical and another the hypogastric region also affected.   The right iliac region was mentioned alone as the site of tenderness in fifteen cases, and in association with other regions, in addition to the cases just mentioned in connection with general abdominal tenderness, three times—with the umbilical once, the left iliac once and the hypogastric and umbilical regions once.   The last-mentioned region was principally affected in one case, 6, in which the tenderness was probably due to castor oil administered; pain in the epigastrium was reported in one case, 17, in which the onset of the disease was characterized by the presence of nausea; lastly, in one case, 48, tenderness was associated at different times with different regions, as the left iliac, epigastric and umbilical, the track of the colon, and on one occasion the right side.

In these thirty-nine cases of abdominal tenderness the general surface is mentioned eighteen times, the right iliac region twenty-eight times, the left iliac seven times, the umbilical seven times, the epigastric three times and the hypogastric once.

---

* MURCHISON has known profuse bleeding to take place into the bowels and the patient die before any blood had been voided,—p. 526.

† "In any case of intestinal hemorrhage the temperature suddenly falls sometimes below the normal standard, but it speedily regains its former height or rises beyond it."—MURCHISON, p. 526.   "If severe hemorrhages supervene in the course of abdominal typhus, particularly hemorrhages from the bowels, a considerable fall of temperature may be met with, even to below normal; but the temperature usually rises again speedily to the previous heights, or even above them."—C. A. WUNDERLICH, *On the Temperature in Diseases*, New Sydenham Society, London, 1869, p. 313.

‡ See notes on pp. 283 and 284, *supra*, indicating the greater frequency of perspirations throughout the attack of typhoid fever in the disease as described by the authorities than in the cases depicted by our medical officers during the war, and the opinion that such perspirations have no favorable influence on the progress of the disease.   Speaking definitely as to a possible relationship between perspiration and diarrhœa LOUIS says, t. II, p. 266, that in grave cases which recovered the skin was ordinarily dry during the day and a part of the night, while during the remainder of the night there was nearly always sweats which were no more influenced by the diarrhœa and had no more influence on it than in the fatal cases; and he had already shown that three-fourths of the latter had been affected with copious perspirations.   He also mentions—p. 267—the case of a patient with obstinate diarrhœa in whom the perspirations lasted for eighteen days.

§ Gurgling, as elicited by pressure with the hand on the lower part of the abdomen and especially in the right iliac region, was regarded by CHOMEL as of diagnostic importance.   In his experience it was as rare in other diseases as it was common in typhoid fever,—t. I, p. 12.   BARTLETT considered it a diagnostic element,—p. 78.   REEVES found it a constant accompaniment of enteric fever,—p. 20.   MURCHISON noted it in 31 of 44 cases, but subsequent experience satisfied him that it is absent in a larger proportion of cases than is indicated by these figures,—p. 523.   WILSON considers that this symptom, when associated with tenderness, has an undoubted diagnostic value, but as it occurs so constantly in other affections attended with diarrhœa it cannot be looked upon as a characteristic phenomenon of enteric fever,—p. 174.

Tenderness, although usually not a source of much complaint, was sometimes very acute; in 10 it was recorded as exquisite, and in 30 the patient objected to having the abdomen touched.

In three of the four cases which were free from diarrhœal tendencies there was nevertheless some tenderness of the abdomen. Among these is included case 29, in which the bowels were moved by the action of castor oil; the only case which presented no clinical sign of an enteric lesion was the mild and apparently unspecific attack recorded as case 2.

Of the ten cases in which there is no record of abdominal tenderness, *four*, 2, 4, 12 and 14, were of a mild type. In *one*, 34, which was more severe, the presence of tympanites on the record suggests that the absence of tenderness may have been due to an omission on the part of the recorder. A similar remark is applicable to the *three* fatal cases, 44, 45 and 51. In *one* case, 39, the gravity of the affection was dependent on chest complications, and in *one*, 41, the record was cut short by the accidental death of the patient.

Distention of the abdomen was usually present in severe cases and absent in those of a mild type.* Generally it was associated with diarrhœa and abdominal tenderness. It was, however, sometimes present in the absence of decided diarrhœa, as in 46, in which an enema was given for its relief. In four cases specified in the last paragraph tympanites appears on the records, while tenderness is not mentioned; but in some of the cases it is stated that although the abdomen was tympanitic there was no tenderness: In case 12 it does not appear that the abdomen was at any time tender, and at one period in the history of 26 there was much tympanites, but no tenderness until some time later when the right iliac region became acutely affected. On the other hand, in 10, with much tenderness the abdomen was reported as scaphoid, a term ambiguous in this connection, but probably used to indicate a concavity of the surface; but in 48 there is no uncertainty as to the condition.— the abdomen became flat shortly before death.

The frequency with which tympanites was present in fatal cases may be seen by a reference to the *post-mortem* records. In case 19 of this series, the only instance in which meteorism is stated as *not* present, hardness and tenderness of the abdomen were associated with symptoms of intestinal perforation. Pain and tenderness in cases fatal by peritonitis, with or without perforation, were usually extreme, but not always confined to the anterior aspect of the abdomen; in 249, the pain, which was so exquisite as to occasion loud outcries, was referred to the back.

In connection with the symptoms referable to the abdomen it may be mentioned that in no case do the clinical records refer to enlargement of the spleen as a characteristic of this fever. That it existed is certain; necroscopic observations leave no doubt of the fact, but the attention of our medical officers does not appear to have been given to its detection during life.†

---

*Hale recognized meteorism in 130 of 197 cases; in 43 it was not present, and in 24 his records did not show whether it was present or absent,—p. 190. Murchison found the distention greatest in the gravest cases; it was present in 20 of 21 fatal cases; of 17 in which it was extreme, death occurred in 7, while of 62 in which it was moderate or slight only 14 died, and of 21 in which it was absent none died,—p. 522. Jenner pointed out that the "convexity is from side to side and not from above downward. The patient is never pot-bellied but tub-shaped, the cause probably being that the flatus occupies the colon, ascending, descending and transverse."—*Monthly Jour. Med. Science*, Edinburgh, Vol. IX, 1849, p. 820.

†Since Louis first called attention to enlargement of the spleen in cases characterized by tumefaction and ulceration of the patches of Peyer this condition of the organ has assumed an increased importance in the opinion of the profession, being generally regarded as one of the most constant and characteristic symptoms of typhoid fever. Jackson in 1838 wrote that: "Enlargement of the spleen was discovered in various cases; some before we were aware of M. Louis's observations on this point, and many more after. But it was not a matter so carefully attended to, in every case, as to give value to our observations,"—p. 57. The tumefied spleen was felt during life in 19 of Enoch Hale's cases, not felt in 21 and not noted on the record in 157 cases. He says: "Enlargement of the spleen, as perceptible during life, is not of much value as a pathognomonic sign. This organ is occasionally felt below the ribs, or by pressing the fingers under the cartilages during a full inspiration; but in many cases it cannot be perceived even where examination after death shows it to be much enlarged. A careful percussion would aid in discovering it. But since there is much uncertainty in regard to the enlargement itself, as a constant occurrence, and some difficulty in ascertaining it when it does occur, we can attach very little importance to it in diagnosis,"—p. 190. But although these observers thus long ago called attention to the enlarged spleen as a symptom and aid to diagnosis in typhoid cases, the changes in the organ were mentioned by Bartlett, Wood and Dickson only as of *post-mortem* interest, and to this is probably due the failure of our medical officers during the war to note splenic enlargement in their clinical records. Murchison says the spleen is often much enlarged and can be felt through the abdominal wall,—p. 523; and Liebermeister, that the enlargement begins early, and can usually be demonstrated after the middle of the first week, increasing in the second week, diminishing in the fourth week, and at the height of the disease reaching to double or treble its normal size,—p. 104. Christian Bäumler—*Can the Mildest Forms of Enteric fever be distinguished from acute Febrile but non-specific Gastro-enteric Catarrh?—Dublin Journal Med. Sciences*, Vol. 70, 1880, p. 384—answers his query in the affirmative by the statement that a decided enlargement of the spleen existing from the beginning of the attack clearly points to the infectious nature of a given disease. His experience leads him to doubt the existence of a "gastric fever," *i. e.*, a catarrh of the mucous membrane of the stomach, or perhaps also of the small intestine, accompanied by pyrexia of a week's duration or

CHEST SYMPTOMS are mentioned in thirty-one of the fifty-one Seminary cases.* Bronchial cough was frequently an early symptom of the attack; sometimes dry, at other times attended with frothy expectoration, it usually continued to the end of the fever, and in occasional instances, as in 35, persisted for some time longer. But in many cases it was not developed until towards the end of the primary fever.

In about two-thirds of the thirty-one cases the cough was slight and did not add much to the sufferings of the patient. In twelve cases the chest symptoms were severe: In 5 and 11 there was marked bronchitis; in 28 cough, which was present from the beginning, became associated at a later period with sibilant râles and hurried respiration; in 39 it was troublesome from the first, and prevented sleep at a later stage; in 45 also sleep was prevented, and the lung complication certainly caused death; in 36 and 46 there was consolidation of the lower lobes of the lungs and bronchitic sounds in the upper lobes; in 42 death occurred from pulmonary congestion; in 50 pleuritic signs and hurried respiration were noted, and in 51 pain in the chest and increased frequency of the respiratory movements; in 38 the cough was slight at first, but the patient from the twenty-fifth to the thirty-second day labored under a pneumonitic attack, manifested by pain in the chest, hurried respiration and rusty sputa, and associated with a recurrence of febrile delirium; lastly, in 40, one of the few cases in which the chest symptoms were of a serious character during the early stages of the disease, an attack of pneumonia preceded the typhoid onset.

It is to be observed, however, with regard to the occurrence of blood-streaked sputa, that this in some instances was not a symptom of an engorged or eroded condition of the pulmonary membrane or tissues, but was considered an accidental result of a trivial epistaxis.†

Bronchial cough was sometimes associated with hoarseness, indicating the participation of the laryngeal mucous membrane in the inflammatory processes. *Post-mortem* observations showed in so many instances the presence of ulceration of this membrane that inflammatory redness in the fauces during life must be regarded as strongly suggestive of the existence of more extensive and dangerous lesions.‡ The voice generally became low-toned or whispering, symptomatic of general prostration, and in the later stages of fatal cases the power of articulation became lost.

In a large number of such of the *post-mortem* records as enumerate more or less of the symptoms, cough is found to have been present with accelerated or difficult respiration and pain in the chest. Generally this affection of the respiration was due to congestive or pneumonitic processes, although in many cases the breathing was hurried during the first stages of the disease as a result of the general febrile condition; but the clinical records do not set forth with sufficient precision the condition of the lungs in these cases. The fatality of this fever among our troops as compared with that of the same disease in the experience of civil practitioners, together with, as will be seen hereafter,§ the great frequency of lung complications in the fatal cases, gives definite testimony as to the greater frequency and severity of such complications among the typhoid cases of the war.

OTHER CLINICAL FEATURES.—*Micturition* was frequently involuntary. Sometimes the urine was passed with difficulty, as in 12, 28 and 35; in the first of these dysuria during the fourth week was accompanied with pain and the passage of blood from the bladder, and in the second the use of the catheter was required to alleviate hypogastric distress. But pain and swelling in the hypogastrium were not always indicative of retention of urine, as may be seen in case 244 of the *post-mortem* records, in which an abdominal abscess was the cause of these symptoms. It may be observed, however, that this case is not recognizable from the record as one of typhoid fever.

The urine was scanty and high-colored during the primary fever, but its characters at a later date were seldom specified. In the Seminary case, 28, the liquid removed had a strongly alkaline reaction and contained blood,

more and by general febrile symptoms. He must therefore have met with few cases in which percussion failed to outline an enlarged spleen. Nevertheless, LIEBERMEISTER observes that enlargement is sometimes absent, especially in old persons, in whom the anomaly is explained by a thickening of the capsule or stroma of the organ, or by the possession of a spleen smaller than the normal before the commencement of the disease; and he cites HOFFMANN as having stated that the essential changes can be, and usually are, present, although the spleen is not strikingly enlarged.

* In LOUIS's experience cough was present in 50 of 57 subjects who had severe attacks of the fever, but it was generally so slight and infrequent, that its existence would not have been recorded had he made note only of that which came under his personal observation; and it was but little less frequent in the cases which were mildly affected,—t. II, p. 283.

† LOUIS indicates blood-tinged sputa as due occasionally to epistaxis,—t. II, p. 283. FLINT also notes—p. 199—that "in three cases sputa expectorated were observed to be streaked with blood, which may have been derived from the posterior nares, but this is not certain."

‡ W. W. KEEN—*On the Surgical complications and sequels of the Continued Fevers*, Washington, Smithsonian Institution, 1877—regards hoarseness and sometimes complete aphonia, followed by paroxysms of dyspnœa, especially at night, as the symptoms of laryngeal implication. But even the first paroxysm may be sudden, unexpected and fatal, particularly in supra-glottic œdema. He shows laryngeal disease to be a cause of dysphagia, which is present in cricoid and arytenoid necroses; for in sixteen such cases the pharynx was normal in ten and inflamed in only six cases,—pp. 25, 26.

§ See *infra*, p. 430.

mucus, pus, epithelial scales and excess of phosphates; in 50 it was acid and albuminous, and in 38 albuminous during the later stages, when pneumonia was present, but normal chemically and microscopically earlier in the attack.*

Diminished secretion of urine, so frequently reported in the early period of the disease, was often followed by delirium or stupor, but it does not appear that any causal relationship existed between these phenomena; the urine was scanty in many cases that were not characterized by prominent head symptoms.

The **parotid glands** became affected in two of the Seminary cases, 44 and 50, and in several of those detailed in the *post-mortem* records.†

The inflammatory action was rapid in its progress to suppuration and disintegration of the glands. As this complication is not mentioned in any of the recoveries its presence must be regarded as significant of extreme gravity; moreover, as it is generally accounted a rare complication of typhoid fever, the frequency of its appearance among our cases during the war must be received as distinguishing them from the typhoid of civil life.‡

Bed-sores were developed on the parts subjected to continued pressure in cases 24, 28 and 36 treated in the Seminary hospital, and in several of the *post-mortem* series.

Pains in the lower extremities were reported in four of the cases as having added much to the sufferings of the patients at an advanced stage of the disease: In the feet, on the subsidence of the primary fever, in 32; in the legs for a few days during convalescence in 33; in the heels and legs about the beginning of the fourth week in 28, and in the legs, which were greatly emaciated, late in the progress of the fatal attack, 46. But as these manifestations belong to the sequelæ of the disease rather than to the primary attack or its complications, they will be referred to hereafter in their appropriate connection.§

RELAPSES.—It need hardly be pointed out at this stage of the analysis that the febrile cases under examination seldom ran a regular course from their accession to the establishment of convalescence. On the contrary diarrhœa and painful meteorism were prone to recur after they had apparently subsided or been controlled by medicine, and latent lung affections were liable to become suddenly aggravated to a dangerous intensity. Coincident with these recrudescences delirium might return, the skin acquire a greater heat and fresh crops of the rose-colored eruption make their appearance. The duration of the attack was thus in many instances either prolonged or brought to a speedy and fatal termination.

---

* According to MURCHISON the urine is scanty, high colored and acid, its specific gravity 1025 to 1030 during the first two weeks, but afterwards, and especially during convalescence, it is copious, pale, feebly acid or even alkaline and of low specific gravity. He has known it as low as 1005 or 1003,—p. 530. The amount of urea excreted during the febrile period is in excess of the normal. PARKES gives the increase at one-fifth or a total daily excretion of 480 grains instead of 400; but it is occasionally greatly in excess of this amount, VOGEL having in one instance found 1200 grains and PARKES 880 grains. An altered condition of the kidney, as shown by the presence of albumen and tube-casts in the urine, may prevent the elimination of urea and induce symptoms of uræmic poisoning, a result which may also be due to reabsorption. MURCHISON found in several instances that the quantity of urea diminished on the advent of cerebral symptoms and increased on their cessation. In one case the quantity, which was 292 grains when the patient was delirious and unconscious, rose to 964 grains when the delirium abated and consciousness returned; in another the quantity which at first was 422 grains, fell to 352 on the appearance of delirium and stupor, and rose to 490 when these symptoms ceased. During the attack uric acid is increased and chloride of sodium diminished. This author holds that albuminous urine coincides with the occurrence of cerebral symptoms. He sums up the observations of PARKES, BRATTLER, BECQUEREL and others, and finds that albumen was present in the urine of 157 of 549 cases of typhoid fever, or in 28.6 per cent. of the cases,—pp. 531–532.

† See *infra*, p. 420.

‡ Parotid swellings and suppuration are more frequently associated with typhus than typhoid fever. Of certain cases studied by W. W. KEEN, typhus was the preceding fever in 352 and typhoid in only 26,—p. 53. MURCHISON met with six cases of parotid bubo, which he regards as a rare complication of typhoid fever, citing LOUIS, CHOMEL and GAIRDNER as each reporting but one case; two of his six cases died,—p. 583. Suppurative parotitis was, however, more frequent and less fatal in HOFFMANN's experience at Basle. Of 1,600 cases of typhoid fever the parotids became inflamed in 19; in 16 of the cases the inflammation ended in suppuration, and of these only 7 proved fatal; the right side was affected in 9 instances, the left in 6, and both sides in 4,—p. 178. Correspondingly in this country, while HALE and REEVES make no mention of parotitis as a complication of their cases, AUSTIN FLINT records 3 cases of parotid inflammation in 73 of fever. In his first series the parotid was inflamed twice in 30 cases; in his third series once in 14 cases, while in his second series of 29 cases this complication was not present. Commenting on these dissimilar results in his first and second series of cases, Dr. FLINT points out that "parotitis is not to be regarded as an intrinsic element of the disease, but one of the events which are due to certain special tendencies incident to the disease at particular times or places—tendencies the nature of which are not susceptible of explanation with our present knowledge of the pathology of fever,"—p. 171. In his first case the right parotid became affected on the tenth day of the attack and the left on the following day. The large livid-red, tender and painful swelling immediately proceeded to suppuration. There was no diarrhœa in this case, and but slight delirium and moderate somnolency. The patient sat up on the twenty-eighth day, and on the thirty-second, when the last entry was made in the record, there was still some discharge from the abscess. In the second case the right parotid began to swell on the seventh day. This case was characterized by mild diarrhœa, tenderness, meteorism, passive delirium and somnolency eventuating in coma, the patient dying on the ninth day while the parotid continued enlarged and resisting to the touch. In the third case the right parotid became affected at the period of convalescence and proceeded to suppuration; the patient recovered. Dr. JACKSON noted four cases, of which one was fatal, in 303 of typhoid fever; suppuration took place in but one of the cases, the issue in this instance being favorable,—p. 57.

§ See *infra*, p. 309.

But cases which with accuracy might be called relapses were not common.* Possibly some which ran a lengthened course may have been instances of what IRVINE has called intercurrent relapse,† but this appears to be a needless refinement in clinical study based upon the assumption of a regularity in the progress of the disease which is not found in nature. Viewing a relapse as a return of the fever with all the symptoms of the primary attack some time after the recognized establishment of convalescence, the Seminary records

---

* MURCHISON records 80 relapses in 2,591 cases of typhoid fever in the wards of the London Fever hospital, or in 3 per cent. of the cases; he cites GRIESINGER as having noted them in 6 per cent. of 463 cases at Zurich, HUMAN in 8 per cent. of 548 at Leipzig, and MACLAGAN in 13 cases or above 10 per cent. of 128 cases at Dundee. It seems clear from these varying percentages that relapses are of more frequent occurrence in some epidemics than in others. JACKSON called attention in this country to the possibility of relapse in typhoid: "An error in diet and regimen is often followed by a new train of symptoms after convalescence from this disease; and these appear to me to be such as belong to this fever. It is, however, true that they are not always so strongly characteristic as to leave no doubt on the subject. If, however, they are carefully noted, they will not be found to accord with any other disease. I hope by these remarks to call such exact attention to the subject as may decide this point hereafter,"—p. 61. But he gives only one case to point his remarks. Dr. FLINT's experience was of greater interest. In his first series of thirty cases there was no relapse, and as, up to that time, he had never witnessed what might properly be called a relapse after the career of continued fever had ended, he was surprised at the statements made by some writers on the subject. But in the second series of cases "my attention was frequently called to the fact that during convalescence, and after patients had so far recovered as to sit up, and even walk about the ward, they were attacked with febrile movement, sometimes preceded by a chill accompanied by anorexia, delirium, etc., these symptoms continuing for several days, when they again began to convalesce. In some instances I was disposed to attribute this recurrence of fever to imprudence in diet, exposure to cold or over exertion, but it appeared to occur when no such cause could be assigned; and as respects the management of convalescence, the patients had the benefit of the same precautions and care as those whose histories were embraced in the first collection, and in the latter this sequence of the disease did not occur in a single instance. Moreover, the febrile movement and associated symptoms were out of proportion to those which might be expected to follow the imprudences just mentioned. The patients in fact appeared to pass through a second febrile career of short duration,"—p. 224. Nine cases of relapse occurred in this series of twenty-nine typhoid cases. In his third series, embracing fourteen cases, relapse occurred in but a single instance. MACLAGAN's experience runs parallel to that of Dr. FLINT. The 13 relapses in his 128 cases occurred within a period of two years, and most of them during one outbreak of the disease spreading over a period of fifteen months,—Edinb. Med. Jour., April, 1871, p. 878. The large percentages mentioned at the commencement of this note are therefore not of general application. Concerning relapses MURCHISON states that after a convalescence of ten or twelve days there is a recurrence of the train of symptoms which the patient experienced on the first attack, but their course is usually more rapid. In fifty-three cases—p. 552—the mean duration of the primary attack was 27 days, the extremes being 14 and 46 days, the mean and extremes of the intermission 11.76, 3 and 25 days, and of the relapse 16.4, 7 and 39 days. The relapse is milder than the first attack; but in one-third of his cases the symptoms of the former were of great severity, and death occurred in seven of the cases. Rose-spots appear on the third, fourth or fifth day, and MURCHISON bases the diagnosis on the presence of this eruption and the absence of any local inflammation to account for the pyrexia. SEGUIN does not describe the thermometric course of relapse, but leads us to infer that it is similar to that of the primary attack by indicating the temperature curve of the first few days as pathognomonic of typhoid processes,—p. 124. Later authorities describe a difference between the accession of the primary fever and that of the relapse: IRVINE (see next note) considers the temperature curve diagnostic: "It is asserted," he says, "by all authorities that the temperature of relapse rises to its highest level more quickly than in the primary disease; and this is true, but it would be more correct (judging by the instances given) to say that there are not in relapse the typical evening exacerbations and morning remissions met with for the first few days in the ordinary fever. The rise in relapse in the great majority of cases is to the fifth day all but uninterrupted, and where great interruptions occur, there are accidents enough to account for them. The maximum evening temperature is reached by the fifth day, as occurs in primary typhoid;"—here the author, recognizing that the experience of most observers indicates the third day as that of highest temperature, invites attention to his own charts in support of his statements, after which he continues: "But afterwards the curve presents a decided contrast to that of the latter, in which to the twelfth day the fever remains high, though with a maximum scarcely so high as in the fourth to sixth days. * * * The second stage in relapse, as compared with that of the primary attack, is cut short; and the same is true of the third stage. In relapse this stage is marked by decided fall of the temperature to the normal, and there is no *fourth week* in which deep curves prove the end of ordinary attacks of primary typhoid. The absence of those exacerbations and remissions met with at the end of typhoid fever, in the cases of relapse, was striking; but in many charts of mild (primary) typhoid which are given by several authorities this absence is met with,"—pp. 131-134. In fact this author represents the temperature curve of a relapse as differing from what is considered the typical curve of typhoid fever only by a lessened development of the diurnal oscillations during the periods of accession and declination, and by a shorter duration of the fastigium. This is well; but the curve of mild cases of typhoid fever being very similar to that of relapse, he does not hesitate to suggest that many of the cases regarded as mild typhoid attacks are in reality relapses in patients by whom the primary fever has been disregarded. Here the argument appears to be pushed to the extreme. According to DA COSTA—*Remarks on Relapses in Typhoid Fever—Trans. Col. Physicians*, Phila., 1877, the relapse generally comes on in the second or third week of assured convalescence, and in the second oftener than the third. Abruptly and almost without warning the patient passes from comparative health into a decided febrile condition. The eruption comes on earlier than in the primary attack, generally about the fourth day, and is as a rule somewhat coarser and redder. It does not disappear so readily on pressure, and the first erupted spots are more likely to last until the whole rash fades. His description of the temperature curve does not agree with that given later by IRVINE: "Unlike the graduated ascending course until the evening of the fourth or fifth day, which is the rule in ordinary instances of typhoid fever, the temperature bounds within twenty-four hours to a decided fever temperature, remits 1 to 1½° the next morning, and by the evening of the second day is a degree or more higher than on the first day, the thermometer very commonly marking 104° degrees. Then for from five to seven days, according to the severity of the attack, the evening figures read about the same; and a morning remission of about 1°, or somewhat more, happens, very similar to what we observe in the first attack after the initial period has passed. Subsequently occur the same more marked morning remissions and less severe evening exacerbations, until the temperature in a zig-zag manner approaches to the normal that we observe during typical cases of the typhoid attack. Yet, as here, until convalescence is established, local complications arrest or reverse the daily descent. Neither do we always find during the height of the relapse that the temperature is as regular as described. It may sink almost continuously for the first three days after it has reached the height occasioned by the returning fever, and then for three or four days more gradually ascend without any morning remission, yet subsequently, as defervescence sets in, show the characteristic zig-zag decline alluded to,"—p. 105. He invites attention to the interference with the growth of the nails in typhoid fever and typhoid relapse, pointing out that "with the relapse of typhoid fever the second ridge of the altered nail growth comes to tell us how completely in every respect the fever has been reproduced; and the first ridge may in obscure cases give us the true meaning of doubtful symptoms, and prove conclusive of the diagnosis." A year after this paper was read Dr. DA COSTA, in a *Clinical Lecture on Relapses in Typhoid Fever*, Philadelphia Med. Times, Vol. VIII, 1877-8, p. 433, is reported as having stated that it is the rule for the eruption to reappear almost coincidently with the first symptoms of relapse. In the case which formed the basis of his remarks convalescence from the primary attack occurred at the end of the third week, and a few days later the temperature was at the normal. Two weeks afterwards, the patient being so far recovered in the mean time as to be allowed to dress and leave the ward, ate very largely of chicken and boiled potatoes. This was followed immediately by abdominal pain; the temperature ran up to 105 and the rose-rash reappeared within twenty-four hours: at the end of the fifth day the temperature was again declining.

† *Relapse of Typhoid Fever*, by J. P. IRVINE, London, 1880.

are found to present but two illustrative cases, 48 and 49, while the *post-mortem* series furnishes but one case, 32. In neither of the former is the history of the primary attack given in detail; but in the latter, the patient, who remained under the observation of the recorder from first to last, was considered convalescent on the thirtieth day; twenty-five days later he was seized with symptoms of typhoid fever which soon became characteristic, death ultimately taking place from chest complications.

The foregoing analysis of the cases set aside as illustrations of pure typhoid, by weeding from the continued fevers of the Seminary hospital such as appeared to present definite indications of a malarial element, has determined the existence of certain differences between the typhoid fever which affected our troops and that recorded by writers of large experience as prevalent among the civil population of this and other countries. These may be summarized as follows:

> *The relative infrequency—*
>   1st. Of nausea and vomiting at an early period;
>   2d. Of a moist skin during the continuance of the primary fever; and
>   3d. Of the pulse during the same period.
>
> *The greater prevalence—*
>   1st. Of diarrhœa during the whole of the attack;
>   2d. Of dangerous congestions of the lungs and grave broncho-pneumonic complications;
>   3d. Of ataxo-adynamic delirium;
>   4th. Of dusky spots and ecchymotic patches, simulating typhus maculæ; and
>   5th. Of suppurative destruction of the parotid glands.

But these differences will be discussed to better advantage after the symptoms of modified typhoid have been considered.

III.—MODIFIED TYPHOID FEVER.

Instead of illustrating typho-malarial fever by febrile cases recorded under that heading, the writer has been constrained in the first instance to determine what ought theoretically to be the probable symptoms of a typho-malarial fever, and, thereafter to collect appropriate illustrations from the records of the camp fevers, whether registered as typhoid, typho-malarial or remittent. This mode of procedure exposes its results to the criticism that the fevers submitted as typho-malarial in this report are not such as were called by that name by the medical officers in attendance on the cases, but merely such as the mental bias of the editor has led him to assign to that class. Undoubtedly the first half of this criticism is well taken, for the cases presented are seldom those which were regarded as typho-malarial in our camps and hospitals. The nature of the reported cases of typho-malarial fever will be investigated hereafter.* But with regard to the latter half of the criticism, certain considerations already suggested† indicate that the method adopted, while the best available for determining the characteristics of the fevers which *should* have been reported as typho-malarial in accordance with Dr. WOODWARD's views, is susceptible of yielding as accurate and trustworthy results as can be obtained in a medical inquiry concerning the consequences of unknown causes; and this is the more gratifying inasmuch as not only are the characteristics of a so-called typho-malarial fever a subject of uncertainty and corresponding interest at the present time, but the more important question of the relationship between the morbid causes of malarial phenomena and febrile conditions attended with a specific intestinal lesion are necessarily to a large extent involved in the discussion.

---

* Infra, p. 372.   *† Supra*, p. 273–5.

ONSET.—The accession of the fever in cases properly typho-malarial was not gradual and progressive as in unmodified typhoid, but was marked by distinct remissions or even intermissions in those having the febrile action of the typhoid poison preceded by a malarial attack. Perspirations or a moist skin formed no part of the clinical record of typhoid until defervescence was in progress; but in cases complicated by the presence of malarial fever the skin was at times hot, dry and rough, and at other times soft, moist or perspiring. In some the remissions seemed but an exaggeration of those which the thermometer always, and the general symptoms frequently, indicate as occurring daily in the progress of typhoid; but in others paroxysmal activity was developed at an unusual hour, as at noon-time on alternate days, or, if occurring at irregular intervals, it was unaccompanied by local conditions to which the sudden access of fever might be attributed. Assuming the alleviation or abatement of these paroxysmal features by a free use of quinine, the febrile action persisted and was associated with many of the symptoms peculiar to typhoid fever, modified in many instances by that deteriorated state of the blood which has been seen to be one of the formidable causes of danger to life in malarial cases. Death from sudden cerebral or pulmonary congestion as in pernicious malarial attacks, not unfrequently cut short the course of the fever at a period when unmodified typhoid rarely proved fatal. But in the absence of such fulminant demonstrations, defervescence began about the end of the second week, usually with exaggerated remissions and profuse perspirations, or the case was prolonged by intestinal, pulmonary or other visceral troubles, at any period of which paroxysmal manifestations were prone to recur.

Of the sixty-four cases of modified typhoid treated in the Seminary hospital, the febrile condition was developed, so far as is shown by the records, without initiatory chills in nineteen, but in five of these the continued type was assumed by cases which at their commencement were regarded as remittents. Of the remaining forty-five cases the continued fever was said to be sequent to the chills of aguish attacks in *seventeen;* it was preceded by chills, fever and perspirations in *eight* and by chills in *nineteen;* in *one* case, 70, there was a chill on the eighth day of the increasing indisposition. From the terms of the record or from the context it appears that in most of these cases the chills recurred on several occasions before the febrile condition reached its acme; but in 59, 66, 67, 74, 93 and 111 it is definitely stated that a single chill preceded the febrile attack.

Five of the nineteen cases that were not characterized by chills, and twelve of the forty-five that showed more or less evidence of a paroxysmal type in the early period, proved fatal. These results manifest, so far as the small number of cases will permit, that typhoid fever was deprived of none of its dangers by the concurrent action of the malarial poison.

The malarial character of these typho-malarial cases is sustained in most instances by other evidence than their paroxysmal onset. Chills are insufficient to establish the malarial presence, since they have been developed in cases of apparently unmodified typhoid. Concerning these, however, it may not be out of place to inquire whether malarial possibilities have been excluded from their causation. The typhoid and malarial influences are so closely allied that it is often impossible to say of a symptom which seems common to both that it is due to one and not to the other; but recurring chills, especially when followed by heat and perspirations, are so essentially manifestations of the malarial poison that when they occur with regularity as a prominent feature of the clinical picture the probable presence of that poison is strongly suggested.*

PULSE.—In one of the sixty-four cases the rate of the pulse was not recorded, and in three it was characterized as rapid, but the number of beats was not stated. In forty-two of the remaining sixty the rate did not exceed 100, except on the occurrence of pulmonary or peritoneal inflammation or in the onward progress of fatal exhaustion, as in 85, 86, 93, 98 and 99. In *eleven* of these cases its quality was not reported; in *one* it was considered thready, in *six* weak or feeble, in *three* quick, in *two* of fair strength, in *five* strong, in *four* quick and strong, in *five* strong and full, in *one* quick and full, in *two* full, in *one* strong and firm and in *one* quick, full and firm.   In the febrile cases already presented as examples of probably pure typhoid, fulness and strength were qualities rarely found in the pulse, but the sthenic character of the arterial excitement in those now under consideration is very notable and appears to have been connected with the existence of the malarial element.   In 79 the pulse, seemingly under the influence of quinine, fell during the first week from 95 to 70 and two days later to 45, while the typhoid element was manifested by the appearance of the specific eruption; in 91 also the pulse-rate fell under the influence of quinine, and in 102, although the rate during the initiatory paroxysms was not stated, it is evident from the history that it must have been higher than later, when the rose-spots were almost the only indication of the presence of typhoid fever.   Strength of pulse is also recorded in many of the cases in which its rate exceeded 100 during the primary fever; and in these the sthenic character seems to have been definitely associated with paroxysmal manifestations. In the onset of the relapse, 91, the pulse was 120, full and strong; in 95 it was rapid, full and bounding in the third week notwithstanding the occurrence of perspirations; in the interesting case, 105, the pulse exceeded 100 during the paroxysmal period of the attack, fell below that rate during the accession of the continued fever and rose to 110 at its acme; in 119 a high rate coincided with remissions and a lower rate with the progress of the continued fever until its termination in fatal peritonitis; in 104 and 110, also, the rate was higher during the early period when the febrile action remitted than later when it was continued, and in 113 and 114 rapidity of pulse was associated with paroxysmal symptoms.

From these observations it may be concluded that although the pulse was not in general more rapid in these cases than in those of pure typhoid, it was fuller, stronger, quicker and firmer in proportion to the activity of the paroxysmal element.

The febrile disturbance was accompanied in its onset by headache, pain in the limbs and back, lassitude, anorexia and thirst.   In a few exceptional instances the appetite was not much impaired: thus in 89 it was good notwithstanding the brown and thickly coated condition of the tongue and the bad taste conveyed by the abnormal secretions of the mouth, and in some mild cases, as 109, it was recorded as fair throughout the attack.

In most of the cases the eyes were injected and the cheeks flushed during the period of accession; in a few instances, as in case 100, one side of the face was more deeply suffused than the other.   Later in the disease, and corresponding with the development of cerebral manifestations, the eyes became dull, and at a later stage, when the patient fortunately emerged from the typhoid narcosis, they were usually clear and bright but sunken, the features pale and the skin cool.

Epistaxis was noted in twenty of the sixty-four cases.   In ten of these it was an early symptom, occurring before the appearance of the rose-colored spots; in six it took place when the fever was at its height; in 74 and 81 it appeared late in the attack, and in 90 when profuse perspirations and vibices were foreshadowing the end; in 6 it was of frequent occurrence for a month before the febrile onset, recurring many times during its progress.

It does not appear that any evil effect was attributed to the loss of blood, even in those cases in which it was a specially marked symptom; nor can any notable benefit be associated with its recurrence: In 67 epistaxis was followed by the development of cerebral symptoms; in 69 its return on alternate days coincided with febrile exacerbations.

Epistaxis occurred perhaps with more frequency, if its recurrences are considered, in these cases than in those of unmodified fever.   From its appearance during the accession or continuance of febrile action, paroxysmal or continued, it would seem due in part at least to circulatory excitement; and since this, as manifested by fulness and strength of pulse, was greater in the typho-malarial cases, the greater frequency of its occurrence among them may be understood.   Its paroxysmal tendency was chiefly manifested at a later period when, coincident with vibices or other signs of alteration of the blood, it occurred on alternate days in conjunction with the heat, dryness of skin, headache and ringing in the ears which betokened the intermittent attack.

THE SKIN, during the continuance of paroxysmal phenomena, was alternately dry and moist, but when the febrile action assumed a continued type moisture ceased to appear. Occasionally defervescence, as in unmodified typhoid, was accompanied with free perspiration. *Sudamina* were frequently observed, but no *herpetic eruptions* were noted in the Seminary cases.

The **rose-colored eruption** was absent, not seen, or not stated as having been seen, in twenty-one of the sixty-four cases. In *three* of the twenty-one there appeared an eruption the characters of which are unspecified; in 95 this probably consisted of the typhoid lenticular spots, and in 98 of the scarlet rash which sometimes accompanies them, but its site on the genitals in 64 throws doubt upon its nature. *Nine* of the cases failed to come under observation until after the end of the second week. Nevertheless, an equal number, cases 60, 83, 85, 88, 99, 101, 104, 117 and 122, were admitted early enough to have shown the eruption had it been present. *Five* of these, however, 83, 85, 101, 117 and 122, had the malarial symptoms strongly developed. Indeed, the absence of rose-colored spots in these cases renders the diagnosis of typhoid fever somewhat doubtful, since it cannot be established that the existence of malarial paroxysms interfered with their development, for cases 102 and 105 presented the rose-rash, although the typhoid attack was mild in comparison with the febrile paroxysms which were its prelude. If these five cases be excluded from consideration there remain but *four* in which the existence of the rose-colored eruption is undetermined,—60, a light febrile attack, the history of which is not given with sufficient detail; 99, in which typhoid fever appears to have been developed on the tenth day after admission with intermittent paroxysms; 104, in which the patient was admitted on the fifth day of an intermittent attack, and 88, the record of which was begun on the ninth day of the disease.

Rose-colored spots in the forty-three cases in which they are mentioned as having been present appeared usually during the second week of the typhoid attack; but by dating the onset of that attack from the commencement of febrile symptoms their appearance was in many cases delayed beyond this period. In cases 108, 109 and 110 they were noticed on the seventeenth, eighteenth and twenty-fifth days respectively, counting from the commencement of the remittent attack. As in pure typhoid they were occasionally few in number, case 115 for instance presenting only two spots, while in other cases they were profuse and occurred in successive crops: In 73 they erupted from the tenth to the thirtieth day and in 75 from the tenth to the thirty-sixth day.

But their appearance was not in every instance that which is usually accepted as characteristic of typhoid fever. There were noted in the typhoid series exceptional cases in which the spots were of a darker color and did not disappear on pressure. Such instances were of more frequent occurrence when the typhoid fever was apparently complicated by a malarial element. In case 62 their appearance on the tenth day was followed by an eruption of a darker color on the fourteenth; in 100, rose-spots appeared on the eleventh and fifteenth days, and were followed two days later by a few dark-red spots which were imperceptible to the touch and disappeared under pressure; in 103, also, rose-spots on the fourteenth day were followed by dark-red spots on the sixteenth, and it is interesting to remark that in both of these cases the skin was jaundiced; in the fatal relapse, 91, the rose-colored eruption was preceded by a few spots of a dark-red color which did not disappear on pressure; late in the progress of 93 there occurred an eruption of dark, almost black, slightly elevated spots somewhat larger than split peas, some of which afterwards became of a light yellow color from purulent accumulations; in case 82 there is said to have been, in addition to the rose-spots, a profuse eruption the characters of which were not recorded; in 83 some pustules appeared on the abdomen about the eighteenth day.

The eruption was seldom mentioned in the defective clinical histories attached to the *post-mortem* records; and the acknowledgment of its presence in the few exceptional instances appears to have been dictated by its peculiar characteristics rather than by its mere presence. Thus in case 115 two or three rose-red spots of doubtful character were observed; in 97 a red papular eruption appeared about the end of the third week; in 51 and 86 rose-spots erupted, which in the latter case became subsequently of a dusky crimson color and unaffected by pressure.

Rose-colored spots usually appeared on the chest and abdomen; but in two cases, 70 and 74 of the Seminary series, they were found as well on the forehead and face.*

It is seen from this analysis that the rose-colored eruption was not observed in so large a proportion of modified as of unmodified typhoid cases; but the conclusion is by no means warranted that the rash was more frequently absent in the one class of cases than in the other. The date of onset of typhoid fever in a patient presenting malarial symptoms was often involved in obscurity. Cases have been instanced in which the rose-colored spots appeared for the first time at a late date, if the initiatory malarial paroxysms were regarded as the period of onset. Cases have also been presented in which the malarial element obscured the symptoms of a mild typhoid affection, the existence of which was manifested during the second week by its specific eruption. It may therefore be assumed that in some instances, as in 99 of the *post-mortem* series, a mild typhoid may have existed for many days in patients subject to ill health from the malarial influence without exciting an apprehension that there was anything unusual the matter, and that these men would date their disease from some subsequent well-marked paroxysm. In such instances the eruption, if

---

* In 8 of 98 cases of typhoid MURCHISON noted the spots as present on the arms and legs, and in one case on the face,—p. 511.

inconspicuous and of short duration, might escape observation, and the cases, owing to an incorrect date of onset, would be regarded as having presented no eruption although under observation at the time when it usually made its appearance. Again, since in many cases the disease was regarded as remittent fever, it is fair to suppose that in some of these the specific eruption was not discovered because it was not looked for until late in the attack, when the fever had assumed a continued type and the prostration, diarrhœa and accompanying tenderness of the bowels suggested the presence of typhoid. The febrile condition lasted in the Seminary hospital case 110 for twenty-five days before the rose-spots made their appearance. Physicians in similar instances of prolonged febrile action may have accepted the absence of the spots and have ceased to look for them, although their presence might have been demonstrated at a later period. Under such circumstances failure to observe the eruption does not imply its non-existence.

Moreover, as has been indicated in the presentation of the records of the 19th Mass. Vols., and as will be shown more definitely hereafter,* there is little doubt that many cases reported as typho-malarial were due solely to the action of the malarial poison. The failure of a close scrutiny to observe the rash in such cases may have led to the opinion that its absence was common in cases of modified typhoid. However this may be, the typho-malarial series of the Seminary hospital presented in so many instances a characteristic or modified eruption as to render it highly probable that when typhoid was present it was manifested by the rash as frequently in the presence as in the absence of malarial complications.

The occurrence of **sudamina** appears frequently on the records; in case 6 of the 27th Connecticut the miliary vesicles coalesced into bullæ containing a turbid yellowish-white liquid, and in 9 they were developed on the site of existing rose-colored spots.

Petechial and **ecchymotic patches.**—Petechial spots were found in two of the Seminary cases, 77 and 118, both of which recovered, and larger patches of an ecchymotic appearance in the seven cases, 68, 69, 73, 74, 90, 98 and 104. Usually these blotches were confined to the chest and abdomen, but in the last-mentioned case they covered the whole body except the face and neck. In 68, 69, 73 and 74 they appeared about the close of the third week; these cases recovered, but the others were fatal. Ecchymosed spots appeared on the abdomen in case 4 of the records of the 27th Connecticut, and spots like small blood blisters on the limbs and trunk in case 6.

It will be observed that these facts do not demonstrate a greater frequency of hemorrhagic exudations in this series of cases than was found in that which has been submitted as representative of unmodified typhoid.

Erysipelas appeared as a complication in several of the cases, as in 92 of the Seminary series and in 74 and 77 of the *post-mortem* records; the ear and side of the face seemed to be its favorite site. In the first-mentioned case it was associated with inflammation of the parotid and became gangrenous in its progress.

Bed-sores are recorded in case 113 as having occurred at a late period, but the circulation at this time fortunately became improved and the patient was soon able to walk. They were found also in 101 of the *post-mortem* series at the end of the third week, over the sacrum, trochanters and angles of the ribs of the right side.

In case 89, during the height of the fever, when the rose-rash was erupting and the patient muttering in his sleep, a **peculiar odor** was reported as emanating from his body. In case 6 of the records of the 27th Connecticut, an odor like that from spoiled meat was perceived about the person of the patient shortly before the occurrence of the fatal event; he was much emaciated and suffered from bed-sores.

CEREBRAL SYMPTOMS.—In the sixty-four cases of the Seminary hospital series headache was reported fifty-two times, wakefulness eleven times, drowsiness eleven times, more or less of dulness or stupor thirty-one times, dizziness seventeen times, ringing in the ears twenty-six times, deafness twenty and delirium twenty-four times.

Delirium occurred in thirteen of the seventeen fatal cases and in twelve of the forty-seven recoveries. Of the four mortal cases in which delirium was unrecorded, one, 85, had the malarial symptoms strongly developed, death being preceded by stupor; 119 was fatal by peritonitis; the two other cases, 94 and 111, were not rendered in full towards their close. Among the forty cases in which delirium was absent or not stated as present, headache was reported thirty-two times, wakefulness six times, drowsiness seven times, more or less of stupor sixteen times, dizziness ten times, ringing in the ears sixteen times and deafness seven times. As the patients in many instances were not received until the disease had made much progress, it is not surprising that in twelve cases there is no evidence that headache constituted one of the symptoms of the attack. In two cases, 102 and 106, neither headache nor any other symptom referable to the cerebral system appears on the record, while in 79, 107 and 120 headache alone; in 59, 94 and 115 wakefulness; in 117 headache and wakefulness; in 60 headache and drowsiness; in 73 headache and dizziness; in 75 and 78 headache and tinnitus, and in 82, 101, 109 and 121 headache, tinnitus and dizziness formed respectively the indications of the cerebral implication. In two instances, 80 and 81, the patients were in a semi-comatose condition, which was associated in the latter case with spasmodic contractions of unusual strength affecting the muscles of the face and extremities. This stupor did not alternate with the low delirium so common in unmodified typhoid fever, but left the patients very deaf in both cases, and with slight delirium and headache in the latter. The *post-mortem* record of case 297 compares the convulsive twitchings of the muscles of the patient to the spasmodic movements produced by moderate shocks from a galvanic battery.

Instead of dilatation of the pupil, which was recorded in several of the typhoid cases, the typho-malarial series of the Seminary hospital presents two cases, 96 and 97, of **contracted pupil.** In one the contraction was associated with delirium preceding the advent of lethal stupor, and in the other with a state of coma vigil which ended fatally. The pupils were also contracted in 86 of the *post-mortem* records during the stupor which was the harbinger of death; nevertheless, in case 12 of the regimental record of the 19th Mass. the pupils were observed to be dilated.

Delirium was generally of the passive character observed in unmodified typhoid, but there appeared to be a greater tendency to lapse into the comatose state than was found in cases of that fever. In some instances, however, the paroxysmal exacerbations were accompanied by more active cerebral manifestations; in 91 of the Seminary series there was what the record calls walking delirium, and the patient afterwards raved and showed much strength; in 6 of the 27th Conn. the delirium was at first violent, then sullen and afterwards of a jocose character. Coma was indeed not unfrequently preceded by continued insomnia, jactitation and active delirium, as in 52 and 111 of the *post-mortem* records, or by intense headache, as in 86 and 94 of the same series. In 56 delirium and coma were apparently connected with inflammatory processes in the middle ear.

Death at an early period was usually due to coma, as in 111 of the *post-mortem* records, which terminated on the ninth day, and in 94 of the same series, which ended on the thirteenth day, although in 122 of the Seminary cases the patient is stated to have been delirious when death took place on the eighth day.

Extreme prostration and **muscular debility,** manifested by the position of the patient in bed, the tremulous tongue, occasional falling of the lower jaw and subsultus tendinum were as frequently noted in these cases as in those of the typhoid series. Occasionally, as in case 6 of the record of the 27th Conn., the patient recovered his intelligence while in this state of extreme debility.

The Seminary records show that delirium, although of less frequent occurrence in typho-malarial cases, was of much more serious import than in cases of pure typhoid. Delirium was present in twenty-one of forty-one favorable cases of typhoid and in only twelve of forty-seven recoveries from typho-malarial fever; but although only eight of twenty-nine cases of typhoid delirium resulted fatally, no less than thirteen of twenty-four cases of typho-malarial delirium had an unfavorable termination. These figures give expression to an increased gravity with which the malarial complication endowed the typhoid disease. It cannot be allowed that the existence of intermittent or remittent fever tended to repress the development of the cerebral symptoms of typhoid, since malarial fevers are themselves associated at times with delirium. Hence it may be inferred that the increased mortality in typho-malarial cases presenting delirium, as compared with typhoid cases having similar cerebral manifestations, was due to the coincidence of malarial disease.

THE DIGESTIVE SYSTEM.—**Vomiting** was noted in twenty-six of the sixty-four cases and **nausea** without vomiting in four cases. In 108, 114 and 122 the nausea occurred early in the attack, but in 86 the fever was at its height when the patient became thus affected. In thirteen of the twenty-six cases the vomiting was recorded during the early period of the attack; four of these, 90, 92, 95 and 96, were fatal, but it does not appear that the vomiting had any prognostic value, for recovery took place in some of the cases in which it was a troublesome symptom, as in 79, in which it continued for several days, and in 82, in which it persisted for two weeks, ceasing only on the occurrence of epistaxis and perspirations. In 98, 101, 107, 110 irritability of the stomach corresponded in time with the full development of the febrile condition, and in 88 it followed the administration of quinine; one of these, 98, was fatal. The vomiting which occurred at a late period in 63, 75 and 80 was not a sign of evil omen, but in 84, 85, 89, 91 and 97 it was connected with fatal peritonitis or collapse.

Nausea and vomiting were of correspondingly frequent occurrence in the cases embraced in the *post-mortem* records. In a few instances gastric irritability was unusually distressing and persistent: In 116 nourishment had to be introduced by enemata; in 95 vomiting was associated with severe epigastric pain and inflammatory processes in the gall-bladder; in 280 it occurred early and persisted to the end.

More or less of **jaundice** was observed in seven of the Seminary cases: The patient's face was slightly tinged in 67 and the skin and conjunctivæ in 121, at the close of a mild febrile attack; in 84 and 100 the eyes and skin were yellowish, this condition having been associated with epigastric pain; in 103 jaundice followed the exhibition of calomel and jalap; it occurred also in 112, in which remittent and typhoid fevers coincided, and in 118, during the activity of a remittent which was followed by a typhoid attack. In addition to these there was some derangement of the liver in 105 during its paroxysmal period. Only one of these cases, 84, was fatal. Jaundice appeared frequently among the symptoms of the *post-mortem* series; it was seen in 54, 65, 81, 95, 96, 97, 98, 100 and 111, and in these, as in those already instanced, the coloration of the skin, conjunctivæ and urine occurred generally in the early period, but sometimes towards the end of the attack.

The greater frequency of nausea, vomiting and jaundice in these cases must be regarded as symptomatic of the action of the malarial poison, since such symptoms are usual in the paroxysmal fevers, while, as has been seen, they are so often absent in typhoid that it is impossible to consider them essential features of its clinical picture.

The tongue was more heavily coated with a white, yellow or grayish fur, especially towards the base, than in unmodified typhoid. Later, as it became dark in color it lost its moisture, but it did not remain dry and brown during the height of the febrile manifestation with such persistency as in pure typhoid. It varied in its condition from day to day, being sometimes more or less moist, and at other times dry or coated with tenacious mucus; but at some period of the disease the red tip and edges, so frequently recorded in the unmodified fever, were also seen in the typho-malarial cases. Before the accession or subsequent to the disappearance of typhoid symptoms the tongue was often pale, flabby and coated as in malarial attacks, and occasionally this flabbiness persisted during the continuance of pathognomonic symptoms of typhoid. In favorable cases the fur sometimes cleaned off in patches, but more generally a white or yellow coating was observed far into the period of convalescence.

In *twenty-two* of the sixty-four cases the **tongue** at some period of the disease was recorded as red at the tip and edges, this characteristic being frequently noted when the rose-colored eruption was visible on the chest and abdomen; seven of these were fatal, 84, 89, 90, 92, 94, 99 and 122. The red tip and edges appeared also in *fourteen* cases, in which the tongue was characterized as flabby or pale and flabby—69, 70, 74, 75, 80, 81, 83, 85, 98, 100, 109, 111, 112 and 118; three of these, 85, 98 and 111, did not recover. In *ten* other cases flabbiness was specially noted: In 59, 62 and 121 the tongue was flabby and slightly coated; in 65 yellow-patched and afterwards white and flabby; in 67 dry, red, white-coated and flabby; in 77 dry and brown, with subsequent flabbiness and prominent papillæ; in 79 red, glossy and dry, becoming afterwards moist and flabby; in 82 white or yellow-coated, and afterwards flabby; in 106 pale, flabby and coated yellowish-brown in the centre, and in 93 pale and flabby. As none of these proved fatal except the last, it would seem that danger diminished with the distinct appreciation of the characteristics of the malarial tongue as distinguished from those of the typhoid tongue. In the remaining *eighteen* cases the tongue was characterized as follows: Coated at the base, but cleaner at the tip and edges in 102 and 108; dry, rough and coated, but cleaner and moist at the edges in 114; coated in the centre, but with the edges moist in 105 and 119; white-coated and moist in 95; heavily coated in 113; yellow-furred and fissured in 115; yellowish in 64; dry and brown in 104; brown and fissured in 107; dry, brown and fissured in 91 and 96; dry, brown and coated in 66 and 97; brown, subsequently becoming white in 86; red, dry and fissured in 71; red and clean in 73. Six of these cases were fatal, viz: 91, 95, 96, 97, 104 and 119.

Notwithstanding the oftentimes foul condition of the tongue the **breath** is said to have been offensive in but two cases, 100 and 113; in the latter it was referred to the existence of ozæna.

The lips, teeth and gums were covered with **sordes** in ten of the seventeen fatal cases, and in eleven of the forty-seven which resulted favorably, so far as the record follows up their history. Of the seven mortal cases in which the mouth was not reported as having been in this foul state, death occurred at an early date in one, 122; in two, 84 and 85, the fatal result was due to peritonitis,—in the former the patient's condition towards the close suggests that sordes may have been present though unrecorded; in 92 death was precipitated by gangrenous erysipelas and in 99 by pulmonary complications; in 94 and 95 the record slurs the details of the last stages of the malady.

The condition of the **mouth, throat** and **larynx** in these cases was sometimes, as in pure typhoid, such as to occasion more or less dysphagia and alteration of voice. The mouth and throat were covered with aphthous spots in 88; the larynx was probably congested in 77 and 81, as it certainly was in 93; in 87, however, aphonia appears to have been due to prostration, and although in 96 and 114 dysphagia must be attributed to cerebral implication, it was in the earlier stages of the latter case probably a result of local inflammatory processes.

Diarrhœa or relaxation of the bowels was present in perhaps the whole of the sixty-four cases of the Seminary series that have been submitted as illustrations of the coincidence of the typhoid and malarial poisons in the same subject. As in the unmodified cases, it was sometimes an early symptom, while at other times it was not developed until late in the attack; it lasted for a few days in some cases, while in others it not only continued throughout the fever, but was prolonged into the period of convalescence. It varied in intensity from an aggravated and exhausting flux to a slight relaxation manifested rather by lessened consistence than frequency of the passages. The stools were thin, yellowish, watery and often fetid. Usually they were passed without pain, notwithstanding the existence of abdominal tenderness; as an exceptional instance, tormina was recorded in case 87.

Diarrhœa was associated with **hemorrhage** from the **bowels** in three of the cases, 85, 92 and 93, all of which were fatal, though not as a direct consequence of the loss of blood; nevertheless, its occurrence probably hastened the fatal event, for in 85 the bloody stools were reported as having caused much depression. Hemorrhage from the bowels forms part of the record of case 109 of the *post-mortem* series.

As in the typhoid cases, several instances occurred in which the diarrhœal tendency was not strongly emphasized: There was no diarrhœa in 68 during the stay of the patient in hospital, but as the intestinal lesion was marked by tenderness and gurgling, it is probable that diarrhœa may have been a symptom during the two weeks of sickness which preceded his admission. In 119 the paroxysmal period was characterized by diarrhœa, but during the progress of the typhoid fever the bowels were comparatively quiet. In 96 also the bowels were quiet, but there was much tympanites. In some cases the use of such purgatives as calomel and jalap, blue pill, compound cathartic pills, Epsom salt or castor oil shows that at the time of their administration the bowels were not loose. In 62, 63, 67 and 108 these cathartics did not produce undue effects, but in 91 and 103 intestinal symptoms were developed or aggravated after their administration. In 75, which was characterized by diarrhœa at first but not throughout its progress, purgative medicines did not intensify the diarrhœal tendency, while in 73, in which the conditions appeared to be similar, full doses of Epsom salt caused frequent stools and iliac tenderness. Lastly, in 79, with constipation present and some tenderness of the bowels, the cathartics administered were not productive of undesirable effects until the twenty-first day of the disease, when violent action was set up. In some cases submitted from regimental records the bowels are said to have been constipated, as in 2, 3, 4, 6 and 9 of the 19th Mass. and 5 and 8 of the 27th Conn.; in two of these, 3 and 5, laxative and even powerful cathartic doses produced but little effect.

Diarrhœa appears with equal frequency in the clinical histories which precede the *post-mortem* records. In 54 and 96 there was a recrudescence of the diarrhœal affection. A few of these fragmentary histories report constipation as the characteristic condition of the bowels during the attack. Thus in 95 there was constipation during the initiatory paroxysmal fever and during ten days of jaundice which followed it, nor did diarrhœa set in when adynamic symptoms were subsequently developed. In 268, also, constipation was present, but in this instance there was cerebral disease sufficient to account for most of the recorded symptoms. The bowels were sluggish in 52, a case characterized by its frequent and copious perspirations. Constipation is mentioned also in the records of 86 and 111; and diarrhœa was certainly absent from the history of 116, in which, on account of the condition of the stomach, nutrient enemata were largely employed.

Sometimes, as in unmodified typhoid, diarrhœa ceased on the occurrence of perspiration at the period of defervescence. Such cases as 72, 80 and 113 are suggestive of a connection between the cessation of the flux and the increased action of the skin, and in 64 and 90 this suggestion is strengthened by alternations of hot skin with diarrhœa and free perspirations with quiescent bowels; but it is doubtful if these bore to each other any closer relationship than that of association as results of the same cause.

***Meteorism, abdominal pain* and *tenderness*.**—Of the sixty-four cases of the Seminary series pain, tenderness and tympanites of the abdomen were mentioned in all except the three mild cases, 60, 102 and 116, the markedly malarial case, 121, and the rapidly fatal paroxysmal case, 122. Pain or tenderness was recorded with tympanites in thirty-eight cases and without tympanites in twenty, while in but one case, 117, was tympanites noted without coincident pain or tenderness. The meteorized condition of the abdomen was generally proportioned to the gravity of the attack, but in 99, in which the fatal result was due to pneumonic complications, the abdomen, which at times had been tympanitic, became soft towards the end.

In thirty-one cases the abdomen generally was assigned as the seat of the tenderness, but in twenty-five of these one or more localities were indicated as particularly affected: In *seven* the right iliac, in *one* the iliac, in *two* both iliac regions and in *one* the right side; in *one* the right iliac and epigastric, and in *one* the right iliac, epigastric and umbilical regions; in *twelve* the umbilical with, in four of these, the right iliac, in one the left iliac, and in five both iliac regions, one of the last having the hypogastric also affected and another the hepatic and epigastric regions. In the cases in which the abdomen was not mentioned in general terms the localities were specified as follows: In *fourteen* the right iliac region with, in two of these, the umbilical, in one the epigastric, in one the umbilical and epigastric, in one the hepatic and in one the hypogastric; in *six* the left iliac region with, in three of these, the umbilical also, and in one the umbilical and epigastric; in *four* both iliac regions with, in one of these, the umbilical, in two the epigastric and in one the epigastric and umbilical; lastly, in *three* the umbilical with, in one of these, the iliac, side not stated, and in one the iliac and hypogastric. Thus, in the sixty-four cases the abdomen was mentioned in thirty-one cases, the right iliac region in thirty-eight, the umbilical in twenty-five, the left iliac in eighteen, the iliac in three, the epigastric in nine, the hypogastric in three and the hepatic region in two cases.

Hypogastric pain was connected in 107 and 119 with retention of urine; in 84 it was probably due to the condition of the bladder in the early period and to peritonitis at a later date. In some of the *post-mortem* records also, as in cases 82 and 83, it was associated with peritoneal inflammation. Epigastric pain was connected in some instances, as 84 and 100, with jaundice; in others, as 85, 101 and 105, with irritability of the stomach; in 78 the morbid feeling experienced in this region was not tenderness but a burning sensation.

Gurgling was frequently observed in connection with abdominal tenderness and distention.

Splenic enlargement was not noted during life in any of these cases, an omission probably due to the cause suggested when referring to this as a symptom of typhoid.

CHEST COMPLICATIONS.—***Cough*** was present in thirty-two of the sixty-four cases. Generally it was slight and yielded a frothy mucous expectoration; but in some cases, as 78, 86 and 101, it was associated with pain in the chest, and in others, as 87, 90 and 93, with definite pneumonitic signs. The expectoration was blood-streaked in 87 and 105 and purulent and blood-streaked in 80; in 114 blood in the sputa was referred to a concurrent epistaxis.

Occasionally, as in 118, mucous and sibilant râles were heard although cough is said to have been absent. The ***respiration*** became accelerated in some, as in 99 and 105; it was hurried also in 106, in which cough did not appear as a symptom; and in the fatal cases, 93, 96 and 97, the breathing became greatly labored towards the end, although in the two last-mentioned instances other symptoms of pneumonic complication were obscured by the intensity of the stupor. Among the cases in the *post-mortem* records pulmonary embarrassment was observed in some, as 100; pneumonia in others, as 53 and 97. In 65 the cough was paroxysmal and prevented sleep. In 115, which was probably an adynamic malarial case, the chest affection was attributed to exposure by throwing off the bedclothes during the night. Accelerated breathing in 111 was probably due in part to pleuritic effusion.

OTHER CLINICAL FEATURES.—The ***urine*** was retained or passed with difficulty in twelve of the sixty-four cases; usually it was scanty and high-colored. No special record was made of its quantity or quality, save in 104 and 113, in the latter of which it was passed in excessive quantity notwithstanding the concurrence of free perspirations; in the former it was acid at first, afterward alkaline, large in quantity and of small specific gravity. From these cases it does not appear that retention or difficult micturition was cotemporaneous with the development of head symptoms: In 65, 73, 78, 82 and 83 the urinary trouble was noted early, but there were no marked cerebral manifestations. In 69 also, micturition was affected at an early date, but delirium did not supervene until after a lapse of ten days. In 70, with difficult micturition on the twelfth day, the only head symptom was some mental dulness, which was shown about six days later. The urinary affection occurred in the middle of the second week in 121, in the third week in 107, in the fourth week in 110, but in none of these was there any delirium. In the fatal case, 84, difficult micturition was followed in a few days by the development of cerebral symptoms, but as the latter appeared and became aggravated the former ceased. In 119, also fatal, headache and slight delirium accompanied a difficulty in retaining the urine, while the opposite condition of retention subsequently developed was not thus accompanied. On the other hand, although in many cases characterized by delirium and stupor there was an involuntary or uncontrolled passage of the urine, case 81 is the only instance in which temporary retention was reported as associated with the comatose condition. In the *post-mortem* series of cases, although delirium followed dysuria in some, as in 65, in others, as 83 and 106, there was no association of head symptoms with retention or dysuria.

Parotitis.—Swelling of the parotid appeared about the end of the third week in 69, 92 and 98; the termination was favorable in the first-mentioned case, but the two others were fatal. In 92 a gangrenous inflammation spread over the face, and death took place four days after the implication of the parotid; in 98 the swelling increased so rapidly that in a few days the patient was unable to protrude his tongue, and in six days death occurred with vibices and aggravated intestinal symptoms. In the *post-mortem* series parotid swelling was found in 53, 65 and 97.

Pains in the ***joints*** and ***muscles,*** especially of the lower extremities, were noted at a late period in the history of 115 of the Seminary series, 8 of the record of the 27th Conn. and 1, 2, 3, 4 and 12 of those belonging to the 19th Mass.; in case 4 of the last-mentioned series these pains were so severe as to cause loss of sleep and slight delirium. ***Gangrene*** of a blistered surface was recorded in case 104; gangrenous erysipelas of the face has already been noted as having been present in 92; gangrene of both feet occurred in 5 of the records of the 27th Conn. and in some of the cases of the *post-mortem* series. These will be referred to hereafter in speaking of the sequelæ of the continued fevers.*

RELAPSES.—The progress of typho-malarial cases was even more irregular than that of typhoid cases, for in addition to the complications and recrudescences to which the typhoid element rendered them obnoxious, their course was liable to interruption and prolongation by intercurrent exacerbations due to their malarial element. But well defined relapses of the typhoid phenomena were as infrequent as in unmodified typhoid.

Relapse was recorded in 59 and 91 of the Seminary series and in 56 of the *post-mortem* series. In the first-mentioned case the relapse was manifested by chill, fever and perspiration, wakefulness, diarrhœa, thirst and some febrile heat, while the pulse, although strong and full, was not accelerated, beating only at the rate of 66 per minute; rose-colored spots appeared on the eighth day, after which defervescence took place, diarrhœa subsided and the appetite returned. The second case presents a different record: Fever, diarrhœa, delirium and unconsciousness were at once developed; modified red spots appeared on the third day, about which time the delirium became violent; this was interrupted by a severe chill with the subsequent establishment of the typhoid condition, during which, on the sixth day, rose-colored spots erupted; death occurred on the seventh day from perforation. In the third case the details of neither the primary fever nor the relapse are given; but it is stated that during the subsidence of the febrile action delirium, coma and death occurred in connection with inflammatory processes in the ear.

FATALITY.—Lastly, it is of importance to point out that the fatality of these cases was considerably greater than that of the typhoid series,—in fact, their percentage of fatality was greater than the sum of the percentages of typhoid and malarial diseases. Of fifty-one Seminary cases of unmodified typhoid ten were fatal or 19.6 per cent., while of sixty-four cases in which this disease was influenced by the coincidence of malarial phenomena seventeen or 26.6 per cent. ended fatally. These results are consistent with medical experience in

---

analogous cases.   No one will deny that when pneumonia occurs in the progress of typhoid or malarial fever the patient's danger is correspondingly enhanced.

In summarizing the differences between the symptoms of the typhoid affection *per se* and the same disease as modified by the intercurrence of active febrile conditions usually attributed to the malarial influence, the following points require mention as generally characteristic of the latter:

1. Paroxysmal invasion with perspirations;
2. Greater strength and frequency of the pulse during the febrile access;
3. Intercurrence of febrile paroxysms at any stage;
4. The paroxysmal recurrence of epistaxis;
5. A doubtful infrequency of the eruption and an undoubted modification of its characters in certain cases;
6. The pale, flabby, moist and coated condition of the tongue;
7. The greater frequency of nausea, vomiting and jaundice;
8. A more defined tendency to constipation in the few cases not characterized by relaxation or positive diarrhœa, and the frequency of abdominal tenderness beyond the limits of the right iliac region, especially towards the epigastric and left iliac regions;
9. The greater gravity of the cerebral symptoms and the earlier period at which death was, in some instances, occasioned by malarial coma;
10. A greater fatality or ratio of deaths to cases.

It appears, therefore, that when these cases as a whole are compared with those of pure typhoid, there are manifested certain clinical differences which were marked in proportion to the activity of the malarial phenomena; when the latter were pronounced there was no difficulty in determining the interference with the course of the typhoid fever, provided the occurrence of the characteristic symptoms of that fever indicated its presence. But, as may be seen in the records of the 19th Mass., there were occasionally presented obscure cases in which it was impossible to say whether the sub-continued fever which prostrated the patient was due solely or chiefly to one or other of these fever-poisons, since the characteristic symptoms of neither were distinctly marked, while well defined cases of each of these febrile conditions were occurring at the same time in neighboring commands and had occurred only a short time before in the regiment itself.

Further inquiry into the nature of the typho-malarial cases of the war must be postponed until after their presentation from the *post-mortem* standpoint.

IV.—TYPHOID FEVER, MODIFIED AND UNMODIFIED.

Sequelæ.—But whether the febrile cases that occurred among our troops were typhoid or typho-malarial certain sequelæ were prone to follow.   Persistent debility, occurring alone or in association with tubercular developments or some local morbid conditions, often incapacitated the soldier for further military service.   Diarrhœa was the most frequent of the engrafted diseases, owing to the prevalence of its causes and the condition of the intestinal lining in convalescents from fever: Following it in order of frequency were inflammatory processes in the lungs.   Diseased conditions of the liver, spleen or kidneys were also found.   Many of the cases already submitted illustrate these occasional consequences of the febrile attack, and others of a similar tenor will be found in the *post-mortem* records.

Perhaps the most interesting sequel presented by the records is the pain in the feet and legs which constituted a prominent and distressing symptom in many of the cases.   It occurred, but not with frequency, in the Seminary cases; it constituted a characteristic of those treated by Surgeons Dyer of the 19th Mass. and Barr of the 36th Ohio,* and it is mentioned in the report of Surgeon McLaren's Board of Inquiry† and in several of the

_____

*See report, *infra*, p. 327.   † *Infra*, p. 365.

cases taken from the records of various general hospitals.   Occasionally it is noted in Sanitary reports, as in the following:

Surgeon HARVEY E. BROWN, 70th N. Y. Vols., Camp Mahan, Va., October 16, 1862.—A number of severe cases of typhoid fever presented the peculiarity that during convalescence there was a remarkable tenderness of the feet and ankles; the patient would cry out with agony at the mere weight of the bedclothes, and a touch of the hand gave excruciating pain.   I found but little relief in this distressing symptom from cooling lotions or poultices; perhaps I was more successful with the use of hog's lard smeared over the foot than with any other remedy.   In most of the cases this soreness gradually disappeared, but loss of power in the feet remained for many weeks, although the patients in other respects grew strong and well.   In one case large abscesses formed on the dorsal surface of the foot; these discharged and the foot got well.

Owing to the meagre character of the records it is difficult to appreciate the cause of this pain in the cases in which it is mentioned.   In some it was probably due to fatigue induced by the first efforts of the convalescent to test his returning strength.   Muscular and rheumatic pains may also be ascribed to degenerative changes arising from mal-nutrition, the poverty or abnormal state of the blood being manifested by an œdematous condition of the feet and ankles or by boils, subcutaneous abcesses or ecchymoses.   But the occurrence of gangrene in cases 40–42, from the records of various hospitals, and in six cases of the *post-mortem* series,* is of importance in this connection.   The severe pain mentioned as the only abnormal phenomenon in some cases, as in those of the 36th Ohio, was associated with swelling in others, in two of Surgeon KENDALL's cases with discoloration, and in certain cases with ulceration, superficial sloughing and even gangrene necessitating amputation above the ankle joint.   Surgeon BARR viewed the occurrence of this pain as a favorable sign indicating the commencement of convalescence, but a larger experience showing its probable connection with a deadly lesion supplies ground for regarding it with much anxiety.

Surgeon J. H. TAYLOR, U. S. Vols., in his report, April 10, 1863, on the occurrence of gangrene of the toes in the Third Army Corps, Army of the Potomac, attributed this morbid condition to exposure to cold.   In the field hospitals of the corps he found six cases, one of which was manifestly a true frost-bite.   In five the gangrene set in during convalescence from typhoid fever, but in the history of each there was detected an exposure to which, in the debilitated condition of the patient, the local injury was ascribed.   In one of these cases, that of Adam Hayerd, 122d Pa., amputation was performed at the upper third of both legs, subsequent to separation of the feet, and at the time of Surgeon TAYLOR's enquiry the stumps were healed.   Gangrene in this case set in during the intensely cold weather that followed the battle of Fredericksburg and while the patient was under treatment for typhoid fever in the regimental hospital.   A suspicion that scurvy was concerned in the development of these cases was not sustained by the results of the investigation.

In the cases above reported the disease has presented a remarkable uniformity in its commencing stages and in the parts attacked, invariably beginning at the ends of the toes and generally with the greatest severity in the little toes.   I failed to detect in a single instance the evidence of its having manifested itself at any point above the ankle joint or anywhere except in the parts immediately involved as already indicated.

In every case the constitutional symptoms have been severe and such as are usually found in mortification supervening on injuries involving sudden loss of vitality.   Great depression of the vital powers, rapid and feeble pulse, with cold sweats in some instances, have marked the course of the disease.   It is true that most of the cases were enfeebled and debilitated by typhoid fever at the time the disease in question manifested itself, and that a great part of the depression might be due to the primary disease; nevertheless the change was decidedly marked, particularly in the pulse, which became more frequent and irritable.   This change took place immediately upon the accession of the gangrene and not, apparently, from the gradual diffusion of any scorbutic taint or latent cachexy.   From the absence in every case of general symptoms indicating scurvy as the cause, and the evidence connecting the gangrenous condition with exposure to cold, I am compelled to assume the latter to be the cause.   It may be alleged that in two of the cases the patients were not exposed to a sufficient degree of cold to produce freezing at the time the disease manifested itself—that they had been in division and regimental hospitals for some time previous, where it was not probable that such an injury would happen. But by noting the facts we find that in one case the patient was sent from regimental to division hospital on the 4th of March, and that immediately after becoming warm in bed he was seized with severe burning pains in the ends of his toes, and that the following morning gangrenous patches were observable. It is reasonable to infer that this patient was frost-bitten while being conveyed from one hospital to another. The case becomes much stronger when we remember the man's condition at the time, and know that such accidents were of frequent occurrence during the Crimean war, even where the sick were transferred to no greater distance than probably intervened between the hospitals in question. The history of the other case is very similar. The patient had been sick in division hospital four weeks with typhoid fever; he was returned to his regiment January 27, where he remained about two/weeks, when he was again sent to division hospital. Within forty-eight hours after his re-admission symptoms of gangrene were manifested in the ends of his toes. The same inference is deducible in this case,—that the man was frost-bitten while being conveyed from one hospital to another. It will be remembered that he was in hospital for six weeks prior to the attack of gangrene; that his diet had been generous and varied; that at the time of his first admission and during the continuance of his stay no symptom of scurvy was discernible, but that immediately after being removed from one hospital to another mortification set in.

In conclusion I will add that it appears to me scarcely possible for scurvy to so affect the system as to produce ten gangrenous spots each in the end of a toe without manifesting itself still further through some one or more of its ordinary concomitant symptoms.—*Surgeon* J. H. TAYLOR'S *Report.*

Sloughing of the cornea occurred in case 39 of the records of various hospitals.*

Swelling of the parotids with frequent suppuration, which has been mentioned in connection with both typhoid and typho-malarial cases, occurred as a sequel or late complication in the cases 43–50 from various hospitals. Surgeon BARR gives the only reference to a similar condition of the submaxillary glands, and records the testicles as having been affected in two instances. Purulent deposits in other parts of the body are noted in cases 34–36 of the series last mentioned and in several of the *post-mortem* records.†

Sequelæ involving impairment of nervous power are illustrated in cases 51–61 from various hospitals. These cases do not differ from those described by MURCHISON, NOTHNAGEL and others, as occasionally occurring after ordinary typhoid fever. They consist of partial paralysis of various parts and include one case, 59, of paralysis agitans, in which the tremors persisted notwithstanding the return of muscular strength, one, 60, of cerebro-spinal fever, with death from coma on the second day of the attack, and one, 61, of paraplegia from spinal meningitis, in which a gradual improvement took place, so that in about four months the patient was able to make very good use of his legs and was strong and healthy in his general condition. In 51 the right leg became œdematous and paralyzed; the œdema disappeared in two weeks, but a considerable time elapsed before the power of free motion was restored. In 52 the lower extremities were partially paralyzed, the result being discharge from service on account of a slow and unsteady gait; in 53 paraplegia was associated with some atrophy of the right leg, but the patient, after a course of crutches and canes, was eventually returned to duty; in 54 there was progressive loss of motion and sensation in the lower limbs until a state of almost complete paraplegia was reached, after which the patient improved, but was discharged at the end of six months as incapable of further service; in 55 hemiplegia improved rapidly, but left the soldier unfit for duty owing to contraction of the right leg; in 56 there was no improvement in a paralyzed left side at the end of four months. All these cases occurred during convalescence; in fact, in 54 the patient is described as having been doing well for seven weeks, when he was taken with the gradually increasing paraplegia. But in 57 and 58 the patients were prostrate at the time of seizure: In the former hemiplegia occurred during the height of a sequent pneumonia; this man was discharged after several months, able to walk with the aid of a cane but with the arm powerless. In the latter the right arm and left leg were paralyzed during the unconsciousness of a late

---

* Dr. WOODWARD says, in the second part of this work, p. 501, that no case of corneal ulcer occurring in the later stages of fever was brought to the notice of the Surgeon General's Office during the war. See also Case 49 of the *post-mortem* records.

† See *infra*, page 432.

period of a severe typhoid attack; the case ended in discharge twelve months afterwards on account of atrophy of the leg and inability to flex the foot.

RELAPSES.—Besides the instances of typhoid relapse in the typhoid and typho-malarial cases, 48 and 49, 59 and 91 of the Seminary series, and 32 and 56 of the *post-mortem* records, 63–65 from various hospitals were regarded by their medical attendants as cases of relapse in typhoid fever. In 63 the details of the primary attack are not given; but the patient died, after passing hemorrhagic stools, on the fourth day from the second access of fever, typhoid symptoms and rose-colored spots having been developed in the meantime. In 64, three weeks after the apparent establishment of convalescence, the patient was seized with severe diarrhœa, which terminated fatally in twenty days; but there is nothing on the record to show that it was a true relapse. In 65, which ended favorably, both the initial and sequent attacks are detailed, but the evidence of the presence of typhoid is by no means convincing.

SECOND ATTACKS.—The records of the series from various hospitals furnish only two cases, 66 and 67, of typhoid attacks in men who had suffered from the disease at a previous period. In one case the second attack was well defined and under observation, but the first rested on the testimony of the patient, corroborated, with some details, by his father; in the other a clear history of the anterior attack is furnished, and the second, typho-malarial in its character, is also described with precision. The patient, in 75 of the Seminary series, is said to have suffered from typhoid fever two years before his admission with a pronounced typho-malarial attack.

EXTRACTS FROM REPORTS, ETC.—A few papers on file in the office of the Surgeon General give clinical descriptions of the continued fevers which prevailed in our camps and hospitals. These are herewith presented. Abstracts of most of the journal articles on this subject are appended as notes.*

---

* J. J. LEVICK,—*Med. and Surg. Reporter*, Phila., Vol. VIII, 1862, p. 283,—in a clinical lecture on six cases of miasmatic typhoid fever from the seat of war summarizes the principal features of the disease. In some there had been an ill-defined forming stage during which the patients, although much troubled with diarrhœa, would attend to their ordinary duties; in others the attack was sudden, coming on with chilliness and intense headache. Diarrhœa was a constant symptom; chilliness or rigors affected all the patients; a flushed face and slight cough, with the usual bronchitic râles, were also noticed in every case. At the beginning there were exacerbations and remissions, and in connection with the latter was found a moistness of the skin at certain periods of the day, the forehead being covered with large drops of perspiration; but this was in no instance critical,—it ceased and recurred. Headache, present in varying degree in every instance, was sometimes described as *splitting* or *battering;* there was always a sense of weight and weariness in the eyes, severe pain in the back of the neck and between the shoulders rather than in the loins, and restless aching in the lower limbs. The tongue was more or less furred, but not heavily coated nor disposed to dryness as in typhoid fever; thirst was moderate; loss of appetite complete. The pulse in two cases reached 120; but with these exceptions it was rarely above 90, and in one it was as low as 60; it was soft although in no case alarmingly feeble. Epistaxis was not always present. The abdomen was more or less prominent, but not decidedly tympanitic. There was none of the mental dulness of enteric fever, so that even in the comparatively advanced stage of the disease questions were answered intelligently and the patient showed interest in what passed around him; in no case was there well-marked delirium. In another article—*Amer. Jour. Med. Science*, Vol. XLVII, 1864, p. 404—he recapitulates the substance of his former lecture, and adverts to the invariable presence of the rose-colored eruption and disease of Peyer's patches, the latter indicated by diarrhœa which was either present or readily induced by a small dose of castor oil. SANFORD B. HUNT, Surgeon U. S. Vols., in a communication to the *Buffalo Med. and Surg. Jour.*, Vol. II, 1862, p. 202, describing the camp fever which he observed in a recently recruited New York regiment, says that for a few days the patients felt weary and stupid, had headache and pain in the back, loss of appetite and fever,—skin hot and dry, pulse 100 or more, tongue dry and brownish. Suffering little pain, they frequently were cheerful throughout, seeming rather lazy than sick. Diarrhœa set in; the pulse reached 120, but seldom rose higher; sordes collected about the teeth and the tongue became cracked. After a time these symptoms declined, the tongue being the last to regain its normal state. A good appetite on a dry tongue was not uncommon. JOSEPH KLAPP, Act. Ass't Surg., U. S. A., in an article on *Typhoid Fever in our Military Hospitals,*—*Med. and Surg. Reporter*, Philadelphia, Vol. IX, 1862–63, p. 18,—says that a large proportion of the fever cases admitted into the hospital in which he served bore a considerable resemblance to ordinary typhoid. In giving a brief notice of the more obvious features of the army fever, he remarks that deafness was infrequent and slight; five cases had the dull, heavy, stolid expression of countenance so often found in pure typhoid; delirium was present only in the most unfavorable cases; sleeplessness was scarcely complained of. In most cases there was diarrhœa, the discharges being thin, yellow and more profuse perhaps than in enteric fever; pain on pressure was felt in the right iliac region and over the abdomen generally, but in a less degree than is usual in typhoid. The rose-colored eruption was present in most instances, sudamina in but few. Convalescence was more rapid, and as soon as it began the countenance acquired a brighter and more cheerful expression; severe cases had a listless, indifferent, yet not stupid expression, a dark mahogany color of the face, sordes about the teeth and a dry tongue disposed to become aphthous in the progress to recovery. Chronic rheumatism, never complained of before, affected many, but not until they had in a great measure recovered their strength. Most of the patients came from the region of the James and Chickahominy rivers and were benefited by quinine. When tenderness of the abdomen, tympanites and acute diarrhœa co-existed with well-marked typhoid symptoms, oil of turpentine was given, with good nourishment, wine, whiskey or milk-punch; warm rubefacient cataplasms over the abdomen afforded great relief. HENRY M. LYMAN, Act. Ass't Surg. U. S. A., writing from University Hospital, Nashville, Tenn., August 6, 1862,—*Amer. Med. Times*, N. Y., Vol. V, p. 109,—says that typhoid fever was of frequent occurrence in the spring of 1862, and that "if all the cases of fever attended with rose-colored spots upon the skin, diarrhœa, etc., are to be reported as

Remarks on the Typhoid Fever of the Army by Ass't Surg. Jos. R. Smith, *U. S. A., Seminary hospital, Georgetown, D. C., Sept.* 30, 1862.—Washington and its environs seem to have been a favorite habitat of intermittent fever for many years past. In common, however, with many other places in this country, the type of prevailing fever has been steadily undergoing a change, intermittents gradually giving place to remittents and the latter in turn to typhoid. Two hundred and eighty-eight cases of fever have been treated during the past quarter in the Seminary hospital; twenty-two were intermittent cases, one hundred and thirty-seven remittent and one hundred and twenty-nine typhoid; one of the remittent and twenty-three of the typhoid cases were fatal.

Intermittent and remittent cases presented no peculiarities, and generally yielded promptly to the free use of quinine. Those cases, however, which proved most obstinate assimilated gradually to typhoid, and in a number there was doubt as to the diagnosis. The cases of remittent fever diminished in frequency during the month of September, and those of typhoid increased in a greater ratio. This was probably owing not simply to a greater prevalence of typhoid, but to the fact that stringent orders were issued prohibiting the sending of light cases of disease from camp to general hospitals; in consequence light remittents were retained for treatment in camp, while those febrile cases that were more unpromising in their appearance were sent to the various general hospitals.

Under the head of typhoid fever I include only those which presented typhoid symptoms from their reception into hospital, though some of them, according to the history obtained from the patients themselves or their former physicians, evidently commenced as remittents. According to my own observation nearly half of the cases originated as remittent fevers,—at all events they presented well-marked daily remissions and exacerbations. In the hospital, where in such cases the utmost attention of the attendant medical officer was given and even the shade of a remission watched for, that the great specific, quinine, might be administered, either only a slight trace of a remission would be discovered, refusing frankly to declare itself under appropriate doses of quinine, or a continued fever would be at once established with all its usual and familiar symptoms. Cases typhoid *ab origine* were usually recognized as such within a very few days. They began with chills or sensations of chilliness, headache, pains in the back and aching limbs, soon followed by a rapid pulse, hot skin and feelings of debility and weakness. Cases of this kind presented in general the greater part of the following symptoms: Chills, headache, pains, feeling of prostration, hebetude, deafness, tinnitus aurium, subsultus tendinum, heat of skin, delirium, capillary congestion, epistaxis, accelerated pulse and hemorrhage, sudamina, petechiæ, eruptions, sweats, tongue foul and coated or dry and harsh, sordes on teeth and lips, meteorism, borborygmus, iliac or abdominal tenderness, constipation or diarrhœa with involuntary evacuations, vomiting and gastric irritability, peritonitis, retention of urine and apparent convalescence followed by relapse. The disease was ordinarily ushered in by a chill with cephalalgia and pain in the back and limbs. Within three or four days, however, these symptoms almost entirely gave place to a sensation of muscular weakness. Hebetude was marked in most of the cases. The patient could be easily roused from a state of stupor to answer questions; he would protrude his tongue if asked to do so, but would often forget to draw it back. The hearing was frequently impaired, although the patient might not recognize his deafness. Delirium was a constant symptom; it was rarely violent, generally low, accompanied by muttering or talking and a desire to leave the bed for some senseless object, a desire which he endeavored to gratify whenever the attention of the nurse was withdrawn; but even when delirious he could often be roused to give a sensible answer. Tinnitus aurium was frequently absent, but subsultus tendinum and general jactitation were among the constant symptoms in severe

cases of typhoid, we must conclude that the disease is modified in many particulars by its intimate relation with the causes of the remittent form which has thus far marked at least nine-tenths of the cases of fever which, during the last three months, have been placed under my observation." The same journal, in its issue of July 12, 1862, has an editorial headed *Reports of Hospitals*, which, in referring to the experience of the Ladies' Home hospital, New York City, states that the malarial fever met with there had its symptoms mingled with those of true typhoid. Diarrhœa and rose-colored spots were almost constantly present, and the fever exhibited a marked disposition to exacerbations and sometimes to collapse,—patients presenting nothing untoward in their condition, and with the mind perfectly clear, would, in three or four hours, and occasionally in less time, be found pulseless, the surface moist and cold and death imminent. When in this condition they would converse intelligently and express themselves well enough to sit up. When asleep the decubitus was dorsal and the appearance of the countenance that peculiar to severe cases of typhoid fever, but the patient could readily be roused, and when awakened showed no bewilderment. In severe cases the tongue was dry and disposed to crack. The appetite generally was not much impaired. Scorbutus was a frequent complication, and suppuration of the parotid gland was present in a few instances. Irving W. Lyon, House Physician, Bellevue hospital, commenting on parotitis as a complication of typhus,—*Amer. Med. Times, N. Y.*, Vol. VIII, 1864, p. 87,—states that in the summer of 1862 he saw in the hospital near Corinth, Miss., about one hundred and fifty cases of typho-malarial fever with parotid swellings in ten per cent. of the cases and on both sides in half of the number affected. Suppuration almost invariably took place if the patient lived long enough. This was regarded as an unfavorable complication. Patients who recovered after having been thus affected were slow in gaining strength, the discharge from the gland continuing for a long time. S. K. Towle, Surgeon 30th Mass., in an article *Notes of Practice in the U. S. A. General Hospital, Baton Rouge, La.,—Boston Med. and Surg. Journal*, Vol. LXX, 1864, p. 49,—speaks of the mixed characters of the fevers prevalent in that section. The remissions in remittent fever were less marked, and often nearly disappeared after two or three days, while, with the continuance of the fever, enteric rather than gastric symptoms became prominent. He holds that cases registered as typhoid fever were without doubt of malarial origin. These had not the rose-colored eruption, and on admission had already lost the early diagnostic features, retaining only the prostrated, low vitiated, semi-conscious condition of the last stage of severe typhoid fever. The mortality was much greater than in pure typhoid, and in those that eventually recovered convalescence was slow and halting. "I do not remember to have seen this season amongst those who had spent last year in this department a single case of typhoid fever such as we see in New England, and most of the cases occurring amongst the new-comers after they had been here two months were decidedly modified by the miasmatic surroundings. Indeed, one could almost tell how long a New England fever patient had been in this section of the country by the type of his disease, a genuine case of uncomplicated typhoid being strictly pathognomonic of a recent down-east Yankee. * * During the spring I saw at the different regimental hospitals, by invitation of the surgeons of several New England nine-months regiments, a great many severe cases of typhoid fever (then quite prevalent in the new regiments here), and although most of them did not exhibit any remissions, and hence had not been thought complicated at all with malaria, yet the fact was indisputable that they did better after the introduction into the treatment of full doses of quinine during the first part of the disease; and in cases in which quinine had not been given at first, it often, though not invariably, was of apparent benefit in somewhat small doses in the later stages." After adverting to the various influences that modify camp fevers he remarks: "Hence it follows that few of the serious cases of malarial disease one is called upon to treat after six months service in the army are either simple, well-defined or exactly described by any of the old terms, as intermittent, remittent or typhoid, but partake in some degree of the nature of all; and from the previous surroundings of the patient are inclined to rapidly assume a decided typhoid type."

cases. In aggravated cases the nervous system seemed entirely prostrated very early in the disease, the above-described symptoms being developed by the fifth or sixth day. Capillary congestion was well marked in the majority of cases; the brown color of the cheeks, disappearing on pressure and but slowly returning after the removal, helped much to impart that expression of the countenance known as the *facies typhosa*. Epistaxis was of rather infrequent occurrence; in two cases, however, it was so severe as to become of serious import. Hemorrhage occurred from no other part except the bowels as an effect of erosion of the walls of a bloodvessel. In every case that I noticed the pulse was accelerated from the beginning of the attack, ranging from about 90 to 110, but in many cases it diminished in frequency coincidently with the disappearance of headache and pain in the back and limbs, so that after three or four days the pulse ranged from 85 to 100 or a little more. I have been accustomed to consider the frequency of the pulse and its strength or weakness as furnishing important prognostic indications. Cases in which the pulse exceeded 128 seldom ended favorably; sometimes in fatal cases it ranged for days beyond this number, gradually running up to 140 or higher, until, with imperceptible pulse, the patient died. An unfavorable result was common also in those cases in which there was a want of correspondence between the force of pulsations in different parts of the body, as indicated by the action of the heart and the beating of the carotids, the abdominal aorta and radial artery, sometimes a labored cardiac action producing but a weak arterial pulsation. Petechiæ and vibices were present in many cases, particularly on the abdomen, less frequently on the chest and but rarely on the limbs. Sudamina were of constant occurrence, profuse all over the abdomen, but in no instance upon the limbs or face. These sweat-vesicles burst shortly after their appearance, and in many cases reappeared in a succession of crops during the whole attack. Their presence or absence seemed of but little value as an index of mildness or severity. The typhoid eruption was not an invariable symptom. When present it appeared usually during the second week, chiefly on the abdomen and thorax. Sometimes only two or three spots were discovered after a careful examination of the surface, and in a certain number of cases no eruption whatever was observed. Some of these non-eruptive cases were as severe as any, and when fatal exhibited no variation from the ordinary *post-mortem* lesions. The digestive system early shared in the morbid actions constituting the febrile condition. From the beginning the tongue was covered with a white coating which seldom disappeared during the disease, or with a black coat, the tip and edges being red and angry-looking; it was often moist, sometimes flabby, and frequently dry and harsh, much fissured and covered, like the teeth and lips, with sordes. In fatal cases this state of the tongue persisted to the end, but in favorable cases it cleaned from the centre to the edges or *vice versa*. One of the most encouraging appearances presented by the tongue, noticed chiefly about the period of convalescence, was the assumption of a delicate film of white on the cleaned surface. Sordes could in general be wiped or washed away, and attention to this apparently trivial act was productive of much comfort to the patient. The pathological changes taking place in the abdominal cavity early invited attention by their local indications. The skin, particularly that of the abdomen, was apparently much raised in temperature, this being sometimes so striking as to constitute the *calor mordax* of the books. I noticed a very frequent connection of this symptom with violent delirium. The abdomen was sometimes flat or cup-shaped, with every pulsation of the abdominal aorta plainly visible, at other times tumid and swollen or meteoric, resonant and rumbling on the slightest pressure. In several instances distention was decidedly relieved by the introduction of flexible tubes *per anum* to allow the gas to escape. Tenderness on pressure was one of the most frequent phenomena, markedly exhibited in the right iliac region. When slight this generally displayed itself by an involuntary shrinking or a contraction of the rectus to protect the parts beneath from pressure. Sometimes the tenderness extended along the course of the colon into the left iliac region, and occasionally the whole abdomen was affected and the patient so sensitive as to shrink from even a motion to bear upon the parts. The bowels were generally irregular, sometimes constipated, but more frequently affected with a persistent and debilitating diarrhœa, the stools usually blackish in color, of a very offensive odor and occasionally bloody. Vomiting and gastric irritability were by no means prominent symptoms; in a few cases, however, it was found impossible to relieve them, the matter vomited being sometimes yellowish and smelling of bile, sometimes watery, sometimes black and in one instance containing blood corpuscles. Toward the end involuntary dejections added to the disagreeable symptoms, though some cases recovered after reaching this stage. The muscular coat of the bladder seemed paralyzed in quite a number of cases and required the regular use of the catheter; this, however, did not indicate their gravity, for many such cases recovered.

The fatality of the disease has been 23 in 129 cases, or one in a little more than five and a half cases; but this rate has presented great variations. Thus, in the first fourteen days of September, 15 deaths occurred. Not only was this owing to the fact before mentioned, that at this time the custom of sending only the most serious cases to general hospitals was strictly adhered to, but it seemed as if some fatal epidemic influence struck suddenly all those who were laboring under this disease. Those who entered the hospital at that date came under its influence, those who had been in hospital a longer time were equal sufferers, and the same mortality extended to the other hospitals in the city, both the neighboring and remote, thus proving its independence of local causes. I have been unable to discover anything to account for this increased mortality, which subsided toward the end of the month.

The question of diagnosis, while of much interest, is one which an elementary report like the present cannot pretend to treat. Where an assemblage of symptoms such as I have enumerated was presented there could be of course no doubt in the diagnosis; but so great was the variety in the nature, number, severity and combination of the symptoms as on several occasions to arouse the suspicion that two distinct diseases were present with certain features in common. The closest and most careful investigation of the symptoms and *post-mortem* appearances failed at the time to confirm such suspicion, and every day and every new observation since has convinced me of its incorrectness. To illustrate: There has entered the hospital a patient whose previous history exhibits all the symptoms of an ordinary pyrexial attack. At present, however, the symptoms are as follows: Pulse 80 to 95; face but little congested;

heat of skin nearly natural or not much increased over abdomen; tongue clean or somewhat dry; very slight or no pain or tenderness in the abdomen; bowels regular; appetite impaired; complaint of slight weakness, much increased by exertion; sudamina and profuse perspirations but no eruption. This assemblage might easily escape recognition as the combined symptoms of a fever case. If this patient be carefully treated, confined to his bed, the state of the secretions watched and regulated and all stimulating food disallowed, the pulse in two or three weeks will fall to or below the natural standard, the tongue assume the delicate whitish appearance I have spoken of as characteristic of convalescence, and with returning appetite, strength and health will reappear. Should, however, the case be neglected and the patient continue his customary or other work, overlooking the premonitions of approaching disease, soon the unheeded warning will speak in language not to be misunderstood. Accelerated pulse, gastric irritability, high febrile action, abdominal tenderness and other typhoid symptoms are speedily developed and death is the usual issue. Now the question arises: What are the elements common to two such dissimilar conditions as are here described? Is there anything that may serve as a connecting link by which these apparently isolated diseases may be joined as one, or are these features of resemblance mere coincidences that might be expected equally in a case of delirium tremens or carcinomatous degeneration? I shall endeavor to give my impression of what is common in all these cases: I have found abdominal tenderness one of the most constant phenomena of some stage of this disease; in fact, without a particular reference to my notes, I do not recall a single instance in which pressure over the right iliac region or some other portion of the abdomen less frequently, did not elicit symptoms of tenderness or uneasiness, either an acknowledgment of pain or an involuntary shrinking from the pressure. The occurrence of sudamina and profuse sweating, without possessing any great pathological significance that I am aware of, has yet seemed to me to possess more or less diagnostic value, and though some cases of fever ran their entire course without them, in the majority several crops have made their appearance, filling up, bursting and leaving the skin in a sort of brawny desquamation. The tongue is generally altered in this disease, presenting the appearance I have before described. To be sure it is sometimes coated in other diseases, but to me the typhoid tongue, with sordes on the teeth and lips, has a pathognomonic appearance. The slight acceleration of the pulse, too, invariably directed my attention to the true state of the case, being neither natural nor yet sufficiently rapid to arouse suspicion of inflammatory pyrexia, but remaining for a number of days at a certain state of moderate acceleration; and here I desire to call attention to a phenomenon in the natural history of the disease which I have hitherto neglected to mention, viz: the occurrence, in frequent cases, of a more or less perfect apyrexial period amounting, in some instances, to almost apparent convalescence, which lasts for several days and is followed by secondary fever sometimes more severe than the preceding stage, but generally milder. This could not be considered a relapse, for generally it seemed one of the natural occurrences, a part and portion of the history of the first attack, whose termination appeared to approach indifferently either by some "crisis," or natural evacuation, or else by some gradual, slow and regular subsidence of the febrile action.

But more conclusive than any of the above symptoms as to the perfect identity of these differently manifested conditions are the *post-mortem* appearances. Autopsies were held in most of the fatal cases, and the lesions in every case diagnosed as typhoid fever were identical and perfectly satisfactory as confirmation of our diagnosis. The following are the principal and most constant lesions that I have noticed—(and here let me state that the *post-mortem* examinations in these cases were directed principally to the condition of the small intestine and cæcum and the presence or absence of lesions usually recognized as typhoid. In quite a number of cases, however, the whole intestinal tube was examined and all the abdominal viscera.) In the ileum: In every case that was examined Peyer's patches presented enlargement and ulceration, generally extending for several feet up the intestine. In only two or three instances was the disease so little advanced as to present nothing more than the shaven-beard appearance; but generally the glands were ulcerated, sometimes only enlarged so as to remind me forcibly of the appearance of "wheals" upon the skin, and in one instance so large as to project over one-third of an inch into the cavity of the intestine. The solitary glands presented similar appearances, being enlarged to the size of a split-pea and many of them ulcerated. Both the solitary and Peyer's glands contained the typhoid matter in the shape of a blackish granular deposit. Sometimes the whole mucous membrane of the ileum seemed covered with a similar adherent material, and at other times it seemed as if the matter were deposited beneath the mucous membrane in great black blotches. In some instances the walls of the intestine were congested both externally and internally between the ulcerated and enlarged patches. The greatest extent of pathological change was found towards the cæcal end of the ileum, gradually diminishing in the upper part of the gut and extending to a greater or less extent in different cases; but in every instance was found enlargement and ulceration of both Peyer's and the solitary glands and typhoid deposit. The upper end of the colon presented similar appearances. The ileo-cæcal valve was often thickened and black. The mesentery and mesenteric glands were generally much congested, the latter enlarged to the size of acorns, and blackish-red from engorgement with venous blood. The omentum often presented an appearance as if it had been for a long time macerated. Sometimes the small intestine was nearly empty and packed down in some corner,—occasionally bound down by inflammatory adhesions; at other times it was much distended with gas. Where perforation had occurred redness and peritoneal effusion were generally present. Nothing pathognomonic was observed in the other viscera; the liver, pancreas and kidneys seemed healthy although sometimes slightly softened; the spleen was generally much congested, enlarged and softened; the stomach occasionally congested and its mucous membrane softened, sometimes over the whole organ.

A few words are needful regarding complications. Bronchitis, pneumonia and inflammation and abscess of the parotid were the principal. In no case was any antiphlogistic treatment directed against the intercurrent inflammation more than blistering, expectorants, dry cups and, distrustfully, tartar-emetic. The treatment adopted in all these cases was stimulating and supporting from the outset. Carbonate of ammonia, wine-whey, milk-punch and essence of beef formed our chief reliance, administered in greater or less quantities according to the prostration of the patient; the pulse was our principal guide to quantity. The regulation of the bowels was generally attempted by opiates and astringents; I have found opium a very reliable remedy not only for this purpose but for calming nervous excitement, relieving jactitation and delirium and producing sleep,—its combination with tartar-emetic in the most violent cases of nervous excitement was sometimes followed by the happiest effects. Quinine was used in many instances, but with little if any benefit. Blisters and other derivative applications to the surface were freely used for the relief of the many distressing abdominal symptoms, sometimes with, sometimes without, success. Emulsion of turpentine was also employed, and in a small proportion of cases with benefit. Hoffmann's anodyne was, next to opium, the best anti-spasmodic. But after all our main object was to support the patient, not to break up the disease, for which latter purpose no medicine was of any avail.

Typhoid fever in this hospital has shown no sign of contagion. Two of my medical officers, as also two medical cadets, were affected during the epidemic with slight symptoms of temporary derangement.

I shall not attempt to discuss the cause of the disease. The change of life from home to camp, and exposure to fatigue and wet under new auspices, seem to have developed it. The season has been a remarkably wet one, but as far as I have been able to ascertain not an unhealthy one among the residents of this vicinity. No epidemics have prevailed save the cases of typhoid fever; and the cases of disease outside of military camps and hospitals have been substantially the same as those occurring in our own experience. The regiments from which our sick were derived have generally been actively employed erecting fortifications, laboring in the trenches, felling trees and standing guard,—not as much exposed to fatigue or inclemency of weather as our troops have ordinarily been on frontier service,—and generally provided with good water and the best of food. Their clothing has been suitable to the season of the year and the men themselves have, as a rule, been clean and temperate.

Surgeon C. J. WALTON, *21st Ky., March 31, 1862, Green River, Taylor County, Ky.*—But the disease from which our troops suffered most was typhoid fever. This is not to be wondered at when we take into consideration their situation with the circumstances attending them. Almost every possible predisposing cause was in operation at the same time: Badly prepared food; sleeping upon the damp ground; unusually warm and wet weather for the season with sudden changes in the temperature of the atmosphere; want of personal cleanliness; camped in the bend of the river and almost surrounded by it; standing guard during rainy nights; leading inactive lives, not drilling one day in seven on account of mud and rain, and, in a word, almost everything that tends to lower the vital energies. We called it typhoid fever, for we could not, as it appeared in our regiment, term it anything else. There seemed to be no essential difference between it and the ordinary typhoid of private practice except that the symptoms were greatly aggravated. Some practitioners whom I have met do not consider it typhoid but camp fever. They contend that it is a disease peculiar to camp life; but I am unable to trace any distinction except as above stated, in the aggravation of the symptoms. Those who were taken down had generally some premonitory symptoms: Diarrhœa, dull headache, pains in the bones, some soreness of the flesh, lassitude, general debility and loss of appetite. After taking to bed many manifested the greatest indifference to their condition, resting quietly and asking for nothing; when enquiry was made how they felt, they would answer *very well*, or *I feel better to-day;* a few, however, became conscious of their danger. Some were delirious from the beginning,—furiously mad, and constantly attempting to get up and leave their tents; others became delirious after a few days. In these cases typho-mania and coma vigil were common symptoms. Hemorrhage from the bowels occurred in two cases. A few cases had no diarrhœa and ran their course to a favorable termination without any alarming symptom and with but little treatment. There was in a large proportion of the cases a very sluggish state of the circulation,—the hands, feet and face presenting a purple-livid appearance which disappeared temporarily on pressure,—a condition which I have seldom seen to any considerable extent in private practice. I attribute it to the greater degree of constitutional depression arising from the peculiar circumstances under which our troops were placed. Our treatment was altogether expectant. After the disease was fully developed we gave nothing but that which seemed plainly indicated. We generally began with a few doses of quinine and opium; but these were discontinued after the disease was fully developed. I am not able to give a favorable opinion of the use of quinine in typhoid fever, although I have, both in private practice and in the army, given it a fair trial. It is often at first impossible to determine to what extent the case is influenced by malaria, and, consequently, to be on the safe side, it is well when doubt is entertained to begin with a few doses of quinine,—if remittent the case will be controlled, but if typhoid, my opinion is that no good will be effected. Acting on the view that it is a self-limited disease I do not attempt its arrest, but endeavor to enable the patient to live through its usual period of eighteen or twenty days. Hence our treatment was opium, tannin and acetate of lead for the diarrhœa, and stimulants with nutritious diet and scrupulous personal cleanliness for the general condition. Every case was well washed at the onset with tepid water and soap. When the fever was at its height the patient was sponged with cold water, which exercised a very salutary effect. Brandy was administered freely from the beginning. In a word, everything calculated to husband the resources of the system was employed. The patients were fed regularly whether they wanted to eat or not. Nitrate of potash was given in solution with some benefit. After all, I think that opium and brandy are the sheet-anchors. The bowels must be controlled and the patient stimulated; I consider him safe when the bowels are properly checked. I feel no uneasiness if they are not moved for three or four days; I have never seen any bad consequences follow their being checked suddenly. I have used turpentine in a few cases in which diarrhœa was obstinate; but this is more applicable to cases that are troubled with tympanites. I gave twenty drops every two hours, apparently with good results, for two or three days; but every case that had tympanites died. In one case tympanites disappeared for two or three days and reappeared before death. In a few cases I gave minute doses of calomel, but they did no good,—I think harm. We had no hospital and had to treat our men in quarters during the first six weeks. After this we had good hospital shelters and nearly all our cases did remarkably well except those that had been on hand for a considerable time.

Surgeon M. R. GAGE, *25th Wis., Columbus, Ky., March* 31, 1863.—Typhoid fever is very insidious in its approach. Many days or even weeks sometimes elapse, during which the patient feels not well nor yet sufficiently ill to give up or take to bed; he will be found more or less complaining, his aspect dull, stupid and anxious. On the occurrence of delirium he is either animated or lost in apathetic bewilderment. Often diarrhœa comes on early, accompanied with pain, tenderness and hardness of the abdomen, which sometimes becomes tympanitic. Usually as the disease progresses the diarrhœa keeps pace with it, and is, no doubt, the result of intestinal irritation, inflammation and ulceration. Epistaxis is frequently present and sometimes troublesome; at first it seems to give relief to the feeling of oppression about the head, but if continued is quite likely to become a source of debility, and needs watching lest, before we are aware, the patient be found succumbing to its depressing influence. Sometimes we observe upon the chest and abdomen the scattered eruption said to be characteristic of typhoid fever.

Surgeon JAS. V. KENDALL, *on the fevers in the camp of the* 149*th N. Y., in the winter of* 1863.—A large number of the cases at the camp at Aquia Creek commenced gradually, the patient scarcely recognizing that he was sick; slight derangement of the bowels; tongue nearly natural; eyes dull or yellow; urine in about one-half the cases nearly natural at first, though many had paid no attention to this; loss of appetite; slight rigor, after which there would be an aggravation of all the symptoms: Prostration great; urine high-colored and in some cases turbid; diarrhœa increased unless checked by anodynes or astringents; tongue red, afterwards dry; some tenderness of bowels and tympanites. Usually there has been no great difficulty in restraining the discharges, which in many cases were liquid and yellowish and in a few cases bloody; tenesmus was present, but seldom. In two there were large inflammatory swellings under the angle of the right jaw; these suppurated and required incision; one proved fatal and the other will probably terminate in the same manner. Three cases, after having been sick for three weeks, complained of severe pain and tenderness of the feet; in two of these the feet began to swell and became purple, as if sphacelation was threatening. By the use of warm applications the pain and swelling diminished and the feet are now but little discolored. But the worst cases have been taken down with much more violence, without derangement of the bowels: Perhaps the first report the surgeon would have of them would be that they were crazy in their tents. It is probable that they had been taken with a sudden congestion; but the fact could not be definitely ascertained. These cases ran their course rapidly to a fatal termination or to convalescence. Some continued wild till near the fatal ending and then became moderately comatose; these appeared like typhus cases, showing early vibices, sordes and a general implication of the nervous system, manifested by involuntary stools and micturition, but without any troublesome diarrhœa. In one case, that of Captain Wheeler, Company D, the patient came in from duty and was suddenly taken with spasms, becoming stupid and remaining so for several days. Gradually his intelligence returned, the febrile symptoms diminished, the urine, which had been thick with sediment, became clear; he had some appetite; his bowels were costive, but easily moved by aperients; in two weeks he was able to undertake the journey to Washington, and has since gone to his home at Syracuse.

Surgeon W. W. GRANGER, *Post hospital, Houston, Mo., Dec.* 31, 1862.—On the character, course or treatment of fevers as developed in this portion of the army I have nothing to add to my report of September 30 except in relation to typhoid fever, of which only a case or two had then fallen into my hands. The largely increased proportion of cases during the last quarter calls for an outline of the symptoms and treatment. The small, frequent pulse, dry skin, continuous but rarely intense pyrexia, narrow-pointed, dry, red-edged and glossy or cracked tongue, sometimes heavily at others slightly furred with shades varying from grayish-white to yellowish-brown or *rhubarb-colored* and even darker, with the sordes-coated teeth, are symptoms too constant to be overlooked. Those which point to the cerebral and epigastric regions are less constant in their occurrence as well as more variable in their character. Great and persisting wakefulness in some cases, which no prudent amount of opiate seems to overcome, is a frequent but by no means regular symptom. An equally unyielding lethargy prevails with as many more. Delirium and perfect clearness of intellect are equally distributed, whether among the comatose or the wakeful, and no greater fatality seems to attend one class of cerebral symptoms than the other. Nausea and emesis are occasional but not frequent symptoms. Tenderness on epigastric pressure is a frequent but by no means certain occurrence, and while some of the patients have diarrhœa in the course of the disease, as large a proportion, from first to last, require purgatives to procure alvine discharges every forty-eight hours, and not a few have regular evacuations throughout. The treatment has been in all cases tonic from the start, with terebinthinate, vinous or, in the absence of the latter, dilute alcoholic stimulants in the low stages, close attention to incidental or transient symptoms and a bland and easily digested diet. Anodynes (opiate when not contraindicated by cerebral symptoms) and diaphoretics have been employed as occasion demanded. Tepid and cold sponging have proved most efficient in soothing the disturbed brain and restoring healthy action to the skin. Mercurials I have rarely had occasion to use in this disease, but in one or two instances decided benefit followed the use of calomel and chalk in small doses for the purpose of exciting the secretions, especially the salivary. In no case has it been necessary to push the remedy to ptyalism or even to fetor of the breath. Quinine, turpentine and wine, cold or tepid sponging and cleanliness of person, bed and clothing, with well ventilated wards, have proved so reliable as curative agents that I have not yet lost a case of this disease.

Ass't Surg. CHARLES E. CADY, *138th Pa., Relay House, Md., Oct.* 31, 1862.—Many of our cases of typhoid fever were of a highly aggravated character. The invasion was frequently most rapid and prostrating. In several cases the men performed duty on the day before reporting themselves ill, and on the third or fourth day all the pathognomonic symptoms would be unmistakably present. Our mortality has been as low as is usual in private practice. The treatment adopted was that in use in the Pennsylvania hospital, Philadelphia: Good, full and easily digested diet; milk and brandy in punch; eggs; Dover's powder, castor oil, sinapisms, neutral mixture, etc.

Surgeon J. T. CALHOUN, *74th N. Y., Dec.* 31, 1861.—One of the patients while convalescing from typhoid fever very imprudently ate a quantity of peanuts and jelly; a fatal relapse ensued. This was the first death from disease that occurred in the regiment.

Surgeon J. B. POTTER, 30th Ohio, Fayetteville, April 2, 1862.—Our typhoid is not the disease so recognized by medical men in private practice, but a continued fever of a typhoid type, modified by change of habits and to a certain extent by climate. Many cases when first reported are delirious, with cold extremities, congestion of the superficial capillaries, free perspirations, rapid and feeble pulse, 120 to 160, and profuse watery diarrhœa. These terminate fatally in forty-eight to seventy-two hours. Such cases require quinia, carbonate of ammonia, brandy, etc., from the commencement.

Surgeon B. ROHRER, 10th Pa. Reserves, Camp Pierpont, Va., December, 1861.—We have had much less disease of malarial origin than was anticipated from our near location to the Potomac. Citizens long resident here say that they have had less ague in their families this season than for many years, and attribute the favorable change to the frequent heavy rains which flooded the streams and thereby removed the cause. Intermittents, with few exceptions, have been of the quotidian type and readily yielded to quinine; recurrences have been infrequent. Remittents have been somewhat peculiar in their character: Many have shown symptoms which are generally considered pathogno-monic of enteric fever, such as rose-colored spots and sudamina, and in consequence have been recorded as typhoid by several surgeons of adjoining regiments. I have been occupying the same apartment with the sick, giving them my whole attention, observing them closely both day and night, and have come to the conclusion that the fever is of malarial origin and of the bilious or remittent type. The grounds for this belief are: 1st. Absence of epistaxis, hemorrhage, obstinate diarrhœa, tympanites, deafness and stupor or delirium after the fifth day, the delirium being invariably an early symptom. 2d. The early convalescence of all and no new cases occurring after one or two heavy frosts. Nearly all when brought to the hospital were delirious, that being the first symptom to attract the atten-tion of their messmates, who thought them either drunk or crazy. In conversation they seemed rational enough, but when left to themselves they would give way to incoherent expressions or endeavor to make their escape. Several succeeded by stratagem in getting out of the hospital and ran to the quarters, half a mile distant, at night with bare feet over the frozen ground. The patients complained of being chilly, although their surface was warm to the touch and they were well covered and surrounded with bottles of hot water; the pulse varied from 100 to 120, the tongue was slightly coated and there was great thirst. This condition lasted from six to thirty hours. The cerebral disturbance in some instances continued two or three days, and as it abated and the patients became more rational they complained of pain in the head, tenderness upon pressure in the epigastrium and general aching and soreness. The skin was hot and dry; there was a tendency to diarrhœa, no matter how mild the purgative, and the evacuations were dark, at times almost black. After the third or fourth day the pulse became less frequent and the tongue dry, smooth, glossy and red or cracked; the tenderness over the epigastrium was aggravated, the urine scanty and high-colored and the eyes slightly tinged with yellow. From the sixth to the ninth day the rose-colored eruption and sudamina made their appearance, also a dry bronchial cough, and by the twelfth or fifteenth day, with one exception, they were sufficiently convalescent to move about the room. If delirious when brought into the hospital wet cups were applied to the back of the neck, and if these afforded no relief a blister was applied over the same place. A purgative of calomel was followed by castor oil, and in the morning from 4 to 10 o'clock, when I could discover a slight remission, from fifteen to forty grains of quinine were administered; during the day, at intervals of four hours, small doses of calomel and ipecacuanha were given. Turpentine was used when the tongue was dry and cracked. Milk diet was employed and barley-water used as a drink.

Surgeon DeWITT C. VAN SLYCK, 35th N. Y., Falls Church, Va., Oct. 20, 1861.—During the months of August and September more than five hundred cases of fever were treated; the duration of these was from four or five days to as many weeks. The first cases were intermitting in type, with a tendency to enteric disease. The fever soon after took on a remitting form and finally assumed a low typhoid grade, in many cases exceedingly malignant. The treat-ment consisted of a mild mercurial laxative, generally blue mass followed by large doses of quinine, and occasionally anodynes and sudorifics. From twenty to sixty grains of sulphate of quinine per day were administered, and if these doses did not entirely eradicate the disease within the first week they modified and reduced its malignancy and duration. No other method of treatment was effective. Mixed and complicated cases were treated according to the indications. During the last stage stimulants were given with manifest advantage. In nearly all the malignant cases sudamina and petechiæ covered the abdomen. From the abdominal tenderness and obstinate diarrhœa which these cases exhibited it was evident that the mucous follicles of the intestines were seriously involved; this condition was frequently protracted and greatly retarded convalescence. It is regretted that no opportunity was afforded for post-mortem examination in the two cases that proved fatal. Convalescence was slow, and in many cases relapse followed imprudence in diet and exercise.

Surgeon A. P. MAYLERT, U. S.V., General Field Hospital, Army of the Ohio, before Corinth, 1862.—The cases of disease treated in this hospital were very similar in character, yet were such as could scarcely be correctly named by any term in nosology. The patient was usually much emaciated, the skin of a light waxen or rather clay color; the pulse small, compressible, variable in character and quickened under the least exertion; the tongue thin and broad, moist, and, with the fauces, almost natural in color, or perhaps of a darker tint than in health; in many the gums were spongy and bled readily upon pressure. The skin was generally moist; there was seldom much fever. The appetite was somewhat capricious—usually no desire for food was manifested, but when fresh vegetables or fresh beef, suitably cooked, were offered they were evidently relished except in the graver cases. The alvine evacuations were more frequent than natural, thin, but otherwise healthy in appearance, except, perhaps, somewhat darker, and in some cases slightly tinged with blood; they were not often attended with pain. There was rarely tympanites, and usually but little tenderness on pressure. In many cases one or both parotid glands were extensively inflamed;

this occurred in the later stages of the disease and terminated occasionally in suppuration. Probably one-half of these were fatal. I know of nothing, in the cases which recovered, to distinguish them from those which terminated fatally except that perhaps in the former suppuration was earlier established. The functions of the brain and nervous system were often considerably impaired: In all cases the patient was languid, weak and disposed to be quiet and sleep as much as possible; there was almost total want of judgment, the memory was defective and the mind wandering; the delirium was always mild in character. In short, this disease was termed variously remittent fever, typhoid fever, diarrhœa, dysentery or scorbutus, according to the symptoms. In each case was a dyscrasia resulting chiefly, as I apprehend, from exposure and lack of suitable nourishment. *Post-mortem* examination usually showed a congested condition of the small intestine, seldom amounting to decided inflammation and rarely attended with ulceration. There was generally a dirty dark-red appearance of the mucous membrane, which was somewhat softened, being readily removed by rubbing with the back of the scalpel. Invaginations of the small intestine were frequently found but were never strangulated. The gall-bladder was often distended with bile. The ventricles of the brain and the pericardial sac contained a little serum than natural. Frequently a fibrinous clot was found in one or both ventricles of the heart, and sometimes this was so large as to distend the heart or at least keep it of normal size. No other abnormal appearances were constant except general emaciation and a flabby and atrophied condition of the muscular system. In many cases the blood appeared thin and uncoagulable in both arteries and veins. A few cases of sudden death showed a degree of pulmonary congestion, or even pulmonary apoplexy, evidently induced by heat exhaustion in patients already greatly reduced by blood-poisoning. The treatment consisted mainly in careful nursing with nourishing diet, where it could be given, and stimulants combined in some cases with quinia.

Surgeon J. B. JACKSON, *121st U. S. Colored Infantry, Maysville, Ky., February,* 1865.—Edward Gray, Taylor Phillips and Robert Nelson were brought to hospital about the same time in a state of collapse, with cold extremities, slow and weak pulse, a vacant stare and mental hallucinations; subsultus tendinum was present, especially on attempting to move. They loathed food and presented a scorbutic appearance. There seemed to be an engorgement of the whole system, particularly of the liver. They would not acknowledge themselves sick, and came to hospital by order of the company commander, who said he considered them nearly dead. Hepatic agents, counter-irritants, stimulants, tonics and anti-scorbutics were employed, without manifest effect except that in Taylor's case heavy bilious stools were procured; but there was no response on the part of the nervous or circulatory system. The patients, if allowed, would rise and walk almost to the hour of their death.* Gray died on the second day after entering hospital and Phillips on the fourth; Nelson lived some days longer: Diarrhœa set in about the sixth day, the most simple diet passing unchanged; injections were tried but none were retained. He continued with little change of mind or body, except emaciation, until death.

These men had been in camp about three weeks. They came from the rural districts and had been accustomed to fresh air and mixed diet. When they joined the weather was intensely cold at night. They were shut up in their tents filled with coal-dust and smoke, and of course lived on the soldier's ration. They suffered severely; subsequently they were removed to a large building, well lighted but with a low ceiling and only one stove. The intensely cold weather made it necessary to partition off a room about 25 by 30 feet, where for about ten days fifty or sixty men were crowded together day and night. During this state of things these three cases were developed, and all cases of measles, fever, diarrhœa, etc., from that company assumed a malignant type and inclined to typhoid or scurvy. The commanding officer was made aware of this, and as soon as possible had his quarters expanded, drilled his men every day in the open air and furnished them with plenty of mixed diet. In little over two weeks all diseases became more amenable to treatment.

Extract from the records of the Chimborazo Hospital, Richmond, Va.—The typhoid fevers observed during the winter 1863–64 have been generally prolonged, but less so as spring approached. There has been almost uniformly a loose state of the bowels, the characteristic thin stools, but less offensive than is usual when turpentine and chlorate of potash, which are the routine here, are not employed. Few have exhibited much abdominal tenderness,

---

* EDWARD BATWELL, Surgeon 14th Mich. Vet. Inf., in an account of a fever that prevailed at Camp Big Springs, Miss., in June, 1862, published in Vol. XIII, *Med. and Surg. Reporter*, Phila., 1865, p. 364 *et seq.*, reports that after the evacuation of Corinth, and during the movement of the pursuing army towards Boonsville, intense heat succeeded to a copious rainfall, during which the soldiers were exposed without tents or sufficient clothing, having left these behind in the camps at Farmington. As there was a dearth of pure water, the stagnant contents of pools were drunk by men and mules alike, the strong sulphuretted water of the artesian wells being used only in urgent necessity. At this time chills and fever appeared among the troops, the febrile action finally becoming continued and of a low type. After falling back to Big Springs an anomalous fever invaded the army. It commenced with malaise; the skin was cool, the tongue moist and natural, the pulse never above 90 and the urinary and alvine secretions regular. There was "no chill, no fever, nothing to indicate anything wrong; the appetite, if anything, was increased; no want of sleep was complained of, nor did a single symptom present itself indicative of diseased action. Despite all this there was a look about your patient, an expression of countenance that firmly convinced you that it was not a case of malingering you had to treat. This condition lasted for some days, when restlessness and a tendency to delirium supervened." There was an irresistible propensity to walk about; nothing but force could keep the patient from leaving his bed, and this peculiarity became more marked as the case approached a fatal termination. From the commencement of the complaint there was a rapid loss of flesh and the pulse became languid and feeble. Restlessness lasted from about the twelfth to the twentieth day, after which there was less disposition to begin walking, but the patient would move over a greater distance. After one of these walks he would express himself as feeling better, go to bed and die in a few minutes. There occurred eighteen of these fatal cases in the regiment, all varying but little in their symptoms. The mortality was also great in other regiments, some of the sick dying on their way to general hospital. The disease was called typhoid fever by army surgeons, but BATWELL says that he "failed to trace a single point of similarity of the symptoms." A local practitioner of whom he made inquiries described the disease accurately, calling it the *walking fever*, and saying "it was peculiar to that section of Mississippi, and that change of location alone exercised any influence over it; that strangers were more especially attacked, and it generally proved fatal." Little benefit was derived from treatment, which, from the absence of anything that might have been considered a positive indication, was "entirely expectant or rather empirical." Quinine, stimulants, counter-irritants, alteratives were resorted to as trial remedies. "*Post-mortem* examinations were made but they failed to develop any lesion; all the internal organs seemed of a healthy character and nothing indicated diseased action."

some none at all. Sub-delirium has been frequent; violent delirium has never occurred. Maculæ have been absent. The gastric type has been rare; few have complained of irritation induced by turpentine, which is given in emulsion in ten-drop doses. Neither cupping nor purging has been employed. In some cases calomel, ipecacuanha and opium have been given, seldom with appreciable benefit. The stimulant method, with whiskey or brandy toddy, egg-nog and animal broths has been employed from the first in nearly all cases, and continued to convalescence. The intervals between the evening and morning meals have been too long for some patients, and it is to be noted that no soups or food other than dry bread is usually kept over night in the wards. It is desirable that attention should be directed to this point and that the intervals of nourishment as well as of stimulation should be distinctly described. Bronchial irritation has been common as a complication and pneumonia not rare. The hospital pharmacy is deficient or has been so in pectoral remedies. Cough mixture often lacked some of its intended elements and afforded but slight palliation. The balsam tar-water, sanguinaria and asclepias tuberosa would form important additions to the pectoral budget. Some cases presented, without violent delirium, the most intense irritation of the nervous centres—continual twitching of features, muscles, etc., and working out of bed and throwing off the bed-clothes. The resources of the hospital in the way of antispasmodics are deplorably limited.

Remarks on the Sequelæ of Chickahominy Fever, Act. Ass't Surg. J. M. Da Costa, *U. S. A., Dec. 31, 1862.*—Among the soldiers returning from the Peninsular campaign a form of fever was observed marked by features of uncommon character. It is not my purpose to attempt a description of this malady, but rather to speak of the morbid states met with after the fever proper has left, and which may therefore be regarded as its consequences or sequelæ; nor can I say that my delineation will include all the possible results of this grave disease. Others may have encountered other issues. I can do no more than sketch what I have seen and endeavor to reproduce those outlines which I believe to be most significant, and which have become familiar to me from personal observation; and first of the—

General appearance.—A striking sign left by the fever is great emaciation. The patient rises from his sick bed the shadow of his former self. In some cases the loss of flesh is so excessive that the muscles of the body appear literally to have been absorbed. The hair falls out in quantities and the whole appearance is that of a person hopelessly reduced; yet, unless diarrhœa be present, the flesh is, under generous diet, rapidly regained. Nay, I have seen individuals soon acquire more than they had lost by the attack of fever. The countenance, produced in part by emaciation and in part by a peculiar hue, is strongly characteristic. No disease has a more remarkable physiognomy. The eye is not heavy nor remarkably languid; the conjunctiva is clear or injected, never yellowish, thus forming a marked contrast with the pallid and yellowish color of the face. The peculiar look may last for a month.

Debility.—Both body and mind remain for a considerable period enfeebled. The weakness of the former shows itself in an inability to bear exercise or undergo fatigue of any kind, whilst the debilitated state of the latter is plainly seen in the loss of memory so constantly complained of. The exhaustion of strength is at times so great that the patient who for a week or two has been able to leave his bed is found to be again losing ground and lapses into a typhoid state in which he perishes:

P. Purcell, 49th N. Y.; age 45; was admitted August 7 from Harrison's Landing. He was just recovering from the fever and was much exhausted by his journey from the James River. After a few days careful nursing he rallied and was soon able to walk about. He continued to gain slowly until the 20th, yet was easily fatigued, and, though craving alcoholic stimulants, was unwilling to eat much. From this time, without any assignable cause, he lost strength daily, and by the 30th was confined to bed. All appetite was gone and it was with the greatest difficulty that he could be persuaded to take any nourishment whatever. He commenced to vomit green matter; his eyes were injected, pulse feeble and skin cool. His stools were at times liquid, at times natural and not of unusual frequency. On September 4 the irritability of the stomach had to a great degree subsided; but a violent diarrhœa set in attended with severe pain and uncontrolled by opiates and astringents. On the 8th he died in a state of utter exhaustion, yet retaining his senses almost to the last. *Post-mortem* examination: Extreme emaciation. Both lungs with old pleuritic adhesions, but the organs themselves healthy. Heart flabby; right ventricle contained a small clot. Spleen lake-red in section. Liver somewhat enlarged and fatty. Stomach and intestines distended with air. Inflammation in patches in the ileum; its glands healthy. Inflammation of cæcum and sigmoid flexure, a less degree in rectum and a feeble degree in ascending and descending colon; there were also a number of small ulcers about the size of a pea in the sigmoid flexure and rectum. Solitary glands with black deposit but otherwise healthy. Kidneys normal.

In looking over the history of this case the question suggests itself, was not this rather a relapse of the original malady? The absence of fever, of cerebral disturbance and the *post-mortem* evidence seem to disprove such an idea. The man's death was, I think, produced by progressive exhaustion, and hastened by an attack of colitis which his enfeebled frame was unable to withstand. In one other case the same result took place, except that there was little or no preceding diarrhœa. Another case recovered, the irritability of the stomach yielding to mercurial purges and repeated doses of dilute sulphuric acid.

Changes in the blood.—In a large number of cases the blood is profoundly altered. The clinical evidence of this is found in the pale look of the tongue, the pallid face, the blood murmurs and the spots that appear on the skin. These spots are like those of purpura; they do not disappear on pressure. Sometimes they are isolated, at others confluent, giving a purple or dark-bluish look to large patches of skin. In the following case this appearance was very marked:

Thomas Rose, 49th Pa.; age 20; was attacked with diarrhœa while on duty on the Chickahominy. This, after the lapse of a month, was followed by fever attended with great prostration and mental wandering. In this condition he came under my care on August 7. He was stimulated and carefully nourished, and by the 14th the fever had subsided, the diarrhœa remaining.· This was treated with pills consisting of the sulphates of morphia and iron, for which, on the 27th, tannic acid was substituted with the happiest effects. From September 1 loose-ness of the bowels ceased to be a prominent symptom. About this time dark-bluish spots were noticed on his chest, unchanged by pressure and of varying size. Soon afterwards they made their appearance on the abdomen and then on the extremities. On the trunk places of a foot in diameter could be found on which no healthy skin could be seen, nothing but dark spots on a variously tinted purple back ground. The gums were firm and healthy-looking, the tongue clean, the abdomen flat, certainly not distended, the skin cool, pulse feeble and 102 per minute. There was very great emaciation and debility and occasionally sore throat; the voice was husky and rarely raised above a whisper. The bowels were on the whole regular, one or two watery passages occurring daily. The patient remained much in this condition until his death, neither the mineral acids, the salts of iron nor a liberal and varied diet checking the spread of the purpurous spots. *Post-mortem* examination: Body considerably emaciated and every-where ecchymosed. Lungs normal. Heart healthy; a white clot in the right ventricle extending into the pulmonary artery, another in the left auricle and a third in the commencement of the aorta. Spleen, liver, kidneys, supra-renal bodies and pancreas natural. Stomach with inflammation of the mucous membrane more or less diffused, mingled with small patches of greater intensity. Inflammation in patches of the mucous membrane of the ileum, increasing in intensity towards the termination; solitary glands enlarged, inflamed and containing black matter; agminated glands with black deposit but otherwise apparently healthy. Colon distended with air, except descend-ing portion, which was narrowly contracted and not inflamed; cæcum, ascending and transverse colon inflamed; solitary glands conspicuous and containing black matter.

Unfortunately no chemical examination was made of the blood in this case—one of a series, including many lighter ones, which have been confounded with typhus fever. But the difference is palpable in spite of the simi-larity of the eruption to that of some of the stages of typhus,—there is an utter absence of the high fever, the cere-bral symptoms, the physiognomy and the early cutaneous rash which mark that disease.

Cardiac disorders.—The wards of all the hospitals are crowded with men complaining of a disease of the heart. What the nature of it commonly is let the following cases answer:

J. B. Waters, corporal, Co. A, 2d N. Y.; age 24; was admitted August 10 from Harrison's Landing, where he had been sick with fever since July 11. The disease was preceded by dysentery. The febrile symptoms subsided within a week after his admission, but the man remained prostrate and was unable to sit up until the last week in August. During this slow convalescence he suffered much from flatulence and was troubled with palpitation and a feeling of uneasiness in the cardiac region. An examination of the heart showed increased action without increased percussion dulness. The second sound was very distinct; the first was replaced by a soft systolic murmur marked at the base but also extending towards the apex. This state of things continued until December, the blowing sound becoming gradually fainter and only being distinctly heard after exercise. The patient is now, the 12th, in good general health, and does not suffer unless he walks much, when his breathing becomes oppressed; the respirations are still quick, thirty a minute, and he cannot sleep on his left side; an examination of the heart shows the trans-verse percussion dulness to be three and three-quarter inches, the longitudinal three and a half inches; the impulse remains forcible and is felt in two intercostal spaces; the second sound is very distinct, but the first dull; a slight hum is yet heard in the cervical veins. The treatment comprised the administration of quinine, iron and strychnia, replaced by veratrum viride when the heart's action was violent; the cardiac uneasiness was much relieved by a belladonna plaster worn over the heart. This case is typical. The appearance of the heart trouble after the fever, its long continuance, the systolic blowing sound and its gradual disappearance, the irritable state of the organ remaining long after the general health was in every other respect fully reëstablished, all form a clinical combina-tion of very great interest and frequency. Many such patients are thought to have hypertrophy and valvular dis-ease, but although here and there a case of doubtful diagnosis may occur, it is generally not difficult to distinguish between these cardiac maladies. The previous history, the absence of increased percussion dulness, the temporary duration of the blowing sound are just the opposite from the visibly augmented size of the heart and the perma-nent murmur of valvular disease. Then, too, the character and site of the murmur are peculiar: It is never rough, always attends the impulse and is very often associated with a hum in the jugular veins. It is plainest at or near midsternum and is thence transmitted in the course of the aorta or pulmonary artery; it is rarely distinct over the apex of the heart. It is frequent, but it would be a mistake to suppose it invariably present in the class of cases just described. Very often the first sound of the heart is dull, short, ill defined and unattended with a murmur; the second sound I have invariably observed to be clear and sharp. In some patients the impulse is very irregular and the cardiac rhythm much changed.

John Bricker, 8th Pa. Cav.; age 24; was taken sick at Fair Oaks Station, June 7, with severe diarrhœa accom-panied with excessive griping pains and followed by the discharge of considerable blood. About the 21st he was seized with fever commencing with rigors, pain on the left side of the chest and in the loins. He noticed that any attempt to stand brought on dimness of sight and dizziness, and also that his tongue was very dark, loaded and dry. About the 29th, while the fever still existed, he was moved to Harrison's Landing, then to Fortress Monroe and thence to this hospital, where he arrived July 7. On his arrival he had little or no fever, but the diarrhœa was still bad, from five to six passages daily, not, however, containing blood. He stated that he had expectorated blood once or twice shortly before he was sent here, and that before the attack of fever he had been in good health. Shortly after his admission he had a slight hemorrhage and complained much of pain in his left breast, which he described as constant, of a sharp cutting character, not increased in intensity by any circumstance he noted, and reaching at times from the lower ribs up to the third or fourth. As soon as he commenced to walk about he observed palpitation of the heart; the action of the organ was very irregular and attended with a blowing sound. He improved much under treatment, and now has a very good appetite and enjoys his food. The diarrhœa has disappeared and he has nearly regained his strength; but any excitement or labor agitates him and brings on violent beating of the heart. Percussion gives him pain; it shows, if performed with care, the transverse diameter to be slightly increased. The apex strikes at its normal position, but the impulse communicated to the finger is every now and then of a throbbing character, extended and intermitting. On auscultation the first sound is dull and a murmur of low pitch is perceived with the systole following the marked intermission; a blowing sound is at the same time heard in the carotid; there is also a continuous hum in the cervical veins. The pulse is about 90, intermitting every third to seventh beat. It is very likely that here the walls of the heart have undergone some change, and that the lack of tone may lead, if it has not already led, to a dilatation of the ventricles. That organic changes may indeed be produced by the unvaried abnormal action I have no doubt. I have seen such cases. One was for months under my observation in the hospital, the signs of dilated hypertrophy developing themselves more and more clearly. If it, then, be possible for organic disease to follow long-continued functional disturbance, the very grave question arises whether men convalescing from fever, with the state of the heart described, are fit for further service. I think not; certainly not when this condition of the organ outlasts a marked improvement in the general health. Amendment is slow, and for perfect recovery to take place long rest of body is essential. Active exercise would be the means most likely to lead to organic disease. The medical treatment which I have found best suited to the class of cases under discussion consists in the administration of iron and nux vomica; to this belladonna, both externally and internally, may be added with advantage, especially if there be much pain in the cardiac region. When the heart's action is very violent I have lowered it by veratrum viride, temporarily suspending the tonic medication, or sometimes employing both agents conjointly.

Phlegmasia alba dolens.—Two cases of this strange morbid condition have come under my notice. Both occurred during convalescence from the fever, and in both recovery took place. In the first the tense smooth swelling occupied the whole thigh of the left side, especially the upper and inner part. It was particularly hard in the course of the saphena vein, which seemed enlarged. A blister was applied over the course of the vein and the swollen thigh kept constantly swathed in lead-water and laudanum. The tumefaction subsided very gradually and did not disappear entirely for several months. In the second case there was much pain along the course of the femoral vein and in the calf of the right leg, which was much increased in size for four or five days, sensitive to the touch, œdematous and partially paralyzed. After that it slowly resumed its natural appearance, but the man does not even now walk without lameness.

Inflammation of the parotid gland tending to suppuration is occasionally encountered in this fever. Of four cases that came under my notice three recovered, one proved fatal. In one of those having a favorable termination both glands became seriously affected. Here the disorder appeared before the febrile signs had left. In the following case the inflammation set in after the commencement of convalescence:

Jacob Risley, Co. F, 6th Pa. Cav., was seized with fever and diarrhœa about July 11 at Harrison's Landing. When admitted into this hospital on August 7 he was very prostrate and suffered much from diarrhœa, but had little or no fever. He soon commenced to improve and after a few days was able to sit up. On the 16th a tumor was observed at the angle of the jaw attended with much pain. It soon increased and appeared to involve the whole right side of the face. It was moderately tender on pressure, not accompanied by much external redness and unassociated with any signs of inflammation of the tonsils or throat. An effort was made to produce resolution by painting with iodine, but it did not succeed. An indistinct fluctuation soon showed that suppuration had taken place. The abscess pointed at the angle of the jaw and was opened, discharging a teacupful of offensive matter. The discharge continued six weeks; the cut then healed, but to this day the patient frequently complains of pain in the region of the duct, which can be felt, hard and round, just below the malar bones. Otherwise he is now in perfect health. The diarrhœa yielded, before the discharge ceased, to the use of sulphates of copper, iron and morphia.

Diarrhœa.—This is one of the most frequent and at the same time one of the gravest sequels of the fever. Indeed, hardly a case of Chickahominy fever recovers without great irritability of the bowels remaining for months afterwards, and under unfavorable circumstances this irritability lapses into uncontrollable diarrhœa. The relation the diarrhœa bears to the fever is very close. It generally precedes it, sometimes by weeks, is a prominent symptom throughout its course and outlasts it. It rarely if ever occurs where it has not been present during the fever. In describing its characteristic traits I shall draw rather from a group of cases that I have noted than give the history of any one in particular: The man who is the subject of the disease convalesces from the fever very slowly. He takes but little nourishment, since if he eats much frequent stools are the result; yet he has scarcely any gastric disturbance, does not vomit, does not loathe food; his tongue is moist and clean. The abdomen is distended with gas, the seat of a dull pain but not painful on pressure. If asked what troubles him most, he generally refers to the flatulency, points to the inability to button his clothes, and may often be heard to declare that he is less annoyed when he has many passages than when they are checked, since in their absence he becomes bloated. His features are pale; his eyes clear; he does not bear fatigue well, though on the whole it is often a matter of wonder that the countenance is so healthy-looking and his strength not more impaired than it is. He may remain in this condition for weeks, either slowly gaining or on the other hand slowly losing ground. In the former case he is liable to the diarrhœa, which has been checked, breaking out from time to time; in the latter he becomes much emaciated, and dies utterly worn out after months of suffering. Among the symptoms mentioned the state of the tongue and gums, the stools and the abdominal pains require a more extended notice. The *tongue* is smooth and moist, sometimes very pale, but almost always clean; only in a few cases is it observed to be coated. The *gums* are generally hard; now and then, probably from antecedent scurvy, they are spongy and red, but this condition is not nearly so frequent as the former, nor can I say that I have found where it existed any difference in the other symptoms,—the diarrhœa did not seem to me either to yield more readily or to be more intractable. The *stools* are always thin and remain so long after they are reduced in frequency. In color they are mostly yellowish, sometimes greenish, rarely dark or very offensive. In not more than one case in fifty do they contain blood. They are frequent, varying from five to twenty or upwards in the twenty-four hours. The passages are not attended with much pain or tenesmus, still there are numerous exceptions to this rule, and then hemorrhoids seem to result from the constant bearing down. *Abdominal pain* is often complained of by the patient. It is, perhaps, a sense of soreness and uneasiness more than of pain, increased from time to time by exacerbations of colic. It is not as a rule augmented by pressure, and this absence of tenderness is very remarkable. When any tender spots exist they are generally discovered in the course of the large intestine. Some few speak of a weighty feeling in the region of the spleen, which organ, on percussion, is found to be increased; yet enlargement of the spleen, contrary to expectation, is not a frequent sequel of the fever. In some cases the urinary organs are deranged: There is a constant disposition to pass water, which becomes a source of great annoyance to the patient. The urine voided is copious and pale, of low specific gravity and contains neither sugar nor albumen. The diagnosis of the diarrhœa is very easy. There is only one complaint with which it may be confounded—dropsy; but careful percussion soon shows that the distention is owing to wind and not to liquid. Dropsy is, indeed, very rarely met with after Chickahominy fever; I have encountered but one instance of the kind, and there it was associated with albumen in the urine. The *post-mortem* appearances are, as far as I have been able to pursue the matter, the same as in the Chickahominy diarrhœa without preceding fever. There is an absence, for the most part, of ulceration or thickening of the mucous membrane, accounting thus for the want of tenderness. There are patches of inflammation near the ileo-cæcal valve, in the colon and sometimes throughout the ileum. The agminated glands are prominent and contain blackish pigment, and so do the solitary glands. The exciting cause of these curious morbid changes is veiled in obscurity. This much, however, appears. There must be in the poison giving rise to the fever something capable at the same time of producing the diarrhœa,—in other words, the same cause may occasion both. The treatment of the diarrhœa consequent upon the fever is the same as that of the diarrhœa without antecedent fever. Both are alike obstinate and difficult to influence. In both all medicines often fail. The best results have in my hands been derived from carefully regulating the diet and administering large doses of tannic acid conjoined with opium, five grains of the former with from one-fourth to one-third of the latter, in pill, four times daily. The medicine can be borne for weeks at a time without nauseating. The subnitrate of bismuth, the sulphate of copper and the nitrate of silver stand next in efficacy, and sometimes succeed where tannic acid fails, The pernitrate of iron, given in from fifteen to thirty-drop doses three times a day, is occasionally of service; but on the whole it has disappointed me. Opium alone does not answer, although useful when joined to other agents. Opium suppositories or enemata give the patient rest at night and are thus of benefit. The tinctures or infusions of catechu and kino only act advantageously in light cases. From acetate of lead, tincture of the chloride of iron, turpentine, the mineral acids, Hope's mixture, quinia, strychnia, saline purgatives and Dover's powder I have seen little or no good effect, although I have given each of them a fair trial. Carminatives exert only a temporary influence on the flatulency. In one case both this troublesome symptom and the diarrhœa yielded to charcoal. Diarrhœa is the last of the issues of Chickahominy fever I shall notice. A few of the less prominent, such as pain in the limbs, the occasional occurrence of tympanites without diarrhœa, I shall merely indicate without specially describing. In taking a survey of the symptoms thus strung together the similarity to those encountered during protracted convalescence from typhoid fever becomes at once apparent, but the dissimilarity is also manifest. Where, for instance, are the pulmonary troubles so common in the latter complaint? Any further discussion is, however, here out of place.

To ascertain whether Chickahominy fever be modified typhoid fever or a distinct disease would require further data and other trains of reasoning than are here admissible. Let, then, this report be accepted as an unbiased clinical contribution to the history of one of the most interesting but unfortunately most destructive forms of fever that this generation of physicians has been called upon to study.

V.—TYPHUS FEVER.

There seems no doubt that occasional cases of typhus fever were treated in the general hospitals during the war, but it is probable that in most of these the disease was due to civic and not to military contagion. We have the high authority of Dr. AUSTIN FLINT for two of the cases, 7 and 8,* that have been submitted, in one of which it is explicitly stated that the fever was contracted while the soldier was at his home in New York City. Cases 5 and 6, treated at the same time in the Cuyler hospital, Philadelphia, Pa., the subject in one instance being a contract nurse, and in the other a patient who had been in hospital for nearly three months with a rheumatic affection, appear also to have been true typhus; and in this connection 389 of the *post-mortem* series may be referred to, as presented by the records of the same hospital, showing restless delirium alternating with comatose quiet, suppression of urine, petechiæ and death on the fourth day with no abnormal condition of the intestines. Case 1, which occurred in a patient recovering from gunshot injury in the hospital at Annapolis, Md., was probably typhus, as the clinical record is supported by the possibility of contact with true typhus then recognized as present in one of the wards. Case 9, in the Lexington avenue hospital, New York City, may also have been typhus, but in 10, from the records of the same hospital, the evidence is insufficient to show that the soldier contracted this fever at Sandy Hook, Md., or in camp prior to the date of his shipment from that point.

In fact the records do not furnish a single instance of undoubted typhus as having occurred among our troops in the field. In cases 12 and 13 there is nothing to substantiate the diagnosis. In 11 the disappearance of the eruption under pressure, the diarrhœa, tympanites, epistaxis and bronchitis suggest typhoid rather than typhus fever. In 3 and 4, both received about the same time from the 119th Ill. regiment at Quincy, Ill., the presumption is in favor of typhoid · in the former a recrudescence is recorded, with death from the gravity of the intestinal lesions, hastened by exhaustion from copious hemorrhages; in the latter a history of typhoid with violent cerebral symptoms, diarrhœa at first but not in the later stages, perspirations, red spots on the body and face on the sixteenth day, and death on the twenty-second. In 2, which may have been typhus, the patient was a hospital inmate convalescing from measles; his face was suffused and spotted, and death occurred on the thirteenth day, but the other symptoms were such as were frequently found in doubtful typhoid cases.

Moreover, the experience of other armies shows definitely that if the contagion of typhus had gained access to our camps, no search of the records of individual cases would have been required to substantiate the fact. The death-roll of our medical officers and hospital nurses would have been a sufficient demonstration.*

Undoubtedly there occurred in our camps a number of febrile cases presenting duskiness of skin, intense cerebral symptoms, dark-colored spots and petechiæ on the chest, abdomen and even on the face, unaccompanied with well defined symptoms of an enteric lesion. It is not surprising that such cases were regarded as typhus by some of our medical officers, for in an epidemic of typhus fever they would certainly have been ascribed to the epidemic cause, and even occurring as they did in isolated cases, their generally rapid and fatal course was sufficiently striking to warrant those who saw them for the first time in fearing that they had before them something dangerously different from the familiar typhoid. But as a larger experience demonstrated the comparative non-contagiousness of these cases, and *post-mortem* examination showed in them the characteristic lesions of typhoid, they became less

---

* See, for instance, Félix Jacquot—*Du Typhus de l'Armée d'Orient*, Paris, 1858, p. 56 et seq.—The two typhus epidemics in the Crimea began with the first hard frosts of December, 1854, and December, 1855. Originating in both years in the Crimea, the disease showed itself in the distant hospitals one month after its outbreak among the troops in the field. These hospitals became in their turn active foci whence the fever was propagated by contagion, and where probably, according to M. Jacquot, it also originated in some instances, in view of the concourse of so many individuals reduced by exhaustion and privation and affected by scurvy and other diseases. The English troops were the first to become infected, but in a little time the French army commenced likewise to suffer. The condition of the latter, though relatively better than that of the English, who became engaged in a great continental war without being prepared for it, was nevertheless far from satisfactory. The Russians, according to Drs. Mœring and Alferief, were tainted with typhus even before the allied armies showed any sign of it. The Russian and Turkish troops in Asia equally fell a prey to it. In a word, typhus was developed wherever were found aggregations of men exposed to fatigue and anxieties, badly quartered, poorly clad, and whose nourishment was not of such a nature as to counteract these hygienic drawbacks. About a month after its development in the Crimea it broke out in all the French hospitals in Constantinople, as also in the English hospital at Scutari. * * * In December, 1855, the English, who in the meantime had completely modified their system and reformed their administration, who were better located and quartered, better clothed and fed, less fatigued and exempt from scurvy, which prevailed fearfully in the French army, escaped visitation from typhus, while the latter suffered from it to a far greater extent than in the previous year. The Italians were a little less affected than the French. In January, 1856, typhus was imported into Constantinople; but the English hospital at Scutari escaped, as did their troops in the Crimea. All the French hospitals were invaded, those situated on the plateau extending from Ramis-Chiflick to Daoud-Pacha and the Candilié hospital on the Bosphorus. There were, including extemporized establishments, twenty hospitals in and around Constantinople, and not one of them escaped. The disease appeared also in the hospitals at Gallipolis and Nagara on the Dardanelles. The crews of merchant and government vessels engaged in the transport of sick and wounded were decimated. Typhus was introduced into the hospitals at Marseilles, Toulon, Porquerolles, Frioul, Avignon and into the Val-de-Grâce in Paris; and isolated cases died in many localities, as at Chalon-sur-Saône, Neufchateau, etc. Fortunately, in Constantinople as well as in France, the disease did not spread outside of the hospitals; but in besieged cities or overcrowded places where troops were quartered in barracks side by side with the population, as for instance in the village of Tchistinakaia near Simféropol, the civil population was more or less affected. In Russia it passed from the Crimea to Odessa, Nicolaïeff and several other localities; Varna, occupied by the French, was likewise affected, and finally the Turkish and Russian armies in Asia Minor paid a heavy tribute to this fever.

frequently reported as typhus. The clinical features of idiopathic febrile affections are not circumscribed but confluent. It has already been shown in this volume that it was not possible in all cases to determine from the symptoms alone that a fever was malarial or typhoid. So in cotemporaneous epidemics of typhus and typhoid, it is not possible in all cases for the clinician to distinguish between them.* Even in typhoid epidemics the practitioner is sometimes at first uncertain in his diagnosis.† The disease in its onset seizing those who have the strongest predisposition, may run a quickly fatal course in individual cases, leaving to future cases or *post-mortem* inquiries the determination of the specific form of fever. The first case may be considered typhus, but when the typhoid nature of the epidemic has been established, other such cases occurring thereafter receive a proper recognition. Again, in malarious districts fulminant febrile cases with cerebral symptoms terminating speedily in death by coma and attended with cutaneous hemorrhagic blotches were, when first seen, regarded doubtfully as typhus, cerebro-spinal meningitis or congestive malarial fevers, until a larger experience showed their etiological relations with malaria rather than with other specific causes of disease. Thus are explained the typhus cases reported by our medical officers in the field during the war. The relatively large number during the first year, 2.84 per thousand of strength, decreased during the second year to 1.44, and continued to decrease to .52, .51 and .30 respectively during the third, fourth and fifth years covered by our statistics, as these fulminant cases were found to lack the contagiousness of true typhus and to be associated, from the etiological point of view, with the typhoid and typho-malarial cases which were prevailing in our camps.‡

Thus, Surgeon ZENAS E. BLISS, U. S. Vols., noted a fatal case of typhus in his command while at Yorktown, the patient dying with superficial ecchymotic blotches and hemorrhages from the nose and bowels; no *post-mortem* examination was held in this instance, but at the same time about forty cases of typhoid fever were under treatment, and in such of these as proved fatal the patches of Peyer were found to be ulcerated.§ Brigade Surgeon J. H. WARREN and Medical Inspector PETER PINEO, U. S. A., reported early in the war the presence of typhus fever in the camps near Washington, D. C. About the same time Surgeon BARR, 36th Ohio, recorded the assumption of a typhus character by fevers prevailing at Summerville, West Va., and Surgeon IRISH, 77th Pa., and Act. Ass't Surg. O. K. REYNOLDS, U. S. A., 15th U. S. Inf., reported similar cases from Camp Wood, Mumfordsville, Ky. At a later date fulminant typhoid among undisciplined recruits at New Albany, Ind., gave rise

---

* Thus a certain number of the cases forming the basis of FLINT's *Clinical Reports on Continued Fevers*, Buffalo, 1852, were reported as *doubtful;* his cases numbered 164, and of these 73 were undoubted cases of typhoid and 65 equally undoubted cases of typhus, but 26 were cases in which the diagnosis as between typhus and typhoid was not positively determined. The official *Medical and Surgical History of the British Army which served in Turkey and the Crimea during the war against Russia in the years 1854-55-56*, London, 1858, does not attempt to differentiate between the malarial and typhoid fevers which prevailed among the troops while operating in Bulgaria, nor between the typhoid and typhus which scourged them during the winter of 1854-55 in the Crimea; but Dr. ROBERT D. LYONS, in his *Report on the Pathology of the Diseases of the Army in the East*, London, 1856, shows that at the time of his visit to the hospitals and camps both typhus and typhoid were prevailing, the latter, however, being the prominent disease. He reached Scutari towards the close of April, 1855, when all but the expiring embers of the terrible epidemic of the previous winter had disappeared. Again, SCRIVE, in his *Relation Médico Chirurgicale de la Campagne d' Orient*, Paris, 1857, describes, p. 418, a *typhus à forme typhoïde.*

† It is at the outbreak of an epidemic that the severest attacks manifest themselves. The first two cases observed at Lyons by M. DUSSOURT differed entirely from the stereotyped typhoid fever. They were consequently considered typhus cases, especially on account of the rapidity of their fatal termination and the absence of intestinal lesions. There existed, no doubt, a co-relation between these two facts, the absence of lesions being due to the shortness of the malady, for in all other autopsies made during the same epidemic, MM. MARMY and ALIX found the usual changes consequent upon typhoid fever. See LÉON COLIN, *De la Fièvre Typhoïde dans l'Armée*, Paris, 1878, p. 18.

‡ JAMES BRYAN, Brigade Surgeon, Burnside's Expedition, New Berne, N. C., *Boston Med. and Surg. Jour.*, Vol. LXV, 1862, p. 394, says, in some observations on the diseases of the army in the Department of North Carolina, that typhus fever was not unfrequently observed, and was in some cases of great malignity, a character which was more particularly noticed in young fleshy subjects. In one such case the patient was brought into the hospital in an insensible condition, with the cellular tissue of the neck filled with air and serum and the legs and feet purple. But we have already seen the pernicious character of the malarial fevers of this military department. On the other hand J. J. LEVICK, in an article on *Miasmatic Typhoid Fever*, *American Jour. Med. Sciences*, Vol. XLVII, 1864, p. 404, when referring to the aggravated character of the cases that arrived at the Pennsylvania hospital from the Army of the Potomac in the autumn of 1862, says that in no case was the true typhus fever-rash observed, nor a single instance in which the disease was known to have been communicated to another, notwithstanding that many cases were much like typhus.

§ Appendix to Part First of this work, p. 85.

to a report of typhus or spotted fever. In 1863 Ass't Surg. WARREN WEBSTER, U. S. A., who had seen European typhus in Boston Harbor from 1853 to 1860, became alarmed at the presence in the 12th Army Corps of some cases which appeared to present all the clinical features of true typhus, and in his report to the Medical Director of the Army the utmost care was enjoined for the protection of the troops against the contagion of this deadly disease. A month later Dr. WEBSTER was called upon to investigate some cases reported from the 11th Army Corps, but etiological considerations were opposed to the recognition of these as inaculated typhus. A few cases of typhus, from two to seven, were reported during the year 1864 from each of eight regiments in the Army of the Potomac. In accordance with instructions from the Medical Director of the Army the history of these cases was investigated, and in every instance in which the surgeon who made the report was still on duty with the command, it was found that he had ceased to consider the disease to have been typhus. Concerning the cases reported from the Army before Corinth, Medical Director R. MURRAY, U. S. A., was of opinion that if the experience of Surgeon MAYLERT, U. S. Vols., who was in charge of the general field hospital, furnished no evidence of typhus, there was assuredly none among the troops. Surgeon MAYLERT's report on the fevers of this army has already been presented.* Those treated at the St. James hospital, New Orleans, La.,† were derived from General BUTLER's regiments, which, with few exceptions, had been crowded to excess on transports from New York to Ship Island, Miss. The passage to the Gulf occupied thirty to forty days, and many of the troops were closely packed on shipboard for sixteen days on the trip up the river to New Orleans. After this some of the regiments were sent to the forts at Carrollton and others to the swamps opposite Vicksburg, Miss. The report of Surgeon EUGENE F. SANGER, U. S. Vols., gives expression to the conditions affecting these men and the probable character of the fevers from which they suffered.

Brigade Surg. J. H. WARREN, 1st Brigade, Casey's Division, Washington, D. C., Jan. 25, 1862.— The 1st brigade is finely situated on Meridian Hill, a very healthy location, the camp well policed and drained. The internal arrangements of the barracks are very bad, as the ventilation is not sufficient, and is obstructed by partitions across the building at intervals of ten or fifteen feet, destroying the free circulation of air. If this defect is not immediately remedied we shall have camp or typhus fever, as it has already made its appearance in the 56th N. Y., and in one case proved fatal.

Brigade Surg. J. H. WARREN, on the condition of the 77th N. Y., Jan. 27, 1862.—This regiment is encamped on the western slope of Meridian Hill. The ground, owing to its gravelly and porous nature, is as well adapted for a camp as any in the vicinity. The atmosphere is impregnated with a malarial odor, arising from an open field where a large number of dead horses are deposited on the surface and allowed to remain and decompose. This, with the rather poor policing of the camp, has given rise to typhus fever, from which, I regret to say, we have lost some ten or twelve men already. The tents are the wedge-tent, and have a wall of boards built up some three feet high, with the tent placed on top. As they have no door, using the fly as such, the men step over the boarding down into this box arrangement, which generates one of the most fetid and vile atmospheres that human beings can possibly be placed in. I suggested that the banking of earth about the boarding should be at once removed, and holes made through the walls near the floor that a free circulation of air may be had. I would also suggest that the regiment be removed to the grounds opposite the Columbian hospital. The men should sleep upon cedar leaves, which can readily be obtained at a short distance from here. They should not be allowed to keep fires in their quarters but a few hours by day and the same at night, nor should they be allowed to wear their overcoats or eat in the tents. A disinfecting agent should be thrown around their quarters and a strong solution of lime inside and out. Should these suggestions be adopted, I think all forms of typhus will speedily disappear from the regiment.

Report on Typhus by Medical Inspector PETER PINEO, U. S. A.—The 23d N. Y. moved Sept. 28, 1861, from Arlington, where it had been encamped some months, to Upton's hill. Because of what was considered a military necessity, the regiment occupied a hillside facing the northeast, the soil being a tenacious clay; the streets were very narrow, the A-shaped tents were close to each other, and the camp confined to the smallest possible space. During October and November I urged unsuccessfully its removal to a more salubrious locality. The importance of striking the tents, careful police and cleanliness was also urged upon the colonel and surgeon of the regiment, but without avail. An almost total neglect of all hygienic precautions ensued, superadded to which was the fact that five or six soldiers slept in each small tent, and as cold weather advanced, their habit was to hermetically seal the tent as

---

nearly as possible, sleeping in a space of but little more than one hundred cubic feet. The circulation of air in such a tent is, it seems to me, of the following character: The canvas permits the ingress and egress of almost no air whatever. The expired air being heated and lighter rises to the top and sides of the tent, where it is immediately condensed, and falling to the bottom is again respired; this process is repeated constantly during the night, producing necessarily a condition scarcely rivalled by the "Black Hole."

This regiment was composed of as fine a body of stout and intelligent young men as any I have seen in the army; yet in November a large sick report was noticed, and in December the sickness and mortality became so alarming that I instituted a careful investigation. In one tent was found a soldier who had kept his tent for a day or two, had scarcely complained at all, but was *in articulo mortis*. The patients generally on first coming under notice of the surgeon presented grave symptoms; they were listless, stupid and greatly depressed, though uncomplaining. Cerebral symptoms were shortly manifested with sordes about the mouth and teeth, rapid and irregular pulse and death by coma often in from twenty-four to seventy-two hours after entering hospital. There was almost no convenience for *post-mortem* observation, yet in two or three cases autopsies were made by Surgeon WILCOX, 21st N. Y., at one of which I was present. The external appearance of the body was darker than usual and slight purpuric spots were present. No organic lesion was discovered, but there was unusual congestion of the internal organs generally. The symptoms above enumerated, with the history of the camp and the pathological appearances, led me to regard the cases as "typhus gravior," the result of "crowd-poison." It should be stated that malarial fever was the prevailing disease in the regiment previous to this alarming condition. It is also worthy of special notice that almost every case of sickness of grave character came from the shady side of the streets where no direct rays of sunlight ever found access. The 21st N. Y. was situated within a few rods of the 23d, in a valley, the situation being nearly or quite as objectionable. This regiment had served in and about Fort Runyon, and had strongly marked manifestations of malarial disease; but the police, cleanliness and ventilation were carefully attended to, and the regiment had only one death from disease in a year.

The camp was at length broken up and removed to a delightful spot; a foundation of logs three or four feet high was built on which was placed the tent; the streets were broad; cleanliness and ventilation were carefully attended to; the hospital, which had been in a small house with low ceilings and much crowded, was moved to a spacious church at Falls Church Village, and from being alarmingly unhealthy the regiment in a short time became one of the healthiest in the army.

Abstract of a Report of Surgeon R. N. BARR, *36th Ohio, for the four months ending Dec. 31, 1861.** [During this period the regiment lost 27 men by death from disease; 16 of the deaths occurred among 344 cases of fever and 7 among 22 cases of typhoid pneumonia. The mean strength of the command in November was 38 officers and 984 enlisted men. It was stationed at Summerville, West Va.] Fever made its appearance in this regiment shortly after its arrival at Summerville in September. The troops relieved by it had suffered from typhoid fever and left behind them in a crowded building about forty cases of the disease. Even in the earlier cases there were differences from typhoid as ordinarily observed: Prostration was greater, and there was severe occipital pain with stiffness and soreness of the muscles of the neck, particularly the sterno-mastoid. The chills in miasmatic cases were slight but came on at regular intervals, usually in the early part of the day; and in the intermittent forms the febrile stage continued until late in the evening. The tongue was large and broad, indented by the teeth along its margin and creased in the centre, thickly and darkly coated on the dorsum and red on the tip and edges; it was tremulous and protruded with difficulty in the severer cases. Diarrhœa was of frequent occurrence but not obstinate. As the season advanced and a typhous condition became more and more developed diarrhœa became less frequent, and oftentimes the bowels would not move spontaneously in two or three days. Antiperiodics, even when remissions were decided, acted but indifferently, often increasing the cerebral and vascular disturbance and the dryness of the tongue and fauces; but during convalescence quinine in small doses, given in conjunction with wine, had a happy effect. By the middle of October cases of what seemed true typhus fever made their appearance. The pulse was frequent and feeble, the skin dry and dusky but not hot, the urine scanty and high-colored and the secretions generally deficient; the sclerotic had a bronzed appearance. From two days to a week from the beginning of the attack delirium or coma, partial or complete, would ensue; sordes collected about the teeth and lips and the tongue became dry and crisped. There was occasionally troublesome gastric irritability, but seldom any tendency to diarrhœa; no tympanites, and, excepting sudamina in rare cases, no eruption. If the patient survived this stage a profuse cold perspiration would come on, the tendency to coma would disappear, and for a few days there might be a partial return to consciousness. Hemorrhage from the bowels was not unusual, recurring at frequent intervals for several days; in these cases tenderness in the iliac regions was found to exist, and occasionally diarrhœa. During this sweating stage glandular swellings were present in almost every case of any severity, generally affecting the parotid and submaxillary glands, and in two cases the testicles; the swellings were large and terminated in suppuration more frequently than in resolution. Abscesses in other localities were also common, and from them would come an incredible amount of purulent discharge. Another singular symptom was the occurrence of an excruciating pain, apparently neuralgic, beginning in the great toe, gradually extending to the other toes and sometimes involving the whole foot and ankle joint; there was no swelling. This pain was invariably the harbinger of convalescence. This was so apparent and uniform as to be observed by the attendants, and Dr. BARR quotes the nurse as saying to him: "Such a man is going to get well, for he has been groaning all night, or all day, with a pain in his big toe." About the beginning of December, while the daily average on the sick-list was 240, an ounce of whiskey was given morning and evening to every man on police or guard duty, and to others engaged in exhausting labor or exposed to inclement weather; this allowance was also given to nurses in hospital. Good results were expected "because of

---

the great depression of the vital energies and impairment of innervation not only of those on the sick-list but of the whole camp." It is asserted that almost immediately after this, new cases of fever became infrequent and of a milder character, and that in three weeks very few occurred. Although the hospital was well ventilated, nurses were frequently attacked before the use of the stimulant, but after its regular issue such cases became rare.

Report on Typhus by Surgeon FRANKLIN IRISH, *77th Pa. Vols.*—During the month of January, 1862, a few cases of genuine typhus fever made their appearance in this regiment while encamped at Mumfordsville, Ky. The cases all occurred in a period of about ten days during a protracted spell of cold and wet weather which confined the men to their tents, the mud being so deep in the vicinity of the camp as to interfere with the usual parades and exercises. The cases presented the regular petechial blotches numerously distributed over the body; they were attended with sudden and excessive physical prostration and terminated fatally, generally from the fifth to the tenth day, death being usually preceded a few hours by delirium. I believe these cases to have been identical with the spotted or petechial fever of the books; in short, typhus fever of a most malignant type. In most instances the disease was perfectly intractable, the most active and vigorous stimulant treatment failing to rally or sustain the terribly depressed vital powers. I am unable to trace it to any malarious origin. It disappeared as suddenly as it came, and I do not know of its having appeared in any of the surrounding camps. I believe it to have been the result of the vitiated air of the tents, together with the depressing influence of long continued cold and wet weather, insufficient exercise and depraved diet surreptitiously bought from camp hucksters.

Report on Typhus in the 15*th U. S. Inf. at Camp Wood, Ky., by Act. Ass't Surg.* O. K. REYNOLDS, *U. S. A.*—During the period of my service with the 1st Battalion of this regiment, four cases of true typhus gravior were observed. No similar cases occurred in the brigade, nor, as I believe, in the division. The diseases prevailing at the time were chronic diarrhœa, dysentery and typhoid fever, and in many of the febrile cases there were evidences of malarial influence seen not only in a tendency to periodicity, but also in the color of the skin and in hepatic derangements. In most cases three things were worthy of remark: 1st. The adynamic condition of patients when first brought to the hospital tent. 2d. Intestinal congestions. 3d. The alvine evacuations, which were generally of a pale dirty-yellow color and quite thin, not offensive at first, but abominably so after a few days exposure in the sinks to a warm sun.

The two hospital tents of the battalion were situated on low ground near the head of a small ravine; there was a shallow sink not more than twenty-five feet behind one of them and above it, the ground being higher behind than in front. The patients lay on old straw which could not be replaced by reason of the scarcity of that article. Vegetation commenced under the straw, which was kept moist by its close proximity to the earth. The four typhus cases occurred in the tent on the low ground near the sink. These, when first brought in, exhibited few symptoms that were not common to every case of camp fever,—there was perhaps rather more debility and nervous prostration than in other cases; but a few days after their admission into the hospital tent stupor and low delirium supervened, and the stools became less frequent and scanty, darker in color and more offensive; the quantity of urine became diminished and the catheter was sometimes required; sudamina were seen in all and the rose-colored eruption in two of the cases, about the end of the first week, continuing until death. In one case epistaxis was troublesome. In all the pulse was small, weak and frequent and the tongue dry, brown and fissured; sordes accumulated rapidly on the teeth, gums and lips, and stupor deepened as the disease progressed. Brigade Surgeon CHARLES SCHÜSSLER, under whose orders I was then acting, regarded these cases as true typhus. In scarcely any other cases of fever at Camp Wood did I observe the disorder of intellect attending these cases; the patients were generally rational even just before death.

Since camp fever prevailed in all the neighboring regimental camps, while few if any other cases of typhus occurred, these four cases may reasonably be attributed to local causes. These I believe to have been the fetid gas arising from the sink and the vapor exhaled from the earth saturated with putrescent fluids under the straw on which the patients lay. But as there were nine men in the tent, it may be asked why did not more cases occur? Probably because some were less reduced upon entering the tent and others remained only a few days exposed to its miasms. I believe that any febrile case, if exposed to similar pathogenic causes for a length of time, would develope symptoms of a true typhus.

Extract from an Inspection Report of Branch Hospital No. 6, New Albany, Ind., by Medical Inspector L. HUMPHREYS, *U. S. A., Jan.* 14, 1864.—[The camp from which the New Albany cases were derived is thus described under date March 8: The troops consisted of seven companies of undisciplined recruits intended for the cavalry service,—present 432, absent with or without leave 219; total 651; number sick in camp hospital 68; severe cases are sent to general hospital at New Albany. The prevailing diseases are measles, pneumonia and intermittent fever,—typhus reported present in January has entirely subsided. The camp is in the fair grounds. There is but little natural drainage and almost no attempt has been made to improve it. The soil is blue water-holding clay which at the present time is worked up into mud. The water-supply is from cisterns and wells; the well-water contains iron and magnesia and produces diarrhœa in those who use it. The quarters are exceedingly filthy; the men cook, eat and sleep in them. The grounds of the camp are covered with garbage and filth. The sinks are so foul from deposited excrement that they cannot be approached without defilement. The unusually large number of sick in hospital is the legitimate result of a want of proper cleanliness and discipline.]

There are a number of cases reported by our medical officers as typhus or spotted fever in this and other branches of the general hospital in this city. The cases have all occurred among the recruits at Camp Noble, a short distance from town. When admitted they present delirium, great depression of the nervous centres, with obstinate vomiting, constipation of bowels and pain in the head; surface of the body cold, with tendency to collapse; pulse over 100 and compressible; petechiæ on the extremities, the spots reddish at first, subsequently turning dark; the attack generally sudden, running to a fatal termination in a few days. I saw one case just received in hospital which had well-marked symptoms of cerebro-spinal meningitis, but *post-mortem* examination affords no evidence of inflammation of these tissues. The blood in the cadaver is reported to be in a liquid state, as in cases of death from electricity. Fifteen or twenty cases of this type of disease have occurred, many of them terminating fatally. Some of the men in Camp Noble, furloughed to their homes, became affected after arriving at their residences, other members of the family, in some instances, taking the disease apparently by contagion. The cases in hospital were all treated with tonics and stimulants. Nearly all under this treatment died. *Post-mortem* appearances indicating the use of an oxidizing remedial agent, cases occurring subsequently were treated by a free use of chlorate of potash conjoined with stimulants, tonics and opiates. Under this mode of treatment nearly all cases of this disease have recovered. Cases have occurred amongst the citizens of the country about New Albany.

In hospital this so-called "spotted fever" is isolated in a ward with 3,000 cubic feet of space to each patient.

Ass't Surg. WARREN WEBSTER, *U. S. A., on Typhus in the* 12th *Army Corps, Army of the Potomac, March* 5, 1863.— [This inspection was occasioned by the reported occurrence during February, 1863, of two fatal cases of typhus fever in the 123d N. Y. and five cases with four deaths in the 149th N. Y. The monthly report of Surgeon JOHN MONEYPENNY, of the former regiment, contains the following remarks: The regiment moved into an old camping ground situated near Stafford Court House, Va. The camp is located in a hollow between two ridges, near the edge of a brook. The soil is porous and the water filtering through it is in my opinion impregnated with an undue quantity of vegetable debris. We brought rubeola with us from our last camp at Fairfax Station. The men had made a hard march through the storms of December. The rations were salt and deficient in quantity. After the first week of camp life here diarrhœa of severe grade showed itself; this was followed by cases of remittent fever, generally assuming a low type; then typho-malarial, typhoid and typhus fevers made their appearance. Two of the cases, reported as typhus, occurred after convalescence from rubeola. Pneumonias were of a typhoid type and dysentery assumed the same sinking character. The health of the camp is bad, the situation is bad and the weather has been unfavorable for us to move; but I have chosen another locality and will probably effect the change next week.]

On my arrival Medical Director McNULTY informed me that the only regiments in which the fever had existed were the 123d and 149th N. Y., and that there was now but one case in each regiment. The case in the latter regiment was not, in his opinion, of so malignant a type as the preceding cases in that regiment, and the case in the other command had, he believed, undergone decided amendment. He also informed me that the camps of the infected regiments had been removed to sites offering in his judgment the best available combination of sanitary conditions. Both patients are isolated in separate hospital tents placed at a considerable distance from the old and new encampments of the respective regiments.

The reports already made by the medical director have given information of the number of cases of typhus reported by regimental surgeons as occurring in these two regiments and the number of deaths resulting therefrom; I therefore need not refer to them except to say in passing that while my inquiries lead me to doubt whether all the cases so reported were genuine typhus, it is undoubted that most of them were distinctly marked cases. Of the two existing instances there cannot be question. My opinions on the subject coincide fully with those of Surgeon McNULTY, whose thorough professional training and extended observation of the disease in New York City make him especially acute in the recognition of the characteristic symptoms.

In compliance with orders to inquire into the causes of this formidable affection, I have to say that I deem the close aggregation of the men of the two regiments in huts of defective construction and on ground having a wet sub-soil imperfectly drained and previously occupied by troops, to be a conspicuous promoter of the disease now under consideration. The 123d regiment was quartered in huts 11×6×4 feet, with eight men to a hut. These huts had been recently abandoned by General Sigel's troops, and the New York regiment arriving upon the ground late at night occupied and remained in them without proper cleaning. Many were within one or two feet of each other. In the intervening spaces human ordure had been deposited; and I learned from the regimental surgeon that much of it had been allowed to remain there up to a recent time. Offal was also deposited from time to time in offensive proximity to the camp. Huts originally intended for the accommodation of a single regiment have been inhabited, since the arrival of the 12th Corps, by two regiments recruited six months ago, and therefore not reduced in numbers. The thin tent-cloth with which the huts were roofed admitted some air of course, when dry, through the interstices of the fabric, but when wet it was almost impervious. No system of ventilation was practiced, and the drainage of the camp was unattended to although the face of the ground presented every facility therefor. The reason assigned for these surprising neglects is that the command was daily expecting to move. This regiment, when organized in northern New York in August, 1862, consisted, I am told, of a fine body of 923 men. It has been in camp at Washington, Arlington Heights, Pleasant Heights, Loudon Valley, Fairfax Station and in the locality I am describing, and at each of these places except the last, camps were generally made on ground not before occupied. Its duty has been picket, fatigue, guard duty, marching and the customary drills, and its sanitary condition has in general been quite good. Diarrhœa, malarial disorders, measles and a few cases of typhoid have occurred. The present typhus patient, who fell sick February 5, was in a partially excavated hut, 6×7 feet in area, in which five men had slept during the first fortnight. More recently the invalid and one or two well men occupied the hut.

On the 3d inst., day before yesterday, the regiment was, with the exception of the sick, removed to a new camping ground selected about a week ago. A new hospital, just obtained, and favorably located near by, contains the typhus patient. On visiting the new camp I found the site good, but the huts built irregularly and much too close together. As the result of a conference with DR. McNULTY and myself, the colonel of the regiment determined to immediately tear down the huts, build anew over a larger area, and allow no excavation of the floors or heaping up of earth on the outside of the walls. He resolved also to drain the camp systematically, protect from surface water by catch-water drains, ventilate the huts thoroughly each day, exercise a rigid police of the camp and interior of the huts, enforce cleanliness by bathing, which had never been attended to, and cause the under-garments of the men to be frequently washed. An inspection of the persons of the men by me was unnecessary, as it was frankly admitted that they were in a filthy state. Their physiognomy, however, did not indicate the cachexy which their wretched habits led me to expect; on the contrary I was surprised by their comparatively healthy appearance. I found in the regiment seven grave cases of typhoid fever, which, although not beset by the same dangerous elements of infection and self-propagation as typhus, still call as loudly for correction of the sanitary negligence which has given rise to both the allied diseases; and now that the insalubrious locality, the defective accommodations of the troops and the tainted atmosphere to which they were subjected have been changed and isolation with improved treatment of the single typhus case secured, we may confidently hope for the speedy erad-ication of these formidable disorders of the regiment.

The existence of typhus fever in the other regiment, the 149th N. Y., is attributable to influences similar to those reported above as having prevailed in the 123d. * * * * Much credit is due Major General SLOCUM for the promptness and energy with which he has employed the measures suggested to arrest the spread of fever and prevent its assuming an epidemic prevalence. He yesterday issued a general order positively prohibiting throughout his command—1st. The habit of sinking the floors of tents and huts below the surface of the ground. 2d. Occu-pation, in encamping troops, of spots recently used for that purpose; and 3d. Employment, in the construction of new huts, of any portion of old ones. The practice of using portions of abandoned huts in the construction of new ones on adjacent ground, in order to avoid the labor of procuring other materials, is so general that it made necessary the third paragraph of this order. Many points of improvement were urged upon the officers of the infected troops; but it was deemed unnecessary to request General SLOCUM to publish them. The troops are now sufficiently aware of their commanding general's earnestness in the matter to insure observance of verbal suggestions, and the intelligence and energy of Surgeon McNULTY will accomplish everything to be desired of the medical officers under his direction. I think the officers with whom we conversed, line as well as medical, are convinced of the general injurious consequences certain to flow from overcrowding and defective ventilation, and more especially how much the prevalency and fatality of typhus depend upon the nature of the in-door accommodation with which the soldier is provided. Inattention to the purity of the air in each tent or hut, to personal cleanliness, constant supplies of fresh clothing and bedding, defective cooking and the accumulation about camps of decomposing vegetable and animal matters have been pointed out to them as potent influences in the production of camp fever. Advice was given to the attending medical officers with reference to the management of the disease, and if fresh cases should occur they will use the promptest means to isolate the patients and will urge the commanding officer to the adoption of any measure, no matter how extreme, necessary to arrest the evil.

Ass't Surg. WARREN WEBSTER, *U. S. A., on supposed Typhus in the* 11th *Army Corps, Army of the Potomac, April* 17, 1863.—I have the honor to report, after careful investigation, that I am not convinced that the sudden death of one of the quartermaster's employés at Hope Landing, reported by Medical Director SUCKLEY, 11th Army Corps, was, as he believes, a case of *maculated typhus;* nor do I think that any active hygienic or precautionary measures need be taken to prevent a spread of the disease existing in the command there.

The two regiments, the 107th and 134th N. Y., composing the command at Hope Landing, have suffered greatly from sickness since their entry into service about eight months ago. Before and since their arrival at that point, two months ago, typhoid fever has been very prevalent and fatal, assuming during the autumn and fall months unusually severe enteric symptoms and during the winter marked cerebral complications. The latter symptoms were by some of the medical officers interpreted to denote typhus, particularly as several of the cases so charac-terized were speedily fatal and the diarrhœa and meteorism usually attending enteric fever were absent or slight. I can learn, however, of two cases only which presented cutaneous eruptions differing materially from those peculiar to typhoid fever, and they were rather extensive ecchymotic patches of subcutaneous extravasation varying in size from a grain of wheat to one's hand, than the peculiar eruption deemed distinctive of contagious typhus: One of these was the case of the quartermaster's clerk; the other occurred in the 107th New York regiment about a week ago. Both were marked by nearly the same course, death resulting in less than twenty-four hours. The patient (a few hours before in apparent good health) complained to the surgeon of violent pain in the head, back and extremities, and the appearance of the countenance and hue of the skin presented evidence of great internal conges-tion. The pulse was small until death, at times almost imperceptible. Persistent vomiting characterized the last case. Delirium was not violent, but comatose symptoms soon prevailed. The patients suffered from involuntary urinal and fæcal discharges. An examination of the first patient a few hours after the attack, and of the other shortly before death, revealed cutaneous ecchymotic patches of extravasated blood varying greatly in form and size, and invading the body, limbs and even the face. No *post-mortem* investigation was made in either case. The treatment consisted primarily of cups, mustard applications to the extremities and a large dose of calomel and rhubarb, with the subsequent employment of camphor, quinine and alcoholic stimulants. This treatment was attended with only partial reaction and improvement of the pulse. The soldier thus affected had been on duty as a teamster for two months previous to the attack, was provided with good and well-prepared food, an abundance of vegetables and ample clothing, was represented to be unusually cleanly in his personal habits, and habitually slept in his wagon, which had no other tenant during the night but himself. The quartermaster's clerk was a man of scrupulous personal cleanliness, lodged in a well-ventilated Sibley tent, and had the reputation of being a free rather than a spare liver. The favorable relations of these men to air, food, clothing and personal attentions certainly con-tradict the supposition that they were victims of typhus. The character and stage of appearance of the cutaneous eruption, and the slight degree of delirium which characterized the cases are also, in my opinion, in opposition to the existence of the supposed disease. If it be claimed that typhus was communicated to them by contagion, I do not understand where was the contagious source. No other cases, answering even as well as these to the characters of typhus, have existed in the command. No exposure to fomites is likely to have occurred; nor was the second sufferer known to have been submitted to contagious propinquity to the first.

Surgeon FLOOD of the regiment in which the first of these mysterious cases occurred informed me that the typhoid fever of the command had, within two weeks, almost completely lost its tendency to cerebral congestion, and that pneumonia was now the prevailing complication. One regiment yesterday removed to near Brook's Station; the other daily expects to change its location. In view of these facts I deem it necessary neither to draw your attention to the objectionable exposure of Hope Landing to vegetable malaria nor to recommend at present any sanitary reforms in the regiments lately composing the command.

Surgeon EUGENE F. SANGER, *U. S. Vols., Third Division,* 19th *Army Corps, on the Fevers that prevailed in New Orleans and its-vicinity in* 1862.—Four important elements entered into the causes of so much disease and such fearful mortality. 1st, *Scorbutus:* The diet had been uniformly salt meat, hard bread and coffee. The transports were too crowded to admit of thorough policing, and the public buildings and cotton presses were too dark, damp or hot. After long confinement, poor diet and habitual uncleanliness, there was nothing in the surroundings of the men to excite their pride or arouse them to a proper appreciation of the importance of attention to hygienic measures. 2d, *Typhus poison:* The entire command had been situated for many months where systematic ablutions could not be performed. The skin was active and performed important functions; it supplied the place of the kidneys largely in carrying off the disintegrated tissues. Men lay down in clothing saturated with effete animal matter and were compelled to breathe constantly the poisonous exhalations of the human body. Reabsorption necessarily followed. 3d, *Typhoid poisoning:* Scorbutic diet soon began to tell upon the stomach, destroying its nervous energy; food fermented, noxious gases formed, the bowels became irritated and imperfect digestion and nutrition followed with emaciation, debility, diarrhœa and fever. 4th, *Malaria:* As early as May dumb agues appeared, and by June intermittents and remittents prevailed generally. The city proper was free from malaria. The 14th Me., while quartered in the city during the months of June and July, suffered badly from typhus but was entirely free from malaria. On the immediate banks of the river at Carrollton the troops were generally exempt from malaria; the 12th Conn. escaped almost entirely. On the other hand, regiments in the fortifications running back from and at right angles to the river, toward the swamps, suffered terribly,—the 14th Me., stationed at Carrollton during September and October, was reduced from 700 strong for duty to 56 in about twenty-eight days. About June 1 six regiments embarked for the swamps opposite Vicksburg and remained exposed to the inclemencies of the weather and pestiferous miasms for more than six weeks.

General Butler's command originally consisted of seventeen regiments with batteries and some cavalry, and in the course of eight months almost the entire force suffered from the causes of disease above enumerated. The 13th Conn. was a noteworthy exception: It embarked at New York late in March, and had a short passage to Ship Island, where it remained until the city surrendered; at New Orleans it was quartered in the custom-house. It had better accommodations at sea, was confined on shipboard for a shorter period and was more rigid in policing. This regiment lost very few men during the summer.

I did not test the accuracy of my diagnosis by *post-mortem* examinations, and I have not the record of a case showing implication or exemption of Peyer's patches, but the symptoms were sufficiently convincing. I invariably found the patients extremely debilitated from the first, with early tendency to slipping down in bed and deafness, dark-brownish and dry tongue, petechial eruption, small and feeble pulse, tense and flat bowels, at first constipated, followed by hemorrhages and diarrhœas. Quinine, whiskey and beef-tea were the only remedial agents admissible. I was in the habit of combining a little opium with the quinine to correct its cinchonizing effects, and ipecacuanha to stimulate the capillaries. The 14th Me., quartered in Lafayette Hall, lost as many as twenty cases of typhus during June; some of these died at their regimental hospital, the others at the St. James. This regiment became so thoroughly used up that over 300 men were discharged from it during the months of June and July on surgeon's certificates, and as many acclimated men enlisted at New Orleans. Other regiments had distinctive typhoid: I remember seeing in one regiment some thirty well-marked cases—beef tongues, rose-red spots and tympanitic bowels.

The regiments that suffered most were the 7th Vt., 30th Mass. and 9th Conn. Arriving at New Orleans worn and debilitated, scorbutic in habit and saturated with zymotic poison, they were allowed but a few days at that city and Carrollton before they were sent to Vicksburg. Thence they returned to Baton Rouge, participated in a brisk fight on August 6, and were compelled to abandon the place about the end of that month. On their return to New Orleans these regiments were a sight to behold. The scenes on board the boats which brought the sick beggar description—the dead and living locked in one embrace. Reduced to shadows by diarrhœa and fever a single paroxysm sufficed to snap the cord. Men put on board at Baton Rouge for simple debility were enveloped in their winding sheets before they reached New Orleans: I counted seven dead bodies on one boat. These remittents or intermittents had but one paroxym; seldom would there be any febrile reaction. The collapse was almost as perfect as in cholera—features sunken, skin cold and livid, voice husky, pulse small and quick, stomach irritable and mind torpid. The patients complained of burning in the stomach and exhaustion; they seemed wholly unconcerned whether they lived or died, and continually tossed to and fro until death relieved them from their sufferings. Warm frictions, stimulants and large doses of quinine occasionally revived them.

The 7th Vt. lost 300 men in the eight months from May to December, the 30th Mass. 215, and the 6th Conn., a small regiment of less than 700 men, 169. During this time I think we must have lost quite 20 per cent. of the entire command by death, to say nothing of those discharged for disability.

Nevertheless, although typhus was fortunately a stranger to our camps, there appears strong ground for believing that an epidemic of this disease prevailed among some rescued and paroled prisoners received at Wilmington from Salisbury, N. C., in the spring of 1865. The number of prisoners was 8,600, and of these 3,400 had to be cared for in Wilmington as they were unable to undertake the voyage northward. The disease spread from them not only to the troops of the garrison but also to the citizens of the town and the residents of the surrounding country. Surgeon D. W. HAND, U. S. Vols., then Medical Director of the Department of North Carolina, furnished a special report of this epidemic, which he considered to be undoubted typhus. It is addressed to the Surgeon-General of the Army and reads as follows:

WILMINGTON, N. C., *March* 10, 1866.

GENERAL: I have the honor to report that, in compliance with your instructions, I have collected all available facts relating to the epidemic fever that prevailed here in the spring of 1865.

Wilmington surrendered February 22 of that year, and our troops on entering found the city in a very filthy condition and the inhabitants that remained in a violent state of alarm. The city up to that time had been quite as healthy as usual, and no epidemic had prevailed among the Confederate troops that formed its garrison.

On the 25th and 26th of February 8,600 Union prisoners were exchanged at Northeast Station and immediately sent down to this city. Of this number about 3,400 were too sick or weak to bear transportation by common transports and had to be cared for in hospital. Under the direction of Surgeon EDWARD SHIPPEN, U. S. Vols., at that time senior medical officer in Wilmington, they were placed in public buildings and deserted dwelling houses in all parts of the town. The sick from the troops on duty near Wilmington, and also those sent from Fayetteville by General Sherman, were admitted indiscriminately to these same hospitals.

During the first week of March or very soon after the arrival of these prisoners an epidemic, which was undoubtedly *typhus* or *jail fever*, appeared in the hospitals and rapidly extended to the citizens in the town.

I find that between February 26 and June 30 about 1,200 white soldiers and 300 colored soldiers died of disease in Wilmington and its vicinity. The epidemic fever prevailed from March 1 to June 1 and caused, so far as can now be ascertained, about 650 of these deaths, viz: 300 exchanged prisoners, 200 other white soldiers and 150 colored soldiers. The records of the Wilmington hospitals are so incomplete that no estimate can be made of the number of soldiers who suffered from an attack of this fever.

Owing to the peculiar state of local affairs at that time the number of deaths among citizens cannot be ascertained; but the resident physicians testify that the fever spread extensively among them and that many died. Among the refugee negroes sent down to Wilmington by General Sherman it was particularly fatal; several thousand of them were put in camp about April 1 near Fort Anderson on the Cape Fear River, and it is thought over 1,000 deaths from typhus fever occurred among them.

It was noticed by the medical officers that the attendants and other soldiers about the hospitals, who contracted the fever from the returned prisoners, had it more violently than the prisoners themselves,—the weak, half starved prisoners having a better chance of recovery than the strong, healthy attendants. Most of the medical officers and attendants contracted the fever. Five surgeons and assistant surgeons, two chaplains and about eighty detailed attendants were among those who died.

The evidence on all sides is conclusive that this fever was brought into Wilmington by the exchanged prisoners. No doubt the crowded and badly ventilated hospitals intensified the poison; but I am satisfied this type of fever existed among the prisoners at the time they were received within our lines.

It was contagious.—Several of the most intelligent physicians in Wilmington think it only prevailed as an epidemic and was no more contagious than yellow fever; but some facts have come to my knowledge which show that it was more than that. Of the officers and men employed on the steamboats that brought the prisoners from Northeast Station to this place nearly all took the fever and several died. They were not known to have been in or about the hospitals after the prisoners were landed in Wilmington. It is known that typhus or a low form of fever prevailed in the families of several planters in this state, conveyed to them by negroes who had recently returned from Wilmington. Particularly was this the case in Richmond and Robinson counties, on the line of General Sherman's march. The negroes followed the army to Fayetteville, and thence passed down to Wilmington; but finding it a hard place to live in many went back to their old masters in May and June and carried with them the fever that was prevailing in the city. Mrs. Gilchrist, living near Montpelier, Richmond county, 104 miles from Wilmington, had some of her negroes come back in this way. Several had the fever after their return. Mrs. Gilchrist suffered a violent attack, but recovered; her son, aged twenty-one years, died. Other white persons in the same family afterwards had the fever but recovered. Mr. McEahan lives on the Lumber River, three miles above Mrs. Gilchrist's place; his negroes carried the fever from Wilmington, and several members of the family took it; one daughter died. Mr. D. St. Clair, in the same neighborhood, had a like experience and lost his daughter. Dr. John Maloy, in Robinson county, had his negroes who remained at home infected in the same way and lost several. His family was mildly attacked.

The physicians in Wilmington estimated the period of incubation of this fever at from four to twenty days.

Symptoms.—It began like an ordinary fever with a chill, followed by more or less heat of skin and great weariness with pain in the back. The languor was excessive. Violent headache does not seem usually to have accompanied it; but the eyes were red, watery and intolerant of light. The tongue was dry in the middle with red tip and edges; sordes appeared early on the gums, and there was great thirst. Almost from the beginning there was uneasiness or pain in the stomach, with tenderness over the whole abdomen; gurgling was heard in the right iliac region, and generally there was diarrhœa. In the later stages hemorrhage from the bowels was not uncommon. The urine was scanty and high-colored, and in bad cases frequently entirely suppressed. The pulse was full and slow, often only 45 to 60 per minute, but easily compressible. The skin was frequently bathed with perspiration without the fever or heat of skin abating. Petechiæ appeared early, and also at times an eruption like urticaria. Towards the end spots like purpura often appeared. Jaundice frequently supervened, the skin and conjunctivæ becoming intensely yellow. Vomiting of a dark-colored fluid, which when dried on a cloth appeared somewhat yellow, was also not uncommon. Sometimes the patient died on the fourth or fifth day with symptoms of congestion of the brain or lungs; but usually the case ran on from fourteen to thirty days.

From the notes of Dr. J. F. KING, a prominent medical man in Wilmington, who served for some months in 1865 as a contract physician in the hospitals there, I select two cases as fair examples of the disease:

CASE 1.—*Severe; resulting in death.*—Mr. Brynim, citizen; age 28 years; weight 175 pounds; moderately temperate; full habit; enjoying good health during whole life, visited a sick friend in hospital. Two days later, March 11, complained of loss of appetite; was languid and oppressed; had soreness of muscles; took a purgative dose of blue mass. That night had a chill with rigors; much prostration; fulness and tenderness in the epigastrium; nausea and vomiting. I saw him next day: Fever; pulse about 90, full, easily compressible; tongue dark, dry, with red edges, attended with urgent thirst; great exhaustion; breathing accelerated, with occasional sighing and bronchial cough; sordes on the teeth and lips; skin hot and husky; bowels loose; discharges yellow, watery and excessively offensive; gurgling in right iliac region; tenderness over the entire abdomen, particularly in the epigastrium; urine very scanty, passing only about a tablespoonful, very dark and offensive; breath extremely fetid. Administered stimulants; potassæ chloras in camphor juleps; mustard, brandy and pepper externally, etc. The above symptoms continued until the fourth day, when the countenance became dingy (livid) with flushed cheeks; injected eyes, dark-yellow in appearance and heavy, with unsteadiness of vision and intolerance of light. The whole surface was covered with a miliary eruption and badly jaundiced; violent delirium; great prostration; passed no urine for eighteen hours; cough dry and frequent; much nausea; bowels loose. *Fifth day:* Somewhat better; retained a little nourishment; voided about two ounces of urine. *Sixth day:* About the same. *Seventh day, early morning:* Skin clear; voided ten ounces of urine during the night; less delirium; retains nourishment and stimulants. 10 *A. M.:* Skin jaundiced; delirium violent; involuntary discharges of clotted blood. 3 *P. M.:* Surface much paler; abatement of delirium; skin hot with slight perspiration; bowels checked; great prostration. 7 *P. M.:* Died. Surface of a greenish-yellow color.

CASE 2.—*Milder; recovery.*—Mr. M. Johnson, Quartermaster's Department, complained April 20 of loss of appetite, languor, soreness, fulness and tenderness in epigastrium, followed by prostration and rigors with fever: Pulse about 100, full, easily compressed; tongue brushed over with a white fur; urgent thirst; nausea and vomiting; breathing somewhat accelerated with slight cough; skin rather hot, but chilly when the covering is removed; occasional attacks of sweating of short duration, unattended with any abatement of the fever; countenance dingy; cheeks flushed; eyes watery and intolerant of light; pain in back of head; deafness; pain in loins; urine free; bowels constipated. *Fifth day:* Not much alteration except red tongue with elevated edges and hard dry centre; restless and somewhat delirious; sleeps only from effects of opiates. *Twelfth day:* Urine rather scanty; bowels in good condition; skin hot with gentle perspiration; delirium; tenderness over the abdomen; pulse 135. *Seventeenth day:* Not much alteration except the tongue more moist; increased quantity of urine; bowels constipated. *Twentieth day:* Decided improvement; tongue slightly coated with a yellowish fur and moist; delirium lessened; sleeps more quietly; pulse 110. After this the patient gradually recovered, having been able to leave his room and go down stairs on the thirty-first day from the beginning of the attack.

No *post-mortem examinations* of an official character were made. This is much to be regretted, but under the circumstances cannot much be wondered at. The physicians of the city were greatly depressed in spirit and many of them sick; and the medical officers of the army were overwhelmed with the vast amount of work so suddenly thrown upon them. But although no systematic autopsical investigations were instituted the intestines were examined in a number of cases in none of which was there any affection of the glands of Peyer. Personally I conducted two examinations for the determination of this point.

Treatment.—Stimulants were required from the beginning, and rarely could a purgative dose of medicine be given with safety. Medical officers at the hospitals noticed that on two occasions, when the supply of stimulants was exhausted for a few days, the mortality became much increased. Chlorate of potash was useful in small doses, and camphor seemed the best anodyne because of its stimulant effect. Those patients apparently did best that received little medicine, but whose strength was sustained by the regular administration of nourishment and brandy or whiskey. Quinine was of no apparent benefit. Oil of turpentine does not seem to have been much used, but in a few cases it was given and appeared to relieve the intestinal irritation.

This fever appears to have prevailed also among those of the released prisoners who were considered able to undertake the journey to New York; but there is no direct reference to a contagious quality in the only sanitary report which speaks of it.

Medical Inspector GEO. H. LYMAN, *U. S. A., on febrile cases at David's Island, New York Harbor, May, 1865.*—A form of low fever with eruption prevails among the recent arrivals from General Sherman's troops. It is unusually fatal, and though differing somewhat from true typhus, bears more resemblance to it in its essential features than any other fever I have met with. The released prisoners from Charlotte and Salisbury arrived in pitiable condition. In some instances both lower extremities were lost from the effects of frost.

IV.—POST-MORTEM RECORDS OF THE CONTINUED FEVERS.

In presenting the *post-mortem* records of the continued fevers it has been deemed advisable to submit, in the first instance, such cases as may be of value in determining the nature of the large number reported as typho-malarial subsequent to June 30, 1862. Since this title was intended to include only modified typhoid fever, the *post-mortem* lesions of that fever should of necessity have been found in all cases.* Dr. Woodward, sixteen months after the introduction of the term, described the intestinal lesions of typho-malarial fever as consisting of tumefaction and ulceration, with the occasional deposit of pigment in the closed follicles of the small intestines;† and from this it may be inferred that all the typho-malarial cases brought to his notice up to that time had presented ulceration of the intestinal glands due to the action of the typhoid poison. But as has already been shown, the mortality statistics of the cases reported as typho-malarial are inconsistent with the idea of an ever-present specific enteric element; and this doubt as to the nature of these febrile cases becomes strengthened by observing that the records of the Seminary hospital attach a higher rate of fatality to typhoid fever when modified by malarial manifestations than when not thus modified.‡

To pursue this inquiry it is needful to compare the anatomical lesions of the two classes of cases. This has been done incidentally while arranging certain of the *post-mortem* records for publication. Submitted below are: 1st, such febrile cases as have the diagnosis *typhoid* more or less sustained by the recorded symptoms; 2d, cases entered as *typho-malarial*, whether accompanied or not by their clinical histories; and 3d, cases which, although recorded as *typhoid*, nevertheless present in their history symptoms suggestive of malarial complications. To permit of the ready comparison of these three sets of cases as well *inter se* as with the remainder of the *post-mortem* records of the continued fevers, they have been arranged in accordance with the characters of the intestinal lesions so far as it has been possible to determine these from the records.

---

* See note, page 273, *supra*.

† In his *Outlines of the Chief Camp Diseases of the United States Army*, Phila., Pa., 1863, pp. 100 *et seq.*: "In the *solitary* follicles of the small intestine the lesion is manifested as a gradual enlargement of these organs, the contents of which become soft, pulpy and very frequently blackened from deposits of pigment. All possible stages may be observed, from a barely perceptible enlargement to a little tumor the size of a pea, or even larger, corresponding to the situation of the follicle; the summits of the larger of these tumid follicles are frequently the seat of a small ulcer. Such ulcers are especially to be observed in the ileum, but the enlarged follicles are encountered throughout the whole length of the small intestine. The ulcer, originating thus in a single closed follicle, may remain of small size (one to three lines in diameter), or it may enlarge, invade the surrounding tissues and produce an ulcer (six lines to an inch, or even more, in diameter) resembling the ulcerations of the patches of Peyer in character, though not in shape or situation. The agminated glands or patches of Peyer undergo similar changes. As a general rule, every patch is more or less involved, those high in the intestine being less affected and the tumefaction being most intense towards the lower part of the ileum. The characteristic ulcer occurring in the patches of Peyer is oval in shape; occupies more or less completely the tumid group of follicles; its edges are jagged and irregular, often undermined. The base of the ulcer is of a dirty ash color, often with a yellowish tinge, occasionally mottled with dark, blackish points from the presence of pigment. It may occupy any fraction of the thickness of the mucous membrane. Sometimes it is limited to the follicular apparatus; in its later stages, however, it usually invades more or less profoundly the submucous connective tissue, and it may even involve the muscular coat. In the latter event, it sometimes penetrates the muscular layers, erodes the subperitoneal connective tissue, and, in extreme cases, penetrates the peritoneum and produces a perforation, through which the intestinal contents may find their way into the general cavity of the abdomen and give rise to a fatal peritonitis." At this time Dr. Woodward was inclined to regard the ulcerations of typho-malarial fever as characterized by certain peculiarities often sufficiently distinctive to enable the anatomist to recognize the fever by the *post-mortem* appearances alone; but a larger experience demonstrated to him that these ulcerations differed in no respect from those produced by typhoid fever. See p. 36 of the pamphlet edition of his *Address on Typho-malarial Fever* in the Section of Medicine, International Medical Congress, Phila., 1876.

‡ *Supra*, p. 308.

CASES IN WHICH THE DIAGNOSIS, TYPHOID, IS MORE OR LESS SUSTAINED BY THE CLINICAL HISTORY—50 CASES.

(A.) Peyer's patches ulcerated and the ileum or small intestine only affected—20 cases.

CASE 1.—Private Joshua Watson, Co. C, 7th Fla.; age 40; was admitted March 22, 1864. He had been sick for some time and was much debilitated; his skin hot, tongue dry, teeth covered with sordes, pulse quick and small, countenance dull, expression vacant; there was tenderness and gurgling in the right iliac region. On the 25th he was suddenly attacked with symptoms of acute laryngitis, resulting in death the same day. *Post-mortem* examination: The glottis and surrounding parts were swollen, apparently from fibrinous exudation beneath the mucous membrane. The patches of Peyer were thickened and ulcerated.—*Act. Ass't Surg. M. K. Gleason, Rock Island Hospital, Ill.*

CASE 2.—Conscript Phineas Moody; age 29; was admitted Sept. 3, 1863. He was taken sick August 6 with diarrhœa which continued a week, and was followed by a chill and fever. On admission the pulse was 96, the tongue dry and brown; he had some diarrhœa, slight delirium, severe and constant cough, with mucous râles in both lungs, but no rose-colored spots. Two days later some red blotches appeared on the face, arms and chest, and there was dulness with subcrepitant râles in the lower lobes of both lungs. Six ounces of whiskey were taken daily, but on account of prostration the quantity on the 10th was increased to sixteen ounces. 12th: Skin moist; tongue furred yellow; no delirium. Whiskey reduced to six ounces. He continued to improve under this treatment until the 25th, when fever, dyspnœa and great prostration set in, with colliquative diarrhœa two days later, and death on October 3. *Post-mortem* examination ten hours after death: Body emaciated; lungs congested; liver enlarged and fatty; spleen enlarged and pulpy; kidneys large and granular; many of Peyer's patches ulcerated, especially those near the ileo-cæcal valve.—*Central Park Hospital, N. Y. City.*

CASE 3.—Private Nathaniel Newell, Co. E, 186th N. Y., was admitted Nov. 30, 1864, from City Point, Va., where he had been sick two weeks with typhoid fever; tongue dry and brown; sordes; anorexia; diarrhœa; involuntary stools; extreme tenderness over small intestine; low delirium; pulse 120, weak, tremulous. He died next day. *Post-mortem* examination: Peyer's patches much ulcerated; spleen enlarged and softened; lungs œdematous posteriorly.—*Third Division Hospital, Alexandria, Va.*

CASE 4.—Private James Foster, Co. A, 139th Pa.; age 20; was admitted March 11, 1864. On the 13th the abdomen became tympanitic and there was gurgling in the right iliac fossa. He died on the 24th. *Post-mortem* examination six hours after death: Peyer's patches extensively ulcerated; solitary follicles enlarged; other organs healthy.—*Third Division Hospital, Alexandria, Va.*

CASE 5.—Private Wm. H. Hartley, Co. G, 22d Pa. Cav., was admitted Oct. 10, 1864. 13th: Delirious at night; petechiæ on abdomen and extremities; pulse 120; tongue moist; slight tympanites; subcrepitant râles and friction sounds on the right side of the chest. Prescribed stimulants, eggs, and twelve grains of sulphate of quinine daily in divided doses. 14th: The soft tissues over the right hip and sacrum began to slough; removed patient to a water-bed. He sank rapidly and died at 10 P. M. *Post-mortem* examination disclosed the lower lobe of the right lung in the third stage of pneumonia and part of the middle of the left lung in the second stage; the right lung was lightly adherent to the walls of the chest, and the cellular tissue in the neighborhood was somewhat emphysematous. The colon, duodenum and jejunum were distended with gas; the ileum contracted; Peyer's glands more or less inflamed, and many of those near the ileo-cæcal valve ulcerated.—*Act. Ass't Surg. W. L. Wells, McClellan Hospital, Philadelphia, Pa.*

CASE 6.—Private Jeremiah O'Brien, Co. G, 24th N. Y. Cav.; age 19; was admitted July 21, 1864, having been sick a week with typhoid fever. On admission his pulse was 88 and full, bowels soluble and tongue moist; but there was pain in the right iliac fossa, with delirium and sleeplessness. The pulse became more frequent and less full, the abdomen tympanitic, the stools involuntary and the urine retained, necessitating catheterization. He died on the 27th. *Post-mortem* examination: The right lung was consolidated posteriorly; the intestines contained five lumbricoid worms and an unusual amount of fæces, natural in color but soft. Peyer's patches were thickened and inflamed, those near the ileo-cæcal valve ulcerated; the solitary follicles also were inflamed.—*Act. Ass't Surg. Henry Gibbons, jr., Douglas Hospital, Washington, D. C.*

CASE 7.—Private Edward Brown, Co. H, 35th Mass.; age 18; was admitted Dec. 16, 1864, with typhoid fever. The patient was but partially conscious, had frequent involuntary stools, epistaxis, quick pulse, tenderness over abdomen, particularly in right iliac region, rose-colored spots and well-marked sudamina; he had muttering delirium and picked at the bedclothes. On the 18th his tongue resembled a piece of unpolished mahogany and his teeth and gums were coated with sordes. He died next day. *Post-mortem* examination five hours and a half after death: The brain was normal. The larynx and trachea were healthy; the right lung weighed twenty ounces and a half, the left seventeen ounces, the lower lobe of each in a state of red hepatization and the inferior portion of the upper lobe of the right lung congested; the heart was normal. The liver weighed seventy-two ounces and was somewhat flabby; the spleen sixteen ounces; several of Peyer's patches were ulcerated; the solitary glands much enlarged and many of them ulcerated; the left kidney somewhat congested.—*Act. Ass't Surg. H. M. Dean, Lincoln Hospital, Washington, D. C.*

CASE 8.—Private Herbert Vaness, Co. D, 171st Pa.; age 20; was admitted July 8, 1863, with typhoid fever of twelve days' duration, which progressed favorably until the 9th, when diarrhœa set in. On the 15th there was delirium, with dry and tremulous tongue, sordes on the teeth and swelling of the abdomen; a troublesome hacking cough was also present. He died on the 17th. *Post mortem* examination ten hours after death: The brain weighed fifty-eight ounces and a half; its membranes were considerably congested and its substance rather soft; a small quantity of fluid was found in its ventricles. The trachea was much congested, of a purplish-red color and filled with bronchial secretion; the lymphatic glands at its bifurcation were enlarged, blackened and softened. The upper lobe of the right lung was highly congested, especially at the apex; the middle lobe was also somewhat congested and presented evidences of bronchitis posteriorly; the lower lobe was intensely engorged, purple in color and in some places almost black. The left lung was generally congested; there was a considerable transudation of blood beneath the pleura at its middle and posterior part; its lower lobe contained splenified lobules, black in color, and separated from each other by permeable tissue. The right lung weighed twenty-four ounces and a half, the left twenty-one ounces and a half. A thin fibrinous clot adhered to the anterior wall of the right auricle and extended through the ventricle into the pulmonary artery; the left auricle also contained a fibrinous clot extending into the ventricle and attached to the mitral valve. The fundus of the stomach was of a dull lake-red and the pyloric portion paler; it contained five lumbricoid worms. The liver was soft but of normal color, its capsule easily torn. The spleen was of a mulberry color and moderately firm. The mucous membrane of the jejunum was rather soft and the villi were easily scraped off. The lining membrane of the three feet of the ileum nearest to the ileo-cæcal valve was greatly congested, and Peyer's patches were ulcerated though not perceptibly thickened; the first ulcer was small, superficial and of a darker color than the surrounding membrane; about a foot above the valve a large patch, softened and very hyperæmic but not elevated, presented near its border an ulceration about the size of a pea, with elevated walls and blackened centre. The kidneys were somewhat injected, the cortical substance firm and pale.—*Ass't Surg. Harrison Allen, U. S. A., Lincoln Hospital, Washington, D. C.*

CASE 9.—Private William Crigger, Co. E, 20th Ind.; age 19; was admitted Nov. 24, 1864, with bronchitis, from which he recovered and was transferred to Convalescent Barracks Jan. 4, 1865. He was readmitted April 8, with pulse 100 to 110, skin hot and dry, tongue brown-coated with red edges, bowels loose, abdomen tympanitic. Active delirium, subsultus tendinum and pneumonic symptoms appeared on the 13th; after the 15th there was continued insomnia and on the 17th involuntary stools. Profuse sweats and coma ushered in death on the 20th. *Post-mortem* examination twelve hours after death: The brain weighed fifty-four ounces; there were six ounces of serum beneath the arachnoid and a large quantity in the lateral ventricles; the cortical portion of the brain was highly congested and the puncta vasculosa prominent. There were pleuritic adhesions on the right side; the lower lobes of the lungs were hepatized. The heart was normal. The spleen was enormously engorged, weight forty-one ounces; liver and kidneys normal; stomach congested in patches; Brünner's glands congested; small intestine congested in lower portion; Peyer's patches near ileo-cæcal valve extensively ulcerated; mesenteric glands greatly enlarged; bladder healthy.—*Hospital, Madison, Ind.*

CASE 10.—Private Daniel L. Keeney, Co. C, 140th Pa.; age 24; was admitted July 11, 1863, with a flesh-wound of the right hand, which granulated kindly until the 22d, when small ulcers were noticed on the inside of the cheek and on the tongue, for which a mouth-wash containing sulphate of zinc and tincture of myrrh was prescribed. During the next few days he became weak and languid, complaining on the 29th of some diarrhœa. Small doses of calomel, opium and ipecacuanha were administered, to which, on August 9, a solution of citrate of potassa was added. On the 12th he had slight cough with sonorous and sibilant râles, and there was iliac tenderness. Next day the red spots of enteric fever appeared on the abdomen and chest and the abdomen became tender all over. On the 13th, as the tongue was very dry and the strength failing, the treatment was changed to turpentine emulsion, wine, milk and beef-essence. Occasional delirium followed, and mucous, sonorous and sibilant râles became audible over the right side of the chest. Four dry cups, carbonate of ammonia and raw eggs were ordered. On the 18th increasing diarrhœa was recorded with subsultus tendinum, stupor, difficulty of swallowing and sloughing of the wound in the hand. Death occurred next day. *Post-mortem* examination seventeen hours after death: Abdomen flat; lungs congested, especially the right; heart, liver and kidneys normal; ileum congested, glands of Peyer thickened and near the cæcum ulcerated; jejunum normal. [Specimens 315 and 316, Med. Sect., Army Medical Museum, ulceration of ileum, are from this case.]—*Act. Ass't Surg. W. L. Wells, McClellan Hospital, Philadelphia, Pa.*

CASE 11.—Private John H. Winland, Co. D, 116th Ohio; age 23; was admitted Nov. 5, 1864, with typhoid fever. On admission the patient's skin was hot, tongue dry and bowels somewhat loose, tympanitic and tender. He was treated with quinine, oil of turpentine and chalk mixture until the 14th, when he seemed very much exhausted, presenting subsultus tendinum, hurried breathing, anxious countenance and a scarcely perceptible pulse. Under milk-punch, beef-tea and camphor and opium improvement took place; on the 24th the tongue was moist, there was some appetite and no delirium. On December 3 he coughed incessantly and his breathing became hurried. He died on the 6th. *Post-mortem* examination thirteen hours after death: Heart soft and flabby; lungs, spleen, kidneys and stomach healthy; liver much enlarged, weighing five pounds and a quarter; ileum inflamed in nearly its whole length and Peyer's patches ulcerated in fifteen places.—*Act. Ass't Surg. Sample Ford, U. S. A., Cumberland Hospital, Md.*

CASE 12.—Private John L. Palmer, 7th Mich. Cav.; age 21; was admitted April 30, 1865, convalescing from measles. On May 22 the nurse reported him as having been ailing for several days; he had headache, flushed cheeks, increased pulse, 90, dry tongue, tympanitic abdomen, pain in right iliac region, a good deal of diarrhœa and some rose-colored spots. Diarrhœa continued troublesome for several days, the pulse becoming more frequent and the teeth covered with sordes; delirium and pneumonic symptoms made their appearance and death occurred June 5. *Post-mortem* examination: The areolar tissue of the front of the neck was œdematous, the epiglottis swollen and the anterior mediastinum filled with lymph and serum. Each pleural sac contained a large quantity of serum; the whole of the right lung and the lower lobe of the left were much congested. The spleen was large; the ileum inflamed and Peyer's patches ulcerated.—*Act. Ass't Surg. H. J. Wiesel, Cumberland Hospital, Md.*

CASE 13.—Private William H. Green, Co. I, 161st N. Y., was admitted Nov. 19, 1862, delirious and greatly prostrated from typhoid fever. He had diarrhœa, sordes on the teeth and lips and a well-marked rose-colored eruption.

He was treated with laudanum and brandy, essence of beef and milk. The diarrhœa was checked and the delirium lessened, but the pulse became more frequent and feeble, the prostration increased and the patient died by asthenia on the 25th. *Post-mortem* examination: An abundant typhoid deposit in the glands of Peyer and solitary glands was in process of sloughing; the mesenteric glands were greatly enlarged.—*Ladies' Home Hospital, N. Y. City.*

CASE 14.—Sergt. Edwin Avery, Co. I, 161st N. Y., was admitted Nov. 19, 1862, with typhoid fever. He had been slightly sick for five days before admission, his case presenting moderate diarrhœa, meteorism and tenderness in the iliac region, rose-colored spots, much prostration and frequent, feeble pulse, but no delirium—indeed, shortly before death he gave directions with regard to certain family matters. He was treated with anodynes in moderate doses, alcoholic stimulants and a sustaining diet. He died by asthenia December 2. *Post-mortem* examination: An abundant typhoid deposit in the glands of Peyer and solitary glands was in process of sloughing; the corresponding mesenteric glands were greatly enlarged.—*Ladies' Home Hospital, N. Y. City.*

CASE 15.—Private John Caillot, Co. L, 4th N. Y. Cav.; age 24; was admitted July 19, 1863, with hot and dry skin, frequent and feeble pulse, diarrhœa, tympanites, abdominal tenderness, taches rouges over chest and abdomen and muttering delirium. He died on the 31st. *Post-mortem* examination eighteen hours after death: Emaciation; abdomen tumid; lower lobe of right lung congested; heart, liver and kidneys healthy; spleen enlarged; greater omentum much injected; mesenteric glands enlarged and inflamed; intestines filled with a liquid resembling pus; mucous membrane of small intestine softened; Peyer's patches thickened and ulcerated.—*Third Division Hospital, Alexandria, Va.*

CASE 16.—Private James Beckwith, Co. F, 2d Me.; age 23; was admitted Sept. 6, 1861, with typhoid fever occurring as a relapse. The patient had a full strong pulse, 120, heavily coated and dry tongue, hot and dry skin. One ounce of sulphate of magnesia was ordered. He rested poorly during the night, having had some head symptoms; his bowels were moved twice, although by mistake the Epsom salt had not been taken. His skin at the midnight visit, September 7, was warm and perspiring, tongue dry and brown in the centre, pulse full, 114. Half an ounce of tincture of rhubarb with ten drops of oil of anise was administered, by which the bowels were moved rapidly. In the evening he was unconscious, and during the night delirious with involuntary stools of a brown color. Next day there was rather less fever; pulse 104. Quinine, which had been given the previous day, was continued in eight-grain doses, with whiskey-punch and beef-essence, and an astringent injection at night. His bowels were moved twice on this day, the 8th, and he had tenderness in the right iliac region. During the following night there was walking delirium, and a few minute red spots were discovered, which did not disappear on pressure. At 11 A. M. of the 9th he had a severe congestive chill; during the paroxysm his pulse was strong and rapid; he raved and showed much strength. Morphia was given to quiet him. His bowels were moved involuntarily during the day, and he was very restless, requiring to be held in bed. On the 10th, after a quiet night, he was dull and stupid, his pulse 117, skin hot, face flushed, teeth covered with sordes; in the evening he became drowsy and was quiet during the night. Turpentine emulsion was given. On the 11th his pulse was quick and weak, 130, tongue cracked and protruded with difficulty, stools involuntary, countenance haggard and eyes fixed; he had also subsultus, grinding of the teeth, rose-colored spots and sudamina. In the evening his skin became cool, the prostration increased and the involuntary stools were large and fetid. On the 12th the symptoms were: Pulse 137, soft, small and weak; respiration 14; skin hot and moist; hands and feet cold and clammy; face pale; nose pinched; eyes and mouth half closed; lips livid; nausea; subsultus; black vomiting. He died at 3 P. M. *Post-mortem* examination: The ileum was much thickened, inflamed and ulcerated for five feet above the ileo-cæcal valve; Peyer's glands were elevated, extensively ulcerated and perforated in two places near the valve. No fæcal matter was found in the peritoneal cavity. The stomach was not examined.—*Seminary Hospital, Georgetown, D. C.*

CASE 17.—Private James D. Prickett, Co. H, 11th Va.; age 21; was admitted Sept. 19, 1864, with typhoid fever. According to the statement of a comrade this man had been in service about two years, during which he had performed his duties with little interruption from ill health. On admission he was delirious and almost moribund. He had apparently been ptyalised by some preparation of mercury before his arrival. Morphia was ordered for the purpose of procuring rest and sleep. On the 21st his pulse was 110, feeble and thread-like, tongue dry, red and glazed, gums spongy, teeth covered with sordes, breath tainted with the fetor of salivation, abdomen tympanitic and tender, countenance darkly flushed, skin cool and dry; there had been delirium during the night. A hot sponge-bath was ordered, with fomentations to the abdomen, quinine, turpentine emulsion, whiskey-punch and solution of chlorate of potassa as a mouth-wash. Under this treatment the tongue became somewhat moist and the sordes disappeared from the teeth, but the delirium continued through the night with drowsiness during the day. He had epistaxis, partly induced by picking at the nose. On the 25th he seemed slightly improved, but next day persistent vomiting set in with slight hiccough, the abdomen continuing distended and extremely sensitive. He died comatose on the 27th. *Post-mortem* examination seventeen hours after death: Body not much emaciated. There were recent peritoneal adhesions and a large quantity of serum in the abdominal cavity. The intestines were distended with flatus. The mucous membrane of the small intestine was congested and of a dark-red color from the pylorus to the ileo-cæcal valve; the glands of Peyer and the solitary glands were inflamed and ulcerated, and there were several minute perforations. The liver was normal; the spleen slightly enlarged and congested; the kidneys congested and greatly enlarged, the right weighing thirteen, the left ten ounces. The brain, thoracic viscera and colon were not examined. *Act. Ass't Surg. A. W. Holden, Cumberland Hospital, Md.*

CASE 18.—Private Abraham Lindsley, Co. E, 15th N. Y. Cav.; age 26; was admitted Sept. 6, 1864, with typhoid fever. This man enlisted in July, 1863, and had good health until March 10 following, when he had an attack of diarrhœa lasting six weeks, for which he was treated in regimental hospital. Exposure in the field during Hunter's raid through West Virginia brought on a recurrence of his diarrhœa, which continued during the whole of that severe campaign and for three weeks after its termination. While slowly improving in the regimental hospital he accompanied his regiment on a forced march, during which his strength utterly gave way, and he was sent to Hancock, Md., and thence to this hospital. On his arrival his symptoms were those of typhoid fever—pulse rapid and irritable, countenance darkly flushed, skin dry, eyes languid and dull, tongue red and dry, abdomen tender and tympanitic. He had frequent slimy, watery stools, with some tenesmus, and was so weak that he could scarcely speak. Morphia and astringent mixtures, quinine and milk-punch were administered, but without improvement. On the 11th his tongue had become brown and dry, his abdomen extremely sensitive and his stools thin and fetid. On the following night he had some delirium, and next day was drowsy and unconscious most of the time, occasionally picking at the bedclothes and fingering the air. He continued thus for two days, his pulse becoming more rapid and feeble and his tongue swollen, glazed and brown, with red margins. On the 14th there was a slight amelioration of the symptoms, but next day the pulse ran up to 140, the eyes became glassy, the pupils dilated, and death occurred after an interval of deep coma. *Post-mortem* examination seventeen hours and a half after death: Body moderately emaciated. Extensive congestion of the omentum, recent adhesions and other indications of peritonitis were observed. The intestinal mucous membrane was red and injected from the duodenum to the ileo-cæcal valve; Peyer's patches were extensively ulcerated and several of the ulcers had penetrated. The liver and kidneys were pale and fatty; the spleen enlarged and dark colored. The colon was not examined.—*Act. Ass't Surg. A. W. Holden, Cumberland Hospital, Md.*

CASE 19.—Private S. C. Cole, Co. F, 77th N. Y.; age 26; was admitted Aug. 1, 1864, with diarrhœa, nausea, vomiting, great prostration, weak voice and feeble pulse, 80, which continued, but with some abatement, until the 10th, when he was seized with a sudden and violent pain in the hypogastric and right iliac regions and became greatly prostrated, the countenance anxious, surface cold and moist, voice coarse and husky, pulse small and increasing in frequency and abdomen hard and tender but not tympanitic. Magendie's solution gave some relief to the pain, but he sank rapidly and died on the 12th. *Post-mortem* examination fourteen hours after death: Peritoneum purple, much congested, unadherent, and cavity containing thirty ounces of a yellow liquid mixed with fæcal matter. Small intestine much congested; ileum within a foot of the ileo-cæcal valve presenting many ulcerations of Peyer's glands, with five circular perforations from three-fourths of an inch to one inch in diameter.—*Surg. Henry K. Steele, 8th Ohio Cav., Hospital, Frederick, Md.*

CASE 20.—Private Henry R. Refior, Co. B, 13th Regulars, was admitted on board hospital steamer D. A. January March 17, 1863, at Young's Point, La. On admission he stated that he had been sick for some weeks, and from his description it was evident that he had suffered from a mild attack of typhoid fever. He was convalescing; he slept well and had a good appetite. When about to leave the boat, on March 23, for transfer to the convalescent hospital at Milliken's Bend, he was suddenly attacked by severe pains in the lower part of the abdomen and was at once carried back to bed. He had a pale, anxious countenance and was bathed in a profuse cold perspiration; pulse 90 and feeble. Half a grain of sulphate of morphia was ordered and hot applications to the abdomen. Castor oil was administered and afterwards an enema, but neither relieved the constipation of the bowels. In the evening there was much pain and distention. Sulphate of morphia was given every two hours. He became intensely prostrated and died at midday of the 26th. There was no vomiting in this case. *Post-mortem* examination ten hours after death: Thoracic viscera normal. The peritoneal sac was inflamed and contained a large quantity of greenish fluid; the abdominal viscera were glued to each other by layers of soft coagulated lymph. The mucous membrane of the ileum was in some places injected, and in its lower part near the cæcum were some cicatrized ulcers of Peyer's glands; one ulcerated patch had perforated the coats of the intestine.—*Surg. Alexander H. Hoff, U. S. V., Hospital Steamer D. A. January.*

(B.) Peyer's patches ulcerated and the large intestine also implicated—13 cases.

CASE 21.—Private Richard Clark, Co. M, 2d Mass. Cav.; age 21; was admitted July 19, 1863, having been sick for an unknown period; tongue dark brown but red along the edges; pulse 130, small; delirium; epistaxis; diarrhœa; abdomen tympanitic and covered with petechiæ. His condition improved under the influence of camphor, valerian, quinine, acetate of ammonia and sponging with alcohol and water, but on the 24th pain was developed in the right lung with dulness and crepitant râles over its lower lobe. Cupping was followed by relief; but his skin continued hot and dry. On August 2 he passed a quart of blood from his bowels and a small quantity on the following day. He died, exhausted, on the 5th. *Post-mortem* examination seven hours after death: Right lung congested throughout; left lung healthy. Stomach bloodless, its coats somewhat thickened and its pyloric orifice contracted; Peyer's patches ulcerated; ileo-cæcal valve extensively ulcerated and disorganized; ascending colon containing a considerable quantity of blood.—*Act. Ass't Surg. T. Turner, Third Division Hospital, Alexandria, Va.*

CASE 22.—Private Henry Royer, Co. C, 148th Pa., died June 30, 1863, from an attack of typhoid fever. *Post-mortem* examination twenty-four hours after death: Slight cadaveric rigidity; much bloody froth issuing from the mouth and nostrils. The mucous lining of the stomach was irregularly colored; it was of a slaty hue at the pylorus, mottled reddish and blackish. Beneath the epithelial lining of the duodenum a quantity of gas was found, supposed to be due to putrefactive changes. Below this point the mucous membrane was of a dull whitish color, very inelastic and easily torn. Eight feet from the ileo-cæcal valve Peyer's patches commenced to be involved; at first the upper and lower parts of the patch were swollen, livid, not ulcerated, the centre being natural; lower down some were entirely livid, with no ulceration; about one foot from the valve was one very large patch with thick high walls, ulcerated centre and numerous small ulcerated points in its area. These portions were of a lighter hue than the non-ulcerated portions, but none of them perforated the gut; the largest patches gave the intestine a honey-combed appearance from the peculiarity of the ulceration. The large intestine was of a grayish-slate color, its mucous membrane softened but not ulcerated.—*Ass't Surg. Harrison Allen, U. S. A., Lincoln Hospital, Washington, D. C.*

CASE 23.—Private Dudley Whitlock, Co. E, 5th Mich. Cav.; age 17; was admitted March 25, 1863. On April 1 his condition was noted as follows: Weak; tongue dry and coated; pulse 144, compressible; respiration 66, difficult; bowels regular; skin hot and dry; bed-sores on back and hips; urine passed involuntarily; dulness on percussion over each lung, most marked posteriorly; greatly increased vocal resonance; bronchial respiration; irritable cough. 3d: Pulse 130; respiration 60; sputa somewhat tenacious. 6th: Stronger; profuse semi-purulent discharge from each ear. 7th: Diarrhœa, seven stools; pulse 140; respiration 44; tongue moist. 10th: Diarrhœa continues; he refuses medicine. Body sponged with whiskey; medicine given by enema. 14th: Pulse 158; respiration 24; weak; death. *Post-mortem* examination twenty hours after death: Rigor mortis; emaciation. Brain normal. Trachea and bronchi filled with white viscid sputa; mucous membrane dark purplish; bronchial glands firm, of a dull liver color mottled blackish in centre. Lungs solidified and dark purple posteriorly, reddish anteriorly; minute whitish points in central portions; pleuritic effusion on left side. Heart contained small white clots on both sides. Liver mottled purple and pale yellow, interlobular areas yellowish; twenty-six drachms of dark bile in gall-bladder. Spleen firm, dark mulberry color. Œsophagus pale; mucous membrane of stomach mottled a delicate pink color; deposit of black pigment on pylorus. Small intestine in upper part pale yellowish; duodenum filled with thick stringy mucus; Peyer's patches normal to within eighteen inches of ileo-cæcal valve, where they were thickened, elevated, congested and in many places indurated and ulcerated, the ulcers having well-defined edges and in some instances reddish bases; solitary follicles the size of small shot. Mucous membrane of large intestine pale, rugæ dark red; solitary glands prominent, dotted with pigment in centre; lower portion of intestine presenting many minute superficial ulcers unconnected with solitary glands. Kidneys pale; suprarenal capsules mottled.—*Ass't Surg. Harrison Allen, U. S. A., Lincoln Hospital, Washington, D. C.*

CASE 24.—Private John North, Co. E, 5th Mich. Cav., was admitted March 25, 1863, having been sick for some time in regimental hospital. He was delirious and had high fever, a tremulous full pulse, sordes upon the mouth and teeth, a typhoid fever tongue, some cough and expectoration, pain in the right iliac fossa and diarrhœa, the evacuations soon becoming involuntary and offensive. He died on the 28th. *Post-mortem* examination twelve hours after death: No emaciation; rigor mortis marked; apparent age 21 years. The brain was healthy. The right lung was congested and weighed twenty-five ounces; the left twenty-six ounces, its lower lobe being intensely engorged and in some parts hepatized. The right side of the heart contained a blackish clot of moderate size; the left ventricle a smaller clot. The liver was pale, its acini well defined, its texture softer than usual, its weight seventy-three ounces and a half; the gall-bladder contained five drachms of deep-yellow flaky bile. The spleen was soft, deep purplish-black and weighed eighteen ounces. The pancreas and kidneys were normal. The stomach was red at the fundus. Peyer's patches were indurated, thickened and in many places ulcerated. The solitary glands were so numerous that on a square inch selected at random fifteen were counted; they were large, about two lines in diameter. The mucous membrane of the large intestine was generally mottled red, but in the ascending colon it was of a light slate color mottled with red; the solitary glands in the cæcum were enlarged and several of them ulcerated.—*Ass't Surg. Harrison Allen, U. S. A., Lincoln Hospital, Washington, D. C.*

CASE 25.—Private Edward E. Rice, Co. D, 123d N. Y., was admitted Jan. 11, 1863. During the interval between his admission and his death on the 14th extreme agitation, hurried respiration, delirium and tenderness in the right iliac fossa were noted. *Post-mortem* examination seven hours after death: The lungs were crowded into the upper part of the thorax by the distended intestines; the left lung was slightly congested posteriorly; the upper and middle lobes of the right lung were partially congested and solidified, apparently the result of hypostasis; the blood was fluid. The liver was large and pale; the spleen large, congested and soft; the kidneys pale and exsanguine. The intestines were inflated with gas; the ileum congested; Peyer's patches enlarged and ulcerated, some to a marked degree; the cæcum congested; the mesenteric glands enlarged.—*Surg. H. Bryant, U. S. Vols., Lincoln Hospital, Washington, D. C.*

CASE 26.—Private Jos. McVaugh, Co. D, 147th Pa.; age 45; was admitted July 28, 1863. He was very feeble and delirious, with an inclination to stupor; his tongue very dry and red; skin cool and clammy; pulse 113, small and weak; bowels moved about ten times daily; abdomen hard and tender, especially in the right iliac region. In the progress of the case the stools became less frequent, but all the other symptoms increased in severity; the passages during the night before death were involuntary. He died August 2. *Post-mortem* examination seven hours after death: The brain weighed forty-five ounces; the pia mater was somewhat congested and the choroid plexuses filled with minute air-bubbles. The trachea was greenish but contained healthy sputa; the mucous membrane of the œsophagus was pale, yellow-stained near the cardiac orifice and presented numerous whitish points. The right lung weighed eleven ounces and was slightly engorged in its upper and middle lobes. The left lung weighed fifteen ounces; its upper lobe was much shrunken and contained but little air; towards its apex was a small circular elevation about the size of a chestnut, surrounded by a livid purplish zone about three inches in diameter; on opening this spot a quantity of air escaped and a few drops of bloody fluid; the lower lobe was engorged with venous blood. The heart contained a small fibrinous clot in the right cavities and a mixed clot in the left; the pericardium contained two drachms of bloody fluid. The stomach was unusually firm and its mucous membrane pale-red in color throughout. The liver weighed fifty-three ounces and was slightly congested; the gall-bladder contained ten ounces of bile of a brownish-ochre color, filled with a flaky substance which did not precipitate. The spleen weighed five ounces and was flabby, soft and of a mulberry color. The right kidney weighed five ounces; its external surface was of a bluish color spotted with numerous dark-blue points; an abscess about the size of a horse chestnut, with ecchymosed walls, containing discolored pus, was found on the anterior surface near the outer margin. The left kidney weighed five ounces and a half; it was much congested; a small cyst containing serum was found on its anterior surface. The small intestine was healthy to within three feet of the ileo-cæcal valve, but from this point downward the mucous membrane was of a reddish-purple color, thin and somewhat softened; Peyer's patches were discolored and ulcerated, especially near the valve, where patches of a dark-blue stone color, fully an inch in diameter, were eroded. The large intestine was greenish but free from ulceration; the solitary glands were white and conspicuous.—*Ass't Surg. Harrison Allen, U. S. A., Lincoln Hospital, Washington, D. C.*

CASE 27.—Private Martin Burnes, Co. G, 164th N. Y.; age 20; admitted July 17, 1865, having been sick about three weeks without medical attendance. Low delirium set in on the 19th; diarrhœa, which was troublesome at first, subsided by the 21st. On the 23d blood to the amount of two pints was passed from the bowels, and he died exhausted four hours thereafter. *Post-mortem* examination nine hours after death: The intestines were half filled with a frothy, semi-fluid, bloody mass; Peyer's patches were ulcerated into deep excavations bounded by thickened and indurated edges; the solitary follicles were ulcerated throughout both small and large intestines; many of the ulcers penetrated to the peritoneum. The spleen was enlarged and softened; the other organs normal.—*Act. Ass't Surg. George P. Hanawalt, Douglas Hospital, Washington, D. C.*

CASE 28.—Private Castor Seebold, Co. E, 51st Pa.; age 19; was admitted May 7, 1864, presenting some emaciation, dry tongue, sordes on teeth, tenderness in right iliac fossa, and restlessness, with a frequent pulse, 120. Next day rose-colored spots were observed, and he had epistaxis and diarrhœa, with a more rapid pulse. He was treated with acetate of ammonia and morphia, milk-punch, eggnog and beef-tea. He died on the 11th. *Post-mortem* examination four hours after death: Lungs congested; heart, liver and kidneys healthy; spleen somewhat softened and congested; ileum and cæcum very much congested; Peyer's patches and the solitary glands in the ileum much enlarged and ulcerated.—*Turner's Lane Hospital, Philadelphia, Pa.*

CASE 29.—Corporal J. B. Richardson, Co. E, 2d Mich.; age 26; admitted Feb. 8, 1863, having been affected for two weeks with anorexia, tympanites, diarrhœa and cough, and presenting a hot and dry skin, furred tongue and injected eyes; delirium and involuntary stools occurred on the 11th, and death took place on the 17th. *Post-mortem* examination: The brain was normal. The bronchial tubes on both sides presented indications of inflammation, and the lower lobes of the lungs contained hepatizations from the size of a chestnut to that of a hen's egg. The liver and spleen were large but unaltered in texture; the gall-bladder was small and half full of dark bile; the kidneys healthy; the pancreas enlarged and somewhat hardened. The mesenteric glands were enlarged and indurated; the mucous membrane of the stomach much injected; the duodenum and jejunum inflamed in patches; the ileum congested, thickened and softened, and its agminated glands ulcerated, the ulcers having thick, hard, prominent edges. The colon was inflamed in patches and its mucous membrane thickened.—*Harewood Hospital, Washington, D. C.*

CASE 30.—Private Edgar Sanborn, Co. D, 6th N. H.; age 15; was admitted July 24, 1864, with feeble and frequent pulse, great heat of body, dry brown tongue, sordes on teeth, slight diarrhœa and great tenderness in the right iliac region. On the 28th his face became dusky and stupor supervened. He died on the 30th. *Post-mortem* examination: Much bronchial secretion; lungs congested; heart and liver normal; lower half of ileum slightly inflamed, with commencing ulceration of Peyer's glands and cicatrices of old ulcers; cæcum presenting two ulcerations; rectum much inflamed.—*Act. Ass't Surg. A. H. Haven, Fairfax Seminary, Va.*

CASE 31.—Private Oscar Snow, Co. H, 3d Vt.; age 20; was admitted Oct. 1, 1861, with typhoid fever. He had been sick a week, but he was so dull that he could give but little information concerning the early part of his sickness. A bath was ordered for him, and Dover's powder at night. Next day his face was flushed, pulse 135, full, skin hot and dry, tongue slightly moist but thickly coated brown; he had slight delirium, some deafness and ten or twelve characteristic rose-colored spots; his bowels were loose, tender and tympanitic. From this time the condition of the patient gradually changed for the worse. His bowels for some time were not loose, but tenderness, meteorism and borborygmus were present throughout; on October 12 he had three involuntary passages. His pulse, which at first was rapid and full, lost its fulness but retained its rapidity, becoming small, weak and fluctuating. His tongue became dry, and on the 9th he was unable to protrude it; on the same day sordes appeared on the teeth. The rose-colored spots disappeared on the 11th. From being somewhat dull mentally, with occasional mild delirium, he fell into a prostrate condition, lying on his back with his lower jaw dropped and his eyes open, taking no notice of anything going on around. On the 8th his breathing became hurried; mucous and sibilant râles were heard in the right lung, and on the 12th a leathery creaking sound was distinguished over both lungs. On the 11th the parotid gland was found to be swollen. The treatment consisted of quinine, turpentine, brown mixture, nourishment and stimulants. On the evening of the 13th his face was ashen-gray in color, lips cold and bloodless, head and extremities cold; there was some deafness and it was very difficult to arouse him; he had also a mild delirium, speaking of going home, and had no idea of his condition. His pulse, about 140, was weak and barely perceptible at the wrist; the superficial circulation was almost suspended—an impression made with the fingers remained a long time. He had no hemorrhage from the nose or bowels; his bowels moved occasionally involuntarily, the passages being very thin; the abdomen was acutely tender and borborygmus frequent. His respiration varied from fifty to sixty per minute; a rattling sound was heard in the throat during expiration, as though from mucus which he had not strength enough to eject; his breath was very offensive for the first time since his illness. His urine, acid and albuminous, had a specific gravity of 1011, and contained mucus, epithelium, urates and a few blood-discs. The parotid gland continued much swollen. On the evening of the 14th he aroused himself and spoke very rationally; his eyes shone brilliantly for a few minutes; he tried to rise from bed, but fell back from weakness; the rattling sound in the bronchial tubes increased, and after a few deep-drawn breaths he was dead. *Post-mortem* examination fourteen hours after death: Side of face swollen; parotid infiltrated with pus. The pleural cavities contained a number of large blood-clots; the derivation of the hemorrhage was not ascertained. The lungs were congested, but were not closely examined for want of time. The stomach contained a pint of very offensive yellowish matter; its mucous membrane was thick and congested. The liver and gall-bladder were enlarged but healthy; the spleen and kidneys enlarged and congested. The peritoneum was much inflamed. The glands of Peyer and the solitary glands of the ileum were much ulcerated. A foot and a half from the ileo-cæcal valve the ileum presented a diverticulum about four inches long, as wide as the gut from which it was derived, and like it, blackened and much ulcerated. The mesenteric glands were enlarged, the mesentery much congested and inflamed. The mucous membrane of the colon was dark in color but not ulcerated.—*Seminary Hospital, Georgetown, D. C.*

CASE 32.—Private Christian Schultz, Co. K, 14th Conn.; age 42; was admitted Dec. 16, 1862, having been sick for two or three months with rheumatism. He complained only of pains in his back and limbs until Jan. 1, 1863, when he was taken with headache, trembling, a full compressible pulse and other manifestations of nervous derangement; his tongue was moist and coated with a white fur. He was ordered a teaspoonful of castor oil, which operated six times in the twenty-four hours. No noticeable change occurred until the 6th, when some tympanites was observed and one tache rouge close to the umbilicus. On the 9th the pulse became small and compressible, the tongue dry, the face flushed and the diarrhœa persistent, while an increasing tendency to drowsiness was manifest. Ten days later the diarrhœa became checked and the tongue dry, raw and cracked; he had herpetic eruptions on the lower lip, a troublesome cough, and was so much prostrated as to slide down in bed. On the 21st his bowels were moved in hard masses after an interval of forty-eight hours; next day his pulse was stronger, tongue cleaning and more moist and skin clammy, but the cough persisted and was distressing. On the 30th he was considered convalescent, and his case, with careful attention to diet, progressed favorably until February 25, when there occurred unmistakable evidence of a relapse. On March 3 the patient presented the taches rouges, and was affected with dulness of hearing, epistaxis, tympanites and diarrhœa; on the 8th he vomited matter which looked like altered blood, and complained of pain in the left hypochondrium. During the next few days the vomiting continued and a cough with bloody sputa was developed. On the 14th the respirations were 56 per minute and the pulse frequent and feeble. He died on the 20th. *Post-mortem* examination: The mucous membrane of the trachea and bronchial tubes was inflamed; the bronchial tubes were filled with muco-purulent matter. In the right lung were several hepatized nodules the size of walnuts, the surfaces of which were attached by recent pseudo-membrane to the costal pleura; the left pleural sac contained about two quarts of yellow serum mingled with pus and thin jelly-like fibrinous coagula. The heart was filled with black and white clots. Peyer's glands were thickened and a number of them ulcerated, three of the latter having perforated; but there was no evidence of peritonitis. The cæcum was moderately inflamed and presented a number of small ulcers; the colon showed a few streaks of inflammation. There was intralobular congestion of the liver. The spleen was soft.—*Act. Ass't Surg. Joseph Leidy, Satterlee Hospital, Philadelphia.*

CASE 33.—Sergt. Gustave Van Ecken, Co. F, Independent battalion, N. Y.; age 30; was admitted from Beaufort, S. C., with typhoid fever: Prostration, pulse 120, tongue dry and brown, sordes, diarrhœa, red eruption, delirium, and, forty-eight hours before death, tympanites. *Post-mortem* examination eighteen hours after death: Peyer's patches extensively ulcerated; mucous membrane of large intestine ulcerated; cæcum perforated at two points; abdominal cavity containing a large quantity of fæcal matter and showing but slight evidences of peritonitis; kidneys fatty; spleen enlarged.—*Act. Ass't Surg. S. Teats, Central Park Hospital, N. Y. City.*

(*C.*) *Condition of Peyer's patches not stated; ileum or small intestine ulcerated—13 cases.*

CASE 34.—Private Benjamin Cunningham, Co. D, 86th N. Y.; age 21; was admitted Feb. 18, 1862, having been sick for some time with chills, headache, pains in back and limbs, loss of appetite, epistaxis, diarrhœa and inability to sleep. On March 4 his pulse was recorded as rapid and weak, skin warm and moist, cheeks flushed, tongue smooth and natural, abdomen tympanitic and covered with vibices and a few sudamina; he had little appetite, great thirst and one or two watery and sometimes involuntary passages; he was somewhat deaf but appeared sensible; respiration was hurried and there was some cough. Treatment: Punch, beef-essence, turpentine emulsion and tincture of iron, with mustard to the abdomen. From this time he improved: His watery passages gave place to more natural and regular discharges,—indeed, on the 10th his bowels were noted as rather constipated, he slept well, his appetite returned and his general appearance and strength seemed improving; but his tongue was considered to be too smooth, and at times his mind did not appear to be clear. He was, however, considered as in a fair way to recovery. On the 15th he complained that his hips were sore from long continued pressure, and next day that he had lost the sense of taste—that he could feel his food when in his mouth but could not taste it. Bed-sores over the sacrum were noted on the 17th, and great debility with enlarging sores over the left trochanter on the 26th, on which day also he was seized with a severe pain in the left side. This pain increased on the 27th, the breathing becoming hurried and prostration extreme; his mind was clear, pupils dilated, the sclerotic showing to an unnatural extent. He died on the 29th, diarrhœa returning a few hours before death. *Post-mortem* examination: The mucous membrane of the ileum was much inflamed and ulcerated eighteen or twenty inches above the ileo-cæcal valve.—*Seminary Hospital, Georgetown, D. C.*

CASE 35.—Private Jacob Davis, Co. I, 63d Pa.; age 21; was admitted Oct. 10, 1863, with emaciation, debility and diarrhœa, a dry, brown tongue, cracked in centre, teeth covered with sordes, respiration quick and feeble and pulse over 90. He lingered without much change until the 18th, when he died. He was given concentrated nourishment and stimulants, sweet spirit of nitre and turpentine emulsion, with nitrate of silver and opium for the diarrhœa. *Post-mortem* examination six hours after death: The small intestine was considerably congested and for several feet was patched with ulcerations, some of which were as large as a quarter dollar; spleen somewhat enlarged. Other organs healthy.—*Act. Ass't Surg. J. E. Smith, Fairfax Seminary, Va.*

CASE 36.—Private Albert Tucker, Co. A, 23d Ohio; age 30; was admitted Oct. 18, 1864, as a convalescent from typhoid fever. He looked pale and weak, had little appetite, but was in good spirits and able to walk about the ward. He had from six to ten stools daily, which were occasionally streaked with blood; his lower extremities were œdematous and there was some slight abdominal effusion; he had a slight cough, and the heart-sounds seemed distant and masked. Astringents, anodynes and diuretics were employed. He died rather suddenly on the 24th after an attack of dyspnœa and severe præcordial pain. *Post-mortem* examination: Head and upper part of body ecchymosed; lower extremities œdematous; brain normal; thoracic cavity containing a pint and a half of serum; lungs congested and lymph-coated posteriorly; pericardium containing considerable effusion; tricuspid valve apparently thickened; omentum almost devoid of fat; liver and stomach healthy; spleen somewhat enlarged; mesenteric glands enlarged; small intestine presenting many and large ulcerations, especially near the ileo-cæcal valve; kidneys very much enlarged but apparently normal in structure.—*Cuyler Hospital, Philadelphia, Pa.*

CASE 37.—Private William H. Harrison, Co. B, 11th Ohio; age 19; was admitted June 22, 1864, presenting a rapid pulse, dry, furred tongue, anorexia, thirst, abdominal tenderness, diarrhœa, restlessness, delirium and the typhoid rose-rash. These symptoms continued, varying in intensity from day to day, until July 2, when they assumed so aggravated a form as to leave no hope of recovery. He died on the 4th. *Post-mortem* examination eight hours after death: Body emaciated; blood oozing from right ear; right lung firmly adherent to costal pleura, its upper lobe congested; spleen three times the usual size; liver enlarged, its right lobe congested; left kidney twice the normal size, its calyx enlarged; lower part of ileum ulcerated, in some places through to its serous coat; mesenteric glands enlarged and inflamed.—*Act. Ass't Surg. C. E. Boyle, Seminary Hospital, Columbus, Ohio.*

CASE 38.—Private Daniel Dewey, Co. E, 196th Ohio; age 23; was admitted April 5, 1865, in a very feeble and emaciated condition: Skin dry and husky, neck and breast covered with sudamina, right elbow and knee joints swollen and very painful, tongue dry and cracked, teeth, lips and gums covered with sordes; he had diarrhœa and a hoarse cough, with difficult respiration but not much expectoration. He died on the 22d. *Post-mortem* examination ten hours after death: Body extremely emaciated. Small deposits of pus were found between the fibres of the pectoralis major of the right side. The epiglottis was œdematous and ulcerated; the vocal cords ulcerated; the mucous membrane of the larynx, trachea and bronchial tubes intensely inflamed; the left lung hepatized; the apex of the right lung engorged and infiltrated with sero-purulent matter. The liver was large, pale and soft; the spleen enlarged and much engorged; the ileum inflamed and ulcerated. There was a large deposit of pus in the cavity of the right knee joint and an effusion of serum in the surrounding parts. The left wrist joint and the right elbow joint also contained pus.—*Act. Ass't Surg. S. B. West, Cumberland Hospital, Md.*

CASE 39.—Private Franklin D. Hicks, Co. K, 157th N. Y., was admitted Nov. 18, 1862, with typhoid fever. The rose-colored spots were very distinct and the sudamina abundant. He died on the 29th. *Post-mortem* examination forty-eight hours after death: In the lower portion of the small intestine the peritoneal coat was much injected and readily peeled off, and the mucous membrane was extensively softened and ulcerated. The mesentery was considerably injected and the mesenteric glands much enlarged.—*Third Division Hospital, Alexandria, Va.*

CASE 40.—Private Josiah Cheever, Co. B, 15th Vt., was admitted April 14, 1863: Headache; occasional delirium; pulse 100, compressible; hot and dry skin; six to eight stools daily; short, dry cough; sibilant rhonchus distinct over chest anteriorly; abdomen tympanitic. Calomel, opium and ipecacuanha in small doses alternating with effervescing mixture ameliorated his condition. The chest and head symptoms subsided, but the abdomen remained distended and tender and the diarrhœa continued. On the 22d his tongue became cracked and pulse feeble, 120. He died on the 28th, notwithstanding the administration of turpentine, alcoholic stimulants and ammonia. *Post-mortem* examination: Thoracic viscera normal. Mucous membrane of small intestine injected, lower ileum presenting eight large ulcers; corresponding mesenteric glands enlarged.—*Third Division Hospital, Alexandria, Va.*

CASE 41.—Private Benjamin Tice, Co. E, 13th N. J.; age 24; was admitted Oct. 29, 1862, with diarrhœa, iliac tenderness, nervous disorder and four taches rouges; the skin was hot and dry, pulse frequent but not very feeble, tongue coated with dark fur; there was also a slight cough, accompanied by very little pain in the chest but with most distressing dyspnœa and almost complete aphonia; the chest was resonant on percussion. Small doses of blue mass, opium and ipecacuanha seemed to relieve the chest symptoms and check the diarrhœa. Later, dulness on percussion was noted over the lower portion of the right lung. Dry cups were applied and stimulants administered. After this the pulse became more frequent and feeble, the tongue fissured, the teeth and gums covered with sordes, diarrhœa profuse and tympanites extreme. He died November 6. *Post-mortem* examination: The heart was healthy; the left lung extensively congested; the middle and lower lobes of the right lung hepatized. The omentum was engorged with dark blood; the liver and spleen enlarged; the mucous membrane of the stomach slightly reddened; the duodenal glands much enlarged; the lower part of the ileum ulcerated in eight large patches. The large intestine was not examined. The kidneys were healthy.—*Third Division Hospital, Alexandria, Va.*

CASE 42.—Private Martin V. Murphy, Co. F, 123d Ohio, was admitted May 4, 1864, from hospital, Alexandria, Va. He had no hereditary tendency to disease and enjoyed excellent health up to fourteen months ago, when he was seized with a cold while on a scout at Winchester, Va., which in a few days was followed by fever. This confined him to bed for six or seven weeks, after which he partially recovered and went home on furlough, where he had a relapse which disabled him for four or five weeks. He so far recovered from this as to be able to walk several miles and continued to improve for two months, when he was taken with dysentery, which lasted two or three weeks, and since that time he has not fully regained his strength. He returned to his regiment and remained with it for about four weeks while it was in camp at Brandy Station, Va., but during that time he was unfit for duty. When the army moved he was sent to hospital at Alexandria, where he remained a month, after which he was transferred, as above stated. When admitted he was suffering from debility consequent on typhoid fever and dysentery. He was put on tonics and astringents, with the best diet the hospital afforded. He improved gradually until the 14th, when he complained of a sharp pain in the lower part of the right breast, aggravated by deep inspiration and coughing; pulse

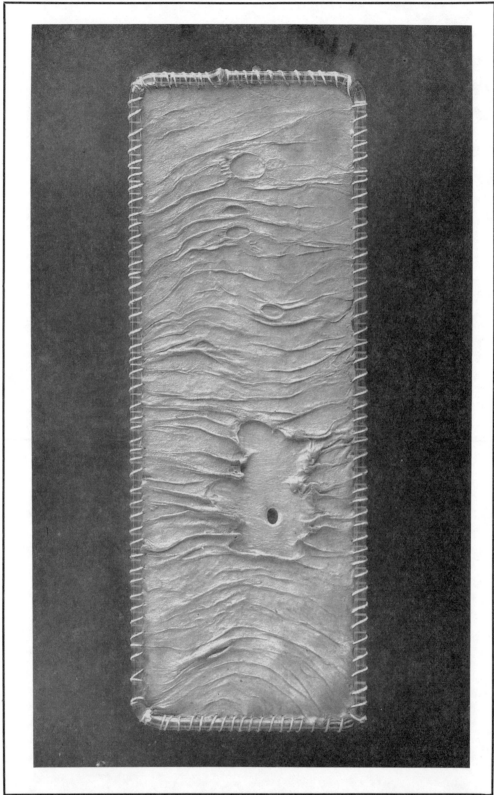

PERFORATING ULCER OF THE ILEUM.

No. 452.   MEDICAL SECTION.

120 and small; tongue moist and red; cough with white frothy expectoration; decubitus on left side; skin very hot. This pleuritic attack lasted until the 25th, after which convalescence progressed satisfactorily until July 11, when he complained of diarrhœa with some tenesmus, which steadily increased, resisting all efforts for its relief. He died July 25th. *Post-mortem* examination sixteen hours after death: Body much emaciated. A large amount of serum was found beneath the dura mater, between the layers of the arachnoid and in the ventricles; the substance of the brain was soft. The right pleural cavity was filled with purulent serum and the pulmonary and costal pleuræ were completely lined with a fibro-albuminous deposit; the lung was consolidated by pressure and bound to the posterior wall of the chest; both lungs were tuberculous; one tubercular ulcer in the right lung had perforated the pulmonary pleura. Tubercles were diffused over the surface of the heart and pericardium. The liver was healthy; spleen small and hard; kidneys small in size but healthy in appearance. Ulcers, with their long diameters at right angles to the length of the gut, were found throughout the small intestine.—*Act. Ass't Surg. Charles P. Tutt, Satterlee Hospital, Philadelphia, Pa.*

CASE 43.—Private E. J. Williamson, Co. C, 179th N. Y.; age 20; was admitted Nov. 30, 1864, having been sick for about twelve months. His tongue was dry, dark and cracked and had a glazed edge; teeth covered with sordes; abdomen tympanitic and tender; bowels loose. There was no rose-colored eruption and but little cerebral excitement. Turpentine emulsion and wine were given, and the case progressed favorably until December 3, when pneumonia set in. Next day the pulse was 120, the delirium marked, cough harassing and expectoration scanty. He died on the 5th. *Post-mortem* examination: Ulceration of the ileum, especially about the ileo-cæcal valve. Posterior portions of both lungs hepatized. [*Specimen* 452, Med. Sect., Army Medical Museum, from this case, shows perforation and peritonitis to have existed.]—*Act. Ass't Surg. W. C. Minor, Third Division Hospital, Alexandria, Va.*

CASE 44.—Private William F. Hart, Co. A, 14th U. S. Inf., was admitted Aug. 14, 1863, with such symptoms of typhoid fever as a dry and cracked tongue, sordes on teeth, small, weak and rapid pulse, quiet delirium and tympanites. Abdominal tenderness became aggravated and he died on the 16th. *Post-mortem* examination: Perforation of the lower ileum; firm adhesions of intestines.—*Third Division Hospital, Alexandria, Va.*

CASE 45.—Private Silas Tomlinson, Co. K, 24th Mich., was admitted Nov. 30, 1864. The patient had been sick for some time in hospital at City Point, Va.; he suffered much and received but little attention during his journey to Alexandria. On admission: Pulse weak, thread-like and from 90 to 100 per minute; skin hot and dry; tongue very dry, red and slightly coated; thirst urgent; appetite small; epistaxis; deafness; expression stupid; delirium; abdomen generally tender, tympanitic and showing a few sudamina and many petechial spots. December 1: No change. 2d: Pulse somewhat stronger, fuller and less frequent; tongue less dry; expression of countenance brighter and hearing improved; diarrhœa less active, but tenderness and tympanites of the abdomen unchanged. 3d: Pulse 80 and decidedly stronger; diarrhœa checked; tongue throwing off its fur; appetite improved; patient intelligent. 4th: The favorable symptoms continued; tenderness of the abdomen lessened. 5th: At 2 A. M. a change for the worse took place; the pulse became weak and ran up to 100; the patient had slight chills; his tongue became dry and red and sordes gathered on his teeth, gums and lips, while the whole surface was bathed in a cold clammy sweat; petechial spots assumed the appearance of purplish blotches, and the abdomen became exceedingly tender, swollen and tympanitic. Ten hours after this change took place the patient had several involuntary stools of a dark-greenish color, after which he fell into a semi-stupor from which he could with difficulty be aroused, and when aroused gave imperfect answers to questions proposed; his face was sunken and there was much twitching of the muscles of the upper extremities. He died on this day. *Post-mortem* examination twenty-three hours after death: A few purple-colored points, said to be of ante-mortem formation, were noticed on the chest and abdomen; there was also purple hypostasis of the posterior part of the body. There was a quantity of fluid under the arachnoid at the vertex of the brain, but the substance of the brain was normal. The heart was dilated on its right side and almost completely filled by a large semi-transparent clot. The left lung was crepitant, although somewhat dark colored posteriorly. The right lung was closely adherent by firm tissue and apparently compressed or drawn over to the right side; the posterior part of its upper lobe was of a dark brown-red color, softened and with minute points, apparently bronchi, filled with a yellow froth; the remainder of the lung was normal. The liver was large and of a uniformly pale clay color; the spleen large and softened; the cortical part of the left kidney of a yellow, semi-fatty appearance. About twelve inches from the colon the small intestine was perforated by a black-margined aperture the size of a small shot; recent lymph glued the perforated coil of the ileum to the bladder and sigmoid flexure. Liquid fæces of a yellow color had to a small extent escaped into the pelvic cavity.—*Act. Ass't Surg. W. C. Minor, General Hospital, Alexandria, Va.*

CASE 46.—Private Thomas Williams, Co. H, 8th Md.; age 32; was taken with fever at Camp Bradford (straggler's camp) Aug. 1, 1863. He was admitted on the 13th: Countenance heavy; face flushed; skin hot; pulse about 100; respiration difficult; diarrhœa with ochre-colored passages; urine scanty and high-colored. Treatment: Acetate of ammonia, camphor and quinine, with opiate enemata. On the 15th he was restless and had considerable subsultus; the tongue was protruded with difficulty; respiration was accelerated; much viscid mucus was brought up; auscultation revealed bronchial breathing, and the right lung was dull on percussion. Extract of valerian, sweet spirit of nitre and carbonate of ammonia were administered and turpentine stupes applied to the chest. On the 19th he was greatly depressed, the diarrhœa frequent and exhausting. Carbonate of ammonia in two-grain doses was given every two hours. Next day the pneumonic symptoms were unchanged, the sputa adhesive and tinged with blood. A blister was applied to the chest. Both iliac regions were tympanitic and tender. On the 21st the patient's extremities were cold. Brandy was substituted for milk-punch, which had been given freely since the 18th. On the 23d his mind was clearer than at any time since his entrance. At 8 A. M. of the following day he was seized with violent pain and tenderness in the abdomen followed by persistent vomiting. He died on the 25th. *Post-mortem* examination shortly after death: The peritoneum showed marks of extensive inflammation and contained about eight ounces of liquid matter similar in character to the dejections during life. The mesenteric glands were enlarged and the ileum, for the distance of three feet above the ileo-cæcal valve, was inflamed and ulcerated; a large perforation was situated fourteen inches above the cæcum. The thoracic and cranial cavities were not opened.—*Med. Cadet W. L. Bradley, McKim's Mansion, Baltimore, Md.*

(D.) Condition of Peyer's patches not stated; ileum or small intestine ulcerated and large intestine affected—4 cases.

CASE 47.—Private Elias Brink, Co. B, 137th N. Y.; age 53; was admitted Jan. 18, 1863, having been sick two weeks. He spoke of having hurt his back and ruptured himself by a fall while on the march, and complained of pain in his back. Symptoms of what was supposed to be pericarditis made their appearance on February 7, and next day veratrum viride was prescribed. On the 11th he was noticed to be very deaf; his pulse was slow and weak, and vomiting had set in. The veratrum viride was discontinued. Next day he lapsed into stupor and when aroused with difficulty from this state his answers were incoherent; his breathing was rapid. On the 14th an eruption like that of typhoid fever made its appearance on his body and extremities; he coughed much and muttered to himself; there appeared to be some iliac tenderness; his urine required to be drawn off by catheter. Next day his evacuations became involuntary. He died on the 19th. *Post-mortem* examination four hours after death: Body emaciated; rigor mortis marked. The brain weighed forty-six ounces; it was light-colored, of firm consistence and contained much fluid in its ventricles. The heart was healthy. The right lung weighed fifteen ounces, the left thirteen ounces; the right was full of blood, the upper lobe being somewhat congested and the lower universally so; the upper lobe of the left lung was congested; collapsed lobules were observed in the lower lobes of both lungs; the bronchial tubes were congested and some of the smaller ones contained pus. The liver weighed fifty-four ounces and was universally congested; the gall-bladder contained eleven drachms of dark-green bile; the spleen weighed five ounces and a half and was of a dark-slate color externally, dark-red internally and moderately firm in consistence; the kidneys weighed four ounces and a half each and were of a rather dark color; the stomach was slightly congested. The mucous membrane of the small intestine was softened, especially near the ileo-cæcal valve; it was slightly congested in the jejunum and upper third of the ileum, decidedly so in the lower two-thirds of the ileum, where a number of ulcers were observed. The cæcum was of a dark-slate color; the rest of the large intestine was normal. The mesenteric and mesocolic glands were enlarged, especially the latter.—*Ass't Surg. George M. McGill, U. S. A., Lincoln Hospital, Washington, D. C.*

CASE 48.—Private William Duryea, Co. I, 109th N. Y.; age 21; was admitted May 14, 1864, with a gunshot flesh wound of the left forearm, which healed kindly. On the 18th he was furloughed for thirty days, and on his return, June 18, he was placed on light hospital duty, his wound unfitting him as yet for active service. On July 28 he was taken with headache and nocturnal delirium; his pulse 100 and his tongue coated with a dark fur. A few days later some difficulty of breathing was noted, with slight diarrhœa and twitchings of the tendons, the delirium having meanwhile become constant. His condition remained unchanged, but for progressive weakness, until August 7, when he died. *Post-mortem* examination six hours after death: The lungs were congested. The heart was pale and contained no clots. The liver was of normal size but congested; the gall-bladder filled with viscid bile; the spleen dark-colored, slightly enlarged and congested; the kidneys normal. The mucous membrane of the stomach was light-colored, thickened and softened. The lining membrane of the small intestine was soft and somewhat thickened down to the lower portion of the ileum, in which there were large ulcers at different points some distance from each other; near the ileo-cæcal valve it was greatly thickened and congested, and presented very large ulcers surrounded by red areolæ and penetrating to the muscular coat. The mucous membrane of the large intestine was greatly congested and its solitary follicles slightly enlarged. The mesenteric glands were enlarged. [*Specimen 352, Med. Sect., Army Medical Museum, ulceration of ileum, was obtained from this case.*]—*Act. Ass't Surg. O. P. Sweet, Carver Hospital, Washington, D. C.*

CASE 49.—Private Hannibal Tichout, Co. H, 2d U. S. Sharpshooters; age 20; was admitted Sept. 16, 1863, having been sick for eight weeks with typhoid fever. His features were sunken, conjunctivæ congested, cornea ulcerated, lips dry and coated with sordes, pulse feeble, 120, and bowels loose; petechial spots on chest and thighs. He sank gradually, dying on the 26th. Treatment consisted of lead and opium for the diarrhœa and of quinine, wine and beef-tea. *Post-mortem* examination twelve hours after death: Extensive peritoneal inflammation and ulceration of ileum and cæcum.—*Act. Ass't Surg. John Flickinger, First Division Hospital, Alexandria, Va.*

CASE 50.—Lieut. J. W. Lowe, Co. B, 9th N. Y. Cav., was admitted Sept. 21, 1863, with his neck somewhat swollen and stiff, the result of a blow from a rebel musket at Brandy Station, Va., Aug. 1, 1863; his general health was good. On the 30th he went home on leave of absence. He returned November 14 much improved, stating that during his absence he had an attack of diarrhœa which lasted only a few days; the attack was preceded by vomiting, and was attributed by him to some error of diet. He felt well and expressed himself as able to join his regiment. But at midnight of the 18th the officer of the day was called to see him as he had been seized with a violent pain in the testicle, without swelling but with great tenderness. An anodyne lotion relieved him and he fell asleep, but awoke about daylight vomiting a pale-green liquid and with great tenderness over the stomach. The abdomen soon became tympanitic, the pulse sank, the vomiting became constant and the countenance livid and anxious. A blister was applied and laudanum given by injection. At noon the vomiting became less frequent and he was able to swallow small quantities of brandy and water with morphia; the pulse, however, was scarcely perceptible and the face and hands were covered with cold sweat. He died at 3.30 P. M. after vomiting as much of a pea-green liquid as half filled a common tin basin. *Post-mortem* examination: The thoracic viscera were healthy. The peritoneal cavity contained two ounces of pus. The whole intestinal canal was in a state of acute inflammation; the ileum was perforated in several places, some of the openings being large enough to admit the end of the little finger. The inflammatory condition extended to all the abdominal viscera. "How this state of things existed without symptoms for a longer period than fifteen hours I am at a loss to explain or even conjecture. The man was not emaciated; on the contrary he had gained in flesh during his visit home. I am informed by his brother, who came for his remains, that he had complained at times of a pain in the bowels, but of so slight a character as not to attract much attention and which was usually relieved by a draught of warm ginger-tea." [*Specimen* 77, Med. Sect., Army Medical Museum, showing typhoid ulceration and perforation, is from this case.]—*Surg. H. W. Ducachet, U. S. V., Seminary Hospital, Georgetown, D. C.*

Cases entered as typho-malarial with or without a record of symptoms to substantiate the
diagnosis—42 cases.

(A.) Peyer's patches ulcerated and the ileum or small intestine only affected—14 cases.

Case 51.—Corporal E. J. Innes, Co. L, 6th Mich. Cav., was admitted July 28, 1863. Diagnosis—typho-malarial fever. On admission he had diarrhœa, debility and slight fever, which was rather remittent in character at first, but became typhoid on August 7. Quinine was given and the diarrhœa was controlled by Dover's powder, lead, tannin and opium; but the prostration increased and a few rose-colored spots appeared on the abdomen. Death took place on the 10th. *Post-mortem* examination: Lungs congested; liver enlarged and softened; Peyer's patches inflamed, thickened and elevated but very little ulcerated.—*Act. Ass't Surg. A. P. Williams, St. Aloysius Hospital, Washington, D. C.*

Case 52.—Private Byron C. Crane, 18th N. Y. Independent Bat'y, was admitted Sept. 22, 1864, from Washington street prison. Diagnosis—typho-malarial fever. He had high fever with daily exacerbations followed by sweating; his tongue was thickly coated and there was much cerebral excitement, with twitchings of the hands and fingers and numbness of the feet and legs. Quinine was given freely and Mindererus' spirit every six hours. On the 26th there was profuse and almost constant sweating, with hot skin, little appetite, increased twitchings, restlessness and but little sleep. Milk-punch was ordered and the acetate of ammonia omitted. The sleeplessness continued until the 30th, on which date constipation was noted. Active delirium set in next day with much jactitation, and continued until death on October 4. *Post-mortem* examination twenty-four hours after death: Small intestine extensively inflamed and Peyer's patches deeply ulcerated; spleen very dark; liver normal; kidneys much congested; lungs normal; pericardium injected and containing an increased quantity of fluid. Other viscera not examined.—*Third Division Hospital, Alexandria, Va.*

Case 53.—Private Henry Williams, Co. D, 141st N. Y.; age 44; was admitted July 28, 1863, having been sick for about a week with fever of a typhoid type. Diagnosis—typho-malarial fever. On admission he had a red, moist tongue, a frequent and feeble pulse, much prostration, abdominal tenderness and slight diarrhœa. Morning remissions were noted on July 31, August 1, 2, 4, 10 and 12, on which days he was treated with from ten to thirty grains of quinine daily—on the other days opiates and aromatic sulphuric acid were given, but the diarrhœa increased to six or seven watery stools daily; râles were heard in the lower lobes of the lungs on the 5th, and the parotid became swollen on the 10th. He became dull and drowsy on the 12th and died next day. *Post-mortem* examination: Pneumonia of lower lobes of lungs; follicular inflammation and softening of mucous membrane of small intestine; two typhoid ulcers in ileum; liver enlarged and fatty; heart hypertrophied, weight sixteen ounces, slight thickening of mitral valve. Other organs healthy.—*Stanton Hospital, Washington, D. C.*

Case 54.—Private Peter A. Beanson, Co. A, 52d N. Y.; age 38; was admitted Nov. 23, 1863, having been sick five weeks with typhoid fever (malarial). There was no tenderness in the right iliac region; the tongue was coated with a black fur and the skin tinged yellow; he had a purulent discharge from the ear. Persistent diarrhœa set in on December 14, with occasional delirium and great prostration. Erysipelas attacked the face on the 17th and the patient became comatose and had convulsive twitchings of the limbs. He died next day. *Post-mortem* examination on the 19th: Body not much emaciated. The pharynx, larynx and trachea were inflamed and ulcerated; the mucous membrane was of a purplish color except about the chordæ vocales, where it was stone-gray; the epiglottis was ulcerated on both sides, the fold of mucous membrane running from it to the cornu major on the left side was also ulcerated; the mucous membrane over the arytenoid cartilages was much tumefied; there was a small abscess between the cricoid cartilage and the pharynx. The lungs were congested posteriorly but otherwise healthy. The liver was healthy. Peyer's patches were ulcerated but not elevated, the ulcers blackish and with thick, sharply defined edges; the bases of some were so discolored that the dark hue was conspicuous through the peritoneum; the solitary glands were not seen.—*Ass't Surg. Harrison Allen, U. S. A., Lincoln Hospital, Washington, D. C.*

Case 55.—Private James Underwood, Co. D, 186th N. Y.; age 19; was admitted Nov. 30, 1864, with remittent fever which became continued on December 3, presenting delirium and typhoid symptoms; afterwards bronchitis occurred, with an uncontrollable and exhausting diarrhœa and great abdominal tenderness. He died on the 15th. *Post-mortem* examination: Lungs œdematous, with indications of pneumonia as well as bronchitis; Peyer's patches extensively ulcerated.—*Surg. E. Bentley, U. S. V., Third Division Hospital, Alexandria, Va.*

Case 56.—Private Chauncey O. Parcher, Co. E, 13th Vt., was admitted Dec. 14, 1862, with typho-malarial fever. This patient had so far convalesced as to sit up a part of the time, when a relapse occurred, from which also he recovered. After this he began to complain of great pain in the right ear, in which an abscess formed and was discharged with relief to the pain. But the ear became a second time the seat of severe pain, which extended to the whole head and was particularly severe in the occiput. Delirium followed and he died Feb. 5, 1863, about forty-eight hours after its accession, coma having in the meantime supervened. *Post-mortem* examination one hundred hours after death: The body was not much emaciated. Nothing abnormal was detected in the brain. The thoracic and abdominal viscera appeared healthy with the exception of the ileum, in which, especially towards the ileo-cæcal valve, a number of Peyer's patches were enlarged, inflamed and ulcerated, the ulcers, however, seemed well advanced in the process of cicatrization.—*Third Division Hospital, Alexandria, Va.*

CASE 57.—Private William Uncapher, Co. H, 140th Pa., was admitted July 22, 1863, with typho-malarial fever. He sank gradually, dying comatose on August 10. *Post-mortem* examination eleven hours after death: There were pleuritic adhesions on the left side and hypostatic congestion in the posterior parts of both lungs, but otherwise the lungs appeared healthy. The heart was flabby. The liver was much enlarged; the spleen weighed a pound and three-quarters; the kidneys were normal; the bladder contracted and nearly empty. Peyer's patches were thickened and ulcerated; the solitary glands of the ileum were enlarged to the size of small shot. The mesenteric glands were greatly swollen; some presented yellow spots of softening and others contained a creamy dark-yellow fluid. —*Jarvis Hospital, Baltimore, Md.*

CASE 58.—Private Jesse Cassel, Co. C, 179th Pa.; age 24; was admitted July 2, 1863, with typho-malarial fever, which, after a few days, became typhoid and accompanied with diarrhœa. Opiates and astringents failed to restrain the diarrhœa, which became colliquative. He died delirious, picking at the bedclothes, on the 26th. *Post-mortem* examination "revealed nothing but slight ulceration of Peyer's glands."—*Ass't Surg. C. C. Lee, U. S. A., Douglas Hospital, Washington, D. C.*

CASE 59.—Private Thomas Hurten, Company C, 140th Ind.; age 18; was admitted Jan. 29, 1865, with typho-malarial fever. He died February 8. *Post-mortem* examination eleven hours after death: Lungs hypostatically congested; posterior pleuritic adhesions on left side; heart flabby. Liver weighed seventy-six ounces; spleen twenty-eight ounces; mesenteric glands greatly swollen, varying from the size of a pea to that of an almond, some containing a creamy dark-yellow fluid, and one presenting some yellow points of softening; Peyer's patches enlarged and ulcerated in the lower part of the ileum,—in the upper part was a patch four inches long; solitary glands much enlarged, feeling like small shot beneath the mucous membrane; kidneys normal.—*Douglas Hospital, Washington, D. C.*

CASE 60.—Private Oscar F. Hunt, Co. H, 9th Mich.; age 20; was admitted Dec. 6, 1864, with typho-malarial fever, and died on the 9th. *Post-mortem* examination twenty hours after death: Thoracic viscera normal; large intestine greatly distended with air; appendix vermiformis inflamed; ileum contracted in its calibre, and Peyer's patches elevated and in various stages of softening and ulceration.—*Hospital No. 8, Nashville, Tenn.*

CASE 61.—Private James Stone, alias Paul Shay, Co. F, 61st N. Y.; admitted March 3, 1864. Died 14th, of typho-malarial fever. *Post-mortem* examination five hours after death: The body was much emaciated. The lungs and heart were healthy, but the pericardium contained a large quantity of serum. The liver weighed sixty-one ounces; the gall-bladder was empty. The spleen, stomach, duodenum, jejunum and large intestine were healthy; the ileum was much congested and inflamed throughout, and many of Peyer's patches presented large ulcers.—*Act. Ass't Surg. Lloyd Dorsey, Harewood Hospital, Washington, D. C.*

CASE 62.—Private Eber Elmer, Co. E, 186th N. Y.; age 17; admitted Oct. 21, 1864. Diagnosis—typho-malarial fever. Died 24th. *Post-mortem* examination thirty hours after death: Body muscular and well developed; sudamina on chest and abdomen; sordes on teeth; slight suggillation posteriorly. Lungs congested; lower lobe of left and upper and lower lobes of right lung hepatized posteriorly; base of left lung covered with recent lymph; each pleural cavity containing two ounces of bloody serum; bronchi congested and filled with frothy mucus; bronchial glands normal. Heart healthy, small clots in the left and a large clot in the right cavities. Stomach filled with air and dark grumous blood; small intestine congested and inflamed; Peyer's patches much thickened, especially near ileo-cæcal valve, where there was one small ulcer; mesenteric glands dark and enlarged; colon and rectum healthy. Liver large, healthy; gall-bladder containing six drachms of dark bile; spleen enlarged, softened, quite dark in color; pancreas, kidneys and bladder healthy.—*Second Division Hospital, Alexandria, Va.*

CASE 63.—Private Edward Martin, Co. H, 12th Vt., admitted Dec. 12, 1862. Diagnosis—typhoid remittent fever. Died 17th. *Post-mortem* examination: The abdomen was moderately tympanitic; recti muscles very much injected and in their sternal third ecchymosed. The anterior portion of the abdominal surface of the diaphragm was coated with plastic lymph; the omentum was greatly injected and adherent by recent lymph to the abdominal parietes; the mesentery was injected; the mesenteric glands greatly enlarged. The mucous membrane of the ileum was congested, especially near the ileo-cæcal valve; Peyer's patches were ulcerated and the peritoneum corresponding to each patch was dark-colored.—*Third Division Hospital, Alexandria, Va.*

CASE 64.—Private Wallace T. Fowler, Co. C, 42d Mass.; age 19; was admitted Oct. 29, 1864, having been taken sick a week before with a decided chill followed by hot skin, thirst, severe headache and backache and a diarrhœa of two or three passages daily. On admission there was no delirium, epistaxis, deafness nor tympanites; pulse 120; tongue furred and dry; some bronchial irritation. Diagnosis—typho-malarial fever. He improved under small doses of blue-pill and ipecacuanha, acetate of potash, squill and spirit of nitre until November 12, when his respiration became hurried and his pulse accelerated. On the 15th he expectorated rusty sputa, although none of the physical signs of pneumonia were present. Until the day of his death, the 17th, he did not appear to be very ill. Pain in the epigastrium, feeble pulse, great prostration and vomiting, at first of green liquid and afterwards of matters resembling coffee-grounds, preceded death for some hours; his mind was clear to the last. *Post-mortem* examination sixteen hours after death: Not much emaciation; suggillation posteriorly. Omentum inflamed; intestines reddened and interadherent; peritoneal cavity containing two pints of a turbid yellow liquid emitting an unpleasant fæcal odor. There was a perforation one-eighth of an inch in diameter about the middle of the ileum, the result of ulceration in one of Peyer's patches [*Specimen* No. 439, Med. Sect., Army Medical Museum], and there were several thickened and ulcerated patches near the perforation and in the lower part of the ileum. Spleen enlarged and softened; liver dark. Other organs not examined.—*Surg. E. Bentley, U. S. V., Second Division Hospital, Alexandria, Va.*

(B.) Peyer's patches ulcerated and the large intestine also implicated—4 cases.

CASE 65.—Private John D. Evans, Co. H, 1st Mich. Cav.; age 28; admitted July 20, 1864, from Camp Distribution, Va. Diagnosis—typho-malarial fever. He had frontal headache, pain in limbs and back, anorexia, sickness at stomach, troublesome diarrhœa, hectic flush on cheeks, irritative cough, deafness of right ear, tongue yellow-coated and eyes suffused and yellowish. Sinapisms were applied over the right lung and liver, and tincture of aconite in acetate of ammonia was given every two hours, with subsequently Hope's mixture and wine bitters. He seemed to improve for some days, but on August 1 he refused food altogether; his cough increased, becoming dry, irritable and paroxysmal, lasting for ten minutes at a time and preventing sleep; his urination became difficult, but this was relieved by extract of buchu and sweet spirit of nitre; and the right parotid became enlarged, indurated and painful. Next day there was a very offensive fetid discharge from the nose and muttering delirium set in, followed by death. *Post-mortem* examination two hours after death: Robust, muscular. Right lung and pleura somewhat inflamed, large abscess in the middle lobe; liver much congested; œsophagus, stomach and intestines inflamed throughout; Peyer's patches, cæcum and colon ulcerated.—*Third Division Hospital, Alexandria, Va.*

CASE 66.—Private Adam Cull, Co. D, 28th Mich.; age 25; admitted Feb. 13, 1865. Diagnosis—typho-malarial fever and congestion of lungs. Died 19th. *Post-mortem* examination fourteen hours after death: Well developed; large deposit of fat; recent blister-marks on neck and chest; slight suggillation posteriorly; great rigidity. Pleuritic adhesions on both sides; right lung congested, crepitant in upper lobe. Stomach distended with air; Peyer's patches inflamed, in many places ulcerated; large intestine congested. Liver nutmeg; spleen enlarged; kidneys small; other viscera normal.—*Third Division Hospital, Alexandria, Va.*

CASE 67.—Private Asa C. Wentworth, Co. H, 19th Me.; was admitted Nov. 26, 1863, with jaundice. [This man appears on the register of the regimental hospital as admitted on the 18th with typho-malarial fever and sent to general hospital on the 22d.] Died Jan. 12, 1864. *Post-mortem* examination twenty-two hours after death: The pharynx and larynx were inflamed; the soft palate hard, stiff and white; the tonsils unaffected; between the pharynx and right arytenoid cartilage was a large abscess with hard, yellowish-white walls; the cartilage mentioned was the seat of a protuberance, probably a collection of pus; there was also a small abscess immediately above the left greater cornu of the hyoid bone; the vocal chords and the upper surface of the epiglottis were œdematous. The pericardium contained seventeen drachms of yellowish fluid; the heart was very soft. The liver was bronzed and mottled with hard lardaceous spots, the gall-bladder full of dark-brown viscid bile; the spleen was rather small and extremely soft; the pancreas soft and of a dull-red color; the kidneys congested. In the ileum the villi were very soft; Peyer's patches were not raised, but one of them presented an ulcer with low rounded edges, at the base of which the transverse muscular fibres could be seen; the ileum had the ironed-out appearance. The colon was slate-colored, its solitary follicles whitish, with conspicuous dark-spotted centres.—*Ass't Surg. Harrison Allen, U. S. A., Lincoln Hospital, Washington, D. C.*

CASE 68.—Private Charles Bangson, Co. I, 14th Conn.; age 27; was admitted Oct. 19, 1863, with typho-malarial fever. He had been sick for twelve days and on admission was in a semi-comatose condition; tongue dry, glazed and red at the tip and edges; pulse 120, full, bounding and incompressible. On the 27th the pulse was 108 and scarcely perceptible at the wrist; the patient had some cough with thick, tenacious yellowish sputa. The ileo-cæcal region was tender, but no eruption was observed. Death occurred on the 29th. At first tincture of aconite was given, for which, on the 25th, quinine, carbonate of ammonia and whiskey were substituted. *Post-mortem* examination four hours after death: The trachea was palish but mottled at its bifurcation; several ecchymotic spots were observed on its posterior surface. The œsophagus was pale and its mucous membrane firm. The right lung was perfectly healthy; the left lung weighed thirty-one ounces and a half, its upper lobe being congested generally and solidified in its central parts and its lower lobe mottled with dark-brown spots about the size of a pea. The heart contained fibrinous clots in its right chambers. The liver was congested and weighed seventy-two ounces; the spleen firm, fourteen ounces and a half; the pancreas normal; the kidneys congested. The small intestine near the ileo-cæcal valve was of a darker color than elsewhere; its mucous membrane was healthy to within ten feet of the valve, at which point it became unusually vascular and softened, Peyer's patches and the solitary glands being of a deep pink color; lower down Peyer's glands became enlarged, whitish and hard, with abrupt edges; still lower down they were ulcerated, which condition frequently existed in the centre of a patch while its margins remained enlarged and hard; the glands near the valve were ulcerated in their whole superfices, some of them looking not unlike Hunterian chancres; the ulceration did not extend deeper than the mucous membrane; the solitary glands were enlarged and of a dark-purple color in the lower part of the ileum, and some near its termination were ulcerated. The mucous membrane of the cæcum and ascending colon was of a dark-bluish color; lower down it was pale and in some places pink; the solitary glands were conspicuous but not elevated, appearing as whitish spots with pigmented centres.—*Ass't Surg. Harrison Allen, U. S. A., Lincoln Hospital, Washington, D. C.*

(C.) Condition of Peyer's patches not stated; the intestines variously affected—15 cases.

CASE 69.—Henry Reynolds, Co. C, 79th N. Y., was admitted Aug. 21, 1863, having been sick ten days with headache and weakness of limbs, followed by fever. Diagnosis—typho-malarial fever. He was weak and somewhat emaciated; his pulse feeble and compressible; tongue slightly coated; appetite poor; bowels regular. He died on the 26th. *Post-mortem* examination thirty-one hours after death: Lungs much congested; a large amount of serum in right pleural cavity; heart normal, containing a large clot; liver somewhat congested; gall-bladder much distended; spleen enlarged, congested and softened; mesenteric glands enlarged.—*West End Hospital, Cincinnati, O.*

Case 70.—Private Joseph E. Hudson, Co. A, Gordon's Ark. regiment; age 19; admitted Dec. 16, 1864; typho-malarial fever. On admission he had fever and diarrhœa; his tongue was slightly coated, pulse 100, appetite fair, respiration normal, legs swollen from the knees down. He rested well and in a few days the swelling of the legs became somewhat reduced, but the diarrhœa persisted. He did not suffer, but grew weaker and died on the 22d. *Post-mortem* examination: There was emaciation with œdema of the legs and feet; the blood was very poor and thin. The lungs and heart were normal; the spleen about three times the normal size; the gall-bladder distended with bile; the mesenteric glands so enlarged that the mesentery had the appearance of being one continuous gland; the solitary glands disorganized and the mucous coat of the rectum inflamed and softened.—*Act. Ass't Surg. H. C. Newkirk, Rock Island Hospital, Ill.*

Case 71.—Private Warren M. Burton, Co. K, 28th Ala.; age 33; was admitted Dec. 7, 1864, with typho-malarial fever. He had been sick for four weeks with diarrhœa and general malaise. On admission his bowels were slightly relaxed, tongue heavily coated with a brown cracked fur, skin hot, pulse frequent and feeble, countenance shrunken; he was inclined to sleep, which he did heavily and with the whites of his eyes exposed. Hiccough speedily came on and he died on the 8th. *Post-mortem* examination ten hours after death: The lower portion of the right pleura was inflamed. The heart contained white clots. The peritoneum was much injected and tinged throughout of a yellow color. The spleen was soft and friable. The stomach contained about a pint of dark liquid with detached shreds of its mucous membrane floating in it; the lining membranes of the œsophagus and duodenum were also softened and disintegrated. The mucous coat of the bowels was much congested throughout; fæcal matter in the rectum was of normal consistence but white and fetid.—*Act. Ass't Surg. J. B. Young, Rock Island Hospital, Ill.*

Case 72.—Private James Bozeman, Co. I, 40th Ala.; age 34; admitted Dec. 22, 1864; typho-malarial fever. This man enlisted in April, 1862; he had measles soon after and since then has had diarrhœa almost constantly and frequent attacks of fever. He was captured in June, 1864. His present attack commenced December 18, with pain in the head and breast and chilly sensations followed by fever. When admitted his tongue was coated brown with red margins; bowels loose; pulse 120; cough and slight expectoration; anorexia and thirst. He died on the 23d. *Post-mortem* examination twelve hours after death: Great emaciation. The lower lobe of the left lung was congested. The liver was pale. The intestinal mucous membrane was congested, and in the rectum softened.—*Act. Ass't Surg. H. C. Newkirk, Rock Island Hospital, Ill.*

Case 73.—Bellfield W. Ferguson, a citizen of Mo.; age 63; typho-malarial fever. Died Dec. 20, 1864. *Post-mortem* examination: The body was greatly emaciated. The posterior part of the left lung was congested and its pleura inflamed. The intestines showed some congestion with disorganization of the solitary glands; the mesenteric glands were enlarged.—*Act. Ass't Surg. J. M. Witherwax, Rock Island Hospital, Ill.*

Case 74.—James Case, citizen of Mo. Typho-malarial fever. Admitted Dec. 1, 1864; died 26th. On the day of his death he had a dry furred tongue which he was unable to protrude; he spoke with difficulty; respiration was quick and labored; the surface dry and cold and the pulse imperceptible. He had a slight erysipelatous swelling of the left ear. *Post-mortem* examination: The lungs were dark and congested posteriorly; the liver was enlarged. "There were commencing ulcerations of the intestines, with general indications of internal congestion."—*Act. Ass't Surg. J. M. Witherwax, Rock Island Hospital, Ill.*

Case 75.—Stockton M. Bayne, Co. H, 3d Ga. Cav.; admitted Dec. 3, 1864; typho-malarial fever. Died 24th. *Post-mortem* examination: Right lung normal; lower lobe of left lung hepatized gray; four ounces of dark yellow serum in pericardium; heart flaccid, both sides containing thrombi extending into the vessels. Liver normal; gall-bladder distended; spleen enlarged, congested and softened; mesenteric glands greatly enlarged. Mucous membrane of small intestine ulcerated in various parts, and that of colon and rectum highly congested and disintegrated.—*Act. Ass't Surg. J. M. Witherwax, Rock Island Hospital, Ill.*

Case 76.—William C. Norton, Co. A, Wood's Missouri battery. Typho-malarial fever. Died Jan. 20, 1865. *Post-mortem* examination: The heart, lungs and liver were normal. The spleen was slightly enlarged; the small intestine congested; the mesenteric glands enlarged; the rectum ulcerated in patches through the mucous and muscular coats, some portions appearing gangrenous.—*Act. Ass't Surg. J. M. Witherwax, Rock Island Hospital, Ill.*

Case 77.—Jesse Eaton, citizen; admitted Dec. 21, 1864; typho-malarial fever. Died 31st. He suffered from sore throat, chills, a slight swelling of the right cheek of an erysipelatous character, and had "many symptoms of a typhoid condition." *Post-mortem* examination six hours after death: Lungs healthy; heart contained white clots in right side; liver and spleen somewhat congested; lower portion of ileum presenting numerous small ulcers; descending colon strictured for six inches of its length, so that an ordinary lead-pencil could scarcely be passed.—*Act. Ass't Surg. W. Matthews, Rock Island Hospital, Ill.*

Case 78.—Private Francis Scott, Co. K, 41st N. Y.; age 35; admitted Feb. 13, 1865; typho-malarial fever and chronic diarrhœa. He was treated with quinia, alcoholic stimulants and turpentine. In the progress of the case the lower extremities became œdematous and signs of valvular disease were discovered. He died March 21. *Post-mortem* examination: Body much emaciated; lower extremities œdematous. The heart was slightly hypertrophied, its aortic valves thickened. The liver was enlarged and deeply bronzed. The mucous membrane of the intestines was softened throughout.—*Third Division Hospital, Alexandria, Va.*

Case 79.—Private Abraham J. Cooper, Co. A, 186th N. Y.; age 20; admitted Nov. 30, 1864; typhoid fever. [The diagnosis at the Ninth Army Corps Field Hospital, on the 24th, was typho-malarial fever, and at the Depot Field Hospital, City Point, Va., on the 26th, remittent fever.] Symptoms on admission: Pulse varying from 90 to 110, feeble and thready; skin hot and dry; tongue dry, extremely red and gashed; teeth, gums and lips incrusted with sordes; deafness; stupor; low delirium. When undisturbed he lay with his eyes half closed muttering broken and unconnected sentences; when aroused he had a vacant expression and was unable to answer correctly. During the first twenty-four hours after admission he had four passages from the bowels; the abdomen was tympanitic, very tender over the small intestine and cæcum, and marked with a few petechiæ and sudamina. Turpentine emulsion, laudanum and milk-punch were administered. Next day there was a slight improvement: The pulse became somewhat stronger, the tongue less tremulous and protruded with more ease; the patient was able to answer a few questions correctly, but the abdominal symptoms continued and there was some epistaxis. On December 2 the pulse became somewhat stronger and less frequent, the tongue quite moist, the sordes partially removed and the diarrhœa checked; but at 9 P. M. the diarrhœa returned, several involuntary stools were passed and the patient fell into a stupor from which he never aroused. He died at 3 A. M. of the 3d. *Post-mortem* examination eight hours after death: Lungs crepitant throughout; liver pale, with well marked nutmeg appearance; spleen of full size and softened; kidneys full of blood, the pyramids of a dark-red color; mesenteric glands enormously enlarged; colon pale and without ulceration; ileum injected.—*Act. Ass't Surg. W. C. Minor, Third Division Hospital, Alexandria, Va.*

CASE 80.—Private Albert Mathews, Co. A, 174th Ohio; age 19; was admitted Jan. 28, 1865, with typho-malarial fever. When admitted his bowels were loose, skin hot and dry, tongue dry and red, pulse 100 and feeble. On February 5 the diarrhœa became profuse. A chill followed by fever and sweating occurred on the 12th and again next day. Quinine was freely administered without apparent benefit. He died on the 27th. *Post-mortem* examination three hours after death: Body much emaciated. Membranes of brain much injected; cerebral hemispheres coated with coagulable lymph; substance of brain much injected and softened; lateral ventricles containing serum and a deposit of lymph. Heart healthy; liver and spleen adherent to diaphragm; gall-bladder distended with dark bile; omentum congested; intestinal mucous membrane extensively diseased and portions of ileum gangrenous.—*Act. Ass't Surg. Sample Ford, Cumberland Hospital, Md.*

CASE 81.—Private William Henry Clay, Co. D, 28th U. S. Colored troops; age 21; was admitted July 21, 1864, on account of inguinal hernia on the right side and enlarged inguinal glands. On April 6, 1865, the records present him as feverish and jaundiced, without giving information as to the period of onset. His pulse was 95, tongue coated with a yellowish fur, skin dry; he had thirst, anorexia, nausea, tenderness in the right iliac region and constipated bowels; there was some mental torpor and considerable muscular debility. On the 8th his pulse was small and frequent; he had a cough and complained of pain in the right side of the chest. He died next day. A mercurial purge operated well on the 6th; subsequently the bowels were so loose that opium was employed. Quinine and stimulants were freely administered. The case is recorded by the attending physician as one of typho-malarial fever. *Post-mortem* examination: The thoracic viscera were normal. The liver was very light-colored and soft; the spleen and kidneys softened and congested. The whole of the intestinal canal was inflamed; the mesenteric glands enlarged. The peritoneum was inflamed and the sac contained about half a pint of sero-purulent liquid.—*Act. Ass't Surg. Frank Buckland, L'Ouvreture Hospital, Alexandria, Va.*

CASE 82.—Private N. Henry Downing, Co. A, 8th Ill. Cav., was admitted June 18, 1864, with typho-malarial fever. He had not been in his usual vigorous health for several weeks, but had continued on duty until admission, when he was suffering from pyrexia, severe headache referred to the temples, diarrhœa and dull pain in the lower extremities; his eyes were suffused and painful and his tongue heavily coated with a dark-yellow fur, the edges being of a livid hue. Quinine, twenty-five grains in the twenty-four hours, and chlorate of potassa were administered. Next day he appeared improved,—pulse 80, headache decreased, tongue less dark; but a little pain and tenderness had developed in the ileo-cæcal and hypogastric regions and there was slight epistaxis. The quinine was continued with a saline, diuretic and diaphoretic mixture. He remained in this condition until the 24th, when his countenance became bright and pleasant and he was free from pain; pulse 120 and full; coating of the tongue lighter and the edges pale; he vomited a little greenish liquid in the morning and had an exacerbation of fever in the afternoon. Twenty-eight grains of quinine with chlorate of potassa were ordered to be taken in the twenty-four hours. Next day his skin was moist and cool, pulse 96, but there remained a little pain in the bowels, which afterwards became a feeling of fulness and was relieved by castor oil and fomentations. On the evening of the 27th he was suddenly seized with a sharp pain in the bladder and penis and inability to void his urine; the catheter showed his bladder to be empty. By next morning the pain had extended over the whole abdomen, which was very tender; his countenance was anxious; pulse 120 and small; tongue moist but with the light-colored fur and pale edges; he lay on the right side with his thighs flexed. On July 1 he became easier under the continued use of morphine, but later in the day the pain again became intense and he died at 2 A. M. of the 2d. *Post-mortem* examination ten hours after death: The liver, spleen and kidneys were healthy. The ileum was perforated about four inches from the ileo-cæcal valve and there was extensive peritoneal inflammation. [*Specimen* 324, Med. Sect., Army Medical Museum, is from this case.]—*Surg. A. Hard, 8th Ill. Cav., Regimental Hospital.*

CASE 83.—Private Daniel Hare, Co. D, 175th Ohio; age 18; was admitted Oct. 15, 1864, with quotidian intermittent fever, which passed into typhoid fever. He was weak and much emaciated from chronic diarrhœa, but his bowels were now regular. He had a chill and fever daily, for which quinine was freely given with beneficial effect; but on the 19th diarrhœa set in and fever was developed in the evening. The bowels remained moderately checked by astringents until the 24th, when, as they became looser, the tongue blackened. Turpentine was given. Three days later retention of urine required relief by catheter and tenderness over the pubes called for fomentations. The suprapubic tenderness continued until the 30th, when a violent chill occurred, lasting for an hour, and followed by high fever, profuse perspiration, great abdominal tenderness, coldness of the extremities and death. *Post-mortem* examination twenty-one hours after death: Heart normal; lungs congested posteriorly. Abdominal viscera generally interadherent; peritoneum congested and containing liquid fæces; ileum ulcerated in patches for three and a half feet above the ileo-cæcal valve, some of the ulcers having reached the peritoneum, and two, about two feet from the valve, having perforated this membrane. Other organs not examined.—*Hospital No. 8, Nashville, Tenn.*

(D.) *Condition of Peyer's patches variously stated, but not ulcerated; intestines more or less affected, but no ulceration of the ileum—9 cases.*

CASE 84.—Serg't John H. Peters, Co. E, 120th Pa.; admitted April 20, 1863. Diagnosis—typho-malarial fever. Died 30th. *Post-mortem* examination nine hours after death: Some rigor mortis. Brain weighed forty-six ounces and a half. Mucous membrane of trachea pale. Right lung fifteen ounces and a half, healthy; left lung thirteen ounces and three-quarters, dark blue, its apex purple. Heart normal; soft black clot in right ventricle; small narrow clot in left ventricle. Liver forty nine ounces and a half, dark purple externally, paler on section, rather soft; capsule of Glisson readily torn. Spleen eight ounces and a quarter, soft, dark mulberry color, trabeculæ conspicuous. Pancreas four ounces and one-quarter, natural. Stomach mottled dark and pale red. Mucous membrane of small intestine generally pale, with irregular patches of congestion; Peyer's patches pale; solitary follicles, especially in lower part, dark purple in color, enlarged and ulcerated; mucous membrane of vermiform appendix dark-colored and presenting two ulcerated patches one-eighth of an inch in length. Large intestine gray throughout; solitary glands conspicuous; three ulcers in the lower part of the bowel—the first, one inch in diameter, in the sigmoid flexure, the others, smaller, in the middle portion of the rectum. Kidneys congested.—*Ass't Surg. Harrison Allen, U. S. A., Lincoln Hospital, Washington, D. C.*

CASE 85.—Private A. C. Starker, Co. D, 15th N. J., was admitted Nov. 23, 1863, as a case of typho-malarial fever: Pulse 115 to 130, irritable; tongue dry as a pine shaving, glossy and red on its edges; sordes on teeth and gums; urine scanty, densely loaded and very fetid; stools involuntary; friction-sound on right side of chest. In answer to questions he talked incoherently for a few seconds and then relapsed into stupor; he picked at the bed-clothes, and drawing his legs up would suddenly straighten them in an apparent effort to kick off the covering. Subnitrate of bismuth controlled the diarrhœa; stimulants were freely administered. He died on the 28th. *Post-mortem* examination ten hours after death: Right lung adherent to costal pleura by a strong and dense false membrane; left lung distended with a black fluid, unadherent; heart normal. Liver very pale, much enlarged and softened; spleen larger than usual and softened; kidneys one-fourth larger than normal and indurated, especially in their lower fourth, where their substance could not be crushed between the thumb and finger. Peyer's patches distinct and elevated, their edges ragged and raised one-tenth inch above the surrounding surface; solitary glands of large intestine ulcerated; lymphatic glands enlarged—one, as large as a walnut, was on section much like the spleen.—*Act. Ass't Surg. W. H. Letterman, Douglas Hospital, Washington, D. C.*

CASE 86.—Private Patrick Conlin, Co. E, 25th Mass.; age 36; was admitted March 11, 1865, with symptoms of typho-malarial fever. He had decided fever with frequent, compressible pulse, hurried breathing, hot dry skin, furred dry tongue, severe headache and costive bowels; his countenance was dusky, his eyes injected, and there was great prostration with considerable mental confusion and hebetude. Numerous red spots, a line in diameter or less, were observed chiefly on the chest and abdomen; they were somewhat elevated and did not disappear completely on pressure. On the 13th the tongue was more thickly coated and brown, the teeth and gums covered with sordes, the urine scanty and high-colored, the abdomen tender and painful; no abnormal condition of the lungs was detected by auscultation or percussion. On the 15th the headache was succeeded by delirium and occasional stupor, with contracted pupils, drooping of the lids and subsultus tendinum; the bowels were constipated. Later the spots on the skin became of a dusky crimson and quite unaffected by pressure. He died comatose on the 17th. *Post-mortem* examination nineteen hours after death: A large quantity of serum was found in the subarachnoid space and a smaller quantity in the ventricles; the membranes and substance of the brain were congested. The heart contained some imperfectly formed clots and fluid blood. The lungs were congested; the lower portion of the right lung was in a condition of gray hepatization; the left lung weighed twenty-one ounces, the right thirty-two ounces. The liver was soft, well filled with blood and weighed sixty-eight ounces; the gall-bladder contained very black bile; the spleen was flaccid and slightly enlarged; the pancreas was reddened and weighed seven ounces. The intestines generally were dark and congested; the glands of Peyer conspicuous and dark-colored. The kidneys were apparently normal.—*Ass't Surg. George M. McGill, U. S. A., National Hospital, Baltimore, Md.*

CASE 87.—Private Niles Ivers, Co. F, 6th Wis., was admitted April 21, 1864, with typho-malarial fever. He stated that he had been sick for a week with fever, which began with chills. He was much prostrated; his bowels were loose and his tongue dry and brown with red edges. Quinine, stimulants and nutriment were ordered. In a few days his respiration became accelerated and he complained of cough and pain in the side, for which he was blistered. Under this treatment he gradually improved, the fever subsiding, but a considerable quantity of liquid remained in the pleural cavity, for the removal of which iodide of potassium was given in free doses and an occasional blister was applied, but without much benefit; the effusion did not embarrass his breathing. Convalescence was slow and he was unable to leave his bed, when, about June 1, symptoms of hectic appeared. He failed gradually and died on the 23d. *Post-mortem* examination twenty-four hours after death: Body much emaciated; rigor mortis moderate. The left pleural cavity contained about a pint and a half of purulent liquid which compressed the lung against the spinal column; the right cavity contained about six ounces of serum; the right lung was healthy. The intestines were distended with gas; the mucous coat of the stomach and of the intestinal canal was thickened and softened; the glands of Brünner and the solitary glands of the ileum were enlarged and prominent but not ulcerated; the patches of Peyer presented the shaven-beard appearance. The liver was about one-third larger than normal and contained a number of minute abscesses; the spleen was enlarged to three times its normal size and also contained abscesses; the kidneys were healthy. [*Specimens* 325–6, Med. Sect., Army Medical Museum, are from the spleen of this case.]—*Ass't Surg. Geo. A. Mursick, U. S. V., Stanton Hospital, Washington, D. C.*

CASE 88.—Private George Pitcher, Co. H, 23d Mich.; age 36; was admitted Feb. 11, 1865, with chronic rheumatism. While under treatment he became attacked, March 18, with symptoms of typho-malarial fever. He progressed favorably until the 23d, when abdominal pains set in; next day he became semi-comatose and died. He was treated with turpentine emulsion and carbonate of ammonia. *Post-mortem* examination twelve hours after death: Liver much enlarged, bronzed; intestines congested, small intestine showing shaven-beard appearance of Peyer's patches and four intussusceptions from four to six inches long.—*Third Division Hospital, Alexandria, Va.*

CASE 89.—Private Lewis Sage, Co. A, 186th N. Y., was admitted Nov. 30, 1864, from City Point, Va., where he had been under treatment for typho-malarial fever. On admission he was in an unconscious condition, with low delirium, troublesome diarrhœa and a harassing cough; pulse 100, soft. He was treated with milk-punch and ammonia, expectorants and turpentine emulsion with laudanum; but he sank gradually and died December 10. *Post-mortem* examination: All the viscera appeared to be healthy except the intestines. The mucous membrane of the ileum was deeply injected throughout and of a dark purple color; its solitary follicles were enlarged and some near the ileo-cæcal valve were ulcerated; Peyer's patches, which were slightly thickened, presented the shaven-beard appearance. The colon presented a number of deep ulcers, especially at its extremities; in the transverse colon several of the ulcers were cicatrizing. An intestinal diverticulum, two inches and a half long, was found in the ileum about three feet and a half from the ileo-cæcal valve. [Nos. 465 and 466, Med. Sect., Army Medical Museum, are from this case.]—*Act. Ass't Surg. W. C. Minor, Third Division Hospital, Alexandria, Va.*

CASE 90.—Private J. T. Pierce, Co. G, 33d Mass., was admitted June 16, 1863, with typho-malarial fever. He had frequently suffered from intermittent fever. When admitted he had been sick for some time and was greatly emaciated; he had some diarrhœa; his tongue was coated in the middle, dry and cracked; pulse 132. After this his breathing became hurried, and coarse mucous râles were heard over both lungs; there was also marked nervous prostration. He died on the 21st. *Post-mortem* examination twenty-six hours after death: Body emaciated; rigor mortis slight. The brain was normal. The mucous membrane of the œsophagus was of a pale purple color. The trachea contained much bronchial secretion; its mucous membrane was purplish. The upper and middle lobes of the right lung were solidified except their anterior free borders, which were pale and healthy; the lower lobe was congested hypostatically but not solidified. The posterior portion of the left lung was in a state of gray hepatization, the anterior part healthy. The right lung weighed twenty-seven ounces and a quarter, the left thirty-seven ounces; the bronchial glands were large, one of them softened. The pericardium was lined by recent lymph roughened by papillary elevations; it contained six drachms of flaky serum. The right cavities of the heart contained a large venous clot, the left cavities a mixed clot which extended into the aorta. The liver weighed fifty-seven ounces, it was pale and slightly softened; the gall-bladder contained a drachm of greenish-brown viscid bile. The spleen was firm and weighed three ounces and three-quarters. The pancreas was firm and white, it weighed two ounces and a half. The right kidney weighed five ounces and a quarter, the left five and a half, both were pale and flabby. No prominent lesion was observed in the intestines; the lower part of the jejunum was contracted and its mucous membrane pale; Peyer's patches were rather pale and dotted with points of black pigment; the large intestine was contracted and its mucous membrane of a pale bluish color.—*Ass't Surg. Harrison Allen, U. S. A., Lincoln Hospital, Washington, D. C.*

CASE 91.—Private Willard Rock, Co. E, 16th N. Y.; age 19; was admitted Aug. 10, 1862. He was convalescing from Chickahominy fever and diarrhœa; but afterwards, from imprudence, was again attacked with diarrhœa and died October 5. *Post-mortem* examination next day: Slight emaciation. The heart and lungs were normal. There were old adhesions of the right half of the right lobe of the liver to the diaphragm, but the organ was sound; the spleen was very small but otherwise natural; the kidneys pale. There was moderate inflammation along the great curvature of the stomach. In the ileum were three large patches, about fourteen inches long, of intense inflammation, with the intervals between them moderately inflamed; these patches presented many small ecchymoses. The colon was much contracted, intensely inflamed at its commencement and moderately inflamed throughout, with here and there small ecchymoses. The agminated and solitary glands of the small and large intestines contained black pigment.—*Act. Ass't Surg. J. Leidy, Satterlee Hospital, Philadelphia, Pa.*

CASE 92.—Lewis G. Baker; age 37; a citizen of Mo., was admitted Dec. 15, 1864, with typho-malarial fever. He stated that he had taken cold in November while making his escape from the rebel service. On admission his tongue was slightly coated, bowels loose, pulse 100, respiration normal, cough and expectoration slight, appetite small and thirst notable. Diarrhœa and increasing prostration were the prominent symptoms during the progress of the case. He died on the 23d. *Post-mortem* examination twelve hours after death: Emaciation. Gray hepatization of right lung; distention of gall-bladder; congestion of bowels and disorganization of the glands.—*Act. Ass't Surg. H. C. Newkirk, Rock Island Hospital, Ill.*

CASES ENTERED AS TYPHOID, BUT THE CLINICAL HISTORIES SUGGESTIVE OF MALARIAL COMPLICATIONS—24 CASES.

(*A.*) *Peyer's patches ulcerated and the ileum or small intestine only affected—5 cases.*

CASE 93.—Private Daniel Plummer, Co. H, 33d Pa.; age 23; was admitted Oct. 2, 1861, with headache, diarrhœa, loss of appetite and strength. He had been sick five days, having had a chill and fever on each day. A bath was given, with quinine at night. Next day his face was flushed, eyes injected, skin hot, dry and rough, tongue coated whitish-gray, pulse 104, full; he had pain in the head and back, slight deafness, tinnitus aurium, insomnia, confusion of thought and muttering; his bowels were tender and had been moved four times. Treatment—Dover's powder and quinine. During the five following days his tongue became dry and brown, pulse less frequent, 84, countenance more anxious and prostration much increased; his bowels were moved about twice daily. On the 8th the treatment was changed to turpentine, Dover's powder and whiskey-punch. A gallon of strongly acid urine, sp. gr. 1009, was passed on the 9th, but later in the disease the urine became alkaline. A blister was applied to the abdomen on the 14th. On the 16th he craved apples, and next day had some appetite; the bowels were quiet, having been moved but once daily for several days back. On the 18th gangrenous spots appeared on the blistered surface, which was dressed with chlorinated soda solution. Three days later an erysipelatous redness extended downward to the thigh and the patient was in extremely low condition, lying on his back with his mouth and eyes open, unable to protrude his tongue, his lips and teeth covered with sordes and his body generally, except the face and neck, with vibices. The gangrenous blistered surface was treated with a solution of one drachm of nitrate of silver in one ounce of water, but without benefit. His throat became sore on the 23d, and he died on the morning of the 24th. *Post-mortem* examination: The lungs were congested; the heart, liver, spleen and pancreas healthy; the kidneys inflamed and suppurating. The peritoneum was inflamed; the mucous membrane of the stomach unusually corrugated; the mesentery and its glands inflamed—of the latter some were ulcerated; the glands of Peyer in the ileum showed cicatrizing ulcerations.—*Seminary Hospital, Georgetown, D. C.*

Case 94.—William L. Layne, Co. G, 2d Ky.; age 28; was admitted Sept. 8, 1864, having been sick one week with feverishness, increased at night, anorexia, great thirst, headache, pain in the back and limbs, somewhat frequent but small stools, scanty urine, occasional epistaxis and increasing debility. On admission the headache was intense; he was listless and disposed to stupor, his sleep dreamful and unrefreshing, eyes congested, complexion venous, breathing slow, pulse 96, tongue brown with red margins, stools frequent, watery and fetid; there was tympanites, iliac and umbilical tenderness and perspirations, with sudamina on the chest and abdomen. He died comatose on the 13th. *Post-mortem* examination: Colon much distended with air; small intestine congested; Peyer's glands greatly congested, enlarged and in two patches immediately above the ileo-cæcal junction ulcerated; liver dark-colored; gall-bladder distended.—*Act. Ass't Surg. M. K. Gleason, Rock Island Hospital, Ill.*

Case 95.—Private Thomas B. Newcomb, Co. M, 11th Vt. Art.; age 26; was admitted Sept 8, 1864, from hospital at Frederick, Md., where his case was recorded on September 6 as one of coup-de-soleil. He stated that he had been very sick with constant nausea, vomiting and general pain for several days. He was treated with hydrocyanic acid and morphine, and on the 11th blue-pill, podophyllin and compound extract of colocynth were given on account of constipation. On the 13th he had occasional spasms, apparently of a hysterical character, and his skin and eyes assumed a yellow hue. Three days later he became much jaundiced, his tongue dry, face flushed and pulse 90, while he had frequent attempts at alvine evacuations but passed little each time. The jaundice disappeared on the 20th and well-marked typhoid symptoms set in, but with no diarrhœa nor abdominal tympanites. His strength failed, his tongue becoming dry and cracked. He complained of much pain over the region of the stomach and transverse colon, and his abdomen, on the 29th, became tympanitic. On the supervention of the typhoid condition he was treated with turpentine, chlorate of potash and Dover's powder, with hot fomentations and sinapisms. He died October 4. *Post-mortem* examination: Lungs healthy; fibrinous clots in both sides of heart; intestines near stomach and liver yellow-colored; gall-bladder disorganized, perforated and with light green bile in and around it; two or three feet of mucous membrane of jejunum and whole of ileum congested; Peyer's glands ulcerated and in some places nearly perforated.—*Act. Ass't Surg. Geo. W. Fay, Hospital Patterson Park, Baltimore, Md.*

Case 96.—Private Charles Perkins, Co. I, 1st Mich. Eng'rs; age 53; was admitted into Hospital No. 6, Nashville, Tenn., in September, 1862. Efforts were made to restrain the debilitating diarrhœa with paregoric, Dover's powder, mercury with chalk, blue mass, ipecacuanha and opium, nitrate of silver and opium, etc.; during the exacerbations of the fever neutral mixture with sweet spirit of nitre was given; during the apyrexia quinia and iron; oil of turpentine was tried, but it disagreed and was discontinued. The patient improved gradually under this treatment conjoined with a bland and nourishing diet, and convalescence seemed to be well established. Tonics and the milder stimulants had been administered for several days, when, all at once, diarrhœa recurred with some tympanites, the tongue became glossy, the pulse 130 to 140, the skin yellowish, and sudamina appeared in great profusion on the neck, breast and groin; he had a hacking cough, low delirium and subsultus tendinum; his countenance became hippocratic and he died October 26. *Post-mortem* examination: Body considerably emaciated. The pericardium contained two ounces of serum. The right lung was collapsed and pale, its lower portion hypostatically congested; the left lung was emphysematous. The heart was large; the right ventricle contained a quantity of uncoagulated blood; the left was empty. The liver was large but normal in texture and color; the gall-bladder filled with thin watery bile; the spleen large and soft. There was much venous congestion of the peritoneal coat of the stomach; its mucous membrane presented a number of soft blackish patches, and at the pyloric end there was some ulceration, which extended an inch and a half into the duodenum. The mucous membrane of the jejunum and ileum presented nothing remarkable except within twenty inches of the ileo-cæcal valve, where Peyer's patches were ulcerated; most of the ulcers were only three or four lines in diameter, but the dark tumefied patches were of considerable size. The mucous membrane of the ileo-cæcal valve was tumefied and the vermiform process filled with pus; the mucous membrane of the colon was normal. The kidneys and bladder were healthy. The blood everywhere was in a fluid state.—*[From Report by E. Swift, U. S. A., Medical Director Department Ohio and Cumberland.]*

Case 97.—Musician William Brandt, 17th U. S. Inf.; age 32; was admitted Dec. 11, 1863. Diagnosis—typhoid fever. He had been sick for two weeks and confined to bed for one week: Delirium at night; stupor; tongue dry and coated; skin dry; pulse 98; thirst; occasional pains in abdomen; bowels relaxed. On the 13th the right parotid gland became painful and much swollen and on the 17th typhoid symptoms were manifested; sordes appeared on the gums; his stupor increased and he was constantly attempting to get out of bed. There was some bronchitis with a little painless expectoration. A red papular eruption was quite distinct. During the next ten days his cough became more troublesome, and on Jan. 6, 1864, jaundice and constipation were added to the symptoms, with increasing stupor, incoherent talking, glazed eyes, thick and tenacious sputa which he was unable to expectorate. He died on the 8th. "The autopsy revealed pneumonia as the cause of death and confirmed the diagnosis of typhoid fever."— *Act. Ass't Surg. Carlos Carvallo, Douglas Hospital, Washington, D. C.*

(B.) *Peyer's patches ulcerated and the large intestine also implicated—6 cases.*

CASE 98.—Private Charles E. Mariner, Co. A, Purnell Legion, was admitted Aug. 16, 1863, having been affected with slight headache and diarrhœa, two or three evacuations daily, for several days. There was no fever on admission, but his tongue was coated and yellow and his eyes jaundiced. Calomel was given as a purgative and small doses of quinine. On the 18th he vomited bile, and next day his tongue was less coated and the sclerotics white. On the 20th signs of prostration were manifested. Delirium occurred on the night of the 22d, after which he failed rapidly and died on the 24th. *Post-mortem* examination eighteen hours after death: The mucous coat of the stomach was softened and almost disintegrated. Peyer's patches were ulcerated and in two places nearly perforated; the solitary glands were greatly ulcerated and in some instances broken down; the ileo-cæcal valve was disorganized, its mucous membrane being converted into a pulpy mass. The rectum was ulcerated in three places, each as large as a dime. A number of the mesenteric glands were enlarged to the size of a pigeon's egg. The liver was pale; the spleen congested and twice its normal size. The left side of the neck was emphysematous and its tissues engorged, the result, probably, of an *ante-mortem* blow.—*Act. Ass't Surg. W. H. Letterman, Douglas Hospital, Washington, D. C.*

CASE 99.—Private Jacob Brewer, Co. D, 15th Ohio; age 19; was admitted April 12, 1864, having had, as reported by himself, a severe chill followed by fever. He was at first regarded as suffering from remittent fever and quinine was given; but as the disease after admission seemed of a continued type, with iliac tenderness and dry, dark and fissured tongue, the quinine was omitted and stimulants administered. He died on the 17th. *Post-mortem* examination thirty hours after death: Brain substance white and softer than might be expected from mere cadaveric change; meninges remarkably pale and anæmic; lungs and heart normal; spleen enlarged, very soft and rotten. Peyer's patches and solitary glands within a foot of the cæcum ulcerated, those nearest the valve most affected, the ulcers raised above the surrounding surface, much thickened and covered with mucus and fæces. Colon ulcerated in small spots in its upper part.—*Chattanooga Hospital, Tenn.*

CASE 100.—Private Hiram Ginder, Co. B, 57th Pa.; age 17; was admitted Nov. 2, 1864, his previous history being unknown. He was deaf but not delirious; skin yellow, cheeks flushed and murky, respiration hurried, pulse 110, teeth covered with sordes, tongue, lips and gums dry, cracked and oozing blood. On the 5th some cough was noted; the respiration became more embarrassed and the cheeks darker. He died on the 7th. He was treated with turpentine, camphor and spirit of nitre, counter-irritation to chest, beef-essence and milk-punch. *Post-mortem* examination: Pleuritic adhesions on left side; four ounces of dark bloody serum in right pleural sac; congestion of lungs posteriorly and hepatization of part of upper lobe of right lung; heart normal. Mesenteric glands enlarged and filled with dark blood; mucous coat of ileum and cæcum thickened and inflamed; fifteen Peyer's patches, from one-fourth inch in diameter to one and a half by two and a half inches, thickened and some showing commencing ulceration. Spleen large and soft; liver normal in size but yellow; gall-bladder large, containing three ounces of bile; kidneys normal.—*Act. Ass't Surg. Thomas Bowen, Second Division Hospital, Alexandria, Va.*

CASE 101.—Private Michael McGowan, Co. A, 154th Ind.; age 18; was admitted May 30, 1865, having been sick for three weeks with a frequent and copious diarrhœa followed by chills and fever, acute pain in chest and dry cough with very little expectoration. On admission he was much emaciated and very feeble; there were large bed-sores over the sacrum, trochanters and angles of the ribs on the right side. His skin was dry and harsh, tongue dry, red and glazed and teeth covered with sordes; he had much thirst, no appetite, pain and tenderness over abdomen, a profuse diarrhœa and hurried breathing. He died on the 7th. *Post-mortem* examination fifteen hours after death: The mucous membrane of the trachea was inflamed and ulcerated. The lower lobe and anterior border of the upper lobe of the left lung, and the upper and lower lobes of the right lung were congested; the middle lobe of the latter was hepatized. The omentum was inflamed and adherent to the abdominal parietes. The spleen weighed twenty-four ounces and was dark and soft. The mucous membrane of the ileum was inflamed and Peyer's patches were ulcerated; there was also some ulceration of the cæcum; the mesenteric glands were enlarged.—*Act. Ass't Surg. S. B. West, Cumberland Hospital, Md.*

CASE 102.—Private Austin Seeley, Co. C, 73d Ohio, was admitted Dec. 18, 1862. He had been treated for intermittent fever in the Harewood hospital, Washington, D. C., from November 19. He died Jan. 30, 1863. *Post-mortem* examination next day: Age about 24; body emaciated. Lungs, excepting a slight bronchial inflammation, healthy; heart contained a large white clot in its right cavities; spleen redder than natural and flabby; liver pale brown and on section pale brown with darker intralobular spots; stomach and upper portion of small intestine apparently healthy; agminated glands in the lower five feet of ileum successively and gradually increasing in enlargement; glands in the terminal foot dark-red and bordered by inflamed mucous membrane, those nearest the ileo-colic valve presenting several small ulcerations; solitary glands apparently healthy; colon greatly distended, its mucous membrane redder than natural, but with no inflamed spots, streaks or patches, and with no visible disease of solitary glands; lymphatic glands of mesentery and mesocolon bluish-black, which color on section formed a circle within the periphery, and under the microscope presented the appearance of exceedingly fine particles similar to the black deposits in the intestinal glands in Chickahominy diarrhœa; kidneys healthy.—[*Specimens* Nos. 99–101, Med. Sect., Army Medical Museum, ulceration of Peyer's patches, are from this case.]—*Act. Ass't Surg. Joseph Leidy, Satterlee Hospital, Philadelphia, Pa.*

CASE 103.—Private James M. Forman, Co. H, 33d Pa.; age 21; was admitted Oct. 2, 1861, having been sick for nine days with pain in the head, back and bones, chills, loss of appetite and strength, diarrhœa, epistaxis, pain in the stomach, nausea and vomiting. A bath was ordered for him with Dover's powder at night. Next morning his face was flushed, eyes injected, pulse 98, full, skin hot, dry and rough, tongue heavily coated, the centre brownish, the tip and edges red; he had anorexia, great thirst, irritability of stomach, diarrhœa, the bowels having been moved four times, tenderness in the right iliac region and four or five characteristic rose-colored spots. The case continued for ten days without much change under treatment by astringents, opiates and whiskey-punch. The nausea and vomiting gradually ceased; some degree of deafness was developed; there was occasional tympanites, and blood appeared in the stools for several days and on the 8th in large quantity. But on the 12th the diarrhœa ceased, the abdominal tenderness was lessened, the tongue became moist and there were indications of returning appetite. About the same time, however, the right parotid gland became inflamed and the face much swollen. There was slight delirium on the 14th, and next day the swelling, which had become erysipelatous, extended over the face, nearly closing both eyes and presenting a small gangrenous spot on the ear and another on the cheek. The patient walked about the ward in high delirium, but towards evening became more quiet. At 10 P. M. he sprang up suddenly, knocked the pitcher containing his punch from the attendant's hand and endeavored to get down stairs. He was got back to bed with some difficulty and immediately thereafter began to fail. At midnight his pulse was rapid and almost imperceptible, his extremities cold, eyes fixed and jaws locked; he took no notice when called or shaken and died at 1 A. M. of the 16th. *Post-mortem* examination: Parotid gland in a state of suppuration; side of face dark-colored and with small patches of gangrene in front of the ear. The mucous membrane of the stomach was congested and softened. The liver and gall-bladder were large but healthy; the spleen congested, enlarged and soft. The ileum was inflamed; its solitary and agminated glands were ulcerated and there was a small perforation in one of the ulcerated patches. The large intestine, from the valve to the rectum, was very much ulcerated. The peritoneum was inflamed; the mesenteric glands enlarged; the kidneys and bladder healthy.—*Seminary Hospital, Georgetown, D. C.*

(C.) Condition of Peyer's patches not stated; the intestines variously affected—7 cases.

CASE 104.—John Freeman, Co. B, 12th Tenn. Cav., was admitted May 7, 1864, in a semi-unconscious state; pulse feeble, respiration normal, tongue dry and dark, teeth covered with sordes, skin jaundiced, pupils natural, stools involuntary. He died next day. *Post-mortem* examination sixteen hours after death: Unusual injection of meningeal vessels; hypostatic congestion of lower lobes of lungs; congestion and discoloration of liver; distention of gallbladder; much congestion of spleen; slight congestion of ileum.—*Act. Ass't Surg. George E. Walton, Hospital No. 8, Nashville, Tenn.*

CASE 105.—Private A. C. Truman, Co. G, 152d N. Y., was admitted April 24, 1863. Diagnosis—typhoid fever. Epigastric pain and tenderness but no diarrhœa; vomiting; marked febrile action; tongue coated dark brown; sordes on teeth and lips; pulse 125; urine scanty; countenance pinched; tinnitus aurium. He was treated with quinine, whiskey and turpentine emulsion, and on the 26th was improving. On the 29th blue mass and colocynth were given for constipation and on May 14 sulphate of magnesia. On the 20th he was seized with a troublesome cough and dull pain in the left side of the chest. A few days later diarrhœa set in, the cough continuing, and he died on June 5. *Post-mortem* examination: Right lung hepatized in its lower lobe; left lung collapsed and containing a few tubercles; heart normal. Ileum extensively congested but not ulcerated; liver, spleen and kidneys normal.—*Act. Ass't Surg. John E. Smith, Douglas Hospital, Washington, D. C.*

CASE 106.—Private Pleasant Willett, Co. E, 135th Ind.; age 28; was admitted Aug. 19, 1864, having suffered from diarrhœa for some time. His pulse was 106 and his tongue dry and furred but not glazed or cracked. Next day a remission was noticed and on the following day nausea and vomiting were recorded. The diarrhœa became profuse, with dysuria and much abdominal tenderness. He died on the 25th. *Post-mortem* examination eight hours after death: Brain and its meninges normal. Lungs healthy; heart normal, right cavities containing a firm clot. Liver much engorged, eighty ounces; spleen intensely engorged, twenty-seven ounces; stomach distended with flatus and fæcal matter; peritoneal cavity containing one pint of purulent serum; colon somewhat thickened and softened; ileum ulcerated in its lower three feet and with a perforation six inches from the ileo-cæcal valve; bladder congested; kidneys together weighing fifteen ounces.—*Act. Ass't Surg. D. W. Flora, Hospital, Madison, Ind.*

CASE 107.—Private Jasper Kemp, Co. H, 11th N. H., was treated in the Fifth Army Corps Field Hospital, City Point, Va., from April 23, 1865, for malarial fever, and transferred May 1 to hospital transport "State of Maine," where his case was diagnosed typhoid fever. He was admitted on the 2d, and two days afterward was seized with acute abdominal pain which increased in severity until he died on the 5th. *Post-mortem* examination: General peritonitis; ulceration of small intestine with seven perforations.—*Campbell Hospital, Washington, D. C.*

CASE 108.—Private Robert Alexander, Co. E, 149th Pa.; age 18; was admitted Dec. 7, 1863, as a fully developed case of typhoid fever, the symptoms stated being a dry and red tongue, laboring pulse, scanty and high-colored urine, with great irritability of stomach and diarrhœa. On the 18th there were involuntary stools and more or less stupor and subsultus. He died on the 22d. *Post-mortem* examination nine hours after death: Softening of the coats of the stomach; thickening and softening throughout the lower course of the colon, but no ulceration of the intestinal membrane. Lungs comparatively healthy. Liver normal.—*Third Division Hospital, Alexandria, Va.*

CASE 109.—Private Myron Balch, Co. B, 9th Mich., was admitted April 2, 1864, with a fever which presented distinct remissions, and was treated with ten grains of quinine during each remission until the 10th, when he became delirious, had iliac tenderness, diarrhœa and hemorrhagic stools. Stimulants were given and persulphate of iron one grain every two hours. He died on the 16th. *Post-mortem* examination twenty-four hours after death: Brain and its membranes anæmic. Posterior three-fourths of upper lobe of right lung hepatized; left lung normal; heart normal, small white clots in both ventricles. Liver fatty; ileum for twelve inches above the ileo-cæcal valve, ulcer-ated in patches varying from the size of a pea to that of a dollar, the largest being nearest the valve; colon injected and ulcerated in its upper part.—*Act. Ass't Surg. C. F. Little, Chattanooga Hospital, Tenn.*

CASE 110.—Private D. F. McLachlan, Co. G, 14th N. Y., was admitted Sept. 20, 1861. He had been taken sick with a chill followed by severe pain in the head, back and sides, with loss of appetite and strength. On admission his skin was warm and perspiring; pulse 92, quick and strong; tongue glossy and pale, slightly colored brown in the centre and at the base; bowels moved eight times in the twenty-four hours; there was tenderness in the iliac and epigastric regions, with meteorism, borborygmus, epistaxis and rose-colored spots (from twenty to thirty) on the abdomen and chest. He was treated with turpentine emulsion, blue pill and opium, and Dover's powder at night. Next day there was slight mental confusion with ringing in the ears, and his tongue was covered with a grayish fur. An eight-grain dose of quinine was added to the treatment. During the week which followed his condition was one of gradual improvement; the pulse did not rise above 90, the meteorism disappeared, his appetite began to return and his tongue lost its fur, becoming moist and pale, but his bowels continued slightly relaxed notwithstanding the use of opiates and astringents. After this his progress was uncertain; at times he felt pretty well. He was treated mainly with wine and quinine in two-grain doses three times daily, but on October 16 the throat and larynx became congested and he had some bronchitic cough. Blisters were applied to the sides of the neck, the throat was swabbed with a strong solution of nitrate of silver and five grains each of calomel and jalap were given. He did not rest well during the night and next day was pale and weak, hoarse and somewhat deaf; his bowels were moved three times and there was tenderness with tympanites and borborygmus. During the day the bowels were again moved three times. He continued thus for three days. On the 21st whiskey-punch was substituted for wine. On the 23d his expression became anxious, pulse 114, skin hot and dry, the tongue continuing pale and flabby; he had six thin evacuations from the bowels; cough was troublesome and the throat symptoms had become so aggravated that he swallowed with difficulty and could not speak above a whisper. The treatment consisted at this time of chlorate of potash, muriate of iron, beef-tea and whiskey-punch. During the following night his pulse rose to 140, and next day sordes appeared on the teeth. Soon after this he became delirious, imagining that some large animal was in bed with him; that he was in camp, etc. On the 27th, having passed a better night, he was not so delirious, but he looked pale and anxious; his pulse was weak and small, 94; skin warm and soft; tongue pale, moist and tremulous; his bowels were moved involuntarily. At this time there was noted on the skin dark, almost black, slightly elevated spots somewhat larger than split-peas, without accompanying inflammation; those which had arisen more recently were whitish-yellow, being full of purulent matter. On the 28th he was almost unconscious; his pulse weak, small and irritable, 120; skin warm and soft; tongue heavily coated; mouth moist and its whole surface covered with white sticky mucus; gums covered with sordes; one side of the face flushed very dark red; his bowels had been quiet since an injection given on the previous evening, but there was tenderness on both sides; submucous and sibilant râles were heard in both lungs. On the evening of this day he was quite unconscious, his eyes and mouth open, pulse 130, respiration 50. During the night hemorrhage from the bowels took place and recurred on the after-noon of the next day, his pulse meanwhile becoming weaker and breathing more rapid. On the 30th his extremities became cold and at 2 P. M. he died. *Post-mortem* examination: The brain, pharynx and œsophagus were not examined. The lungs were much congested and hepatized. The heart contained fibrinous clots in both ventricles. The liver and pancreas were normal; the spleen soft and somewhat enlarged. The right kidney was small and transformed into a thin-walled cyst containing a yellowish liquid; the left kidney presented several large cavities containing pus. "The small intestine showed that inflammation had been rife there some time ago, but no ulcers were seen that had been formed lately; there were places where large and recently healed sores were evidently indicated." The mucous membrane of the colon was broken by several large ulcers. The mesentery was quite healthy.—*Semi-nary Hospital, Georgetown, D. C.*

(D.) Condition of Peyer's patches variously stated, but not ulcerated; intestines more or less affected—6 cases.

CASE 111.—Private Charles Lewis, Co. G, 23d U. S. Colored troops; age 21; was admitted Oct. 20, 1865, on which day he had a chill followed by fever. Dover's powder was given in the evening, but the chill recurring next day quinine in five-grain doses was administered. There was no chill on the following day; but the febrile action con-tinued and increased so that on the 24th his pulse was 120, quick and full, respiration 60, skin hot and dry, tongue furred; and he was weaker, sleepless and slightly delirious. Small doses of eggnog, chlorate of potash and tur-pentine with Dover's powder were administered. Next day his condition was unchanged; castor oil was given to move the bowels. On the 26th the insomnia and delirium continued; the tongue was dry, brown and coated; the eyes jaundiced; the urine passed involuntarily, staining the linen yellow; the abdomen tender and tympanitic; a thin yellow-colored discharge was procured by the oil. Next day the pulse was not so strong, the tongue continued dry and brown, but the skin became somewhat moist and the patient slept a little. One grain of calomel and two of ipecacuanha were given every hour for six hours, with mustard to the back of the neck and chest. He died on the 28th. *Post-mortem* examination thirty hours after death: The arachnoid over the interpeduncular space was thickened and opaque and there was serous effusion in the cerebral ventricles. The lungs and heart were normal, but there was effusion in the left thoracic cavity. The liver was large, its right lobe honey-combed, full of air and of a very peculiar appearance, and its left lobe normal in texture but of a yellow color. The pancreas was large; the kidneys normal; the spleen large, soft and dark-colored. The colon and rectum were normal; Peyer's patches were enlarged, as were also the mesenteric glands. [*Specimen* 639, Med. Sect., Army Medical Museum, from this case, shows the honey-combing of the liver by dilated gall-ducts.]—*Surg. E. Bentley, U. S. V., Slough Hospital, Alexandria, Va.*

CASE 112.—Private F. Binder, Co. G, 131st Pa.; age 27; was admitted Dec. 30, 1862, with gangrene of both feet after typhoid fever. About eight weeks prior to admission he was attacked with chills and fever, but the disease afterwards assumed the character of typhoid fever. The condition of his feet was supposed to be due to frost-bite while sick in camp. On Jan. 7, 1863, the skin of both feet was reported as blue from the toes to above the ankles, where was an irregular border of redness; below the malleoli the parts were cold and a pin could be inserted without being felt. Lines of demarcation were formed on the 9th just above the malleoli; at this time the patient's appetite was improving and his tongue looking well, but his skin was slightly yellow and he complained of much pain, which he referred to his feet. On the 22d his bowels became loose, there having been five stools during the day, and next day the tongue was somewhat dry. He slept well at night and had no night-sweats, but he lost flesh and continued to suffer from pain in the feet. The right foot separated at the ankle-joint on the 26th, the stump having bled quite freely. Next day both legs were amputated by "Le Noir's" operation, after which the patient reacted fairly and rested well. On the 30th the stumps looked badly and discharged a grayish pus, while vomiting, hiccough and extreme depression were developed. Death took place February 2. *Post-mortem* examination twenty-four hours after death: There were clots in all the arteries of the stumps except the right anterior tibial. On pressing the medulla of the left tibia a yellowish liquid exuded from the vascular foramina in the compact substance of the bone. The brain was healthy. The right lung weighed thirty-three ounces and three-quarters; in its lower lobe was a circumscribed, light-colored, consolidated mass and numerous light-colored points, about the size of pinheads, surrounded by irregular areas of congestion; a portion of this lobe was in the state of gray hepatization. The left lung weighed eighteen ounces and a quarter; on the posterior surface of its lower lobe and in the substance of the upper lobe were a number of discolored spots beneath which the lung-tissue was infiltrated with serum. The heart was pale and contained a small fibrinous clot in the right ventricle. The liver was pale and firm; the gall-bladder small; the spleen weighed seven ounces and a half and was very soft; the pancreas was of a grayish color; both kidneys were small and light-colored. The stomach was large, its mucous membrane slightly softened; the upper part of the jejunum was slate-colored; the whole of the ileum congested and its valvulæ conniventes indistinct; Peyer's patches were slightly thickened and some of them congested. The large intestine was congested.—*Ass't Surg. George M. McGill, U. S. A., Lincoln Hospital, Washington, D. C.*

CASE 113.—Private John Frink, Co. K, 40th N. J.; age 19; admitted June 4, 1865. Typhoid fever. Severe diarrhœa, gastric irritability and nervous disorder were the prominent phenomena. Died 23d. *Post-mortem* examination twenty-four hours after death: The lungs were emphysematous; the small intestine much inflamed; the glands of Peyer congested; the spleen normal.——*Third Division Hospital, Alexandria, Va.*

CASE 114.—Private Benjamin Brady, Co. I, 24th N. Y. Cav.; age 23; was admitted June 5, 1865, with chronic diarrhœa and intermittent fever. Typhoid symptoms soon became apparent, including delirium and petechial spots on the abdomen. He died on the 14th. *Post-mortem* examination nine hours after death: Body much emaciated. Lungs normal; spleen enlarged and softened; small intestine ulcerated; Peyer's patches much inflamed and corresponding mesenteric glands enlarged and indurated.—*Slough Hospital, Alexandria, Va.*

CASE 115.—Private David E. Martin, Co. K, 137th Pa.; age 32; was admitted May 17, 1863, with irregular chills followed by fever from which he had suffered for some weeks. A chill followed by fever and perspiration occurred on the evening of his admission, but next day he was feeling pretty well. This was repeated on the following evening, but on the third day there was no recurrence, quinine having been administered meanwhile. On the 21st he was found for the first time with hot skin, active pulse and headache, his tongue remaining as heretofore, yellow-furred but comparatively clean at the tip. Signs of nervous agitation were also observed, as tremulousness of the lower lip and twitching of the hands. Neutral mixture, cold drinks and low diet were substitued for the quinine. He continued in this condition, some diarrhœa meanwhile appearing, until the 25th, when, having thrown off the bed-clothes during the night, an oppression of the breathing was developed, with sonorous and sibilant râles and some sluggishness of mind. Acetate of ammonia and wine-whey were given with sinapisms to the chest. A blister was applied next day, and on the day following infusion of serpentaria and carbonate of ammonia were given. On the 28th, in view of the continued cerebral disturbance, indicated by heat of head, some confusion of ideas, and injection of the right conjunctiva, a blister was applied to the back of the neck. Next day two or three rose-colored spots of doubtful character were noticed and there was slight abdominal distention. Perspirations were added to the list of symptoms on the 30th and involuntary discharges on the 31st. He died June 3. *Post-mortem* examination next day: Body somewhat emaciated. Heart normal; mucous membrane of trachea and bronchi inflamed, the inflammation extending to the smaller tubes and in several instances to the pulmonary lobules. About four feet of lower portion of ileum showing slight irregularly diffused inflammation; glands of Peyer generally healthy, but a few of the lower ones containing some black deposit; ileum, for eight inches above ileo-cæcal valve, and cæcum intensely inflamed, the mucous membrane liver-colored, thickened and in many places ulcerated, the ulcers varying from the size of a pea to that of the thumb-nail and the largest extending through to the muscular coat; colon distended with air and its mucous membrane here and there slightly inflamed and presenting a few scattered ulcers about the size of pepper-corns; rectum more intensely inflamed and with large and numerous ulcers. Liver large and rather soft; spleen soft and flabby; kidneys darker than usual, their pelves somewhat injected; suprarenal bodies and pancreas healthy. The muscular system and blood appeared to be in sound condition; a large translucent clot occupied the right cavities of the heart.—*Act. Ass't Surg. Joseph Leidy, Satterlee Hospital, Philadelphia, Pa.*

CASE 116.—Private Darius Greenlaw, Co. I, 7th Me., was admitted Aug. 10, 1862. He rejected all nourishment, and was sustained by injections of milk, brandy and beef-tea. He vomited frequently a dark-greenish, fetid liquid; there was no fever nor diarrhœa; the alvine evacuations were slight and infrequent. He died September 1. *Post-mortem* examination: Body not much wasted; apparently about 20 years of age. In consequence of the patient having had a swollen eye and bleeding at the ears the brain and skull were examined, but both appeared to be normal. Lungs and heart normal. Stomach much contracted and empty; its mucous membrane inflamed from œsophageal orifice into cul-de-sac and a short distance along greater curvature; rugæ of stomach and summits of valvulæ conniventes of duodenum also inflamed. Ileum presenting four small inflamed patches; upper agminated glands healthy, lower glands thickened and containing black pigment, several of the latter, from one to two inches long, presenting two or three little ulcers not more than one or two lines in diameter; lower solitary glands enlarged and containing black pigment. Mucous membrane of cæcum and of part of ascending colon inflamed and, in a less degree, that of the descending colon; solitary glands blackened.—*Act. Ass't Surg. Joseph Leidy, Satterlee Hospital, Philadelphia, Pa.*

Among the one hundred and sixteen cases submitted above there are fifty that, in view of their clinical history, and the information already gathered concerning the symptomatology of the continued fevers, must be regarded as cases of undoubted typhoid. The *post-mortem* observations in some of these instances were insufficient and loosely expressed, but, as in others they were more extensive and entered with precision on the record, there is no difficulty in appreciating the associated anatomical changes. The brain and its membranes were oftentimes found in a normal condition; the thoracic viscera were frequently affected, but in many cases no morbid alteration was discovered in them; the abdominal contents were variously changed from the healthy state. The character of these changes will be examined hereafter on presentation of the remainder of the *post-mortem* records. It is sufficient for the present to point out that an ulcerated condition of the small intestine, particularly of its lower part, and perhaps specifically of that part of its extent which corresponds to the position of the agminated glands, was the only constant anatomical lesion. In some instances the stomach and upper part of the intestinal tract presented traces of inflammation, in others the large intestine bore similar marks; but all these had at the same time an ulceration of some part of the lower portion of the small intestine. Of the fifty cases Peyer's glands were ulcerated in thirty-three; and in seventeen, in which the condition of these patches is not stated, the ileum or small intestine was said to have been ulcerated.

Had the typho-malarial cases reported by our medical officers consisted of typhoid fever modified by the activity of a malarial element, there should have been discovered in all fatal cases the constant anatomical lesion of typhoid fever with such changes in the cadaver as are known to be occasioned by the presence of the malarial poison. It has been seen in a previous chapter that fatal cases of malarial fever presented no constant or characteristic lesion. Inflammatory conditions, observed perhaps more frequently in the small than in the large intestine, were noted, and these had often progressed to ulceration; but as in some cases the intestinal canal was apparently healthy, such conditions could not be regarded as pathognomonic. Ulceration of the intestines, of the small intestine especially, is therefore to be expected in the typho-malarial cases as the constant accompaniment of their typhoid essential and as an occasional result of their malarial complication.

Nevertheless, of forty-two cases recorded as typho-malarial, there were nine in which the patches of Peyer were reported as having been found in various conditions, but not ulcerated, and in which the intestines were more or less affected, but without ulceration of the ileum, except perhaps in two instances. Moreover, of the forty-two cases there were fifteen in which, while the condition of the patches was not stated, the intestines were variously affected, but in only one-third of these is it stated in terms or inferentially that ulceration was present.   The remaining eighteen cases were characterized by ulceration of the patches of Peyer.

Of the nine cases, 84–92, in which the condition of the agminated glands was variously reported, case 84 had the elliptical patches pale, the solitary glands and the rectum ulcerated.   These are not the generally accepted lesions of typhoid.   In 85 the patches were distinct and elevated and the solitary glands of the large intestine ulcerated, while in 86 the patches were dark-colored and conspicuous and the mucous lining of the small intestine congested.   These may be set aside as indicating by the glandular tumefaction the possibility of a typhoid element.   In 87–91 the patches presented the shaven-beard appearance; in 87 the solitary glands were prominent; in 89 these glands, near the ileocæcal valve, were ulcerated, as was also the colon; in 88 the intestines were congested, and in 90, according to Dr. HARRISON ALLEN, they presented no special lesion other than pigmentation of the patches.   In Dr. LEIDY's case, 91, there was, in addition to deposits of pigment in the agminated and solitary glands, large inflamed and ecchymosed patches in the small intestine and similar but more diffused conditions in the large intestine.   In case 92 the record is indefinite; the expression "congestion of the bowels and disorganization of the glands" leaves an uncertainty as to whether the glands of the mesentery or the closed glands of the intestinal mucous membrane were thus affected.   Six of the nine cases presumed by the diagnosis to have both a typhoid and a malarial element may thus be regarded as having offered no *post-mortem* evidence of the existence of a typhoid factor.

Of the fifteen cases, 69–83, in which the condition of Peyer's patches was not stated, the small intestine was ulcerated in five instances: In case 74, the patient having been under treatment in hospital for twenty-six days before death, there was congestion and commencing ulceration of the intestines; in 75 the mucous membrane of the small intestine was ulcerated in various parts and that of the large intestine congested and disintegrated; in 77 there were small ulcerations in the lower part of the ileum, and in 82 and 83 this part of the intestine was perforated.   Allowing the ulceration in these cases to represent the enteric lesion of typhoid fever, there remain ten cases in which the small intestine was not ulcerated.   In 71, 72, 73, 78 and 81 the intestinal mucous membrane was congested, inflamed or softened; in the first-mentioned case the œsophagus, stomach and duodenum participated in the inflammatory action; in 73 the solitary glands were disorganized and in 81 there was also peritoneal inflammation.   In 76 the small intestine was congested and the rectum ulcerated and gangrenous.   In 79 the ileum was injected and in 80 gangrenous.   In 70 the solitary glands were disorganized and the mucous coat of the rectum inflamed and softened.   In 69 nothing is said of the condition of the small intestine, possibly because it presented nothing of importance.   Negative, as contradistinguished from positive, testimony has its value: The record of case 76 of the paroxysmal fevers does not take cognizance of the condition of the small intestine; but as the diagnosis was remittent fever, few pathologists would doubt its negative testimony as to the absence of ulceration of the ileum.   In 69 of the present series the diagnosis typho-malarial sustains rather than invalidates a similar negative evidence.   That typhoid symptoms may be present without the co-existence of an enteric lesion is evident from the following case of mistaken diagnosis:

Private William McMillan, Co. I, 15th Ill. Cav.; age 16; was admitted from Washington street prison Feb. 9, 1865, with typhoid fever. He complained of frontal headache and was delirious at times; his tongue was dry and coated with dark-brown fur, teeth covered with sordes, skin hot, dry and sallow, pulse 120 and weak, bowels tympanitic and tender. He died on the 13th. *Post-mortem* examination twenty-one hours after death: The pericardium was full of serum and-flakes of lymph. The left lung was coated with recent deposits of lymph; similar deposits glued together the intestines and other abdominal viscera. The liver was pale. The mucous membrane of the ileum was quite normal.—*Third Division Hospital, Alexandria, Va.*

But even were case 69 thrown out as indefinite in its evidence, there would be no modification of the general conclusion drawn from this series of cases, to wit: that among them are to be found cases in which the symptoms warranted a typho-malarial diagnosis in the absence of the lesion considered pathognomonic of typhoid fever.

This conclusion is sustained by an examination of the *post-mortem* records of those cases which, though recorded as typhoid fever, showed by their clinical history that their course was probably modified by the concurrent action of the malarial poison. Twenty-four such cases have been submitted,* in eleven of which the patches of Peyer were referred to definitely as ulcerated. In six of the twenty-four cases, 111–116, the condition of these glands was mentioned, and if the enlargement in 111, the thickening and congestion in 112, the inflamed condition with ulceration of the small intestine in 114 and the commencing ulceration of the pigmented glands in 116 be regarded as representing the anatomical lesions of typhoid fever, there remain two cases in which those lesions cannot be recognized. These are 113, in which, although the patient was under treatment in hospital for twenty days prior to death, the patches of Peyer presented no other characteristic than a participation in the general congestion of the small intestine, and 115, in which, although, according to the testimony of Dr. LEIDY, the ileum near the valve and the cæcum beyond it were intensely inflamed, the patches were healthy except that a few of the lower ones contained some black pigment. The condition of the agminated glands was not stated in seven, 104–110, of the twenty-four cases. Four of these may be set aside as presenting probable typhoid lesions, but the remaining three cannot be so regarded. In 104 the ileum was but slightly congested; in 105 it was extensively congested but not ulcerated; and in 108 the mucous membrane of the stomach was reported softened, of the lower part of the colon thickened and softened, but no mention is made of the condition of the ileum or small intestine, and it is hardly admissible to suppose that the characteristic lesion, in a case admitted as fully developed typhoid fever, would have been omitted from the record while details were given of other and apparently less important lesions.

It is evident from these records that among the fatal cases reported as typho-malarial were some which, while presenting the inflammatory conditions recognized as the frequent

* Among the forty-two cases entered as typho-malarial and the twenty-four which, although showing in their clinical history a probable malarial complication, were nevertheless regarded as typhoid, are to be found those of which Dr. WOODWARD spoke as follows in his remarks on *Typho-malarial Fever, before the International Medical Congress,* Phila., 1876, pamphlet, pages 34–35: "In the group of cases in which the malarial phenomena predominated the disease began as a simple intermittent or remittent fever, of quotidian, tertian or quartan type, the most frequent form being a simple or double tertian; but after a week or ten days the fever assumed a more or less completely continued type, with many of the phenomena characteristic of typhoid fever, such as diarrhœa, abdominal tenderness, meteorism, muttering delirium, subsultus tendinum, dry, brown tongue and the like. But even when the typhoid phenomena were most pronounced some of the most characteristic of them were often wanting. Thus, sometimes there was no diarrhœa at all, but constipation instead. The characteristic tache rouge, or rose-colored eruption, was generally entirely absent; gastric disturbance, hepatic tenderness and an icteroid hue of the countenance were much more generally present than in simple typhoid fever. Now, a large proportion of these cases terminated favorably, especially, as I think, because quinine was so freely used in their treatment; the occurrence of ordinary paroxysms of ague was a frequent accident during the convalescence. And, just because of the frequency with which they recovered, I suppose, the number of autopsies in cases of this kind which I have been able to collect is much less than in cases of the second group, of which I shall presently speak. Still, I have collected a number of autopsies of cases of this kind, in which diarrhœa had been present during the fever and in which, after it had assumed a continuous type, it had strikingly resembled typhoid fever, but in which dissection showed no other lesion in the alimentary canal than a smart intestinal catarrh. Patches of inflammation, scattered irregularly throughout both small and large intestines, and enlargement of the closed glands, often associated with pigment deposits, were the characteristic lesions. The solitary glands of the small intestine appeared as little projecting tumors the size of pinheads, which often had constricted necks, so that they resembled tiny polypi. The agminated glands of Peyer, slightly prominent, were often the seat of pigment deposit, which gave them the so-called shaven-beard appearance. Sometimes the villi of the small intestines were hypertrophied; sometimes they had pigment deposits at their apices. In the large intestine the slightly swollen solitary glands were often the seat of pigment deposits, seated either in the glands alone or sometimes also in the surrounding mucosa, in which case the central dot of pigment was surrounded by a little pigmentary ring. When the fever had supervened, as often happened, upon a chronic flux, or where dysentery had been developed during the course of the fever or of the convalescence and had been the immediate cause of death, the characteristic follicular ulcerations of the colon or the phenomena of the diphtheritic process complicated the picture. Great enlargement of the spleen and congestion of the liver, with or without fatty degeneration, were frequent concomitants."

attendant of acute malarial poisoning, did not have associated with them the morbid condition which daily experience shows to be the invariable accompaniment of typhoid fever. Certain cases of the paroxysmal fevers, as for instance 58, 63, 81 and 82, indicated that a clinical history suggestive of typhoid fever might be presented without the discovery of typhoid lesions on *post-mortem* examination. This indication has been fully sustained by the records just submitted. They demonstrate that there were sometimes developed in the progress of a malarial fever, and in the absence of the local intestinal lesions characteristic of typhoid, certain symptoms which are so generally the manifestations of typhoid fever that they are technically known as typhoid symptoms. As these cases are too numerous and well authenticated to be disposed of by the assumption that they were exceptional cases of mistaken diagnosis, it follows that our medical officers applied the term typho-malarial to cases which Dr. WOODWARD did not have in view on its introduction. Adynamic malarial remittents swelled the list of febrile cases reported as typho-malarial, and to a greater extent than would be supposed from the small number of *post-mortem* records that support this statement. Most of the recorded cases presented the characteristic lesion of typhoid, or such ulcerative changes in the mucous membrane of the small intestine as might be claimed to represent the typhoid lesion, although malarial fevers are also productive of such changes. But it has already been shown that malarial cases rarely reached the general hospitals in the rear, where facilities existed for *post-mortem* observation and record. Such cases occurring at the front recovered under the influence of quinine, or died, if the disease was pernicious, before reaching the general hospitals. Hence the paucity of malarial changes as compared with the frequency of typhoid lesions in the recorded cases. Had the *post-mortem* records of typho-malarial fever been preserved in the field-books of the regimental surgeons as in the case-books of the general hospitals, it is highly probable that the number of cases presenting lesions not definitely typhoid would have been largely increased.

When anomalous febrile cases were first observed in the autumn of 1861 they were viewed by our medical officers as remittent fevers which, owing to depressing influences operating on the newly levied troops, tended to assume a continued type and adynamic character. This is expressed in a large number of sanitary reports furnished at that early period of the war, a few of which are herewith submitted:

Surgeon J. M. CUYLER, *U. S. A., Fortress Monroe, Va., August* 17, 1861.—Continued fever of malarial origin, by many here called "typhoid," is the most formidable disease we have to contend with; the number of fatal cases has as yet been comparatively few, but patients are long in recovering their strength.

Surgeon ISAAC J. CLARK, *12th Pa. Reserves.*—Our camp at Tennallytown, Md., in August, 1861, was on a hillside with a gravelly surface but a wet clayey subsoil, near a piece of low ground suitable for the generation of malaria. The prevailing disease was remittent fever, which almost invariably in a few days changed to a mild typhoid fever; most of the cases recovered, but convalesced quite slowly.

Surgeon A. P. FRICK, *103d Pa.*—During our sojourn at White Oak Swamp, June 1862, there was much and serious sickness, principally typhoid fever, or we may more properly say remittent fever of a typhoid form. The prolonged exposure, continued watching and great mental depression after the battle (Fair Oaks), united with the malarial influences of the region in giving a low form to disease and in making cases alarmingly fatal. Stimulants, quinine, chlorate of potash and opium were the remedies chiefly relied on.

Surgeon SAMUEL G. LANE, *5th Pa. Reserves.*—Disease during the winter 1861–62 was of a decidedly typhoid type, death being usually sudden and from local inflammatory complications. We had but few cases of enteric fever; all others were purely miasmatic. The treatment was simple: Depletion, even local, was pernicious; quinine in full and repeated doses, stimulants, nutritious diet and cleanliness constituted the general treatment, with oil of turpentine, nitrate of silver, acetate of lead and opiates for diarrhœa, which was a usual accompaniment, and dry cupping, blistering and counter-irritants to subdue inflammatory action.

Surgeon S. N. SHERMAN, *34th N. Y., Seneca Mills, Md., Sept.* 30, 1861.—The 34th N. Y. was mustered into service June 15 at Albany, N. Y. It reached Washington July 6 and went into camp on Kalorama heights. There it remained until the 30th, when the sick were ordered to the Georgetown hospital and the regiment to Seneca Mills, Md., where it arrived on August 2. While encamped at Kalorama the diseases were almost exclusively diarrhœa and rheumatism, but since it occupied its present location there have been superadded intermittent and remittent fevers, which in a few cases have assumed a typhoid type. I was detained at Washington and did not rejoin my regiment until August 11, when I found it encamped in the Seneca bottom, half a mile from the Potomac. Immediately the camp was removed to an elevation half a mile from and one hundred and fifty feet above the creek and about the same distance from and height above the Potomac. All possible attention has been paid to police regulations. The location is airy and descends in all directions. The water from a spring adjacent is both pure and abundant. The rations furnished are sufficient in quantity and of unexceptionable quality. Ardent spirits are excluded. Among the duties assigned the regiment is that of guarding the river for four miles above and below the camp; this has required the constant services of two companies, with generally four on picket on the banks of the river or the tow-path of the canal. Chills and fever have resulted, but only among those doing guard duty on the river; and of those attacked few fail of a rapid recovery when quinine is liberally used and strict confinement to camp enjoined. As the frosts of autumn approach the number of attacks decrease and the recoveries are more speedy.

Ass't Surg. S. COMPTON SMITH, *4th Wis. Cav., Relay House, Md., Sept.* 30, 1861.—We had been in our present encampment but a few days when fevers of a remittent and typhoid type supervened, three patients having died of the last-named disease. Until the present time these fevers, accompanied with the various forms of intermittent, have been attendant upon us, latterly, however, assuming more the forms of remittent and tertian. They are generally controlled by the sulphate of quinia administered early in from ten to twenty-grain doses at intervals of two or three hours and preceded by the usual cathartics. At this date our hospital wards are filled with patients laboring under the two last-named forms of fever with a few cases of dysentery.

Surgeon D. WADSWORTH WAINWRIGHT, *4th N. Y., Havre de Grace, Md., Sept.* 30, 1861.—On August 13 the regiment was ordered to guard the bridges on the Philadelphia, Wilmington and Baltimore Railroad: Company H at Back river, B and I at Gunpowder river, E and D at Bush river, K at Perrymanville, A, C and G at Havre de Grace and F at Perryville. We have had many cases of malarial fever, mostly from Back, Gunpowder and Bush rivers; some of these were intermittent, others remittent, and all had a tendency to a typhoid state. Most of them yielded readily to treatment, ten grains of calomel with castor oil followed by quinine, twenty-four grains in twenty-four hours.

Ass't Surg. HENRY S. SCHELL, *U. S. A., on the condition of the Light Batteries of Fitz-John Porter's Division, Hall's Hill, Va., Sept.* 30, 1861.—Fort Corcoran is situated about one-fourth of a mile from the Potomac river on the Virginia side, opposite Georgetown, D. C. It is upon the brow of the first hill from the river, and is a recently constructed earthwork exposing a large amount of freshly upturned and moist soil to the action of the sun. Besides this, the woods which at one time intervened between its site and the marsh below were felled during the summer in the construction of abatis. Hence miasmatic diseases are prevalent and characterized to some extent by a typhoid tendency.

Surgeon N. F. MARSH, *4th Pa. Cav., Washington, D. C., Dec.* 30, 1861.—During the past two months the tendency of every disease has been to assume a typhoid character; a simple attack of diarrhœa would in twenty-four hours render a vigorous man perfectly prostrate, and he would then present all the incipient symptoms of typhoid fever.

Surgeon JOSEPH P. COLGAN, *59th N. Y., Camp Sherman, Fort Good Hope, D. C., January,* 1862.—The weather for the season of the year has been favorable, yet the temperature is variable and the transitions quick, which is productive perhaps of more respiratory disease than a colder and less variable season might be. Coughs and catarrhal affections have prevailed to a considerable extent in consequence. Another cause of the prevalence of such complaints is found in the fact that the Sibley tents in which the men sleep are furnished with small sheet-iron stoves of poor quality, easily and quickly heated and as quickly cooled again, and unless they are constantly supplied with fuel the temperature speedily falls to a low point, so that it is all the time too hot or too cold. Previous to day-break, when the mercury ordinarily falls lower than at any other hour and the men are all asleep, the fires die out, and as the top of the tent is open to the atmosphere, dew, frost, snow or rain, as the case may be, causes surgeon's call to be well attended with invalids complaining of pains, coughs, colds, fevers, etc. Some of the stoves have pipes reaching out at the top, but others, and these the majority, have pipes reaching but half way up, so that the smoke ascending deposits soot on the slope of the canvas from which at every blast of the wind it is shaken off, covering the faces and hands of the men, adhering to their clothes and giving them, previous to ablution in the morning, a dirty and unbecoming appearance. This is, however, unavoidable when troops have to take up winter quarters in tents, sleeping on the ground. I may as well say here that men so situated are too scantily supplied with covering, each man being provided with but a single blanket for covering and protection from the cold and damp ground. This scanty covering compels them always to sleep in their clothes, the overcoat being the only garment removed, and this only to be converted into a bedcover or quilt. It must not be forgotten that when they retire to their canvas quarters their clothes are often wet. There can be no question as to the consequence of men sleeping in garments and in such quarters, huddled together in crowds of twenty to a tent; that it tends to demoralize them to a certain extent I entertain no doubt, and think it should be practiced only when unavoidable. As a consequence of these conditions our prevailing diseases are affections of the respiratory organs and fevers. Intermittents are seldom well marked, but remittents are frequent and various in their character from the most simple to the most complicated, some soon assuming the typhoid type; for which reason they have been by many surgeons named "typhoid fevers," so that nearly all have been compelled to adopt the nomenclature, while many are of the opinion that the disease is "bilious remittent," which sometimes, of course, runs into continued and congestive fevers. The pathological conditions are so various that no organ escapes being involved in all cases. Quinine and stimulants are necessary and in very large doses; in a few instances the disease refused to yield to these remedies until the system was brought slightly under the influence of calomel.

Act. Ass't Surg. EDWARD T. WHITTINGHAM, *on the condition of the Artillery Brigade of Kearny's Division, near Harrison's Landing, Va., June 30, 1862.*—I joined the command May 17, at Cumberland Landing on the Pamunkey river. Since that time we have been constantly exposed to the fatigue of marching and the emanations from swamps lying on our route. We have also been obliged to use water so muddy and impure as to be unfit for drinking. These causes, in conjunction with the previous exposure of the troops in the marshes about Yorktown, produced a general tendency to malarial fevers and dysenteric affections severe in their type and exceedingly unmanageable. Quinine in very large doses and opium have been the remedies employed. Though the mortality has not been large, yet the average duration of sickness has been extremely long.

Surgeon J. M. BOISNOT, *U. S. V., Gaines' Mill Hospital, near Mechanicsville, Va., June, 1862.*—The seven cases of typhoid fever which we report were of unusual severity, four of them original and three sequences of remittent fever. All diseases in the army, of the class of fevers particularly, have a typhoid tendency. I believe that circumstances producing frequent and rapid changes in the temperature of the body, as a rapid march and then a halt, a hot and quickly eaten meal of soup and coffee, etc., then lying down on the cool ground, have mainly to do in bringing about this condition. My plan of treatment in the seven cases treated in this hospital was to give strong but digestible food and stimulants in small quantities, administered nearly every hour; six recovered and one died.

Surgeon DAVID MERRITT, *55th Pa., Edisto Island, S. C., June 30, 1862.*—Edisto Island, upon which this regiment is stationed, abounds in swamps or salt-water marshes. The climate is warm and generally sultry, but modified by a cool sea-breeze in the afternoon from North Edisto river. The prevalent diseases are bilious remittent fever, which tends to assume a typhoid character, and dysentery, bilious in character and mild, easily managed by the prompt use of mercurials followed by full doses of saline cathartics. The duties of the troops are light; they are quartered in tents and the sick in hospital tents. The diet, clothing and general habits of the men as to cleanliness, temperance, etc., are good. The water, however, is bad, being generally sulphurous.

Surgeon A. B. SNOW, *N. Y. Engineers, Hilton Head, S. C., June 30, 1862.*—During the winter the fevers were of an intermittent character, but since the warm weather has set in they have assumed more of a bilious typhoid type.

Surgeon ALEXANDER M. SPEER, *7th Pa. Cav., Bardstown, Ky., Feb. 3, 1862.*—The diseases to which the men were most susceptible were a remittent form of fever with a strong tendency to assume a typhoid character, diarrhœas arising from change of food and water, and mild bronchial affections, which have been, however, with a few exceptions, amenable to treatment.

Surgeon W. J. CHENOWITH, *35th Ill., near Rolla, Mo., Dec. 1, 1861.*—Here also [Otterville, Mo.] was our largest list of intermittents and remittents, and to add to our trouble we had no quinine nor could we procure any. Frequent requisitions were made on St. Louis, and in the space of two weeks as many as five messengers were dispatched for it; but as the medicine had been forwarded to us by the purveyor it was supposed we would receive it. This supply, however, was lost, and we were compelled to resort to arsenite of potash and other antiperiodics, but our sick-list steadily increased from fifty a day up to one hundred and fifty. Many cases assumed a typhoid type, and two men died. A marked case, showing the efficacy of quinine in the arrest of the disease, was exhibited in the person of Lowery, Co. E: One of our officers on rejoining the regiment brought with him a solution of quinine. This we concluded to give to any of the graver cases that still showed a remission. Lowery had a dry cracked tongue, frequent pulse, and his fever manifested every indication of falling, as in other cases, into the continued form. We gave him twenty grains of quinine and repeated the dose during the next remission, with the result of arresting the disease.

Surgeon JAMES L. KIERNAN, *6th Mo. Cav., June 30, 1862.*—The prevailing diseases in the Southwest are bronchial and thoracic affections, typhoid fever in the low alluvial districts, and in the army, amongst those who have seen service, that peculiar train of symptoms, induced by malaria, exposure and privations and characterized by lassitude, emaciation and a low irritative fever, which can scarcely be classified. I observed the same phenomena amongst the troops comprising the Army of the Potomac last year, but not to the same extent.

Typhoid fever of undoubted character broke out in many of the regiments soon after their organization, and it is highly probable that many cases of this disease were mistaken for adynamic developments in malarial cases where remittents and intermittents were the prevailing fevers. It is equally probable that during these regimental epidemics adynamic remittents were occasionally classed with the prevailing fever. After the presentation of so many cases of undoubted typhoid from the case-books of the Seminary hospital and the *post-mortem* records of various general hospitals it is needless to occupy space with a selection of reports indicating the presence of this fever. Some extracts showing its prevalence will be embraced in the section discussing the etiology of the continued fevers.* Brigade Surgeon DAVID PRINCE, under the impression that the Army Medical Board of which Surgeon

* See *infra*, p. 486 *et seq.*

McLaren was president had concluded, as the result of its investigations, that there was no typhoid fever in the army,* filed, in protest at the office of the Surgeon General, a detailed account of cases of this fever that had been treated in his command.

But although typhoid fever was recognized by so many regimental medical officers, it was not held by them to constitute the prevailing army fever. Surgeon Zenas E. Bliss, U. S. V., appears to have been the only officer whose recorded experience was opposed to the general view. While on duty with the 3d Mich. at Yorktown, in 1862, he had a few cases of intermittent and remittent fever and about forty cases of typhoid. These were treated at a hospital where were also many fever cases from other regiments, and nearly all were regarded by Dr. Bliss as cases of typhoid, although some of them might easily have been classed as low remittents. Death was caused by hemorrhage in many instances, and in six cases in which *post-mortem* observations were made the glands of Peyer were ulcerated.†

Even at this early date, however, cases of true typho-malarial fever were observed and reported in general terms. When the troops had been exposed—using the language of the accepted theory of a distinct pathogenesis for the typhoid and remittent fevers—to the causes of both these morbid conditions the resulting epidemic presented such a complexity and variability of symptoms that an accurate diagnosis could not be expressed by a term in which but one of the etiological factors was represented. Surgeon James King, 1st Brigade Pa. Reserves, in a published article,‡ dated Dec. 23, 1861, on the sanitary condition of the troops in his command, says that it was impossible to classify either as pure malarial or pure typhoid all the cases of fever that occurred. He regarded them as mixed affections, combining in varying degrees the characteristics of both the diseases named: In some the diagnostic symptoms of malarial fever predominated, in others those of the typhoid affection, while in others again there was such a blending of symptoms that it was difficult to say which was the prominent disease.

Similar views had already been expressed by some regimental medical officers in their sanitary reports.

Surgeon James Collins, *3d Pa. Reserves, Camp Tennally, Va., Dec. 31, 1861.*—During the month of October the health of the regiment continued tolerably good. There was, however, a slight and general increase of sickness, and the type of disease seemed to indicate a malarial origin. Early in November diseases of an undoubted malarial nature began to assume a more malignant type than had been noticed since the regiment had been organized. The prevalent diseases were remittent and typhoid fever, catarrh and acute bronchitis. Cases of typhoid fever have without doubt many if not all the symptoms of the same disease as seen in New England and Pennsylvania; yet, as seen in this camp, malarial influence exercises a modifying tendency upon the disease. In some cases the line between intermittent and typhoid could not be sharply drawn. In all cases quinia has been given with advantage; it has seemed to produce peculiarly happy effects even in those of a marked typhoid type.

Surgeon W. H. Thorne, *12th Pa. Reserves, Camp Pierpoint, Va., Nov. 1, 1861.*—The camp of this regiment is located on the slope of a hill well adapted for surface drainage; a streamlet drains the bottom of all superfluous water and carries off the refuse matter of the camp. The soil is clay mixed with pebbles and does not retain moisture to any great extent. The prevailing diseases are remittent and typhoid fevers, with some dysentery, but almost no diarrhœa. The former fever scarcely ever occurs as pure remittent, being rather of the asthenic type and not so amenable to antiperiodics.

Surgeon Wm. Faulkner, *83d Pa., Hall's Hill, Va., Dec. 31, 1861.*—It was during the first days of November that typhoid and remittent fevers began to show themselves, and indicated a most important change in the type and character of disease. The worst cases were complicated with extensive disease of the mucous membrane, which called for the early and free use of quinine and alcoholic stimulants. They were doubtless of a malarial origin and contracted perhaps when in camp near the river in the latter part of September.

Surgeon David Minis, *48th Pa., Camp Winfield, N. C., Dec. 31, 1861.*—The 1st of October, 1861, found us encamped at Camp Hamilton, near Fortress Monroe, and laboring under the usual epidemic of diarrhœa and dysentery to which

---

* For report of this Board, see *infra,* page 365.
† See his report, p. 86 of the Appendix to the first part of this volume.
‡ *Medical and Surgical Reporter*, Philadelphia, Pa., Vol. VII, p. 306.

new troops are liable. These diseases were at this time almost universal but manageable, no case terminating fatally. After their subsidence the health of the troops was excellent and continued so until the last week in October, when an epidemic of catarrh set in, having its origin in the exposure incident to the service during inclement weather. This disease, although very general in its manifestations and exceedingly painful in its symptoms, yielded readily to treatment. During the first week of November typhoid fever made its appearance, following immediately in the footsteps of the epidemic catarrh, many cases of the latter appearing to glide by almost imperceptible gradations into a typhoid condition with all the physical signs of the specific fever. On the 11th the regiment left Camp Hamilton and next day encamped at Fort Clark, near Hatteras Inlet. Immediately after our arrival numerous cases of typhoid fever, which had been in their incipient stage on leaving Camp Hamilton, became fully developed, and being modified by the miasm of the island assumed a malignant and unmanageable aspect such as I had never witnessed in any cases of the disease previously falling under my observation. In fact in these cases typhoid fever, epidemic catarrh, remittent and intermittent fevers were so commingled and mutually complicated one another as to render the diagnosis obscure, the treatment unsatisfactory and the prognosis unfavorable. The most striking characteristic of this epidemic has been, in the graver cases, the almost total absence of tongue-symptoms. In some, and those terminating fatally in a few days after the access of the disease, there was no abnormal appearance of the tongue during the whole progress of the attack; while those cases in which the tongue became heavily coated, dry and red, made good recoveries. Between the 1st and 20th of December the regiment was removed from Fort Clark to this station, Camp Winfield, about four miles north of Fort Clark. The general health of the regiment is good at present. Either from the prevalence of cool weather for the last two weeks or because the troops are becoming acclimated, diseases having a malarious origin have almost disappeared. We have but few cases of severe aspect now under treatment.

No doubt the opinion that the fevers then prevailing in the army were adynamic remittents was based primarily on etiological and clinical considerations,—the absence of a special typhoid infection and of symptoms indicative of a typhoid lesion, the presence of malarial influences, the sequence of the adynamic or so-called typhoid symptoms to an intermittent or remittent attack and in many instances the notable efficacy of quinine. But since deaths were unfortunately of frequent occurrence it must be concluded that the general opinion did not continue long without support from *post-mortem* observations.

The only official investigation into the nature of the fevers which prevailed in our camps was made when the Seminary hospital was receiving and treating the typhoid cases that have been presented in a previous section, *i. e.*, at a time when typhoid fever was unusually prevalent among the troops. A Board specially instituted to ascertain whether the existing fever was to be considered "an intermittent or bilious remittent fever in its inception assuming in its course a typhoid type, or a typhoid fever primarily," proceeded to the field, and as the result of personal observation and inquiry concluded that, although a certain number of cases of ordinary typhoid existed in the army, the large majority of the cases were bilious remittent fevers which "had assumed that adynamic type which is present in enteric fever."

The report of this Board is as follows:*

---

* Some official documents bearing on the nature of the fevers that prevailed in the Hooghly District during the years 1870–73 have been published in the *Indian Med. Gazette*, Vol. IX, 1874, p. 74 *et seq.* These are of interest, as the question at issue was similar to that submitted to the Board mentioned in the text. Whole families, we are told, were prostrated at the same time by the Hooghly fever; from twelve to eighteen or more members of joint families would be laid up at the same time, though not all suffering from the same type of fever. For instance, of eighteen cases three would present the symptoms of typhoid, four or five of remittent, five or six of intermittent and the remainder of common continued fever. JAMES A. GREENE, Civil Medical Officer, Serampore, having seen and treated at least 2,000 cases during the epidemic in the town and suburbs under his care, arrived at the conclusion that "the fever we have to deal with is typhoid, complicated, no doubt, with malaria, but the first outburst in any place is typhoid, and this is the formidable fever which kills as it victims so prostrated that they suffer thereafter for months and years from relapses of malarious fever ending in enlargement of the spleen, liver, etc." Unfortunately in Dr. GREENE's practice *post-mortem* examination was never allowed owing to caste prejudice. His reports on these fevers were sent to Surgeon-Major NORMAN CHEVERS, with a request for his opinion on the subject. In reply this officer refers to the want of precision involved in the use of the word typhoid. "Having paid considerable attention to the recent discussion upon typhoid fever in India, it has appeared clear that much confusion and vain dispute would be avoided if we strictly confined ourselves to the designations 'paludal fever' and 'enteric fever,' never again using the word 'typhoid.' Every practitioner is aware that, in Bengal, cases of cholera and remittent fever frequently take on a condition so 'typhoid' or typhus-like in its character that no physician, seeing a case for the first time, could immediately determine, by the symptoms alone, whether it was one of true typhus or (when, as frequently happens in the congestive, paludal, remittent of the cold season, there is bowel complication) one of the true enteric fever as described by JENNER." Dr. CHEVERS then discusses the typical cases given in the reports, showing that the "patients may have been the subjects of 'typhoid'—that is, true enteric fever, but Dr. GREENE has not at all proved that they were." He acknowledges that enteric fever has taken a defined position among the diseases of Bengal, but claims that this malady has never during the last eleven years become at all extremely prevalent in Calcutta, although a typhus-like fever (often attended with diarrhœa), demonstrably of paludal origin and amenable to the antidotal action of quinine in nearly all but the moribund cases, has been almost daily among the chief subjects of his clinical practice. "Dr. GREENE has shown that cases somewhat resembling enteric fever occur in these districts [Burdwan, Hooghly and Serampore], but such cases also occur in Calcutta, where these causative elements are nearly equally rife. Still, when thoroughly sifted, very few of the multitude of grave Calcutta fever

HEADQUARTERS OF THE ARMY, ADJUTANT GENERAL'S OFFICE,
Washington, Dec. 6th, 1861.

SPECIAL ORDERS, ⎫
    No. 323.   ⎬

* * * * * * * * * * * * * * *

6. A Board to consist of Surgeon A. N. MCLAREN, U. S. A., Brigade Surgeon G. H. LYMAN, U. S. Volunteer service and Ass't Surg. M. J. ASCH, U. S. Army, is hereby instituted for the following object: To visit as many of the camps in the vicinity of Washington as they may consider necessary to obtain sufficient data to make a report to the Surgeon General on the character of the disease termed by the Medical Officers of the Brigades and Regiments "Typhoid Fever," and as far as practicable the causes of its adynamic type and whether it is to be considered an intermittent or bilious remittent fever in its inception, assuming in its course the typhoidal type or a typhoid fever primarily.

The Board will be regulated in its sessions and movements by its President so as least to interfere with the other operations of the service. The junior member will act as recorder.

* * * * * * * * * * * * * *

BY COMMAND OF MAJ. GEN'L MCCLELLAN.

(Signed) L. THOMAS,
Adjutant General.

In obedience to the above order the Board convened on Monday the 16th day of December, 1861, at the quarters of Brigade Surgeon LYMAN and proceeded to examine the brigade and regimental hospitals of the division commanded by Brigadier General Fitz-John Porter with a view to the observation of such cases as might exist, and to the comparison of such symptoms and tendencies of the disease as at present prevailing with a similar affection that had already occurred and had been reported as typhoid fever.

The regimental hospitals of the 17th and 25th New York, the 83d Pennsylvania, the 18th Massachusetts and the 2d Maine regiments were observed, together with the brigade hospital connected with General Morell's brigade; but few cases were discovered which could be designated correctly as of a typhoid character. Of the cases so marked the majority had been received into hospital as suffering from bilious remittent fever which in its progress assumed the typhoid type so well known to those whose experience in malarial fevers has been gleaned in the South. No case of enteric fever was observed. The disease was evidently of malarial origin and was so considered by the medical officers. As a general rule in this division, quinine given in large doses in the remission, with mercurials as required, had the effect of checking the fevers. The typhoid state only appeared as a result of a continuous neglect of hygienic precautions when in health or in those persons who had been exposed to unusually severe and prolonged duty. In the cases assuming the typhoid type which the Board examined, although symptoms of prostration and sinking were present, together with the dry glazed tongue, collection of sordes on the teeth and gums and subsultus tendinum which characterize the state, still the absence of any enteric symptoms and of the taches rouges, which are the almost invariably constant symptoms in true typhoid fever, as well as of any pulmonary complication, was sufficient to warrant the Board in concluding that the cases before them were not of the enteric fever so common in the Northern States and generally known as typhoid fever, while the previous location of the regiments in regions notoriously malarious justified them in attributing malarial origin in the febrile cases brought to their notice. The camps and hospitals of this division with one exception were remarkably neat and clean and are deserving of the highest encomium. It must be noticed as a medical curiosity, which it would be scarcely safe to take as a precedent for any similar rule of action, that the camp in which police regulations had not been enforced and which, in consequence, was in an eminently filthy condition, was in the most satisfactory sanitary state and, at the period of the visit of the Board, had not a seriously ill patient in its hospital. It is but just to the surgeon of this regiment to state that he had already instituted measures which in a very brief period would cause his camp to compare favorably with any other in the division. There was observed in one of the regimental hospitals a number of cases of superficial gangrene of the toes resulting in some cases from fever, although present in others where no such primary cause existed but where the patient was in an adynamic condition.

On the 18th of December the Board again convened and visited the divisions commanded by Gen'ls McCall and Smith. Here were found some cases of typhoid fever with the enteric and pulmonary symptoms which distinguish it in the North, but by far the majority of the cases were of bilious remittent fever resulting from the encampment

cases turn out to be instances of true enteric fever. The true nature of many of the cases which occur in the Serampore district may be inferred from the fact mentioned by Dr. GREENE that, when patients struggle through the first violence of the malady, they ultimately fall victims to debility, enlargement of the spleen and liver, anæmia and dropsy. These are not the proper sequelæ of enteric or of relapsing fever, and they clearly point to a paludal cause. Hence, I submit, our first course is to ascertain, by at least some half dozen carefully performed *post-mortem* examinations in well-chosen cases, whether the disease is, in reality, true enteric fever or a typhus-like fever of paludal origin, complicated in some cases with diarrhœa, which symptom, I need scarcely say, is very common in the true marsh fevers of India whenever, as in very cold weather, the state of the skin does not allow of free critical sweating." Here Dr. CHEVERS attaches the following note: "Since I wrote this a very characteristic case of this type of malarious fever has terminated fatally in my ward. A khansamah, of Toltolah, was attended on the 4th instant, complaining that he had suffered from intermittent fever for about 15 days. Tongue moist and clean, temperature 105°, splenic fulness, a little cough and bronchitic râles. On the next day there was jaundice with constipation. On the day after that pleuro-pneumonia of the right lung set in. Some might consider this a primary feature in the case, I recognized it as a secondary lesion common in the severe malarious fever of this cold weather. The daily evening temperature was 105 ; 103 ; 100 ; 102 ; 99 ; 101 ; 100, sordes on tongue and lips ; 98 m., 99 e ; 101 ; 102 ; 102 ; 100 ; 101, rather constipated ; 99 m., 100.8 e. ; 101 m., 100 e., tongue, lips and teeth dry, loose yellow stools ; 102 m. and e., tongue moist and clean, three stools of the consistence and appearance of thick dal, no gurgling in the iliac fossa ; 102 ; three stools ; 98 m., 100 e. ; 97.8 m., tongue moist and clean, three diarrhœal stools, 101 e., frequent diarrhœal stools, incoherence, death. Here the stools had very much the appearance of those in enteric fever, but they did not contain blood or mucus. The character of the moderate head symptoms, the range of the temperature and the state of the tongue, except for a time, did not indicate enteric fever ; and yet I could not feel quite satisfied on this point until I had ascertained that the small intestine was perfectly healthy."

of the regiments during the autumn months in a malarious district. In Gen'l Smith's division nearly all diseases assumed a typhoid type, which was attributed by the surgeons to ochlesis or crowd-poisoning produced by the over-crowding of men in their quarters, and also to the fatigue induced by excessive drilling and the unnecessary length of time which the men are occasionally required to pass on duty, as well as the depressing influence of camp life on persons not habituated to it. In Gen'l Hancock's brigade a number of cases of typhoid fever had occurred which Brigade Surgeon HAVEN attributed to causes belonging to the men themselves and not to the condition of the camp. This brigade is composed of Vermont troops, who are the most thoroughly provincial of any in the service, and who, accustomed to their native mountains, feel acutely the depressing influence of nostalgia and malaria when absent from them and on this account, probably, are more liable to disease of an adynamic type than those from other local-ities. The same fact is noticed among those Pennsylvania troops coming from the mountainous region of the Alle-ghanies. In the division commanded by Gen'l McCall a number of cases of typhoid fever were reported, but, as in Gen'l Smith's division, the majority of the patients were laboring under bilious remittent fever; some cases of gastro-enteric fever were found. As want of time precluded the Board from examining thoroughly all the hospitals of this division, the following interrogations were propounded to the various medical officers, the answers to which will be found appended, viz:

1. What number of cases of bilious remittent and of typhoid fever have occurred in your regiment?
2. Is the so-called typhoid fever the typhoid fever of the North or is it of malarial origin?
3. What do you consider to be its cause?
4. Describe the symptoms of the fever occurring under your care?
5. The treatment adopted?
6. The locality of the regiment before the appearance of the disease?
7. The percentage of the disease?
8. Have any cases of gangrene of the toes been observed as the result of fever or otherwise?

From the information afforded by the answers to these questions the Board found nothing to justify an opinion that typhoid fever existed as an epidemic or otherwise than in a very small proportion in this part of the army. The majority of cases of fever were clearly of malarial origin and in some cases from the causes above enumerated they assumed a typhoid type. The gangrene of the toes which had been observed in other divisions was found here also from the same supposed cause and in but small ratio. In Heintzleman's division the brigades of Sedgwick and Jamison were examined: In the former no case of enteric fever was found and but few of bilious remittent; in the latter there were a few cases presenting the appearance of typhoid fever in which were the taches rouges and intestinal symptoms, pathognomonic of the disease, accompanied with pulmonary and cerebral disturbances, but the cases were convalescing and no new ones were appearing.

From the data furnished by the investigations stated above the Board feel justified in concluding:

First. That the large majority of febrile diseases which have been reported as "typhoid fever" are not cases of that fever which is characterized by the eruption of rose-colored spots about the seventh day and has for its pecu-liar lesion inflammation and ulceration of the glands of Peyer and is known in the Northern States as typhoid or gastro-enteric fever, but they are bilious remittent fevers, which not having been controlled in their primary stage have assumed that adynamic type which is present in enteric fever, on which account they have been erroneously termed "typhoid," whereas in reality those lesions which invariably accompany true "typhoid fever" have been wanting. There is undoubtedly present in some patients low delirium, subsultus tendinum, sordes on the teeth and gums with occasionally a black, dry and glazed tongue, but the tender and tympanitic abdomen, the taches rouges and the diarrhœa, which are almost constant symptoms in enteric fever, are absent. Cases of typhoid fever certainly exist in the army, but it is so far from being epidemic that the ratio of its occurrence is less than it would be in civil life amongst the same number of individuals.

Secondly. The cause of the bilious remittent fever that exists in the Army of the Potomac is undoubtedly the malaria generated in the vicinity of the river to which it has been exposed during the late summer and autumn months, but the causes of the typhoid condition that it takes on are different and probably within our reach to be guarded against. The hygienic measures instituted by the Medical Director of the Army of the Potomac are proving effectual in lessening the number of cases of malarial fever, and it is possible that measures may be adopted which will lessen the tendency of diseases to take on the low forms that they have lately assumed. This tendency may originate from blood-poisoning induced by the crowding together of men in close and illy ventilated quarters, from fatigue occasioned by excessive drilling, from over-exertion resulting from a too protracted tour of duty, from nos-talgia and from a want of attention to personal cleanliness. If it occur from these causes, and in the opinion of the Board it does, the prevention is in the hands of the proper authorities. Sufficient space should be given for quarters; a proper discretion exercised in the allotment of time for drill; consideration should be shown for those engaged in laborious and fatiguing duty; cleanliness should be rigidly enforced and nostalgia avoided by diversion of mind brought about by proper gymnastic and other sports, and it may be that the depressing influences now operating will be obviated and as a necessary result the adynamic type of disease will be changed.

The Board takes this occasion to remark that the sanitary condition of the army generally is eminently satis-factory as far as it has come under observation, the number of cases of disease being proportionally few and of these but a small ratio are of a serious character.

Papers appended to the Report of the Board.

Brigade Surgeon JAMES KING, *U. S. Vols.*—**1st.** The last three monthly reports of the surgeons show in the four regiments of the brigade 539 cases of remittent fever and 37 of typhoid fever, the mean strength of the brigade being about 3,200, officers and men. **2d.** The surgeons represent two forms of fever as prevailing—one, bilious remittent, a fever of malarial origin, the other typhoid, "the typhoid of the North." In my opinion it is impossible to draw such a line of distinction respecting these fevers as to divide the cases into two well-defined classes, one exhibiting in its group of symptoms the ordinary diagnostic marks of typhoid and the other of remittent fever. On the contrary, there is a certain *tout ensemble* or general form belonging to all by which we recognize one affection, though varying in its features in different cases, just as we know the physiognomy of man in all its diversified modes of expression. I have observed the following characters or so-called diagnostic signs of the two diseases apparently expressed and variously coexisting in the same subject. It would be easy to arrange the facts observed in a tabular statement showing in one column the distinguishing marks of the "malarial" and in the other of the "typhoid" disease, but the facts are so commingled and united in many cases that if required to classify them with one or the other disease it would be difficult to say to which they belong. The following facts, for example, I have observed as variously coexisting in many cases:

Evidences of remittent fever or disease of "malarial origin."

1st. The disease made its appearance in autumn and on the Potomac (malarial region).

2d. Many of the subjects have the disease developed suddenly.

3d. Rare cases begin with epistaxis.

4th. No special tendency to diarrhœa manifested, at least I have not observed this.

5th. We very seldom see much tympanites, often none.

6th. The fever has distinct remissions and is found in company with true intermittents.

7th. In the first stages the tongue is furred white or yellow, enlarged and indented at the edges.

8th. Numerous cases of other malarial disease occurring, as neuralgia and jaundice, fever patients showing jaundiced urine.

9th. Certain marked effects of quinine in relieving headache, stupor and delirium in the early stages, in cutting some cases short and occasionally in affording speedy benefit when the cases are characterized by dry tongue, rose-spots and other signs of the typhoid condition.

10th. Certain *post-mortem* appearances, as loss of color in the liver and distention of the gall-bladder; the liver was very pale in two cases examined.

11th. Exposure to night-air before the attack in localities where intermittents arise, as on night marches, picket duty, etc.

Evidences of typhoid, the "typhoid fever of the North."

1st. It continues to prevail after the heavy frosts and in winter.

2d. Most cases have a protracted convalescence though they have not been attacked with particular violence.

3d. Many show rose-colored spots.

4th. Few cases, none that I have known, have shown much nausea and bilious vomiting.

5th. Many of the cases have suffusion of the eyes, dusky countenance and mental hebetude.

6th. The duration of the disease when fully marked mostly runs on to the third or fourth week.

7th. In the last stages the tongue is dry and glazed, often cracked and covered with sordes.

8th. The occurrence of troublesome suppurations, as abscess about the parotid glands, following the fever in a number of cases.

9th. Certain good effects of turpentine in cases with glazed tongue and tympanitic abdomen, the decided advantage of nutritious stimulants, as brandy-punch, in all cases, and the apparent necessity of supporting means to relieve the adynamic state and resist the tendency to death by asthenia.

10th. Certain *post-mortem* appearances, as thickening, inflammation and ulceration of Peyer's glands in three cases examined, and affection of mesenteric glands. Ulceration of the elliptical plates was noticed where there was no gaseous distention of the bowels.

11th. Previous crowding of men in badly ventilated tents in filthy camps, for as yet it has been impossible to enforce proper police regulations.

I cannot pursue this analysis further in the present report, but I will ask, are we justified in regarding all the facts above noted as entitled to weight, as I think we are, and in determining from the combination in the same cases of many of these characteristics of two diseases that we have a mixed affection? Or, if not, shall we take the "rose-colored eruption" and affection of Peyer's glands as pathognomonic of the disease and say it is typhoid fever, or take the influence of quinine in the treatment as specific for the malarial poison or some such characteristic and say the fever is a "bilious remittent?" In my judgment it is only by carefully collecting the facts noted by regimental and hospital surgeons who have made diligent observation of their cases that we can arrive at just conclusions on this subject, the investigation of which, by a competent officer detailed for the purpose, would not be without its uses to the public service. **3d.** As to treatment, I have observed most satisfactory results from the use of quinine, beginning with a dose of sixteen or twenty grains in the morning and the remedy continued in smaller doses for several successive mornings in the early stages of the disease, the occasional use of blue mass, febrifuge mixtures when indicated, the early resort to nutritious stimulants and fluid nourishment with nitrate of silver, sugar of lead and spirit of turpentine administered for certain enteric symptoms when particularly indicated. The inflammatory and congestive complications are treated successfully in the usual way by sinapisms and cupping. **4th** and **5th.** As to the symptoms and cause of the fever, I have no other report than that given above to indicate its character. **6th.** As to the localities of regiments, I have to refer to the reports of the regimental surgeons. **7th.** As to percentage of sick, I suppose that is sufficiently answered with the 1st point. **8th.** As to gangrene of the toes: This I observed in one case; in another great pain was complained of, but I observed no discoloration or sloughing of the skin. In both the fever was protracted, but as I had not the opportunity of watching the progress of the disease in the first case I have no further remarks on the subject.

Surgeon H. K. NEFF, *8th Pa.*—**1st.** This regiment has at the present time ten or twelve cases of bilious remittent and typhoid fever under treatment. **2d.** The so-called typhoid fever here is not the same in all particulars as that of the North. I consider it emphatically of malarial origin. **3d.** Treatment has been in all cases anti-periodic, tonic and stimulant. Large doses of quinine are given at the outset and followed by decreased doses throughout the course of the attack. Blue mass is also frequently given in combination with the quinine when indicated. Ordinarily after the first dose, which is usually from fifteen to twenty grains, the patient gets the quinine in divided doses so as to receive from ten to twelve grains in 24 hours. In addition to this he gets tonics such as the tincture of iron and, when indicated, diuretics, febrifuges, etc. The usual plan of treatment is that pursued in the North in like cases except the quinine and stimulants during the early stages. **4th.** The symptoms are similar to those of ordinary fevers. The tongue, however, is flabby, watery and pale, remaining so, except in the most malignant cases, throughout the whole course of the disease; when the fever is of the malignant type the tongue is dark, dry and in some cases fissured. The pulse is generally feeble from the start. In many cases for several days after its onset the disease assumes a decided remittent and in some cases intermittent form; but in most instances it afterwards becomes continued. **5th.** The supposed cause is malaria. Exciting causes: Exposure, irregularities in diet, drink, etc., and an indifference to the established rules of hygiene generally. **6th.** Last locality: A northern slope near the Potomac on the Virginia side, Fairfax Co. Present locality: Southern slope of opposite hill facing former location. **7th.** Percentage of sick: 4½. **8th.** Gangrene of toes: no remarks.

Ass't Surg. D. McKINNEY, *10th Pa.*—**1st.** The number of cases of bilious remittent fever treated in our hospital has been 38, of which 13 occurred at Camp Tennally and 25 at Pierpont; we had three cases of typhoid fever. **2d.** From my observation I am led to believe that the army typhoid is of malarious origin. Our first case had just recovered from an attack of bilious remittent fever and the two other cases showed decided remissions at first. Quite a number of our bilious remittent fevers exhibited for a time a typhoid character, although yielding readily to large doses of quinine. **3d.** In the treatment of typhoid fever quinine, solution of the acetate of lead, mucilage of turpentine, wine and brandy were used. **4th.** The early symptoms were those of remittent fever, but after a few days decided symptoms of typhoid fever were displayed. The disease yields much earlier to treatment than the typhoid fever of the North. **5th.** Malaria is the supposed cause, aided by the entire change of habits of the volunteer from the comforts of home to excitement, exposure, badly prepared food and crowded tents incident to camp life. **6th.** Camp Tennally, two cases; Camp Pierpont, one case. **7th.** Four per cent. for the past thirty days.

Surgeon S. G. LANE, *5th Pa.*—**1st.** We have had from December 1 to date 24 cases of remittent and one of typhoid fever. **2d.** The typhoid reported is properly so called, and is the typhoid or enteric fever of the North. **3d.** Our treatment consists of quinine, gentle purgatives when needed, alteratives, turpentine, nourishment, stimulants and cleanliness; local complications are treated as their character demands. The large and repeated doses of quinine, so highly lauded by many authorities, have failed in our hands to effect the promised good results, and, I believe, when given thus heroically, it is apt to oppress the nervous powers, mask the symptoms and aggravate local congestions into inflammations. **4th.** The symptoms vary as the case may be remittent or enteric fever. In the remittent the disease usually makes its appearance suddenly with a chill, followed by fever and perspiration; sometimes the patient has a sallow, sickly appearance, with impaired appetite, nausea, diarrhœa and the tongue covered with yellowish or whitish fur. This diseased condition intensifies and breaks into a distinct remittent, or an intermittent may pass into a remittent. When the fever is fully formed the patient has slight remissions, quick pulse, hot skin, headache, tenderness of abdomen and more or less delirium; the tongue soon becomes dry and cracked, the bowels relaxed and the stools various. Many cases pass early into a low or typhoid condition with the usual symptoms. The local affections are numerous, occurring in the head, chest and abdomen. Usually the enteric cases begin insidiously: Nervous derangement is an early symptom; fever, sometimes at first remittent; epistaxis; pulse quick and feeble; headache, confusion of mind and dulness of hearing; stools characteristic; dry glazed tongue; sordes on teeth; appetite often not affected; hemorrhage from bowels; rose-colored eruption on abdomen; tympanites not always present; slow and tedious recovery; patients generally young men; deaths sudden; ulcerations of glands of intestines discovered on *post-mortem* examination; strong tendency to local inflammations. **5th.** The supposed causes of remittent fever are miasmata, but as our cases tend so rapidly to the typhoid condition I believe them also influenced by the causes which develop enteric fever. Our camp is located on a narrow tongue of land until within a short time densely wooded and surrounded by woods. A slow, boggy spring, in which four regiments wash, runs along one side, and at the point of the strip upon which we are encamped it meets another purer stream running along our other side. The tents are crowded together, preventing proper drainage. Six men sleep in one A tent. They have no straw, insufficient blankets, sleep in their clothes, which they can seldom change, disregard cleanliness, cook badly, take no gymnastic exercise and are discouraged. Log houses are being built by the men, but they are close and crowded. Here is a process of impairing the vital forces which must make our diseases adynamic. **6th.** These diseases have prevailed in this regiment since September (when I joined), but are now more severe. **7th.** Percentage of sick of aggregate force to-day 13.11. **8th.** Have had no gangrene of toes.

Surgeon L. W. READ, *1st Pa.*—**1st.** Number of fever cases from August to December inclusive: Remittent 526, typhoid 7. **2d.** Many of the cases treated were well defined remittent fever, but the majority presented various grades of complication, manifested by a sense of great weakness, exhaustion or prostration indicating the presence of some depressing or epidemic influence; and as they did not present the characteristics of genuine typhoid they were regarded and treated as remittent fever. Only seven cases, two of which died, gave evidence of pure typhoid fever. **3d.** The great change in the habits of the men, such as exposure to rain and night-air in the performance of picket and guard duty, lying on the ground, sleeping in wet clothes, etc. **4th.** Many of the cases were ushered in without any premonition, but the majority were preceded for one or two days by a feeling of great fatigue or disinclination to exertion, with pain in the head and back; tongue coated and the circulation accelerated; about the third day there was a decided chill and fever with an aggravation of all the symptoms. There was generally a combination of these conditions in the morning. A number of the cases yielded readily to treatment and were convalescent in five or six days. Those that persisted were characterized by a feeling of exhaustion or prostration, heavily coated or dry tongue, pain in the head and back, loss of appetite, occasionally nausea and diarrhœa with slight tympanites. The urine was turbid or highly colored, with a strong ammoniacal odor. **5th.** When the case was seen during the remission quinine was freely given, and during the day blue-pill followed by castor or croton oil was administered. When seen during the presence of fever, quinine was preceded by purgatives; as a febrifuge neutral mixture or muriate of ammonia was given; when the tongue was dry turpentine was used, and when there was much depression an emulsion of carbonate of ammonia, brandy-punch and beef-tea; restlessness was treated with anodynes. **6th.** The locality of the regiment before the breaking out of the disease was Camp Wayne, West Chester, Pa. **7th.** Percentage: Remittent fever 526, typhoid 7. **8th.** I have had no case of gangrene of the toes but have treated a number of cases in which there was great pain and acute sensibility of the toes, several of which have persisted for more than three months.

Brigade Surg. W. G. LOWMAN, *U. S. V.*—**1st.** I am of opinion that all the cases of fever in my brigade are bilious remittents. **2d.** The typhoid fever here is not the typhoid of the North. Although there are many of the symptoms, as slight diarrhœa and tympanites, rose-spots, delirium, etc., the disease comes on too rapidly for typhoid and there is not that hebetude of body and mind, tenderness or tympanites of the bowels, nor the red pointed tongue that we have in the North. The disease assumes a typhoid type in cases that run on for ten days or two weeks, and in constitutions that have been broken down by previous disease, in drunkards, etc. I am of opinion that if the use of quinine be commenced early the disease will be broken up in from three days to a week, at least in the majority of cases. Those of my surgeons who use quinine early and freely have few cases of the so-called typhoid,—it is almost always cut short. Hence I look upon the disease as remittent in character and caused by malaria. Indeed all diseases here are, I think, influenced more or less by malaria. If a man takes a bad cold, sufficient to produce a little fever, icterus shows itself and he will in all probability have remittent fever. **3d.** The treatment is blue-pill and quinine; and those who give these freely have the best success. When the disease runs on for ten days or two weeks and the tongue becomes red, dry and chapped, the treatment consists of stimulants and alteratives, as turpentine, brandy, wine-whey, punch, etc. The turpentine acts admirably on the dry, chapped tongue. **4th.** The symptoms generally come on rapidly with chilliness or rigors followed by heat, full pulse, dry tongue, slightly furred and soon becoming brown, constipated bowels, tenderness in epigastric region, frequent vomiting, jaundiced skin often preceding the attack, flushed eyes and face and congested surface; and in all these cases the patient is quite delirious. The remission is well marked in some cases, but in others it is not—in either event quinine generally acts well; but if the disease be not arrested in the course of a week, typhoid symptoms make their appearance. I suppose the cause of the disease to be malaria. **6th.** The location of the brigade at the breaking out of the disease was Camp Tennally. **8th.** I have not seen any gangrenous toes in my brigade. Permit me further to state that the prevailing disease at present is a catarrh of a peculiar character. There is seldom any coryza or lachrymation. It commences with a dry, tickling cough with little expectoration, no fever or loss of appetite except in a few cases which run into bronchitis. The patient feels well generally, but coughs almost incessantly. The disease began about a month ago after a few foggy nights followed by hard frosts. Since the frost our remittent fever (or so-called typhoid) has decreased very much. There has not been a new case in my brigade for about three weeks, which is additional evidence to my mind that it is caused by malaria and is not typhoid.

Surgeon W. H. THORNE, *12th Pa.*—**1st.** Of bilious fever we have had but one case in our regiment; of typhoid we have had four, in all of which there was more or less tendency to inflammation of the lungs. **2d.** This typhoid is the same as that of the North; it is not malarial and does not yield to antiperiodics. A spurious typhoid, which prevailed during the summer and fall, presented many of the symptoms of true typhoid, but there was a marked remission generally in the forenoon, and although the tongue indicated more or less intestinal irritation in some of the cases, the bowels were mostly constipated. This disease was of malarial origin and yielded readily to alteratives and antiperiodics—blue mass and quinine; none of the cases were fatal. **3d.** The treatment of typhoid has been alterative, supporting and stimulant; turpentine was given in nearly every case and with marked benefit. **4th.** Symptoms: More or less nervous derangement, headache, furred tongue and diarrhœa; in some cases epistaxis, tympanites, sordes on the teeth and delirium; the taches rouges were mostly present. **5th.** Cause: Impure and confined air, cold and damp, and irregularities in diet added to an improper location. **6th.** Locality: Near the bottom of a hill with a marsh on one side and low, damp ground on the other. **7th.** Now sick, 10 per cent. of the command, the majority being catarrhal affections. **8th.** We have had several cases of wounds of toes, but no gangrene.

Surgeon J. A. PHILLIPS, *9th Pa. Reserves.*—**1st.** During the last three months I have treated 56 cases of remittent and 14 of typhoid fever. **2d.** The majority of the idiopathic fevers which have come under my observation were of the remittent type and differed from the enteric or typhoid fever of the North in these particulars: The disease was not often preceded by headache, dulness or feelings of malaise, but began abruptly, nor was it preceded by epistaxis or diarrhœa; the bowels were generally constipated during the course of the attack; in most cases rose-colored spots and sudamina were not developed; there were distinct remissions though not at any particular time in the day; lastly, the fever could often be checked in a few days by the free use of quinine. Patients were generally convalescent in ten or twelve days; but if the disease was not subdued within two weeks, it often ran into an adynamic form resembling typhoid in some respects. **3d.** A mercurial cathartic was first administered followed in a few hours by fifteen, twenty or thirty grains of quinia. Refrigerant diaphoretics were freely given during the fever. I was not deterred from the liberal exhibition of quinine by the absence of a distinct remission nor by symptoms of gastric or cerebral disturbance. If the disease assumed a low form quinine, ammonia, milk-punch and the most nutritious diet, beef-tea and beef-essence, were given. It may be proper to add that I have often seen a dry, brown tongue become clean and moist in twenty-four hours after the administration of what would be called in the Northern States a heroic dose of quinine. **4th.** In a few instances the attack was preceded by languor, loss of appetite, etc., but in most cases it began with a chill and pain in the head, back and limbs, followed by smart febrile excitement. There was generally a remission of the fever daily, sometimes twice a day; the tongue covered with a pasty fur such as I have seen accompanying yellow fever; bowels constipated; skin dry and pungent except during the remissions; conjunctivæ of a yellow tinge; pain in epigastric and hypochondriac regions; urine highly colored. **5th.** The effects of miasmata. Three months ago the regiment for strategic reasons was encamped in its present position. The tents were pitched on low ground with hills rising on either side. The camp, from the nature of its site, cannot be properly drained and policed. **6th.** Tennallytown, D. C. **7th.** The monthly reports show an average of 2½ per cent. **8th.** I have not seen a case of gangrene of the toes; convalescents from remittent fever have complained occasionally of stiffness and soreness of the toes, but these symptoms yielded promptly to emollient applications.

Brigade Surg. A. E. STOCKER, *U. S. V.*—**1st.** In answer to the first query, as the cases I have seen, although numerous, have been only in consultation with the regimental surgeons, I can give no additional information. **2d.** Such of the cases as I have examined and designated as typhoid fever were clearly cases of the true typhoid fever of the North, characterized by all the usual symptoms and phenomena of that disease as it there exists. There have, however, been a great number of cases which in their commencement and progress were true bilious remittent fevers, although they subsequently put on a low or typhoid type; these were undoubtedly due to malarious influences. **3d.** I have advised quinine and iron, the former in doses of two or three grains every two hours, with milk-punch and strong essence of beef; when the tongue became dry, brown and cracked, turpentine was used with excellent effect. **4th.** The cases I have designated as typhoid have had, in addition to the usual symptoms of febrile disease, the low compressible pulse, extinguishable by pressure, so characteristic of this fever, with epistaxis, deafness, flushed and besotted appearance, diarrhœa and taches rouges. If I should say one symptom of typhoid was less marked than those usually found in this disease it would be the want of special tenderness and gurgling in the right iliac fossa, while in many cases the tenderness on pressure seemed to be equally diffused over the abdominal cavity. **5th.** The cause of the disease is yet undetermined. I am not prepared to say that there is even a greater number of cases of this disease in the camps of this division than would exist were the same number of men placed under the care of one or two physicians in any city of the North. **6th.** As the manifestation of the disease does not seem to have been sudden at any time in my experience here, it would be impossible for me to designate the locality of the regiments when it broke out. **7th.** As no time has been specified for the calculation of the number of cases the regimental reports cannot be expected to approach uniformity in their calculation of the percentage of typhoid cases. **8th.** I have seen two cases of gangrene of the toes in the regiments under my charge. They were consequent upon attacks of typhoid fever; the issue of them I cannot tell as they were removed to general hospital before entire convalescence had taken place.

Surgeon D. STANTON, *1st Pa. Cav.*—**1st.** We have now five cases of remittent fever, all mild and amenable to quinine in five-grain doses three times daily; of typhoid fever we have one case now convalescent and one case in division hospital. **2d.** With perhaps one or two exceptions the typhoid cases we have had this fall have been clearly of a malarious origin. **3d.** A mild purgative and quinine in five-grain doses every three hours during the remission; during the febrile paroxysm sweet spirit of nitre with acetate of ammonia. When about the eighth or tenth day the remissions become less marked and typhoid symptoms appear, the quinine is continued in doses of two or three grains every four hours, with brandy, beef-tea and wine-whey, and when the tongue becomes dry and parched and the bowels tympanitic I give castor oil and turpentine every four hours. I have found blisters upon the abdomen to be of great advantage in the second stage of the disease. **4th.** Nearly all of our cases have been of a remittent character at first. About the sixth or eighth day the fever became of a more-continued form, with more or less delirium and subsultus, tympanites, hot skin, compressible pulse, tongue at first furred and afterwards smooth or cracked and dry, and on the ninth or tenth day the characteristic eruption of rose-spots would appear on the body. About the end of the second week, in favorable cases, the tongue becomes moist and clean at the tip and edges; in more protracted cases it cleans off from the centre, becoming dry, parched and cracked. Diarrhœa occurred in most of the cases, but was not attended with hemorrhage. The mortality of the cases treated in the regimental hospital has been about twenty per cent. **5th** and **6th** may be conjoined, for the locality of our camp was certainly the cause of two-thirds of our typhoid cases. We were located at first on damp, low ground, not susceptible of drainage. Two weeks after this our sick-list was doubled, and ten or twelve of our typhoid cases originated. The camping ground was certainly pregnant with causes of malarial and typhoid fevers. In addition to this cause there were also those resulting from the mode of life in camp, and especially in the camps of recruits who have not yet learned and practiced the most salutary police regulations. Bad cooking and want of cleanliness in their persons, clothes and quarters, the change and irregularity of diet, exposure, etc., may be named amongst the causes of typhoid fever and diseases in general. **7th.** Sick 84, mean strength 909, giving about 9.25 per cent., including about 25 who have been recommended for discharge, and also those injured by horses, gunshot wounds, etc. **8th.** But one case of gangrene of the toes has occurred,—in a severe and tedious case of typhoid fever. The predisposing cause was, I think, the low vital powers of the system and the exciting cause the pressure of bed-clothes. As this was the only case we were not sufficiently on the alert; perhaps had more care been taken the gangrene might have been prevented. Bathing in warm water or with hot whiskey and the application of artificial heat might prevent this trouble in a measure, if not altogether.

Surgeon J. COLLINS, 3*d Pa.*—**1st.** Cases of bilious remittent 52, of typhoid fever 16, taken sick during the month of November. **2d.** There has been a striking similarity between the febrile cases observed in camp and those I have seen in Pennsylvania and New England. A few cases have begun as well-marked remittents and ended as typhoid fever of a malignant type. Moreover, the fact that quinine is well borne in all typhoid cases would seem to indicate that malarial influences operated in them. **3d.** The treatment has not been uniform. As a rule in a case of remittent fever a mercurial purge is given, followed by oil or a saline and afterwards by quinine and tincture of iron. Should the case prove persistent, alterative doses of blue-pill are given. During the paroxysm great relief is afforded by neutral mixture or acetate of ammonia. Hoffmann's anodyne is valuable, and in the later stages good milk-punch plays an important part. The sequelæ of the disease, debility, diarrhœa and jaundice, need particular attention. Typhoid cases require strict watching as the symptoms are in many cases insidious and deceptive. After the first stage these bear stimulants and quinia quite well; in fact stimulants are absolutely necessary. Carbonate of ammonia, milk-punch with generous diet of beef-tea and animal broths, and in certain cases turpentine emulsion, are given with great advantage. In the obstinate and debilitating diarrhœa of typhoid I have found catechu most efficient. **4th.** In remittent fever, besides the ordinary febrile symptoms, may be noted a peculiar brown or bluish-black coating of the tongue. This peculiar shade I have never noticed before. In other cases the conjuntivæ are injected, often yellow and the tongue of a reddish tint. The paroxysm generally occurs towards evening. In typhoid cases there is generally a greater tenderness or gurgling in the line of the colon; the discharges are dark or watery; the pulse has a hollow vanishing beat; the tongue is dry; the fever continued; rose-colored spots, etc. **5th.** The supposed cause is concealed in the two terms used with scientific flippancy, viz: predisposition and malaria. **6th.** The regiment has never been quite free from the disease. I think the violent and malignant form assumed in November due to location in the swamp just in advance of our present encampment. **7th.** During the month 32 per cent. of the whole regiment were sick at one period or another. **8th.** One case of gangrene of the toes was sent to division hospital. Another, a patient suffering from a violent attack of typhoid fever, occurred in the regimental hospital: On the morning of the tenth day he complained of intense pain in the toes. The feet were cold, the toes quite blue or bluish-black. I immediately ordered stimulation, and heat to be applied externally, with large doses of tincture of iron, milk-punch and good diet. In a few days the patient ceased to complain and the symptoms yielded.

Surgeon J. S. DE BENNEVILLE, 11*th Pa.*—**1st.** From August to December inclusive we have had 20 cases of remittent fever and 19 of typhoid. **2d.** The cases of typhoid were similar to those called typhoid or enteric fever at the North. **3d.** Treatment was by gentle purgatives when necessary and diaphoretics of neutral mixture or acetate of ammonia combined with sweet spirit of nitre, tartrate of antimony or ipecacuanha in the first stage. Mecurials combined with diaphoretics were used as the secretions diminished and the tongue became furred and dry; cold applications to the head, dry cups to the temples and back of the neck and blisters to the temples or scalp when fever and delirium were present. In the advanced stages, when the tongue became dry and fissured and the abdomen tympanitic, turpentine was employed with advantage. Dry cupping, mustard poultices and stimulating liniments to the chest were used in treating bronchitis and pulmonary complications. The diet was at first arrow-root gruel, farina and barley, but as the disease advanced beef-tea, essence of beef, milk-punch and wine-whey were given with cinchona or quinine. **4th.** The patient usually suffered from a feeling of general uneasiness and discomfort, headache, alternate sensations of heat and chilliness, diarrhœa, in some cases epistaxis, furred tongue, etc. These symptoms became aggravated with dry skin and tongue, pain in the iliac region, tympanites, bronchitis or pneumonia. Rose-colored spots and sudamina were found in nearly all cases; marked cerebral disorder with delirium occurred in many. **5th.** It is probably the endemic fever of this region, its increase being favored by overcrowding in small tents and neglect of cleanliness. **6th.** The first case occurred while the troops were at Camp Tennally, about a month after they had removed from a camp one mile north of Washington. **7th.** The number of sick daily averaged 5.0 per cent. in July and August, 4.5 in September, 5.0 in October, 5.75 in November and 6.75 in December. **8th.** The only case of gangrene that came under my notice was at the division hospital. The patient had been sick in this regiment for seventeen days with a low form of remittent fever in which the prominent symptoms were cerebral; the lower limbs became œdematous and the gangrenous condition appeared soon after his entrance into hospital.

Surgeon S. D. FREEMAN, 13*th Pa. Reserves.*—**1st.** During the last three months we have had 91 cases of bilious remittent and 9 cases of typhoid fever. **2d.** The typhoid fever is not the typhoid of the North, but originates in bilious remittent, attributed to malaria. **3d.** Treatment is alterative, tonic and stimulating by blue mass, carbonate of ammonia, turpentine, quinine and brandy. The disease does not yield to quinine. **4th.** Headache, with chills, backache, general malaise, tongue coated, at first yellow then dark, crusting and cracking in the centre—in short, the usual symptoms. **5th.** The cause is supposed to be the change from a high and dry to a low and moist climate, as that portion of the regiment coming from the Alleghany mountains suffers most. **6th.** The regiment was encamped at Harrisburg, Pa.; Cumberland, Md.; New Creek, Va.; then again at Harrisburg, Sandy Hook, Buckeyestown and Hyattstown, where fevers first made their appearance. **7th.** The percentage of sick from all causes is at present 7.25. **8th.** There is no gangrene of the toes.

Surgeon A. W. GREEN, 7*th Pa. Reserves.*—**1st.** Six cases for the present month. **2d.** I do not consider it the same as the typhoid fever of the North; it commences as a bilious remittent, running rapidly into a typhoid condition, and almost invariably with strongly marked cerebral symptoms. I think the heavy fogs overhanging us almost every night, the nature of the soil, vegetable mould with clay subsoil, and the constant digging connected with camp improvements serve to indicate a malarial origin. **3d.** Quinine in doses of three to ten grains every two hours generally succeeds in breaking up the fever; but at this time we have to be exceedingly careful, else the disease will assume the typhoid form. The treatment in this event consists of turpentine emulsion, opium or Dover's powder, beef-tea, milk-punch, brandy, carbonate of ammonia, etc. **4th.** Chilliness, restlessness, fever, headache, pain in back and bones, general uneasiness, torpor of the bowels, pain in bowels, tenderness on pressure, tympanites, diarrhœa, hemorrhage, dilated pupils, entire adynamic condition, death. **5th.** The supposed causes are miasm and exposure. **6th.** Camp Tennally. **7th.** Three and one-half per cent. **8th.** Convalescents complain very much of their feet, but I have not met with a case of gangrene.

Brigade Surg. S. R. HAVEN, *U. S. V.*—The report of sick and wounded shows in October 1,794 cases of disease and in November 2,918 cases. Most of those included in the report for October have been of a distinctly malarial type: Remittent, intermittent and continued fevers; also a large number of cases of measles.

Camp Advance is situated on the bluffs forming the southwest bank of the Potomac at Chain bridge. These bluffs vary from 180 to 200 feet in height. The Potomac at this point and for a considerable distance above and below flows over a rocky bed with steep banks on both shores, extending back in rolling hills with sharp gulches intervening. The region is, therefore, apparently non-malarious. The intermittent and remittent fevers that have prevailed here during the last month are attributable, I think, to the extensive felling of timber and clearing up of a new country required by the military necessities of the camp. This division was moved to its present camp October 10. Its topography is not unlike that of Camp Advance except that it is four miles distant from the Potomac. It will be observed that the diseases reported indicate a gradual deepening into more serious forms as the season advances. These forms, I think, are not correctly designated typhoid, the condition being rather that of a low form of bilious remittent incident to the depressing influence of camp life upon those wholly unaccustomed to it.

Brigade Surg. J. H. WARREN, *U. S. V.*—As far as I have visited the various camps in this division I have not been able to find more than six or eight cases of true typhoid fever as I have been accustomed to see it at the North. These cases were, I think, brought with the troops from the North here. We have a great many cases of bilious remittent fever assuming the typhoid type. Quinine, opium and camphor seem to be the best agents for the treatment of this form of fever. The surgeons unite in this statement, that all cases begin with the usual form of remittent fever and end with the typhoid type. The common diagnostic signs of typhoid fever as we see it farther North are wanting in the incipient stage of the disease.

In the face of this testimony acknowledging the existence of typhoid fever in our camps, but pronouncing the prevailing camp-fever to be essentially a malarial fever of an adynamic character, it is difficult to conceive that the insertion of the term typho-malarial in the monthly sick reports, without a word of explanation as to its scope, could have so influenced medical officers in the field as to cause them to change their views and regard these fevers as typhoid modified by active malarial phenomena. As a matter of fact their opinions remained unchanged. This is fully evidenced by the sanitary reports that were filed subsequent to June 30, 1862, the date of the introduction of the new term. Thus, Surgeon JONATHAN LETTERMAN, U. S. A., Medical Director of the Army of the Potomac, in a report covering the first six months after the date stated, referred the prevailing typhoid type of fevers to the action of the deadly malarial poison.[*] His successor, Surgeon THOMAS A. McPARLIN, U. S. A., makes use of the new term, but does not explain the value attached to it when he says[†] that "during the advance from the Rapidan to Petersburg malarial and typho-malarial fevers and diarrhœa were the prevailing diseases," and he is equally indefinite, so far as the use of the new term is concerned, when later in the same report he mentions "fevers of the intermittent and typhoid type" among the diseases prevalent during the siege of Petersburg.

The large number of cases, 23,346, reported as typho-malarial during the year following the introduction of this term, shows how generally it was accepted by medical officers in the field; but it has no bearing on their views as to the essential nature of the fevers thus reported.[‡] The term, when used outside of the monthly reports of sick and wounded, was seldom accompanied by any data indicating whether a modified typhoid or an adynamic remittent was intended. There is on the files of the Surgeon General's Office but one report which attaches to typho-malarial the value which Dr. WOODWARD had in view on its official introduction. It reads as follows:

---

[*] P. 93, Appendix to the First Part of this volume.   [†] *Loc. cit.*, p. 161.

[‡] "As it was, the term went upon the sick report without any explanation or a word of comment. But even under these circumstances 23,346 cases were reported as typho-malarial fever during the following year, showing how widely the opinions I had formed were shared by the medical officers of the Army."—Dr. WOODWARD's paper on *Typho-malarial Fever, Section of Medicine, International Medical Congress,* Philadelphia, 1876, p. 12.

Surgeon WM. O'MEAGHER, 37*th N. Y.*, *Edward's Ferry, Md., Sept.* 30, 1862.—But notwithstanding all our efforts, aided by abundance of nourishment and stimulants, several died of a mixed disease which is, to my mind, accurately named in the new monthly reports of sick and wounded as typho-malarial fever. The two cases of this nature recorded in my report for August exhibited very marked evidence of typhoid fever and miasmatic poisoning, and the treatment was adapted accordingly. In one case the delirium was so violent as to approach the character of mania; cerebro-spinal meningitis was the prominent condition, and to this the treatment was mainly directed, the remote and exciting cause being, however, kept in view. But the patient died exhausted in a few days. The second case partook more of the typhoid condition and the delirium was of the usual character. He also died in an equally short space. A third man recovered, but I am satisfied his constitution is permanently impaired. He is still in the regiment and under observation, being on light duty only. I should have mentioned that the daily exacerbations in each case varied considerably. In the first there was violent delirium, almost maniacal; in the second a mere shudder with low muttering; and in the third a convulsive tremor, with gurgling in the throat and a hissing expiration accompanied by the expulsion of some frothy mucus between the teeth.

On the other hand Ass't Surg. J. T. CALHOUN, U. S. A., believed the fevers of the Peninsula to be not enteric but miasmatic, and appropriately denominated typho-malarial.* "The form of fever termed by the negroes swamp fever, but which should be known, perhaps, in scientific nosology as typho-malarial fever, was very frequent."† Dr. CALHOUN bore testimony also to the absence of intestinal glandular lesions in certain adynamic fevers.‡

Surgeon J. M. RICE, 25*th Mass.*, *New Berne, N. C., March* 10, 1863.—The intermittents, unless controlled by the administration of cinchona or other antiperiodics, passed into remittent, and the remittents frequently assumed that type of disease now named in our reports typho-malarial. In the commencement there was usually cephalalgia; pain in the eyes; severe aching pain in the back and limbs, very noticeable even in the milder cases; sometimes nausea and vomiting; generally slight desire for food. The condition of the bowels was variable—diarrhœa when present being readily controlled. During the remissions the debility was quite marked, with indisposition to the slightest exertion. In a number of cases I had the most satisfactory evidence that the production of cinchonism cut short the disease in its early stages, and, as it appeared to me, without causing any unsatisfactory result when this was not accomplished. In some cases there was a tendency to the congestive form, and this, when occurring in those debilitated by frequent attacks of intermittent or by recent remittents, was always dangerous and in some instances fatal. Nearly all were remarkable for the long and unsatisfactory period of convalescence. Treatment consisted of mercurials combined with other cathartics; sometimes emetics; counter-irritation when required; the exhibition of quinine in full doses in the early remissions; diaphoretics during the febrile paroxysms, accompanied with a dry skin, and later in the disease quinine in small doses, with stimulants when needed.

But perhaps the strongest evidence of the undetermined value attached to the term typho-malarial by our medical officers is afforded by a report of Surgeon GEORGE A. OTIS, afterwards for many years the colleague of Dr. WOODWARD in the preparation of this history:

Remarks on the Monthly Report of Surgeon GEORGE A. OTIS, 27*th Mass.*, *New Berne, N. C., June*, 1863.—There were three cases of typho-malarial fever (so-called)—cases in which it was impracticable for me to decide whether the disease should be pronounced remittent or typhoid fever. One (Hall) entered on the 21st instant with high fever, delirium, excessive prostration. He had been reported at surgeon's call for ten or twelve days previously with diarrhœa, but his bowels were confined when he was admitted. There was abdominal tenderness, especially near the cæcum. There was no remission in his fever, and the administration of quinine was not ventured upon, for signs of rapid sinking were speedily noticed. He died three days after admission. It was not practicable to make an autopsy. The other fatal case was similar in many respects, save that the cerebral complications were less prominent. Although a remission was anxiously looked for, none could be detected. At last tentative doses of quinine were given. They did not apparently aggravate the symptoms, but they failed to relieve any of them appreciably. In the third case, the only one of recovery, quinine was administered before an absolute remission was observed. The next day there was a fair remission, and the antiperiodic was given immediately in full doses with the happiest effect.

This able officer made use of the term one year after its introduction, not as embodying his views of the pathology of the febrile cases, but as indicating his inability to discriminate between a typhoid modified by malarial manifestations and a remittent with typhoid symptoms.

The general acceptance of the term typho-malarial fever, as indicated by the large number of cases reported under it, shows manifestly that it filled a nosonomial want which had been sorely felt. It may be fairly claimed that it was made use of in all febrile cases not purely

---

* In his report, p. 91, Appendix, Part 1st.   † *Op. cit.*, p. 92.

‡ In the *Med. and Surg. Reporter*, Vol. X, Phila., 1863, p. 97, he says that besides cases of pure enteric fever which differed in no manner from those seen in civil life, there frequently occurred cases of an adynamic fever in which there were no enteric symptoms, no rose-colored spots and no epistaxis; and in these *post-mortem* examination failed to reveal any ulceration or change of structure in the glands of Peyer.

enteric, which presented the so-called typhoid symptoms, by those who regarded such symptoms as indicative of enteric fever, by those who regarded them as developed during the
persistence of a malarial fever irrespective of the presence of typhoid, and lastly, by those
who, in the absence of *post-mortem* investigation in individual cases, were ready, like Dr.
OTIS, to confess their inability to determine whether a specific typhoid element was or was
not present.

From the frequency with which ulceration of Peyer's patches was found in the *post-
mortem* researches conducted at the general hospitals, the officers forming the staff of these
institutions very generally concluded that the prevailing fevers of the Army were essentially
typhoid.   The cases which occasionally presented an unaltered intestinal mucous membrane,
or one changed only by an apparently unspecific congestion, were accepted as showing that
death had resulted from the malarial influences to which our troops were almost constantly
exposed.   But these cases, as has already been explained, seldom lived to reach the general hospitals, or if they did so died subsequently, not from the primary fever, but from
secondary pneumonic or intestinal complications, the latter of which offered to view extensive ulcerations of the intestines simulating the appearances of typhoid fever.   Typho-malarial fever, therefore, to the medical officers of these hospitals generally, implied an enteric
lesion.   Positive results were obtained at the necropsies, and specimens were forwarded to
the Army Medical Museum in such numbers as seemed to the pathological anatomist to
leave no doubt of the character of the prevailing fever.

But fatality and prevalence are not synonymous.   Fevers presenting ulceration of the
small intestine, and particularly of its closed glands, certainly occasioned more deaths than
those unassociated with such anatomical changes, but the universal testimony of the medical
men who treated the fever cases that recovered or died at an early period after the onset of
the disease, is to the effect that the prevailing fevers were essentially paroxysmal.   The
hospital pathologists did not give due weight to these assertions.   They found that the field
surgeons reported large numbers of typho-malarial cases, and assuming that these cases were
characterized by pathological conditions similar to those with which their experience had
made them familiar, they conceived their view of the enteric nature of the fevers reported
as typho-malarial to be correct because based upon *post-mortem* research instead of on symptomatology and therapeusis.

But, as has been indicated by certain of the *post-mortem* records of typho-malarial cases,
this term was applied by the field surgeons to fevers which in its absence would have been
returned as malarial remittents.   Inasmuch as no instructions had been issued limiting the
applicability of the term to enteric fever with malarial complications, these officers were
fully justified in including under it those malarial cases which had typhoid, *i. e.*, adynamic
tendencies, particularly as there was nothing in the first part of the compound term to limit
its significance to one specific cause of typhoidal symptoms.   Undoubtedly, also, the new
term was accepted by many as enabling them to dispose of their anomalous cases without
committing themselves to certain etiological and pathological doctrines.

The pathologists were therefore in error in supposing that enteric fever was present in
all the cases reported as typho-malarial by our medical officers.   This view is sustained by
a study of the monthly changes in the curve of prevalence; and on it only can the singular death-rate of typho-malarial fever be understood.   It has been shown by the records
of the Seminary hospital that the fatality of typhoid cases which were complicated with

active manifestations of the malarial influence was much greater than that of uncomplicated cases: and such a result is consistent with our general experience of the action of morbific agencies on the system, especially when these agencies have similar destructive tendencies. But the statistics of the white troops show that although the mortality caused by typhoid subsequent to the introduction of the new term was 40 per cent. of the cases, the fatality of the cases reported as typho-malarial was only 8 per cent. This is convincing proof that the medical officers who placed these cases on the monthly reports did not restrict the term to cases in which there was a coincidence of both fevers. Had they done so an antagonism between the action of the typhoid and malarial poisons on the human system would have been immediately established. But there was no evidence of an antagonism of this character. On the contrary, typhoid fever was deadly in proportion to its modification by other deteriorating agencies, chief among which was the malarial influence.*

In true typho-malarial fever at least 41.4 per cent. of cases among the white troops should have terminated fatally, since typhoid gave 40 per cent. of fatality and remittents 1.4 per cent. from June 30, 1862, to the end of the period covered by the statistics. But as the cases reported under the term typho-malarial were fatal at the rate of only 8 per cent., it may be inferred that for one case thus reported which was really characterized by the specific typhoid element, there were 4.85 cases which could not have been typhoid as they lacked its gravity and were so amenable to specific treatment that they furnished only the mortality which would have occurred among an equal number of malarial remittents. In other words, 83 per cent. of the cases reported among the white troops as typho-malarial were remittents or febrile attacks attended with no greater mortality than the remittents. Speaking approximatively, of the 49,871 cases thus reported more than 41,393 were remittent and less than 8,478 were true typho-malarial cases.

A similar calculation on corresponding data furnished by the statistics of the colored troops—to wit: Percentage of typhoid cases which ended fatally 55.69, of remittents 3.27, of cases reported as typho-malarial 17.27—shows that 73 per cent. of the cases entered on the reports under the new term were remittents or febrile attacks which had no larger mortality than the malarial remittents.

Typhoid fever, including typhus, occasioned during the war 181 cases of sickness and 59.6 deaths among every thousand of our white soldiers. The remittent-malarial fevers caused 664 cases and 8.2 deaths. There were also 115 cases and 8.6 deaths attributed to typho-malarial fever. But the cases last mentioned have been seen to consist of one truly typho-malarial case to 4.85 malarial remittents. Were the typho-malarial figures duly distributed among the typhoid and the remittent fevers the former would number 200 per thousand of strength with 67.16 deaths, and the latter 759 per thousand with 9.24 deaths. There were thus more than seven deaths attributable to typhoid fever for every death caused by adynamic remittent or other low fevers not specifically typhoid or enteric. In other words, seven cases of fever with typhoid symptoms presented typhoid ulcerations for one case of fever with typhoid symptoms which had no ulceration of the closed glands. Hence the opinion of the pathologists that a specific typhoid was the prevalent fever. The relative prevalence of these fevers was, however, 3.7 of malarial remittent to one of true typhoid; most of the former were treated in camp, of the latter in general hospitals. Hence

---

* Dr. JAS. J. LEVICK is the only observer who, while denying any antagonism between the poison of typhoid and that of malarial fever, considers that the malarial complication did not add to the gravity of the typhoid affection; but, on the contrary, it, or the remedies employed to control it, seemed to render the disease more tractable and less fatal.—*American Journal Med. Sci.*, 1864, Vol. XLVII, p. 407.

the opinion of the field surgeons that the prevailing fever was a malarial remittent. These figures include the vast number of typhoid fever cases that occurred after the organization of the volunteer armies. Had they been excluded by making use of the statistics of the third year of the war, that ending June 30, 1864, the remittents would have been found to have outnumbered the enteric cases in the proportion of 6.5 : 1, although the chances of finding typhoid ulcerations in a fatal case of low fever would yet have remained as high as 5.4 : 1.

It is to be regretted that the applicability of the new term was not fully explained and limited on its introduction. Had this been done, the attention of our medical officers would have been directed to the differentiation of typhoid fever with malarial complications and remittents with adynamic symptoms, and our knowledge of this clinically obscure subject would have been materially improved. As it was, the new term was productive of undesirable results. It dissociated cases of typhoid and malarial fevers from their etiological, pathological and therapeutic associates, thus injuring the totality of the statistics of both the classes, and massed them in uncertain proportions in a separate group which could be analysed only at the close of the war on the presentation of all the materials relating to it. Instead of conducing to discrimination and simplification in the study of the camp fevers its use tended to admixture and confusion. It appears, also, to have been responsible for the lack of material illustrative of itself, as by affording a local habitation and a name to obscure cases it relieved medical officers from the official necessity of maturely considering them prior to formulating a diagnosis or of entering into the details of their peculiarities and difficulties. Moreover, the term was carried by our medical men into civil practice at the close of the war, where it has perpetuated the uncertainties attaching to the cases that have been classed under it.*

But while the cases reported under the heading typho-malarial comprised so small a proportion of such as were really typho-malarial in the views of the originator of the term, it by no means follows that true typho-malarial fever was a rare occurrence in our camps. On the contrary, it may be said with certainty that it occurred with greater frequency than unmodified typhoid; and owing to its tedious and uncertain course, the typhoid affection being often prolonged by preliminary malarial attacks, and the return to health interrupted by relapses of the malarial essential or prevented by the development of diarrhœal, dysenteric, pneumonic or other sequelæ common to both its elements, it assumed prominence among the fevers of our camps as being the most destructive to the army as well as to the life of the individual, although by no means the most prevalent fever.

In the early months of the war typhoid fever was to be expected from the aggregation of young and susceptible subjects under unhygienic conditions. But as the men at this time had not become so thoroughly affected by the malarial poison as was the case at a later date, their typhoid epidemics ought to have been of a comparatively unmodified character. Nevertheless it has been shown by the clinical records of the Seminary hospital that many of the cases which then occurred were distinctly impressed by the malarial poison and on that account entitled to be ranked as typho-malarial fevers. Later in the war the frequency of such cases undoubtedly increased, but as the typhoid element was recognized by some symptom regarded as pathognomonic or by *post-mortem* observation in a sample case of the series, the fever was reported as typhoid and not as typho-malarial. It is impossible to

---

* See page 509, *infra.*

say how many of those so reported were modified by malarial influences, but the number must have been very great. Dr. WOODWARD was correct in assigning importance to the true typho-malarial fevers, but he erred in regarding the numbers reported under the typho-malarial heading as giving expression to that importance. The true typho-malarial cases were usually reported under the term typhoid. The sanitary reports indicate that when typhoid became epidemic among men on duty in a malarious section the disease did not present the characteristics common to it in the civil population of the Northern States. Only in regiments newly levied and as yet unexposed to malarial influences was the typhoid disease similar to that with which their medical officers had been familiar in civil life. In the first-mentioned commands the disease was always of a grave character; while in those last referred to the mortality from typhoid was generally light, in some instances a hundred cases having been reported with only a few deaths. Correspondingly the rate of fatality of typhoid was only 18.8 per cent. among the white troops during the first eight months of the war, while it rose later, as the disease became modified, to an average of 38.3 per cent. The greater fatality during the later years may not be wholly attributed to the malarial influence, but that it was due in part to this is obvious from the evidence already presented. These considerations imply a relative paucity of cases of unmodified typhoid fever and a large proportion of cases which, had the term typho-malarial been properly applied, would have been dropped from the reports as typhoid and recorded as typho-malarial.

It has been shown that the cases reported as typho-malarial were chiefly composed of malarial remittents with a comparatively small percentage of true typho-malarial cases. It has been shown also that of the cases reported as typhoid the majority were really complicated with malarial phenomena, and were thus in fact typho-malarial cases, while the minority were cases of unmodified typhoid. But among those reported as typhoid was another group in which typhoid symptoms were associated with no anatomical lesions other than those attributable to the action of the malarial poison. In other words, adynamic remittents and malarial fevers assuming a sub-continued form and typhoidal tendency, while forming the mass of the cases reported as typho-malarial, constituted also a portion of those fevers reported as typhoid. The following series of cases will amply sustain the latter part of this statement. In most of these there is no clinical history to show what were the symptoms during life, but the diagnosis presumes the existence of more or less of the so-called typhoid symptoms, while in a minority of the cases some of these typhoid symptoms are specified. A certain number of these cases, so far as can be learned from the *post-mortem* records, were instances of pure typhoid; others were instances of true typho-malarial fever; but a third set, comprising no inconsiderable number, were cases which offered to view no other lesion than those which have been construed as indicating the presence of malarial disease. These cases, like those which preceded them, have been arranged for convenience of study in accordance with the character and situation of the changes in the intestinal canal:

CASES REPORTED AS TYPHOID FEVER, THE CLINICAL HISTORY INSUFFICIENT OR ABSENT—182 CASES.

(A.) Peyer's patches ulcerated and the ileum or small intestine only affected—43 cases.

CASE 117.—Private Levi Schietz, Co. I, 47th Pa., was admitted April 3, 1864, with a hot and dry skin, brown, dry and cracked tongue and lips, slightly dilated pupils, quick pulse, 112 to 120, and muttering delirium. Two days thereafter, under the influence of small doses of turpentine and laudanum, the delirium subsided, the tongue became somewhat moist and the pulse fell to 100–112; but the improvement was only temporary,—diarrhœa set in and the skin over the sacrum became painful and reddened. He died on the 14th. *Post-mortem* examination fifteen hours after death: "Slight ulceration but extensive inflammation of Peyer's patches; also a slight degree of arachnitis." —*Act. Ass't Surg. Charles Carter, Turner's Lane Hospital, Philadelphia, Pa.*

Case 118.—Private Henry H. Whitney, Co. D, 53d Mass., was admitted Aug. 16, 1863, having been sick a week with diarrhœa, great prostration, dry and furred tongue, sordes on teeth, sudamina on abdomen and chest, suffusion of face and tympanites of abdomen. Gave beef-tea and sherry wine. 19th: Severe chill. 20th: Mumps; pulse 110, quick and feeble. 21st: Great prostration; rusty sputa; crepitant râles; death. *Post-mortem* examination ten hours after death: Both lungs congested posteriorly and partly adherent to thoracic walls, with slight effusion into each pleural cavity; heart healthy; stomach much distended; bowels purple-spotted on their serous surface; Peyer's patches in several instances prominent, much congested and slightly ulcerated.—*Union Hospital, Memphis, Tenn.*

Case 119.—Private John H. Beckwith, Co. C, 79th N. Y.; age 33; admitted June 6, 1865. Diagnosis—typhoid fever. Died 26th. The only symptoms mentioned are delirium, almost constant, and much jactitation. *Post-mortem* examination twelve hours after death: Lungs adherent to pleuræ by fibrinous bands; spleen enlarged and softened; Peyer's patches ulcerated.—*Slough Hospital, Alexandria, Va.*

Case 120.—Private Robert Booth, Co. A, 147th Pa.; age 21; was admitted Nov. 4, 1863, delirious, with dry tongue and sordes, and on the second day after admission involuntary discharges from the bowels. He died on the 13th. *Post-mortem* examination showed "that condition of the intestinal glands usually found in typhoid cases."—*Act. Ass't Surg. James Robertson, 1st Division Hospital. Alexandria, Va.*

Case 121.—Private Albert Graff, Co. D, 4th N. Y., was admitted Nov. 30, 1864, with typhoid fever, much exhausted by his journey from City Point, Va. His tongue was dry and brown, teeth covered with sordes, bowels tender; he was affected with low delirium and subsultus. He died December 3, having had involuntary fæcal passages and retention of urine for twenty-four hours before death. *Post-mortem* examination: Extensive ulceration of Peyer's patches.—*Third Division Hospital, Alexandria, Va.*

Case 122.—Private Aaron T. Ward, Co. B, 20th Me.; age 25; was admitted Oct. 29, 1862, with diarrhœa following typhoid fever. He was feeble and emaciated; the stools were generally natural in color, but liquid and occasionally streaked with blood. On November 11, the diarrhœa still continuing, he was attacked with diphtheria characterized by suffocative paroxysms; he died next day. *Post-mortem* examination eighteen hours after death: The larynx was œdematous and lined with pseudo-membrane. The lungs were congested. The heart was normal, its right ventricle filled with a large firm clot. The stomach, liver and kidneys were normal. The glands of Brünner were enlarged; Peyer's glands thickened and in the lower portion of the ileum ulcerated.—*Third Division Hospital, Alexandria, Va.*

Case 123.—Private William Martin, Co. M, 17th Pa.; age 23; was admitted July 19, 1863, delirious and with a hot and dry skin, frequent and feeble pulse, dry and brown tongue, tender bowels and some diarrhœa. He died on the 21st. *Post-mortem* examination twenty-four hours after death: Mucous membrane of the small intestine inflamed; glands of Peyer ulcerated; mesenteric glands enlarged; lower lobes of both lungs congested; heart and liver normal. —*Act. Ass't Surg. S. Upson, Third Division Hospital, Alexandria, Va.*

Case 124.—Corp'l Charles S. Benedict, Co. B, 144th N. Y., was admitted April 14, 1863, moribund: Pulse 130, very feeble; respiration 28; tongue dry, brown, cracked; bowels relaxed; skin moist; extremities cold, clammy. He died next day. *Post-mortem* examination twenty-four hours after death: Mucous membrane of larger bronchi abnormally red; liver and spleen enlarged and softened; stomach injected; mucous membrane of small intestine much injected; Peyer's patches enlarged, some deeply ulcerated.—*Third Division Hospital, Alexandria, Va.*

Case 125.—Private Anthony Duchey, Co. C, 195th Ohio; age 18; was admitted April 6, 1865, much emaciated and very weak, his mind much impaired. A number of small abscesses on his thighs and legs, on being punctured, discharged a quantity of thin milky pus. He had a large deep bedsore over the sacrum and one over each trochanter, great thirst, anorexia and a red, dry, transversely fissured tongue. He died on the 24th. *Post-mortem* examination four hours after death: Large deposits of pus were found beneath the skin and between the muscles of the lower extremities; the right parotid gland was infiltrated with pus. The liver adhered to the diaphragm and the abdominal parietes; its substance was softened; the gall-bladder was enormously distended with black bile; the spleen was enlarged and softened. The stomach was contracted and its mucous membrane inflamed; the ileum inflamed and Peyer's patches ulcerated.—*Act. Ass't Surg. S. B. West, Cumberland Hospital, Md.*

Case 126.—Private John S. Hall, 17th Ind. Bat'y; age 18; was admitted Nov. 10. 1862, with typhoid fever, and died on the 20th. *Post-mortem* examination: The only lesion found was an extensive inflammation and ulceration of Peyer's patches.—*Ass't Surg. H. Pierce, 150th N. Y., Stewart's Mansion Hospital, Baltimore, Md.*

Case 127.—Private William O'Brien, Co. D, 38th Mass.; age 19; was admitted Nov. 5, 1862, with typhoid fever, and died on the 9th. *Post-mortem* examination: Heart, lungs, stomach, liver and kidneys normal; inflammation of Peyer's glands: intussusception in the middle third of the ileum.—*Act. Ass't Surg. T. F. Murdoch, Stewart's Mansion Hospital, Baltimore, Md.*

Case 128.—Private Patrick Farmer, Co. B, 38th Mass., was admitted Oct. 7, 1864, from City Point, Va., with typhoid fever, and died next day. *Post-mortem* examination sixteen hours after death: Ulceration of Peyer's glands; much pleuritic effusion.—*Act. Ass't Surg. John T. Myers, Beverly Hospital, N. J.*

Case 129.—Private William J. Roberts, 26th Ohio Bat'y; age 22; was admitted Nov. 29, 1864, with typhoid fever. He died December 10. *Post-mortem* examination twenty hours after death: The spleen weighed thirty-four ounces; Peyer's glands were inflamed and ulcerated throughout the ileum and for some distance up in the jejunum. —*Natchez Hospital, Miss.*

Case 130.—Private John Prall, Co. K, 160th Ohio; age 22; was admitted Aug. 29, 1864, greatly prostrated and almost unconscious. He died next day. *Post-mortem* examination: Extensive ulceration of Peyer's patches and an intussusception of one portion of the ileum.—*Seminary Hospital, Columbus, Ohio.*

CASE 131.—Private Jonathan Heaman, Co. H, 57th Pa.; admitted April 30, 1864. Died May 10. *Post-mortem* examination twenty hours after death: Body much emaciated. Lungs and spleen congested; Peyer's glands ulcerated.—*Act. Ass't Surg. C. W. Fillmore, Harewood Hospital, Washington, D. C.*

CASE 132.—Private Joseph J. Reed, Co. B, 8th Ill. Cav.; admitted April 16, 1864. Typhoid fever. Died May 6. *Post-mortem* examination five hours after death: Body slightly emaciated. The lower lobe of the left lung and the lower border of the right lung were much congested and sank in water. The heart was normal. The liver was slightly enlarged; the gall-bladder full; the spleen much congested, weighing forty-one ounces; Peyer's patches were enlarged and many of them ulcerated; the mesenteric glands were much enlarged.—*Act. Ass't Surg. J. D. Linton, Harewood Hospital, Washington, D. C.*

CASE 133.—Private Jno. Bender, Co. G, 67th Pa., was admitted May 10, 1865, with typhoid fever, and died next day. *Post-mortem* examination twenty-eight hours after death: Lungs normal; heart pale; liver pale; spleen much enlarged; Peyer's patches ulcerated; kidneys normal.—*Depot Field Hospital, Sixth Army Corps, Army of Potomac.*

CASE 134.—Private James McLoon, Co. E, 40th N. J., was admitted May 10, 1865, with typhoid fever, and died on the 13th. *Post-mortem* examination seventy-two hours after death: Lungs, heart, liver, spleen and stomach normal; mesenteric glands enlarged; Peyer's patches ulcerated.—*Depot Field Hospital, Sixth Army Corps, Army of Potomac.*

CASE 135.—Private William D. Ebaugh, Co. F, 39th Ind.; age 18; was admitted Dec. 14, 1863, with typhoid fever, and died March 2, 1864. *Post-mortem* examination twenty-four hours after death: Much emaciation; pleuritic adhesions on both sides; right lung hepatized red and gray, left lung partly hepatized; heart weighed ten ounces; liver sixty-four ounces, fatty; spleen fifteen ounces and a half; right kidney six ounces, left six ounces and a half; mucous membrane of stomach somewhat congested; lower ileum showing a few large cicatrizing ulcers in Peyer's patches; large intestine normal.—*Hospital No. 1, Nashville, Tenn.*

CASE 136.—Private Jacob Spangles, Co. M, 1st Mich. Eng'rs, was admitted Dec. 3, 1863, with typhoid fever, and died on the 11th. *Post-mortem* examination fourteen hours after death: Pericardium containing six to eight ounces of serum; heart filled with large cadaveric clots; lungs hepatized posteriorly, the right containing a few hard isolated tubercles; liver and kidneys normal; spleen weighing fourteen ounces; mesenteric glands enlarged; Peyer's patches deeply ulcerated; stomach and large intestine normal; anterior abdominal wall much contused inferiorly and presenting some blood-clots beneath the peritoneum.—*Hospital No. 1, Nashville, Tenn.*

CASE 137.—Private W. H. Slingland, Co. H, 14th U. S. Inf., was admitted June 15, 1863, and died on the 17th. *Post-mortem* examination twenty-one hours after death: Body not emaciated. Brain healthy. Æsophageal mucous membrane yellow-tinged and presenting superficial ulcers in its lower portion, the ulcers having their greatest diameter parallel to the axis of the tube. Lymphatic glands at bifurcation of trachea much softened and blackish; upper and middle lobes of right lung and upper lobe of left lung slightly congested, lower lobes intensely congested. Heart flabby, containing no clots; pericardium everywhere firmly attached to the heart, obliterating the sac. Liver very flabby, dull greenish in color, evolving a peculiar chicken-coop odor and so soft that the finger could be inserted in every direction; gall-bladder containing eight drachms of dark ochre-colored bile; spleen dark, soft, pultaceous, weight seven ounces. Lower fifth of small intestine ulcerated, the ulcers confined to Peyer's patches and presenting ragged surfaces, purplish walls and congestion of the surrounding mucous membrane—the patches higher up in the intestine being pale and not elevated or congested. Kidneys congested.—*Ass't Surg. Harrison Allen, U. S. A., Lincoln Hospital, Washington, D. C.*

CASE 138.—Private Stephen Cornwright, 18th N. Y.; age 23; was admitted Nov. 30, 1864, with fever and feet gangrenous from frost-bite. He died December 20. *Post-mortem* examination two hours after death: Body much emaciated. The larynx, trachea, œsophagus and heart were normal. The right lung weighed twenty-two ounces and the left thirty ounces; the lower and middle lobes of the right lung and the lower lobe and lower portion of the upper lobe of the left lung were solidified and studded with small abscesses. The liver weighed seventy-one ounces and a half and the spleen seven ounces and a half; Peyer's patches were ulcerated; the kidneys appeared to be normal. [The attending physician remarks: "This man was admitted with both feet in a gangrenous condition. According to his own statement he had them frozen; but my opinion is that their condition was a result of his fever." This opinion is supported by the register of the hospital at Giesboro Point, Md., in which the patient appears as admitted November 25 with typhoid fever, and as sent to General hospital on the 29th. No reference is made to frost-bite.]—*Lincoln Hospital, Washington, D. C.*

CASE 139.—Private Nathan Upton, Co. B, 1st D. C. Cav.; age 32; was admitted Sept. 6, 1863, with typhoid fever, and died on the 19th. *Post-mortem* examination eight hours after death: Rigor mortis well marked. The brain substance was healthy; the pia mater slightly congested; half a drachm of fluid was found in the ventricles. The right lung weighed twenty-four ounces, the left fifteen ounces; the lower lobes of both were much congested. The right auricle of the heart contained a venous clot which extended into the ventricle; the left auricle contained a small fibrinous clot; the pericardium was everywhere firmly attached to the heart, so that its separation was almost impossible without tearing the muscular tissue. The liver was healthy; the gall-bladder contained three ounces of a thin straw-colored liquid; the spleen was firm and dark purple on section, weight thirteen ounces and a half. The mucous membrane of the stomach was congested. The small intestine was healthy in its upper portion, but in its lower part the solitary glands were enlarged and Peyer's patches ulcerated. The large intestine was healthy. The kidneys were congested; weight of right six ounces and a half, of left seven ounces.—*Ass't Surg. Harrison Allen, U. S. A., Lincoln Hospital, Washington, D. C.*

CASE 140.—Private Charles B. Beams, Co. B, 146th N. Y.; age 26; admitted Nov. 23, 1863; died 27th. *Post-mortem* examination twelve hours after death: Rigor mortis extremely marked; body moderately emaciated. The brain was unusually firm and weighed forty-nine ounces; its ventricles contained one drachm and a half of fluid. The larynx, trachea and œsophagus were natural. The right lung weighed eleven ounces and a half and the left twelve ounces; the lower lobes were engorged, softened, friable and charged with frothy bronchial secretion. The heart was healthy and contained a large fibrinous clot in its right cavities; the pericardial liquid was pale and measured fourteen drachms. The liver was healthy, weight sixty-eight ounces; the spleen firm, natural in size and of normal color. The small intestine was much distended with air; within five feet of the ileo-cæcal valve its mucous membrane was deeply congested, the solitary and agminated glands prominent, and the latter ulcerated in parts of their surface. The kidneys were congested.—*Ass't Surg. H. Allen, U. S. A., Lincoln Hospital, Washington, D. C.*

CASE 141.—Private Thomas Butler, Co. H, 137th N. Y., was admitted Jan. 11, 1863, with typhoid fever, and died during the night. He came from Fairfax Court House, Va., to Washington in an ambulance without covering, so that he was thoroughly chilled. Stimulants were employed without effect. *Post-mortem* examination: The thoracic viscera, the liver, spleen and kidneys were normal. The small intestine was inflamed; Peyer's patches were thickened and ulcerated; the solitary glands were much swollen, especially in the jejunum, where they stood out from the mucous membrane, attaining the size of medium-sized shot and having their apices pigmented or, in some cases, ulcerated.—*Lincoln Hospital, Washington, D. C.*

CASE 142.—Private Milton Striker, Co. C, 188th N. Y., was admitted Feb. 1, 1865, and died on the 3d. *Post-mortem* examination: Upper lobe of right lung hepatized, middle lobe healthy, lower lobe congested, weight of lung fifty-four ounces; upper lobe of left lung healthy, lower lobe congested, weight fourteen ounces. Heart normal. Weight of liver seventy ounces; of spleen fourteen ounces. Stomach healthy; Peyer's patches and solitary follicles ulcerated; mesenteric glands enlarged. Kidneys healthy.—*Fifth Army Corps Field Hospital, Army of Potomac.*

CASE 143.—Private James Loveland, Co. G, 4th Vt., was admitted Nov. 23, 1863, moribund. *Post-mortem* examination: Toes and anterior portion of metatarsus of both feet gangrenous. [*Specimens* 79 and 80, Med. Sect., Army Medical Museum, constitute the only record: 79, a portion of the upper part of the ileum, shows a single oblong and thickened Peyer's patch; 80, a portion of the lower part, presents two thickened and ulcerated patches and two small ulcers, corresponding probably to solitary follicles.]—*Ass't Surg. W. Thomson, U. S. A., Douglas Hospital, Washington, D. C.*

CASE 144.—Private Michael Kennedy, Co. I, 32d N. Y.; age 24; was admitted Aug. 10, 1862, and died on the 11th. *Post-mortem* examination next day: The body presented a vigorous appearance, with but slight emaciation. Thoracic organs healthy. Liver cirrhosed, much enlarged, of a yellowish brown color and granular, the granules about the size of pepper-corns; spleen enlarged, nine by five and a half by two and a half inches, but natural in color and consistence. Mucous membrane of ileum reddened, the lower agminated glands thickened and ulcerated, the upper unaffected. Other organs apparently healthy. [*Specimens* 60, 61 and 62, Med. Sect., Army Medical Museum, ulcerated patches and enlarged spleen, are from this case.]—*Act. Ass't Surg. Joseph Leidy, Satterlee Hospital, Philadelphia, Pa.*

CASE 145.—Private Joseph Terry, 1st N. J. Cav.; age 19; was admitted Jan. 14, 1864, in a state of low delirium from typhoid fever. He died on the 19th. *Post-mortem* examination: Lungs congested; liver softened; Peyer's patches ulcerated.—*Third Division Hospital, Alexandria, Va.*

CASE 146.—Private N. G. Carey, 1st N. J. Cav.; age 18; admitted Jan. 14, 1864. Diagnosis—continued fever. Died 18th. *Post-mortem* examination: Lower lobe of left lung hepatized; Peyer's patches ulcerated; one inch and a half of ileum gangrenous.—*Third Division Hospital, Alexandria, Va.*

CASE 147.—H. Russell, citizen; colored. Died June 24, 1865. *Post-mortem* examination: The lungs and heart were normal. The spleen was large and hard; the mesenteric glands enlarged. A series of elevated Peyer's patches of all sizes, honey-combed and with constricted bases, extended from the ileo-cæcal valve along the ileum; the solitary glands for eight or ten inches from the valve were elevated and had softened white centres. [*Specimen* 565, Med. Sect., Army Medical Museum, taken from this case, shows also hypertrophied villi, giving the ileum a velvety appearance, seen in plate facing this page.]—*Act. Ass't Surg. W. C. Minor, L'Ouverture Hospital, Alexandria, Va.*

CASE 148.—Private William T. Barrett, Co. K, 39th Mass., was admitted Dec. 24, 1862, with typhoid fever. Bronchitis set in about a week before his death, which occurred Jan. 29, 1863. *Post-mortem* examination twelve hours after death: The brain was pale, firm and weighed forty-three ounces. There were pleuritic adhesions on both sides. The lungs were marked by black pigment in the course of the ribs. The left lung weighed nineteen ounces and a half; its lower lobe was much congested and friable and its bronchial tubes congested, especially in their finer ramifications. The right lung weighed twenty-five ounces and three-quarters; there was a mass of solidified tissue in the posterior part of its lower lobe, the centre of which was occupied by fluid and opened into an inflamed bronchial tube of the third magnitude; several condensed pulmonary lobules were found also in the upper part of the lung; the bronchial glands were mottled black and white and were quite firm. The heart was flabby and contained clots. The liver, seventy-four ounces, was firm and of a light brown color, its acini comparatively distinct; the spleen, eleven ounces and a half, was soft and presented inferiorly a cyst containing half a drachm of fluid; the left kidney, five ounces, was slightly flabby and full of blood; the right kidney, four ounces and a half, was normal. The mucous membrane of the stomach was softened and free from folds. There were patches of intense congestion in the small intestine; some of Peyer's patches were ulcerated in the centre, some were neither ulcerated nor thickened and others near the valve contained black pigment and were ulcerated through to the peritoneum. The large intestine was quite thin.—*Lincoln Hospital, Washington, D. C.*

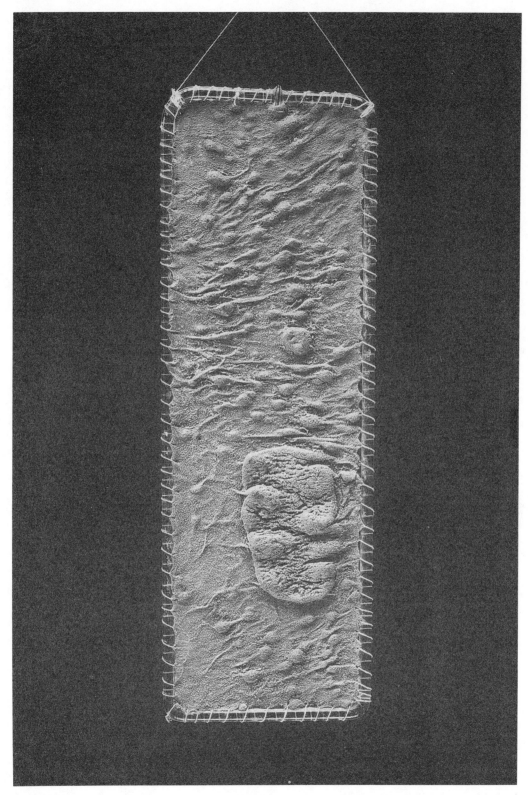

 James R. Osgood & Co., Boston.

THICKENED PEYER'S PATCH AND ENLARGED SOLITARY FOLLICLES.

No. 565.   MEDICAL SECTION.

CASE 149.—Private George Kiahl, Co. F, 39th N. J.; age 36; was admitted June 28, 1865, delirious and much exhausted. He had been sick ten days. The tympanites, which was present on admission, diminished, but was succeeded by profuse involuntary stools, with extreme exhaustion. He died July 9. *Post-mortem* examination twelve hours after death: The solitary follicles of the lower ileum were enlarged, congested and in some cases ulcerated; Peyer's patches were enlarged, pigmented and ulcerated. The remaining viscera were normal.—*Act. Ass't Surg. George P. Hanawalt, Douglas Hospital, Washington, D. C.*

CASE 150.—Private David Cline, Co. H, 191st Ohio; age 24; was admitted June 21, 1865, in a state of collapse, having been sick about ten days with diarrhœa. His mind was obtuse; his pulse slow and almost imperceptible; tongue dry and white; skin bathed in cold clammy sweat. Stimulants were freely administered and he rallied somewhat, but nausea and hiccough supervened, and he died on the 23d. *Post-mortem* examination: Heart pale and flabby; blood uncoagulated and very thin; peritoneum over ileum covered with a deposit of coagulable lymph; mucous membrane of ileum inflamed; glands of Peyer ulcerated; corresponding mesenteric glands highly inflamed.—*Act. Ass't Surg. H. J. Wiesel, Cumberland Hospital, Md.*

CASE 151.—Private Andrew M. Hyland, Co. D, 38th Mass.; age 21; was admitted Nov. 6, 1862, with typhoid fever, and died on the 10th. *Post-mortem* examination: Purulent effusion within the sheath of the rectus abdominis; exudation of lymph on the peritoneum, gluing the intestines together; ulceration of Peyer's patches; distention of gall-bladder by about four ounces of bile.—*Ass't Surg. H. Pierce, 150th N. Y., Stewart's Mansion Hospital, Baltimore, Md.*

CASE 152.—Private William N. Peake, Co. C, 19th Wis.; age 18; was admitted from the Army of the Potomac Sept. 9, 1864, having been sick two weeks with typhoid fever. On the 13th a pain, which had developed on the preceding day in the left iliac region, became diffused over the abdomen and was accompanied with much tympanites. He died next day. *Post-mortem* examination two hours after death: The intestines were adherent; more than two quarts of a yellowish-colored liquid, which had escaped in part from the intestinal tube, were found in the peritoneal cavity. The glands of Peyer near the ileo-cæcal valve were indurated at the edges and soft in the centre; in one of these patches the ulceration had perforated the peritoneum. [*Specimen* 810, Med. Sect., Army Medical Museum.]—*Act. Ass't Surg. J. H. Butler, West's Building Hospital, Baltimore, Md.*

CASE 153.—Private S. Emmons, 26th Ohio Bat'y; age 19; admitted Nov. 9, 1864, with typhoid fever. Died Dec. 11. *Post-mortem* examination: Body much emaciated. Peyer's patches extensively ulcerated, in many places as far as the peritoneum, which in some places was perforated.—*Act. Ass't Surg. J. T. Warner, Natchez Hospital, Miss.*

CASE 154.—Private J. C. Morrow, Co. E, 110th Ohio; admitted Nov. 23, 1863. Died 28th. *Post-mortem* examination thirty-nine hours after death: The brain was healthy. The lungs were somewhat engorged posteriorly. The heart was flabby and contained a small clot in both sides, larger in the right than in the left. The liver was firm and somewhat congested, its surface of an intense bluish-slate color, which coloration extended two lines into the parenchyma; the gall-bladder contained an ounce of dark-brown bile; the spleen was of a purple color with an admixture of brown and was extremely firm; the pancreas was white and not very firm. The ileum, in its six lower feet, was extensively ulcerated; about two feet above the ileo-cæcal valve was a Peyer's patch of an irregular circular shape, presenting three distinct ulcers with high blackish walls and stone-gray bases, in one of which was a small perforation which had caused some exudation of lymph on the peritoneal coat. The kidneys were healthy.—*Ass't Surg. H. Allen, U. S. A., Lincoln Hospital, Washington, D. C.*

CASE 155.—Sergeant James Geddis, Co. L, 6th Mich. Cav.; age 33; admitted Aug. 18, 1863. Died 22d. *Post-mortem* examination nineteen hours after death: The brain was firm and healthy. The trachea was of a dark-purple color, tinged with ochre on the rings; the bronchial tubes contained a dark grumous secretion. The œsophagus was yellowish throughout. The lungs were somewhat œdematous, the right weighing twenty ounces and the left twenty-one ounces. The heart was pushed upwards by the intestines; the right ventricle contained a fibrinous clot which extended some distance into the pulmonary artery; the left cavities contained a soft venous clot; the aorta was highly colored. The liver and stomach were concealed by the intestines; the liver was firm; the gall-bladder contained twelve drachms of dark-colored bile with a yellow flocculent deposit; the spleen was compact and of a dark-purple color; the pancreas was dark-green externally, hard and white internally. The intestines were much distended, evidently from cadaveric changes; the lower third of the small intestine was ulcerated in several places, in one of which there was a circular perforation with pale white edges, and the peritoneum surrounding it blackened to the extent of the Peyer's patch affected and covered with tough yellowish lymph for some distance beyond; the large intestine was healthy except that its solitary glands were conspicuous. The kidneys were dark-purple in color. —*Ass't Surg. H. Allen, U. S. A., Lincoln Hospital, Washington, D. C.*

CASE 156.—Private W. S. Doyle, Co. H, 3d Mich. Cav.; admitted June 14, 1863; died October 15. *Post-mortem* examination: Sudamina were observed, especially on the abdomen and arms. The brain-substance was very firm; the lining membrane of the ventricles was roughened, especially over the corpora striata and the descending crura of the fornix, where the roughness seemed like an exudation of lymph, but it could not be detached without destroying the cerebral substance; there was no meningitis. The trachea, dark purplish-red in color, presented numerous minute whitish points of exudation on the surface of the mucous membrane at its upper part. The œsophagus was of a pale purple color superiorly and of a brownish hue below; an abscess the size of a chestnut was found in its walls. Both lungs were congested; the right weighing sixteen ounces and one-quarter, the left twelve ounces and a half. The heart contained fibrinous clots in both sides. The liver was firm, its capsule easily torn, its acini distinct; the spleen was pultaceous. The stomach was mottled and filled with liquid greenish fæcal-like matter. The intestines were distended with air; patches of the peritoneal surface were of a bright crimson color and the coils of the small intestine were glued together with recent lymph; the duodenum was of a dark color, its villi softened and readily detached; the ileum was passively congested, its solitary glands enlarged, its agminated glands elevated and whitish, those near the ileo-cæcal valve forming elliptical ulcerated patches with high thickened walls and smooth pale bases, in many instances covered by a whitish adherent exudation, while in one instance the peritoneum formed the base and in another perforation had taken place; the large intestine was healthy. The kidneys were normal.—*Ass't Surg. H. Allen, U. S. A., Lincoln Hospital, Washington, D. C.*

CASE 157.—Corporal Cyrus B. Clark, Co. B, 15th Vt.; admitted Dec. 14, 1862, with continued fever; died 21st. *Post-mortem* examination: Peyer's glands were ulcerated and one of the ulcers had perforated. There was general peritonitis and a large quantity of serum in the abdominal cavity. The recti muscles, in their lower third, contained much extravasated blood.—*Third Division Hospital, Alexandria, Va.*

CASE 158.—Private John Clark, Co. E, 16th Va.; age 21; was admitted Nov. 13, 1862, presenting a hot skin, frequent feeble pulse, dry, dark and furred tongue, diarrhœa, tympanitic and tender bowels and slight dulness on percussion over the lower lobes of the lungs; there were no rose-spots nor sudamina. The patient apparently did well during the day and slept comfortably the greater part of the night, but towards morning he became delirious, after which he sank rapidly, and died during the day. *Post-mortem* examination: The middle and lower lobes of the right lung were engorged; the left lung was slightly congested. The heart was normal. The peritoneal cavity contained a large quantity of serum mingled with fæcal matter; the great omentum was engorged and the mesenteric glands enlarged. The small intestine was greatly discolored, in some places nearly black; its mucous membrane was reddened and engorged with black blood; the patches of Peyer were inflamed and ten of them ulcerated, two of the ulcers having perforated. The liver and spleen were enlarged but of normal consistence; the kidneys were normal.—*Third Division Hospital, Alexandria, Va.*

CASE 159.—Private Martin Hogle, Co. B, 5th N. Y. Cav.; age 27; was admitted Aug. 12, 1864, with well-marked symptoms of typhoid fever. He was delirious, the abdomen tympanitic and tender, the tongue furred and the pulse accelerated. He died on the 29th. There was no diarrhœa until within four days of death. *Post-mortem* examination on the day of death: Rigor mortis well marked; body moderately emaciated. The trachea was lined with frothy sputa of a molasses color; the right lung normal externally, was studded internally with melanic spots about the size of peas, it weighed twelve ounces; the left lung was healthy, it weighed seven ounces and a half. The right side of the heart contained a large firm black clot. A considerable quantity of pus was observed on the omentum; the spleen, fourteen ounces and a half, was firm and of a bluish-slate color; the liver, seventy-eight ounces, appeared to be normal; the kidneys were healthy. Peyer's patches were extensively ulcerated and the ulcers had perforated in five places; the large intestine was normal. [See Med. Sect., Army Medical Museum, 369 to 373, and also plate facing this page.]—*Act. Ass't Surg. H. M. Dean, Lincoln Hospital, Washington, D. C.*

(B.) Peyer's patches ulcerated and the large intestine also implicated—45 cases.

CASE 160.—Private James Kilgore, Co. D, 150th Ind.; age 30; was admitted April 25, 1865. It was at first supposed that this man was crazy, and his bed-card was marked accordingly: His manner was strange, his face flushed, his breath exceedingly offensive and his habits filthy; when asked his age he answered "about a hundred." On May 1 his pulse and respiration became frequent and he presented the physical signs of pneumonia. He died on the 3d. *Post-mortem* examination four hours after death: Suggillation on the chest and posteriorly; sudamina on the skin. There was some injection of the meninges and a moderate quantity of serum at the base of the brain. The right lung was engorged with blood and adherent to the thoracic parietes. The transverse colon was much constricted, not measuring more than eight lines in diameter; the mucous membrane of the ileum was inflamed and the patches of Peyer ulcerated. The spleen was very soft and enlarged to three times its ordinary size.—*Act. Ass't Surg. H. J. Wiesel, Cumberland Hospital, Md.*

CASE 161.—Private Norman Boyd, Co. B, 1st Conn. Heavy Art., was admitted July 25, 1864, in moribund condition; tongue dark brown, dry and cracked; sordes on teeth; involuntary passages from bowels. He died comatose next day. *Post-mortem* examination five hours after death: Body not much emaciated. The lungs were engorged and the pleuræ adherent. Peyer's glands were slightly ulcerated for the space of eight inches above the ileo-cæcal valve, and extending for six inches below it were twenty or thirty ulcers, several of which nearly perforated the intestine; the rest of the intestine was apparently healthy.—*Fairfax Seminary Hospital, Va.*

CASE 162.—Private Patrick Lynch, Co. A, 65th Ill.; age 17; was admitted July 20, 1865, with diarrhœa and constant delirium; he died on the 27th. *Post-mortem* examination: There was about an ounce of clear serum in each lateral ventricle and two ounces in the sub-arachnoid space. The posterior portions of both lungs were congested. Peyer's patches were greatly enlarged and ulcerated and the solitary glands enlarged. In the colon minute oval purpura-like spots were observed.—*Ass't Surg. Geo. M. McGill, U. S. A., Hicks Hospital, Baltimore, Md.*

CASE 163.—Private O. J. Richardson, Co. C, 108th N. Y., was admitted Nov. 23, 1863, in a comatose condition; pulse 120, just perceptible; tongue dry and fissured; breast and abdomen covered with sudamina and feet and legs cold. Stimulants were freely given and warmth applied to the feet. He died on the 27th. *Post-mortem* examination thirteen hours after death: Much emaciation; feet becoming gangrenous. Lungs, heart and spleen normal; Peyer's glands enlarged and ulcerated; solitary glands of large intestine enlarged and ulcerated; mesenteric glands enlarged.—*Act. Ass't Surg. W. H. Letterman, Douglas Hospital, Washington, D. C.*

CASE 164.—Private John Hutton, Co. D, 1st Vt. Cav., was admitted Nov. 23, 1863, delirious. He rolled from side to side in bed and picked at the bedclothes; his tongue and skin were dry, his pulse small and his feet cold;

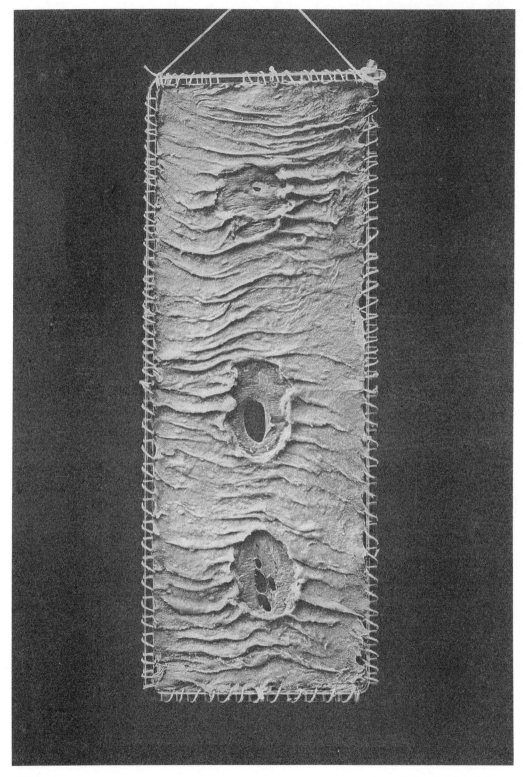

Heliotype.   *James R. Osgood & Co., Boston.*

PERFORATING ULCERS OF THE ILEUM.

No. 370. MEDICAL SECTION.

involuntary stools were passed frequently. Stimulants were given and warmth and mustard applied to his feet and legs. He died on the 27th. *Post-mortem* examination twelve hours after death: Body not emaciated; both feet gangrenous. Heart and lungs healthy. Spleen enlarged and of a dark-purple color; kidneys healthy; mesenteric glands enlarged; Peyer's glands enlarged and ulcerated; solitary glands of large intestine ulcerated.—*Act. Ass't Surg. W. H. Letterman, Douglas Hospital, Washington, D. C.*

CASE 165.—Sergeant Frank Donohue, Co. A, 17th Pa. Cav., was admitted Feb. 19, 1863, having been sick for two months with typhoid fever. He was completely deaf. On March 1 he had sore throat, severe headache and constipation. On the 15th his stomach became irritable and there was soreness in the bowels with diarrhœa. Later the stools became dark-looking but less frequent. He died on the 25th. *Post-mortem* examination forty-eight hours after death: Body well developed and not emaciated. The right lung weighed sixteen ounces and a half and the left twenty-one ounces and a quarter; posteriorly the lower lobe of the right lung was full of blackish-brown fluid, which also filled the bronchi; similar appearances were found in spots in the left lung. The heart weighed nine ounces and contained no clots; the aorta was somewhat contracted, deeply congested, and three inches beyond the semilunar valves was a cicatrix-like puckering with intense surrounding congestion. The liver was pale and weighed fifty-eight ounces and a half; the spleen soft, reddened, weighed twelve ounces and a half; the pancreas natural, three ounces and three-quarters; the stomach healthy. The mucous membrane of the upper part of the small intestine was yellowish and presented several roundish ulcers with well-defined edges in Peyer's patches and one patch, a half inch in diameter, enlarged and indurated; lower down the ulcers were more ragged and apparently did not involve Peyer's patches; in the last fifteen inches of the ileum the mucous membrane was of a reddish-slate color, the solitary glands brownish, and there were ragged excoriating ulcers in many of which was a thick yellowish exudation. The mucous membrane of the large intestine was of a dull slate color, presenting one ulcer on the ileo-cæcal valve, one at the commencement of the cæcum and a third four inches beyond. The kidneys were flabby and much congested.—*Ass't Surg. Harrison Allen, U. S. A., Lincoln Hospital, Washington, D. C.*

CASE 166.—Private John F. Chapman, Co. I, 32d Me.; age 35; was admitted July 2, 1864, with some irritability of the bowels, soreness of abdomen, slight tympanites, fever, great thirst, a dry furred tongue and a pulse of 110. He became afflicted with a troublesome cough on the 5th, which continued for some days, but on the 11th he was reported as improving. Two days later the stomach became irritable and the skin showed a tendency to slough. On the 14th he refused food and medicine, and next day he died. *Post-mortem* examination three hours after death: The right lung weighed fourteen ounces, the left fourteen ounces and a half; both were healthy except that there were a few softened tubercles in the upper lobe of each. The heart weighed eight ounces; its right ventricle contained a small fibrinous clot. The stomach was healthy. Peyer's patches were extensively ulcerated; the solitary glands showed many ulcers; the ileo-cæcal valve was much congested; the ascending colon presented two ulcers—the upper one, about the size of a pea, was superficial, the lower, five-eighths of an inch in diameter, penetrated to the peritoneum. The liver weighed sixty-nine ounces and was slightly congested; the gall-bladder contained five or six ounces of thin bile; the spleen weighed thirteen ounces.—*Act. Ass't Surg. James T. Logan, Lincoln Hospital, Washington, D. C.*

CASE 167.—Private Everett H. Felton, Co. G, 187th Pa.; age 28; was admitted Aug. 30, 1864, with an apparently mild attack of typhoid fever; but on September 20 a profuse diarrhœa supervened, and he died October 5. *Post-mortem* examination ten hours after death: Body much emaciated. Brain and thoracic viscera normal; a fibrinous clot in each side of the heart; spleen and kidneys normal; several Peyer's patches and solitary follicles ulcerated; numerous small ulcers in the large intestine.—*Act. Ass't Surg. H. M. Dean, Lincoln Hospital, Washington, D. C.*

CASE 168.—Private Lewis Weir, Co. A, 202d Pa.; age 18; admitted Nov. 2, 1864. Typhoid fever. Died on the 7th. *Post-mortem* examination forty hours after death: Rigor mortis well marked; suggillation posteriorly; no emaciation. On the upper surface of the cerebral hemispheres, anteriorly along the course of the large bloodvessels, there was in several places a gelatinous subarachnoid deposit; the subarachnoid space contained one ounce and a half of serum. The right pleural cavity contained two ounces and the left four ounces of dark bloody serum; the posterior part of the right lung was engorged and small portions of its upper and middle lobes were hepatized; the left lung was congested posteriorly. The intestines were distended with air; Peyer's patches in the lower part of the ileum were ulcerated in several places; the solitary follicles of the cæcum and of the first six inches of the colon were ulcerated; the remainder of the large intestine was normal; the mesenteric glands adjacent to the ulcerated intestinal glands were enlarged and dark-colored. The spleen was enlarged and softened.—*Act. Ass't Surg. Thomas Bowen, Second Division Hospital, Alexandria, Va.*

CASE 169.—Private Joseph Gilly, Co. D, 6th Pa. Heavy Art.; age 47; was admitted Oct. 30, 1864, with typhoid fever, and died November 3. *Post-mortem* examination nine hours after death: Marked rigor mortis; slight emaciation; suggillation posteriorly. Lungs very dark, filled with blood; bronchi slightly congested; bronchial glands normal; ventricles of heart dilated and containing small dark clots; liver enlarged, pale; spleen enlarged, darkened, much softened; mucous coat of stomach and jejunum normal; Peyer's patches in the lower two feet of ileum and solitary follicles of first six inches of colon thickened and ulcerated; mesenteric glands enlarged, filled with dark matter, especially three near the cæcum; kidneys congested.—*Second Division Hospital, Alexandria, Va.*

CASE 170.—Private John Verberson, Co. B, 35th Mass.; age 33; was admitted Nov. 30, 1864, convalescing from typhoid fever. He was much debilitated and had a severe diarrhœa. He died December 16. *Post-mortem* examination ten hours after death: Sudamina on legs and breast; slight suggillation posteriorly. Some pleuritic adhesions on the right side; emphysema of both lungs; puckering of middle lobe of right lung; three ounces of pale serum in pericardium; enlargement of liver; congestion and in some places ulceration of Peyer's patches; congestion of cæcum.—*Third Division Hospital, Alexandria, Va.*

CASE 171.—Private George Wood, Co. B, 1st Bat'y, 2d Me. Light Art.; age 24; was admitted July 25, 1864, in very low condition. He died comatose on the following day. *Post-mortem* examination twenty-two hours after death: Body extremely emaciated. Stomach and intestinal canal greatly inflamed; large intestine much ulcerated; liver fatty; gall-bladder enormously distended; other organs healthy. [*Specimen* 420, Med. Sect., Army Medical Museum, which is from this case, shows several large ulcers of Peyer's patches just above the ileo-cæcal valve, penetrating in some places to the transverse muscle and in others to the peritoneum, as also some enlarged and ulcerated solitary follicles.]—*Surg. E. Bentley, U. S. V., Third Division Hospital, Alexandria, Va.*

CASE 172.—Private Joseph Swartz, Co. M, 2d U. S. Cav.; age 22; was admitted June 12, 1863, for a contusion of the chest. On July 5 he was placed on duty as nurse, but on the 26th he became attacked with typhoid fever which proved fatal on August 10. *Post-mortem* examination seventeen hours after death: Slight emaciation; commencing decomposition. Lungs slightly congested; heart healthy, a fibrinous clot in the left ventricle. Stomach and liver healthy; spleen firm but nearly double its normal size. Peyer's patches in the lower part of the ileum ulcerated, the surrounding mucous membrane much congested and the corresponding mesenteric glands enlarged. Cæcum presenting one ulcer; the remainder of the large intestine healthy.—*Act. Ass't Surg. J. H. Hutchinson, Satterlee Hospital, Philadelphia, Pa.*

CASE 173.—Private John Flowers, Co. M, 5th Pa. Cav., was admitted June 9, 1862, with rheumatism, and died July 29 of typhoid fever. *Post-mortem* examination on the day of death: Effusion of serum into the pericardium, amounting to about one-third of a pint or more; no evidence of pericarditis except a more than usual redness of the surface of the left ventricle; indications of a recent pleurisy, with the formation of pseudo-membrane on the right side, the corresponding pleural cavity filled with serous effusion. The mucous membrane of the large intestine presented patches of inflammation but no ulceration; that of the ileum was more intensely inflamed and all the agminated glands were ulcerated, in most instances as far as the muscular coat and in two instances to the peritoneum, though the latter was not inflamed.—*Act. Ass't Surg. Joseph Leidy, Satterlee Hospital, Philadelphia, Pa.*

CASE 174.—Private George Young, Co. and Reg't not recorded, was admitted Aug. 10, 1862, and died on the 13th. He was delirious from the time of his admission. *Post-mortem* examination same day: Age apparently between 35 and 40; body much emaciated; about a dozen scattered rose-colored spots on thorax and abdomen. The organs of the chest, the stomach, liver, spleen, pancreas and kidneys appeared natural. The small intestine was inflamed throughout; its agminated glands were ulcerated, the ulceration exposing the muscular coat; the mucous membrane of the lower part of the ileum was of a livid purple; the agminated glands, together with a portion of the surrounding mucous and sub-mucous tissue, were completely destroyed, leaving patches of exposed transverse muscular fibre inclosed by thickened ridges of the mucous membrane. [*Specimen* 239, Med. Sect., Army Medical Museum.] The lining membrane of the colon was slightly inflamed and of a slate-color. The solitary glands of the small and large intestines were not conspicuously diseased.—*Act. Ass't Surg. Joseph Leidy, Satterlee Hospital, Philadelphia, Pa.*

CASE 175.—Private Benjamin Allen, Co. H, 1st Ohio, was admitted Dec. 23, 1862, with typhoid fever and erysipelas of head and face; he died on the 26th. *Post-mortem* examination next day: Body fat; left side of head and neck discolored by erysipelas. Brain healthy but pia mater somewhat injected on left side and slight effusion in subarachnoid space. Lungs and heart, liver, stomach, pancreas and kidneys healthy. Spleen enlarged, seven by five by two and a half inches, very flabby, bluish on the surface and marked with dark reticular lines; mucous membrane of ileum and colon moderately inflamed; intestinal glands healthy except in the lower three feet of the ileum, where the agminated glands were much enlarged and ulcerated. [*Specimens* 112–114, Med. Sect., Army Medical Museum, are from this case.]—*Act. Ass't Surg. Joseph Leidy, Satterlee Hospital, Philadelphia, Pa.*

CASE 176.—Private Sidney Church, Co. A, 189th N. Y.; admitted Jan. 17, 1865; died 21st. *Post-mortem* examination: Lungs normal; heart flabby; liver healthy; spleen fourteen ounces, softened; duodenum and jejunum healthy; Peyer's patches of ileum ulcerated, the ulcers cup-shaped and round; ileo-cæcal valve much thickened; colon for eighteen inches filled with clotted blood, below which the solitary follicles were not enlarged.—*Ass't Surg. H. Loewenthal, U. S. V., Fifth Army Corps Field Hospital, Army of Potomac.*

CASE 177.—Private Silas N. Peterson, Co. D, 38th Mass.; age 25; was admitted Nov. 5, 1862, with typhoid fever, and died on the 10th. *Post-mortem* examination: Inflammation and ulceration of Peyer's patches and of the colon near the caput; much enlargement of the mesenteric glands.—*Act. Ass't Surg. T. F. Murdoch, Stewart's Mansion Hospital, Baltimore, Md.*

CASE 178.—Private C. M. Kelsey, Co. M, 14th N. Y. Heavy Art., was admitted July 24, 1864, having been sick since the 7th with diarrhœa and fever. He died on the 28th. *Post-mortem* examination on day of death: Lungs and heart healthy. Peyer's patches were inflamed and slightly ulcerated; several ulcers were found in the large intestine; the mesenteric glands were much enlarged and softened. The spleen was five inches long by three broad and rather soft; the kidneys were large and fatty.—*Fairfax Seminary Hospital, Va.*

CASE 179.—Private H. Richardson, Co. C, 13th E. Tenn. Cav., was admitted Jan. 22, 1864, with typhoid fever, and died February 6. *Post-mortem* examination forty-eight hours after death: Body emaciated; rigor well marked. The brain, lungs, heart and solid abdominal viscera were healthy. The stomach was injected; Peyer's patches ulcerated throughout the entire length of the ileum; the mucous membrane of the large intestine inflamed and thickened; the mesenteric glands enlarged.—*Act. Ass't Surg. G. W. Roberts, Hospital No. 19, Nashville, Tenn.*

CASE 180.—Private Robert Traut, Co. A, 10th E. Tenn. Cav., was admitted Jan. 29, 1864, with typhoid fever. He died February 6. *Post-mortem* examination twenty hours after death: Body emaciated; rigor slight. The membranes of the brain were slightly injected. The lungs weighed sixty ounces and the pleural cavities contained two ounces of liquid; the heart was healthy. The liver was pale but seemingly healthy; the spleen congested, weighing fifteen ounces; the kidneys, especially the left, congested. The mucous membrane of the stomach was inflamed and softened, as was that of the small intestine and colon; Peyer's glands were ulcerated and the mesenteric glands, in some instances, as large as a chestnut.—*Act. Ass't Surg. G. W. Roberts, Hospital No. 19, Nashville, Tenn.*

CASE 181.—Private Ira A. Sperry, Co. D, 147th N. Y.; age 24; was admitted June 15, 1863, with typhoid fever, and died on the 22d. *Post-mortem* examination twenty-five hours after death: Body not emaciated. Brain healthy. Mucous membrane of trachea much congested; upper lobe of right lung somewhat congested, middle lobe more natural, lower lobe extremely congested, weight of lung sixteen ounces; upper lobe of left lung congested, weight of lung fifteen ounces and a half. Right cavities of heart contained fibrinous clots; left mixed clots. Liver, sixty-five ounces, flabby, mottled cineritious and deep purple; about the middle of the anterior surface of the right lobe was a large white spot coated with lymph, indicative probably of previous inflammation. Œsophagus normal; stomach of a dull gray color; spleen firm, dark mahogany colored, weight eleven ounces and a quarter, an opaque spot covered with recent lymph on its upper surface; pancreas firm and white, weight two ounces and a half. Duodenum somewhat congested; jejunum and upper part of ileum normal; mucous membrane of lower part of ileum thin, pale and easily torn; Peyer's patches elevated, dark slate-colored; solitary glands prominent; ulceration present but nowhere extensive. Large intestine dull greenish in color but not ulcerated. Left kidney flabby, slightly injected, somewhat friable and with many ecchymosed blotches on pelvis; bladder much distended with urine.—*Ass't Surg. Harrison Allen, U. S. A., Lincoln Hospital, Washington, D. C.*

CASE 182.—Private William Gibbings, Co. F, 5th Mich.; age 35; was admitted April 21, 1864, with typhoid fever, and died May 12. *Post-mortem* examination twenty-three hours after death: The brain weighed fifty ounces. The mucous membrane of the larynx and trachea was somewhat congested. The right lung weighed thirty-two ounces, its lower lobe hepatized red, its upper lobe gray and the pleural surfaces adherent; the left lung weighed nineteen ounces. The heart was flabby; there were three drachms of light-red fluid in the pericardium. The œsophagus was healthy; the cardiac end of the stomach reddish-brown and much softened; the mucous membrane of the duodenum much congested; the solitary follicles of the ileum and Peyer's patches ulcerated, some of the ulcers penetrating to the peritoneum; a small triangular piece of bone was found in the appendix vermiformis; the mucous membrane of the large intestine was much congested and softened. The liver, fifty-nine ounces and a half, was flabby and anæmic; there were six drachms of gamboge-colored liquid in the gall-bladder; the spleen eleven ounces and a half, was pulpy, its capsule easily separated and presenting on its superior surface a "round white body resembling bone." The right kidney weighed five ounces, the left five ounces and a half; both were soft and flabby.—*Act. Ass't Surg. A. Ansell, Lincoln Hospital, Washington, D. C.*

CASE 183.—Private Peter W. Backoven, Co. G, 8th N. Y. Cav.; age about 21; admitted Aug. 18, 1863; died 26th. *Post-mortem* examination: Body not much emaciated; rigor mortis great. The brain weighed fifty-one ounces and a half; the surface of the cerebellum was slightly red and the vessels of the pia mater filled with a purplish fluid; the interior of the brain was normal. The larynx and trachea were pale, the portions between the rings of a light purple hue. The œsophageal mucous membrane was pale gray in the upper part, becoming tawny or purplish further down, and considerably corrugated both longitudinally and transversely. The right lung weighed eleven ounces and a half, the left twelve ounces and a half; both were somewhat congested in their lower lobes. The heart was healthy, its right ventricle contained a fibrinous clot; the liquid of the pericardium was decidedly reddish in color and measured six drachms. The liver weighed fifty-seven ounces, its surface purple with a few scattered yellowish maculæ, its section paler than usual but firm; the mucous membrane of the stomach near the pylorus was somewhat marbled; the spleen, nineteen ounces and a half, was firm and of a chocolate color; the pancreas was normal. Peyer's patches in the lower part of the ileum were elevated, white and covered with small ulcerations, a few of the patches were congested; the large intestine was purple in its upper part, becoming paler towards the rectum. The kidneys were firm; on section a small quantity of venous blood flowed from the cut edges of the pyramids; the right supra-renal capsule was yellowish-white internally and did not contain the usual brown fluid; the left capsule was darker in color and contained a small quantity of brownish fluid.—*Ass't Surg. Harrison Allen, U. S. A., Lincoln Hospital, Washington, D. C.*

CASE 184.—Private Abram Beeker, Co. H, 14th U. S. Inf.; age 39; was admitted May 11, 1864, with a gunshot flesh wound of the left heel. He contracted typhoid fever while in hospital, but had apparently convalesced; his appetite improved, and he gained strength during the last two days of his life; he was walking about within ten minutes of his death on July 30. *Post-mortem* examination seventeen hours after death: Body well nourished. The lungs contained much frothy, bloody fluid; the right weighed nineteen ounces and three-quarters, the left nineteen ounces. The heart was flabby and contained a small soft fibrinous clot in the right ventricle. The liver was flabby and dark-colored; the spleen weighed thirteen ounces and three-quarters. In the ileum Peyer's patches were congested, near the ileo-cæcal valve ulcerated; some of the solitary glands also were ulcerated. The large intestine was somewhat congested in its upper portion.—*Act. Ass't Surg. H. M. Dean, Lincoln Hospital, Washington, D. C.*

CASE 185.—Private Jos. S. Nelson, 6th Me. Bat'y; age 45; was admitted Oct. 19, 1863, with typhoid fever, and died Nov. 24. *Post-mortem* examination next day: Body greatly emaciated. The brain was healthy. The epiglottis was lined on the posterior surface with an exudation and ulcerated on either side of the free border, the ulceration being confined to the mucous membrane, which was of a palish pink color and thickened around the edges of the ulcers; an irregular ulcer, with pinkish walls, was seen on the left side of the larynx immediately below the vocal cord and a smaller ulceration of similar appearance in the angle of the thyroid cartilage. The posterior portion of the pharynx opposite the epiglottis was the seat of a superficial ulcer; the œsophagus was pale and filled with a whitish curd-like mass, at first supposed to be a retained portion of ingesta, but on careful examination found to be a true exudation. The right lung weighed twenty-seven ounces; the posterior part of its upper lobe was quite œdematous, its bronchi prominent, feeling like millet-seed under the fingers, and their mucous lining everywhere of a dark-purple color; the posterior surface of the lobe was coated to the extent of an inch and a half with a thick whitish membrane; the lower lobe posteriorly was much compressed by a circumscribed pleuritic effusion measuring fourteen ounces. The weight of the left lung was thirty-two ounces; its upper lobe presented the same general appearance as that of the right side; the bronchial tubes were everywhere prominent, in some parts giving the feel of a cirrhosed liver; the lower portion of the lung was of a dark-purple flesh-color, friable and heavier than water. The heart contained but little clot in its right side and none in its left. The liver was dark and tolerably firm, weighing fifty-seven ounces; the gall-bladder was very prominent and contained twenty drachms of thin brown bile; the spleen weighed seven ounces and was of a dark mahogany color and quite firm. Peyer's patches and the lower portion of the small intestine were ulcerated; the large intestine was also ulcerated and of a stone-gray hue alternating with patches of a dull lardaceous appearance; the ulceration was of the punctated form. A large gangrenous abscess was found on the right of the anus extending deeply into the right buttock; its external opening was small. Just before death a severe hemorrhage had taken place from this abscess; several very large, firm, blackish clots were found in its cavity. It was supposed from the examination that this communicated with the rectum, but the passage to that gut was obtained with some difficulty, and it is not improbable that the force used in manipulation produced the communication. No flatus or excrementitious matter had escaped during life.—*Ass't Surg. Harrison Allen, U. S. A., Lincoln Hospital, Washington, D. C.*

CASE 186.—Private Martin Stevens, Co. D, 7th N. C.; age 33; was admitted May 20, 1864, with typhoid fever, and died on the 24th. *Post-mortem* examination sixteen hours after death: Body rather spare. Lungs congested throughout; left ventricle of heart dilated; small intestine much inflamed; solitary follicles and Peyer's patches ulcerated; large intestine inflamed; mesenteric glands enlarged and softened; liver and kidneys normal; spleen much enlarged and congested.—*Lincoln Hospital, Washington, D. C.*

CASE 187.—Sergeant John Link, Co. A, 107th Ohio, was admitted June 15, 1863, delirious, and died on the 17th. *Post-mortem* examination ten hours after death: The brain was normal. The trachea was purple; its mucous membrane firm; the bronchial glands at its bifurcation large. The lower part of the œsophagus was of a pale yellowish color and presented ulcers of the same hue; its mucous membrane was not softened. The right lung weighed nineteen ounces and a half and was congested in its lower and in part of its upper lobe; the lower lobe of the left lung was somewhat engorged. The heart was normal and contained a fibrinous clot in its right side. The liver was large and dark-colored, extending entirely across the body; the gall-bladder contained three ounces and six drachms of bile. The stomach was immensely distended and occupied the greater portion of the abdomen in an oblique position; its mucous membrane was softened and presented several minute black spots towards the pylorus; between its superior curvature and the gall-bladder was a small quantity of recent lymph. The small intestine was contracted; its mucous membrane was softened and varied in color from light pink to deep purple; the jejunum was filled with a glairy tenacious mass; the last two feet of the ileum presented well defined ulceration of Peyer's patches, the ulcers being mostly circular with ragged walls and an irregular base, which was generally stained of a dull-ochre color by the intestinal contents; near the ileo-cæcal valve several of the ulcers ran together, forming a large ulcerated area, which, with its black indurated walls and yellowish base, stood out in strong relief against the purple, livid and congested mucous membrane. The large intestine was also much contracted, its rugæ elevated and coated with a tenacious mucoid secretion; no ulcers were found in it. The right kidney was congested, and several small spots of transuded blood were noticed on its external surface; the pelvis of the left kidney was similarly discolored.—*Ass't Surg. H. Allen, U. S. A., Lincoln Hospital, Washington, D. C.*

CASE 188.—Private John Walford, Co. F, 2d U. S. Colored troops, was admitted Jan. 17, 1866, in a moribund condition; tongue parched; teeth and lips covered with sordes. Stimulants were freely used, but he died next day. There is no detailed record of the autopsy, but the whole intestinal canal was received at the Museum. The ileum showed hypertrophied villi and progressive thickening and ulceration of the solitary follicles and Peyer's patches; many solitary glands in the colon were enlarged to the size of peas and ulcerated on their summits. [See Med. Sect., Army Medical Museum, 707 and 708.]—*Surg. R. B. Bontecou, U. S. V., Harewood Hospital, Washington, D. C.*

CASE 189.—Corporal Walter Angel, Co. K, 10th N. Y. Cav.; admitted Aug. 17, 1863, with typhoid fever. Died 20th. *Post-mortem* examination: Body slightly emaciated. The lungs, heart and pericardium were normal. The liver was congested; the gall-bladder somewhat distended; the spleen enlarged and congested, weight eleven ounces. The mesenteric and meso-colic glands were much enlarged and there was considerable venous congestion of the intestinal peritoneum. The mucous membrane of the lower jejunum and ileum was congested in patches, the congestion increasing progressively downwards, the last two feet being much congested, with, in the last six inches, several deep circular ulcers having yellow bases and raised edges; Peyer's patches were not elsewhere ulcerated. The colon was of a deep mahogany color, especially in the ascending portion. The pyramids of the kidneys were congested, the cortical substance pale.—*Harewood Hospital, Washington, D. C.*

CASE 190.—Private H. G. W. Stoner, Co. A, 14th U. S. Inf.; admitted Oct. 10, 1863, with typhoid fever. Died 13th. *Post-mortem* examination: The lungs were normal excepting a slight adhesion to the pericardium on the left side. The right cavities of the heart were dilated and filled with fluid blood; their walls were thinned. The liver weighed sixty-four ounces; the spleen twelve ounces. The stomach and the upper part of the duodenum were much congested. The ileum was congested, especially in its lower part, which was thickened and inflamed and in Peyer's patches ulcerated; the ileo-cæcal valve was much thickened and ulcerated. The mucous membrane of the colon was congested and softened and hundreds of its solitary follicles were ulcerated; the rectum also was congested and softened. The kidneys were congested.—*Harewood Hospital, Washington, D. C.*

CASE 191.—Private Martin Riley, Co. C, 122d Pa.; admitted April 21, 1863. Continued fever. Died May 24. *Post-mortem* examination twenty hours after death: The body was much emaciated. The lungs were healthy, but the bronchial tubes contained a purulent secretion. The heart was softened and pale; a small point of pus was found at its apex; the mitral valve was thickened and slightly roughened. The stomach was nearly filled with bile. The liver was healthy; the gall-bladder nearly empty. The duodenum and jejunum were normal; the ileum inflamed and Peyer's patches ulcerated; the ascending colon congested in spots, the transverse and descending portions healthy. The kidneys were normal.—*Act. Ass't Surg. A. H. Haven, Harewood Hospital, Washington, D. C.*

CASE 192.—Private John Hause, Co. H, 175th Pa.; age 35; admitted July 6, 1863. Died 12th. *Post-mortem* examination: Body slightly emaciated. Liver healthy; gall-bladder distended with bile; spleen somewhat enlarged, much congested and very soft; duodenum and jejunum healthy; ileum much inflamed and its agminated and solitary glands ulcerated, but some of the ulcers appeared to be healing; solitary follicles of ascending colon enlarged and ulcerated. Kidneys healthy.—*Act. Ass't Surg. Lloyd Dorsey, Harewood Hospital, Washington, D. C.*

CASE 193.—Private Frederick Wolfanger, Co. C, 93d N. Y.; age 43; was admitted Oct. 24, 1863, and died November 18. *Post-mortem* examination thirty hours after death: Body much emaciated. Brain healthy. The left parotid gland was the seat of suppurative inflammation; the pus had discharged from two openings, one in the mouth, between the tongue and the inferior maxilla, the other externally, between the mastoid process and clavicle. The left lobe of the thyroid gland contained a calcareous mass as large as a walnut, and in its upper portion a cyst the size of a pea, filled with a dark-brown fluid; the right lobe contained a cyst the size of a small chestnut, and in its lower portion an apoplectic extravasation one inch and a half long by one inch in width. The right lung weighed forty-seven ounces and a half; its lobes were interadherent but not attached to the ribs; the lateral and posterior parts were œdematous. The left lung resembled the other, but contained a greater quantity of blood in many places, the parenchyma being of a darker hue. The bronchial tubes were thickened and their mucous membrane reddish; a yellow tenacious mucus was contained in the smaller tubes, giving a granular appearance to a section of the lung. Both sides of the heart contained mixed fibrinous and dark clots; its muscular tissue was much softer than usual. The liver was normal; the spleen soft, flabby and of a turbid purple color. The intestines were of a dark grayish color; Peyer's patches were ulcerated in places but were not elevated. The kidneys were slightly congested.—*Ass't Surg. H. Allen, U. S. A., Lincoln Hospital, Washington, D. C.*

CASE 194.—Private Walter Wisner, Co. F, 6th Mich. Cav.; age 28; was admitted July 30, 1863, with typhoid fever, and died August 3. *Post-mortem* examination eighteen hours after death: The brain weighed fifty-three ounces; both lobes of the cerebrum were highly congested, especially in their superior and anterior portions, which were in part of a brilliant crimson color. The tracheal mucous membrane was of a deep dull-purplish red; the trachea and bronchi contained a thin bloody liquid instead of the normal secretion; the veins under the mucous membrane of the larynx were distended; the lymphatic glands at the bifurcation of the trachea were large, soft and engorged with black blood. The lungs were of a delicate pink color; the external and lateral portions of the upper lobes and the whole of the lower lobes were doughy, semi-solidified and engorged with dark blood mixed with a frothy bronchial secretion; the right lung weighed twenty-five ounces, the left twenty-four ounces. The cavities of the heart were free from clots, except a very thin wafer-like formation on the tricuspid valve. The liver was flabby and somewhat congested; the spleen, sixteen ounces, was grayish-purple in color and unusually firm. The intestines were diseased throughout: the mucous membrane of the upper portion was flaccid, softened and easily torn, the valvulæ conniventes of an orange-ochre color; Peyer's patches were enlarged, elevated above the surrounding mucous membrane, whitish in color and ulcerated, none of the ulcerated points being larger than the head of a pin; the solitary glands were also affected and, in the neighborhood of the valve, the mucous membrane was completely nodulated with shot-like eminences; the mucous membrane of the last six feet of the ileum, which was the part chiefly involved, was of a dark-red color and its veins were very prominent. The kidneys were slightly congested, soft and flaccid.—*Ass't Surg. Harrison Allen, U. S. A., Lincoln Hospital, Washington, D. C.*

CASE 195.—Private Vincent Hogle, Co. E, 5th Mich.; age 33; was admitted March 24, 1864, and died on the 26th. *Post-mortem* examination: Lungs and pleuræ inflamed; much effusion in right cavity. Intestines inflamed nearly throughout; Peyer's patches ulcerated.—*Third Division Hospital, Alexandria, Va.*

CASE 196.—Private John Sullivan, Co. B, 1st Mass. Cav., was admitted July 2, 1864, and died on the 11th. *Post-mortem* examination: Much emaciation. Lungs extensively inflamed; heart, liver and spleen healthy; stomach and intestines much inflamed; Peyer's patches slightly ulcerated.—*Third Division Hospital, Alexandria, Va.*

CASE 197.—Private James Foster, Co. I, 83d Pa.; age 19; admitted April 19, 1864; died 22d. *Post-mortem* examination twenty-four hours after death: The lungs, liver and spleen were normal. The glands of the intestines were enlarged, ulcerated and almost disintegrated.—*Third Division Hospital, Alexandria, Va.*

CASE 198.—Private Alonzo Wilkinson, Co. A, 20th Me., was admitted Aug. 21, 1864, having about five or six alvine evacuations daily, with some pain in the right side and slight dyspnœa; pulse 120; tongue dry and covered with a brown fur. The patient continued with but little change in his symptoms other than a temporary abatement of the diarrhœa and aggravation of the lung trouble, together with increasing prostration, until delirium came on, and death occurred on the 27th. *Post-mortem* examination six hours after death; Body not emaciated; rigor mortis great. The right lung was generally congested and its middle lobe hepatized; the left lung was congested posteriorly. The pericardium contained two ounces of liquid; the right cavities of the heart were filled with a large partially washed clot. The liver was enlarged and pale; the gall-bladder distended with viscid bile; the spleen enlarged and soft. The stomach was inflated with gas, dilated and flabby, and its mucous membrane was reddened near the pylorus. In the lower half of the ileum the agminated glands were congested, enlarged and prominent, and those near the ileo-cæcal valve showed small ulcers; the mucous membrane around the glands was more or less congested according to its proximity or distance from the valve; the solitary follicles were enlarged and prominent. No ulcers were found in the large intestine, which, however, was congested throughout and dotted with black pigment, particularly in the descending colon, where an occasional large black spot appeared. [*Specimens* 398 and 399, Med. Sect., Army Medical Museum, were taken from this case.]—*Act. Ass't Surg. O. P. Sweet, Carver Hospital, Washington, D. C.*

CASE 199.—Private Wm. S. Armstrong, Co. B, 7th Me.; age 21; was admitted June 14, 1863, with high fever and delirium, a furred and fissured tongue, sordes on the teeth, frequent retching and diarrhœa, the stools numbering about twenty daily. He was much emaciated and so weak as to be unable to sit up. During the next few days his stools became less frequent, but on the 19th the passages were involuntary, the delirium continued, the pulse, which had fallen from 120 to 80, was very weak, the countenance pinched, the extremities cool, the perspiration cold. He died on the 20th. *Post-mortem* examination fourteen hours after death: The brain was healthy. The mucous membrane of the œsophagus was of a bright-ochre color and rather softened; the trachea was of a dark-purple color, its mucous membrane slightly softened. The lower lobe of the right lung and the whole of the left lung were congested. The endocardium was somewhat darkened; the right ventricle contained a fibrinous clot; the aorta was reddish. The surface of the liver was generally of a grayish-blue color, but anteriorly the right lobe presented a more healthy appearance; minute collections of air were disseminated throughout the parenchyma of this organ, which was softened, of the color of sanious pus and possessed of a disagreeable odor; the air-cavities and the transverse section of the portal veins gave a honey-combed appearance to the interior; Glisson's capsule was smooth and easily torn. The mucous lining of the stomach was of a dark-slate color but healthy. The spleen, fifteen ounces and a half, was unusually firm and of a deep mulberry color; the pancreas was healthy. The intestines were distended with air; the mucous membrane of the upper portion of the small intestine was of a light-yellow color; in the lower third Peyer's patches were ulcerated and the mucous membrane, in some places very pale, was in others intensely injected; at the ileo-cæcal valve it was indurated, thickened and blackened and in the large intestine pale and irregularly dotted with blackish spots. A cavity containing about four drachms of pus was found between the peritoneum and the cellular tissue on the right side of the abdomen, about two inches below the diaphragm; the omentum was healthy. The kidneys resembled the liver in having air-cavities disseminated through their parenchyma; the distinction between the cortical and pyramidal portions was almost obliterated, the latter being purplish; the organs generally were tumid and flabby. Two large bed-sores were noted, one over the sacrum, the other over the great trochanter of the right femur.—*Ass't Surg. Harrison Allen, U. S. A., Lincoln Hospital, Washington, D. C.*

CASE 200.—Private R. L. Tyler, Co. E, 17th U. S. Inf.; age 23; was admitted Aug. 10, 1862, and died on the 16th. *Post-mortem* examination: The mucous membrane of the ileum was not generally inflamed, being of a pinkish-cream color; there were twenty-two agminated glands, varying in size from half an inch to one which was four inches in length; the twelve upper patches were healthy, the thirteenth ulcerated, the fourteenth healthy and the remainder ulcerated, some even through to the peritoneum; the last of the series, near the ileo-cæcal valve, formed a blackish-brown, irregular eschar about an inch and a quarter square and the fourth of an inch thick [see plate facing this page]; in the vicinity of the ulcerated glands the mucous membrane was inflamed. The colon was inflamed in patches, and its solitary glands were prominent and contained a deposit of black pigment, which was observed also in the agminated and solitary glands of the ileum. [*Specimens* 240 and 241, Med. Sect., Army Medical Museum, are from this case.]—*Act. Ass't Surg. Joseph Leidy, Satterlee Hospital, Philadelphia, Pa.*

CASE 201.—Private Lorenzo H. Cox, Co. C, 6th Vt.; admitted August 10, 1862. Typhoid fever. Died Sept. 7. *Post-mortem* examination next day: Age about 25 years; emaciation extreme; diffuse ecchymoses on skin of body. Lungs healthy; heart natural, containing some liquid blood and a soft black clot in the right ventricle. Spleen small, lake-red on section; liver dull-brown above, slate-color below and uniformly brown on section. Stomach moderately distended, its mucous membrane dirty gray with some vascular injection; ileum and colon inflamed in patches; agminated glands containing black deposit, but otherwise healthy, except two near the colon, which were slightly ulcerated; solitary glands everywhere pigmented.—*Act. Ass't Surg. J. Leidy, Satterlee Hospital, Philadelphia, Pa.*

CASE 202.—Sergeant Samuel Kelley, Co. E, 23d N. Y., was admitted Dec. 23, 1862, with a gunshot wound, and died Jan. 15, 1863. *Post-mortem* examination next day: Age about 30 years; no emaciation; a few faint reddish spots on the abdomen. Vessels of brain distended with blood. Lungs and heart healthy. Liver pale Indian-red on surface and on section; spleen enlarged, six by four by two and a half inches, rather soft and on section like black currant-jelly. Colon pale gray with slate-colored streaks and reddish spots, its solitary glands containing black matter; ileum generally pale, but with streaks and patches of moderate inflammation, its solitary glands enlarged, some to the size of pepper grains, and its agminated glands enlarged, several ulcerated and with ochre-yellow adherent granulations.—*Act. Ass't Surg. Joseph Leidy, Satterlee Hospital, Philadelphia, Pa.*

CASE 203.—Private Moses Burkett, Co. A, 12th U. S. Inf.; admitted Aug. 10, 1862. Typhoid fever. Died Sept. 9. *Post-mortem* examination same day: Age about 20 years; emaciation; slight petechial marks on breast and abdomen. Right lung with old pleuritic adhesions throughout; left with adhesions at apex of upper lobe; small tubercles, few in number, from the size of hempseed to that of a pea, deposited in the pleura pulmonalis, pleura costalis and superficial tissue of both lungs. Heart flabby, with a large, transparent, fibrinous clot in the left ventricle but none in the right.

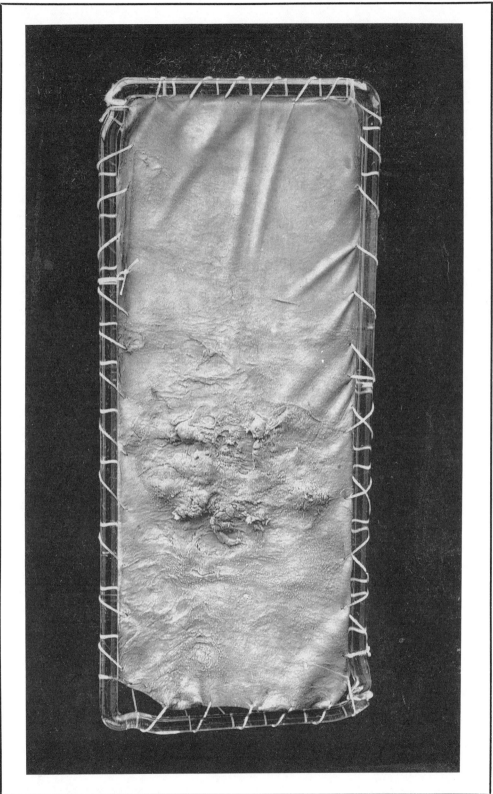

Am. Photo-Relief Printing Co.,   1002 Arch St., Philadelphia.

SLOUGHING PEYER'S PATCH.

No. 241. MEDICAL SECTION.

Peritoneum everywhere strewed with small tubercles from the size of mustard-seed to that of hempseed, in greatest abundance in the pelvis, where they were accompanied with peritonitis, the bowels adhering by recent pseudo-membranous matter; mesenteric glands and, indeed, all the abdominal lymphatic glands, enlarged but not tubercular. Liver fatty, the acini in section appearing large, dull yellowish with brown centres; spleen natural. Stomach moderately contracted and not inflamed. Ileum with several small patches of moderate inflammation and one ecchymosed patch; agminated glands slightly thickened and the lower ones superficially ulcerated; solitary glands enlarged. Moderate inflammation in the cæcum and sigmoid flexure of the colon, the mucous membrane of the latter with a blackish blush, apparently from deposits of fine black pigment in the epithelial cells; solitary glands healthy and not blackened.—*Act. Ass't Surg. Joseph Leidy, Satterlee Hospital, Philadelphia, Pa.*

CASE 204.—Thomas James, a nurse of ward 7, died Oct. 30, 1863, of peritonitis. *Post-mortem* examination eight hours after death: Age about fifty years; body well nourished; thyroid body enlarged on one side to the size of a hen's egg. Heart and lungs healthy; capacity of chest diminished by pressure of abdominal contents. Peritoneal surface everywhere reddened by turgid vessels and covered by thin, recent, cream-colored pseudo-membrane, with interstitial sero-purulent liquid; abdominal lymphatic glands not palpably diseased. Liver large, yellowish-brown, soft and somewhat fatty; gall-bladder small and partially collapsed; spleen flabby, on the surface bluish-white and with an old white cicatrix-like mark, which, together with the sub-serous tissue, was spotted with black maculæ, on section light Indian-red, remarkably bloodless and for half a line from the surface black from pigment deposited in molecular granules and round masses the size of blood corpuscles. Stomach, pancreas and kidneys healthy. Ileum and colon slightly more pink than normal; upper agminated glands healthy; glands of lower three feet of ileum ulcerated, the ulcers occupying only part of the surface, but extending to the muscular and serous coats and in one instance perforating the latter, the hole being circular and about a line in diameter. The blood contained, if anything, fewer white corpuscles than usual. [*Specimens* 234 to 236, Med. Sect., Army Medical Museum, are from this case.]—*Act. Ass't Surg. Joseph Leidy, Satterlee Hospital, Phila., Pa.*

(G.) Condition of Peyer's patches not stated; the ileum or the small intestine ulcerated—22 cases.

CASE 205.—Private Benjamin McCoy, Co. H, 46th Pa., was admitted Sept. 16, 1863, in low condition and cyanotic. Next day he became delirious, and soon afterwards ecchymoses appeared on the chest and abdomen. He died on the 22d. *Post-mortem* examination: Heart sound; parenchymatous organs healthy; a portion of the ileum ulcerated.—*Act. Ass't Surg. W. Leon Hammond, First Division Hospital, Alexandria, Va.*

CASE 206.—Private Richard Boyer, Co. F, 149th Ohio National Guard; age 43; delirious and with a feeble intermitting pulse; diarrhœa profuse. Died August 31, 1864. *Post-mortem* examination sixteen hours after death: Lungs somewhat emphysematous on their periphery; pericardium thickened and containing four ounces of yellow liquid; heart enlarged but with no valvular derangement; lower third of ileum ulcerated, some of the ulcers nearly perforating, others almost cicatrized.—*Seminary Hospital, Columbus, Ohio.*

CASE 207.—Private Levi Bentley, Co. E, 14th N. Y. Art.; age 18; was admitted June 11, 1864, with typhoid fever, and died on the 25th. *Post-mortem* examination twenty-four hours after death: Miliary tubercles in both lungs; ulceration of the ileo-cæcal valve and of the whole of the ileum. Heart, liver, spleen and kidneys normal.—*Act. Ass't Surg. B. B. Miles, Jarvis Hospital, Baltimore, Md.*

CASE 208.—Private William Park, Co. F, 149th Ohio National Guards; age 37; was admitted May 30, 1864, and died June 26. *Post-mortem* examination twenty-four hours after death: Adhesions of the membranes of the brain and slight effusion of serum under the arachnoid. Lungs normal; heart natural, but the pericardium contained some effusion; liver much mottled; spleen normal. The lower part of the ileum was much congested but showed only one ulcer.—*Act. Ass't Surg. B. B. Miles, Jarvis Hospital, Baltimore, Md.*

CASE 209.—Private James M. Cammell, Co. G, 11th Va.; age 22; was admitted Aug. 31, 1864, with typhoid fever, and died September 10. *Post-mortem* examination twenty-four hours after death: Effusion in the ventricles of the brain. Twenty-five ulcers in the ileum, which, for two feet above the ileo-cæcal valve, was intensely inflamed; the valve was one mass of ulcers.—*Act. Ass't Surg. B. B. Miles, Jarvis Hospital, Baltimore, Md.*

CASE 210.—John Henry, contraband; age 22; was admitted Aug. 27, 1864, with typhoid fever, and died on the 30th. *Post-mortem* examination: Lungs congested; heart, liver and kidneys normal; spleen softened; small intestine congested and extensively ulcerated, especially near the ileo-cæcal valve.—*Chattanooga Field Hospital, Tenn.*

CASE 211.—Spencer Jonaque, contraband; age 29; was admitted Aug. 18, 1864, with typhoid fever, and died on the 27th. *Post-mortem* examination: Lungs congested; heart, liver and kidneys normal; spleen softened; small intestine congested, softened and showing many minute ulcers.—*Chattanooga Field Hospital, Tenn.*

CASE 212.—Private James Lock, Co. K, 22d Mich.; age 19; was admitted Aug. 10, 1864, with typhoid fever, and died on the 19th. *Post-mortem* examination on day of death: Lungs congested and lower lobe of left lung hepatized; heart flabby; liver and kidneys normal; spleen large and softened; mucous membrane of ileum softened and showing many ulcers of various sizes.—*Chattanooga Field Hospital, Tenn.*

CASE 213.—Private David Cantwell, Co. A, 42d U. S. Colored troops; age 37; admitted Aug. 17, 1864; died 29th. *Post-mortem* examination on the day of death: Lungs universally and firmly adherent; heart, liver and kidneys normal; spleen one and a half ounces; mucous membrane of small intestine thickened, softened and showing several ulcers one-fourth to one-half inch in diameter.—*Chattanooga Field Hospital, Tenn.*

CASE 214.—Private Fielding Childers, Co. D, 16th U. S. Colored troops; age 22; was admitted Sept. 2, 1864, and died on the 8th. *Post-mortem* examination on the day of death: The lower lobe of the right lung and part of the upper lobe were hepatized; the lower lobe of the left lung was congested; the heart was flabby. The liver was softened; the spleen, eighteen ounces, was softened and had two large cysts on its surface. The mucous membrane of the small intestine was softened, congested and studded with numerous small ulcers. The kidneys were normal.—*Field Hospital, Chattanooga, Tenn.*

CASE 215.—Private Henry W. Shedron, Co. E, regiment not stated, was admitted Oct. 14, 1864, as a convalescent from typhoid fever. He was greatly emaciated and had slight chills every day followed by high fever and night-sweats. On the 16th he complained of pain in the chest; diarrhœa set in next day, and he died on the 22d. *Post-mortem* examination eight hours after death: Right lung hepatized throughout; ulcers and an old cicatrix in the small intestine.—*Hospital No. 8, Nashville, Tenn.*

CASE 216.—Private Simeon M. Van Horn, Co. F, 141st Pa.; admitted Oct. 14, 1862; died 24th. *Post-mortem* examination: The mucous membrane of the small intestine was much softened and presented many ulcerated patches. The mesentery was highly congested; the mesenteric glands enlarged; the spleen twice the usual size, much engorged and easily broken down; the liver enlarged and friable.—*Third Division Hospital, Alexandria, Va.*

CASE 217.—Recruit John H. Skillington, 49th Pa.; age 25; was admitted Sept. 9, 1864, with typhoid fever. He fell into an unconscious state, and died on the 14th. *Post-mortem* examination one hour and a half after death: Slight effusion beneath arachnoid at apex; three small, flat, strong deposits in anterior part of posterior commissure in front of pineal gland; a dirty looking clot in the heart; gray hepatization of posterior part of upper lobe of right lung and minute red-brown interlobular infiltrations in posterior part of lower lobe; liver large; spleen large, dark and hard; kidneys pale; ileum, near ileo-cæcal valve, showing patches of congestion and ulcers with thickened and reddened borders; colon normal.—*Third Division Hospital, Alexandria, Va.*

CASE 218.—Private Benedict Gehrich, Co. D, 67th Pa.; admitted April 24, 1865. Typhoid fever. Died 29th. *Post-mortem* examination: Rigor mortis well marked; integuments excoriated; patches of denuded muscle here and there. Lungs, heart and stomach healthy. Spleen enlarged to three times the usual size, congested; small intestine slightly ulcerated at several points.—*Depot Field Hospital, Sixth Army Corps, City Point, Va.*

CASE 219.—Private Frederick Wombeyer, Co. F, 41st N. Y., was admitted March 15, 1865, and died on the same day. *Post-mortem* examination twenty-four hours after death: The lungs were filled with blood and frothy serum; there were adhesions on the right side, and eight ounces of serum in each pleural sac; the heart was pale and contained a small clot. The liver was normal; the lower portion of the ileum was entirely denuded; the kidneys were inflamed and contained pus.—*Depot Field Hospital, Sixth Army Corps, City Point, Va.*

CASE 220.—Private John Fitzsimmons, Co. D, 102d Pa.; admitted March 15, 1865. Diagnosis—typhoid fever. Died 28th. *Post-mortem* examination forty-eight hours after death: The lungs were healthy, but there were pleuritic adhesions on the left side; the heart contained large fibrinous clots in all its cavities. The liver was pale, almost fatty; the spleen normal. The intestines were normal except the last two feet of the ileum; near the ileo-cæcal valve the gut was entirely denuded of membrane and covered with greenish slime. The left kidney was pale; the right contained a large abscess.—*Depot Field Hospital, Sixth Army Corps, City Point, Va.*

CASE 221.—Private Robert E. Shaw, Co. K, 111th N. Y.; age 23; was admitted June 26, 1863, with typhoid fever, and died August 10. *Post-mortem* examination twenty-five hours after death: Body rigid, not emaciated. Lungs normal excepting cadaveric changes, right weighing eighteen ounces, left seventeen ounces; right cavities of heart containing a large clot, fibrinous with a bloody admixture, extending a long distance into the pulmonary artery. Liver pale and flabby; spleen soft and decomposing; small intestine healthy to within four feet of the ileo-cæcal valve, below this point extensive typhoid ulceration existed, the ulcers being superficial and situated for the most part in the centre of large congested patches; large intestine healthy; kidneys very soft and flabby, congested in their cortical substance.—*Ass't Surg. H. Allen, U. S. A., Lincoln Hospital, Washington, D. C.*

CASE 222.—Private H. Mortenson, Co. G, 27th Wis.; age 32; was admitted May 10, 1863, with parotitis, a sequel of fever. An infusion of frostwort (*Helianthemum Canadense*) was given and the affected parts painted with tincture of iodine. The patient would not permit any poultices or other applications to be used. An ichorish matter was discharged from both ears until death on the 18th. "*Autopsy* revealed softening of kidneys and a cavity containing fluid in right kidney; intussusception and ulceration of small intestine."—*Act. Ass't Surg. W. A. McMurray, City General Hospital, St. Louis, Mo.*

CASE 223.—Private Wendilin Griesbaum, Co. F, 16th Ill. Cav.; age 43; was admitted Sept. 12, 1863, having had fever for ten days. As he was unable to speak English and was rather dull withal, but little account of his case could be obtained. Simple febrifuge remedies with quinine were ordered. Castor oil was administered on the 15th, as the bowels were constipated, painful, somewhat distended and hard. The abdominal symptoms were aggravated on the 16th, although the bowels had been moved in the meantime; the pulse was 100 and feeble. He died on the evening of this day. Dr. F. K. BAILEY, attending surgeon, reports that "on inquiry among his comrades I learn that this man had been kicked, some six or eight months ago, in the abdomen by a fellow-soldier, and that he has been sick ever since." *Post-mortem* examination fourteen hours after death: Body emaciated; abdomen hard and very much distended; large quantities of bloody liquid oozing from mouth; skin in dependent regions livid. The thoracic viscera were normal. The peritoneal cavity contained a large quantity of bloody serum, pus and fæces; the omentum was livid and so tender as to scarcely hold together; the liver was twice the usual size and could be easily broken down by the finger; the spleen was discolored but not enlarged. The stomach was distended to double the normal size; the ileum perforated near its union with the large intestine. The kidneys were healthy.—*Hospital, Quincy, Ill.*

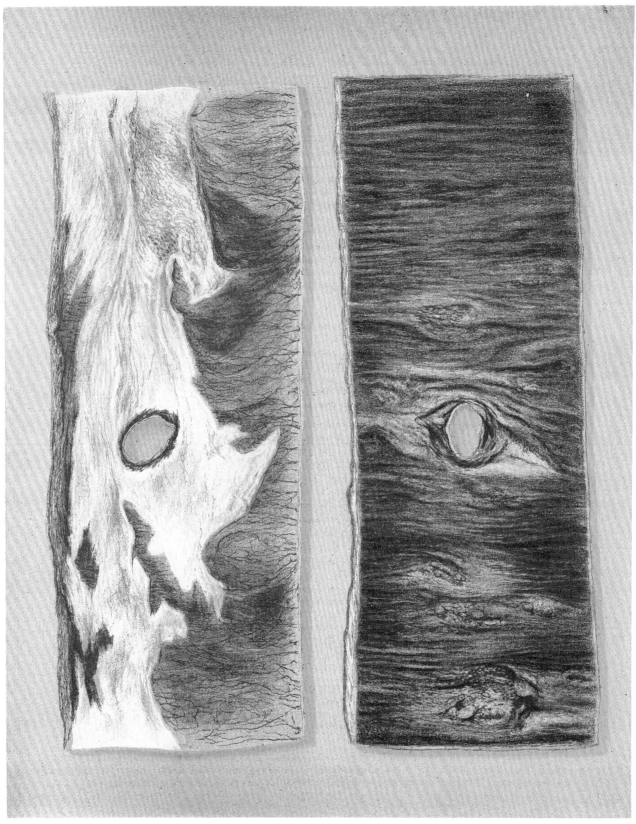

H. Faber pinx.^t   F. Moras chromolith. Phila.

PERFORATING ULCER OF THE ILEUM.

The right hand piece shows the mucous, the left the peritoneal surface.

CASE 224.—Private Eli W. Whiting, 5th Me. Bat'y, was admitted Sept. 1, 1862, with a gunshot wound received at the battle of Bull Run. He was sent to his home on furlough November 12, and was there taken very sick. He returned to hospital February 6, 1863, in a debilitated condition. On March 18 he was attacked by fever and a severe pain in the præcordial region. On the morning of the 24th he had a chill, and the seat of the pain changed to the umbilical and hypogastric regions; he lay on his back with his knees drawn up and the abdominal walls motionless in respiration; his face was pale and contracted, showing great distress and anxiety; pulse frequent and small; tongue red at the tip and edges and furred with yellow in the centre; thirst extreme; bowels constipated; he had much nausea and vomited a greenish offensive matter. He was conscious until within an hour of his death, which took place on the evening of the 25th. *Post-mortem* examination: A large quantity of serum and pus was found in the peritoneal cavity; the peritoneum was thickened and congested; it presented a brilliant red appearance over some parts of the small intestine and a deep-red, almost black, appearance over other parts. The ileum for about five feet from the cæcum was more or less ulcerated; it was perforated by a large ulcer at a point eighteen inches from the ileo-cæcal valve. [See *specimen* 147, Med. Sect., Army Medical Museum, and plate facing this page.]—*Med. Cadet Abner Thorp, U. S. A., Columbian Hospital, Washington, D. C.*

CASE 225.—Private Joseph Fair, Co. L, 14th Pa. Cav.; age 52; was admitted July 25, 1863, with delirium, tremors and diarrhœa. He died August 3. *Post-mortem* examination ten hours after death: Lower lobe of right lung hepatized; liver hypertrophied; gall-bladder enormously enlarged, six to eight inches long; ileum ulcerated and perforated. [Gall-bladder forms *specimen* 37, Med. Sect., Army Medical Museum.]—*Ass't Surg. DeWitt C. Peters, U. S. A., Jarvis Hospital, Baltimore, Md.*

CASE 226.—Corp'l Paul Granvet, Co. D, 1st N. J., was admitted Aug. 9, 1862, having suffered from diarrhœa and fever at Harrison's Landing. After his admission he did well, recovered his appetite, increased in flesh and strength, and appeared in fact entirely convalescent; but during the afternoon of the 31st he was suddenly seized with violent pain in the abdomen, quick pulse, prostration and vomiting. Under the use of opiates and restoratives he was relieved from pain, but the abdomen became tumid. He continued to sink, and died during the night. On the day of this attack the patient took an unusually large meal of meat, which he did not chew sufficiently, and which he vomited in pieces as large as a shellbark. "The *autopsy* revealed three large patches of ulceration, two of which had perforated the small intestine, producing intense peritonitis."—*Satterlee Hospital, Philadelphia, Pa.*

(D.) Condition of Peyer's patches not stated; the ileum or the small intestine ulcerated and the large intestine also affected—19 cases.

CASE 227.—Private Albert Turner, Co. A, 42d U. S. Colored troops; age 48; was admitted Aug. 31, 1864, with typhoid fever, and died September 2. *Post-mortem* examination on day of death: Right lung congested and at points hepatized; left lung normal; heart pale and flabby. Liver congested and somewhat softened; spleen enlarged and softened; kidneys enlarged but firm, weight of each nine ounces. Lower ileum ulcerated in patches; mucous membrane of ascending and transverse colon thickened and softened.—*Chattanooga Field Hospital, Tenn.*

CASE 228.—Charles Lancaster, contraband; age 28; was admitted Sept. 2, 1864, with typhoid fever, and died on the 10th. *Post-mortem* examination next day: Left lung partly hepatized; lower lobe of right lung congested; heart normal. Liver congested and softened; spleen weighing two ounces; left kidney presenting a small cyst filled with pus. Large intestine congested and softened; ileum ulcerated, the ulcers measuring two to three inches in their long diameter.—*Chattanooga Field Hospital, Tenn.*

CASE 229.—Private Ire Campbell, Co. K, 16th U. S. Colored troops; age 20; was admitted Aug. 27, 1864, with typhoid fever, and died on the 30th. *Post-mortem* examination on day of death: Lungs somewhat congested; heart normal. Liver congested and softened; spleen much softened; kidneys normal. Large and small intestines ulcerated, some of the ulcers being one-fourth inch in diameter.—*Chattanooga Field Hospital, Tenn.*

CASE 230.—Private Richard Weatherford, Co. D, 42d U. S. Colored troops, was admitted Aug. 14, 1864, with typhoid fever, and died on the 17th. *Post-mortem* examination: Lungs congested; heart flabby. Liver and kidneys normal; spleen softened. Intestines congested and softened, ileum ulcerated.—*Chattanooga Field Hospital, Tenn.*

CASE 231.—Private Frederick H. A. Steel, Co. D, 15th Pa. Cav., was admitted Aug. 16, 1864, with typhoid fever, and died on the 18th. *Post-mortem* examination next day: Lungs much congested; heart and liver normal; spleen softened; right kidney somewhat congested, left kidney congested and fatty; mucous membrane of intestines softened and congested, that of ileum presenting ulcers, some small and others with a long diameter of two inches and a half.—*Chattanooga Field Hospital, Tenn.*

CASE 232.—Private Samuel Hurto, Co. B, 10th U. S. Inf.; age 21; was admitted July 2, 1864, from City Point. Diagnosis—typhoid fever. Died 11th. *Post-mortem* examination eleven hours after death: Extreme emaciation. The intestinal canal was inflamed and presented several indurated ulcers in the cæcum, colon, rectum and ileum. The other organs were in a normal condition. [*Specimen* 421, Med. Sect., Army Medical Museum, is from this case.]—*Surg. E. Bentley, U. S. V., Third Division Hospital, Alexandria, Va.*

CASE 233.—Private George Martin, Co. B, 110th Ohio, was admitted Aug. 10, 1864, unconscious, and died next day. *Post-mortem* examination: Much emaciation. Considerable thickening of the intestinal mucous membrane and extensive ulceration of the ileum, cæcum and colon.—*Third Division Hospital, Alexandria, Va.*

CASE 234.—Corporal William Powell, Co. K, 10th N. Y. Cav.; age 43; admitted July 13, 1864. Diagnosis—typhoid fever. Died 24th. *Post-mortem* examination: Great emaciation. Slight adhesions of right pleura and extensive inflammation of lower lobe of right lung. Numerous and large ulcers in the intestines, extending from about two feet above the cæcum to the anus, and two intussusceptions of the ileum, recent in appearance. Liver enlarged and fatty; spleen very much enlarged and congested.—*Third Division Hospital, Alexandria, Va.*

CASE 235.—Private George Fox, Co. K, 2d N. Y. Mounted Rifles; admitted July 23, 1864; typhoid fever. This patient was delirious on admission, and continued so until he died comatose on the 29th; vibices appeared on the chest on the 27th and became darker and more extensive during the following day. *Post-mortem* examination twenty hours after death: Much emaciation. Inflammation and ulceration of the mucous coat of the ileum and colon, in some places nearly perforating; other organs not seriously diseased.—*Third Division Hospital, Alexandria, Va.*

CASE 236.—Private Frederick Bingal, Co. I, 5th U. S. Cav.; age 24; was admitted June 26, 1863, in the last stage of typhoid fever—pulse 110 to 140; muttering delirium, with subsultus. *Post-mortem* examination twenty-four hours after death showed "considerable hepatization of the lungs, with extensive softening of the mesenteric glands and ulceration of the intestines."—*Act. Ass't Surg. A. P. Crafts, Third Division Hospital, Alexandria, Va.*

CASE 237.—Private Isaac F. Blasdale, Co. C, 156th Ind.; age 18; was admitted June 16, 1865, in an extremely weak and exhausted condition, having been sick in camp for ten days before admission. His tongue and lips were pale and dry, the former covered with a white fur; he had great thirst; his pulse was very quick, small and feeble; his respiration hurried, and his dejections small, liquid and frequent. He died on the 20th. *Post-mortem* examination sixteen hours after death: The spleen was large, soft and very dark; the mucous membrane of the ileum and cæcum was inflamed and ulcerated.—*Act. Ass't Surg. S. B. West, Cumberland Hospital, Md.*

CASE 238.—Private William Fowler, Co. D, 91st Ohio; age 21; was admitted Aug. 21, 1864, with typhoid fever, and died September 22. *Post-mortem* examination twenty-four hours after death: Hypostatic congestion of both lungs; a quantity of serum in the left pleural cavity, two ounces in the pericardium, four ounces in the peritoneum. The liver was large and light-brown in color and the spleen large and congested. The whole of the large intestine was much thickened and its mucous surface covered with large elevated, hard and ragged ulcers; the ileum was softened, thinned and, for two feet from the ileo-cæcal valve, intensely congested, showing traces of numerous ulcers, some of which were healed.—*Act. Ass't Surg. B. B. Miles, Jarvis Hospital, Baltimore, Md.*

CASE 239.—Private Alson Breedlove, Co. D, 13th E. Tenn. Cav., was admitted Jan. 22, 1864, with typhoid fever, and died February 4. *Post-mortem* examination twelve hours after death: Body much emaciated; cadaveric rigidity marked. The brain was healthy. The lungs weighed forty-one ounces; their apices were emphysematous and thin; bronchial tubes inflamed; heart healthy. The stomach contained two ounces of matter like coffee-grounds; its mucous membrane was inflamed and softened. The upper part of the small intestine was softened and ulcerated in small patches and contained two lumbricoid worms; the mucous membrane of the large intestine was thickened and softened in patches; the mesenteric glands were much enlarged. The liver was somewhat fatty; the spleen congested, weighing fifteen ounces; the kidneys normal; the prostate enlarged and containing one drachm of pus. —*Act. Ass't Surg. G. W. Roberts, Hospital No. 19, Nashville, Tenn.*

CASE 240.—Serg't H. C. Rogers, Co. C, 16th Pa. Cav.; age 28; was admitted Aug. 18, 1863, with typhoid fever, and died on the 20th. *Post-mortem* examination fourteen hours after death: Body but little emaciated. Trachea slightly congested, purplish between the rings; right lung weighing seventeen ounces, its upper lobe greatly congested and its lower lobe almost solidified but lighter than water; left lung, eighteen ounces and a half, congested generally, emphysematous in lower part of upper lobe; right ventricle containing a fibrinous clot which extended into the pulmonary artery. Liver dark colored, its parenchyma stained around the portal veins; spleen firm, purple and conspicuously mottled on its surface with a darker hue. Ileum congested and extensively ulcerated, the upper ulcers being small, blackish and with depressed centres, while those near the ileo-cæcal valve had a long diameter of one and a half inches, in one of which the ulceration had penetrated to the muscular coat; cæcum and ascending colon, especially between the longitudinal bands, studded with superficial ulcers having dark-blue borders and an elliptic form, their long diameter, one to five lines, at right angles to the axis of the bowel. Right kidney anæmic and firm; left somewhat congested.—*Ass't Surg. H. Allen, U. S. A., Lincoln Hospital, Washington, D. C.*

CASE 241.—Private David C. Hollenbeck, Co. E, 188th N. Y.; age 37; was admitted Jan. 30, 1865, having been under treatment for fever with his command for seven days before admission. He died February 5. *Post-mortem* examination: The lower lobe of each lung was congested; the right weighed twenty-two ounces, the left fourteen ounces. The liver, spleen and kidneys were healthy. The mesenteric glands were enlarged and congested. The stomach was congested and contracted; the duodenum and jejunum healthy, except that there was an intussusception, two inches long, about seven feet and a half from the stomach; there was a good deal of ulceration in the neighborhood of the ileo-cæcal valve; a few ulcers were scattered through the colon.—*Ass't Surg. M. L. Lord, 140th N. Y., Depot Field Hospital, Fifth Army Corps, City Point, Va.*

CASE 242.—Private Charles Brown, Co. H, 9th Pa., was admitted Sept. 28, 1862, convalescing from typhoid fever. The patient was greatly debilitated with diarrhœa, but under a tonic treatment he improved slowly until within three or four days of his death, when he began to complain occasionally of faintness. On October 17, after visiting the water-closet, he lay down on bed and expired almost immediately. *Post-mortem* examination: Brain, lungs and stomach normal; walls of right ventricle of heart very thin and soft; intestines ulcerated to a moderate extent and showing signs of former ulceration.—*Ward Hospital, Newark, N. J.*

CASE 243.—Private Jeremiah Thorndyke, Co. C, 12th Mass., was admitted Nov. 4, 1863, having been sick for some time. On admission his bowels were loose and he had pain in the chest and abdomen. Pills of tannin and opium were given, with opiate enemata, but on the 10th nausea and vomiting came on and continued with failing pulse, dyspnœa and hiccough until death on the 15th. *Post-mortem* examination: The right lung was congested, the left hepatized; the walls of the right ventricle of the heart were as thin as glove-leather. The right lobe of the liver, posteriorly, was softened, and the contiguous hepatic flexure of the colon was gangrenous. The mucous membrane of the stomach and of the duodenum, from the pyloric orifice to the valvulæ conniventes, was pultaceous; the ileum was ulcerated; the lower end of the sigmoid flexure constricted. The left kidney was normal; the right kidney and suprarenal capsule showed traces of inflammation; the fundus of the bladder was very much thickened.—*Act. Ass't Surg. W. Leon Hammond, First Division Hospital, Alexandria, Va.*

CASE 244.—Corp'l P. S. Nottingham, Co. D, 149th N. Y.; age 32; was admitted April 22, 1863, with a profuse diarrhœa which resisted remedies, intense pain and swelling in the hypogastric region and difficulty of micturition; he was in low condition, pulse 130. As the distention of the abdomen did not depend on accumulated urine hot fomentations were applied, and on the 25th, fluctuation being apparent, an abdominal abscess was opened, giving issue to a sero-purulent discharge which continued for five days. He died May 1 with symptoms of peritonitis. *Post-mortem* examination: Ulceration of a large portion of the intestines and perforation in several places; fatty degeneration of the kidneys.—*Armory Square Hospital, Washington, D. C.*

CASE 245.—Private Simon Fogg, Co. C, 20th Me., was admitted Jan. 3, 1865, and died on the 30th. *Post-mortem* examination: Lungs collapsed and pale; left adherent to pericardium, weight ten ounces and a half; bronchi filled with pus; right sixteen ounces, middle lobe inflamed; heart ten ounces, clot in right ventricle. Liver, sixty-one ounces, healthy; gall-bladder filled with bile; spleen five ounces, healthy. Stomach and jejunum normal; ileum ulcerated, perforated in eight places, its walls surrounded with pus and interadherent; colon slightly inflamed at its upper end; mesenteric glands enlarged, filled with cheesy matter. Kidneys four ounces each; suprarenal capsules much softened.—*Fifth Army Corps Field Hospital, Army of Potomac.*

(E.) *Condition of Peyer's patches not stated; the intestines congested or inflamed but not ulcerated—11 cases.*

CASE 246.—Private Daniel McCloud, Co. C, 17th U. S. Inf., was admitted Aug. 14, 1863, with typhoid fever. Tongue dry and cracked; sordes on teeth; muttering delirium; pulse weak and frequent; extreme emaciation. He died on the 16th. *Post-mortem* examination: Lower portion of ileum highly congested and contracted, its submucous coat thickened and its mucous coat softened.—*Third Division Hospital, Alexandria, Va.*

CASE 247.—Private Mark E. Robinson, Co. E, 13th W. Va.; age 21; was admitted Feb. 16, 1865, complaining of severe pain in the left side and in the back of the head. His skin was hot, pulse 110, frequent, small and compressible, face darkly flushed, tongue dry, red and cracked; his dejections were frequent, copious and liquid, his abdomen tympanitic and tender on pressure. A diaphoretic mixture was ordered, with tepid sponging of the body, cold to the head and mustard to the ankles and nape of the neck. He became delirious during the night, his pulse increased, and his teeth, gums and lips became covered with sordes. Quinine, oil of turpentine and carbonate of ammonia were given, with chlorate of potash as a mouth-wash. He died on the 20th. *Post-mortem* examination twenty-four hours after death: Body slightly emaciated. The vessels of the pia mater were filled with dark blood; the cerebrum and cerebellum were congested posteriorly. The lungs were congested; the lower lobe of the left lung was hepatized. The stomach and intestines were distended with gas; extensive patches of inflammation were found in the jejunum and ileum. The spleen was very large.—*Act. Ass't Surg. S. B. West, Cumberland Hospital, Md.*

CASE 248.—Private Theophilus Gillespie, Co. A, 13th W. Va.; age 23; was admitted Feb. 3, 1865, with typhoid fever. He was very feeble and aphonic, his tongue dry, skin hot, pulse 100, bowels loose and abdomen swollen and painful. Quinine, oil of turpentine, lead, opium and whiskey were given. Vomiting set in on the 7th and he died next day. *Post-mortem* examination two hours after death: Slight emaciation; good muscular development. The epiglottis was thickened and ulcerated; the lining membrane of the larynx and of the trachea as far as the bifurcation was similarly affected; the vocal cords were almost obliterated. The lungs and heart were healthy. The spleen was very large, weighing nineteen ounces; the liver enlarged and congested; the gall-bladder enormously distended with bile. There was no intestinal ulceration, but scattered patches of inflammation were found in the ileum. A large quantity of coagulated blood was extravasated in the lower portion of the abdominal recti muscles and in the intermuscular septa.—*Act. Ass't Surg. Sample Ford, Cumberland Hospital, Md.*

CASE 249.—Philip Fisher, recruit, 9th Ohio; age 18; was admitted Nov. 30, 1864, with typhoid fever. There was much febrile action, dusky countenance, parched tongue, cough, diarrhœa and tenderness over the abdomen. A grain of quinine was given every four hours, and on December 5 half an ounce of brandy three times daily was ordered, with glycerine to moisten the tongue and morphine to allay abdominal pain, which had become severe. After a few days the cough became more annoying and there was dulness on percussion over the left side of the chest; the pulse became rapid and feeble and the diarrhœa troublesome. Acetate of lead with opium was added to the treatment. On the 12th the tongue, lips and mouth were very dry, the countenance livid, and bronchial râles were heard over the left lung; but on the 14th an improvement took place, the tongue becoming moist and the diarrhœa quieting; pulse 120 and feeble. Next day he was apparently much better than at any time since his admission; but in the afternoon he was seized with intense pain in the back which caused him to make loud outcries. Hot cloths were applied and morphine administered. In an hour he seemed relieved, and remained comfortable until midnight, when his breathing became hurried. He died comatose two hours thereafter. *Post-mortem* examination thirty-six hours after death: The pericardium contained four ounces of serum. The right lung was healthy; the left was firmly adherent to the costal pleura and diaphragm; the bronchial mucous membrane was inflamed throughout on the left and in the larger tubes on the right. The under surface of the diaphragm, the abdominal walls, the stomach, intestines and left lobe of the liver were coated with a thick layer of straw-colored lymph. The spleen was of normal size but contained several cavities filled with a soft, white, cheesy substance; two of these had ruptured into the peritoneal cavity. The mucous membrane of the ileum was slightly inflamed; the colon was largely distended with gas.—*Ass't Surg. H. C. May, 145th N. Y., Hospital No. 8, Nashville, Tenn.*

CASE 250.—Private George Lubenk, Co. K, 4th Mich. Cav.; age 34; admitted Feb. 1, 1864. Typhoid fever. Died 17th. *Post-mortem* examination: Body moderately emaciated. Lungs, heart, stomach, liver, spleen and large intestine healthy; the small intestine and kidneys highly congested.—*Hospital No. 1, Nashville, Tenn.*

CASE 251.—Theodore Jeter, 4th Ind.; age 22; was admitted March 21, 1863. He became sick January 16, at Vicksburg, Miss., with typhoid fever, mild in form, but with a tendency to diarrhœa. Suppuration occurred in the parotid gland, and he died April 12. *Post-mortem* examination: Pleuritic adhesions on right side; heart fatty, right ventricle thinned. Ileum congested; colon congested and softened. Right parotid gland entirely broken down by suppuration, leaving the external carotid bare but intact.—*City Hospital, St. Louis, Mo.*

CASE 252.—Thomas J. Slaton, private of an Alabama regiment, admitted Oct. 29, 1864, with typhoid fever. Bowels tender and somewhat loose; tongue narrow, tremulous, dry, slightly furred and red; pulse 110, weak; he was dull and drowsy and became gradually weaker until death took place December 5. *Post-mortem* examination: Great emaciation. Abscess in left lung; atrophy of heart; congestion of bowels and enlargement of mesenteric and solitary glands; fatty degeneration of the liver; spleen small.—*Act. Ass't Surg. H. C. Newkirk, Rock Island Hospital, Ill.*

CASE 253.—Private William Brown, Co. I, 1st Ark.; died March 16, 1865. *Post-mortem* examination: The spleen was much enlarged; the bowels distended and in many places disorganized; the mesenteric glands enlarged. An abscess of the arm and shoulder had discharged a large amount of pus for some days before death; on incision great disorganization of the muscles was revealed.—*Act. Ass't Surg. H. H. Russell, Rock Island Hospital, Ill.*

CASE 254.—Private Milton L. Coon, Co. I, 85th N. Y.; age 23; was admitted Aug. 19, 1862, with typhoid fever. Died suddenly November 18. *Post-mortem* examination: Extensive inflammation of the lower part of the ileum and cæcum, with pin-head enlargement of the solitary follicles, [*Specimen* 153, Med. Sect., Army Medical Museum]; mesenteric glands enlarged; liver and kidneys fatty.—*Surg. A. C. Bournonville, U. S. V., Hospital Fifth and Buttonwood streets, Philadelphia, Pa.*

CASE 255.—Private Lewell Cates, Co. A, 12th Ky.; admitted April 24, 1865. Died May 7. The course of the disease was that of typhoid fever; shortness of breath was the only pneumonic symptom observed. *Post-mortem* examination thirty-six hours after death: No emaciation. Both lungs were congested, the left partially hepatized; the heart normal. The liver was enlarged, friable and resembled that of yellow fever; the spleen and kidneys were normal. The intestines were immensely distended with gas, and the mucous membrane of the ileum and colon was congested.—*Act. Ass't Surg. E. Holden, Ward Hospital, Newark, N. J.*

CASE 256.—Private Patrick Cady, Co. B, 35th Ill.; admitted July 23, 1864. Typhoid fever. Died September 22. *Post-mortem* examination: Body much emaciated. The intestinal mucous membrane was congested and inflamed, but not ulcerated, in the lower third of the ileum and in the colon. An abscess holding two ounces of light-colored pus was found in the right lobe of the liver. The other organs were normal.—*Hospital No. 8, Nashville, Tenn.*

(F.) Condition of Peyer's patches stated variously, but not ulcerated, and generally without ulceration of the intestines—42 cases.

(a.) Peyer's patches normal or healthy.

CASE 257.—Private Edwin A. Maxfield, Co. G, 7th Me.; age 27; was admitted Aug. 14, 1864, with remittent fever. On admission the patient had a weak, frequent pulse, a dry, coated tongue and loose passages of a light color. Next day he had fever and headache. On the 16th he became delirious and somewhat drowsy, and on the 18th he died comatose. He was treated with citrate of potash and nitre, cold lotions to the head, and afterwards with calomel, ipecacuanha, camphor and blisters to the back of the neck. *Post-mortem* examination nine hours and a half after death: Body not much emaciated; rigor mortis well marked. The base of the brain was covered with a thin layer of lymph, the pia mater was injected, the liquid in the ventricles opaque. The trachea contained a considerable quantity of whitish frothy sputa streaked with the color of prune-juice; the right lung weighed twenty-five ounces, its posterior portion much congested, its anterior margin normal; the left lung weighed twenty-three ounces and a half, its posterior and lower part in the state of red hepatization, the rest of the lung healthy. The pericardium contained two ounces of straw-colored serum; the right side of the heart a small fibrinous clot. The stomach, liver and spleen were normal in appearance; the last weighed nine ounces and a quarter. The kidneys were somewhat injected. The mucous membrane of nearly the whole of the small and large intestines was congested, but Peyer's patches and the solitary glands were normal.—*Act. Ass't Surg. H. M. Dean, Lincoln Hospital, Wash'n, D. C.*

CASE 258.—Private James H. Morrison, Co. B, 151st Pa.; age 26; was admitted June 17, 1863, with typhoid fever. [He entered Kalorama hospital, Washington, D. C., Dec. 1, 1862, with small-pox, and was returned to duty Feb. 17, 1863; Douglas hospital, Washington, D. C., June 14, with diarrhœa, and was transferred to Philadelphia next day.] He was much debilitated and had severe diarrhœa which continued throughout the case. On July 4 there was swelling of the right parotid gland and on the 6th constant vomiting. He died on the 14th. Astringents, quinine and iron, turpentine, beef-tea, wine and milk-punch were prescribed. *Post-mortem* examination: Body much emaciated; skin marked with variolous scars. The bronchial mucous membrane was inflamed; the left lung was covered with a thin pseudo-membrane stained with blood, the surface laterally, posteriorly and at the base was darkly ecchymosed and there was a large clot with a quart of bloody serum in the pleura, but no rupture of the lung. There were four ounces of liquid in the pericardium and white fibrinous clots in the cavities of the heart. The spleen contained three soft tubercular masses the size of hickory nuts. The mesenteric glands were somewhat enlarged and many of them blackened. Four intussusceptions were found in the ileum, the mucous membrane of which showed irregularly diffused inflammation with black deposits; the solitary glands were somewhat congested; Peyer's patches were healthy.—*Satterlee Hospital, Philadelphia, Pa.*

CASE 259.—Private George Stone, Co. F, 73d Ohio; age 20; admitted June 15, 1863, with phthisis and typhoid fever. Died July 25. *Post-mortem* examination eleven hours after death: Emaciation. Brain forty-eight ounces, soft; lateral ventricles filled with effusion. Mucous membrane of trachea easily torn, slightly discolored, delicate purple at its lower portion; tube containing tough, tenacious sputa; lymphatic glands at bifurcation healthy. Mucous lining of œsophagus pale and extensively eroded, especially below. Right lung eight ounces, uniformly pale, lower lobe slightly injected; left lung seven ounces and a half, lower lobe slightly injected and containing a consolidation about the size of a horse-chestnut, with a central cavity as large as a hazel-nut; walls of cavity well defined and enclosing a secretion similar to that found in the trachea. Pericardium large and containing twelve drachms of pale, limpid, straw-colored liquid; a small fibrinous clot in the right ventricle. Liver firm, of a dark-purple color externally and showing portal engorgement on section; spleen four ounces and a half, firm and of a dark mulberry color; omentum crowded up under lower edge of liver, well supplied with adipose tissue. Upper part of the small intestine congested, lower portion empty and much congested; Peyer's patches perfectly healthy; large intestine normal and filled with healthy fæces. Kidneys firm and congested internally, a blackish blood exuding on section.—*Ass't Surg. H. Allen, U. S. A., Lincoln Hospital, Washington, D. C.*

CASE 260.—Private George H. Grover, Co. C, 7th Me.; admitted Aug. 10, 1863; typhoid fever. Died 21st. *Post-mortem* examination: Body much emaciated; apparently about 20 years of age; skin of trunk minutely ecchymosed. The lungs, heart, stomach and spleen were healthy; the liver was bright colored and exhibited distinctly the outlines of its acini. The mucous membrane of the lower part of the jejunum and of the ileum was inflamed, the inflammation being most intense in the lower part of the latter; the solitary and agminated glands appeared healthy and contained no deposit of black pigment; the ascending and descending portions of the colon were moderately inflamed but not ulcerated.—*Act. Ass't Surg. J. Leidy, Satterlee Hospital, Philadelphia, Pa.*

CASE 261.—Private W. C. Swails, Co. I, 49th Pa.; admitted Aug. 10, 1862; typhoid fever. Died September 8. *Post-mortem* examination next day: Age about 40 years; body extremely emaciated; skin ecchymosed. Lungs filled with bloody liquid; heart presenting an opaque-white membranous spot on the surface of the right ventricle and containing a large white clot in the right and a soft black clot with liquid blood in the left ventricle. Stomach presenting three large inflamed patches; its cul-de-sac softened. Liver dull-brown in color but otherwise natural; kidneys healthy. Ileum inflamed in patches; its glands not diseased; mesenteric glands opaque, cream-colored and somewhat enlarged; large intestine diffusely inflamed in the colon, particularly in the cæcum and sigmoid flexure, and extending into the rectum along its rugæ.—*Act. Ass't Surg. J. Leidy, Satterlee Hospital, Philadelphia, Pa.*

(b.) Peyer's patches not ulcerated.

CASE 262.—Private Thomas Ward, Co. D, 42d N. Y.; age 30; was admitted Sept. 20, 1862, with a shell wound of the right cheek and typhoid fever. He died November 17. *Post-mortem* examination ten hours after death: Great emaciation. Lungs and pleuræ healthy; pericardium distended with serum; heart paler than natural. Liver, spleen and kidneys healthy. Mucous membrane of stomach pale, softened and with spots of extravasated blood; of ileum injected but not softened and Peyer's patches not ulcerated; of colon and rectum greatly injected, thickened, but neither softened nor ulcerated.—*Ass't Surg. C. H. Andrus, 128th N. Y., Stewart's Mansion Hospital, Baltimore, Md.*

CASE 263.—Corp'l Daniel Landis, Co. C, 212th Pa.; age 22; admitted Oct. 21, 1864. Diagnosis—typhoid fever. Died November 2. *Post-mortem* examination twenty hours after death: Marked rigor mortis; some emaciation; bed-sores; two very large abscesses under each ear. Lower lobe of right lung hepatized posteriorly. Heart, liver, pancreas and kidneys normal; gall-bladder containing two ounces of bile; spleen enlarged, black, softened; mucous coat of small and large intestines much congested but no thickening or ulceration of Peyer's patches or the solitary follicles. The reporter, Dr. THOMAS BOWEN, says that, in view of the diagnosis being typhoid fever, a very careful examination of the small intestine was made.—*Second Division Hospital, Alexandria, Va.*

(c.) Peyer's patches prominent, conspicuous, enlarged, thickened, etc.

CASE 264.—Private Henry Clay, Co. I, 179th N. Y., was admitted May 11, 1865, much emaciated, very weak and unable to speak; his teeth and gums covered with sordes; pulse thready and irregular; respiration labored. He was washed with tepid water and whiskey, and treated with stimulants and nutritives, turpentine, quinine and opiate enemata. He died on the 19th. *Post-mortem* examination: Emaciation extreme. Membranes of brain anæmic. Lower lobe of left lung congested; heart containing a few small coagula; blood generally diffluent. Liver of normal size, showing fat-cells under the microscope; spleen large, soft. Ileum and cæcum much congested and inflamed, in a few places ulcerated; Peyer's patches quite prominent by a soft, friable deposit; mesenteric glands large, filled with similar deposits. Kidneys congested, somewhat fatty; urine albuminous.—*Augur Hospital, Alexandria, Va.*

CASE 265.—Private William Plomb, Co. I, 4th N. J.; admitted Aug. 9, 1862; typhoid fever. Died 10th. *Post-mortem* examination next day. Body well formed and robust. The lungs were healthy; the heart flabby but otherwise normal. The liver, stomach, pancreas, spleen and kidneys were healthy. The ileum was deeply reddened, and the agminated and solitary glands more than ordinarily conspicuous, but without apparent disease; the colon was slate-colored, with patches of redness, and presented a number of scattered ulcers about the size of peas.—*Act. Ass't Surg. J. Leidy, Satterlee Hospital, Philadelphia, Pa.*

CASE 266.—Private Eugene Mason, Co. G, 157th N. Y.; age 16; admitted Sept. 19, 1864; typhoid fever. Died October 3. *Post-mortem* examination eighteen hours after death: Slight rigor mortis; much emaciation. Brain fifty-six ounces. Right lung nine ounces, somewhat compressed and adhering firmly to the thoracic wall; left lung seven ounces; heart six ounces and a half, containing fibrinous clots in right and black clots in left cavities. Liver forty ounces, normal; spleen three ounces and a half, firm. Small intestine congested, some of its solitary follicles ulcerated and Peyer's patches thickened; large intestine studded with small ulcers a quarter of an inch in diameter. Kidneys normal.—*Act. Ass't Surg. H. M. Dean, Lincoln Hospital, Washington, D. C.*

CASE 267.—Serg't K. A. Babcock, Co. H, 27th Mich., was admitted Aug. 12, 1863, having been suffering for six weeks from fever and diarrhœa. Under opium, camphor, blue-pill and subsequently quinine, aromatic sulphuric acid and morphine, he improved until the 20th, when the diarrhœa became profuse, and was followed by prostration and delirium which terminated in death on the 25th. *Post-mortem* examination: Heart flabby, pale; spleen enlarged, softened; mesenteric glands enlarged; elliptical patches near the ileo-cæcal valve hypertrophied but not ulcerated. —*Act. Ass't Surgs. C. T. Simpson and J. F. White, West End Hospital, Cincinnati, Ohio.*

CASE 268.—Private Jacob Walder, Co. E, 2d Mass. Cav., was admitted Sept. 27, 1864, in a semi-conscious condition; pulse 90 and feeble, tongue brown and slightly cracked, bowels constipated, right iliac region tender and urine retained. Three pints of urine were withdrawn by catheter, and oil of turpentine and milk-punch were ordered. On the 29th his urine passed involuntarily, his condition otherwise remaining the same. On October 5 the tympanites had subsided and the tongue was cleaning. The turpentine was omitted, and as the bowels continued constipated an enema was given. On the 12th the patient fell into a state of almost complete stupor. As there was much difficulty in swallowing, beef-essence and whiskey were administered per rectum. He died on the 17th. *Post-mortem* examination twelve hours after death: Body much emaciated. A tumor about the size of an orange was found between the posterior portions of the cerebral hemispheres; it was quite firm and cut like soft cartilage. [*Specimen* 535, Med. Sect., Army Medical Museum.] The lungs were congested; the heart, liver and kidneys healthy; the spleen and glands of Peyer enlarged.—*Act. Ass't Surg. W. S. Adams, Hospital, Frederick, Md.*

CASE 269.—Musician John Hummel, 4th N. Y. Cav.; age 29; was admitted June 28, 1863, having suffered for an unknown time with typhoid fever. He appeared to be doing well until July 7, when he began to sink, and died next day. *Post-mortem* examination nine hours after death: Spleen greatly enlarged; glands of Brünner, Peyer and of the mesentery enlarged; mucous and muscular coats of small intestine ulcerated throughout their whole length.—*Act. Ass't Surg. A. P. Crafts, Third Division Hospital, Alexandria, Va.*

CASE 270.—Private Leonard Snell, Co. C, 2d N. Y. Cav.; age 27; was admitted Nov. 29, 1862, with enteric fever: Hot skin, frequent feeble pulse, dry tongue, coated with dark fur, dry cough and severe dyspnœa, delirium, slight diarrhœa, tympanitic distention of bowels and dulness on percussion over the lower lobe of the right lung. He died December 1. *Post-mortem* examination: The lower lobe of the left lung was hepatized; the upper portion of the left lung and the lower lobe of the right lung were congested; the heart, liver and spleen were normal. The small intestine was injected and the glands of Peyer enlarged.—*Third Division Hospital, Alexandria, Va.*

CASE 271.—Private Jefferson Perkins, Co. F, 3d Ky. Cav.; age 21; was admitted Feb. 22, 1864, with typhoid fever. His case progressed favorably till one day, after sitting on the close-stool for a long time, he grew worse, failed rapidly, and died March 6. *Post-mortem* examination twenty-three hours after death: Lungs healthy; right cavities of heart containing a large clot which extended into the great vessels; liver somewhat pale; Peyer's patches enlarged.—*Hospital No. 8, Nashville, Tenn.*

CASE 272.—Private Benjamin Ostrander, Co. H, 91st N. Y.; admitted May 6, 1865. Diagnosis—typhoid fever. Died 11th. *Post-mortem* examination fourteen hours after death: Lungs and heart normal; liver enlarged and softened; ileum congested; Peyer's patches much enlarged.—*Sixth Army Corps Field Hospital, Army of Potomac.*

CASE 273.—Private James Roberts, Co. B, 67th Ohio; admitted Oct. 27, 1862; typhoid fever. Died Jan. 27, 1863. *Post-mortem* examination: Age about 22; no emaciation; a purplish color from gravitation of blood into the skin of the occiput; a number of reddish spots on the front of the abdomen and chest. Lungs and heart healthy. Spleen enlarged and flabby; liver healthy. Ileum presenting diffused redness with a few ecchymosed spots; lower agminated glands moderately enlarged, upper glands healthy; lowest solitary glands enlarged and in a few instances slightly ulcerated on the summit; large intestine with a grayish aspect of the mucous membrane accompanied with a few inflamed streaks. [*Specimens* 102–5, Med. Sect., Army Medical Museum, from this case, show various degrees of enlargement and ulceration of the agminated glands, 105 being specially noteworthy as exhibiting an extensive sloughing patch.]—*Act. Ass't Surg. J. Leidy, Satterlee Hospital, Philadelphia, Pa.*

(d.) Peyer's patches reddened, congested or inflamed.

CASE 274.—Private William Eckard, Co. E, 149th N. Y.; admitted Jan. 18, 1863; typhoid fever. About a week before his death, February 21, pneumonic symptoms were observed. *Post-mortem* examination: Body slightly emaciated; apparent age 20 years. The brain weighed fifty ounces and a half; it was light colored and of normal consistence. The right lung weighed nineteen ounces and three-quarters, the left seventeen ounces and three-quarters; on both melanic matter was conspicuously arranged in lines corresponding to the course of the ribs. The left lung contained a deposit of tubercle and there were several consolidated lobules in its upper lobe; similar lobules were observed scattered through the right lung; a few cretefied tubercles were found in both; the bronchial tubes of the left lung were intensely congested and contained purulent matter; several of the bronchial glands contained calcareous deposits. There was a white fibrinous clot in the right side of the heart extending into the pulmonary artery; in the left side a black clot from which a white fibrinous branch extended into the aorta. The liver weighed sixty-seven ounces; its acini were distinctly marked; the gall-bladder was empty. The spleen weighed six ounces and a quarter; it was of a light brick-red color and very soft. The pancreas weighed three ounces and a quarter; it was firm and of a light pinkish color. The kidneys and suprarenal capsules were natural. The mucous membrane of the stomach was very soft; that of the small intestine was generally softened, especially in the jejunum, where it had a velvety appearance; the ileum was thin, dilated in places and somewhat congested; Peyer's patches were reddened; the large intestine was slate-colored except in the rectum, where it was congested; the mesenteric and mesocolic glands were normal.—*Ass't Surg. George M. McGill, U. S. A., Lincoln Hospital, Washington, D. C.*

CASE 275.—Private George P. Thomas, Co. G, 43d Ohio; age 26; was admitted Feb. 4, 1865, with the eruption of measles well developed. In a few days the eruption had almost entirely disappeared; but symptoms of typhoid fever were manifested, and he died on the 12th. *Post-mortem* examination: The brain was normal. The lungs were congested posteriorly and presented nodulated inflammation, the substance of which was heavier than water; great numbers of miliary tubercles filled the posterior and inferior portions of the lungs; the right lung weighed thirty-seven ounces. Clots were found in both sides of the heart. The liver and pancreas were normal; the spleen, six ounces, contained miliary tubercles; the kidneys were somewhat enlarged and lobulated, each weighing eight ounces. The stomach was contracted and its mucous membrane somewhat congested. In the ileum small raised points were observed, which were hard to the feel, Peyer's patches were generally tumid and dark; about the middle of the ileum its mucous folds were deeply congested, and above these a long Peyer's patch, enlarged and reddened, was situated in the midst of another congested region; among the valvulæ conniventes, surrounded by congestion, was a patch a foot in length resembling a Peyer's patch in structure and enlarged, as were such patches in the ileum. The transverse and descending portions of the colon were reddened; the rectum congested.—*Ass't Surg. Geo. M. McGill, U. S. A., National Hospital, Baltimore, Md.*

CASE 276.—Private Phineas Wooster, Co. E, 137th N. Y.; age 35; admitted Jan. 11, 1863. Diagnosis—typhoid fever. The clinical history is meagre, consisting of only one entry dated February 4: Pulse frequent, easily compressed; tongue dry, edges white; skin dry and harsh; night-sweats; bowels loose, stools thin and offensive. Treated by wine and porter with opiates at bedtime. He died on the 10th. *Post-mortem* examination twenty-eight hours after death: Body much emaciated. The brain was anæmic. The right lung weighed seventeen ounces and a quarter, its upper lobe congested posteriorly and its lower hepatized and containing small abscesses which communicated with the bronchial tubes; the left lung weighed eleven ounces. The pericardium adhered to the surface of the heart, on which were dark spots and exuded lymph; the heart was flabby and contained fibrinous clots in both ventricles. The liver, forty-four ounces and a quarter, was flabby and light colored; the gall-bladder contained two ounces of thin green bile; the spleen was small and tough. The duodenum was much congested in its upper part, its serous coat was slate-colored; the jejunum in its upper part was slate-colored without and highly congested within, and lower down the color of the serous membrane was darker; Peyer's patches were congested, the valvulæ softened and the coats of the ileum generally thinned and reddened; the ascending colon was slate-colored. The left kidney was slightly congested.—*Lincoln Hospital, Washington, D. C.*

CASE 277.—Private M. W. Reese, Co. H, 42d Miss.; rebel; age 28; admitted Aug. 3, 1863; typhoid fever. Died 11th. *Post-mortem* examination: Body rigid, not emaciated. Brain forty-seven ounces, healthy; lateral ventricles distended. Trachea pale above, purple and congested towards the bronchi; œsophagus pale, with light purplish patches in its upper third and ochre-colored below. Right lung eighteen ounces, much congested, several of the lobules of the upper lobe surrounded by a dark-reddish material resembling clotted blood; left lung seventeen ounces and a half, engorged with semi-solidified blood in the posterior part of its lower lobe. Heart nine ounces, no clot. Liver sixty-four ounces, mottled light and dark purple externally, slightly pale internally; gall-bladder containing an ounce of bile; spleen fourteen ounces, dark but firm; pancreas four ounces, healthy. Intestines healthy except near the ileo-cæcal valve, where Peyer's patches seemed to be congested, but they were not swollen nor ulcerated. Both kidneys were anæmic, with the pelves pale and the pyramidal bodies of a dark-purple color.—*Ass't Surg. Harrison Allen, U. S. A., Lincoln Hospital, Washington, D. C.*

CASE 278.—Serg't Alexander Beatty, Co. I, 15th N. J.; age 22; was admitted Jan. 2, 1863, with gangrene of the toes following typhoid fever. The gangrenous condition was attributed to frost-bite while sick in camp. Both feet were amputated through the metatarso-phalangeal articulation. On February 3, the day after the operation, delirium set in and continued, with occasional lucid intervals, until death on the 10th. *Post-mortem* examination an hour and a half after death: No rigor mortis; skin sallow; in the sole of the right foot was an abscess with offensive grayish contents, and over the external malleolus of the left foot was another which communicated with the wound of operation; the cartilages exposed by the amputation were much eroded, and those of the cuboid and internal cuneiform bones were nearly destroyed. The subarachnoid space and the ventricles of the brain contained an unusual quantity of serum. The right lung weighed eleven ounces, the left nine and a quarter; in the upper lobe of the left lung were two small round masses of cheesy tubercle and an abscess the size of a chestnut, which contained offensive pus; a similar, rather smaller, abscess was found in the middle lobe of the right lung; the bronchial tubes contained a whitish exudation; the bronchial glands were dark-colored externally and contained a white calcareous deposit. The heart was flabby. The liver was of firm consistence and somewhat congested; the spleen, sixteen ounces, was dark-colored, firm and congested; the pancreas was of a light-red color and firm. Both kidneys were of firm consistence; in the lower part of the right kidney was a small cavity containing whitish cheesy pus. The stomach was healthy; the jejunum darkly congested; the lower part of the ileum intensely congested, its solitary glands enlarged and inflamed and Peyer's patches congested and somewhat prominent; there was a region of congestion in the ascending colon.—*Ass't Surg. George M. McGill, U. S. A., Lincoln Hospital, Washington, D. C.*

CASE 279.—Corp'l John Schaffner, Co. B, 14th Vet. Res. Corps; admitted March 28, 1864; typhoid fever. Died April 3. *Post-mortem* examination eighteen hours after death: Body much emaciated. The duodenum was congested; the jejunum slightly congested in patches; the ileum congested throughout; Peyer's patches congested but not ulcerated; there was one congested spot in the lower colon, which was otherwise healthy.—*Act. Ass't Surg. C. T. Trautman, Harewood Hospital, Washington, D. C.*

CASE 280.—Private Conrad Hold, Co. D, 52d N. Y., was admitted Feb. 13, 1863, with fever and persistent vomiting. Epistaxis occurred on the 17th, and with the vomiting continued to the end, the bleeding usually recurring at night. The patient became stupid on the 21st, and there was some diarrhœa, which did not last beyond the 28th. Creasote, acetate of morphia and blisters had no effect on the vomiting. Medicine was discarded towards the end, stimulants and nourishment only being used. He lingered until March 7. *Post-mortem* examination: The glands of Peyer were congested and swollen and there were some signs of recent pericarditis. The spleen, liver, kidneys and lungs were normal.—*Act. Ass't Surg. John E. Smith, Douglas Hospital, Washington, D. C.*

CASE 281.—Private Henry G. Howell, Co. I, 27th N. J., was admitted Feb. 15, 1863, in a prostrate and delirious condition. He had frequent fits of coughing and expectorated a viscid, transparent, frothy mucus. During the following night his face became purplish, his delirium increased, and a clammy perspiration bedewed his skin. He died next day. *Post-mortem* examination four hours after death: Body robust; apparent age 25 years. The brain weighed forty-six ounces and was soft and congested to redness. There were pleuritic adhesions on both sides; the right lung weighed forty ounces and a half, the left thirty-three ounces; the lower lobes of both lungs and portions of the upper lobes were in a state of red hepatization, approaching gray; the bronchial tubes were congested and in some instances plugged with a fibrinous deposit. The heart contained large fibrinous clots on both sides. The liver weighed twenty-eight ounces and a half, its acini were distinct; the spleen, four ounces and three-quarters, was light-colored and soft, with distinct trabeculæ; the right kidney weighed five ounces and a half, the left five and a quarter; the suprarenal capsules were small, dark and tough. The stomach was large and its fundus congested; the glands of the duodenum were slightly enlarged; the upper third of the jejunum was irregularly congested; the ileum was congested, its solitary glands enlarged and reddened and the patches of Peyer irregularly inflamed and thickened. The large intestine was distended with gas, the solitary glands swollen and reddened— twelve of these enlarged glands were counted in a square inch selected at random; the mesenteric glands were enlarged and inflamed.—*Ass't Surg. George M. McGill, U. S. A., Lincoln Hospital, Washington, D. C.*

CASE 282.—Private Henry Campbell, Co. H, 20th Mich., was admitted Jan. 24, 1863, with typhoid fever, and died February 2. *Post-mortem* examination sixty-eight hours after death: Body well developed and fat. The brain, forty ounces and a half, was of light color and firm consistence. The heart contained clots. The lungs were congested hypostatically; the left lung weighed eighteen ounces, the right twenty-four ounces. The liver weighed forty-five ounces; the spleen ten ounces; the kidneys seven ounces each; the pancreas two ounces and three-quarters; the gall-bladder was empty. The mucous membrane of the stomach was congested; a lumbricoid worm was found in the jejunum, which was irregularly congested; its lower part and the upper part of the ileum were much thinned; Peyer's patches were enlarged and inflamed, especially near the ileo-cæcal valve; the coats of the large intestine were very thin and the mucous membrane congested, especially in the upper portion of the colon.—*Ass't Surg. George M. McGill, U. S. A., Lincoln Hospital, Washington, D. C.*

CASE 283.—Private Martin Dusenbery, recruit, 9th Ohio Cav.; age 20; was admitted Oct. 14, 1863, with typhoid fever. He had been sick four or five days. His fever was slight, but there was some delirium and cough with mucous sputa; his bowels were open, and there was slight tenderness in the epigastric and right iliac regions. Next day the delirium had disappeared and he was otherwise better. On the 18th his tongue was more coated, bowels open, abdomen tender, cough aggravated and respiration hurried. During the night of the 19th he was actively delirious, requiring restraint; and next day there was severe pain in the right lung, with dulness and crepitant râles. He died on this day. *Post-mortem* examination three hours after death: Left lung congested; lower two-thirds of right lung hepatized, with pleuritic adhesions especially of the diaphragm, and twelve ounces of serum in the pleural cavity. Intestines congested; Peyer's patches enlarged and inflamed but not ulcerated.—*Dennison Hospital, Ohio.*

CASE 284.—Private George W. Harvey, Co. H, 24th Maine; age 31; was admitted July 24, 1863. This patient was a deserter, and although rational on admission his mind was much exercised on the subject of his capture and probable punishment. This had an evident influence on the progress of his disease. Low delirium followed and continued until death on the 30th. *Post-mortem* examination: Heart, lungs and liver healthy; mesenteric glands and those of Brünner and Peyer extensively enlarged and inflamed; mucous coat of small intestine softened and ulcerated throughout its entire length.—*Act. Ass't Surg. A. P. Craft, Third Division Hospital, Alexandria, Va.*

CASE 285.—Corp'l William H. Glattz, Co. K, 4th Del.; age 23; was admitted July 23, 1863, in an advanced stage of typhoid fever. He died on the 26th. *Post-mortem* examination: Lower lobe of right lung congested; Peyer's patches inflamed and elevated; mucous follicles of the colon much enlarged; spleen congested; liver and kidneys normal.—*Act. Ass't Surg. T. Turner, Third Division Hospital, Alexandria, Va.*

CASE 286.—Private Peter A. Wayman, Co. B, 91st N. Y.; admitted May 6, 1865. Diagnosis—typhoid fever. Died on the 11th. *Post-mortem* examination sixty hours after death: Upper lobe of right lung hepatized and adherent; left lung and heart normal; spleen double the usual size; stomach healthy; Peyer's patches swollen and inflamed; colon normal.—*Sixth Army Corps Field Hospital, Army of Potomac.*

(e.) Peyer's patches pigmented.

CASE 287.—Private William Sibley, Co. A, 2d Mass. Heavy Art.; age 25; was admitted Sept. 10, 1865, having, from his own statement, been sick for a long time with fever and diarrhœa. He had a hot skin, dry and coated tongue and feeble intermittent pulse; he became delirious during the night, and died next day. *Post-mortem* examination ten hours after death: Not much emaciation; no rigor mortis. The subarachnoid space contained about two ounces of serum, and a small quantity was found in the ventricles; the pia mater was congested; ecchymosed spots were observed on the summit of the right cerebral hemisphere and on the right side of the floor of the fourth ventricle; the section of the hemispheres showed numerous puncta vasculosa. A large portion of the lower lobe of the left lung was in the first stage of pneumonia; the right lung was congested posteriorly and weighed twenty-two ounces, the left thirty-two ounces. The heart weighed twelve ounces; the auricular septum was perforated; there was a mixed clot in the right side, a little fluid blood in the left. The liver was firm, dark-colored and weighed fifty-eight and a quarter ounces; the gall-bladder contained a small quantity of thin brown bile; the spleen was soft and weighed six ounces. The stomach was thin and discolored; the ileum congested in regions, its solitary glands enlarged and Peyer's patches prominent and speckled with blood; the large intestine flaccid and in part discolored. The kidneys were large and soft.—*Ass't Surg. George M. McGill, U. S. A., Hick's Hospital, Baltimore, Md.*

CASE 288.—Private Henry H. Joyce, Co. B, 6th Va. (rebel) Inf.; admitted Aug. 3, 1863; typhoid fever. Died 7th. *Post-mortem* examination sixteen hours after death: Body not emaciated; rigor mortis slight; apparent age 23. The brain was firm and weighed forty-eight ounces; the pia mater was congested over the posterior portion of both hemispheres. The mucous membrane of the trachea was congested, the congestion extending into the bronchial tubes; the lymphatic glands at the bifurcation of the trachea were firm and black. There were pleuritic adhesions on both sides; the right lung weighed nineteen ounces, its upper lobe slightly congested and a frothy secretion exuding on pressure, its middle lobe congested hypostatically and having on its surface numerous spots of transuded blood; the left lung weighed twenty ounces, its upper lobe normal, but the lower ecchymosed and greatly congested. The right auricle of the heart contained a thin fibrinous clot which extended into the ventricle and thence into the pulmonary artery and its branches for a distance of three or four inches; the endocardium in the right auricle was purplish. The liver was somewhat congested and rather flabby; the gall-bladder contained half a drachm of thick bile; the spleen, nineteen ounces, was firm and of a rich mahogany color; both kidneys were moderately firm, the surface somewhat greenish, the cortical substance pale except at the superior extremities of the organs, where it was congested, the pyramidal bodies purplish; the pancreas, three ounces, was purplish and of normal firmness. The mucous membrane of the fundus of the stomach was dark-colored, in the rest of the organ it was pale. The small intestine presented nothing remarkable except a dark-purplish congestion in the lower third of the ileum; Peyer's patches were pale with conspicuous black spots in their follicles, but nowhere were they thickened or ulcerated. The large intestine was healthy.—*Ass't Surg. Harrison Allen, U. S. A., Lincoln Hospital, Washington, D. C.*

CASE 289.—Private Jacob Henson, Co. G, 16th Pa. Cav.; age 18; was admitted March 25, 1864, very weak and much emaciated, with a frequent and feeble pulse and hurried respiration. He was quite deaf; he had a bedsore two inches square, with highly inflamed margins, over the lower part of the sacrum; his right knee-joint was acutely inflamed, quite red over the internal condyle, very hot and exquisitely painful. From the testimony of a comrade it was learned that the patient had been affected with erysipelas and typhoid fever, and that the inflammation of the knee-joint occurred as a sequel to these diseases. Cold water was applied to the knee and extension kept up by Gurdon Buck's apparatus with a three-pound weight. Opium and whiskey were administered. Next day the condition of the knee-joint was improved; but the patient's eyes were yellow, his skin purpuric and dry and his face flushed; he had pain in the left side with some dulness, bronchial respiration and increased vocal resonance, a hacking cough but no expectoration; he had also some diarrhœa. On the 28th he had a severe chill, which recurred next day and was followed by profuse perspiration. After this, although there was manifest improvement in the condition of the knee-joint and lung, his strength failed gradually, and he died on April 7. *Post-mortem* examination fourteen hours after death: Body much emaciated; skin dingy with many purpuric spots; rigor mortis well marked. The brain was healthy. The right lung was healthy but firmly adherent on all sides; the left pleural cavity contained two pints of serum; the lower lobe of the left lung was covered with fibrin, at one point nearly half an inch thick, and in its lower and posterior part was an abscess the size of a large walnut surrounded by much solidified tissue. The pericardium contained two ounces of serum. The liver, seventy-one ounces, was firm and waxy and had pale spots scattered over its surface; the gall-bladder was empty; the pancreas, spleen and kidneys were healthy. The solitary and agminated glands of the intestines were prominent and dotted with dark points. The knee-joint contained two ounces of pus mixed with fibrinous flakes, one of which was over an inch and a half in diameter; the cartilage on the lateral aspects of the femoral articulating surface was destroyed, laying bare the cancellous structure of the bone; the synovial membrane was vascular, especially above the patella, where also it was covered with shreds of fibrin; the bursa beneath the extensor tendon of the thigh communicated with the joint by several orifices and was filled with pus and lymph.—*Lincoln Hospital, Washington, D. C.*

CASE 290.—Private Daniel Crum, Co. C, 61st N. Y.; admitted July 26, 1862; typhoid fever. Died August 24. *Post-mortem* examination next day: Organs generally healthy except that the agminated and solitary glands were thickened and of a most remarkable black color, resembling the bluish-black marks of tatooing; the surrounding parts of the mucous membrane were pale and devoid of anything like congestion.—*Act. Ass't Surg. J. Leidy, Satterlee Hospital, Philadelphia, Pa.*

CASE 291.—Private Thomas J. Crumb, Co. D, 44th N. Y.; admitted Aug. 10, 1862; typhoid fever. The patient had diarrhœa on admission, and during the last few days of life was delirious. Died 27th. *Post-mortem* examination next day: Body much emaciated; age about 25 years. Brain natural in appearance except that the pia mater was unusually bloodless, opaque and wrinkled. Heart small, contracted, without a vestige of adipose tissue, liquid blood in its right side, the left empty except a small coagulum of fibrin attached to the chordæ tendineæ. Lungs healthy. Liver small, dusky-purple above and slate-colored below; spleen small, in section dull-brown. Stomach and intestines distended with air and presenting no evidence of inflammation; agminated glands healthy except that they contained a deposit of black matter; solitary glands unusually prominent and containing black matter; mucous membrane of the colon cream-colored, remarkably bloodless, solitary glands barely perceptible.—*Act. Ass't Surg. J. Leidy, Satterlee Hospital, Philadelphia, Pa.*

CASE 292.—Private Thomas Rose, Co. A, 49th Pa.; admitted Aug. 10, 1862; typhoid fever. Died September 23d. *Post-mortem* examination: Age about 20; body considerably emaciated and everywhere ecchymosed. Lungs and heart healthy, the latter containing a white clot in the right ventricle extending into the pulmonary artery, another in the left auricle and a third in the commencement of the aorta. Spleen, liver, kidneys, suprarenal bodies and pancreas natural. Mucous membrane of stomach inflamed more or less diffusely and with occasional small patches of greater intensity. Ileum inflamed in patches, increasing in intensity towards the lower end; solitary glands enlarged, inflamed and containing black matter; agminated glands with black deposit but otherwise apparently healthy. Colon distended with air, except descending portion, which was narrowly contracted but not inflamed; cæcum, ascending and transverse colon inflamed; solitary glands conspicuous and containing black pigment.—*Act. Ass't Surg. J. Leidy, Satterlee Hospital, Philadelphia, Pa.*

CASE 293.—Private A. W. Parris, Co. H, 2d Vt.; admitted Aug. 10, 1862; typhoid fever. Died 26th. *Post-mortem* examination next day: Body large, somewhat wasted, aged about 30 years; skin bronzed and upon the trunk somewhat ecchymosed. Heart normal, containing a fibrinous clot and much liquid blood. Lungs, liver and spleen healthy. Stomach distended with air and liquid, its mucous membrane dusky-gray and with an inflamed patch near the pylorus. Ileum highly inflamed in patches; agminated glands, thirty-six in number, all dotted with black pigment but otherwise natural; solitary glands inconspicuous. Colon contracted, gray, with a few small red patches, and with black pigment in the solitary glands.—*Act. Ass't Surg. J. Leidy, Satterlee Hospital, Philadelphia, Pa.*

CASE 294.—Private James B. Hendricks, Co. F, 49th Pa.; admitted Aug. 10, 1862; typhoid fever. Died 14th. *Post-mortem* examination: The organs of the chest and abdomen appeared to be healthy except the ileum and colon, in both of which the mucous membrane was inflamed. The agminated and solitary glands contained points of black pigment, but otherwise seemed natural.—*Act. Ass't Surg. J. Leidy, Satterlee Hospital, Philadelphia, Pa.*

CASE 295.—Private Joseph Robbins, Co. H, 49th Pa.; admitted Aug. 10, 1862; typhoid fever. Died 14th. *Post-mortem* examination next day: The body was much emaciated; the skin of the trunk in some places appeared as if ecchymosed. The heart, lungs, liver, stomach, spleen, pancreas and kidneys were healthy. The mucous membrane of the ileum was inflamed throughout, but near the lower end, for about ten inches, the inflammation was most aggravated and had attached small but numerous shreds of opaque-white pseudo-membranous matter, which under the microscope was found to consist of a fibro-granular matrix and granular corpuscles resembling ordinary pus corpuscles; the solitary glands were invisible or absent, except a few scattered here and there in the jejunum; the agminated glands were conspicuous, dotted with black pigment, but not perceptibly diseased. The colon was exceedingly contracted; within the cæcum and ascending colon the mucous membrane was red and the solitary glands large and conspicuous by the presence of black pigment; the lower two-thirds of the colon presented a mingled red and slate-color, with many small ulcers apparently resulting from the destruction of the solitary glands.—*Act. Ass't Surg. J. Leidy, Satterlee Hospital, Philadelphia, Pa.*

CASE 296.—Private Thomas Elder, Co. D, 14th U. S. Inf.; age 18; was admitted Aug. 10, 1862, with typhoid fever, and died on the 18th. *Post-mortem* examination next day: Body not much wasted. Heart and inner surface of pericardial sac roughened with old pseudo-membranes; right lung engorged. Liver large; gall-bladder nearly empty; mucous membrane of stomach presenting a large reddened patch on the lower part of its cardiac extremity; spleen showing an inflamed condensation of its tissue about the size of a nutmeg at its upper end, with the omentum in contact also inflamed. The mucous membrane of the ileum was inflamed in regions, one of which was two feet long and stopped about six inches from the ileo-colic valve. There were thirty-two agminated glands ranging from half an inch to three inches in length; a large patch on each fold of the ileo-colic valve was dotted with black pigment, but appeared otherwise healthy; the next gland above also appeared healthy; the others, except the first two, were much thickened, opaque and white, or thickened and reddened by inflammation, but none were ulcerated; the solitary glands generally were invisible in the jejunum and were few in the ileum, but where obvious in the latter, they were quite prominent and red. The colon was much contracted; its mucous membrane was of a slate-color mingled with small patches of inflammation, and the solitary glands were black. [*Specimens* 228 to 231, Med. Sect.. Army Medical Museum, are from this case.]—*Act. Ass't Surg. Joseph Leidy, Satterlee Hospital, Philadelphia, Pa.*

CASE 297.—Private Daniel Eaton, Co. H, 3d N. J. Cav.; age 20; was admitted April 29, 1865: Pulse 150; tongue dry, brown and glazed; teeth and lips covered with sordes; pupils considerably dilated; mouth, nose, cheeks and hands stained with blood; respiration frequent and deglutition difficult. He moaned constantly and lay in a state of low muttering delirium, from which he could be partly aroused, but was unable to articulate; there were frequent slight convulsive movements of the body somewhat like those produced by moderate shocks of an electric battery; his urine was passed involuntarily and there was a very offensive ammoniacal odor about his person. He died May 1. *Post-mortem* examination five hours after death: Body but little emaciated. The vessels of the pia mater were engorged. The upper lobe of the left lung was hepatized, and hepatized patches were found here and there through both lungs; the rest of the lung-tissue was congested. The pericardium contained about an ounce and a half of serum. The spleen was enlarged. Peyer's glands were enlarged but not ulcerated; slate-colored patches, having a peculiar punctated appearance, were scattered here and there in the lower portion of the ileum and in the colon in the vicinity of the ileo-cæcal valve.—*Act. Ass't Surg. G. Ellis Porter, Cumberland Hospital, Md.*

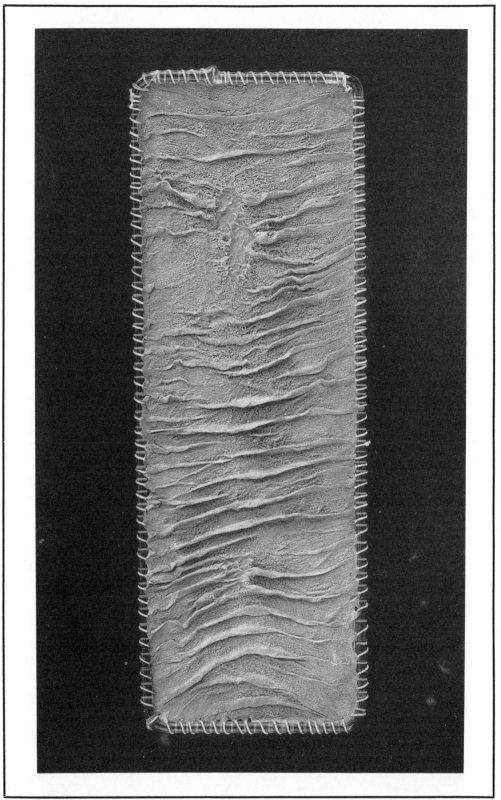

Am. Photo-Relief Printing Co.,   1002 Arch St., Philadelphia.

CICATRICES OF ULCERATED PEYER'S PATCHES.

No. 490.   MEDICAL SECTION.

(f.) Peyer's patches cicatrized.

CASE 298.—Recruit Joseph Hughes, 7th N. Y. Cav.; age 16; was admitted Jan. 31, 1865, with phthisis consecutive to camp fever. He had been sick five months. He complained of palpitation of the heart and pain in the left breast just below the nipple, with cough and slight expectoration. Sinapisms were applied to the chest and brown mixture prescribed, with Dover's powder at night. Stimulants seemed to aggravate the chest symptoms. He died February 8. *Post-mortem* examination: The brain was quite firm. The right lung was small and had a few tubercles at the apex; in the left there were numerous vomicæ. The abdominal cavity contained a quantity of serum rendered turbid with curdy flakes of lymph; the viscera were coated with soft white lymph. The mucous membrane of the ileum was of a grayish-slate color, its villi were hypertrophied and at the apex of each was a deposit of black pigment; Peyer's patches, which had been ulcerated away, were in every stage of cicatrization, the ulcers being smooth and the gut around them puckered. [See *specimens* 489–491, Med. Sect., Army Medical Museum, and the plate facing this page.] The colon was cream-colored, its solitary follicles black and with minute central depressions.—*Act. Ass't Surg. W. C. Minor, Third Division Hospital, Alexandria, Va.*

Overlooking for the present the eighty-eight cases in which the patches of Peyer were said to have been ulcerated as indicating the presence of the typhoid poison, and the forty-one cases of ulceration of the ileum or small intestine as failing to exclude the possibility of typhoid from a want of precision in the language used, attention is invited to a brief consideration of the intestinal lesions in the remaining fifty-three cases: In eleven of these, 246–256, the condition of Peyer's patches was not stated, and the intestine is said to have been congested or inflamed but not ulcerated, and in forty-two, cases 257–298, various conditions of the patches, not, however, including ulceration, were reported, and the intestines also were found to be generally free from ulceration.

Case 253, one of the eleven, may be set aside as implying in the disorganization of the intestine a possibility of typhoid sloughing of the closed glands. The history in seven of the cases, 249–252 and 254–256, shows that the patients lived long enough for notable changes to have taken place in the agminated glands had typhoid fever been really present; but the records refer only to a congestion of the intestines; in 252 the solitary glands were enlarged and in 254 their apices were ulcerated, but the agminated glands were unaffected; in 249 there was no typhoid lesion, but whether the changes in the spleen, which caused the fatal peritonitis, were malarial or not is uncertain. In one other case, 248, time was afforded before death for the development of typhoid ulceration of the glands had the typhoid poison been the primary cause of the fatal sickness, for the patient lived long enough to present extensive ulcerations of the larynx and trachea. In two cases the duration of the sickness is unknown; but in one of these, 246, the condition of the ileum is expressed in language that admits of no doubt of the absence of typhoid, and as in the other case, 247, the *post-mortem* appearances indicated typhus or a malarial fever, the inference is that the disease was malarial.

Of the forty-two cases presenting various conditions of the agminated glands, not, however, including ulceration, the glands were *normal, healthy* or *not diseased* in *five* cases, 257–261. In the first of these the patient was only five days in hospital when death occurred with symptoms of cerebral implication which, if not due to a malarial cause, was certainly not owing to typhoid fever. A tumefaction of the glands of Peyer has, since the time of LOUIS, been regarded as the initial and essential lesion of this fever; but in the case in question these glands were healthy while the brain presented signs of inflammation. In the four other cases there was ample time afforded before death for well-developed ulceration of the patches, but a congestion of the lining membrane was the only morbid intestinal appearance, and in 259 this was mainly found in the upper portion of the small intestine.

In *two* of the forty-two cases the patches were reported as *not ulcerated*, and in both the patients were in hospital long enough to permit of the occurrence of well-marked changes if typhoid fever had been the cause of their sickness.   In one of these, case 263, it is recorded that, in view of the diagnosis, special attention had been paid to the *post-mortem* condition of the small intestine.

In accordance with pathological doctrines which are generally accepted, the prominent condition of the patches in the *ten* cases, 264–273, must be regarded as indicating the presence of enteric fever at the time of death.   But since the fatal illness in most of these cases lasted long enough for sloughing of the patches to have taken place had it been typhoid fever from its inception, some morbid cause must have been in operation before the influence of the typhoid poison was manifested; and there is nothing in the *post-mortem* lesions to contraindicate, but on the contrary much to sustain the opinion, derived from clinical observation in other and concurrent cases, that this antecedent disease was an active malarial affection.   These cases may therefore be viewed as truly typho-malarial, the typhoid affection supervening on the malarial attack.

Of the *thirteen* cases, 274–286, in which the vascular supply of the patches had undergone notable changes, these were associated with tumefaction in seven cases, 275, 279, 281–284 and 286, in most of which the short period elapsing before the fatal issue suggests death from typhoid fever in advance of the period when sloughing usually takes place.   It may be remarked, however, that if tumefaction and congestion of the patches are ever developed, in the absence of enteric fever, as a consequence of morbid vascular action affecting the intestinal canal as a whole,* the claims of some of these cases, to wit: 275 and 279, as illustrative of this condition might be entitled to consideration.   Two of the thirteen cases, 280 and 285, may be regarded as truly typho-malarial, since they presented the glands swollen but entire at a period when in pure typhoid the eliminative process would have been in operation.   In 277 there was no tumefaction of the agminated glands, although the patient was eight days in hospital and sick for probably a longer time.   In 274 and 276, in which the fever lasted long enough for the establishment of the ulcerative process if a typhoid element had been present, the plaques were altered only in so far as they participated in a general and long continued congestion of the intestinal membrane.   Lastly, in 278, which ended fatally at a late period, the patches were not ulcerated but only congested and somewhat prominent in an intestine which was darkly injected throughout.

In *twelve* of the forty-two cases, 287–298, the intestinal lining was pigmented, but the agminated glands were not ulcerated.   In the first of these there was neither ulceration nor sloughing, although the patient was sick for a long time; the ileum was congested in regions, its patches prominent and speckled with blood and its solitary follicles conspicuous.   In the eight cases, 288–295, the solitary and agminated glands were dotted with black pigment, and in most of these there was ample time before death for ulceration of the patches to have taken place, for even in 295, which had been only five days in hospital, the patient had lived long enough for the development of ulceration in the solitary follicles; nevertheless the agminated glands were intact but for the pigmentary deposit.   But in the remaining three cases, 296–298, an enteric element was superadded to the pigmented condition; in 296 certain of Peyer's glands were thickened, opaque and white or reddened by congestion; in 297 they were enlarged, and in 298 the ulcerated glands had become cicatrized.

In summing up the analytical results briefly enumerated in the above paragraphs it is found that, of fifty-three cases characterized by so many of the so-called typhoid symptoms

---

* See *infra*, page 456.

that the attending medical officers formed a diagnosis of typhoid fever, no less than thirty failed to present at the *post-mortem* examination those anatomical changes which from the time of LOUIS have been generally regarded as pathognomonic of the disease; but showed, on the contrary, a series of lesions in perfect harmony with our knowledge of the frequently occurring but not essential incidence of the malarial poison on the intestinal canal. It is submitted that these cases fully sustain the statement that among those reported as typhoid fever were many which were purely and simply malarial fevers; and since similar cases have been presented from the typho-malarial records, and even from those of the paroxysmal fevers, the conclusion that typhoid symptoms were not necessarily associated with a specific enteric poison must be admitted.

The *post-mortem* records contain also a series of seventy-nine cases variously reported at first, but from their later symptoms or necroscopic appearances afterwards regarded as typhoid fever. These are of interest as showing the relations of typhoid to various other diseases. Three cases, 301, 347 and 366, admitted by the attending medical officers as malarial fevers, should have been presented in a previous part of this section; but their absence from the series of cases reported as typho-malarial does not alter the conclusions that have been derived from an investigation of that series, while in their present connection they serve as delegates from the typho-malarial cases, each illustrative or typical of its kind; 301 as instancing true typho-malarial fever—typhoid modified by malarial complications; 347 as representing malarial fever with typhoid symptoms, the record of which fails to show whether the intestinal ulceration was due to the malarial or the typhoid element,—such cases have in this report been set aside as probably typhoid; and 366 as illustrating paroxysmal fever with typhoid symptoms, but with no *post-mortem* lesion to indicate the presence of a specific enteric poison.

These seventy-nine cases have been arranged in accordance with the anatomical changes in the intestinal canal.

(A.) PEYER'S PATCHES ULCERATED—42 CASES.

(a.) No diagnosis.

CASE 299.—Private George H. Rimer, Co. I, 24th N. Y. Cav.; age 16; was admitted June 24, 1864, with a gun-shot flesh wound of the left leg. On July 1 signs of congestion of the brain made their appearance; the pupils were largely dilated, the right being larger than the left; the head was hot and with the chest was covered with a copious perspiration; the fæces and urine were passed involuntarily; articulation was indistinct. He died on the 3d. *Post-mortem* examination twelve hours after death: The body was somewhat emaciated. The brain weighed sixty ounces; its bloodvessels were much injected, and the liquid in the ventricles and subarachnoid spaces was increased in quantity. The lungs were slightly adherent at their apices by recent lymph; the right weighed eleven ounces and a half, the left thirteen ounces; the lobes of the left lung were interadherent and the posterior part of the lower lobe was hepatized. The heart weighed seven ounces and a half, the liver fifty-nine ounces, and the spleen nine ounces and a half. The stomach was normal. Many of Peyer's patches were extensively ulcerated, the others thickened; the solitary glands were much enlarged; the large intestine was congested and in its lower portion ulcerated.—*Act. Ass't Surg. H. M. Dean, Lincoln Hospital, Washington, D. C.*

CASE 300.—Private John Rice, Co. F, 10th Vt.; age 23; was admitted from field hospital at Sandy Hook, Aug. 27, 1864, in a low condition, lying dull and inattentive, complaining of exquisite pain in the abdomen and having frequent mucous discharges from the bowels. Hoffmann's anodyne was prescribed and a large poultice applied over the abdomen. On the 30th there was much headache, which continued on the 31st; on this day the discharges were controlled by enemata containing lead and opium. September 1 the symptoms were more favorable, the skin less harsh and sometimes perspiring, the pulse less rapid and not so weak, but there were occasional recurrences of febrile action. Beef-tea, wine and citrate of iron and quinine were given, with opiate enemata and woolen packing to the abdomen instead of the poultice; turpentine was also administered. The patient's appetite was good, but he remained very weak and his tongue continued red and dry. Towards the end of September the febrile symptoms returned, assuming the tertian type, and the diarrhœa continued. On October 3 the patient became dull and was aroused with diffi-culty; the dejections were passed involuntarily and were mixed with blood and pus; bed-sores appeared on the hips. Wine and stimulants were freely given, but the patient grew worse rapidly, and died on the 14th. *Post-mortem* inves-tigation showed the coats of the large intestine extensively thickened, its calibre diminished and its mucous tissue destroyed in patches by ulceration; these patches were most numerous in the sigmoid flexure, where perforation had taken place, the orifice being two-thirds of an inch in diameter. The mucous coat of the ileum was eroded and the agminated and solitary glands ulcerated; the jejunum was inflamed in patches. [See *specimens* 459 and 460, Med. Sect., Army Medical Museum, and plate facing this page.]—*Ass't Surg. C. Bacon, jr., U. S. A., Annapolis Hospital, Md.*

(b.) Diagnosis: Remittent fever.

CASE 301.—Private Jesse Steiner, Co. D, 167th Pa.; age 30; was admitted July 12, 1863, with debility and remittent fever, and died on the 21st. *Post-mortem* examination twelve hours after death: Body well developed; rigor mortis well marked. The brain-substance was firm and slightly congested; half a drachm of bloody fluid was found in the lateral ventricles. The trachea was discolored and filled with viscid, dark-brown sputa; its mucous membrane was rather soft and the lymphatic glands at its bifurcation were enlarged, blackened and softened, except in the centre, where there was a calcareous degeneration. The œsophagus was pale and rather contracted; numerous dark-colored spots were found at the lower portion, one of which was the seat of superficial ulceration. The right lung weighed twenty ounces; its upper lobe was covered with fibrinous adhesions; this lobe and the lower lobe were slightly congested, but the middle lobe was healthy; the bronchial tubes were filled with a secretion similar to that found in the trachea. The left lung weighed twenty-three ounces and was somewhat congested at its apex and of a dark-purple color from venous engorgement in its lower lobe. The heart contained a very small clot in the right ventricle. The liver was of a delicate purplish hue externally, its acini pale, capsule readily torn and parenchyma firm; the spleen was mulberry-purple and moderately firm. The small intestine was perfectly healthy to within a few inches of the ileo-cæcal valve, where several Peyer's patches were ulcerated. Numerous ecchymosed spots were found in the upper portion of the large intestine; the lower third contained an immense quantity of unripe blackberry seeds, and its mucous membrane, purple in color and rather firm, was lined with an extensive black clot.—*Ass't Surg. H. Allen, U. S. A., Lincoln Hospital, Washington, D. C.*

(c.) Diagnosis: Gastritis.

CASE 302.—Private Lorenzo Weakley, Co. C, 7th Va.; age 19; was admitted Aug. 21, 1864, his previous history being unknown. He was emaciated and exhausted from epigastric pain and incessant vomiting, his food and drink being almost instantly rejected; he had a slight diarrhœa; his pulse was feeble and his tongue covered with a gray moist coating. The vomiting and diarrhœa continued until the 23d, when there was some abatement; but the surface of the body became cold and clammy, and he died on the 25th. He was treated with brandy, morphine, mild astringents and sinapisms. *Post-mortem* examination six hours after death: Abdomen tympanitic. The lungs were emphysematous and in their posterior parts congested; the right side of the heart contained a large fibrinous clot, the left was empty; the pericardium contained about six ounces of liquid. The liver was slightly enlarged and pale; the gall-bladder nearly filled with dark viscid bile; the spleen normal in size but dark-colored. The pericardium and omentum were congested; the mesenteric glands enlarged. The mucous membrane of the stomach was thickened and of a deep red color at its cardiac end. The small intestine was healthy to the middle of the ileum, below which point it was congested and ulcerated, the ulcers being larger and more numerous at the lower end; the apertures of the solitary follicles and tubuli were colored with black pigment, giving the mucous membrane the appearance of being covered with small black spots; the lower portion of the descending colon was considerably thickened and softened. The kidneys had a large deposit of fat about the pelves and their medullary substance was abnormally pale. [*Specimens* 407 and 408, Med. Sect., Army Medical Museum, are from this case.]—*Act. Ass't Surg. O. P. Sweet, Carver Hospital, Washington, D. C.*

(d.) Diagnosis: Cerebro-spinal meningitis.

CASE 303.*—Private Davis N. Hosmer, Co. F, 45th Mass.; age 18; was admitted Jan. 30, 1863. Two days before admission he had a slight chill, which was succeeded by violent headache, slight epistaxis and pain in the back and limbs. On admission he had severe occipital headache, fever and delirium; his head was thown back. Diarrhœa set in, but was controlled by acetate of lead and opium; cough also was troublesome, and sibilant râles were heard over both sides of the chest. On February 4 the pulse declined to 100, the skin became cool and moist and the ability to answer questions returned. Next day there was gurgling in the right iliac region. On the 6th the patient became rather stupid and affected with low delirium, but there was no diarrhœa. Several spots appeared on the abdomen on the 7th. He became comatose on the 8th and died on the 10th. *Post-mortem* examination fourteen hours after death: The cerebral membranes were slightly injected; the lateral ventricles were distended with turbid serum; a firm deposit of lymph from a quarter to three-eighths of an inch in thickness covered the inferior aspect of the cerebellum and medulla oblongata. The lungs were congested posteriorly. The heart, liver, stomach, spleen, pancreas, kidneys and bladder were normal. The solitary glands of the intestines were enlarged and Peyer's patches thickened and in one or two places ulcerated.—*Ass't Surg. J. B. Treadwell, 45th Mass., Stanley Hospital, New Berne, N. C.*

(e.) Diagnosis: Diarrhœa.†

CASE 304.—Private Milo Holmes, Co. G, 37th Mass.; age 38; was admitted July 28, 1863, having been suffering more or less from diarrhœa for the previous twelve months. He was much emaciated but was able to sit up and

---

* This case was published by J. B. UPHAM, *Boston Med. and Surg. Journal*, Vol. LXVIII, 1863, p. 191, as one of cerebro-spinal meningitis.

† CHARLES H. RAWSON, Surg. 5th Iowa Vols., *American Medical Times*, Vol. IV, 1862, p. 129, briefly enumerates the symptoms of two fatal cases of camp typhoid fever. These were at first regarded as diarrhœas and treated as such in quarters without any beneficial result. At the end of five days they were taken to hospital, where soon after fever of a remittent type was developed, presenting in its course a dry, red tongue; subsultus; delirium forty-eight hours before death; a pulse ranging from 120 to 160 and feeble, imperceptible at the wrist for two days preceding the fatal termination. The abdomen was tender in the first case but not in the other. Both patients succumbed ten days after the attack. The treatment consisted of the administration of stimulants and nourishment. The mucous membrane of the alimentary tract from the cardiac extremity of the stomach to the anus was

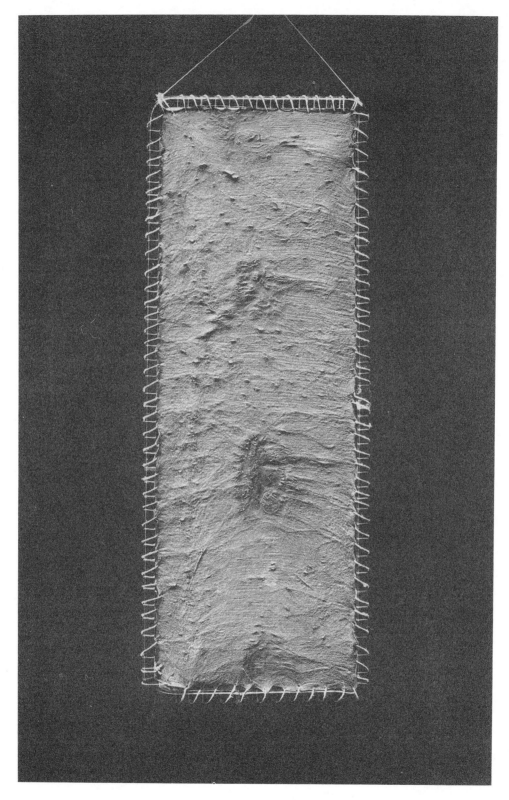

Heliotype.

James R. Osgood & Co., Boston.

CICATRICES OF ULCERATED PEYER'S PATCHES.

No. 459. MEDICAL SECTION.

walk around a little. He had no appetite; had several thin stools daily; his pulse was quick and weak, tongue furred, temperature of body low and breathing slow and labored. There was no marked change in these symptoms until August 6, when the stools became involuntary and he appeared to be sinking. Coma supervened on the 8th, and he died next day. *Post-mortem* examination twenty hours after death: The body was very much emaciated. The brain weighed forty ounces and a quarter; the posterior part of the cerebrum was hypostatically congested; one drachm and a half of clear serum was contained in the lateral ventricles; the brain-substance was rather firm. The trachea was pale and somewhat purplish between the rings; the lymphatic glands at its bifurcation were small and not softened, but of a moderately blackish color; the œsophageal lining was firm and of a yellowish-ochre color. The upper lobe of the right lung was hypostatically congested posteriorly, but its anterior portion was healthy; the middle lobe was of a dark-purple color and its central portion was splenified posteriorly; the weight of this lung was thirteen ounces and a half. The left lung weighed fourteen ounces and a half; it was of a dark-purple hue posteriorly and its lower lobe was considerably engorged with venous blood. The heart was normal; its cavities contained a soft jelly-like clot; a large fibrinous clot was found in the pulmonary artery, extending a long distance beyond its bifurcation, and lying on the posterior surface of the vessel surrounded by a thin venous fluid. The liver was somewhat congested; Glisson's capsule was readily torn; the gall-bladder contained six drachms of bile; the spleen was firm and of a mulberry color. The small intestine presented nothing remarkable except in the neighborhood of the ileo-cæcal valve, where were several ulcers of Peyer's patches, evidently of long standing, circular in form and penetrating to the transverse muscular fibres. The kidneys were soft and anæmic but somewhat injected on their external surface.—*Ass't Surg. H. Allen, U. S. A., Lincoln Hospital, Washington, D. C.*

CASE 305.—Private Charles Jillson, Co. G, 146th Ind., was admitted Aug. 2, 1865, with chronic diarrhœa. He had pain in the hypogastric region and very frequent stools. He died on the 6th. *Post-mortem* examination: Brain normal. Lungs œdematous posteriorly, weight of each twenty-six ounces; heart normal, a black clot in the left ventricle, a mixed one in the right. Liver somewhat dark-colored and quite full of blood; spleen dark-colored, weight six ounces; pancreas and kidneys normal. The fundus of the stomach was congested, and there were longitudinal streaks of congestion in the œsophagus. The ileum was congested and Peyer's patches thickened and ulcerated, especially near the ileo-cæcal valve. The contents of the large intestine were semi-fluid and of a dark-green color mixed with a yellowish granular matter.—*Ass't Surg. George M. McGill, U. S. A., Hicks Hospital, Baltimore, Md.*

CASE 306.—Private Richard Parker, Co. K, 133d Pa., was admitted Dec. 30, 1862, having been sick three weeks. When the first notes were taken, Jan. 1, 1863, the diagnosis recorded was typhoid fever, but this was afterwards changed to chronic diarrhœa. The patient was sleepless, his mouth dry and his tongue smooth, glazed and red; his emaciation was progressive and ultimately became extreme. A loose cough set in on the 12th, and a few days later he became jaundiced. He died on the 17th, having vomited a good deal of yellow matter the day before his death. *Post-mortem* examination twenty-three hours after death: There were strong pleuritic adhesions on the anterior surface of the upper lobe of the right lung; the parenchyma of the lung was congested and a purulent secretion issued from its bronchi upon pressure. The left lung was less congested, but the purulent discharge from the smaller ramifications of its tubes was of a thicker consistence than that found on the other side; cheesy tubercles were thickly scattered throughout the parenchyma of this lung except in its upper portion. The right cavities of the heart contained fibrinous clots. The liver had a nutmeg appearance and weighed forty ounces; the spleen was of a dark color and weighed three ounces and a half. The mucous membrane of the lesser curvature of the stomach was injected in points; the jejunum exhibited irregular patches of congestion in its lower part; Peyer's patches were almost destroyed. The kidneys weighed five ounces and a half each.—*Lincoln Hospital, Washington, D. C.*

CASE 307.—Private Matthias Koon, Co. E, 8th N. Y.; age 50; was admitted Dec. 1, 1864, in a partially comatose condition. Diagnosis—diarrhœa and anasarca. He died on the 15th. *Post-mortem* examination: Rigor mortis marked; sudamina on left breast. Trachea congested; bronchi filled with bloody fluid; lungs congested; the middle and lower lobes of the right lung sank in water; the right lung and upper lobe of the lung were adherent to the parietal pleura. Pericardium thickened and containing six ounces of straw-colored serum. Peritoneum thickened and containing sixteen ounces of straw-colored serum. Liver mottled light-brown, fatty; two ounces and a half inspissated bile in gall-bladder. Brünner's glands and Peyer's patches ulcerated; ileum inflamed; mesenteric glands filled with chalky concretions. Kidneys large and fatty.—*Third Division Hospital, Alexandria, Va.*

CASE 308.—Corp'l Joseph Cole, Co. B, 2d N. Y. Mounted Rifles, was admitted July 24, 1864, much emaciated from chronic diarrhœa. Under treatment by wine, opium, catechu and milk diet he improved, and his stools were natural, August 7–9, but on the 10th his throat became swollen and covered with false membrane. He died on the 12th. *Post-mortem* examination eleven hours after death: Larynx thickly covered with false membrane; glottis œdematous. Lungs, heart, liver, spleen and kidneys normal; Peyer's patches ulcerated, especially near the ileo-cæcal valve; large intestine healthy.—*Fairfax Seminary Hospital, Va.*

---

red and thickened; Peyer's glands were thickened but not ulcerated. In a third case the patches were extensively ulcerated. The nature and extent of the intestinal affection revealed by *post-mortem* examination led to the abandonment of the stimulant mode of treatment in the thirty cases which speedily followed. Cups and blisters to the abdomen, with turpentine emulsion containing opium, and, in the presence of diarrhœa, castor oil, were successfully employed. But one fatal case occurred after this, and in it the intestinal mucous membrane was red as in the previous cases. "Every one of Peyer's patches was ulcerated to its fullest size, enormously raised and spread out like a full-blown rose, if I may use the expression. They would range from a five-cent piece to the size of a dollar. Every mucous follicle and duct was thickened, raised and ulcerated from the size of a pin's head to a pea. On passing through into the cæcum, at the junction of the ileum, was an ulcer as large as a teacup. The whole mucous membrane to the rectum was in a frightful state of disorganization." [The three cases briefly sketched by Dr. RAWSON appear on his Monthly Report of Sick and Wounded for December, 1861, as cases of gastro-enteritis. The thirty cases said to have terminated favorably cannot be identified on the official reports unless they are included among seventeen cases of typhoid fever, three of which were fatal, and forty-three cases of remittent fever, none of which were fatal, specified on his monthly reports for December, 1861, and January, 1862.]

Case 309.—Private Smith Byerly, Co. C, 57th Pa.; age 22; was admitted Feb. 4, 1865, with chronic diarrhœa, and died on the 28th. *Post-mortem* examination: Right lung adherent for the upper two-thirds of its extent; eight ounces of a sero-purulent liquid in the pleural sac; pericardium inflamed and its cavity literally filled with pus. Liver, spleen and kidneys very much softened. Ileum perforated at its junction with the colon, the aperture being about the size of a Spanish half-dollar; small intestine much inflamed, with some degree of ulceration scattered throughout and well-marked ulceration of the glands of Peyer.—*Act. Ass't Surg. B. B. Miles, Jarvis Hospital, Baltimore, Md.*

Case 310.—Private Charles M. Delano, Co. I, 7th Me., was admitted Aug. 10, 1862, with diarrhœa, and died on the 20th. *Post-mortem* examination next day: Body exceedingly emaciated; apparently about thirty-five years of age. Lungs healthy although adherent to the costal pleura throughout; heart, liver and spleen normal. The mucous membrane of the stomach presented numerous injected points about the size of mustard-seed, and the rugæ along the great curvature near the pylorus were inflamed. The ileum was inflamed in patches, some of them intensely; the lower fifteen agminated glands were ulcerated, some completely, others with from one to three small ulcers; the upper glands were inflamed but not ulcerated. The colon was inflamed, especially in its descending portion, which presented many small black stellate ulcers in positions formerly occupied by solitary glands; a patch of intense inflammation, extending from the sigmoid flexure into the rectum, was covered with an opaque-white membranous matter which the microscope exhibited as a fibro-granular substance mingled with desquamated epithelium.—*Act. Ass't Surg. Joseph Leidy, Satterlee Hospital, Philadelphia, Pa.*

Case 311.—Private J. R. Everts, Co. G, 2d E. Tenn.; age 22; was admitted from Richmond, Va. (a paroled prisoner), April 18, 1864, with diarrhœa. He died May 3d. *Post-mortem* examination twenty-four hours after death: Large vomica in left lung with two quarts of effusion in pleural cavity, pushing the heart to the right side; vomica in middle lobe of right lung and tubercular deposit in upper lobe with adhesion of pleural surfaces. Heart flabby and pale; aortic valves thickened. Spleen soft and friable; gall-bladder empty. Peritoneum inflamed; omentum, lower part of ileum and whole of rectum gangrenous.—[*Specimens* 307 and 308, Med. Sect., Army Medical Museum, showing ulceration of the solitary follicles and Peyer's patches, with exuded lymph on the peritoneal surface, are from this case.]—*Act. Ass't Surg. B. B. Miles, Jarvis Hospital, Baltimore, Md.*

Case 312.—Private Gilbert F. Sherwood, Co. K, 144th N. Y., was admitted July 20, 1863, with chronic diarrhœa. Typhoid symptoms set in about August 1. The low delirium was conceived to have been favorably influenced by a large blister over the epigastrium. He died on the 21st. *Post-mortem* examination twelve hours after death: The whole of the intestines were inflamed, especially the caput coli and twenty inches of the ileum, the mucous membrane presenting a deep-red, velvety appearance with many ulcerated patches. [*Specimen* 76, Med. Sect., Army Medical Museum, shows the ulcerated patches of the ileum and the follicular ulcers of the cæcum in this case.]—*Act. Ass't Surg. F. Hinkle, Jarvis Hospital, Baltimore, Md.*

Case 313.—Private John Weiant, Co. E, 118th Pa.; age 23; was admitted Aug. 30, 1864, with diarrhœa. On September 13 he became much prostrated by constant vomiting and diarrhœa. He died on the 20th. *Post-mortem* examination eighteen hours after death: Some emaciation. The brain was normal. The larynx and trachea contained a large quantity of frothy rose-colored sputa. The right lung weighed thirty-one ounces and a half and was much congested and hepatized posteriorly, exuding on section much frothy, rust-colored sputa; the left lung weighed fourteen ounces and contained a similar frothy, reddish fluid. The heart inclosed a medium-sized fibrinous clot in its right side and a small one in the left. The liver weighed eighty-one ounces; the spleen sixteen ounces. The stomach was normal; the solitary follicles of the lower ileum were enlarged and Peyer's patches ulcerated, there were a few small ulcers in the cæcum, but the large intestine was otherwise normal; the left kidney was much congested.—*Act. Ass't Surg. H. M. Dean, Lincoln Hospital, Washington, D. C.*

Case 314.—Corp'l Andrew Richardson, Co. K, 189th N. Y., was admitted Jan. 17, 1865, with chronic diarrhœa, and died on the 29th. *Post-mortem* examination: The right lung weighed forty ounces and the left twenty ounces; the right pleural sac contained pus, and the lung was adherent and hepatized; the heart weighed eight ounces, the liver seventy-four ounces and the spleen eight ounces and a half. The stomach was injected at its cardiac end; the jejunum much inflamed; the ileum injected and Peyer's patches thickened and ulcerated; there were some small ulcers in the upper part of the colon.—*Fifth Army Corps Field Hospital.*

Case 315.—Private Orlow Lawrence, Co. F, 140th N. Y., was admitted Jan. 17, 1865, with chronic diarrhœa, having previously suffered from what was supposed to be remittent fever. He died on the 26th. *Post-mortem* examination: The right lung weighed eighteen ounces, the left thirteen ounces and a half; there was an abscess in the lower lobe of the left lung, and the left pleura contained twenty-four ounces of serum with much plastic lymph. The liver weighed seventy-two ounces and presented the nutmeg appearance; the spleen weighed six ounces. The ileum was injected throughout; Peyer's patches were thickened and ulcerated as was also the colon; the mesenteric glands were much enlarged.—*Fifth Army Corps Field Hospital.*

Case 316.—Private John H. Benjamin, Co. H, 127th N. Y., was admitted July 29, 1863, with chronic diarrhœa of three months' standing. A few days after admission it was discovered that he was also laboring under a tertian ague; this was controlled by quinine, but the diarrhœa continued. He had a scorbutic appearance; his gums were spongy and he was feeble and emaciated. He gradually sank, and died comatose August 27. *Post-mortem* examination: Peyer's patches were extensively ulcerated and the solitary follicles enlarged. The mucous membrane of the rectum was converted into a pulpy mass.—*Act. Ass't Surg. W. H. Letterman, Douglas Hospital, Washington D. C.*

CASE 317.—Private J. W. Foreman, Co. M, 5th U. S. Art.; admitted Oct. 10, 1863; chronic diarrhœa. Died 17th. *Post-mortem* examination: Body somewhat emaciated. Lungs normal; heart atrophied. Liver slightly hypertrophied; gall-bladder distended; spleen enlarged. Stomach congested; duodenum congested and thickened; jejunum normal; Peyer's patches enlarged, congested and in some instances ulcerated; colon congested, thickened and ulcerated in patches; rectum thickened. Right kidney normal, left fatty.—*Harewood Hospital, Washington, D. C.*

CASE 318.—Corp'l Charles M. Mosher, Co. A, 122d N. Y.; admitted April 21, 1863. Chronic diarrhœa. Died May 7. *Post-mortem* examination: Body much emaciated. The right lung, heart and pericardium were healthy; the lower lobe of the left lung was hepatized and a portion of its pleura thickened. The liver was mottled and fatty; the spleen mottled and double the usual size. The stomach was healthy; the duodenum injected in patches; the jejunum slightly injected and presenting small ulcers; the mucous membrane of the ileum was congested in patches, thinned and softened, and Peyer's glands were reddened and ulcerated. The ascending and descending portions of the colon presented small purple spots with, in the former, several small distinct ulcers, some of which were healed; there was one large inflamed patch in the transverse colon and a purple spot three inches long in the rectum. Some cysts were observed in the kidneys.—*Act. Ass't Surg. H. Hirshfield, Harewood Hospital, Washington, D. C.*

CASE 319.—Private William Green, Co. B, 6th Mich. Cav., was admitted July 30, 1863, with chronic diarrhœa. Under treatment he seemed to improve until August 10, when sudden prostration came on. Next day he felt better, but in the evening the prostration recurred with slight delirium, lasting until death, on the 12th. *Post-mortem* examination eighteen hours after death: Lungs somewhat congested. Solitary follicles of intestines ulcerated; Peyer's glands enlarged, inflamed and ulcerated.—*Third Division Hospital, Alexandria, Va.*

CASE 320.—Private David Rumbaley, Co. A, 32d Mass.; age 20; was admitted August 30, 1864, having been sick for two weeks at City Point, Va., with diarrhœa and occasional rigors. He was emaciated, had anorexia, pain in both hypochondriac regions and severe diarrhœa with involuntary stools; his tongue was coated in the centre with a dark fur. On September 4 there was intense pain in the right side of the chest, with slight cough, accelerated pulse and breathing and continuance of the anorexia, diarrhœa and progressive debility. Delirium, with great prostration, set in next day, and he died on the 6th. *Post-mortem* examination: The larynx and trachea were healthy; the lungs were congested, the left markedly so, and while both were in part closely and firmly adherent to the parietes the right had a coating of recent lymph on its pleura. The pericardium was firmly adherent to the costal cartilages and sternum; the right side of the heart contained a large fibrinous clot, but the left was nearly empty. The liver was enlarged and soft and connected by recent lymph to the abdominal wall and the diaphragm; the spleen was enlarged, soft, of a dark-brown color, coated with recent lymph and adherent to the abdominal wall. The stomach was red and congested towards the cardia, thickened and softened at the pylorus. The small intestine, distended with flatus, was healthy in its upper part, but toward the ileum the agminated glands and the mucous membrane around them were congested; lower down these glands and the solitary follicles were enlarged and prominent, occasionally presenting deep ulcers with red areolæ, which became more numerous and stained with yellow pigment near the ileo-cæcal valve. [*Specimens* 424 and 425, Med. Sect., Army Medical Museum.] The large intestine was distended with air; the ascending colon congested and presenting a few small ulcers; the transverse and descending portions slightly congested and the orifices of their solitary follicles covered with black pigment; the mesenteric glands enlarged. The kidneys were normal.—*Act. Ass't Surg. O. P. Sweet, Carver Hospital, Washington, D. C.*

(f.) Diagnosis: Dysentery.

CASE 321.—Private Thomas Jones, Co. A, 1st U. S. Art., was admitted March 16, 1865, with dysentery, and died on the 23d. *Post-mortem* examination: Rigor mortis well marked. Right lung completely hepatized; left lung, heart and pericardium normal. Stomach inflamed along its lower border and pyloric orifice; lower part of ileum slightly inflamed and Peyer's glands ulcerated, the ulcers surrounded by a red areola.—*Fort Strong, Va.*

CASE 322.—Private William H. Morse, Co. H, 147th N. Y.; age 33; was admitted Aug. 20, 1864, with dysentery of four weeks' standing. He had about twelve passages daily, with tormina and tenesmus. The disease did not yield to treatment. He died on the 30th. *Post-mortem* examination: Peyer's patches were much ulcerated, some to the muscular coat and one perforating the intestine, [*Specimens* 374 and 375, Med. Sect., Army Medical Museum,] but there was no liquid in the abdominal cavity; a small cul-de-sac existed in the ileum.—*Act. Ass't Surg. D. L. Haight, Douglas Hospital, Washington, D. C.*

CASE 323.—Private Addison Griffin, Co. G, 144th N. Y., was admitted July 29, 1863, with typhoid dysentery. He was much prostrated for two hours after his entry, but he rallied and seemed in fair condition; pulse 88 but feeble; much tormina and tenesmus; abdomen tender upon pressure, especially over the ileo-cæcal valve; tongue smooth, glossy and red in front and coated white with a greenish-yellow tinge behind. On the day of admission the discharges consisted of glairy mucus specked in a few places with blood. Pills of lead acetate, opium and blue mass, with an opiate enema, gave him a rather quiet night, with only four passages, so that next morning his condition was encouraging; but at 4 P. M. he passed a large quantity of blood from his bowels and died within an hour. *Post-mortem* examination fifteen hours after death: The mucous coat of the small intestine was softened in its whole course and in many places not able to bear its own weight; the glands of Peyer were softened and ulcerated, some completely disorganized; the mesenteric glands were enlarged to the size of a pigeon's egg. The large intestine in its whole length was softened and disorganized.—*Act. Ass't Surg. W. H. Letterman, Douglas Hospital, Washington, D. C.*

CASE 324.—Private Gustavus Frank, Co. B, 20th N. Y., was admitted July 26, 1862, with chronic dysentery, and died August 9. *Post-mortem* examination the same day: The body was much emaciated. The heart was pale and flabby, with opaque, white patches on the right ventricle about the size of a dime and similar but quite small patches on both auricles, together with some roughness of the corresponding portions of the pericardium. The lungs, liver, stomach, pancreas and spleen were healthy. The mucous membrane of the ileum was inflamed and the agminated glands, with the exception of the upper ones, were thickened and inflamed and in several instances presented small ulcerations, [*Specimens* 242 and 243, Med. Sect., Army Medical Museum;] the mesenteric glands were tumefied. The mucous membrane of the colon was inflamed, especially towards its extremities.—*Act. Ass't Surg. Joseph Leidy, Satterlee Hospital, Philadelphia, Pa.*

(g.) Diagnosis: Typhoid debility.

CASE 325.—Private Howard Rice, Co. H, 206th Pa.; age 27; was admitted Oct. 14, 1864, with debility, and died on the 30th from gastric and intestinal hemorrhage. *Post-mortem* examination forty-two hours after death: Muscles well developed. The spleen was dark-colored, enlarged and softened. Peyer's patches in the lower part of the ileum and a few solitary follicles in the cæcum and in the first six inches of the colon were thickened and ulcerated, but beyond this the large intestine was normal. The lungs, heart, liver and kidneys were normal; the stomach was healthy but contained four ounces of grumous liquid.—*Act. Ass't Surg. Thomas Bowen, Second Division Hospital, Alexandria, Va.*

CASE 326.—Private Jeremiah Blair, Co. C, 202d Pa.; age 38; was admitted Nov. 4, 1864, with debility, and died on the 6th. *Post-mortem* examination: Peyer's patches near the ileo-cæcal valve were thickened and ulcerated in two or three places; the mesenteric glands were enlarged; the liver dark-colored; the spleen enlarged; the other organs healthy.—*Second Division Hospital, Alexandria, Va.*

CASE 327.—Private Isaac H. Cole, Co. M, 6th Pa. Art.; age 40; admitted Oct. 17, 1864; died November 7. *Post-mortem* examination twenty-six hours after death: Marked rigor mortis; no emaciation; extensive suggillation posteriorly. The left lung was congested posteriorly and a small portion of its upper lobe was hepatized; there was an ounce of serum in the right pleural cavity and two ounces in the left. The pericardium, which was slightly reddened, contained four ounces of serum. The great omentum was inflamed and adherent to the small intestine, the coils of which were interadherent; there were extensive deposits of lymph on the peritoneum, and the cavity contained two pints of a thick straw-colored liquid having a fæcal odor and some floating shreds and small masses, apparently fæcal, about the size of barley-grains. The liver was enlarged; the coats of the gall-bladder were disorganized from extension of the peritonitis; the pancreas normal; the spleen enlarged and softened. Several of Peyer's patches in the lower ileum were thickened and ulcerated, one ulcer about two feet from the ileo-cæcal valve having perforated; the mucous coat of the cæcum and of the first few inches of the colon was inflamed and thickened; the mesenteric glands were much enlarged and quite dark.—*Second Division Hospital, Alexandria, Va.*

CASE 328.—Private William DePraley, Co. I, 118th Pa.; admitted Oct. 10, 1863. Debility. Symptoms of peritonitis were observed on the evening of the 28th. Died 29th. *Post-mortem* examination: Body much emaciated. The lungs and heart were normal; the pericardium contained four ounces of liquid. The abdominal cavity contained a large quantity of serum; the liver was adherent to the adjoining viscera; the gall-bladder, spleen, stomach, duodenum, jejunum and kidneys were normal. The ileum was inflamed and Peyer's glands ulcerated; one of the ulcers just above the ileo-cæcal valve had perforated the peritoneum; the colon and rectum were much inflamed. —*Harewood Hospital, Washington, D. C.*

(h.) Diagnosis: Bronchitis.

CASE 329.—Private John Connor, Co. B, 28th Mass.; age 22; was admitted Oct. 18, 1863, with acute bronchitis, and died November 8. *Post-mortem* examination twenty-two hours after death: The brain was natural. The larynx and trachea were inflamed; the mucous membrane above the chordæ vocales was greenish-brown in color and much puffed out and thickened, particularly on the right side; a slight exudation was observed on the cords and under surface of the epiglottis; the sub-epiglottidean follicles were enlarged, softened and blackened; the mucous membrane below was of a paler color but still greenish, becoming grayish in the bronchi. The œsophagus was inflamed, its lower part dark purplish-red and presenting numerous purpura-like spots which invaded the sub-mucous tissue, its upper part greenish-brown and very much softened and thickened. The right lung weighed fifteen ounces, contained much pigmentary matter, was well filled with air and on section exuded little or no bronchial secretion; the left lung weighed twelve ounces and was healthy, excepting the slate-color of the bronchial membrane; the pleural cavities contained three pints of serum. The heart was firm and almost free from clots; three ounces of fluid were found in the pericardium. The liver was perfectly healthy; the spleen was firm and weighed three ounces and three-quarters; the pancreas four ounces. The small intestine was thin and the valvulæ conniventes almost obliterated; the solitary follicles were not enlarged; Peyer's patches were of a deep-brown color and but little elevated—such as were ulcerated were surrounded by a light-red areola, but the ulcerations were in no place deep and had everywhere the appearance of undergoing the healing process. The large intestine was of a darkish gray color, its solitary glands normal. Both kidneys were somewhat congested.—*Ass't Surg. Harrison Allen, U. S. A., Lincoln Hospital, Washington, D. C.*

CASE 330.—Private E. B. Dolph, Co. B, 27th Conn., was admitted March 9, 1863, having been suffering for six weeks from a rather severe attack of bronchitis, for which he had been treated in quarters. On admission his pulse was 108, tongue clean and moist; he had considerable cough with white frothy sputa and some substernal soreness; his stools were rather infrequent (not daily) but loose and watery. Next day he seemed better; pulse 84. On the 11th his pulse was 108, respiration 20, tongue furred and a little tinged with brown, and he had one watery passage in the preceding twenty-four hours. He continued in this condition until the 14th, when he had three loose passages and complained of some tenderness over the whole course of the colon. Next day the pulse and respiration became slightly accelerated and the tongue dry; he had two loose passages. On the 16th the pulse was 120, the respiration 28, the lips dark in patches, the tongue dry and dark; he did not answer questions sensibly; the abdomen was tender all over; his cough was loud, dry and very annoying; the respiratory murmur was absent and there was dulness on percussion from the lower extremity of the scapula downwards on the right side, but elsewhere the murmur was loud and dry. Tubular breathing was heard on the 17th below the fifth rib on the right side anteriorly and laterally. He died on the 20th. The cough ceased during the last three days of life. The abdomen was at no time tympanitic nor were any rose-colored spots observed. *Post-mortem* examination: [The condition of the thoracic viscera is not recorded.] There were about twenty-five indurated Peyer's patches in the ileum, six of which were ulcerated; the ileo-cæcal valve was thickened and presented an indurated, slightly ulcerated patch on its cæcal surface; the neighboring parts of the ileum and colon were much congested; the mesenteric glands were enlarged. [*Specimen* 150, Med. Sect., Army Medical Museum, is from this case.]—*Surg. W. O. McDonald, Hospital, 27th Conn. Vols.*

(i.) Diagnosis: Pneumonia or typhoid pneumonia.

CASE 331.—Private Orlando Stevens, Co. A, 5th Vt., was admitted Jan. 2, 1863, with pneumonia. As marked typhoid symptoms were present a supporting treatment was adopted. He improved to within a day or two before his death, when prostration set in. He complained at one time of a dull pain in the left breast and of some difficulty in breathing; he had also a slight diarrhœa. He died on the 16th. *Post-mortem* examination six hours after death: Body much emaciated; skin sallow and tightly stretched. The lower part of the upper lobe of the left lung contained a few small masses of hepatized tissue; the lower lobe was hepatized, its small bronchi filled with false membrane and its whole surface covered with a thin layer of exuded lymph. The spleen was small but of normal consistence and color; the kidneys and liver were natural. The stomach was contracted, its greater curvature having strongly marked rugæ in front and towards the pyloric orifice; the fundus was injected, particularly at the lowest point and near the cardiac orifice; the mucous membrane to the right of the cardiac and towards the pyloric orifice was mammillated. The small intestine was healthy to the upper end of the ileum; below that point it was congested in patches which occupied about half the surface for two feet and a half in length, thence it was uniformly congested to the ileo-cæcal valve. Peyer's patches were punctated—some were reddish; they were slightly swollen and much softened; within a foot of the ileo-cæcal valve were eight or ten over which the mucous membrane was eroded, while the muscular tissue beneath was much congested; the ulcers as a rule did not occupy the whole of these patches, but in the middle third of the ileum there were several in which this was the case; the mesenteric glands were normal. The peritoneal surface of the cæcum was congested; the mucous membrane of the descending colon was slightly congested near its commencement, then slaty in color to the sigmoid flexure; in the lower two-thirds of the gut the solitary glands were distinctly marked and filled with a dark-blue deposit: in the sigmoid flexure were several small ulcerations not exceeding a line in diameter, but the mucous membrane was of normal consistence.—*Act. Ass't Surg. T. R. Dunglison, Lincoln Hospital, Washington, D. C.*

CASE 332.—Private M. W. Knowles, Co. D, 67th Pa., was admitted Feb. 3, 1864, with pneumonia, and died on the 8th. *Post-mortem* examination: The right lung, excepting a part of its anterior margin, was hepatized; the left was congested. The liver was slightly granular and fatty; the spleen large, soft and of a dull purple color internally; the kidneys congested. Peyer's patches in the lower part of the ileum were ulcerated but the surrounding villi were not affected. [*Specimen* 201, Med. Sect., Army Medical Museum.] The large intestine presented isolated ulcers mostly confined to the cæcum; the mucous membrane was of a dull whitish-blue color.—*Ass't Surg. Harrison Allen, U. S. A., Lincoln Hospital, Washington, D. C.*

CASE 333.—Private L. M. Cole, Co. E, 16th Me.; age 20; was admitted March 26, 1864, with pneumonia, and died on the 28th. *Post-mortem* examination twenty-three hours after death: Body much emaciated. Brain healthy. Trachea much congested; right lung twenty-six ounces, left twenty ounces—both congested; bronchi filled with bloody mucus and each pleural sac containing a small quantity of bloody serum. Heart pale. Liver anæmic, weighing fifty ounces; spleen healthy, nine ounces. Œsophagus and stomach normal; small intestine much congested, especially towards the ileo-cæcal valve, where the mucous membrane was of a bluish-slate color; Peyer's patches and the solitary follicles prominent, several showing points of ulceration; large intestine congested near the caput coli. Mucous membrane of bladder around orifices of ureters dark-bluish colored in spots, varying in size from a pea to a large cent.—*Act. Ass't Surg. H. M. Dean, Lincoln Hospital, Washington, D. C.*

CASE 334.—Private Henry Shrum, Co. F, 2d Md.; age 55; was admitted Sept. 6, 1865, with pneumonia. Two weeks before his entry he had a chill lasting for half an hour, followed by oppression in the chest, with complete anorexia for five days. On admission he had diarrhœa, a suffocative feeling on taking a deep breath, a purple pustular eruption on his body and coldness of the hands and feet. He died on the 8th. *Post-mortem* examination: Left lung adherent and collapsed posteriorly; right lung congested generally and solidified posteriorly. Spleen enlarged and softened. Peyer's patches of ileum elevated, enlarged and in some instances ulcerated; solitary glands of colon and rectum enlarged and presenting the shaven-beard appearance. Kidneys with many superficial cysts containing a transparent light-brown fluid.—*Act. Ass't Surg. Carlos Carvallo, Douglas Hospital, Washington, D. C.*

CASE 335.—Private John Strickland, Co. E, 103d Ill.; age 34; was admitted June 21, 1863, with typhoid pneumonia. He was delirious on admission, but it was learned that he had been seriously ill for two or three weeks. His pulse was small, tongue dry, thirst excessive; he had not much diarrhœa, but expectorated large quantities of purulent matter. His condition remained unchanged until the morning of the 23d, when a large pool of bright-red blood, which had flowed from his bowels, was discovered under the bed. Ten drops of solution of perchloride of iron were ordered to be taken every thirty minutes, and the patient was placed on another bed; but he continued to bleed so freely that this also became speedily soaked. By the time the third dose of the iron was given the bleeding had ceased, but the patient was extremely exhausted and almost pulseless. He rallied, however, and seemed to be doing well until the evening of the 26th, when he suddenly became restless and his pulse accelerated. He died next morning. *Post-mortem* examination ten hours after death: The mesenteric glands were enlarged, softened and in some cases nearly broken down. Only two ulcerated Peyer's patches were found; these were large and ragged, situated a short distance from the ileo-cæcal valve; there was no blood in the intestines.—*Lawson Hospital, St. Louis, Mo.*

CASE 336.—Private Morris Hyatt, Co. A, 142d Ohio National Guard; age 21; was admitted July 28, 1864, with typhoid pneumonia. He was delirious and had a slight cough, without expectoration, and an infrequent diarrhœa. In the progress of the case the pulse became rapid and weak, the breathing hurried and the countenance dusky. He died August 1. *Post-mortem* examination six hours after death: Rigor mortis marked. The lungs were engorged posteriorly and some of the lobules hepatized. The liver was engorged, enlarged and softened; the spleen softened. The mucous membrane of the stomach in the region of the greater curvature was much softened and easily torn. Peyer's patches and the solitary glands of the small intestine were extensively diseased, this condition becoming more marked toward the lower end of the ileum; for three or four feet above the ileo-cæcal valve the morbid patches were circular, from the size of a pinhead to that of a two-cent piece, or oval, some of the latter having the greater axis over two inches long with a thickness in some cases of three-sixteenths of an inch; they were firm, the edges smooth and regular, the surfaces in those most advanced slightly excavated and in all more or less covered with a yellowish-green, easily detached coating or deposit. [See *specimens* 376–380, Med. Sect., Army Medical Museum, and plates facing pages 410, 412 and 436, *infra*.] The mesentery was greatly thickened and the glands enlarged, some to the size of a large peach-stone, [*Specimen* 381, Army Medical Museum.] The large intestine was generally healthy. The kidneys were normal.—*Douglas Hospital, Washington, D. C.*

CASE 337.—Private Frederick Brand, Co. E, 11th Pa.; admitted Jan. 7, 1865; typhoid pneumonia. Died February 1. *Post-mortem* examination ten hours after death: Both lungs were hepatized (gray) and closely adherent to the costal pleura. Slight adhesions existed between the liver, diaphragm, ascending colon and small intestine; the intestines were covered with plastic lymph; the abdominal cavity contained twelve ounces of a colorless liquid; the mesentery was thickened and congested throughout and contained large, soft, white deposits which resembled tubercle. The duodenum was healthy; the upper part of the jejunum was slightly congested in spots and its lower part presented a large ulcer; the ileum was congested throughout and Peyer's patches ulcerated. The ascending colon was healthy; the rest of the colon and the rectum much congested but not ulcerated. The other viscera were normal.—*Act. Ass't Surg. C. T. Trautman, Harewood Hospital, Washington, D. C.*

CASE 338.—Serg't Alexander M. Elgin, Co. B, 139th Pa.; admitted April 21, 1863; typhoid pneumonia. Died May 21. *Post-mortem* examination: The left parotid gland and surrounding cellular tissue formed the site of an abscess which penetrated to the œsophagus. The lungs and heart were normal. The duodenum and jejunum were dark-lead colored and contained fresh bile; the ileum was thin and dark colored, its mucous membrane much injected; Peyer's patches and certain of the solitary glands were deeply colored, softened and in some instances ulcerated. The large intestine exhibited large black spots scattered over its surface. The liver was black on its under surface, its parenchyma fatty; the gall-bladder distended with bile; the spleen and kidneys normal.—*Act. Ass't Surg. Thos. H. Elliott, Harewood Hospital, Washington, D. C.*

CASE 339.—Private H. F. Wardwall, Co. D, 33d Mass., was admitted Feb. 9, 1863, with great dyspnœa and complete aphonia. Death occurred from suffocation on the 15th. There was no indication during life of any intestinal lesion, nor was the patient emaciated as he would probably have been if just recovering from typhoid fever or chronic diarrhœa. *Post-mortem* examination: The lungs were much congested, but there seemed to be enough of comparatively healthy tissue to have enabled respiration to go on. The trachea was highly inflamed, the larynx ulcerated and the glottis occluded by œdema. The mucous membrane of the small intestine, and especially of the ileum, presented the softened and tumefied aspect usually found in cases of chronic diarrhœa, and there were numerous ulcers, one near the cæcum being two inches in diameter. [*Specimen* 207, Med. Sect., Army Medical Museum, showing ulceration of Peyer's glands, is derived from this case.]—*Med. Cadet E. Coues, U. S. A., Mount Pleasant Hospital, Washington, D. C.*

(k.) Diagnosis: Pleurisy.

CASE 340.—Private Henry Mead, Co. D, 10th N. Y. Cav.; age 19; was admitted April 7, 1865, with pleurisy. [He entered the cavalry corps hospital, City Point, Va., March 27, diagnosis chronic diarrhœa, and was transferred to Lincoln hospital, Washington, D. C., April 1, where his case was registered bronchitis.] He was pale and much debilitated; tongue white; bowels loose; appetite poor; pulse full, weak, not frequent, intermittent and sometimes resembling the whir-r-r of an aneurism; breathing hurried and difficult; he was unable to lie on his right side. Physical examination discovered dulness over the left lung and inferiorly over the right lung, crepitation over the right lung posteriorly, with a large moist râle over its middle lobe and a sibilant râle over its lower lobe and displacement of the heart four inches towards the right, its apex seeming to be under the right nipple. He died on the 12th. *Post-mortem* examination: There were two gallons of bloody liquid in the left thoracic cavity; the left lung was compressed against the spinal column and so dense as to sink in water; the right was passively congested, especially in its lower lobe. The heart was displaced to the right and contained a soft coagulum in its left cavities, a fibrinous one in the right; there was slight effusion into the pericardium. The liver was somewhat congested. The small intestine was congested and some of Peyer's patches were ulcerated.—*Satterlee Hospital, Philadelphia, Pa.*

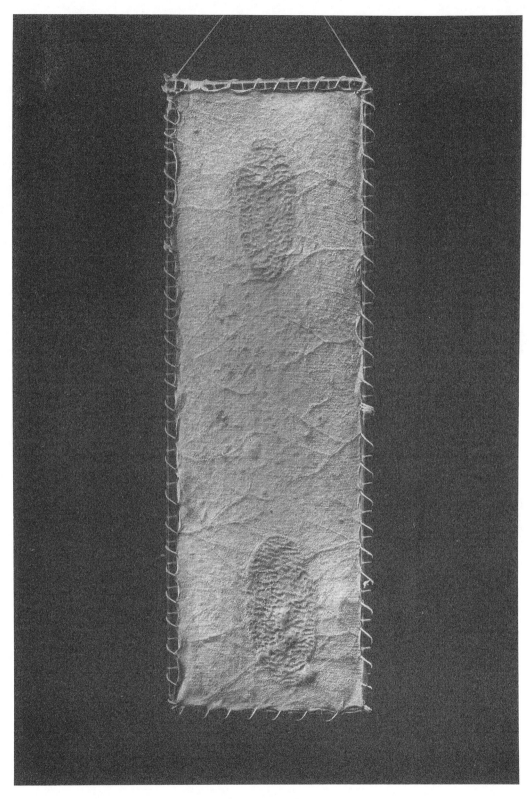

James R. Osgood & Co., Boston.

SLIGHTLY THICKENED PEYER'S PATCHES.

No. 377. MEDICAL SECTION.

(B.) CONDITION OF PEYER'S PATCHES NOT STATED; THE ILEUM OR THE SMALL INTESTINE SAID TO HAVE BEEN ULCERATED—21 CASES.

(a.) Diagnosis: Intermittent fever.

CASE 341.—Private Jacob Shoulders, Co. B, 15th Va.; age 26; was admitted Aug. 31, 1864, with intermittent fever, and died September 13 with typhoid symptoms. *Post-mortem* examination: Hypostatic congestion of both lungs. Liver large, weighing five pounds; spleen very large, twenty-six ounces; left kidney small, three ounces; ileum for three feet above the ileo-cæcal valve intensely inflamed and containing thirty ulcers, some of the size of a silver dollar.—*Act. Ass't Surg. B. B. Miles, Jarvis Hospital, Baltimore, Md.*

(b.) Diagnosis: Cerebral disease.

CASE 342.—Private Zebulon F. Whittaker, Co. B, 16th Me., was admitted Feb. 1, 1865, as a convalescent from typhoid fever. He was hypochondriacal and nostalgic, complaining ot severe headache, intense lumbar pain and constipation. Blisters were applied behind the ears and dry and wet cups to the back with but temporary relief. He vomited large quantities of a greenish watery liquid, and later had involuntary stools and paralysis of the bladder necessitating catheterism. He became very restless and noisy, and on the 20th had to be fastened to his bed to prevent his leaving it. He died on the 24th. *Post-mortem* examination: Brain normal. Lungs congested, softened and friable. Stomach showing numerous ecchymoses; ileum and ileo-cæcal valve presenting a few isolated ulcers. Bladder thick, small, ecchymosed.—*Act. Ass't Surg. Carlos Carvallo, Douglas Hospital, Washington, D. C.*

(c.) Diagnosis: Diarrhœa.

CASE 343.—Private R. M. Hapman, Co. F, 150th N. Y.; age 41; was admitted July 9, 1863, with chronic diarrhœa and general debility. He was doing well up to August 22, when meningitis supervened, and he died on the 25th. *Post-mortem* examination: Close adhesion between the pia mater and the hemispheres of the cerebrum, with an unusual quantity of serum in the subarachnoid spaces; ossification of a Pacchionian granulation, [*Specimen 41, Med. Sect., Army Medical Museum.*] Lungs and heart healthy; liver and spleen softened and congested; ileum inflamed and ulcerated in patches.—*Act. Ass't Surg. B. B. Miles, Jarvis Hospital, Baltimore, Md.*

CASE 344.—Private Franklin Sollans, Co. E, 122d Ohio; age 22; was admitted Aug. 12, 1864, with diarrhœa, and died on the 19th. *Post-mortem* examination: The vessels of the pia mater were anæmic and seemed to contain globules of air; there were two ounces of serous effusion at the base of the brain; the third ventricle contained one ounce of liquid; the brain-substance was natural. There was extensive interlobular emphysema of both lungs, which were congested posteriorly; the areolar tissue of the anterior mediastinum was infiltrated with air. The heart and kidneys were natural; the liver large; the spleen congested. There were three ulcers in the ileum; two of which were one inch and the other eight inches above the ileo-cæcal valve; the mucous membrane to the extent of a foot from the valve was very much congested.—*Act. Ass't Surg. B. B. Miles, Jarvis Hospital, Baltimore, Md.*

CASE 345.—Private Charles A. Taylor, Co. A, 9th Mich. Cav.; age 18; admitted dead, March 1, 1864, having died in the ambulance on the way to hospital. *Post-mortem* examination fourteen hours after death: Body greatly emaciated. The lungs were healthy; the heart small and flabby. The liver was large but of normal consistence; the left kidney engorged with blood, the right small and apparently fatty. The omentum had lost its fat; the mesenteric glands were enlarged and there were indications of former peritonitis. The stomach was healthy; the mucous membrane of the ileum was destroyed by ulceration in many places and thickened in others.—*Surg. Wm. C. Otterson, U. S. V., Hospital No. 8, Nashville, Tenn.*

CASE 346.—Private Martin O'Neil, Co. E, 14th N. J.; age 40; was admitted Nov. 5, 1864. He had been sick for two weeks with diarrhœa complicated with kidney disease and œdema of the hands and feet. He died Jan. 30, 1865. *Post-mortem* examination nineteen hours after death: Mucous membrane of ileum and cæcum ulcerated in a dozen patches, two of which perforated the gut about two feet above the ileo-cæcal valve; abdominal cavity contained about six ounces of pus. Left kidney somewhat enlarged, pale and mottled; right normal in size but congested.—*Act. Ass't Surg. S. P. White, Ward Hospital, Newark, N. J.*

CASE 347.—Private Rudolph Norman, Co. G, 28th Mass.; age 28 (a paroled prisoner); was admitted from Richmond, Va., April 18, 1864, with chronic diarrhœa. He died June 4. *Post-mortem* examination twenty-four hours after death: Lungs healthy; heart flabby and anæmic, filled with white clots; liver adhering by its entire upper surface to diaphragm; spleen large; mucous coat of intestines much congested and thickened; ileum perforated in ten or twelve places by ulcers; peritoneum congested and adherent in many places.—*Act. Ass't Surg. B. B. Miles, Jarvis Hospital, Baltimore, Md.*

CASE 348.—Private Alfred A. King, Co. F, 2d Pa. Cav.; age 16; admitted Aug. 9, 1864, from Army of Potomac; chronic diarrhœa. Died next day. *Post-mortem* examination: Much emaciation; enlargement and suppuration of parotid glands. Ulceration of ileum, cæcum and part of colon; a half-pint of lumbricoid worms scattered through the intestinal canal and quite a lot of them in the cæcum.—*Third Division Hospital, Alexandria, Va.*

(d.) Diagnosis: Debility.

CASE 349.—Private Henry C. Davis, Co. C, 9th N. Y. Cav.; age 32; was admitted July 23, 1863, with debility. He was appointed an assistant nurse, but symptoms of meningitis came on, for which cups, blisters and enemata were employed. He died August 3. *Post-mortem* examination fourteen hours after death: "On removing the cerebrum slight adhesion was found on the left side with some effusion, the meninges of the brain being softer than usual. The liver was congested and weighed four pounds and six ounces, and an ulcer was found in it near the gall-bladder; the spleen weighed two pounds and four ounces. There was ulceration along the ileum."—*Act. Ass't Surg. B. B. Miles, Jarvis Hospital, Baltimore, Md.*

CASE 350.—Private Lyman Avery, Co. I, 9th N. Y. Cav.; age 23; was admitted July 20, 1863, with debility, and died August 14. *Post-mortem* examination twenty hours after death: Brain, lungs, heart and liver healthy; ileum showing cicatrices of old ulcers in their different stages.—*Act. Ass't Surg. B. B. Miles, Jarvis Hospital, Baltimore, Md.*

CASE 351.—Private Henry Lott, Co. D, 173d N. Y.; age 22; was admitted Oct. 29, 1863, suffering from cough and typhoid debility. Next day it was noted that his abdomen was covered with purple spots, and on November 2 that he had dysentery but with little tenesmus. He was treated with carbonate of ammonia, whiskey, nourishment and hot applications to his extremities. He died on the 3d. *Post-mortem* examination twenty-six hours after death: Inflammation and ulceration of the intestines.—*Act. Ass't Surg. W. W. Royal, Hospital, Annapolis, Md.*

(e.) Diagnosis: Rheumatism.

CASE 352.—Private Daniel Repplogel, Co. A, 61st Pa.; age 28; was admitted Aug. 23, 1864, with rheumatism, and died September 22. *Post-mortem* examination twenty-four hours after death: The middle lobe of the right lung was hepatized and infiltrated with pus. The ileum was intensely congested in spots and presented four large ulcers at a little distance from the ileo-cæcal valve. The bladder was very much thickened and contracted.—*Act. Ass't Surg. B. B. Miles, Jarvis Hospital, Baltimore, Md.*

(f.) Diagnosis: Pneumonia or typhoid pneumonia.

CASE 353.—Private Richard Vaughn, Co. F, 146th Ind.; age 26; was admitted June 8, 1865, having been sick for ten days with pneumonia. On admission his bowels were rather loose and he had some cough with free expectoration. He improved steadily until the 13th, when permission was given him to go to Cumberland to be mustered out; but he became much exhausted by the way, was abandoned by his friends, and returned to the hospital on the 14th in a prostrate condition. He died on the 17th. *Post-mortem* examination eight hours after death: There were pleuritic adhesions on both sides. The abdominal cavity contained a quantity of serum and the intestines were coated with coagulable lymph. The liver was large, intensely congested and softened; the spleen large, congested, softened and of a black color. The mucous membrane of the jejunum, ileum and cæcum was inflamed, softened and ulcerated.—*Act. Ass't Surg. S. B. West, Cumberland Hospital, Md.*

CASE 354.—Private Philip Dick, Co. A, 187th N. Y.; age 28; was admitted Feb. 20, 1865, with pneumonia. He died March 4. *Post-mortem* examination eight hours after death: Purpuric spots, the largest one-fourth of an inch in diameter, were scattered on the lower extremities. The lower lobe of each lung was deeply congested and on the outside of the left was a sunken star-shaped cicatrix, with beneath it a collection of tubercular matter about as large as a butternut, connected at its inner side with one of the bronchial tubes. The heart was healthy and contained a large white clot in the right ventricle and a smaller one in the left. The liver and kidneys were healthy. The spleen weighed twelve ounces and adhered strongly to the diaphragm; in its substance beneath the adhesion was a cavity, partly divided by a partition extending to its bottom and containing about an ounce of viscid greenish fluid, [*Specimen* 523, Med. Sect., Army Medical Museum.] The stomach was inflamed and exhibited one ulcer about the middle of its greater curvature; the duodenum was congested; the jejunum injected in patches, its lower three feet healthy, as was the first foot of the ileum; the rest of the ileum ulcerated; the mesenteric glands inflamed; the large intestine healthy.—*Surg. W. L. Faxon, 32d Mass., Depot Hospital, Fifth Army Corps, City Point, Va.*

CASE 355.—Private Charles Hackett, Co. D, 129th Ind.; age 26; was admitted May 26, 1864, with pneumonia. When first seen by the reporter June 5, the patient was feeble, delirious and had diarrhœa with involuntary stools. He died June 10. *Post-mortem* examination: There were recent adhesions and a large serous effusion in the left pleural cavity; the upper lobe of the left lung was congested, the lower partially consolidated and coated with pseudo-membrane; the right lung was comparatively healthy. The heart was flabby and soft. The spleen was enlarged, congested and easily torn. The ileum was much inflamed and ulcerated in a number of places. The left kidney was slightly inflamed.—*Act. Ass't Surg. L. A. Walton, Hospital No. 8, Nashville, Tenn.*

CASE 356.—Private Edwin Preston, Co. D, 5th N. Y. Cav.; age 20; was admitted Oct. 13, 1864, with typhoid pneumonia, and died on the 24th. *Post-mortem* examination twenty-four hours after death: Adhesion and almost complete consolidation of both lungs, which did not, however, sink in water; a band of lymph connecting the two surfaces of the pericardium; twelve ulcers in the ileum penetrating to the serous coat. Other organs normal.—*Act. Ass't Surg. B. B. Miles, Jarvis Hospital, Baltimore, Md.*

CASE 357.—Private Meredith P. Osborn, Co. I, 9th Tenn. Cav., was admitted with typhoid pneumonia, and died Oct. 27, 1864. *Post-mortem* examination: The right lung was healthy; the left was in a state of gray hepatization with effusion of about one pint of serum in the pleural cavity. There was a large white clot in the right side of the heart. The liver was much congested; the ileum ulcerated; the mesenteric glands enlarged.—*Act. Ass't Surg. J. E. Brooke, Rock Island Hospital, Ill.*

CASE 358.—Private William Walters, Co. I, 17th Ohio; age 34; was admitted Aug. 27, 1864, with typhoid pneumonia. He died September 4. *Post-mortem* examination on the day of death: The lower lobe of the left lung was in the state of red hepatization. The heart, liver and kidneys were normal. The spleen was softened and enlarged; the lower portion of the ileum ulcerated in patches.—*Field Hospital, Chattanooga, Tenn.*

CASE 359.—Private Ansel Fraley, Co. F, 33d Ohio; age 16; was admitted Aug. 21, 1864, with typhoid pneumonia, and died September 8. *Post-mortem* examination next day: Both lungs were congested and several lobules of the lower lobe of the right lung were hepatized. The mitral valve was thickened. The liver was somewhat softened;

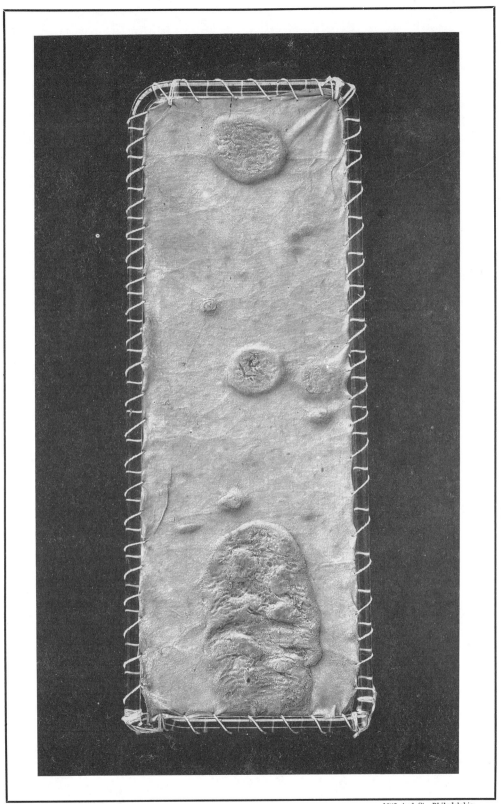

Am. Photo-Relief Printing Co., 1002 Arch St., Philadelphia.

THICKENED PEYER'S PATCHES.

No. 380. MEDICAL SECTION.

the spleen and kidneys normal. The mucous membrane of the lower portion of the ileum was deeply congested, softened and presented a number of ulcers.—*Field Hospital, Chattanooga, Tenn.*

CASE 360.—Private Elcy Hall, Co. D, 3d Va. Cav.; age 17; was admitted Dec. 27, 1864, with pneumonia of the left lung, and died Jan. 6, 1865. *Post-mortem* examination twenty-four hours after death: About three ounces of liquid and some recent adhesions in each pleural cavity; lower lobe of each lung deeply congested and slightly hepatized. Heart and liver normal; spleen large and soft; kidneys congested. Peritoneal cavity containing about two pints of a turbid liquid; ileum above the ileo-cæcal valve presenting many deep and large ulcers, one of which had perforated the gut; colon slightly ulcerated.—*Act. Ass't Surg. B. B. Miles, Jarvis Hospital, Baltimore, Md.*

(g.) Diagnosis: Peritonitis.

CASE 361.—Private William Riley, alias Cohen, Co. C, 14th Conn., was admitted Feb. 13, 1865, with peritonitis. Large doses of anodynes were given per rectum, the stomach being too irritable to retain anything. He died on the 17th. *Post-mortem* examination five hours after death: Peritoneum thickened and inflamed, containing twelve ounces of pale serum; small intestine adherent by bands of lymph; lower ileum showing many large, deep, irregular ulcers and containing three living lumbricoid worms; large intestine inflamed and in the rectum presenting ulcerated hemorrhoidal tumors; liver normal; spleen enlarged; kidneys small.—*Third Division Hospital, Alexandria, Va.*

(C.) CONDITION OF PEYER'S PATCHES NOT STATED; THE INTESTINAL MUCOUS MEMBRANE NOT ULCERATED—4 CASES.

(a.) Diagnosis: Pneumonia.

CASE 362.—Private Garrison North, Co. E, 5th Mich. Cav.; admitted March 25, 1863. Diagnosis—pneumonia. Died April 9 of typhoid fever. *Post-mortem* examination two hours after death: Brain forty-seven ounces. Right lung eighteen ounces, some pleuritic adhesions of upper lobe; left lung twenty-ounces, lower lobe much congested; bronchi of both lungs, especially of upper lobes, thickened and indurated, feeling on section like nodules. Heart thirteen ounces and a half. Liver eighty ounces, dark-purple, adherent to diaphragm, acini not well marked, capsule easily torn; two drachms and a half of pale bile, with white flakes, in gall-bladder; spleen fourteen ounces and a half, slate-colored externally, mulberry colored internally, softened. Stomach of a delicate pink color; duodenum and jejunum yellowish, mucous membrane tough; ileum pink, much congested, and solitary glands enlarged, especially in the lower part. Large intestine greenish at the cæcum and rather pale in other parts, with hyperæmic spots irregularly distributed over the surface; solitary glands dotted with black pigment.—*Ass't Surg. Harrison Allen, U. S. A., Lincoln Hospital, Washington, D. C.*

CASE 363.—Elim Bess, Mo., guerilla; age 30; was admitted Nov. 2, 1864, with typhoid pneumonia: Tongue dry, slightly furred and red, bowels regular, pulse 100; he had no cough or expectoration, nor did he complain of pain or discomfort, but was so drowsy he could not be aroused to give his history; the lower lobe of his right lung was considered to be hepatized. During the last two or three days of life the bowels were tympanitic and tender. He died December 2. *Post-mortem* examination two hours after death: Lower lobe of right lung hepatized; spleen enlarged and softened; mesentery inflamed and glands much enlarged; solitary glands disorganized; bowels congested.—*Act. Ass't Surg. H. C. Newkirk, Rock Island Hospital, Ill.*

(b.) Diagnosis: Rheumatism.

CASE 364.—Private Salem Brocket, 1st Kans. Bat'y; age 16; admitted June 9, 1864. A liniment of fluid extract of aconite, chloroform and tincture of camphor gave relief; but typhoid symptoms supervened, with cough, pain in the right side and expectoration of tenacious mucus; the stools were passed involuntarily. Pills of acetate of lead and opium were given with carbonate of ammonia and brandy. He failed gradually, became delirious and died on the 20th. *Post-mortem* examination: Lungs much congested, right partially adherent; pericardium containing two ounces of serum; liver and spleen enlarged; lower ileum inflamed; kidneys nearly double the normal size.—*Hospital No. 8, Nashville, Tenn.*

CASE 365.—Private Aaron Dudley, Co. E, 31st Me.; age 31; was admitted June 6, 1864, with rheumatism, and died of typhoid fever August 8. *Post-mortem* examination twenty-four hours after death: Lungs congested posteriorly; liver normal; gall-bladder distended; kidneys much congested; spleen large and rather soft; intestines congested in spots; ileum near the ileo-cæcal valve much congested and presenting many ecchymoses; mesenteric glands very much enlarged.—*Act. Ass't Surg. B. B. Miles, Jarvis Hospital, Baltimore, Md.*

(D.) PEYER'S PATCHES VARIOUSLY STATED, BUT NOT ULCERATED—12 CASES.

(a.) Peyer's patches healthy.

Diagnosis: Intermittent.

CASE 366.—Private Francis Bleakley, Co. E, 6th Pa. Heavy Art.; age 24; was admitted Oct. 10, 1864, with intermittent fever. He died November 14 of typhoid fever. *Post-mortem* examination thirty hours after death: Emaciation; bedsores and suggillation posteriorly. Right lung normal anteriorly, congested and indurated posteriorly, splenified in a small portion of the lower lobe; left lung normal in its upper but congested in its lower lobe. Lower ileum congested in patches, but Peyer's patches were healthy. Kidneys slightly congested; pancreas, liver and spleen normal.—*Act. Ass't Surg. Thomas Bowen, Second Division Hospital, Alexandria, Va.*

Diagnosis: Peritonitis.

CASE 367.—Private James Wynn, Co. D, 175th Pa.; admitted July 6, 1863, with fever and peritonitis. Died 7th. *Post-mortem* examination: Body not much emaciated. Lungs and heart healthy. Liver large and mottled, adherent to the diaphragm and intestines. The cavity of the abdomen contained much yellowish serum in which flakes of yellowish lymph floated. The intestines were injected and interadherent by recent lymph; the mesenteric glands much enlarged and the mesentery thickened; the ileum was slightly injected and presented in its lower portion two perforating ulcers, one as large as a pea, the other the size of a ten-cent piece; Peyer's glands were free from disease.—*Act. Ass't Surg. Lloyd Dorsey, Harewood Hospital, Washington, D. C.*

(b.) Peyer's patches thickened and prominent.

Diagnosis: Pericarditis.

CASE 368.—Hiram Bailey, colored; age 24; was admitted on the evening of Dec. 22, 1865, complaining of pain in the stomach and bowels. He came to hospital on foot without apparent difficulty. A dose of opium, with ginger and capsicum, was administered and he rested well during the night. Next day cathartic pills were given, with castor oil in the evening. On the 24th the patient had a copious stool, but in the meantime he had fallen into a lethargic condition; eyes open and staring; pulse 80, weak; skin natural; head cool; mucous râles heard over the large bronchi; chest resonant; no swelling or tenderness of the abdomen. Quinine was given freely and at short intervals, with mustard to the spine, feet and chest, but death took place on the morning of the 25th. *Post-mortem* examination six hours after death: The brain was normal. The right pleural sac contained ten ounces of serum; the lungs were normal but for the presence of a few scattered tubercles. The pericardium and heart were firmly adherent except at a small space where was an ounce of serum; the heart substance was normal. The liver and spleen were somewhat enlarged. In the ileum several of Peyer's patches were slightly elevated and quite dark, nearly black in color. The other abdominal viscera were normal.—*L'Ouverture Hospital, Alexandria, Va.*

Diagnosis: Pleurisy.

CASE 369.—Private Charles A. Hoadley, Co. I, 3d Vt., was admitted Jan. 2, 1863, with pleurisy, and died on the 8th. *Post-mortem* examination thirty-six hours after death: The brain weighed forty-seven ounces. The right lung weighed fifty ounces; between its lobes was a deposit of yellowish semi-organized fibrinous lymph; posteriorly it was consolidated and in part hepatized, the consolidated portions being readily reduced to a pulp and exuding a reddish-gray puruloid matter. The left lung weighed fifty-two ounces; its lower lobe and the lower and posterior portions of its upper lobe were infiltrated with puruloid matter. The right auricle of the heart contained a fibrinous clot which extended through the ventricle into the pulmonary artery; the left cavities contained a black clot; about the middle of the thoracic aorta were some transverse yellow bands which were supposed to be atheromatous. The liver, sixty-nine ounces, was finely mottled and of a light reddish-brown color; the spleen, nine ounces, was light-colored, hardened in small portions and softened near the hilus, whence a thick reddish puruloid matter was readily pressed; the right kidney weighed seven ounces, the left six ounces and a half. The stomach was softened and congested; the jejunum was irregularly congested towards its termination; the ileum was very thin and there were spots of intense congestion in its middle third; Peyer's patches were enormously thickened, especially towards the cæcum.—*Ass't Surg. George M. McGill, U. S. A., Lincoln Hospital, Washington, D. C.*

Diagnosis: Pneumonia.

CASE 370.—Private John Mosner, Co. B, 149th N. Y., was admitted Jan. 18, 1863, with typhoid pneumonia. The patient was very deaf and almost unconscious; his skin was hot and dry, respiration hurried, tongue dry and pulse 95; there was dulness on percussion and fine crepitation on the right side of the chest. He was ordered blue-pill, ipecacuanha and tartar emetic in small doses with dry cups to the chest. On the 22d the tongue became dryer, the pulse more rapid and the expectoration bloody and of a dark color. Stimulants and beef-essence were employed, with a blister to the right side, but they were unavailing; death took place on the 27th. *Post-mortem* examination four hours after death: Body finely developed. The brain weighed forty-nine ounces and a half. The right lung weighed thirty-two ounces and a quarter, the left twenty-eight and a half; the right lung was much congested, the lower part of its upper lobe in the state of gray hepatization and parts of its lower lobe in the state of red hepatization; the lobes of the left lung were interadherent, the lower congested and partly solidified; the bronchial glands were large, soft and black. The heart weighed nine ounces; there was much adipose tissue about the auriculo-ventricular rings; the cavities on both sides contained small clots. The liver weighed eighty ounces, its acini were distinct; the spleen weighed nine ounces and a half; the right kidney eight ounces, the left seven and three-quarters. The fundus of the stomach was extremely congested, as was the mucous membrane of the whole intestinal tract; in the lower part of the large intestine the congestion was so intense as to resemble ecchymosis; the glands of Peyer were large.—*Ass't Surg. George M. McGill, U. S. A., Lincoln Hospital, Washington, D. C.*

CASE 371.—Private John Beaton, Co. D, 1st Vt. Cav.; admitted Nov. 2, 1862, with typhoid pneumonia: Hot dry skin, pulse 85, compressible, tongue coated with brown fur, moderate diarrhœa, sudamina profusely distributed about the neck and thorax, gurgling and some tenderness in the right iliac region, dry cough, severe dyspnœa and almost complete aphonia; dulness on percussion and bronchial respiration over the lower portion of both lungs; no rose-colored spots. Treatment: Small doses of calomel, ipecacuanha and opium; dry cups and turpentine stupes to the chest; a mustard cataplasm to the abdomen. Died 5th. *Post-mortem* examination eighteen hours after death: The lower portion of both lungs was hepatized. The heart, stomach, spleen, liver, kidneys and large intestine were normal. The glands of Peyer were enlarged and inflamed.—*Third Division Hospital, Alexandria, Va.*

CASE 372.—Private Charles Whitten, Co. K, 20th Me.; age 16; was admitted Nov. 18, 1862, with typhoid pneumonia. He complained of a dull pain below the right nipple; his pulse was frequent and feeble; his tongue covered with a white fur; skin hot and dry; bowels constipated. There was dulness on percussion over the right side, and crepitus was distinctly heard both anteriorly and posteriorly. Small doses of calomel, opium and ipecacuanha were given, with dry cups to the right side of the chest. In the progress of the case the cough became more troublesome and the respiration hurried; diarrhœa supervened, accompanied by great tympanites of the abdomen; the tongue became dry and fissured and the lips and teeth covered with sordes. Stimulants were freely administered, but he died on the 26th. *Post-mortem* examination: The surface of the body was bluish from capillary congestion; the abdomen tumid. The upper lobes of both lungs were congested and the lower lobes, with the middle lobe on the right side, hepatized. The stomach and colon were immensely distended with gas; the mucous membrane of the small intestine was highly injected; the glands of Peyer enlarged. The liver, spleen and kidneys appeared to be normal. —*Third Division Hospital, Alexandria, Va.*

(c.) Peyer's patches congested or inflamed.

Diagnosis: Rheumatism.

CASE 373.—Private James Makin, Co. B, 124th Pa.; age about 25; admitted Dec. 26, 1862. Died Feb. 17, 1863. *Post-mortem* examination forty-eight minutes after death: Rigor mortis marked; hypostasis general. Brain forty-four ounces, light-colored, moderately firm. Pharynx purple, congested; tonsils yellow, enlarged to the size of an almond. Right lung twenty ounces, left seventeen and a half, congested; bronchial glands black. Heart eleven ounces and three-quarters; fibrinous clots in both sides extending into vessels. Liver sixty-eight ounces, light-colored, firm; gall-bladder light-colored, containing seventeen drachms of watery bile; spleen seventeen ounces and a quarter, soft, of a dark-purple color, intensely congested; pancreas three ounces and a half, dark-colored, slightly congested. Duodenum slightly congested, stained with bile, valvulæ thinned; jejunum light brownish-yellow, thinned in lower two-thirds, solitary glands slightly enlarged in upper third; ileum thinned, solitary glands somewhat enlarged and Peyer's patches in upper third slightly congested; large intestine generally congested. Suprarenal capsules light-colored, soft, decidedly fatty; right kidney six ounces and a quarter, left six and three-quarters, somewhat congested.—*Ass't Surg. George M. McGill, U. S. A., Lincoln Hospital, Washington, D. C.*

Diagnosis: Diarrhœa.

CASE 374.—Private Cyrus G. Chatterton, Co. C, 24th N. Y. Cav., was admitted July 24, 1864. He was greatly emaciated, having suffered from diarrhœa for some time. The stools were frequent, quite watery, clay-colored and accompanied with griping pains in the abdomen; he had no appetite; his tongue was red and had marked elevations of the papillæ; pulse 100 and very weak. In a few days the passages became less frequent and of a dark-green color, but although thus improving he continued depressed in mind. On August 3 the right side of the face became much swollen and the gums swollen and red but not bleeding, the general appearance of the patient being scorbutic. Chlorate of potash was given internally and as a wash. Next day he had much difficulty in opening his mouth, and complained of sore throat; the fauces became much inflamed, the tonsils covered with pseudo-membrane, portions of which were expectorated, and mucous râles were developed in the chest. He died on the 6th. *Post-mortem* examination: Body very much emaciated. The larynx and fauces were covered with patches of false membrane. The right lung was slightly adherent; the left lung and heart normal. The liver was normal; the spleen measured five inches and a half by four inches; the right kidney was seven inches and a half long, its substance firm and healthy; the left kidney and suprarenal capsule were absent, their place being occupied by a closed cyst, one inch and a half long, in which no kidney structure could be detected. Peyer's patches were much inflamed; the mesenteric glands healthy.—*Act. Ass't Surg. E. David, Fairfax Seminary Hospital, Va.*

CASE 375.—Private Elias Zimmerman, Co. D, 48th Pa.; age 18; admitted July 24, 1864, from City Point hospital, Va. Died August 5. *Post-mortem* examination: Body much emaciated. Peyer's patches inflamed; solitary follicles extensively ulcerated. Other organs normal.—*Act. Ass't Surg. G. W. Peer, Fairfax Seminary Hospital, Va.*

CASE 376.—Private Franklin Dougherty, Co. D, 100th Pa.; age 18; admitted July 5, 1864, with chronic rheumatism and diarrhœa. He was considerably emaciated, had anorexia and severe diarrhœa, with pulse weak and frequent and tongue coated in the centre with a thick gray fur; the left parotid was painful and much swollen. The parotid abscess was opened on the 15th and a small quantity of dark fetid pus was obtained; meanwhile the diarrhœa persisted and the patient seemed to be sinking gradually; he had a slight remission of fever in the forenoon of every day. In the progress of the case the integuments covering the parotid sloughed, delirium set in, at first chiefly at night, his face became more flushed and the daily remissions less marked. He died on the 22d. *Post-mortem* examination six hours after death: Body greatly emaciated, rigor mortis well marked. Lungs much congested, heart pale and flabby. Liver slightly congested; gall-bladder distended with bile; spleen enlarged and pale; kidneys healthy. Stomach reddened in patches, which were more numerous near the pylorus; duodenum and jejunum healthy; Peyer's glands congested slightly in the upper portion of the ileum and the solitary follicles in the lower portion considerably enlarged, many having incipient ulcers on their summits. Mucous membrane of the large intestine puckered, softened and presenting several small ulcers in the cæcum and in the lower portion of the descending colon. Upper portion of left parotid gland exposed by sloughing of integument and superficial fascia; dark fetid pus had burrowed a short distance down the side of the neck. [*Specimens 385 to 390, Med. Sect., Army Medical Museum, are from this case.*]—*Act. Ass't Surg. O. P. Sweet, Carver Hospital, Washington, D. C.*

No diagnosis: Death from heart-clot.

CASE 377.—Private Nicholas Sassaman, Co. E, 50th Pa., was admitted Oct. 11, 1861, at noon. His pulse was weak and intermittent, breathing hurried, difficult and mainly abdominal; his extremities were cold and he complained of severe pain over the præcordia and epigastrium. In the evening two wet cups were applied over each lung, after which he arose from bed and walked to the chair to stool: he expired as he sat down. *Post-mortem* examination ten hours after death: Body well developed and not emaciated; rigor mortis strongly marked. There were old pleuritic adhesions on the right side; the lower lobe of the lung was congested, the upper contained tubercles; the left lung was healthy. The heart weighed twelve ounces and a half; fibrinous clots were found in the right ventricle, the walls of which were hypertrophied; the mitral valve was thickened and its right segment studded on the margin with roundish fibrinous bodies, some about the size of a pin-head, others as large as a pea. The liver was enlarged and fatty; the spleen was triple its normal size and mottled with spots surrounded by reddish areolæ, exuding on section a sero-purulent liquid; the kidneys were enlarged and fatty. Peyer's patches were inflamed and the mesenteric glands enlarged.—*Armory Square Hospital, Washington, D. C.*

Of the above seventy-nine cases, *forty-two* in which Peyer's patches were ulcerated, and *twenty-one* in which the ileum was ulcerated, may be set aside as being distinctly or probably cases of typhoid fever. In four, 362–365, of the remaining *sixteen* the intestinal lining was congested or inflamed. It is not stated that the membrane was *not* ulcerated or that Peyer's patches were *not* affected; for these *post-mortem* records seldom embody negative evidence in terms so positive. It must be inferred that if the membrane had been ulcerated the inquirer who noted its ecchymosed condition would have observed its ulceration, and that had the agminated glands been implicated the anatomist who took note of the enlarged, pigmented and disorganized condition of the solitary follicles would not have overlooked the condition of the others, particularly in cases in which typhoid fever was in question. Now, as there was no *post-mortem* evidence of typhoid fever in these cases, the change in the diagnosis must have been occasioned by the occurrence of typhoid symptoms, *i. e.*, in these cases typhoid symptoms were present although typhoid fever was not. Of the remaining twelve cases five, 368–372, presented appearances of the patches consistent with the theory of death at an early period of the progress of typhoid fever; but in the others the presence of that fever cannot be considered established: In 366 and 367 Peyer's glands were healthy. In 373–377 they are said to have been congested or inflamed, but this condition alone may not be accepted as pathognomonic of typhoid, since in 376 the ulceration of the solitary follicles, with which it was associated, while giving assurance that had the patches been ulcerated their condition would have been stated, indicates that the patient had lived long enough for this change to have taken place; indeed the prolonged duration of the fatal illness is sufficiently attested by the disorganization of the parotid glands. But for the congestion of the agminated glands the case of death from heart-clot, 377, would have found place in the malarial series in company with its cases 95 and 96.

In the absence of clinical histories it is impossible in many cases of the above series to say whether the change in the diagnosis was based on clinical or *post-mortem* considerations. It is certain, however, that in sixty-eight of the seventy-nine cases the *post-mortem* lesions authorized the change, while in eleven their testimony was less positive. In some of the latter clinical observation must have suggested the presence of typhoid fever, as the intestinal appearances were inadequate to sustain the diagnosis, but in others the presence of typhoid seems to have been based on a mistaken view of the import of these appearances.

A few cases illustrative of accidents in the course of typhoid fever or morbid conditions following it complete the *post-mortem* records of cases reported under this heading; but from the condition of the intestines in some of these cases it is doubtful if typhoid was the antecedent fever.

Case 378.—*Lumbricoid worm in larynx.*—Private Joseph Shuman, Co. M, 1st N. J. Cav.; age 17; was admitted Jan. 16, 1864, with typhoid fever. The patient was doing very well under tonics and stimulants when, on the 18th, he suddenly died asphyxiated. At the autopsy a lumbricoid worm nine inches long was found extending from the trachea into the right bronchus.—[See *specimen* 290, Med. Sect., Army Medical Museum.]—*Act. Ass't Surg. S. B. Ward, Third Division Hospital, Alexandria, Va.*

Case 379.—*Sudden death during convalescence; heart-clot; cerebral congestion.*—Private James F. Wilson, Co. C, 16th Me.; age 21; was admitted Feb. 8, 1865, convalescing from typhoid fever. He had a slight cough, but was otherwise well and continued to gain strength until the 24th. At 3 A. M. on this day the nurse, in passing through the ward, found him awake, put the blankets over him and gave him some water to drink. He was then well. Three hours later he was found dead, having apparently died without a struggle. *Post-mortem* examination: No lividity about the face; pupils dilated; rigor mortis well marked on the right side, slight on the left. A considerable quantity of venous blood escaped on opening the cranium; some exudation was found on the arachnoid; the substance of the cerebrum and cerebellum was highly engorged, and bright blood welled up in unusual quantities when sections were made; the lateral ventricles were distended with a sero-sanguineous liquid. The lower lobe of the right lung was engorged. The right ventricle contained a large fibrinous clot. There were no other unusual appearances.—*Act. Ass't Surg. W. Kempster, Patterson Park Hospital, Baltimore, Md.*

CASE 380.—*Destructive inflammation of lungs.*—Private Richard H. Nelson, Co. A, 8th Mich., was admitted Dec. 30, 1862, with typhoid fever. On Jan. 24, 1863, he appeared to be convalescent and was walking about the ward, complaining occasionally, however, of pain in the right side of the chest. On February 18 he had headache, slight irritation of the fauces, constipation, difficulty of micturition and severe pain in the right side of the chest. He was ordered to bed, a laxative administered and warm fomentations applied to the chest. Next day, feeling better, he got up and went out of doors, after which the pain in the side returned and he began to cough and expectorate a muco-purulent matter. His cheeks were flushed, pulse 120, respiration 22; a friction sound with sibilant râles was heard over the lateral portion of the right lung; the respiratory murmur was absent in front. On the 22d he seemed much improved; the pain was not so severe; his appetite was good and bowels regular, but the expectoration remained copious. Two days later he had chills followed by fever and increasing prostration. He died March 8. *Post-mortem* examination twenty-eight hours after death: Body slightly rigid, not emaciated; apparent age 21 years. The brain was healthy. There was a white fibrinous clot in the right side of the heart extending into the pulmonary artery, and a small white clot with some dark blood in the left side. The right lung weighed thirty-four ounces and a half; it was congested generally and consolidated on the posterior and inner part of its lower lobe; its bronchial tubes, especially those proceeding from the consolidated portions, were somewhat congested and contained a puruloid matter; its anterior surface was coated with a thick layer of fibrinous lymph and the pleural sac contained sixteen ounces of pus. The left lung weighed twenty-seven ounces; portions of it were carnified; its bronchial tubes were congested and contained a purulent matter; the pleural cavity was sacculated and contained twenty-two ounces of straw-colored serum. The liver was firm, coarsely mottled, of a light reddish-brown externally and covered with numerous blood-spots; on section it was slate-colored; the gall-bladder was empty. The spleen, twenty ounces and three-quarters, was of firm consistence, dark-purple in color and with prominent trabeculæ; in its inferior border was a hard nodule about the size of a hazel-nut. The pancreas was firm and of a light-straw color. The kidneys were of a purplish-slate color; the suprarenal capsules firm, large and of a reddish-ash color. The mesenteric glands were much enlarged. The stomach was softened and congested along the longitudinal folds and in the lesser curvature; the duodenum and jejunum were irregularly congested; the ileum decidedly congested; Peyer's patches apparently healthy; the solitary glands slightly enlarged and congested. The ascending colon and cæcum were dilated, their mucous membrane thin and soft; the transverse colon was somewhat contracted and covered with black specks; the sigmoid flexure congested; the rectum normal.—*Ass't Surg. George M. McGill, U. S. A., Lincoln Hospital, Washington, D. C.*

CASE 381.—*Inflammation of the parotid; paralysis and hyperæsthesia of the limbs.*—Private John Parker, Co. B, 3d Ohio Cav., was admitted March 4, 1864, as a convalescent from typhoid fever. His tongue was very much coated and the parotid gland was slightly swollen. In a few days the swelling had almost disappeared but he continued feeble, lost the use of his arms and legs and complained when they were touched; this sensitiveness was especially marked in the right arm and left leg. Diarrhœa set in on the 11th, when his tongue became dry and pulse small; death took place on the 13th. *Post-mortem* examination eighteen hours after death: Body not much emaciated. The lungs, heart, stomach and intestines appeared to be healthy. The liver was pale, much enlarged, and showed evidence of a local peritonitis; its right lobe was congested; the gall-bladder was empty. Both kidneys were much congested.—*Act. Ass't Surg. L. A. Walton, Hospital No. 8, Nashville, Tenn.*

CASE 382.—*Psoas abscess.*—Private S. E. Robinson, Co. A, 3d Md.; age 26; was admitted from Patterson Park hospital Sept. 21, 1864, as a convalescent from typhoid fever. On the 28th he had a chill and two days later there was pain in the upper part of the right thigh, where redness, swelling and fluctuation were observed. On October 1 flatus and fæcal matter were brought away by an exploring needle, and the case was regarded as one of typhlitis with perforation and adhesion of the bowel to the abdominal walls. A free incision was made and a considerable quantity of pus escaped mixed with fæcal matter. The patient became delirious on the 4th and had obstinate hiccough. He died on the 6th, after having been unconscious for thirty-six hours. *Post-mortem* examination: A large psoas abscess had dissected the muscles of the thigh as far as the middle third. "No perforation of the bowel was discovered, so that what was supposed to have been fæcal matter must have been altered pus. It is but right, however, to state that several medical men present at the time concurred in the opinion then formed." [The condition of the mucous membrane of the intestine was not recorded.]—*Mower Hospital, Philadelphia, Pa.*

CASE 383.—*Purulent collections.*—Private J. W. Cunningham, Co. I, 170th Ohio; age 26; was admitted from hospital, Frederick, Md., Aug. 7, 1864; diarrhœa following typhoid fever. He died September 8. *Post-mortem* examination twenty-four hours after death: Abscesses were found under the right arm, on the anterior aspect of the right forearm and on the dorsum of the left foot. Both lungs contained abscesses; the lower lobe of the left lung was one immense cavity which had opened into the pleural sac, filling its lower half with pus, but adhesions of the parietal and pulmonary pleuræ around the upper part of the lobe separated this purulent collection from the upper half of the pleura; on the right side the abscess under the arm communicated freely with the pleural cavity, which was filled with pus. The pericardium was distended with serum. The liver was normal; the gall-blader distended. —*Act. Ass't Surg. B. B. Miles, Jarvis Hospital, Baltimore, Md.*

CASE 384.—*Diphtheria and inflammation of the submaxillary gland.*—Private Charles Williams, Co. F, 52d Pa.; age 21; was admitted Sept. 22, 1864, with typhoid pneumonia. He was recovering from an attack of typhoid fever and was thin and broken down; his skin presented a peculiar bronzed appearance in spots, from which the epidermis was easily peeled off, leaving an abnormally white surface beneath; he suffered considerably from diarrhœa. There was dulness on percussion and an absence of the respiratory murmur over the base of the right lung, with slight nocturnal cough. His condition did not change much until the middle of November, when he had an attack of diphtheria, followed, after a few days, by inflammation of the left submaxillary gland, which suppurated and was opened about December 1. On the 6th he complained of cough, difficult expectoration and constant pain through the lower part of both lungs, with occasional paroxysms of pain of a more lancinating character. There was dulness on percussion and bronchitic râles at the base of both lungs with friction sounds superadded; these signs afterwards gave place to blowing respiration with entire absence of the vesicular murmur, and finally to loose mucous and submucous râles. He died December 24. *Post-mortem* examination: Both lungs were bound to the thoracic parietes by extensive and firm adhesions; the lower portion of each lung was in a state of gray hepatization. [There is no record of the condition of the intestinal mucous membrane.]—*Cuyler Hospital, Philadelphia, Pa.*

Of the fevers reported as typhus the records furnish but five cases in which the *post-mortem* appearances are described. In one of these, 385, extensive disease of the agminated glands sufficiently indicates its typhoid character. Case 386 appears to have been an example of pernicious malarial fever, for although the disease had lasted some time, most of the patches were healthy, a few only being inflamed and somewhat thickened and none ulcerated, while the large intestine was ecchymosed and ulcerated. Case 387, with its prominent and pigmented solitary glands, was apparently of a similar nature. Many cases presenting intestinal lesions of this character have already been noted as referable to the malarial rather than to the typhoid influence. From the necroscopic appearances 388 seems related to the suddenly fatal cases which were reported as cerebro-spinal meningitis.* Case 389 is the only instance in which the *post-mortem* lesions, so far as determined, were consistent with the diagnosis, and as the case occurred in the city of Philadelphia, it is probable that it is the representative of that veritable typhus which occurred among soldiers exposed to circumscribed foci of infection during a temporary residence in the large cities.

CASE 385.—Private Burton White, Co. E, 147th N. Y., was admitted April 22, 1863, with an incised wound of the right leg. He died May 26, of pneumonia supervening on an obscure disease resembling typhus. *Post-mortem* examination: Body plump and full; depending parts dark-colored. The adjoining halves of the lower and middle lobes of the right lung were infiltrated with pus. The lower part of the ileum was extensively ulcerated in patches, in one of which was a small perforation closed by adhesion to the peritoneum covering the bladder; there had been no escape of intestinal contents and there was no indication of peritonitis. The spleen and the mesenteric glands were enlarged and softened. [*Specimens* 180 to 183, Med. Sect., Army Medical Museum, are from this case: see also plate facing this page.]—*Surg. Thomas R. Crosby, U. S. V., Columbian Hospital, Washington, D. C.*

CASE 386.—Private Charles B. Dorr, Co. B, 17th U. S. Inf.; admitted Aug. 10, 1862, from the Army of the Potomac. Typhus fever. Died 22d. *Post-mortem* examination: Age about 22 years; body moderately emaciated and with diffused ecchymoses on the skin of the trunk; the muscles were of their ordinary character, but the viscera of the chest and abdomen were generally softer than usual. The lungs and heart were normal except that there were two ecchymosed spots about a quarter of an inch in diameter near the base of the latter. The blood presented nothing unusual. The liver and spleen were natural. The mucous membrane of the stomach was inflamed near the pylorus and presented a number of small ulcers, about a line in diameter, along the lesser curvature. [*Specimen* 272, Med. Sect., Army Medical Museum.] The ileum was inflamed in patches, some of which were intensely affected; the solitary glands were enlarged and inflamed; most of the agminated glands were healthy, some were inflamed and slightly thickened, but none were ulcerated. [*Specimens* 273–276.] The mucous membrane of the colon was more or less slate-colored, with patches of inflammation, a number of ecchymoses about half an inch in diameter, and in the descending portion a number of stellate, blackened ulcers.—*Act. Ass't Surg. J. Leidy, Satterlee Hospital, Philadelphia, Pa.*

CASE 387.—Private John Mills, Co. C, 43d N. Y.; vigorous looking, but somewhat emaciated; admitted Aug. 10, 1862. Died 14th. [Case supposed by Dr. ATLEE, the attending physician, to be typhus.] *Post-mortem* examination next day: The skin of the front and sides of the chest and abdomen was slightly ecchymosed. The lower lobe of the left lung was affected with recent pleuro-pneumonia; the upper lobe was inflamed; the right lung was somewhat congested. The heart, stomach and spleen were natural, and the liver exhibited a healthy color and texture, but presented an unusually lobular appearance (as in the rat). The mucous membrane of the small intestine was of

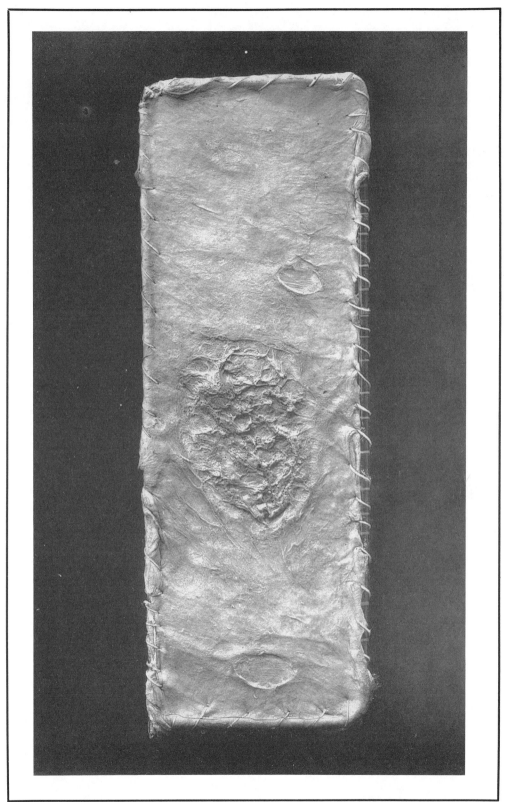

SLOUGHING PEYER'S PATCH.

No. 182. MEDICAL SECTION.

a pinkish-cream color and tinged with bile; the solitary glands of the jejunum were opaque-white and those of the ileum unusually prominent and dotted with black pigment; the agminated glands were slightly thicker than usual but did not appear positively diseased. The colon was much contracted and its mucous membrane slightly inflamed; the solitary glands were large and prominent, especially in the cæcum, and were marked by a deposit of black pigment.—*Act. Ass't Surg. J. Leidy, Satterlee Hospital, Philadelphia, Pa.*

CASE 388.—Jeremiah Saulsburg, a colored soldier, died of typhus Jan. 24, 1864. *Post-mortem* examination eight hours after death: Body stout and well developed. There were well-marked deposits of viscid pus between the convolutions of the frontal lobes and of the parietal lobes near the longitudinal fissure, as also over the pons medulla and crura; a mass of pus overlaid the anterior corpora quadrigemina, and the membrane covering them was finely injected; the substance of the brain was gorged with blood, but the choroid plexus was pale and the ventricles not enlarged although containing some effusion. The pericardium was full of serum and the right cavities of the heart contained fibrinous clots. The lower lobe of the left lung was congested by hypostasis, but there were also some spots of proper hepatization. The liver was darker than usual and full of blood. The colon and ileum were inflated. (There had been strabismus during the last three or four days of this patient's life.)—*Act. Ass't Surg. W. C. Minor, Knight General Hospital.*

CASE 389.—Private William W. Fenno, Co. K, 145th Pa.; age 19; was admitted Dec. 13, 1862, with chronic rheumatism and debility, and so far recovered as to be able for guard duty; but on Feb. 17, 1863, he was taken with diarrhœa and next day he had a high fever, quick breathing, tremulous voice and a dark furred tongue. 19th: Diagnosis—typhus fever; dyspnœa greatly increased; diarrhœa almost ceased; stupid, but could be aroused by a loud voice; abdomen tympanitic; capillary circulation feeble; no eruption. 20th: Suppression of urine. 1.30 P. M., vomited a large lumbricoid worm and other matters; restless delirium alternating with comatose quiet. Died at 4 P. M. *Post-mortem* examination: Suggillation distinct; no vibices; petechiæ over epigastrium, stated by the nurse to have existed during life. Brain not examined. Lungs congested posteriorly. Left ventricle of heart filled with black fluid blood; right containing two fibrinous clots. Liver large but healthy; spleen much enlarged and lobulated; kidneys and intestines healthy.—*Cuyler Hospital, Philadelphia, Pa.*

V.—ON THE PATHOLOGICAL ANATOMY AND PATHOLOGY OF THE CONTINUED FEVERS.

I.—THE CASES AND THEIR ANALYSIS.

Three hundred and eighty-nine cases from the *post-mortem* records have been submitted. These were regarded by the medical officers in attendance as fatal instances of continued fever. They have been presented as—

1st. *Fifty* cases, 1-50, presumed from their symptoms to have been unmodified typhoid;

2d. *Sixty-six* cases, 51-116, of an adynamic continued fever, which might from the symptoms or diagnosis have been individually either cases of modified typhoid or of adynamic malarial fever;

3d. *Two hundred and sixty-eight* cases, 117-384, of fever which, although reported as typhoid, might individually have been typhoid, typho-malarial or adynamic malarial, in view of the uncertainty attaching to the diagnosis;

4th. *Five* cases, 385-389, reported as typhus, but which, in like manner, might have been due to other pernicious causes than the typhus or the typhoid poison.

The study of the intestinal lesions, as conducted in the last section, has modified antemortem views as to the relationship of these cases one to the other, and rendered a rearrangement advisable to facilitate further investigation into their pathological anatomy. The diagnosis of the fifty cases presumed to be unmodified typhoid was confirmed by the evidence of the agminated glands or by such conditions of the ileum as were suggestive of a glandular involvement. The sixty-six continued febrile cases of an adynamic or typhoid type consisted of *forty-six* in which the lesions of typhoid were associated with malarial symptoms and of *twenty* in which the absence of these lesions indicated the malarial influence as the sole cause of the morbid phenomena. The two hundred and sixty-eight cases of reported typhoid comprised *fifteen* cases in which the *post-mortem* appearances testified that some febrile cause, which from its symptoms was of a malarial nature, had preceded the onset of a typhoid attack, *forty-one* in which typhoid lesions were not discovered, and *two hundred and twelve* in which these lesions were present or such ulceration of the small intestine as might be attributed to either typhoid fever alone or to typhoid as modified by the concurrence of malarial fever, thus constituting a mixed series of typhoid and typho-malarial cases. The five cases reported as typhus were similarly found to consist of one typhoid case, two malarial cases, one case related to cerebro-spinal fever and one of probably true typhus.

Aggregating these in accordance with clinical history, diagnosis and intestinal lesions, there appear—

Fifty cases of unmodified typhoid, cases 1–50;

Sixty-three cases of malarial fever with typhoid or adynamic symptoms but without typhoid lesions, cases 70–73, 76, 78–81, 84, 87–91, 104, 105, 108, 113, 115, 246–252, 254–263, 274, 276–278, 287–295, 362–367, 373–377, 386 and 387;*

Sixty-one cases of true typho-malarial fever, cases 51–69, 74, 75, 77, 82, 83, 85, 86, 92–103, 106, 107, 109–112, 114, 116, 264–273, 280, 285 and 296–298;†

Two hundred and thirteen cases of a mixed class, consisting chiefly of typho-malarial fever, but probably containing some instances of typhoid alone and of malarial fever alone, cases 117–245, 253, 275, 279, 281–284, 286, 299–361, 368–372, 378–384 and 385;

One case of cerebro-spinal fever, (?) case 388;

One case of typhus, (?) case 389.

The results of an analysis of the *post-mortem* appearances in these cases is herewith submitted; and, to admit of a comparison between the anatomical details of the typhoid cases of the war and those of civil life, a summary of the lesions in the cases so carefully observed by LOUIS is given below.‡

ANALYSIS OF THE POST-MORTEM APPEARANCES.

The SALIVARY GLANDS.—In but one of the continued febrile cases was mention made of an inflamed condition of the submaxillary or sublingual glands, but a destructive inflammation occurred with some frequency in the parotid region. It was present in sixteen of the recorded cases; in six the glands were swollen and indurated and in ten destroyed by suppuration. In three cases the morbid action affected both sides, while in thirteen it was confined to one side; the right gland was involved in five cases, the left in three; in five the record does not specify the side.

Parotid abscess occurred in but one case, 31, of the fifty *typhoid* cases; one side only was affected. In 258 of the *malarial* series the right parotid was swollen, and in three cases abscess was formed,—on the right side in 251, on the left in 376 and on both sides in 263. Parotitis occurred in four of the *typho-malarial* series: In 53 on one side and in 65 and 97 on the right side; suppuration was present on one side, in 103. In the *mixed* series of cases swelling existed in two cases and suppuration in five: The swelling in 118 and 381 does not appear to have culminated in abscess; the right gland suppurated in 125; the left in 193 and 338, and both glands in 222 and 348. Suppuration occurred in the submaxillary glands in case 384 of this series.

The condition of the PHARYNX and ŒSOPHAGUS appears to have been seldom observed by our medical officers. The mucous membrane was reported pale in case 23 of the *typhoid* series. It presented morbid appearances in six of the *malarial* cases,—purplish coloration in 90 and 277, deep congestion in 373, erosion without accompanying con-

---

*To these might with propriety be added certain cases reported as typho-malarial fever by the attending officers, but submitted in the second part of this work as cases of diarrhœa and dysentery. Thus, in case 313, entered as typho-malarial fever, the small intestine was found healthy; in 363, reported as typhoid-remittent fever, the duodenum was of a dark-purple color, but the remainder of the small intestine was healthy except near the valve, where were many small circular superficial ulcers, the solitary glands being prominent and the patches of Peyer pale but neither ulcerated nor elevated; in 518, reported typho-malarial, the mucous membrane of the ileum was somewhat inflamed; in 832, at first regarded as remittent fever and afterwards as typhoid dysentery, the ileum was congested and studded with small ulcerations, while the large intestine was more extensively ulcerated and almost gangrenous. Perhaps also case 783 should be added to these, as the patient had an adynamic fever from the time he entered the hospital, yet *post-mortem* investigation showed the small intestine to be in a healthy condition. In fact many cases of the diarrhœal series, in which the typhoid lesion was not found after death, presented more or less of a clinical resemblance to typhoid fever.

†To these might be added the case submitted in the second part of this work as 825 of the diarrhœal series; the diagnosis was typho-malarial fever, and *post-mortem* examination revealed the ileum and colon studded with ulceration. Perhaps 436, presenting fever of an adynamic type, with hemorrhage from the bowels, and showing at the autopsy the small intestine ulcerated in patches and the large intestine perforated, may also have been a true typho-malarial case. For a discussion of the connection between the diarrhœal cases and the continued fevers, see *infra*, p. 615 *et seq*.

‡The following abstract of the *post-mortem* appearances found by LOUIS in his forty-six cases may be of interest in connection with the lesions observed in the fifty typhoid cases of the text:

The SALIVARY GLANDS.—The submaxillary and sublingual glands were not altered in any of the cases; but in two there was suppuration in the parotid region, due in one instance to inflammation of the surrounding cellular tissue and in the other to inflammation of the glandular structure.

The PHARYNX was affected in eight cases; ulcerated in six and covered with false membranes associated with purulent infiltration of the submucous cellular tissue in two. The ulcerations were few, three to eight lines in their greatest, the vertical, diameter and situated on the lower and lateral aspects of the sac. As no such ulceration was found in seventy cases of other acute diseases, LOUIS considered it an important lesion and one of the secondary anatomical characteristics of the typhoid affection.

The ŒSOPHAGUS was ulcerated in seven cases, only two of which were included among those having the pharynx affected. The ulcers, when few, were situated near the cardia, when numerous they extended throughout the whole of the tube, but were more frequent and larger towards the lower end. LOUIS associated these ulcers with those of the pharynx as peculiar to typhoid fever.

gestion in 259, softening and denudation in 71, and diphtheritic exudation in 374. In the *typho-malarial* series a morbid condition is mentioned in but three instances: In 65 the mucous membrane was inflamed; in 54 inflamed and ulcerated; in 67 abscesses were found on the left side in front of the hyoid bone. In the *mixed* series morbid appearances were noted in twelve instances: The œsophageal lining was of a pale color and ulcerated in its lower part in 137 and 187, while in the same region in 301 it presented dark-colored spots, one of which was eroded; it was congested in longitudinal streaks in 305; inflamed, purplish, and in its lower part ecchymosed in 329; in 156 the œsophagus was of a purple or brown color and its walls contained an abscess as large as a chestnut, and in 185 there was an ulceration on its posterior wall on a level with the larynx, while the tube below was filled with a whitish exudation; in 155, 199 and 304 the mucous membrane was yellowish and in 183 purple; in 338 the pharyngeal coats were perforated by matter from the parotid region.

The STOMACH was normal in four of the *typhoid* cases, 11, 27, 35 and 36, and in one, 16, it was not examined. Of twelve cases in which a morbid change was reported its mucous membrane in 24, 26, 29, 41 and 47 was reddened from congestion; in 9 the congestion was in circumscribed patches; in 8 the fundus, which was of a dull-red color, contained five lumbricoid worms; in 21 the mucous membrane was pale and thickened; in 22 slaty and mottled; in 23 mottled, congested and blackened from pigmentary deposits near the pylorus; in 48 thickened and softened, and in 31 thickened and congested, the viscus containing about a pint of an offensive yellow liquid. Of the sixty-three *malarial* cases the condition of the stomach was not stated in thirty-four, and in the remaining twenty-nine it was normal in fourteen, congested in six, thickened and softened in three, inflamed on its peritoneal surface in 249 and along the great curvature in 91; ulcerated along the small curvature in 386; flaccid, thin and greatly discolored in 287; ecchymosed but uncongested in 262, and in 71 the organ contained a pint of dark-colored liquid in which floated shreds of its disintegrated mucous membrane. Of the *typho-malarial* series the condition of the stomach was mentioned in sixteen cases: It was normal in six, congested in two, 103 and 296; softened in two, 98 and 112, in the former of which the lining membrane was almost disintegrated; in 93 it was unusually corrugated; in 65 and 116 inflamed; in 96 it presented black patches and was ulcerated near the pylorus; in 62 it was filled with dark grumous blood, and in 106, in which death resulted from peritonitis, it contained fæcal matter. In the *mixed* series of cases the state of the stomach was mentioned seventy-four times: In thirty-three it was normal, but in one of these, 325, it contained a grumous liquid; in four it was merely distended. Of the remaining thirty-seven cases its mucous membrane was congested and more or less softened in sixteen; softened in four, to pultaceousness in 243; injected in five; inflamed in six, in one of which, 354, there was ulceration, and in another, 239, the viscus contained matter like coffee-grounds; grayish, slate-colored or marbled in three; ecchymosed in one, 342; in 191 the stomach was filled with bile and in 156 with a liquid of a greenish color and fæcal-like odor.

The DUODENUM was distended in case 5 of the *typhoid* series, normal in 26, filled with thick tenacious mucus in 23 and undergoing putrefactive changes in 22; its mucous membrane was congested or inflamed in 17, 18, 29 and 50, softened and thickened in 48; in 41 its glands were enlarged and in 9 congested. Morbid changes were defined in four of the *malarial* series: In 87 the glands of Brünner were enlarged; in 276 and 373 the lining membrane was congested and in 71 disintegrated; but in other instances, as 81, 113 and 259, a congested or inflamed condition of the duodenum may be inferred. Ten observations were recorded in precise terms or by inference in the *typho-malarial* series: In four a normal condition was indicated; in 269 the glands were enlarged; in 53 there was follicular inflammation with softening; in 86 the lining membrane was dark-colored and congested; in 65 and 116 inflamed and in 96 ulcerated. Twenty-six observations were noted in the *mixed* series of cases: In ten a healthy condition was stated; in four the glands alone were mentioned, enlarged in 122 and 281, inflamed in 284 and ulcerated in 307; in nine, 181, 182, 190, 279, 317, 318, 354, 370 and 380 the mucous membrane was congested; in one, 243, pultaceous; and in two, 156 and 338, dark-colored.

The JEJUNUM was distended in case 5 of the *typhoid* series; normal in 10 and 26 and probably also in 23. In 17, 18, 29, 47 and 50 it was more or less congested; its mucous membrane was softened in 8 and 48 and white, inelastic and easily torn in 22. Its condition was altered in seven of the *malarial* cases: In 90 its calibre was contracted and its mucous membrane pale; in 247, 259, 260, 276 and 278 there was more or less of congestion or inflammation, in some general, in others affecting the lower portion only; in 274 the mucous membrane was softened and velvety. It was mentioned as normal in six cases. Eleven observations were made in the *typho-malarial* cases: In five the jejunum was normal; it was congested in 86 and 95; softened in 53; inflamed in 65; ulcerated in 269 and slate-colored in 112. In many of the *mixed* series a healthy condition of the jejunum may be inferred; in others, as 171, 174, 180, 195, 196, 210, etc., the inflammation which affected the ileum appears to have extended upward. But in forty-two instances its condition is specified in precise terms: In seventeen of these it was normal; in fourteen, 141, 187, 189, 279, 281, 282, 300, 306, 314, 321, 354, 369, 370 and 380, congested; in three, 191, 323 and 339, softened; in seven, 165, 239, 284, 309, 318, 337 and 353, ulcerated, and in one, 338, lead-colored. It was normal in 181, although the duodenum and ileum were implicated, and in 241, notwithstanding the existence of an intussusception; in 354 its lower part only was congested; in 239 and 282, respectively ulcerated and congested, there were lumbricoid worms.

INTUSSUSCEPTION OF THE SMALL INTESTINE was not recorded as having been observed in any of the *typhoid* or

---

The STOMACH was healthy in thirteen cases and in the others more or less altered by hyperæmic conditions; in four there were small ulcerations or erosions; but similar changes, and in nearly the same proportion, were found in seventy-two patients who died of other diseases.

The DUODENUM.—The notes on the condition of this portion of the alimentary canal are restricted to twenty-two cases, in eight of which it was healthy. Of the remaining fourteen the mucous membrane was red in four, the redness being diffused or circumscribed; grayish in two; soft in three, in which it was also red; Brünner's glands were much enlarged near the pyloric end in three, two of which had the mucous membrane softened and in two there was slight ulceration near the valve. With the exception of the ulceration similar conditions were found in thirty-six cases of death from acute diseases other than typhoid.

INTUSSUSCEPTION of the small intestine was found in three cases.

typho-malarial cases; but it was noted in 88 and 258 of the *malarial* series, and in five cases, 127, 130, 222, 234 and 241, of the *mixed* series of febrile cases.

LUMBRICOID WORMS were noted in cases 6 and 8 of the *typhoid*, in 239, 282, 348, 361 and 378 of the *mixed* series, and in the *typhus* case 389. Their presence was not observed or recorded in any of the *malarial* or *typho-malarial* cases.

The PATCHES OF PEYER were ulcerated in thirty-three of the fifty *typhoid* cases, while in seventeen their condition was not stated; but, as will be seen in referring to the occurrence of perforation, the ulceration of the intestine in the latter cases was of the same circumscribed and penetrating character as that definitely stated in the former as having its site in the patches. Since all febrile cases presenting adynamic symptoms have been in this volume classified as typhoid when *post-mortem* examination revealed in them a tumefied or ulcerated condition of the patches, it necessarily follows that in the sixty-three cases submitted as examples of *malarial* fever the agminated glands were not found to be thus affected. Their condition was not stated in twenty-six cases; they were healthy in seven cases, 257–261, 366 and 367, and reported not ulcerated in 262 and 263; in the remaining twenty-eight cases they were pale, white, reddened, congested or pigmented. Their condition was not stated in ten of the sixty-one *typho-malarial* cases; they were enlarged, congested, inflamed or pigmented in twenty-one cases and ulcerated in thirty. Of the two hundred and thirteen *mixed* cases their condition was not reported in sixty-eight. They were ulcerated in one hundred and thirty-one and tumid and inflamed in twelve; they were healthy in one, 380, and indirectly stated to have been so in one, 379,—in the former death occurred from pneumonia six weeks after the patient had so far convalesced from his typhoid attack as to be able to walk about the ward; in the latter, as the object of the *post-mortem* examination seems to have been an explanation of sudden and unexpected death during convalescence, the appearances presented by the agminated glands were not referred to except in so far as they may be included in the general statement that there were no other unusual appearances than those recorded as having been observed in the brain, heart and lungs.

The condition of the MUCOUS MEMBRANE OF THE ILEUM, in the intervals between the ulcerated patches, was not stated in twenty-two of the fifty *typhoid* cases. What may have been its condition in these instances is uncertain. If credit be given to the records as well for what is not said as for what is stated, the mucous membrane presented no morbid appearance of note beyond its destruction over the site of the affected glands. But such negative evidence is of doubtful value, and has not heretofore been admitted in these analytical observations. Nevertheless, it seems probable that in at least some of these cases there was no general congestion of the membrane, for, as will be seen immediately, congestion when present in other cases was confined to the vicinity of the affected patches, and in cases 23 and 48 the bases of the ulcers are said to have been of a reddish color, which distinction could not well have been made had the general lining of the intestine, including the part surrounding the ulcers, been in a highly injected condition. In twenty-five cases the ileum was reported congested, but in nine of these, 8, 9, 16, 26, 30, 34, 39, 40 and 46, the congestion was confined to the lower part of the intestine or to that part in which the destruction of the patches was greatest, and in many of those in which a general congestion is intimated it was more intense at this part than higher up, where the disease of the patches was less advanced. The mucous membrane was softened in two cases, 15 and 29, and of a dull whitish color in one case, 22. In 5 the ileum was contracted and in 27 it contained a frothy semi-liquid sanguinolent matter.

LUMBRICOID WORMS were noted in two cases; but this does not express the frequency of their presence, for some instances of their passage from the body during life and others of their detection after death were not recorded.

The PATCHES OF PEYER were altered in structure in the lower 2–8 feet of the small intestine in all the cases; in the whole length of the canal in one case only. Those nearest the cæcum were most altered, those farthest from it least altered; whence it is inferred that the morbid process did not commence simultaneously in all the patches, but was progressive in an upward direction, and that the changes to which an individual plaque is subject may be appreciated by a study of the various patches from above downwards. They were at first slightly elevated and of a pale-rose color, the elevation being due to a hyperplasia of the parts or an exaggeration of the normal structure. Afterwards they became redder, thicker, larger, softer and adherent to the submucous tissue, which was reddened and thickened beneath them. Then ulceration took place, or a process of absorption without ulceration. The destruction of the mucous membrane covering a patch was due to the union of many ulcerative points or to the extension of one; hence the ulcerations differed from each other considerably in appearance. Their outline was generally regular, oval or rounded, but sometimes angular; in some the edges were perpendicular, in others they sloped gradually into the central and deeper parts of the ulcer; the muscular coat was exposed in some, and in a certain number the serous coat was perforated. On the establishment of recuperative action the red color became tinged with gray or blue, and a thin cicatricial pellicle was developed from the surrounding mucous surface. In those that had not undergone ulceration a similar change in color was accompanied by a diminution of the tumefaction and softness. LOUIS gave the name of soft patches (*plaques molles*) to the agminated glands when affected as has been described, applying the term hard patches (*plaques dures*) to them when, superadded to the conditions present in the soft patches, there was a transformation of the submucosa by an interstitial exudation of a homogeneous, unorganized and more or less friable substance of a faint rose or yellowish color which attained a thickness of two or three lines. When the mucous membrane over these plates was unbroken they had a smooth uniform appearance; but when ulcerated their appearance was uneven, furrowed and stained with bile. This substance was also formed beneath some of the irregular patches intervening between the patches of Peyer, and in some cases it appeared in the form of prominences two or three lines in diameter and of equal height. These hard patches were found in thirteen of the forty-six cases, in ten of which they alone constituted the local lesion, while in three they were associated with the plaques molles. The SOLITARY GLANDS of the small intestine were affected in twelve cases, but generally only within a few feet of the cæcum. They were flattened and white or rounded and of a grayish color. In one instance they had a grayish point in their centres; in three others they were ulcerated. Louis considered it doubtful if all the small white elevations present in some of the cases were really enlarged crypts. Setting aside the condition of the patches of Peyer, these changes in the small intestine, the result of congestive or inflammatory processes in its mucous membrane, were found in other acute diseases and in nearly the same proportion as in typhoid fever. Even the changes in the solitary glands may not be excepted, as in five cases, three of which were cases of scarlet fever, those near the cæcum were enlarged and reddened. Hence these morbid changes, like those affecting the stomach, were considered by Louis as the result of a continuance of febrile action on the system. But as the affection of the agminated glands was not found in any other disease it was conceived to be the primary and pathognomonic lesion of typhoid fever.

In seventeen cases the mucous membrane of the JEJUNUM and ILEUM preserved its natural color, white or yellow from a tinge of bile, throughout nearly their whole length; in sixteen it was red, and while in six of these the redness extended throughout the length of the tube, in ten it was confined to the lower half or third; in thirteen patients in whom death took place late in the attack the membrane was of a grayish color. Of forty-two cases the mucous lining was of normal consistence in nine, softened throughout in thirteen and in its lower portion only in twenty.

Of the sixty-three *malarial* cases the condition of the mucous membrane of the ileum was not stated in eight; congested in patches in thirteen; generally injected or inflamed in thirty-two, and variously stated in ten. Of the thirteen in which the injection was circumscribed in patches the lower part of the ileum was chiefly affected in three, 115, 292 and 366, the upper part in one, 259, while in nine a general distribution of the patches throughout the ileum is indicated: In 247 these localized congestions were extensive; in 248 scattered; in 287, 293 and 386 intensely affected, and in 91 and 365 ecchymosed; in 84 and 261 the agminated glands were not diseased notwithstanding the existence of these inflamed patches. Of the thirty-two cases in which the congestion of the membrane was general throughout the ileum it is expressly stated in some, as in 105, 256 and 263, that no ulceration was present; in 367 the intestine was perforated by ulceration, but the patches of Peyer were not involved. Of the ten cases in which the condition of the membrane was variously reported it was thinned in 373; thinned and reddened in 274 and 276; of a pinkish-cream color in 387; softened in 78; thickened and softened in 87; gangrenous in 80; and free from congestion or other lesion than pigmentary deposits in the closed glands in 90, 290 and 291. In the eight cases, 70, 108, 277, 289, 374–377, in which the condition of the mucous membrane was not stated, it is probable that there was no marked congestion, for in several, as in the pyæmic case, 289, the attention of the operator was certainly directed to this part of the intestinal canal, since the condition of its closed glands was observed and recorded. Moreover, as has been already shown, the *post-mortem* appearances in the paroxysmal fevers do not necessarily include congestion or inflammation of the lining membrane of the small intestine.

Of the sixty-one *typho-malarial* cases the condition of the ileum, exclusive of its glands, was not stated in thirty-three. It was more or less congested or inflamed in twenty-four; but in three of these, 63, 68 and 96, the morbid condition was confined to the neighborhood of the ileo-cæcal valve; in one, 102, it constituted only a border to the inflamed or ulcerated patches of Peyer; in two, 116 and 296, it was arranged in circumscribed patches, and in one, 273, darkened by spots of ecchymosis. In one, 53, of the remaining four cases the mucous membrane of the ileum was softened, in a second, 67, thinned, in a third, 297, pigmented in punctated slate-colored patches, and in the last, 298, of a grayish-slate color from deposits in the villi.

The condition of the mucous membrane of the ileum was not stated in one hundred and seven of the two hundred and thirteen *mixed* febrile cases; it was more or less reddened, congested or inflamed in eighty-two and variously affected by inflammatory action in twenty-four. In some the injection was slight; thus in 204 it gave only a faintly pink tinge to the membrane. In the seven cases, 137, 172, 198, 200, 320, 321 and 329, the congestion was confined to the vicinity of the inflamed and ulcerated patches of Peyer, around each of which it formed an areola; in the last-mentioned case the mucous membrane of the upper part was thinned and its valvulæ almost obliterated. In the nine cases, 140, 208, 217, 221, 302, 341, 344, 359 and 238, the congested or inflamed condition was found only in the lower part of the ileum; in the last-mentioned case the membrane was thinned and softened in the upper part of its track. In the five cases, 190, 209, 312, 331 and 333, the congestion, although affecting also the upper part, was noted as especially intense towards the ileo-cæcal junction. It was disposed in scattered patches or streaks in the twelve cases, 148, 189, 199, 201, 203, 275, 310, 318, 343, 352 and 369, in one of which, 203, an ecchymosed patch was observed, while the congested spots in 369 were thinned and in 318 thinned and softened. Thickening was usually associated with the congestion, but in the four cases already mentioned and in 338 the membrane was thinned. In the remaining forty-seven of the eighty-two cases the congestion was general throughout the ileum. Of the twenty-four cases in which various conditions of the mucous membrane were recorded it was said to have been softened in 194, 212, 213, 216, 239, 284, 323 and 339; thickened in 233 and 345; thinned in 282; thin, pale and easily torn in the lower part in 181, and of a dark-grayish color in 193. It was said to have been ulcerated, apart from the ulcerations of the agminated glands, in 165, and the erosions in 300 appear also to have been in addition to the destruction of the membrane at the site of the ulcerated glands. The ileum is said to have been denuded in its lower part in 219 and 220 and gangrenous in 311. In five cases, 139, 161, 301, 304 and 354, it was healthy in its upper part, while in its lower part the condition of the glands only is stated; but in case 332 it is said that the surrounding villi were not affected. From these last observations it seems probable that in many of the large number of cases in which the condition of the mucous membrane was not recorded the failure to report its appearance arose from the fact that it presented nothing of importance apart from the condition of the glands.

The LARGE INTESTINE.—Of the fifty *typhoid* cases the inflammatory processes affected both the large and small intestine in seventeen, and the small intestine alone, so far as can be learned from the records, in thirty-three, but in two of these, 18 and 41, it is stated that the large intestine was not examined. The large intestine was therefore congested, inflamed or ulcerated in seventeen of forty-eight cases, or in 35.4 per cent. In one of these cases, 27, ulceration of the solitary glands was the only abnormity mentioned; but in six other cases the general appearance of the mucous membrane was recorded in addition to the condition of the crypts, which will be considered here-

---

In the LARGE INTESTINE distention was observed with much more frequency than in the small intestine. It was present in twenty-two of thirty-nine cases, and in sixteen of the twenty-two it was considerable. Notwithstanding a great distention of the gut its coats were not thinned, but on the contrary rather thickened, a result considered due to the reaction of the membranes on the distending gases. Its mucous membrane was white in thirteen of forty-three cases and yellow-tinged from fæces in two; its color was uniformly red in fifteen cases, in three of which the redness was general and in twelve localized; in four cases there were circumscribed red patches; the membrane was grayish in color in nine cases, all of which were fatal at a late date. The mucous lining was of normal consistence in thirteen of the forty-three cases; softened throughout its whole extent in sixteen; throughout its first or second half in eight; in the cæcum and rectum in one; in the cæcum only in two, and at different points in the extent of the intestine in three cases. Enlargement of the SOLITARY GLANDS, usually not numerous and with no manifest change in the mucous membrane of the locality occupied by them, was found in eight cases; in a ninth case the enlarged glands were numerous, scattered over the whole extent of the canal, ulcerated at their summits and with the submucous and muscular coats near them considerably thickened. Four other cases presented hard patches like those occurring in the small intestine, but only from three to four lines in diameter, and ulcerated only in one instance. Ulcerations were found in fourteen cases, but they were rarely numerous—they varied from four to thirty lines in length and affected the cæcum alone, or, in conjunction with other parts of the intestine,

after: Thus in 22 it was soft and of a grayish-slate color, in 24 mottled red and slate-colored, in 26 greenish, in 31 dark-colored, in 48 greatly congested and in 50 inflamed. In two cases, 25 and 28, the cæcum was congested; in one, 47, dark slate-colored, and in four, 30, 32, 33 and 49, ulcerated; in the first mentioned of these four there was also an inflamed condition of the rectum, in the second of the colon, while in the third the cæcum had become perforated. Ulceration was also found in 23, in the lower part of the intestine, where it was unconnected with the state of the solitary glands. The mucous membrane of the colon was inflamed and thickened in 29. Lastly, in 21, the colon is said to have contained a considerable quantity of blood.

Of the sixty-three *malarial* cases the large and small intestines were affected in thirty-eight, the large alone in two, and the small alone, so far as is shown by the records, in nineteen. The intestines in the four cases not accounted for in the preceding statement presented no lesion other than pigmentary deposits confined, in case 291, to the agminated and solitary glands of the small intestine, but involving also the walls of the large intestine in cases 90, 289 and 290. The large intestine was thus implicated in forty-three of sixty-three cases, or in 68 per cent. In thirteen of these cases, 71, 73, 78, 81, 88, 252, 257, 261, 263, 362, 363, 365 and 373, the mucous membrane of the large intestine was generally congested or inflamed; in 87 softened; in 90 bluish; in 287 discolored, and in 80 diseased, while in 289 and 290 pigmentation of the solitary glands was the only abnormal appearance recorded. The mucous membrane of the colon was congested or inflamed in ten cases, 91, 251, 254–256, 260, 278, 292, 294 and 387, in the first of which the inflamed membrane was also ecchymosed; it was thickened and softened in 108, slate-colored in 276, and gray with a few red patches in 293. The rectum was affected in four cases: In 72 its lining was softened; in 70 inflamed and softened; in 262 injected and thickened, the colon being similarly affected; and in 274 congested, the large intestine generally being slate-colored. Ulceration was mentioned in seven of the cases: In 386 the lining membrane of the intestine was slate-colored, with patches of congestion, ecchymosis and ulceration; it was inflamed and ulcerated throughout, but particularly in the rectum, in 115; the lower part of the bowel was ulcerated in 84, ulcerated and gangrenous in 76; the colon was ulcerated in 89, slate-colored, injected and ulcerated in 295, and thickened, softened and ulcerated at its commencement and termination in 376.

Of the sixty-one *typho-malarial* cases the large intestine was affected in twenty-nine, the small intestine alone in thirty-one, but in three of these, 52, 64 and 83, the large intestine was not examined. In one case, 69, nothing is said concerning an intestinal lesion. The large intestine was thus involved in twenty-nine of fifty-seven cases, or in 51 per cent. In three of these cases the glands only were mentioned: In 285 as enlarged, in 298 as pigmented and in 85 as ulcerated. The membranous lining of the intestine generally was congested or inflamed in the five cases, 66, 86, 92, 112 and 273; in 296 it was slate-colored and injected in patches; in 297 the dark coloration was confined to the cæcum and in 67 and 68 to the colon. The colon was congested or inflamed in 100, 102, 106 and 116, and strictured in 77. Ulceration was present in twelve cases; generally throughout the intestine in 74, 103 and 266; in the colon in 65, 99, 101, 109, 110, 264 and 265; in the colon and rectum in 75, and in the rectum alone in 98.

Of the two hundred and thirteen *mixed* cases the large intestine was more or less affected in one hundred and six, the small alone, so far as can be learned from the records, in one hundred and one. In six cases, 378, 379, 381–384, the record is silent concerning the condition of the intestinal tract. The large intestine was thus implicated in one hundred and six of two hundred and seven cases, or in 51.2 per cent. of the cases. In fourteen of these cases, 163, 164, 168, 169, 188, 192, 193, 197, 199, 281, 319, 329, 334 and 338, the recorded statements as to the condition of the large intestine refer only to enlargement or ulceration of its glands or pigmentation of its walls. The intestine was more or less congested or inflamed in twenty-one cases, in one of which, 173, the congestion was disposed in patches; in another, 282, it was particularly intense in the cæcum, while in a third, 370, in the lower part of the bowel it resembled ecchymosis. In addition to these twenty-one instances of congestion the lining membrane of the large intestine as a whole was recorded as greenish in 181; thickened and softened in 239; thinned, softened, pigmented and slightly congested in 380; soft and disorganized in 323; ecchymosed in 301; while in 187 its rugæ were elevated and its calibre contracted. The colon was constricted in two cases, 160 and 243; in 176 it contained coagulated blood; in 227 and 302 its mucous membrane was thickened and softened; in 162 dotted with minute oval purpuric spots; in twenty-two cases it was congested or inflamed: In ten of these this condition appears to have been general, while in seven, 170, 184, 245, 312, 327, 330 and 333, it was more particularly observed at the commencement; in three, 279, 310 and 337, towards the lower end of the bowel, and in two, 203 and 324, at both of the extremities. Ulceration was present in thirty-seven of the cases. It affected the intestine generally in the thirteen cases, 167, 171, 178, 185, 229, 232, 234, 236, 238, 242, 244, 300 and 351, but in 300 the action was especially manifested in the sigmoid flexure, where perforation had taken place; it affected the cæcum in the eleven cases, 161, 165, 172, 177, 237, 313, 314, 325, 332, 348 and 353; the colon in ten cases, 166, 233, 235, 240, 241, 315, 317, 318, 320 and 360, in one of which, 318, there were purpuric spots; the rectum in one case, 299, but in addition to this the lower end of the bowel was gangrenous in one case, 311, and disorganized in another, 316.

The condition of the SOLITARY GLANDS was observed and stated in thirteen of the fifty *typhoid* cases. They were inflamed in one; ulcerated in six; sloughing in two; in most of the cases they were unusually prominent,

---

in ten cases. The ulcers were in some cases evidently an affection of the solitary glands, but in others their site was the mucous membrane in the intervals between these crypts. In one of the cases an ulcer near the anus communicated with a small submucous abscess. Excepting the hard plaques the morbid changes in the large intestine were the same in those who died of typhoid as in those who died of other acute affections, and the difference of proportion was considerable only in the instances of meteorism and ulceration of the mucous membrane. Thus, in forty-five cases of typhoid fever the membrane was generally red in three, partially red in ten, grayish in nine, generally softened in sixteen and partially softened in fourteen, while in sixty-nine cases of other acute maladies there was general redness in three, partial redness in twelve, a gray color in seven, general softening in twenty-two and partial softening in twenty-five cases. Meteorism was observed only in three cases and in none of them to the extent found in typhoid fever; while excluding one case of dysentery, in which the colon presented many ulcers, erosion of the membrane was discovered in three cases only, all of them instances of lung inflammation.

and in four this enlargement was the only abnormal condition reported. In some instances it is uncertain from the terms of the record whether the glands of the large intestine were involved in the morbid processes: Thus, in 4, 6, 7, 13, 14 and 17, the changes in the solitary glands were mentioned in connection with those of the patches of Peyer, while nothing was specified with regard to the glands of the cæcum or colon; and in 28 and 31 the solitary glands of the ileum were particularized, while those of the large intestine and even the intestine itself were not mentioned. On the other hand, in the three cases, 23, 24 and 27, the glands of the large intestine were affected as well as those of the ileum, although in one of these, 23, the appearances were not similar, the glands of the latter being prominent only, while those of the former were blackened by pigmentary deposits. Again, in the two cases, 26 and 48, the glands affected were confined to the large intestine. Hence, so far as the indefinite terms of the *post-mortem* records permit of a knowledge of the locality of the altered glands, those of the ileum were affected in eleven cases and those of the large intestine in five.

The condition of the glands was observed in a larger proportion of the *malarial* than of the typhoid cases. Twenty-nine observations were made, in four of which, 257, 260, 261 and 263, the glands of both the large and small intestines were normal. Of the remaining twenty-five the glands were reported congested in one, 258; inflamed in two, 278 and 386; ulcerated in five, 84, 89, 295, 375 and 376; disorganized in three, 70, 73 and 363, and pigmented in nine. In most of these there was coexisting enlargement, but in five cases, 87, 252, 254, 287 and 373, prominence of the glands was the only abnormal condition stated. In some instances the same difficulty is found in determining the site of the affected glands that was experienced in certain of the typhoid cases. They were mentioned in general terms, but in connection with the patches of Peyer in two cases; those of the ileum were reported altered in seven cases, in which more or less uncertainty attaches to the condition of the large intestine; those of both intestines were affected in thirteen, while in three the glands of the large intestine alone are mentioned. Hence, so far as the terms of the record permit of a knowledge of the locality of the glands affected, those of the ileum were implicated in twenty-two cases and those of the large intestine in sixteen. In 290 and 291, of the nine in which the change consisted in the deposit of pigmentary matter in the glands, with or without enlargement, congestion or ulceration, the altered glands were those of the ileum; in 91, 289, 292, 294 and 387 all the solitary glands were thus affected; in one, 362, those of the large intestine were pigmented, while those above the ileo-cæcal valve were simply enlarged, and in 293 the black deposit was reported present in the large intestine only. Usually the glands in the large and the small intestine were similarly affected, 362, already instanced, being exceptional in this regard, and also 84, in which the glands of the large intestine were prominent while those of the small intestine were ulcerated.

Seventeen observations were recorded in the sixty-one *typho-malarial* cases. Of these there was no unhealthy condition in two, 54 and 102; simple enlargement in three, inflammation or ulceration in eight and pigmentation in four. The glands of both the large and small intestines were affected in three cases; of the large intestine alone in three cases; and of the ileum in nine cases, in which more or less uncertainty exists as to the condition of the large intestine. Hence, the crypts of the ileum were altered in twelve cases; of the large intestine in six cases. In but one instance, 116, were the glands of the ileum said to have been pigmented, although in 297 the mucous membrane was slate-colored and in 298 deposits in the villi darkened its color. The solitary glands of the colon were pigmented in five cases,—in 116 and 298, just mentioned, in 67, in which the crypts of the ileum were not mentioned, and in 68 and 296, in which they were inflamed or ulcerated.

The condition of the solitary glands was observed and noted in fifty-one of the two hundred and thirteen *mixed* febrile cases, and in one of these, 329, the crypts were normal throughout the whole of the intestinal canal. The glands were enlarged in eighteen cases, ulcerated in twenty-three and pigmented in nine cases, in some of which enlargement and ulceration were also present. The site of the affected glands is uncertain in some instances and in others definitely stated: In twelve cases the glands were mentioned in connection with the patches of Peyer, whence it may be inferred that those of the small intestine were certainly affected; the ileum appears indicated as the site in eighteen cases, in the majority of which the condition of the glands of the large intestine is more or less uncertain, as in only one, 203, are they stated to have been normal; both the ileum and large intestine were involved in nine cases, while the large intestine alone was mentioned in eleven. Hence it may be said with certainty that the solitary glands of the ileum were implicated in at least thirty-nine cases and those of the large intestine in at least twenty cases. Pigmentation was found in the glands of the ileum in 141 and 302, in which no reference was made to those of the large intestine, and in 200 and 201, in which the glands of the large intestine also contained the deposit; in 203, 320 and 380, in which the crypts of the ileum were enlarged or congested, those of the large intestine were pigmented; the latter glands were pigmented also in 331 and 334, in which those of the ileum were not mentioned.

PERFORATION OF THE INTESTINE AND PERITONITIS.—In twelve of the fifty *typhoid* cases, or in 24 per cent., the intestine was perforated by the ulcerative processes, the situation of the perforation being in Peyer's patches in the six cases, 16–20 and 32; in the ileum and probably in the patches in the five cases, 43–46 and 50, and in the cæcum in case 33. Peritoneal inflammation generally followed this accident, but in 32 it is said that there was no evidence of inflammatory action. In 19 and 23 fæces had escaped into the peritoneal cavity. Peritonitis occurred in the absence of perforation in cases 31 and 49, apparently without any other immediate or determining cause than the morbid condition of the glands of the mucous membrane and mesentery. In striking contrast with this record, there was but one case of perforated intestine among the sixty-three *malarial* cases. In this instance, 367, the ileum had given way, while Peyer's patches were reported free from disease. Peritonitis was present in 80, in which the intestines were in a gangrenous condition, and in 249, in which it was apparently due to a rupture of splenic cysts. Perforation occurred in six of the sixty-one *typho-malarial* cases, or in 9.8 per cent.: In 107 the small intestine was recorded as the site, in 82, 83 and 106 the ileum, and in 64 and 103 the ulcerated aggregated glands. Peritonitis occurred without perforation in the five cases, 63, 93, 101, 296 and 298; in 63 it may have been connected with the degenerated condition of the recti muscles, and in 296 with morbid changes in the spleen. Perforation of the intestine was observed in twenty-four of the two hundred and thirteen *mixed* cases. The accident is stated as having taken place in the intestines in case 244; in the large intestine in 300; in the small intestine in 226; in the ileum in nine cases, 223–225, 245, 309, 346, 347, 360 and 385, and in the patches of Peyer in twelve cases, 152–159, 204, 322, 327 and 328. Case 385 is exceptional as showing a possibility of recovery even after perforation; in it there was neither escape of the intestinal contents nor peritonitis, on account of the occlusion of the aperture by adhesion to the serous covering of the bladder. Peritonitis was reported as having occurred in seven cases in which no mention was made of perforation; in 203 and 337 it was probably tubercular; in 151 connected with the condition of the abdominal recti muscles; and in the others, 150, 311, 353 and 361, with the state of the interior tunics of the intestinal canal.

PIGMENTARY DEPOSITS in the intestine are mentioned in only two of the fifty *typhoid* cases; in 23 near the pylorus and in the solitary glands of the large intestine, and in 26 in which the ulcerated glands near the ileo-cæcal valve were of a dark-blue color. The colon, however, was slate-colored, greenish or dark-colored in cases 22, 24, 26, 31 and 47. Pigmentation was found in twenty of the sixty-three *malarial* cases, or in 31.7 per cent. of the cases: The patches of Peyer were dotted with dark-colored spots presenting what has been called the shaven-beard appearance in the six cases, 87–90, 115 and 288, as also in the eight cases, 91 and 289–295, in which the solitary glands are mentioned as involved in the pigmentation; the ileum and mesenteric glands were blackened in 258, although the patches of Peyer were healthy; in 287 the patches were prominent and speckled with blood and the mucous membrane of the colon discolored; the interior of the colon was slate-colored in 274 and 386, and its solitary crypts blackened in 362 and 387. The intestines were blackened by deposited pigment in ten of the sixty-one *typho-malarial* cases, or in 16.4 per cent.: Peyer's patches were affected in 54, 86 and 96, and the solitary glands also in 116 and 296; the ileum and colon in 297 and 298; the colon alone in 265, and its solitary glands in 67 and 68. Peyer's patches presented dark-colored ulcerations or deposits in the four cases 148, 149, 181 and 368 of the *mixed* series. The colon or its glands are alone mentioned as pigmented in the twelve cases, 168, 169, 174, 198, 202, 203, 302, 310, 320, 329, 334 and 380, while Peyer's patches were also affected according to the records of 200, 201, 331 and 338, and the ileum according to that of 199. The solitary glands of the small intestine were pigmented in 141 and 165, and the ileum was of a blue-slate color in 333, which also presented dark-blue spots in the bladder near the orifices of the ureters. The intestines were of a dark-gray color in 193. These twenty-five instances of deposited pigment form 11 per cent. of the total of two hundred and thirteen mixed febrile cases. But there should be mentioned in this connection the ecchymoses or purpuric spots in the large intestine in cases 162, 183, 189, 301, 318 and 370.

The condition of the MESENTERIC GLANDS is mentioned in but fourteen cases of the *typhoid* series, in all of which there was notable enlargement. In the *malarial* series the glands are mentioned fourteen times; in twelve cases they were enlarged and more or less altered in color, while in the two others, 274 and 374, they are said to have been healthy although Peyer's patches were much affected; in 70 the enlargement was so great and general that the mesentery had the appearance of being one continuous gland. In the *typho-malarial* series their condition is recorded seventeen times; enlarged and more or less deeply colored or affected with yellow softening in sixteen cases, and ulcerated in one case, 93. In the *mixed* series they were inflamed, enlarged and softened in all of forty-five cases except two, 307, which contained chalky concretions, and 331, normal notwithstanding the affection of the agminated glands.

The appearance of the SPLEEN is stated in thirty of the fifty *typhoid* cases, in only two of which was it normal. The alteration consisted of enlargement and softening, sometimes to pulpiness, frequently associated with a darkened color. In case 37 the spleen was three times its usual size; in 9 it weighed forty-one ounces; in one case only, 42, one of sequent consumption, was it small and hard. Its condition was reported in fifty-two of the *malarial* cases. It was normal in eighteen and small in six cases, 90, 91, 252, 259, 276 and 291; it weighed only three ounces and a quarter in one of these, and was tough and of a dark color in most of them. In the other instances it was enlarged, congested, soft, flabby or friable; in 70 it was three times its usual size; in 87 it was similarly enlarged and

---

The LYMPHATIC GLANDS.—All of the *mesenteric* glands corresponding to altered plaques suffered a modification of size, color or consistence. They were enlarged and rose-colored, subsequently becoming softened, of a darker red and developing yellowish points or purulent foci in their tissues; and even the glands corresponding to apparently healthy patches in ten of the forty-six cases were found to be enlarged and reddened. The *mesocolic* glands were marked by inflammatory changes in fourteen of nineteen cases in which they were examined, and although these changes were associated with redness, softening or ulceration of the membrane in most cases, in others the membrane was healthy; nevertheless, these glands in no case contained purulent deposits. Enlargement and reddening of the glands of the *stomach* corresponded in three cases with inflammatory conditions of the mucous lining of that viscus, but in a fourth case, in which the glands were affected, the lining was healthy, and in a fifth case this want of correspondence was reversed. LOUIS considered that this latter condition was of frequent occurrence, although not recorded by him. He argued that while the stomach was very frequently altered, he could scarcely in his *post-mortem* work have failed to notice corresponding enlargement of the glands had such a change been present. The *lumbar* glands were large and firm in two cases, in one of which the patient succumbed to a sequent erysipelas of the lower extremities. In a similar case the *inguinal* glands were large, red and contained white pus; in three others, in which the legs had been blistered, these glands were inflamed but had not suppurated. The *cervical* glands were enlarged and reddened in nine of twelve cases in which they were examined. Six of the nine had concurrent ulceration of the pharynx, but in the three others there was no marked lesion of the organ corresponding to the glands. In patients who died of other acute maladies the mesenteric glands were large and red in six cases of small-pox, scarlet fever, pneumonia and erysipelas, and somewhat softened in one case of small-pox, but in none of these was the change comparable with that suffered by the glands of the lower part of the mesentery in typhoid fever. The cervical glands were affected in four cases, three of which were eruptive fevers, and in only two of these was there a manifest alteration of the air-passages. It is inferred from these facts that while the condition of the glands does not in all instances depend on that of the organs with which they are connected, the typhoid affection establishes a marked predisposition to inflammatory changes in the mesenteric and cervical glands.

The SPLEEN was unaltered in four only of the forty-six cases. It was more than three times its usual size in seventeen cases; more than double its usual size in nineteen, but slightly enlarged in nine and apparently small in one case. It was softened in thirty-four, and in seven of these, in which the softening was extreme, the organ was largely increased in volume; but in no instance was pus found in its tissues. It was observed that the tumefaction and softening specially characterized those cases that were speedily fatal, while the organ was more frequently normal or but

contained abscesses; in 377 its surface was mottled with spots surrounded by reddish areolæ and its section exuded a sero-purulent liquid; in 258 it contained tubercular masses and in 249 cysts, the cheesy contents of which had in part escaped into the peritoneal cavity. Its condition was not stated or not observed in nineteen, normal in eight and altered in thirty-four of the sixty-one *typho-malarial* cases. In case 266 it weighed three ounces and a half and was firm; in 67 it was small but extremely soft. With these exceptions it was enlarged, congested, softened and often darkened in color. In case 99 it is said to have been rotten; in 296 it had an inflamed condensation of its tissue about the size of a nutmeg at its upper end and the contiguous omentum was also inflamed. In the *mixed* series the spleen was normal in thirty-six and variously changed in one hundred and seven cases. It was small in seven of these, 201, 213, 228, 281, 306, 329 and 331, varying in weight from one ounce and a half in 213 to four ounces and three-quarters in 281. It was discolored but not enlarged in a few instances. Generally the organ was large, congested, dark-colored and more or less softened; in 132 it weighed forty-one ounces, in 349 thirty-six ounces and in 129 thirty-four ounces; in 137 and 221 the alteration of the tissue approached decomposition, and in 137 it was pultaceous; in 369 it was light-colored and hardened in portions of its substance, but softened and suppurating near the hilus; in 354, underlying a diaphragmatic adhesion, was a cavity containing an ounce of viscid green liquid; 148 and 214 also contained cysts; in 204 the superficial layer of the splenic parenchyma was colored slate-blue by molecular deposits.

The appearance of the LIVER was recorded in twenty-nine of the fifty *typhoid* cases: It was normal in eleven, leaving only eighteen in which the attention was called to diseased conditions. The liver was large in four of these, soft in one, large and flabby in one, large and pale in two, large, pale and soft in two, large and fatty in one, pale and fatty in one, large and congested in one, congested in four and mottled in one. In the sixty-three *malarial* cases the condition of the liver was recorded fifty-three times; in twenty-one it was normal and in thirty-two altered. Enlargement is indicated in most of the cases; but there was generally more than this, for enlargement alone is mentioned in but one of them. The organ was soft, flabby or friable in five cases; pale in four, in one only of which it was firm; fatty in four; waxy in one; congested in five; dark-colored or bronzed in seven; in 249 it was covered with exuded lymph; in 80 it adhered to the diaphragm and in 367 to the intestines also; in 87 it contained minute abscesses and in 256 a single abscess of large size. In the sixty-one *typho-malarial* cases the liver was reported normal in nineteen and variously changed in appearance in twenty-six cases; in sixteen its condition was not examined or not stated. Enlargement was generally observed, and in four cases this was the only change mentioned. The organ was pale in four cases; soft in four, in which this condition is stated alone or with enlargement; fatty in four and of the nutmeg appearance in one; dark or bronzed in three; congested in five and emphysematous in one. In the *mixed* series of febrile cases the condition of the liver was not stated in seventy-one, normal in fifty-five and altered in eighty-seven. Enlargement alone is mentioned in eighteen and in conjunction with various changes in many of the others. The organ was pale in twelve, in two of which it was reported flabby and in one firm. It was anæmic in one case, 333; granular in 144; fatty in nine; of the nutmeg appearance in two, 306 and 315; soft, flabby or friable in eleven, in one of which, 199, its substance was emphysematous, of the color of sanious pus and possessed of a disagreeable odor, while in another, 137, in which the parenchyma was of a greenish color, a chicken-coop odor was instanced. It was soft also in five of fifteen cases which were reported congested, and in two, 125 and 320, in which there were adhesions; in three others, 328, 337 and 347, the serous coat adhered to contiguous organs. It was brown or dark-colored in eight, mottled in 181 and 208, of a blue-slate color in 154, ecchymosed on its surface and slate-colored on section in 380, and small, weighing only twenty-eight ounces and a half, in 281.

The GALL-BLADDER OR ITS CONTENTS were observed in seven of the *typhoid* cases: The viscus was small in 29 and large in 31,—in the former it was half filled with bile; it was completely filled with viscid bile in 48; it contained five drachms of yellow bile in 24; eleven drachms of dark-green bile in 47; twenty-six drachms in 23 and ten ounces of brown bile in 26. Observations were made in sixteen of the *malarial* cases: The viscus was distended with dark-green or yellow-colored bile in the six cases, 70, 80, 104, 248, 365 and 376; one ounce was said to have been present in 90 and 277, and about two ounces in 263, 276 and 373, the bile in the last-mentioned case having been watery; the gall-bladder in 274 and 289 was empty, and in 287, 288 and 362 the quantity of its thick or flaky contents was small. Among the *typho-malarial* cases fourteen observations were made: The gall-bladder was normal in 103, small in 112, empty or nearly so in 61 and 296; it contained six drachms of bile in 62, three ounces in 100, and was distended in the seven cases, 67, 69, 75, 86, 92, 94 and 96; generally the bile was of a dark or black color and of some viscidity, but in the last-mentioned case it was described as watery. In 95 the walls of the gall-bladder were disorganized and perforated, the bile in this instance having been of a light-green color. Thirty observations were made in the *mixed* series: The bladder was healthy in one case, 328, large in one, 225, small and collapsed in one, 204, and empty or nearly so in 191, 282, 311, 380 and 381. It contained one fluid ounce or less of bile in the four cases, 137, 154, 182 and 304, dark-brown in the second instance, and gamboge-colored in the third. In 155 it contained twelve drachms of dark bile, and in 185, 139, 187 and 166, respectively, two and a half, three, three and three-quarters and five ounces of liquid. It was distended also in the twelve cases, 125, 132, 151, 171, 189, 192, 198, 245, 302, 317, 338 and 383. In 327 the walls of the gall-bladder were disorganized by their participation in a general peritonitis.

Only two observations on the PANCREAS were recorded in the *typhoid* series: In case 29 the gland was said to have been enlarged and somewhat hard; in 24 it was normal. Of thirteen observations in the *malarial* cases the pancreas was normal in eight, 84, 115, 263, 277, 289, 292, 295 and 366; it was soft in one case, 67, in which it was of a reddish color, and firm in three, 90, 274 and 278, in the first of which its color was white and in the others somewhat reddened; in 288 it was of a purple-flesh color, and in 373 dark-colored and slightly congested; its weight varied from two and a half to four and a quarter ounces. Nine observations were recorded in the *typho-malarial* cases: In 62, 68, 93, 110 and 265 it was normal; in 111 large; in 112 of a grayish color; in 67 soft and of a dull-red color, and in 86 reddened and increased in weight to seven ounces. Of seventeen observations in the *mixed* series the organ was normal, so far as can be learned from the records, in thirteen cases, its weight ranging from two and a half to four ounces; it was recorded as white in color in 154, 155, 181 and 380, not very firm in the first-mentioned case, hard or firm in the three others.

The KIDNEYS in thirteen of twenty-seven cases of *typhoid* were normal. In five of the remaining fourteen they were congested, with concomitant enlargement in two instances; in three others they were enlarged and in one of these granular; in five they were pale or fatty, and in one, 26, the right kidney was pigmented on its surface and contained an abscess with ecchymosed walls, while the left was merely congested. In sixteen of thirty-seven *malarial* cases the kidneys were normal; in thirteen they were congested, with softening superadded in one instance; enlargement was noted in three, in one of which the organs were soft and in another fatty; they were pale in one, flabby in one, fatty in one; in 278 the right kidney contained a small abscess, and in 374 the left was represented by a closed cyst in which no glandular tissue could be detected. Of twenty-eight *typho-malarial* cases they were normal in eighteen; congested in four, in one of which they were said to have been fatty; large in two; small in one; small and pale in one; in one case, 110, the right kidney was small and transformed into a thin-walled cyst, while the left contained large abscesses, and in 93 both were inflamed to suppuration. In sixty-two of one hundred and eight cases of the *mixed* series in which the kidneys were examined they were pronounced normal. Of the remaining forty-six cases they were congested in twenty-two, in one of which, 187, there were ecchymosed spots; large in four, 227, 275, 369 and 370; pale in two, 217 and 302; fatty in five, 178, 244, 307, 317 and 345; soft or flabby in six, 199, 181, 148, 182, 304 and 309, and in the first-mentioned of these they were tumid and emphysematous, like the liver in the same case, while in the second the left kidney was ecchymosed; in 243 traces of inflammation were said to have been present in the right kidney, and in 219 and 220 suppuration had taken place; in 228, 222, 318 and 334 there were cysts which, in the first-mentioned case, contained purulent matter.

The SUPRARENAL CAPSULES were mottled in case 23 of the *typhoid* series. They were reported healthy in three *malarial* cases, 115, 274 and 292; soft and fatty in 373. Their condition was reported in five cases of the *mixed* series: Yellow in 183, soft in 245, small, dark and tough in 281, firm, large and of a reddish-ash color in 380, and showing traces of inflammation in 243.

URINARY BLADDER.—The only observations of interest respecting the condition of this viscus occur in the *mixed* cases: Its mucous membrane presented bluish spots in case 333 and was ecchymosed in 342; the prostate in 239 was enlarged and contained pus.

The PERICARDIUM was seldom altered. It contained an unusual quantity of effused liquid in case 36 of the *typhoid* series, a small quantity of bloody liquid in 26, and in 42 the sac was tuberculous. A manifest excess of liquid was found in three of the *malarial* cases, coinciding with effusion into the pleura in 258, with bronchial inflammation on the left side in 249 and with a healthy condition of the lungs and pleuræ in 262. No indication of inflammatory action was recorded in these cases of effusion; but in 90, in which only six drachms had exuded, the contained flocculi and the fibrinous coating over the serous surfaces testified to an intercurrent pericarditis; in 276 there were adhesions and the surface of the heart was covered with dark spots and exuded lymph. In the *typho-malarial* series three cases, 52, 61 and 75, presented an excess of serum, with some injection of the sac in the first-mentioned instance; in 280 there were signs of recent pericarditis, and in 296 the serous surface was roughened by exudation unconnected with the fatal illness. In the *mixed* series five cases presented evidence of a pericarditis which antedated the typhoid attack: In 324 the opposing pericardial surfaces showed some small roughened patches; in 356 they were united by a fibrinous band; in 368 the adhesion was more intimate, leaving only a small sac at the apex in which was an ounce of serum, while in 137 and 139 the sac was wholly obliterated. Moreover, in 320 the pericardium was firmly united to the costal cartilages and sternum. On the other hand, in 182 and 183 the effused liquid, although not large in quantity, was of a red color, and in 309 the sac is said to have been filled with

---

The KIDNEYS were seldom and slightly affected. They were somewhat enlarged in three cases and of diminished consistence in six of thirty-six cases. Their color was darker than usual in seventeen of forty-two cases, and this coloration was more frequent in those who died early. The mucous membrane of the pelves was thickened and injected in one case, and in a second, presenting similar injection, it was bathed in pus.

The lining of the BLADDER was injected in six cases, somewhat softened in two, and in one slightly ulcerated near the urethral entrance.

The PERICARDIUM was seldom altered; in seven cases it contained a little serous liquid, which, in one instance, was sanguinolent. None of the cases presented the slightest trace of recent inflammation, in this differing from cases of other acute maladies and especially from cases of pneumonia.

purulent matter. Excess of liquid, from three to six or eight ounces, was found in ten cases, 136, 170, 173, 206, 302, 307, 327, 328, 329 and 383, in two of which, 206 and 307, the pericardium is said to have been thickened, and in two others, 173 and 327, somewhat injected; the lungs were more or less engorged in four of these cases; in three the pleural cavities contained effusion, while in three, 170, 206 and 328, there was no concurrent inflammation of the lungs or pleuræ.

The condition of the HEART is recorded in seventeen of the fifty *typhoid* cases, in thirteen of which it was normal; in one, 48, pale; in one, 11, soft and flabby; in one, 42, tuberculous on its surface, and in one, 45, having its right cavities dilated. In addition to these observations the contents of the heart were noted in five instances in which no intimation is given of any abnormity of texture. In the *malarial* series the heart was mentioned as normal in twenty-six cases, and in ten others in which reference was made to its covering or contents no alteration of texture was indicated. In twelve cases there were morbid changes: In 252 and 291 the heart was small; in 78 and 377 it presented thickened valves and hypertrophied walls, and in 261 an opaque-white membranous spot on the surface of the right ventricle; it was pale in 262; flabby in 278; pale and flabby in 376; fatty in 251; slightly softened and ecchymosed in 386, and in 90 and 276 there were evidences of pericardial inflammation. In the *typho-malarial* series it was recorded as normal in twenty cases, and in eleven others in which its covering or contents were mentioned its condition does not seem to have called for remark. Its texture or appearance was altered in nine cases: It was large and hypertrophied in 53 and 96; pale in 112; soft in 67; flabby in 57, 59 and 265; pale and flabby in 267, and flaccid in 75. The heart is said to have been normal in seventy-one of the *mixed* cases, and in thirty-three, in which its coverings or contents were mentioned, the condition of its tissue does not appear to have been materially altered. Morbid changes were noted in thirty-one instances: In 317 the heart was reported atrophied; in 340 displaced; in 206 enlarged; its ventricles dilated in 169, 186 and 190, and its mitral valve thickened in 359; in the remaining twenty-four cases the organ had lost its normal color and tonicity: In 193 it was softened; in 242 and 243 thinned and softened, the right ventricle in the latter case being said to have been as thin as glove-leather; in 133, 219 and 333 pale; in 191 pale and soft, this case presenting a small purulent deposit near the apex; and flabby in seventeen, in ten of which, 137, 148, 154, 176, 182, 184, 203, 212, 214 and 230, no other qualification was stated; but in four, 150, 227, 311 and 324, the organ was also said to have been pale; in one, 345, small; in one, 347, anæmic, and in one, 355, soft. In addition to these, antecedent inflammation is indicated by the appearance of the pericardial lining and contents in certain of the cases mentioned in the last paragraph.

The CONTENTS OF THE HEART were stated in only seven of the *typhoid* cases, and in one of these, 48, there was no clot. Both sides of the heart in five cases contained clots, which were fibrinous in 8 and 23, black in 24, mixed in 32, fibrinous in the right and mixed in the left cavities in 26. In case 45 there were fibrinous clots in the right side, but the contents of the left cavities were not recorded. Of the sixty-three *malarial* cases the cardiac contents were specified in eighteen: In one of these, 277, there were no clots. Fibrinous deposits were observed in thirteen, in two of which, 71 and 293, the side of the heart was not particularized; in four, 258, 276, 292 and 373, they were present in both sides; in seven, 115, 257, 259, 261, 274, 288 and 377, in the right side only, one of these, 274, containing a mixed clot in the left side, and another, 261, a venous or black clot. In 287 there were mixed clots in the right and fluid blood in the left cavities; in 84 and 90 the right side contained black clots, the left in the former presenting a narrow clot of unstated color and in the latter a mixed coagulum; in 291 the right ventricle contained fluid blood, the left being empty but for a small fibrinous clot attached to the chordæ tendineæ. The contents of the chambers of the heart were recorded in sixteen of the *typho-malarial* cases: Fibrinous coagula were reported in ten— in the right side only in six, in one of which, 266, there were venous clots in the left side; in the four others the fibrin was deposited in both sides. Clots of unspecified color were noted as present in the heart in 69, 86 and 264, —small and imperfectly formed, in a black and diffluent blood, in the two cases last mentioned. Clots were also found in the right side in 106 and in both sides in 62, but in neither is the character of the coagulum stated; in 96 the right chambers contained fluid blood while the left were empty. The cardiac contents are stated in fifty-three of the *mixed* series, in four of which, 137, 165, 194 and 329, there were no clots. In three cases clots of an unspecified character, in one mixed clots, in one black clots and in one uncoagulated blood were reported as having been observed in the heart, but the containing cavity is not stated; in three cases unspecified clots were found in the right side and in three in both sides; in one instance mixed clots were found in both sides. Fibrinous coagula were noted in the right side in twenty-seven instances, in twelve of which the contents of the left side were not recorded, but in nine cases similar coagula were found in this side—in one an unspecified and in one a mixed coagulum, in two venous clots and in two no coagulum of any kind. The right chambers contained fluid blood in 190 and a mixed clot in 221 and 305, the left chambers of the latter instance being filled with dark clots. The right cavities contained venous coagula in four cases, 159, 169, 139 and 201, associated with similar clots in the opposite side of the heart in the second case mentioned, with a fibrinous deposit in the third, while in the first and last the contents of the left side were not recorded. In 172 and 203 the heart presented a fibrinous clot in the left ventricle only.

LARYNX and TRACHEA.—These parts appear to have met with as little attention at the hands of our medical officers as the contiguous section of the digestive system. Morbid appearances were noted in only six of the *typhoid*

The HEART was normal in size, consistence and color in twenty-three of the forty-six cases. Its tissue was softer than natural in seventeen cases, in some to so marked a degree that the organ was flaccid and easily torn. Loss of color and thinning of the walls were generally associated with the softening. These changes were usually more distinct on the left than on the right side; and, like the alterations in the liver and spleen, were more prominent in patients who died at an early period of the attack. Similar changes were found, but with less frequency, in cases of other acute diseases. In the typhoid affection when the heart was but little softened its cavities, especially those of the right side, contained fibrinous clots; whereas when the softening was greater the inclosed clots were black, and when the highest degree of flaccidity was present the cavities contained only a few drops of blood mixed with air-bubbles. While these facts seem to indicate a connection between the state of the blood and that of the heart it does not appear to be a necessary one, as in certain cases of pneumonia, in which the heart was very evidently softened, it contained fibrinous clots in its right cavities.

cases: In 12 the epiglottis was swollen; in 30 ulcerated and œdematous, the vocal chords being similarly affected; in 1 the lining of the larynx was thickened by an exudation in the submucous cellular tissue; in 8, 23 and 32 the mucous membrane of the trachea was congested. In the *malarial* series the mucous lining of the trachea was pale in 84; inflamed, congested or purplish in 90, 115, 259, 277 and 288; the larynx was covered with false membrane in 374; the epiglottis ulcerated, the lining membrane of the larynx and trachea thickened and the vocal chords nearly destroyed in 248. In the *typho-malarial* series only four observations were recorded: In 68 ecchymosed spots were found on the posterior surface of the trachea, and in 101 its mucous membrane was inflamed and ulcerated; in 54 the laryngeal membrane was congested and ulcerated and a small abscess was observed between the cricoid cartilage and the pharynx, and in 67 the epiglottis and chords were œdematous and an abscess was connected with the right arytenoid cartilage. Seventeen observations were made in the *mixed* series: The trachea was congested in 181, 240, 307 and 333, and in 182 the larynx also was involved. The lining membrane of the trachea was soft and dark-colored in 301; of a purple color in 155, 183, 187, 199 and 304, and to this, in 156, some spots of whitish exudation were added. In 329 the mucous membrane, which was thick, soft and discolored, presented a slight exudation on the vocal chords and the laryngeal surface of the epiglottis; while in 122 and 308 the larynx was lined with false membrane. In 185 there was an ulceration below the vocal chords on one side and another in the thyroidean angle. Lastly, in 339 the trachea was inflamed, the larynx ulcerated and the glottis occluded by œdema.

The THYROID BODY was mentioned in but two of the cases, both belonging to the *mixed* series: In 204 it was enlarged on one side, and in 193 the left lobe contained a calcareous mass as large as a walnut and a small cyst filled with dark-brown liquid.

The condition of the BRONCHIAL TUBES was seldom reported. They were inflamed in a few cases, as 29, 32, 38 and 47 of the *typhoid* series; 115, 249, 258, 274, 283 and 362 of the *malarial;* 55, 62 and 102 of the *typho-malarial,* and 124, 148, 169, 185, 191, 193, 239, 245 and 380 of the *mixed* series. In 281 and 331 the smaller tubes were plugged with fibrinous exudation, and in 362 they were so thickened and indurated as to appear on section like small prominences.

The LUNGS were pronounced normal in only five of thirty-four *typhoid* cases in which their condition was stated. They were engorged or congested in fourteen cases; œdematous in one, 3; more or less hepatized or solidified in twelve, 5, 6, 7, 9, 23, 24, 29, 32, 38, 41, 43 and 45; splenified in one, 8, and in one, 42, tubercular. Generally the engorgement and hepatization were in the lower and posterior parts, but sometimes the whole of a lung is said, as in 38, to have been affected. Generally, also, both lungs participated in the pneumonitic processes, but in some, as in 6, one lung only was involved. The third stage of inflammation was reached in case 5. In 29 and 32, hepatization was localized in nodular masses from the size of a chestnut to that of a hen's egg; splenization in 8 was also lobular. It is probable that the term engorgement, congestion or hepatization was used in some instances to indicate that condition of the lung-tissue recognized by LOUIS as splenization, for in case 25 the solidification is evidently distinguished from that caused by inflammatory processes. The lungs were altered in thirty-two of fifty-eight observations in the *malarial* series, normal in twenty-three, and unrecorded in three in which pleuritic adhesions are mentioned. They were engorged, splenified or hepatized in thirty cases, two of which, 258 and 288, were marked by subpleural ecchymoses, three, 252, 276 and 289, contained abscesses, and four, 105, 274, 278 and 377, tubercle; in 113 the lungs were emphysematous, and in 87 the left lung was compressed by a purulent collection in the pleural sac. In the *typho-malarial* series the lungs in nineteen of fifty-one cases were normal and in thirty-two altered. Of the latter they were tubercular in one, emphysematous in a second, œdematous in a third and congested, splenified or hepatized in twenty-nine, in one of which, 65, there was a large abscess in the middle lobe of the right lung. They were normal in forty-seven of one hundred and sixty-three cases of the *mixed* series; congested, splenified, hepatized or infiltrated in one hundred and four, in three of which purulent collections had formed, multiple and small in 138, single in 315 and 383 and of large size in the last-mentioned case; emphysematous in four, tubercular in seven and in one, 340, compressed by a large quantity of bloody liquid in the left pleural sac.

The PLEURÆ.—Adhesions in three of the *typhoid* series, 9, 37 and 45, probably antedated the typhoid attack; but in 5 and 32 they were certainly associated with the fatal sickness. The pleural cavity in 12, 23, 32, 36 and 42 contained serous effusion which was connected in all except, perhaps, 23, with other and distinctly marked signs of

---

The EPIGLOTTIS was covered with false membrane in two cases in which the pharynx was similarly affected; in one there was a red spot on its inferior aspect and in seven it was more or less ulcerated, the pharynx participating in the ulceration in three of the cases. From the rarity of ulceration of the epiglottis in other acute diseases LOUIS regarded this lesion like the similar affection of the pharynx and œsophagus as of a character peculiar to typhoid fever.

The GLOTTIS was œdematous in two cases, but this condition was found to be equally common in pneumonia.

The MUCOUS MEMBRANE OF THE LARYNX was blackish and softened in one case, covered with false membrane in three and slightly ulcerated in one.

The LINING OF THE TRACHEA was seldom altered in color and in no case ulcerated.

The BRONCHIAL MUCOUS MEMBRANE was often of a red color; but it was thickened in only one case. Generally the tubes contained a thin bright-red mucus; in three cases they were enlarged.

The LUNGS in fifteen cases were healthy or only a little darker in color posteriorly, with or without some rounded spots a few lines in diameter and depth. In two cases they were somewhat emphysematous. There was splenization in nineteen cases, generally in one or both of the lower lobes, the splenified part being heavier than water, firm, of a dark bluish-red color, giving issue on section to a thick dark-red liquid and destitute of the granular aspect of hepatized lung. Congestion or hepatization was present in seventeen cases, some of which had the lower lobes splenified; the congestion was sometimes lobular, more frequently so than the hepatization, but generally both were continuous, although not occupying in any case a large portion of the organ. Abscesses were found in one of the hepatized lungs. In one case the lung contained a filamentous tumor one inch in diameter; in four cases some semitransparent granulations, and in one case crude tubercle.

The PLEURÆ.—Although adhesions were present in nineteen of the forty-six cases, there were signs of recent inflammation in two only, in one a soft false membrane and in the other a flocculent effusion; the pleural sacs, however, in nineteen cases contained a reddish serosity varying in quantity in individual cases from three to thirty ounces. But similar conditions of the bronchial tubes, pulmonary tissue and pleural membranes were observed in thirty-five cases of other acute maladies exclusive of pneumonia and pleurisy.

inflammation of the membrane, and in 42 with tubercular disease of the lungs; blood was effused into the pleural cavity in 31. In the *malarial* series adhesions were found in the five cases, 251, 362, 364, 374 and 377, but their recent character is not indicated; on the other hand, in 71, 73, 87, 249, 258, 288, 289 and 387 there is evidence of pleuritic complication. The adhesions in 57, 59, 66 and 266 of the *typho-malarial* series are also of old or uncertain date; but in 85 the clinical history shows their recent formation, and in 62 the lymph on the base of the lung connects the small quantity of bloody liquid in the pleura with inflammatory action, although it is not certain that the larger quantity of serum in 69 was the result of other than passive processes; in 65 the right pleura was inflamed, and in 100 the right sac contained four ounces of sanguinolent serum. Pleuritic adhesions, without other indications of pleural inflammation, are mentioned in twenty-three of the *mixed* series; in about half of this number they certainly ante-dated the fatal attack and probably also in others. In four cases, 128, 238, 329 and 368, effused liquid was found in the pleural cavities, but whether as the result of active or passive processes is uncertain. In three cases, 118, 219 and 283, which presented both adhesion and effusion, the date of neither is defined. Thirteen cases showed decided indications of recent inflammation of the serous membrane—173, 185, 195, 309, 314, 315, 318, 331, 355, 357, 360 and 380. In addition to these 168 and 333 had in each pleural sac a small quantity of dark sanguineous serum, apparently connected with pulmonary engorgement and hepatization, while 340 presented on one side a large effusion of a similar character, which compressed and consolidated the corresponding lung. Pleuritic adhesions in 203 and effusion in 311 were of tubercular origin. The presence of purulent matter in the pleural sacs of 383 was due to the rupture of pulmonary and intermuscular abscesses into them.

The BRAIN AND ITS MEMBRANES were normal in five of eleven *typhoid* cases in which their condition was stated: The membranes were congested in two cases, 8 and 26; in the former the cerebral substance was soft and there was a small quantity of liquid in the ventricles; in the latter the brain was apparently normal. In neither of these is mention made of effusion in connection with the meningeal congestion; but in three others there was a quantity of serum in the subarachnoidal spaces, especially at the vertex, and this was associated in 45 with a normal brain-substance, in 42 with softening of the brain and serum in its cavities, and in 9 with congestion of the cortical substance, marked vascular puncta in the medullary tissue and effused liquid in the ventricles; in 47 there was much serum in the ventricles. The condition of the brain or its membranes was mentioned in seventeen of the *malarial* cases, and in six of these both were normal. Of the eleven in which attention was directed to abnormal appearances the brain alone was mentioned in three—in 276 as anæmic, in 84 as softened, and in 259 as softened and with the ventricles distended with effused serum; in two others the membranes alone were mentioned, the meningeal vessels being injected in 104 and the pia mater anæmic, opaque and wrinkled in 291; in one case, 288, the pia mater was congested in its posterior part while the brain was firm. Of the five cases remaining the subarachnoid spaces and ventricles contained effused liquid in 278; the pia mater and posterior part of the brain were congested in 247; the membranes congested, the subarachnoid spaces distended with liquid and the surface of the cerebrum and the floor of the fourth ventricle ecchymosed in 287; while two cases only, 80 and 257, presented definite evidence of recent inflammation—in the former lymph on the surface of the hemispheres, in the latter on the base of the brain and in both in the ventricles. The brain or its membranes were affected in seven of thirteen *typho-malarial* cases in which they were examined: In 268 attention was directed to the brain only as containing a tumor; in 264 and 297 the condition of the brain was not stated, probably because in neither did it present any abnormity—in both the meningeal vessels were engorged; in 99 and 109 the membranes were anæmic, in the latter the cerebral matter was also anæmic, in the former white and soft; in 86 there was general congestion with effusion into the subarachnoid spaces and ventricles, while in 111 effusion into the ventricles was associated with thickening and opacity of the arachnoid over the interpeduncular space. The brain or its membranes were normal or healthy in twenty-eight of the *mixed* cases, and in two others, 140 and 148, the firmness of the cerebral substance may not be regarded as morbid. Changes from the normal were reported in twenty-one instances: In 202 the cerebral vessels were engorged; in four the condition of the brain alone was stated—as firm and congested in its posterior parts in 304, congested and with a small quantity of bloody liquid in the ventricles in 301, congested and softened in 281, and congested to a crimson color in its upper and anterior portions in 194; in 156 there was some roughness of the ventricular lining but no meningitis. In eight cases the condition of the membranes alone is stated, the brain substance inferentially being normal; in four of these, 168, 208, 343 and 349, there was a slight subarachnoidal effusion; in 344 the meningeal vessels were anæmic and seemed to contain air-bubbles; in 160 and 180 these vessels were congested, and in 117 there was a slight degree of arachnitis, but the facts on which this conclusion was based were

---

The CEREBRAL MEMBRANES.—Four cases had two or three small spoonfuls of clear serum in the upper part of the arachnoid; and in one of these some albuminous particles adhered to the visceral layer, while in a fifth case the corresponding part of the parietal layer was similarly affected. In four cases there was some opacity, but no effusion, at the upper part of the membrane, a lesion regarded by Louis as antedating the typhoid attack. The subarachnoid cellular tissue contained serosity in twenty-eight cases; copious in four but slight in the others, and in some occupying only the occipital sulci. In no case was there adhesion between the arachnoidal layers. The pia mater was injected in a number of cases and remarkably so in eleven, in most of which the upper cerebral veins were distended; in one case some air-bubbles were observed in these veins.

The CEREBRUM.—The cortical substance was of a uniform roseate hue in seventeen cases, speckled with blackish points in one case, and in two others darkened almost to violet; the medullary substance was deeply congested in seven cases and slightly injected in thirty-two. In general this congestion of the brain-tissue was proportioned to the injection of the pia mater. The cerebral matter was firmer than usual in six cases, softer than usual in five; but these alterations had no relation to existing conditions of congestion. Louis hence concluded that increased firmness represented merely physiological differences in the tissues of the organ, but that diminished consistence, which was more distinctly marked, might be considered a morbid lesion analagous to the softening found in many cases in the liver and heart. No serosity was found in the third ventricle in any of the cases; in the lateral ventricles there was in six cases no effusion, in twenty-eight slight effusion and in twelve several spoonfuls of liquid which in two was turbid.

The CEREBELLUM participated, but not in all cases, in the changes which affected the cerebrum. Similar encephalic lesions and in nearly the same proportion were found in patients who died of acute diseases other than typhoid.

not recorded. In four cases, 139, 175, 183 and 217, in which the brain was reported healthy, there was injection of the pia mater with subarachnoid effusion. Lastly, in three cases in which the brain and its membranes were both mentioned as having undergone alteration, there was in 299 effusion into the subarachnoid spaces and ventricles, with congestion of the brain-tissue, in 379 some exudation on the arachnoid, with engorgement of the brain-substance and distention of the lateral ventricles with blood-tinged serum, and in 303 lymph at the base of the brain, with injection of the membranes and turbid serum in the ventricles.

The BLOOD was found in an unusually fluid condition in the *typhoid* case 25, in the *malarial* case 70, in the *typho malarial* cases 96 and 264 and in case 150 of the *mixed* series; in 204 of the last series the blood was said to have contained few white corpuscles.

ŒDEMA was noted in few cases: the neck was affected in 12 and the legs in 36 of the *typhoid* series; the lower extremities in 70 and 78 of the *malarial* series; the hands and feet in 346, and the body generally in 307 of the *mixed* series.

PURULENT INFILTRATIONS AND DEPOSITS.—In one of the *typhoid* cases, 38, pus was deposited in the greater pectoral muscle and in the knee, elbow and wrist joints. The articular cartilage of the knee was destroyed and the joint and synovial bursa filled with lymph and pus in 289 of the *malarial* series. Purulent deposits were found in several of the *mixed* series: Within the sheath of the rectus abdominis in 151; in the abdominal walls in 244; in the subperitoneal cellular tissue on the left side a little below the diaphragm in 199; in the muscles of the arm and shoulder in 253; in the pectoral region opening into the pleural sac in 383; along the track of the psoas magnus in 382; between the muscles of the lower extremities in 125; in the right buttock, communicating externally by a small aperture near the anus, in 185, and in the prostate in 239.

EXTRAVASATIONS OF BLOOD IN THE VOLUNTARY MUSCLES.—Blood-clots were found within the sheath of the rectus abdominis in 248 of the *malarial* series, in 63 of the *typho-malarial* and 157 of the *mixed* series; the upper third of the muscle was affected in 63, the lower third in the others. To these may be added 136 of the last-mentioned series, in which the anterior abdominal wall was said to have presented contusions and subperitoneal blood-clots, and 98 of the *typho-malarial* series, in which an emphysematous and engorged condition of the tissues of the left side of the neck was believed to have been the result of an ante-mortem blow.

PETECHIAL OR ECCHYMOSED SPOTS OR BLOTCHES on the skin were noted in the *post-mortem* records of two of the *typhoid* cases, 36 and 45; but in six others the clinical history refers to their existence during the course of the disease: Thus, in 5, 21 and 49 there were petechiæ on the chest, abdomen and thighs; in 16 a few minute reddish spots which did not disappear on pressure; in 2 blotches on the face, abdomen and chest, and in 34 vibices on the abdomen. In eight of the *malarial* cases, 260, 261, 289, 292, 293, 295, 386 and 387, the surface of the trunk or of the body generally was more or less ecchymosed; in 292 and 293 the skin was reported also as dingy or bronzed. Of the *typho-malarial* series 273 is the only case in which the record notes the *post-mortem* appearance of spots of this character, in this instance situated on the abdomen and chest; but the clinical history of 86 and 114 indicates their existence, while that of 93 shows the body generally, except the face and neck, covered with vibices. In the *mixed* series of cases only nine instances were recorded of ecchymosed or purpuric spots on the skin. In two of these, 205 and 235, the clinical history is the source of the information that ecchymoses appeared on the chest and abdomen. In the others the *post-mortem* records show diffused ecchymoses on the body in 201, a few faint reddish spots or petechiæ on the chest or abdomen in 202 and 203, purpuric spots in 351, 354 and perhaps 303, and a purple pustular eruption in 334. Petechiæ were noted on the epigastrium in the *typhus* case 389.

BED-SORES formed on the back and hips in cases 5, 23 and 34 of the *typhoid* series, in 289 and 366 of the *malarial* series and in 101 of the *typho-malarial* series; in the last case they were developed also over the angles of the ribs on the right side. In the *mixed* series the clinical history of 117 and 166 states that the skin over the sacrum became red and painful, manifesting a tendency to slough; in 125, 199 and 300 large sores were developed over the sacrum and trochanters, and in 218 the skin is said to have been excoriated and denuded.

GANGRENOUS SPOTS appeared on a blistered surface in case 93 and in connection with parotitis in 103 of the *typho-malarial* series.

GANGRENE OF THE FEET is recorded in six of the cases: 278, a *malarial* case in which amputation was performed at the metatarso-phalangeal articulations; 112, *typho-malarial*, in which amputation was effected by the circular method above the ankle, and 138, 143, 163 and 164 of the *mixed* series. In all the cases both feet were affected; in the three first mentioned the condition was attributed to frostbite.

SUPPURATION IN THE EAR occurred in many cases, but in 56, *typho-malarial*, it appeared to be intimately connected with the fatal event.

ULCERATION OF THE CORNEA was mentioned in but one case, 49, of the *typhoid* series.

In connection with the above the following abstract of a synopsis of autopsies in thirty-five typho-malarial cases is submitted. The examinations were made by Assistant Surgeons H. ALLEN and GEORGE M. McGILL, U. S. Army, at the Lincoln hospital, Washington, D. C., during 1863 and 1864. The report was filed in the Surgeon General's Office,

---

The SKIN was jaundiced in two cases, affected with erysipelas in four cases and with eschars in eight. The cellular tissue of the neck was emphysematous and the skin of the part greenish in one case. This condition was found in eight cases of death from other acute diseases; and in some of these the emphysema was general, but specially marked in the intermuscular septa of the lower extremities. As the heart and liver were softened in all these cases and the latter organ itself emphysematous in three, LOUIS attributed the condition to a morbid change in the fluids of the body.

The VOLUNTARY MUSCLES were healthy in all of the forty-six cases.

but the general results of the observations were published in the *American Journal of the Medical Sciences*.* It may be stated that most of these cases are to be found in the *post-mortem* records that have just been analyzed.

In one case the *fauces* and *epiglottis* were covered with diphtheritic membranes, the margins of the epiglottis and lining of the *larynx* ulcerated; in another there was thickening of the membrane but no ulceration. In one instance the *trachea* was decidedly inflamed, but without coincident laryngitis or pneumonia. The *œsophagus* and *pharynx* were healthy in twenty-seven cases, inflamed in three and ulcerated in five. Several of the ulcers were covered with a greenish exudation, and two, which had perforated the mucous coat, exhaled a gangrenous odor. In one of the cases of inflammation without ulceration an abscess about the size of a hazelnut was found where the tube is crossed by the left bronchus.

The *lungs* were mottled in every case, owing to the deposit of black pigmentary matter; congestion was found in fifteen and red hepatization in ten. Under the heading of congestion is embraced every variety of engorgement from simple excess of blood to a turgidity of the parenchyma, absence of crepitation and the presence of an excessive amount of sero-sanguineous liquid; all the specimens on section gave issue to a thin dark-red and frothy fluid. This condition differed from splenization, as under pressure the lung collapsed when the liquid was expressed, while a splenified lung would break down when subjected to this treatment. But splenization was frequently found associated with this sero-sanguineous engorgement. In three of the ten pneumonitic cases both lungs were affected and in seven one only; of the latter two were on the right side and five on the left. One case was tuberculous, one showed capillary bronchitis and the remaining eight were normal. *Pleurisy* was observed in three cases, in two of which it was simple and in the other complicated with pneumonia.

The *heart* was generally pale; in twenty-nine cases firm and in six soft. It contained clots in all except three cases, and the larger clots were invariably associated with pneumonic complications. Pericardial adhesions were found in two cases; the quantity of effused liquid varied from one fluid drachm to three fluid ounces.

The *liver* was firm in twenty-four cases and flabby in eleven, but three were fatty, four congested and two bronzed. Bile was generally present, in quantity from two to twenty fluid drachms. It was usually black, thick and tar-like, occasionally dark-greenish, brown or ochre-colored, and in other cases of a more yellowish tinge. While frequently viscid it was sometimes thin, with a light flocculent deposit.

The *spleen* in twenty-one cases was firm and healthy; in fourteen flabby or pultaceous. It was generally grayish-purple externally and bluish-gray or dark-brown internally. In some the softening was so extreme that the organ would break under the handling necessary to remove it from the body, and when squeezed the pulp would flow out in a thick continued stream as from a sponge.

The *intestines.*—In twenty-eight cases the morbid conditions were confined to the *small intestine;* in seven the colon was also involved. The mucous membrane was more or less softened, and in protracted cases of illness its folds in the lower third of the ileum were obliterated. The parts immediately around the ileo-cæcal valve were uniformly the seat of greater pathological changes than elsewhere. From this point the glandular evidence of disease extended several feet up the canal, in one instance reaching the distance of ten feet above the valve. No ulceration was detected above the jejunum. The greater lesions were invariably observed in the closed glands. These in the earlier stages were tumid, thickened, of a whitish color, with high abrupt walls. Of the whole number of specimens eighteen presented ulceration in tumefied patches; fourteen in patches not tumefied; in three the condition of the patches was unnoticed. The character of the ulcer varied as it existed in the swollen or the shrunken gland: In the former its walls were high, its base red, its form generally circular or sub-oval, with occasionally a low form of exudation on its surface. This form was never confluent, and in no instance was the entire surface of a patch the seat of ulcerative change. Several distinct ulcers, however, were seen in one patch, and in three instances the whole area was pitted with punctate ulcers, giving the gland a honey-combed appearance. This condition of the agminated glands was always accompanied with a similar change in the solitary follicles; the enlarged follicles were frequently so numerous as to give the surface of the gut a mammillated appearance. In the shrunken gland the ulcers were always of a duller hue, the walls seldom high, and if so, only in the periphery of the affected patch, forming a rounded subeverted border, the area within constituting the ulcer. The base was chiefly of a dark-blackish color, due to the presence of pigment. The form of the ulcer was, as a rule, irregular, a condition resulting from the unequal ravages of the undermining process which had taken place at the base of the individual follicles. In eight cases the borders of the patches were scooped out to the depth of a line by this action; in two perforation of the intestine had taken place in ulcers near the ileo-cæcal valve, and in both of these peritonitis was extensive. The *colon* was congested in seven cases, in four of which there was follicular enlargement and in three ulceration; in one case its mucous membrane was thickened and its solitary glands ulcerated, and in another, in which the immediate cause of death was hemorrhage, large quantities of blackberry seeds were found in the actively inflamed tissues of the alimentary canal.

Gluteal abscess was observed in one case. The parotid glands were inflamed in six cases, in two of which suppuration was noticed. Inflammation of the thyroid gland with thyroid apoplexy and abscess of the salivary glands was observed in one case. In another an abscess containing a drachm of healthy pus was detected in the cellular tissue beneath the diaphragm at the epigastrium.

The scattered facts presented by the records of individual cases having been, for convenience in study, consolidated in the above analytical summary, some remarks suggested by their consideration, and references to matters of interest untouched upon in the analysis, are herewith submitted.

II.—THE ALIMENTARY TRACT AND ABDOMINAL VISCERA.

THE SALIVARY GLANDS.—The parotid gland was inflamed in 4.1 per cent. of the cases. No predilection was shown for either side, and in several instances both glands became involved. In some cases the inflammation subsided after a continuance of many days; but in the greater number purulent infiltration speedily resulted. As an illustration of the rapidity with which this was effected case 31 may be instanced,—the gland was observed to be swollen on the eleventh day of the month, and on the fourteenth, when death occurred, disorganization had already taken place. In 222 the matter escaped by the ears; in 193 by apertures in the mouth between the root of the tongue and the inferior maxilla, and also externally a little below the mastoid process. Parotid swelling occurred only after a prolonged attack of fever, and was recorded among the malarial as well as the typhoid cases. It must therefore be considered a result not so much of the direct action of the fever-poison as of the lessened vitality and deteriorated condition of the blood produced by the continuance of the febrile state. Its occurrence in the later stages of typhus* also indicates its independence of a specific febrile cause. The frequency of parotid swelling in the continued fevers of the war, as compared with those of civil life, has already been noticed in the section on symptomatology.† It seems of interest as one of several morbid phenomena that occurred in our camp fevers intimating a tendency to typhus, or rather to a return of the clinical features that characterized the fevers of the unsanitary camps, ships and prisons of the middle ages. The rarity of notable inflammation of the submaxillary (suppuration having occurred in this gland in but one case, 384) or sublingual glands or of the pancreas was in marked contrast with the frequency of these parotid abscesses. HOFFMANN‡ ascribes the destructive character of the inflammation in the parotid after typhoid to peculiarities in the anatomical situation of the gland. The density and inelasticity of its fascia and the bony structures among which it is embedded prevent expansion during the congestion and corpuscular accumulation attending the process, so that impaction and necrobiosis are more readily produced. But although this is true in part, and corresponds with our knowledge of inflammatory results in similarly situated localities, as in the familiar example of paronychia, the febrile poison appears to exercise a certain influence on the progress of parotid swellings in view of the infrequency of suppuration as a result of the inflammatory condition in mumps.

That the PHARYNX and ŒSOPHAGUS were not more frequently observed to have suffered from inflammatory action appears due to the fact that their condition was seldom examined by our medical officers. Dr. HARRISON ALLEN's notes afford the only data for estimating the frequency of their morbid appearances. The mucous membrane was normal in twenty-seven of his thirty-five cases,—when altered its changes were such as have been recorded by Louis in his typhoid cases; it was inflamed in three and ulcerated in five. The *post-*

---

* MURCHISON, p. 216, reports the appearance of parotid swellings in 211 of 14,676 patients admitted into the London Fever Hospital in the ten years 1861-70, and refers to their presence in the typhus of military writers, as noted by MONRO in the British army operating in Germany in 1761 and by JACQUOT in the typhus of the French army in the Crimea.

† See *supra*, p. 298.

‡ *Untersuchungen über die Pathologisch-Anatomischen Veranderungen der organe beim Abdominaltyphus.*—C. E. E. HOFFMANN, Leipzig, 1869, p. 189.

mortem records presented above show in addition the occurrence of ecchymoses, diphtheritic exudation, and abscess.

The observations on the STOMACH were not numerous. This organ was altered in appearance in 75 per cent. of sixteen typhoid cases, in 51.7 per cent. of twenty-nine malarial, in 62.5 per cent. of sixteen typho-malarial, and in 50 per cent. of seventy-four mixed febrile cases. In most of these there was more or less congestion, sometimes general, at other times circumscribed in patches and in a few cases punctiform; this was often associated with softening and thickening of the mucous membrane and in three cases with ulceration. The ulcers were minute and situated along the small curvature in 386, near the middle of the large curvature in 354 and near the pylorus in 96. These hyperæmic conditions are essentially the same as those found by LOUIS in his typhoid cases, and considered by him to be of secondary importance as he had encountered them in death from acute diseases other than typhoid fever. But it is evident that the changes found in the malarial series of continued fevers were occasionally of a more intensely congestive character than those of the typhoid series; ecchymoses and thorough disintegration of the mucous lining of the stomach, which was filled with a dark grumous liquid, may be mentioned in illustration. Similar conditions were observed in the cases submitted in the last chapter as belonging to the paroxysmal fevers. There appears, therefore, some warrant for referring them to the presence of the malarial poison when they are discovered in certain cases of the typho-malarial and mixed series.

The condition of the lining membrane of the DUODENUM was seldom specially recorded, but when noted in the typhoid cases the lesions were similar to those observed by LOUIS and regarded by him as of minor importance since they had been found with equal frequency in other acute diseases. The duodenum was seldom affected alone; generally it participated in the morbid affection of the stomach. Thus both of these portions of the alimentary tract were inflamed in 29, 116 and 354, ulcerated in 96, and disintegrated in 71 and 243. When only a part of the duodenum was affected the morbid action was restricted to the upper third; and even when the whole of this portion of the canal was implicated the jejunum was frequently, as in 317, healthy. On the other hand there occurred some cases, as 276 and 354, in which the duodenum was affected while the stomach was considered in a healthy condition; in these the morbid action had extended from below. Brünner's glands were noted as enlarged in some instances and in one case, 307, as ulcerated.

The JEJUNUM was mentioned with sufficient frequency to show that it became altered by the extension of the diseased action from below and not from above.* The lowest part of the tube was affected when only one portion was said to have suffered, and when the whole was implicated the action in its lower part was more diffuse and intense than in its upper. In addition to congestion there was sometimes a softened and thickened condition of the membrane with enlargement of the solitary glands, and in rare cases ulceration. In many instances, however, in which the record states only an ulcerated condition of the small intestine, it is probable that the ulceration affected the jejunum as well as the part of the canal lying below it.

INTUSSUSCEPTION of the small intestine was occasionally found, but not with the frequency recorded by LOUIS in his typhoid cases. It cannot be regarded as having a special

---

*HOFFMANN—*Op. cit.*, p. 96—says that he has but seldom found disease of the jejunum in typhoid; that when it does occur it is extremely rare for its upper portion to be involved, and that the duodenum is exempt in a still greater degree.

relation to the febrile cases, as it was found with perhaps equal frequency in the diarrhœal series.*

LUMBRICOID WORMS were also noted in a few cases, but it does not appear that they had any special connection with the continued fevers.† In 378 a worm crawled into the larynx of the patient and caused death by suffocation. Specimen 290, Army Medical Museum, exhibits this worm extended in the larynx, trachea and right bronchus. In 348 the intestinal canal was extensively colonized.

A tumefied, inflamed or ulcerated condition of the PATCHES of PEYER or deep and circumscribed ulcerations of the intestine which, in view of our knowledge of the typhoid intestinal lesion, might be ascribed to the destruction of these patches, were found in all the cases of continued fever except those that have been separately presented as probably due solely to the action of the malarial poison and two of those that were regarded clinically as typhus. It is evident that the glands in the vicinity of the ileo-cæcal valve were especially prone to become affected, for in some cases it is stated that the diseased action was in progress only in those occupying the lower part of the ileum; while in cases in which the whole of the intestine was involved the ulcerative process had made greater progress in the glands near its termination than in those of the jejunum. This is illustrated by many of the specimens that have been preserved in the Museum. Three, four or more pieces from different convolutions of the same ileum invariably show a progressive increase of the diseased action as the ileo-cæcal valve is approached. Thus the seven successive portions of the ileum constituting specimens 171–177 present the most gradual transitions from the slightest thickening of Peyer's patches in the first piece to the large ulcerations just above the valve in the last. Thus also the five portions of the ileum, specimens 376–380, present from above downwards a gradual enlargement of the agminated glands, the summits of which are more or less ulcerated in the last three pieces; many of the solitary glands are also diseased, forming in the lower pieces oval, ulcerated elevations similar in character to those in the patches of Peyer but smaller in size. The plate facing this page, prepared from a watercolor drawing of the fresh intestine, reproduces the appearance of the second and last of these specimens. The section of the intestine on the left side, taken from high up in the ileum, shows two of Peyer's patches somewhat thickened, rising from the surface of the mucous membrane with abrupt edges, the lower decidedly thicker than the upper, but neither ulcerated; the tawny-yellow mucous membrane is considerably injected and a few slightly enlarged solitary follicles are scattered over its surface. The section on the right side of the plate, taken from just above the ileo-cæcal valve, shows in its lower part a large patch much thickened, with abrupt edges, its surface ulcerated and stained with biliary pigment; eight similar but smaller ulcerations of various sizes seem to have originated in the solitary glands, and a number of these glands are enormously enlarged but not ulcerated; the pale cream-colored mucous membrane is highly injected in patches, which appear as irregular red stains. The case from which these specimens were obtained is given as 336 of the *post-mortem* records.‡ Prints from negatives of the mounted specimens are submitted (facing pages 410 and 412) for comparison with the chromo-lithographs of the fresh intestine.

It is also evident that the diseased action had a progressive upward movement, for in but few instances were the upper glands affected while those below were in a healthy con-

---

* See p. 313, Part Second of this work.   † See *infra*, p. 591.   ‡ See *ante*, p. 410.

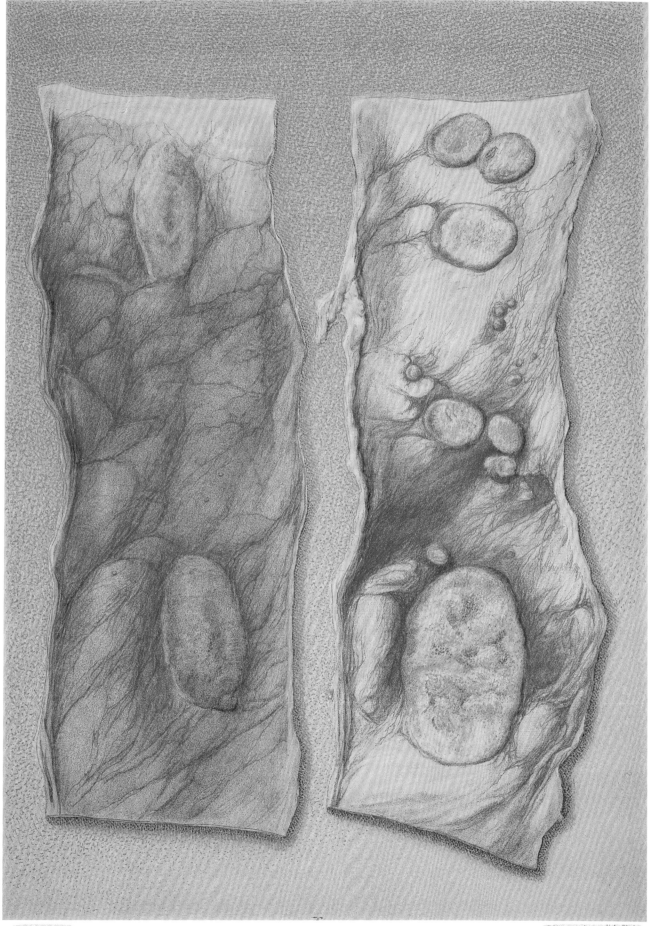

H.Faber pinx.   F.Moras chromolith.Phila

TYPHOID THICKENING OF PEYER'S PATCHES.

dition. In case 296 there were thirty-two patches of Peyer varying from half an inch to three inches in length, and twenty-seven of these were much thickened and generally inflamed but not ulcerated; the first two patches of the series were not thickened; a large patch dotted with black pigment but otherwise healthy was found on each fold of the ileo-cæcal valve, and the next patch above these appeared to be healthy. In another exceptional case, 200, the twelve upper patches were healthy, the thirteenth ulcerated, the fourteenth healthy and the remainder ulcerated and sloughing, some even through to the peritoneum.

The affected patches in the continued fever cases were usually circular or oval, from half an inch in diameter to three or four inches in their longest measurement, that parallel with the long axis of the tube. Occasionally, however, they were of unusual size. Thus specimen 399, Army Medical Museum, from case 198, exhibits in the ileum immediately above the ileo-cæcal valve a patch eight inches long, the upper extremity of which is covered with minute ulcerations.

The thickening of the patches varied from a just perceptible tumefaction, such as is seen in the upper part of specimen 377, to a prominent node rising gradually from the surface of the surrounding mucous membrane; but in many instances the margins of the nodes, as seen in the plate of specimen 380, were abrupt, and in some, as in 565 (see plate facing page 380), the patches were so constricted at the base as to present the appearance of flat sessile fungoid growths. The enlargement was opaque, soft and of a white, yellow or grayish color, more or less reddened by congestion. In some the mucous membrane covering the patch presented a slightly reticulated appearance from the irregularity of the underlying surface; this is well seen in the lower part of specimen 377, as shown in the photographic print.

When the morbid action had made further progress in such plaques, ulcers appeared on the prominences and afforded escape to the softened and broken-down portion of the contents. These ulcerations became enlarged by the destruction of the interlying glandular and mucous tissue and the coalescence of adjoining ulcerations until the greater part or whole of the node was removed, leaving a shallow cavity containing the remains of the glands and the infiltrated submucous tissue usually stained of a dark or greenish color by the intestinal contents. Patches seen in various stages of this destructive process presented a variety of appearances: In some a few minute ulcerations on the apices of individual glands; in others one or more larger ulcerations at some points, with the remaining surface intact or only minutely penetrated; and in others again a large irregular ulcerated surface more or less stained and perhaps bridged in part or overlaid by fragments of the softened mucous covering. The edges of the completed ulcer were sometimes ragged from the persistence of shreds of the mucous membrane, but generally they were well defined by a thickening of this membrane and its underlying tissue. Some of these appearances are admirably shown in the chromo-lithographs of specimens 177, 185 and 189, Army Medical Museum, herewith submitted. The first of these has already been referred to as one of seven successive portions of the ileum showing a gradual transition from the slightest thickening of the patches of Peyer in the upper part of the canal to·extensive ulceration in the lower part. It is from the case of a soldier of the 6th Pennsylvania Cavalry who was admitted into the Judiciary Square hospital April 26, 1863, and died May 2. The details of the case were not furnished. The chromo-lithograph facing page 440 represents the ileum in the vicinity of the ileo-cæcal valve; the mucous membrane is reddened by congestion except near the valve, where it is grayish, with occasional stains of brownish pigment; the patches of Peyer and several of the solitary glands are thickened and ulcerated, the contour and surface of the ulcers being irregular from the imperfect destruction of the overlying mucous membrane.

The specimens 185 and 189, plate facing this page, were taken from a soldier who died of fever in the Finley hospital, Washington, D. C., during the summer of 1863. His history was not recorded. The left piece, representing a portion of the upper part of the ileum, shows four typhoid ulcers, two evidently based on Peyer's patches and two apparently on diseased solitary glands. A number of slightly thickened follicles are scattered under the cream-colored mucous membrane, which is lightly streaked with an arborescent redness. The contour of the ulcers is irregularly rounded or oval, their surfaces dark colored with a greenish tinge and their edges thickened and pale but in parts somewhat injected. The right piece, taken from just above the ileo-cæcal valve, shows two large ulcerated Peyer's patches and five ulcers apparently due to disease of the solitary glands. The mucous membrane is thickened, of a livid crimson color and raised at several points into small rounded elevations by enlargement of the solitary crypts. The contour of the ulcers is irregularly round or oval, but in some of the smaller lesions the long diameter is at right angles to the axis of the tube. The surface is stained of a dark-green color, but in the lowest, the largest ulceration, there are some spots of reddish congestion. The edges are abrupt and thickened and participate more or less in the dark injection of the mucous lining.

In many cases, however, some of the ulcers, particularly in the lower part of the ileum, extended through the submucous tissue and exposed the transverse fibres of the muscular tunic in the bottom of the cavity. In many cases, also, the muscular coat became involved in the process of disintegration, and the serous covering of the intestine gave way at the weakened point. But in a small proportion of the cases the nodes, instead of breaking down in this gradual manner, sloughed away *en masse;* or a part of the thickened patch became subject to progressive ulceration while another part was removed by sloughing. The patches are sometimes stated in the record to have been converted into soft pultaceous sloughs. Thus in cases 13 and 14 of the typhoid series the so-called typhoid deposit was removed by sloughing, as also in cases 200 and 385 of the mixed series. In 200, according to the record, one of the patches of Peyer was converted into a blackish-brown irregular eschar one and one-fourth inches square and one-fourth of an inch thick. In 385 the patches were blackish in color, marked with livid-red and their margins indistinctly defined. Photographic prints of a portion of the ileum in each of the last two cases accompany this report, facing pages 388 and 418. The first, representing specimen 241, Army Medical Museum, shows a large irregular pulpy slough, its transverse diameter measuring three inches and its longitudinal diameter one inch and a half; several small shallow ulcerations may also be observed on the specimen. The second, representing specimen 182, shows a large, thickened, sloughing patch, several oval ulcers based on the solitary glands being also present. When the destructive process was effected in this rapid and general way the tendency to perforation was obviously increased.

In the analysis given above of the *post-mortem* records of the series of fifty pure typhoid cases there is ample ground for the assertion that the mucous membrane of the small intestine was affected chiefly, and not unfrequently solely, over and immediately around the tumefied or ulcerated patches of Peyer. The absence of a general congestion of the mucous membrane in some cases proves that its presence was not essential to the

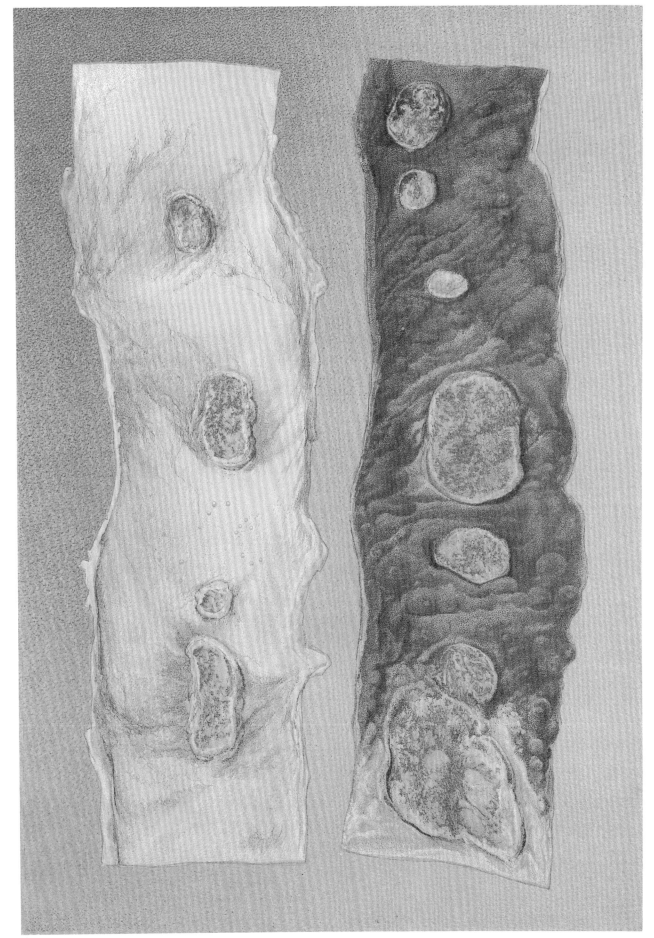

H Faber pinx!.   F.Moras cromolith.Philad?

ULCERATED PEYER'S PATCHES.-FEVER.

The left piece from the upper, the right from the lower part of the ileum.

diseased condition of the glands. Their affection must therefore be considered the primary lesion, and any extension of inflammatory processes to the general mucous surface must be regarded as secondary and as much a consequence of the morbid action in the glands as its extension to the serous membrane after the destruction of the muscular tunic. This secondary congestion of the membrane between the ulcerated patches was usually confined to the lower part of the ileum, where the diseased action had made most progress. In some cases, however, it was more generally diffused, but in these it was invariably, so far as the records show, less intense in proportion to its distance from the ileo-cæcal valve. Specimens from some of the cases of this series, as from 10, 43, 48 and 50, were received at the Museum and have been preserved, but unfortunately none of them were submitted to the artist for the preservation in colors of their appearance when recent. Nevertheless the absence of a diffuse congestion of the mucous membrane in the vicinity of typhoid ulcerations, at least in the upper part of the ileum, is shown by the chromo-lithograph of specimen 185 on the left side of the plate facing page 438. As the history of the case from which this specimen was obtained is not on record, it is uncertain whether it was or was not modified by a malarial element. But even had the case been so modified the value of the drawing as an illustration of typhoid ulceration, unaccompanied by diffuse inflammation of the lining membrane, is by no means impaired. As will be seen directly, a diffusely congested or inflamed condition of the membrane was more frequently met with in modified than in unmodified cases; hence, while the general congestion of 189, shown on the right side of the same plate, may be viewed as due to a malarial complication, the absence of a similar congestion in 185 cannot be ascribed to an interference of that nature.

In the malarial series of continued fever cases presenting adynamic symptoms the condition of the patches of Peyer was not reported in twenty-six instances; and as in most of these some details are given of the appearances presented by the mucous membrane of the small intestine, it may be inferred that the patches were not so altered as to attract special attention, or in other words, that they or the membrane covering them were healthy, congested or inflamed according to the condition of the general mucous lining. They were healthy in seven cases and not ulcerated in two cases, although in six of these, 257, 260–263 and 367, the membrane was more or less congested or inflamed, and in the last-mentioned case ulcerated at one point to perforation. When special attention was given by the reporters to the condition of the patches they were generally said to be reddened or altered in color by deposits of black or bluish pigment: They were reddened, congested or inflamed in ten cases, in four of which the state of the mucous membrane of the small intestine remained unnoted, while in six it was more or less hyperæmic; it is to be observed also that in one of these cases, 373, contrary to what is found in typhoid fever, the glands and mucous membrane of the upper part of the intestinal tract were the seat of the congestion. In case 84, in which the agminated glands were reported pale, the mucous membrane of the small intestine, although showing some streaks of congestion, was generally bloodless. In 386 most of the glands were healthy, but a few were inflamed and slightly thickened, while the ileum was inflamed in patches, some of which were intensely affected. In 387 the glands were opaque-white and slightly thickened, but did not appear positively diseased, and the mucous membrane generally was of a pale-cream color. In the remaining fifteen of the sixty-three cases the patches of Peyer were colored by deposits of pigment, which will be more particularly referred to hereafter.*

* See *infra*, p. 455.

The mucous lining of the ileum was congested in nearly two-thirds of the cases of this series. In some the congestion formed streaks and patches, and in these there appeared no marked partiality for the lower part of the intestine; generally, however, the congestion was diffused throughout the whole of the ileum. The mucous membrane was frequently darkened by the intensity of the engorgement and occasionally spotted with ecchymosis; in one instance the ileum is said to have been gangrenous; nevertheless ulceration was rarely present. In a few cases the membrane was softened, thickened or thinned. In some it is stated that there was no congestion of the membrane, and in others the absence of any statement with regard to its condition, although the changes in its glands were noted, leads to the belief that it was not materially affected. In fact the condition of the mucous lining of the ileum in these continued malarial fevers did not differ from that found in the paroxysmal malarial cases submitted in the preceding chapter. The hyperæmia of the membrane in the malarial series differed from that met with in the typhoid cases not only in its greater extent and intensity but in its mode of development. In the latter it was a secondary result of the morbid action in the closed glands; in the former, on the contrary, it must be regarded as a direct result of the virulence of the febrile cause,—a primary lesion because unconnected with any antecedent focus of inflammation. The agminated and solitary glands were frequently healthy or participated only in the general congestion. In one exceptional case the gut was perforated, but usually no circumscribed areas of special activity appear to have been developed, although the engorgement was such that in two cases ecchymotic blotches, and in one gangrene, were recorded as its consequences. In fact, while the inflammation in the typhoid cases was confined to the glands, penetrating deeply on account of their anatomical relations, and spreading laterally along the continuity of the membrane to but a limited extent from these primary foci, the hyperæmia in the malarial cases was general and primary, differing as much in appearance and distribution from that in the typhoid cases as the developments on the skin in erythema or erysipelas differ from those in small-pox during its period of maturation.

In the sixty-one cases of the typho-malarial series the patches of Peyer were tumefied and more or less congested, as in the earlier stages of the progress of typhoid fever, in twenty-one instances. They were ulcerated, as in the later stages of typhoid, in thirty cases; in some of these, as 56, 93, 110 and 298, they were in process of healing, while in one, 92, their disorganized condition is suggestive of that removal by sloughing which has been mentioned as occasionally occurring. In ten cases in which the condition of the patches was not entered on the record, the ileum or small intestine was congested or ulcerated and in several instances perforated. Deposits of black pigment were found in some of the glands in three of these typho-malarial cases.

In this series the mucous membrane of the ileum, exclusive of that covering the affected glands, was generally congested or inflamed throughout its whole extent; but in a few cases the hyperæmic condition was confined to its lower portion, and in one it was reported as forming only an areola around each enlarged and ulcerated patch. In a few cases, also, softening, thickening, thinning or pigmentation was noted.

Conditions of the mucous membrane and patches of the ileum similar to those observed in the typho-malarial cases were found in the mixed series. Some difference in the frequency of certain observations may, however, be noted. Thus, it has been seen that twenty-one of the sixty-one typho-malarial cases proved fatal at a time when the disease of the agmi-

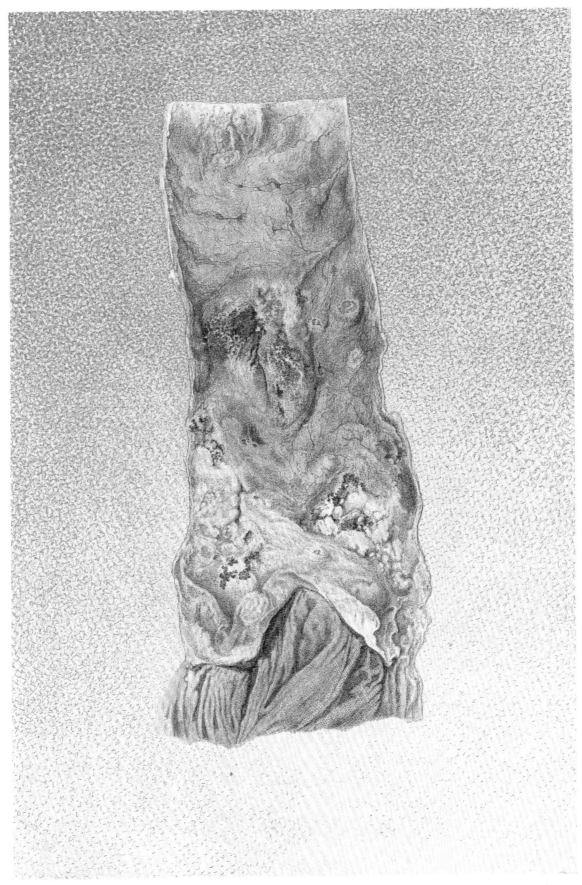

ULCERATED PEYER'S PATCH.-FEVER

taken near the Ileo-coecal valve.

nated glands had not advanced beyond the stage of hyperæmia and tumefaction. Death occurred in these modified typhoid cases at an earlier period of the typhoid career than is usual, and this result must be ascribed to the influence of a concurrent and probably antecedent malarial fever. But only twelve of two hundred and thirteen cases of the mixed series are reported as having presented tumefied but unulcerated glands. This accords with our knowledge of the constitution of this group of cases. It consisted of pure and modified typhoid cases in unknown proportions, but the proportion of coincident malarial fevers was necessarily less than in the typho-malarial series, in which every case was modified by a malarial complication. The relative infrequency of unulcerated patches of Peyer in the mixed series of cases may thus be readily understood.

The LARGE INTESTINE was recorded as more or less altered from the normal or healthy condition in 35.4 per cent. of the typhoid cases, 68 per cent. of the malarial and in 51 per cent. of the typho-malarial and the mixed series of cases. These figures, however, express only approximately the relative frequency of the implication of the large intestine, as in many cases in which its condition was not stated there is an uncertainty as to whether or not it was examined. The appearances indicated that congestive or inflammatory processes had been in progress during the fatal sickness or at some period shortly anterior to it. The mucous membrane was reddened in erythematous patches or more diffusely and deeply congested. The latter condition was frequently found at or near the extremities of the gut; the former in the intermediate parts. With or without this congested condition in their vicinity the solitary glands were in many instances observed as prominences sometimes as large as small shot and frequently ulcerated. Occasionally the presence of larger ulcerations was recorded, but whether these were based upon the glandular substance or a result of the inflammation of the membrane independent of the condition of its crypts is uncertain.* In some, however, as in case 23, it is said that the ulceration was unconnected with the state of the solitary glands. Sometimes the more deeply congested parts were spotted with ecchymoses, and in a few cases the canal contained extravasated blood. Those parts of the mucous membrane that were but slightly congested were frequently mottled with patches and streaks of a slate-gray, bluish, greenish or other dark color. Frequently, also, and particularly in these cases of mottling, the solitary glands, whether prominent or not, presented points of black pigmentary deposit in their apices. In a few cases softening with thickening, or rarely thinning of the mucous membrane, was recorded. Ulceration without specially noted congestion appears frequently in the reports of the typhoid cases, while congestion without ulceration seems to have characterized the majority of the malarial cases. Only 30 per cent. of the large intestines that were observed in the typhoid series presented congestion without ulceration, while 35 per cent. presented ulceration without particularized congestion; but in the malarial series 63 per cent. showed congestion without ulceration, while only 16 per cent. were ulcerated, and the mucous membrane in these was inflamed, ecchymosed, congested or mottled with slate-colored patches.

It may reasonably be supposed that the lesions of the large intestine in a few of the cases were those of diphtheritic dysentery, as for instance in 323, in which the intestine was softened and disorganized; in 80, in which it was said to have been diseased, and in 311 and 316, in which its lower end and lining membrane were reported respectively as gangrenous and converted into a pulpy mass. Dr. WOODWARD has instanced cases 141, 192, 226,

---

* See *infra*, p. 450.

278 and 800 of his diarrhœal series as examples of the coincidence of typhoid fever and diphtheritic dysentery.

The SOLITARY GLANDS were reported altered from the normal or healthy condition in 26 per cent. of the typhoid cases, 38 per cent. of the malarial, 24.6 per cent. of the typho-malarial and 23.5 per cent. of the mixed series. These figures cannot be regarded as accurate expressions of the frequency of such changes in the glands owing to the obvious imperfection of some of the records. Nevertheless a more frequent involvement in the malarial cases seems to be indicated. This deduction may be accepted the more readily as it has already been shown that in these cases the congestion of the mucous membrane was more diffuse and intense than in unmodified typhoid. Not that the affection of the glands was always associated with existing congestion, for in many instances their tumefaction or ulceration is the only abnormity mentioned, and in the chromo-lithograph of specimen 185, facing page 438, they may be seen enlarged on a mucous surface which is not reddened; but from our knowledge of the histology of catarrhal diarrhœa it is certain that tumefaction of the follicles originates in hyperæmic conditions of the membrane, which at a later period may subside before the glands have returned to their normal condition. Moreover, pigmentation of the glands was more frequently found in the malarial cases than in the typhoid; thus, while in the latter deposits of pigment were reported in but two of thirteen cases in which attention was given to this point, they were noted in ten of twenty-eight malarial cases, in five of fifteen typho-malarial cases, and in nine of fifty-one cases of the mixed series; and, as will be shown hereafter, this pigmentation was dependent on an antecedent congestion.

The records show also, with some uncertainty, however, owing to their occasional want of precision, that the glands of the ileum were more commonly affected than those of the large intestine, and that while the former were altered with nearly equal frequency in all the series of cases the latter appeared more liable to become changed in the malarial than in the typhoid cases. Thus, the solitary glands of the small intestine were in an abnormal or unhealthy condition in 84.6 per cent. of thirteen typhoid cases, in 92 per cent. of twenty-four malarial cases, in 70 per cent. of seventeen typho-malarial cases and in 78 per cent. of fifty of the mixed series; while those of the large intestine were similarly altered in 38.4 per cent. of the typhoid, 62.5 per cent. of the malarial, 35.5 per cent. of the typho-malarial and 40 per cent. of the mixed cases.

LOUIS, while setting aside the changes in the patches of Peyer as peculiar to the typhoid affection, regarded the congested or inflammatory condition of the intestinal lining, including also the enlargement and ulceration of the solitary glands, as of an accidental or secondary character, since he had observed them in cases of death from other acute diseases. In the present section they have been found of even more frequent occurrence in fevers that did not exhibit the specific lesions of typhoid than in those that did, but evidently constituting an essential of the disease in neither of these classes. Dr. WOODWARD,* however, has shown the invariable presence of congestion and the frequent occurrence of an affection of the solitary glands in catarrhal diarrhœa; and since, in the cases of continued fever which were characterized by these appearances, there had invariably been an antecedent diarrhœa, it is not surprising to find that the changes in the solitary glands in these cases were precisely those that have been described as characteristic of the simple diarrhœal affection. In fact the case reported as 300 of the *post-mortem* records of the continued fevers furnished the

_____

* Page 326, Second Part of this work.

specimen which was used in the microscopic delineation of the changes in the mucous membrane and its solitary glands in cases of acute diarrhœa,—see, in the Second Part of this work, the steel engraving facing page 326 and the photographic print facing page 328. The patient died of a complicating dysentery associated with a febrile movement of a paroxysmal character.

The plate facing page 380 of the present volume shows the solitary glands enlarged to the size of small peas. The portion of the ileum represented, constituting specimen 565, Army Medical Museum, was taken from near the valve, the case being that reported as 147 of the *post-mortem* records. The patch of aggregated glands in the lower half of the specimen is much and irregularly thickened, and the villi are so enlarged as to give the mucous surface a plush-like aspect. In connection with the marked enlargement of both the solitary and agminated glands in this case, it may be stated that in general the solitary glands in typhoid cases presented characters similar to those of the patches of Peyer, as if they had been involved in the same morbid action; when the latter were largely tumefied, extensively ulcerated or in a sloughing condition, the former were in most instances similarly affected.

But tumefaction and ulceration commencing in the solitary glands of the ileum not unfrequently extended beyond their boundaries. The surrounding mucous and submucous tissues became involved, and by the coalescence of neighboring morbid areas ulcers of comparatively large size were produced. When small the ulcers were round or oval, when large they were less regular in form and not unfrequently their greater diameter lay across rather than along the intestine. Their edges were usually abrupt and their cavities stained like those resulting from the disorganization of the patches of Peyer,—see the chromo-lithographs of the specimens submitted on the right of the plates facing pages 436 and 438.

The morbid action in the solitary follicles of the colon resulted in similar enlargements and ulcerations. In some cases the mucous surface was raised by minute rounded prominences; in others pin-hole apertures, produced by the sloughing of the apices of the glands, permitted their softened stroma with its recent abnormal deposit to be extruded, leaving small cavities in its place; in others again the extension and coalescence of neighboring ulcers gave rise to larger patches of irregular outline, sometimes even an inch in diameter, and in these the muscular coat was frequently exposed. The appearance of the colon when altered by follicular ulceration has been illustrated in the Second Part of this work,—see the photographic prints of specimens 206, Army Medical Museum, facing page 516, and of 195, facing page 526. The former exhibits ulcers varying in size from a mere puncture to a break one-tenth of an inch in diameter, with a series near the centre of the specimen enlarged by progressive ulceration and coalescence to a diameter of over half an inch. The latter shows a more extensive ulceration, which originated apparently in a morbid condition of the solitary glands.

The changes in the minute anatomy of the mucous membrane* in typhoid, whether

---

*To permit of ready comparison with the statements in the text, a summary of the views and observations of some recent investigators is herewith submitted. ROKITANSKY—*Lehrbuch der Pathologischen Anatomie*, Vienna, 1861, Vol. III—says that two stages may be observed in the typhoid process affecting the mucous membrane of the small intestine. In the first there is an acute catarrhal inflammation of the ileum, chiefly of its lower half; the membrane is injected, its villi turgescent and its agminated and solitary glands visibly enlarged. In the second the hyperæmia is concentrated upon the glands, which become swollen in consequence of exudation and hyperplasia of their structural elements. An injected vascular network surrounds the patches, which are thickened and have an abruptly rising margin; sometimes a constriction around the base gives them a fungus-like appearance. The glands are firm and have a grayish, yellowish or pale-red color, visible not only through the mucous coat but also through the outer layers of the intestine; or they are softer, more yielding and of a darker or bluish-red color. A section of one of these tumefied patches shows a uniform degeneration of its glandular structure and its bed of connective tissue into a marrow-like substance, which invades the overlying membrane, and in some instances penetrates beyond the submucous layer into the muscular coat. This degeneration is the result of an excessive development of the exuded plastic elements. The solitary follicles are in like manner enlarged, firm and surrounded by a vascular zone. The diseased process has two modes of termination—resolution and sloughing. When resolution takes place the swollen glands become less dense and resistant; a grayish opaque liquid replaces the firm

pure or modified, appear to have depended wholly on a condition of hyperplasia. The first of the observed changes was a congestion of the capillaries and small veins, particularly noticeable in the vascular circlets surrounding the closed glands. This was followed by an increase of the lymphoid elements of the adenoid tissue of the mucosa and the submucous connective. These elements accumulated in the mucous membrane between the follicles of Lieberkühn, which were pushed apart, and in some instances occluded, giving rise to the appearance of closed cysts embedded in the prominent mass of the new elements. They accumulated also in the solitary and agminated glands or at particular points in or beneath the membrane, which, when thus raised into prominence by the newly-developed mass, were undistinguishable from enlarged glands. Numerous swarms of these lymphoid corpuscles were found also around the swollen glands or pseudo-glands in the vicinity of the small veins, and disposed in irregular stellate groups corresponding in outline to the serous canals of the connective tissue. Accompanying these aggregations of the corpuscular elements was an infiltration of plasma which relaxed the cohesion of the reticular matrix and increased the size of the lymph-spaces.

The tumefaction caused by this accumulation of the lymphoid elements disappeared gradually, the site of the aggregation resuming its normal aspect as resorption of the plasma and broken-down corpuscles was effected; or the swelling continued to increase until by pressure on the nutrient vessels a necrosis occurred at various points, leading to the development of ulcers varying in size with that of the necrosed tissues. In some instances these ulcerations, beginning as mere points, became extended and coalesced into larger areas by the progressive infiltration of the surrounding tissues and the concomitant interference with nutrition. In other cases in which tumefaction was suddenly developed the whole mass

elements and, after the absorption of this, there remains a slate-gray or black pigmentation of the mucous membrane and glandular plexus. Sloughing of the agminated glands not only involves wholly or in part the membrane covering them, but also other and otherwise normal adjacent tissues through which the typhous product has become diffused. The portion to be thrown off has meanwhile been converted into a yellow or yellowish-brown substance like yellow tubercle, deriving its surface coloring from the presence of bile. The process seizes upon the part uniformly throughout, or frequently distinct portions of a patch are removed by sloughing while other parts undergo a simple resolution. The solitary glands pursue the same course; but they are slower in their progress and their sloughs are small and round. When the muscular coat is involved the peritoneal coat thus laid bare soon becomes gangrenous and peritonitis ensues; even when the muscular coat has not been originally implicated a necrosis of its tissue in layers may take place at a later period and the process extend to the serous coat with the same consequences. Perforation is generally effected at some distance above the ileo-cæcal valve. Sometimes the development of the agminated glands is inconsiderable; the swellings do not rise much above the general surface; they are relaxed, and occasionally their individual cysts become disorganized and burst through the mucous membrane, giving by the numerous resulting depressions a net-like appearance to the surface. In rare cases only a single group of glands attains to an extreme stage of the typhoid process, while in others there is no glandular involvement and the intestinal affection is limited to a catarrh of the mucous membrane. In other cases there are present thick, hard, glandular tumors passing into a fungoid condition at the intestinal surface and accompanied with intense hyperæmia of the surrounding parts, which gives rise to hemorrhage; or in some instances the typhoid matter developing towards the exterior penetrates the muscular tunic and gives origin to a pseudomembranous efflorescence on the peritoneal surface. After the separation of the slough the mucous membrane around the margin of the ulcer sinks to the level of the latter and appears, in proportion to the original thickness of the gland, as a more or less broad, free and movable border, at first rather elevated, red and injected, and afterwards more relaxed and of a dark-gray color. Healing proceeds from the circumference towards the centre; the overlying mucous border unites with the exposed layer of submucous cellular tissue, from which a cell-growth springs up and the surface becomes transformed into a facet having a lustre like that of a serous membrane. Over this the advancing edges of the surrounding mucous membrane are gradually extended, though not with equal rapidity from all parts, until they finally meet. Occasional instances are met with in which a membrane furnished with villi and crypts is found to cover an extraordinarily large area where loss of substance had taken place, and imperfect villi may be observed in the very centre of the facet-like cicatrix; these circumstances render it probable that a mucous formation takes place from the cicatrix itself. After the healing of the ulcers a shallow depression remains, due to the thinned mucous membrane adhering more intimately to the defective layer beneath; and not unfrequently there is seen in the centre a small portion of the smooth lustrous cicatrix still uncovered by mucous membrane; in other instances the mucous coat is smooth, without folds, less pliable and in comparison with the surrounding tissue less vascular, and in patches less rich in villi. These appearances are sometimes found after a lapse of thirty years. Only in rare cases, in which there has been an extensive loss of substance, does contraction of the cicatrix give rise to a noticeable stenosis. Occasionally the mucous margin around the ulcers becomes hypertrophied and remains permanently raised, contributing nothing to the covering of the cicatrix, while sometimes it has no connection with the subjacent layer and projects into the hollow of the bowel. HARLEY—in *Reynold's System of Medicine*, Vol. I, London, 1866, p. 572 *et seq.*—says that in the earliest stage of typhoid inflammation the patches of Peyer are slightly swollen and a little more vascular than in health. The swelling implicates the network of mucous membrane chiefly, the ridges between the crypts becoming more vascular, wider and prominent, and the intervening depressions more contracted and deeper, while the glands themselves appear unaltered. The inflammatory products are therefore formed around the closed glands and not in their interior. Careful observation leads him to speak positively on this point; but an examination of the illustration on page 449, *infra*, suffices to disprove this. He has never seen the glands project on the surface of the patch; they are placed below and between the swollen mucous ridges, and in the later stages are completely buried beneath the inflamed surface. When this covering becomes disintegrated they are discovered lying deeply in the abundant submucous tissue and exhibiting little or no increase of size. The cellular texture is infiltrated with finely granular corpuscles of various sizes, chiefly spherical and averaging $\frac{1}{3000}$ of an inch in diameter. In the more advanced and ulcerated patches the cells are equally numerous, but are large and of more uniform size, averaging $\frac{1}{2100}$ of an inch, and a little more darkly granular. In still more advanced stages the enlarged

Photographed by Dr. E. Curtis, U.S.A.   on steel by H. Faber.

THREE PERPENDICULAR SECTIONS OF ILEUM
showing
enlargement softening and ulceration.
of the solitary glands.
Magnified 12 diameters.

of an infiltrated and impacted patch, with much of the underlying and surrounding submucous tissue, was involved in the necrosis and separated as a slough. Many of the microscopic sections that have been preserved show the vessels of the affected parts filled with blood corpuscles and their periphery surrounded by swarms of the new corpuscular elements, but in none of these sections, nor in those recently cut for examination, were those plugs of micrococci observed which KLEIN invested with the important rôle of causing the death of the tumefied parts.

Enlargement, softening and ulceration, as affecting the solitary glands of the ileum and their site in the mucous and submucous tissues, are illustrated by the plate facing page 444. This is an engraving on steel from photographs of specimens in the microscopic collection. The section on the left of the plate represents specimen 1745, the middle section 1747 and that on the right 1750. These are three of a series of six specimens, 1745–1750, showing various stages of the ulceration of a solitary gland in the ileum from a case the history of which is unknown, but in which the patches of Peyer were thickened at their edges and destroyed in their interior by eroding ulcers, and the solitary glands the subject of what has been called pinhead enlargement and ulceration. The gland in the section on the left of the plate is slightly enlarged and elevated, and embedded in a mass of the new lymphoid cells which appear as a well-defined and darkened setting. In the middle section the outline of the gland has become obscured by the impaction of the surrounding tissue with corpuscular elements, which have also extended through the submucous connective in more or less dense swarms as far as the muscular tunic. In the section on the right the mucous membrane has given way, forming an aperture into a small cavity containing and surrounded by the altered tissues of the mucous and submucous coats.

---

capsules contain spherules of oil and there is much intercorpuscular molecular matter. Swelling of the individual glands at this period is due to the enlargement of the corpuscles forming their parenchyma. HOFFMANN—*Untersuchungen über die Pathologisch-Anatomischen veränderungen der Organe beim Abdominal typhus*, Leipzig, 1869, p. 105 *et seq.*—states that typhoid fever is ushered in by acute catarrhal changes in the intestinal mucous membrane, the capillaries becoming dilated and the circulation retarded, while marked exudation takes place in the mucous tissue. Frequently after death the affected capillaries of the earlier stages of the disease, together with those of the deeper layers of the mucous coat with which they connect, are still found enlarged and filled with blood corpuscles, the red as a rule predominating, although sometimes white corpuscles aggregated in spots are observed in considerable numbers. Towards and within the follicles the vessels diminish in calibre. The thickness of the vascular walls corresponds to their enlargement, so that while the vessels in the immediate vicinity of the follicles show a double contour, in those more distant this condition becomes less distinct and is often wanting. Upon the dilatation of the vessels and the engorgement in connection with it depend in part the morbid appearances in the early stages of the disease; the turgid vascular network around the follicles and other fully-charged vessels throughout the tumefied tissues give to the mucous surface its red color. Resulting from these vascular conditions is a slowness of circulation with a corresponding exudation into the mucous tissues, promoting an abundant shedding of the epithelium. The dilated state of the vessels is often associated with small extravasations, and occasionally, in severe cases, with more extensive ecchymotic blotches; moreover, the pigmentation frequently observed in the later stages points to the fact that such extravasations had occurred. While this enlargement of the capillaries is found very generally in the early period it subsides gradually as tumefaction increases. Although the swelling of the glands is ushered in with an exudation into the mucous tissue, it is dependent upon this only in a slight degree; it is due in great part to the excessive development and increase of the structural elements. In recent cases large cell-structures are seen, some similar in appearance to lymph corpuscles, but twice, three times and even eight times as large, and others poly-nucleated and occasionally notched in one or more places as if in the act of division. This occurring not only in the patches of Peyer and solitary follicles, but also in the adjacent mucous tissue, seems to point to an enormous increase and enlargement of the original lymph-cells; the new cell-structures are the progeny of the old lymph corpuscles and possess nothing specific. The enlarged follicles elevate the membrane covering them and impart to the surface a mammillated aspect; sometimes they project so much as to assume a polypoid appearance, and occasionally by their enlargement in an opposite direction they press upon the muscular coat and give rise to an infiltration of cell elements through its interstices to the serous coat, where they form small grayish bodies beneath the peritoneum. To this infiltration of the cell elements is also due the occasional tuberculated condition of the edges of ulcerated patches. Resolution is ushered in with a diminished afflux of blood. Its simplest form is observed in the upper portion of the bowel and preferably in the least tumefied patches, where it occurs as a rule in connection with others, and may even be so associated with them that one part of a plaque is subject to it and the rest to another, or what is of more common occurrence different portions of the bowel are respectively subject to different forms of retrograde change. In the simpler process great numbers of cells undergo disintegration; among these are included the large structures so abundant in the follicles and contiguous tissue before the diseased process had reached its height. When resorption goes on with uniformity throughout all the structural elements of a patch the tumefaction subsides evenly; but when the contrary obtains inequalities remain on its surface. Absorption, for instance, may go on more energetically within the follicles than in the intervening thickened areolar tissue, which, through the sinking in of the more rapidly diminishing follicles, becomes more prominent and thus gives rise to a reticulated appearance of the surface of the plaque. Sometimes the contents of the glands, including the stroma as well as the altered mass, undergo fatty degeneration, become dissolved and are evacuated; the small cavities which result also give rise to the reticulated appearance just noted. After the evacuation of the follicles numerous minute bloodvessels are seen to pass through their cavities like vessels traversing the hollow of a pulmonary abscess. This condition has an intimate connection with the punctate pigmentation frequently seen in the glands. This coloration is due to little bleedings into the empty follicles from rupture of the minute permeating vessels during the process of disorganization and evacuation; and the extravasations, at first of a red color, become later dark-blue, probably from the action of the intestinal gases. The process of follicular destruction just described constitutes one of the less grave forms of ulcer-formation. Sometimes fatty degeneration commences at superficial points of limited size, where separation from the tissues beneath takes place and a more extensive ulcer is formed, which finds its limit ultimately in neighboring

The plate facing this page shows an extension of the follicular ulcer in all directions by the impaction and subsequent necrosis of the tissues. The interior layer of the muscular coat has been almost reached. Laterally the morbid action has progressed more rapidly in the submucous tissue than in the mucous membrane, so that the latter is left as a thickened edge overhanging the cavity in the former. This is a steel engraving of a photograph of specimen 1756 of the microscopic collection, the section having been derived from the same source as the three that have just been presented.

In the colon the solitary glands usually began to ulcerate before any considerable enlargement or protrusion above the surface of the mucous membrane had taken place. When the corpuscular elements were set free a minute cavity was formed, which became enlarged by progressive ulcerative action in the infiltrated submucous tissue and the caving in of the undermined mucous membrane. This process has already been illustrated by the plates facing pages 568, 570 and 572 of the Second Part of this History.

The changes in the agminated glands were essentially of the same character. The plate facing page 448, *infra*, shows the typhoid thickening of a patch the mucous membrane over which has been in a great measure destroyed, while the glands and submucous connective are converted into a somewhat uniform cellular mass by the dense aggregation of the corpuscles. This plate was engraved from a photograph of specimen 1704, one of a series of thirty-two perpendicular sections of the ileum of a dark mulatto woman who died in the Freedman's hospital, Washington, D. C.

This patient, twenty-six years of age and nursing an infant three months old, was admitted Sept. 5, 1865, with typhoid fever. She had been suffering for four weeks from fever, headache, anorexia, thirst and pain in the abdomen; pulse feeble and rapid, 120; skin hot and dry and tongue coated with a thick yellow fur; the bowels were moved once daily, the passages being of a greenish color, but diarrhœa set in prior to death on the 13th. At the

mucous structures supplied with normally abundant bloodvessels and organically unaltered. Such ulcers have moderately elevated edges and are often of considerable extent; occasionally they penetrate the muscular tunic and lead to perforation. When in process of healing, there spring up on the floor of the ulcerated cavities fine granulations which become covered with a transparent and sometimes pigmented membrane. The more frequent and dangerous process of ulcer-formation proceeds with greater energy: The tissues which by cell-multiplication and enlargement have been deprived of their nutrition separate in defined patches by sloughing. After the detachment of the slough the surface is in many cases moderately red with strongly injected edges; in others dark-red and often ecchymosed from the presence of a capillary network on the surface of an extremely delicate granulating tissue in which a lesion readily leads to hemorrhage. These sloughing ulcers sometimes extend to the submucous, muscular and even to the serous coat of the bowel. Sometimes the two modes of ulcer-formation occur in the same plaque, the milder attacking the margin of sloughing ulcers and forming confluent sores of large size. Sometimes, too, the destructive and reparative processes are present in the same ulcer, the former going on in the centre and the latter at the circumference. While this is generally difficult to demonstrate, instances have been observed in which the marginal structure bears so decidedly the characters of new tissue that there can hardly be any doubt of attempts at repair. The tissues which border the ulcers towards the exterior aspect of the bowel have generally their natural firmness increased by the effusion of plastic elements, but occasionally these structures become brittle or gangrenous and either lead to perforation or predispose to peritoneal inflammation. Typhoid cicatrices present themselves in the form of smooth formations, red at first but later deeply pigmented, a peculiarity occasionally observed even after the lapse of years. No villi are found on these cicatrices, and even the mucous tissue itself fails to be developed from the granulating material when the ulceration had penetrated to the muscular coat. Gangrene as a rule makes its appearance in spots of limited size in parts that have been excessively infiltrated. In some cases of extensive ulceration diphtheritic inflammation complicates the typhoid process and affects both the small and large intestine to a variable extent. This is seldom confined to one locality, but fixes at the same time upon several portions of the digestive tube; frequently it starts from the larger ulcers and is a cause of recurring hemorrhages; sometimes no relation to existing ulcers can be determined, and in these instances secondary ulcerations, resulting from the diphtheritic inflammation, often appear at a late period. According to RINDFLEISCH—*Pathological Histology*, New Sydenham Society, London, 1872, Vol. I, p. 438 *et seq.*—the closed glands of the small and large intestine participate in a catarrhal inflammation of the mucous membrane. The solitary glands appear as dull-gray pearly nodules the size of a pinhead, surrounded by a hyperæmic plexus of vessels; and each of the individual glands of the patches of Peyer become similarly affected. After this the glands pass into the stage of medullary infiltration in which the solitary follicles attain a size even six times greater than the normal, and the perifollicular connective becomes infiltrated. The aggregated follicles of a patch coalesce with the interstitial tissue to form a soft, rose-colored, seemingly homogeneous mass resembling the medullary substance of the fœtal brain, the entire patch appearing as a flattened elevation two lines in height, of an elongated oval outline and marked off from the surrounding mucous membrane by a precipitous edge. The infiltration is composed of a numerical increase of the corpuscular elements and an increase in the size of these individually. They contain a larger proportionate quantity of protoplasm than the simple lymph corpuscle; the protoplasm of the latter scarcely equals the contained nucleus in amount, but in the typhous cell it usually takes up more space than the nucleus. The morbid product is removed by a process of colliquative softening, the cells becoming disintegrated into oily matters which are absorbed; or failing this the deposit passes into a state of cheesy necrosis and is removed by ulcerative action. KLEIN—in his *Report on the Intimate Anatomical Changes in Enteric or Typhoid Fever*, in the Report of the Local Government Board, London, 1875, pp. 80-124 —describes the changes in the intestinal mucous membrane as beginning with a distention of the vessels surrounding the lymphatic follicles. This is followed by swelling of the solitary glands due to an accumulation of ordinary nucleated lymph corpuscles. Similar accumulations in the mucosa exercise a destructive compression on the crypts of Lieberkühn, detaching their epithelium and converting it into masses of cells, which by the occasional occlusion of the follicular aperture appear sometimes to be contained in a closed cyst. The lymphoid corpuscles are also increased in the submucosa, particularly in and around the bases of the solitary and agminated glands. But this observer objected to consider all the minute prominences on the mucous membrane to be enlarged glands, as he had been able to trace back their development to small accumulations of the lymph corpuscles in the mucosa, and moreover, the solitary glands are not so numerous in man as are frequently the minute tumefactions found in typhoid fever. Following

Photographed by Dr. E. Curtis U.S.A.   on steel by H. Faber.

PERPENDICULAR SECTION OF ILEUM
showing a
FOLLICULAR ULCER.

which has penetrated nearly to the muscular coat.

Magnified 12 diameters.

post-mortem examination sixteen hours after death great emaciation and marked rigor mortis were noted. The lower lobes of the lungs were somewhat congested. The duodenum and ileum were inflamed throughout, the jejunum in patches. The agminated glands were enlarged and thickened gradually from above downwards; each of those in the lower third of the ileum presented one or more points of ulceration; some near the valve were completely ulcerated away, leaving the fibres of the muscular coat exposed, while on the valve and for about four inches above it the whole mucous surface was a mass of enlarged and thickened patches, each presenting several points of ulceration. The ascending colon was inflamed and deeply ulcerated in transverse oval patches, some of them two inches in diameter and with overhanging edges,—there were also a few enlarged solitary follicles the size of peas, some of which were ulcerated on the apex; the transverse colon presented a few small round ulcers which had penetrated to the muscular coat; the descending colon was inflamed in patches and had in the sigmoid flexure a group of small oval ulcers and slightly enlarged solitary follicles with specks of pigment in each; the rectum also presented a few small ulcers.—*Hospital Steward A. J. Shafhirt, U. S. Army, Freedman's Hospital, Washington, D. C.*

The photo-engraving which follows this paragraph illustrates the appearance of a perpendicular section of a patch when its superficial layers have been removed by necrobiotic processes. The section shows a shallow ulcer with abrupt edges, involving the whole patch. The glandular stroma and intervening submucous tissue are indistinguishable on account of the great accumulation of the corpuscular elements. The tissues around the impacted portions are freely beset with swarms of new cells and liberally supplied with vessels which are generally filled with blood corpuscles.

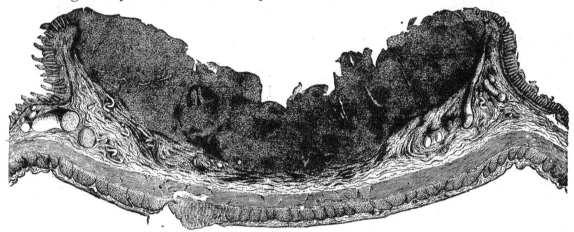

Section of a typhoid patch : Specimen 7489, microscopic collection, Army Medical Museum, magnified 13 diameters and subsequently reduced one-third.

The record of the case from which this specimen was obtained reads as follows:

Private George Hayes, Co. B, 12th U. S. Inf.; age 25; was admitted from Russell Barracks, Washington, D. C., Aug. 25, 1866, with typhoid fever. [He had been confined to the guard-house at the barracks from May 10. About August 1 he complained of diarrhœa and was excused from fatigue duty. Afterwards, symptoms of typhoid fever having appeared, he was sent to the post hospital.] On admission he was quite stupid, but could readily be aroused. On the afternoon of the 26th he became delirious and during the night required constant watching and restraint to keep him in bed. This continued until the forenoon of the 27th, when, almost complete loss of sensibility ensued. He could not swallow; an attempt was made to give him a spoonful of beef-tea, but it nearly strangled him. Heavy stupor continued until about noon of the 28th, when death took place. *Post-mortem* examination five hours after death: There was an opacity of the arachnoid at the base of the brain, with some effusion of lymph just below the medulla oblongata on the posterior portion of the spinal cord. Peyer's patches were much thickened and ulcerated, especially in the lower part of the ileum; the villi were hypertrophied and the solitary follicles enlarged to the size of peas, many of them ulcerated at their apices. The solitary follicles of the large intestine were similarly affected.

---

this enlargement there appear in the swollen tissues some cells two to four times as large as the lymphoid corpuscles, but with a larger nucleus than the latter; and sometimes this nucleus is apparently undergoing division. As intermediate forms are observed between these large cells and the lymphatic corpuscles it seems that the whole of the corpuscular mass originates in the lymphoid elements. Gradually the ordinary lymphatic corpuscles become enlarged or the enlarged cells incorporate the smaller ones, until the adenoid tissue contains only cells of the larger size, each enclosing an ovoid, transparent nucleus situated peripherally, and a variable number of spherical nuclei either isolated or in groups embedded in the substance of the cell or enclosed in a vacuole. In the centre of the tumefied gland many of the cells assume the characters of true giant-cells, each containing from ten to thirty nuclei; but the giant-cells of typhoid tumefaction differ from those of tubercle in that their stroma is provided with bloodvessels. A change was also observed to take place in some of the arterial capillaries of the impacted follicles; they became more or less obstructed by a deposit of yellowish colloid substance between the lining endothelium and an adventitial thin nucleated membrane; their walls were thickened and their lumina distorted. In addition to these appearances in the stage of tumefaction, KLEIN observed in the crypts of Lieberkühn some highly refractive greenish-

A section of a patch, constituting No. 7479 of the microscopic collection, from the case just reported, is represented below. The lymphoid elements are densely packed in the glands and adjoining stroma, and freely distributed in the mucous and submucous layers of the surrounding parts of the intestine; the vessels in the submucous tissue are distended with coagulated blood.

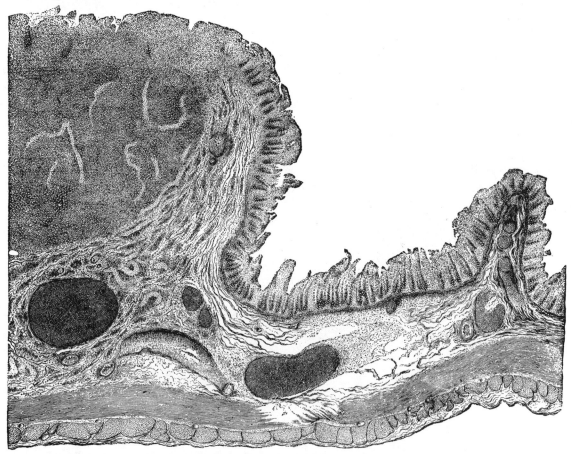

Section of a typhoid patch: Specimen 7479, microscopical collection, Army Medical Museum.

The illustrations submitted above show the affection of the interlying tissue of the submucosa to be as strongly marked as that of the glands themselves, so that had necrosis taken place it would have affected the patch as a whole, the surface continuing to break down and be carried away with the intestinal contents until the disintegrated mass was completely removed. But it is evident from the reticulated appearance of many ulcerated typhoid patches that certain parts were more susceptible to the morbid process than others. The parts specially liable to impaction and consequent necrosis were the follicular components of the patches. This is illustrated by the following photo-engraving of a specimen,

yellow corpuscles, varying from the size of a mere granular point to that of a human red-blood corpuscle. They were mostly spherical, hour-glass or kidney-shaped, and seemed to be held together by a transparent connecting substance; some of them, particularly the terminal cells, contained minute bodies resembling spores or micrococci. He regarded these as joints of the mycelial threads of an organism similar to the Crenothrix polyspora, described by Cohn in 1870 as characteristic of the vegetation discovered by him in the well-water of a district of Breslau noted for the prevalence of enteric fever. Klein found the micrococci as zooglæa masses in the lymph-spaces adjoining the tubular follicles, and also impacting the veins and venous capillaries of the affected solitary and agminated glands and of the adjacent mucous and submucous tissues; he found them also in the alvine discharges. When the tumefaction reached its height the corpuscular elements appeared to fade, break down and become absorbed or detached as a slough, while the stroma was converted into a dense felt-work of stiff highly refractive fibres. He did not consider this due wholly to compression of the bloodvessels by the surrounding accumulation of new elements and the encroachments on their lamina by the colloid deposit; on the contrary, as he had observed a fading of the corpuscular elements and other signs of a retrograde change specially marked in the neighborhood of vessels impacted with micrococci, he regarded these organisms as the chief cause of the necrotic developments.

PERPENDICULAR SECTION OF ILEUM
Showing
Typhoid thickening of a Peyer's Patch.
Magnified 12 diameters.

7454 of the microscopical series, contributed by Dr. W. W. Johnston, of Washington, D. C. The cellular elements, while freely scattered throughout the mucous layer and the adenoid tissue of the submucosa, are so densely aggregated in the glands that each is converted into a distinct and separate cellular tumor.

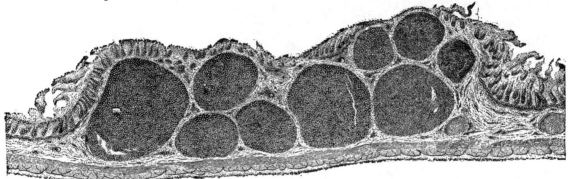

Section of a typhoid patch : Specimen 7454, microscopical collection, Army Medical Museum.

The case from which this specimen was obtained was that of a child three years of age, who had suffered for almost a week with slight fever and diarrhœa. He died apparently of syncope about an hour after swallowing, through the carelessness of attendants, eighteen sugar-coated pills each said to contain three grains of quinine. *Post-mortem* examination found the heart relaxed, the right cavities empty, the left containing fluid blood. The lungs were congested posteriorly. The liver and pancreas were normal; the Malpighian bodies of the spleen were well marked. The stomach was congested and ecchymosed; the duodenum and jejunum congested, their glands conspicuous and villi hypertrophied. In the ileum also the villi were hypertrophied; the solitary and agminated glands were progressively enlarged, and the serous surface corresponding to the bases of the latter was patched with arborescent congestion; the contents of the intestinal glands were dark and granular. The mucous membrane of the large intestine was congested and its follicles enlarged. The examination was made by Dr. D. S. Lamb, of the Army Medical Museum, Surgeon General's Office.

The plate facing page 450 further illustrates the special liability of the glands, as distinguished from that of the surrounding adenoid tissue, to impaction and disintegration. It is etched on steel from a photograph of specimen 455 of the microscopic collection, one of a series of nine perpendicular sections of the ileum, showing the ulcers to have originated in the individual glands of the patch. These sections are from the case submitted as 323 of the *post-mortem* records of the continued fevers. They show admirably the softening and discharge of the glands each by its own aperture, the gradual enlargement of the resulting cavities and the coalescence of these, embracing the whole of the patch in the irregularly ulcerated area.

To illustrate the minute anatomy of the corpuscular elements the two figures on the following page have been introduced. The lower represents the deeper portion of a section of an enlarged agminated gland, from the case which furnished the specimen delineated in the figure on this page; the upper is a view of a more superficial portion of the same section. These were drawn under a magnifying power of 700 diameters by Dr. J. C. McConnell of this office, and afterwards reduced by the photo-electrotype process to two-thirds the size of the original drawing. In the deeper portion the endothelial cells are principally confined to the vessels; the intervascular spaces are occupied by a variety of lymph corpuscles, some of which, by their aggregation, suggest a multiplication by fission, while others are possibly passing into the round, mononucleated vesicular form which is the prevailing type in the superficial parts of the affected patches. Instances suggesting the transition of the ordinary lymphoid corpuscle into the nucleated cell may be observed on the field This transition seems the more probable, as nearer the surface or in more advanced stages the true lymphoid cells are found to have been to a great extent replaced by the

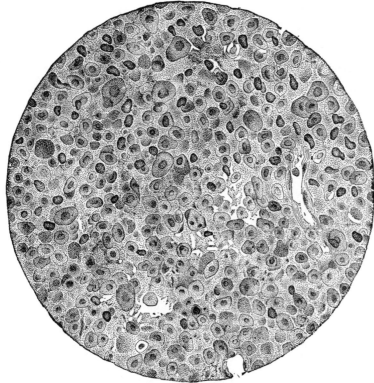

Matter from the superficial part of a typhoid patch.

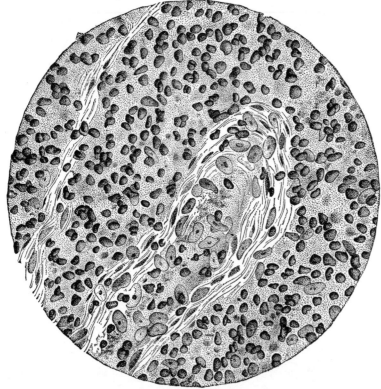

Matter from the deeper parts of a typhoid patch.

larger nucleated and granular cellular bodies. These appear to become larger, hazier in outline and ultimately to disintegrate into a molecular or granular mass.

EROSION OF THE INTESTINAL MUCOUS MEMBRANE.—In case 23 of the *post-mortem* records it is stated that the ulceration of the mucous membrane was unconnected with the state of the solitary glands. It seems that the aggregation of the corpuscular elements in the mucous membrane, aside from the situation of the closed glands, sometimes gave rise to an erosion of the membrane. The destruction of the epithelium left the underlying infiltrated tissues with an abraded surface, which became extended and deepened by the removal of the softening and disintegrating corpuscles. When such ulcers were small and shallow their mode of origin could usually be determined; but when large and deep it was often impossible to discriminate between them and those that followed the separation of a diphtheritic slough or the necrosis of a follicle and its surrounding tissue.

HEMORRHAGE, PERFORATION AND PERITONEAL INFLAMMATION.—The necrobiotic processes occurring in the diseased agminated glands, or in patches usually involving one or more of the solitary glands, were attended in their progress by an increasing liability to hemorrhage from the intestinal

Photographed by Dr. Curtis U.S.A.   on steel by H. Faber.

PERPENDICULAR SECTION OF ILEUM.
through an
ULCERATED PEYER'S PATCH.

The softened contents of several follicles have escaped from the section.

Magnified 12 diameters.

vessels and to an extension of the inflammatory action to the serous lining of the abdominal cavity. Manifestly these dangers were proportioned to the rapidity of the processes, for although the records are not sufficiently explicit to give a numerical expression to this proportion, the disorganized condition of the intestine, in many cases characterized by clinical or *post-mortem* evidence of hemorrhage or peritonitis, indicates that a sloughing of the diseased patches rather than a progressive ulceration was under observation.

In some cases, particularly such as were due wholly or chiefly to the malarial influence, the occurrence of hemorrhage may be ascribed to that extreme congestion of the parts which led to the extravasation of blood even into the submucous tissues. In cases also that were purely typhoid it is probable that the slight hemorrhages which were observed in the early period of the disease were due to congestion.* But when bleeding took place later, and especially when it was profuse, it could with propriety be ascribed to no other cause than a break in the walls of the vessels by the separating tissues of the small intestine in typhoid cases and of the large or small intestine in those due to malaria or complicated by dysenteric processes. Hemorrhage from the bowels was probably the cause of death in the cases 21, 27, 110, 176, 323, 325 and 335.

Peritoneal inflammation in continued febrile cases was sometimes due to other causes than the extension of the intestinal ulcerations. The condition of the mesenteric glands was in some instances the determining cause; this, however, may be regarded as an indirect extension from the ulcerated mucous membrane. The degeneration of the abdominal recti muscles in cases 63 and 151 probably gave rise to the peritonitis from which the patients suffered, while in 249 it resulted from the rupture of a degenerated spleen. When due, as was usually the case, to an extension of the morbid action from the ulcerated intestines, the peritoneal inflammation was generally associated with perforation of the intestinal wall. Nevertheless, a number of cases have been instanced in the analytical summary in which peritonitis was present, although none of the ulcers had perforated; and several specimens preserved in the museum show plastic exudation on the peritoneal surface in cases which had no record of perforating ulcers. But while in some cases a local peritonitis may have preceded the perforation with which general peritonitis was usually found associated after death, the sudden advent of acute pain, tenderness, vomiting, hiccough and extreme prostration indicates that the serous coat seldom became largely involved until the occurrence of perforation and extravasation of the intestinal contents. On the other hand, perforation sometimes occurred without giving rise to the symptoms or *post-mortem* appearances of peritoneal inflammation. Either the perforation was effected while the patient was in his dying agony, so that there was no time for the development of the morbid appearances that generally attend extravasation of the intestinal contents, as may have been the case in 32, or the adhesion of contiguous serous surfaces strengthened the point of impending rupture and limited the area of inflammation by preventing communication with the peritoneal cavity, as appears to have been the case in 385.

From what has been said of the circumscribed character of the diseased processes in typhoid, as compared with the extent and diffusion of the hyperæmia in the cases attributed to malaria, it is not surprising that perforation should have proved so frequent a result in the former and so rare in the latter. Case 367 is the only example of perforation in which typhoid ulceration of the patches of Peyer was not discovered at the *post-mortem* exam-

---

*See *supra*, p. 294.

ination.   Forty-three cases of perforation have been submitted to analysis, and as these
occurred in three hundred and eighty-nine cases of continued fever, perforation took place in
11 per cent. of the cases.   But if the sixty-three malarial cases which furnished but one
instance of perforated bowel be withdrawn from the calculation the frequency of this accident in probably typhoid cases will be increased to 12.9 per cent.   MURCHISON, as the result
of a tabulation of 1,721 cases recorded by various observers, found that perforation occurred
in 196 or in 11.38 per cent.*   In twenty of the forty-three cases the site of the perforation
was reported to have been the patches of Peyer; in eighteen the ileum; in two the small
intestine; in one the intestine; in one the cæcum, and in one the sigmoid flexure of the
colon.   It is evident from these figures that ulceration of the agminated glands was generally, and of the solitary glands rarely, the cause of the perforation, notwithstanding the
frequency with which the latter were affected by the morbid processes.   Had perforation at
the site of the solitary glands been a common occurrence it would have been reported in the
large intestine with greater frequency than twice, cases 33 and 300, in forty-three cases.

As the sloughing or ulcerative action progressed at so many points in the same intestine it not unfrequently happened that more than one break was found at the *post-mortem*
examination.   Thus, in the series of pure typhoid cases there were two perforations in 16,
three in 32, five in 19 and several in 17, 18 and 50.   Furthermore, on account of the irregularity of the advance of the destructive process in the same area of ulceration it sometimes
happened that more than one break was found on its floor, as may be seen in one of the
ulcers represented in the plate facing page 382.   The specimen, 370, Army Medical Museum,
from which this was photographed was taken from the patient whose case appears as 159
of the *post-mortem* series already submitted.   The clinical record says that this soldier had
well-marked symptoms of typhoid fever; he was delirious and extremely prostrated, and there
was much distention and tenderness of the abdomen, but no diarrhœa until a few days before
death.   Five of the ulcers in the ileum had perforated.   Five specimens, 369–373, Army
Medical Museum, from this case have been preserved.   The first, taken from high up in the
ileum, presents five irregular ulcerations from one-quarter to half an inch in diameter,
penetrating nearly through the muscular coat.   The second, represented in the plate to which
attention has been invited, shows three irregular oval ulcers, each about an inch in diameter,
their edges thickened, their bases formed by the muscular coat except where perforation has
been effected; the perforation in the upper ulcer is small, but a little to the left is a point
at which a break through the serous coat was about to take place; the middle ulcer presents
an oval perforation nearly half an inch long, having shreds of the peritoneal coat attached
to its margin, while immediately above the perforation is a point where the serous coat has
been exposed; the lower ulcer presents in its centre an oval patch one inch in its long diameter, in the upper part of which the serous coat retains its position, forming the floor of the
cavity, while in its lower portion this coat has given way, forming four oval apertures separated from each other by shreds of the serous membrane; the solitary follicles are slightly
prominent, and there is pseudomembranous exudation on the peritoneal surface of the specimen.   The third and fourth specimens, 371 and 372, present ulcers similar to those represented in the plate, one of which in each instance has perforated the intestinal wall; some

---

* His table shows that this undesirable result was of more frequent occurrence in the experience of English observers than in that of Continental
physicians.   Thus, of 412 fatal cases recorded by himself, BRISTOWE, JENNER and WATERS, perforation was found in 80 cases or 19.41 per cent.; of 270
cases by the French observers, LOUIS, BRETONNEAU, CHOMEL, MONTAULT and FORGET, perforation was discovered in 25 or 9.25 per cent., and of 1,039 cases
by the German observers, GRIESINGER, HOFFMANN, LEBERT and others, 91 or 8.75 per cent. had the intestine perforated.   See his treatise, p. 566.

minute punched-out ulcerations, corresponding to the solitary glands, are also seen in these sections. The last specimen, 373, taken from just above the valve, has the mucous membrane considerably thickened and studded with enlarged solitary follicles; there are also several irregular ulcerations, one of which measures fully two inches in its long diameter, the floors formed by the muscular coat of the intestine. These specimens may be accepted as illustrations of the fact that the part of the ileum usually perforated in typhoid fever lies more frequently some distance above the valve than immediately adjacent to it.

Perforation of the site of the agminated glands is also illustrated by the plate facing page 343. The specimen, 452, Army Medical Museum, from which this was photographed was obtained from the patient whose case is recorded as 43 of the *post-mortem* records of the continued fevers. In this instance the perforated part of the ileum was not far above the ileo-cæcal valve. The aperture, small and oval, appears near the centre of a large irregularly shaped ulcer with overhanging edges and a smooth and even floor, formed by the muscular coat; its margins are as sharply defined as if the piece had been punched out. The specimen shows also some small ulcers of the solitary glands situated between the transverse mucous folds and extending through the submucous tissue to the muscular tunic, while on its peritoneal surface is a coating of pseudomembranous lymph.

The inflammatory condition of the ileum in a case of death from peritonitis consequent on perforation is well shown on the chromo-lithograph facing page 391. The specimen, 147, Army Medical Museum, from which this drawing was made was taken from the case recorded above as 224 of the *post-mortem* records. The peritoneal cavity contained a large quantity of pus and serum. The serous membrane was generally thickened and congested; over the intestine in some parts it was of a brilliant red color, in other parts deep red or almost black. The ileum for five feet above the cæcum was more or less ulcerated, and at a point about eighteen inches above the valve it was perforated. The drawing on the right of the plate shows the mucous surface in the vicinity of this point: The perforation, large and oval, occupies nearly the whole of the site of the original ulceration, and the mucous membrane, of a livid-brown color, lies in closely set transverse folds and shows several ulcerated patches above and below the perforated point. The drawing on the left of the plate represents the serous surface of the same specimen: The intensely injected peritoneum is coated in yellowish patches with pseudomembranous lymph.

REPARATION OF THE INTESTINAL ULCERATIONS.—But when, instead of extension and penetration through the walls of the intestine, a reparative process was initiated after the removal of the necrosed and disintegrated tissues, the vessels adjacent to the lesions became enlarged and the ulcerated cavities filled with granulations over which the mucous membrane advanced from the edges to the centre as a thin and glistening covering. The area of the cicatrized surface was much less than that of the original ulceration, as the mucous membrane became drawn over it by the subsequent contraction of the connective tissue of the granulations. In the solitary glands the cicatrix appeared as a smooth central spot around which the mucous membrane between the tubular follicles was thrown into radiating ridges, giving the whole a stellate appearance, which has been illustrated by the photograph of specimen 603, Army Medical Museum, facing page 528 of the Second Part of this work. The contraction of cicatrized patches of Peyer was manifested by puckering of the surrounding membrane and occasionally by the disposition of the transverse folds in the neighborhood of each to radiate from it. Cicatrices left in the intestines after the healing of ulcerated patches have been illustrated by five plates,—one a chromo-lithograph of a recent specimen, and the others photographic reproductions of preserved specimens.

Nothing is known of the history of the case represented by the chromo-lithograph. The plate facing this page shows the lower portion of the ileum and part of the cæcum. On the mucous surface of the former are a number of oval ulcers similar to those frequently left after typhoid fever; the cream-colored membrane is injected in reddish patches; the colon, also somewhat injected, shows several follicular ulcers.

The photographic reproduction of specimen 597, Army Medical Museum, facing page 456, shows a portion of the ileum with the ileo-cæcal valve and part of the cæcum. A Peyerian patch, one and a half inches above the valve, presents an oval cicatrix which is somewhat obscured by the pseudomembrane covering the whole of the mucous surface; there are some small ulcerations near the valve. This specimen was taken from a soldier who died of dysentery, apparently subsequent to his recovery from an attack of typhoid fever.

Private William Henry, Co. G, 8th N. Y. Cav.; age 18; was admitted July 22, 1865, with chronic diarrhœa. [This man appears on the records of the Augur hospital, near Alexandria, Va., as admitted from regimental hospital June 24 with acute rheumatism, and sent to Slough hospital July 22.] He died on the 29th. *Post-mortem* examination: Body not much emaciated. The lungs were collapsed, of a gray color and without pleuritic adhesions. The heart was normal. Externally the liver was clay-colored; internally it presented the nutmeg appearance. The spleen was lake-red on section. The sigmoid flexure was folded down against the anterior wall of the pelvis, to which it adhered by a layer of yellow semi-transparent lymph. Portions of the ileum were also adherent, the adhesions enclosing a little yellow serum in the lower part of the pelvic cavity; the peritoneal surface of the last foot of the ileum was much injected and its mucous membrane coated with whitish pseudomembrane; Peyer's patches were tumid and reticulated. The large intestine was thickened and its mucous lining, which was dirty and blackish, presented a number of shallow irregular ulcers and patches of pseudomembrane.—*Act. Ass't Surg. W. C. Minor, Slough Hospital, Alexandria, Va.*

Specimen 459, Army Medical Museum, which is represented in the plate facing page 404, is from the case reported as 300 of the *post-mortem* records of the continued fevers. The large intestine was said to have been thickened and ulcerated, and in the sigmoid flexure perforated, while the mucous lining of the ileum was eroded and the agminated and solitary glands ulcerated. The portion of the ileum represented was taken from just above the ileo-cæcal valve. It shows cicatrices in four of the patches of Peyer,—in the upper two the process has been completed; in the lower two the ulcers are not wholly cicatrized. The solitary glands are enlarged and prominent. Sections of the follicles from this specimen have been presented in the plates facing pages 326 and 328 of the Second Part of this History as illustrative of the follicular changes in acute diarrhœa.

The plate facing page 401 represents a portion of the ileum from the tract of the valvulæ conniventes, taken from the patient whose case is reported as 298 of the *post-mortem* records of the continued fevers. The record states that the mucous membrane of the ileum was of a grayish-slate color, its villi hypertrophied and dotted at their apices with black pigment, and that the patches of Peyer were in every stage of cicatrization, the ulcers smooth and the gut around them puckered. On the specimen represented hypertrophied villi are seen on all parts except the cicatrices, which are marked by their smoothness and the breaks in the transverse folds of the mucous membrane. Three sections of a cicatrized patch from this ileum, constituting specimens 470–472 of the microscopic collection, show it to consist of condensed connective tissue, embedded in which are a few of the original glands of the locality.

The contraction of the cicatrix is so strongly marked in the plate facing page 458 that the interrupted and adjacent valvulæ tend to radiate from the newly-formed tissue;

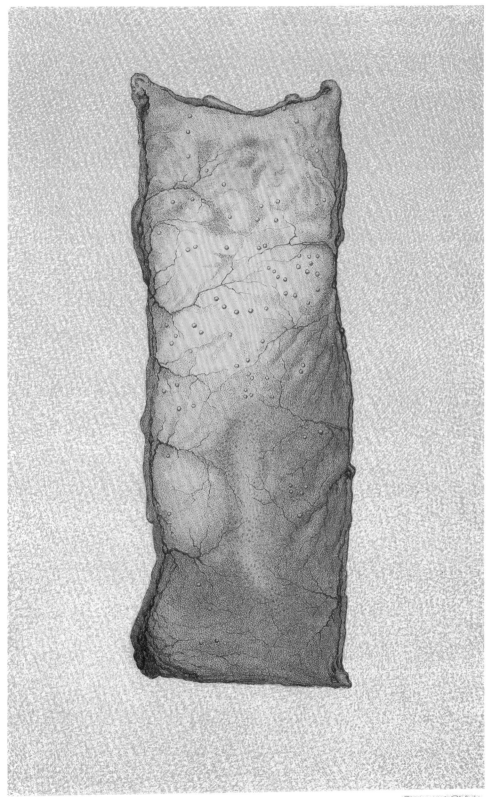

PIGMENTATION of the ILEUM
in CAMP FEVERS.

some small tubercles are situated on the peritoneal surface. The specimen, 887, Army Medical Museum, which furnished this illustration has, unfortunately, no recorded history.

PIGMENTATION OF THE INTESTINAL LINING.—There remain for consideration the pigmentary deposits sometimes observed in the intestinal walls. This pigment was seen only on the fresh intestine; it disappeared under the treatment adopted for the preservation of the specimen. Usually it occurred in streaks or patches of a gray, greenish, bluish or other dark color, affecting the general surface of the mucous membrane of the small or large intestine. Sometimes it was aggregated in the apices of the hypertrophied villi of the small intestine, giving a dark tinge to its plush-like surface. Large accumulations were found in the solitary follicles and in the glands of the patches of Peyer, constituting what was known as the *shaven-beard* appearance in the affected area of the latter.

The diffused streaks of pigment on the general surface of the mucous membrane consisted of minute brown granules deposited in the lymphoid cells of the stroma between the follicles of Lieberkühn, and most abundant about midway between the epithelial layer and the muscle of Brücke. The deposits in the solitary and aggregated glands consisted of similar granules in the cells of their parenchyma. But in all these instances the pigment was occasionally observed in larger agglomerations, situated apparently between the corpuscular elements rather than within them.

Dark colorations of the mucous membrane had long been recognized as due to antecedent hyperæmic conditions. LOUIS regarded them as vestiges of an extinct enteritis, and assigned a similar origin and meaning to the dark color of the mesenteric glands after typhoid. But the shaven-beard patches were wholly misunderstood by our medical officers during and after the war. They were regarded as pathognomonic of the malarial form of typho-malarial fever. Indeed a chromo-lithograph, reproduced in the present volume, and facing page 460, was published in Circular No. 6, Surgeon General's Office, Washington, D. C., Nov. 1, 1865, as an illustration of the characteristic lesion of this form of fever.* The plate represents the congested condition of the membrane, the injection of the vessels, the enlargement of the solitary follicles and the shaven-beard appearance of the patches of Peyer. The case from which this specimen was taken is reported as 89 of the *post-mortem* records of the continued fevers.

No further light was thrown upon this pigmentation of the closed glands of the intestine until, in his remarks on typho-malarial fever, read before the Section of Medicine of the International Medical Congress, Philadelphia, 1876, Dr. WOODWARD gave an outline of what he considered to be the clinical course of the malarial form of typho-malarial fever, to which was added an acknowledgment that *post-mortem* examination of the diseased intestines in these cases showed no other lesion than those which were the invariable accompaniment

---

* "The most characteristic specimens may be thus described: In the fresh intestine as received at the Museum the ileum presents patches of deep congestion of variable extent; the solitary follicles, enlarged to the size of large pinheads, are frequently black with pigment deposits. The Peyer's patches sometimes quite healthy are more generally the seat of pigment deposits in the individual follicles composing the patch, which appears of a gray color dotted over with blackish points, presenting a resemblance to the freshly-shaven chin. The name "shaven-beard appearance" has been quite currently bestowed upon this condition. In other cases the Peyer's patches are somewhat thickened and occasionally as much so as in ordinary cases of enteric fever. In the preparations as preserved in the Museum the color of the pieces, including that of the pigment deposit, gradually disappears. The enlarged solitary follicles and the alterations in the Peyer's patches are, however, well preserved. The solitary follicles are not ulcerated in these cases except rarely some of the largest, which may present a minute point of ulceration on the apex. The form of fever from which these specimens are obtained is that which attracted attention in 1862, under the designation of Chickahominy fever, but which before and since has prevailed whenever our armies have operated in malarial regions. It is a continued fever which presents also a more or less decidedly remittent type at the beginning at least. It is accompanied by diarrhœa and abdominal tenderness, but usually without tympanites. Cerebral and pulmonary complications are common as in ordinary enteric fever. Enlargement of the spleen is frequent and often excessive. The fever usually lasts from three to five weeks and terminates in a lingering and protracted convalescence. This variety I have proposed to designate as the Malarial form of Typho-malarial Fever."—Dr. WOODWARD in Circular No. 6, p. 140.

of a smart intestinal catarrh, to wit: Patches of congestion, enlargement, with sometimes ulceration and pigmentation of the solitary follicles, and frequently a slight tumefaction of the patches of Peyer with such pigmentary deposits as gave them the shaven-beard appearance.[*]

The next reference to the meaning of these accumulations is contained in the Second Part of this work,[†] published in 1879. At this stage of his investigation Dr. WOODWARD showed officially the connection of the pigment with those hyperæmic conditions of the membrane that are manifested clinically by continued diarrhœal attacks. In view of the testimony then presented there appears no ground for doubting the origin of the deposits in minute extravasations into the mucous membrane or in the plugging of its capillary loops. They were of more common occurrence in the patches of Peyer than in the solitary follicles, notwithstanding the frequent and decided enlargement of the latter. The former, although seldom much swollen, were often more distinct than normal from participation in the general hyperæmia of the mucous and submucous tissues. Occasionally, indeed, a diarrhœal case presented such morbid changes, including ulceration of the agminated glands, as were suggestive of the presence of typhoid fever: In the plate facing page 300 is a thickened patch which appears as a dark elliptical spot two inches long by an inch in its transverse measurement, its surface not materially elevated above that of the surrounding membrane, but thicker than normal, and by transmitted light more opaque than any of the other patches observed in this subject. In the plate facing page 302 is a plaque which shows a greater advance towards a morbid condition; its surface, which is not materially raised above the surrounding level, is marked by narrow broken lines studded with hypertrophied villi similar to those on the general surface of the specimen, and between these are irregular areas which, being destitute of villi, seem depressed below the adjacent level and give the patch a somewhat reticulated appearance; in its centre is a shallow oval ulcer an eighth of an inch in diameter; half an inch below this, near the right margin, is a similar ulcer, and a third may be observed near the upper end of the patch. But in cases of non-specific intestinal congestion pigmented villi and the shaven-beard appearance of the patches were more frequent *post-mortem* observations than tumefaction and ulceration of the glands of Peyer.

These results of a completed study of the accumulated material relating to diarrhœa necessarily deprived this pigmentation of the patches of its assumed significance in connection with typho-malarial fever. Dr. WOODWARD was prompt to recognize this fact. He observed:[‡] "The discussion of the interesting question of the relation of the lesion just described to a particular form of malarial fever must be postponed to a subsequent chapter; it must suffice at present to express the conviction that the intestinal lesion in the class of fever cases referred to presents nothing by which it can be distinguished from the lesions observed in other cases in which the febrile phenomena are not well marked or at least present no specific characters."

This intimates that there is no specific intestinal lesion by which the malarial form of typho-malarial fever may be distinguished from the malarial fever which, beginning as an intermittent or a remittent, becomes, like typhoid, subcontinuous, and in its later stages is attended with typhoid, *i. e.*, adynamic symptoms.

Had Dr. WOODWARD been spared to complete his work one or other of two courses was open to him in the discussion of his malarial group of typho-malarial fevers: Either to relegate this group to the class of purely malarial fevers or to argue that typhoid fever is non-

---

[*] See page 35 of the pamphlet, Philadelphia, 1876.   [†] See pp. 298 *et seq.*   [‡] Page 302.

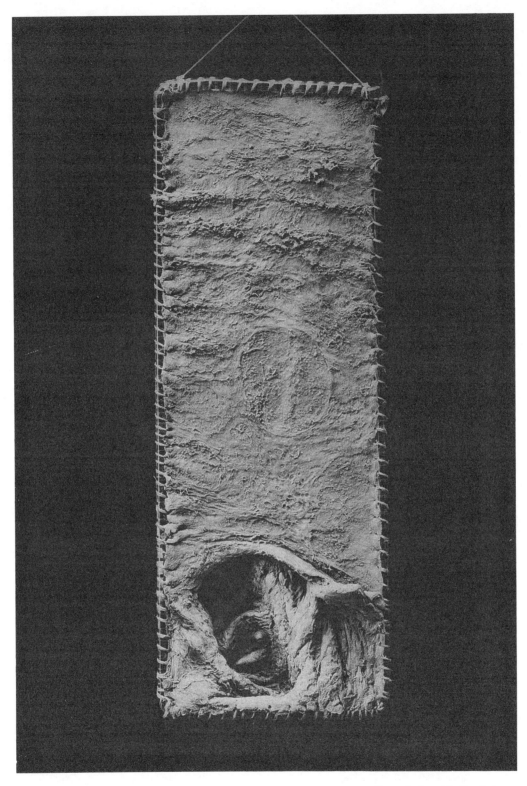

Heliotype. *James R. Osgood & Co., Boston.*

CICATRIX OF AN ULCERATED PEYER'S PATCH.

No. 597. MEDICAL SECTION.

specific in its character and may supervene on an intestinal congestion such as may be due to the incidence of the malarial poison when sufficiently prolonged to involve the patches of Peyer, or in the presence of constitutional abnormities or peculiarities in the environment tending to the development of that typhoid state which is the usual accompaniment of an ulcerated condition of these patches.

It is needless to say that the correct course appears to the writer to be that first indicated, as he has been led to adopt it by a clinical and pathological analysis, the various processes of which have been carried on in full view of the reader of the preceding pages. Moreover, if the argument be continued on the basis of the similarity between the condition of the patches in intestinal catarrh and in the malarial group of the typho-malarial fevers it is equally conclusive: The cases in question were either examples of a subcontinued malarial fever with adynamic symptoms, showing on *post-mortem* examination—if the intestines were implicated, which was by no means the case in every instance—the anatomical lesions which characterized cases of intestinal catarrh and not those of typhoid fever, or they were cases of typhoid fever so modified by the presence of malaria that the full action on the aggregated glands was prevented. But while, as has been shown in the course of this report, there is ample testimony in support of the former alternative, the latter is based on the assumption that typhoid fever may be present without showing its existence by its usual action on the aggregated glands of the intestine. If this assumption were allowed, typhoid fever, as known to the medical profession for the past sixty years, would itself cease to exist, and in the clinical and pathological chaos that would result it would manifestly be useless to attempt the identification of a typho-malarial fever when its typhoid element was acknowledged to be unrecognizable. Fortunately the assumption is suggested by facts which may be used instead to strengthen and sustain views that are in accord with our present knowledge and past experience: Undoubted malarial fever may assume clinically the appearance of typhoid, while at the *post-mortem* examination the lesions of typhoid are not present. The general experience that has found a particular lesion in all cases of typhoid naturally concludes that in these malarial cases there was no typhoid element. It requires a forced rendition of the facts to construe them into a proof of the modification of the typhoid lesion by the coexisting malaria. If malaria exert such an interference in one case it should do so to a greater or less extent in all the cases of typhoid which it complicates; yet the *post-mortem* records that have been submitted contain many cases in which, although the malarial complication was strongly marked clinically, the typhoid lesions were as distinct as in a specially selected case of unmodified typhoid. It must therefore be concluded that the absence of the typhoid lesion implies an absence of the febrile condition which is its cause, and not an interference with the development of morbid changes in glands that are known to be not recessarily affected by the poison which is assumed to have caused the interference.

The only course open for an attempt to sustain the malarial group of the typho-malarial fevers in their position of modified typhoid fevers is to deny the specific character of typhoid fever and show that there is a more intimate relationship between malarial and typhoid fevers than has hitherto been allowed. This involves the subversion of the generally accepted views of typhoid fever and the establishment of typho-malarial fever as the typical and central figure of the subcontinued fever series, which becomes paroxysmal or continued according as certain inflammatory processes are restricted to the general surface of the intestinal mucous membrane or invade the substance of the agminated glands, results which are due not to specific differences in the febrile cause but to accidental circumstances pertaining to the constitution, age and hygienic surroundings of the affected individuals. To sustain this position in the face of our present knowledge of the malarial and typhoid febrile conditions is impossible. The natural history of the causes of these conditions must be shown to be wholly at variance with our present conceptions before any attempt of this kind can be other than a work of the imagination.

If the cases that have been instanced in the analytical summary as presenting pigmentation of the mucous membrane of the intestine be examined it will be found that, where the patient's condition for some time before death is mentioned, diarrhœal attacks form invariably a part of his history. Notable pigmentation was of much greater frequency in the continued malarial cases than in those which presented a distinct typhoid element; in the former pigmentation existed in nearly one-third of the cases, and in the greater proportion of these the deposits were specially marked in the patches of Peyer. This corresponds with what has already been observed concerning the intensity of the congestion in such cases. In the true typho-malarial and the mixed series the proportion of pigmented cases was much smaller; while in the typhoid series there occurred no instance in which deposits had formed in the patches, and but two in which the solitary glands were their site, although the mucous membrane of the colon presented in five cases an alteration of color which must be ascribed to an antecedent hyperæmia. This absence of the shaven-beard appearance from the patches in typhoid is susceptible of explanation on the one hand by the rarity of that intense congestion which tends to relief by extravasation, and on the other by the removal of each ecchymosed spot by subsequent ulceration or sloughing.

The prevalence of the pigmented intestine in the continued malarial fevers that were reported as typhoid or typho-malarial is worthy of remark as compared with its infrequency in the fatal cases of paroxysmal fever. Thus, while, as has been stated, 31.7 per cent. of the former presented pigmentary deposits in which the aggregated glands were generally participants, only one, case 98, of twenty-five paroxysmal cases, in which the intestines were morbidly affected, had the patches of Peyer blackened, and in only two, 57 and 94, was the mucous membrane of the large intestine the site of these deposits. It will be remembered, however, that death in the paroxysmal cases occurred usually after a short illness, while in the continued malarial cases that were reported as typhoid or typho-malarial the fatal attack was prolonged. Time was afforded in the latter for the development of a pigmented condition, which in the former was represented by an existing congestion such as led to ecchymoses in the pernicious cases 97–99, or gave a deeper color to the apices of the solitary glands in 69, or produced in 59 an extravasation of blood. If these cases are taken into consideration as presenting the earlier stages of the development of the pigmented condition it will be found that the proportion of such cases in the paroxysmal fevers did not differ from that in the continued malarial series.

THE MESENTERIC GLANDS.—The writers of the *post-mortem* records seldom gave a detailed account of the condition of the mesenteric glands; but enough has been said to show that their affection was similar to that observed by LOUIS* in his classical typhoid

---

* See note, p. 426, *supra*. ROKITANSKY, *op. cit., supra*, page 443, describes the mesenteric glands as congested and swollen during the initial stage of acute catarrhal inflammation of the ileum. Their tumefaction is progressive with that of the closed glands of the intestinal lining. They attain the size of a bean or pigeon's egg and sometimes that of a hen's egg, those nearest the bowel showing the most enlargement; their greatest size is reached during the congestion attending the destruction of the intestinal follicles, when they are often so soft as to fluctuate under pressure. They appear to degenerate into a medullary substance, sometimes firm and white, at other times softer and of a grayish-red or pale-red color. The areolar tissue enveloping them shows a varicose vascular network; occasionally their serous covering becomes inflamed and perhaps ruptured, giving rise to hemorrhage and peritoneal inflammation, and their parenchyma is converted into a yellow or yellowish-red, thick and diffluent mass. When the necrosed

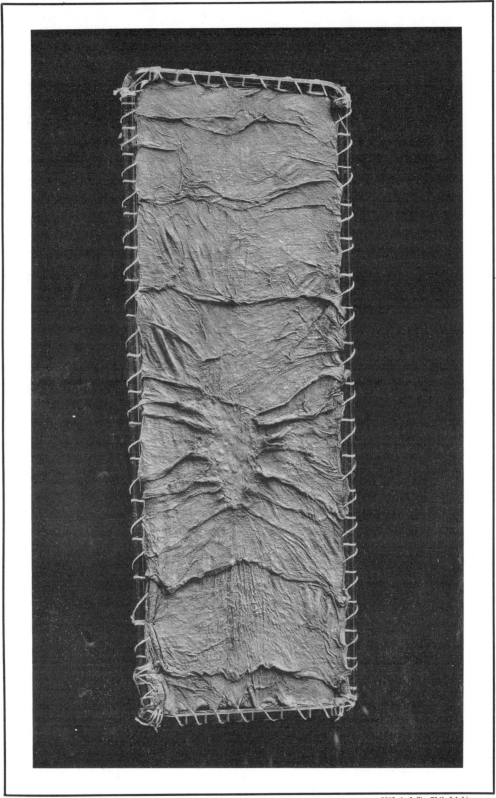

Am. Photo-Relief Printing Co., 1002 Arch St., Philadelphia.

CICATRIX OF AN ULCERATED PEYER'S PATCH.

No. 887. MEDICAL SECTION.

cases. Their increasing tumefaction and redness, their dark coloration and subsequent softening, absorption and pigmentation as the general result, with rarely the formation of pus and its escape into the peritoneal cavity, or its inspissation and transformation into a calcareous deposit, have all been illustrated by the cases submitted. The occasional exceptions to the general rule, that the most severely affected glands were those in direct communication with the diseased patches of Peyer, have also been noted in the analytical summary. Sections of the diseased glands have been prepared in the Museum showing the occlusion of the lymph passages by corpuscular elements differing in no respect from those found in the closed glands of the intestinal mucous membrane.*

THE SPLEEN.—The enlargement, softening and occasional darkening of the spleen found by LOUIS in his typhoid cases were observed also by our medical officers in their fatal cases of that disease; and as he found one instance of diminished volume in his forty-six cases, so in the fifty cases that have been reported in this work there also occurs an exceptional case of this character.†

In a majority of their continued malarial cases our medical officers reported the spleen as large, soft and darkened, and their records bear testimony to the existence of more actively destructive changes in these cases than in those of the typhoid series. Thus, in three of the cases noted in the anatomical summary there were purulent or caseous cysts or circumscribed sero-purulent infiltrations, with escape in one instance of the morbid product into the cavity of the peritoneum. Specimens 325 and 326, Army Medical Museum, two perpendicular sections of the spleen, from a case recorded as 87 of this series, show the organ

portions of the intestinal patches have been removed the mesenteric glands begin to decrease in size, though still retaining an abnormal dark bluish-red color; but by the time that the intestinal ulcers are healed the glands have regained their normal size, and are frequently smaller than usual, wilted, tough, pale and often pigmented. The swollen glands are, according to HARLEY, almost entirely constituted of corpuscles of various sizes, for the most part spherical and nucleated; the most numerous average $\frac{1}{3600}$ of an inch in diameter; the larger present well-formed nuclei and average $\frac{1}{2300}$ of an inch. HOFFMANN states that the locality of the glands most deeply implicated does not always correspond with that of the bowel in like condition, for in some instances the mesenteric glands may be decidedly enlarged while the intestinal affection is slight, and in others the tumefied glands may be found higher up and away from the seat of the intestinal disease. The tumefaction is often so rapid that in a few days the glands acquire double their natural size, and by the time the disease has reached its height it is not uncommon to find them as large as a hazelnut or walnut, and in some instances even as large as a hen's egg. In the initial stage they are hyperæmic; internally the periphery is of a deeper tinge than the remainder of the section, but more frequently the interior is of a uniform rose-color, or of this color mottled with lighter shades of the same tint or with gray. The coloration and swelling continue for some time, and then decline; as a rule the fading of the medullary substance proceeds towards the cortical portion, and the latter commonly retains its pronounced red coloring after the centre has become pale-gray; gradually, however, the redness of the entire gland disappears and the tumefaction becomes reduced, constituting the most simple and frequent mode of resolution. In many cases, however, the glands take on a yellowish or even an intense yellow color, developing foci of puriform softening, mostly small except in the centre, where they often acquire greater dimensions. When the softening is of limited extent absorption readily takes place; but when considerable the liquid components disappear leaving a dry, cheese-like, yellow mass in which, at a later period, calcareous matter may be deposited. All the structural elements of the gland are subject to enlargement, the stroma as well as the other constituents; large cells, resembling those found in Peyer's patches, are observed in all parts of the glandular tissue, but most abundantly in the lymph sinuses. Atrophy may follow both forms of resolution. As the changes coincide in general with those in the intestinal follicles, and as both are developed simultaneously and in corresponding localities, HOFFMANN suggests a pathological connection between the processes,—that the changes in the mesenteric glands are caused by matter brought into them by the lymph-current. According to RIND-FLEISCH the histological characters of the primary infiltration are faithfully reproduced in the mesenteric glands. Catarrhal swelling is followed by excessive enlargement from medullary infiltration. The follicles and their prolongations are the principal seats of the morbid changes, while the lymph sinuses and the connective are only moderately infiltrated. The vessels are enlarged and many of the capillary loops plugged. The trabeculæ become three or four times thicker than usual, the nodal points especially are swollen and the nuclei vesicular. Proliferation, chiefly fissiparous, but also endogenous, so fills every space, not already occupied by the vessels, with corpuscular elements that it is impossible to inject the lymphatic path of the gland. Degeneration and absorption follow, leaving the gland shrunken and sometimes pigmented by extravasations that had occurred during the antecedent congestion. Cheesy necrosis is regarded as a rare phenomenon. Peritonitis may be caused by the resulting suppurative inflammation, or the pus may become inspissated, calcareous and encysted. The changes observed in the mesenteric glands, according to KLEIN, were similar to those described as occurring in the closed glands of the mucous membrane of the intestine; micrococci, formed in the proper glandular tissue and in the capillary branches, were always connected with the necrotic changes.

* See supra, page 449.

† ROKITANSKY describes the spleen in typhoid as sometimes enlarged to six times its normal size, its pulp consisting of a soft pultaceous matter, cherry-red or pale-red in color and similar to that of the typhoid substance of the mesenteric glands; occasionally the splenic parenchyma becomes reduced to a fluctuating mass. HARLEY detected under the higher powers only "minute granular corpuscles, fibre-cells and molecular branched fibres." HOFFMANN says that changes in the spleen are as regularly observed in autopsies in typhoid fever cases as changes in the intestines, and among them an increase of volume is the most frequent and striking. Nevertheless, in every epidemic, cases occur in which this condition is not present, particularly in persons over forty years of age, in whom expansion is restrained by the firmness and thickness of the stroma; similar restraints are imposed when a capsule has become thickened and unyielding as a result of previous disease, and when extensive adhesions between the organ and its surroundings have previously taken place; but it sometimes happens that in young persons splenic enlargement is wanting, even in the culminating stage of the disease, without the appearance of any conditions that might be considered as explanatory. In general the spleen in typhoid gains rapidly in size at an early period, and continues to increase until the height of the disease is reached, when it remains without change for a time, and then subsides by a slower process than that

enlarged and considerably infiltrated with metastatic masses. When fresh this spleen was so soft as to be easily torn with the finger; it was partly bluish-black in color and partly of a livid blood-color, while the so-called metastatic masses were bright yellow; these foci consisted of granular matter in which were embedded the partly disintegrated anatomical elements of normal splenic structure. Nevertheless the proportion of cases in which the spleen was small or normal in size and consistence was greater in the malarial than in the typhoid cases. Similar conditions were found in the fatal cases of the paroxysmal fevers.* The spleen presented abnormal changes in 93.3 per cent. of those typhoid cases in which its condition was observed and recorded and in only 65.4 per cent. of the malarial cases. In the typho-malarial and mixed series a medium as to frequency is found, the former furnishing 81 and the latter 75 per cent.; but although the proportion of abnormities in these cases was greater than in the continued malarial series, the proportion of cases in which a pulta-ceous or purulent degeneration had taken place was not so great.

The LIVER in our typhoid cases differed from that of LOUIS's observations in the very general presence of an augmentation of volume: Although noted in but five of his forty-six cases, enlargement is mentioned in a majority of such of our records as call attention to abnormities. The somewhat enlarged, pale, perhaps fatty, softened and sometimes con-gested state of the liver in typhoid was present also, to a certain extent, in the malarial cases, a result probably due in both instances to the action of the disease-poisons; for since these manifest their operation by similar pyrexial symptoms and disordered secre-tions a similarity in the secondary morbid lesions might naturally be expected. But among the malarial cases was found a larger proportion of congested livers, and instances of adhe-sion and suppuration give evidence that the inflammatory conditions were more intense as well as more general; there was also found that darkening or bronzing of its substance which was observed in the paroxysmal but not in the typhoid fevers. The liver was altered in eighteen of twenty-nine typhoid cases in which its condition was observed and recorded, i. e., in 62 per cent., in thirty-two of fifty-three cases, or 60 per cent. of the malarial, in twenty-six of forty-five cases, or 58 per cent. of the typho-malarial, and in eighty-seven of one hundred and forty-two, or 61 per cent. of the mixed series. The bronzing and occa-sional disorganization found in continued malarial cases were found also in the typho-mala-rial and mixed cases.

---

by which its augmentation was effected. While enlarging the organ is tense, firm and uniformly dark bluish-red, with the trabecular structure barely seen in the outswelling pulp-mass; but as the disease advances its substance becomes softer, the pulp assumes a pultaceous character and the stroma has less cohesion. Later the capsule becomes wrinkled, white, cloudy and thickened, while the spleen itself diminishes in size. These changes depend upon an alteration of the blood-contents and of the constituent elements of the spleen. In their entire character they exhibit great similarity to those observed in the lymphatic system of the small intestine. There appear single nucleated lymph-cells of normal size and larger, together with great numbers of large many-nucleated cells, which latter compose in great part the contents of the venous sinuses and are profusely distributed in the larger splenic veins. This is especially the case in the commencing stage of the splenic swelling; in the second and third weeks the large cells are found in vast numbers in a state of partial division, while in later stages the single nucleated cells preponderate. The original lymph-cells are supposed to be the source of the cellular development. Coincident with the increased cell formation the trabeculæ become extended and the vessels tense. The Malpighian bodies are mostly distinct, somewhat enlarged and well supplied with blood; at first they are abundantly filled with cells, among which are a moderate number of the larger many-nucleated corpuscles. As long as cell proliferation continues active the firmness of the splenic tissue is maintained, but when it begins to subside, about the end of the third week, the tissue becomes soft. With the evacuation of the cell-structures the tension and volume of the splenic substance diminish and the larger trabeculæ contract; but the fibrous reticulum and capsule remain thickened during the further progress of the resolu-tion. The cell elements leave the spleen by the vessels leading from the organ; but as comparatively few of the large many-nucleated cells are seen in those vessels it is inferred that, considering their abundance in the splenic tissue, they are broken up into small cells in the efferent channels. At this period dark-red and even black hemorrhagic foci are occasionally found scattered throughout the substance of the organ. Infarction is generally con-fined to one portion, a wedge-shaped mass, having its base directed towards the splenic periphery. So long as the infarcted portion continues firm its tissue preserves its ability to undergo a progressive fading, shrinkage and isolation from the surrounding parts by a dense capsule of connective tissue; but when the infarction is large it is prone to become softened into a pultaceous grayish-brown mass. If the capsular tissue has already been formed the portion within it, as a rule, alone becomes disorganized, but if it is unformed the softening process may extend beyond the infarction and lead to peritonitis. According to KLEIN, the cells in the distended blood-paths of the spleen in typhoid cases resemble lymphoid cells changed in the same manner as those of the intestinal and mesenteric glands.

    * See ante, page 146.

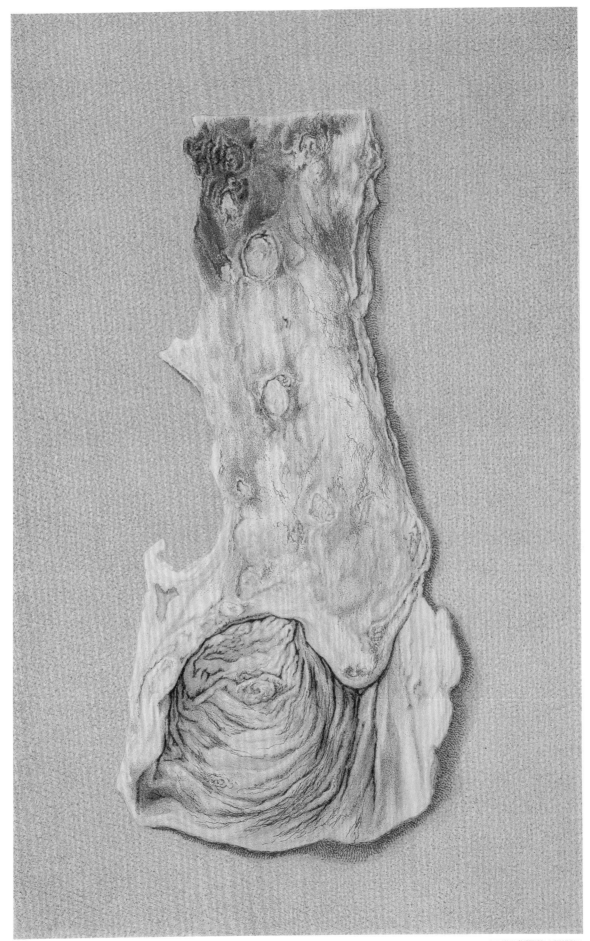

H. Faber p[illegible] F. Moras [illegible] Ph. [illegible]

ULCERATION OF THE ILEUM AND CÆCUM.

The two cases 111 and 199 are of interest in connection with that rare *post-mortem* condition emphysema of the liver. In the first case, which occurred in the service of Surgeon E. B. BENTLEY, U. S. Vols., at the Slough hospital, Alexandria, Va., the patient had recurring chills followed by fever, sleeplessness, delirium and jaundice, with death on the ninth day after admission. The patches of Peyer and mesenteric glands were enlarged and the liver increased in size, its right lobe honey-combed, "full of air and of a very peculiar appearance," and its left lobe normal in texture but of a yellow color; the kidneys were normal. Specimen 639, Army Medical Museum, is a section of the right lobe of the liver from this case, showing the honey-combing of the organ by dilated ducts which, according to the statement of the Catalogue of the Museum, was filled when recent with a yellowish serum-like fluid. This statement makes no mention of the presence of emphysema. The second case was reported by Assistant Surgeon HARRISON ALLEN, U. S. Army, in charge of the Lincoln hospital, Washington, D. C. The patient died on the seventh day after admission, but the existence of bed-sores over the sacrum and trochanters showed that he must have been sick for several weeks. He suffered from high fever and delirium, frequent retching and violent diarrhœa. The patches of Peyer were ulcerated; the mucous membrane at the ileo-cæcal valve thickened, indurated and blackened and in the colon pale but dotted with spots of black pigment. On the left side of the abdomen, about two inches below the diaphragm, was a subperitoneal abscess containing four drachms of pus. The surface of the liver was generally of a grayish-blue color, but anteriorly the right lobe had a more healthy appearance; minute collections of air were disseminated through its parenchyma, which was soft, of the color of sanious pus and possessed of a disagreeable odor; the air-cavities and the transverse sections of the portal veins gave a honey-combed appearance to the interior. The kidneys were in a similar emphysematous condition, the distinction between the pyramidal and cortical portions being almost obliterated.

Perhaps to these might be added case 137, as presenting the color, odor and consistence of the fully-developed emphysematous case, although no air is mentioned as present in the tissues. This case, also reported by Dr. ALLEN of the Lincoln hospital, died on the third day after admission, but no clinical history has been preserved. The patches of Peyer in the lower part of the ileum were surrounded by congestion and had ragged surfaces and purplish edges. The liver, of a dull greenish color, evolved a peculiar chicken-coop odor and was so soft that the finger could be passed through it in every direction; the gall-bladder contained an ounce of dark ochre-colored bile. The kidneys were congested.

FRERICHS* refers to *emphysema hepatis*, and cites GRAVES and HASPEL as instancing cases in which an abscess or hydatid cyst, after the discharge of its contents into the stomach or intestine, became filled with gases from the gastro-intestinal canal owing to pressure exerted by the abdominal walls or muscular tunics of the intestine; but he acknowledges that it is more difficult to account for those cases in which air-cavities, from the size of a millet-seed to that of a pea, are found permeating the hepatic substance. He met an instance of this kind in the body of a woman who died from purulent inflammation of the joints, death having been preceded a short time by abortion and the appearance of petechiæ. He also cites some cases observed by others,—by STOKES in a person who died from the rupture of an aneurism into the œsophagus, by LOUIS in a tubercular patient, by CAMBAY after dysentery and peritonitis and by PIORRY after small-pox.

---

* *A Clinical Treatise on Diseases of the Liver*—New Sydenham Society, London, 1861, Vol. II, p. 369.

In addition to his tubercular case above cited Louis* found this emphysema of the liver in certain cases of acute disease; but in the typhoid affection he never encountered it, and he comments with astonishment on what seems to him a fact, that this apparently putrefactive condition of the liver should be absent in a disease which has been long known as putrid fever while present in other acute maladies that are not so intimately associated with the idea of putridity. Emphysema of the liver in his cases coincided with a similar condition of the neck and limbs.

J. Forsyth Meigs has reported a case in which the liver was found in this condition after typhoid fever.† In this case there was much exhaustion, which was regarded as due to an unusual destruction of the red corpuscles of the blood indicated by the amount of their coloring matter in the urine. The patient died after profuse hemorrhage from the bowels about the eighteenth day of his attack. The patches of Peyer and many of the solitary glands were ulcerated and the mesenteric glands enlarged, vascular and softened. The liver was much enlarged, brownish-yellow, spongy and crepitant, so light as to float in water and so soft that the finger could readily be thrust through it; on pressure much dirty, frothy, thin liquid escaped, which looked like ichor but not like pus; the gall-bladder was filled with thin yellowish bile. The kidneys were enlarged, dark colored and congested; they crepitated distinctly but did not float in water. There was subcutaneous emphysema of the sides of the neck and thorax, and much discoloration from stasis in the dependent parts of the body. On microscopic examination, the liver was found to be fatty; fat in large drops was scattered over the field, and all the small angulated and irregular cells contained much fat in minute refractive points. On the other hand, the kidneys were not fatty, but the tubes were large, swollen and crowded with dark cloudy cells. Dr. Meigs remarks that there was no emphysema of the neck before death, or at least none was observed, as he believes it would have been had it existed; but he considers it difficult to suppose that the singular cribriform and spongy character of the liver could have been produced in the eleven hours and a half which elapsed between death and *post-mortem* observation, especially as there was no decomposition of the tissues in other parts of the body, and assuredly none in the kidney, which also, although to a less extent, was emphysematous.

The honey-combing of the liver in case 111 was certainly due to dilatation of the ducts, by a serum-like fluid, according to the statement in the Catalogue, connected with which was the jaundice of the clinical history; but the language of the reporter leaves no room for doubt that emphysema was associated with this condition. Without additional cases and more precise details it is difficult to say what may have been the origin of the emphysema; but in view of similar conditions in the kidneys in some of these cases, and in the muscles of the neck in case 98, it seems probable that it was the result of *post-mortem* changes. In tissues that have become so profoundly altered from the normal condition during life it is not surprising that chemical reactions, in advance of bacterial or putrefactive changes, should have given rise to the evolution of gaseous products as soon as vitality ceased to act as a preservative.

---

* Paris, 1829, t. I, p. 309.

† *Philadelphia Medical Times*, 1872–73, Vol. III, p. 1.—Referring to the rarity of this condition of the liver Dr. Meigs says: "In that great treasure-house of pathological medicine, Rokitansky's Pathological Anatomy, I cannot find a single specific reference to it. I have looked through seven volumes of the Year-Books of the Sydenham Society and did not find a case. Bamberger, in Virchow's Hand-book of Pathology and Therapeutics, in the chapter on the liver, makes no mention of it. Neither Budd in his Treatise on the Liver, nor Watson in his Practice, nor Graves, who saw so much typhus in Dublin, in his great work on the Science of Medicine, nor the writers on Typhoid Fever and Diseases of the Liver in Reynold's System of Medicine, nor the Compendium de Médecine Pratique even glance at it."

The GALL-BLADDER in the continued fever cases presented no special characteristics. It was large or small, empty, distended or charged with various quantities of bile, usually dark-colored and viscid, but sometimes thin, straw-colored or watery. As accidental complications may be mentioned the perforation of its walls in case 95, in which constant nausea and vomiting, jaundice and subsequent peritonitis obscured the symptoms of typhoid, and its disorganization in 327 as the result of its participation in a general peritonitis.

The PANCREAS was normal in twenty-seven of forty-one observations and but slightly altered in the remaining fourteen, the alteration consisting of an asserted hardness, softness or change of tint. The resistance of this gland to the typhoid and malarial poisons may be fairly assumed from a consideration of the many cases in which it was healthy, although the other abdominal organs were extensively diseased. Even when the parotid gland became affected it does not appear that the susceptibility of the pancreas was increased, for while the condition of the latter was stated in but one of the cases in which the parotids were inflamed it was normal in that case, 263. But the inference that on this account there is a greater difference between these glands than is generally supposed is hardly warranted, since the submaxillary glands were so rarely affected.

The KIDNEYS were less frequently affected in the continued fevers than the liver or spleen, but the morbid changes that were observed were of a similar character. The large number of instances in which their condition was not stated detracts from the value of the statistics for certain purposes; but of the cases that were examined about one-half were reported as in a healthy condition. In 52 per cent. of the typhoid series the kidneys were more or less altered; in 57 per cent. of the continued malarial cases; in 35.7 of the typho-malarial, and 42.6 of the mixed series of cases. It is inferred from these figures that although an altered condition of the kidneys was as frequent an attendant of malarial as of typhoid fever, the conjunction of these was not expressed by an increased frequency in the lesions of this organ. Nevertheless an examination of the analytical summary, by showing a somewhat greater prevalence of acutely inflamed cases in the typho-malarial and mixed series, suggests that the coincidence of the febrile poisons may have been manifested by an increased gravity of the lesions. The kidneys were congested, in many cases soft and flabby and in some pale and fatty; occasionally the congestion resulted in ecchymoses, and at times the inflammatory action proceeded to suppuration. The emphysematous kidney in case 199 has already been referred to in speaking of the lesions of the liver.

As has been shown in a previous part of this chapter,* no general connection was observable between dysuria or retention, and delirium or stupor, although it is probable, as argued by MURCHISON, that cerebral symptoms are in some instances the result of an accumulation of urea in the blood.

III.—THE ORGANS OF RESPIRATION AND CIRCULATION.

As the condition of the LARYNX and TRACHEA was observed in so few of the cases, the relative frequency of their lesions can be ascertained only by the figures supplied by Dr. HARRISON ALLEN.† In only three of his cases of camp fever was the trachea or larynx implicated. In one the fauces and epiglottis were covered with false membrane, and the margins of the latter and mucous lining of the larynx were ulcerated; in a second there was thickening of the membrane but no ulceration, and in the third a decided inflammation of

* See *ante*, pages 298 and 308. † See *ante*, page 433.

the trachea unaccompanied by laryngitis or pneumonia. From the paucity of such lesions in thirty-five cases it seems probable that the reason why the larynx and trachea were not more frequently mentioned in our *post-mortem* records was the absence of morbid appear-ances in these parts. Observations were made in six of the typhoid, eight of the malarial, four of the typho-malarial and seventeen of the mixed cases. The alterations consisted of thickening of the lining membrane by congestion, œdema, exudation into the submucous tissue or the development of false membranes on its surface; not unfrequently the membrane was ulcerated,* and occasionally small abscesses were formed in connection with the laryn-geal cartilages. Unquestionably these conditions were frequently the causes of the alter-ation or loss of voice and the dysphagia that were at times present in the progress of the fever. Œdema was a dangerous lesion in some instances, as in 339, in which it caused death by occluding the rima glottidis. Perhaps also this was the cause of the sudden death in 36; in this case, as there was œdema of the lower extremities and effusion into the serous sacs, the fatal result may have been occasioned by the pericardial effusion, which suffices to account for the masking of the heart-sounds, the dyspnœa and præcordial pain; but it is not certain, in the absence of *post-mortem* observations directed to the larynx, that an œdematous con-dition of the glottis arising from the anæmia may not have been the immediate cause of death. Generally, however, œdema glottidis was connected with local congestive processes. Occa-sionally pseudomembranes were the proximate cause of the fatal issue, as in cases 122 and 308; but it does not appear that diphtheria was specially a complication of typhoid or other continued fevers, for it appeared in patients enfeebled by other diseases and, indeed, by gun-shot wounds. Its occurrence seems to have been determined by the deteriorated condition rather than by the specific cause of the deterioration.†

Emphysema of the neck has been attributed to the existence of ulcers in the larynx;‡ but in the only instance, case 98, in which this condition of the cervical cellular tissue was noted, the larynx does not seem to have been examined, and the emphysema, on account of a coexisting ecchymosis, was referred to a hypothetical ante-mortem violence. In case 12 the œdematous condition of the neck was apparently connected with processes affecting the throat, as the epiglottis was much swollen.

The condition of the BRONCHIAL TUBES was seldom observed or noted, but they occa-sionally appear to have been congested irrespective of the condition of the pulmonary tissue. In a few cases, as 281, 331 and 362, there were distinct evidences of inflammation.

The condition of the LUNGS was variously reported by our medical officers as engorged, congested, œdematous, splenified or hepatized. They weighed more than in the healthy state from the afflux and stagnation of the blood and the subsequent exudation or transuda-tion of its elements in certain parts, generally their lower and posterior portions. Undoubt-edly this condition arose, in many instances, during the great prostration that immediately preceded death, for it was found in cases in which there had been no symptomatic manifesta-tion of its presence; but in other cases the morbid action was of a more active character, leading to a true hepatization. Generally the sanguineous condensation was diffuse, but it was

---

* According to LIEBERMEISTER, *Ziemssen's Cyclopedia,* Am. Ed., Vol. 1, p. 166, laryngeal ulcers are of comparatively frequent occurrence in typhoid. He cites HOFFMANN as having found them in 28 of 250 autopsies of typhoid fever, and GRIESINGER in 26 per cent. of his fatal cases.

† See diphtheria, *infra,* p. 739.

‡ MURCHISON refers to WILKS as having demonstrated the association of emphysema of the neck with ulcer. "A boy, aged 12, became emphysema-tous on the twelfth day of an attack of enteric fever, the emphysema commencing in the neck, spreading to the face, arms and chest, and greatly impeding deglutition. Death occurred on the twenty-second day, when it was found that the air had escaped through a sloughing ulcer of the larynx, situated at the posterior junction of the vocal cords."—*Op. cit.,* p. 558.

occasionally circumscribed in lobular masses as if the result of catarrhal processes.   Owing to want of definition in the records it is uncertain to what extent hemorrhagic infarction conduced to the production of the morbid appearances.

The lungs presented a larger proportion of morbid changes in the typhoid-than in the malarial cases.   They were altered from the normal in 85.3 per cent. of thirty-four typhoid cases in which their condition was noted, and in but 55.2 per cent. of fifty-eight malarial cases, the typho-malarial and mixed cases taking a middle position in this respect, the former presenting 62.7 per cent. of fifty-one cases and the latter 71.2 per cent. of one hundred and sixty-three cases; but while the lungs, like the spleen, were less frequently affected in continued malarial than in typhoid fever, they presented in the individual cases of the former more extensive or aggravated diseased conditions, as manifested by the occurrence of ecchymosis with congestion and by the greater frequency of purulent collections.   Hurried respiration, although generally due to local hyperæmic conditions, was in some instances attributable to nervous agitation, to febrile excitement, to pressure on the lungs by the tympanitic abdomen, or, as in case 25, to a combination of these conditions.

THE PLEURÆ.—As compared with the frequency of congestive and inflammatory processes in the parenchyma of the lungs, morbid changes in the pleural membrane were of great rarity.   Adhesions unconnected with the febrile attack are of course excluded from the list of abnormal appearances.   The pleural cavity sometimes contained a serous effusion, due in some instances to a transudation from engorged capillaries, but in others to more active processes, as may be inferred from the flakes of lymph or purulent turbidity described as present; recent lymph appeared occasionally on the surface of the membrane and the serous effusion was sometimes tinged with blood.

This rarity of the pleural affection in continued fevers among the white troops is strongly contrasted, according to the published statements of Surgeon ROBERT REYBURN, U. S. Vols., by its frequency and fatality among the negroes.   In a report* which gives the results of the treatment of 7,949 cases of sick and wounded freedmen in the District of Columbia from June 1 to December 31, 1865, he states that typhoid fever constituted the most fatal although by no means the most numerous class of cases; there were one hundred and sixteen cases, of which forty-nine, or nearly 41 per cent., proved fatal.   He considered that pneumonia, which so often occurred in the progress of typhoid fever affecting the Caucasian race, became in the negro pleuro-pneumonia of a low grade, and was generally accompanied with a large serous or sero-sanguineous effusion, which after death was found filling the pleural cavities. In fact, inflammation of the serous membranes seemed to be more frequent and dangerous among negroes than among whites.   That the effusion was not a *post-mortem* transudation was proved by its quantity, which entirely precluded that idea, and by the fact that in many of the cases percussion revealed its existence during life.

The PERICARDIUM was less frequently affected than the pleuræ.   Sometimes an excess of serum was present, and occasionally this was tinged with blood or associated with a slight redness of the membrane.   Rarely, as in 90, 206, 276 and 307, there were such indications of inflammatory action as fibrinous flocculi in the effused liquid, exuded lymph on the serous surface or a thickening of the membrane.   Many of the cases presenting these pericardial changes had the lungs or pleural cavities in a morbid state, but in some, as 170, 206, 262 and 328, there was no coincident implication of these parts.

* See *American Journal of the Medical Sciences*, 1866, p. 364 *et seq.*

The condition of the HEART was mentioned in less than one-half of the cases; and in these it was frequently said to have been normal or healthy, as, for instance, in 82 per cent. of twenty-two typhoid cases, in 75 per cent. of forty-eight malarial cases, in 77.5 per cent. of forty typho-malarial and in 77 per cent. of one hundred and thirty-five cases of the mixed series. Usually, when described as altered from the normal, the words pale, anæmic, soft, flabby, flaccid or atrophied were employed to express its condition; in a few cases it was said to have been fatty. From these observations it would be difficult to infer the frequency and great importance of the degenerative changes in the muscular tissue of the heart induced by the continuance of the febrile movement as demonstrated by the investigations of HAYEM,* VALLIN† and others; but it is known that these changes, involving a cloudiness of the striæ of the muscular tissue apparently by albuminous granules in the fibres and inter-fibrillar protoplasm, and even a fatty degeneration of the muscle, are gradual in their progress and may be shown by microscopic examination to be notably advanced although the organ may not attract attention by changes in its macroscopic characters.

But although the heart was so frequently reported in a healthy condition by the *post-mortem* observers, the attending medical officers recognized in the symptoms a tendency to a failure in the powers of this organ, and were inclined to attribute cases of sudden or otherwise unexplained death to this cause. Nevertheless, in the series of cases that have been submitted there is not one case that may with certainty be instanced as having proved fatal by the sudden failure of a degenerated heart. In case 184, which had a suddenly fatal termination during an apparently favorable convalescence, the heart was flabby. In the large number of cases in which death was the result of progressive prostration, and which were unmarked at the autopsy by the presence of a particular lesion known to be mortal, it is possible that the heart was materially implicated, but the records do not say so. Thus, in cases 13 and 14, in which it is stated in terms that the cause of death was asthenia, the condition of the heart is not mentioned. On the other hand, while there is no certainty that this degenerated condition of the heart was the cause of death in the cases in which it was present, it is deserving of note that in a large proportion of them there was no lesion of the viscera that could be cited as the immediate cause of the fatal result. In about one-third of the three hundred and eighty-nine cases that have been presented the cause of death could be ascribed to some particular complication or lesion, as coma, hemorrhage, perforation, pneumonia, etc.; but of the thirty-nine cases in which the heart was stated to have been pale, anæmic, softened, flabby, atrophied or fatty, a lesion to which death might with probability be assigned was found only in six or seven cases,—gangrene of the feet in 112 and 278, gangrene of the intestines in 311, perforation of the bowels in 347 and pneumonia in 243, 333 and perhaps 182. In view of what is known concerning the degeneration of the muscular tissue of the heart in continued fevers it is not unlikely that death in many of these thirty-nine cases may have been due, to a certain extent, to the special influence of this morbid change.

Physiological considerations lead to the expectation of a greater frequency of congestion of the lungs in connection with a degenerated condition of the heart than in those cases in which this organ was reported healthy; but this expectation is not sustained by an examination

---

* *Recherches sur les Rapports existant entre la Mort Subite et les altérations vasculaires du Cœur dans la Fièvre Typhoïde*, par GEORGES HAYEM.—Archives de Physiologie Normale et Pathologique, Paris, 1869, t. 2d, p. 699.

† *Des Altérations Histologiques du Cœur et des Muscles Volontaires dans les fièvres pernicieuses et remittentes*, par M. E. VALLIN.—Memoires de Médecine, &c., Militaries, 3me serie, t. XXX, Paris, 1874.

of the records. The condition of the lungs was not stated in four of the thirty-nine cases in which the heart was said to have been degenerated; in twelve the lungs were normal and in twenty-three congested or more actively diseased; they were, therefore, altered in 66 per cent. of the cases in which their condition was reported. On the other hand, in looking at the cases in which the records do not state the heart to have presented this flabby condition of its walls, the lungs were hyperæmic in one hundred and eighty-six, normal in eighty-five, while in seventy-nine their condition was not stated, i. e., they were congested or otherwise altered in 68.7 per cent. of the cases in which their condition was recorded. In view of these figures, showing the association of a larger proportion of congested lungs with hearts that did not attract attention by their morbid conditions than with those that were reported as more or less degenerated, it is to be inferred that pulmonary congestion in these fevers was unconnected with the condition of the heart or that the naked-eye appearances of the latter organ gave by no means a true impression of its actual condition.

The contents of the chambers of the heart were noted in ninety-six of the three hundred and eighty-nine cases of continued fever. In nine of these it is stated that no clots were present: In 48 the heart was pale; in 329 firm; in 137 flabby; in 165 and 277 it was said to have weighed nine ounces; in 96 it was reported large, the left ventricle empty and the right containing uncoagulated blood; in 150 and 190 the blood was uncoagulated; in 194 there was a thin wafer-like formation on the tricuspid valve. Manifestly, from the small number of cases in which the heart was reported as having been found free from clots, its contents were specially noted, as a rule, only when the attention of the recorder was attracted by these coagula.

Clots occurred with greater frequency in the cavities of the right side than in those of the left. In a few instances the records do not specify whether the coagula or fibrinous concretions were formed in the right or left side or in both sides, the statement being simply as to their presence in the heart. But if their existence in the chambers of both sides be assumed in these cases, it will be found that of eighty-seven recorded cases of heart-clot both sides were affected in forty-nine. Of the remaining thirty-eight cases the right side contained clots in thirty-five and the left in three instances. Of those containing clots in the right chambers only, the left side contained fluid blood in two and no clot in two, while in thirty-one assurance is conveyed of the absence of clots by the fact that their presence was not recorded. In the cases containing clots in the left chambers only, the right side contained fluid blood in one instance and no clot in another; in the third no statement of its contents is given. The greater liability of the right side of the heart to the accumulation of coagula may be gathered from these figures. Clots were noted in the right cavities of eighty-four and in the left cavities of fifty-two hearts.

But the character of the coagulum had a tendency to vary according as the right or left chambers of the heart were its seat. Of the eighty-four coagula noted in the right cavities fifty-six consisted of fibrinous concretions or deposits, frequently filling the chambers and projecting into the great vessels, eight were venous or black clots, six a mixture of fibrinous deposits and venous coagula, while in fourteen the appearance of the clot was not entered on the record. Of the fifty-two coagula in the left cavities twenty-five were fibrinous, eight venous, seven mixed and twelve of unstated appearance.

Dr. WOODWARD has discussed the general question of heart-clot in connection with its occurrence in diarrhœa and dysentery.* He concluded that although fibrinous coagula may be formed during life they must be regarded in the vast majority of instances as occurring during the death agony. He pointed out that no facts had been presented to show that clots were formed more frequently in cases of sudden death than in cases of the same disease in which death took place in the usual way and without any symptoms referable to the heart; and that there was no evidence that the clots in the one group of cases differed from those that occurred in the others as to size, texture, adhesions, etc. Dr. WOODWARD dealt with this question before the whole of the data relating to it had been submitted. It is true the further evidence contained in the records does not unsettle his conclusions; but if there had been before him the cases of heart-clot recorded in the chapter on the paroxysmal fevers,† with cases 271 and 377 of the continued fevers and 34 of the secondary pneumonias,‡ it is probable that he would have given a more emphatic acknowledgment of the existence of heart-clots of ante-mortem development, and conceded them as a whole a higher place in the scale of importance. The clots being manifestly of ante-mortem formation in some cases, it is assumed that they must have had a similar history in other cases unless it can be shown that in the latter they were of *post-mortem* origin. It is admitted that in most instances these clots were formed when the patient was about to succumb. The question at issue is their relation to the death agony. If they were formed during the agony and because of it, they had only a *post-mortem* value; but if, as seems likely from the cases presented, they were due to some cause which induced a temporary stasis or retardation of the flow of the blood through the chambers of the heart and brought about the agony by the rapidity of their development, they become of importance as the determining cause of the fatal issue in a large number of cases and as indicating the necessity of preserving patients from such influences as are known to be efficient in precipitating the deposition. When the predisposing conditions were not strongly marked, as in a case of typhoid in which the patient apparently retained strength sufficient to enable him to help himself in many of the necessities incident to his condition, a notable impress on the system might be required to constitute the immediate or determining cause of the fibrinous deposits, as the faintness which followed the exertion of rising to stool in cases 271 and 379, or the chill in 96 of the paroxysmal series. But on the other hand, in the presence of strongly predisposing conditions, such as were constituted by the prolonged duration of the fever, the existence of pulmonary hyperæmia, the exhaustion of diarrhœa or hemorrhage or the collapse attendant on perforation, the agency that determined the deposit and the closely-following fatal result might have been so slight as to have passed unnoticed; yet it may not be allowed that there was no exciting cause to occasion the deposit and death at that particular time.

In the majority of cases in which heart-clots were formed there was no lesion of the abdominal viscera, brain or lungs obviously inconsistent with the continuance of life. To no one in particular of the morbid changes in these organs could the rôle of executioner be assigned. The patients died from the totality of the morbid changes produced by the fever, typhoid or malarial, as the case may have been, or from the asthenic conditions bearing on the thread of life in the diarrhœal, pneumonic or other cases in which heart-clot was found as a *post-mortem* appearance;—or they died from heart-clot. But while the totality of the morbid changes was an inconstant quantity and of an uncertain value, the heart-clot was constant and efficient. In view of these considerations it is not surprising that our medical

---

* See p. 539 *et seq.* of the Second Part of this work.   † See *supra*, page 138.   ‡ See *infra*, page 788.

officers came to regard the fibrinous coagula as the immediate cause of the fatal issue in the cases presenting them. If a patient manifestly died, as in 110, from exhaustion consequent on repeated hemorrhage from the bowels, what may be conceived to have been the *modus operandi* of the cause? The hemorrhage predisposed to death by syncope, but the patient did not die until a clot had formed in his heart. He might have lingered for some time longer, notwithstanding the weakened action of the heart and the altered condition of the blood, had not some slight exciting cause determined the deposition of the fibrinous coagulum, which speedily interfered with the continuance of the cardiac flow. In case 112, in which the patient may be said to have died of gangrene of the feet, there was no condition, so far as is learned from the record, to occasion the immediate extinction of life until the deposition of fibrin was effected by some trifling, but under the circumstances all-sufficient cause. In some of the cases of peritonitis from perforation, as 45, 106, 156, 245 and 347, or that in which the gall-bladder was perforated, case 95, there appears no cause for the destruction of life at one particular moment rather than at another, if the fibrinous coagula in the heart are excluded from consideration. So, too, in such pneumonitic cases as 62, 198, 281, 357 and 369, in the pleuritic effusion of 340, and in the cases 217 and 304, which passed into death from a condition of coma, the agency that determined the occurrence of the fatal event at one time rather than another must be conceived to have been the development of these clots, owing to some temporary, and but for this not necessarily permanent, stasis in the passage of the blood through the chambers of the heart. Even in such a case as 122, in which the occlusion of the larynx by diphtheritic membranes may be readily assigned as the cause of death, it is probable that the immediate cause was the fibrin deposited in the heart during the stasis occasioned by the last of the suffocative paroxysms; since, if this had not occurred, the patient might have lived to have added another to the suffocative paroxysms that he had already experienced. The proposition that certain cardiac concretions are formed during life does not therefore rest exclusively, as it appeared to Dr. WOODWARD, upon the anatomical characteristics of the concretions;* but in some cases very clearly on the symptoms, and in others less clearly on positive and negative pathological evidences. These, indeed, suggest that sometimes the ordinary black coagulum may have an ante-mortem formation and be the cause of the death agony.†

Theoretically, one of the conditions provocative of the deposition of fibrin in the heart

---

* Page 541, Part II.

† The three following cases are briefly presented as illustrating the ante-mortem occurrence of all the varieties of clots that have been found in the heart: 1st. Fibrillated clots with central softening and arterial projections into their roots, which manifest with certainty their ante-mortem origin; 2d. Fibrinous clots which sometimes by their symptoms, as in the cases already given in the text, are known to precede and cause the death agony; 3d. Ordinary blood coagula, which are usually ascribed to *post-mortem* changes, but which may, in some cases, be the immediate cause of death. The first is related by JOHN G. M. KENDRICK, *Edinburgh Med. Jour.*, Vol. XV, 1869, p. 396. The patient, a woman of 19, was admitted Feb. 23, 1869, and died March 1. She was low-spirited and anxious, but complained only of slight cough and frontal headache, particularly towards evening. The most remarkable phenomenon of the case was a constant moaning of the patient during sleep, which was usually disturbed by frightful dreams. Nothing relieved this distressing symptom except propping her head and shoulders high with pillows. One morning, having been in her usual state till breakfast time, she suddenly became worse, dying at 10 A. M., apparently from congestion of the lungs. In the right auricle there was a white irregularly pear-shaped clot about the size of a large walnut, attached by several band-like processes at its narrow end to the musculi pectinati in the apex of the appendage. This clot, of firm consistence and slightly floccular appearance, had a cavity in its centre communicating with the exterior by a small rent in its substance. In the left auricle a firm white clot, attached to the columnæ carneæ, divided into two branches, one of which occluded the mitral orifice and the other extended into the aorta. Hypertrophy of the left ventricle, thickening of the anterior flap of the tricuspid valve and imperfect closure of the foramen ovale, were also observed. The lungs were much congested, and a few ounces of serum were found in the left pleural cavity together with a little serum in the pericardium, but there was no pericarditis. The clots, on microscopical examination, were found to be of fibrillated structure, holding in its meshes numerous corpuscular bodies with corrugated edges; several minute bloodvessels from the endocardium entered the root of one of the band-like processes of the clot in the right auricle, but, as far as could be observed, did not penetrate its substance; the epithelial layer of the endocardium, with the subjacent one of elastic tissue, seemed to be reflected upon the root of the clot and to run along with it for a few lines. The second case is given by Dr. PLAYFAIR, in the *Trans. Path. Soc.*, London, Vol. XVIII, 1867, pp. 68–70, as having occurred at King's College hospital. The patient had complained of pain in the right knee, but there was no swelling or tenderness of the part, nor feverishness. An alkaline mixture was prescribed. She was not seen next day. On the third morning she expressed herself free from pain and said she had passed a good night; but shortly after this she complained of feeling weak, and asked for a bed-pan that she might not have to leave her bed. She was then seized with hurried breathing and died before the house physician, who was sent for, could arrive. On *post-mortem* examination all the organs and structures of the body were found to be healthy. A firm solid clot of fibrin of

is that degeneration of its muscular fibre which in prolonged fever gives rise to the charac-teristic feebleness of the pulse. But the records do not show a greater frequency of clots in hearts reported pale, flabby, flaccid, etc., than in those reported healthy or which did not attract attention by any abnormal appearances. Of thirty-nine cases in which a degenera-tion of the heart was noted it was free from clots in two cases, its contents were not stated in twenty-nine cases, and it contained clots in eight cases, or in 20.5 per cent. of the number observed. The eight cases were 75, 276 and 347, in which fibrinous clots were present in both sides of the heart; 112 and 184, in which they were confined to the right side, and 148, 154 and 219, in which coagula, the character of which was not specified, were found, pre-sumably, in both the right and left chambers. Of three hundred and fifty cases in which the condition of the heart was not stated or stated to be healthy, seventy-nine, or 22.5 per cent. of the whole number, contained clots. In view of what has already been advanced concerning the difficulty of deciding upon the actual condition of the heart from its micro-scopic appearances, this similarity in the percentages of heart-clot in the two sets of cases might be construed as indicating that the heart was possibly as much weakened in the cases in which its condition was not stated or said to have been healthy as in those in which the observers considered it flabby or otherwise degenerated.

As congestion of the lungs was so commonly present in the final hours of continued fever, occurring in as many as 68.3 per cent. of the cases, the frequent coincidence of clots in the heart with such congestion was to be expected. On questioning the cases for a possible connection between the presence of fibrinous clots in the right chamber of the heart and an engorged or other condition of the lungs interfering with the circulation of the blood through their tissues the following information is obtained:

In the five cases of typhoid in which separation of fibrin took place there were pulmonary conditions during the last stage of the fatal illness involving stasis of the blood-current.

In four of the fourteen cases of the malarial series in which there were fibrinous coagula in the right chambers the lungs were not seriously affected: In 259 some injection and a small nodular consolidation was recorded, but the weight of the lungs was inconsistent with any material engorgement; in 71 the lower part of the pleura on one side was said to have been inflamed, whence it may be inferred that had the pulmonary tissue presented any notable abnormity it would have been observed and recorded: in the two cases, 292 and 293, the lungs were expressly stated as having been in a healthy condition.

Of the ten typho-malarial cases presenting fibrinous clots in the right side the lungs were normal in four, 77, 95, 102 and 271, while in a fifth, 266, old pleuritic adhesions constituted the only abnormity. Moreover, 106, in which clots of an unspecified character were found in the heart, had the lungs in a healthy state.

Lastly, of the thirty-one cases of the mixed series in which fibrinous or partly fibrinous clots were observed in the right side of the heart, the lungs were normal in four, 167, 220, 221 and 347, while in a fifth, 166, the pulmonary disease consisted merely of a few softened tubercles in the apex of each lung.

From the above figures it may be calculated that congestion of the lungs was present in 75.4 per cent. of those fever cases in which the heart was found to contain fibrinous or mixed clots in the cavities of its right side. This increase in the percentage of lung disease in the heart-clot cases may be considered an expression of the influence of pulmonary

a pale-yellow color was found in the right side of the heart and pulmonary artery, adhering to the valves and fleshy columns. If this clot was formed during the death agony, why did the death agony occur? If the woman did not die of heart-clot, what was the cause of death? Dr. PLAYFAIR's theory was that the clot had probably been forming during the night preceding the fatal result, and that so long as the patient remained quiet sufficient blood passed through the obstructed vessels to carry on the organic functions, but when she was obliged to exert herself there was a sudden call for blood, which could not be supplied through the occluded artery, and death resulted. Dr. JOHN A. LIDELL, of New York, gives the third case,—Am. Jour. of Med. Sci., Vol. XLIV, 1872, p. 328,—that of an intemperate woman, who, when recovering from an attack of epileptic convulsions, was seized with dyspnœa, and died in an hour. The left pulmonary artery was obstructed with coagula. The heart was enlarged, fatty externally and flabby; its cavities were dilated and those of the right side filled with dark-colored clotted blood. The right lung was much congested and œdematous and the left intensely congested. It was supposed that the coagula in the artery had at first formed a part of the mass found in the right side of the heart, which was conceived to have originated in the stasis of the blood attending the epileptic convulsion, and that these, after the patient had recovered her consciousness, had been carried to the point where they were found. It is true the opinions of PLAYFAIR and LIDELL are merely conjectures, but they are conjectures founded on *post-mortem* and negative pathological evidences, in view of the history of the patient during the later hours of life.

conditions as predisposing to the formation of clots; but, in view of the relatively large number of these cases in which the lungs were in a healthy or comparatively healthy condition, the clots may not be referred for causation to the pulmonary congestion alone.

The opinion is very generally entertained that in the course of continued fevers the blood becomes progressively altered by the diminished nutrition of the patient and the abnormal action of the various organs concerned in elaboration and elimination, irrespective of the morbid changes that may be produced in it by the more or less direct action of a specific fever-poison. But the character of the blood-changes has not been sufficiently studied. When inflammatory conditions prevail in the system the fibrin, as is well known, becomes largely augmented. In such cases there would be no difficulty in appreciating the existence of a predisposition to coagulation. But the deterioration in fevers that are not symptomatic of acute inflammatory processes seems rather to tend to a *dissolutio sanguinis* manifested by the fluid and disorganized condition in which the blood is sometimes found after death, and by the ecchymoses, hæmaturia, epistaxis and other hemorrhages that appear in the progress of the disease. The one series of changes offsets the other so far as relates to the proportion of fibrin in the blood, and involves the occurrence of fibrinous coagula in the heart in corresponding obscurity.

Since *post-mortem* observations on the pale, weak and flaccid heart fail, as has been seen, to connect it as a strongly predisposing element with the heart-clot of fever; since pulmonary congestion and inflammation give but a slight increase in the percentage of these clots, and since the condition of the blood itself does not appear to be notably favorable to their development, it follows that for their production there is needful an immediate or exciting cause of an intensity proportioned to the inadequacy of the predisposing factors. Generally, no doubt, this is constituted by some unusual exertion on the part of the patient, perhaps sometimes by mental impressions; but accurate details of death scenes in fever are necessary to complete our knowledge of the immediate causes and progress of these fibrinous depositions.

THE BLOOD.—Few observations were made on the condition of the blood in the continued fevers. It was said to have been thin, uncoagulated or unusually fluid in the five cases, 25, 70, 96, 150 and 264. It is singular, in view of the general belief in the connection between a disorganized condition of the blood, such as exists in scurvy, and cutaneous blotches of a hemorrhagic nature, that in none of these cases is there a record of petechial spots or cutaneous or internal ecchymoses. In one case, 70, the liquidity of the blood was associated with œdema of the lower extremities. In case 204, in which a decrease in the number of white corpuscles was recorded, it is observed that the spleen was remarkably bloodless and the thyroid gland enlarged.

According to the records ecchymoses of the internal organs were rarely coincident with ecchymoses of the skin; whence it may be inferred that the former were in general the result of local congestions rather than of a deteriorated condition of the blood, and similarly, that the latter were frequently due to local rather than general conditions. Thus, in the typhoid series there were blood-clots in the pleural cavity in 31 and a bloody or reddish serum in the pericardium in 26. In the malarial series the lungs were ecchymosed in 258 and 288, and in the former the pleura contained a quantity of bloody serum; the stomach was ecchymosed in 262, the intestines in 91 and 365, and the upper surface of the cerebral hemispheres in 287. In the typho-malarial series the ileum was affected in 273, and in this instance the skin also was implicated.   In the mixed series of cases the pericardium contained reddish serum in 182 and 183; a similar effusion was found in the pleural cavities in 168, 333 and 340; the œsophagus was ecchymosed in 301 and 329, the stomach and bladder in 342, the ileum in 203, the colon in 162, 301, 318 and 370, the liver in 380 and the kidneys in 181 and 187.   But in none of these cases, except 203 and 273, was the passage of the blood from the vessels of the internal organs associated with a similar leakage from those of the skin.   The *post-mortem* records are, however, very defective so far as relates to the condition of the skin.   This is shown by the number of typhoid cases in which, although petechiæ were present according to the clinical record, no mention was made of their existence by the *post-mortem* observer.   It may be claimed, therefore, that in the cases instanced above there is no evidence that the skin was free from petechiæ, purpuric spots or ecchymotic blotches.

If, however, the cases which presented such spots or blotches be examined for concurrent leakage in the internal organs, it will be found that few instances of coincidence are recorded.   The eight typhoid cases in which the skin was more or less spotted had no internal ecchymoses.   The eight malarial cases that presented superficial blotches showed similar internal appearances in but one case, 386, in which the heart and the colon were affected.   Of the four cases, 86, 93, 114 and 273, of the typho-malarial series that had the skin ecchymosed, the last mentioned had the ileum also spotted.   Finally, of the nine cases of the mixed series that showed purpuric spots on the cutaneous surface only one, 203, had ecchymoses of the internal organs.   Although petechiæ or other superficial colorations may have been overlooked by the recorders in cases presenting internal ecchymoses, it is not likely that the latter would have been overlooked where the record preserves the existence of the former.   Thus it may be concluded that internal ecchymoses were not invariably associated with cutaneous transudation, and that in many instances each of these was due rather to local conditions than essentially to the deteriorated condition of the blood.

But perhaps the facts would be expressed with greater accuracy by the statement that while the situation of the extravasations and transudations was dependent on local conditions their existence was rendered possible only by the changes which had taken place in the blood.   An abnormal state of the blood, frequently manifested by petechiæ, vibices, blood-colored urine and passive hemorrhages has already been noted as characterizing pernicious cases of the paroxysmal fevers.   In cases of continued fever of malarial origin a similar condition might naturally be expected.   In typhoid cases it is difficult to assume a healthy condition of the blood, in view of the prolonged interference with the normal action of the various organs concerned in its preservation at a particular standard.   Assuming this unhealthy condition to have existed, it would probably have been especially marked in prolonged or pernicious cases; but since, as has been shown by the records of the Seminary and other hospitals, it was precisely in such cases that petechiæ and vibices were of frequent occurrence, it may be concluded that a connection existed in typhoid between the condition of the blood and these ecchymotic appearances, although the few observations on the blood in the *post-mortem* records of the continued fever fail to show it.   This view is sustained by the hemorrhagic blotches of scurvy, which are known to depend on a deterioration of the blood constituting the essence of the disease, by the ecchymoses of typhus and by the transudations which, occurring in association with a liquid and uncoagulable state of the blood, gave the name of spotted fever to those febrile cases characterized by a special implication of the cerebro-spinal system. It is sustained also by the extravasations of altered blood observed in the paroxysmal fevers; and as in these there was the same want of coincidence between external and internal hemorrhagic manifestations that was found in typhoid, it follows that ecchymotic spots were probably as much due to an altered condition of the blood in the latter as in the former cases.

But although the connection between a degenerated blood and its escape from the vessels may require argument, in view of the non-coincidence of superficial and internal ecchymoses in the recorded cases of the continued fevers, it is scarcely needful to argue the existence of an abnormal condition of the blood in them. This has been shown in the malarial cases to have been the immediate consequence of the pervasion of the system by the febrile poison. Not one of the typhoid cases that have been presented demonstrates the disorganized condition of the blood as the direct result of the febrile cause; but this was observed in the following rapidly fatal case which, in this respect, was precisely analagous to the pernicious malarial cases that have been submitted. The patient died after a delirious attack of twenty-four hours, and *post-mortem* observation discovered the blood in a liquid state, the skin covered with purpuric spots, the patches of Peyer thickened and some of those near the ileo-cæcal valve remarkable for their pultaceous character, the spleen enlarged and the lungs engorged or hepatized. In this instance the disease did not last long enough for the blood to become deteriorated by gradual processes based on the imperfect operations of the organic functions. The fluidity of the blood must therefore be referred to the action of the fever-poison. The case has already been published* as 163 of the diarrhœal series. Dr. WOODWARD presented it, along with several other cases of fever that had been similarly recorded as diarrhœa, in order to illustrate a class of errors of diagnosis which were no doubt of frequent occurrence;† but as it illustrates matters of greater consequence‡ than these errors, its presentation in this connection has been deemed advisable:

Private Thomas Kelley, Co. A, 124th N. Y.; admitted Dec. 12, 1862. Diarrhœa. The patient was not confined to bed. On the 18th he was moving about and in the evening ate his supper with other patients. The same night he was slightly delirious. Died December 19, at 11 P. M. *Autopsy* next day: Body not emaciated; apparent age about 28 years; upon the body, especially the thighs, there were a number of irregular spots of purpura from the size of a flea-bite to that of a dime. The blood was very liquid and poured forth from incisions of the skin and all the internal organs. The brain was examined but exhibited no unhealthy marks. Pleuritic adhesions throughout, on both sides, of not very old date; left lung crepitant but engorged with a bloody liquid; the upper lobe of the right lung hepatized, the lower lobe congested. There was slight atheroma throughout the course of the aorta. Liver soft, Indian-red in color and large; spleen large, flabby and on section dark Indian-red, its convex surface exhibiting the remains of a former inflammation. Stomach, pancreas, kidneys and suprarenal bodies healthy. Small intestine pink in color; the agminated glands thickened and mostly bright-red in color; the lower glands were a line in thickness and contained a white cellular deposit; none of them were ulcerated. Mesenteric glands somewhat enlarged. Mucous membrane of the large intestine dirty slate-colored, with streaks of inflammation here and there.—*Act. Ass't Surg. Joseph Leidy.* [Nos. 88 to 90, Med. Sect., Army Medical Museum, from this case, are successive portions of the ileum, in each of which is a large thickened Peyer's patch; in 90 the patch is remarkable for its great size and the pultaceous character of the thickening, there are also several large solitary follicles in this specimen.]

MURCHISON§ recognizes two conditions of the blood in typhoid fever: One rare, in which it is dark-colored and liquid, the other of more frequent occurrence, in which it is disposed to concrete in firm white coagula. He conceives that a close relation exists between the state of the blood and the symptoms during life; that when death has been preceded for some days by the typhoid state the blood is usually dark and fluid; while in other cases, as when due to perforation or pneumonia, it often contains fibrinous coagula. The first of these observations does not apply to the typhoid cases observed during the war; for, of those

---

* In the Second Part of this work, page 117.   † Id., page 521.   ‡ See *infra*, page 480.   § Page 631 of his Treatise.

submitted as constituting the *post-mortem* records of the continued fevers, many presenting fibrinous heart-clots were not cut off by pneumonia or peritonitis, but died while in the typhoid state. The dark-colored and fluid condition of the blood appears rather to have been characteristic of rapidly fatal cases, such as that given in the preceding paragraph; and this observation is sustained by analogous changes found in fulminant cases of malarial, cerebro-spinal and typhus fevers.

The condition of the blood in typhoid fever has not been made the subject of special study by medical observers or physiological chemists. CHOMEL, while recognizing that the blood in this disease differed from that of pneumonia and other acute inflammations, concluded from his observations that its changes did not constitute a primitive lesion whence the symptoms of the disease were derived, nor even a secondary phenomenon.* LEHMANN states that during the first eight days of a typhoid attack the blood is like that of plethora, in which the corpuscles are increased, the fibrin normal and the albumen but little above the usual proportion; but that later it resembles the blood of anæmia, in which the corpuscles are diminished in number and the serum watery and deficient in albumen and other organic constituents although richer in salts.† VIRCHOW holds that in typhoid the fibrin is diminished; but as he states also that an increase of the colorless corpuscles may be looked for in diseased conditions attended with a notable swelling of the glands of the lymphatic system, this increase must be inferred as present in typhoid. In cases presenting a large black spleen he found pigment-cells resembling colorless blood corpuscles, spherical, often elongated and having granular contents, among which appeared black particles of various sizes; these pigmented bodies were observed also in other diseases attended with a rapid exhaustion of the vital properties of the blood and productive of cachectic and anæmic conditions.‡ ALONZO CLARK is of opinion that the most important of the lesions of typhoid fever is found in the blood; and from some experiments at Bellevue hospital he concludes that the blood-change is characterized by a progressive loss of coagulability.§

But although so few observations on the quality of the blood in typhoid fever appear in the records of medicine, the belief is generally entertained that a depraved condition is invariably present in this and other continued fevers. Sir WILLIAM JENNER deduces the existence of a deteriorated condition of the blood from the suppurations which are consecutive to the disease. He argues that the exudation of a blastema possessing the same properties in so many places at the same time, indicates the existence of a definitely diseased condition of the fluid from which that blastema is formed, just as the deposit of many masses of cancer-blastema in the same body at the same time is held to indicate the existence of a definite disease of the blood in the person who is the seat of them.‖

The degeneration of the blood, at first due to the more or less direct influence of the fever-poison, becomes afterward increased and modified by the retention in the system of the products of that retrogressive metamorphosis of the tissues which appears to constitute the essential of the febrile condition, no matter what may have been its exciting cause.¶ Urea

---

* He drew blood from thirty patients, each of whom was in the early stage of the disease. In six the clot was firm and buffed; in twenty it was firm but not coated; in four diffluent and curdled. His conclusion, as given in the text, was based on the small number of cases in which the blood was *diffluent et caillboté*, and the fact that a similar condition is found in diseases other than typhoid, some of which indeed are not of a serious character. From the firmness of the clot in the twenty-six cases he opposed the belief of those who held that in grave cases of fever the blood suffered a loss of coagulability.—A. F. CHOMEL, *Leçons de Clinique Médicale—Fièvre Typhoïde*, Paris, 1834, p. 50.

† C. G. LEHMANN—*Handbuch der Physiologischen Chemie*, Leipzig, 1859, pp. 230 and 232.

‡ VIRCHOW—*Cellular Pathologie*, Berlin, 1858, p. 201.

§ See *Medical Record*, New York, Vol. XIII, 1878, p. 262.

‖ *Medical Times and Gazette*, Vol. XXVII, London, 1853, p. 463.

¶ J. MILNER FOTHERGILL has a suggestive article on *The Typhoid Condition*, in the *Edinburgh Medical Journal*, 1873, Vol. XIX, Pt. 1, p. 225.

and carbonic acid are the ultimate products of this metabolism; but between these and the organized albuminous matters of the living system are a vast number of complex transition products concerning which little is known either chemically or physiologically. When the skin and kidneys are inactive, as is generally the case during the febrile continuance, these products accumulate in the blood, and coincident with this accumulation the patient falls into what is known as the typhoid condition. As urea is susceptible of quantitative determination, its retention in the blood and its pernicious influence on the system can be demonstrated. The poisonous action of carbonic acid, or of the concomitant deprivation of oxygen, as shown by the circulation of venous blood, is manifested by the insensibility and convulsions of asphyxia. Other products of tissue-waste, concerning which our knowledge is meagre, are plausibly assumed to be detrimental to the system in which they are retained. There is no proof that they are the cause of the typhoid condition; but the invariable appearance of the latter after a prolonged period of unusual change in the tissues and its more rapid development when the eliminative organs are inactive, are strongly suggestive of a causative relation between the metabolic products and the typhoid state. If this view of the occurrence of the typhoid condition be correct there is no difficulty in understanding the supervention of the so-called typhoid symptoms in malarial or other fevers* uncomplicated by the special poison of typhoid fever.

The great prostration which was characteristic of the continued fevers not only in their early stages but even from their onset, must be attributed to the condition of the blood, depraved primarily by the influence of the fever-poison and secondarily by the disorder of the functions of the body. The latter will readily be admitted as a debilitating cause. The former has been well argued by LOUIS as regards specific typhoid cases, in which the primary debility was more marked than in malarial cases: We cannot attribute it to the diarrhœa, as it is often present before the flux has developed, nor to the abdominal pain, which is often slight, nor to the cephalalgia, which is generally dull and which, when severe in other acute affections, is not accompanied by a like loss of strength, nor to any appreciable lesion of the brain or stomach, as shown by *post-mortem* observations; hence it is needful to recur for its explanation to the special changes in the small intestine as acting sympathetically on the brain, or still further, to the typhoid fever-poison which produced these changes.†

The intense prostration of the later stages of continued fever is the result of a complexus of causes originating in the disordered state of the blood. Prominent, however, among them is that degeneration of the muscular system which has already been mentioned in the paroxysmal and continued fevers as affecting the substance of the heart. ZENKER‡ first called the attention of the profession to the frequency and extent of these changes in the muscles. He considered them wholly unconnected with inflammation; but by WALDEYER§ and HAYEM‖ they were on the contrary viewed as resulting from inflammatory processes. The latter attributed them to the morbid condition of the blood, placing them among those

* See Pneumonic Fever, *infra*, page 613. † See his *Recherches*, t. II, p. 203.
‡ ZENKER—*Ueber die Veränderungen der willkürlichen muskeln im Typhusabdominalis*, Leipzig, 1864.
§ WALDEYER—*Die Veränderungen der quergestreiften Muskeln bei der Entzündung und dem Typhusprozess, etc.* VIRCHOW'S *Arch.*, t. XXXIV, 1865, p. 473.
‖ HAYEM—*Etudes sur les Myositis Symptomatiques—Archives de Physiologie*, Paris, 1870. He considers (page 581) that he has established three degrees or successive phases in the progress of the muscular lesions. The first is characterized by hyperæmia, the commencement of vitreous and granular degenerations of the fibres and sometimes a slight degree of alteration of the walls of the vessels. In the second is found the complete development of the vitreous and granular degenerations of the striated contents, with a proliferation of the cellular elements in the interior of the sarcolemma, which activity sometimes extends to the vascular walls. The third degree includes on the one hand the atrophy, disorganization and complete disappearance of the degenerated fibres, and on the other the work of regeneration or reparation, involving the return of the muscles to their normal condition. The new muscular fibres formed during this last period originate in pre-existing muscular cells, the proliferation of which was evident in the second phase of the morbid changes.

disorders of nutrition that are produced in many of the tissues by diseases attended with a notable dyscrasia.

Connected with the deterioration of the blood and the degeneration of the muscles were those ecchymoses simulating contusions, and the large extravasations that were in some cases found in the voluntary muscles, particularly in the lower part of the rectus abdominis and in the muscles of the neck, as in 63, 98, 136, 157 and 248. To these causes may also be attributed the purulent infiltration of the muscles sometimes observed, as in 151, in which the sheath of the rectus abdominis was the affected locality, and in other instances noted in the analytical summary.

Scurvy has been by some considered a very important cause of the peculiar characters exhibited by the fevers that affected our troops; but this opinion is not sustained by the records that have been preserved. In but one case, 316, was a notable scorbutic element present. If the ecchymoses, purpuric spots and hemorrhages that supervened during fever be regarded as symptoms of scurvy, this complication was of frequent occurrence; but there is no ground for supposing that these phenomena were dependent on the scorbutic taint, except in so far as it formed one of many influences which tended to their production, the determining factor being the great and sudden impress on the blood effected by the febrile poison. Certainly these extravasations occurred in cases in which, prior to the febrile attack, there was no suspicion of scurvy. They may not therefore be regarded as scorbutic symptoms when observed in the progress of fever.*

Diminished vitality resulting from disordered nutrition led to the formation of sloughs and gangrenous patches in situations determined by local conditions of impeded circulation, as on the sacrum and hips from continued pressure, in the parotid region and on blistered surfaces. Probably the absorption of morbific detritus from these gave rise to pyæmic developments in some instances, as bedsores were present in three of the cases, 125, 199 and 289, in which purulent deposits were found in other parts of the body. In some pyæmic cases, however, as in 38, which presented purulent collections in the joints and pectoralis major muscle, there is no record of the existence of bedsores or parotid abscess. Excluding these cases of purulent accumulations in the joints, there is no instance of disease of the bones following continued fever to be found among the *post-mortem* records, although the clinical accounts of severe rheumatic pain endured by convalescents render it probable that the periosteum and bones occasionally became affected, and that the large burrowing abscesses sometimes observed were associated with caries or necrosis.† A single instance of

* See *infra*, p. 622.

† Sir JAMES PAGET has observed that periostitis following typhoid fever generally affected the tibia, but occasionally the femur, ulna and parietal bones. It was always circumscribed in a space of one to three inches in area. When necrosis occurred its extent was less than that of the inflammation over it, and generally only the compact structure or outer table perished; it was never attended with the delirium, fever or other severe symptoms associated with acute necrosis. Periostitis of the ribs so resembles ordinary scrofulous periostitis that he sometimes thought it should be regarded as an evidence of scrofula educed by the feebleness of the nutrition consequent on the fever; but it has occurred after typhoid in patients of so robust and apparently unblemished constitutions that it would seem absurd to impute scrofula to them. The swelling, painful and tender, is usually on the front of the chest, and suppuration slowly occurs in it, the thin, pale pus making its exit through small openings in the skin; but he has seen pus burrow between the abdominal muscles, forming a great abscess, which had to be opened in the groin. See *St. Bartholomew's Hospital Reports*, Vol. XII, London, 1876, p. 2. KEEN, page 12 of his paper cited in note, page 297, *supra*, says that of 47 cases of disease of the bones 10 arose during the first two weeks of the fever, 27 in from three to six weeks and 10 followed ten months after the fever. He attributed the earlier cases to thrombosis or embolism, and the later cases to enfeebled nutrition, whose effects, especially in structures which vary so slowly as the bones, may readily extend over such long periods. Quoting AITKEN's remark that "No man can be considered fit for work or for general military service for three or four months after an attack of severe typhoid fever,"—*Holmes' System of Surgery*, 1st ed., Vol. IV, p. 50,—he gives a case in which extensive necrosis of the long bones, disabling the patient for three or four years, was the result of hard work in the use of a ten-pound hammer, undertaken before the system had sufficiently recovered from the effects of the febrile attack. He also describes a monarticular form of inflammation, a subacute synovitis, which affects the larger joints and especially the hip, where the swelling is sometimes obscured by the muscles. Usually it arises spontaneously, but occasionally from periostitis or necrosis invading the joint. It rarely produces suppurative or fistulous openings, the result being generally a gradual return to usefulness. These joint troubles are very infrequent. He cites GÜTERBOCK as responsible for the statement that in the Charité (Berlin) and in the Hamburg hospitals not a case

destruction of bone, possibly connected with fever, is furnished by the case of Carleton Bergan, private Co. B, Purnell's Maryland Legion.*

When admitted into hospital at Frederick, Md., this patient had a bedsore over the sacrum; his body was bathed in sweat and covered with sudamina; tongue dry and covered with sordes. It was reported that he had been treated in camp with large doses of mercurials, but the record does not show that he was salivated on admission. Two days afterwards a ragged ulcer was observed on the right edge of the tongue, which in ten days extended to the cheek and roof of the mouth, exposing by sloughing the entire upper maxilla. Six weeks later the whole of this bone, the vertical plate of the palate bone and a narrow strip of the left maxilla were removed, they being at the time quite separated from the healthy bone. The right eye was destroyed and sunken; the right half of the upper lip, the right ala of the nose, the adjacent portion of the cheek and the right superior maxillary bone were gone, leaving an extensive opening directly into the cavity of the mouth and right nasal fossa.†

But the most striking of the uncommon results of the disordered condition of the blood was the gangrene of the feet, recorded in six of the three hundred and eighty-nine cases constituting the *post-mortem* records. These numbers perhaps exaggerate the frequency of this occurrence, inasmuch as the unusual nature of the complication may have led to the preservation of the cases presenting it, when otherwise they might have remained unnoticed. Its uncommon character is evidenced by the fact that in one-half of the cases in which it occurred it was regarded as the result of exposure to cold.

Spontaneous gangrene, usually of parts in which the circulation is languid, is rare in the general experience of typhoid fever, but of greater frequency in typhus. In some epidemics the nose has been the site of the gangrenous attack,‡ in others the feet have suffered, as in the cases from our war records.§

---

occurred in a series of years, and in the Vienna General hospital from 1868 to 1871 only two cases among 3,130. MURCHISON does not mention this complication, nor any other of our text writers on surgery or practice except VOLKMANN, who gives a few lines to it in *Pitha und Billroth's Handbuch*. Sometimes the distension of the synovial cavity gives rise to conditions in which spontaneous dislocation occurs, and in a majority of the cases studied the actual dislocation was the first fact observed relative to the condition of the joint; this arose from the subacute nature of the lesion and the apathetic state of the patient.

* An account of this case is given in the First Part of the Surgical volume of this History, pp. 375–377.

† This frightful deformity was successfully treated by Dr. GURDON BUCK.—See *Transactions of the New York Medical Society*, 1864, p. 173.

‡ M. J. GUTBERLET—*Ueber die blaue Nase bei dem Typhus bellicus*—in *Hufeland's Journal*, Bd. XLII, 1816, part VI, p. 101—says that the "blue nose" was seen only in overcrowded military hospitals infected with the typhus contagion. Exposure to cold was not concerned in its production. It was met with during the hottest months of 1809 in the Austrian hospitals at Nickolsburg; during the mild damp winter of 1809–10 at Erlau in upper Hungary, and during the rigorous winter of 1813–14 in the military hospitals near Würzburg. The patients were generally convalescents from fever who, although so far improved as to have a good appetite, did not gain in strength; they had at the same time an excited pulse, a hot dry skin, and were always tired, languid and disinclined to leave their beds even in the warmest weather. Some were soldiers with their systems completely exhausted by colliquative diarrhœa of many weeks or months continuance; these were attacked immediately on their admission. Nurses were seldom affected, even though they had by a long stay in hospital acquired the sallow, cachectic appearance or so-called "hospital complexion." The graver symptoms of nervous fever, such as delirium and stupor, never accompanied the "blue nose." The associated fever was not severe; the patient was languid, indifferent, spoke little and unwillingly, but answered questions correctly; he had mostly a frequent watery but not particularly offensive diarrhœa, and always a fixed though not very severe pain, increased by pressure in the umbilical region; he made no complaint, but his countenance was anxious and he objected to any tactile examination of his abdomen, which was sunken, retracted and had a soft doughy feel; respiration was mostly thoracic. The disease did not spread from the particular hospital, but its occurrence was regarded as a sign of the presence of a high degree of the typhus contagion. GUTBERLET saw between two and three hundred cases during the years 1809 and 1810, and subsequently during the winter of 1813–14, *all of which were fatal*. Death generally ensued in from twenty-four to thirty-six hours after the attack, but sometimes it was delayed to the third, fourth or fifth day. No *post-mortem* observations were made, but the disease was thought to be connected with a gangrenous affection of the intestine. In BARKER and CHEYNE's *Account of the Fever lately Epidemic in Ireland*—London, 1821—Dr. BRACKEN of Waterford reports from his hospital, during the winter of 1818–19, eighteen cases in which death quickly followed a lividity which, affecting first the nose, extended in a short time over the face and ears. The fever prevailing in Ireland at this time had been preceded by excessively rigorous winters and cold damp summers. During the first of these unpropitious harvest seasons much of the grain remained uncut and was altogether lost; and a greater part of that which was saved had germinated in the husk and become in proportion impaired as an article of food. The potatoes of that year were small, wet and deficient in nutriment; turf or peat, constituting the chief fuel of the poor, could not be cut and dried, so that dampness of clothes and bedding, imperfect cooking of food and ventilation of apartments, deficient cleanliness of person and dwelling, co-operated with a deficiency of food in lowering the vitality of the people. "The failure of the crops in 1816 was not much felt till the spring of the following year, but scarcity then becoming general, attained its greatest height about midsummer, and extending to all the productions of the earth occasioned extreme distress. In some places the poorer classes were compelled to the sad necessity of collecting various esculent wild vegetables, nettles, wild mustard, navew and others of the same kind to sustain life; and in places distant from Dublin wretched beings were often seen exploring the fields with the hope of obtaining a supply of this miserable food. In districts contiguous to the sea various marine plants were had recourse to for the purpose of allaying the cravings of hunger; and we have been informed that on the seacoast of Ballyshannon many of the poor during several months at this period subsisted either chiefly or altogether on cockles, muscles, limpets or even the putrefying fish they could procure on the shore. In some districts seed-potatoes were taken up from the ground and the hopes of the future year thus destroyed for the relief of present necessity; and the blood drawn from the cattle in the fields and mixed with oatmeal, when this could be procured, has not unfrequently supplied a meal to a starving family. So general was the distress and insufficient the supply in some parts of the country that a few unhappy sufferers are said to have died of absolute want of food, and many must have sunk under the combined impressions of hunger, damp, cold and the anguish of mind necessarily attendant on sad anticipations of the future."—*Op. cit.*, pp. 34–5.—The connection between these conditions and the unusual prevalence and peculiarities of the continued fevers that afterwards scourged the country was acknowledged by all the reporters.

§ Mortification of the toes and feet occurred in a few instances in the epidemic described by BARKER and CHEYNE.—See Vol. I, page 349. J. A. ESTLANDER, in an article in *Langenbeck's Archiv. für Klinische Chirurgie*, Berlin, Vol. XII, pp. 453–517—on *Gangrene of the lower extremities in Typhus Fever*—

An impoverished condition of the blood, resulting from a deficiency of food, and the other co-operating influences to which a poverty-stricken people are subject have been so generally present not only in epidemics but in individual cases of fever characterized by gangrenous tendencies, that the appearance of the latter warrants a strong belief in the pre-existence of the former.   The deprivations and exposures to which our soldiers were liable, together with the prostration incident to repeated attacks of antecedent diarrhœa or other lowering diseases, render it probable that in occasional febrile seizures the specific cause of the fever found the patient in a condition as favorable for the development of spontaneous gangrene as if he had undergone the preliminary course of starvation so common in Ireland during the years of famine and fever.   On this view of the conditions associated with gangrene Dr. KEEN's summary of the causes may be accepted as accurate.   He attributed it to an altered blood, a weakened heart and the mechanical difficulties in carrying on the circulation, especially in distant parts; but in view of the usual seat of the affection in the lower extremities he concluded that the last two causes were the more immediately determining factors.*   To these, perhaps, should be added exposure to cold, as the six reported cases occurred during months when frostbite from exposure on active field service was not uncommon, although unknown amid the comparative comforts of camp and hospital life.   A degree of coldness of the feet resulting from displaced blankets, which, under ordinary conditions, would have been immediately succeeded by healthy reaction, may in these devitalized cases have sufficed to determine the development of gangrenous phenomena.†

Nevertheless it is to be noted that in none of the six cases is there any record of special deprivations; on the contrary, in one, 164, the body of the patient was said to have been not emaciated.   Hence it is probable that in certain cases something more than depression of the vital powers was needful to the occurrence of gangrene.   MURCHISON‡ speaks of spontaneous gangrene as a result of arterial thrombosis, and ESTLANDER found the clot in many of his cases.   Case 112 of our *post-mortem* records is the only instance in which the arteries are said to have been occluded.

IV.—THE BRAIN AND ITS MEMBRANES.

Cases of the continued fevers in which the condition of the brain and its membranes was examined constitute but a small percentage of the whole number.   In some of the hospitals where *post-mortem* investigations were systematically pursued the brain was examined

based upon observations made during an epidemic which prevailed in Finnland during the famine of 1866–68, states that the affection was no doubt due to the intensity of the typhus contagion, aggravated by a want of food and proper care during the disease.   With regard to its immediate cause it is said that of twenty-one cases met with there were thrombi in the principal artery of the limb in fourteen; and it is held that these were plainly the cause of the gangrene, as their presence was established by examination of the artery during life and after death.   Generally no pulsation could be felt in the vessel of the affected limb, while that of the vessel of the opposite side could be readily detected.   The obstructed artery felt like a hard cord and was wholly without sensation.   Now and then, below the knee, it would feel harder and more resisting than usual, and in the vicinity of Poupart's ligament would still pulsate feebly and obscurely, yet so evidently as to render it uncertain whether any obstruction actually existed; but on amputation the hemorrhage was trifling,—no blood came from the femoral or popliteal, and only a little from the smaller muscular branches, while a fibrinous plug filled the vessel and projected beyond its retracted end.   Most of the thrombi were examined; they generally terminated below where an abrupt narrowing occurred, as at the division of the popliteal artery, or as was the case in one instance, at the origin of the profunda femoris, from which the thrombus extended upward.   In one case in which the part removed by amputation was not wholly disorganized and a plug was formed at the bifurcation of the popliteal, the vessels below this point were completely free and sound; in another case in which amputation had been performed at the upper third of the leg, the anterior and posterior tibial and the peroneal arteries were found empty.   ESTLANDER was of opinion that when the obstructing coagulum did not extend from the popliteal artery higher than the tendon of the adductor magnus gangrene either did not result or involved only a toe or a small portion of the foot; but when it extended beyond the origin of the profunda femoris the disease involved the upper third of the leg; this was illustrated in eight or ten cases.   The emboli were believed to have originated in the left ventricle of the heart when, owing to debility, contraction was imperfect and evacuation incomplete.   Afterwards, when the heart became stronger, the coagula were expelled and occluded the vessels.   This gangrene from obstruction was observed only at the end of the fever or after the commencement of convalescence.   Gangrene, where no obstruction was found, showed itself by peculiar symptoms even at the beginning of the fever and attacked both sides, being confined generally to some of the toes or to other small portions of the foot and only in the severest cases extending as far as the ankle-joint.

* See page 35 of his *Lecture*, cited *supra*, note to page 297.
† See report of Surg. J. H. TAYLOR, U. S. V., *supra*, p. 310.   ‡ Page 559 of his *Treatise*.

as a matter of course, but in others where apparently the object of the examination was merely to verify a diagnosis or find an adequate cause for death, the intracranial examination was frequently omitted unless specially called for by clinical manifestations. Hence it may be assumed that the cases in which time was devoted to opening the calvaria and examining its contents were as a whole characterized by a prominence of the cerebral symptoms. Nevertheless, in a large proportion of these no abnormal appearance was observed. The brain and its membranes were considered normal in 45.5 per cent. of the purely typhoid cases; congestion and effusion were present, but none of the cases presented undeniable evidence of the existence of inflammatory action. Of the malarial cases in which the cranium was opened abnormal appearances were observed in 64.7 per cent. The hyperæmic tendency attained a higher development in these cases than in typhoid; and this was shown as well by the intensity of its manifestions as by their frequency, for in one case, 287, the cerebrum was ecchymosed, and in two, 80 and 257, the active character of the hyperæmia was evidenced by the lymph that had been exuded. Morbid changes were found in 54 per cent. of the typho-malarial cases and in 41.2 per cent. of the mixed series of cases.

In a large number of cases in which the brain and its membranes were said to have presented a healthy appearance nothing is known of the associated symptoms; in certain other of these cases, as 23, 36, 106, 112, 116, 289 and 380, no mention was made of head symptoms, although what must be regarded as the clinical characteristics of each case were stated by way of preface to the *post-mortem* record. There remain, however, some important observations which show that very notable disturbances of the cerebral functions occurred without leaving in the brain or its membranes any trace by which their existence could have been predicated. Thus, in 7, 24, 29 and 199 delirium was present, prolonged in the last-mentioned case for a week before death; in 370 the patient was deaf and unconscious; in 368 he fell into a lethargic state twenty-four hours before death; and in 56 coma and delirium were reported, apparently in connection with inflammation of the middle ear.

Looking now at the cases in which some abnormity was discovered in the brain or its membranes, it is found that in many of these no record of the associated symptoms has been preserved, while in others, as 42, 80, 99, 264 and 276, although certain symptoms were reported, no mention was made of any referable to the encephalic lesions. Delirium was mentioned in ten cases, 8, 109, 111, 117, 247, 278, 281, 287, 291 and 297, as the prominent cerebral symptom. Generally it occurred as the precursor of death, supervening, as in 287, a few hours before the fatal issue, or lasting, as in 278, for several days with occasional lucid intervals. This was associated in the majority of these instances with congestion of the pia mater, leading in case 287 to ecchymosis, with or without congestion of the cerebral substance or effused serum in the subarachnoid space and ventricles. In one case, 111, in which delirium was associated with insomnia, the arachnoid at the base of the brain was thickened and opaque and the ventricles filled with effused liquid. But in contrast with these hyperæmic appearances the brain and its membranes in 109 were pale and anæmic, and in 291, in which delirium lasted for several days, the brain was normal and the pia mater anæmic, opaque and wrinkled.

In nine cases, 9, 26, 45, 47, 86, 104, 257, 303 and 304, the cerebral implication was marked by unconsciousness, usually succeeding to delirium or insomnia, and passing into death by coma: In 45 and 47 the only abnormal appearance consisted of a serous transudation into the arachnoidal sac or ventricles, and in 26 and 104 of a simple injection of the membranes, while in 9 and 86 both injection and effusion were said to have been present. In 304 the condition of the membranes was not stated, but the cerebral substance was firm and slightly congested posteriorly. In two cases only, 257 and 303, were definite signs of inflammatory action presented—a coating of lymph on the base of the brain and a turbidity of the ventricular serosity.

In two cases, 343 and 349, the encephalic symptoms were said to have been those of meningitis, but the prominent *post-mortem* lesion in each case consisted of subarachnoid effusion. In 299 signs of cerebral congestion, noted clinically, were verified by *post-mortem* examination. In 160, in which the cerebral disturbance was manifested by craziness, the usual hyperæmia of the membranes and subarachnoid effusion were observed. Lastly, in 379, in which death overtook the patient suddenly and quietly while in bed and supposed to have been asleep, the brain and its membranes were engorged with bright blood and the ventricles distended with sero-sanguinolent serum.

Although headache, dizziness, insomnia, delirium, dulness, stupor and coma were in some instances associated with changes in the brain and its membranes, to which they might with propriety be attributed, the encephalic lesions were in other cases wholly incommensurate with the intensity of the cerebral symptoms; and in many cases noted the latter were, indeed, unaccompanied by any observed lesion. LOUIS long ago demonstrated that the existence of delirium in typhoid could not be in all cases explained by the condition of the brain. He argued also that the intestinal lesion could not be regarded as the cause of the delirium, for although there is delirium in pneumonia there is no concomitant intestinal lesion, and it is unlikely that the sympathetic action on the brain of organs so different in function and structure as the lungs and alimentary canal should be similar.* He attributed the delirium to the pyrexia, as it was the only pathological factor common to all the cases. It has already been shown, in speaking of the alteration of the blood resulting from the persistence of fever, that the febrile condition may develop delirium by an accumulation in the blood of the noxious transition products of tissue-waste. The coma that was the frequent prelude of death may also have been due in many cases to this altered blood, for free effusions were often discovered in the serous and subserous spaces without a concomitant congestion. Effusions unconnected with inflammatory processes were observed in other serous cavities, particularly in the pericardium, and these must be referred to that watery condition of the blood which occasioned œdema of the legs in the paroxysmal fevers and in some, as 70 of the malarial series, of the continued fevers.

But cerebral symptoms unconnected with notable hyperæmic conditions of the brain or its membranes were not in all cases due to that alteration of the blood which resulted from the continuance of the fever, for in some instances they were developed from the beginning of the attack.† The patient in the case presented on page 473, *supra*, died after an illness of twenty-four hours marked by slight delirium; and while the brain exhibited no unhealthy appearances the blood was so liquid that it had become extravasated subcutaneously in irregular purpuric spots and issued freely from *post-mortem* incisions into the skin and internal organs. Here the disordered condition of the blood was evidently a primary lesion manifested by cerebral phenomena.

---

* LOUIS,—*Recherches, &c.*, t. II, p. 176.

† Speaking of delirium in typhoid, BARTLETT, in his *Treatise on the Fevers of the United States*, Philadelphia, 1852, p. 65, says: "In a small number of cases this symptom is present at the commencement or very early in the disease. * * * As a general rule, it appears early in proportion to the gravity and rapid progress of the disease." MURCHISON gives two cases, one of which was fatal on the first and the other on the second day. "The symptoms in these rapid cases are usually severe headache and acute delirium, with profuse diarrhœa or great engorgement of the lungs."—*The Continued Fevers of Great Britain*, London, 1873, p. 548.

For Reference

Not to be taken from this room